David Ingham

NEWS OF THE WORLD

G000079999

Published by Invincible Press
77-85 Fulham Palace Road, Hammersmith, London W6 8JB

First published 1887

© Invincible Press 2002

Editorial compilation by Hayters, Humatt House, 146-148 Clerkenwell Road, London EC1R 5DP

Typesetting by Letterpart Limited, Reigate, Surrey

Printed and bound in Great Britain by Clays Ltd, St Ives plc, Bungay, Suffolk

Distributed by The Magazine Marketing Company, Octagon House, White Hart Meadows, Ripley, Woking, Surrey GU23 6HR. Telephone (01483) 211222

ISBN 0 00 714137 8

FRONT COVER

Ronaldo scores his second, and decisive, goal ensuring Brazil win the 2002 World Cup.

CONTENTS

STILL A LONG WAY TO GO FOR ENGLAND

BY ROB BEASLEY, CHIEF FOOTBALL WRITER, NEWS OF THE WORLD

So Sven's nearly men must try again in Portugal and by then it will be 36 years of hurt for England. After the thrills, spills and upsets of Japan and Korea 2002, what chance do they really have of emerging as European champions in 2004?

Of course we'd love it to happen, but the bottom line is how realistic is it to envisage England sweeping all before them? First, let's forget the partisan, wishful thinking and blind allegiance. Let's take off the rose-tinted specs and examine where they can go from here.

Yes, at face value, the World Cup was something of a success. We reached the quarter-finals, so we can rightly claim to be one of the best eight teams in the world. You could even argue we are even better than that because we lost to the eventual winners, Brazil. And remember that in the Final Brazil beat Germany, a team we trounced 5-1 in Munich in qualifying. So we must be the second best team on the planet, right? We didn't have Steven Gerrard, while David Beckham, Michael Owen and Kieron Dyer were only half-fit; Brazil's winner was a fluke; Ronaldinho didn't mean it . . . . . . blah, blah.

Can we even claim to be the second best team in Europe? How can we be when two European sides progressed further than us? After Germany came Turkey, who finished third by beating South Korea, in the play-off match after they had lost to Brazil in the semis. And while, this time, we may have avoided meeting the Germans, we do have to take on the Turks in the Euro qualifiers. That won't be easy.

Sure, Sven's young side will be older and wiser for the experience. But where is the new blood bristling and battling to come through? Who is going to push veteran David Seaman? Who is going to provide the creative invention, the unscripted stroke of genius, the genuine class that we were so sadly lacking? And who is going to weigh in with the goals when Owen is out-of-form or struggling for fitness? Most importantly, can coach Eriksson shake off the shackles of his oh-so-rigid 4-4-2 formation and allow a bit of freedom for his team?

That was arguably the biggest disappointment of all. OK, beating Argentina and safely negotiating our way through the Group of Death were achievements in themselves. We wasted no time ruthlessly despatching the not so great Danes. The nation celebrated. Everything was going to plan and we screamed 'Bring on Brazil.' But that's the trouble with getting caught up in and carried away by all the hype. For when push came to shove, England were found badly wanting. Worse, Eriksson was found wanting and we weren't expecting that.

The Brazilians proved too good, far too good. Even playing against ten men and 2-1 down, we were unable to muster a single shot on goal when the game, and our World Cup dream, was slipping away fast. We did not have the leadership – on or off the pitch – to turn the tide. Eriksson sat impassive as England wilted. He swapped like for like with his substitutions, still strangely protecting his precious formation. And in the end he looked not just beaten but bamboozled.

On the pitch there wasn't a player seemingly capable of rising to the challenge, let alone the occasion. We didn't have the technique or skill to exploit our numerical advantage. More upsetting, we didn't seem to have the drive or the desire.

So we went out with a whimper and looking for all the world like a regimented team of pre-programmed plodders who could not switch their style or tactics when Plan A patently was not working. There did not appear to be a Plan B, unless you call using Rio Ferdinand as a striker a carefully-considered option. We'll need a bit more than that in Portugal – assuming we qualify of course.

BRAZIL AGAIN AS A NEW ORDER EMERGES

Everyone recognised that the game's order at international level was changing. Out of Africa had come discipline to supplement natural flair and finesse. From Asia there was organisation to accompany running power and sheer enthusiasm. From North America an enhanced level of experience of competing at the highest level. The coaches, most of them European, had done a good job.

Yet no-one would have predicted that four of the World Cup quarter-final places would be filled by rank outsiders – South Korea, Senegal, the United States and Turkey – or that two of them would make it to the last four. That Brazil were eventually crowned champions for a record fifth time after beating Germany 2-0 with two goals by Ronaldo did not alter the fact that this will be remembered, more than anything, as the tournament of the underdog. As Graham Taylor, the Aston Villa and former England manager, observed: 'It's truly a world game now, belonging to no one country or continent.'

A lack of great teams and outstanding players may have left the purists wanting. For the rest of us, the first Finals to be held in Asia proved totally absorbing and hugely entertaining. Yes, there were occasions when a referee's red card, or his assistant's raised flag, unfairly penalised some of the bigger teams. But at the same time a flawed attitude and questionable tactics displayed by those same teams in crucial situations contributed just as much to their failure.

The pattern was set in the 30th minute of the opening game when Papa Bouba Diop's strike for Senegal sent defending champions France sliding towards elimination from their group without a single goal on the board. Argentina and Portugal joined them on the plane home. Then, ten-man Italy lost to South Korea by a golden goal in the second round after Christian Vieri scored first for them and later missed a sitter.

The Koreans ousted Spain on penalties before falling to Germany in the semi-finals, where Turkey, Europe's most improved side, lost by the same 1-0 margin to Brazil. Oliver Kahn, goalkeeper and captain, had been largely responsible for Germany's progress and his formidable presence looked to be the biggest threat to Brazil in the Final.

But once again the sheer unpredictability of the tournament came to the fore, Kahn spilling a shot from Rivaldo and Ronaldo accepting the gift. A brilliantly worked second by Ronaldo confirmed Brazil's superiority and finally erased the player's memory of defeat by France four years earlier when he had a seizure before the Final and contributed nothing to it.

Turkey beat South Korea 3-2 in the third place play-off, which produced one of the abiding memories when players of both teams linked arms to salute spectators, whose warmth and passion for the month's action had helped make it so enjoyable.

England flattered to deceive after Sol Campbell's first international goal against Sweden, falling away badly in the second half and conceding an equaliser. There was nothing half-hearted about the performance against Argentina, David Beckham's penalty delivering a deserved victory, but a goalless draw with Nigeria left something to be desired.

The roller-coaster continued. Denmark were despatched 3-0 in the second round, with the outstanding Rio Ferdinand scoring his first for his country, and Michael Owen's goal against Brazil suggested great things. But Rivaldo equalised on the stroke of half-time, Ronaldinho's long-range free-kick sailed over David Seaman's head and although Ronaldinho was sent off soon afterwards, England failed miserably to exploit their numerical advantage.

The Republic of Ireland overcame the loss of captain Roy Keane, sent home for abusing manager Mick McCarthy, to win plenty of praise. They came from behind to equalise against Cameroon through Matt Holland, did the same against Germany thanks to Robbie Keane's last-minute effort and qualified by beating Saudi Arabia 3-0.

The end came in a penalty-shoot-out against Spain, but not before the Irish had again risen to the occasion, with Damien Duff continuing to confirm his emergence as a genuine world-class player.

STUART BARNES

QUALIFYING FOR 2002 WORLD CUP FINALS

EUROPE

GROUP 1

	P	W	D	L	F	A	Pts
RUSSIA	10	7	2	1	18	5	23
SLOVENIA	10	5	5	0	17	9	20
Yugoslavia	10	5	4	1	22	8	19
Switzerland	10	4	2	4	18	12	14
Faroe Islands	10	2	1	7	6	23	7
Luxembourg	10	0	0	10	4	28	0

Results: Switzerland 0, Russia 1; Faroe Islands 2, Slovenia 2; Luxembourg 0, Yugoslavia 2; Luxembourg 1, Slovenia 2; Switzerland 5, Faroe Islands 1; Russia 3, Luxembourg 0; Slovenia 2, Switzerland 2; Luxembourg 0, Faroe Islands 2; Russia 1, Slovenia 1; Yugoslavia 1, Switzerland 1; Russia 1, Faroe Islands 0; Switzerland 5, Luxembourg 0; Slovenia 1, Yugoslavia 1; Yugoslavia 0, Russia 1; Faroe Islands 0, Switzerland 1; Russia 1, Yugoslavia 1; Slovenia 2, Luxembourg 0; Faroe Islands 0, Yugoslavia 6; Luxembourg 1, Russia 2; Switzerland 0, Slovenia 1; Yugoslavia 2, Faroe Islands 0; Faroe Islands 1, Luxembourg 0; Slovenia 2, Russia 1; Switzerland 1, Yugoslavia 2; Faroe Islands 0, Russia 3; Luxembourg 0, Switzerland 3; Yugoslavia 1, Slovenia 1; Russia 4, Switzerland 0; Slovenia 3, Faroe Islands 0; Yugoslavia 6, Luxembourg 2.

GROUP 2

	P	W	D	L	F	A	Pts
PORTUGAL	10	7	3	0	33	7	24
REP OF IRELAND	10	7	3	0	23	5	24
Holland	10	6	2	2	30	9	20
Estonia	10	2	2	6	10	26	8
Cyprus	10	2	2	6	13	31	8
Andorra	10	0	0	10	5	36	0

Results: Estonia 1, Andorra 0; Andorra 2, Cyprus 3; Holland 2, **Republic of Ireland** 2; Estonia 1, Portugal 3; Andorra 1, Estonia 2; Cyprus 0, Holland 4; Portugal 1, **Republic of Ireland** 1; Holland 0, Portugal 2; **Republic of Ireland** 2, Estonia 0; Cyprus 5, Andorra 0; Portugal 3, Andorra 0; Andorra 0, Holland 5; Cyprus 0, **Republic of Ireland** 4; Andorra 0, **Republic of Ireland** 3; Cyprus 2, Estonia 2; Portugal 2, Holland 2; Holland 4, Cyprus 0; **Republic of Ireland** 3, Andorra 1; Estonia 2, Holland 4; **Republic of Ireland** 1, Portugal 1; Estonia 0, **Republic of Ireland** 2; Portugal 6, Cyprus 0; Estonia 2, Cyprus 2; Andorra 1, Portugal 7; **Republic of Ireland** 1, Holland 0; Cyprus 1, Portugal 3; Holland 5, Estonia 0; Holland 4, Andorra 0; Portugal 5, Estonia 0; **Republic of Ireland** 4, Cyprus 0.

GROUP 3

	P	W	D	L	F	A	Pts
DENMARK	10	6	4	0	22	6	22
CZECH REPUBLIC	10	6	2	2	20	8	20
Bulgaria	10	5	2	3	14	15	17
Iceland	10	4	1	5	14	20	13
Northern Ireland	10	3	2	5	11	12	11
Malta	10	0	1	9	4	24	1

Results: Bulgaria 0, Czech Republic 1; Iceland 1, Denmark 2; **Northern Ireland** 1, Malta 0; Bulgaria 3, Malta 0; Czech Republic 4, Iceland 0; **Northern Ireland** 1, Denmark 1; Denmark 1, Bulgaria 1; Iceland 1, **Northern Ireland** 0; Malta 0, Czech Republic 0; Bulgaria 2, Iceland 1; Malta 0, Denmark 5; **Northern Ireland** 0, Czech Republic 1; Bulgaria 4, **Northern Ireland** 3; Czech Republic 0, Denmark 0; Malta 1, Iceland 4; Denmark 2, Czech Republic 1; Iceland 3, Malta 0; **Northern Ireland** 0, Bulgaria 1; Czech Republic 3, **Northern Ireland** 1; Denmark 2, Malta 1; Iceland 1, Bulgaria 2; Denmark 1, **Northern Ireland** 1; Iceland 3, Czech Republic 1; Malta 0, Bulgaria 2; Bulgaria 0, Denmark 2; Czech Republic 3, Malta 2; **Northern Ireland** 3, Iceland 0; Czech Republic 6, Bulgaria 0; Denmark 6, Iceland 0; Malta 0, **Northern Ireland** 1.

GROUP 4

	P	W	D	L	F	A	Pts
SWEDEN	10	8	2	0	20	3	26
TURKEY	10	6	3	1	18	8	21
Slovakia	10	5	2	3	16	9	17
Macedonia	10	1	4	5	11	18	7
Moldova	10	1	3	6	6	20	6
Azerbaijan	10	1	2	7	4	17	5

Results: Azerbaijan 0, Sweden 1; Turkey 2, Moldova 0; Slovakia 2, Macedonia 0; Macedonia 2, Azerbaijan 0; Moldova 0, Slovakia 1; Sweden 1, Turkey 1; Azerbaijan 0, Turkey 1; Moldova 0, Macedonia 0; Slovakia 0, Sweden 0; Azerbaijan 0, Moldova 0; Sweden 1, Macedonia 0; Turkey 1, Slovakia 1; Macedonia 1, Turkey 2; Moldova 0, Sweden 2; Slovakia 3, Azerbaijan 1; Macedonia 2, Moldova 2; Sweden 2, Slovakia 0; Turkey 3, Azerbaijan 0; Azerbaijan 2, Slovakia 0; Sweden 6, Moldova 0; Turkey 3, Macedonia 3; Macedonia 1, Sweden 2; Moldova 2, Azerbaijan 0; Slovakia 0, Turkey 1; Azerbaijan 1, Macedonia 1; Slovakia 4, Moldova 2; Turkey 1, Sweden 2; Macedonia 0, Slovakia 5; Moldova 0, Turkey 3; Sweden 3, Azerbaijan 0.

GROUP 5

	P	W	D	L	F	A	Pts
POLAND	10	6	3	1	21	11	21
Ukraine	10	4	5	1	13	8	17
Belarus	10	4	3	3	12	11	15
Norway	10	2	4	4	12	14	10
Wales	10	1	6	3	10	12	9
Armenia	10	0	5	5	7	19	5

Results: Belarus 2, **Wales** 1; Norway 0, Armenia 0; Ukraine 1, Poland 3; Armenia 2, Ukraine 3, Poland 3, Belarus 1; **Wales** 1, Norway 1; Belarus 2, Armenia 1; Norway 0, Ukraine 1; Poland 0, **Wales** 0; Armenia 2, **Wales** 2; Norway 2, Poland 3; Ukraine 0, Belarus 0; Belarus 2, Norway 1; Poland 4, Armenia 0; **Wales** 1, Ukraine 1; Armenia 0, Belarus 0; Ukraine 0, Norway 0; **Wales** 1, Poland 2; Armenia 1, Norway 1; Belarus 1, Ukraine 1, **Wales** 1; Belarus 0, Ukraine 2; Poland 3, Norway 0; **Wales** 0, Armenia 0; Belarus 4, Poland 1; Norway 3, **Wales** 2; Ukraine 3, Armenia 0; Armenia 1, Norway 4; Poland 1, Ukraine 1; **Wales** 1, Belarus 0.

GROUP 6

	P	W	D	L	F	A	Pts
CROATIA	8	5	3	0	15	2	18
BELGIUM	8	5	2	1	25	6	17
Scotland	8	4	3	1	12	6	15
Latvia	8	1	1	6	5	16	4
San Marino	8	0	1	7	3	30	1

Results: Belgium 0, Croatia 0; Latvia 0, **Scotland** 1; Latvia 0, Belgium 4; San Marino 0, **Scotland** 2; Croatia 1, **Scotland** 1; San Marino 0, Latvia 1; Belgium 10, San Marino 1; Croatia 4, Latvia 1; **Scotland** 2, Belgium 2; **Scotland** 4, San Marino 0; Latvia 1, San Marino 1; Belgium 3, Latvia 1; Croatia 4, San Marino 0; Latvia 0, Croatia 1; San Marino 1, Belgium 4; **Scotland** 0, Croatia 0; Belgium 2, **Scotland** 0; San Marino 0, Croatia 4; Croatia 1, Belgium 0; **Scotland** 2, Latvia 1.

GROUP 7

	P	W	D	L	F	A	Pts
SPAIN	8	6	2	0	21	4	20
Austria	8	4	3	1	10	8	15
Israel	8	3	3	2	11	7	12
Bosnia	8	2	2	4	12	12	8
Liechtenstein	8	0	0	8	0	23	0

Results: Bosnia 1, Spain 2; Israel 2, Liechtenstein 0; Liechtenstein 0, Austria 1; Spain 2, Israel 0; Austria 1, Spain 1; Israel 3, Bosnia 1; Bosnia 1, Austria 1; Spain 5, Liechtenstein 0; Austria 2, Israel 1; Liechtenstein 0, Bosnia 3; Austria 2, Liechtenstein 0; Liechtenstein 0, Israel 3; Spain 4, Bosnia 1; Israel 1, Spain 1; Bosnia 0, Israel 0; Spain 4, Austria 0; Austria 2, Bosnia 0; Liechtenstein 0, Spain 2; Bosnia 5, Liechtenstein 0; Israel 1, Austria 1.

GROUP 8

	P	W	D	L	F	A	Pts
ITALY	8	6	2	0	16	3	20
Romania	8	5	1	2	10	7	16
Georgia	8	3	1	4	12	12	10
Hungary	8	2	2	4	14	13	8
Lithuania	8	0	2	6	3	20	2

Results: Hungary 2, Italy 2; Romania 1, Lithuania 0; Italy 3, Romania 0; Lithuania 0, Georgia 4; Italy 2, Georgia 0; Lithuania 1, Hungary 6; Hungary 1, Lithuania 1; Romania 0, Italy 2; Georgia 0, Romania 2; Italy 4, Lithuania 0; Georgia 1, Italy 2; Romania 2, Hungary 0; Hungary 4, Georgia 1; Lithuania 1, Romania 2; Georgia 3, Hungary 1; Lithuania 0, Italy 0; Georgia 2, Lithuania 0; Hungary 0, Romania 2; Italy 1, Hungary 0; Romania 1, Georgia 1.

GROUP 9

	P	W	D	L	F	A	Pts
ENGLAND	8	5	2	1	16	6	17
GERMANY	8	5	2	1	14	10	17
Finland	8	3	3	2	12	7	12
Greece	8	2	1	5	7	17	7
Albania	8	1	0	7	5	14	3

Results: Finland 2, Albania 1; Germany 2, Greece 0; **England** 0, Germany 1; Greece 1, Finland 0; Albania 2, Greece 0; Finland 0, **England** 0; **England** 2, Finland 1; Germany 2, Albania 1, **England** 1; Greece 2, Germany 4; Finland 2, Germany 2; Greece 1, Albania 0; Albania 0, Germany 2; Greece 0, **England** 2; Albania 0, Finland 2; Germany 1, **England** 5; **England** 2, Abania 0; Finland 5, Greece 1; **England** 2, Greece 2; Germany 0, Finland 0.

SOUTH AMERICA

	P	W	D	L	F	A	Pts
ARGENTINA	18	13	4	1	42	15	43
ECUADOR	18	9	4	5	23	20	31
BRAZIL	18	9	3	6	31	17	30
PARAGUAY	18	9	3	6	29	23	30
URUGUAY	18	7	6	5	19	13	27
Colombia	18	7	6	5	20	15	27
Bolivia	18	4	6	8	21	33	18
Peru	18	4	4	10	14	25	16
Venezuela	18	5	1	12	18	44	16
Chile	18	3	3	12	15	27	12

Results: Colombia 0, Brazil 0; Argentina 4, Chile 1; Ecuador 2, Venezuela 0; Peru 2, Paraguay 0; Uruguay 1, Bolivia 0; Bolivia 1, Colombia 1; Brazil 3, Ecuador 2; Chile 1, Peru 1; Paraguay 1, Uruguay 0; Venezuela 0, Argentina 4; Paraguay 3, Ecuador 1; Uruguay 2, Chile 1; Argentina 1, Bolivia 0; Colombia 3, Venezuela 0; Peru 0, Brazil 1; Brazil 1, Uruguay 1; Venezuela 4, Bolivia 2; Colombia 1, Argentina 3; Chile 3, Paraguay 1; Colombia 1, Argentina 3; Ecuador 2, Peru 1; Paraguay 2, Brazil 1; Uruguay 3, Venezuela 1; Argentina 2, Ecuador 0; Bolivia 1, Chile 0; Peru 0, Colombia 1; Ecuador 0, Colombia 0; Venezuela 0, Chile 2; Brazil 3, Argentina 1; Uruguay 0, Peru 0; Bolivia 0, Paraguay 0; Chile 3, Brazil 0; Colombia 1, Uruguay 0; Argentina 1, Paraguay 1; Ecuador 2, Bolivia 0; Peru 1, Venezuela 0; Chile 1, Colombia 1; Paraguay 3, Venezuela 0; Brazil 5, Bolivia 0; Peru 1, Argentina 0; Uruguay 4, Ecuador 0; Colombia 0, Paraguay 2; Argentina 2, Uruguay 1; Bolivia 1, Peru 0; Ecuador 1, Chile 0; Venezuela 0, Brazil 6; Bolivia 0, Uruguay 0; Brazil 1, Colombia 0; Chile 0, Argentina 2; Paraguay 5, Peru 1; Venezuela 1, Ecuador 2; Colombia 2, Bolivia 0; Peru 3, Chile 1; Argentina 5, Venezuela 0; Ecuador 1, Brazil 0; Uruguay 0, Paraguay 1; Chile 1, Uruguay 1; Ecuador 2, Paraguay 1; Venezuela 2, Colombia 2; Bolivia 3, Argentina 3; Brazil 1, Peru 1; Paraguay 1, Chile 0; Peru 1, Ecuador 2; Argentina 3, Colombia 0; Bolivia 5, Venezuela 0; Uruguay 1, Brazil 0; Chile 2, Bolivia 2; Venezuela 2, Uruguay 0; Brazil 2, Paraguay 0; Ecuador 0, Argentina 2; Colombia 0, Peru 1; Chile 0, Venezuela 2; Peru 0, Uruguay 2; Argentina 2, Brazil 1; Colombia 0, Ecuador 0; Paraguay 5, Bolivia 1; Bolivia 1, Ecuador 5; Brazil 2, Chile 0; Paraguay 2, Argentina 2; Uruguay 1, Colombia 1; Venezuela 3, Peru 0; Argentina 2, Peru 0; Bolivia 3, Brazil 1; Colombia 3, Chile 1; Ecuador 1, Uruguay 1; Venezuela 3, Paraguay 1; Brazil 3, Venezuela 0; Chile 0, Ecuador 0; Paraguay 0, Colombia 4; Peru 1, Bolivia 1; Uruguay 1, Argentina 1.

AFRICA

GROUP 1

	P	W	D	L	F	A	Pts
CAMEROON	8	6	1	1	14	4	19
Angola	8	3	4	1	11	9	13
Zambia	8	3	2	3	14	11	11
Togo	8	2	3	3	10	13	9
Libya	8	0	2	6	7	19	2

Results: Angola 2, Zambia 1; Libya 0, Cameroon 3; Zambia 2, Togo 0; Cameroon 3, Angola 0; Angola 3, Libya 1; Togo 0, Cameroon 2; Libya 3, Togo 3; Cameroon 1, Zambia 0; Zambia 2, Libya 0; Togo 1, Angola 1; Zambia 1, Angola 1; Cameroon 1, Libya 0; Angola 2, Cameroon 0; Togo 3, Zambia 2; Libya 1, Angola 1; Cameroon 2, Togo 0; Zambia 2, Cameroon 0; Togo 2, Libya 0; Libya 2, Zambia 4; Angola 1, Togo 1.

GROUP 2

	P	W	D	L	F	A	Pts
NIGERIA	8	5	1	2	15	3	16
Liberia	8	5	0	3	10	8	15
Sudan	8	4	0	4	8	10	12
Ghana	8	3	2	3	10	9	11
Sierra Leone	8	1	1	6	2	15	4

Results: Nigeria 2, Sierra Leone 0; Sudan 2, Liberia 0; Ghana 5, Sierra Leone 0; Liberia 2, Nigeria 1; Nigeria 3, Sudan 0; Ghana 1, Liberia 3; Liberia 1, Sierra Leone 0; Sudan 1, Ghana 0; Ghana 0, Nigeria 0; Sierra Leone 0, Sudan 2; Sierra Leone 1, Nigeria 0; Liberia 2, Sudan 0; Nigeria 2, Liberia 0; Sierra Leone 1, Ghana 1; Liberia 1, Ghana 2; Sudan 0, Nigeria 4; Sierra Leone 0, Liberia 1; Ghana 1, Sudan 0; Nigeria 3, Ghana 0; Sudan 3, Sierra Leone 0.

GROUP 3

	P	W	D	L	F	A	Pts
SENEGAL	8	4	3	1	14	2	15
Morocco	8	4	3	1	8	3	15
Egypt	8	3	4	1	16	7	13
Algeria	8	2	2	4	11	14	8
Namibia	8	0	2	6	3	26	2

Results: Algeria 1, Senegal 1; Namibia 0, Morocco 0; Morocco 2, Algeria 1; Senegal 0, Egypt 0; Algeria 1, Namibia 0; Egypt 0, Morocco 0; Morocco 0, Senegal 0; Namibia 1, Egypt 1; Senegal 4, Namibia 0; Egypt 5, Algeria 2; Morocco 3, Namibia 0; Senegal 3, Algeria 0; Algeria 1, Morocco 2; Egypt 1, Senegal 0; Morocco 1, Egypt 0; Namibia 0, Algeria 4; Egypt 8, Namibia 2; Senegal 1, Morocco 0; Algeria 1, Egypt 1; Namibia 0, Senegal 5.

GROUP 4

	P	W	D	L	F	A	Pts
TUNISIA	8	6	2	0	23	4	20
Ivory Coast	8	4	3	1	18	8	15
DR Congo	8	3	1	4	7	16	10
Madagascar	8	2	0	6	5	15	6
Congo	8	1	2	5	5	15	5

Results: Ivory Coast 2, Tunisia 2; Madagascar 3, DR Congo 0; Tunisia 1, Madagascar 0; DR Congo 2, Congo 0; Congo 1, Tunisia 2; Madagascar 1, Ivory Coast 3; Tunisia 6, DR Congo 0; DR Congo 1, Ivory Coast 2; DR Congo 1, Madagascar 0; Ivory Coast 2, Congo 0; Congo 2, Madagascar 0; Madagascar 0, Tunisia 2; Congo 1, DR Congo 1; Tunisia 1, Ivory Coast 1; Ivory Coast 6, Madagascar 0; Tunisia 6, Congo 0; Congo 1, Ivory Coast 1; DR Congo 0, Tunisia 3; Ivory Coast 1, DR Congo 2; Madagascar 1, Congo 0.

GROUP 5

	P	W	D	L	F	A	Pts
SOUTH AFRICA	6	5	1	0	10	3	16
Zimbabwe	6	4	0	2	7	5	12
Burkina Faso	6	1	2	3	7	8	5
Malawi	6	0	1	5	4	12	1

(Guinea expelled, record expunged)

Results: Malawi 1, Burkina Faso 1; Zimbabwe 0, South Africa 2 (abandoned 82 mins, score stood); South Africa 1, Burkina Faso 0; Burkina Faso 1, Zimbabwe 2; Malawi 1, South Africa 2; Zimbabwe 2, Malawi 0; Burkina Faso 4, Malawi 2; South Africa 2, Zimbabwe 1; Burkina Faso 1, South Africa 1; South Africa 2, Malawi 0; Zimbabwe 1, Burkina Faso 0; Malawi 0, Zimbabwe 1.

FOOTBALL CONFEDERATION

	P	W	D	L	F	A	Pts
COSTA RICA	10	7	2	1	17	7	23
MEXICO	10	5	2	3	16	9	17
USA	10	5	2	3	11	8	17
Honduras	10	4	2	4	17	17	14
Jamaica	10	2	2	6	7	14	8
Trinidad & Tobago	10	1	2	7	5	18	5

Results: Costa Rica 2, Honduras 2; Jamaica 1, Trinidad & Tobago 0; USA 2, Mexico 0; Mexico 4, Jamaica 0; Costa Rica 3, Trinidad & Tobago 0; Honduras 1, USA 2; Jamaica 1, Honduras 1; Trinidad & Tobago 1, Mexico 1; USA 1, Costa Rica 1; Jamaica 0, USA 0; Mexico 1, Costa Rica 2; Trinidad & Tobago 2, Honduras 4; Costa Rica 2, Jamaica 1; Honduras 3, Mexico 1; USA 2, Trinidad & Tobago 0; Trinidad & Tobago 1, Jamaica 2; Honduras 2, Costa Rica 3; Mexico 1, USA 0; Trinidad & Tobago 0, Costa Rica 2; USA 2, Honduras 3; Jamaica 1, Mexico 2; Costa Rica 2, USA 0; Honduras 1, Jamaica 0; Mexico 3, Trinidad & Tobago 0; Costa Rica 0, Mexico 0; Honduras 0, Trinidad & Tobago 1; USA 2, Jamaica 1; Jamaica 0, Costa Rica 1; Mexico 3, Honduras 0; Trinidad & Tobago 0, USA 0.

OCEANIA

GROUP 1

	P	W	D	L	F	A	Pts
Australia	4	4	0	0	66	0	12
Fiji	4	3	0	1	27	4	9
Tonga	4	2	0	2	7	30	6
Samoa	4	1	0	3	9	18	3
American Samoa	4	0	0	4	0	57	0

Results: Samoa 0, Tonga 1; Fiji 13, American Samoa 0; Tonga 0, Australia 22; American Samoa 0, Samoa 8; Samoa 1, Fiji 6; Australia 31, American Samoa 0; Fiji 0, Australia 2; American Samoa 0, Tonga 5; Australia 11, Samoa 0; Tonga 1, Fiji 8. (All games played at Coffs Harbour, Australia).

GROUP 2

	P	W	D	L	F	A	Pts
New Zealand	4	4	0	0	19	1	12
Tahiti	4	3	0	1	14	6	9
Solomon Islands	4	2	0	2	17	10	6
Vanuatu	4	1	0	3	11	21	3
Cook Islands	4	0	0	4	2	25	0

Results: Vanuatu 1, Tahiti 6; Solomon Islands 9, Cook Islands 1; Tahiti 0, New Zealand 5; Cook Islands 1, Vanuatu 8; Vanuatu 2, Solomon Islands 7; New Zealand 2, Cook Islands 0; Solomon Islands 1, New Zealand 5; Cook Islands 0, Tahiti 6; New Zealand 7, Vanuatu 0; Tahiti 2, Solomon Islands 0. (All games played in Auckland, New Zealand).

Group play-off: New Zealand 0, Australia 2; Australia 4, New Zealand 1 (Australia won 6-1 on agg).

ASIA

GROUP 1

	P	W	D	L	F	A	Pts
SAUDI ARABIA	8	5	2	1	17	8	17
Iran	8	4	3	1	10	7	15
Bahrain	8	2	4	2	8	10	10
Iraq	8	2	1	5	9	8	7
Thailand	8	0	4	4	5	15	4

Results: Iraq 4, Thailand 0; Saudi Arabia 1, Bahrain 1; Bahrain 2, Iraq 0; Iran 2, Saudi Arabia 0; Saudi Arabia 1, Iraq 0; Thailand 0, Iran 0; Bahrain 1, Thailand 1; Iraq 1, Iran 2; Iran 0, Bahrain 0; Thailand 1, Saudi Arabia 3; Bahrain 0, Saudi Arabia 4; Thailand 1, Iraq 1; Iraq 1, Bahrain 0; Saudi Arabia 2, Iran 2; Iran 1, Thailand 0; Iraq 1, Saudi Arabia 2; Iran 2, Iraq 1; Thailand 1, Bahrain 1; Bahrain 3, Iran 1; Saudi Arabia 4, Thailand 1.

GROUP 2

	P	W	D	L	F	A	Pts
CHINA	8	6	1	1	13	2	19
Uae	8	3	2	3	10	11	11
Uzbekistan	8	3	1	4	13	14	10
Qatar	8	2	3	3	10	10	9
Oman	8	1	3	4	7	16	6

Results: Qatar 0, Oman 0; United Arab Emirates 4, Uzbekistan 1; China 3, United Arab Emirates 0; Uzbekistan 2, Qatar 1; United Arab Emirates 0, Qatar 2; Oman 0, China 2; Qatar 1, China 1; Uzbekistan 5, Oman 0; Oman 1 United Arab Emirates 1; China 2, Uzbekistan 0; Oman 0, Qatar 3; Uzbekistan 0, United Arab Emirates 1; United Arab Emirates 0, China 1; Qatar 2, Uzbekistan 2; Qatar 1, United Arab Emirates 2; China 1, Oman 0; Oman 4, Uzbekistan 2; China 3, Qatar 0; United Arab Emirates 2, Oman 2; Uzbekistan 1, China 0.

Group play-off: Iran 1, United Arab Emirates 0; United Arab Emirates 0, Iran 3 (Iran won 4-0 on agg).

QUALIFYING PLAY-OFFS

Europe, first legs: Austria 0, Turkey 1; Belgium 1, Czech Republic 0; Slovenia 2, Romania 1; Ukraine 1, Germany 1. **Second legs:** Czech Republic 0, Belgium 1 (Belgium won 2-0 on agg); Germany 4, Ukraine 1 (Germany won 5-2 on agg); Romania 1, Slovenia 1 (Slovenia won 3-2 on agg); Turkey 5, Austria 0 (Turkey won 6-0 on agg).

Europe/Asia, first leg: Republic of Ireland 2, Iran 0. **Second leg:** Iran 1, Republic of Ireland 0 (**Republic of Ireland won** 2-1 on agg).

South America/Oceania first leg: Australia 1, Uruguy 0. **Second leg:** Uruguay 3, Australia 0 (Uruguay won 3-1 on agg.

• France qualified as holders, along with Japan and South Korea as joint hosts.

WORLD CUP FINALS
MATCH-BY-MATCH SUMMARIES

Match 1 – Friday, May 31 (Group A, Seoul, 62,561)
FRANCE 0, SENEGAL 1

France (4-2-3-1): Barthez, Thuram, Leboeuf, Desailly, Lizarazu, Vieira, Petit, Wiltord (D. Cisse 80), Djorkaeff (Dugarry 59), Henry, Trezeguet. **Booked:** Petit.

Senegal (4-1-4-1): Sylva, Coly, Diatta, P. M. Diop, Daf, A. Cisse, N'Diaye, P. B. Diop, Diao, Fadiga, Diouf. **Scorer:** Diop (30). **Booked:** A. Cisse.

Referee: A. Bujsaim (United Arab Emirates). **Half-time:** 0-1.

Match 2 – Saturday, June 1 (Group E, Niigata, 33,679)
REPUBLIC OF IRELAND 1, CAMEROON 1

Rep. of Ireland (4-4-2): Given, Kelly, Breen, Staunton, Harte (Reid 77), McAteer (Finnan 46), Holland, Kinsella, Kilbane, Keane, Duff. **Scorer:** Holland (52). **Booked:** McAteer, Finnan, Reid.

Cameroon (3-5-2): Alioum, Kalla, Song, Tchato, Geremi, Lauren, Foe, Olembe, Wome, Mboma (Suffo 69), Eto'o. **Scorer:** Mboma (39). **Booked:** Kalla.

Referee: T. Kamikawa (Japan). **Half-time:** 0-1.

Match 3 – Saturday, June 1 (Group A, Ulsan, 30,157)
URUGUAY 1, DENMARK 2

Uruguay (4-3-1-2): Carini, Mendez, Sorondo, Montero, Rodriguez (Magallanes 87), Varela, Garcia, Guigou, Recoba (Regueiro 80), Abreu (Morales 88), Silva. **Scorer:** Rodriguez (47). **Booked:** Mendez.

Denmark (4-4-2): Sorensen, Helveg, Laursen, Henriksen, Heintze (Jensen 58), Rommedahl, Tofting, Gravesen, Gronkjaer (Jorgensen 70), Tomasson, Sand (Poulsen 89). **Scorer:** Tomasson (45, 83). **Booked:** Heintze, Laursen.

Referee: S. Mane (Kuwait). **Half-time:** 0-1.

Match 4 – Saturday, June 1 (Group E, Sapporo, 33,679)
GERMANY 8, SAUDI ARABIA 0

Germany (3-5-2): Kahn, Metzelder, Ramelow (Jeremies 46), Linke, Frings, Hamann, Schneider, Ballack, Ziege, Jancker (Bierhoff 67), Klose (Neuville 77). **Scorers:** Klose (20, 25, 69), Ballack (40), Jancker (45), Linke (73), Bierhoff (84), Schneider (90). **Booked:** Ziege, Hamann.

Saudi Arabia (4-4-2): Al-Deayea, Tukar, Sulaimane, Al-Solaimani, A. Al-Dosari, K. Al-Dosari (Al-Shahrani 46), Noor, Al-Temyat (Al-Khathran 46), Al-Waked, Al-Jaber, Al-Yami (Al-Dosary 77). **Booked:** Noor.

Referee: U. Aquino (Paraguay). **Half-time:** 4-0.

Match 5 – Sunday, June 2 (Group F, Ibaraki, 34,050)
ARGENTINA 1, NIGERIA 0

Argentina (3-4-3): Cavallero, Pochettino, Samuel, Placente, Zanetti, Veron (Aimar 78), Simeone, Sorin, Ortega, Batistuta (Crespo 81), Claudio Lopez (Kily Gonzalez 46). **Scorer:** Batistuta (63). **Booked:** Samuel, Simeone.

Nigeria (4-4-2): Shorunmu, Sodje (Christopher 73), West, Okoronkwo, Babayaro, Okocha, Yobo, Kanu (Ikedia 48), Lawal, Ogbeche, Aghahowa. **Booked:** Sodje.

Referee: G. Veissiere (France). **Half-time:** 0-0.

Match 6 – Sunday, June 2 (Group B, Busan, 25,186)
PARAGUAY 2, SOUTH AFRICA 2

Paraguay (3-5-2): Tavarelli, Ayala, Gamarra, Caniza, Alvarenga (Gavilan 66), Struway (Franco 86), Acuna, Caceres, Arce, Campos (Morinigo 72), Santa Cruz. **Scorers:** Santa Cruz (39), Arce (55). **Booked:** Caceres, Caniza, Tavarelli, Franco.

South Africa (4-4-2): Arendse, Nzama, Radebe, Issa (Mukasi 27), Carnell, T. Mokoena, A. Mokoena, Sibaya, Fortune, McCarthy (Koumantarakis 78), Zuma. **Scorers:** Struway (64 og), Fortune (90 pen). **Booked:** Issa, McCarthy, Zuma, A.Mokoena.

Referee: L. Michel (Slovakia). **Half-time:** 1-0.

Match 7 – Sunday, June 2 (Group F, Saitama, 52,721)
ENGLAND 1, SWEDEN 1

England (4-4-2): Seaman, Mills, Ferdinand, Campbell, A. Cole, Beckham (Dyer 63), Scholes, Hargreaves, Heskey, Owen, Vassell (J. Cole 73). **Scorer:** Campbell (24). **Booked:** Campbell.

Sweden (4-4-2): Hedman, Mellberg, Mjallby, Jakobsson, Lucic, Linderoth, Alexandersson, Ljungby, M. Svensson (A. Svensson 55), Allback (Andersson 80), Larsson. **Scorer:** Alexandersson (59). **Booked:** Allback, Jakobsson.

Referee: C. Simon (Brazil). **Half-time:** 1-0.

Match 8 – Sunday, June 2 (Group B, Gwangju, 28,598)
SPAIN 3, SLOVENIA 1

Spain (4-4-2): Iker Casillas, Puyol, Hierro, Nadal, Juanfran (Romero 83), Luis Enrique (Helguera 73), Baraja, Valeron, De Pedro, Tristan (Morientes 66), Raul. **Scorers:** Raul (44), Valeron (74), Hierro (88 pen). **Booked:** Valeron.

Slovenia (3-4-2-1): Simeunovic, Milinovic, Galic, Knavs, Novak (Gajser 77), Ceh, Pavlin, Karic, Zahovic (Acimovic 62), Osterc (Cimirotic 56), Rudonja. **Scorer:** Cimirotic (82). **Booked:** Karic, Cimirotic.

Referee: M. Guezzaz (Morocco). **Half-time:** 1-0.

Match 9 – Monday, June 3 (Group G, Niigata, 32,239)
CROATIA 0, MEXICO 1

Croatia (4-3-1-2): Pletikosa, Zivkovic, R. Kovac, Simunic, Jarni, N. Kovac, Tomas, Soldo, Prosinecki (Rapaic 46), Suker (Saric 64), Boksic (Stanic 67). **Sent-off:** Zivkovic.

Mexico (3-5-2): Perez, Vidrio, Marquez, Carmona, Mercado, Caballero, Torrado, Morales, Luna, Blanco (Palencia 79), Borgetti (Hernandez 68). **Scorer:** Blanco (60 pen).

Referee: Lu Jun (China). **Half-time:** 0-0.

Match 10 – Monday, June 3 (Group C, Ulsan, 33,842)
BRAZIL 2, TURKEY 1

Brazil (4-3-2-1): Marcos, Cafu, Edmilson, Lucio, Roberto Carlos, Roque Junior, Juninho (Vampeta 73), Rivaldo, Gilberto Silva, Rivaldo, Ronaldinho (Denilson 67), Ronaldo (Luizao 73). **Scorers:** Ronaldo (50), Rivaldo (87 pen). **Booked:** Denilson.

Turkey (4-3-1-2): Rustu, Alpay, Umit Ozat, Bulent (Ilhan 65), Hakan Unsal, Fatih, Tugay (Arif 88), Emre Belozoglu, Basturk, (Umit Davala 65), Hasan Sas, Hakan Sukur. **Scorer:** Hasan Sas (45). **Booked:** Fatih, Hakan Unsal, Alpay. **Sent-off:** Alpay, Hakan Unsal.

Referee: Kim Young-joo (South Korea). **Half-time:** 0-1.

Match 11 – Monday, June 3 (Group G, Sapporo, 31,081)
ITALY 2, ECUADOR 0

Italy (4-4-2): Buffon, Panucci, Nesta, Cannavaro, Maldini, Zambrotta, Di Biagio (Gattuso 70), Tommasi, Doni (Di Livio 65), Totti (Del Piero 74), Vieri. **Scorer:** Vieri (7, 27). **Booked:** Cannavaro.

Ecuador (4-4-1-1): Cevallos, De La Cruz, Hurtado, Porozo, Guerron, Chala (Asencio 85), E. Tenorio (Ayovi 60), Obregon, Mendez, Aguinaga (C. Tenorio 46), Delgado. **Booked:** Poroso, De La Cruz, Chala.

Referee: B. Hall (USA). **Half-time:** 2-0.

Match 12 – Tuesday, June 4 (Group C, Gwangju, 27,217)
CHINA 0, COSTA RICA 2

China (4-4-2): Jiang Jin, Xu Yunlong, Fan Zhiyi (Yu Genwei 73), Li Weifeng, Wu Chengying, Sun Jihai (Qu Bo 26), Li Xiaopeng, Li Tie, Ma Mingyu, Yang Chen (Su Maozhen 65), Hao Haidong. **Booked:** Li Tie, Xu Yunlong, Li Xiaopeng.

Costa Rica (4-4-2): Lonnis, Marin, Wright, Martinez, Castro, Wallace (Bryce 69), Solis, Centeno, Gomez, Fonseca (Medford 56), Wanchope (Lopez 79). **Scorers:** Gomez (61), Wright (65). **Booked:** Marin, Solis, Gomez, Centeno.

Referee: K. Vassaras (Greece). **Half-time:** 0-0.

Match 13 – Tuesday, June 4 (Group H, Saitama, 55,256)
JAPAN 2, BELGIUM 2

Japan (3-5-2): Narazaki, Matsuda, Morioka (Miyamoto 72), K. Nakata, Ichikawa, Inamoto, Toda, H. Nakata, Ono (Alex 64), Suzuki (Morishima 70), Yanagisawa. **Scorers:** Suzuki (59), Inamoto (67). **Booked:** Toda, Inamoto.

Belgium (3-5-2): De Vlieger, Van Buyten, Van Meir, Van der Heyden, Peeters, Vanderhaeghe, Simons, Walem (Sonck 70), Goor, Wilmots, Verheyen (Strupar 83). **Scorers:** Wilmots (57), Van der Heyden (75). **Booked:** Van der Heyden, Verheyen, Van Meir.

Referee: W. Mattus Vega (Costa Rica). **Half-time:** 0-0.

Match 14 – Tuesday, June 4 (Group D, Busan, 55,982)
SOUTH KOREA 2, POLAND 0

South Korea (3-4-3): Lee Woon-jae, Choi Jin-cheul, Hong Myung-bo, Kim Tae-young, Song Chong-gug, Kim Nam-il, Yoo Sang-chul (Lee Chun-soo 62), Lee Eul-yong, Park Ji-sung, Hwang Sun-hong (Ahn Jung-hwan 50), Seol Ki-hyeon (Cha Doo-ri 90). **Scorers:** Hwang Sun-hong (26), Yoo Sang-chul (53). **Booked:** Park Ji-sung, Ch Doo-ri.

Poland (4-4-2): Dudek, Hajto, Bak (Klos 51), Waldoch, Michal Zewlakow, Kozminski, Kaluzny (Marcin Zewlakow 65), Swierczewski, Krzynowek, Olisadebe, Zurawski (Kryszalowicz 46). **Booked:** Krzynowek, Hajto, Swierczewski.

Referee: O. Ruiz (Colombia). **Half-time:** 1-0.

Match 15 – Wednesday, June 5 (Group H, Kobe, 30,957)
RUSSIA 2, TUNISIA 0

Russia (3-5-2): Nigmatullin, Kovtun, Onopko, Nikiforov, Solomatin, Semshov (Khokhlov 46), Karpin, Titov, Izmailov (Alenichev 78), Beschastnykh (Sychev 55), Pimenov. **Scorers:** Titov (59), Karpin (64 pen). **Booked:** Semshov, Alenichev.

Tunisia (5-3-2): Boumnijel, Badra (Zitouni 84), Mkacher, Trabelsi, Bouzaiane, Jaidi, Gabsi (Mhadhebi 67), Bouazizi, Ben Achour, Jaziri, Sellimi (Baya 67). **Booked:** Jaziri, Gabsi.

Referee: P. Prendergast (Jamaica). **Half-time:** 0-0.

Match 16 – Wednesday, June 5 (Group D, Suwon, 37,306)
UNITED STATES 3, PORTUGAL 2

United States (4-1-3-2): Friedel, Agoos, Pope (Llamosa 79), Mastroeni, Sanneh, Hejduk, O'Brien, Beasley, Donovan (Moore 75), Stewart (Jones 46), McBride. **Scorers:** O'Brien (4), Jorge Costa (30 og), McBride (36). **Booked:** Beasley.

Portugal (5-3-2): Vitor Baia, Jorge Costa (Jorge Andrade 73), Beto, Fernando Couto, Rui Jorge (Paulo Bento 68), Sergio Conceicao, Rui Costa (Nuno Gomes 80), Petit, Figo, Joao Pinto, Pauleta. **Scorers:** Beto (40), Agoos (71 og). **Booked:** Beto, Petit.

Referee: B. Moreno (Ecuador). **Half-time:** 3-1.

Match 17 – Wednesday, June 5 (Group E, Ibaraki, 35,854)
GERMANY 1, REPUBLIC OF IRELAND 1

Germany (3-5-2): Kahn, Linke, Ramelow, Metzelder, Frings, Schneider (Jeremies 90), Hamann, Ballack, Ziege, Jancker (Bierhoff 74), Klose (Bode 86). **Scorer:** Klose (19).

Rep. of Ireland (4-4-2): Given, Kelly (Quinn 72), Breen, Staunton (Cunningham 88), Harte (Reid 72), Finnan, Holland, Kinsella, Kilbane, Keane, Duff. **Scorer:** Keane (90).

Referee: K. Nielsen (Denmark). **Half-time:** 1-0.

Match 18 – Thursday, June 6 (Group A, Daegu, 43,500)
DENMARK 1, SENEGAL 1

Denmark (4-4-2): Sorensen, Helveg, Laursen, Henriksen, Heintze, Gronkjaer (Jorgensen 49), Gravesen (Poulsen 62), Tofting, Rommedahl (Lovernkrands 86), Tomasson, Sand. **Scorer:** Tomasson (16 pen). **Booked:** Sand, Tomasson, Helveg, Poulsen.

Senegal (4-4-2): Sylva, Coly, P. M. Diop, Diatta, Sarr (S. Camara 46) (Beye 82), Diao, N'Diaye (H. Camara 46), P. B. Diop, Fadiga, Daf, Diouf. **Scorer:** Diao (52). **Booked:** Fadiga, Diao. **Sent-off:** Diao.

Referee: C. Batres (Guatemala). **Half-time:** 1-0.

Match 19 – Thursday, June 6 (Group E, Saitama, 52,328)
CAMEROON 1, SAUDI ARABIA 0

Cameroon (4-4-2): Alioum, Wome (Njanka 80), Tchato, Song, Kalla, Geremi, Lauren, Foe, Ngom Kome (Olembe 46), Eto'o, Mboma (Ndiefi 63). **Scorer:** Eto'o (65). **Booked:** Wome.

Saudi Arabia (3-5-2): Al-Deayea, Al-Jahani, Tukar, Zubromawi (A. Al-Dosari 62), Al-Shehri, I. Al-Shahrani, Sulamani, Khathran (Moor 81), A. Al-Shahrani, Al-Temyat, O. Al-Dosari (Al-Yami 35). **Booked:** Al-Yami.

Referee: T. Hauge (Norway). **Half-time:** 0-0.

Match 20 – Thursday, June 6 (Group A, Busan, 38,289)
FRANCE 0, URUGUAY 0

France (4-2-3-1): Barthez, Thuram, Lebouef (Candela 16), Desailly, Lizarazu, Vieira, Petit, Wiltord (Dugarry 90), Micoud, Henry, Trezeguet (Cisse 81). **Booked:** Petit. **Sent-off:** Henry.

Uruguay (3-4-1-2): Carini, Lembo, Sorondo, Montero, Varela, Romero (De Los Santos 71), Garcia, Rodriguez (Guigou 73), Recoba, Silva (Magallanes 60), Abreu. **Booked:** Garcia, Abreu, Romero, Silva.

Referee: F. Ramos Rizo (Mexico). **Half-time:** 0-0.

Match 21 – Friday, June 7 (Group F, Kobe, 36,194)
SWEDEN 2, NIGERIA 1

Sweden (4-4-2): Hedman, Mellberg, Jakobsson, Mjallby, Lucic, Alexandersson, Linderoth, A. Svensson (M. Svensson 84), Ljungberg, Allback (Andersson 64), Larsson. **Scorers:** Larsson (35, 63 pen). **Booked:** Mjallby, Alexandersson.

Nigeria (4-4-2): Shorunmu, Yobo, West, Okoronkwo, Udeze, Christopher, Okocha, Utaka, Babayaro (Kanu 66), Ogbeche (Ikedia 71), Aghahowa. **Scorer:** Aghahowa (27). **Booked:** West.

Referee: R. Ortube (Bolivia). **Half-time:** 1-1.

Match 22 – Friday, June 7 (Group B, Jeonju, 24,000)
SPAIN 3, PARAGUAY 1

Spain (4-4-2): Iker Casillas, Puyol, Hierro, Nadal, Juanfran, Luis Enrique (Helguera 46), Baraja, Valeron (Xavi 85), De Pedro, Tristan (Morientes 46), Raul. **Scorers:** Morientes (53, 69), Hierro (83 pen). **Booked:** Baraja.

Paraguay (3-4-1-2): Chilavert, Caceres, Ayala, Gamarra, Arce, Acuna, Paredes, Caniza (Struway 78), Gavilan, Santa Cruz, Cardozo (Campos 63). **Scorer:** Puyol (10 og). **Booked:** Arce, Gavilan, Santa Cruz.

Referee: G. Ghandour (Egypt). **Half-time:** 0-1.

Match 23 – Friday, June 7 (Group F, Sapporo, 35,927)
ARGENTINA 0, ENGLAND 1

Argentina (3-4-1-2): Cavallero, Pochettino, Samuel, Placente, Zanetti, Simeone, Sorin, Kily Gonzalez (Claudio Lopez 65), Veron (Aimar 46), Ortega, Batistuta (Crespo 59). **Booked:** Batistuta.

England (4-4-2): Seaman, Mills, Ferdinand, Campbell, A. Cole, Beckham, Butt, Hargreaves (Sinclair 19), Scholes, Owen (Bridge 80), Heskey (Sheringham 55). **Scorer:** Beckham (44 pen). **Booked:** Cole, Heskey.

Referee: P. Collina (Italy). **Half-time:** 0-1.

Match 24 – Saturday, June 8 (Group B, Daegu, 47,226)
SOUTH AFRICA 1, SLOVENIA 0

South Africa (4-4-2): Arendse, Nzama, A. Mokoena, Radebe, Carnell, Zuma, T. Mokoena, Sibaya, Fortune (Pule 83), Nomvethe (Buckley 71), McCarthy (Koumantarakis 80). **Scorer:** Nomvethe (4). **Booked:** Radebe.

Slovenia (3-5-2): Simeunovic, Milinovic, Vugdalic, Knavs (Bulajic 60), Novak, Acimovic (N. Ceh), A. Ceh, Pavlin, Karic, Cimerotic (Osterc 41), Rudonja. **Booked:** Vugdalic, Milinovic, A.Ceh, Pavlin.

Referee: A. Sanchez (Argentina). **Half-time:** 1-0.

Match 25 – Saturday, June 8 (Group G, Ibaraki, 36,472)
ITALY 1, CROATIA 2

Italy (4-4-1-1): Buffon, Panucci, Nesta (Materazzi 24), Cannavaro, Maldini, Zambrotta, Tommasi, Zanetti, Doni (Inzaghi 79), Totti, Vieri. **Scorer:** Vieri (56). **Booked:** Vieri.

Croatia (4-3-2-1): Pletikosa, Saric, R. Kovac, Simunic, Jarni, N. Kovac, Tomas, Soldo (Vranjes 63), Vugrinec (Olic 57), Rapaic (Simic 79), Boksic. **Scorers:** Olic (73), Rapaic (76). **Booked:** R. Kovac.

Referee: G. Poll (England). **Half-time:** 0-0.

Match 26 – Saturday, June 8 (Group C, Seogwipo, 36,750)
BRAZIL 4, CHINA 0

Brazil (3-3-3-1): Marcos, Lucio, Roque Junior, Anderson Polga, Cafu, Gilberto Silva, Roberto Carlos, Rivaldo, Juninho (Ricardinho 70), Ronaldinho (Denilson 46), Ronaldo (Edilson 71). **Scorers:** Roberto Carlos (15), Rivaldo (32), Ronaldinho (45 pen), Ronaldo (55). **Booked:** Ronaldinho, Roque Junior.

China (4-4-2): Jiang Jin, Xu Yunlong, Du Wei, Li Weifeng, Wu Chengying, Li Xiaopeng, Zhao Junzhe, Li Tie, Ma Mingyu (Yang Pu 62), Hao Haidong (Qu Bo 75), Qi Hong (Shao Jiayi 66).

Referee: A. Frisk (Sweden). **Half-time:** 3-0.

Match 27 – Sunday, June 9 (Group G, Miyagi, 45,601)
MEXICO 2, ECUADOR 1

Mexico (4-4-2): Perez, Vidrio, Marquez, Carmona, Morales, Arellano, Rodriguez (Caballero 86), Torrado, Luna, Borgetti (Hernandez 76), Blanco (Mercado 90). **Scorers:** Borgetti (28), Torrado (57). **Booked:** Torrado.

Ecuador (4-4-2): Cevallos, De La Cruz, Hurtado, Poroso, Guerron, Obregon (Aguinaga 58), Mendez, E. Tenorio (Ayovi 34), Chala, Delgado, Kaviedes (C. Tenorio 48). **Scorer:** Delgado (5). **Booked:** Kaviedes, Cevallos, Guerron, C. Tenorio, Delgado,

Referee: M. Daami (Tunisia). **Half-time:** 1-1.

Match 28 – Sunday, June 9 (Group C, Incheon, 42,229)
COSTA RICA 1, TURKEY 1

Costa Rica (3-4-3): Lonnis, Martinez, Wright, Marin, Wallace (Bryce 77), Solis, Centeno (Medford 67), Castro, Gomes, Wanchope, Lopez (Parks 77). **Scorer:** Parks (86). **Booked:** Martinez, Castro.

Turkey (4-3-1-2): Rustu, Fatih, Umit Ozat, Emre Asik, Ergun, Umit Davala, Tugay (Arif 88), Emre Belozoglu, Basturk (Kahveci 79), Hasan Sas, Hakan Sukur (Ilhan 75). **Scorer:** Emre Belozoglu (56). **Booked:** Emre Asik, Tugay, Emre Belozoglu.

Referee: C. Codjia (Benin). **Half-time:** 0-0.

Match 29 – Sunday, June 9 (Group H, Yokohama, 66,108)
JAPAN 1, RUSSIA 0

Japan (3-5-2): Narazaki, Matsuda, Miyamoto, K. Nakata, Myojin, Inamoto (Fukunishi 85), Toda, H. Nakata, Ono (Hattori 75), Suzuki (Nakayama 72), Yanagisawa. **Scorer:** Inamoto (51). **Booked:** Myamoto, K. Nakata, Nakayama.

Russia (3-5-2): Nigmatullin, Kovtun, Nikiforov, Onopko, Solomatin, Karpin, Titov, Smertin (Beschastnykh 57), Semshov, Izmailov (Khokhlov 52), Pimenov (Sychev 46). **Booked:** Pimenov, Solomatin, Khokhlov.

Referee: M. Merk (Germany). **Half-time:** 0-0.

Match 30 – Monday, June 10 (Group D, Daegu, 60,778)
SOUTH KOREA 1, UNITED STATES 1

South Korea (3-5-2): Lee Woon-jae, Choi Jin-cheol, Hong Myung-bo, Kim Tae-young, Song Chong-gug, Kim Nam-il, Yoo Sang-chul (Choi Yong-soo 69), Lee Eul-yong, Park Ji-sung (Lee Chun-soo 37), Seol Ki-hyeon, Hwang Sun-hong (Ahn Jung-hwan 55). **Scorer:** Ahn Jung-hwan (78). **Booked:** Hong Myung-bo.

United States (4-4-2): Friedel, Sanneh, Pope, Agoos, Hejduk, Donovan, Reyna, O'Brien, Beasley (Lewis 74), Mathis (Wolff 82), McBride. **Scorer:** Mathis (24). **Booked:** Hejduk, Agoos.

Referee: U. Meier (Switzerland). **Half-time:** 0-1.

Match 31 – Monday, June 10 (Group H, Oita, 37,900)
TUNISIA 1, BELGIUM 1

Tunisia (4-4-1-1): Boumnijel, Trabelsi, Jaidi, Badra, Bouzaine, Gabsi (Sellimi 67), Bouazizi, Ghodhbane, Melki (Baya 89), Ben Achour, Jaziri (Zitouni 78). **Scorer:** Bouzaine (17). **Booked:** Gabsi, Ghodhbane, Trabelsi, Melki.

Belgium (4-3-2-1): De Vlieger, Deflandre, De Boeck, Van Buyten, Van der Heyden, Vanderhaeghe, Simons (Mpenza 74), Goor, Verheyen (Vermant 46), Wilmots, Strupar (Sonck 46). **Scorer:** Wilmots (13). **Booked:** Van Buyten.

Referee: M. Shield (Australia). **Half-time:** 1-1.

Match 32 – Monday, June 10 (Group D, Jeonju, 31,000)
PORTUGAL 4, POLAND 0

Portugal (4-4-2): Vitor Baia, Frechaut (Beto 63), Fernando Couto, Jorge Costa, Rui Jorge, Sergio Conceicao (Capucho 69), Petit, Paulo Bento, Figo, Pauleta, Joao Pinto (Rui Costa 60). **Scorers:** Pauleta (14, 65, 77), Rui Costa (88). **Booked:** Frechaut, Jorge Costa, Rui Jorge.

Poland (4-4-2): Dudek, Kozminski, Hajto, Waldoch, Kaluzny (Bak 16), Zurawski (Marcin Zewlakow 56), Swierczewski, Krzynowek, Michal Zewlakow (Rzasa 71), Olisadebe, Kryszalowicz. **Booked:** Swierczewski, Bak.

Referee: H. Dallas (Scotland). **Half-time:** 1-0.

Match 33 – Tuesday, June 11 (Group A, Incheon, 48,100)
DENMARK 2, FRANCE 0

Denmark (4-1-4-1): Sorensen, Helveg, Laursen, Henriksen, Jensen, Poulsen (Bogelund 75), Rommedahl, Tofting (Nielsen 80), Gravesen, Jorgensen (Gronkjaer 46), Tomasson. **Scorers:** Rommedahl (22), Tomasson (67). **Booked:** Poulsen, Jensen.

France (4-2-3-1): Barthez, Candela, Thuram, Desailly, Lizarazu, Vieira (Micoud 71), Makelele, Wiltord (Djorkaeff 84), Zidane, Dugarry (Cisse 54), Trezeguet. **Booked:** Dugarry.

Referee: V. Melo Pereira (Portugal). **Half-time:** 1-0.

Match 34 – Tuesday, June 11 (Group A, Suwon, 33,681)
SENEGAL 3, URUGUAY 3

Senegal (4-5-1): Sylva, Coly (Beye 63), Diatta, P. M. Diop, Daf, Camara (N'Diaye 67), Ndour (Faye 76), Cisse, P. B. Diop, Fadiga, Diouf. **Scorers:** Fadiga (20 pen), Diop (26, 38). **Booked:** Camara, Daf, Coly, P. B. Diop, Diouf, Fadiga, Beye.

Uruguay (3-5-2): Carini, Lembo, Montero, Sorondo (Regueiro 31), Varela, Garcia, Romero (Forlan 46), Rodriguez, Recoba, Abreu (Morales 46), Silva. **Scorers:** Morales (47), Forlan (69), Recoba (89 pen). **Booked:** Romero, Carini, Garcia, Rodriguez, Montero.

Referee: J. Wegereef (Holland). **Half-time:** 3-0.

Match 35 – Tuesday, June 11 (Group E, Shizuoka, 47,085)
CAMEROON 0, GERMANY 2

Cameroon (4-4-2): Alioum, Wome, Tchato (Suffo 53), Song, Kalla, Geremi, Lauren, Foe, Olembe (Ngom Kome 64), Eto'o, Mboma (Job 80). **Booked:** Foe, Song, Tchato, Geremi, Olembe, Suffo, Lauren. **Sent-off:** Suffo.

Germany (3-5-2): Kahn, Linke, Metzelder, Ziege, Ramelow, Hamann, Ballack, Schneider (Jeremies 80), Frings, Jancker (Bode 46), Klose (Neuville 84). **Scorers:** Bode (50), Klose (79). **Booked:** Jancker, Hamann, Ballack, Ramelow, Kahn, Ziege, Frings. **Sent-off:** Ramelow.

Referee: A. Lopez Nieto (Spain). **Half-time:** 0-0.

Match 36 – Tuesday, June 11 (Group E, Yokohama, 65,320)
SAUDI ARABIA 0, REPUBLIC OF IRELAND 3

Saudi Arabia (5-4-1): Al-Deayea, Al-Jahani (A. Al-Dosari 78), Tukar, Zubromawi (Al-Dosary 67), Al-Shehri, Sulimani, Al-Shahrani, Al-Temyat, K. Al-Dosari, Khathran (Al-Shlhoub 66), Al-Yami. **Booked:** Al-Temyat.

Rep. of Ireland (4-4-2): Given, Finnan, Breen, Staunton, Harte (Quinn 46), Kelly (McAteer 79), Holland, Kinsella (Carsley 88), Kilbane. Keane, Duff. **Scorers:** Keane (7), Breen (62), Duff (87). **Booked:** Staunton.

Referee: F. Ndoye (Senegal). **Half-time:** 0-1.

Match 37 – Wednesday, June 12 (Group F, Miyagi, 45,777)
SWEDEN 1, ARGENTINA 1

Sweden (4-4-2): Hedman, Lucic, Mellberg, Mjallby, Jakobsson, Alexandersson, M. Svensson, A. Svensson (Jonsson 68), Linderoth, Allback (Andersson 46), Larsson (Ibramimovic 88). **Scorer:** A. Svensson (59). **Booked:** Larsson, M. Svensson.

Argentina (3-5-2): Cavallero, Pochettino, Samuel, Chamot, Sorin (Veron 63), Aimar, Almeyda (Kily Gonzalez 63), Zanetti, Ortega, Claudio Lopez, Batistuta (Crespo 58). **Scorer:** Crespo (88). **Booked:** Chamot, Almeyda, Kily Gonzalez. **Sent-off:** Caniggia.

Referee: A. Bujsaim (United Arab Emirates). **Half-time:** 0-0.

Match 38 – Wednesday, June 12 (Group F, Osaka, 44,864)
NIGERIA 0, ENGLAND 0

Nigeria (4-4-2): Enyeama, Sodje, Yobo, Okoronkwo, Udeze, Okocha, Christopher, Obiorah, Opabunmi (Ikedia 86), Aghahowa, Akwuegbu.

England (4-4-2): Seaman, Mills, Ferdinand, Campbell, A. Cole (Bridge 85), Beckham, Butt, Scholes, Sinclair, Owen (Vassell 77), Heskey (Sheringham 69).

Referee: B. Hall (United States). **Half-time:** 0-0.

Match 39 – Wednesday, June 12 (Group B, Daejeon, 31,024)
SOUTH AFRICA 2, SPAIN 3

South Africa (4-4-2): Arendse, Nzama, A. Mokoena, Radebe (Molefe 79), Carnell, Zuma, Sibaya, T. Mokoena, Fortune (Lekgetho 83), Nomvethe (Koumantarakis 74), McCarthy. **Scorers:** McCarthy (31), Radebe (53). **Booked:** Nomvethe, Nzama, Carnell, A. Mokoena.

Spain (4-4-2): Iker Casillas, Curro Torres, Helguera, Nadal, Romero, Joaquin, Albelda (Sergio 53), Xavi, Mendieta, Morientes (Luque 75), Raul (Luis Enrique 82). **Scorers:** Raul (4, 56), Mendieta (45).

Referee: S. Mane (Kuwait). **Half-time:** 1-2.

Match 40 – Wednesday, June 12 (Group B, Seogwipo, 30,176)
SLOVENIA 1, PARAGUAY 3

Slovenia (4-4-2): Dabanovic, Bulajic, Milinovic, Karic, Tavcar, D. Novak, A. Ceh, Pavlin (Rudonja 40), Acimovic (N. Ceh 63), Cimirotic, Osterc (Tiganj 78). **Scorer:** Acimovic (45). **Booked:** Pavlin, Karic, Rudonja, Milinovic. **Sent-off:** N. Ceh.

Paraguay (3-5-2): Chilavert, Caceres, Ayala, Gamarra, Arce, Paredes, Acuna, Alvarenga (Campos 54), Caniza, Cardozo (Cuevas 61) (Franco 90), Santa Cruz. **Scorers:** Cuevas (66, 84), Campos (73). **Booked:** Paredes. **Sent-off:** Paredes.

Referee: F. Ramos Rizo (Mexico). **Half-time:** 1-0.

Match 41 – Thursday, June 13 (Group C, Suwon, 38,524)
COSTA RICA 2, BRAZIL 5

Costa Rica (3-5-2): Lonnis, Martinez (Parks 74), Wright, Marin, Wallace (Bryce 46), Solis (Fonseca 65), Lopez, Centeno, Castro, Wanchope, Gomez. **Scorers:** Wanchope (40), Gomez (56).

Brazil (3-5-2): Marcos, Lucio, Edmilson, Anderson Polga, Cafu, Juninho (Ricardinho 60), Gilberto Silva, Junior, Rivaldo (Kaka 72), Ronaldo, Edilson (Kleberson 57). **Scorers:** Ronaldo (10, 13), Edmilson (38), Rivaldo (62), Junior (64). **Booked:** Cafu.

Referee: G. Ghandour (Egypt). **Half-time:** 1-3.

Match 42 – Thursday, June 13 (Group C, Seoul, 43,605)
TURKEY 3, CHINA 0

Turkey (4-3-1-2): Rustu (Catkic 35), Fatih, Bulent, Emre Asik, Hakan Unsal, Umit Davala, Tugay (Havutcu 84), Emre Belozoglu, Basturk (Ilhan 70), Hasan Sas, Hakan Sukur. **Scorers:** Hasan Sas (6), Bulent (9), Umit Davala (85). **Booked:** Emre Asik, Emre Belozoglu, Hasan Sas.

China (4-4-1-1): Jiang Jin, Xu Yunlong, Du Wei, Li Weifeng, Wu Chengying (Shao Jiayi 46), Li Xiaopeng, Zhao Junzhe, Li Tie, Yang Pu, Yang Chen (Yu Genwei 73), Hao Haidong (Qu Bo 73). **Booked:** Yang Pu, Li Weifeng. **Sent-off:** Shao Jiayi.

Referee: O. Ruiz (Colombia). **Half-time:** 2-0.

Match 43 – Thursday, June 13 (Group G, Oita, 39,291)
MEXICO 1, ITALY 1

Mexico (3-5-2): Perez, Vidrio, Marquez, Carmona, Arellano, Rodriguez (Caballero 75), Torrado, Luna, Morales (Garcia 75), Borgetti (Palencia 80), Blanco. **Scorer:** Borgetti (34). **Booked:** Arellano, Perez.

Italy (3-4-1-2): Buffon, Cannavaro, Nesta, Maldini, Zambrotta, Tomassi, Zanetti, Panucci (Coco 63), Totti (Del Piero 78), Vieri, Inzaghi (Montella 56). **Scorer:** Del Piero (85). **Booked:** Cannavaro, Panucci, Totti, Montella, Zambrotta.

Referee: C. Simon (Brazil). **Half-time:** 1-0.

Match 44 – Thursday, June 13 (Group G, Yokohama, 65,862)
ECUADOR 1, CROATIA 0

Ecuador (4-4-2): Cevallos, De La Cruz, Hurtado, Porozo, Guerron, Mendez, Obregon (Aguinaga 40), Ayovi, Chala, Tenorio (Kaviedes 75), Delgado. **Scorer:** Mendez (48). **Booked:** Chala.

Croatia (3-5-2): Pletikosa, Simic (Vugrinec 52), N. Kovac (Vranjes 59), Simunic, Saric (Stanic 67), Tomas, Rapaic, R. Kovac, Jarni, Olic, Boksic. **Booked:** Tomas, Simunic.

Referee: W. Mattus (Costa Rica). **Half-time:** 0-0.

Match 45 – Friday, June 14 (Group H, Osaka, 45,213)
TUNISIA 0, JAPAN 2

Tunisia (4-5-1): Boumnijel, Badra, Trabelsi, Bouzaiane (Zitouni 77), Jaidi, Clayton (Mhadhebi 60), Bouazizi, Ben Achour, Ghodhbane, Melki (Baya 46), Jaziri. **Booked:** Bouazizi, Badra.

Japan (3-5-2): Narazaki, Matsuda, Miyamoto, K. Nakata, Myojin, Inamoto (Ichikawa 46), Toda, H. Nakata (Ogasawara 84), Ono, Suziki, Yanagisawa (Morisima 46). **Scorers:** Morishima (48), H. Nakata (75).

Referee: G. Veissiere (France). **Half-time:** 0-0.

Match 46 – Friday, June 14 (Group H, Shizuoka, 46,640)
BELGIUM 3 RUSSIA 2

Belgium (4-4-2): De Vlieger, Peeters, De Boeck (Van Meir 90), Van Buyten, Van Kerckhoven, Mpenza (Sonck 71), Vanderhaeghe, Walem, Goor, Verheyen (Simons 79), Wilmots. **Scorers:** Walem (7), Sonck (78), Wilmots (82). **Booked:** Vanderhaeghe.

Russia (3-5-2): Nigmatullin, Nikiforov (Sennikov 44), Onopko, Kovtun, Karpin (Kerzhakov 83), Solomatin, Titov, Smertin (Sychev 35), Alenichev, Khokhlov, Beschastnykh. **Scorers:** Beschastnykh (52), Sychev (88). **Booked:** Solomatin, Smertin, Alenichev, Sennikov.

Referee: K. Nielsen (Denmark). **Half-time:** 1-0.

Match 47 – Friday, June 14 (Group D, Incheon, 50,239)
PORTUGAL 0, SOUTH KOREA 1

Portugal (4-4-1-1): Vitor Baia, Beto, Fernando Couto, Jorge Costa, Rui Jorge (Xavier 73), Sergio Conceicao, Petit (Nuno Gomes 77), Paulo Bento, Figo, Joao Pinto (Jorge Andrade 68), Pauleta. **Booked:** Beto, Jorge Costa. **Sent-off:** Joao Pinto, Beto.

South Korea (3-1-3-3): Lee Woon-jae, Song Chong-gug, Choi Jin-cheol, Hong Myung-bo, Kim Tae-young, Yoo Sang-chul, Kim Nam-il, Lee Young-pyo, Park Ji-sung, Ahn Jung-hwan (Lee Chun-soo 90), Seol Ki-hyeon. **Scorer:** Park Ji-sung (70). **Booked:** Kim Tae-young, Seol Ki-hyeon, Kim Nam-il, Ahn Jung-hwan.

Referee: A. Sanchez (Argentina). **Half-time:** 0-0.

Match 48 – Friday, June 14 (Group D, Daejeon, 26,482)
POLAND 3, UNITED STATES 1

Poland (4-4-2): Majdan, Klos (Waldoch 89), Glowacki, Zielinski, Kozminski, Zurawski, Kucharski (Zewlakow 65), Murawski, Krzynowek, Kryszalowicz, Olisadebe (Sibik 86). **Scorers:** Olisadebe (3), Kryszalowicz (5), Zewlakow (66). **Booked:** Majdan, Kozminski, Kucharski, Olisadebe.

United States (4-3-3): Friedel, Sanneh, Pope, Agoos (Beasley 36), Hejduk, Mathis, Reyna, O'Brien, Stewart (Jones 68), McBride (Moore 58), Donovan. **Scorer:** Donovan (83). **Booked:** Hejduk.

Referee: Lu Jun (China). **Half-time:** 2-0.

HOW THE GROUPS FINISHED

GROUP A

	P	W	D	L	F	A	Pts
DENMARK	3	2	1	0	5	2	7
SENEGAL	3	1	2	0	5	4	5
Uruguay	3	0	2	1	4	5	2
France	3	0	1	2	0	3	1

GROUP B

	P	W	D	L	F	A	Pts
SPAIN	3	3	0	0	9	4	9
PARAGUAY	3	1	1	1	6	6	4
South Africa	3	1	1	1	5	5	4
Slovenia	3	0	0	3	2	7	0

GROUP C

	P	W	D	L	F	A	Pts
BRAZIL	3	3	0	0	11	3	9
TURKEY	3	1	1	1	5	3	4
Costa Rica	3	1	1	1	5	6	4
China	3	0	0	3	0	9	0

GROUP D

	P	W	D	L	F	A	Pts
SOUTH KOREA	3	2	1	0	4	1	7
UNITED STATES	3	1	1	1	5	6	4
Portugal	3	1	0	2	6	4	3
Poland	3	1	0	2	3	7	3

GROUP E

	P	W	D	L	F	A	Pts
GERMANY	3	2	1	0	11	1	7
REP. OF IRELAND	3	1	2	0	5	2	5
Cameroon	3	1	1	1	2	3	4
Saudi Arabia	3	0	0	3	0	12	0

GROUP F

	P	W	D	L	F	A	Pts
SWEDEN	3	1	2	0	4	3	5
ENGLAND	3	1	2	0	2	1	5
Argentina	3	1	1	1	2	2	4
Nigeria	3	0	1	2	1	3	1

GROUP G

	P	W	D	L	F	A	Pts
MEXICO	3	2	1	0	4	2	7
ITALY	3	1	1	1	4	3	4
Croatia	3	1	0	2	2	3	3
Ecuador	3	1	0	2	2	4	3

GROUP H

	P	W	D	L	F	A	Pts
JAPAN	3	2	1	0	5	2	7
BELGIUM	3	1	2	0	6	5	5
Russia	3	1	0	2	4	4	3
Tunisia	3	0	1	2	1	5	1

SECOND ROUND

Match 49 – Saturday, June 15 (Seogwipo, 25,176)
GERMANY 1, PARAGUAY 0

Germany (4-4-2): Kahn, Frings, Linke, Rehmer (Kehl 46), Metzelder (Baumann 60), Schneider, Jeremies, Ballack, Bode, Klose, Neuville (Asamoah 90). **Scorer:** Neuville (88). **Booked:** Schneider, Baumann, Ballack.

Paraguay (5-3-2): Chilavert, Arce, Gamarra, Ayala, Caceres, Caniza, Bonet (Gavilan 84), Acuna, Struway (Cuevas 90), Cardozo, Santa Cruz (Campos 29). **Booked:** Acuna, Cardozo. **Sent-off:** Acuna.

Referee: C. Batres (Guatemala). **Half-time:** 0-0.

Match 50 – Saturday, June 15 (Niigata, 40,582)
DENMARK 0, ENGLAND 3

Denmark (4-4-2): Sorensen, Helveg (Bogelund 7), Laursen, Henriksen, N. Jensen, Rommedahl, Tofting (C. Jensen 58), Gravesen, Tomasson, Sand, Gronkjaer. **Booked:** Tofting.

England (4-4-2): Seaman, Mills, Ferdinand, Campbell, A. Cole, Beckham, Butt, Scholes, (Dyer 49), Sinclair, Owen (Fowler 46), Heskey (Sheringham (69). **Scorers:** Ferdinand (5), Owen (22), Heskey (44). **Booked:** Mills.

Referee: M. Merk (Germany). **Half-time:** 0-3.

Match 51 – Sunday, June 16 (Oita, 39,747)
SWEDEN 1, SENEGAL 2
(aet, Senegal won with golden goal)

Sweden (4-4-2): Hedman, Lucic, Mellberg, Mjallby, Jakobsson, Alexandersson (Ibrahimovic 76), M. Svensson (Jonsson 99), A. Svensson, Linderoth, Allback (Andersson 65), Larsson. **Scorer:** Larsson (11).

Senegal (4-3-3): Sylva, Daf, P. M. Diop (Beye 66), Diatta, Coly, Faye, Cisse, P. B. Diop, Diouf, Camara, Thiaw. **Scorers:** Camara (37, 104). **Booked:** Coly, Thiaw.

Referee: U. Aquino (Paraguay). **Half-time:** 1-1.

Match 52 – Sunday, June 16 (Suwon, 38,926)
SPAIN 1, REPUBLIC OF IRELAND 1
(aet, Spain won 3-2 on pens)

Spain (4-4-2): Iker Casillas, Puyol, Hierro, Helguera, Juanfran, Luis Enrique, Baraja, Valeron, Javi, De Pedro (Mendieta 65), Morientes (Albelda 71), Raul (Luque 80). **Scorer:** Morientes (8). **Booked:** Juanfran, Baraja, Hierro.

Rep. of Ireland (4-4-2): Given, Finnan, Breen, Staunton (Cunningham 49), Harte (Connolly 82), Kelly (Quinn 54), Kinsella, Holland, Kilbane, Keane, Duff. **Scorer:** Keane (90 pen).

Penalties – Keane (0-1), Hierro (1-1), Holland (missed), Baraja (2-1), Connolly (saved), Juanfran (missed), Kilbane (saved), Valeron (missed), Finnan (2-2), Mendieta (3-2).

Referee: A. Frisk (Sweden). **Half-time:** 1-0.

Match 53 – Monday, June 17 (Jeonju, 36,380)
MEXICO 0, UNITED STATES 2

Mexico (3-5-2): Perez, Vidrio (Mercado 46), Marquez, Carmona, Arellano, Rodriguez, Torrado (Garcia Aspe 78), Luna, Morales (Hernandez 28), Borgetti, Blanco. **Booked:** Vidrio, Hernandez, Blanco, Garcia Aspe, Carmona. **Sent-off:** Marquez.

United States (3-5-2): Friedel, Sanneh, Pope, Berhalter, Reyna, Mastroeni (Llamosa 90), Donovan, O'Brien, Lewis, Wolff (Stewart 59), McBride (Jones 79). **Scorers:** McBride (8), Donovan (65). **Booked:** Pope, Mastroeni, Wolff, Berhalter, Friedel.

Referee: V. Melo Pereira (Portugal). **Half-time:** 0-1.

Match 54 – Monday, June 17 (Kobe, 40,440)
BRAZIL 2, BELGIUM 0

Brazil (3-5-2): Marcos, Lucio, Roque Junior, Edmilson, Cafu, Gilberto Silva, Rivaldo (Ricardinho 90), Juninho (Denilson 57), Roberto Carlos, Ronaldo, Ronaldinho (Kleberson 81). **Scorers:** Rivaldo (67), Ronaldo (87). **Booked:** Roberto Carlos.

Belgium (3-5-2): De Vlieger, Van Kerckhoven, Van Buyten, Peeters (Sonck 73), Verheyen, Simons, Vanderhaeghe, Walem, Goor, Mpenza, Wilmots. **Booked:** Vanderhaeghe.

Referee: P. Prendergast (Jamaica). **Half-time:** 0-0.

Match 55 – Tuesday, June 18 (Miyagi, 45,666)
JAPAN 0, TURKEY 1

Japan (3-4-1-2): Narazaki, Matsuda, Miyamoto, K. Nakata, Myojin, Toda, Inamoto (Ichikawa 46) (Morishima 86), Ono, H. Nakata, Santos (Suzuki 46), Nishizawa. **Booked:** Toda.

Turkey (4-4-2): Rustu, Hakan Unsal, Bulent, Alpay, Fatih, Ergun, Tugay, Basturk (Ilhan 90), Umit Davala (Nihat 74), Hasan Sas (Tayfur 85), Hakan Sukur. **Scorer:** Umit Davala (12). **Booked:** Alpay, Ergun, Hakan Sukur.

Referee: P. Collina (Italy). **Half-time:** 0-1.

Match 56 – Tuesday, June 18 (Daejeon, 38,588)
SOUTH KOREA 2, ITALY 1
(aet, South Korea won with golden goal)

South Korea (3-4-3): Lee Woon-jae, Choi Jin-cheul, Hong Myung-bo (Cha Du-ri 82), Kim Tae-young (Hwang Sun-hong 63), Song Chong-gug, Yoo Sang-chul, Kim Nam-il (Lee Chun-soo 68), Lee Young-pyo, Park Ji-sung, Ahn Jung-hwan, Seol Ki-hyeon. **Scorers:** Seol Ki-hyeon (88), Ahn Jung-hwan (117). **Booked:** Kim Tae-young, Song Chong-gug, Lee Chun-soo, Choi Jin-cheul.

Italy (4-3-2-1): Buffon, Panucci, Iuliano, Maldini, Coco, Zambrotta (Di Livio 72), Tommasi, Zanetti, Del Piero (Gattuso 61), Totti, Vieiri. **Scorer:** Vieri (18). **Booked:** Coco, Totti, Tommasi, Zanetti. **Sent-off:** Totti.

Referee: B. Moreno (Ecuador). **Half-time:** 0-1.

QUARTER-FINALS

Match 57 – Friday, June 21 (Shizuoka, 47,436)
ENGLAND 1, BRAZIL 2

England (4-4-2): Seaman, Mills, Ferdinand, Campbell, A. Cole (Sheringham 80), Beckham, Butt, Scholes, Sinclair (Dyer 56), Owen (Vassell 79), Heskey. **Scorer:** Owen (23). **Booked:** Scholes, Ferdinand.

Brazil (3-5-2): Marcos, Lucio, Edmilson, Roque Junior, Cafu, Kleberson, Gilberto Silva, Ronaldinho, Roberto Carlos, Ronaldo (Edilson 70), Rivaldo. **Scorers:** Rivaldo (45), Ronaldinho (50). **Sent-off:** Ronaldinho.

Referee: F. Ramos Rizo (Mexico). **Half-time:** 1-1.

Match 58 – Friday, June 21 (Ulsan, 37,337)
GERMANY 1, UNITED STATES 0

Germany (3-5-2): Kahn, Linke, Kehl, Metzelder, Frings, Schneider (Jeremies 61), Hamann, Ballack, Ziege, Neuville (Bode 79), Klose (Bierhoff 88). **Scorer:** Ballack (39). **Booked:** Kehl, Neuville.

United States (3-4-1-2): Friedel, Sanneh, Pope, Berhalter, Hejduk (Jones 65), Mastroeni (Stewart 79), O'Brien, Lewis, Reyna, Donovan, McBride (Mathis 58). **Booked:** Lewis, Pope, Reyna, Mastroeni, Berhalter.

Referee: H. Dallas (Scotland). **Half-time:** 1-0.

Match 59 – Saturday, June 22 (Gwangju, 42,114)
SPAIN 0, SOUTH KOREA 0
(aet, South Korea won 5-3 on pens)

Spain (4-4-2): Iker Casillas, Puyol, Hierro, Nadal, Romero, Joaquin, Helguera (Xavi 93), Baraja, De Pedro (Mendieta 70), Morientes, Valeron (Luis Enrique 80). **Booked:** De Pedro, Morientes.

South Korea (3-4-3): Lee Woon-jae, Choi Jin-cheol, Hong Myung-bo, Kim Tae-young (Hwang Sun-hong 90), Song Chong-gug, Kim Nam-il (Lee Eul-yong 32), Yoo Sang-chul (Lee Chun-soo 60), Lee Young-pyo, Park Ji-sung, Ahn Jung-hwan, Seol Ki-hyeon. **Booked:** Yoo Sang-chul.

Penalties – Hwang Sun-hong (0-1), Hierro (1-1), Park Ji-sung (1-2), Baraja (2-2), Seol Ki-hyeon (2-3), Xavi (3-3), Ahn Jung-hwan (3-4), Joaquin (missed), Hong Myung-bo (3-5).

Referee: G. Ghandour (Egypt). **Half-time:** 0-0.

Match 60 – Saturday, June 22 (Osaka, 44,233)
SENEGAL 0, TURKEY 1
(aet, Turkey won with golden goal)

Senegal (4-5-1): Sylva, Coly, Diatta, P. M. Diop, Daf, Camara, Cisse, P. B. Diop, Diao, Fadiga, Diouf. **Booked:** Daf, Cisse.

Turkey (3-4-2-1): Rustu, Alpay, Bulent, Fatih, Ergun, Basturk, Tugay, Umit Davala, Emre Belozoglu (Arif 90), Hasan Sas, Hakan Sukur (Ilhan 67). **Scorer:** Ilhan (94). **Booked:** Emre Belozoglu, Ilhan.

Referee: O. Ruiz (Colombia). **Half-time:** 0-0.

SEMI-FINALS

GERMANY 1, SOUTH KOREA 0

Germany (4-4-2): Kahn, Frings, Linke, Ramelow, Metzelder, Schneider (Jeremies 84), Hamann, Ballack, Bode, Klose (Bierhoff 69), Neuville (Asamoah 87). **Scorer:** Ballack (75). **Booked:** Ballack, Neuville.

South Korea (3-4-3): Lee Woon-jae, Choi Jin-cheul (Lee Min-sung 55), Hong Myung-bo (Seol Ki-hyeon 80), Kim Tae-young, Song Chong-gug, Park Ji-sung, Yoo Sang-chul, Lee Young-pyo, Cha Du-ri, Hwang Sun-hong (Ahn Jung-hwan 54), Lee Chun-soo. **Booked:** Lee Min-sung.

Referee: U. Meier (Switzerland). **Half-time:** 0-0.

Match 62 – Wednesday, June 26 (Saitama, 61,058)
BRAZIL 1, TURKEY 0

Brazil (3-4-3): Marcos, Lucio, Edmilson, Roque Junior, Cafu, Kleberson (Belletti 85), Gilberto Silva, Roberto Carlos, Edilson (Denilson 75), Ronaldo (Luizao 68), Rivaldo. **Scorer:** Ronaldo (49). **Booked:** Gilberto Silva.

Turkey (4-5-1): Rustu, Fatih, Bulent, Alpay, Ergun, Umit Davala (Izzet 74), Tugay, Basturk (Arif 88), Hasan Sas, Emre Belozoglu (Ilhan 62), Hakan Sukur. **Booked:** Tugay, Hasan Sas.

Referee: K. Nielsen (Denmark). **Half-time:** 0-0.

THIRD PLACE PLAY-OFF

Match 63 – Saturday, June 29 (Daegu, 63,483)
SOUTH KOREA 2, TURKEY 3

South Korea (3-4-3): Lee Woon-jae, Lee Min-sung, Hong Myung-bo (Kim Tae-young 46), Lee Eul-yong, Song Chong-gug, Yoo Sang-chul, Lee Young-pyo, Lee Chun-soo (Cha Doo-ri 64), Park Ji-sung, Ahn Jung-hwan, Seol Ki-hyeon (Choi Tai-uk 79). **Scorers:** Lee Eul-yong (9), Song Chong-gug (90). **Booked:** Lee Eul-yong.

Turkey (4-4-2): Rustu, Fatih, Alpay, Bulent, Ergun, Umit Davala (Okan 75), Tugay, Basturk (Tayfur 85), Emre Belozoglu (Hakan Unsal 41), Ilhan, Hakan Sukur. **Scorers:** Hakan Sukur (1), Ilhan (13, 32). **Booked:** Tugay, Rustu.

Referee: S. Mane (Kuwait). **Half-time:** 1-3.

FINAL

Match 64 – Sunday, June 30 (Yokohama, 69,029)
GERMANY 0, BRAZIL 2

Germany (3-5-2): Kahn (capt), Linke, Ramelow, Metzelder, Frings, Jeremies (Asamoah 77), Hamann, Schneider, Bode (Ziege 84), Klose (Bierhoff 74), Neuville. **Booked:** Klose. **Coach:** Rudi Voeller.

Brazil (3-4-2-1): Marcos, Lucio, Edmilson, Roque Junior, Cafu (capt), Kleberson, Gilberto Silva, Roberto Carlos, Ronaldinho (Juninho 85), Rivaldo, Ronaldo (Denilson 90). **Scorer:** Ronaldo (67,79). **Booked:** Roque Junior. **Coach:** Luiz Felipe Scolari.

Referee: P. Collina (Italy). **Half-time:** 0-0.

2002 WORLD CUP FACTS AND FIGURES

• **England squad:** 1 Seaman (Arsenal), 2 Mills (Leeds Utd.), 3 Ashley Cole (Arsenal), 4 Sinclair (West Ham Utd.), 5 Ferdinand (Leeds Utd.), 6 Campbell (Arsenal), 7 Beckham (Manchester Utd., capt), 8 Scholes (Manchester Utd.), 9 Fowler (Leeds Utd.), 10 Owen (Liverpool), 11 Heskey (Liverpool), 12 Brown (Manchester Utd.), 13 Martyn (Leeds Utd.), 14 Bridge (Southampton), 15 Keown (Arsenal), 16 Southgate (Middlesbrough), 17 Sheringham (Tottenham), 18 Hargreaves (Bayern Munich), 19 Joe Cole (West Ham Utd.), 20 Vassell (Aston Villa), 21 Butt (Manchester Utd.), 22 James (West Ham Utd.), 23 Dyer (Newcastle Utd.).

• **Republic of Ireland squad:** 1 Given (Newcastle Utd.), 2 Finnan (Fulham), 3 Harte (Leeds Utd.), 4 Cunningham (Wimbledon), 5 Staunton (Aston Villa, capt), *6 Roy Keane (Manchester Utd.), 7 McAteer (Sunderland), 8 Holland (Ipswich Town), 9 Duff (Blackburn Rov.), 10 Robbie Keane (Leeds Utd.), 11 Kilbane (Sunderland), 12 Kinsella (Charlton Athletic), 13 Connolly (Wimbledon), 14 Breen (unattached), 15 Dunne (Manchester City), 16 Kiely (Charlton Athletic), 17 Quinn (Sunderland), 18 Gary Kelly (Leeds Utd.), 19 Morrison (Crystal Palace), 20 O'Brien (Newcastle Utd.), 21 Reid (Millwall), 22 Carsley (Everton), 23 Alan Kelly (Blackburn Rov.). *Roy Keane sent home before the Finals.

• **Match venues:** Japan – Ibaraki (42,000), Kobe (42,000), Miyagi (49,000), Niigata (43,000), Oita (43,000), Osaka (45,000), Saitama (64,000), Sapporo (42,000), Shizuoka (51,000), Yokohama (71,000). South Korea – Daegu (70,000), Daejeon (42,000), Gwangju (43,000), Incheon (52,000), Jeonju (42,000), Busan (56,000), Seogwipo (42,000), Seoul (64,000), Suwon (44,000), Ulsan (43,000).

• **Ton up:** Steve Staunton became the first Republic of Ireland player to win 100 caps in the group match against Germany. He made his debut in a friendly against Tunisia in 1988 when the team was captained by Mick McCarthy. Staunton and Niall Quinn, the Republic's leading all-time scorer, announced their retirements from international football after the second round defeat by Spain.

• **Bowing out:** Mohammed Al Deayea, the Saudi Arabia goalkeeper, announced his retirement from international football after winning a record 165th cap against the Republic of Ireland.

• **Sacre bleu:** France's record of one point and no goals was the worst of any team defending the World Cup. They were also the first holders to be knocked out at the first stage since Brazil in England in 1966.

• **Yellow peril:** The record total of bookings in a Finals match (10) was broken twice in one day. There were 12 yellow cards handed out by Dutch referee Jan Wegereef in the Senegal-Uruguay game, followed by 16 – along with two sendings-off – when Cameroon played Germany in a game refereed by Antonio Lopez Nieto, of Spain.

• **Going home:** Zlatko Zahovic, Slovenia midfield player, suffered the same fate as Roy Keane when he was sent home for directing 'deeply personal abuse' at coach Srecko Katanec after being substituted against Spain.

• **Hit in the pocket:** Rivaldo was fined £5,180 by FIFA's disciplinary committee for pretending to be hit in the face by a ball struck at his shin by Hakan Unsal, the Blackburn Rovers' player who was sent off in the Brazil-Turkey match.

• **Goals galore:** Germany's 8-0 win over Saudi Arabia was the biggest in the Finals since Hungary beat El Salvador 10-1 in 1982.

• **Goal spree:** The Republic of Ireland scored more than once in a Finals game for the first time when beating Saudi Arabia 3-0.

• **Quick off the mark:** Hakan Sukur's goal after 11 seconds for Turkey against South Korea in the third place play-off was the fastest-ever in the Finals. The previous quickest was scored in 15 seconds by Czechoslovakia's Vaclav Masek against Mexico in 1962. San Marino's Davide Gualtieri holds the record for any World Cup game – seven seconds against England in 1993.

• **Dream team:** FIFA's all-time best World Cup team, the result of an international poll on its website, was: Yashin (USSR), Maldini (Italy), Beckenbauer (West Germany), Roberto Carlos (Brazil), Platini (France), Baggio (Italy), Zidane (France), Maradona (Argentina), Romario (Brazil), Cruyff (Holland), Pele (Brazil).

• **Hat-trick:** FIFA made a presentation to Cafu for becoming the first man to appear in three World Cup Finals, the Brazilian captain having come on as a substitute in 1994 against Italy and played the whole game against France four years later. This was a record fifth triumph for his country after victories in 1958, 1962, 1970 and 1994, and Brazil achieved another 'first' by winning all their seven games. But a change of rules means they will have to qualify for 2006. Hosts Germany will not.

• **Mixed fortunes:** Brazil defender Lucio had that winning feeling at last after three major defeats with Bayer Leverkusen last season. But there was more disappointment for club colleagues Michael Ballack, Oliver Neuville, Carsten Ramelow, Bernd Schneider and reserve goalkeeper Jorg Butt. They were all in the Leverkusen side that lost to Real Madrid in the Champions League Final, were beaten to the Bundesliga title by Borussia Dortmund and went down to Schalke in the German Cup. Ballack missed the Final through suspension.

• **Final officials:** Scotland referee Hugh Dallas was the fourth official and Premiership linesman Philip Sharp was one of Pierluigi Collina's two assistants for the Final. Dallas had previously taken charge of the Germany-United States quarter-final and the Portugal-Poland group game and was the fourth official at two other matches. Sharp ran the line at four other fixtures. Premiership referee Graham Poll, who disallowed two Italy goals against Croatia on his Danish linesman's flag, was criticised by the Italians and did not receive another match. Poll was twice named the fourth official.

• **Golden Ball:** Oliver Kahn, Germany's captain, became the first goalkeeper to win the Golden Ball for the best player at the Finals. Kahn, also named top keeper at the tournament, was chosen by the media before the Final, when his mistake presented Ronaldo with Brazil's first goal. Ronaldo came second in the poll and Hong Myung-bo of South Korea third.

• **Golden Boot:** Ronaldo's tally of eight goals was the highest since Gerd Muller's 10 for Germany in the 1970 Finals. Other leading scorers this time were: 5 – Klose (Germany), Rivaldo (Brazil); 4 – Tomasson (Denmark), Vieri (Italy). 3 – Ballack (Germany), Bouba Diop (Senegal), Robbie Keane (Republic of Ireland), Larsson (Sweden), Morientes (Spain), Pauleta (Portugal), Raul (Spain), Wilmots (Belgium).

• **Sportsmanship:** Belgium won FIFA's Fair Play award with Sweden second and Japan third. Fans around the world voted South Korea the most entertaining team ahead of Turkey and Brazil.

• **All Stars:** FIFA's all-star squad, chosen from teams reaching the quarter-finals was: Goalkeepers – Kahn (Germany), Rustu (Turkey). Defenders – Roberto Carlos (Brazil), Campbell (England), Hong Myung-bo (South Korea), Alpay (Turkey), Hierro (Spain). Midfielders – Rivaldo (Brazil), Ronaldinho (Brazil), Reyna (United States), Ballack (Germany), Yoo Sang-chul (South Korea). Strikers – Ronaldo (Brazil), Diouf (Senegal), Hasan Sas (Turkey), Klose (Germany).

WORLD CUP QUOTE UNQUOTE

'You were a crap player and you are a crap manager. The only reason I have any dealings with you is that somehow you are the manager of my country and you're not even Irish' – **Roy Keane**'s training camp tirade against Mick McCarthy which resulted in him being sent home by the Republic of Ireland manager.

'This is a huge decision, but I'm happy to go to the World Cup one man down rather than with a man who shows utter disregard and disrespect for me. I will not tolerate being spoken to with that level of abuse. He's one of the best players in the world, but he's a disruptive influence' – **Mick McCarthy**.

'I've never witnessed anything like it in my life. There is a line you can't cross and unfortunately Roy has crossed it' – **Steve Staunton** who took over the captaincy.

'I feel drained and shattered, so how do you feel the younger players feel? I can't understand why Roy didn't apologise' – **Niall Quinn**, the squad's senior player.

'Are you watching Roy Keane' – Irish fans after the 1-1 draw against Cameroon.

'I told the players after the game we were not at a funeral. This is only the start of the World Cup' – **Sven Goran Eriksson** on England's stuttering start against Sweden.

'Football is a game and people have to be cunning' – **Rivaldo** refusing to apologise for feigning injury in Brazil's match against Turkey which brought him a £5,180 FIFA fine and widespread condemnation.

'The thin dividing line between flamboyance and madness' – **Jon Champion**, ITV commentator, as Paraguay goalkeeper Jose Luis Chilavert came forward to take a free-kick just outside the Spain penalty area.

'It's marvellous isn't it? One minute I'm a complete buffoon, the next I'm a tactical and technical genius' – **Mick McCarthy** after substitute Niall Quinn sets up Ireland's equaliser against Germany.

'I've never felt pressure like it. I just held my breath and hit it as hard as I could' – **David Beckham** on his penalty winner for England against Argentina.

'I'm going to sleep with a coat-hanger in my mouth to keep the smile on my face for the next four days' – **Mick McCarthy** after his team qualified from their group by beating Saudi Arabia.

'We got what we deserved' – **Patrick Vieira** on France finishing bottom of their group and going out.

'Practising penalties is garbage. You stand up and take them if you fancy it on the night' – **Mick McCarthy** after the Republic of Ireland lost a shoot-out to Spain.

'My feelings of disappointment are mixed with immense pride and satisfaction for the way we have conducted ourselves' – **Mick McCarthy** as Ireland headed home.

'Shock after shock after shock' – **Alan Hansen**, BBC pundit, on South Korea's win over Italy.

'We are normal, human, hard-working people' – **Guus Hiddink**, the South Korea coach.

'I want to say sorry to the people I've let down today' – **David Seaman** whose mistake condemned England to defeat against Brazil.

'It will be an absolute disgrace if David is made the scapegoat' – **David Beckham**, the England captain.

'My biggest victory is that I can play again' – **Ronaldo**, Brazil's matchwinner, thanking the French doctor who saved his career when it was threatened by a knee injury.

'You make your one mistake of the whole tournament and you get punished like that. Nothing can console me, but life goes on' – **Oliver Kahn**, Germany's goalkeeper, who gifted Ronaldo the first goal in the Final.

'Finishing second in Brazil is like finishing last and I tried to pass that on to the players' – **Luiz Felipe Scolari**, the winning coach.

WORLD CUP SUMMARIES 1930-98

1930 IN URUGUAY

WINNERS: Uruguay. RUNNERS-UP: Argentina. THIRD: U.S.A.
Other countries taking part: Belgium, Bolivia, Brazil, Chile, France, Mexico, Paraguay, Peru, Rumania, Yugoslavia. **Total entries:** 13.
Venue: All matches played in Montevideo.
Top scorer: Stabile (Argentina) 8 goals.
Final (30.7.30): **Uruguay 4** (Dorado 12, Cea 55, Iriarte 64, Castro 89), **Argentina 2** (Peucelle 29, Stabile 35). **Att:** 90,000.
Uruguay: Ballesteros; Nasazzi (Capt.), Mascheroni, Andrade, Fernandez, Gestido, Dorado, Scarone, Castro, Cea, Iriarte.
Argentina: Botasso; Della Torre, Paternoster, Evaristo (J.), Monti, Suarez, Peucelle, Varallo, Stabile, Ferreira (Capt.), Evaristo (M.).
Referee: Langenus (Belgium). **Half-time:** 1-2.

1934 IN ITALY

WINNERS: Italy. RUNNERS-UP: Czechoslovakia. THIRD: Germany.
Other countries in finals: Argentina, Austria, Belgium, Brazil, Egypt, France, Holland, Hungary, Romania, Spain, Sweden, Switzerland, U.S.A. **Total entries:** 29 (16 qualifiers).
Venues: Bologna, Florence, Genoa, Milan, Naples, Rome, Trieste, Turin.
Top scorers: Conen (Germany), Nejedly (Czechoslovakia), Schiavio (Italy), each 4 goals.
Final (Rome, 10.6.34): **Italy 2** (Orsi 82, Schiavio 97), **Czechoslovakia 1** (Puc 70), **after extra time. Att:** 50,000.
Italy: Combi (Capt.); Monzeglio, Allemandi, Ferraris, Monti, Bertolini, Guaita, Meazza, Schiavio, Ferrari, Orsi.
Czechoslovakia: Planicka (Capt.); Zenisek, Ctyroky, Kostalek, Cambal, Krcil, Junek, Svoboda, Sobotka, Nejedly, Puc.
Referee: Eklind (Sweden). **Half-time:** 0-0. **90 mins:** 1-1.

1938 IN FRANCE

WINNERS: Italy. RUNNERS-UP: Hungary. THIRD: Brazil.
Other countries in finals: Belgium, Cuba, Czechoslovakia, Dutch East Indies, France, Germany, Holland, Norway, Poland, Rumania, Sweden, Switzerland. **Total entries:** 25 (15 qualifiers).
Venues: Antibes, Bordeaux, Le Havre, Lille, Marseilles, Paris, Reims, Strasbourg, Toulouse.
Top scorer: Leonidas (Brazil) 8 goals.
Final (Paris, 19.6.38): **Italy 4** (Colaussi 6, 36, Piola 15, 81), **Hungary 2** (Titkos 7, Sarosi 65). **Att:** 45,000.
Italy: Olivieri; Foni, Rava, Serantoni, Andreolo, Locatelli, Biavati, Meazza (Capt.), Piola, Ferrari, Colaussi.
Hungary: Szabo; Polgar, Biro, Szalay, Szucs, Lazar, Sas, Vincze, Sarosi (Capt.), Szengeller, Titkos.
Referee: Capdeville (France). **Half-time:** 3-1.

1950 IN BRAZIL

WINNERS: Uruguay. RUNNERS-UP: Brazil. THIRD: Sweden.
Other countries in finals: Bolivia, Chile, England, Italy, Mexico, Paraguay, Spain, Switzerland, U.S.A., Yugoslavia. **Total entries:** 29 (13 qualifiers).
Venues: Belo Horizonte, Curitiba, Porto Alegre, Recife, Rio de Janeiro, Sao Paulo.
Top scorer: Ademir (Brazil) 9 goals.
Deciding Match (Rio de Janeiro, 16.7.50): **Uruguay 2** (Schiaffino 64, Ghiggia 79), **Brazil 1** (Friaca 47). **Att:** 199,850.

(For the only time, the World Cup was decided on a final pool system, in which the winners of the four qualifying groups met in a six-match series. So, unlike previous and subsequent tournaments, there was no official Final as such, but Uruguay v Brazil was the deciding final match in the final pool).

Uruguay: Maspoli; Gonzales, Tejera, Gambetta, Varela (Capt.), Andrade, Ghiggia, Perez, Miguez, Schiaffino, Moran.

Brazil: Barbosa; Augusto (Capt.), Juvenal, Bauer, Danilo, Bigode, Friaca, Zizinho, Ademir, Jair, Chico.

Referee: Reader (England). **Half-time**: 0-0.

1954 IN SWITZERLAND

WINNERS: West Germany. RUNNERS-UP: Hungary. THIRD: Austria.
Other countries in finals: Belgium, Brazil, Czechoslovakia, England, France, Italy, Korea, Mexico, Scotland, Switzerland, Turkey, Uruguay, Yugoslavia. **Total entries**: 35 (16 qualifiers).
Venues: Basle, Berne, Geneva, Lausanne, Lugano, Zurich.
Top scorer: Kocsis (Hungary) 11 goals.
Final (Berne, 4.7.54): **West Germany 3** (Morlock 12, Rahn 17, 84), **Hungary 2** (Puskas 4, Czibor 9). **Att**: 60,000.
West Germany: Turek; Posipal, Kohlmeyer, Eckel, Liebrich, Mai, Rahn, Morlock, Walter (O.), Walter (F.) (Capt.), Schaefer.
Hungary: Grosics; Buzansky, Lantos, Bozsik, Lorant, Zakarias, Czibor, Kocsis, Hidegkuti, Puskas (Capt.), Toth (J.).
Referee: Ling (England). **Half-time**: 2-2.

1958 IN SWEDEN

WINNERS: Brazil. RUNNERS-UP: Sweden. THIRD: France.
Other countries in finals: Argentina, Austria, Czechoslovakia, England, Hungary, Mexico, Northern Ireland, Paraguay, Scotland, Soviet Union, Wales, West Germany, Yugoslavia. **Total entries**: 47 (16 qualifiers).
Venues: Boras, Eskilstuna, Gothenburg, Halmstad, Helsingborg, Malmo, Norrkoping, Orebro, Sandviken, Stockholm, Vasteras.
Top scorer: Fontaine (France) 13 goals.
Final (Stockholm, 29.6.58): **Brazil 5** (Vava 10, 32, Pele 55, 88, Zagalo 76), **Sweden 2** (Liedholm 4, Simonsson 83). **Att**: 49,737.
Brazil: Gilmar; Santos (D.), Santos (N.), Zito, Bellini (Capt.), Orlando, Garrincha, Didi, Vava, Pele, Zagalo.
Sweden: Svensson; Bergmark, Axbom, Boerjesson, Gustavsson, Parling, Hamrin, Gren, Simonsson, Liedholm (Capt.), Skoglund.
Referee: Guigue (France). **Half-time**: 2-1.

1962 IN CHILE

WINNERS: Brazil. RUNNERS-UP: Czechoslovakia. THIRD: Chile.
Other countries in finals: Argentina, Bulgaria, Colombia, England, Hungary, Italy, Mexico, Soviet Union, Spain, Switzerland, Uruguay, West Germany, Yugoslavia. **Total entries**: 53 (16 qualifiers).
Venues: Arica, Rancagua, Santiago, Vina del Mar.
Top scorer: Jerkovic (Yugoslavia), 5 goals.
Final (Santiago, 17.6.62): **Brazil 3** (Amarildo 17, Zito 69, Vava 77), **Czechoslovakia 1** (Masopust 16). **Att**: 68,679.
Brazil: Gilmar; Santos (D.), Mauro (Capt.), Zozimo, Santos (N.), Zito, Didi, Garrincha, Vava, Amarildo, Zagalo.
Czechoslovakia: Schroiff; Tichy, Novak, Pluskal, Popluhar, Masopust (Capt.), Pospichal, Scherer, Kvasnak, Kadraba, Jelinek.
Referee: Latychev (Soviet Union). **Half-time**: 1-1.

1966 IN ENGLAND

WINNERS: England. RUNNERS-UP: West Germany. THIRD: Portugal.
Other countries in finals: Argentina, Brazil, Bulgaria, Chile, France, Hungary, Italy, Mexico, North Korea, Soviet Union, Spain, Switzerland, Uruguay. **Total entries**: 53 (16 qualifiers).
Venues: Birmingham (Villa Park), Liverpool (Goodison Park), London (Wembley and White City), Manchester (Old Trafford), Middlesbrough, Sheffield (Hillsborough), Sunderland.
Top scorer: Eusebio (Portugal) 9 goals.
Final (Wembley, 30.7.66): **England 4** (Hurst 19, 100, 120, Peters 78), **West Germany 2** (Haller 13, Weber 89), **after extra time. Att**: 93,802.
England: Banks; Cohen, Wilson, Stiles, Charlton (J.), Moore (Capt.), Ball, Hurst, Hunt, Charlton (R.), Peters.
West Germany: Tilkowski; Hottges, Schnellinger, Beckenbauer, Schulz, Weber, Haller, Held, Seeler (Capt.), Overath, Emmerich.
Referee: Dienst (Switzerland). **Half-time**: 1-1. **90 mins**: 2-2.

1970 IN MEXICO

WINNERS: Brazil. RUNNERS-UP: Italy. THIRD: West Germany.
Other countries in finals: Belgium, Bulgaria, Czechoslovakia, El Salvador, England, Israel, Mexico, Morocco, Peru, Romania, Soviet Union, Sweden, Uruguay. **Total entries**: 68 (16 qualifiers).
Venues: Guadalajara, Leon, Mexico City, Puebla, Toluca.
Top scorer: Muller (West Germany) 10 goals.
Final (Mexico City, 21.6.70): **Brazil 4** (Pele 18, Gerson 66, Jairzinho 71, Carlos Alberto 87), **Italy 1** (Boninsegna 38). **Att**: 107,412.
Brazil: Felix; Carlos Alberto (Capt.), Brito, Piazza, Everaldo, Clodoaldo, Gerson, Jairzinho, Tostao, Pele, Rivelino.
Italy: Albertosi; Burgnich, Facchetti (Capt.), Cera, Rosato, Bertini (Juliano 72), Domenghini, De Sisti, Mazzola, Boninsegna (Rivera 84), Riva.
Referee: Glockner (East Germany). **Half-time**: 1-1.

1974 IN WEST GERMANY

WINNERS: West Germany. RUNNERS-UP: Holland. THIRD: Poland.
Other countries in finals: Argentina, Australia, Brazil, Bulgaria, Chile, East Germany, Haiti, Italy, Scotland, Sweden, Uruguay, Yugoslavia, Zaire. **Total entries**: 98 (16 qualifiers).
Venues: Berlin, Dortmund, Dusseldorf, Frankfurt, Gelsenkirchen, Hamburg, Hanover, Munich, Stuttgart.
Top scorer: Lato (Poland) 7 goals
Final (Munich, 7.7.74): **West Germany 2** (Breitner 25 pen., Muller 43), **Holland 1** (Neeskens 2 pen.). **Att**: 77,833.
West Germany: Maier; Vogts, Schwarzenbeck, Beckenbauer (Capt.), Breitner, Bonhof, Hoeness, Overath, Grabowski, Muller, Holzenbein.
Holland: Jongbloed; Suurbier, Rijsbergen (De Jong 69), Haan, Krol, Jansen, Van Hanegem, Neeskens, Rep, Cruyff (Capt.), Rensenbrink (Van der Kerkhof (R.) 46).
Referee: Taylor (England). **Half-time**: 2-1.

1978 IN ARGENTINA

WINNERS: Argentina. RUNNERS-UP: Holland. THIRD: Brazil.
Other countries in finals: Austria, France, Hungary, Iran, Italy, Mexico, Peru, Poland, Scotland, Spain, Sweden, Tunisia, West Germany. **Total entries**: 102 (16 qualifiers).
Venues: Buenos Aires, Cordoba, Mar del Plata, Mendoza, Rosario.
Top scorer: Kempes (Argentina) 6 goals.

Final (Buenos Aires, 25.6.78): **Argentina 3** (Kempes 38, 104, Bertoni 115), **Holland 1** (Nanninga 82), **after extra time. Att:** 77,000.
Argentina: Fillol; Passarella (Capt.), Olguin, Galvan, Tarantini, Ardiles (Larrosa 66), Gallego, Ortiz (Houseman 74), Bertoni, Luque, Kempes.
Holland: Jongbloed; Krol (Capt.), Poortvliet, Brandts, Jansen (Suurbier 73), Haan, Neeskens, Van der Kerkhof (W.), Rep (Nanninga 58), Van der Kerkhof (R.), Rensenbrink.
Referee: Gonella (Italy). **Half-time:** 1-0. **90 mins:** 1-1.

1982 IN SPAIN

WINNERS: Italy. RUNNERS-UP: West Germany. THIRD: Poland.
Other countries in finals: Algeria, Argentina, Austria, Belgium, Brazil, Cameroon, Chile, Czechoslovakia, El Salvador, England, France, Honduras, Hungary, Kuwait, New Zealand, Northern Ireland, Peru, Scotland, Soviet Union, Spain, Yugoslavia. **Total entries:** 109 (24 qualifiers).
Venues: Alicante, Barcelona, Bilbao, Coruna, Elche, Gijon, Madrid, Malaga, Oviedo, Seville, Valencia, Valladolid, Vigo, Zaragoza.
Top scorer: Rossi (Italy) 6 goals.
Final (Madrid, 11.7.82): **Italy 3** (Rossi 57, Tardelli 69, Altobelli 81), **West Germany 1** (Breitner 84). **Att:** 90,089.
Italy: Zoff (Capt.); Bergomi, Scirea, Collovati, Cabrini, Oriali, Gentile, Tardelli, Conti, Rossi, Graziani (Altobelli 18 – Causio 88).
West Germany: Schumacher; Kaltz, Stielike, Forster (K-H.), Forster (B.), Dremmler (Hrubesch 63), Breitner, Briegel, Rummenigge (Capt.) (Muller 70), Fischer, Littbarski.
Referee: Coelho (Brazil). **Half-time:** 0-0.

1986 IN MEXICO

WINNERS: Argentina. RUNNERS-UP: West Germany. THIRD: France.
Other countries in finals: Algeria, Belgium, Brazil, Bulgaria, Canada, Denmark, England, Hungary, Iraq, Italy, Mexico, Morocco, Northern Ireland, Paraguay, Poland, Portugal, Scotland, South Korea, Soviet Union, Spain, Uruguay. **Total entries:** 118 (24 qualifiers).
Venues: Guadalajara, Irapuato, Leon, Mexico City, Monterrey, Nezahualcoyotl, Puebla, Queretaro, Toluca.
Top scorer: Lineker (England) 6 goals.
Final (Mexico City, 29.6.86): **Argentina 3** (Brown 23, Valdano 56, Burruchaga 85), **West Germany 2** (Rummenigge 74, Voller 82). **Att:** 115,026.
Argentina: Pumpido; Cuciuffo, Brown, Ruggeri, Olarticoechea, Batista, Giusti, Maradona (Capt.), Burruchaga (Trobbiani 89), Enrique, Valdano.
West Germany: Schumacher; Berthold, K-H.Forster, Jakobs, Brehme, Briegel, Eder, Matthaus, Magath (Hoeness 62), Allofs (Voller 45), Rummenigge (Capt.).
Referee: Filho (Brazil). **Half-time:** 1-0.

1990 IN ITALY

WINNERS: West Germany. RUNNERS-UP: Argentina. THIRD: Italy.
Other countries in finals: Austria, Belgium, Brazil, Cameroon, Colombia, Costa Rica, Czechoslovakia, Egypt, England, Holland, Rep. of Ireland, Romania, Scotland, Spain, South Korea, Soviet Union, Sweden, United Arab Emirates, U.S.A., Uruguay, Yugoslavia. **Total entries:** 103 (24 qualifiers).
Venues: Bari, Bologna, Cagliari, Florence, Genoa, Milan, Naples, Palermo, Rome, Turin, Udine, Verona.
Top scorer: Schillaci (Italy) 6 goals.
Final (Rome, 8.7.90): **Argentina 0, West Germany 1** (Brehme 85 pen.). **Att:** 73,603.
Argentina: Goycochea; Ruggeri (Monzon 45), Simon, Serrizuela, Lorenzo, Basualdo, Troglio, Burruchaga (Calderon 53), Sensini, Maradona (Capt.), Dezotti. **Sent-off:** Monzon (65), Dezotti (86) – first players ever to be sent off in World Cup Final.

West Germany: Illgner; Berthold (Reuter 75), Buchwald, Augenthaler, Kohler, Brehme, Matthaus (Capt.), Littbarski, Hassler, Klinsmann, Voller.
Referee: Codesal (Mexico). **Half-time:** 0-0.

1994 IN U.S.A.

WINNERS: Brazil. RUNNERS-UP: Italy. THIRD: Sweden.
Other countries in finals: Argentina, Belgium, Bolivia, Bulgaria, Cameroon, Colombia, Germany, Greece, Holland, Mexico, Morocco, Nigeria, Norway, Rep. of Ireland, Romania, Russia, Saudi Arabia, South Korea, Spain, Switzerland, U.S.A. **Total entries:** 144 (24 qualifiers).
Venues: Boston, Chicago, Dallas, Detroit, Los Angeles, New York City, Orlando, San Francisco, Washington.
Top scorers: Salenko (Russia), Stoichkov (Bulgaria), each 6 goals.
Final (Los Angeles, 17.7.94): **Brazil 0, Italy 0,** after extra time; **Brazil** won 3-2 on pens. **Att:** 94,194.
Brazil: Taffarel; Jorginho (Cafu 21), Aldair, Marcio Santos, Branco, Mazinho, Mauro Silva, Dunga (Capt.), Zinho (Viola 105), Romario, Bebeto.
Italy: Pagliuca; Mussi (Apolloni 35), Baresi (Capt.), Maldini, Benarrivo, Berti, Albertini, D. Baggio (Evani 95), Donadoni, R. Baggio, Massaro.
Referee: Puhl (Hungary).
Shoot-out: Baresi over, Marco Santos saved, Albertini 1-0, Romario 1-1, Evani 2-1, Branco 2-2, Massaro saved, Dunga 2-3, R Baggio over.

1998 IN FRANCE

WINNERS: France. RUNNERS-UP: Brazil. THIRD: Croatia.
Other countries in finals: Argentina, Austria, Belgium, Bulgaria, Cameroon, Chile, Colombia, Denmark, England, Germany, Holland, Iran, Italy, Jamaica, Japan, Mexico, Morocco, Nigeria, Norway, Paraguay, Romania, Saudi Arabia, Scotland, South Africa, South Korea, Spain, Tunisia, U.S.A., Yugoslavia. **Total entries:** 172 (32 qualifiers).
Venues: Bordeaux, Lens, Lyon, Marseille, Montpellier, Nantes, Paris (St Denis, Parc des Princes), Saint-Etienne, Toulouse.
Top scorer: Davor Suker (Croatia) 6 goals.
Final (Paris St Denis, 12.7.98): **Brazil 0, France 3** (Zidane 27, 45, Petit 90). **Att:** 75,000.
Brazil: Traffarel; Cafu, Junior Baiano, Aldair, Roberto Carlos; Dunga, Leonardo (Denilson 46), Cesar Sampaio (Edmundo 74), Rivaldo; Bebeto, Ronaldo.
France: Barthez; Thuram, Leboeuf, Desailly, Lizarazu; Karembeu (Boghossian 56), Deschamps, Petit, Zidane, Djorkaeff (Viera 75); Guivarc'h (Dugarry 66). **Sent-off:** Desailly (68).
Referee: S Belqola (Morocco). **Half-time:** 0-2.

CHANGE OF NAME FOR CHARITY SHIELD

The Charity Shield, traditional curtain-raiser to the domestic season, will be known as the Community Shield from now on. The F.A. decided on the change to recognise and reward the work of an estimated 250,000 volunteers in amateur football.

WIMBLEDON END MIDWEEK HOODOO

Wimbledon scored their first midweek League victory at Selhurst Park for four-and-a-half years when beating Crewe Alexandra 2-0.

NEW SEASON, NEW HOPE, SAME OLD OUTCOME

BY STUART BARNES

If one thing is certain about the new season it is that before too many matches have been decided the first of many managers will either be sacked, has resigned or, in that euphemistic way much loved by football, has left 'by mutual consent.' Such are the demands of directors, fans and, increasingly the City, that what was once a steady turnover has now turned into a torrent.

Witness last season. Before the end of August, Paul Bracewell had gone from Halifax Town, quickly followed by Gordon Strachan (Coventry City), Swansea City's John Hollins and Wrexham's Brian Flynn, the third longest-serving manager after Dario Gradi and Sir Alex Ferguson. By the end of the season there had been a change – in some cases more than one – at nearly half the 92 clubs. And by the time that Leeds United dispensed with the services of David O'Leary at the end of June, that total had risen to 49 in the space of 12 months.

Admittedly, it was not all one-way. Some managers were quick to jump ship when a bigger club, or a better offer, beckoned. Yet the overwhelming majority were sent packing, even though in some cases a measure of success – or at least a degree of stability – had been achieved.

Gudjon Thordarson was dismissed by Stoke City five days after winning promotion. Huddersfied Town got rid of Lou Macari despite reaching the play-offs. And for all the problems which piled in on Leeds, was fifth place in the Premiership – or for that matter O'Leary's tough-talking over the Rio Ferdinand issue – all that unacceptable?

Not everything was so gloomy. Flynn may have gone after 12 years in the job, but glasses were raised to Gradi when he celebrated 1,000 games in charge last November. What a pity that the season ended in relegation for a man who has overseen a renowned youth academy and built a reputation for playing passing football in his 19 years at Crewe Alexandra.

Ferguson is coming up for 16 years at Old Trafford, having decided against relinquishing the reins just yet, while Charlton Athletic, under Alan Curbishley's 11-year stewardship, have built a team, a ground and a standing in the game to be proud of.

But we are clearly in an era of diminishing patience, the quick fix or a lack of loyalty. 'More so than ever, the days of someone staying at a football club for eight or ten years are few and far between,' observed Martin O'Neill, the Celtic manager, while contemplating, and then deciding against, walking out at Celtic to take the Leeds job eventually filled by Terry Venables.

The other sure thing about the season ahead is that there will be no shortage of applicants for every vacancy arising. 'You know all about the pressures and the pitfalls and you know there is every chance it will end in the sack,' one manager confided recently. 'But the game is in your blood. You can't get it out of your system. You know there is no other place to be on a Saturday afternoon.'

Of all the men preparing for 2002-03, Kevin Keegan carries, arguably, the biggest weight of expectancy. His promoted Manchester City side are not expected to figure in what could prove another gripping championship race, but a summer spending spree, notably on Nicolas Anelka, means that he will be expected, at least, to provide some stability for a team notorious for going up and down.

George Burley knows he must mount a challenge for an immediate return to the Premiership for Ipswich Town, while Wolves fans will expect nothing less than promotion from Dave Jones after last season's fall from grace. Among the younger brigade, Steve Cotterill tests himself in the First Division with Stoke City after leaving Cheltenham Town, while Paul Sturrock attempts to build on Third Division championship success with Plymouth Argyle, a club intent on going places with a redeveloped ground and a capacity now beyond 20,000.

SOCCER DIARY 2001-02

JULY 2001

1 Howard Wilkinson steps down as **England U-21** manager. **Joe Fagan**, who led **Liverpool** to an unprecedented treble of the Championship, League Cup and European Cup in his first season in charge in 1984, dies aged 80. **3** The **Sol Campbell** saga ends with a free transfer from **Tottenham** to **Arsenal**. **Billy Liddell**, **Liverpool**'s finest player in the immediate post-war years, dies aged 79. **4 Gianluigi Buffon** becomes the world's most expensive goalkeeper after a £32.6m. switch from **Parma** to **Juventus**. **Charlton Athletic** pay a club record £4.75m. for **Wimbledon**'s **Jason Euell**. **5 Richard Wright** joins **Arsenal** from **Ipswich Town** for £5m. **Aston Villa** sign **Moustapha Hadji** from **Coventry City** in a £4.5m. deal which takes **Julian Joachim** to Highfield Road. **Birmingham City** announce what is believed to be the biggest shirt sponsorship in Football League history – a £3m. agreement with Phones 4u. **9 Real Madrid** sign **Zinedine Zidane** from **Juventus** for a world record £48m. **11** Two players leave **Aston Villa** – **Gareth Southgate** goes to **Middlesbrough** for £6.5m. and **David James** to **West Ham Utd.** for £3.5m. **Southampton** pay a club record £4m. for **Rory Delap** from **Derby Co. 12 Manchester Utd.** break the British transfer record again with the £28.1m. signing of **Lazio**'s **Juan Sebastian Veron**, who joins £19m. **Ruud van Nistelrooy** at Old Trafford. **Peter Schmeichel** makes a surprise return to the Premiership with **Aston Villa** after completing his contract with **Sporting Lisbon**. **David Platt** becomes **England U-21** manager and is replaced as **Nott'm. Forest** manager by **Paul Hart**, youth team boss at the City Ground. **Ian Atkins** is sacked as **Carlisle Utd.** manager. **13 Manchester Utd.** announce that **Sir Alex Ferguson** will stay on as a consultant when he retires as manager at the end of the 2001-02 season. **17 Everton** sign **Tomasz Radzinski** from **Anderlecht** for £4.5m. **Christian Karembeu** leaves **Middlesbrough** for **Olympiakos** for £3.5m. **18 Barry Town** become the first club from Wales to win a Champions League round, beating **Shamkir** from Azerbaijan 3-0 on aggregate at the first qualifying stage. **19 Aston Villa** pay £5m. for **Olof Mellberg** from **Racing Santander**. **Christian Ziege** leaves **Liverpool** for **Tottenham** for £4m. **20 Roy McFarland**, former **Bolton Wand.**, **Derby Co.** and **Cambridge Utd.** manager, takes charge at **Torquay Utd. 23 Junichi Inamoto** becomes the first Premiership player from Japan, joining **Arsenal** from **Gamba Osaka** for £4m. **Everton** get the go-ahead to build a £155m. stadium, with a 55,000 capacity, on the Mersey waterfront at King's Dock. **26 Charlton Athletic** pay £3m. for **Tottenham**'s **Luke Young. 27** The Premier League rule out the possibility of **Rangers** and **Celtic** joining their ranks. Four years after leaving **Middlesbrough**, **Fabrizio Ravanelli** returns to English football with **Derby Co.** on a free transfer from **Lazio. 28 Celtic** open their defence of the Scottish Premier League title with a 3-0 win over **St Johnstone. 30 Leicester City** sign **James Scowcroft** from **Ipswich Town** for £3m. **31 Fulham** pay £7m. – more than double their record fee – for **Edwin van der Sar** from **Juventus**. A £10.5m. fee takes **Laurent Robert** from **Paris St-Germain** to **Newcastle Utd.**

AUGUST 2001

1 As **Ryan Giggs** nets £1m. from his testimonial match against **Celtic**, watched by nearly 67,000 at Old Trafford, Sports Minister **Richard Caborn** plans to ask the Treasury whether such windfalls for top players should remain tax-free. **John Hartson** leaves **Coventry City** for **Celtic** for £6.5m. **2 Chelsea** take their summer spending past £30m. with the £7.5m. acquisition of **Barcelona**'s **Boudewijn Zenden. 3** A £30m. prize fund for the F.A. Cup is announced. **Swindon Town** appoint former **Liverpool** manager **Roy Evans** as director of football and ex-Anfield defender **Neil Ruddock** as player-coach following the sacking of manager **Andy King. Fulham** sign **Steed Malbranque** from **Lyon** for £5m. **4 Portsmouth** goalkeeper **Aaron Flahavan** (25) dies in a car crash. **8 Coventry City** pay £5m. for **Lee Hughes** from **W.B.A. Jon Harley** moves across west London from **Chelsea** to **Fulham** for £3.5m. **9 Middlesbrough** sign **Manchester Utd.** pair **Jonathan Greening** and **Mark Wilson** for a combined £3.5m. **12** In the first match between English clubs under a roof,

Liverpool beat **Manchester Utd.** 2-1 in the Charity Shield at the Millennium Stadium. **15** **England**'s 100% record under **Sven Goran Eriksson** comes to an end with a 2-0 defeat by **Holland**. The **Republic of Ireland** surrender a two-goal lead in the final 10 minutes to draw 2-2 with **Croatia**. **16** **Wimbledon**'s bid to relocate to Milton Keynes is turned down by the Football League. **Finidi George** moves to **Ipswich Town** from **Mallorca** for £3m. **17** **Everton**'s **Michael Ball** joins **Rangers** for £6.5m. **Ipswich Town** pay a club record £4.5m. for **Matteo Sereni** from **Sampdoria**. **18** **Jamie Redknapp** returns to the Premiership after a season's absence with a knee injury in **Liverpool**'s 2-1 opening day win over **West Ham Utd.** Promoted **Bolton Wand.** take the honours, beating **Leicester City** 5-0 away from home. **19** **Manchester Utd.** open their defence of the title with a 3-2 victory over **Fulham** after twice falling behind. **Robbie Fowler** apologises to assistant manager **Phil Thompson** a week after a training ground row and is restored to the first team squad at **Liverpool**. **Les Sealey**, former **Luton Town**, **Manchester Utd.** and **West Ham Utd.** goalkeeper, dies from a heart attack aged 43. **Tom Staniforth**, 20-year-old **Sheffield Wed.** defender, collapses and dies on a night out. **21** **Leeds Utd.** have **Lee Bowyer** and **Danny Mills** sent off but win 2-1 at **Arsenal** in the season's first big match. In the Worthington Cup first round, **Rushden & Diamonds** knock out **Burnley** 3-2, while **Notts Co.** goalkeeper **Steve Mildenhall** scores with a free-kick inside his own half in the 4-3 victory over **Mansfield Town**. **Fulham** continue their spending spree with the £3.3m. signing of **Sylvain Legwinski** from **Bordeaux**. **22** **Rangers** fail to make the group stage of the **Champions League**, losing 2-1 on aggregate to **Fenerbahce**. **24** **Liverpool** win their fifth trophy in sixth months by beating **Bayern Munich** 3-2 in the European Super Cup. **Aston Villa** sign **Bosko Balaban** from **Dynamo Zagreb** for £6m. **25** **Patrick Vieira** is sent off for the seventh time in his **Arsenal** career after a head-to-head with **Leicester City**'s **Dennis Wise**, himself dismissed for the 12th time. **Sir Alex Ferguson**, unhappy with **Jaap Stam**'s form and his comments about **Manchester Utd.** in a controversial autobiography, sells the **Holland** defender to **Lazio** for £16m. **28** **Fulham** break their club record for the second time in a month, paying **Lyon** £11.5m. for **Steve Marlet** to take their summer spending to £34m. **Tottenham**'s **Gary Doherty** has the red card received at **Everton** rescinded. **29** **Don Hutchison** leaves **Sunderland** for **West Ham Utd.**, who pay a club record £5m. **30** **Manchester Utd.** replace **Jaap Stam** with 35-year-old **Laurent Blanc** on a free transfer from **Inter Milan**. **Paul Bracewell** becomes the first managerial casualty of the season, resigning at **Halifax Town**. **31** **Liverpool** buy two goalkeepers, **Chris Kirkland** from **Coventry City** for £5m. – rising with appearances to a British record £8m. – and **Feyenoord**'s **Jerzy Dudek** for £4.9m. **Silvinho** leaves **Arsenal** for **Celta Vigo** for £5m.

SEPTEMBER 2001

1 **Michael Owen** scores a hat-trick in **England**'s remarkable 5-1 win over **Germany** in Munich. **Jason McAteer**'s goal gives the **Republic of Ireland** a 1-0 victory over **Holland**. Other World Cup qualifiers: **Scotland** 0, **Croatia** 0; **Wales** 0, **Armenia** 0; **Denmark** 1, **Northern Ireland** 1. **Brian Moore**, ITV's voice of football for 30 years, dies aged 69. **4** **Francis Jeffers** scores a hat-trick in a 5-0 win by the **England U-21** side against **Albania**. **5** **Michael Owen** is on the mark again as **England** close in on the finals of the **World Cup** with a 2-0 win over **Albania**, but **Scotland** hopes fade with a 2-0 defeat by **Belgium**. **George McCartney** scores on his debut for **Northern Ireland**, who beat **Iceland** 3-0. **Ryan Giggs**, captaining **Wales**, is sent off for the first time in his career in a 3-2 defeat by **Norway**. **7** **Leeds Utd.** announce plans to build a new 50,000-capacity stadium on the outskirts of the city for the start of the 2004-05 season. **10** Manager **Gordon Strachan** leaves struggling **Coventry City** by mututal consent. **12** UEFA postpone Champions League and UEFA Cup games following the terrorist attacks on New York and Washington. **Swansea City** dismiss **John Hollins** and appoint **Colin Addison** as manager. **West Ham Utd.** lose a Worthington Cup second round tie to **Reading** on penalties. **13** Second Division **Cardiff City** pay £1.8m. for **Stoke City**'s **Peter Thorne**. **15** **Tomas Repka**, signed for a club record £5.5m. from **Fiorentina** the previous day, is sent off on his **West Ham Utd.** debut at **Middlesbrough**. **18** **Danny Cadamarteri**, fined £2,000 at Liverpool Crown Court for punching a woman, is told he can leave **Everton**. **Neil Harris** make his comeback for **Millwall** after treatment for testicular cancer. **Billy Davies** resigns as

Motherwell manager. **21** Tottenham sign **Dean Richards** from **Southampton** for £8.1m. Red cards received by **Matteo Sereni (Ipswich Town)** and **Lee Marshall (Leicester City)** in separate incidents in the match at Filbert Street are rescinded. So is the one shown to **Chelsea's Jimmy Floyd Hasselbaink** against **Arsenal**. **Celtic** manager **Martin O'Neill** is banned from the touchline for one match by UEFA for remarks about a last-minute penalty to **Juventus** in a Champions League fixture. **22 Chelsea** players **Frank Lampard, Jody Morris, John Terry** and **Eidur Gudjohnsen** are fined two weeks' wages by the club for drunken behaviour at a hotel near Heathrow the day after terrorists attacked New York and Washington. Former team-mate **Frank Sinclair**, also part of the group, is later fined the same by his club, **Leicester City. Norwich City** apologise to East Anglian rivals **Ipswich Town** for an insulting message — Manchester United. 1 Scum 0 – displayed on the Carrow Road electronic scoreboard. **23 Paul Gascoigne**, in an interview with *The Observer*, admits he is an alcoholic. **Exeter City** sack manager **Noel Blake. 24 Brian Flynn**, third longest-serving manager behind **Dario Gradi** and **Sir Alex Ferguson**, parts company with **Wrexham** by mutual consent after 12 years in the job. **25** The F.A. fine **Birmingham City** manager **Trevor Francis** £1,500 and his players **Michael Johnson** and **Danny Sonner** £1,200 and £1,000 respectively for incidents at the end of last season's play-off semi-final with **Preston N.E. St Johnstone** dismiss manager **Sandy Clark. 26 Northampton Town** sack manager **Kevin Wilson. 27 Michael Owen**, sidelined with another hamstring injury, signs a new four-year contract with **Liverpool. 27 Aston Villa, Hibernian** and **Kilmarnock** go out in the first round of the UEFA Cup. **29 Manchester Utd.** produce a remarkable comeback to win 5-3 at **Tottenham** after trailing 3-0 at half-time. **30** Peter **Taylor**, sacked by **Leicester City**, becomes the first Premiership managerial casualty of the season. **Frank Lampard** is left out of **England's** squad to play **Greece** following that drinking session with team-mates.

OCTOBER 2001

2 Amid growing concern that some players are feigning injury, **Aston Villa's Dion Dublin**, sent off at **Southampton**, and **Leicester City's Junior Lewis**, dismissed against **Charton Athletic**, become the fifth and sixth players to have red cards rescinded by the F.A. **3** **Steven Gerrard** apologises to coach **Sven Goran Eriksson** for a late-night drinking session hours before joining **England's** squad to play **Greece. 5 England** reach the play-offs for the European U-21 Championship by beating **Greece** 2-1 to top their group. Former **Aberdeen** and **Celtic** player **Billy Stark** is appointed manager of **St Johnstone. 6** A stoppage-time free-kick by captain **David Beckham** salvages a 2-2 draw against **Greece** and puts **England** into the finals of the World Cup. **Scotland** coach **Craig Brown** resigns after his side miss out, despite a 2-1 victory over **Latvia**. The **Republic of Ireland** reach the play-offs and **Niall Quinn** celebrates his 35th birthday by becoming their highest scorer with his 21st international goal in the 4-0 success against **Cyprus. Northern Ireland**, who have manager **Sammy McIlroy** and his assistant **Jim Harvey** sent off following touchline incidents, and **Wales** round off disappointing campaigns with 1-0 wins over **Malta** and **Belarus** respectively. **7** Manager **Jim Smith** leaves **Derby Co.** after refusing to become director of football. He is replaced by assistant **Colin Todd**, a former long-serving player with the club. **8 Denis Smith**, former **Sunderland, W.B.A.** and **Oxford Utd.** manager, takes over at **Wrexham. Gil Prescott** quits as manager of **Macclesfield Town** to concentrate on the job of director of football. **9 Liverpool** surrender the **Worthington** Cup at the first hurdle, losing 2-1 at home to **Grimsby Town. David Webb** resigns as manager of **Southend Utd. 10 Dave Bassett** is appointed manager of **Leicester City**, his seventh club, with **Micky Adams**, the **Brighton & H.A.** manager, as assistant. **Notts Co.** sack **Jocky Scott** and replace him with former manager **Gary Brazil** in the new role of head coach. **12 Alan Little**, former **Southend Utd.** and **York City** manager, takes charge at **Halifax Town** where he was once a player. **13 Liverpool** manager **Gerard Houllier** undergoes 11 hours of life-saving heart surgery after being taken ill at half-time of his team's match against **Leeds Utd.** In an attempt to increase attendances, **Brentford** stage the first completely free League fixture, with 11,000 watching the match against **Peterborough Utd. 15** Two more managerial departures. **Tommy Taylor**, longest-serving boss in Division Three with nearly five years at **Leyton Orient**, resigns and is replaced by coach **Paul Brush**. Then, **Trevor Francis**, second longest-serving manager in Division One, leaves by mutual consent after five-and-a-half years with **Birmingham City**. 16 Caretaker **Roland Nilsson** becomes **Coventry City** manager. **Eric Black**, former **Aberdeen** stalwart, is named **Motherwell** manager with ex-**England** defender **Terry Butcher** as assistant. 17 **Peter Shreeves** resigns as **Sheffield Wed.** manager. **Peter Taylor** makes a rapid return to management with **Brighton & H.A.** Worried about their safety, **Marcel Desailly**, **Albert Ferrer**, **Graeme Le Saux**, **Emmanuel Petit**, **Eidur Gudjohnsen** and **William Gallas** pull out of **Chelsea**'s trip to **Israel** for a UEFA Cup tie against **Hapoel Tel Aviv**, a game they lose 2-0. 18 **David O'Leary** takes his spending at **Leeds Utd.** to £83m. with the signing of **Seth Johnson** from **Derby Co.** for £7m., a figure that could eventually rise to £9m. After six months of deadlock, BBC and ITV agree a £160m. deal to show the finals of the 2002 and 2006 World Cup. 20 Goalkeeper **Peter Schmeichel** volleys a last-minute goal for **Aston Villa** in their 3-2 defeat at **Everton**. 21 **Stuart Gray** is sacked as **Southampton** manager after eight League games and is replaced by **Gordon Strachan**, who left **Coventry City** the previous month. 22 **Bertie Mee**, manager of the **Arsenal** double-winning side in 1971, dies aged 82. **Graeme Le Saux** publicly apologises for a two-footed tackle on **Danny Mills** in the **Leeds Utd.** – **Chelsea** match. **Leeds Utd.** manager **David O'Leary**, sent to the stands for protesting about the challenge, escapes F.A. disciplinary action. Poor viewing figures force ITV to move the Saturday Premiership highlights programme from its 7pm slot to 10.30. Caretaker **Rob Newman**, a former club captain, is appointed manager of **Southend Co.** 23 Three goals in the final 12 minutes give **Manchester Utd.** a 3-0 win over **Olympiakos** and a place in the second group stage of the **Champions League**. 24 **Thierry Henry**'s last-minute goal earns **Arsenal** a 3-1 victory over **Mallorca** and the necessary two-goal margin for a place in the second stage of the competition. **Gary Bennett** resigns as **Darlington** manager and is replaced by **Tommy Taylor**, who parted company with **Leyton Orient** the previous week. 25 **Barnsley** sack their manager **Nigel Spackman**. Caretaker **Kevin Broadhurst** gets the job at **Northampton Town**. **Andy Todd** is put on the transfer list by **Charlton Athletic** after a training ground incident which leaves **Dean Kiely** with a black eye. 29 **Stockport Co.** dismiss manager **Andy Kilner**. Referee **Dermot Gallagher** is dropped from the Premiership list for a spell after failing to send off **Robbie Keane** for pushing over **David Beckham** in the **Manchester Utd.**– **Leeds Utd.** match. 30 **Liverpool** join **Manchester Utd.** and **Arsenal** in the second group stage of the Champions League by beating **Borussia Dortmund** 2-0. Caretaker **John Cornforth** is appointed **Exeter City** manager. 31 Despite beating **Juventus** 4-3 in their final group match, **Celtic** fail to reach the second stage of the Champions League. **Andy Ritchie**, sacked by **Oldham Athletic**, becomes the 13th managerial departure in October and the 20th of the season.

NOVEMBER 2001

1 **Chelsea** suffer an embarrassing 3-1 aggregate defeat by **Hapoel Tel Aviv** in the second round of the UEFA Cup. **Liverpool** manager **Gerard Houllier** leaves hospital after heart surgery. 2 **Steve Bruce** resigns as **Crystal Palace** manager, but chairman **Simon Jordan** blocks his move to **Birmingham City**. 5 **Derby Co.** pay £3m. for **Francois Grenet** from **Bordeaux**. 6 Four **Newcastle Utd.** players, **Craig Bellamy**, **Kieron Dyer**, **Carl Cort** and **Andy Griffin**, are sent home from their Spanish training camp and fined two weeks' wages for failing to appear at a tribute dinner for club president **Sir John Hall**. After playing for eight clubs, **Carlton Palmer** breaks into management with **Stockport Co.** Mark Wright, the **Oxford Utd.** manager, is fined £1,750 and given a four-match touchline ban by the F.A. after being dismissed from the dug-out for abusive language towards referee **Joe Ross** during the home game against **Scunthorpe Utd.** 7 **Paul Scholes** is fined by **Manchester Utd.** after failing to turn up for the Worthington Cup tie against **Arsenal**. **Mick Wadsworth**, former assistant manager at **Newcastle Utd.** and **Southampton**, takes over at **Oldham Athletic**. 8 **David Moss**, former **Stockport Co.** assistant manager, takes charge at **Macclesfield Town**. 9 Members of the Professional Footballers' Association vote 99% for strike action in a dispute with the Premier League and Football League over television money. **Steve Parkin** leaves **Rochdale** to become **Barnsley** manager. Portuguese club **Boavista** are fined £9,200 by UEFA for racist chants of supporters against **Emile Heskey** during the Champions League game against **Liverpool**. 10 The **Republic of Ireland** beat

Iran 2-0 in the first leg of their World Cup qualifying play-off. **England** and **Sweden** draw 1-1 in a friendly. **13 England** reach the finals of the European U-21 Championship with a 3-2 aggregate win over **Holland. Southampton** sign **Agustin Delgado** from Mexican club **Necaxa** for £3.2m. **15** The **Republic of Ireland** reach the finals of the World Cup with a 2-1 aggregate win over **Iran** in the play-offs. Caretaker **Terry Yorath** is appointed **Sheffield Wed.** manager. **16 Jaap Stam,** Lazio's former **Manchester Utd.** defender, becomes the latest high-profile sportsman to test positive for the banned steroid, nandrolone. **17 Canvey Island** take the day's F.A. Cup first round honours with a 1-0 away win over **Wigan Athletic. 18** Hereford utd. follow suit by putting out **Wrexham** by the same scoreline. **20** The Professional Footballers' Association serve notice of a strike on December 1 after rejecting a new £50m., three-year offer of television money from the Premier League and Football League. **Dario Gradi** completes 1,000 games as **Crewe Alexandra** manager. **22 Crystal Palace** win a temporary injunction in the High Court preventing manager **Steve Bruce** from leaving without serving nine months' notice. **John Beck** resigns as manager of **Cambridge Utd.** Manager **Mark Wright** is suspended on full pay by **Oxford Utd.** pending further consideration by the club of his dismissal from the dug-out during the home game against **Scunthorpe Utd. 23** Strike action by the Professional Footballers' Association is called off after a new £52.5m., three-year offer of television money is accepted. **Ipswich Town** pay £3m. for **Marcus Bent** from **Blackburn Rov. 27 Alan Shearer** scores his 100th goal for **Newcastle Utd.. 28 Robbie Fowler** joins **Leeds Utd.** from **Liverpool** for £11m. After 24 penalties, **Macclesfield Town** win the longest-ever F.A. Cup shoot-out 11-10 against **Forest Green Rov.** in a first round replay. **29** Amid proposals by a group of first division clubs for a second tier for the Premiership, Football League chairmen agree to conduct a review of the game's structure with the F.A. **Paolo Di Canio** wins FIFA's 2001 Fair Play Award for spurning a match-winning chance for **West Ham Utd.** by halting play for attention to injured **Everton** goalkeeper **Paul Gerrard. 30 Trevor Francis,** who parted company with **Birmingham City** last month, becomes manager of **Crystal Palace. Mark Wright** resigns as **Oxford Utd.** manager and is replaced by **Ian Atkins,** formerly with **Carlisle Utd.** and **Northampton Town.** Accountants Deloitte and Touche declare **Manchester Utd.** the richest club in the world for the fourth successive year with a turnover of £117m. FIFA break with tradition and decide that the World Cup winners will have to qualify for the 2006 finals in Germany.

DECEMBER 2001

1 Sir Alex Ferguson writes off **Manchester Utd.'s** chances of retaining the title after a 3-0 home defeat by **Chelsea. 3 Alan Shearer,** sent off in the **Newcastle Utd.-Charlton Athletic Athletic** game, has the red card rescinded by the F.A. **4** The F.A. fine **Watford** £5,000 and **W.B.A.** £2,500 for a brawl between their players. **Manchester City** manager **Kevin Keegan** is dismissed from the dug-out for disputing a **Millwall** penalty. **6 Arsenal** manager **Arsene Wenger** ends months of speculation about his future by signing a new four-year contract. **Ipswich Town** are knocked out of the UEFA Cup by **Christian Vieri's** hat-trick for **Inter Milan** and **Celtic** lose on penalties to **Valencia. 7 Sunderland** equal their club record signing with the £4.5m acquisition of **Claudio Reyna** from **Rangers. Swindon Town** are taken over by a consortium headed by former champion jockey **Willie Carson,** who becomes club chairman. **9 England** coach **Sven Goran Eriksson** rules out any chance of succeeding **Sir Alex Ferguson** as **Manchester Utd.** manager. **England** captain **David Beckham** pledges his future to Old Trafford after being voted BBC Sports Personality of the Year. **Canvey Island** spring the weekend's F.A. Cup second round surprise, beating **Northampton Town** 1-0. **10 Arsenal** receive approval from Islington Council for a new, 60,000-capacity stadium half-a-mile from Highbury. **Cardiff City** are refused permission to switch their F.A. Cup third round tie against **Leeds Utd.** to the Millennium Stadium. **11** Hibernian manager **Alex McLeish** takes over at **Rangers,** succeeding **Dick Advocaat** who becomes director of football. **12** Premiership clubs rule out proposals for a second division which would have included **Celtic** and **Rangers.** A managerial 'swop' is completed. **Steve Bruce** becomes **Birmingham City** manager, a fortnight after **Trevor Francis's** appointment at **Crystal Palace,** a compensation package having been agreed for Bruce's release. **John Hollins,** dismissed by **Swansea City** in September, is named the new **Rochdale** manager. **Leeds Utd.** absolve new-signing **Robbie Fowler** of any wrong-doing for his arrest, and release without charge, over an incident with a photographer following the players' Christmas party. **13** **Wolves** sign **Kenny Miller** from **Rangers** for £3m. **14** **Leeds Utd.** player **Jonathan Woodgate** is found guilty, at Hull Crown Court, of affray and ordered to undertake 100 hours of community service. He is cleared of causing grievous bodily harm to a 21-year-old student. Team-mate **Lee Bowyer** is found not guilty of both charges. **Hibernian** name club captain **Franck Sauzee** as their new manager. **16** Manager **David O'Leary** defends his decision to write a book, *Leeds United On Trial*, which includes a chapter on the trial of Woodgate and Bowyer. **17** **Michael Owen** is named European Footballer of the Year, the first English player since **Kevin Keegan** in 1979. **David Beckham**, placed fourth, is runner-up to **Portugal's Luis Figo** in FIFA's World Player of the Year poll. **Les Ferdinand** scores the Premiership's 10,000th goal, wins a Barclaycard cheque for £10,000 for charity and sparks **Tottenham's** 4-0 win over **Fulham**. **Jonathan Woodgate**, **Lee Bowyer** and **Leeds Utd.** learn that they face private legal action by Sarfraz Najeib, the Asian student the players were cleared of assaulting. **17** **Luis Boa Morte**, sent off in **Fulham's** match against **Everton**, has the red card rescinded. **18** **Lee Bowyer** is placed on the transfer list after refusing to pay four weeks' wages for breaching the club's code of conduct. **Jonathan Woodgate** accepts a fine of eight weeks' wages imposed by the club. **Newcastle Utd.** end a run of 29 matches without a victory in London by beating **Arsenal** 3-1. **19** The F.A. announce that Wembley remains the preferred choice for a new national stadium, but lukewarm support from the Government casts further doubt on the project. **Dagenham & Redbridge** reach round three of the F.A. Cup for the second successive season by beating **Exeter City** 3-0 in a replay. **20** **Lee Bowyer** backs down, agrees to a club fine of four weeks' wages and is taken off the transfer list by **Leeds Utd.** After four months in the job, **Roy Evans** resigns as director of football at **Swindon Town** and **Andy King** begins his second spell as manager. **21** **Liverpool** acquire former **Arsenal** and **Real Madrid** player **Nicolas Anelka** on loan from **Paris St-Germain** and complete the £3.2m. signing of **Milan Baros** from **Banik Ostrava** after he obtains a work permit. **22** **Clyde Wijnhard**, who almost died in a car crash in September 2000, makes his comeback for **Huddersfield Town**. **24** Two managerial resignations – **Jim Jefferies** at **Bradford City** and **Gerry Francis** at **Bristol Rov. 28** **Grimsby Town** sack their manager **Lennie Lawrence** and appoint **Paul Groves** player-manager. Caretaker **Garry Thompson** takes over as manager of **Bristol Rov. Newcastle Utd.'s Craig Bellamy** appeals successfully against his sending-off against **Arsenal**. **29** **Andy Cole** joins **Blackburn Rov.** from **Manchester Utd.** for £7.5m. **Michael Owen** scores his 100th goal for **Liverpool**. **Paul Warhurst** and **Dean Holdsworth (Bolton Wand.)** and **Muzzy Izzet (Leicester City)** are sent off at the Reebok Stadium. Former **England** manager **Graham Taylor** receives an OBE and **Liverpool** veteran **Gary McAllister** gets an MBE in the New Year's Honours List. **Arsenal** end the year on top of the table, ahead of **Newcastle Utd.** on goal difference, with **Manchester Utd.** having restored their challenge after five straight wins. In Scotland, **Celtic** lead **Rangers** by 10 points. **31** **Nicky Law** leaves **Chesterfield** to become **Bradford City** manager.

JANUARY 2002

2 **Sir Alex Ferguson** dismisses speculation that he will stay on as **Manchester Utd.** manager beyond the end of the season. **3** **Jim Smith** returns to management as assistant to **Roland Nilsson** at **Coventry City**. **5** F.A. Cup third round surprises: **Sunderland** 1, **W.B.A.** 2; **Portsmouth** 1, **Leyton Orient** 4. **6** Crowd violence overshadows **Cardiff City's** 2-1 F.A. Cup win over **Leeds Utd.** In another shock, **Derby Co.** lose 3-1 at home to a **Nathan Ellington** hat-trick for **Bristol Rov. Manchester Utd.** score three times in six minutes to retrieve a two-goal deficit and beat **Aston Villa** 3-2, but this victory is also marred by a pitch invasion. **7** **John Carew's** £7m. move from **Valencia** to **Fulham** is called off after he fails a medical. Twenty four hours after resigning as **Mansfield Town** manager, **Billy Dearden** takes over at **Notts Co.**, replacing **Gary Brazil** who stays on as coach. Caretaker **John Taylor** is appointed manager of **Cambridge Utd.** England's **Graham Poll** and Scotland's **Hugh Dallas** are chosen to referee at the World Cup in Japan and South Korea. **8** **Chelsea** fine **John Terry** and **Jody Morris** two weeks' wages each for breaking a nightclub ban. Following crowd trouble at the F.A. Cup tie against **Leeds Utd., Cardiff City** owner **Sam Hammam** promises to stop walking around the pitch during games. A consortium headed by former manager and chairman **Jim McLean** takes control of **Dundee Utd. 9** Bottles and coins thrown during the **Chelsea-Tottenham** Worthington Cup semi-final raise further fears of a return to the bad old days of hooliganism. Assistant manager **Stuart Watkiss** is appointed manager of **Mansfield Town. 10** Managers **Mark McGhee** and **Steve Bruce** are both sent to the stands in a heated game between **Millwall** and **Birmingham City. 12** Leeds Utd. are fined £25,000 by the F.A. for six bookings against **Newcastle Utd. 14** Derby Co. dismiss manager **Colin Todd** after three months in the job. **16** Southampton lose 2-1 to **Rotherham Utd.** in the F.A. Cup third round. **19** Ruud van Nistelrooy sets a Premiership record by scoring for **Manchester Utd.** for the eighth successive match. Crowd trouble causes a 17-minutes interruption of the **Aberdeen-Rangers** game. Jeff Astle, former **W.B.A.** and **England** striker, dies aged 59. **22** Manchester Utd. sign Uruguayan **Diego Forlan** from **Independiente** for £6.9m. **Walsall** sack manager **Ray Graydon. 24** John Gregory resigns as **Aston Villa** manager. **Villa's David Ginola** is fined £22,000 by the F.A. and banned for two games for misconduct. **Carlisle Utd.** are fined £25,000 for fielding an ineligible player against **Mansfield Town**, but escape a points deduction. So do **Luton Town**, fined £20,000 for failing to fulfil a fixture against **Kidderminster Harriers** because of illness. A consortium headed by former player **Mel Nurse** takes over **Swansea City**. Former **Wolves** manager **Colin Lee** takes over at **Walsall. 25** A case of mistaken identity results in **Jimmy Floyd Hasselbaink's** red card against **Tottenham** in the Worthington Cup semi-final being transferred to his **Chelsea** team-mate **Mario Melchiot. Dick Advocaat** is appointed **Holland** coach for the second time, but continues as director of football at **Rangers. 26** Walsall take pride of place in round four of the F.A. Cup with a 2-1 away win over **Charlton Athletic. Middlesbrough's** 2-0 win over **Manchester Utd.** is overshadowed by the death, only hours later, of defender **Colin Cooper's** two-year-old son. **27** Jamie Carragher is sent off for throwing a coin back into the crowd as F.A. Cup holders **Liverpool** lose 1-0 to **Arsenal**, who have **Martin Keown** and match-winner **Dennis Bergkamp** dismissed for fouls. **29** An F.A. arbitration panel refers **Wimbledon's** proposal to move to Milton Keynes back to the Football League. **30** John Gregory takes over as **Derby Co.** manager, six days after quitting **Aston Villa**. Following a vote of no-confidence by the **Coventry City** board, **Bryan Richardson** is removed as chairman and chief executive. **31** Manchester Utd. admit defeat after a month-long bid to sign **Paolo Di Canio** from **West Ham Utd. Benito Carbone** is fined two weeks' wages by **Bradford City** for refusing to be a substitute against **Preston N.E.**

FEBRUARY 2002

2 Arsenal set a Premiership record. by scoring for the 26th successive match. **4** Newcastle Utd. pay £5m. for 18-year-old **Jermaine Jenas** from **Nott'm. Forest. Fulham** announce they will ground-share with **Q.P.R.** while Craven Cottage is redeveloped. Conference officials refuse permission for **Stevenage Borough** to take part in a Channel 4 programme in which fans would have a say in team selection. **5** Nine months after retiring from management, **Graham Taylor** takes charge at **Aston Villa. Derby Co.** manager **John Gregory** receives a three-match touchline ban and is fined £12,000 by the F.A. for abusive language to linesman **Ray Gould** during the **Aston Villa-Liverpool** match. **Lee Bowyer** is banned for six games and fined £10,000 for elbowing **Liverpool's Gary McAllister** and using abusive language to referee **Jeff Winter.** His Leeds Utd. team-mate **Danny Mills** is fined £7,500 along with a two-match ban for abusive language to fourth official **Andy D'Urso** at **Arsenal. Ade Akinbiyi**, much-criticised **Leicester City** striker, joins **Crystal Palace** for £2.2m. **6** Fabien Barthez is fined by **Manchester Utd.** for a late night-out in London before training. **8** David Ginola ends an unhappy spell at **Aston Villa** with a no-fee move to **Everton**, who also sign **Lee Carsley** from **Coventry City** for £1.9m. **11** West Ham Utd. manager **Glenn Roeder** signs a three-year extension to his contract. **13** Darius Vassell scores a spectacular goal on his **England** debut in a 1-1 draw with **Holland**. Other friendly international results: **Wales** 1, **Argentina** 1; **Poland** 4, **Northern Ireland** 1; **Republic of**

Ireland 2, **Russia** 0. **Berti Vogts**, who guided **Germany** to victory in Euro 96, takes over as **Scotland** coach. **Youri Djorkaeff**, a World Cup winner with **France**, joins **Bolton Wand.** from **Kaiserslautern** until the end of the season. **Newcastle Utd.** fine **Jamie McClen** after he was cautioned by police for being drunk and disorderly. **14 Halifax Town** are put up for sale. **Newcastle Utd.** fine **Craig Bellamy** after he was cautioned by police for assaulting a woman student. **17 Sir Walter Winterbottom**, the first and longest-serving **England** manager, dies aged 89. **18 Alan Cork** resigns as manager of **Cardiff City** and is replaced by director of football **Lennie Lawrence**. **19 Chelsea**'s **Roberto Di Matteo**, who suffered a badly broken leg in September 2000, is forced to retire. **21 Hibernian** manager **Franck Sauzee** is sacked after two months in the job. **22 Chesterfield** name club physio **David Rushbury** as manager. **24** In the first domestic final to be played indoors, **Blackburn Rov.** beat **Tottenham** 2-1 to win the **Worthington Cup** under the closed Millennium Stadium roof. **25 Manchester City** fine **Nicky Weaver**, **Richard Dunne** and **Jeff Whitley** over an incident at a night-club. **Bobby Williamson** quits **Kilmarnock** to become **Hibernian** manager. **26** After changing his mind about retiring from management at the end of the season, **Sir Alex Ferguson** signs a new three-year deal with **Manchester Utd.** The F.A. fine **Millwall** manager **Mark McGhee** £7,500 and **Steve Bruce**, of **Birmingham City**, £5,000 following confrontations with referee **Phil Dowd** during their teams' match at the New Den. **27 Hull City** part company with manager **Brian Little** by mutual consent. **28** British interest in the UEFA Cup ends at the fourth round stage, with **Leeds Utd.** conceding a last-minute goal to lose 1-0 on aggregate to **PSV Eindhoven** and **Rangers** going down 4-3 to **Feyenoord**. Scotland and Ireland launch a joint bid for the finals of the 2008 European Championship. **Portsmouth** chairman **Milan Mandaric** backs down after refusing to pay his players, manager **Graham Rix** and the coaching staff because of poor performances. **Jim Jefferies**, former **Bradford City** and **Hearts** manager, takes charge at **Kilmarnock**.

MARCH 2002

1 Bury, faced with closure because of large debts, go into administration. **2 Roy Keane** effectively commits the rest of his career to **Manchester Utd.** by signing a new four-year contract. **3 Peter Ridsdale**, the **Leeds Utd.** chairman, is rebuked by police after remonstrating with supporters for abusing coach **Brian Kidd** at **Everton**. **4** A Charity Commission inquiry criticises the F.A. for breaking fund-raising regulations in the distribution of profits from the Charity Shield match. **5** The F.A. fine **Fulham** £30,000 and **Everton** £25,000 for a brawl involving their players at Craven Cottage. **Kevin Keegan** follows up the £2m. signing of Chinese defender **Sun Jihai** by paying a club record £5m. to bring **Jon Macken** to **Manchester City** from **Preston N.E. 6 Thierry Henry** is banned for three matches for confronting referee **Graham Poll** at the end of **Arsenal**'s home defeat by **Newcastle Utd.** American businessman **Albert Scardino** takes over **Notts Co. Andy Clarke**, of **Peterborough Utd.**, is banned for a month after failing a drugs test. **Leicester City** sell their Filbert Street ground to a development company for £3.75m. ahead of moving to a new stadium. **7 Swansea City** sack manager **Colin Addison**. **10 W.B.A.**, the last Nationwide League side left in the F.A. Cup, lose 1-0 to **Fulham** in the quarter-finals. **12 Everton** dismiss manager **Walter Smith**. **13 Manchester Utd.** qualify for the quarter-finals of the Champions League. **14 David Moyes**, the **Preston N.E.** manager, takes over at **Everton**. **Patrick Vieira** (**Arsenal**) and **Leeds Utd.** pair **Mark Viduka** and **Alan Smith** are cleared by the F.A. of misconduct charges. A Premier League commision fines **Liverpool** £20,000 and **Christian Ziege** £10,000 for an illegal approach which led to the German player leaving **Middlesbrough** for Anfield. **15 York City** are saved from closure by motor racing tycoon **John Batchelor** and **Bury**'s short-term future is secured by High Court approval to extend the club's period of administration. **16** On a black day for English football, referee **Eddie Wolstenholme** takes the unprecedented step of abandoning the **Sheffield Utd.**- **W.B.A.** match after the Bramall Lane side, losing 3-0, are reduced to six men by the dismissals of **Simon Tracey**, **George Santos** and **Patrick Suffo** and injuries. A total of 16 red cards, two in the Premiership and 14 in the Nationwide League, overtakes the previous one-day highest of 15. First division **Stockport Co.** become the first side to be relegated. **17 Paul Gascoigne** joins **Burnley** from **Everton** on a short-term contract. **19** Five months after life-saving heart surgery, **Gerard Houllier** returns to the **Liverpool** dug-out and sees his team reach the quarter-finals of the Champions League by beating **Roma** 2-0. **Tottenham**'s **Mauricio Taricco** is fined £5,000 by the F.A. for improper conduct against **Chelsea**, who have **Jimmy Floyd Hasselbaink** cleared of misconduct during the match with **Southampton**. **Manchester Utd.** manager **Sir Alex Ferguson** is awarded £7,500 libel damages in the High Court over an allegation by columnist **David Mellor** in the *London Evening Standard* about match interviews. **20 Arsenal** fail to reach the Champions League quarter-finals, but **Patrick Vieira** offers some consolation by ruling out a move abroad. **21** The Football League rule that the 3-0 scoreline to **W.B.A.** in their abandoned match against **Sheffield Utd.** should stand as the result. **Jan Molby**, the **Kidderminster Harriers** manager, and **Northampton Town** player **Marco Gabbiadini** are fined £500 each by the F.A. for improper conduct in separate matches. **23 Jonathan Woodgate** is omitted from **England**'s World Cup plans because of his conviction for affray. **25 Robert Pires** is ruled out of the remainder of **Arsenal**'s season and of **France**'s defence of the World Cup by a cruciate knee ligament injury. **Portsmouth** sack **Graham Rix** and appoint director of football **Harry Redknapp** as manager. **26** Commentator **Kenneth Wolstenholme** dies aged 81. Third division **Plymouth Argyle** become the first side to win promotion. **27 Berti Vogts** suffers a 5-0 defeat by **France** in his first game as **Scotland** manager. Other friendly international results: **England** 1, **Italy** 2; **Wales** 0, **Czech Republic** 0; **Liechtenstein** 0, **Northern Ireland** 0; **Republic of Ireland** 3, **Denmark** 0. Some clubs relying on television money say they face ruin after ITV Digital goes into administration with £178m. outstanding on its contract with the Football League. **Peter Crouch** joins **Aston Villa** from **Portsmouth** for £5m. The No 10 shirt worn by **Pele** in the 1970 World Cup Final is auctioned for a record £157,750 at Christie's in London. **28 Matthew Le Tissier** announces his retirement after 16 years at his only club, **Southampton**. **29 Jan Molby** resigns as **Kidderminster Harriers** manager to take over at **Hull City**. **30 Cambridge Utd.** are relegated from the Second Division and **Luton Town** gain promotion from Division Three.

APRIL 2002

1 Halifax Town become the first club to be relegated twice to the Conference. Three **Kidderminster Harriers** players, **Abdou Sall**, **Gary Montgomery** and **Ian Foster** are sent off against **Bristol Rov. 3 Worthington** calls time on sponsorship of the League Cup after next season. **4 Graeme Souness**, the **Blackburn Rov.** manager, is fined £10,000 and banned for one match for comments to referee **Graham Barber. 6 Celtic** retain the Scottish Premier League title with a month of the season to go. **St. Johnstone** are relegated. **Leicester City** go down from the Premiership. **Manchester City** are champions of Division One and top 100 goals. **Wrexham** are relegated from the Second Division, despite a 5-0 win over **Cambridge Utd.** in which **Lee Jones** scores all their goals. **Roddy Collins**, manager of **Carlisle Utd.**, is sacked for upsetting owner **Michael Knighton** with comments about a takeover of the club. **7 Brighton & H.A.** go up to Division One. **8** Manager **Alan Little** leaves **Halifax Town. 9 Liverpool** lose 4-3 on aggregate to **Bayer Leverkusen** in the Champions League quarter-finals. **Jonathan Woodgate**, the **Leeds Utd.** defender, sustains a broken jaw in a street incident. **Garry Thompson** is sacked as manager of **Bristol Rov.** Protests by supporters force **Leicester City** to change the name of their new ground from the Walkers Bowl to the Walkers Stadium. **10** A broken bone in his left foot threatens to put **England** captain **David Beckham** out of the World Cup. The injury overshadows a 5-2 aggregate win for **Manchester Utd.** over **Deportivo La Coruna** in the Champions League quarter-finals. **12 Chelsea** coach **Claudio Ranieri** ends speculation about his future by signing a new five-year contract. The Football League turn down £60m. to settle their dispute with ITV Digital. **13 Brighton & H.A.** win the Division Two title – their second successive championship success. **Barnsley** are relegated from the First Division. **14 Arsenal** and **Chelsea** reach the F.A. Cup Final with 1-0 wins over **Middlesbrough** and **Fulham** respectively. **Manchester Utd.**'s **Ruud van Nistelrooy** is named P.F.A. Players' Player of the Year. **15 Tottenham** follow up a £4m. shirt advertising deal with Thomson with a £15m. kit manufacturing agreement with Italian company Kappa. **Plymouth Argyle** are Division Three champions. **16 Roland Nilsson** is sacked after six months as **Coventry City** manager, along with his assistant **Jim Smith**. Tottenham sign **Liverpool** club captain **Jamie Redknapp** on a free transfer. Ten clubs threaten to resign from the Scottish Premier League in two seasons' time following the rejection by **Celtic** and **Rangers** of proposals for the League to have a TV channel. **17** Bury coach **Billy Ayre**, a former **Blackpool** and **Halifax Town** manager, dies of cancer aged 49. **17 Michael Owen**, at 22 the youngest **England** captain since Bobby Moore, leads a 4-0 win over **Paraguay**. Other friendly international results: **Scotland** 1, **Nigeria** 2; **Northern Ireland** 0, **Spain** 5; **Republic of Ireland** 2, **United States** 1. **19** Arsenal sign a £10m. shirt sponsorship deal with mobile phone operator mmO2. **20** Alan Shearer becomes the first player to score 200 Premiership goals. **Derby Co.** are relegated. **Reading** pip **Brentford** for the second automatic promotion spot in Division Two. **Bournemouth** and **Bury** go down. **Mansfield Town** go up from the Third Division. The Football Writers' Association Player of the Year award goes to **Arsenal's Robert Pires**. **21** W.B.A. are promoted from the First Division. **Crewe Alexandra** go down. **Stuart Pearce** misses a penalty in his final match for **Manchester City** before retiring. **John Hartson** and **Johan Mjallby**, of **Celtic**, and **Fernando Ricksen** (**Rangers**) are sent off in the Old Firm match. **23** Fulham announce the biggest annual loss in British football – £24m. **Roy McFarland** resigns as manager of Torquay Utd. over cost-cutting caused by the ITV Digital affair. **Robbie Savage** is fined two weeks' wages by **Leicester City** for using the referee's toilet before the match against **Aston Villa**. **24 Gary McAllister** signs up to become **Coventry City** manager after completing the season with **Liverpool**. **Terry Butcher**, a former manager at Highfield Road, becomes manager of **Motherwell** when **Eric Black** resigns, along with chief executive **Pat Nevin**, after the club goes into administration. **25** Wimbledon manager **Terry Burton** is sacked. **Alan Buckley** loses his job at **Lincoln City**, another casualty of the ITV Digital dispute. Caretaker **Ian Britton** is appointed **Kidderminster Harriers** manager. **26** Barclays Bank pull out of the project to rebuild Wembley Stadium. **Celtic's John Hartson** has the red card received against **Rangers** rescinded. **27** A pitch invasion by protesting **Airdrie** fans causes their game against **Ayr Utd.** to be abandoned. The scoreline, 1-0 to **Ayr**, stands. **28 Boston Utd.** are promoted from the Conference, pipping **Dagenham & Redbridge** on goal difference. Former **Scotland** coach **Craig Brown** is appointed **Preston N.E.** manager. **Rangers** defender **Lorenzo Amoruso** is named the Scottish P.F.A. Player of the Year. **29** A fortnight after winning the Second Division title, **Peter Taylor** resigns as manager of **Brighton & H.A.** **30** Manchester **City** lose to **Bayer Leverkusen** on away goals in the semi-finals of the Champions League. Nine days after celebrating promotion, **W.B.A.** chairman **Paul Thompson** resigns over a dispute with manager **Gary Megson**.

MAY 2002

1 Scottish First Division club **Airdrie**, founded in 1878, go out of business with debts of nearly £3m. Fans clash with police after the **Cardiff City-Stoke City** play-off semi-final. **2** More violent scenes after the **Millwall-Birmingham City** game, with 47 police injured. Following the abandoned match against **W.B.A.**, **Sheffield Utd.** are fined £10,000 and individual fines are imposed on manager **Neil Warnock** (£300) and players **Patrick Suffo** (£3,000) and **Keith Curle** (£500). **Neil Warnock** is fined a further £1,000 by the F.A. and banned for two matches over an incident at Barnsley. **3** England's **Gary Neville** is ruled out of the World Cup with a broken bone in his left foot. **Lincoln City**, with a new manager in **Keith Alexander**, go into adminstration. **Rushden & Diamonds** claim one of their players, **Ritchie Hanlon**, is struck with a police baton after the play-off semi-final at **Rochdale**. **4** Arsenal beat **Chelsea** 2-0 in the F.A. Cup Final. **Rangers** add the Tennents Cup to the CIS Cup with a last-minute goal which gives them a 3-2 win over **Celtic**. **6 Cheltenham Town** beat **Rushden & Diamonds** 3-1 in the Division Three Play-off Final. **Gary Kelly** donates around £700,000 from his **Leeds Utd.** testimonial to a cancer charity. Manager **Mick McCarthy** stays loyal to the players who qualified when naming his **Republic of Ireland** World Cup squad. **7** Arsenal complete the Double by winning at 1-0 Old Trafford. Two goals by former **Celtic** and **Nott'm. Forest** player **Pierre van Hooijdonk** and one by **Jon Dahl Tomasson**, once of **Newcastle Utd.**, give **Feyenoord** a 3-2 victory over **Borussia Dortmund** in the UEFA Cup Final. **9** The inclusion of **Martin Keown** is the only real surprise in **England's** 23 for the World Cup. **10 Marlon King**, top scorer with

Gillingham, is jailed for 18 months for handling a stolen car. **11** **Liverpool** beat **Manchester Utd.** to the Premiership runners-up spot. **Ipswich Town** are relegated. **Stoke City** defeat **Brentford** 2-0 in the Division Two Play-off Final. **Yeovil Town** are F.A. Trophy winners by 2-0 against **Stevenage Borough**. **12** **Birmingham City** win the Division One Play-off Final on penalties against **Norwich City**. **Tahar El Khalej** apologises for the red-card tackle in the **Southampton-Newcastle Utd.** match which threatens the World Cup place of **Kieron Dyer**. **13** **Steven Gerrard** is ruled out of the World Cup by a groin injury. Another double success for **Arsenal**, with **Arsene Wenger** named Premiership Manager of the Year and **Freddie Ljungberg** Player of the Year. **Tony Adams** raises around £500,000 for his Sporting Chance charity from his Arsenal testimonial match. **14** A goal by **Robert Earnshaw**, of **Cardiff City**, on his international debut gives **Wales** a 1-0 win over **Germany**. **Niall Quinn's** testimonial at **Sunderland** raises about £750,000 of his £1m. target for children's hospital charities. **Matthew Le Tissier's** testimonial at **Southampton** nets about £500,000. **15** A spectacular goal by **Zinedine Zidane** gives **Real Madrid** a 2-1 win over **Bayer Leverkusen** in the European Cup Final at Hampden Park. The F.A. overturn a £30,000 fine imposed on **Fulham** for a players' brawl in the match against **Everton**. **Mark Kennedy (Wolves)** is forced out of the **Republic of Ireland** squad for the World Cup with a groin injury and there is a call-up for **Steven Reid**, of **Millwall**. **16** **Bradford City** go into administration, the first high-profile casualty of the collapse of ITV Digital. **Stoke City** sack manager **Gudjon Thordarson** five days after promotion to Division One. **Cardiff City** are fined £20,000 by the F.A. of Wales for crowd trouble at their F.A. Cup tie against **Leeds Utd.** The **Republic of Ireland** lose 2-1 to **Nigeria** in World Cup warm-up. **Scotland** are beaten 4-1 by **South Korea**. **Liverpool** pay £3.7m. for **Lille** striker **Bruno Cheyrou**. **17** **Liverpool** unveil plans for a new 55,000-capacity stadium in Stanley Park, 300 yards from Anfield. **England** beat **Switzerland** 2-1 in their opening group match of the European U-21 Championship Finals. **19** **Sylvain Distin**, on loan at **Newcastle Utd.** last season, joins **Manchester City** from **Paris St-Germain** for £4m. **Aston Villa** beat **Everton** 4-2 on aggregate in the F.A. Youth Cup Final. **20** **England** lose 2-1 to **Italy** in the European U-21 Championship. **Scotland** go down 2-0 to **South Africa**. **21** Captain **Roy Keane**, unhappy with the **Republic of Ireland's** World Cup preparations, withdraws from the squad, then has a change of heart. **England** are held 1-1 by **South Korea** in their first World Cup warm-up. **22** **England** go out of the European U-21 Championship after a 3-1 defeat by **Portugal**. **23** **Roy Keane** is sent home from the **Republic of Ireland's** World Cup training camp after directing abuse at manager **Mick McCarthy**. Administrators at **Bradford City** cancel the contracts of 19 players, nearly half the squad, in an effort to save the club. **Franco Baresi**, former **AC Milan** and **Italy** defender, joins **Fulham** as technical director. **Derby Co.** manager **John Gregory** is fined £5,000 by the F.A. for abusive language towards the fourth official during the game against **Newcastle Utd. 24** **Danny Murphy** becomes another **England** World Cup casualty with a broken bone in his left foot. **Trevor Sinclair**, who returned home 48 hours earlier, flies out to rejoin the squad. **26** A last-minute goal by **Robbie Fowler** gives **England** a 2-2 draw with **Cameroon** in their final match before the World Cup. **27** **Steve Cotterill** who led **Cheltenham Town** into the Second Division, becomes **Stoke City** manager. **Q.P.R.** come out of administration. **Northern Ireland** manager **Sammy McIlroy** and his assistant **Jim Harvey** are banned for one match and fined a total of £4,000 after being ordered from the dug-out during the World Cup qualifier against **Malta**. **28** **Roy Keane** rules out any chance of returning to the **Republic Ireland's** World Cup squad by refusing to apologise to manager **Mick McCarthy**. **Wimbledon** are given the go-ahead to move to Milton Keynes by an F.A. independent commission. Relegated **Ipswich Town** win a UEFA Cup place through the Fair Play League. **Sir Elton John** resigns as **Watford** chairman, ending a 29-year involvement with the club. **29** The F.A. oppose his re-election but **Sepp Blatter** overcomes serious allegations of mismanagement and continues as president of FIFA. **Rochdale** appoint midfielder **Paul Simpson** player-manager. **30** Coach **Graham Allner** becomes manager of **Cheltenham Town**. **31** The World Cup opens with a shock 1-0 win for **Senegal** over **France**, the holders. **Oldham Athletic** sack manager **Mick Wadsworth** and replace him with coach **Iain Dowie**.

JUNE 2002

1 The **Republic of Ireland** come from behind to draw 1-1 with **Cameroon** in their opening World Cup game. **2 England** are held 1-1 by **Sweden** in their first match. **5 The Republic of Ireland**, with Steve Staunton winning his 100th cap, equalise in stoppage time through **Robbie Keane** to draw 1-1 with **Germany**. The **USA** surprise **Portugal** with a 3-2 win. **6** **Thierry Henry** is sent off in **France**'s goalless draw with **Uruguay**. **Steve Coppell** resigns as **Brentford** manager. Former **Portugal** and **South Africa** coach **Carlos Queiroz** becomes **Sir Alex Ferguson**'s No 2 at **Manchester Utd**. **7 England** beat **Argentina** 1-0 with a **David Beckham** penalty. **Manchester City** pay a club-record £13m. for **Nicolas Anelka**, who was on loan at **Liverpool** from **Paris St-Germain** last season. **8** Promotion and relegation between the Conference and Football League is increased to two teams. **11 The Republic of Ireland** beat **Saudi Arabia** 3-0 to reach the knock-out stages of the World Cup. Holders **France**, without a goal to their credit, go out after losing 2-0 to **Denmark**. In an attempt to confront hooliganism, **Millwall** bar away supporters from matches against six clubs. **Carlisle Utd.** go into voluntary administration. **12 England** reach the second round with a goalless draw against **Nigeria**. **Argentina** fail to qualify. **14** Another shock as **Portugal** fail to go through from one of the weaker groups. **Gianluca Vialli** is sacked as **Watford** manager, 24 hours after his assistant **Ray Wilkins** and backroom staff are dismissed. **Huddersfield Town** oust their manager **Lou Macari** and his assistant **Joe Jordan**. **Newcastle Utd.** manager **Bobby Robson** is knighted and there is a CBE for **Scotland**'s FIFA vice-president **David Will**. **15 England** reach the World Cup quarter-finals by beating **Denmark** 3-0. **16 The Republic of Ireland** go out on penalties against **Spain**. **17 Notts Co.**, the oldest Football League club, go into administration. **18 South Korea** topple **Italy** in the latest World Cup upset. **21 England** go out, beaten 2-1 by **Brazil** in the quarter-finals. **22 South Korea** reach the semi-finals, beating **Spain** on penalties. **24 Charlton Athletic** announce a club-record sponsorship deal with sports retailer all:sports worth up to £4.3m. **25 South Korea**'s run ends with a 1-0 defeat by **Germany**. **Senegal** World Cup striker **El Hadji Diouf** joins **Liverpool** from **Lens** for £10m. **27 David O'Leary** is sacked as **Leeds Utd.** manager. **28 Wimbledon** appoint goalkeeper coach **Stuart Murdoch** their new new manager. First team coach **Wally Downes** becomes **Brentford** manager. **30 Brazil** beat **Germany** 2-0 in the World Cup Final with two goals by **Ronaldo**.

QUOTE UNQUOTE

'I don't miss Wembley one bit. It was a tired old stadium, with a tired old atmosphere and a lot of cynical old fans' – **Gary Neville** urging the F.A. to continue taking England games around the country.

'I am not a dreamer. United will win it because they will put the power in when they need it' – **Gerard Houllier**, Liverpool manager, conceding the championship to Manchester United before the start of the season.

'Obviously he's using a bit of psychology and trying to take the pressure off his team' – **Sir Alex Ferguson**, dismissing Houllier's comments.

'I don't think we will win it now' – **Sir Alex Ferguson** after the 3-0 home defeat by Chelsea midway through the campaign.

'I didn't take what Alex Ferguson said seriously when you saw him putting Beckham, Giggs and Veron on the bench. United won the championship last year, then spent £50m., so do you expect them to finish bottom?' – **Arsene Wenger**, Arsenal manager.

'It's out of our hands now – Arsenal look favourites,' **Sir Alex Ferguson** after Manchester United suffered a fifth home defeat of the season against Middlesbrough.

'Under past England managers I was not exactly flavour of the month' – **Michael Owen** after his hat-trick in the 5-1 win over Germany.

FOOTBALLER OF THE YEAR

(Original award by the Football Writers' Association to the 'player who, by precept and example, on the field and off, shall be considered to have done most for football').

1948 Stanley Matthews (Blackpool); **1949** Johnny Carey (Manchester Utd.); **1950** Joe Mercer (Arsenal); **1951** Harry Johnston (Blackpool); **1952** Billy Wright (Wolves); **1953** Nat Lofthouse (Bolton Wand.); **1954** Tom Finney (Preston N.E.); **1955** Don Revie (Manchester City); **1956** Bert Trautmann (Manchester City); **1957** Tom Finney (Preston N.E.); **1958** Danny Blanchflower (Tottenham); **1959** Syd Owen (Luton Town); **1960** Bill Slater (Wolves); **1961** Danny Blanchflower (Tottenham); **1962** Jimmy Adamson (Burnley); **1963** Stanley Matthews (Stoke City); **1964** Bobby Moore (West Ham Utd.); **1965** Bobby Collins (Leeds Utd.); **1966** Bobby Charlton (Manchester Utd.); **1967** Jack Charlton (Leeds Utd.); **1968** George Best (Manchester Utd.); **1969** Tony Book (Manchester City) & Dave Mackay (Derby Co.) – shared; **1970** Billy Bremner (Leeds Utd.); **1971** Frank McLintock (Arsenal); **1972** Gordon Banks (Stoke City); **1973** Pat Jennings (Tottenham); **1974** Ian Callaghan (Liverpool); **1975** Alan Mullery (Fulham); **1976** Kevin Keegan (Liverpool); **1977** Emlyn Hughes (Liverpool); **1978** Kenny Burns (Nott'm Forest); **1979** Kenny Dalglish (Liverpool); **1980** Terry McDermott (Liverpool); **1981** Frans Thijssen (Ipswich Town); **1982** Steve Perryman (Tottenham); **1983** Kenny Dalglish (Liverpool); **1984** Ian Rush (Liverpool); **1985** Neville Southall (Everton); **1986** Gary Lineker (Everton); **1987** Clive Allen (Tottenham); **1988** John Barnes (Liverpool); **1989** Steve Nicol (Liverpool); Special award to the Liverpool players for the compassion shown to bereaved families after the Hillsborough Disaster; **1990** John Barnes (Liverpool); **1991** Gordon Strachan (Leeds Utd.); **1992** Gary Lineker (Tottenham); **1993** Chris Waddle (Sheff. Wed.); **1994** Alan Shearer (Blackburn Rov.); **1995** Jurgen Klinsmann (Tottenham); **1996** Eric Cantona (Manchester Utd.); **1997** Gianfranco Zola (Chelsea); **1998** Dennis Bergkamp (Arsenal); **1999** David Ginola (Tottenham); **2000** Roy Keane (Manchester Utd.); **2001** Teddy Sheringham (Manchester Utd.); **2002** Robert Pires (Arsenal).

P.F.A. AWARDS

Player of the Year: 1974 Norman Hunter (Leeds Utd.); **1975** Colin Todd (Derby Co.); **1976** Pat Jennings (Tottenham); **1977** Andy Gray (Aston Villa); **1978** Peter Shilton (Nott'm Forest); **1979** Liam Brady (Arsenal); **1980** Terry McDermott (Liverpool); **1981** John Wark (Ipswich Town); **1982** Kevin Keegan (Southampton); **1983** Kenny Dalglish (Liverpool); **1984** Ian Rush (Liverpool); **1985** Peter Reid (Everton); **1986** Gary Lineker (Everton); **1987** Clive Allen (Tottenham); **1988** John Barnes (Liverpool); **1989** Mark Hughes (Manchester Utd.); **1990** David Platt (Aston Villa); **1991** Mark Hughes (Manchester Utd.); **1992** Gary Pallister (Manchester Utd.); **1993** Paul McGrath (Aston Villa); **1994** Eric Cantona (Manchester Utd.); **1995** Alan Shearer (Blackburn Rov.); **1996** Les Ferdinand (Newcastle Utd.); **1997** Alan Shearer (Newcastle Utd.); **1998** Dennis Bergkamp (Arsenal); **1999** David Ginola (Tottenham); **2000** Roy Keane (Manchester Utd.); **2001** Teddy Sheringham (Manchester Utd.); **2002** Ruud van Nistelrooy (Manchester Utd.).

Young Player of the Year: 1974 Kevin Beattie (Ipswich Town); **1975** Mervyn Day (West Ham Utd.); **1976** Peter Barnes (Manchester City); **1977** Andy Gray (Aston Villa); **1978** Tony Woodcock (Nott'm Forest); **1979** Cyrille Regis (W.B.A.); **1980** Glenn Hoddle (Tottenham); **1981** Gary Shaw (Aston Villa); **1982** Steve Moran (Southampton); **1983** Ian Rush (Liverpool); **1984** Paul Walsh (Luton Town); **1985** Mark Hughes (Manchester Utd.); **1986** Tony Cottee (West Ham Utd.); **1987** Tony Adams (Arsenal); **1988** Paul Gascoigne (Newcastle Utd.); **1989** Paul Merson (Arsenal); **1990** Matthew Le Tissier (Southampton); **1991** Lee Sharpe (Manchester Utd.); **1992** Ryan Giggs (Manchester Utd.); **1993** Ryan Giggs (Manchester Utd.); **1994** Andy Cole (Newcastle Utd.); **1995** Robbie Fowler (Liverpool); **1996** Robbie Fowler (Liverpool); **1997** David Beckham (Manchester Utd.);

1998 Michael Owen (Liverpool); **1999** Nicholas Anelka (Arsenal); **2000** Harry Kewell (Leeds Utd.); **2001** Steven Gerrard (Liverpool); **2002** Craig Bellamy (Newcastle Utd.).

Merit Awards: 1974 Bobby Charlton & Cliff Lloyd; **1975** Denis Law; **1976** George Eastham; **1977** Jack Taylor; **1978** Bill Shankly; **1979** Tom Finney; **1980** Sir Matt Busby; **1981** John Trollope; **1982** Joe Mercer; **1983** Bob Paisley; **1984** Bill Nicholson; **1985** Ron Greenwood; **1986** England 1966 World Cup-winning team; **1987** Sir Stanley Matthews; **1988** Billy Bonds; **1989** Nat' Lofthouse; **1990** Peter Shilton; **1991** Tommy Hutchison; **1992** Brian Clough; **1993** Manchester Utd., 1968 European Champions; Eusebio (Benfica & Portugal); **1994** Billy Bingham; **1995** Gordon Strachan; **1996** Pele; **1997** Peter Beardsley; **1998** Steve Ogrizovic; **1999** Tony Ford; **2000** Gary Mabbutt; **2001** Jimmy Hill; **2002** Niall Quinn.

MANAGER OF THE YEAR (1)

(Chosen by a panel including managers, players, media, fan representatives, referees, the England coach and representatives of the Premier League and Football Association.)

1966 Jock Stein (Celtic); **1967** Jock Stein (Celtic); **1968** Matt Busby (Manchester Utd.); **1969** Don Revie (Leeds Utd.); **1970** Don Revie (Leeds Utd.); **1971** Bertie Mee (Arsenal); **1972** Don Revie (Leeds Utd.); **1973** Bill Shankly (Liverpool); **1974** Jack Charlton (Middlesbrough); **1975** Ron Saunders (Aston Villa); **1976** Bob Paisley (Liverpool); **1977** Bob Paisley (Liverpool); **1978** Brian Clough (Nott'm Forest); **1979** Bob Paisley (Liverpool); **1980** Bob Paisley (Liverpool); **1981** Ron Saunders (Aston Villa); **1982** Bob Paisley (Liverpool); **1983** Bob Paisley (Liverpool); **1984** Joe Fagan (Liverpool); **1985** Howard Kendall (Everton); **1986** Kenny Dalglish (Liverpool); **1987** Howard Kendall (Everton); **1988** Kenny Dalglish (Liverpool); **1989** George Graham (Arsenal); **1990** Kenny Dalglish (Liverpool); **1991** George Graham (Arsenal); **1992** Howard Wilkinson (Leeds Utd.); **1993** Alex Ferguson (Manchester Utd.); **1994** Alex Ferguson (Manchester Utd.); **1995** Kenny Dalglish (Blackburn Rov.); **1996** Alex Ferguson (Manchester Utd.); **1997** Alex Ferguson (Manchester Utd.); **1998** Arsene Wenger (Arsenal); **1999** Alex Ferguson (Manchester Utd.); **2000** Sir Alex Ferguson (Manchester Utd.); **2001** George Burley (Ipswich Town); **2002** Arsene Wenger (Arsenal).

MANAGER OF THE YEAR (2)

(As chosen by the League Managers' Association and awarded to 'the manager who has made best use of the resources available to him'.)

1993 Dave Bassett (Sheff. Utd.); **1994** Joe Kinnear (Wimbledon); **1995** Frank Clark (Nott'm Forest); **1996** Peter Reid (Sunderland); **1997** Danny Wilson (Barnsley); **1998** David Jones (Southampton); **1999** Alex Ferguson (Manchester Utd.); **2000** Alan Curbishley (Charlton Athletic); **2001** George Burley (Ipswich Town); **2002** Arsene Wenger (Arsenal).

SCOTTISH FOOTBALL WRITERS' ASSOCIATION

Player of the Year: 1965 Billy McNeill (Celtic); **1966** John Greig (Rangers); **1967** Ronnie Simpson (Celtic); **1968** Gordon Wallace (Raith); **1969** Bobby Murdoch (Celtic); **1970** Pat Stanton (Hibernian); **1971** Martin Buchan (Aberdeen); **1972** David Smith (Rangers); **1973** George Connelly (Celtic); **1974** World Cup Squad; **1975** Sandy Jardine (Rangers); **1976** John Greig (Rangers); **1977** Danny McGrain (Celtic); **1978** Derek Johnstone (Rangers); **1979** Andy Ritchie (Morton); **1980** Gordon Strachan (Aberdeen); **1981** Alan Rough (Partick Thistle); **1982** Paul Sturrock (Dundee Utd.); **1983** Charlie Nicholas (Celtic); **1984** Willie Miller (Aberdeen); **1985** Hamish McAlpine (Dundee Utd.); **1986** Sandy Jardine (Hearts); **1987** Brian McClair (Celtic); **1988** Paul McStay (Celtic); **1989** Richard Gough (Rangers); **1990** Alex McLeish (Aberdeen); **1991** Maurice Malpas

(Dundee Utd.); **1992** Ally McCoist (Rangers); **1993** Andy Goram (Rangers); **1994** Mark Hateley (Rangers); **1995** Brian Laudrup (Rangers); **1996** Paul Gascoigne (Rangers); **1997** Brian Laudrup (Rangers); **1998** Craig Burley (Celtic); **1999** Henrik Larsson (Celtic); **2000** Barry Ferguson (Rangers); **2001** Henrik Larsson (Celtic); **2002** Paul Lambert (Celtic).

SCOTTISH P.F.A. AWARDS

Player of the Year: 1978 Derek Johnstone (Rangers); **1979** Paul Hegarty (Dundee Utd.); **1980** Davie Provan (Celtic); **1981** Mark McGee (Aberdeen); **1982** Sandy Clarke (Airdrieonians); **1983** Charlie Nicholas (Celtic); **1984** Willie Miller (Aberdeen); **1985** Jim Duffy (Morton); **1986** Richard Gough (Dundee Utd.); **1987** Brian McClair (Celtic); **1988** Paul McStay (Celtic); **1989** Theo Snelders (Aberdeen); **1990** Jim Bett (Aberdeen); **1991** Paul Elliott (Celtic); **1992** Ally McCoist (Rangers); **1993** Andy Goram (Rangers); **1994** Mark Hateley (Rangers); **1995** Brian Laudrup (Rangers); **1996** Paul Gascoigne (Rangers); **1997** Paolo Di Canio (Celtic) **1998** Jackie McNamara (Celtic); **1999** Henrik Larsson (Celtic); **2000** Mark Viduka (Celtic); **2001** Henrik Larsson (Celtic); **2002** Lorenzo Amoruso (Rangers).

Young Player of Year: 1978 Graeme Payne (Dundee Utd.); **1979** Ray Stewart (Dundee Utd.); **1980** John McDonald (Rangers); **1981** Charlie Nicholas (Celtic); **1982** Frank McAvennie (St. Mirren); **1983** Paul McStay (Celtic); **1984** John Robertson (Hearts); **1985** Craig Levein (Hearts); **1986** Craig Levein (Hearts); **1987** Robert Fleck (Rangers); **1988** John Collins (Hibernian); **1989** Billy McKinlay (Dundee Utd.); **1990** Scott Crabbe (Hearts); **1991** Eoin Jess (Aberdeen); **1992** Phil O'Donnell (Motherwell); **1993** Eoin Jess (Aberdeen); **1994** Phil O'Donnell (Motherwell); **1995** Charlie Miller (Rangers); **1996** Jackie McNamara (Celtic); **1997** Robbie Winters (Dundee Utd.); **1998** Gary Naysmith (Hearts); **1999** Barry Ferguson (Rangers) ; **2000** Kenny Miller (Hibernian); **2001** Stilian Petrov (Celtic); **2002** Kevin McNaughton (Aberdeen).

SCOTTISH MANAGER OF THE YEAR

1987 Jim McLean (Dundee Utd.); **1988** Billy McNeill (Celtic); **1989** Graeme Souness (Rangers); **1990** Andy Roxburgh (Scotland); **1991** Alex Totten (St. Johnstone); **1992** Walter Smith (Rangers); **1993** Walter Smith (Rangers); **1994** Walter Smith (Rangers); **1995** Jimmy Nicholl (Raith); **1996** Walter Smith (Rangers); **1997** Walter Smith (Rangers); **1998** Wim Jansen (Celtic); **1999** Dick Advocaat (Rangers); **2000** Dick Advocaat (Rangers); **2001** Martin O'Neill (Celtic); **2002** John Lambie (Partick Thistle).

EUROPEAN FOOTBALLER OF THE YEAR

(Poll conducted by *France Football*) 1956 Stanley Matthews (Blackpool); **1957** Alfredo di Stefano (Real Madrid); **1958** Raymond Kopa (Real Madrid); **1959** Alfredo di Stefano (Real Madrid); **1960** Luis Suarez (Barcelona); **1961** Omar Sivori (Juventus); **1962** Josef Masopust (Dukla Prague); **1963** Lev Yashin (Moscow Dynamo); **1964** Denis Law (Manchester Utd.); **1965** Eusebio (Benfica); **1966** Bobby Charlton (Manchester Utd.); **1967** Florian Albert (Ferencvaros); **1968** George Best (Manchester Utd.); **1969** Gianni Rivera (AC Milan); **1970** Gerd Muller (Bayern Munich); **1971** Johan Cruyff (Ajax); **1972** Franz Beckenbauer (Bayern Munich); **1973** Johan Cruyff (Barcelona); **1974** Johan Cruyff (Barcelona); **1975** Oleg Blokhin (Dynamo Kiev); **1976** Franz Beckenbauer (Bayern Munich); **1977** Allan Simonsen (Borussia Moenchengladbach); **1978** Kevin Keegan (SV Hamburg); **1979** Kevin Keegan (SV Hamburg); **1980** Karl-Heinz Rummenigge (Bayern Munich); **1981** Karl-Heinz Rummenigge (Bayern Munich); **1982** Paolo Rossi (Juventus); **1983** Michel Platini (Juventus); **1984** Michel Platini (Juventus); **1985** Michel Platini (Juventus); **1986** Igor Belanov (Dynamo Kiev); **1987** Ruud Gullit (AC Milan); **1988** Marco Van Basten (AC Milan); **1989** Marco Van Basten (AC Milan); **1990** Lothar Matthaus (Inter Milan); **1991** Jean-Pierre Papin (Marseille); **1992** Marco Van Basten (AC Milan); **1993** Roberto Baggio (Juventus); **1994** Hristo Stoichkov (Barcelona);

1995 George Weah (AC Milan); 1996 Matthias Sammer (Borussia Dortmund); 1997 Ronaldo (Inter Milan); 1998 Zinedine Zidane (Juventus); 1999 Rivaldo (Barcelona); 2000 Luis Figo (Real Madrid); 2001 Michael Owen (Liverpool).

FIFA WORLD FOOTBALLER OF YEAR

(Voted by national coaches): 1991 Lothar Matthaus (Inter Milan and Germany); 1992 Marco van Basten (AC Milan and Holland); 1993 Roberto Baggio (Juventus and Italy); 1994 Romario (Barcelona and Brazil); 1995 George Weah (AC Milan and Liberia); 1996 Ronaldo (Barcelona and Brazil); 1997 Ronaldo (Barcelona, Inter Milan and Brazil); 1998 Zinedine Zidane (Juventus and France); 1999 Rivaldo (Barcelona and Brazil); 2000 Zinedine Zidane (Juventus and France); 2001 Luis Figo (Real Madrid and Portugal).

QUOTE UNQUOTE

'Whatever the court decided, they were guilty in my eyes for failing to exercise control, lacking in responsibility and for failing to behave as professional footballers should. What did they think they were doing, boozed up and running through the streets? Was that not inviting trouble?' – **David O'Leary**, Leeds United manager, after the trial verdicts on Jonathan Woodgate and Lee Bowyer.

'It would have made it easier if they had gone inside. After the courts had dealt with it, we got the backlash' – **David O'Leary**.

'From being the second favourite club of most neutral supporters, we seem to have become the most hated club in the country' – **David O'Leary**.

'If I knew then what I know now I would not have signed him' – **Peter Ridsdale**, Leeds United chairman, on Lee Bowyer.

'Under past England managers I was not exactly flavour of the month' – **Michael Owen** after his hat-trick in the 5-1 win over Germany.

'It has been quite a good week, I think' – **Sven Goran Eriksson** after victories over Germany and Albania.

'They were totally out of order, irresponsible and a bad example to youngsters for whom they are role models' – **Colin Hutchinson**, Chelsea's managing director, after Frank Lampard, Jody Morris, John Terry and Eidur Gudjohnsen were fined two weeks' wages for drunken behaviour at a hotel near Heathrow the day after September 11.

'The players are well rewarded and have got to take the responsibility that goes with it' – **Peter Taylor**, Leicester City manager, fining Frank Sinclair two weeks' wages for his part in incident.

'He must ask himself if he wants to follow the path which is littered with drunks and wrecks of former players, or emerge from this episode stronger and better for it' – **Ken Bates**, Chelsea chairman, after John Terry was charged with affray and causing actual bodily harm at a London club.

'The gaffer has bombed me' – **Robbie Fowler**, Liverpool striker, dropped for the Charity Shield match against Manchester United following a training ground spat with assistant manager Phil Thompson.

'Just because you are a class act does not give you the right to act like a scoundrel' – **Gerard Houllier**, Liverpool manager, after Fowler apologised to Thompson.

'Rivaldo is not for sale. Must I say it in Chinese?' – **Joan Gaspart**, Barcelona president.

LEAGUE CLUB MANAGERS

Figure in brackets = number of managerial changes at club since the War.
Date present manager took over shown on right.
Dario Gradi, appointed by Crewe Alexandra in June, 1983, currently has the longest service with one club.

F.A. BARCLAYCARD PREMIERSHIP

Arsenal (11)	Arsene Wenger	October 1996
Aston Villa (17)	Graham Taylor	February 2002
Birmingham City (21)	Steve Bruce	December 2001
Blackburn Rov. (21)	Graeme Souness	March 2000
Bolton Wand. (17)	Sam Allardyce	October 1999
Charlton Athletic (12)	Alan Curbishley	July 1991
Chelsea (18)	Claudio Ranieri	September 2000
Everton (16)	David Moyes	March 2002
Fulham (22)	Jean Tigana	April 2000
Leeds Utd. (18)	Terry Venables	July 2002
Liverpool (9)	Gerard Houllier†	July 1998
Manchester City (24)	Kevin Keegan	May 2001
Manchester Utd. (8)	Sir Alex Ferguson	November 1986
Middlesbrough (16)	Steve McClaren	June 2001
Newcastle Utd. (17)	Sir Bobby Robson	September 1999
Southampton (14)	Gordon Strachan	October 2001
Sunderland (17)	Peter Reid	March 1995
Tottenham (16)	Glenn Hoddle	March 2001
W.B.A. (24)	Gary Megson	March 2000
West Ham Utd. (8)	Glenn Roeder	June 2001

(† Joint manager until Roy Evans resigned in November 1998).

NATIONWIDE LEAGUE – FIRST DIVISION

Bradford City (26)	Nicky Law	December 2001
Brighton & H.A. (24)	Martin Hinshelwood	July 2002
Burnley (19)	Stan Ternent	June 1998
Coventry City (23)	Gary McAllister	April 2002
Crystal Palace (29)	Trevor Francis	November 2001
Derby Co. (16)	John Gregory	January 2002
Gillingham (16)	Andy Hessenthaler	June 2000
Grimsby Town (25)	Paul Groves	December 2001
Ipswich Town (8)	George Burley	December 1994
Leicester City (18)	Micky Adams	April 2002
Millwall (21)	Mark McGhee	September 2000
Norwich City (21)	Nigel Worthington	January 2001
Nott'm. Forest (12)	Paul Hart	July 2001
Portsmouth (21)	Harry Redknapp	March 2002
Preston N.E. (21)	Craig Brown	April 2002
Reading (15)	Alan Pardew	October 1999
Rotherham Utd. (18)	Ronnie Moore	May 1997
Sheffield Utd. (29)	Neil Warnock	December 1999
Sheffield Wed. (21)	Terry Yorath	November 2001
Stoke City (19)	Steve Cotterill	May 2002
Walsall (27)	Colin Lee	January 2002
Watford (23)	Ray Lewington	July 2002
Wimbledon (10)	Stuart Murdoch	June 2002
Wolves (18)	David Jones	January 2001

(Number of Wimbledon changes since club elected to Football League in 1977)

SECOND DIVISION

Barnsley (14)	Steve Parkin	November 2001
Blackpool (21)	Steve McMahon	January 2000
Brentford (24)	Wally Downes	June 2002
Bristol City (18)	Danny Wilson	June 2000
Cardiff City (25)	Lennie Lawrence	February 2002
Cheltenham Town (1)	Graham Allner	May 2002
Chesterfield (15)	Dave Rushbury	February 2002
Colchester Utd. (19)	Steve Whitton	August 1999
Crewe Alexandra (17)	Dario Gradi	June 1983
Huddersfield Town (20)	Mick Wadsworth	July 2002
Luton Town (18)	Joe Kinnear	February 2001
Mansfield Town (21)	Stuart Watkiss	January 2002
Northampton Town (22)	Kevin Broadhurst	October 2001
Notts Co. (25)	Bill Dearden	January 2002
Oldham Athletic (19)	Iain Dowie	May 2002
Peterborough Utd. (20)	Barry Fry	May 1996
Plymouth Argyle (25)	Paul Sturrock	October 2000
Port Vale (17)	Brian Horton	January 1999
Q.P.R. (21)	Ian Holloway	February 2001
Stockport Co. (29)	Carlton Palmer	November 2001
Swindon Town (20)	Andy King	December 2001
Tranmere Rov. (14)	Dave Watson	May 2001
Wigan Athletic (15)	Paul Jewell	June 2001
Wycombe Wand. (4)	Lawrie Sanchez	February 1999

(Number of changes since elected to Football League: Peterborough Utd. 1960; Wigan Athletic 1978; Wycombe Wand. 1993; Cheltenham Town 1999).

THIRD DIVISION

Boston Utd. (–)	Steve Evans	October 1998
Bournemouth (18)	Sean O'Driscoll	August 2000
Bristol Rov. (20)	Ray Graydon	April 2002
Bury (19)	Andy Preece	December 2000
Cambridge Utd. (13)	John Taylor	January 2002
Carlisle Utd. (27)	–	–
Darlington (28)	Tommy Taylor	October 2001
Exeter City (23)	John Cornforth	October 2001
Hartlepool Utd. (25)	Chris Turner	February 1999
Hull City (20)	Jan Molby	April 2002
Kidderminster Harr. (1)	Ian Britton	April 2002
Leyton Orient (19)	Paul Brush	October 2001
Lincoln City (23)	Keith Alexander	May 2002
Macclesfield Town (3)	David Moss	November 2001
Oxford Utd. (17)	Ian Atkins	November 2001
Rochdale (26)	Paul Simpson	May 2002
Rushden & Diamonds (–)	Brian Talbot	April 1997
Scunthorpe Utd. (21)	Brian Laws	February 1997
Shrewsbury Town (16)	Kevin Ratcliffe	November 1999
Southend Utd. (24)	Rob Newman	October 2001
Swansea City (25)	Nick Cusack	March 2002
Torquay Utd. (28)	Leroy Rosenior	May 2002
Wrexham (19)	Denis Smith	October 2001
York City (18)	Terry Dolan	February 2000

(Number of changes since elected to Football League: Oxford Utd. 1962; Macclesfield Town 1997; Kidderminster Harr. 2000; Rushden & Diamonds 2001; Boston Utd. 2002).

SKY ADD NATIONWIDE GAMES TO ITS PORTFOLIO

The Football League secured a partial 'reprieve' following the collapse of ITV Digital by agreeing a four-year deal with Sky Sports for the rights to screen live matches. The agreement is worth £95m. and will deliver more than 300 games by the end of the 2005-06 season.

Sky, which also shows the Premiership, will cover 60 Nationwide League fixtures a season, 50 from Division One and the remainder from the Second and Third Divisions. There will be up to nine matches in the end-of-season play-offs, including all three Finals, up to two Worthington Cup ties from each round, both semi-finals and the Final, and the LDV Vans Trophy Final. Games are scheduled for Friday, Saturday and Sunday.

ITV Digital went into administration in March after admitting it could not afford to pay the £178.5m. owed to the League for the remaining two years of its contract. Fears were expressed for the future of several clubs relying on a share of the money for survival. At the time of going to press, the League was continuing to fight parent companies Carlton and Granada for a settlement. It previously turned down an offer of £60m.

LIVE ON SKY

AUGUST: Sat 10: Walsall v Ipswich Town. **Sun 11:** Bradford City v Wolves. **Tues 13:** Reading v Sheffield Wed. **Wed 14:** Stoke City v Leicester City. **Sat 17:** Grimsby Town v Derby Co. **Sun 18:** Arsenal v Birmingham City. **Wed 21:** Scotland v Denmark. **Fri 23:** Chelsea v Manchester Utd. **Sat 24:** Manchester City v Newcastle Utd. **Mon 26:** Watford v Coventry City. **Wed 28:** Fulham v West Ham Utd. **Sat 31:** Coventry City v Nott'm Forest.
SEPTEMBER: Sun 1: Chelsea v Arsenal, Sheffield Wed. v Sheffield Utd. **Mon 2:** Liverpool v Newcastle Utd. **Sat 7:** Wolves v Preston N.E. **Tues 10:** Arsenal v Manchester City. **Sat 14:** Leeds Utd. v Manchester Utd. **Sun 15:** Birmingham City v Aston Villa, Ipswich Town v Norwich City. **Mon 16:** Tottenham v West Ham Utd. **Tue 17:** Burnley v Millwall. **Sat 21:** Derby Co. v Preston N.E. **Sun 22:** Newcastle Utd. v Sunderland. **Mon 23:** Fulham v Chelsea. **Sat 28:** Leeds Utd. v Arsenal. **Sun 29:** Crystal Palace v Gillingham. **Mon 30:** W.B.A. v Blackburn Rov.
OCTOBER: Sun 6: Liverpool v Chelsea. **Mon 7:** Manchester Utd. v Everton. **Tues 15:** Scotland v TBA. **Wed 16:** England v Macedonia. **Sun 20:** Charlton Athletic v Middlesbrough. **Mon 21:** Aston Villa v Southampton. **Sun 27:** West Ham Utd. v Everton. **Mon 28:** Bolton Wand. v Sunderland.
NOVEMBER: Sun 3: Charlton Athletic v Sunderland. **Mon 4:** Newcastle Utd. v Middlesbrough. **Sat 9:** Manchester City v Manchester Utd. **Sun 10:** Sunderland v Tottenham. **Sun 17:** West Ham Utd. v Manchester Utd. **Wed 20:** Scotland v TBA. **Sat 23:** Manchester Utd. v Newcastle Utd. **Sun 24:** Charlton Athletic v Blackburn Rov.
DECEMBER: Sun 1: Liverpool v Manchester Utd. **Mon 2:** West Ham Utd. v Southampton. **Sat 7:** Manchester Utd. v Arsenal. **Sun 8:** Tottenham v W.B.A. **Sun 15:** Sunderland v Liverpool. **Mon 16:** Bolton Wand. v Leeds Utd. **Sun 22:** Liverpool v Everton. **Mon 23:** Manchester City v Tottenham. **Thurs 26:** Middlesbrough v Manchester Utd. **Sun 29:** Arsenal v Liverpool.
JANUARY: Sun 1: Newcastle Utd. v Liverpool.
APRIL: Wed 2: England v Turkey, Albania v Republic of Ireland. **Wed 30:** Scotland v Republic of Ireland.
JUNE: Sat 7: Scotland v Germany, Republic of Ireland v Albania. **Wed 11:** England v Slovakia, Republic of Ireland v Georgia.

PAY-PER-VIEW

AUGUST: Sun 18: Aston Villa v Liverpool. **Sat 24:** W.B.A. v Leeds Utd. **Tues 27:** Arsenal v W.B.A.
SEPTEMBER: Sun 1: Bolton Wand. v Aston Villa. **Tues 3:** Manchester Utd. v Middlesbrough. **Wed 11:** Newcastle Utd. v Leeds Utd. **Sun 15:** Manchester City v Blackburn Rov. **Sun 22:** Aston Villa v Everton. **Sat 28:** Birmingham City v Newcastle Utd.
OCTOBER: Sun 6: Arsenal v Sunderland. **Sat 19:** Leeds Utd. v Liverpool. **Sun 27:** Southampton v Fulham.
NOVEMBER: Sun 3: Tottenham v Chelsea.

F.A. BARCLAYCARD PREMIERSHIP RESULTS 2001-02

	Arsenal	Aston Villa	Blackburn Rov.	Bolton Wand.	Charlton Athletic	Chelsea	Derby Co.	Everton	Fulham	Ipswich Town	Leeds Utd.	Leicester City	Liverpool	Manchester Utd.	Middlesbrough	Newcastle Utd.	Southampton	Sunderland	Tottenham	West Ham Utd.
Arsenal	–	3-2	3-3	1-1	2-4	2-1	1-0	4-3	4-1	2-0	1-2	4-0	1-1	3-1	2-1	1-3	1-1	3-0	2-1	2-0
Aston Villa	1-2	–	2-0	3-2	1-0	1-1	2-1	0-0	2-0	2-1	0-1	0-2	1-2	1-1	0-0	1-1	2-1	0-0	2-1	2-1
Blackburn Rov.	2-3	3-0	–	1-1	4-1	0-0	0-1	0-1	3-0	1-2	1-2	3-1	1-1	2-2	0-1	2-2	2-0	0-3	1-1	7-1
Bolton Wand.	0-2	3-2	1-1	–	0-0	2-2	1-3	2-2	0-0	4-1	0-3	2-2	2-1	0-4	0-0	0-4	0-1	0-2	1-1	1-0
Charlton Athletic	0-3	1-2	0-2	1-2	–	2-1	1-0	1-2	3-2	3-2	0-2	2-0	0-2	0-3	0-0	1-1	2-4	2-2	3-1	4-4
Chelsea	1-1	1-3	0-0	5-1	1-1	–	2-1	3-4	0-1	1-1	2-0	2-0	4-0	0-3	2-2	1-1	2-4	4-0	4-0	5-1
Derby Co.	1-1	3-1	2-1	3-1	1-1	1-1	–	3-4	0-1	1-3	0-0	2-3	0-1	2-2	2-0	0-1	0-1	1-0	4-0	0-0
Everton	0-1	3-2	1-2	3-1	0-3	0-0	1-0	–	2-1	1-2	0-0	2-2	1-3	0-2	2-0	1-3	2-0	1-0	1-1	5-0
Fulham	1-3	0-0	2-0	3-0	0-0	1-1	1-0	2-0	–	1-1	0-0	2-0	0-2	2-3	2-1	3-1	2-0	2-0	0-2	0-1
Ipswich Town	0-2	0-0	1-1	1-2	0-0	0-0	1-1	0-0	1-0	–	1-2	0-0	0-6	0-1	0-0	0-1	3-1	5-0	1-2	3-1
Leed Utd.	1-3	1-1	3-1	0-0	0-0	0-0	1-0	3-2	1-0	2-2	–	2-0	1-4	3-4	2-2	3-4	2-0	2-0	2-1	3-0
Leicester City	1-3	2-2	2-1	0-5	1-2	2-3	3-0	2-2	0-0	1-1	1-2	–	1-4	0-1	1-2	0-0	0-4	2-0	2-1	1-3
Liverpool	1-1	1-3	1-1	1-1	0-0	1-0	1-4	1-1	0-0	5-0	1-1	1-0	–	3-1	2-0	1-3	1-1	1-0	1-0	2-1
Manchester Utd.	0-1	1-0	4-3	1-2	2-0	0-3	5-0	4-1	3-2	4-0	1-1	2-0	0-1	–	0-1	3-1	6-1	4-1	4-0	5-1
Middlesbrough	0-4	2-1	1-3	1-1	0-0	0-2	5-1	1-0	1-1	2-2	2-2	1-0	1-2	0-1	–	0-1	1-3	4-1	1-1	2-0
Newcastle Utd.	0-2	3-0	2-1	3-2	3-0	1-2	3-1	6-2	1-1	2-2	3-1	1-0	0-2	4-3	3-0	–	3-1	1-1	3-1	3-1
Southampton	0-2	1-3	1-2	0-0	1-1	0-2	1-2	0-1	1-1	3-3	0-1	2-2	2-0	1-3	1-1	3-1	–	1-1	0-1	2-0
Sunderland	1-1	1-1	1-0	3-2	2-2	0-0	1-1	1-0	1-1	1-0	0-1	2-1	1-1	1-3	0-1	1-1	2-0	–	1-2	1-1
Tottenham	1-1	0-0	1-0	3-2	0-1	2-3	3-1	4-0	4-0	1-2	2-1	2-1	1-0	3-5	2-1	1-3	1-1	2-1	–	1-1
West Ham Utd.	1-1	1-1	1-1	2-1	2-0	2-1	4-0	1-0	0-2	3-1	0-0	1-0	1-1	3-5	1-0	3-0	2-0	3-0	0-1	–

Read across for home results, down for away

NATIONWIDE LEAGUE RESULTS 2001-02 – FIRST DIVISION

Home \ Away	Barnsley	Birmingham City	Bradford City	Burnley	Coventry City	Crewe Alexandra	Crystal Palace	Gillingham	Grimsby Town	Manchester City	Millwall	Norwich City	Nott'm. Forest	Portsmouth	Preston N.E.	Rotherham Utd.	Sheffield Utd.	Sheffield Wed.	Stockport Co.	Walsall	Watford	W.B.A.	Wimbledon	Wolves
Barnsley	–	1-3	3-3	3-3	4-0	4-0	1-0	3-0	5-1	2-1	2-1	1-1	2-1	4-4	2-2	1-1	1-1	3-1	1-3	3-0	3-0	0-1	0-1	4-1
Birmingham City	1-0	–	1-1	2-3	2-0	0-0	1-0	4-1	1-2	1-2	0-1	4-0	2-1	0-1	1-0	2-2	1-2	1-2	2-1	1-0	3-2	0-1	0-2	2-2
Bradford City	4-0	1-1	–	1-0	1-1	2-0	1-0	5-1	3-2	1-1	0-2	1-1	2-1	3-1	2-1	3-1	1-2	0-2	2-4	2-1	4-3	0-1	0-2	0-3
Burnley	3-3	0-1	1-1	–	2-4	3-3	1-0	1-0	1-0	2-4	0-2	1-1	3-0	0-2	2-1	3-0	2-0	0-2	5-2	5-2	0-2	0-1	3-3	2-3
Coventry City	4-0	0-2	4-0	0-2	–	2-0	2-0	1-0	2-0	1-4	1-0	1-0	0-1	2-0	2-2	1-0	2-0	0-1	4-0	2-1	0-2	1-1	3-1	2-3
Crewe Alexandra	2-0	2-2	2-0	0-2	1-6	–	3-0	1-2	1-3	1-3	1-3	3-2	0-3	0-0	1-0	2-1	2-2	0-2	0-0	1-1	0-1	1-1	1-4	0-2
Crystal Palace	1-0	0-0	2-0	1-0	2-1	4-1	–	1-2	5-0	2-1	2-2	0-2	0-0	4-1	3-0	2-1	2-2	4-1	3-1	2-2	0-3	0-1	4-0	0-2
Gillingham	3-0	3-1	2-0	3-0	0-1	3-1	3-0	–	4-0	0-4	3-2	2-0	1-1	3-1	0-1	0-1	1-0	2-1	3-0	2-1	3-1	0-0	4-0	1-0
Grimsby Town	1-0	3-1	2-2	2-0	1-3	1-0	5-2	1-2	–	1-4	1-1	0-2	0-3	3-1	0-0	0-2	0-0	0-2	3-1	2-2	0-3	0-1	6-2	1-1
Manchester City	5-1	3-0	2-0	4-1	4-2	5-2	2-1	4-1	4-0	–	0-2	3-0	3-1	4-2	2-1	2-0	2-0	0-4	3-1	2-0	3-0	4-0	0-4	2-2
Millwall	2-1	0-1	3-0	0-2	1-0	2-2	2-2	2-1	2-0	0-2	–	4-0	3-3	0-0	3-0	4-0	0-0	4-0	2-0	1-1	1-0	0-0	1-1	0-1
Norwich City	2-1	0-1	0-0	1-1	2-2	2-0	3-0	2-1	4-0	1-2	1-0	–	0-0	1-0	0-1	1-1	1-0	2-0	2-0	1-0	1-1	0-2	1-0	1-0
Nott'm. Forest	2-1	2-1	1-1	2-1	0-3	0-0	1-1	2-2	5-0	1-0	1-0	1-2	–	0-1	2-0	1-2	0-0	0-1	3-0	2-1	3-1	2-0	1-2	1-0
Portsmouth	4-4	0-0	1-0	2-3	1-0	4-0	1-3	2-1	2-1	1-1	1-2	2-1	3-2	–	2-0	3-1	3-0	4-2	6-0	2-3	1-2	1-2	2-3	1-2
Preston N.E.	2-2	1-0	2-0	1-1	1-1	1-0	1-3	0-2	3-1	2-0	3-0	0-2	3-0	0-1	–	2-0	2-0	1-1	3-0	1-1	2-1	1-2	2-0	0-3
Rotherham Utd.	1-1	4-0	2-0	1-1	1-1	1-0	2-1	3-2	3-1	0-0	3-2	2-1	0-0	4-3	0-2	–	1-1	1-2	3-2	2-0	0-2	1-1	3-2	2-2
Sheffield Utd.	1-1	4-0	1-0	3-1	1-3	1-0	2-1	1-0	3-1	0-2	3-2	2-1	0-0	4-3	0-0	1-1	–	3-0	3-0	1-1	0-1	0-1	3-1	1-1
Sheffield Wed.	3-1	0-1	0-2	0-2	1-3	2-0	4-1	0-0	4-0	0-5	0-4	1-1	0-2	2-3	2-1	1-2	0-0	–	5-0	1-0	1-3	0-1	1-0	0-1
Stockport Co.	1-3	1-2	0-3	3-1	3-1	0-1	0-2	2-0	3-3	2-6	0-4	2-0	1-3	2-1	2-1	0-1	1-2	1-2	–	2-1	0-3	1-2	1-2	2-2
Walsall	3-0	1-2	2-2	1-0	2-1	2-2	1-0	0-0	4-0	0-0	1-4	1-0	1-0	3-0	1-0	1-1	0-2	3-1	1-0	–	2-1	2-1	1-2	2-1
Watford	3-0	3-3	4-0	0-2	0-1	1-0	1-0	2-3	4-0	1-2	2-2	2-0	1-2	5-0	1-2	4-0	3-1	0-3	4-0	1-0	–	0-3	3-0	0-1
W.B.A.	0-1	1-0	3-1	1-2	1-0	4-1	0-1	1-0	2-1	0-0	0-0	1-2	1-0	1-0	0-1	0-0	1-0	1-0	3-1	1-0	1-0	–	1-0	1-1
Wimbledon	3-1	3-1	1-2	2-1	0-1	2-0	1-1	3-1	0-1	0-4	2-2	2-2	2-0	3-3	2-0	1-0	1-1	1-1	3-1	2-2	3-0	0-1	–	0-1
Wolves	4-1	2-1	3-1	2-1	2-1	2-2	2-1	2-0	2-1	0-2	1-0	3-0	2-3	2-0	3-0	2-1	1-0	2-1	2-2	3-0	1-0	0-1	1-0	–

Read across for home results, down for away

NATIONWIDE LEAGUE RESULTS 2001-02 – SECOND DIVISION

	Blackpool	Bournemouth	Brentford	Brighton & H.A.	Bristol City	Bury	Cambridge Utd.	Cardiff City	Chesterfield	Colchester Utd.	Huddersfield Town	Northampton Town	Notts Co.	Oldham Athletic	Peterborough Utd.	Port Vale	Q.P.R.	Reading	Stoke City	Swindon Town	Tranmere Rov.	Wigan Athletic	Wrexham	Wycombe Wand.
Blackpool	-	4-3	1-3	2-2	5-1	0-1	1-1	0-3	2-1	2-1	1-2	1-2	0-0	2-1	2-2	4-0	2-2	0-2	2-2	1-0	1-1	3-1	3-0	2-2
Bournemouth	0-1	-	0-2	0-2	1-0	3-2	2-2	2-2	2-1	1-1	2-3	5-1	4-2	6-0	0-2	0-0	1-2	1-1	3-1	0-0	1-1	2-0	3-0	1-2
Brentford	2-0	1-0	-	4-0	1-2	3-2	2-1	2-1	1-1	0-1	3-0	2-1	4-2	1-0	0-0	0-1	1-0	1-1	1-1	0-0	2-0	0-1	0-0	1-0
Brighton & H.A.	2-1	4-0	1-2	-	0-1	2-1	4-3	1-1	1-2	1-2	1-2	2-0	2-2	0-2	2-0	1-1	2-0	3-3	2-0	2-1	4-0	2-1	2-2	4-0
Bristol City	2-1	0-1	2-0	2-2	-	2-0	2-2	2-1	2-1	3-1	1-2	2-2	3-2	0-4	2-1	1-1	1-3	1-1	1-2	3-1	1-0	2-2	0-1	0-1
Bury	1-1	2-1	2-0	3-1	2-2	-	2-2	2-0	1-0	4-1	1-2	2-0	3-0	0-2	3-1	0-1	2-0	2-2	1-1	0-3	0-1	2-2	0-2	1-1
Cambridge Utd.	0-3	2-2	2-1	2-1	0-3	3-1	-	2-1	3-0	1-1	2-1	2-1	3-1	2-2	2-1	1-1	1-1	2-2	1-2	1-2	1-1	2-2	3-2	2-0
Cardiff City	2-2	2-1	0-1	1-1	1-3	2-1	2-1	-	0-1	1-2	2-0	2-2	0-2	0-1	3-1	0-1	2-3	1-1	3-0	1-2	0-2	2-1	3-2	2-0
Chesterfield	2-1	2-1	1-1	1-2	2-1	1-0	3-0	0-1	-	0-0	0-0	1-2	2-2	2-2	0-0	1-3	3-1	2-3	1-2	4-0	2-1	0-0	5-1	0-1
Colchester Utd.	1-1	1-4	1-2	1-0	0-2	3-1	2-1	3-6	0-0	-	2-1	2-3	4-2	2-0	3-1	1-3	0-0	3-1	2-0	1-3	1-1	1-1	4-1	2-2
Huddersfield Town	2-4	1-0	1-1	1-2	1-2	1-2	2-1	2-0	0-2	0-1	-	2-0	0-2	1-1	1-1	1-3	0-2	1-0	1-3	3-1	4-1	1-1	2-2	4-1
Northampton Town	1-3	1-0	0-0	2-0	2-2	2-0	2-1	2-2	1-2	2-3	3-0	-	4-1	2-1	0-1	1-0	2-0	2-2	0-0	2-0	1-1	1-0	1-3	2-0
Notts Co.	1-0	3-3	3-2	2-2	3-2	3-0	3-1	0-2	0-3	4-2	0-1	4-1	-	4-2	3-2	0-0	2-2	3-4	1-0	1-1	5-0	1-1	2-3	2-0
Oldham Athletic	2-1	6-0	1-0	0-2	0-4	0-2	2-2	0-1	2-2	2-0	1-1	2-1	4-2	-	4-1	3-0	1-0	0-1	1-2	4-0	1-1	2-0	2-0	1-1
Peterborough Utd.	1-1	0-1	0-0	2-0	2-1	3-1	2-1	3-1	0-0	3-1	1-1	0-1	3-2	2-2	-	3-0	4-1	0-0	2-1	2-1	1-0	1-2	3-0	3-0
Port Vale	2-0	1-1	0-1	2-0	3-1	4-0	1-0	3-1	1-2	1-3	1-3	1-0	3-1	2-2	2-1	-	1-0	0-0	0-3	1-2	3-0	1-0	2-0	1-1
Q.P.R.	3-0	2-0	1-0	1-0	5-0	2-1	5-0	2-0	4-1	1-0	0-2	2-0	4-2	1-0	1-0	0-1	-	1-0	1-1	4-0	1-0	2-2	1-0	2-0
Reading	2-0	3-0	2-2	2-2	5-0	3-0	1-2	0-0	0-1	0-2	1-0	2-0	1-1	0-0	0-0	0-1	1-0	-	0-0	1-3	4-1	0-0	5-0	5-1
Stoke City	2-0	2-0	3-1	1-0	6-1	4-0	2-2	0-3	0-1	1-0	0-0	0-0	4-2	2-2	2-1	3-1	2-0	0-3	-	0-0	2-2	1-0	2-3	1-1
Swindon Town	4-0	0-0	1-0	2-1	4-1	3-1	4-0	1-2	3-0	3-0	3-1	3-0	1-1	4-0	2-1	1-0	2-3	2-2	0-0	-	1-2	2-2	1-0	1-0
Tranmere Rov.	0-1	4-0	0-0	1-2	2-2	0-0	4-1	0-2	1-1	2-2	4-1	3-2	5-0	1-0	1-0	1-0	1-0	0-2	6-1	0-0	-	1-1	1-2	1-0
Wigan Athletic	0-1	0-0	1-0	0-2	0-2	6-1	5-0	2-2	1-0	1-0	1-1	1-1	1-0	3-3	1-2	1-3	1-0	0-2	0-1	2-2	2-2	-	2-0	0-0
Wrexham	1-2	1-1	1-1	1-0	1-3	4-0	5-0	3-1	2-1	1-3	2-2	3-2	2-3	1-2	3-0	3-1	1-0	0-2	1-0	2-1	2-1	2-0	-	0-0
Wycombe Wand.	1-4	1-1	5-3	1-1	0-1	0-2	0-1	1-0	0-0	0-2	4-1	2-1	2-0	2-1	3-0	3-1	1-0	0-2	1-0	1-1	2-1	1-0	5-2	-

Read across for home results, down for away

56

NATIONWIDE LEAGUE RESULTS 2001-02 – THIRD DIVISION

Home \ Away	Bristol Rov.	Carlisle Utd.	Cheltenham Town	Darlington	Exeter City	Halifax Town	Hartlepool Utd.	Hull City	Kidderminster H.	Leyton Orient	Lincoln City	Luton Town	Macclesfield Town	Mansfield Town	Oxford Utd.	Plymouth Argyle	Rochdale	Rushden & D.	Scunthorpe Utd.	Shrewsbury Town	Southend Utd.	Swansea City	Torquay Utd.	York City
Bristol Rov.	–	0-0	1-2	0-0	0-0	2-0	0-1	1-1	2-1	5-3	2-1	3-2	0-2	0-1	1-1	0-2	0-2	0-3	0-3	0-1	0-1	4-1	1-0	2-2
Carlisle Utd.	1-0	–	2-0	1-3	1-0	2-0	0-2	0-0	1-1	6-1	2-2	0-2	3-1	1-1	2-1	0-2	1-2	3-0	3-3	0-1	0-1	3-1	2-0	2-1
Cheltenham Town	0-0	2-0	–	0-0	3-1	5-0	3-0	0-1	1-0	1-0	2-1	1-1	4-1	2-3	1-0	1-4	1-0	0-0	3-3	3-0	0-0	2-2	2-2	4-0
Darlington	1-0	0-2	0-2	–	4-0	0-0	3-0	0-1	2-0	1-0	2-1	3-2	1-1	0-1	1-0	1-4	1-0	0-0	2-1	2-1	2-2	0-0	2-3	3-1
Exeter City	1-0	1-0	0-2	4-2	–	3-0	2-2	0-1	3-0	0-0	3-0	1-2	0-0	1-0	1-0	1-4	1-2	2-4	0-4	2-1	1-1	0-3	1-1	3-1
Halifax Town	0-2	2-0	4-1	1-2	2-0	–	0-0	4-0	1-1	0-0	3-0	1-2	0-0	0-1	3-2	0-1	2-4	2-4	3-1	2-1	1-1	0-3	4-1	2-1
Hartlepool Utd.	1-1	3-1	5-1	1-2	2-0	3-0	–	4-0	1-1	1-0	5-0	1-0	1-0	4-1	0-1	1-0	3-1	5-1	3-2	2-0	5-1	7-1	4-1	3-0
Hull City	0-0	0-2	0-2	1-0	3-1	3-0	2-0	–	1-3	0-1	5-0	1-0	2-0	1-1	0-0	1-0	4-2	1-0	0-0	2-0	0-0	2-1	2-1	4-0
Kidderminster H.	3-1	2-2	0-2	0-0	3-1	0-0	2-2	0-0	–	2-0	1-1	1-4	0-1	2-0	3-0	4-1	4-2	1-0	0-3	2-4	2-1	1-2	1-1	4-0
Leyton Orient	0-1	2-2	0-1	0-1	1-1	3-1	2-0	0-0	1-3	–	1-1	1-4	0-1	0-1	1-1	0-0	1-1	1-0	1-0	2-4	0-0	2-2	2-1	1-2
Lincoln City	3-1	1-1	3-1	5-2	2-0	5-0	2-2	1-1	0-1	2-0	–	1-4	0-1	1-1	0-0	2-1	4-2	3-0	3-0	0-2	1-1	2-1	1-0	1-3
Luton Town	3-0	1-1	0-1	1-1	1-2	3-0	2-2	0-0	2-0	5-3	5-0	–	2-1	4-1	1-1	2-0	4-2	1-0	3-2	2-4	0-0	2-1	5-1	1-2
Macclesfield Town	2-1	1-1	3-0	4-2	1-2	6-1	0-1	0-1	3-0	2-0	3-2	1-2	–	0-1	3-0	1-0	0-0	2-1	3-2	1-0	2-0	2-1	1-1	2-1
Mansfield Town	2-0	3-0	4-2	2-1	1-2	2-1	2-2	0-1	1-0	3-2	1-1	1-2	4-0	–	1-1	2-0	1-1	1-4	2-3	2-0	2-0	3-0	2-2	2-1
Oxford Utd.	1-0	0-0	2-0	3-1	3-0	6-1	1-0	0-0	2-1	3-0	3-0	1-2	4-0	3-2	–	1-1	1-1	1-0	4-3	0-1	2-0	2-1	1-1	2-1
Plymouth Argyle	3-1	1-1	3-1	2-1	2-0	2-0	3-3	3-1	2-1	3-0	1-1	1-2	1-0	3-1	4-2	–	0-0	0-0	2-1	3-0	4-0	2-0	1-1	3-0
Rochdale	3-1	1-1	1-0	7-1	3-4	4-0	1-1	2-0	0-2	4-1	0-2	0-2	1-1	0-0	1-0	2-3	–	1-1	0-1	1-0	0-0	1-0	1-1	1-0
Rushden & D.	1-2	2-1	1-2	1-0	0-1	3-1	1-3	1-1	4-0	1-2	1-1	1-2	3-0	3-1	1-0	3-1	1-0	–	1-1	3-1	3-0	2-1	1-1	2-1
Scunthorpe Utd.	2-1	0-1	0-1	1-0	3-1	4-1	2-0	2-0	4-0	1-2	2-1	0-2	1-0	0-0	1-0	3-1	2-2	4-2	–	0-2	0-0	4-2	2-0	0-1
Shrewsbury Town	2-1	3-2	0-1	1-0	0-1	4-1	0-1	1-1	2-0	1-1	1-1	0-2	3-0	1-0	1-0	3-1	2-2	2-2	2-2	–	2-0	3-0	0-1	2-1
Southend Utd.	2-1	0-0	2-1	2-0	4-2	2-4	1-1	1-1	0-0	1-3	0-0	1-3	0-1	0-0	3-3	3-1	1-3	4-2	2-2	0-2	–	4-2	0-1	0-1
Swansea City	2-1	0-1	0-1	2-0	0-2	1-0	1-0	1-1	1-0	1-1	2-0	0-1	1-1	2-2	3-3	2-0	3-0	1-1	3-3	0-2	3-2	–	2-2	0-1
Torquay Utd.	2-1	1-0	2-1	0-2	2-3	1-0	1-0	2-1	1-4	1-1	0-0	1-1	1-0	0-0	3-3	1-1	3-0	0-0	0-0	3-3	2-1	1-2	–	0-3
York City	3-0	2-1	1-0	2-0	1-0	1-0	2-1	2-1	2-1	2-1	2-0	1-2	1-0	3-1	0-0	0-0	0-0	0-1	0-2	1-1	2-1	0-2	1-1	–

Read across for home results, down for away

57

FINAL TABLES 2001-02

F.A. BARCLAYCARD PREMIERSHIP

		P	W	D	L	F	A	W	D	L	F	A	Pts	GD
				HOME						AWAY				
1	Arsenal	38	12	4	3	42	25	14	5	0	37	11	87	+43
2	Liverpool	38	12	5	2	33	14	12	3	4	34	16	80	+37
3	Manchester Utd.	38	11	2	6	40	17	13	3	3	47	28	77	+42
4	Newcastle Utd.	38	12	3	4	40	23	9	5	5	34	29	71	+22
5	Leeds Utd.	38	9	6	4	31	21	9	6	4	22	16	66	+16
6	Chelsea	38	11	4	4	43	21	6	9	4	23	17	64	+28
7	West Ham Utd.	38	12	4	3	32	14	3	4	12	16	43	53	−9
8	Aston Villa	38	8	7	4	22	17	4	7	8	24	30	50	−1
9	Tottenham	38	10	4	5	32	24	4	4	11	17	29	50	−4
10	Blackburn Rov.	38	8	6	5	33	20	4	4	11	22	31	46	+4
11	Southampton	38	7	5	7	23	22	5	4	10	23	32	45	−8
12	Middlesbrough	38	7	5	7	23	26	5	4	10	12	21	45	−12
13	Fulham	38	7	7	5	21	16	3	7	9	15	28	44	−8
14	Charlton Athletic	38	5	6	8	23	30	5	8	6	15	19	44	−11
15	Everton	38	8	4	7	26	23	3	6	10	19	34	43	−12
16	Bolton Wand.	38	5	7	7	20	31	4	6	9	24	31	40	−18
17	Sunderland	38	7	7	5	18	16	3	3	13	11	35	40	−22
18	Ipswich Town	38	6	4	9	20	24	3	5	11	21	40	36	−23
19	Derby Co.	38	5	4	10	20	26	3	2	14	13	37	30	−30
20	Leicester City	38	3	7	9	15	34	2	6	11	15	30	28	−34

(Arsenal and Liverpool go straight into the Champions League first group stage; Manchester Utd. and Newcastle Utd. into the qualifying stage. Leeds Utd., Chelsea, Blackburn Rov. and Ipswich Town qualify for the UEFA Cup.)

Prize-money: 1 £8.8m; 2 £8.36m; 3 £7.92m; 4 £7.48m; 5 £7.04m; 6 £6.6m; 7 £6.16m; 8 £5.72m; 9 £5.28m; 10 £4.84m; 11 £4.4m; 12 £3.96m; 13 £3.52m; 14 £3.08m; 15 £2.64m; 16 £2.2m; 17 £1.76m; 18 £1.32m; 19 £880,000; 20 £440,000.

Biggest win: Blackburn Rov. 7, West Ham Utd. 1; Ipswich Town 0, Liverpool 6.
Highest attendance: 67,683 (Manchester Utd. v Middlesbrough).
Lowest attendance: 15,412 (Leicester City v Middlesbrough).
Barclaycard Manager of Year: Arsene Wenger (Arsenal).
Player of Year: Freddie Ljungberg (Arsenal).
Golden Boot: 24 Thierry Henry (Arsenal).
Golden Glove: Jussi Jaaskelainen (Bolton Wand.).
Football Writers' Association Player of Year: Robert Pires (Arsenal).
PFA Player of Year: Ruud van Nistelrooy (Manchester Utd.).
PFA Young Player of Year: Craig Bellamy (Newcastle Utd.).
PFA divisional team of season: Given (Newcastle Utd.), Finnan (Fulham), Ferdinand (Leeds Utd.), Hyypia (Liverpool), Bridge (Southampton), Pires (Arsenal), Keane (Manchester Utd.), Vieira (Arsenal), Giggs (Manchester Utd.), Van Nistelrooy (Manchester Utd.), Henry (Arsenal).
Fair Play award: Manchester Utd.
Best Behaved Supporters' award: Liverpool.
Barclaycard Groundsman of year: Paul Burgess (Arsenal).
Leading scorers (all competitions): 36 Van Nistelrooy (Manchester Utd.); 32 Henry (Arsenal); 29 Hasselbaink (Chelsea); 28 Owen (Liverpool); 27 Shearer (Newcastle Utd.); 25 Solskjaer (Manchester Utd.); 23 Gudjohnsen (Chelsea); 21 Crouch (Aston Villa – 19 for Portsmouth), Ormerod (Southampton – 20 for Blackpool); 18 Cole (Blackburn Rov. – 5 for Manchester Utd.); 17 Ljungberg (Arsenal), Wiltord (Arsenal).

NATIONWIDE LEAGUE

FIRST DIVISION

			HOME				AWAY						
		P	W	D	L	F	A	W	D	L	F	A	Pts	GD
1	Manchester City	46	19	3	1	63	19	12	3	8	45	33	99	+56
2	W.B.A.	46	15	4	4	36	11	12	4	7	25	18	89	+32
3	Wolves	46	13	4	6	33	18	12	7	4	43	25	86	+33
4	Millwall	46	15	3	5	43	22	7	8	8	26	26	77	+21
5	Birmingham City*	46	14	4	5	44	20	9	7	7	26	29	76	+21
6	Norwich City	46	15	6	2	36	16	7	3	13	24	35	75	+9
7	Burnley	46	11	7	5	39	29	10	5	8	31	33	75	+8
8	Preston N.E.	46	13	7	3	45	21	7	5	11	26	38	72	+12
9	Wimbledon	46	9	8	6	30	22	9	5	9	33	35	67	+6
10	Crystal Palace	46	13	3	7	42	22	7	3	13	28	40	66	+8
11	Coventry City	46	12	4	7	33	19	8	2	13	26	34	66	+6
12	Gillingham	46	12	5	6	38	26	6	5	12	26	41	64	-3
13	Sheffield Utd.	46	8	8	7	34	30	7	7	9	19	24	60	-1
14	Watford	46	10	5	8	38	30	6	6	11	24	26	59	+6
15	Bradford City	46	10	1	12	41	39	5	9	9	28	37	55	-7
16	Nott'm. Forest	46	7	11	5	26	21	5	7	11	24	30	54	-1
17	Portsmouth	46	9	6	8	36	31	4	8	11	24	41	53	-12
18	Walsall	46	10	6	7	29	27	3	6	14	22	44	51	-20
19	Grimsby Town	46	9	7	7	34	28	3	7	13	16	44	50	-22
20	Sheffield Wed.	46	6	7	10	28	37	6	7	10	21	34	50	-22
21	Rotherham Utd.	46	7	13	3	32	29	5	6	14	20	37	49	-14
22	Crewe Alexandra	46	8	8	7	23	32	4	5	14	24	44	49	-29
23	Barnsley	46	9	9	5	37	33	2	6	15	22	53	48	-27
24	Stockport Co.	46	5	1	17	19	44	1	7	15	23	58	26	-60

(* Also promoted via play-offs)

Biggest win: Preston N.E. 6, Stockport Co. 0.
Highest attendance: 34,407 (Manchester City v W.B.A.).
Lowest attendance: 4,086 (Stockport Co. v Watford).
Top League scorer: 28 Shaun Goater (Manchester City).
Manager of Year: Gary Megson (W.B.A.).
PFA divisional team of season: Hoult (W.B.A.), Alexander (Preston N.E.), Moore (W.B.A.), Lescott (Wolves), Clement (W.B.A.), Berkovic (Manchester City), Kennedy (Wolves), Benarbia (Manchester City), Prosinecki (Portsmouth), Goater (Manchester City), Freedman (Crystal Palace).
Fair Play award: Crewe Alexandra.
Groundsman of Year: Steve Welch (Nott'm. Forest).
Leading scorers (all domestic competitions): 32 Goater (Manchester City); 26 Huckerby (Manchester City); 24 Morrison (Crystal Palace), Sturridge (Wolves – 3 for Leicester City); 22 John (Birmingham City – 14 for Nott'm. Forest); 21 Freedman (Crystal Palace); 20 King (Gillingham); 18 Claridge (Millwall), Connolly (Wimbledon), Dyer (Barnsley); 17 Sadlier (Millwall).

OLD TRAFFORD SUBS' BENCH WORTH £70M

Manchester United fielded a substitutes' bench worth around £70m. against Ipswich Town – a game they won 4-0. It comprised the club's two most expensive signings, Juan Veron (£28m.) and Ruud van Nistelrooy (£19m.), Paul Scholes valued at about £15m., Gary Neville (£8m.) and £2.5m. goalkeeper Roy Carroll.

SECOND DIVISION

			HOME					AWAY					
		P	W	D	L	F	A	W	D	L	F	A	Pts	GD

		P	W	D	L	F	A	W	D	L	F	A	Pts	GD
1	Brighton & H.A.	46	17	5	1	42	16	8	10	5	24	26	90	+24
2	Reading	46	12	7	4	36	20	11	8	4	34	23	84	+27
3	Brentford	46	17	5	1	48	12	7	6	10	29	31	83	+34
4	Cardiff City	46	12	8	3	39	25	11	6	6	36	25	83	+25
5	Stoke City*	46	16	4	3	43	12	7	7	9	24	28	80	+27
6	Huddersfield Town	46	13	7	3	35	19	8	8	7	30	28	78	+18
7	Bristol City	46	13	6	4	38	21	8	4	11	30	32	73	+15
8	Q.P.R.	46	11	10	2	35	18	8	4	11	25	31	71	+11
9	Oldham Athletic	46	14	6	3	47	27	4	10	9	30	38	70	+12
10	Wigan Athletic	46	9	6	8	36	23	7	10	6	30	28	64	+15
11	Wycombe Wand.	46	13	5	5	38	26	4	8	11	20	38	64	−6
12	Tranmere Rov.	46	10	9	4	39	19	6	11	24	41	63	+3
13	Swindon Town	46	10	7	6	26	21	5	7	11	20	35	59	−10
14	Port Vale	46	11	6	6	35	24	5	4	14	16	38	58	−11
15	Colchester Utd.	46	9	6	8	35	33	6	6	11	30	43	57	−11
16	Blackpool	46	8	9	6	39	31	6	5	12	27	38	56	−3
17	Peterborough Utd.	46	11	5	7	46	26	4	5	14	18	33	55	+5
18	Chesterfield	46	9	3	11	35	36	4	10	9	18	29	52	−12
19	Notts Co.	46	8	7	8	28	29	5	4	14	31	42	50	−12
20	Northampton Town	46	9	4	10	30	33	5	3	15	24	46	49	−25
21	Bournemouth	46	9	4	10	36	33	1	10	12	20	38	44	−15
22	Bury	46	6	9	8	26	32	5	2	16	17	43	44	−32
23	Wrexham	46	7	7	9	29	32	4	3	16	27	57	43	−33
24	Cambridge Utd.	46	7	7	9	29	34	0	6	17	18	59	34	−46

(* Also promoted via play-offs)

Biggest win: Peterborough Utd. 6, Bournemouth 0; Oldham Athletic 1, Cardiff City 7.
Highest attendance: 23,019 (Stoke City v Port Vale).
Lowest attendance: 2,379 (Cambridge Utd. v Port Vale).
Top League scorer: 28 Bobby Zamora (Brighton & H.A.).
Manager of Year: Peter Taylor (Brighton & H.A.).
PFA divisional team of season: Tyler (Peterborough Utd.), Murty (Reading), De Zeeuw (Wigan Athletic), Cullip (Brighton & H.A.), Bell (Bristol City), Kavanagh (Cardiff City), Koumas (Tranmere Rov.), Murray (Bristol City), Evans (Brentford), Zamora (Brighton & H.A.), Forster (Reading).
Fair Play award: Colchester Utd.
Groundsman of Year: Jem Fox (Reading).
Leading scorers (all domestic competitions): 32 Zamora (Brighton & H.A.); 29 Allsopp (Notts Co.); 23 Ellington (Wigan Athletic – 21 for Bristol Rov.); 22 Owusu (Brentford) 21 Thomson (Q.P.R.); 20 McKenzie (Peterborough Utd.), Murphy (Blackpool); 18 Burgess (Brentford), Forrester (Northampton Town), Forster (Reading), Thorpe (Bristol City).

FREE FOR ALL AT BRENTFORD

As part of an attempt to increase attendances at Griffin Park, Brentford staged the League's first free match. A crowd of 11,097, twice the average, saw them beat Peterborough United 2-1 and go, briefly, top of the Second Division.

THIRD DIVISION

		P	W	D	L	F	A	W	D	L	F	A	Pts	GD
				HOME					**AWAY**					
1	Plymouth Argyle	46	19	2	2	41	11	12	7	4	30	17	102	+43
2	Luton Town	46	15	5	3	50	18	15	2	6	46	30	97	+48
3	Mansfield Town	46	17	3	3	49	24	7	4	12	23	36	79	+12
4	Cheltenham Town*	46	11	11	1	40	20	10	4	9	26	29	78	+17
5	Rochdale	46	13	8	2	41	22	8	7	8	24	30	78	+13
6	Rushden & Diamonds	46	14	5	4	40	20	6	8	9	29	33	73	+16
7	Hartlepool Utd.	46	12	6	5	53	23	8	5	10	21	25	71	+26
8	Scunthorpe Utd.	46	14	5	4	43	22	5	9	9	31	34	71	+18
9	Shrewsbury Town	46	13	4	6	36	19	7	6	10	28	34	70	+11
10	Kidderminster Harriers	46	13	6	4	35	17	6	3	14	21	30	66	+9
11	Hull City	46	12	6	5	38	18	4	7	12	19	33	61	+6
12	Southend Utd.	46	12	5	6	36	22	3	8	12	15	32	58	−3
13	Macclesfield Town	46	7	7	9	23	25	8	6	9	18	27	58	−11
14	York City	46	11	5	7	26	20	5	4	14	28	47	57	−13
15	Darlington	46	11	6	6	37	25	4	5	14	23	46	56	−11
16	Exeter City	46	7	9	7	25	32	7	4	12	23	41	55	−25
17	Carlisle Utd.	46	11	5	7	31	21	1	11	11	18	35	52	−7
18	Leyton Orient	46	10	7	6	37	25	3	6	14	18	46	52	−16
19	Torquay Utd.	46	8	6	9	27	31	4	9	10	19	32	51	−17
20	Swansea City	46	8	5	8	26	26	6	4	13	27	51	51	−24
21	Oxford Utd.	46	8	7	8	34	28	3	7	13	19	34	47	−9
22	Lincoln City	46	8	4	11	25	27	2	12	9	19	35	46	−18
23	Bristol Rov.	46	8	7	8	28	28	3	5	15	12	32	45	−20
24	Halifax Town	46	5	9	9	24	28	3	3	17	15	56	36	−45

(* Also promoted via play-offs)

Biggest win: Hartlepool Utd. 7, Swansea City 1; Scunthorpe Utd. 7, Darlington 1.
Highest attendance: 18,517 (Plymouth Argyle v Cheltenham Town).
Lowest attendance: 1,227 (Halifax Town v Kidderminster Harriers).
Top League scorer: 24 Steve Howard (Luton Town).
Manager of Year: Paul Sturrock (Plymouth Argyle).
PFA divisional team of season: Larrieu (Plymouth Argyle), Duff (Cheltenham Town), Wotton (Plymouth Argyle), Coughlan (Plymouth Argyle), Taylor (Luton Town), Beagrie (Scunthorpe Utd.), Friio (Plymouth Argyle), Hodges (Scunthorpe Utd.), Williamson (Mansfield Town), Greenacre (Mansfield Town), Ellington (Bristol Rov.).
Fair Play award: Plymouth Argyle.
Groundsman of Year: Mark Patterson (Macclesfield Town).
Leading scorers (all domestic competitions): 28 Greenacre (Mansfield Town); 26 Alsop (Cheltenham Town); 24 Howard (Luton Town); 23 Alexander (Hull City); 22 Rodgers (Shrewsbury Town); 20 Lowe (Rushden & Diamonds); 18 Naylor (Cheltenham Town), Watson (Hartlepool Utd.); 17 Carruthers (Scunthorpe Utd.), Townson (Rochdale); 16 Foran (Carlisle Utd.).

KEEPER SENT OFF IN SUCCESSIVE GAMES

League newcomers Rushden and Diamonds had goalkeeper Billy Turley sent off in back-to-back matches. Turley was dismissed for two yellow cards in a Worthington Cup tie against Crewe Alexandra. Four days later, he brought down Leyton Orient's Scott Houghton in a Division Three game, conceded a penalty and was shown red again.

NATIONWIDE LEAGUE PLAY-OFFS 2002

Holding their nerve in a penalty shoot-out, Birmingham City wiped away the memory of three successive defeats in the semi-finals of the play-offs to return to the top division after a 16-year absence.

In front of a 71,000 crowd under the closed roof of the Millennium Stadium, they beat Norwich City 4-2 on spot-kicks, with 18-year-old substitute Darren Carter completing a fairy-tale first season as a professional by scoring the fourth. Carter, who was cheering his team on from the stands in the previous season's Worthington Cup Final against Liverpool, followed up successful efforts by Stern John, Paul Devlin and Stan Lazaridis after Phil Mulryne and Daryl Sutch had missed for Norwich.

Birmingham fell behind in the first minute of extra-time when substitute Iwan Roberts headed in Alex Notman's cross. John headed Devlin's far-post centre back across the face of goal for Geoff Horsfield to equalise and his team finished the stronger with Michael Johnson hitting a post.

The previous day, Stoke City became the first successful team to come from the south dressing room in 12 finals since football was adopted by the home of Welsh rugby, beating Brentford 2-0 in the Second Division decider. Deon Burton put them ahead after Arnar Gunnlaugsson's corner was headed on by Chris Iwelumo and Ben Burgess deflected a free-kick by manager's son Bjarni Gudjonsson into his own net on the stroke of half time.

Brentford, whose ability to defend set-pieces had been a key factor throughout the season, pressed strongly in the second half without having the same degree of good fortune in front of goal.

Julian Alsop's 26th goal of the season pointed Cheltenham Town to a 3-1 victory over League newcomers Rushden and Diamonds in the Third Division Final. Alsop scored four minutes into the second half after Martin Devaney's opener was cancelled out a minute later by Paul Hall, and John Finnigan made sure late on.

The semi-finals were marred by crowd trouble after matches at Rushden, Rochdale, Cardiff City and Millwall – the most serious occuring at the New Den when police were attacked, horses injured and cars set alight.

SEMI-FINALS, FIRST LEGS

DIVISION 1

Birmingham City 1 (Hughes 56), **Millwall** 1 (Dublin 80). Att: 28,282. **Norwich City** 3 (Rivers 56, McVeigh 73, Mackay 90), **Wolves** 1 (Sturridge 22). Att: 20,127.

DIVISION 2

Huddersfield Town 0, **Brentford** 0. Att: 16,523. **Stoke City** 1 (Burton 84), **Cardiff City** 2 (Earnshaw 12, Fortune-West 59). Att: 21,245.

DIVISION 3

Hartlepool Utd. 1 (Williams 45), **Cheltenham Town** 1 (Grayson 89). Att: 7,135. **Rushden & Diamonds** 2 (Wardley 34, Butterworth 73), **Rochdale** 2 (McEvilly 8, Simpson 57). Att: 6,015.

SEMI-FINALS, SECOND LEGS

DIVISION 1

Millwall 0, **Birmingham City** 1 (John 90). Att: 16,391 (**Birmingham City** won 2-1 on agg). **Wolves** 1 (Cooper 77), **Norwich City** 0. Att: 27,418 (**Norwich City** won 3-2 on agg).

DIVISION 2

Brentford 2 (Powell 14, Owusu 46), **Huddersfield Town** 1 (Booth 2). Att 11,191 (**Brentford** won 2-1 on agg). **Cardiff City** 0, **Stoke City** 2 (O'Connor 90, Oulare 115). Att: 19,367 (aet, **Stoke City** won 3-2 on agg).

DIVISION 3

Cheltenham Town 1 (Williams 26), **Hartlepool Utd.** 1 (Arnison 17). Att: 7,165 (aet, agg 2-2, **Cheltenham Town** won 5-4 on pens). **Rochdale** 1 (Turley 65 og), **Rushden & Diamonds** 2 (Lowe 67, Hall 76). Att: 8,547 (**Rushden & Diamonds** won 4-3 on agg).

FINALS – MILLENNIUM STADIUM

DIVISION 1 – MAY 12, 2002

Birmingham City 1 (Horsfield 102), **Norwich City** 1 (Roberts 91). Att: 71,597 (aet, **Birmingham City** won 4-2 on pens).
Birmingham City (4-4-2): Vaesen, Kenna, Vickers (Carter 71), M. Johnson, Grainger, Devlin, Hughes, Tebily, Mooney (Lazaridis 69), John, Horsfield (A. Johnson 113). **Subs not used:** Bennett, D. Johnson. **Booked:** Grainger, Carter. **Penalties:** Scored – John, Devlin, Lazaridis, Carter. **Manager:** Steve Bruce.
Norwich City (4-4-2): Green, Kenton, Fleming, Mackay, Drury, Rivers (Notman 90), Mulryne, Holt, Easton, Nielsen (Roberts 83), McVeigh (Sutch 102). **Subs not used:** Crichton, Libbra. **Penalties:** Scored – Roberts, Easton. Missed – Mulryne, Sutch. **Manager:** Nigel Worthington.
Referee: G. Barber (Tring). **Half-time:** 0-0.

DIVISION 2 – MAY 11, 2002

Brentford 0, **Stoke City** 2 (Burton 15, Burgess 45 og). Att: 42,523.
Brentford (4-4-2): Smith, Dobson, Powell, Ingimarsson, Anderson, Rowlands (K. O'Connor 78), Sidwell, Evans, Hunt, Burgess (McCammon 70), Owusu. **Subs not used:** Gottskalksson, Boxall, Theobald. **Manager:** Steve Coppell.
Stoke City (4-3-1-2): Cutler, Thomas, Handyside, Shtaniuk, Clarke, Gudjonsson, Dinning (Brightwell 85), J. O'Connor, Gunnlaugsson (Vandeurzen 75), Iwelumo (Cooke 57), Burton. **Subs not used:** Viander, Oulare. **Manager:** Gudjon Thordarson.
Referee: G. Laws (Whitley Bay). **Half-time:** 0-2.

DIVISION 3 – MAY 6, 2002

Cheltenham Town 3 (Devaney 27, Alsop 49, Finnigan 80), **Rushden & Diamonds** 1 (Hall 28). Att: 24,368.
Cheltenham Town (4-4-2): Book, Griffin, Duff, Walker, Victory, Williams, Yates, Finnigan, Devaney (Grayson 75), Alsop, Naylor. **Subs not used:** Muggleton, Howarth, Lee, Tyson. **Manager:** Steve Cotterill.
Rushden & Diamonds (4-4-2): Turley, Mustafa, Peters, Tillson, Underwood, Hall, Butterworth, Wardley, Gray (Brady 69), Lowe, Partridge (Angell 69). **Subs not used:** Pennock, Setchell, Hunter. **Manager:** Brian Talbot.
Referee: A. Leake (Darwen). **Half-time:** 1-1.

PLAY-OFF FINALS – HOME & AWAY

1987 Divs. 1/2: Charlton Athletic beat Leeds Utd. 2-1 in replay (Birmingham City) after 1-1 agg (1-0h, 0-1a). Charlton Athletic remained in Div. 1. Losing semi-finalists: Ipswich Town and Oldham Athletic. **Divs. 2/3: Swindon Town** beat Gillingham 2-0 in replay (Crystal Palace) after 2-2 agg (0-1a, 2-1h). Swindon Town promoted to Div. 2. Losing semi-finalists: Sunderland and Wigan Athletic; Sunderland relegated to Div. 3.

Divs. 3/4: Aldershot beat Wolves 3-0 on agg (2-0h, 1-0a) and promoted to Div. 3. Losing semi-finalists: Bolton Wand. and Colchester Utd.; Bolton Wand. relegated to Div.4.

1988 Divs. 1/2: Middlesbrough beat Chelsea 2-1 on agg (2-0h, 0-1a) and promoted to Div. 1; Chelsea relegated to Div. 2. Losing semi-finalists: Blackburn Rov. and Bradford City. **Divs. 2/3: Walsall** beat Bristol City 4-0 in replay (h) after 3-3 agg (3-1a, 0-2h) and promoted to Div. 2. Losing semi-finalists: Sheffield Utd. and Notts Co; Sheffield Utd. relegated to Div. 3. **Divs. 3/4: Swansea City** beat Torquay Utd. 5-4 on agg (2-1h, 3-3a) and promoted to Div. 3. Losing semi-finalists: Rotherham Utd. and Scunthorpe Utd.; Rotherham Utd. relegated to Div.4.

1989 Div. 2: Crystal Palace beat Blackburn Rov. 4-3 on agg (1-3a, 3-0h). Losing semi-finalists: Watford and Swindon Town. **Div. 3: Port Vale** beat Bristol Rov. 2-1 on agg (1-1a, 1-0h). Losing semi-finalists: Fulham and Preston N.E. **Div.4: Leyton Orient** beat Wrexham 1-0 on agg (0-0a, 2-1h). Losing semi-finalists: Scarborough and Scunthorpe Utd.

PLAY-OFF FINALS AT WEMBLEY

1990 Div. 2: Swindon Town 1, Sunderland 0 (att: 72,873). Swindon Town promoted, then demoted for financial irregularities; Sunderland promoted. Losing semi-finalists: Blackburn Rov. and Newcastle Utd. **Div. 3: Notts Co.** 2, Tranmere Rov. 0 (att: 29,252). Losing semi-finalists: Bolton Wand. and Bury. **Div.4: Cambridge Utd.** 1, Chesterfield 0 (att: 26,404). Losing semi-finalists: Maidstone and Stockport Co.

1991 Div. 2: Notts Co. 3, Brighton & H.A. 1 (att: 59,940). Losing semi-finalists: Middlesbrough and Millwall. **Div. 3: Tranmere Rov.** 1, Bolton Wand. 0 (att: 30,217). Losing semi-finalists: Brentford and Bury. **Div.4: Torquay Utd.** 2, Blackpool 2 – Torquay Utd. won 5-4 on pens (att: 21,615). Losing semi-finalists: Burnley and Scunthorpe Utd.

1992 Div. 2: Blackburn Rov. 1, Leicester City 0 (att: 68,147). Losing semi-finalists: Derby Co. and Cambridge Utd. **Div. 3: Peterborough Utd.** 2, Stockport Co. 1 (att: 35,087). Losing semi-finalists: Huddersfield Town and Stoke City. **Div.4: Blackpool** 1, Scunthorpe Utd. 1 – Blackpool won 4-3 on pens (att: 22,741). Losing semi-finalists: Barnet and Crewe Alexandra.

1993 Div. 1; Swindon Town 4, Leicester City 3 (att: 73,802). Losing semi-finalists: Portsmouth and Tranmere Rov. **Div. 2: W.B.A.** 3, Port Vale 0 (att: 53,471). Losing semi-finalists: Stockport Co. and Swansea City. **Div. 3: York City** 1, Crewe Alexandra 1 – York City won 5-3 on pens (att: 22,416). Losing semi-finalists: Bury and Walsall.

1994 Div. 1: Leicester City 2, Derby Co. 1 (att: 73,671). Losing semi-finalists: Millwall and Tranmere Rov. **Div. 2: Burnley** 2, Stockport Co. 1 (att: 44,806). Losing semi-finalists: Plymouth Argyle and York City. **Div. 3: Wycombe Wand.** 4, Preston N.E. 2 (att: 40,109). Losing semi-finalists: Carlisle Utd. and Torquay Utd.

1995 Div. 1: Bolton Wand. 4, Reading 3 (att: 64,107). Losing semi-finalists: Tranmere Rov. and Wolves. **Div. 2: Huddersfield Town** 2, Bristol Rov. 1 (att: 59,175). Losing semi-finalists: Brentford and Crewe Alexandra. **Div. 3: Chesterfield** 2, Bury 0 (att: 22,814). Losing semi-finalists: Mansfield Town and Preston N.E.

1996 Div. 1: Leicester City 2, Crystal Palace 1, aet (att: 73,573). Losing semi-finalists: Charlton Athletic and Stoke City. **Div. 2: Bradford City** 2, Notts Co. 0 (att: 39,972). Losing semi-finalists: Blackpool and Crewe Alexandra. **Div. 3: Plymouth Argyle** 1, Darlington 0 (att: 43,431). Losing semi-finalists: Colchester Utd. and Hereford.

1997 Div. 1: Crystal Palace 1, Sheffield Utd. 0, (att: 64,383). Losing semi-finalists: Ipswich Town and Wolves. **Div. 2: Crewe Alexandra** 1, Brentford 0 (att: 34,149). Losing semi-finalists: Bristol City and Luton Town. **Div. 3: Northampton Town** 1, Swansea City 0 (att: 46,804). Losing semi-finalists: Cardiff City and Chester City.

1998 Div. 1: Charlton Athletic 4, Sunderland 4, aet Charlton Athletic won 7-6 on pens. (att: 77, 739). Losing semi-finalists: Ipswich Town and Sheffield United. **Div. 2: Grimsby Town** 1, Northampton Town 0 (att: 62,988). Losing semi-finalists: Bristol Rov. and Fulham. **Div. 3: Colchester Utd.** 1, Torquay Utd. 0 (att: 19,486). Losing semi-finalists: Barnet and Scarborough.

1999 Div. 1: Watford 2, Bolton Wand. 0, (att. 70,343). Losing semi-finalists: Ipswich Town and Birmingham City. **Div. 2: Manchester City** 2, Gillingham 2, aet Manchester City won 3-1 on pens. (att. 76,935). Losing semi-finalists: Preston N.E. and Wigan Athletic. **Div. 3: Scunthorpe Utd.** 1, Leyton Orient 0, (att. 36,985). Losing semi-finalists: Rotherham Utd. and Swansea City.

2000 Div. 1: Ipswich Town 4, Barnsley 2 (att: 73,427). Losing semi-finalists: Birmingham City and Bolton Wand. **Div. 2: Gillingham** 3, Wigan Athletic 2, aet (att: 53,764). Losing semi-finalists: Millwall and Stoke City. **Div. 3: Peterborough Utd.** 1, Darlington 0 (att: 33,383). Losing semi-finalists: Barnet and Hartlepool Utd.

PLAY-OFF FINALS AT MILLENNIUM STADIUM

2001 Div. 1: Bolton Wand. 3, Preston N.E. 0 (att: 54,328). Losing semi-finalists: Birmingham City and W.B.A. **Div. 2: Walsall** 3, Reading 2, aet (att: 50,496). Losing semi-finalists: Stoke City and Wigan Athletic. **Div. 3: Blackpool** 4, Leyton Orient 2 (att: 23,600). Losing semi-finalists: Hartlepool Utd. and Hull City.

HISTORY OF THE PLAY-OFFS

Play-off matches were introduced by the Football League to decide final promotion and relegation issues at the end of season 1986-87.

A similar series styled "Test Matches" had operated between Divisions One and Two for six seasons from 1893-98, and was abolished when both divisions were increased from 16 to 18 clubs.

Eighty-eight years later, the play-offs were back in vogue. In the first three seasons (1987-88-89), the Finals were played home-and-away, and since they were made one-off matches in 1990, they have featured regularly in Wembley's spring calendar, until the old stadium closed its doors and the action switched to the Millennium Stadium in Cardiff in 2001.

Through the years, these have been the ups and downs of the play-offs:

1987 Initially, the 12 clubs involved comprised the one that finished directly above those relegated in Divisions One, Two and Three and the three who followed the sides automatically promoted in each section. Two of the home-and-away Finals went to neutral-ground replays, in which **Charlton Athletic** clung to First Division status by denying Leeds Utd. promotion while **Swindon Town** beat Gillingham to complete their climb from Fourth Division to Second in successive seasons, via the play-offs, **Sunderland** fell into the Third and **Bolton Wand.** into Division Four, both for the first time. **Aldershot** went up after finishing only sixth in Division Four; in their Final, they beat Wolves, who had finished nine points higher and missed automatic promotion by one point.

1988 Chelsea were relegated from the First Division after losing on aggregate to Middlesbrough, who had finished third in Division Two. So Middlesbrough, managed by Bruce Rioch, completed the rise from Third Division to First in successive seasons, only two years after their very existence had been threatened by the bailiffs. Also promoted via the play-offs: **Walsall** from Division Three and **Swansea City** from the Fourth. Relegated, besides Chelsea: **Sheffield Utd.** (to Division Three) and **Rotherham Utd.** (to Division Four).

1989 After two seasons of promotion-relegation play-offs, the system was changed to involve the four clubs who had just missed automatic promotion. That format has remained. Steve Coppell's **Crystal Palace**, third in Division Two, returned to the top flight after eight years, beating Blackburn Rov. 4-3 on aggregate after extra time. Similarly, **Port Vale** confirmed third place in Division Three with promotion via the play-offs. For **Leyton Orient**, promotion seemed out of the question in Division Four when they stood 15th. on March 1. But eight wins and a draw in the last nine home games swept them to sixth in the final table, and two more home victories in the play-offs completed their season to triumph.

1990 The play-off Finals now moved to Wembley over three days of the Spring Holiday week-end. On successive afternoons, **Cambridge Utd.** won promotion from Division Four and **Notts County** from the Third. Then, on Bank Holiday Monday, the biggest crowd for years at a Football League fixture (72,873) saw Ossie Ardiles' **Swindon Town** beat Sunderland 1-0 to reach the First Division for the first time. A few weeks later, however, Wembley losers **Sunderland** were promoted instead, by default; Swindon Town were found guilty of "financial irregularities" and stayed in Division Two.

1991 Again, the season's biggest League crowd (59,940) gathered at Wembley for the First Division Final in which **Notts Co.** (having missed promotion by one point) still fulfilled their ambition, beating Brighton & H.A. 3-1. In successive years, County had climbed from Third Division to First via the play-offs – the first club to achieve double promotion by this route. Bolton Wand. were denied automatic promotion in Division Three on goal difference, and lost at Wembley to an extra-time goal by **Tranmere Rov.** The Fourth Division Final made history, with Blackpool beaten 5-4 on penalties by **Torquay Utd.** – first instance of promotion being decided by a shoot-out. In the table, Blackpool had finished seven points ahead of Torquay Utd.

1992 Wembley that Spring Bank Holiday was the turning point in the history of **Blackburn Rov.** Bolstered by Kenny Dalglish's return to management and owner Jack Walker's millions, they beat Leicester City 1-0 by Mike Newell's 45th-minute penalty to achieve their objective – a place in the new Premier League. Newell, who also missed a second-half penalty, had recovered from a broken leg just in time for the play-offs. In the Fourth Division Final **Blackpool** (denied by penalties the previous year) this time won a shoot-out 4-3 against Scunthorpe Utd., who were unlucky in the play-offs for the fourth time in five years. **Peterborough Utd.** climbed out of the Third Division for the first time, beating Stockport Co. 2-1 at Wembley.

1993 The crowd of 73,802 at Wembley to see **Swindon Town** beat Leicester City 4-3 in the First Division Final was 11,000 bigger than that for the F.A. Cup Final replay between Arsenal and Sheffield Wed. Leicester City rallied from three down to 3-3 before Paul Bodin's late penalty wiped away Swindon Town's bitter memories of three years earlier, when they were denied promotion after winning at Wembley. In the Third Division Final, **York City** beat Crewe Alexandra 5-3 in a shoot-out after a 1-1 draw, and in the Second Division decider, **W.B.A.** beat Port Vale 3-0. That was tough on Vale, who had finished third in the table with 89 points – the highest total never to earn promotion in any division. They had beaten Albion twice in the League, too.

1994 Wembley's record turn-out of 158,586 spectators at the three Finals started with a crowd of 40,109 to see Martin O'Neill's **Wycombe Wand.** beat Preston N.E. 4-2. They thus climbed from Conference to Second Division with successive promotions. **Burnley's** 2-1 victory in the Second Division Final was marred by the sending-off of two Stockport Co. players, and in the First Division decider **Leicester City** came from behind to beat

Derby Co. and end the worst Wembley record of any club. They had lost on all six previous appearances there – four times in the F.A. Cup Final and in the play-offs of 1992 and 1993.

1995 Two months after losing the Coca-Cola Cup Final to Liverpool, Bruce Rioch's **Bolton Wand.** were back at Wembley for the First Division play-off Final. From two goals down to Reading in front of a crowd of 64,107, they returned to the top company after 15 years, winning 4-3 with two extra-time goals. **Huddersfield Town** ended the first season at their new £15m. home with promotion to the First Division via a 2-1 victory against Bristol Rov. – manager Neil Warnock's third play-off success (after two with Notts Co.). Of the three clubs who missed automatic promotion by one place, only **Chesterfield** achieved it in the play-offs, comfortably beating Bury 2-0.

1996 Under new manager **Martin O'Neill** (a Wembley play-off winner with Wycombe Wand. in 1994), **Leicester City** returned to the Premiership a year after leaving it. They had finished fifth in the table, but in the Final came from behind to beat third-placed Crystal Palace by Steve Claridge's shot in the last seconds of extra time. In the Second Division **Bradford City** came sixth, nine points behind Blackpool (3rd), but beat them (from two down in the semi-final first leg) and then clinched promotion by 2-0 v Notts Co. at Wembley. It was City's greatest day since they won the Cup in 1911. **Plymouth Argyle** beat Darlington in the Third Division Final to earn promotion a year after being relegated. It was manager **Neil Warnock**'s fourth play-off triumph in seven seasons after two with Notts Co. (1990 and 1991) and a third with Huddersfield Town in 1995.

1997 High drama at Wembley as **Crystal Palace** left it late against Sheffield Utd. in the First Division play-off final. The match was scoreless until the last 10 seconds when David Hopkin lobbed Blades' keeper Simon Tracey from 25 yards to send the Eagles back to the Premiership after two seasons of Nationwide action. In the Second Division play-off final, **Crewe Alexandra** beat Brentford 1-0 courtesy of a Shaun Smith goal. **Northampton Town** celebrated their first Wembley appearance with a 1-0 victory over Swansea City thanks to John Frain's injury-time free-kick in the Third Division play-off final.

1998 In one of the finest games ever seen at Wembley, **Charlton Athletic** eventually triumphed 7-6 on penalties over Sunderland. For Charlton Athletic, Wearside-born Clive Mendonca scored a hat-trick and Richard Rufus his first career goal in a match that lurched between joy and despair for both sides as it ended 4-4. Sunderland defender Michael Gray's superb performance ill deserved to end with his weakly struck spot kick being saved by Sasa Ilic. In the Third Division, the penalty spot also had a role to play, as **Colchester Utd.**'s David Gregory scored the only goal to defeat Torquay Utd., while in the Second Division a Kevin Donovan goal gave **Grimsby Town** victory over Northampton Town.

1999: Elton John, watching via a personal satellite link in Seattle, saw his **Watford** side overcome **Bolton Wand.** 2-0 to reach the Premiership. Against technically superior opponents, Watford prevailed with application and teamwork. They also gave Bolton a lesson in finishing through match-winners by Nick Wright and Allan Smart. **Manchester City** staged a reamrkable comeback to win the Second Division Final after trailing to goals by Carl Asaba and Robert Taylor for **Gillingham**. Kevin Horlock and Paul Dickov scored in stoppage time and City went on to win on penalties. A goal by Spaniard Alex Calvo-Garcia earned **Scunthorpe Utd.** a 1-0 success against **Leyton Orient** in the Third Division Final.

2000: After three successive play-off failures, **Ipswich Town** finally secured a place in the Premiership. They overcame the injury loss of leading scorer David Johnson to beat **Barnsley** 4-2 with goals by 36-year-old Tony Mowbray, Marcus Stewart and substitutes Richard Naylor and Martijn Reuser. With six minutes left of extra-time in the Second Division Final, **Gillingham** trailed **Wigan Athletic** 2-1. But headers by 38-year-old player-coach Steve Butler and fellow substitute Andy Thomson gave them a 3-2 victory. Andy Clarke, approaching his 33rd birthday, scored the only goal of the Third Division decider for **Peterborough Utd.** against **Darlington**.

2001: Bolton Wand., unsuccessful play-off contenders in the two previous seasons, made no mistake at the third attempt. They flourished in the new surroundings of the Millennium Stadium to beat **Preston N.E.** 3-0 with goals by Gareth Farrelly, Michael Ricketts – his 24th of the season – and Ricardo Gardner to reach the Premiership. **Walsall**, relegated 12 months earlier, scored twice in a three-minute spell of extra time to win 3-2 against **Reading** in the Second Division Final, while **Blackpool** capped a marked improvement in the second half of the season by overcoming **Leyton Orient** 4-2 in the Third Division Final.

PLAY-OFF CROWDS YEAR BY YEAR

YEAR	MATCHES	AGG. ATT.
1987	20	310,000
1988	19	305,817
1989	18	234,393
1990	15	291,428
1991	15	266,442
1992	15	277,684
1993	15	319,907
1994	15	314,817
1995	15	295,317
1996	15	308,515
1997	15	309,085
1998	15	320,795
1999	15	372,969
2000	15	333,999
2001	15	317,745
2002	15	327,894
	252	4,906,807

QUOTE UNQUOTE

'The system is a hangover from the past when players had a testimonial to supplement what were not high earnings in a short career' – **Richard Caborn**, Minister for Sport, asking the Treasury to rule whether benefit games should continue to be tax-free.

'I have to admit that it looks as though the ball didn't cross the line' – **Sir Geoff Hurst** on THAT goal in the 1966 World Cup Final.

'I think it is overkill. I don't think people can consume all the matches that are now on offer' – **John Motson**, BBC commentator, maintaining there is too much football on television.

'This is not the Albanian League' – **Paolo Di Canio** warning that his West Ham United team needed strengthening.

'What is a bank full of money if you have no team' – **Arsene Wenger**, Arsenal manager, ruling out a move to Real Madrid for Patrick Vieira.

'I let the club, the fans, my team-mates and myself down' – **Jamie Carragher**, Liverpool defender, sent off for throwing a coin back into the crowd during an F.A. Cup tie at Highbury.

OTHER COMPETITIONS 2001-02

LDV VANS TROPHY

FIRST ROUND

Northern: Blackpool 3, Stoke City 2; Darlington 2, Macclesfield Town 1; Doncaster Rov. 0, Kidderminster Harriers 1; Hartlepool Utd. 0, Bury 1 (aet, golden goal); Huddersfield Town 0, Halifax Town 0 (aet, Huddersfield Town won 4-3 on pens); Leigh RMI 2, Scarborough 1 (aet, golden goal); Notts Co. 2, York City 0; Port Vale 2, Carlisle Utd. 1; Rochdale 2, Southport 0; Scunthorpe Utd. 3, Lincoln City 1; Shrewsbury Town 0, Chesterfield 1; Wrexham 5, Wigan Athletic 1.
Southern: Barnet 2, Bournemouth 1 (aet, golden goal); Bristol City 1, Torquay Utd. 0 (aet, golden goal); Cardiff City 7, Rushden & Diamonds 1; Cheltenham Town 2, Plymouth Argyle 1; Colchester Utd. 1, Swindon Town 0; Dagenham & Redbridge 3, Leyton Orient 2 (aet, golden goal); Exeter City 1, Cambridge Utd. 2 (aet, golden goal); Northampton Town 2, Oxford Utd. 0; Stevenage Borough 1, Southend Utd. 4; Swansea City 1, Brighton & H.A. 2; Wycombe Wand. 1, Brentford 0; Yeovil Town 3, Q.P.R. 0.

SECOND ROUND

Northern: Bury 2, Notts Co. 3 (aet, golden goal); Chesterfield 1, Kidderminster Harriers 0 (aet, golden goal); Hull City 3, Leigh RMI 0; Mansfield Town 0, Blackpool 4; Oldham Athletic 2, Tranmere Rov. 0; Rochdale 1, Port Vale 2; Scunthorpe Utd. 3, Darlington 0; Wrexham 0, Huddersfield Town 1.
Southern: Brighton & H.A. 2, Wycombe Wand. 1 (aet, golden goal); Bristol Rov. 1, Yeovil Town 1 (aet, Bristol Rov. won 5-4 on pens); Cambridge Utd. 1, Cheltenham Town 1 (aet, Cambridge Utd. won 5-4 on pens); Cardiff City 1, Peterborough Utd. 3; Dagenham & Redbridge 3, Luton Town 2 (aet, golden goal); Northampton Town 0, Barnet 1; Reading 2, Colchester Utd. 1; Southend Utd. 0, Bristol City 2.

THIRD ROUND

Northern: Chesterfield 0, Blackpool 3; Huddersfield Town 4, Scunthorpe Utd. 1; Hull City 2, Port Vale 1; Notts Co. 0, Oldham Athletic 1.
Southern: Barnet 4, Reading 1; Bristol City 2, Peterborough Utd. 1 (aet, golden goal); Bristol Rov. 4, Dagenham & Redbridge 1; Cambridge Utd. 2, Brighton & H.A. 1.

SEMI-FINALS

Northern: Hull City 0, Huddersfield Town 1; Oldham Athletic 2, Blackpool 5.
Southern: Bristol City 3, Bristol Rov. 0; Cambridge Utd. 2, Barnet 0.

AREA FINALS

Northern first leg: Blackpool 3 (Wellens 3, Murphy 38, Taylor 70), Huddersfield Town 1 (Schofield 56). Att: 4,573. **Second leg:** Huddersfield Town 2 (Wijnhard 5 pen, Schofield 33), Blackpool 1 (Bullock 103). Att: 7,736 (aet, Blackpool won 4-3 on agg with golden goal).
Southern first leg: Cambridge Utd. 0, Bristol City 0. Att: 3,470. **Second leg:** Bristol City 0, Cambridge Utd. 2 (One 38, 60). Att: 12,264 (Cambridge Utd. won 2-0 on agg).

FINAL

BLACKPOOL 4, CAMBRIDGE UNITED 1

Millennium Stadium, (20,287), Sunday, March 24, 2002

Blackpool (4-4-2): Barnes; O'Kane, Clarke, I. Marshall (Hughes 39), Jaszczun, Bullock, Collins, Wellens (Simpson 85), Hills, Murphy, Taylor (Walker 85). **Subs not used:** Pullen, Fenton. **Scorers:** Murphy (6), Clarke (54), Hills (77), Taylor (82). **Booked:** Jaszczun. **Manager:** Steve McMahon.

Cambridge Utd. (4-4-2): Perez; Angus (Goodhind 85), Tann, Duncan, Murray, Tudor (Jackman 61), Wanless, Ashbee, Guttridge, Youngs, Kitson (One 73). **Subs not used:** Fleming, S. Marshall. **Scorer:** Wanless (28 pen). **Booked:** Guttridge. **Manager:** John Taylor.

Referee: R. Furnandiz (Doncaster). **Half-time:** 1-1.

FINALS – RESULTS

Associated Members' Cup
1984   (Hull City) Bournemouth 2, Hull City 1
Freight Rover Trophy
1985   (Wembley) Wigan Athletic 3, Brentford 1
1986   (Wembley) Bristol City 3, Bolton Wand. 0
1987   (Wembley) Mansfield Town 1, Bristol City 1 (aet; Mansfield Town won 5-4 on pens.)
Sherpa Van Trophy
1988   (Wembley) Wolves 2, Burnley 0
1989   (Wembley) Bolton Wand. 4, Torquay Utd. 1
Leyland Daf Cup
1990   (Wembley) Tranmere Rov. 2, Bristol Rov. 1
1991   (Wembley) Birmingham City 3, Tranmere Rov. 2
Autoglass Trophy
1992   (Wembley) Stoke City 1, Stockport Co. 0
1993   (Wembley) Port Vale 2, Stockport Co. 1
1994   (Wembley) Huddersfield Town 1, Swansea City 1 (aet; Swansea City won 3-1 on pens.)
Auto Windscreens Shield
1995   (Wembley) Birmingham City 1, Carlisle Utd. 0 (Birmingham City won in sudden-death overtime)
1996   (Wembley) Rotherham Utd. 2, Shrewsbury Town 1
1997   (Wembley) Carlisle Utd. 0, Colchester Utd. 0 (aet; Carlisle Utd. won 4-3 on pens.)
1998   (Wembley) Grimsby Town 2, Bournemouth 1 (Grimsby Town won with golden goal in extra time)
1999   (Wembley) Wigan Athletic 1, Millwall 0
2000   (Wembley) Stoke City 2, Bristol City 1
LDV Vans Trophy
2001   (Millennium Stadium) Port Vale 2, Brentford 1
2002   (Millennium Stadium) Blackpool 4, Cambridge Utd. 1

OTHER LEAGUE CLUBS' CUP COMPETITIONS

FINALS – AT WEMBLEY

Full Members' Cup (Discontinued after 1992)
1985-86   Chelsea 5, Manchester City 4
1986-87   Blackburn Rov. 1, Charlton Athletic 0

Simod Cup
1987-88   Reading 4, Luton Town 1
1988-89   Nott'm. Forest 4, Everton 3

Zenith Data Systems Cup
1989-90   Chelsea 1, Middlesbrough 0
1990-91   Crystal Palace 4, Everton 1
1991-92   Nott'm. Forest 3, Southampton 2

ANGLO-ITALIAN CUP (Discontinued after 1996: * Home club)

1970   *Napoli 0, Swindon Town 3
1971   *Bologna 1, Blackpool 2 (aet)
1972   *AS Roma 3, Blackpool 1
1973   *Fiorentina 1, Newcastle Utd. 2
1993   Derby Co. 1, Cremonese 3 (at Wembley)
1994   Notts Co. 0, Brescia 1 (at Wembley)
1995   Ascoli 1, Notts Co. 2 (at Wembley)
1996   Port Vale 2, Genoa 5 (at Wembley)

F.A. CHALLENGE VASE FINALS

At Wembley
1975   Hoddesdon Town 2, Epsom & Ewell 1
1976   Billericay Town 1, Stamford 0*
1977   Billericay Town 2, Sheffield 1 (replay Nottingham, after a 1-1 draw at Wembley)
1978   Blue Star 2, Barton Rov. 1
1979   Billericay Town 4, Almondsbury Greenway 1
1980   Stamford 2, Guisborough Town 0
1981   Whickham 3, Willenhall Town 2*
1982   Forest Green Rov. 3, Rainworth Miners' Welfare 0
1983   V.S. Rugby 1, Halesowen Town 0
1984   Stansted 3, Stamford 2
1985   Halesowen Town 3, Fleetwood Town 1
1986   Halesowen Town 3, Southall 0
1987   St. Helens Town 3, Warrington Town 2
1988   Colne Dynamoes 1, Emley 0*
1989   Tamworth 3, Sudbury Town 0 (replay Peterborough Utd., after a 1-1 draw at Wembley)
1990   Yeading 1, Bridlington 0 (replay Leeds Utd., after 0-0 draw at Wembley)
1991   Guiseley 3, Gresley Rov. 1 (replay Bramall Lane, Sheffield, after a 4-4 draw at Wembley)
1992   Wimborne Town 5, Guiseley 3
1993   Bridlington Town 1, Tiverton Town 0
1994   Diss Town 2, Taunton Town 1*
1995   Arlesey Town 2, Oxford City 1
1996   Brigg Town 3, Clitheroe 0
1997   Whitby Town 3, North Ferriby Utd. 0
1998   Tiverton Town 1, Tow Law Town 0
1999   Tiverton Town 1, Bedlington Terriers 0
2000   Deal Town 1, Chippenham Town 0

At Villa Park
2001   Taunton Town 2, Berkhamsted 1
2002   Whitley Bay 1, Tiptree Utd. 0*

(Sponsors: Carlsberg since 1995; * After extra time)

F.A. UMBRO TROPHY

THIRD ROUND

Bashley 2, Bognor Regis Town 1; Burton Albion 3, Blyth Spartans 0; Cambridge City 1, Hendon 1; Canvey Island 2, Purfleet 2; Chesham Utd. 2, Hereford Utd. 2; Chester City 1, Stourport Swifts 1; Dagenham & Redbridge 1, Eastbourne Borough 0; Doncaster Rov. 2, Harrogate Town 0; Dulwich Hamlet 3, Braintree Town 4; Farnborough 1, Carshalton Athletic 1; Fisher Athletic 0, Barnet 5; Forest Green Rov. 1, Aldershot Town 1;

Grantham Town 2, Moor Green 1; Grays Athletic 2, Welling Utd. 4; Hampton & Richmond Borough 2, Newport Co. 0; Histon Town 1, Gravesend & Northfleet 1; Ilkeston Town 0, Telford Utd. 2; Leigh RMI 2, Emley 2; Mangotsfield Utd. 3, Tooting & Mitcham Utd. 2; Margate 3, Hayes 1; Morecambe 2, Kings Lynn 0; North Ferriby Utd. 3, Altrincham 2; Northwich Victoria 3, Boston Utd. 1; Scarborough 2, Hednesford Town 0; Solihull Borough 3, Runcorn 0; Southport 1, Gresley Rov 1; Stalybridge Celtic 1, Nuneaton Borough 1; Stevenage Borough 5, Dover Athletic 1; Tiverton Town 1, Yeovil Town 3; Vauxhall Motors 4, Lancaster City 0; Woking 2, Kingstonian 1; Worksop Town 4, Tamworth 5. **REPLAYS:** Aldershot Town 2, Forest Green Rov. 3; Carshalton Athletic 0, Farnborough 5; Emley 1, Leigh RMI 4; Gravesend & Northfleet 3, Histon Town 1; Gresley Rov. 1, Southport 0; Hendon 2, Cambridge City 0; Hereford Utd. 4, Chesham Utd. 0; Nuneaton Borough 1, Stalybridge Celtic 2 (aet); Purfleet 0, Canvey Island 1 (aet); Stourport Swifts 0, Chester City 3.

FOURTH ROUND

Barnet 0, Scarborough 0; Chester City 0, Solihull Borough 0; Dagenham & Redbridge 0, Telford Utd. 2; Farnborough 1, Burton Albion 1; Forest Green Rov. 1, Worksop Town 0; Grantham Town 1, Canvey Island 4; Gravesend & Northfleet 2, Hendon 1; Hereford Utd. 4, Hampton & Richmond Borough 2; Mangotsfield Utd. 0, Stalybridge Celtic 1; Margate 2, Leigh RMI 0; Morecambe 5, Gresley Rov. 0; North Ferriby Utd. 4, Braintree Town 4; Stevenage Borough 1, Bashley 0; Woking 4, Welling Utd. 2; Yeovil Town 1, Doncaster Rov. 1. **REPLAYS:** Braintree Town 2, North Ferriby 2 (aet, Braintree Town won 5-4 on pens); Burton Albion 3, Farnborough 2; Doncaster Rov. 4, Yeovil Town 5; Scarborough 2, Barnet 2 (aet, Scarborough won 5-3 on pens); Solihull Borough 2, Chester City 4.

FIFTH ROUND

Burton Abion 3, Woking 0; Chester City 2, Hereford Utd. 1; Gravesend & Northfleet 0, Stalybridge Celtic 2; Margate 1, Braintree Town 1; Northwich Victoria 3, Telford Utd. 2; Scarborough 1, Morecambe 1; Stevenage Borough 3, Forest Green Rov. 2; Yeovil Town 2, Canvey Island 1. **REPLAYS:** Braintree Town 1, Margate 2; Morecambe 3, Scarborough 0.

SIXTH ROUND

Burton Albion 2, Chester City 0; Margate 1, Morecambe 2; Northwich Victoria 0, Yeovil Town 2; Stevenage Borough 1, Stalybridge Celtic 0.

SEMI-FINALS

First legs: Morecambe 1, Stevenage Borough 2; Yeovil Town 4, Burton Albion 0. **Second legs:** Burton Albion 2, Yeovil Town 1 (Yeovil Town won 5-2 on agg); Stevenage Borough 2, Morecambe 0 (Stevenage Borough won 4-1 on agg).

FINAL

STEVENAGE BOROUGH 0, YEOVIL TOWN 2
Villa Park, (18,809), Sunday, May 12, 2002

Stevenage Borough (4-3-3): Wilkerson, Hamsher, Goodliffe, Trott, Fraser, Evers (Williams 56), Fisher, Wormull (Sterling 70), Sigere (Campbell 74), Jackson, Clarke. **Subs not used:** Greygoose, Campbell. **Booked:** Fisher. **Manager:** Wayne Turner.

Yeovil Town (4-4-2): Weale, Lockwood, Skiverton, Pluck (White 50), Tonkin, Crittenden (Lindegaard 83), Johnson, Way, McIndoe, Alford (Giles 86), Stansfield. **Subs not used:** Sheffield, O'Brien. **Scorers:** Alford (12), Stansfield (66). **Manager:** Gary Johnson.

Referee: N. Barry (Scunthorpe). **Half-time:** 0-1.

F.A. CHALLENGE TROPHY FINALS

At Wembley
1970 Macclesfield Town 2, Telford Utd. 0
1971 Telford Utd. 3, Hillingdon Borough 2
1972 Stafford Rangers 3, Barnet 0
1973 Scarborough 2, Wigan Athletic 1*
1974 Morecambe 2, Dartford 1
1975 Matlock Town 4, Scarborough 0
1976 Scarborough 3, Stafford Rangers 2*
1977 Scarborough 2, Dagenham 1
1978 Altrincham 3, Leatherhead 1
1979 Stafford Rangers 2, Kettering Town 0
1980 Dagenham 2, Mossley 1
1981 Bishop's Stortford 1, Sutton Utd. 0
1982 Enfield 1, Altrincham 0*
1983 Telford Utd. 2, Northwich Victoria 1
1984 Northwich Victoria 2, Bangor City 1 (replay Stoke City, after a 1-1 draw at Wembley)
1985 Wealdstone 2, Boston Utd. 1
1986 Altrincham 1, Runcorn 0
1987 Kidderminster Harriers 2, Burton Albion 1 (replay W.B.A., after a 0-0 draw at Wembley)
1988 Enfield 3, Telford Utd. 2 (replay W.B.A., after a 0-0 draw at Wembley)
1989 Telford Utd. 1, Macclesfield Town 0*
1990 Barrow 3, Leek Town 0
1991 Wycombe Wand. 2, Kidderminster Harriers 1
1992 Colchester Utd. 3, Witton Albion 1
1993 Wycombe Wand. 4, Runcorn 1
1994 Woking 2, Runcorn 1
1995 Woking 2, Kidderminster 1
1996 Macclesfield Town 3, Northwich Victoria 1
1997 Woking 1, Dagenham & Redbridge 0*
1998 Cheltenham Town 1, Southport 0
1999 Kingstonian 1, Forest Green Rov. 0
2000 Kingstonian 3, Kettering Town 2

At Villa Park
2001 Canvey Island 1, Forest Green Rov. 0
2002 Yeovil Town 2, Stevenage Borough 0

(Sponsors: Umbro since 1995; * After extra time)

F.A. YOUTH CUP WINNERS

Year	Winners	Runners-up	Aggregate
1953	Manchester Utd.	Wolves	9-3
1954	Manchester Utd.	Wolves	5-4
1955	Manchester Utd.	W.B.A.	7-1
1956	Manchester Utd.	Chesterfield	4-3
1957	Manchester Utd.	West Ham Utd.	8-2
1958	Wolves	Chelsea	7-6
1959	Blackburn Rov.	West Ham Utd.	2-1
1960	Chelsea	Preston N.E.	5-2
1961	Chelsea	Everton	5-3
1962	Newcastle Utd.	Wolves	2-1
1963	West Ham Utd.	Liverpool	6-5
1964	Manchester Utd.	Swindon Town	5-2

1965	Everton	Arsenal	3-2
1966	Arsenal	Sunderland	5-3
1967	Sunderland	Birmingham City	2-0
1968	Burnley	Coventry City	3-2
1969	Sunderland	W.B.A.	6-3
1970	Tottenham	Coventry City	4-3
1971	Arsenal	Cardiff City	2-0
1972	Aston Villa	Liverpool	5-2
1973	Ipswich Town	Bristol City	4-1
1974	Tottenham	Huddersfield Town	2-1
1975	Ipswich Town	West Ham Utd.	5-1
1976	W.B.A.	Wolves	5-0
1977	Crystal Palace	Everton	1-0
1978	Crystal Palace	Aston Villa	*1-0
1979	Millwall	Manchester City	2-0
1980	Aston Villa	Manchester City	3-2
1981	West Ham Utd.	Tottenham	2-1
1982	Watford	Manchester Utd.	7-6
1983	Norwich City	Everton	6-5
1984	Everton	Stoke City	4-2
1985	Newcastle Utd.	Watford	4-1
1986	Manchester City	Manchester Utd.	3-1
1987	Coventry City	Charlton Athletic	2-1
1988	Arsenal	Doncaster Rov.	6-1
1989	Watford	Manchester City	2-1
1990	Tottenham	Middlesbrough	3-2
1991	Millwall	Sheffield Wed.	3-0
1992	Manchester Utd.	Crystal Palace	6-3
1993	Leeds Utd.	Manchester Utd.	4-1
1994	Arsenal	Millwall	5-3
1995	Manchester Utd.	Tottenham	†2-2
1996	Liverpool	West Ham Utd.	4-1
1997	Leeds Utd.	Crystal Palace	3-1
1998	Everton	Blackburn Rov.	5-3
1999	West Ham Utd.	Coventry City	9-0
2000	Arsenal	Coventry City	5-1
2001	Arsenal	Blackburn Rov.	6-3
2002	Aston Villa	Everton	4-2

(* One match only; † Manchester Utd. won 4-3 on pens.)

WELSH CUP FINAL

Barry Town 4, Bangor City 1 (at Aberystwyth).

WOMEN'S F.A. CUP FINAL

Fulham 2, Doncaster Belles 1 (at Selhurst Park).

WOMEN'S PREMIER LEAGUE CUP FINAL

Fulham 7, Birmingham City 1 (at Adams Park).

F.A. SUNDAY CUP FINAL

Britannia 2, Little Paxton 0.

F.A. CHARITY SHIELD
(Sponsor: One2One)

LIVERPOOL 2, MANCHESTER UNITED 1
Millennium Stadium, (70,227), Sunday, August 12, 2001

Liverpool (4-4-2): Westerveld, Babbel, Henchoz, Hyypia, Riise (Carragher 83), Barmby (Biscan 71), McAllister, Hamann, Murphy (Berger 71), Heskey, Owen. **Subs not used:** Arphexad, Traore, Redknapp, Litmanen. **Scorers:** McAllister (2 pen), Owen (16). **Booked:** Murphy, Hamann.

Manchester Utd. (4-4-1-1): Barthez, Irwin, G. Neville, Stam, Silvestre, Beckham, Keane, Butt (Yorke 66), Giggs, Scholes, Van Nistelrooy. **Scorer:** Van Nistelrooy (51). **Subs not used:** Carroll, Johnsen, P. Neville, Blomqvist, Solskjaer, Brown. **Booked:** Scholes.

Referee: A. D'Urso (Billericay). **Half-time:** 2-0.

CHARITY SHIELD RESULTS

Year	Winners	Runners-up	Score
1908	Manchester Utd.	Q.P.R.	4-0
			(after 1-1 draw)
1909	Newcastle Utd.	Northampton Town	2-0
1910	Brighton & H.A.	Aston Villa	1-0
1911	Manchester Utd.	Swindon Town	8-4
1912	Blackburn Rov.	Q.P.R.	2-1
1913	Professionals	Amateurs	7-2
1920	W.B.A.	Tottenham	2-0
1921	Tottenham	Burnley	2-0
1922	Huddersfield Town	Liverpool	1-0
1923	Professionals	Amateurs	2-0
1924	Professionals	Amateurs	3-1
1925	Amateurs	Professionals	6-1
1926	Amateurs	Professionals	6-3
1927	Cardiff City	Corinthians	2-1
1928	Everton	Blackburn Rov.	2-1
1929	Professionals	Amateurs	3-0
1930	Arsenal	Sheffield Wed.	2-1
1931	Arsenal	W.B.A.	1-0
1932	Everton	Newcastle Utd.	5-3
1933	Arsenal	Everton	3-0
1934	Arsenal	Manchester City	4-0
1935	Sheffield Wed.	Arsenal	1-0
1936	Sunderland	Arsenal	2-1
1937	Manchester City	Sunderland	2-0
1938	Arsenal	Preston N.E.	2-1
1948	Arsenal	Manchester Utd.	4-3
1949	Portsmouth	Wolves	*1-1
1950	England World Cup XI	F.A. Canadian Tour Team	4-2
1951	Tottenham	Newcastle Utd.	2-1
1952	Manchester Utd.	Newcastle Utd.	4-2
1953	Arsenal	Blackpool	3-1
1954	Wolves	W.B.A.	*4-4
1955	Chelsea	Newcastle Utd.	3-0
1956	Manchester Utd.	Manchester City	1-0
1957	Manchester Utd.	Aston Villa	4-0
1958	Bolton Wand.	Wolves	4-1

1959	Wolves	Nott'm. Forest	3-1
1960	Burnley	Wolves	*2-2
1961	Tottenham	F.A. XI	3-2
1962	Tottenham	Ipswich Town	5-1
1963	Everton	Manchester Utd.	4-0
1964	Liverpool	West Ham Utd.	*2-2
1965	Manchester Utd.	Liverpool	*2-2
1966	Liverpool	Everton	1-0
1967	Manchester Utd.	Tottenham	*3-3
1968	Manchester City	W.B.A.	6-1
1969	Leeds Utd.	Manchester City	2-1
1970	Everton	Chelsea	2-1
1971	Leicester City	Liverpool	1-0
1972	Manchester City	Aston Villa	1-0
1973	Burnley	Manchester City	1-0
1974	Liverpool	Leeds Utd.	1-1
	(Liverpool won 6-5 on penalties)		
1975	Derby Co.	West Ham Utd.	2-0
1976	Liverpool	Southampton	1-0
1977	Liverpool	Manchester Utd.	*0-0
1978	Nott'm. Forest	Ipswich Town	5-0
1979	Liverpool	Arsenal	3-1
1980	Liverpool	West Ham Utd.	1-0
1981	Aston Villa	Tottenham	*2-2
1982	Liverpool	Tottenham	1-0
1983	Manchester Utd.	Liverpool	2-0
1984	Everton	Liverpool	1-0
1985	Everton	Manchester Utd.	2-0
1986	Everton	Liverpool	*1-1
1987	Everton	Coventry City	1-0
1988	Liverpool	Wimbledon	2-1
1989	Liverpool	Arsenal	1-0
1990	Liverpool	Manchester Utd.	*1-1
1991	Arsenal	Tottenham	*0-0
1992	Leeds Utd.	Liverpool	4-3
1993	Manchester Utd.	Arsenal	1-1
	(Manchester Utd. won 5-4 on penalties)		
1994	Manchester Utd.	Blackburn Rov.	2-0
1995	Everton	Blackburn Rov.	1-0
1996	Manchester Utd.	Newcastle Utd.	4-0
1997	Manchester Utd.	Chelsea	1-1
	(Manchester Utd. won 4-2 on penalties)		
1998	Arsenal	Manchester Utd.	3-0
1999	Arsenal	Manchester Utd.	2-1
2000	Chelsea	Manchester Utd.	2-0
2001	Liverpool	Manchester Utd.	2-1

(Fixture played at Wembley since 1974. Millennium Stadium since 2001.
*Trophy shared)

HAT-TRICK IN FIVE MINUTES

Wayne Purser scored three times in five minutes – one of the fastest hat-tricks in F.A. Cup history – to give Barnet a 3-0 victory over Havant and Waterlooville in a fourth qualifying round replay.

76

ATTENDANCES 2001-02

Premiership attendances reached a new high last season, accompanied by significant increase in the Football League. Bigger capacities, greater comfort and championship and relegation issues stretching to the final few matches kept the game booming. A total of 13m. watched matches in the top flight, more than 500,000 up on the previous record from the 2000-01 season. Half the clubs were operating at near capacity. With Arsenal, Leeds United, Liverpool, Everton, Fulham and Manchester City all planning new stadiums, there is every reason to believe that the upward trend will continue.

The Division One aggregate of 8.4m. was the highest since 1958-59, Division Two reversed a recent downward trend with 3.9m., while the Third Division figure of 2.4m. was the best since 1971-72. Combined Premiership and Nationwide gates of 27.8m. was the biggest since 1971-72.

LEAGUE CROWDS SINCE 1980

	Total	Div. One	Div. Two	Div. Three	Div. Four
1979-80	24,623,975	12,163,002	6,112,025	3,999,328	2,349,620
1980-81	21,907,569	11,392,894	5,175,442	3,637,854	1,701,379
1981-82	20,006,961	10,420,793	4,750,463	2,836,915	1,998,790
1982-83	18,766,158	9,295,613	4,974,937	2,943,568	1,552,040
1983-84	18,358,631	8,711,448	5,359,757	2,729,942	1,557,484
1984-85	17,849,835	9,761,404	4,030,823	2,667,008	1,390,600
1985-86	16,498,868	9,037,854	3,555,343	2,495,991	1,409,680
1986-87	17,383,032	9,144,676	4,168,131	2,354,784	1,715,441
1987-88	17,968,887	8,094,571	5,350,754	2,751,275	1,772,287
1988-89	18,477,565	7,809,993	5,827,805	3,048,700	1,791,067
1989-90	19,466,826	7,887,658	6,884,439	2,803,551	1,891,178
1990-91	19,541,341	8,618,709	6,297,733	2,847,813	1,777,086
1991-92	20,487,273	9,989,160	5,809,787	2,993,352	1,694,974

New format	Total	Premier	Div. One	Div. Two	Div. Three
1992-93	20,657,327	9,759,809	5,874,017	3,483,073	1,540,428
1993-94	21,693,889	10,655,059	6,487,104	2,972,702	1,579,024
1994-95	21,856,223	11,213,371	6,044,293	3,037,752	1,560,807
1995-96	21,844,416	10,469,107	6,566,349	2,843,652	1,965,308
1996-97	22,791,527	10,804,762	6,804,606	3,332,451	1,849,708
1997-98	24,679,527	11,091,773	8,330,018	3,503,264	1,767,220
1998-99	25,435,981	11,620,765	7,543,369	4,169,697	2,102,150
1999-2000	25,342,478	11,668,222	7,811,420	3,700,433	2,162,403
2000-01	26,067,729	12,503,732	7,912,046	3,490,250	2,161,701
2001-02	27,835,107	13,043,118	8,402,142	3,981,252	2,408,595

Note: All-time record Football League attendance aggregate: 41,271,414 in season 1948-49 (88 clubs). The average was 22,333.

LANDMARK GOALS FOR FERDINAND AND NIELSEN

Les Ferdinand and David Nielsen scored landmark League goals last season. Ferdinand's goal for Tottenham against Fulham was the 10,000th in the Premiership and earned him a £10,000 cheque for charity from sponsor Barclaycard. When Nielsen scored for Norwich City against Walsall, it was the 50,000th in the Football League since the formation of the Premiership in 1992.

HONOURS LIST

F.A. PREMIER LEAGUE

	First	Pts.	Second	Pts.	Third	Pts.
1992-3*a*	Manchester Utd.	84	Aston Villa	74	Norwich City	72
1993-4*a*	Manchester Utd.	92	Blackburn Rov.	84	Newcastle Utd.	77
1994-5*a*	Blackburn Rov.	89	Manchester Utd.	88	Nott'm Forest	77
1995-6*b*	Manchester Utd.	82	Newcastle Utd.	78	Liverpool	71
1996-7*b*	Manchester Utd.	75	Newcastle Utd.	68	Arsenal	68
1997-8*b*	Arsenal	78	Manchester Utd.	77	Liverpool	65
1998-9*b*	Manchester Utd.	79	Arsenal	78	Chelsea	75
1999-00*b*	Manchester Utd.	91	Arsenal	73	Leeds Utd.	69
2000-01*b*	Manchester Utd.	80	Arsenal	70	Liverpool	69
2001-02*b*	Arsenal	87	Liverpool	80	Manchester Utd.	77

Maximum points: *a*, 126; *b*, 114.

FOOTBALL LEAGUE

FIRST DIVISION

1992-3	Newcastle Utd.	96	West Ham Utd.	88	††Portsmouth	88
1993-4	Crystal Palace	90	Nott'm Forest	83	††Millwall	74
1994-5	Middlesbrough	82	††Reading	79	Bolton Wand.	77
1995-6	Sunderland	83	Derby Co.	79	††Crystal Palace	75
1996-7	Bolton Wand.	98	Barnsley	80	††Wolves	76
1997-8	Nott'm Forest	94	Middlesbrough	91	††Sunderland	90
1998-9	Sunderland	105	Bradford City	87	††Ipswich Town	86
1999-00	Charlton Athletic	91	Manchester City	89	Ipswich Town	87
2000-01	Fulham	101	Blackburn Rov.	91	Bolton Wand.	87
2001-02	Manchester City	99	W.B.A.	89	††Wolves	86

Maximum points: 138. ††Not promoted after play-offs.

SECOND DIVISION

1992-3	Stoke City	93	Bolton Wand.	90	††Port Vale	89
1993-4	Reading	89	Port Vale	88	††Plymouth Argyle	85
1994-5	Birmingham City	89	††Brentford	85	††Crewe Alexandra	83
1995-6	Swindon Town	92	Oxford Utd.	83	††Blackpool	82
1996-7	Bury	84	Stockport Co.	82	††Luton Town	78
1997-8	Watford	88	Bristol City	85	Grimsby Town	72
1998-9	Fulham	101	Walsall	87	Manchester City	82
1999-00	Preston N.E.	95	Burnley	88	Gillingham	85
2000-01	Milwall	93	Rotherham Utd.	91	††Reading	86
2001-02	Brighton & H.A.	90	Reading	84	††Brentford	83

Maximum points: 138. †† Not promoted after play-offs.

THIRD DIVISION

1992-3*a*	Cardiff City	83	Wrexham	80	Barnet	79
1993-4*a*	Shrewsbury Town	79	Chester City	74	Crewe Alexandra	73
1994-5*a*	Carlisle Utd.	91	Walsall	83	Chesterfield	81
1995-6*b*	Preston N.E.	86	Gillingham	83	Bury	79
1996-7*b*	Wigan Athletic	87	Fulham	87	Carlisle Utd.	84
1997-8*b*	Notts County	99	Macclesfield Town	82	Lincoln City	75
1998-9*b*	Brentford	85	Cambridge Utd.	81	Cardiff City	80
1999-00*b*	Swansea City	85	Rotherham Utd.	84	Northampton Town	82

| 2000-01b | Brighton & H.A. ..... 92 | Cardiff City .... 82 | *Chesterfield .... 80 |
| 2001-02b | Plymouth Argyle ... 102 | Luton Town .... 97 | Mansfield Town ...... 79 |

Maximum points: a, 126; b, 138; * Deducted 9 points for financial irregularities.

FOOTBALL LEAGUE 1888-1992

	First	Pts.	Second	Pts.	Third	Pts.
1888-89a	Preston N.E.	40	Aston Villa	29	Wolves	28
1889-90a	Preston N.E.	33	Everton	31	Blackburn Rov.	27
1890-1a	Everton	29	Preston N.E.	27	Notts Co.	26
1891-2b	Sunderland	42	Preston N.E.	37	Bolton Wand.	36

OLD FIRST DIVISION

	First	Pts.	Second	Pts.	Third	Pts.
1892-3c	Sunderland	48	Preston N.E.	37	Everton	36
1893-4c	Aston Villa	44	Sunderland	38	Derby Co.	36
1894-5c	Sunderland	47	Everton	42	Aston Villa	39
1895-6c	Aston Villa	45	Derby Co.	41	Everton	39
1896-7c	Aston Villa	47	Sheffield Utd.	36	Derby Co.	36
1897-8c	Sheffield Utd.	42	Sunderland	39	Wolves	35
1898-9d	Aston Villa	45	Liverpool	43	Burnley	39
1899-1900d	Aston Villa	50	Sheffield Utd.	48	Sunderland	41
1900-1d	Liverpool	45	Sunderland	43	Notts Co.	40
1901-2d	Sunderland	44	Everton	41	Newcastle Utd.	37
1902-3d	The Wednesday	42	Aston Villa	41	Sunderland	41
1903-4d	The Wednesday	47	Manchester City	44	Everton	43
1904-5d	Newcastle Utd.	48	Everton	47	Manchester City	46
1905-6e	Liverpool	51	Preston N.E.	47	The Wednesday	44
1906-7e	Newcastle Utd.	51	Bristol City	48	Everton	45
1907-8e	Manchester Utd.	52	Aston Villa	43	Manchester City	43
1908-9e	Newcastle Utd.	53	Everton	46	Sunderland	44
1909-10e	Aston Villa	53	Liverpool	48	Blackburn Rov.	45
1910-11e	Manchester Utd.	52	Aston Villa	51	Sunderland	45
1911-12e	Blackburn Rov.	49	Everton	46	Newcastle Utd.	44
1912-13e	Sunderland	54	Aston Villa	50	Sheffield Wed.	49
1913-14e	Blackburn Rov.	51	Aston Villa	44	Middlesbrough	43
1914-15e	Everton	46	Oldham Athletic	45	Blackburn Rov.	43
1919-20f	W.B.A.	60	Burnley	51	Chelsea	49
1920-1f	Burnley	59	Manchester City	54	Bolton Wand.	52
1921-2f	Liverpool	57	Tottenham	51	Burnley	49
1922-3f	Liverpool	60	Sunderland	54	Huddersfield Town	53
1923-4f	*Huddersfield Town	57	Cardiff City	57	Sunderland	53
1924-5f	Huddersfield Town	58	W.B.A.	56	Bolton Wand.	55
1925-6f	Huddersfield Town	57	Arsenal	52	Sunderland	48
1926-7f	Newcastle Utd.	56	Huddersfield Town	51	Sunderland	49
1927-8f	Everton	53	Huddersfield Town	51	Leicester City	48
1928-9f	Sheffield Wed.	52	Leicester City	51	Aston Villa	50
1929-30f	Sheffield Wed.	60	Derby Co.	50	Manchester City	47
1930-1f	Arsenal	66	Aston Villa	59	Sheffield Wed.	52
1931-2f	Everton	56	Arsenal	54	Sheffield Wed.	50
1932-3f	Arsenal	58	Aston Villa	54	Sheffield Wed.	51
1933-4f	Arsenal	59	Huddersfield Town	56	Tottenham	49
1934-5f	Arsenal	58	Sunderland	54	Sheffield Wed.	49
1935-6f	Sunderland	56	Derby Co.	48	Huddersfield Town	48
1936-7f	Manchester City	57	Charlton Athletic	54	Arsenal	52
1937-8f	Arsenal	52	Wolves	51	Preston N.E.	49
1938-9f	Everton	59	Wolves	55	Charlton Athletic	50
1946-7f	Liverpool	57	Manchester Utd.	56	Wolves	56

Year	First	Pts.	Second	Pts.	Third	Pts.
1947-8f	Arsenal	59	Manchester Utd.	52	Burnley	52
1948-9f	Portsmouth	58	Manchester Utd.	53	Derby Co.	53
1949-50f	*Portsmouth	53	Wolves	53	Sunderland	52
1950-1f	Tottenham	60	Manchester Utd.	56	Blackpool	50
1951-2f	Manchester Utd.	57	Tottenham	53	Arsenal	53
1952-3f	*Arsenal	54	Preston N.E.	54	Wolves	51
1953-4f	Wolves	57	W.B.A.	53	Huddersfield Town	51
1954-5f	Chelsea	52	Wolves	48	Portsmouth	48
1955-6f	Manchester Utd.	60	Blackpool	49	Wolves	49
1956-7f	Manchester Utd.	64	Tottenham	56	Preston N.E.	56
1957-8f	Wolves	64	Preston N.E.	59	Tottenham	51
1958-9f	Wolves	61	Manchester Utd.	55	Arsenal	50
1959-60f	Burnley	55	Wolves	54	Tottenham	53
1960-1f	Tottenham	66	Sheffield Wed.	58	Wolves	57
1961-2f	Ipswich Town	56	Burnley	53	Tottenham	52
1962-3f	Everton	61	Tottenham	55	Burnley	54
1963-4f	Liverpool	57	Manchester Utd.	53	Everton	52
1964-5f	*Manchester Utd.	61	Leeds Utd.	61	Chelsea	56
1965-6f	Liverpool	61	Leeds Utd.	55	Burnley	55
1966-7f	Manchester Utd.	60	Nott'm Forest	56	Tottenham	56
1967-8f	Manchester City	58	Manchester Utd.	56	Liverpool	55
1968-9f	Leeds Utd.	67	Liverpool	61	Everton	57
1969-70f	Everton	66	Leeds Utd.	57	Chelsea	55
1970-1f	Arsenal	65	Leeds Utd.	64	Tottenham	52
1971-2f	Derby Co.	58	Leeds Utd.	57	Liverpool	57
1972-3f	Liverpool	60	Arsenal	57	Leeds Utd.	53
1973-4f	Leeds Utd.	62	Liverpool	57	Derby Co.	48
1974-5f	Derby Co.	53	Liverpool	51	Ipswich Town	51
1975-6f	Liverpool	60	Q.P.R.	59	Manchester Utd.	56
1976-7f	Liverpool	57	Manchester City	56	Ipswich Town	52
1977-8f	Nott'm Forest	64	Liverpool	57	Everton	55
1978-9f	Liverpool	68	Nott'm Forest	60	W.B.A.	59
1979-80f	Liverpool	60	Manchester Utd.	58	Ipswich Town	53
1980-1f	Aston Villa	60	Ipswich Town	56	Arsenal	53
1981-2g	Liverpool	87	Ipswich Town	83	Manchester Utd.	78
1982-3g	Liverpool	82	Watford	71	Manchester Utd.	70
1983-4g	Liverpool	80	Southampton	77	Nott'm Forest	74
1984-5g	Everton	90	Liverpool	77	Tottenham	77
1985-6g	Liverpool	88	Everton	86	West Ham Utd.	84
1986-7g	Everton	86	Liverpool	77	Tottenham	71
1987-8h	Liverpool	90	Manchester Utd.	81	Nott'm Forest	73
1988-9j	†Arsenal	76	Liverpool	76	Nott'm Forest	64
1989-90j	Liverpool	79	Aston Villa	70	Tottenham	63
1990-1j	Arsenal	83	Liverpool	76	Crystal Palace	69
1991-2g	Leeds Utd.	82	Manchester Utd.	78	Sheffield Wed.	75

Maximum points: a, 44; b, 52; c, 60; d, 68; e, 76; f, 84; g, 126; h, 120; j, 114.
*Won on goal average. †Won on goal diff. No comp. 1915-19 – 1939-46

OLD SECOND DIVISION 1892-1992

Year	First	Pts.	Second	Pts.	Third	Pts.
1892-3a	Small Heath	36	Sheffield Utd.	35	Darwen	30
1893-4b	Liverpool	50	Small Heath	42	Notts Co.	39
1894-5c	Bury	48	Notts County	39	Newton Heath	38
1895-6c	*Liverpool	46	Manchester City	46	Grimsby Town	42
1896-7c	Notts Co.	42	Newton Heath	39	Grimsby Town	38
1897-8c	Burnley	48	Newcastle Utd.	45	Manchester City	39
1898-9d	Manchester City	52	Glossop	46	Leicester Fosse	45
1899-1900d	The Wednesday	54	Bolton Wand.	52	Small Heath	46

1900-1d	Grimsby Town 49	Small Heath 48	Burnley 44
1901-2d	W.B.A. 55	Middlesbrough 51	Preston N.E. 42
1902-3d	Manchester City 54	Small Heath 51	Woolwich Arsenal 48
1903-4d	Preston N.E. 50	Woolwich Arsenal 49	Manchester Utd. 48
1904-5d	Liverpool 58	Bolton Wand. 56	Manchester Utd. 53
1905-6e	Bristol City 66	Manchester Utd. 62	Chelsea 53
1906-7e	Nott'm Forest 60	Chelsea 57	Leicester Fosse 48
1907-8e	Bradford City 54	Leicester Fosse 52	Oldham Athletic 50
1908-9e	Bolton Wand. 52	Tottenham 51	W.B.A. 51
1909-10e	Manchester City 54	Oldham Athletic 53	Hull City 53
1910-11e	W.B.A. 53	Bolton Wand. 51	Chelsea 49
1911-12e	*Derby Co. 54	Chelsea 54	Burnley 52
1912-13e	Preston N.E. 53	Burnley 52	Birmingham City 46
1913-14e	Notts County 53	Bradford City P.A. .. 49	Woolwich Arsenal 49
1914-15e	Derby Co. 53	Preston N.E. 50	Barnsley 47
1919-20f	Tottenham 70	Huddersfield Town .. 64	Birmingham City 56
1920-1f	*Birmingham City 58	Cardiff City 58	Bristol City 51
1921-2f	Nott'm Forest 56	Stoke City 52	Barnsley 52
1922-3f	Notts County 53	West Ham Utd. 51	Leicester City 51
1923-4f	Leeds Utd. 54	Bury 51	Derby Co. 51
1924-5f	Leicester City 59	Manchester Utd. 57	Derby Co. 55
1925-6f	Sheffield Wed. 60	Derby Co. 57	Chelsea 52
1926-7f	Middlesbrough 62	Portsmouth 54	Manchester City 54
1927-8f	Manchester City 59	Leeds Utd. 57	Chelsea 54
1928-9f	Middlesbrough 55	Grimsby Town 53	Bradford City 48
1929-30f	Blackpool 58	Chelsea 55	Oldham Athletic 53
1930-1f	Everton 61	W.B.A. 54	Tottenham 51
1931-2f	Wolves 56	Leeds Utd. 54	Stoke City 52
1932-3f	Stoke City 56	Tottenham 55	Fulham 50
1933-4f	Grimsby Town 59	Preston N.E. 52	Bolton Wand. 51
1934-5f	Brentford 61	Bolton Wand. 56	West Ham Utd. 56
1935-6f	Manchester Utd. 56	Charlton Athletic 55	Sheffield Utd. 52
1936-7f	Leicester City 56	Blackpool 55	Bury 52
1937-8f	Aston Villa 57	Manchester Utd. 53	Sheffield Utd. 53
1938-9f	Blackburn Rov. 55	Sheffield Utd. 54	Sheffield Wed. 53
1946-7f	Manchester City 62	Burnley 58	Birmingham City 55
1947-8f	Birmingham City 59	Newcastle Utd. 56	Southampton 52
1948-9f	Fulham 57	W.B.A. 56	Southampton 55
1949-50f	Tottenham 61	Sheffield Wed. 52	Sheffield Utd. 52
1950-1f	Preston N.E. 57	Manchester City 52	Cardiff City 50
1951-2f	Sheffield Wed. 53	Cardiff City 51	Birmingham City 51
1952-3f	Sheffield Utd. 60	Huddersfield Town .. 58	Luton Town 52
1953-4f	*Leicester City 56	Everton 56	Blackburn Rov. 55
1954-5f	*Birmingham City 54	Luton Town 54	Rotherham Utd. 54
1955-6f	Sheffield Wed. 55	Leeds Utd. 52	Liverpool 48
1956-7f	Leicester City 61	Nott'm Forest 54	Liverpool 53
1957-8f	West Ham Utd. 57	Blackburn Rov. 56	Charlton Athletic 55
1958-9f	Sheffield Wed. 62	Fulham 60	Sheffield Utd. 53
1959-60f	Aston Villa 59	Cardiff City 58	Liverpool 50
1960-1f	Ipswich Town 59	Sheffield Utd. 58	Liverpool 52
1961-2f	Liverpool 62	Leyton Orient 54	Sunderland 53
1962-3f	Stoke City 53	Chelsea 52	Sunderland 52
1963-4f	Leeds Utd. 63	Sunderland 61	Preston N.E. 56
1964-5f	Newcastle Utd. 57	Northampton Town . 56	Bolton Wand. 50
1965-6f	Manchester City 59	Southampton 54	Coventry City 53
1966-7f	Coventry City 59	Wolves 58	Carlisle Utd. 52
1967-8f	Ipswich Town 59	Q.P.R. 58	Blackpool 58
1968-9f	Derby Co. 63	Crystal Palace 56	Charlton Athletic 50

	First	Pts.	Second	Pts.	Third	Pts.
1969-70f	Huddersfield Town .. 60		Blackpool 53		Leicester City 51	
1970-1f	Leicester City 59		Sheffield Utd. 56		Cardiff City 53	
1971-2f	Norwich City 57		Birmingham City 56		Millwall 55	
1972-3f	Burnley 62		Q.P.R. 61		Aston Villa 60	
1973-4f	Middlesbrough 65		Luton Town 50		Carlisle Utd. 49	
1974-5f	Manchester Utd. 61		Aston Villa 58		Norwich City 53	
1975-6f	Sunderland 56		Bristol City 53		W.B.A. 53	
1976-7f	Wolves 57		Chelsea 55		Nott'm Forest 52	
1977-8f	Bolton Wand. 58		Southampton 57		Tottenham 56	
1978-9f	Crystal Palace 57		Brighton & H.A. 56		Stoke City 56	
1979-80f	Leicester City 55		Sunderland 54		Birmingham City 53	
1980-1f	West Ham Utd. 66		Notts Co. 53		Swansea City 50	
1981-2g	Luton Town 88		Watford 80		Norwich City 71	
1982-3g	Q.P.R. 85		Wolves 75		Leicester City 70	
1983-4g	†Chelsea 88		Sheffield Wed. 88		Newcastle Utd. 80	
1984-5g	Oxford Utd. 84		Birmingham City 82		Manchester City 74	
1985-6g	Norwich City 84		Charlton Athletic 77		Wimbledon 76	
1986-7g	Derby Co. 84		Portsmouth 78		††Oldham Athletic .. 75	
1987-8h	Millwall 82		Aston Villa 78		Middlesbrough 78	
1988-9j	Chelsea 99		Manchester City 82		Crystal Palace 81	
1989-90j	†Leeds Utd. 85		Sheffield Utd. 85		†† Newcastle Utd. .. 80	
1990-1j	Oldham Athletic 88		West Ham Utd. 87		Sheffield Wed. 82	
1991-2j	Ipswich Town 84		Middlesbrough 80		†† Derby Co. 78	

Maximum points: *a*, 44; *b*, 56; *c*, 60; *d*, 68; *e*, 76; *f*, 84; *g*, 126; *h*, 132; *j*, 138. * Won on goal average. † Won on goal difference. †† Not promoted after play-offs.

THIRD DIVISION 1958-92

	First	Pts.	Second	Pts.	Third	Pts.
1958-9	Plymouth Argyle 62		Hull City 61		Brentford 57	
1959-60	Southampton 61		Norwich City 59		Shrewsbury Town ... 52	
1960-1	Bury 68		Walsall 62		Q.P.R. 60	
1961-2	Portsmouth 65		Grimsby Town 62		Bournemouth 59	
1962-3	Northampton Town . 62		Swindon Town 58		Port Vale 54	
1963-4	*Coventry City 60		Crystal Palace 60		Watford 58	
1964-5	Carlisle Utd. 60		Bristol City 59		Mansfield Town 59	
1965-6	Hull City 69		Millwall 65		Q.P.R. 57	
1966-7	Q.P.R. 67		Middlesbrough 55		Watford 54	
1967-8	Oxford Utd. 57		Bury 56		Shrewsbury Town ... 55	
1968-9	*Watford 64		Swindon Town 64		Luton Town 61	
1969-70	Orient 62		Luton Town 60		Bristol Rov. 56	
1970-1	Preston N.E. 61		Fulham 60		Halifax Town 56	
1971-2	Aston Villa 70		Brighton & H.A. 65		Bournemouth 62	
1972-3	Bolton Wand. 61		Notts Co. 57		Blackburn Rov. 55	
1973-4	Oldham Athletic 62		Bristol Rov. 61		York City 61	
1974-5	Blackburn Rov. 60		Plymouth Argyle 59		Charlton Athletic 55	
1975-6	Hereford 63		Cardiff City 57		Millwall 56	
1976-7	Mansfield Town 64		Brighton & H.A. 61		Crystal Palace 59	
1977-8	Wrexham 61		Cambridge Utd. 58		Preston N.E. 56	
1978-9	Shrewsbury Town ... 61		Watford 60		Swansea City 60	
1979-80	Grimsby Town 62		Blackburn Rov. 59		Sheffield Wed. 58	
1980-1	Rotherham Utd. 61		Barnsley 59		Charlton Athletic 59	
†1981-2	*Burnley 80		Carlisle Utd. 80		Fulham 78	
†1982-3	Portsmouth 91		Cardiff City 86		Huddersfield Town .. 82	
†1983-4	Oxford Utd. 95		Wimbledon 87		Sheffield Utd. 83	
†1984-5	Bradford City 94		Millwall 90		Hull City 87	
†1985-6	Reading 94		Plymouth Argyle 87		Derby Co. 84	
†1986-7	Bournemouth 97		Middlesbrough 94		Swindon Town 87	
†1987-8	Sunderland 93		Brighton & H.A. 84		Walsall 82	

†1988-9	Wolves	92	Sheffield Utd.	84	Port Vale	84
†1989-90	Bristol Rov.	93	Bristol City	91	Notts Co.	87
†1990-1	Cambridge Utd.	86	Southend Utd.	85	Grimsby Town	83
†1991-2	Brentford	82	Birmingham City	81	††Huddersfield T	78

* Won on goal average. † Maximum points 138 (previously 92). †† Not promoted after play-offs.

FOURTH DIVISION 1958-92

	First	Pts.	Second	Pts.	Third	Pts.	Fourth	Pts.
1958-9	Port Vale	64	Coventry City	60	York City	60	Shrewsbury Town	58
1959-60	Walsall	65	Notts Co.	60	Torquay Utd.	60	Watford	57
1960-1	Peterborough Utd.	66	Crystal Palace	64	Northampton Town	60	Bradford City P.A.	60
1961-2	Millwall	56	Colchester Utd.	55	Wrexham	53	Carlisle Utd.	52
1962-3	Brentford	62	Oldham Athletic	59	Crewe Alexandra	59	Mansfield Town	57
1963-4	*Gillingham	60	Carlisle Utd.	60	Workington	59	Exeter City	58
1964-5	Brighton & H.A.	63	Millwall	62	York City	62	Oxford Utd.	61
1965-6	*Doncaster Rov.	59	Darlington	59	Torquay Utd.	58	Colchester Utd.	56
1966-7	Stockport Co.	64	Southport	59	Barrow	59	Tranmere Rov.	58
1967-8	Luton Town	66	Barnsley	61	Hartlepool Utd.	60	Crewe Alexandra	58
1968-9	Doncaster Rov.	59	Halifax Town	57	Rochdale	56	Bradford City	56
1969-70	Chesterfield	64	Wrexham	61	Swansea City	60	Port Vale	59
1970-1	Notts Co.	69	Bournemouth	60	Oldham Athletic	59	York City	56
1971-2	Grimsby Town	63	Southend Utd.	60	Brentford	59	Scunthorpe Utd.	57
1972-3	Southport	62	Hereford	58	Cambridge Utd.	57	Aldershot	56
1973-4	Peterborough Utd.	65	Gillingham	62	Colchester Utd.	60	Bury	59
1974-5	Mansfield Town	68	Shrewsbury Town	62	Rotherham Utd.	59	Chester City	57
1975-6	Lincoln City	74	Northampton Town	68	Reading	60	Tranmere Rov.	58
1976-7	Cambridge Utd.	65	Exeter City	62	Colchester Utd.	59	Bradford City	59
1977-8	Watford	71	Southend Utd.	60	Swansea City	56	Brentford	59
1978-9	Reading	65	Grimsby Town	61	Wimbledon	61	Barnsley	61
1979-80	Huddersfield Town	66	Walsall	64	Newport	61	Portsmouth	60
1980-1	Southend Utd.	67	Lincoln City	65	Doncaster Rov.	56	Wimbledon	55
†1981-2	Sheffield Utd.	96	Bradford City	91	Wigan Athletic	91	Bournemouth	88
†1982-3	Wimbledon	98	Hull City	90	Port Vale	88	Scunthorpe Utd.	83
†1983-4	York City	101	Doncaster Rov.	85	Reading	82	Bristol City	82
†1984-5	Chesterfield	91	Blackpool	86	Darlington	85	Bury	84
†1985-6	Swindon Town	102	Chester City	84	Mansfield Town	81	Port Vale	79
†1986-7	Northampton Town	99	Preston N.E.	90	Southend Utd.	80	††Wolves	79
†1987-8	Wolves	90	Cardiff City	85	Bolton Wand.	78	††Scunthorpe Utd.	77
†1988-9	Rotherham Utd.	82	Tranmere Rov.	80	Crewe Alexandra	78	††Scunthorpe Utd.	77
†1989-90	Exeter City	89	Grimsby Town	79	Southend Utd.	75	††Stockport Co.	74
†1990-1	Darlington	83	Stockport Co.	82	Hartlepool Utd.	82	Peterborough Utd.	80
1991-2a	Burnley	83	Rotherham Utd.	77	Mansfield Town	77	Blackpool	76

* Won on goal average. Maximum points: †, 138; a, 126; previously 92. †† Not promoted after play-offs.

THIRD DIVISION – SOUTH 1920-58

	First	Pts.	Second	Pts.	Third	Pts.
1920-1a	Crystal Palace	59	Southampton	54	Q.P.R.	53
1921-2a	*Southampton	61	Plymouth Argyle	61	Portsmouth	53
1922-3a	Bristol City	59	Plymouth Argyle	53	Swansea City	53
1923-4a	Portsmouth	59	Plymouth Argyle	55	Millwall	54
1924-5a	Swansea City	57	Plymouth Argyle	56	Bristol City	53
1925-6a	Reading	57	Plymouth Argyle	56	Millwall	53
1926-7a	Bristol City	62	Plymouth Argyle	60	Millwall	56
1927-8a	Millwall	65	Northampton Town	55	Plymouth Argyle	53
1928-9a	*Charlton Athletic	54	Crystal Palace	54	Northampton Town	52

	First	Pts.	Second	Pts.	Third	Pts.
1929-30a	Plymouth Argyle	68	Brentford	61	Q.P.R.	51
1930-31a	Notts Co.	59	Crystal Palace	51	Brentford	50
1931-2a	Fulham	57	Reading	55	Southend Utd.	53
1932-3a	Brentford	62	Exeter City	58	Norwich City	57
1933-4a	Norwich City	61	Coventry City	54	Reading	54
1934-5a	Charlton Athletic	61	Reading	53	Coventry City	51
1935-6a	Coventry City	57	Luton Town	56	Reading	54
1936-7a	Luton Town	58	Notts Co.	56	Brighton & H.A.	53
1937-8a	Millwall	56	Bristol City	55	Q.P.R.	53
1938-9a	Newport	55	Crystal Palace	52	Brighton & H.A.	49
1946-7a	Cardiff City	66	Q.P.R.	57	Bristol City	51
1947-8a	Q.P.R.	61	Bournemouth	57	Walsall	51
1948-9a	Swansea City	62	Reading	55	Bournemouth	52
1949-50a	Notts Co.	58	Northampton Town	51	Southend Utd.	51
1950-1d	Nott'm Forest	70	Norwich City	64	Reading	57
1951-2d	Plymouth Argyle	66	Reading	61	Norwich City	61
1952-3d	Bristol Rov.	64	Millwall	62	Northampton Town	62
1953-4d	Ipswich Town	64	Brighton & H.A.	61	Bristol City	56
1954-5d	Bristol City	70	Leyton Orient	61	Southampton	59
1955-6d	Leyton Orient	66	Brighton & H.A.	65	Ipswich Town	64
1956-7d	*Ipswich Town	59	Torquay Utd.	59	Colchester Utd.	58
1957-8d	Brighton & H.A.	60	Brentford	58	Plymouth Argyle	58

THIRD DIVISION – NORTH 1921-58

	First	Pts.	Second	Pts.	Third	Pts.
1921-2b	Stockport Co.	56	Darlington	50	Grimsby Town	50
1922-3b	Nelson	51	Bradford P.A.	47	Walsall	46
1923-4a	Wolves	63	Rochdale	62	Chesterfield	54
1924-5a	Darlington	58	Nelson	53	New Brighton	53
1925-6a	Grimsby Town	61	Bradford P.A.	60	Rochdale	59
1926-7a	Stoke City	63	Rochdale	58	Bradford P.A.	57
1927-8a	Bradford P.A.	63	Lincoln City	55	Stockport Co.	54
1928-9a	Bradford City	63	Stockport Co.	62	Wrexham	52
1929-30a	Port Vale	67	Stockport Co.	63	Darlington	50
1930-1a	Chesterfield	58	Lincoln City	57	Wrexham	54
1931-2c	*Lincoln City	57	Gateshead	57	Chester City	50
1932-3a	Hull City	59	Wrexham	57	Stockport Co.	54
1933-4a	Barnsley	62	Chesterfield	61	Stockport Co.	59
1934-5a	Doncaster Rov.	57	Halifax Town	55	Chester City	54
1935-6a	Chesterfield	60	Chester City	55	Tranmere Rov.	54
1936-7a	Stockport Co.	60	Lincoln City	57	Chester City	53
1937-8a	Tranmere Rov.	56	Doncaster Rov.	54	Hull City	53
1938-9a	Barnsley	67	Doncaster Rov.	56	Bradford City	52
1946-7a	Doncaster Rov.	72	Rotherham Utd.	64	Chester City	56
1947-8a	Lincoln City	60	Rotherham Utd.	59	Wrexham	50
1948-9a	Hull City	65	Rotherham Utd.	62	Doncaster Rov.	50
1949-50a	Doncaster Rov.	55	Gateshead	53	Rochdale	51
1950-1d	Rotherham Utd.	71	Mansfield Town	64	Carlisle Utd.	62
1951-2d	Lincoln City	69	Grimsby Town	66	Stockport Co.	59
1952-3d	Oldham Athletic	59	Port Vale	58	Wrexham	56
1953-4d	Port Vale	69	Barnsley	58	Scunthorpe Utd.	57
1954-5d	Barnsley	65	Accrington	61	Scunthorpe Utd.	58
1955-6d	Grimsby Town	68	Derby Co.	63	Accrington	59
1956-7d	Derby Co.	63	Hartlepool Utd.	59	Accrington	58
1957-8d	Scunthorpe Utd.	66	Accrington	59	Bradford City	57

Maximum points: a, 84; b, 76; c, 80; d, 92. * Won on goal average.

CHAMPIONSHIP WINNERS

F.A. PREMIER LEAGUE
Manchester Utd. 7
Arsenal 2
Blackburn Rov. 1

FOOTBALL LEAGUE
DIV.1 (NEW)
Sunderland 2
Bolton Wand. 1
Charlton Athletic 1
Crystal Palace 1
Fulham 1
Manchester City 1
Middlesbrough 1
Newcastle Utd. 1
Nott'm Forest 1

DIV.1 (ORIGINAL)
Liverpool 18
Arsenal 10
Everton 9
Aston Villa 7
Manchester Utd. 7
Sunderland 6
Newcastle Utd. 4
Sheffield Wed. 4
Huddersfield Town 3
Leeds Utd. 3
Wolves 3
Blackburn Rov. 2
Burnley 2
Derby Co. 2
Manchester City 2

Portsmouth 2
Preston N.E. 2
Tottenham 2
Chelsea 1
Ipswich Town 1
Nott'm Forest 1
Sheffield Utd. 1
W.B.A. 1

DIV.2 (NEW)
Birmingham City 1
Brighton & H.A. 1
Bury 1
Fulham 1
Millwall 1
Preston N.E. 1
Reading 1
Stoke City 1
Swindon Town 1
Watford 1

DIV.2 (ORIGINAL)
Leicester City 6
Manchester City 6
Sheffield Wed. 5
Birmingham City 4
Derby Co. 4
Liverpool 4
Ipswich Town 3
Leeds Utd. 3
Middlesbrough 3
Notts County 3

Preston N.E. 3
Aston Villa 2
Bolton Wand. 2
Burnley 2
Chelsea 2
Grimsby Town 2
Manchester Utd. 2
Norwich City 2
Nott'm Forest 2
Stoke City 2
Tottenham 2
W.B.A. 2
West Ham Utd. 2
Wolves 2
Blackburn Rov. 1
Blackpool 1
Bradford City 1
Brentford 1
Bristol City 1
Bury 1
Coventry City 1
Crystal Palace 1
Everton 1
Fulham 1
Huddersfield Town 1
Luton Town 1
Millwall 1
Newcastle Utd. 1
Oldham Athletic 1
Oxford Utd. 1
Q.P.R. 1
Sheffield Utd. 1
Sunderland 1

APPLICATIONS FOR RE-ELECTION
(System discontinued 1987)

14 Hartlepool Utd.	4 Norwich City	2 Oldham Athletic
12 Halifax Town	3 Aldershot	2 Q.P.R.
11 Barrow	3 Bradford City	2 Rotherham Utd.
11 Southport	3 Crystal Palace	2 Scunthorpe Utd.
10 Crewe Alexandra	3 Doncaster Rov.	2 Southend Utd.
10 Newport	3 Hereford	2 Watford
10 Rochdale	3 Merthyr Tyd.	1 Blackpool
8 Darlington	3 Swindon Town	1 Brighton & H.A.
8 Exeter City	3 Torquay Utd.	1 Bristol Rov.
7 Chester City	3 Tranmere Rov.	1 Cambridge Utd.
7 Walsall	2 Aberdare	1 Cardiff City
7 Workington	2 Ashington	1 Carlisle Utd.
7 York City	2 Bournemouth	1 Charlton Athletic
6 Stockport Co.	2 Brentford	1 Mansfield Town
5 Accrington	2 Colchester Utd.	1 Port Vale
5 Gillingham	2 Durham C.	1 Preston N.E.
5 Lincoln City	2 Gateshead	1 Shrewsbury Town
5 New Brighton	2 Grimsby Town	1 Swansea City
4 Bradford P.A.	2 Millwall	1 Thames
4 Northampton Town	2 Nelson	1 Wrexham

RELEGATED CLUBS (TO 1992)

1892-3	In Test matches, Darwen and Sheffield Utd. won promotion in place of Accrington and Notts Co.
1893-4	Tests, Liverpool and Small Heath won promotion. Darwen and Newton Heath relegated.
1894-5	After Tests, Bury promoted, Liverpool relegated.
1895-6	After Tests, Liverpool promoted, Small Heath relegated.
1896-7	After Tests, Notts Co. promoted, Burnley relegated.
1897-8	Test system abolished after success of Burnley and Stoke City, League extended. Blackburn Rov. and Newcastle Utd. elected to First Division. Automatic promotion and relegation introduced.

FIRST DIVISION TO SECOND DIVISION

1898-9	Bolton Wand., Sheffield Wed.
1899-00	Burnley, Glossop
1900-1	Preston N.E., W.B.A.
1901-2	Small Heath, Manchester City
1902-3	Grimsby Town, Bolton Wand.
1903-4	Liverpool, W.B.A.
1904-5	League extended. Bury and Notts Co., two bottom clubs in First Division, re-elected.
1905-6	Nott'm Forest, Wolves
1906-7	Derby Co., Stoke City
1907-8	Bolton Wand., Birmingham City
1908-9	Manchester City, Leicester Fosse
1909-10	Bolton Wand., Chelsea
1910-11	Bristol City, Nott'm Forest
1911-12	Preston N.E., Bury
1912-13	Notts Co., Woolwich Arsenal
1913-14	Preston N.E., Derby Co.
1914-15	Tottenham, *Chelsea
1919-20	Notts Co., Sheffield Wed.
1920-1	Derby Co., Bradford P.A.
1921-2	Bradford City, Manchester Utd.
1922-3	Stoke City, Oldham Athletic
1923-4	Chelsea, Middlesbrough
1924-5	Preston N.E., Nott'm Forest
1925-6	Manchester City, Notts Co.
1926-7	Leeds Utd., W.B.A.
1927-8	Tottenham, Middlesbrough
1928-9	Bury, Cardiff City
1929-30	Burnley, Everton
1930-1	Leeds Utd., Manchester Utd.
1931-2	Grimsby Town, West Ham Utd.
1932-3	Bolton Wand., Blackpool
1933-4	Newcastle Utd., Sheffield Utd.
1934-5	Leicester City, Tottenham
1935-6	Aston Villa, Blackburn Rov.
1936-7	Manchester Utd., Sheffield Wed.
1937-8	Manchester City, W.B.A.
1938-9	Birmingham City, Leicester City
1946-7	Brentford, Leeds Utd.
1947-8	Blackburn Rov., Grimsby Town
1948-9	Preston N.E., Sheffield Utd.
1949-50	Manchester City, Birmingham City
1950-1	Sheffield Wed., Everton
1951-2	Huddersfield Town, Fulham

1952-3	Stoke City, Derby Co.
1953-4	Middlesbrough, Liverpool
1954-5	Leicester City, Sheffield Wed.
1955-6	Huddersfield Town, Sheffield Utd.
1956-7	Charlton Athletic, Cardiff City
1957-8	Sheffield Wed., Sunderland
1958-9	Portsmouth, Aston Villa
1959-60	Luton Town, Leeds Utd.
1960-61	Preston N.E., Newcastle Utd.
1961-2	Chelsea, Cardiff City
1962-3	Manchester City, Leyton Orient
1963-4	Bolton Wand., Ipswich Town
1964-5	Wolves, Birmingham City
1965-6	Northampton Town, Blackburn Rov.
1966-7	Aston Villa, Blackpool
1967-8	Fulham, Sheffield Utd.
1968-9	Leicester City, Q.P.R.
1969-70	Sheffield Wed., Sunderland
1970-1	Burnley, Blackpool
1971-2	Nott'm Forest, Huddersfield Town
1972-3	W.B.A., Crystal Palace
1973-4	Norwich City, Manchester Utd., Southampton
1974-5	Chelsea, Luton Town, Carlisle Utd.
1975-6	Sheffield Utd., Burnley, Wolves
1976-7	Tottenham, Stoke City, Sunderland
1977-8	Leicester City, West Ham Utd., Newcastle Utd.
1978-9	Q.P.R., Birmingham City, Chelsea
1979-80	Bristol City, Derby Co., Bolton Wand.
1980-1	Norwich City, Leicester City, Crystal Palace
1981-2	Leeds Utd., Wolves, Middlesbrough
1982-3	Manchester City, Swansea City, Brighton & H.A.
1983-4	Birmingham City, Notts Co., Wolves
1984-5	Norwich City, Sunderland, Stoke City
1985-6	Ipswich Town, Birmingham City, W.B.A.
1986-7	Leicester City, Manchester City, Aston Villa
1987-8	Chelsea**, Portsmouth, Watford, Oxford Utd.
1988-9	Middlesbrough, West Ham Utd., Newcastle Utd.
1989-90	Sheffield Wed., Charlton Athletic, Millwall
1990-1	Sunderland, Derby Co.
1991-2	Luton Town, Notts Co., West Ham Utd.

* Subsequently re-elected to First Division when League extended after the war.
** Relegated after play-offs.

SECOND DIVISION TO THIRD DIVISION

1920-1	Stockport Co.
1921-2	Bradford City, Bristol City
1922-3	Rotherham Utd., Wolves
1923-4	Nelson, Bristol City
1924-5	Crystal Palace, Coventry City
1925-6	Stoke City, Stockport Co.
1926-7	Darlington, Bradford City
1927-8	Fulham, South Shields
1928-9	Port Vale, Clapton Orient
1929-30	Hull City, Notts County
1930-1	Reading, Cardiff City
1931-2	Barnsley, Bristol City
1932-3	Chesterfield, Charlton Athletic

1933-4	Millwall, Lincoln City
1934-5	Oldham Athletic, Notts Co.
1935-6	Port Vale, Hull City
1936-7	Doncaster Rov., Bradford City
1937-8	Barnsley, Stockport Co.
1938-9	Norwich City, Tranmere Rov.
1946-7	Swansea City, Newport
1947-8	Doncaster Rov., Millwall
1948-9	Nott'm Forest, Lincoln City
1949-50	Plymouth Argyle, Bradford P.A.
1950-1	Grimsby Town, Chesterfield
1951-2	Coventry City, Q.P.R.
1952-3	Southampton, Barnsley
1953-4	Brentford, Oldham Athletic
1954-5	Ipswich Town, Derby Co.
1955-6	Plymouth Argyle, Hull City
1956-7	Port Vale, Bury
1957-8	Doncaster Rov., Notts Co.
1958-9	Barnsley, Grimsby Town
1959-60	Bristol City, Hull City
1960-1	Lincoln City, Portsmouth
1961-2	Brighton & H.A., Bristol Rov.
1962-3	Walsall, Luton Town
1963-4	Grimsby Town, Scunthorpe Utd.
1964-5	Swindon Town, Swansea City
1965-6	Middlesbrough, Leyton Orient
1966-7	Northampton Town, Bury
1967-8	Plymouth Argyle, Rotherham Utd.
1968-9	Fulham, Bury
1969-70	Preston N.E., Aston Villa
1970-1	Blackburn Rov., Bolton Wand.
1971-2	Charlton Athletic, Watford
1972-3	Huddersfield Town, Brighton & H.A.
1973-4	Crystal Palace, Preston N.E., Swindon Town
1974-5	Millwall, Cardiff City, Sheffield Wed.
1975-6	Portsmouth, Oxford Utd., York City
1976-7	Carlisle Utd., Plymouth Argyle, Hereford Utd.
1977-8	Hull City, Mansfield Town, Blackpool
1978-9	Sheffield Utd., Millwall, Blackburn Rov.
1979-80	Fulham, Burnley, Charlton Athletic
1980-1	Preston N.E., Bristol City, Bristol Rov.
1981-2	Cardiff City, Wrexham, Orient
1982-3	Rotherham Utd., Burnley, Bolton Wand.
1983-4	Derby Co., Swansea City, Cambridge Utd.
1984-5	Notts Co., Cardiff City, Wolves
1985-6	Carlisle Utd., Middlesbrough, Fulham
1986-7	Sunderland**, Grimsby Town, Brighton & H.A.
1987-8	Sheffield Utd.**, Reading, Huddersfield Town
1988-9	Shrewsbury Town, Birmingham City, Walsall
1989-90	Bournemouth, Bradford City, Stoke City
1990-1	W.B.A., Hull City
1991-2	Plymouth Argyle, Brighton & H.A., Port Vale

** Relegated after play-offs.

THIRD DIVISION TO FOURTH DIVISION

| 1958-9 | Rochdale, Notts Co., Doncaster Rov., Stockport Co. |
| 1959-60 | Accrington, Wrexham, Mansfield Town, York City |

1960-1	Chesterfield, Colchester Utd., Bradford City, Tranmere Rov.
1961-2	Newport, Brentford, Lincoln City, Torquay Utd.
1962-3	Bradford City P.A., Brighton & H.A., Carlisle Utd., Halifax Town
1963-4	Millwall, Crewe Alexandra, Wrexham, Notts Co.
1964-5	Luton Town, Port Vale, Colchester Utd., Barnsley
1965-6	Southend Utd., Exeter City, Brentford, York City
1966-7	Doncaster Rov., Workington, Darlington, Swansea City
1967-8	Scunthorpe Utd., Colchester Utd., Grimsby Town, Peterborough Utd. (demoted)
1968-9	Oldham Athletic, Crewe Alexandra, Hartlepool Utd., Northampton Town
1969-70	Bournemouth, Southport, Barrow, Stockport Co.
1970-1	Gillingham, Doncaster Rov., Bury, Reading
1971-2	Mansfield Town, Barnsley, Torquay Utd., Bradford City
1972-3	Scunthorpe Utd., Swansea City, Brentford, Rotherham Utd.
1973-4	Cambridge Utd., Shrewsbury Town, Rochdale, Southport
1974-5	Bournemouth, Watford, Tranmere Rov., Huddersfield Town
1975-6	Aldershot, Colchester Utd., Southend Utd., Halifax Town
1976-7	Reading, Northampton Town, Grimsby Town, York City
1977-8	Port Vale, Bradford City, Hereford, Portsmouth
1978-9	Peterborough Utd., Walsall, Tranmere Rov., Lincoln City
1979-80	Bury, Southend Utd., Mansfield Town, Wimbledon
1980-1	Sheffield Utd., Colchester Utd., Blackpool, Hull City
1981-2	Wimbledon, Swindon Town, Bristol City, Chester City
1982-3	Reading, Wrexham, Doncaster Rov., Chesterfield
1983-4	Scunthorpe Utd., Southend Utd., Port Vale, Exeter City
1984-5	Burnley, Orient, Preston N.E., Cambridge Utd.
1985-6	Lincoln City, Cardiff City, Wolves, Swansea City
1986-7	Bolton Wand.**, Carlisle Utd., Darlington, Newport
1987-8	Doncaster Rov., York City, Grimsby Town, Rotherham Utd.**
1988-9	Southend Utd., Chesterfield, Gillingham, Aldershot
1989-90	Cardiff City, Northampton Town, Blackpool, Walsall
1990-1	Crewe Alexandra, Rotherham Utd., Mansfield Town
1991-2	Bury, Shrewsbury Town, Torquay Utd., Darlington

** Relegated after plays-offs.

DEMOTED FROM FOURTH DIVISION TO CONFERENCE

1987	Lincoln City
1988	Newport
1989	Darlington
1990	Colchester Utd.
1991	No demotion
1992	No demotion

DEMOTED FROM THIRD DIVISION TO CONFERENCE

1993	Halifax Town
1994-6	No demotion
1997	Hereford
1998	Doncaster Rov.
1999	Scarborough
2000	Chester City
2001	Barnet
2002	Halifax Town

RELEGATED CLUBS (SINCE 1993)

1993

Premier League to Div. 1: Crystal Palace, Middlesbrough, Nott'm Forest
Div. 1 to Div. 2: Brentford, Cambridge Utd., Bristol Rov.
Div. 2 to Div. 3: Preston N.E., Mansfield Town, Wigan Athletic, Chester City

1994

Premier League to Div. 1: Sheffield Utd., Oldham Athletic, Swindon Town
Div. 1 to Div. 2: Birmingham City, Oxford Utd., Peterborough Utd.
Div. 2 to Div. 3: Fulham, Exeter City, Hartlepool Utd., Barnet

1995

Premier League to Div. 1: Crystal Palace, Norwich City, Leicester City, Ipswich Town
Div. 1 to Div. 2: Swindon Town, Burnley, Bristol City, Notts Co.
Div. 2 to Div. 3: Cambridge Utd., Plymouth Argyle, Cardiff City, Chester City, Leyton Orient

1996

Premier League to Div. 1: Manchester City, Q.P.R., Bolton Wand.
Div. 1 to Div. 2: Millwall, Watford, Luton Town
Div. 2 to Div. 3: Carlisle Utd., Swansea City, Brighton & H.A., Hull City

1997

Premier League to Div. 1: Sunderland, Middlesbrough, Nott'm Forest
Div. 1 to Div. 2: Grimsby Town, Oldham Athletic, Southend Utd.
Div. 2 to Div. 3: Peterborough Utd., Shrewsbury Town, Rotherham Utd., Notts Co.

1998

Premier League to Div. 1: Bolton Wand., Barnsley, Crystal Palace
Div. 1 to Div. 2: Manchester City, Stoke City, Reading
Div. 2 to Div. 3: Brentford, Plymouth Argyle, Carlisle Utd., Southend Utd.

1999

Premier League to Div. 1: Charlton Athletic, Blackburn Rov., Nott'm Forest
Div. 1 to Div. 2: Bury, Oxford Utd., Bristol City
Div. 2 to Div. 3: York City, Northampton Town, Lincoln City, Macclesfield Town

2000

Premier League to Div. 1: Wimbledon, Sheffield Wed., Watford
Div. 1 to Div. 2: Walsall, Port Vale, Swindon Town
Div. 2 to Div. 3: Cardiff City, Blackpool, Scunthorpe Utd., Chesterfield

2001

Premier League to Div. 1: Manchester City, Coventry City, Bradford City
Div. 1 to Div. 2: Huddersfield Town, Q.P.R., Tranmere Rov.
Div. 2 to Div. 3: Bristol Rov., Luton Town, Swansea City, Oxford Utd.

2002

Premier League to Div. 1: Ipswich Town, Derby Co., Leicester City
Div. 1 to Div. 2: Crewe Alexandra, Barnsley, Stockport Co.
Div. 2 to Div. 3: Bournemouth, Bury, Wrexham, Cambridge Utd.

AXA F.A. CUP 2001-02

FIRST ROUND

Aldershot Town 0, Bristol Rov. 0
Altrincham 1, Lancaster City 1
Barnet 0, Carlisle Utd. 0
Bedford Town 0, Peterborough Utd. 0
Blackpool 2, Newport Co. 2
Bournemouth 3, Worksop Town 0
Brentford 1, Morecambe 0
Brighton & H.A. 1, Shrewsbury Town 0
Bristol City 0, Leyton Orient 1
Cambridge Utd. 1, Notts Co. 1
Colchester Utd. 0, York City 0
Dagenham & Redbridge 1, Southport 0
Doncaster Rov. 2, Scunthorpe Utd. 3
Exeter City 3, Cambridge City 0
Grays Athletic 1, Hinckley Utd. 2
Halifax Town 2, Farnborough Town 1
Hayes 3, Wycombe Wand. 4
Hereford Utd. 1, Wrexham 0
Huddersfield Town 2, Gravesend &
   Northfleet 1
Kettering Town 1, Cheltenham Town 6
Kidderminster Harriers 0, Darlington 1
Lewes 0, Stoke City 2 (played at Stoke)
Lincoln City 1, Bury 1
Macclesfield Town 2, Forest Green Rov. 2
Mansfield Town 1, Oxford Utd. 0
Northwich Victoria 2, Hull City 5
Oldham Athletic 1, Barrow 1
Port Vale 3, Aylesbury Utd. 0
Reading 1, Welling Utd. 0
Southend Utd. 3, Luton Town 2
Stalybridge Celtic 0, Chesterfield 3
Swansea City 4, Q.P.R. 0
Swindon Town 3, Hartlepool Utd. 1
Tamworth 1, Rochdale 1
Tiverton Town 1, Cardiff City 3
   (played at Cardiff)
Torquay Utd. 1, Northampton Town 2
Tranmere Rov. 4, Brigg Town 1
Whitby Town 1, Plymouth Argyle 1
Wigan Athletic 0, Canvey Island 1
Worcester City 0, Rushden & Diamonds 1

FIRST ROUND REPLAYS

Barrow 0, Oldham Athletic 1
Bristol Rov. 1, Aldershot Town 0

Bury 1, Lincoln City 1†
   (Lincoln City won 3-2 on pens)
Carlisle Utd. 1, Barnet 0
Forest Green Rov., 1 Macclesfield Town 1†
   (Macclesfield Town won 11-10 on pens)
Lancaster City 1, Altrincham 4†
Newport Co. 1, Blackpool 4†
Notts Co. 2, Cambridge Utd. 0
Peterborough Utd. 2, Bedford Town 1
Plymouth Argyle 3, Whitby Town 2
Rochdale 1, Tamworth 0
York City 2, Colchester Utd. 2†
   (York City won 3-2 on pens)

SECOND ROUND

Altrincham 1, Darlington 2
Blackpool 2, Rochdale 0
Brighton & H.A. 2, Rushden & Diamonds 1
Canvey Island 1, Northampton Town 0
Cardiff City 3, Port Vale 0
Chesterfield 1, Southend Utd. 1
Exeter City 0, Dagenham & Redbridge 0
Halifax Town 1, Stoke City 1
Hinckley Utd. 0, Cheltenham Town 2
Hull City 2, Oldham Athletic 3
Leyton Orient 2, Lincoln City 1
Macclesfield Town 4, Swansea City 1
Mansfield Town 4, Huddersfield Town 0
Peterborough Utd. 1, Bournemouth 0
Plymouth Argyle 1, Bristol Rov. 1
Scunthorpe Utd. 3, Brentford 2
Swindon Town 3, Hereford Utd. 2
Tranmere Rov. 6, Carlisle Utd. 1
Wycombe Wand. 1, Notts Co. 0
York City 2, Reading 0

SECOND ROUND REPLAYS

Bristol Rov. 3, Plymouth Argyle 2
Dagenham & Redbridge 3, Exeter City 0
Southend Utd. 2, Chesterfield 0
Stoke City 2, Halifax Town 0

† After extra-time

ARSENAL COMPLETE FIRST PART OF THE DOUBLE

THIRD ROUND	FOURTH ROUND	FIFTH ROUND	SIXTH ROUND	SEMI-FINALS	FINAL
Arsenal 4	*Arsenal 1	*Arsenal 1	Arsenal 5	Arsenal 1	Arsenal 2
*Watford 2	Liverpool 0	Gillingham 2	Gillingham 2		
*Liverpool 3	*Gillingham 1	*Newcastle Utd. 1	*Newcastle Utd. 1:0		
Birmingham City 0	Bristol Rov. 0	Manchester City 0	Middlesbrough 3	Middlesbrough 0	
Gillingham 1	Newcastle Utd. 4	*Middlesbrough 1	*Middlesbrough 3		
*Wolves 0	*Peterborough Utd. 2	Blackburn Rov. 0			
Bristol Rov. 3	Manchester City 4	*Everton 0:2			
*Derby Co. 1	*Ipswich Town 1	Crewe Alexandra 0:1			
*Newcastle Utd. 2	*Middlesbrough 1				
Crystal Palace 0	Manchester Utd. 0				
Peterborough Utd. 2:2	Blackburn Rov. 1				
*Darlington 2:0	*Millwall 0				
*Manchester City 0	*Everton 4				
Swindon Town 0	Leyton Orient 1				
Ipswich Town 4	Crewe Alexandra 4				
*Dag & Redbridge 1	*Rotherham Utd. 2				
Middlesbrough 0:2					
*Wimbledon 0:0					
Manchester Utd. 3					
*Aston Villa 1:3					
Blackburn Rov. 1:1					
*Barnsley 1:1					
*Millwall 2					
Scunthorpe Utd. 1					
Everton 1					
*Stoke City 0					
Leyton Orient 4					
*Portsmouth 1					
*Crewe Alexandra 2					
Sheffield Wed. 1					
*Rotherham Utd. 2					
Southampton 1					

F.A. CUP FINAL

Round 1				
Fulham 2:1				
*Wycombe Wand. .. 2:0	Fulham 2			
York City 0:1	*York City 0	Fulham 1		
*Grimsby Town 0:0				
*Walsall 2	*Walsall 2			
Bradford City 0	*Charlton Athletic ... 1	*Walsall 1	Fulham 0	
*Charlton Athletic 2				
Blackpool 1				
W.B.A. 2	*W.B.A. 1			
*Sunderland 1	Leicester City 0	*W.B.A. 1		
Leicester City 2				
Mansfield Town 1			*W.B.A. 0	Chelsea 0
*Cheltenham Town 2	*Cheltenham Town ... 2			
Oldham Athletic 1	Burnley 1	Cheltenham Town ... 0		
*Burnley 4				
Canvey Island 1				
Tottenham 4	*Tottenham 4			
*Coventry City 0	Bolton Wand. 0	*Tottenham 4		
Bolton Wand. 4				
*Stockport Co. 0			*Tottenham 0	
Tranmere Rov. 3	Tranmere Rov. 3			
*Southend Utd. 1	Cardiff City 1	Tranmere Rov. ... 0		
*Cardiff City 2				
Leeds Utd. 1				Chelsea 1
*Preston N.E. 2	*Preston N.E. 2			
*Brighton & H.A. 1	Sheffield Utd. 1	*Preston N.E. ... 1		
*Sheffield Utd. 1				
Nott'm. Forest 0			Chelsea 1	
*Macclesfield Town 3	West Ham Utd. ... 1:2	Chelsea 4		
*Norwich City 0:0	*Chelsea 1:3			
Chelsea 0:4				

* Drawn at home. Semi-finals: Arsenal v Middlesbrough (Old Trafford); Chelsea v Fulham (Villa Park).

93

AXA F.A. CUP FINAL

ARSENAL 2, CHELSEA 0

Millennium Stadium, (73,963), Saturday, May 4, 2002

Arsenal (4-4-2): Seaman, Lauren, Campbell, Adams (capt), Cole, Wiltord (Keown 90), Parlour, Vieira, Ljungberg, Bergkamp (Edu 72), Henry (Kanu 81). **Subs not used:** Wright, Dixon. **Scorers:** Parlour (70), Ljungberg (80). **Booked:** Vieira, Henry. **Manager:** Arsene Wenger.

Chelsea (4-4-2): Cudicini, Melchiot (Zenden 77), Desailly (capt), Gallas, Babayaro (Terry 46), Gronkjaer, Lampard, Petit, Le Saux, Hasselbaink (Zola 68), Gudjohnsen. **Subs not used:** De Goey, Jokanovic. **Booked:** Le Saux, Terry, Gudjohnsen. **Manager:** Claudio Ranieri.

Referee: M. Riley (Leeds Utd.). **Half-time:** 0-0. **Man-of-the-match:** Freddie Ljungberg. **Presentation:** Lennart Johansson (president of UEFA).

SHOOTING STARS WIN IT FOR ARSENAL

Down the years, the F.A. Cup Final has produced many memorable goals, but rarely has there been a brace as good as the ones which Ray Parlour and Freddie Ljungberg struck late on to give Arsenal this victory.

With extra-time looking a distinct possibility, Sylvain Wiltord accepted a pass out of defence from Tony Adams to release Parlour, a player who, like Adams, had spent all his professional career at Highbury.

Twelve months earlier after coming on as a substitute for Wiltord, Parlour gave away the free-kick from which Michael Owen scored the first of his two goals for Liverpool in their 2-1 win. This time he was the hero of the hour, striding on, cutting inside and finding the top corner of the net from 30 yards.

Carlo Cudicini got a hand to the ball without being able to keep it out and 10 minutes later the goalkeeper was beaten again. The Brazilian Edu, brought on for Dennis Bergkamp, fed Ljungberg just inside his own half. Off went Ljungberg through the Chelsea defence, finally shaking off John Terry's challenge before curling a beauty inside the far upright from the edge of the penalty box.

It was Ljungberg's seventh goal in seven games of a purple patch at the end of the season, made him the first man to score in two successive F.A. Cup Finals since Tottenham's Bobby Smith 40 years earlier and left no leeway for a Chelsea comeback.

The goals came, ironically, when Chelsea were having their best spell of a match which came to life after a cagey, largely sterile first half. Frank Lampard worked tirelessly in midfield and Eidur Gudjohnsen forced an excellent stretching save from David Seaman, whom Arsene Wenger had entrusted with the Final after using Richard Wright in earlier rounds. But there were not too many other occasions when Chelsea threatened to repeat Wembley victories in 1997 under Ruud Gullit and in 2000 under Gianluca Vialli.

They were handicapped by Jimmy Floyd Hasselbaink's lack of mobility caused by a calf strain, and his eventual replacement Gianfranco Zola had little opportunity to influence the outcome once Parlour's sharpness more than compensated for rare blunt displays by Bergkamp and Thierry Henry. How Chelsea could have done with the silky touches and shooting power of the man who led the team out following his enforced retirement from the game – Robert Di Matteo.

So it was Tony Adams lifting the trophy for the third time after another resolute performance alongside the man set to replace him as the bedrock of the Arsenal defence – Sol Campbell.

HOW THEY REACHED THE FINAL

ARSENAL

Round 3: 4-2 away to Watford (Henry, Ljungberg, Kanu, Bergkamp)
Round 4: 1-0 home to Liverpool (Bergkamp)
Round 5: 5-2 home to Gillingham (Wiltord 2, Kanu, Adams, Parlour)
Round 6: 1-1 away to Newcastle Utd. (Edu); 3-0 home to Newcastle Utd. (Pires, Bergkamp, Campbell)
Semi-final (Old Trafford): 1-0 v Middlesbrough (Festa og)

CHELSEA

Round 3: 0-0 away to Norwich City; 4-0 home to Norwich City (Stanic, Lampard, Zola, Forssell)
Round 4: 1-1 home to West Ham Utd. (Hasselbaink); 3-2 away to West Ham Utd. (Hasselbaink, Forssell, Terry)
Round 5: 3-1 home to Preston N.E. (Gudjohnsen, Hasselbaink, Forssell)
Round 6: 4-0 away to Tottenham (Gallas, Gudjohnsen 2, Le Saux)
Semi-final (Aston Villa Park): 1-0 v Fulham (Terry)

LEADING SCORERS (COMPETITION PROPER)

5 Greenacre (Mansfield Town), Naylor (Cheltenham Town)
4 Alsop (Cheltenham Town), Ellington (Bristol Rov.), Koumas (Tranmere Rov.), Price (Tranmere Rov.)
3 Ashton (Crewe Alexandra), Bergkamp (Arsenal), Bramble (Southend Utd.), Carruthers (Scunthorpe Utd.), Currie (Wycombe Wand.), Defoe (West Ham Utd.), Eyres (Oldham Athletic), Flynn (Tranmere Rov.), Forssell (Chelsea), Gudjohnsen (Chelsea), Hasselbaink (Chelsea), Marlet (Fulham), Moore I (Burnley), Poyet (Tottenham), Whelan (Middlesbrough), Watts (Leyton Orient).

KEEPER ROBERTS MAKE F.A. CUP HISTORY

Persistence paid dividends for Tony Roberts when he became the first-ever goalkeeper to score an F.A. Cup goal. It came for Dagenham and Redbridge in a fourth qualifying tie at Basingstoke which his team were losing 2-1. Roberts, who spent 11 seasons at Q.P.R. and won a Wales cap, joined his attack for three late, unsuccessful corners. From a fourth, three minutes into stoppage time, Roberts swung his boot at a Danny Shipp knock-down for the equaliser. The Conference team won the replay, beat Southport in the first round proper, then knocked out Exeter City in a replay to reach round three for the second successive season before losing 4-1 to Ipswich Town. Two other goalkeepers were on the scoresheet last season. Peter Schmeichel volleyed a last-minute goal for Aston Villa in their 3-2 defeat at Everton. And Steve Mildenhall helped Notts County to a 4-3 Worthington Cup first round victory at Mansfield with a free-kick from inside his own half which was misjudged by his opposite number, Kevin Pilkington.

F.A. CUP FINAL TEAMS 1900-2002

1900 BURY – Thompson; Darrock, Davidson, Pray, Leeming, Ross, Richards, Wood, McLuckie, Sagar, Plant. **SOUTHAMPTON** – Robinson; Meehan, Durber, Meston, Chadwick, Petrie, Turner, Yates, Farrell, Wood, Milward. **Scorers:** Bury – McLuckie 2, Wood, Plant.

1901 TOTTENHAM – Clawley; Erentz, Tait, Norris, Hughes, Jones, Smith, Cameron, Brown, Copeland, Kirwan. **SHEFFIELD UTD.** – Foulke; Thickett, Boyle, Johnson, Morren, Needham, Bennett, Field, Hedley, Priest, Lipsham. **Scorers:** (first match) Tottenham – Brown 2, Sheff. Utd. – Bennett, Priest. **Scorers:** (second match) Tottenham – Cameron, Smith, Brown, Sheff. Utd. – Priest.

1902 SHEFFIELD UTD. – Foulke; Thickett, Boyle, Needham, Wilkinson, Johnson, Barnes, Common, Hedley, Priest, Lipsham. (Bennett injured in first match and Barnes took his place in the replay). **SOUTHAMPTON** – Robinson; A. C. B. Fry, Molyneux, Bowman, Lee, A. Turner, Wood, Brown, Chadwick, J. Turner, Metson. **Scorers:** (first match) Sheff. Utd. – Common, Southampton – Wood. **Scorers:** (second match) Sheff. Utd. – Hedley, Barnes, Southampton – Brown.

1903 BURY – Monteith; Lindsey, McEwan, Johnson, Thorpe, Ross, Richards, Wood, Sagar, Leeming, Plant. **DERBY CO.** – Fryer; Methven, Morris, Warren, Goodall (A.) May, Warrington, York, Boag, Richards, Davis. **Scorers:** Bury – Ross, Sagar, Leeming 2, Wood, Plant.

1904 MANCHESTER CITY – Hillman; McMahon, Burgess, Frost, Hynde, S. B. Ashworth, Meredith, Livingstone, Gillespie, Turnbull (A.), Booth. **BOLTON WAND.** – D. Davies; Brown, Struthers, Clifford, Greenhalgh, Freebairn, Stokes, Marsh, Yenson, White, Taylor. **Scorer:** Manchester City – Meredith.

1905 ASTON VILLA – George; Spencer, Miles, Pearson, Leake, Windmill, Brawn, Garratty, Hampton, Bache, Hall. **NEWCASTLE UTD.** – Lawrence; McCombie, Carr, Gardner, Aitken, McWilliam, Rutherford, Howie, Appleyard, Veitch, Gosnell. **Scorer:** Aston Villa – Hampton 2.

1906 EVERTON – Scott; Balmer (W.), Crelly, Makepeace, Taylor, Abbott, Sharp, Bolton, Young, Settle, H. P. Hardman. **NEWCASTLE UTD.** – Lawrence; McCombie, Carr, Gardner, Aitken, McWilliam, Rutherford, Howie, Veitch, Orr, Gosnell. **Scorer:** Everton – Young.

1907 SHEFFIELD WED. – Lyall; Layton, Burton, Brittleton, Crawshaw, Bartlett, Chapman, Bradshaw, Wilson, Stewart, Simpson. **EVERTON** – Scott; Balmer (W.), Balmer (R.), Makepeace, Taylor, Abbott, Sharp, Bolton, Young, Settle, H. P. Hardman. **Scorers:** Sheff. Wed. – Stewart, Simpson, Everton – Sharp.

1908 WOLVES – Lunn; Jones, Collins, Rev. K. R. G. Hunt, Wooldridge, Bishop, Harrison, Shelton, Hedley, Radford, Pedley. **NEWCASTLE UTD.** – Lawrence; McCracken, Pudan, Gardner, Veitch, McWilliam, Rutherford, Howie, Appleyard, Speedie, Wilson. **Scorers:** Wolves – Hunt, Hedley, Harrison, Newcastle Utd. – Howie.

1909 MANCHESTER UTD. – Moger; Stacey, Hayes, Duckworth, Roberts, Bell, Meredith, Halse, Turnbull (J.), Turnbull (A.), Wall. **BRISTOL CITY** – Clay; Annan, Cottle, Hanlin, Wedlock, Spear, Staniforth, Hardy, Gilligan, Burton, Hilton. **Scorer:** Manchester Utd. – Turnbull (A.).

1910 NEWCASTLE UTD. – Lawrence; McCracken, Carr, Veitch, Low, McWilliam, Rutherford, Howie, Shepherd, Higgins, Wilson. (Whitson was injured in first match and Carr took his place in the replay). **BARNSLEY** – Mearns; Downs, Ness, Glendinning, Boyle, Utley, Bartrop, Gadsby, Lillycrop, Tufnell, Forman. **Scorers:** (first match) Newcastle Utd. – Rutherford, Barnsley – Tufnell. **Scorer:** (second match) Newcastle Utd. – Shepherd 2 (1 pen.).

1911 BRADFORD CITY – Mellors; Campbell, Taylor, Robinson, Torrance, McDonald, Logan, Spiers, O'Rourke, Devine, Thompson. (Gildea played centre half in the first match). **NEWCASTLE UTD.** – Lawrence; McCracken, Whitson, Veitch, Low, Willis, Rutherford, Jobey, Stewart, Higgins, Wilson. **Scorer:** Bradford City – Spiers.

1912 BARNSLEY – Cooper; Downs, Taylor, Glendinning, Bratley, Utley, Bartrop, Tufnell, Lillycrop, Travers, Moore. **W.B.A.** – Pearson; Cook, Pennington, Baddeley, Buck, McNeal, Jephcott, Wright, Pailor, Bower, Shearman. **Scorer:** Barnsley – Tufnell.

1913 ASTON VILLA – Hardy; Lyons, Weston, Barber, Harrop, Leach, Wallace, Halse, Hampton, Stephenson (C.), Bache. **SUNDERLAND** – Butler; Gladwin, Ness, Cuggy, Thompson, Low, Mordue, Buchan, Richardson, Holley, Martin. **Scorer:** Aston Villa – Barber.

1914 BURNLEY – Sewell; Bamford, Taylor, Halley, Boyle, Watson, Nesbit, Lindley, Freeman, Hodgson, Mosscrop. **LIVERPOOL** – Campbell; Longworth, Pursell, Fairfoul, Ferguson, McKinlay, Sheldon, Metcalfe, Miller, Lacey, Nicholl. **Scorer:** Burnley – Freeman.

1915 SHEFFIELD UTD. – Gough; Cook, English, Sturgess, Brelsford, Utley, Simmons, Fazackerley, Kitchen, Masterman, Evans. **CHELSEA** – Molyneux; Bettridge, Harrow, Taylor, Logan, Walker, Ford, Halse, Thompson, Croal, McNeil. **Scorers:** Sheff. Utd. – Simmons, Fazackerley, Kitchen.

1920 ASTON VILLA – Hardy; Smart, Weston, Ducat, Barson, Moss, Wallace, Kirton, Walker, Stephenson (C.), Dorrell. **HUDDERSFIELD TOWN** – Mutch; Wood, Bullock, Slade, Wilson, Watson, Richardson, Mann, Taylor, Swan, Islip. **Scorer:** Aston VIlla – Kirton.

1921 TOTTENHAM – Hunter; Clay, McDonald, Smith, Walters, Grimsdell; Banks, Seed, Cantrell, Bliss, Dimmock. **WOLVES** – George; Woodward, Marshall, Gregory, Hodnett, Riley, Lea, Burrill, Edmonds, Potts, Brooks. **Scorer:** Tottenham – Dimmock.

1922 HUDDERSFIELD TOWN – Mutch; Wood, Wadsworth, Slade, Wilson, Watson, Richardson, Mann, Islip, Stephenson, Smith (W.H.). **PRESTON N.E.** – J. F. Mitchell; Hamilton, Doolan, Duxbury, McCall, Williamson, Rawlings, Jefferis, Roberts, Woodhouse, Quinn. **Scorer:** Huddersfield Town – Smith (pen.).

1923 BOLTON WAND. – Pym; Haworth, Finney, Nuttall, Seddon, Jennings, Butler, Jack, Smith (J. R.), Smith (J.), Vizard. **WEST HAM UTD.** – Hufton; Henderson, Young, Bishop, Kay, Tresadern, Richards, Brown, Watson (V.), Moore, Ruffell. **Scorers:** Bolton Wand. – Jack, Smith (J. R.).

1924 NEWCASTLE UTD. – Bradley; Hampson, Hudspeth, Mooney, Spencer, Gibson, Low, Cowan, Harris, McDonald, Seymour. **ASTON VILLA** – Jackson; Smart, Mort, Moss, Dr. V. E. Milne, Blackburn, York, Kirton, Capewell, Walker, Dorrell. **Scorers:** Newcastle Utd. – Harris, Seymour.

1925 SHEFFIELD UTD. – Sutcliffe; Cook, Milton, Pantling, King, Green, Mercer, Boyle, Johnson, Gillespie, Tunstall. **CARDIFF CITY** – Farquharson; Nelson, Blair, Wake, Keenor, Hardy, Davies (W.), Gill, Nicholson, Beadles, Evans (J.). **Scorer:** Sheff. Utd. – Tunstall.

1926 BOLTON WAND. – Pym; Haworth, Greenhalgh, Nuttall, Seddon, Jennings, Butler, Jack, Smith (J. R.), Smith (J.), Vizard. **MANCHESTER CITY** – Goodchild; Cookson, McCloy, Pringle, Cowan, McMullan, Austin, Browell, Roberts, Johnson, Hicks. **Scorer:** Bolton Wand. – Jack.

1927 CARDIFF CITY – Farquharson; Nelson, Watson, Keenor, Sloan, Hardy, Curtis, Irving, Ferguson, Davies (L.), McLachlan. **ARSENAL** – Lewis; Parker, Kennedy, Baker, Butler, John, Hulme, Buchan, Brain, Blyth, Hoar. **Scorer:** Cardiff City – Ferguson.

1928 BLACKBURN ROV. – Crawford; Hutton, Jones, Healless, Rankin, Campbell, Thornewell, Puddefoot, Roscamp, McLean, Rigby. **HUDDERSFIELD TOWN** – Mercer; Goodall, Barkas, Redfern, Wilson, Steele, Jackson (A.), Kelly, Brown, Stephenson, Smith (W.H.). **Scorers:** Blackburn Rov. – Roscamp 2, McLean, Huddersfield Town – Jackson.

1929 BOLTON WAND. – Pym; Haworth, Finney, Kean, Seddon, Nuttall, Butler, McCleland, Blackmore, Gibson, Cook (W.). **PORTSMOUTH** – Gilfillan; Mackie, Bell, Nichol, McIlwaine, Thackeray, Forward, Smith (J.), Weddle, Watson, Cook (F.). **Scorers:** Bolton Wand. – Butler, Blackmore.

1930 ARSENAL – Preedy; Parker, Hapgood, Baker, Seddon, John, Hulme, Jack, Lambert, James, Bastin. **HUDDERSFIELD TOWN** – Turner; Goodall, Spence, Naylor, Wilson, Campbell, Jackson (A.), Kelly, Davies, Raw, Smith (W. H.). **Scorers:** Arsenal – James, Lambert.

1931 W.B.A. – Pearson; Shaw, Trentham, Magee, Richardson (W.), Edwards, Glidden, Carter, Richardson (W. G.), Sandford, Wood. **BIRMINGHAM CITY** – Hibbs; Liddell, Barkas, Cringan, Morrall, Leslie, Briggs, Crosbie, Bradford, Gregg, Curtis. **Scorers:** W.B.A. – Richardson (W. G.) 2, Birmingham City – Bradford.

1932 NEWCASTLE UTD. – McInroy; Nelson, Fairhurst, McKenzie, Davidson, Weaver, Boyd, Richardson, Allen, McMenemy, Lang. **ARSENAL** – Moss; Parker, Hapgood, Jones (C.), Roberts, Male, Hulme, Jack, Lambert, Bastin, John. **Scorers:** Newcastle Utd. – Allen 2, Arsenal – John.

1933 EVERTON – Sagar; Cook, Cresswell, Britton, White, Thomson, Geldard, Dunn, Dean, Johnson, Stein. **MANCHESTER CITY** – Langford; Cann, Dale, Busby, Cowan, Bray, Toseland, Marshall, Herd, McMullan, Brook. **Scorers:** Everton – Stein, Dean, Dunn.

1934 MANCHESTER CITY – Swift; Barnett, Dale, Busby, Cowan, Bray, Toseland, Marshall, Tilson, Herd, Brook. **PORTSMOUTH** – Gilfillan; Mackie, Smith (W.), Nichol, Allen, Thackeray, Worrall, Smith (J.), Weddle, Easson, Rutherford. **Scorers:** Manchester City – Tilson 2, Portsmouth – Rutherford.

1935 SHEFFIELD WED. – Brown; Nibloe, Catlin, Sharp, Millership, Burrows, Hooper, Surtees, Palethorpe, Starling, Rimmer. **W.B.A.** – Pearson; Shaw, Trentham, Murphy, Richardson (W.), Edwards, Glidden, Carter, Richardson (W. G.), Sandford, Boyes. **Scorers:** Sheff. Wed. – Rimmer 2, Palethorpe, Hooper, W.B.A. – Boyes, Sandford.

1936 ARSENAL – Wilson; Male, Hapgood, Crayston, Roberts, Copping, Hulme, Bowden, Drake, James, Bastin. **SHEFFIELD UTD.** – Smith; Hooper, Wilkinson, Jackson, Johnson, McPherson, Barton, Barclay, Dodds, Pickering, Williams. **Scorer:** Arsenal – Drake.

1937 SUNDERLAND – Mapson; Gorman, Hall, Thomson, Johnston, McNab, Duns, Carter, Gurney, Gallacher, Burbanks. **PRESTON N.E.** – Burns; Gallimore, Beattie (A.), Shankly, Tremelling, Milne, Dougal, Beresford, O'Donnell (F.), Fagan, O'Donnell (H). **Scorers:** Sunderland – Gurney, Carter, Burbanks, Preston N.E. – O'Donnell (F.).

1938 PRESTON N.E. – Holdcroft; Gallimore, Beattie (A.), Shankly, Smith, Batey, Watmough, Mutch, Maxwell, Beattie (R.), O'Donnell (H.) **HUDDERSFIELD TOWN** – Hesford; Craig, Mountford, Willingham, Young, Boot, Hulme, Isaac, McFadyen, Barclay, Beasley. **Scorer:** Preston N.E. – Mutch (pen.).

1939 PORTSMOUTH – Walker; Morgan, Rochford, Guthrie, Rowe, Wharton, Worrall, McAlinden, Anderson, Barlow, Parker. **WOLVES** – Scott; Morris, Taylor, Galley, Cullis, Gardiner, Burton, McIntosh, Westcott, Dorsett, Maguire. **Scorers:** Portsmouth – Barlow, Anderson, Parker 2, Wolves – Dorsett.

1946 DERBY CO. – Woodley; Nicholas, Howe, Bullions, Leuty, Musson, Harrison, Carter, Stamps, Doherty, Duncan. **CHARLTON ATHLETIC** – Bartram; Phipps, Shreeve, Turner (H.), Oakes, Johnson, Fell, Brown, A. A. Turner, Welsh, Duffy. **Scorers:** Derby Co. – Turner (H.) (o.g.), Doherty, Stamps 2, Charlton Athletic – Turner (H.).

1947 CHARLTON ATHLETIC – Bartram; Croker (P.), Shreeve, Johnson, Phipps, Whittaker, Hurst, Dawson, Robinson (W.), Welsh, Duffy. **BURNLEY** – Strong; Woodruff, Mather, Attwell, Brown, Bray, Chew, Morris, Harrison, Potts, F. P. Kippax. **Scorer:** Charlton Athletic – Duffy.

1948 MANCHESTER UTD. – Crompton; Carey, Aston, Anderson, Chilton, Cockburn, Delaney, Morris, Rowley, Pearson, Mitten. **BLACKPOOL** – Robinson; Shimwell, Crosland, Johnston, Hayward, Kelly, Matthews, Munro, Mortensen, Dick, Rickett. **Scorers:** Manchester Utd. – Rowley 2, Pearson, Anderson, Blackpool – Shimwell (pen.), Mortensen.

1949 WOLVES – Williams; Pritchard, Springthorpe, Crook (W.), Shorthouse, Wright, Hancocks, Smyth, Pye, Dunn, Mullen. **LEICESTER CITY** – Bradley; Jelly, Scott, Harrison (W.), Plummer, King, Griffiths, Lee, Harrison (J.), Chisholm, Adam. **Scorers:** Wolves – Pye 2, Smyth, Leicester City – Griffiths.

1950 ARSENAL – Swindin; Scott, Barnes, Forbes, Compton (L.), Mercer, Cox, Logie, Goring, Lewis, Compton (D.). **LIVERPOOL** – Sidlow; Lambert, Spicer, Taylor, Hughes, Jones, Payne, Baron, Stubbins, Fagan, Liddell. **Scorer:** Arsenal – Lewis 2.

1951 NEWCASTLE UTD. – Fairbrother; Cowell, Corbett, Harvey, Brennan, Crowe, Walker, Taylor, Milburn, Robledo (G.), Mitchell. **BLACKPOOL** – Farm; Shimwell, Garrett, Johnston, Hayward, Kelly, Matthews, Mudie, Mortensen, W. J. Slater, Perry. **Scorer:** Newcastle Utd. – Milburn 2.

1952 NEWCASTLE UTD. – Simpson; Cowell, McMichael, Harvey, Brennan, Robledo (E.), Walker, Foulkes, Milburn, Robledo (G.), Mitchell. **ARSENAL** – Swindin; Barnes, Smith (L.), Forbes, Daniel, Mercer, Cox, Logie, Holton, Lishman, Roper. **Scorer:** Newcastle Utd. – Robledo (G.).

1953 BLACKPOOL – Farm; Shimwell, Garrett, Fenton, Johnston, Robinson, Matthews, Taylor, Mortensen, Mudie, Perry. **BOLTON WAND.** – Hanson; Ball, Banks (R.), Wheeler, Barrass, Bell, Holden, Moir, Lofthouse, Hassall, Langton. **Scorers:** Blackpool – Mortensen 3, Perry, Bolton Wand. – Lofthouse, Moir, Bell.

1954 W.B.A. – Sanders; Kennedy, Millard, Dudley, Dugdale, Barlow, Griffin, Ryan, Allen, Nicholls, Lee. **PRESTON N.E.** – Thompson; Cunningham, Walton, Docherty, Marston, Forbes, Finney, Foster, Wayman, Baxter, Morrison. **Scorers:** W.B.A. – Allen 2 (1 pen.), Griffin, Preston N.E. – Morrison, Wayman.

1955 NEWCASTLE UTD. – Simpson; Cowell, Batty, Scoular, Stokoe, Casey, White, Milburn, Keeble, Hannah, Mitchell. **MANCHESTER CITY** – Trautmann; Meadows, Little, Barnes, Ewing, Paul, Spurdle, Hayes, Revie, Johnstone, Fagan. **Scorers:** Newcastle Utd. – Milburn, Mitchell, Hannah, Manchester City – Johnstone.

1956 MANCHESTER CITY – Trautmann; Leivers, Little, Barnes, Ewing, Paul, Johnstone, Hayes, Revie, Dyson, Clarke. **BIRMINGHAM CITY** – Merrick; Hall, Green, Newman, Smith, Boyd, Astall, Kinsey, Brown, Murphy, Govan. **Scorers:** Manchester City – Hayes, Dyson, Johnstone, Birmingham City – Kinsey.

1957 ASTON VILLA – Sims; Lynn, Aldis, Crowther, Dugdale, Saward, Smith, Sewell, Myerscough, Dixon, McParland. **MANCHESTER UTD.** – Wood; Foulkes, Byrne, Colman, Blanchflower, Edwards, Berry, Whelan, Taylor (T.), Charlton, Pegg. **Scorers:** Aston Villa – McParland 2, Manchester Utd. – Taylor.

1958 BOLTON WANDERERS – Hopkinson; Hartle, Banks (T.), Hennin, Higgins, Edwards, Birch, Stevens, Lofthouse, Parry, Holden. **MANCHESTER UTD.** – Gregg; Foulkes, Greaves, Goodwin, Cope, Crowther, Dawson, Taylor (E.), Charlton, Viollet, Webster. **Scorer:** Bolton Wand. – Lofthouse 2.

1959 NOTT'M FOREST – Thomson; Whare, McDonald, Whitefoot, McKinlay, Burkitt, Dwight, Quigley, Wilson, Gray, Imlach. **LUTON TOWN** –. Baynham; McNally, Hawkes, Groves, Owen, Pacey, Bingham, Brown, Morton, Cummins, Gregory. **Scorers:** Nott'm. Forest – Dwight, Wilson, Luton Town – Pacey.

1960 WOLVES – Finlayson; Showell, Harris, Clamp, Slater, Flowers, Deeley, Stobart, Murray, Broadbent, Horne. **BLACKBURN ROV.** – Leyland; Bray, Whelan, Clayton, Woods, McGrath, Bimpson, Dobing, Dougan, Douglas, MacLeod. **Scorers:** Wolves – McGrath (o.g.), Deeley 2.

1961 TOTTENHAM – Brown; Baker, Henry, Blanchflower, Norman, Mackay, Jones, White, Smith, Allen, Dyson. **LEICESTER CITY** – Banks; Chalmers, Norman, McLintock, King, Appleton, Riley, Walsh, McIlmoyle, Keyworth, Cheesebrough. **Scorers:** Tottenham – Smith, Dyson.

1962 TOTTENHAM – Brown; Baker, Henry, Blanchflower, Norman, Mackay, Medwin, White, Smith, Greaves, Jones. **BURNLEY** – Blacklaw; Angus, Elder, Adamson, Cummings, Miller, Connelly, McIlroy, Pointer, Robson, Harris. **Scorers:** Tottenham – Greaves, Smith, Blanchflower (pen.), Burnley – Robson.

1963 MANCHESTER UTD. – Gaskell; Dunne, Cantwell, Crerand, Foulkes, Setters, Giles, Quixall, Herd, Law, Charlton. **LEICESTER CITY** – Banks; Sjoberg, Norman, McLintock, King, Appleton, Riley, Cross, Keyworth, Gibson, Stringfellow. **Scorers:** Manchester Utd. – Law, Herd 2, Leicester City – Keyworth.

1964 WEST HAM UTD. – Standen; Bond, Burkett, Bovington, Brown, Moore, Brabrook, Boyce, Byrne, Hurst, Sissons. **PRESTON N.E.** – Kelly; Ross, Smith, Lawton, Singleton, Kendall, Wilson, Ashworth, Dawson, Spavin, Holden. **Scorers:** West Ham Utd. – Sissons, Hurst, Boyce, Preston N.E. – Holden, Dawson.

1965 LIVERPOOL – Lawrence; Lawler, Byrne, Strong, Yeats, Stevenson, Callaghan, Hunt, St. John, Smith, Thompson. **LEEDS UTD.** – Sprake; Reaney, Bell, Bremner, Charlton, Hunter, Giles, Storrie, Peacock, Collins, Johanneson. **Scorers:** Liverpool – Hunt, St. John, Leeds Utd. – Bremner.

1966 EVERTON – West; Wright, Wilson, Gabriel, Labone, Harris, Scott, Trebilcock, Young, Harvey, Temple. **SHEFFIELD WED.** – Springett; Smith, Megson, Eustace, Ellis, Young, Pugh, Fantham, McCalliog, Ford, Quinn. **Scorers:** Everton – Trebilcock 2, Temple. Sheff. Wed. – McCalliog, Ford.

1967 TOTTENHAM – Jennings; Kinnear, Knowles, Mullery, England, Mackay, Robertson, Greaves, Gilzean, Venables, Saul. **CHELSEA** – Bonetti; Harris (A.), McCreadie, Hollins, Hinton, Harris (R.), Cooke, Baldwin, Hateley, Tambling, Boyle. **Scorers:** Tottenham – Robertson, Saul, Chelsea – Tambling.

1968 W.B.A. – Osborne; Fraser, Williams, Brown, Talbut, Kaye (Clarke), Lovett, Collard, Astle, Hope, Clark. **EVERTON** – West; Wright, Wilson, Kendall, Labone, Harvey, Husband, Ball, Royle, Hurst, Morrissey. **Scorer:** W.B.A. – Astle.

1969 MANCHESTER CITY – Dowd; Book, Pardoe, Doyle, Booth, Oakes, Summerbee, Bell, Lee, Young, Coleman. **LEICESTER CITY** – Shilton; Rodrigues, Nish, Roberts, Woollett, Cross, Fern, Gibson, Lochhead, Clarke, Glover (Manley). **Scorer:** Manchester City – Young.

1970 CHELSEA – Bonetti; Webb, McCreadie, Hollins, Dempsey, Harris (R.) (Hinton), Baldwin, Houseman, Osgood, Hutchinson, Cooke. **LEEDS UTD.** – Sprake; Madeley, Cooper, Bremner, Charlton, Hunter, Lorimer, Clarke, Jones, Giles, Gray. **Scorers:** Chelsea – Houseman, Hutchinson, Leeds Utd. – Charlton, Jones. **Replay: CHELSEA** – Bonetti; Harris (R.), McCreadie, Hollins, Dempsey, Webb, Baldwin, Cooke, Osgood (Hinton), Hutchinson, Houseman. **LEEDS UTD.** – Harvey; Madeley, Cooper, Bremner, Charlton, Hunter, Lorimer, Clarke, Jones, Giles, Gray. **Scorers:** Chelsea – Osgood, Webb, Leeds Utd. – Jones.

1971 ARSENAL – Wilson; Rice, McNab, Storey (Kelly), McLintock, Simpson, Armstrong, Graham, Radford, Kennedy, George. **LIVERPOOL** – Clemence; Lawler, Lindsay, Smith, Lloyd, Hughes, Callaghan, Evans (Thompson), Heighway, Toshack, Hall. **Scorers:** Arsenal – Kelly, George, Liverpool – Heighway.

1972 LEEDS UTD. – Harvey; Reaney, Madeley, Bremner, Charlton, Hunter, Lorimer, Clarke, Jones, Giles, Gray. **ARSENAL** – Barnett; Rice, McNab, Storey, McLintock, Simpson, Armstrong, Ball, Radford (Kennedy), George, Graham. **Scorer:** Leeds Utd. – Clarke.

1973 SUNDERLAND – Montgomery; Malone, Guthrie, Horswill, Watson, Pitt, Kerr, Hughes, Halom, Porterfield, Tueart. **LEEDS UTD.** – Harvey; Reaney, Cherry, Bremner, Madeley, Hunter, Lorimer, Clarke, Jones, Giles, Gray (Yorath). **Scorer:** Sunderland – Porterfield.

1974 LIVERPOOL – Clemence; Smith, Lindsay, Thompson, Cormack, Hughes, Keegan, Hall, Heighway, Toshack, Callaghan. **NEWCASTLE UTD.** – McFaul; Clark, Kennedy, McDermott, Howard, Moncur, Smith (Gibb), Cassidy, Macdonald, Tudor, Hibbitt. **Scorers:** Liverpool – Keegan (2), Heighway.

1975 WEST HAM UTD. – Day; McDowell, Lampard, Bonds, Taylor (T.), Lock, Jennings, Paddon, Taylor (A.), Brooking, Holland. **FULHAM** – Mellor; Cutbush, Fraser, Mullery, Lacy, Moore, Mitchell, Conway, Busby, Slough, Barrett. **Scorer:** West Ham Utd. – Taylor (A.) 2.

1976 SOUTHAMPTON – Turner; Rodrigues, Peach, Holmes, Blyth, Steele, Gilchrist, Channon, Osgood, McCalliog, Stokes. **MANCHESTER UTD.** – Stepney; Forsyth, Houston, Daly, Greenhoff (B.), Buchan, Coppell, McIlroy, Pearson, Macari, Hill (McCreery). **Scorer:** Southampton – Stokes.

1977 MANCHESTER UTD. – Stepney; Nicholl, Albiston, McIlroy, Greenhoff (B.), Buchan, Coppell, Greenhoff (J.), Pearson, Macari, Hill (McCreery). **LIVERPOOL** – Clemence; Neal, Jones, Smith, Kennedy, Hughes, Keegan, Case, Heighway, McDermott, Johnson (Callaghan). **Scorers:** Manchester Utd. – Pearson, Greenhoff (J.), Liverpool – Case.

1978 IPSWICH TOWN – Cooper; Burley, Mills, Talbot, Hunter, Beattie, Osborne (Lambert), Wark, Mariner, Geddis, Woods. **ARSENAL** – Jennings; Rice, Nelson, Price, O'Leary, Young, Brady (Rix), Sunderland, Macdonald, Stapleton, Hudson. **Scorer:** Ipswich Town – Osborne.

1979 ARSENAL – Jennings; Rice, Nelson, Talbot, O'Leary, Young, Brady, Sunderland, Stapleton, Price (Walford), Rix. **MANCHESTER UTD.** – Bailey; Nicholl, Albiston,

McIlroy, McQueen, Buchan, Coppell, Greenhoff (J.), Jordan, Macari, Thomas. **Scorers:** Arsenal – Talbot, Stapleton, Sunderland, Manchester Utd. – McQueen, McIlroy.

1980 WEST HAM UTD. – Parkes; Stewart, Lampard, Bonds, Martin, Devonshire, Allen, Pearson, Cross, Brooking, Pike. **ARSENAL** – Jennings; Rice, Devine (Nelson), Talbot, O'Leary, Young, Brady, Sunderland, Stapleton, Price, Rix. **Scorer:** West Ham Utd. – Brooking.

1981 TOTTENHAM – Aleksic; Hughton, Miller, Roberts, Perryman, Villa (Brooke), Ardiles, Archibald, Galvin, Hoddle, Crooks. **MANCHESTER CITY** – Corrigan; Ranson, McDonald, Reid, Power, Caton, Bennett, Gow, Mackenzie, Hutchison (Henry), Reeves. **Scorer:** Tottenham – Hutchison (o.g.), Manchester City – Hutchison. **Replay: TOTTENHAM** – Aleksic; Hughton, Miller, Roberts, Perryman, Villa, Ardiles, Archibald, Galvin, Hoddle, Crooks. **MANCHESTER CITY** – Corrigan; Ranson, McDonald (Tueart), Reid, Power, Caton, Bennett, Gow, Mackenzie, Hutchison, Reeves. **Scorers:** Tottenham – Villa 2, Crooks, Manchester City – Mackenzie, Reeves (pen.).

1982 TOTTENHAM – Clemence; Hughton, Miller, Price, Hazard (Brooke), Perryman, Roberts, Archibald, Galvin, Hoddle, Crooks. **Q.P.R.** – Hucker; Fenwick, Gillard, Waddock, Hazell, Roeder, Currie, Flanagan, Allen (Micklewhite), Stainrod, Gregory. **Scorers:** Tottenham – Hoddle, Q.P.R. – Fenwick. **Replay: TOTTENHAM** – Clemence; Hughton, Miller, Price, Hazard (Brooke), Perryman, Roberts, Archibald, Galvin, Hoddle, Crooks. **Q.P.R.** – Hucker; Fenwick, Gillard, Waddock, Hazell, Neill, Currie, Flanagan, Micklewhite (Burke), Stainrod, Gregory. **Scorer:** Tottenham – Hoddle (pen.).

1983 MANCHESTER UTD. – Bailey; Duxbury, Albiston, Wilkins, Moran, McQueen, Robson, Muhren, Stapleton, Whiteside, Davies. **BRIGHTON & H.A.** – Moseley; Ramsey (Ryan), Pearce, Grealish, Gatting, Stevens, Case, Howlett, Robinson, Smith, Smillie. **Scorers:** Manchester Utd. – Stapleton, Wilkins, Brighton & H.A. – Smith, Stevens. **Replay: MANCHESTER UTD.** – Bailey; Duxbury, Albiston, Wilkins, Moran, McQueen, Robson, Muhren, Stapleton, Whiteside, Davies. **BRIGHTON & H.A.** – Moseley; Gatting, Pearce, Grealish, Foster, Stevens, Case, Howlett (Ryan), Robinson, Smith, Smillie. **Scorers:** Manchester Utd. – Robson 2, Whiteside, Muhren (pen.).

1984 EVERTON – Southall; Stevens, Bailey, Ratcliffe, Mountfield, Reid, Steven, Heath, Sharp, Gray, Richardson. **WATFORD** – Sherwood; Bardsley, Price (Atkinson), Taylor, Terry, Sinnott, Callaghan, Johnston, Reilly, Jackett, Barnes. **Scorers:** Everton – Sharp, Gray.

1985 MANCHESTER UTD. – Bailey; Gidman, Albiston (Duxbury), Whiteside, McGrath, Moran, Robson, Strachan, Hughes, Stapleton, Olsen. **EVERTON** – Southall; Stevens, Van den Hauwe, Ratcliffe, Mountfield, Reid, Steven, Sharp, Gray, Bracewell, Sheedy. **Scorer:** Manchester Utd. – Whiteside. **Sent-off:** Moran.

1986 LIVERPOOL – Grobbelaar; Lawrenson, Beglin, Nicol, Whelan, Hansen, Dalglish, Johnston, Rush, Molby, MacDonald. **EVERTON** – Mimms; Stevens (Heath), Van den Hauwe, Ratcliffe, Mountfield, Reid, Steven, Lineker, Sharp, Bracewell, Sheedy. **Scorers:** Liverpool – Rush 2, Johnston, Everton – Lineker.

1987 COVENTRY CITY – Ogrizovic; Phillips, Downs, McGrath, Kilcline (Rodger), Peake, Bennett, Gynn, Regis, Houchen, Pickering. **TOTTENHAM** – Clemence; Hughton (Claesen), Thomas (M.), Hodge, Gough, Mabbutt, Allen (C.), Allen (P.), Waddle, Hoddle, Ardiles (Stevens). **Scorers:** Coventry City – Bennett, Houchen, Mabbutt (o.g.), Tottenham – Allen (C.), Mabbutt.

1988 WIMBLEDON – Beasant; Goodyear, Phelan, Jones, Young, Thorn, Gibson (Scales), Cork (Cunningham), Fashanu, Sanchez, Wise. **LIVERPOOL** – Grobbelaar; Gillespie, Ablett, Nicol, Spackman (Molby), Hansen, Beardsley, Aldridge (Johnston), Houghton, Barnes, McMahon. **Scorer:** Wimbledon – Sanchez.

1989 LIVERPOOL – Grobbelaar; Ablett, Staunton (Venison), Nicol, Whelan, Hansen, Beardsley, Aldridge (Rush), Houghton, Barnes, McMahon. **EVERTON** – Southall; McDonald, Van den Hauwe, Ratcliffe, Watson, Bracewell (McCall), Nevin, Steven, Sharp, Cottee, Sheedy (Wilson). **Scorers:** Liverpool – Aldridge, Rush 2, Everton – McCall 2.

1990 MANCHESTER UTD. – Leighton; Ince, Martin (Blackmore), Bruce, Phelan, Pallister (Robins), Robson, Webb, McClair, Hughes, Wallace. **CRYSTAL PALACE** – Martyn; Pemberton, Shaw, Gray (Madden), O'Reilly, Thorn, Barber (Wright), Thomas, Bright, Salako, Pardew. **Scorers:** Manchester Utd. – Robson, Hughes 2, Crystal Palace –

O'Reilly, Wright 2. **Replay: MANCHESTER UTD.** – Sealey; Ince, Martin, Bruce, Phelan, Pallister, Robson, Webb, McClair, Hughes, Wallace. **CRYSTAL PALACE** – Martyn; Pemberton, Shaw, Gray, O'Reilly, Thorn, Barber (Wright), Thomas, Bright; Salako (Madden), Pardew. **Scorer:** Manchester Utd. – Martin.

1991 TOTTENHAM – Thorstvedt; Edinburgh, Van den Hauwe, Sedgley, Howells, Mabbutt, Stewart, Gascoigne (Nayim), Samways (Walsh), Lineker, Allen. **NOTT'M FOREST** – Crossley; Charles, Pearce, Walker, Chettle, Keane, Crosby, Parker, Clough, Glover (Laws), Woan (Hodge). **Scorers:** Tottenham – Stewart, Walker (o.g.), Nott'm. Forest – Pearce.

1992 LIVERPOOL – Grobbelaar; Jones (R.), Burrows, Nicol, Molby, Wright, Saunders, Houghton, Rush (I.), McManaman, Thomas. **SUNDERLAND** – Norman; Owers, Ball, Bennett, Rogan, Rush (D.) (Hardyman), Bracewell, Davenport, Armstrong (Hawke), Byrne, Atkinson. **Scorers:** Liverpool – Thomas, Rush (I.).

1993 ARSENAL – Seaman; Dixon, Winterburn, Linighan, Adams, Parlour (Smith), Davis, Merson, Jensen, Wright (O'Leary), Campbell. **SHEFFIELD WED.** – Woods; Nilsson, Worthington, Palmer, Hirst, Anderson (Hyde), Waddle (Bart-Williams), Warhurst, Bright, Sheridan, Harkes. **Scorers:** Arsenal – Wright, Sheff. Wed. – Hirst. **Replay: ARSENAL** – Seaman; Dixon, Winterburn, Linighan, Adams, Davis, Jensen, Merson, Smith, Wright (O'Leary), Campbell. **SHEFFIELD WED.** – Woods; Nilsson (Bart-Williams), Worthington, Palmer, Hirst, Wilson (Hyde), Waddle, Warhurst, Bright, Sheridan, Harkes. **Scorers:** Arsenal – Wright, Linighan, Sheff. Wed. – Waddle.

1994 MANCHESTER UTD. – Schmeichel; Parker, Bruce, Pallister, Irwin (Sharpe), Kanchelskis (McClair), Keane, Ince, Giggs, Cantona, Hughes. **CHELSEA** – Kharine; Clarke, Johnsen, Kjeldbjerg, Sinclair, Burley (Hoddle), Newton, Wise, Peacock, Stein (Cascarino), Spencer. **Scorers:** Manchester Utd. – Cantona 2 (2 pens.), Hughes, McClair.

1995 EVERTON – Southall; Jackson, Watson, Unsworth, Ablett, Horne, Parkinson, Hinchcliffe, Stuart, Limpar (Amokachi), Rideout (Ferguson). **MANCHESTER UTD.** – Schmeichel; Neville (G.), Bruce (Giggs), Pallister, Irwin, Butt, Keane, Ince, Sharpe (Scholes), McClair, Hughes. **Scorer:** Everton – Rideout.

1996 MANCHESTER UTD. – Schmeichel; Irwin, May, Pallister, Neville (P.), Beckham (Neville, G.), Keane, Butt, Giggs, Cantona, Cole (Scholes). **LIVERPOOL** – James; McAteer, Scales, Wright, Babb, Jones (Thomas), McManaman, Redknapp, Barnes, Collymore (Rush), Fowler. **Scorer:** Manchester Utd. – Cantona.

1997 CHELSEA – Grodas; Sinclair, Lebouef, Clarke, Minto, Petrescu, Di Matteo, Newton, Wise, Zola (Vialli), Hughes (M.). **MIDDLESBROUGH** – Roberts; Blackmore, Pearson, Festa, Fleming, Stamp, Emerson, Mustoe (Vickers), Hignett (Kinder), Juninho, Ravanelli, (Beck). **Scorers:** Chelsea – Di Matteo, Newton.

1998 ARSENAL – Seaman; Dixon, Adams, Keown, Winterburn, Parlour, Petit, Vieira, Overmars, Wreh (Platt), Anelka. **NEWCASTLE** – Given; Barton (Watson), Dabizas, Howey, Pearce (Andersson), Pistone, Batty, Lee, Speed, Shearer, Ketsbaia (Barnes). **Scorers:** Arsenal – Overmars, Anelka.

1999 MANCHESTER UTD. – Schmeichel; Neville (G.), Johnsen, May, Neville (P.); Beckham, Scholes (Stam), Keane (Sheringham), Giggs; Cole (Yorke), Solskjaer. **NEWCASTLE UTD.** – Harper; Griffin, Charvet, Dabizas, Domi; Lee, Hamann (Ferguson), Speed, Solano (Maric); Ketsbaia (Glass), Shearer. **Scorers:** Manchester Utd. – Sheringham, Scholes.

2000 CHELSEA – De Goey; Melchiot, Desailly, Lebouef, Babayaro, Di Matteo, Wise, Deschamps, Poyet, Weah (Flo), Zola (Morris). **ASTON VILLA** – James; Ehiogu, Southgate, Barry, Delaney. Taylor (Stone), Boateng, Merson, Wright (Hendrie), Dublin, Carbone (Joachim). **Scorer:** Chelsea – Di Matteo.

2001 LIVERPOOL – Westerveld; Babbel, Henchoz, Hyypia, Carragher, Murphy (Berger), Hamann (McAllister), Gerrard, Smicer (Fowler), Heskey, Owen. **ARSENAL** – Seaman; Dixon (Bergkamp), Keown, Adams, Cole, Ljungberg (Kanu), Grimandi, Vieira, Pires, Henry, Wiltord (Parlour). **Scorers:** Liverpool – Owen 2, Arsenal – Ljungberg.

2002 ARSENAL – Seaman; Lauren, Campbell, Adams, Cole, Wiltord (Keown), Parlour, Vieira, Ljungberg, Bergkamp (Edu), Henry (Kanu). **CHELSEA** – Cudicini; Melchiot, Desailly, Gallas, Babayaro (Terry), Gronkjaer, Lampard, Petit, Le Saux, Hasselbaink (Zola), Gudjohnsen. **Scorers:** Arsenal – Parlour, Ljungberg.

F.A. CUP FINALS – COMPLETE RESULTS

AT KENNINGTON OVAL
1872   The Wanderers beat Royal Engineers (1-0)

AT LILLIE BRIDGE, LONDON
1873   The Wanderers beat Oxford University (2-1)

AT KENNINGTON OVAL
1874   Oxford University beat Royal Engineers (2-0)
1875   Royal Engineers beat Old Etonians (2-0 after a 1-1 draw)
1876   The Wanderers beat Old Etonians (3-0 after a 0-0 draw)
1877††   The Wanderers beat Oxford University (2-1)
1878*   The Wanderers beat Royal Engineers (3-1)
1879   Old Etonians beat Clapham Rov. (1-0)
1880   Clapham Rov. beat Oxford University (1-0)
1881   Old Carthusians beat Old Etonians (3-0)
1882   Old Etonians beat Blackburn Rov. (1-0)
1883††   Blackburn Olympic beat Old Etonians (2-1)
1884   Blackburn Rov. beat Queen's Park (Glasgow) (2-1)
1885   Blackburn Rov. beat Queen's Park (Glasgow) (2-0)
1886†a   Blackburn Rov. beat W.B.A. (2-0 after a 0-0 draw)
1887   Aston Villa beat W.B.A. (2-0)
1888   W.B.A. beat Preston N.E. (2-1)
1889   Preston N.E. beat Wolves (3-0)
1890   Blackburn Rov. beat Sheffield Wed. (6-1)
1891   Blackburn Rov. beat Notts Co. (3-1)
1892   W.B.A. beat Aston Villa (3-0)

AT FALLOWFIELD, MANCHESTER
1893   Wolves beat Everton (1-0)

AT GOODISON PARK
1894   Notts Co. beat Bolton Wand. (4-1)

AT CRYSTAL PALACE
1895   Aston Villa beat W.B.A. (1-0)
1896   Sheffield Wed. beat Wolves (2-1)
1897   Aston Villa beat Everton (3-2)
1898   Nott'm. Forest beat Derby Co. (3-1)
1899   Sheffield Utd. beat Derby Co. (4-1)
1900   Bury beat Southampton (4-0)
1901††† Tottenham beat Sheffield Utd. (3-1 after a 2-2 draw)
1902   Sheffield Utd. beat Southampton (2-1 after a 1-1 draw)
1903   Bury beat Derby Co. (6-0)
1904   Manchester City beat Bolton Wand. (1-0)
1905   Aston Villa beat Newcastle Utd. (2-0)
1906   Everton beat Newcastle Utd. (1-0)
1907   Sheffield Wed. beat Everton (2-1)
1908   Wolves beat Newcastle Utd. (3-1)
1909   Manchester Utd. beat Bristol City (1-0)
1910** Newcastle Utd. beat Barnsley (2-0 after a 1-1 draw)
1911b   Bradford City beat Newcastle Utd. (1-0 after a 0-0 draw)
1912c   Barnsley beat W.B.A. (1-0 after a 0-0 draw)
1913   Aston Villa beat Sunderland (1-0)
1914   Burnley beat Liverpool (1-0)

AT OLD TRAFFORD
1915   Sheffield Utd. beat Chelsea (3-0)

AT STAMFORD BRIDGE
1920††   Aston Villa beat Huddersfield Town (1-0)
1921   Tottenham beat Wolves (1-0)
1922   Huddersfield Town beat Preston N.E. (1-0)

AT WEMBLEY
1923   Bolton Wand. beat West Ham Utd. (2-0)
1924   Newcastle Utd. beat Aston Villa (2-0)
1925   Sheffield Utd. beat Cardiff City (1-0)
1926   Bolton Wand. beat Manchester City (1-0)
1927   Cardiff City beat Arsenal (1-0)
1928   Blackburn Rov. beat Huddersfield Town (3-1)
1929   Bolton Wand. beat Portsmouth (2-0)
1930   Arsenal beat Huddersfield Town (2-0)
1931   W.B.A. beat Birmingham City (2-1)
1932   Newcastle Utd. beat Arsenal (2-1)
1933   Everton beat Manchester City (3-0)
1934   Manchester City beat Portsmouth (2-1)
1935   Sheffield Wed. beat W.B.A. (4-2)
1936   Arsenal beat Sheffield Utd. (1-0)
1937   Sunderland beat Preston N.E. (3-1)
1938††   Preston N.E. beat Huddersfield Town (1-0)
1939   Portsmouth beat Wolves (4-1)
1946††   Derby Co. beat Charlton Athletic (4-1)
1947††   Charlton Athletic beat Burnley (1-0)
1948   Manchester Utd. beat Blackpool (4-2)
1949   Wolves beat Leicester City (3-1)
1950   Arsenal beat Liverpool (2-0)
1951   Newcastle Utd. beat Blackpool (2-0)
1952   Newcastle Utd. beat Arsenal (1-0)
1953   Blackpool beat Bolton Wand. (4-3)
1954   W.B.A. beat Preston N.E. (3-2)
1955   Newcastle Utd. beat Manchester City (3-1)
1956   Manchester City beat Birmingham City (3-1)
1957   Aston Villa beat Manchester Utd. (2-1)
1958   Bolton Wand. beat Manchester Utd. (2-0)
1959   Nott'm. Forest beat Luton Town (2-1)
1960   Wolves beat Blackburn Rov. (3-0)
1961   Tottenham beat Leicester City (2-0)
1962   Tottenham beat Burnley (3-1)
1963   Manchester Utd. beat Leicester City (3-1)
1964   West Ham Utd. beat Preston N.E. (3-2)
1965††   Liverpool beat Leeds Utd. (2-1)
1966   Everton beat Sheffield Wed. (3-2)
1967   Tottenham beat Chelsea (2-1)
1968††   W.B.A. beat Everton (1-0)
1969   Manchester City beat Leicester City (1-0)
1970††•   Chelsea beat Leeds Utd. (2-1 after a 2-2 draw)
1971††   Arsenal beat Liverpool (2-1)
1972   Leeds Utd. beat Arsenal (1-0)
1973   Sunderland beat Leeds Utd. (1-0)
1974   Liverpool beat Newcastle Utd. (3-0)
1975   West Ham Utd. beat Fulham (2-0)

1976	Southampton beat Manchester Utd. (1-0)
1977	Manchester Utd. beat Liverpool (2-1)
1978	Ipswich Town beat Arsenal (1-0)
1979	Arsenal beat Manchester Utd. (3-2)
1980	West Ham Utd. beat Arsenal (1-0)
1981	Tottenham beat Manchester City (3-2 after a 1-1 draw)
1982	Tottenham beat Q.P.R. (1-0 after a 1-1 draw)
1983	Manchester Utd. beat Brighton & H.A. (4-0 after a 2-2 draw)
1984	Everton beat Watford (2-0)
1985††	Manchester Utd. beat Everton (1-0)
1986	Liverpool beat Everton (3-1)
1987††	Coventry City beat Tottenham (3-2)
1988	Wimbledon beat Liverpool (1-0)
1989††	Liverpool beat Everton (3-2)
1990	Manchester Utd. beat Crystal Palace (1-0 after a 3-3 draw)
1991††	Tottenham beat Nott'm. Forest (2-1)
1992	Liverpool beat Sunderland (2-0)
1993††	Arsenal beat Sheffield Wed. (2-1 after a 1-1 draw)
1994	Manchester Utd. beat Chelsea (4-0)
1995	Everton beat Manchester Utd. (1-0)
1996	Manchester Utd. beat Liverpool (1-0)
1997	Chelsea beat Middlesbrough (2-0)
1998	Arsenal beat Newcastle Utd. (2-0)
1999	Manchester Utd. beat Newcastle Utd. (2-0)
2000	Chelsea beat Aston Villa (1-0)

AT MILLENNIUM STADIUM

2001	Liverpool beat Arsenal (2-1)
2002	Arsenal beat Chelsea (2-0)

†† After extra time. * Won outright but restored to the Association. a Replayed at Baseball Ground, Derby Co. † A special trophy was awarded for the third consecutive win. ††† Replayed at Burnden Park, Bolton Wand. ** Replayed at Goodison Park, Liverpool. b Replayed at Old Trafford, Manchester, new trophy provided. c Replayed at Bramall Lane, Sheffield. • Replayed at Old Trafford.
(All replays since 1981 played at Wembley.)

SUMMARY OF F.A. CUP WINS

Manchester Utd.	10	Chelsea	3	Charlton Athletic	1
Arsenal	8	Sheffield Wed.	3	Clapham Rov.	1
Tottenham	8	West Ham Utd.	3	Coventry City	1
Aston Villa	7	Bury	2	Derby Co.	1
Blackburn Rov.	6	Nott'm Forest	2	Huddersfield Town	1
Liverpool	6	Old Etonians	2	Ipswich Town	1
Newcastle Utd.	6	Preston N.E.	2	Leeds Utd.	1
Everton	5	Sunderland	2	Notts Co.	1
The Wanderers	5	Barnsley	1	Old Carthusians	1
W.B.A.	5	Blackburn Olympic	1	Oxford University	1
Bolton Wand.	4	Blackpool	1	Portsmouth	1
Manchester City	4	Bradford City	1	Royal Engineers	1
Sheffield Utd.	4	Burnley	1	Southampton	1
Wolves	4	Cardiff City	1	Wimbledon	1

APPEARANCES IN FINALS

(Figures do not include replays)

Arsenal	15	The Wanderers*	5	Clapham Rov.	2
Manchester Utd.	15	Derby Co.	4	Notts Co.	2
Newcastle Utd.	13	Leeds Utd.	4	Queen's Park (Glas.)	2
Everton	12	Leicester City	4	Blackburn Olympic*	1
Liverpool	12	Oxford University	4	Bradford City*	1
Aston Villa	10	Royal Engineers	4	Brighton & H.A.	1
W.B.A.	10	Sunderland	4	Bristol City	1
Tottenham	9	West Ham Utd.	4	Coventry City*	1
Blackburn Rov.	8	Blackpool	3	Crystal Palace	1
Manchester City	8	Burnley	3	Fulham	1
Wolves	8	Nott'm Forest	3	Ipswich Town*	1
Bolton Wand.	7	Portsmouth	3	Luton Town	1
Chelsea	7	Southampton	3	Middlesbrough	1
Preston N.E.	7	Barnsley	2	Old Carthusians*	1
Old Etonians	6	Birmingham City	2	Q.P.R.	1
Sheffield Utd.	6	Bury*	2	Watford	1
Sheffield Wed.	6	Cardiff City	2	Wimbledon*	1
Huddersfield Town	5	Charlton Athletic	2	(* Denotes undefeated)	

APPEARANCES IN SEMI-FINALS

(Figures do not include replays)

Everton 23, Arsenal 22, Manchester Utd. 22, Liverpool 21, Aston Villa 19, W.B.A. 19, Tottenham 17, Blackburn Rov. 16, Newcastle Utd. 16, Sheffield Wed. 16, Chelsea 15, Wolves 14, Bolton Wand. 13, Derby Co. Co. 13, Nott'm Forest 12, Sheffield Utd. 12, Sunderland 11, Manchester City 10, Preston N.E. 10, Southampton 10, Birmingham City 9, Burnley 8, Leeds Utd. 8, Huddersfield Town 7, Leicester City 7, Fulham 6, Old Etonians 6, Oxford University 6, West Ham Utd. 6, Notts Co. 5, Portsmouth 5, The Wanderers 5, Luton Town 4, Queen's Park (Glasgow) 4, Royal Engineers 4, Blackpool 3, Cardiff City 3, Clapham Rov. 3, *Crystal Palace 3, Ipswich Town 3, Millwall 3, Norwich City 3, Old Carthusians 3, Oldham Athletic 3, Stoke City 3, The Swifts 3, Watford 3, Barnsley 2, Blackburn Olympic 2, Bristol City 2, Bury 2, Charlton Athletic 2, Grimsby Town 2, Middlesbrough 2, Swansea City Town 2, Swindon Town 2, Wimbledon 2, Bradford City 1, Brighton & H.A. 1, Cambridge University 1, Chesterfield 1, Coventry City 1, Crewe Alexandra 1, Darwen 1, Derby Co. Junction 1, Hull City 1, Marlow 1, Old Harrovians 1, Orient 1, Plymouth Argyle 1, Port Vale 1, Q.P.R. 1, Rangers (Glasgow) 1, Reading 1, Shropshire Wand. 1, Wycombe Wand. 1, York City 1.

(*A previous and different Crystal Palace club also reached the semi-final in season 1871-72)

QUOTE UNQUOTE

'The clubs say it's sabre-rattling, a bluff about market forces. We say it's about people's lives' – **Gordon Taylor**, chief executive of the PFA, after his members voted 99 per cent for strike action in a dispute about television money.

'They are not so much killing the goose that laid the golden egg as tearing out its entrails and throwing them on the field of dreams' – **Barry Hearn**, Leyton Orient chairman.

'Gordon Taylor is becoming increasingly like Arthur Scargill and if he's not careful he'll end up like Arthur Scargill' – **Ken Bates**, Chelsea chairman.

'It's just like winning the F.A. Cup' – **Gordon Taylor** after agreeing a £175m., 10-year deal with the Premier and Nationwide Leagues.

FOOTBALL'S CHANGING HOMES

Plans have advanced for six Premiership clubs to build new stadiums. **Arsenal** received approval from Islington Council for a £250m., 60,000-capacity ground at Ashburton Grove, half-a-mile from Highbury, scheduled to open in August, 2004.

Everton are aiming to have their 55,000-seater all-events stadium in the city's prestigious Kings Dock ready for the beginning of the 2005-06 season. One of the aims is to be able to stage a major entertainment event hours before a Premiership match.

Liverpool unveiled their plans to leave Anfield and move to nearby Stanley Park for 2005-06. Original plans for an arena holding 70,000 were shelved when costs were estimated to exceed £120m. Instead, it will cost up to £70m. and seat 55,000.

Leeds United announced their intention to leave Elland Road for a 50,000-capacity stadium on the outskirts of the city for 2004-05.

Fulham will share Loftus Road with Q.P.R. for the next two seasons while Craven Cottage is redeveloped at a cost of £70m. **Manchester City**, meanwhile, are starting their final season at Maine Road before switching to the City of Manchester Stadium, built for the Commonwealth Games.

Anxious not to be left behind by their North London neighbours, **Tottenham** have plans to rebuild the West Stand and extend the East Stand to reach a capacity of between 50,000 and 60,000. But worries about whether the transport infrastructure can cope may persuade the club to think about moving from White Hart Lane.

Wimbledon, given permission to relocate to Milton Keynes, will continue to share Selhurst Park with **Crystal Palace** this season after plans for a temporary home at the National Hockey Stadium fell through. The club hope to have a new 30,000-capacity ground ready for 2003-04.

Promoted as champions for the last two seasons, **Brighton and Hove Albion** have the backing of local councillors for a £44m. stadium, seating 22,000 at Falmer, to be ready for 2004-05.

Relegated **Leicester City** start the season in new surroundings – the 32,000-seater, £35m. Walkers Stadium a stone's throw from Filbert Street, their home for 111 years. The club agreed to change the original name, the Walkers Bowl, because of local opposition.

Scaled-down plans for a new ground holding 32,000 – 13,000 fewer than originally intended – moved forward for **Coventry City** when the City Council and partners Advantage West Midlands teamed up to buy the former Foleshill gas works site near the M6.

With **Bristol City** and **Bristol Rovers** both wanting bigger capacities, the City Council has looked at a number of possible sites for a £40m., 40,000-capacity stadium which could also house the local rugby club.

Promoted **Luton Town** want to leave cramped Kenilworth Road, while **Brentford** hope to sell Griffin Park and move, possibly to Feltham.

Owner George Reynolds has a declared ambition to take **Darlington** from Division Three to the Premiership. He has paid for a £20m., 25,000 all-seater stadium, but the club will kick-off 2002-03 still at Feethams. The new ground could be ready by mid-season.

Hull City are also ambitious and their new Kingston Communications Stadium is scheduled for completion in December 2002. It is costing £43m., will house the city's football and rugby clubs and other facilities include an indoor sports centre, library and skate park.

Motor racing magnate John Batchelor, who took over **York City** last season when the club's future was under threat, insists that a move away from Bootham Crescent is crucial to continued survival. He has unveiled plans for a new, multi-purpose use ground.

Swansea City, another under-pressure club confident of a brighter future with a new Board, aim to move to the new Morfa Stadium in September 2003.

BLACKBURN'S FIRST MAJOR TROPHY FOR 74 YEARS

SECOND ROUND	THIRD ROUND	FOURTH ROUND	FIFTH ROUND	SEMI-FINALS	FINAL
*Tottenham 2	Tottenham 4	Tottenham 2	*Tottenham 6	Tottenham 1:5	Tottenham 1
Torquay Utd. 0	*Tranmere Rov. 0	*Fulham 1	Bolton Wand. 0	*Chelsea 2:1	
*Tranmere Rov. 4	*Fulham 5	*Bolton Wand. ...... †H2	*Chelsea 1		
Preston N.E. 1	Derby Co. 2	Southampton 2	Newcastle Utd. 0		
*Rochdale 2	*Bolton Wand. 1	Chelsea 2			
Fulham ...... †A2	Nott'm. Forest 0	*Leeds Utd. 0			
*Derby Co. 3	Southampton 2	*Newcastle Utd. 4			
Hull City 0	*Gillingham 0	Ipswich Town 1			
*Bolton Wand. ...... †4	Chelsea 2				
Walsall 3	*Coventry City 0				
*Nott'm. Forest .... †B1	Leeds Utd. 6				
Stockport Co. 1	*Leicester City 0				
*Brighton & H.A. ... 0	Newcastle Utd. 1				
Southampton 3	*Barnsley 0				
*Gillingham 0	Ipswich Town 3				
Millwall 1	*Crewe Alexandra 2				
Chelsea 2					
*Peterborough Utd. ... 2					
Coventry City ...... †C2					
● Bye					
Leeds Utd. 6					
*Leicester City 0					
● Bye					
*Blackpool 0					
Leicester City 1					
*Newcastle Utd. .... †4					
Brentford 1					
*Colchester Utd. 1					
Barnsley 0					
● Bye					
Ipswich Town 3					
*Crewe Alexandra ... †2					
Rushden & Diamonds . 0					

Round 1

- *Sheffield Wed. ..... †4
- Sunderland 2
- *Everton 1
- Crystal Palace ..... †D1
- ● Bye
- *Reading ..... †E0
- West Ham Utd. 0
- *Bristol City 2
- Watford 4
- *Rotherham Utd. 3
- Bradford City 4
- *Charlton Athletic 1
- Port Vale 0
- *W.B.A. ..... †2
- Swindon Town 0
- ● Bye
- ● Bye
- *Grimsby Town ..... †F3
- Sheffield Utd. 3
- ● Bye
- *Notts Co. 2
- Manchester City ..... †4
- *Bristol Rov. 3
- Birmingham City 0
- *Middlesbrough 1
- Northampton Town 1
- *Oldham Athletic 2
- *Blackburn Rov. ..... †2

Round 2

- *Sheffield Wed. ..... †G2
- Crystal Palace 2
- *Aston Villa 1
- Reading 0
- Watford ..... †3
- Bradford City 1
- Charlton Athletic 1
- *W.B.A. 0
- *Arsenal 4
- Manchester Utd. 0
- *Grimsby Town ..... †2
- *Liverpool 0
- *Manchester City 6
- Birmingham City 0
- Middlesbrough 1
- *Blackburn Rov. 2

Round 3

- Sheffield Wed. 1
- *Aston Villa 4
- *Watford 0
- Charlton Athletic 2
- *Arsenal 0
- Grimsby Town 0
- Manchester City 0
- *Blackburn Rov. 4

Round 4

- *Sheffield Wed. 4
- Watford 0
- Arsenal 0
- Blackburn Rov. 2:4

Semi-finals

- *Sheffield Wed. 1:2
- Blackburn Rov. 2

Final

- Blackburn Rov. 2

* Drawn at home; in semi-finals drawn at home in first leg. † After extra-time. A – Fulham won 6-5 on pens. B – Nott'm. Forest won 8-7 on pens. C – Coventry City won 4-2 on pens. D – Crystal Palace won 5-4 on pens. E – Reading won 6-5 on pens. F – Grimsby Town won 4-2 on pens. G – Sheffield Wed. won 3-1 on pens. H – Bolton Wand. won 6-5 on pens.

WORTHINGTON CUP 2001-02

FIRST ROUND

Barnsley 2, Halifax Town 0; Birmingham City 3, Southend Utd. 0; Blackpool 3, Wigan Athletic 2; Bournemouth 0, Torquay Utd. 2; Brentford 1, Norwich City 0; Brighton & H.A. 2, Wimbledon 1; Bristol City 2, Cheltenham Town 1; Burnley 2, Rushden & Diamonds 3; Bury 1, Sheffield Wed. 3; Cambridge Utd. 1, W.B.A. 1 (aet W.B.A. won 4-3 on pens); Darlington 0, Sheffield Utd. 1; Exeter City 0, Walsall 1; Grimsby Town 2, Lincoln City 1; Hartlepool Utd. 0, Nott'm. Forest 2; Huddersfield Town 0, Rochdale 1; Kidderminster Harriers 2, Preston N.E. 3 (aet); Leyton Orient 2, Crystal Palace 4; Macclesfield Town 1, Bradford City 2 (aet); Mansfield Town 3, Notts Co. 4; Millwall 2, Cardiff City 1; Northampton Town 2, Q.P.R. 1 (aet); Oxford Utd. 1, Gillingham 2 (aet); Port Vale 2, Chesterfield 1; Portsmouth 1, Colchester Utd. 2; Reading 4, Luton Town 0; Scunthorpe Utd. 0, Rotherham Utd. 2; Stockport Co. 3, Carlisle Utd. 0; Stoke City 0, Oldham Athletic 0 (aet, Oldham Athletic won 6-5 on pens); Swansea City 0, Peterborough Utd. 2; Tranmere Rov. 3, Shrewsbury Town 1; Watford 1, Plymouth Argyle 0; Wolves 1, Swindon Town 2; Wrexham 2, Hull City 3; Wycombe Wand. 0, Bristol Rov. 1; York City 2, Crewe Alexandra 2 (aet, Crewe Alexandra won 6-5 on pens).

WORTHINGTON CUP FINAL

BLACKBURN ROVERS 2, TOTTENHAM 1

Millennium Stadium, (72,500), Sunday, February 24, 2002

Blackburn Rov. (4-4-2): Friedel, Taylor, Berg, Johansson, Bjornebye, Gillespie (Hignett 77); Hughes, Dunn, Duff, Cole, Jansen (Yordi 74). **Subs not used:** Miller, Curtis, Mahon. **Scorers:** Jansen (25), Cole (69).

Tottenham (3-5-2): Sullivan, King, Perry, Thatcher, Taricco (Davies 78), Anderton, Sherwood, Poyet (Iversen 83), Ziege, Sheringham, Ferdinand. **Subs not used:** Keller, Gardner, Rebrov. **Scorer:** Ziege (33). **Booked:** Sherwood, Taricco, Ziege.

Referee: G.Poll (Tring). **Half-time:** 1-1. **Man-of-the-match:** Brad Friedel.

FULL SET FOR COLE AS THE UNDERDOGS PREVAIL

If nothing else, this match was a statistician's delight – the first domestic final to be played indoors; Blackburn Rovers' first major trophy for 74 years; Andy Cole completing a full set of winners' medals; an American goalkeeper winning the man-of-the-match award. In the event, it produced much more under the closed roof of the Millennium Stadium – an entertaining, absorbing affair in which Rovers upset the odds with a 69th minute goal by Cole.

Signed from Manchester United for £7.5m. two months earlier with Blackburn already through the semi-finals, Cole completed a mistake by Ledley King to add to his Premiership, F.A. Cup and Champions League honours gained at Old Trafford.

Tottenham were left protesting – with some justification – about Graham Poll's refusal to award a late penalty when Teddy Sheringham went down under the challenge of Nils-Eric Johansson, although Sheringham certainly made the most of his fall. They also pointed to a shot from Gustavo Poyet which struck the angle of post and crossbar.

What was beyond any argument was the fact that too many of their players had an off-day, most significantly Les Ferdinand whose touch in front of goal deserted him. Brad Friedel certainly deserved the man-of-the-match award, yet Ferdinand knew he should have done better with two close-range headers and a one-on-one with the goalkeeper. How ironic that manager Glenn Hoddle, during his time in charge of England, had maintained that Cole 'needed five chances to score a goal.'

Rovers made more of fewer openings, Matt Jansen putting them ahead on 25 minutes when Keith Gillespie's shot was deflected into his path off Ben Thatcher and so finishing as the competition's leading scorer on six. Christian Ziege equalised eight minutes later after Poyet released Ferdinand to cross low to the far post. But Tottenham failed to build on the impetus of the goal and in the end paid the price for their overall failings.

The final was also notable for two splendid touches by the Rovers manager Graeme Souness. He insisted that Tony Parkes lead the team out, a gesture to mark Parkes's 32 years as a player, coach and occasional caretaker manager at Ewood Park.

Then, as his side celebrated, Souness pushed 38-year-old Mark Hughes to the head of the queue for medals, rewarding the midfield contribution of the Wales manager who was a surprise choice to start the game and an even bigger surprise to finish it.

HOW THEY REACHED THE FINAL

BLACKBURN ROVERS

Round 2: 2-0 home to Oldham Athletic (Jansen, Dunning)
Round 3: 2-1 (aet) home to Middlesbrough (Hignett, Short)
Round 4: 2-0 home to Manchester City (Johansson, Johnson)
Round 5: 4-0 home to Arsenal (Jansen 3, Hughes)
Semi-finals: v Sheffield Wed. – first leg 2-1 away (Hignett, Cole); second leg 4-2 home (Jansen, Duff, Cole, Hignett)

TOTTENHAM

Round 2: 2-0 home to Torquay Utd. (King, Ferdinand)
Round 3: 4-0 away to Tranmere Rov. (Sheringham pen, Anderton, Poyet, Rebrov)
Round 4: 2-1 away to Fulham (Rebrov, Davies)
Round 5: 6-0 home to Bolton Wand. (Ferdinand 3, Davies, Iversen, Barness og)
Semi-finals: v Chelsea – first leg, 1-2 away (Ferdinand); second leg 5-1 home (Iversen, Sherwood, Sheringham, Davies, Rebrov)

LEADING SCORERS

6 – Jansen (Blackburn Rov.)
5 – Ekoku (Sheffield Wed.), Ferdinand (Tottenham), Huckerby (Manchester City)
4 – Allsopp (Notts Co.), Bellamy (Newcastle Utd.), Wiltord (Arsenal)
3 – Cole (Blackburn Rov.), Davies (Tottenham), Dyer (Barnsley), Gudjohnsen (Chelsea), Hasselbaink (Chelsea), Hignett (Blackburn Rov.), Keane (Leeds Utd.), Ormerod (Blackpool), Rebrov (Tottenham), Taylor (Stockport Co.).

RECORD SUM FOR PELE WORLD CUP SHIRT

A record £157,750 was paid for the No 10 shirt worn by Pele in the 1970 World Cup Final when it was auctioned at Christie's. It had been expected to go for about £50,000. The anonymous telephone bid overtook the £91,750 paid for Sir Geoff Hurst's 1966 World Cup-winning shirt. It also surpassed the £124,750 which netted the winners' medal of Hurst's team-mate Gordon Banks.

LEAGUE CUP – COMPLETE RESULTS

LEAGUE CUP FINALS

1961*   Aston Villa beat Rotherham Utd. 3-2 on agg. (0-2a, 3-0h)
1962   Norwich City beat Rochdale 4-0 on agg. (3-0a, 1-0h)
1963   Birmingham City beat Aston Villa 3-1 on agg. (3-1h, 0-0a)
1964   Leicester City beat Stoke City 4-3 on agg. (1-1a, 3-2h)
1965   Chelsea beat Leicester City 3-2 on agg. (3-2h, 0-0a)
1966   W.B.A. beat West Ham Utd. 5-3 on agg. (1-2a, 4-1h)

AT WEMBLEY

1967   Q.P.R. beat W.B.A. (3-2)
1968   Leeds Utd. beat Arsenal (1-0)
1969*   Swindon Town beat Arsenal (3-1)
1970*   Manchester City beat W.B.A. (2-1)
1971   Tottenham beat Aston Villa (2-0)
1972   Stoke City beat Chelsea (2-1)
1973   Tottenham beat Norwich City (1-0)
1974   Wolves beat Manchester City (2-1)
1975   Aston Villa beat Norwich City (1-0)
1976   Manchester City beat Newcastle Utd. (2-1)
1977†*   Aston Villa beat Everton (3-2 after 0-0 and 1-1 draws)
1978††   Nott'm. Forest beat Liverpool (1-0 after 0-0 draw)
1979   Nott'm. Forest beat Southampton (3-2)
1980   Wolves beat Nott'm. Forest (1-0)
1981††† Liverpool beat West Ham Utd. (2-1 after 1-1 draw)

MILK CUP

1982*   Liverpool beat Tottenham (3-1)
1983*   Liverpool beat Manchester Utd. (2-1)
1984**   Liverpool beat Everton (1-0 after *0-0 draw)
1985   Norwich City beat Sunderland (1-0)
1986   Oxford Utd. beat Q.P.R. (3-0)

LITTLEWOODS CUP

1987   Arsenal beat Liverpool (2-1)
1988   Luton Town beat Arsenal (3-2)
1989   Nott'm. Forest beat Luton Town (3-1)
1990   Nott'm. Forest beat Oldham Athletic (1-0)

RUMBELOWS CUP

1991   Sheffield Wed. beat Manchester Utd. (1-0)
1992   Manchester Utd. beat Nott'm. Forest (1-0)

COCA-COLA CUP

1993   Arsenal beat Sheffield Wed. (2-1)
1994   Aston Villa beat Manchester Utd. (3-1)
1995   Liverpool beat Bolton Wand. (2-1)
1996   Aston Villa beat Leeds Utd. (3-0)
1997   Leicester City beat Middlesbrough (*1-0 after *1-1 draw) ★
1998   Chelsea beat Middlesbrough (2-0)

WORTHINGTON CUP (AT MILLENNIUM STADIUM FROM 2001)

1999   Tottenham beat Leicester City (1-0)
2000   Leicester City beat Tranmere Rov. (2-1)
2001   Liverpool beat Birmingham City (5-4 on pens after *1-1 draw)
2002   Blackburn Rov. beat Tottenham (2-1)

* After extra time. † First replay at Hillsborough, second replay at Old Trafford. ††
Replayed at Old Trafford. ††† Replayed at Aston Villa Park. ** Replayed at Maine
Road. ★ Replayed at Hillsborough

SUMMARY OF LEAGUE CUP WINNERS

Liverpool 6	Manchester City 2	Manchester Utd. 1
Aston Villa 5	Norwich City 2	Oxford Utd. 1
Nott'm. Forest 4	Wolves 2	Q.P.R. 1
Leicester City 3	Blackburn Rov. 1	Sheffield Wed. 1
Tottenham 3	Birmingham City 1	Stoke City 1
Arsenal 2	Leeds Utd. 1	Swindon Town 1
Chelsea 2	Luton Town 1	W.B.A. 1

LEAGUE CUP FINAL APPEARANCES

8 Liverpool; **7** Aston Villa; **6** Nott'm. Forest; **5** Arsenal, Leicester City, Tottenham; **4**
Manchester Utd., Norwich City; **3** Chelsea, Manchester City, W.B.A.; **2** Birmingham City,
Everton, Leeds Utd., Luton Town, Middlesbrough, Q.P.R., Sheffield Wed., Stoke City,
West Ham Utd., Wolves; **1** Blackburn Rov., Bolton Wand., Newcastle Utd., Oldham
Athletic, Oxford Utd., Rochdale, Rotherham Utd., Southampton, Sunderland, Swindon
Town, Tranmere Rov. **(Figures do not include replays).**

LEAGUE CUP SEMI-FINAL APPEARANCES

11 Aston Villa, Liverpool; **10** Tottenham; **9** Arsenal; **7** Chelsea, Manchester Utd., West
Ham Utd.; **6** Nott'm. Forest; **5** Leeds Utd., Leicester City, Manchester City, Norwich
City; **4** Birmingham City, Middlesbrough, Sheffield Wed., W.B.A.; **3** Blackburn Rov.,
Bolton Wand., Burnley, Crystal Palace, Everton, Ipswich Town, Q.P.R., Sunderland,
Swindon Town, Wolves; **2** Bristol City, Coventry City, Luton Town, Oxford Utd., Plymouth
Argyle, Southampton, Stoke City, Tranmere Rov., Wimbledon; **1** Blackpool, Bury, Cardiff
City, Carlisle Utd., Chester City, Derby Co., Huddersfield Town, Newcastle Utd., Oldham
Athletic, Peterborough, Rochdale, Rotherham Utd., Shrewsbury Town, Stockport Co.,
Walsall, Watford. **(Figures do not include replays).**

LONG-PLAYING FORD CALLS IT A DAY

Tony Ford, one of football's finest servants, brought the curtain down on a career
spanning 27 seasons after making his 931st League appearance in Rochdale's 2-0
home win over Torquay United. He was still going strong in the Third Division, having
been an ever-present up to that point of the campaign in early November. But when
manager Steve Parkin took his assistant with him to Barnsley following the dismissal of
Nigel Spackman, 42-year-old Ford recognised that playing at the higher level was
beyond him. His career began in the 1975-76 season with home-town club Grimsby
Town and took in Sunderland on loan, Stoke City (£35,000), W.B.A. (£145,000), back
to Grimsby (£50,000), Bradford City on loan and then free transfers to Scunthorpe
Utd., Mansfield Town and Rochdale. He scored 108 League goals and made a further
141 appearances (13 goals) in other competitions. Ford won the Division Three
championship with Grimsby in 1980, played in two England B internationals on a tour
of Scandinavia in 1989 and received the MBE for services to football in the 2000 New
Year's Honours List. Only Peter Shilton (1,005 League appearances, 1387 overall) can
better his record.

IT'S NEW THIS SEASON

End-of-season play-offs have been introduced by the **Nationwide Conference** after a decision to increase promotion and relegation with the **Football League** to two teams. The Conference champions go automatically into the Third Division and the next four will contest a knock-out format along the lines of the system in Divisions One, Two and Three.

The change, which received overwhelming backing at the League's Annual General Meeting, was made possible by a funding package worth £6m. agreed with the **F.A.** It means all Division Three clubs will receive £50,000 at the start of the next five seasons as a compensatory payment for the increased likelihood of losing League status. The two promoted clubs will receive £35,000, while 'parachute' payments will be made to the two relegated clubs for one season.

David Burns, the League's chief executive said: 'Twelve months earlier this step was rejected because of the absence of a suitable financial package. This is no longer the case. The Conference has been a national league for over twenty years, with crowds now averaging over 1,500. There is no doubt that this extra promotion place will enable it to enhance its appeal and this can only be good for football as a whole.'

John Moules, chief executive of the Conference, said: 'A lot of hard work has now come to fruition. For our clubs and supporters, this landmark decision brings their dreams to fruition. Over the past two to three seasons, supporters around the country have seen, through our clubs' F.A. Cup exploits, just how far standards of players and facilities have improved. Along with future **F.A.** plans for the restructuring of the national leagues' system, a whole new avenue of opportunity has opened up for players in English football.'

The **League**'s AGM also approved major changes to the loan system in a move aimed at helping clubs share the burden of escalating player costs and increasing the scope for player development. They will still be able to take eight players on short-term loan during the season. But the number permitted at any one time rises from two to four, the limit for long-term loans increases from two to four months and so does the maximum number that can be taken from one club (short and long term). A maximum of five loan players (short and long term) can now be included in the 16 listed on the team sheet on match day.

The **Conference** will fall in line with the **League** and the **Premiership** by having squad numbers. The 2002-03 season will also see the F.A. Cup Final back in its traditional place on the last Saturday of the domestic season. For the last two years it has been followed by a **Premiership** programme.

Law-makers underlined their determination to crack down on divers and cheats when the **International Board**'s annual meeting in Zermatt, Switzerland, backed **FIFA's** call to referees at the World Cup to deal firmly with players seeking an unfair advantage by pretending to be fouled. After the previous year's decision to clear players to remove their shirts when celebrating a goal – providing there was no provocation or time-wasting – the Board expressed concern that some were taking advantage to display advertising slogans or political and religious messages. This will not be permitted, with under-shirts restricted to a plain colour.

It was also agreed that advertising on players' kit should be restricted to the front of the shirt only. The Board decided to continue the experiment, pioneered in England, of advancing free-kicks by 10 yards if the defending team encroaches, and possibly include it in a **FIFA** tournament like the 2003 World Youth Championship in the United Arab Emirates. Law 5 is to be amended to make it clear that an injured player leaving the pitch for treatment may return only when the game has restarted, and it was decided to endorse **FIFA's** stance that there should be no provision for interruptions in play to allow players to take drinks.

UEFA has scrapped the golden goal rule. If a European club match is level after 90 minutes, 15 minutes of extra-time is played and a team leading at that point are the winners. If not, a further 15 minutes will be played and then, if necessary, penalties decide the outcome. There is also a change in the Champions League from 2003-04 in an attempt to reduce fixture congestion. The second group stage will be replaced by a two-leg knock-out system for the last 16 teams leading to the quarter-finals.

CLUBS' DEMISE CLOUDS SUCCESSFUL SEASON

An intriguing season's football in Scotland gave way to a summer of turmoil in which two clubs went out of business for financial reasons and another struggled for survival. Only days after finishing runners-up in the First Division Airdrie, founded in 1878, were placed in liquidation with huge reported debts. It meant a reprieve from relegation for Falkirk and Stenhousemuir, who finished second from bottom in Divisions One and Two, and a vacancy in the Third that was awarded to the Borders club Gretna. After 55 years playing in England, latterly in the Unibond League, Gretna were voted in ahead of the newly-formed Airdrie United and five other challengers.

The second to go under were Second Division Clydebank, who had been forced to spend recent years sharing with Partick Thistle and then Morton after losing their own ground. Administrators approved a buy-out bid by Airdrie United and the League gave permission for the club to take over Clydebank's fixtures. They will play at the same ground as the original side, although its name will be changed from the Shyberry Excelsior to the New Broomfield Stadium, an echo of the past.

Meanwhile, players and staff at another financially-stricken club, Second Division Hamilton Academicals, walked out after not being paid in full for some time. At the time of going to press, takeover talks were taking place to try to save the club.

Martin O'Neill had guided Celtic to their second successive SPL championship even more emphatically than he had done in his first season in charge. They had it all wrapped up with a month of the campaign to run, finishing 18 points ahead of Rangers. Alex McLeish could do little to alter the balance of power after leaving Hibernian in mid-December to take over as Ibrox manager from Dick Advocaat, who became director of football and later Holland coach as well. But McLeish and his team certainly made their mark in the cup competitions.

First, an extra-time goal by Bert Konterman gave Rangers a 2-1 success over the old enemy in the semi-finals of the CIS Insurance Cup. Then, they overcame brave resistance from Ayr United to win the Final 4-0. The Division One side, roared on by 14,000 fans celebrating the first Final in the club's history, forced two fine saves from Stefan Klos before Tore Andre Flo scored in the 44th minute, and Rangers pulled away in the second half with a Barry Ferguson penalty and two goals from Claudio Caniggia.

The Tennents Cup Final was a classic, swaying one way and then the other before Peter Lovenkrands headed in Neil McCann's cross to give Rangers the verdict 3-2 seconds from the end of injury-time. It did not look to be their day when players' Player of the Year Lorenzo Amoruso, hindered by a back injury which needed pain-killing injections, gifted goals to John Hartson and Bobo Balde. But Lovenkrands and Ferguson came up with two equalisers, and while the Celtic captain Paul Lambert was forced to bow out with a recurrence of an ankle injury, his opposite number Ferguson went on to be the game's biggest influence.

While O'Neill and McLeish were polishing the silverware, a 61-year-old scooped the Tennents Manager of the Year award and is now looking forward to pitting his wits against them in the top division. John Lambie, who began his second spell in charge at Partick Thistle with the club struggling in Division Two, gained the accolade for championship wins in successive seasons.

KENNEDY CORNERS PAVE THE WAY FOR WIGAN

When Wigan Athletic beat Cardiff City 4-0 at the JJB Stadium last season, all four goals were headed in from corners taken by Northern Ireland international Peter Kennedy. Two were scored by Canadian Jason De Vos and one each by Dutchman Arjan De Zeeuw and Scot Lee McCulloch. Alan Cork, ironically a good header of the ball in his playing days with Wimbledon, resigned as Cardiff manager the day after the match.

SCOTTISH FINAL TABLES 2001-02

BANK OF SCOTLAND PREMIER LEAGUE

		P		HOME					AWAY				Pts	GD
			W	D	L	F	A	W	D	L	F	A		
1	Celtic	38	18	1	0	51	9	15	3	1	43	9	103	+76
2	Rangers	38	14	4	1	42	11	11	6	2	40	16	85	+55
3	Livingston	38	9	5	4	23	17	7	5	8	27	30	58	+3
4	Aberdeen	38	12	2	5	31	19	4	5	10	20	30	55	+2
5	Hearts	38	8	3	8	30	27	6	3	10	22	30	48	−5
6	Dunfermline	38	9	4	6	25	24	3	5	11	16	40	45	−23
7	Kilmarnock	38	7	6	6	24	26	6	4	9	20	28	49	−10
8	Dundee Utd.	38	6	5	8	18	30	6	5	8	20	29	46	−21
9	Dundee	38	8	5	6	23	24	4	3	12	18	31	44	−14
10	Hibernian	38	6	6	7	35	30	4	5	10	16	26	41	−5
11	Motherwell	38	8	5	6	30	25	3	2	14	19	44	40	−20
12	St. Johnstone	38	2	3	15	11	32	3	3	12	13	30	21	−38

(League split after 33 matches. Teams stay within top six or bottom six regardless of points won).

Leading scorers (all competitions): 35 Larsson (Celtic); 25 Flo (Rangers); 24 Hartson (Celtic); 17 Arveladze (Rangers); 15 Winters (Aberdeen); 13 Sara (Dundee); 11 Elliott (Motherwell), Wilson (Livingston); 10 Fuller (Hearts), Luna (Hibernian), McFadden (Motherwell).

BELL'S FIRST DIVISION

		P		HOME					AWAY				Pts	GD
			W	D	L	F	A	W	D	L	F	A		
1	Partick Thistle	36	12	6	0	38	15	7	3	8	23	23	66	+23
2	Airdrie	36	8	6	4	31	19	7	5	6	28	21	56	+19
3	Ayr Utd.	36	8	6	4	25	16	5	7	6	28	28	52	+9
4	Ross Co.	36	10	2	6	33	21	4	8	6	18	22	52	+8
5	Clyde	36	8	6	4	27	21	5	4	9	24	35	49	−5
6	Inverness CT	36	11	3	4	47	22	2	6	10	13	29	48	+9
7	Arbroath	36	9	3	6	22	28	5	3	10	20	31	48	−17
8	St. Mirren	36	6	8	4	19	19	5	4	9	24	34	45	−10
9	Falkirk	36	8	5	5	24	36	5	4	9	25	37	39	−24
10	Raith Rov.	36	7	5	6	31	25	1	6	11	19	37	35	−12

(Falkirk not relegated because of Airdrie going out of business)

Leading scorers (all competitions): 27 Coyle (Airdrie); 22 Novo (Raith Rov.), Wyness (Inverness CT); 21 Annand (Ayr Utd.); 20 Ritchie (Inverness CT); 17 Hislop (Ross Co.); 16 Hardie (Patrick Thistle), Roberts (Airdrie); 15 Britton (Patrick Thistle); 12 Keogh (Clyde).
Manager of Year: John Lambie (Patrick Thistle). **Player of Year:** Owen Coyle (Airdrie).

BELL'S SECOND DIVISION

		P	W	D	L	F	A	W	D	L	F	A	Pts	GD
			HOME					**AWAY**						
1	Queen of South	36	12	2	4	33	19	8	5	5	31	23	67	+22
2	Alloa Athletic	36	8	8	2	35	17	7	6	5	20	16	59	+22
3	Forfar Athletic	36	8	3	7	25	25	7	5	6	26	22	53	+4
4	Clydebank	36	8	4	6	25	23	6	5	7	19	22	51	−1
5	Hamilton Acad.	36	9	5	4	26	15	4	4	10	23	29	48	+5
6	Berwick Rangers	36	6	4	8	19	28	6	7	5	25	24	47	−8
7	Stranraer	36	7	5	6	27	25	3	10	5	21	26	45	−3
8	Cowdenbeath	36	5	8	5	27	28	6	3	9	22	23	44	−2
9	Stenhousemuir	36	3	8	7	15	25	5	4	9	18	32	36	−24
10	Morton	36	3	8	7	20	28	4	6	8	28	35	35	−15

(Stenhousemuir not relegated because of Airdrie going out of business)

Leading scorers (all competitions): 23 Tosh (Forfar Athletic); 21 O'Neill (Queen of the South); 18 Harty (Stranraer); 16 Brown (Cowdenbeath), Hutchison (Alloa Athletic), Weatherson (Queen of the South); 13 Moore (Hamilton Acad.); 11 Byers (Forfar Athletic), Wood (Berwick Rangers).
Manger of Year: John Connolly (Queen of South). **Player of Year:** John O'Neill (Queen of South).

BELL'S THIRD DIVISION

		P	W	D	L	F	A	W	D	L	F	A	Pts	GD
			HOME					**AWAY**						
1	Brechin City	36	12	4	2	38	14	10	3	5	29	24	73	+29
2	Dumbarton	36	10	4	4	30	22	8	3	7	29	26	61	+11
3	Albion Rov.	36	8	5	5	28	23	8	6	4	23	19	59	+9
4	Peterhead	36	9	4	5	36	26	8	1	9	27	26	56	+11
5	Montrose	36	9	2	7	25	20	7	5	6	18	19	55	+4
6	Elgin City	36	9	3	6	26	20	4	5	9	19	27	47	−2
7	East Stirling	36	8	1	9	27	27	4	3	11	24	31	40	−7
8	East Fife	36	6	4	8	23	26	5	3	10	16	30	40	−17
9	Stirling Albion	36	6	4	8	23	29	3	6	9	22	39	37	−23
10	Queen's Park	36	4	6	8	17	21	5	2	11	21	32	35	−15

Leading scorers (all competitions): 22 Williams (Stirling Albion); 21 Stewart (Peterhead); 19 Flannery (Dumbarton); 18 Johnston (Peterhead); 16 Laidlaw (Montrose), McManus (East Fife), Templeman (Brechin City); 13 Gilzean (Elgin City), Grant (Brechin City), McLean (Albion Rov.).
Manager of Year: Dick Campbell (Brechin City). **Player of Year:** Paul McManus (East Fife).

FIVE REDS FOR REFEREE ALCOCK

Referee Paul Alcock sent off five opposition players in two matches at Scunthorpe. Alcock dismissed three from Carlisle United in the space of nine minutes in April 2001, and in his next game in charge at Glanford Park seven months later, showed red cards to two Darlington players.

SCOTTISH HONOURS LIST

PREMIER DIVISION

	First	Pts.	Second	Pts.	Third	Pts.
1975-6	Rangers	54	Celtic	48	Hibernian	43
1976-7	Celtic	55	Rangers	46	Aberdeen	43
1977-8	Rangers	55	Aberdeen	53	Dundee Utd.	40
1978-9	Celtic	48	Rangers	45	Dundee Utd.	44
1979-80	Aberdeen	48	Celtic	47	St. Mirren	42
1980-81	Celtic	56	Aberdeen	49	Rangers	44
1981-2	Celtic	55	Aberdeen	53	Rangers	43
1982-3	Dundee Utd.	56	Celtic	55	Aberdeen	55
1983-4	Aberdeen	57	Celtic	50	Dundee Utd.	47
1984-5	Aberdeen	59	Celtic	52	Dundee Utd.	47
1985-6	*Celtic	50	Hearts	50	Dundee Utd.	47
1986-7	Rangers	69	Celtic	63	Dundee Utd.	60
1987-8	Celtic	72	Hearts	62	Rangers	60
1988-9	Rangers	56	Aberdeen	50	Celtic	46
1989-90	Rangers	51	Aberdeen	44	Hearts	44
1990-1	Rangers	55	Aberdeen	53	Celtic	41
1991-2	Rangers	72	Hearts	63	Celtic	62
1992-3	Rangers	73	Aberdeen	64	Celtic	60
1993-4	Rangers	58	Aberdeen	55	Motherwell	54
1994-5	Rangers	69	Motherwell	54	Hibernian	53
1995-6	Rangers	87	Celtic	83	Aberdeen	55
1996-7	Rangers	80	Celtic	75	Dundee Utd.	60
1997-8	Celtic	74	Rangers	72	Hearts	67

PREMIER LEAGUE

	First	Pts.	Second	Pts.	Third	Pts.
1998-99	Rangers	77	Celtic	71	St. Johnstone	57
1999-2000	Rangers	90	Celtic	69	Hearts	54
2000-01	Celtic	97	Rangers	82	Hibernian	66
2001-02	Celtic	103	Rangers	85	Livingston	58

Maximum points: 72 except 1986-8, 1991-4 (88), 1994-2000 (108), 2001-02 (114).
* Won on goal difference.

FIRST DIVISION (Scottish Championship until 1975-76)

	First	Pts.	Second	Pts.	Third	Pts.
1890-1a	††Dumbarton	29	Rangers	29	Celtic	24
1891-2b	Dumbarton	37	Celtic	35	Hearts	30
1892-3a	Celtic	29	Rangers	28	St Mirren	23
1893-4a	Celtic	29	Hearts	26	St Bernard's	22
1894-5a	Hearts	31	Celtic	26	Rangers	21
1895-6a	Celtic	30	Rangers	26	Hibernian	24
1896-7a	Hearts	28	Hibernian	26	Rangers	25
1897-8a	Celtic	33	Rangers	29	Hibernian	22
1898-9a	Rangers	36	Hearts	26	Celtic	24
1899-1900a	Rangers	32	Celtic	25	Hibernian	24
1900-1c	Rangers	35	Celtic	29	Hibernian	25
1901-2a	Rangers	28	Celtic	26	Hearts	22
1902-3b	Hibernian	37	Dundee	31	Rangers	29
1903-4d	Third Lanark	43	Hearts	39	Rangers	38
1904-5a	†Celtic	41	Rangers	41	Third Lanark	35

118

Year	1st		2nd		3rd	
1905-6a	Celtic	46	Hearts	39	Rangers	38
1906-7f	Celtic	55	Dundee	48	Rangers	45
1907-8f	Celtic	55	Falkirk	51	Rangers	50
1908-9f	Celtic	51	Dundee	50	Clyde	48
1909-10f	Celtic	54	Falkirk	52	Rangers	49
1910-11f	Rangers	52	Aberdeen	48	Falkirk	44
1911-12f	Rangers	51	Celtic	45	Clyde	42
1912-13f	Rangers	53	Celtic	49	Hearts	41
1913-14g	Celtic	65	Rangers	59	Hearts	54
1914-15g	Celtic	65	Hearts	61	Rangers	50
1915-16g	Celtic	67	Rangers	56	Morton	51
1916-17g	Celtic	64	Morton	54	Rangers	53
1917-18f	Rangers	56	Celtic	55	Kilmarnock	43
1918-19f	Celtic	58	Rangers	57	Morton	47
1919-20h	Rangers	71	Celtic	68	Motherwell	57
1920-1h	Rangers	76	Celtic	66	Hearts	56
1921-2h	Celtic	67	Rangers	66	Raith	56
1922-3g	Rangers	55	Airdrieonians	50	Celtic	40
1923-4g	Rangers	59	Airdrieonians	50	Celtic	41
1924-5g	Rangers	60	Airdrieonians	57	Hibernian	52
1925-6g	Celtic	58	Airdrieonians	50	Hearts	50
1926-7g	Rangers	56	Motherwell	51	Celtic	49
1927-8g	Rangers	60	Celtic	55	Motherwell	55
1928-9g	Rangers	67	Celtic	51	Motherwell	50
1929-30g	Rangers	60	Motherwell	55	Aberdeen	53
1930-1g	Rangers	60	Celtic	58	Motherwell	56
1931-2g	Motherwell	66	Rangers	61	Celtic	48
1932-3g	Rangers	62	Motherwell	59	Hearts	50
1933-4g	Rangers	66	Motherwell	62	Celtic	47
1934-5g	Rangers	55	Celtic	52	Hearts	50
1935-6g	Celtic	68	Rangers	61	Aberdeen	61
1936-7g	Rangers	61	Aberdeen	54	Celtic	52
1937-8g	Celtic	61	Hearts	58	Rangers	49
1938-9f	Rangers	59	Celtic	48	Aberdeen	46
1946-7f	Rangers	46	Hibernian	44	Aberdeen	39
1947-8g	Hibernian	48	Rangers	46	Partick	46
1948-9i	Rangers	46	Dundee	45	Hibernian	39
1949-50i	Rangers	50	Hibernian	49	Hearts	43
1950-1i	Hibernian	48	Rangers	38	Dundee	38
1951-2i	Hibernian	45	Rangers	41	East Fife	37
1952-3i	*Rangers	43	Hibernian	43	East Fife	39
1953-4i	Celtic	43	Hearts	38	Partick	35
1954-5f	Aberdeen	49	Celtic	46	Rangers	41
1955-6f	Rangers	52	Aberdeen	46	Hearts	45
1956-7f	Rangers	55	Hearts	53	Kilmarnock	42
1957-8f	Hearts	62	Rangers	49	Celtic	46
1958-9f	Rangers	50	Hearts	48	Motherwell	44
1959-60f	Hearts	54	Kilmarnock	50	Rangers	42
1960-1f	Rangers	51	Kilmarnock	50	Third Lanark	42
1961-2f	Dundee	54	Rangers	51	Celtic	46
1962-3f	Rangers	57	Kilmarnock	48	Partick	46
1963-4f	Rangers	55	Kilmarnock	49	Celtic	47
1964-5f	*Kilmarnock	50	Hearts	50	Dunfermline	49
1965-6f	Celtic	57	Rangers	55	Kilmarnock	45
1966-7f	Celtic	58	Rangers	55	Clyde	46
1967-8f	Celtic	63	Rangers	61	Hibernian	45
1968-9f	Celtic	54	Rangers	49	Dunfermline	45
1969-70f	Celtic	57	Rangers	45	Hibernian	44

119

1970-1f	Celtic	56	Aberdeen	54	St Johnstone	44
1971-2f	Celtic	60	Aberdeen	50	Rangers	44
1972-3f	Celtic	57	Rangers	56	Hibernian	45
1973-4f	Celtic	53	Hibernian	49	Rangers	48
1974-5f	Rangers	56	Hibernian	49	Celtic	45

* Won on goal average. †Won on deciding match. ††Title shared.
Competition suspended 1940-46 (Second World War).

SCOTTISH CHAMPIONSHIP WINS

Rangers	*49	Hibernian	4	Kilmarnock	1
Celtic	38	Dumbarton	*2	Motherwell	1
Aberdeen	4	Dundee	1	Third Lanark	1
Hearts	4	Dundee Utd.	1	(* Incl. 1 shared)	

FIRST DIVISION

(Since formation of Premier Division)

	First	Pts.	Second	Pts.	Third	Pts.
1975-6d	Partick	41	Kilmarnock	35	Montrose	30
1976-7j	St. Mirren	62	Clydebank	58	Dundee	51
1977-8j	*Morton	58	Hearts	58	Dundee	57
1978-9j	Dundee	55	Kilmarnock	54	Clydebank	54
1979-80j	Hearts	53	Airdrieonians	51	Ayr	44
1980-1j	Hibernian	57	Dundee	52	St. Johnstone	51
1981-2j	Motherwell	61	Kilmarnock	51	Hearts	50
1982-3j	St. Johnstone	55	Hearts	54	Clydebank	50
1983-4j	Morton	54	Dumbarton	51	Partick	46
1984-5j	Motherwell	50	Clydebank	48	Falkirk	45
1985-6j	Hamilton	56	Falkirk	45	Kilmarnock	44
1986-7k	Morton	57	Dunfermline	56	Dumbarton	53
1987-8k	Hamilton	56	Meadowbank	52	Clydebank	49
1988-9j	Dunfermline	54	Falkirk	52	Clydebank	48
1989-90j	St. Johnstone	58	Airdrieonians	54	Clydebank	44
1990-1j	Falkirk	54	Airdrieonians	53	Dundee	52
1991-2k	Dundee	58	Partick	57	Hamilton	57
1992-3k	Raith	65	Kilmarnock	54	Dunfermline	52
1993-4k	Falkirk	66	Dunfermline	65	Airdrieonians	54
1994-5l	Raith	69	Dunfermline	68	Dundee	68
1995-6l	Dunfermline	71	Dundee Utd.	67	Greenock Morton	67
1996-7l	St. Johnstone	80	Airdrieonians	60	Dundee	58
1997-8l	Dundee	70	Falkirk	65	Raith	60
1998-9l	Hibernian	89	Falkirk	66	Ayr	62
1999-2000l	St. Mirren	76	Dunfermline	71	Falkirk	68
2000-01l	Livingston	76	Ayr Utd.	69	Falkirk	56
2001-02l	Partick Thistle	66	Airdie	56	Ayr Utd.	52

Maximum points: a, 36; b, 44; c, 40; d, 52; e, 60; f, 68; g, 76; h, 84; i, 60; j, 78; k, 88; l, 108. * Won on goal difference.

SECOND DIVISION

	First	Pts.	Second	Pts.	Third	Pts.
1921-2a	Alloa	60	Cowdenbeath	47	Armadale	45
1922-3a	Queen's Park	57	Clydebank	52	St. Johnstone	50
1923-4a	St. Johnstone	56	Cowdenbeath	55	Bathgate	44
1924-5a	Dundee Utd.	50	Clydebank	48	Clyde	47
1925-6a	Dunfermline	59	Clyde	53	Ayr	52

	First	Pts.	Second	Pts.	Third	Pts.
1926-7a	Bo'ness	56	Raith	49	Clydebank	45
1927-8a	Ayr	54	Third Lanark	45	King's Park	44
1928-9b	Dundee Utd.	51	Morton	50	Arbroath	47
1929-30a	*Leith Athletic	57	East Fife	57	Albion	54
1930-1a	Third Lanark	61	Dundee Utd.	50	Dunfermline	47
1931-2a	*East Stirling	55	St. Johnstone	55	Stenhousemuir	46
1932-3c	Hibernian	55	Queen of South	49	Dunfermline	47
1933-4c	Albion	45	Dunfermline	44	Arbroath	44
1934-5c	Third Lanark	52	Arbroath	50	St. Bernard's	47
1935-6c	Falkirk	59	St. Mirren	52	Morton	48
1936-7c	Ayr	54	Morton	51	St. Bernard's	48
1937-8c	Raith	59	Albion	48	Airdrieonians	47
1938-9c	Cowdenbeath	60	Alloa	48	East Fife	48
1946-7d	Dundee Utd.	45	Airdrieonians	42	East Fife	31
1947-8e	East Fife	53	Albion	42	Hamilton	40
1948-9e	*Raith	42	Stirling	42	Airdrieonians	41
1949-50e	Morton	47	Airdrieonians	44	St. Johnstone	36
1950-1e	*Queen of South	45	Stirling	45	Ayr	36
1951-2e	Clyde	44	Falkirk	43	Ayr	39
1952-3e	Stirling	44	Hamilton	43	Queen's Park	37
1953-4e	Motherwell	45	Kilmarnock	42	Third Lanark	36
1954-5e	Airdrieonians	46	Dunfermline	42	Hamilton	39
1955-6b	Queen's Park	54	Ayr	51	St. Johnstone	49
1956-7b	Clyde	64	Third Lanark	51	Cowdenbeath	45
1957-8b	Stirling	55	Dunfermline	53	Arbroath	47
1958-9b	Ayr	60	Arbroath	51	Stenhousemuir	46
1959-60b	St. Johnstone	53	Dundee Utd.	50	Queen of South	49
1960-1b	Stirling	55	Falkirk	54	Stenhousemuir	50
1961-2b	Clyde	54	Queen of South	53	Morton	44
1962-3b	St. Johnstone	55	East Stirling	49	Morton	48
1963-4b	Morton	67	Clyde	53	Arbroath	46
1964-5b	Stirling	59	Hamilton	50	Queen of South	45
1965-6b	Ayr	53	Airdrieonians	50	Queen of South	47
1966-7b	Morton	69	Raith	58	Arbroath	57
1967-8b	St. Mirren	62	Arbroath	53	East Fife	49
1968-9b	Motherwell	64	Ayr	53	East Fife	48
1969-70b	Falkirk	56	Cowdenbeath	55	Queen of South	50
1970-1b	Partick	56	East Fife	51	Arbroath	46
1971-2b	*Dumbarton	52	Arbroath	52	Stirling	50
1972-3b	Clyde	56	Dunfermline	52	Raith	47
1973-4b	Airdrieonians	60	Kilmarnock	58	Hamilton	55
1974-5b	Falkirk	54	Queen of South	53	Montrose	53

SECOND DIVISION (MODERN)

	First	Pts.	Second	Pts.	Third	Pts.
1975-6d	*Clydebank	40	Raith	40	Alloa	35
1976-7f	Stirling	55	Alloa	51	Dunfermline	50
1977-8f	*Clyde	53	Raith	53	Dunfermline	48
1978-9f	Berwick Rangers	54	Dunfermline	52	Falkirk	50
1979-80f	Falkirk	50	East Stirling	49	Forfar	46
1980-1f	Queen's Park	50	Queen of South	46	Cowdenbeath	45
1981-2f	Clyde	59	Alloa	50	Arbroath	50
1982-3f	Brechin	55	Meadowbank	54	Arbroath	49
1983-4f	Forfar	63	East Fife	47	Berwick Rangers	43
1984-5f	Montrose	53	Alloa	50	Dunfermline	49
1985-6f	Dunfermline	57	Queen of South	55	Meadowbank	49
1986-7f	Meadowbank	55	Raith	52	Stirling	52
1987-8f	Ayr	61	St. Johnstone	59	Queen's Park	51

1988-9f	Albion	50	Alloa	45	Brechin	43
1989-90f	Brechin	49	Kilmarnock	48	Stirling	47
1990-1f	Stirling	54	Montrose	46	Cowdenbeath	45
1991-2f	Dumbarton	52	Cowdenbeath	51	Alloa	50
1992-3f	Clyde	54	Brechin	53	Stranraer	53
1993-4f	Stranraer	56	Berwick Rangers	48	Stenhousemuir	47
1994-5g	Greenock Morton	64	Dumbarton	60	Stirling	58
1995-6g	Stirling	81	East Fife	67	Berwick Rangers	60
1996-7g	Ayr	77	Hamilton	74	Livingston	64
1997-8g	Stranraer	61	Clydebank	60	Livingston	59
1998-9g	Livingston	77	Inverness Cal.	72	Clyde	53
1999-2000g	Clyde	65	Alloa	64	Ross County	62
2000-01g	Partick Thistle	75	Arbroath	58	Berwick Rangers	54
2001-02g	Queen of South	67	Alloa Athletic	59	Forfar Athletic	53

Maximum points: *a*, 76; *b*, 72; *c*, 68; *d*, 52; *e*, 60; *f*, 78; *g*, 108. * Won on goal average.

THIRD DIVISION (MODERN)

	First	Pts.	Second	Pts.	Third	Pts.
1994-5	Forfar	80	Montrose	67	Ross County	60
1995-6	Livingston	72	Brechin	63	Caledonian Th.	57
1996-7	Inverness Cal.T.	76	Forfar	67	Ross County	77
1997-8	Alloa	76	Arbroath	68	Ross County	67
1998-9	Ross County	77	Stenhousemuir	64	Brechin	59
1999-2000	Queen's Park	69	Berwick Rangers	66	Forfar	61
2000-01	*Hamilton	76	Cowdenbeath	76	Brechin	72
2001-02	Brechin City	73	Dumbarton	61	Albion Rov.	59

Maximum points: 108. * Won on goal difference.

RELEGATED FROM PREMIER DIVISION

1975-6	Dundee, St. Johnstone	1989-90	Dundee
1976-7	Kilmarnock, Hearts	1990-1	No relegation
1977-8	Ayr, Clydebank	1991-2	St. Mirren, Dunfermline
1978-9	Hearts, Motherwell	1992-3	Falkirk, Airdrieonians
1979-80	Dundee, Hibernian	1993-4	St. J'stone, Raith, Dundee
1980-1	Kilmarnock, Hearts	1994-5	Dundee Utd.
1981-2	Partick, Airdrieonians	1995-6	Falkirk, Partick Thistle
1982-3	Morton, Kilmarnock	1996-7	Raith
1983-4	St. Johnstone, Motherwell	1997-8	Hibernian
1984-5	Dumbarton, Morton	1998-9	Dunfermline
1985-6	No relegation	1999-2000	No relegation
1986-7	Clydebank, Hamilton	2000-01	St. Mirren
1987-8	Falkirk, Dunfermline, Morton	2001-02	St. Johnstone
1988-9	Hamilton		

RELEGATED FROM FIRST DIVISION

1975-6	Dunfermline, Clyde	1982-3	Dunfermline, Queen's Park
1976-7	Raith, Falkirk	1983-4	Raith, Alloa
1977-8	Alloa, East Fife	1984-5	Meadowbank, St. Johnstone
1978-9	Montrose, Queen of South	1985-6	Ayr, Alloa
1979-80	Arbroath, Clyde	1986-7	Brechin, Montrose
1980-1	Stirling, Berwick Rangers	1987-8	East Fife, Dumbarton
1981-2	East Stirling, Queen of South	1988-9	Kilmarnock, Queen of South

1989-90	Albion, Alloa	1995-6	Hamilton, Dumbarton
1990-1	Clyde, Brechin	1996-7	Clydebank, East Fife
1991-2	Montrose, Forfar	1997-8	Partick, Stirling Alb.
1992-3	Meadowbank, Cowdenbeath	1998-9	Hamilton, Stranraer
1993-4	Dumbarton, Stirling Alb.,	1999-2000	Clydebank
	Clyde, Morton, Brechin	2000-01	Morton, Alloa
1994-5	Ayr, Stranraer	2001-02	Raith Rov.

RELEGATED FROM SECOND DIVISION

1993-4	Alloa, Forfar, E. Stirling,	1996-7	Dumbarton, Berwick Rangers
	Montrose, Queen's Park,	1997-8	Stenhousemuir, Brechin
	Arbroath, Albion,	1998-9	East Fife, Forfar
	Cowdenbeath	1999-2000	Hamilton
1994-5	Meadowbank, Brechin	2000-01	Queen's Park, Stirling Alb.
1995-6	Forfar, Montrose	2001-02	Morton

QUOTE UNQUOTE

'The ball ends up with Arsenal's man-of-the-match Fabien Barthez . . . . . .' **Mike Ingham**, Radio 5 Live commentator, choking on his desciption as the goalkeeper presented Arsenal's Thierry Henry with the first of two gift goals at Highbury.

'When I cross that white line I am prepared to do what it takes to win the match for my team' – **Iwan Roberts**, Norwich City striker, responding to a question at a sports forum about players diving or putting the ball in the net with a hand or an arm.

'The Phoenix League breakaway proposals are firmly established at the top of football's agenda' – *Daily Mail*.

'The so-called Phoenix League has bitten the dust' – *Mail on Sunday* the following day.

'It was the most evil game in the five years I have done in the Premiership' – **Neale Barry** after refereeing Leeds United against Aston Villa.

'He knows the club, players and chairman. He has every confidence in his ability to do the job' – **Jonathan Crystal**, agent for Stan Collymore, on his client's application – unsuccessful – for the vacant manager's job at Bradford City.

'Thank God my chairman and three directors were with me' – **David O'Leary**, Leeds United manager, admitting he lost his cool with Cardiff City owner Sam Hammam after crowd violence at the clubs' F.A. Cup tie.

'Rabid dogs and rats' – **Sam Hammam** berating the media over coverage of the trouble at Ninian Park.

'It must have been close because I could smell the beer that came out of it' – **Les Ferdinand**, Tottenham striker, who was almost hit by a bottle in the Worthington Cup semi-final against Chelsea at Stamford Bridge.

'This is the saddest moment in my football career. It should have been 13 or 14' – **Paolo Di Canio** after West Ham United's 7-1 defeat by Blackburn Rovers.

'I have an inflammation of an achilles tendon, a problem related to a dental infection' – **Marcel Desailly** giving his reason for pulling out of Chelsea's trip to Israel for a UEFA Cup tie against Hapoel Tel Aviv.

SCOTTISH LEAGUE RESULTS 2001-02

BANK OF SCOTLAND PREMIER LEAGUE

	Aberdeen	Celtic	Dundee	Dundee Utd.	Dunfermline	Hearts	Hibernian	Kilmarnock	Livingston	Motherwell	Rangers	St. Johnstone
Aberdeen	–	2-0	0-0	2-1	3-2	3-2	2-0	2-0	0-3	4-2	0-3	1-0
	–	0-1	–	4-0	1-0	2-3		1-1	3-0	1-0	0-1	–
Celtic	2-0	–	3-1	5-1	3-1	2-0	3-0	1-0	3-2	2-0	2-1	3-0
	1-0	–	–	1-0	5-0	2-0	–	–	5-1	–	1-1	2-1
	–	–	–	–	5-0	–	–	–	–	–	–	–
Dundee	1-4	0-4	–	1-1	2-2	1-1	2-1	1-2	1-0	3-1	0-0	1-1
	2-3	0-3	–	0-1	–	–	1-0	2-0	2-0	2-0	–	1-0
Dundee Utd.	1-1	0-4	2-2	–	3-2	0-2	3-1	0-2	0-0	1-1	1-6	2-1
	–	–	1-0	–	0-2	–	1-2	0-2	–	1-0	0-1	0-0
	–	–	–	–	–	2-1	–	–	–	–	–	–
Dunfermline	1-0	0-4	1-0	1-1	–	0-1	1-0	0-2	1-2	5-2	1-4	2-1
	0-0	–	2-0	–	–	1-1	–	2-0	1-0	3-1	2-4	–
	–	–	–	–	–	–	–	–	–	–	1-1	–
Hearts	1-0	0-1	3-1	1-2	1-1	–	1-1	2-0	1-3	3-1	2-2	3-0
	3-1	1-4	2-0	1-2	2-0	–	–	–	2-3	–	0-2	1-3
Hibernian	2-0	1-4	1-2	0-1	5-1	2-1	–	2-2	0-3	1-1	0-3	4-0
	3-4	1-1	2-2	–	1-1	1-2	–	2-2	–	4-0	–	3-0
Kilmarnock	3-1	0-1	0-1	2-0	0-0	1-0	0-0	–	1-5	2-0	2-2	2-1
	–	0-2	3-2	2-2	–	3-3	1-0	–	1-1	1-4	–	0-1
Livingston	2-2	0-0	1-0	2-0	0-0	2-1	1-0	0-1	–	3-1	0-2	2-1
	0-0	1-3	–	1-1	4-1	2-0	0-3	–	–	–	2-1	–
Motherwell	3-2	1-2	4-2	0-0	1-0	2-0	1-3	2-2	0-0	–	2-2	1-2
	–	0-4	2-1	2-0	–	1-2	4-0	2-0	1-2	–	–	1-1
Rangers	2-0	0-2	2-0	3-2	4-0	3-1	2-2	3-1	0-0	3-0	–	1-0
	2-0	1-1	2-1	–	–	2-0	1-1	5-0	3-0	3-0	–	–
St. Johnstone	1-1	1-2	0-2	0-1	0-2	0-2	0-0	1-0	2-2	2-3	0-2	–
	0-1	–	0-1	1-4	0-1	–	0-1	0-3	3-0	0-2	0-2	–

Read across for home results, down for away. After 33 matches, League split into top six and bottom six teams, each playing five further games.

BELL'S FIRST DIVISION

	Airdrie	Arbroath	Ayr Utd.	Clyde	Falkirk	Inverness CT	Partick Thistle	Raith Rov.	Ross Co.	St. Mirren
Airdrie	–	3-1	2-1	1-2	2-1	6-0	1-0	2-2	1-1	0-0
	–	2-0	1-2	2-2	1-0	3-0	1-1	1-1	0-2	2-3
Arbroath	0-6	–	3-2	2-1	1-0	3-2	1-3	1-1	2-1	0-2
	2-1	–	0-2	2-0	0-1	1-0	1-0	2-2	1-1	0-3
Ayr Utd.	1-3	0-1	–	2-1	2-2	3-0	0-2	1-1	2-0	4-2
	1-0	0-0	–	0-1	0-0	1-0	1-1	3-1	0-0	4-1
Clyde	0-3	1-0	2-2	–	1-1	1-1	3-1	3-2	3-0	1-1
	0-1	1-0	2-2	–	2-3	1-0	2-1	1-2	0-0	3-1
Falkirk	1-2	3-2	1-2	1-1	–	1-2	1-1	1-0	4-2	3-2
	2-2	1-3	0-2	1-6	–	0-0	1-4	2-1	1-4	0-0
Inverness CT	1-2	5-1	3-1	5-1	1-2	–	1-2	5-2	3-0	1-2
	1-0	3-2	1-1	1-1	3-2	–	3-0	5-0	1-1	4-2
Partick Thistle	1-1	4-1	2-1	3-0	5-1	1-0	–	2-1	0-0	3-3
	1-1	2-2	2-1	2-1	3-0	4-1	–	1-0	1-1	1-0
Raith Rov.	2-2	3-1	1-1	1-2	5-2	1-5	1-2	–	1-3	3-0
	2-1	0-0	3-3	0-1	5-1	0-0	2-0	–	0-1	1-0
Ross Co.	0-1	0-2	3-2	4-0	1-2	2-1	3-2	1-0	–	0-1
	4-1	0-1	1-1	2-1	4-2	0-0	0-1	4-2	–	4-1
St. Mirren	0-0	1-0	0-1	4-1	1-5	1-1	1-0	1-1	1-0	–
	2-1	2-3	1-1	2-2	0-0	0-0	0-2	1-0	1-1	–

Read across for home results, down for away.

BELL'S SECOND DIVISION

	Alloa Athletic	Berwick Rangers	Clydebank	Cowdenbeath	Forfar Athletic	Hamilton Acad.	Morton	Queen of South	Stenhousemuir	Stranraer
Alloa Athletic	–	2-2	1-0	5-1	1-2	2-1	1-1	2-0	0-1	2-2
	–	1-1	2-2	0-0	2-1	2-2	4-0	4-1	4-0	0-0
Berwick Rangers	0-4	–	0-2	2-5	1-1	0-2	2-0	0-4	1-1	2-2
	0-1	–	1-2	1-0	0-2	2-0	0-0	1-0	2-1	4-1
Clydebank	1-0	1-2	–	3-2	1-1	3-2	3-2	3-0	3-2	1-3
	1-1	0-2	–	1-0	1-0	1-1	1-2	0-1	0-0	1-2
Cowdenbeath	1-2	2-1	1-1	–	3-2	2-1	1-1	1-1	1-1	2-2
	1-2	1-1	2-1	–	1-2	2-1	2-2	1-2	2-4	1-1
Forfar Athletic	0-1	2-1	1-2	2-1	–	3-0	2-1	0-3	1-2	1-1
	4-1	0-0	1-2	0-0	–	1-4	2-1	0-3	2-0	3-2
Hamilton Acad.	1-0	0-1	3-0	1-0	1-1	–	2-2	1-1	2-3	0-1
	1-1	3-1	2-0	0-2	2-0	–	2-1	3-1	0-0	2-0
Morton	1-1	1-2	0-2	0-2	1-3	1-1	–	2-2	4-1	1-1
	0-0	3-2	3-1	0-0	1-4	0-0	–	0-3	0-1	2-2
Queen of South	2-1	2-2	1-0	1-3	1-2	0-1	6-5	–	2-0	1-0
	0-1	0-0	1-0	2-1	3-1	3-1	4-0	–	1-0	3-1
Stenhousemuir	1-1	3-0	2-2	0-3	1-1	2-0	0-3	1-1	–	0-0
	1-0	1-3	0-0	0-1	0-0	0-3	2-3	1-4	–	0-0
Stranraer	1-1	0-2	0-1	3-0	2-0	2-1	1-4	2-2	6-1	–
	0-2	2-2	1-1	2-1	0-3	3-2	0-0	1-2	1-0	–

Read across for home results, down for away.

BELL'S THIRD DIVISION

	Albion Rov.	Brechin City	Dumbarton	East Fife	East Stirling	Elgin City	Montrose	Peterhead	Queen's Park	Stirling Albion
Albion Rov.	–	1–2	0–2	3–0	0–4	4–4	0–0	1–0	2–1	1–3
	–	0–1	1–1	2–1	5–1	2–2	0–0	2–1	2–0	2–0
Brechin City	4–1	–	3–2	6–0	1–2	1–0	0–0	4–3	2–1	3–1
	0–0	–	0–1	1–1	2–0	1–0	2–0	1–1	5–0	2–1
Dumbarton	1–1	1–2	–	1–0	2–2	2–2	0–1	0–3	2–1	4–1
	2–0	2–1	–	2–0	2–1	3–1	0–5	3–0	1–1	2–0
East Fife	0–0	3–1	4–1	–	0–4	3–0	1–2	0–1	1–4	1–1
	2–3	1–1	1–0	–	1–0	0–1	2–0	2–3	0–3	1–1
East Stirling	1–2	3–4	2–4	1–2	–	2–1	0–1	2–3	0–1	1–1
	1–2	2–0	1–0	2–1	–	0–3	2–1	1–0	3–1	3–0
Elgin City	2–0	0–1	0–3	1–1	2–1	–	1–2	4–1	2–0	2–3
	0–0	3–1	2–0	2–0	2–2	–	1–0	0–3	0–1	2–1
Montrose	1–2	0–1	1–3	2–1	2–0	0–2	–	0–3	3–1	4–0
	2–0	0–0	1–1	0–1	2–0	1–0	–	2–1	3–1	1–3
Peterhead	0–0	4–2	0–3	1–3	3–2	1–1	4–0	–	2–1	3–3
	0–2	1–3	4–0	1–1	2–1	1–0	3–1	–	1–2	5–1
Queen's Park	1–2	1–3	0–0	1–2	2–3	0–0	2–2	0–1	–	2–2
	0–3	0–0	0–2	2–0	1–0	3–0	0–1	2–0	–	0–0
Stirling Albion	2–2	1–3	4–5	2–1	1–1	0–1	1–1	2–1	0–0	–
	0–3	1–3	2–1	0–1	1–0	3–1	0–1	0–2	3–2	–

Read across for home results, down for away.

RANGERS COMPLETE SCOTTISH CUP DOUBLE

THIRD ROUND	FOURTH ROUND	FIFTH ROUND	SEMI-FINALS	FINAL
Celtic 5	Celtic 2	Celtic 2	Celtic 3	Celtic 2
*Alloa Athletic 0				
*Kilmarnock 3	*Kilmarnock 0			
Airdrie 0				
Aberdeen 2	*Aberdeen 2	*Aberdeen 0		
*St Johnstone 0				
Livingston 4	Livingston 0			
*Albion Rov. 1				
*Dundee Utd. 3	*Dundee Utd. 4	*Dundee Utd. 2:0		
Forres Mechs. 0				
*Hamilton Acad. 1	Hamilton Acad. 0			
Raith Rov. 0				
Ayr Utd. 6	*Ayr Utd. 3	Ayr Utd. 2:2	Ayr Utd. 0	
*Deronvale 0				
*Dunfermline 3	Dunfermline 0			
Motherwell 1				
Partick Thistle 4	*Partick Thistle 1:2	*Partick Thistle 2:1	Partick Thistle 0	
*East Fife 2				
*Dundee 1:1 1:0	Dundee 1:1			
Falkirk				
*Hearts 2	*Hearts 1	Inverness CT 2:0		
Ross Co. 1				
Inverness CT 2	Inverness CT			
*Arbroath 0				

128

| *Clyde | 1 |
| St Mirren | 0 |

| Forfar Athletic | 5 |
| *Gala Fairydean | 0 |

| Hibernian | 0:4 |
| *Stranraer | 0:0 |

| *Berwick Rangers | 0:0 |
| Rangers | 0:3 |

| *Clyde | 1 |
| Forfar Athletic | 2 |

| Hibernian | 1 |
| *Rangers | 4 |

| *Forfar Athletic | 0 |
| Rangers | 3 |

| Rangers | 6 |

| Rangers | 3 |

FIRST ROUND: Albion Rov. 0, Elgin City 0; Alloa Athletic 3, Dumbarton 1; Brechin City 4, Stenhousemuir 0; Clydebank 1; Peterhead 0; Morton 1, Queen of the South 2; Stirling Albion 2, Buckie Thistle 1; Tarff 1, Montrose 4; Wick Academy 2, Threave Rov. 3.

REPLAY: Elgin City 0, Albion Rov. 1.

SECOND ROUND: Alloa Athletic 1, Queen of the South 0; Berwick Rangers 1, Cowdenbeath 0; Brechin City 0, Albion Rov. 1; Clydebank 0, Stranraer 1; Deronvale 0, Spartans 0; East Stirling 1, Forres Mechs. 1; Forfar Athletic 2, Threave Rov. 0; Gala Fairydean 1, Stirling Albion 0; Hamilton Acad. 4, Montrose 0; Queen's Park 0, East Fife 0.

REPLAYS: East Fife 2, Queen's Park 2 (East Fife won 4-2 on pens); Forres Mechs. 3, East Stirling 1; Spartans 1, Deronvale 2.
*Drawn at home. Semi-finals at Hampden Park.

TENNENTS SCOTTISH CUP FINAL

CELTIC 2, RANGERS 3

Hampden Park, (51,138); Saturday, May 4, 2002

Celtic (3-5-2): Douglas, Mjallby, Sutton, Balde, Agathe, Lambert (McNamara 44), Lennon, Petrov, Thompson, Larsson, Hartson. **Subs not used:** Gould, Boyd, Moravcik, Guppy. **Scorers:** Hartson (19), Balde (50). **Booked:** Balde, Hartson, Lennon. **Manager:** Martin O'Neill.

Rangers (4-3-3): Klos, Ross, Moore, Amoruso, Numan, Ricksen, De Boer, Ferguson, Caniggia (Arveladze 20), Lovenkrands, Flo. **Scorers:** Lovenkrands (21, 90), Ferguson (69). **Booked:** Amoruso, Moore. **Manager:** Alex McLeish.

Referee: H. Dallas. **Half-time:** 1-1.

SCOTTISH LEAGUE CUP FINALS

1946	Aberdeen beat Rangers (3-2)
1947	Rangers beat Aberdeen (4-0)
1948	East Fife beat Falkirk (4-1 after 0-0 draw)
1949	Rangers beat Raith Rov. (2-0)
1950	East Fife beat Dunfermline Athletic (3-0)
1951	Motherwell beat Hibernian (3-0)
1952	Dundee beat Rangers (3-2)
1953	Dundee beat Kilmarnock (2-0)
1954	East Fife beat Partick Thistle (3-2)
1955	Hearts beat Motherwell (4-2)
1956	Aberdeen beat St. Mirren (2-1)
1957	Celtic beat Partick Thistle (3-0 after 0-0 draw)
1958	Celtic beat Rangers (7-1)
1959	Hearts beat Partick Thistle (5-1)
1960	Hearts beat Third Lanark (2-1)
1961	Rangers beat Kilmarnock (2-0)
1962	Rangers beat Hearts (3-1 after 1-1 draw)
1963	Hearts beat Kilmarnock (1-0)
1964	Rangers beat Morton (5-0)
1965	Rangers beat Celtic (2-1)
1966	Celtic beat Rangers (2-1)
1967	Celtic beat Rangers (1-0)
1968	Celtic beat Dundee (5-3)
1969	Celtic beat Hibernian (6-2)
1970	Celtic beat St. Johnstone (1-0)
1971	Rangers beat Celtic (1-0)
1972	Partick Thistle beat Celtic (4-1)
1973	Hibernian beat Celtic (2-1)
1974	Dundee beat Celtic (1-0)
1975	Celtic beat Hibernian (6-3)
1976	Rangers beat Celtic (1-0)
1977†	Aberdeen beat Celtic (2-1)
1978†	Rangers beat Celtic (2-1)
1979	Rangers beat Aberdeen (2-1)
1980	Dundee Utd. beat Aberdeen (3-0 after 0-0 draw)
1981	Dundee Utd. beat Dundee (3-0)
1982	Rangers beat Dundee Utd. (2-1)
1983	Celtic beat Rangers (2-1)
1984†	Rangers beat Celtic (3-2)
1985	Rangers beat Dundee Utd. (1-0)
1986	Aberdeen beat Hibernian (3-0)
1987	Rangers beat Celtic (2-1)
1988†	Rangers beat Aberdeen (5-3 on pens. after 3-3 draw)
1989	Rangers beat Aberdeen (3-2)
1990†	Aberdeen beat Rangers (2-1)
1991†	Rangers beat Celtic (2-1)
1992	Hibernian beat Dunfermline Athletic (2-0)
1993†	Rangers beat Aberdeen (2-1)
1994	Rangers beat Hibernian (2-1)
1995	Raith Rov. beat Celtic (6-5 on pens. after 2-2 draw)
1996	Aberdeen beat Dundee (2-0)
1997	Rangers beat Hearts (4-3)
1998	Celtic beat Dundee Utd. (3-0)
1999	Rangers beat St. Johnstone (2-1)

2000	Celtic beat Aberdeen (2-0)
2001	Celtic beat Kilmarnock (3-0)
2002	Rangers beat Ayr Utd. (4-0)

(† After extra time; Skol Cup 1985-93, Coca-Cola Cup 1995-97, CIS Insurance 1999)

SUMMARY OF SCOTTISH LEAGUE CUP WINNERS

Rangers	22	Dundee	3	Motherwell	1
Celtic	12	East Fife	3	Partick Thistle	1
Aberdeen	6	Dundee Utd.	2	Raith Rov.	1
Hearts	4	Hibernian	2		

BELL'S SCOTTISH CHALLENGE CUP 2001-02

First round: Airdrie 2, Queen of the South 0; Albion Rov. 2, Montrose 0; Berwick Rangers 3, Elgin City 0; Brechin City 4, Stirling Albion 1; Cowdenbeath 0, Ross Co. 2; East Fife 2, Raith Rov. 3; East Stirling 0, Alloa Athletic 1; Falkirk 4, Arbroath 1; Inverness CT 3, Forfar Athletic 2; Morton 1, Clyde 3; Partick Thistle 5, Queen's Park 0; Peterhead 2, Hamilton Acad. 0; Stenhousemuir 1, Stranraer 4; St Mirren 1, Ayr Utd. 3.

Second round: Albion Rov. 1, Airdrie 4; Alloa Athletic 3, Inverness CT 2 (aet); Brechin City 4, Peterhead 0; Clyde 5, Berwick Rangers 0; Dumbarton 0, Ross Co. 2; Falkirk 0, Clydebank 0 (aet, Clydebank won 5-4 on pens); Raith Rov. 3, Partick Thistle 5 (aet); Stranraer 3, Ayr Utd. 2.

Third round: Alloa Athletic 4, Stranraer 3 (aet); Clyde 1, Partick Thistle 0; Clydebank 1, Airdrie 2; Ross Co. 0, Brechin City 2.

Semi-finals: Airdrie 1, Brechin City 1 (aet, Airdrie won 4-3 on pens); Clyde 0, Alloa Athletic 1.

FINAL

AIRDRIE 2, ALLOA ATHLETIC 1
Broadwood Stadium, (4,548), Sunday, October 14, 2001

Airdrie: Ferguson, Armstrong, Stewart, McManus, James, McPherson, Gardner (Dunn 73), McFarlane, Taylor, Coyle, Roberts. **Subs not used:** McDonald, Beesley, Docherty, Bennett. **Scorers:** Coyle (76), Roberts (85).

Alloa Athletic: Soutar, Seaton, Watson, Thomson, Knox (Curran 79), Valentine, Fisher (Christie 72), Little, Walker, (Evans 57), Hutchison, Hamilton. **Subs not used:** Irvine, McQueen. **Scorer:** Evans (90).

Referee: M. McCurry. **Half-time:** 0-0.

SATURATION COVERAGE AT ST MARY'S

A total of 351 journalists, mainly from Japan, watched their touring national team draw 2-2 with Nigeria at St Mary's Stadium, Southampton. The match attracted a crowd of 11,801.

RANGERS WIN LEAGUE CUP FOR 22ND TIME

SECOND ROUND	THIRD ROUND	FOURTH ROUND	SEMI-FINALS	FINAL
● Bye	*Rangers 3	Rangers 2	Rangers ...... †2	Rangers 4
*Airdrie ...... 2 / Motherwell 1	Airdrie 0			
*Ross Co. ...... †B0 / Hearts 0	*Ross Co. 2	*Ross Co. 1		
*Hamilton Acad. ...... 0 / Dundee 2	Dundee 1			
*Queen of the South ...... 1 / Aberdeen 2	*Aberdeen 1	*Livingston 0		
*Livingston ...... 3 / East Fife 0	Livingston 6			
● Bye	*Celtic 8	Celtic 2	Celtic 1	
*Stirling Albion ...... 2 / St. Mirren 1	Stirling Albion 0			
*Falkirk ...... 0 / Raith Rov. 2	Raith Rov. 0	*Hibernian 2	Hibernian 0	
● Bye	Hibernian 2			
*Dundee Utd. ...... 3 / Dumbarton 0	*Dundee Utd. ...... †3	Dundee Utd. 0		
*Clyde ...... 1 / St. Johnstone 2	St. Johnstone 2			

*Dunfermline ... 3	
Alloa Athletic ... 0	*Dunfermline ... 1
	Inverness CT ... 1
*Inverness CT ... †C3	
Partick Thistle ... 3	Inverness CT ... †D1
	Ayr Utd. ... 0
• Bye	
	Kilmarnock ... 0
	*Ayr Utd. ... †E0
Stranraer ... 0	
*Ayr Utd. ... 4	*Ayr Utd. ... †5

FIRST ROUND: Airdrie 3, Morton 0; Albion Rov. 0, Inverness CT 2; Alloa Athletic 4, Peterhead 0; Berwick Rangers 0, Partick Thistle 3; †A Clyde 2, Stenhousemuir 2; Dumbarton 2, Clydebank 0; East Fife 1, Arbroath 0; East Stirling 0, Queen of the South 3; Elgin City 2, Stranraer 3; Forfar Athletic 1, Falkirk 2; Queens Park 0, Hamilton Acad. 1; Raith Rov. 1, Montrose 0; Ross Co. 3, Brechin City 0; Stirling Albion 3, Cowdenbeath 2.

* Drawn at home. † After extra-time. A – Clyde won 4-2 on pens. B – Ross Co. won 5-4 on pens. C – Inverness CT won 4-2 on pens. D – Inverness CT won 4-2 on pens. E – Ayr Utd. won 5-4 on pens. Both semi-finals at Hampden Park.

CIS INSURANCE CUP FINAL

RANGERS 4, AYR UNITED 0

Hampden Park, (50,076), Sunday, March 17, 2002

Rangers (4-3-3): Klos, Ricksen, Amoruso, Vidmar (S. Hughes 74); Numan, Latapy (W. Dodds 77), Ferguson, Konterman, Caniggia, Flo, Lovenkrands (McCann 64). **Subs not used:** McGregor, Kanchelskis. **Scorers:** Flo (44), Ferguson (49 pen), Caniggia (75, 90).

Ayr Utd. (4-4-2): Nelson, Robertson, J. Hughes, Craig, Duffy, Wilson (Chaplain 88), McGinlay, Sheerin, Lovering, McLaughlin (Kean 81), Grady. **Subs not used:** McEwan, Sharp, J. Dodds. **Booked:** Lovering.

Referee: H. Dallas. **Half-time:** 1-0. **Man-of-the-match:** Claudio Caniggia.

SCOTTISH CUP FINALS

1874	Queen's Park beat Clydesdale (2-0)
1875	Queen's Park beat Renton (3-0)
1876	Queen's Park beat Third Lanark (2-0 after 1-1 draw)
1877	Vale of Leven beat Rangers (3-2 after 0-0, 1-1 draws)
1878	Vale of Leven beat Third Lanark (1-0)
1879	Vale of Leven awarded Cup (Rangers withdrew after 1-1 draw)
1880	Queen's Park beat Thornlibank (3-0)
1881	Queen's Park beat Dumbarton (3-1)
1882	Queen's Park beat Dumbarton (4-1 after 2-2 draw)
1883	Dumbarton beat Vale of Leven (2-1 after 2-2 draw)
1884	Queen's Park awarded Cup (Vale of Leven withdrew from Final)
1885	Renton beat Vale of Leven (3-1 after 0-0 draw)
1886	Queen's Park beat Renton (3-1)
1887	Hibernian beat Dumbarton (2-1)
1888	Renton beat Cambuslang (6-1)
1889	Third Lanark beat Celtic (2-1)
1890	Queen's Park beat Vale of Leven (2-1 after 1-1 draw)
1891	Hearts beat Dumbarton (1-0)
1892	Celtic beat Queen's Park (5-1)
1893	Queen's Park beat Celtic (2-1)
1894	Rangers beat Celtic (3-1)
1895	St. Bernard's beat Renton (2-1)
1896	Hearts beat Hibernian (3-1)
1897	Rangers beat Dumbarton (5-1)
1898	Rangers beat Kilmarnock (2-0)
1899	Celtic beat Rangers (2-0)
1900	Celtic beat Queen's Park (4-3)
1901	Hearts beat Celtic (4-3)
1902	Hibernian beat Celtic (1-0)
1903	Rangers beat Hearts (2-0 after 0-0, 1-1 draws)
1904	Celtic beat Rangers (3-2)
1905	Third Lanark beat Rangers (3-1 after 0-0 draw)
1906	Hearts beat Third Lanark (1-0)
1907	Celtic beat Hearts (3-0)
1908	Celtic beat St. Mirren (5-1)
1909	Cup withheld because of riot after two drawn games in Final between Celtic and Rangers (2-2, 1-1)
1910	Dundee beat Clyde (2-1 after 2-2, 0-0 draws)
1911	Celtic beat Hamilton Academical (2-0 after 0-0 draw)
1912	Celtic beat Clyde (2-0)
1913	Falkirk beat Raith Rov. (2-0)
1914	Celtic beat Hibernian (4-1 after 0-0 draw)
1915-19	No competition (World War 1)
1920	Kilmarnock beat Albion Rov. (3-2)
1921	Partick Thistle beat Rangers (1-0)
1922	Morton beat Rangers (1-0)
1923	Celtic beat Hibernian (1-0)
1924	Airdrieonians beat Hibernian (2-0)
1925	Celtic beat Dundee (2-1)
1926	St. Mirren beat Celtic (2-0)
1927	Celtic beat East Fife (3-1)
1928	Rangers beat Celtic (4-0)
1929	Kilmarnock beat Rangers (2-0)
1930	Rangers beat Partick Thistle (2-1 after 0-0 draw)
1931	Celtic beat Motherwell (4-2 after 2-2 draw)
1932	Rangers beat Kilmarnock (3-0 after 1-1 draw)

1933	Celtic beat Motherwell (1-0)
1934	Rangers beat St. Mirren (5-0)
1935	Rangers beat Hamilton Academical (2-1)
1936	Rangers beat Third Lanark (1-0)
1937	Celtic beat Aberdeen (2-1)
1938	East Fife beat Kilmarnock (4-2 after 1-1 draw)
1939	Clyde beat Motherwell (4-0)
1940-6	No competition (World War 2)
1947	Aberdeen beat Hibernian (2-1)
1948†	Rangers beat Morton (1-0 after 1-1 draw)
1949	Rangers beat Clyde (4-1)
1950	Rangers beat East Fife (3-0)
1951	Celtic beat Motherwell (1-0)
1952	Motherwell beat Dundee (4-0)
1953	Rangers beat Aberdeen (1-0 after 1-1 draw)
1954	Celtic beat Aberdeen (2-1)
1955	Clyde beat Celtic (1-0 after 1-1 draw)
1956	Hearts beat Celtic (3-1)
1957†	Falkirk beat Kilmarnock (2-1 after 1-1 draw)
1958	Clyde beat Hibernian (1-0)
1959	St. Mirren beat Aberdeen (3-1)
1960	Rangers beat Kilmarnock (2-0)
1961	Dunfermline Athletic beat Celtic (2-0 after 0-0 draw)
1962	Rangers beat St. Mirren (2-0)
1963	Rangers beat Celtic (3-0 after 1-1 draw)
1964	Rangers beat Dundee (3-1)
1965	Celtic beat Dunfermline Athletic (3-2)
1966	Rangers beat Celtic (1-0 after 0-0 draw)
1967	Celtic beat Aberdeen (2-0)
1968	Dunfermline Athletic beat Hearts (3-1)
1969	Celtic beat Rangers (4-0)
1970	Aberdeen beat Celtic (3-1)
1971	Celtic beat Rangers (2-1 after 1-1 draw)
1972	Celtic beat Hibernian (6-1)
1973	Rangers beat Celtic (3-2)
1974	Celtic beat Dundee Utd. (3-0)
1975	Celtic beat Airdrieonians (3-1)
1976	Rangers beat Hearts (3-1)
1977	Celtic beat Rangers (1-0)
1978	Rangers beat Aberdeen (2-1)
1979†	Rangers beat Hibernian (3-2 after two 0-0 draws)
1980†	Celtic beat Rangers (1-0)
1981	Rangers beat Dundee Utd. (4-1 after 0-0 draw)
1982†	Aberdeen beat Rangers (4-1)
1983†	Aberdeen beat Rangers (1-0)
1984†	Aberdeen beat Celtic (2-1)
1985	Celtic beat Dundee Utd. (2-1)
1986	Aberdeen beat Hearts (3-0)
1987†	St. Mirren beat Dundee Utd. (1-0)
1988	Celtic beat Dundee Utd. (2-1)
1989	Celtic beat Rangers (1-0)
1990†	Aberdeen beat Celtic (9-8 on pens. after 0-0 draw)
1991†	Motherwell beat Dundee Utd. (4-3)
1992	Rangers beat Airdrieonians (2-1)
1993	Rangers beat Aberdeen (2-1)
1994	Dundee Utd. beat Rangers (1-0)
1995	Celtic beat Airdrieonians (1-0)
1996	Rangers beat Hearts (5-1)

1997	Kilmarnock beat Falkirk (1-0)
1998	Hearts beat Rangers (2-1)
1999	Rangers beat Celtic (1-0)
2000	Rangers beat Aberdeen (4-0)
2001	Celtic beat Hibernian (3-0)
2002	Rangers beat Celtic (3-2)

(† After extra time; Cup sponsored by Tennents since season 1989-90)

SUMMARY OF SCOTTISH CUP WINNERS

Celtic 31, Rangers 30, Queen's Park 10, Aberdeen 7, Hearts 6, Clyde 3, Kilmarnock 3, St. Mirren 3, Vale of Leven 3, Dunfermline Ath. 2, Falkirk 2, Hibernian 2, Motherwell 2, Renton 2, Third Lanark 2, Airdrieonians 1, Dumbarton 1, Dundee 1, Dundee Utd. 1, East Fife 1, Morton 1, Partick Thistle 1, St. Bernard's 1.

QUOTE UNQUOTE

'To write a book like that means he was badly advised' – **Sir Alex Ferguson**, Manchester United manager, on Jaap Stam's controversial autobiography in which he was criticial of Ferguson and some of his team-mates.

'The incidents I described were not, in my eyes, things to shock the world' – **Jaap Stam**.

'Believe me, trust me, it was absolutely a football decision and nothing to do with that (book) nonsense' – **Sir Alex Ferguson** on why he sold Stam to Lazio for £16m.

'It was a bolt from the blue. I never wanted to leave this club. I love it here' – **Jaap Stam**'s reaction.

'I suspect it will be a slap in the face to our fans who voted Dean player of the year and raised him to icon status' – **Rupert Lowe**, Southampton chairman, after Dean Richards got the move he wanted to Tottenham.

'It might not have been too good for the blood pressure, but I'll be able to look back on this day and remember it vividly for the rest of my life' – **Sir Alex Ferguson** after Manchester United retrieved a 3-0 half-time deficit at Tottenham to win 5-3.

'I don't think we went behind Stuart's back. We were loyal to him. If you're not aware of something, you don't worry about it' – **Rupert Lowe**, Southampton chairman, after replacing manager Stuart Gray with Gordon Strachan.

'The fact that they had their new manager sitting in the stand at the match on Saturday before Stuart had even been told he was being sacked is disgraceful' – **John Barnwell**, chief executive of the League Managers' Association.

'Micky's the young sexy one and I'm the old codger' – **Dave Bassett** after being appointed Leicester City manager with Micky Adams as his assistant.

SPONSORSHIP FOR INJURY-TIME

Injury-time sponsorship made its debut last season in a deal between Leeds United and the Accident Group, a personal injury compensation company, whose advertisements appeared along the length of the Elland Road pitch at the end of both halves.

IRISH FOOTBALL 2001-02

EIRCOM LEAGUE

PREMIER DIVISION

		P	W	D	L	F	A	Pts
1	Shelbourne	33	19	6	8	50	28	63
2	Shamrock Rov.	33	17	6	10	54	32	57
3	*St Patrick's Ath.	33	20	8	5	59	29	53*
4	Bohemians	33	14	10	9	57	32	52
5	Derry City	33	14	9	10	42	30	51
6	Cork City	33	14	7	12	48	39	49
7	UCD	33	12	12	9	40	39	48
8	Bray Wand.	33	12	10	11	54	45	46
9	Longford Town	33	10	10	13	41	51	40
10	Dundalk	33	9	12	12	37	46	39
11	Galway Utd.	33	5	4	24	28	73	19
12	Monaghan Utd.	33	2	6	25	19	85	12

* St Patrick's Ath. deducted 15 points.

Leading scorer: 21 Glen Crowe (Bohemians). **Player of Year:** Owen Heary (Shelbourne). **Young Player of Year:** Robert Martin (UCD). **Personality of Year:** Paul Doolin (UCD).

FIRST DIVISION

		P	W	D	L	F	A	Pts
1	Drogheda Utd.	32	14	16	2	53	28	58
2	Finn Harps	32	15	9	8	51	47	54
3	Dublin City	32	15	8	9	55	46	53
4	*Waterford Utd.	32	13	12	7	47	35	48*
5	Kilkenny City	32	12	9	11	47	39	45
6	Sligo Rov.	32	8	9	15	35	48	33
7	Athlone Town	32	7	11	14	40	53	32
8	Cobh Ramblers	32	8	7	17	32	42	31
9	Limerick F.C.	32	8	7	17	32	54	31

* Waterford deducted 3 points.

Leading scorer: 24 Kevin McHugh (Finn Harps). **Player of Year:** Kevin McHugh.

FAI CARLSBERG CUP FINAL

Dundalk 2 (Haylock 2), **Bohemians** 1 (O'Connor) – Tolka Park, April 7, 2002

Dundalk: Connolly, Whyte, Crawley, Broughan, McGuinness, Flanagan, Kavanagh, Reilly, Haylock (Malone), Hoey, Lawless (McArdle).

Bohemians: Russell, O'Connor, Webb, Hunt, Hawkins, Caffrey, Morrison (Hill), Harkin (Byrne), Molloy (O'Neill), Crowe, Rutherford. **Sent-off:** Webb.

Referee: P. McKeon (Dublin).

EIRCOM LEAGUE CUP FINAL

First Leg: Limerick 2 (Foley, Whyte pen.), **Derry City** 1 (Deery) – Jackman Park, April 6, 2002.
Second Leg: Derry City 1 (Coyle pen), **Limerick** 0 – The Brandywell, April 11, 2002 (agg 2-2, **Limerick** won 3-2 on pens).

SMIRNOFF IRISH LEAGUE

PREMIER DIVISION

		P	W	D	L	F	A	Pts
1	Portadown	36	22	9	5	75	34	75
2	Glentoran	36	21	11	4	63	23	74
3	Linfield	36	17	11	8	64	35	62
4	Coleraine	36	19	2	15	64	58	59
5	Omagh Town	36	15	9	12	55	55	54
6	Cliftonville	36	9	11	16	37	46	38
7	Glenavon	36	9	9	18	37	57	36
8	Newry Town	36	8	12	16	40	62	36
9	Crusaders	36	9	7	20	41	65	34
10	Ards	36	6	9	21	30	71	27

(No clubs relegated from Premier Division).

Leading scorer: 30 Vinny Arkins (Portadown). **Player of Year:** Vinny Arkins. **Young Player of Year:** Peter McCann (Portadown). **Manager of Year:** Ronnie McFall (Portadown).

FIRST DIVISION

		P	W	D	L	F	A	Pts
1	Lisburn Distillery	36	24	4	8	64	26	76
2	Institute	36	22	8	6	76	35	74
3	Dungannon Swifts	36	17	8	11	55	42	59
4	Larne	36	14	11	11	52	42	53
5	Ballymena Utd.	36	14	11	11	59	56	53
6	Bangor	36	10	12	14	40	45	42
7	Limavady Utd.	36	10	7	19	49	68	37
8	Carrick Rangers	36	9	9	18	34	55	36
9	Ballyclare Com.	36	7	12	17	40	73	33
10	Armagh City	36	8	8	20	40	67	32

Leading scorer: 18 Stuart Bratton (Institute), Mark Holland (Lisburn Distillery). **Player of Year:** Mark Holland. **Manager of Year:** Paul Kee (Institute).

NATIONWIDE IRISH CUP FINAL

Linfield 2 (Morgan 2), **Portadown** 1 (Neill), Windsor Park – May 11, 2002

Linfield: Mannus, Collier, McShane (N. Kelly), Hunter, King (Murphy), R. Kelly, Morgan (McBride), Gorman, Ferguson, Marks, Bailie.

Portadown: Keenan, Douglas, O'Hara, McCann, Feeney (Ogden), Major, Clarke (Hamilton), Collins, Hamilton, Arkins, Neill.

Referee: M. Ross (Carrickfergus).

CIS LEAGUE CUP FINAL

Linfield 3 (Morgan, Gorman, Kelly), **Glentoran** 1 (Haylock) – Windsor Park, November 27, 2001.

OTHER LEAGUES 2001–02

NATIONWIDE CONFERENCE

		P	W	D	L	F	A	W	D	L	F	A	Pts	GD
1	†Boston Utd.	42	12	5	4	53	24	13	4	4	31	18	84	42
2	Dag & Redbridge	42	13	6	2	35	20	11	6	4	35	27	84	23
3	Yeovil Town	42	6	7	8	27	30	13	6	2	39	23	70	13
4	Doncaster Rov.	42	11	6	4	41	23	7	7	7	27	23	67	22
5	Barnet	42	10	4	7	30	19	9	6	6	34	29	67	16
6	Morecambe	42	12	5	4	30	27	5	6	10	33	40	62	-4
7	Farnborough Town	42	11	3	7	38	23	7	4	10	28	31	61	12
8	Margate	42	7	9	5	33	22	7	7	7	26	31	58	6
9	Telford Utd.	42	8	6	7	34	31	6	9	6	29	27	57	5
10	Nuneaton Borough	42	9	3	9	33	27	7	6	8	24	30	57	0
11	Stevenage Borough	42	10	4	7	36	30	5	6	10	21	30	55	-3
12	*Scarborough	42	9	6	6	27	22	5	8	8	28	41	55	-8
13	Northwich Victoria	42	9	4	8	32	34	7	3	11	25	36	55	-13
14	Chester City	42	7	7	7	26	23	8	2	11	28	28	54	3
15	Southport	42	9	6	6	40	26	4	8	9	13	23	53	4
16	Leigh RMI	42	6	4	11	29	29	9	4	8	27	29	53	-2
17	Hereford Utd.	42	9	6	6	28	15	5	4	12	22	38	52	-3
18	Forest Green Rov.	42	7	7	7	28	32	5	8	8	26	44	51	-22
19	Woking	42	7	5	9	28	29	6	4	11	31	41	48	-11
20	Hayes	42	6	2	13	27	45	7	3	11	26	35	44	-27
21	Stalybridge Celtic	42	7	6	8	26	32	4	4	13	14	37	43	-29
22	Dover Athletic	42	6	5	10	20	25	5	1	15	21	40	39	-24

*Scarborough deducted 1 point for ineligible player †Boston Utd. promoted to Football League

Manager of Year: Steve Evans (Boston Utd.) and Garry Hill (Dagenham & Redbridge).
Player of Year: Daryl Clare (Boston Utd.). **Goalscorer of Year:** 25 Daryl Clare.
Relegated: Stalybridge Celtic (Unibond League); Dover Athletic (Dr Martens League); Hayes (Ryman League).
Promoted to Conference: Burton Albion (Unibond League); Kettering Town (Dr Martens League); Gravesend & Northfleet (Ryman League).
Leading scorers (all competitions): 26 Clare (Boston Utd.); 25 Stein (Dagenham & Redbridge); 21 Charlery (Dagenham & Redbridge – 8 for Boston Utd.), Cooper (Forest Green Rov.); 19 Beesley (Chester City), Piper (Farnborough Town); 18 Blundell (Northwich Victoria), Paterson (Doncaster Rov.); 17 Twiss (Leigh RMI).

CONFERENCE CHAMPIONS

1979-80	Altrincham	1991-92*	Colchester Utd.
1980-81	Altrincham	1992-93*	Wycombe Wand.
1981-82	Runcorn	1993-94	Kidderminster H.
1982-83	Enfield	1994-95	Macclesfield Town
1983-84	Maidstone Utd.	1995-96	Stevenage Borough
1984-85	Wealdstone	1996-97*	Macclesfield Town
1985-86	Enfield	1997-98*	Halifax Town
1986-87*	Scarborough	1998-99*	Cheltenham Town
1987-88*	Lincoln City	1999-2000*	Kidderminster Harriers
1988-89*	Maidstone Utd.	2000-01*	Rushden & Diamonds
1989-90*	Darlington	2001-02*	Boston Utd.
1990-91*	Barnet		

(* Promoted to Football League)
Conference – Record Attendance: 9,432, Lincoln City v Wycombe Wand., May 2, 1988.

DR MARTENS LEAGUE

PREMIER DIVISION

		P	W	D	L	F	A	Pts
1	Kettering Town	42	27	6	9	80	41	87
2	Tamworth	42	24	13	5	81	41	85
3	Havant & Waterboville	42	22	9	11	74	50	75
4	Crawley Town	42	21	10	11	67	48	73
5	Newport Co.	42	19	9	14	61	48	66
6	Tiverton Town	42	17	10	15	70	63	61
7	Moor Green	42	18	7	17	64	62	61
8	Worcester City	42	16	12	14	65	54	60
9	Stafford Rangers	42	17	9	16	70	62	60
10	Ilkeston Town	42	14	16	12	58	61	58
11	Weymouth	42	15	11	16	59	67	56
12	Hinckley Utd.	42	14	13	15	64	62	55
13	Folkestone Invicta	42	14	12	16	51	61	54
14	Cambridge City	42	12	16	14	60	70	52
15	Welling Utd.	42	13	12	17	69	66	51
16	Hednesford Town	42	15	6	21	59	70	51
17	Bath City	42	13	11	18	56	65	50
18	Chelmsford City	42	13	11	18	63	75	50
19	Newport I.O.W.	42	12	12	18	38	61	48
20	King's Lynn	42	11	13	18	44	57	46
21	Merthyr Tydfil	42	12	8	22	53	71	44
22	Salisbury City	42	6	8	28	36	87	26

RYMAN LEAGUE

PREMIER DIVISION

		P	W	D	L	F	A	Pts
1	Gravesend	42	31	6	5	90	33	99
2	Canvey Island	42	30	5	7	108	41	95
3	Aldershot Town	42	22	7	13	76	51	73
4	Braintree Town	42	23	4	15	66	61	73
5	Purfleet	42	19	15	8	67	44	72
6	Grays Athletic	42	20	10	12	65	55	70
7	Chesham Utd.	42	19	10	13	69	53	67
8	Hendon	42	19	5	18	66	55	62
9	Billericay Town	42	16	13	13	59	60	61
10	St Albans City	42	16	9	17	71	60	57
11	Hitchin Town	42	15	10	17	73	81	55
12	Sutton Utd.	42	13	15	14	62	63	54
13	Heybridge Swifts	42	15	9	18	68	85	54
14	Kingstonian	42	13	13	16	50	56	52
15	Borehamwood	42	15	6	21	50	62	51
16	Maidenhead Utd.	42	15	5	22	52	63	50
17	Bedford Town	42	12	12	18	64	69	48
18	Basingstoke Town	42	11	15	16	50	67	48
19	Enfield	42	11	9	22	48	77	42
20	Hampton & Richmond	42	9	13	20	51	71	40
21	Harrow Borough	42	8	10	24	50	89	34
22	Croydon	42	7	5	30	35	94	26

UNIBOND LEAGUE

PREMIER DIVISION

		P	W	D	L	F	A	Pts
1	Burton Albion	44	31	11	2	106	30	104
2	Vauxhall Motors	44	27	8	9	86	55	89
3	Lancaster City	44	23	9	12	80	57	78
4	Worksop Town	44	23	9	12	74	51	78
5	Emley	44	22	9	13	69	55	75
6	Accrington Stanley	44	21	9	14	89	64	72
7	Runcorn	44	21	8	15	76	53	71
8	Barrow	44	19	10	15	75	59	67
9	Altrincham	44	19	9	16	66	58	66
10	Bradford Park	44	18	5	21	77	76	59
11	Droylsden	44	17	8	19	65	78	59
12	Blyth Spartans	44	14	16	14	59	62	58
13	*Frickley Athletic	44	16	11	17	63	69	58
14	Gateshead	44	14	14	16	58	71	56
15	Whitby Town	44	15	8	21	61	76	53
16	Hucknall Town	44	14	9	21	50	68	51
17	Marine	44	11	17	16	62	71	50
18	Burscough	44	15	5	24	69	86	50
19	Gainsborough Trinity	44	13	10	21	61	76	49
20	Colwyn Bay	44	12	11	21	49	82	47
21	Bishop Auckland	44	12	8	24	46	68	44
22	Hyde Utd.	44	10	10	24	61	87	40
23	**Bamber Bridge	44	7	10	27	38	88	30

*Frickley deducted 1 point
**Bamber Bridge deducted 1 point

F.A. BARCLAYCARD PREMIERSHIP RESERVE LEAGUE

NORTH

		P	W	D	L	F	A	Pts
1	Manchester Utd.	24	12	7	5	47	28	43
2	Newcastle Utd.	24	13	3	8	46	28	42
3	Middlesbrough	24	12	6	6	38	27	42
4	Sunderland	24	12	4	8	43	28	40
5	Bolton Wand.	24	12	3	9	45	39	39
6	Blackburn Rov.	24	11	4	9	41	29	37
7	Manchester City	24	10	7	7	40	28	37
8	Leeds Utd.	24	10	4	10	25	33	34
9	Liverpool	24	9	6	9	55	52	33
10	Everton	24	7	8	8	30	30	32
11	Aston Villa	24	7	4	13	25	49	25
12	Bradford City	24	5	6	13	27	56	21
13	Sheffield Wed.	24	2	4	18	26	61	10

SOUTH

		P	W	D	L	F	A	Pts
1	Ipswich Town	26	17	5	4	51	23	56
2	Arsenal	26	15	5	6	48	27	50
3	Derby Co.	26	15	5	6	47	31	50
4	Fulham	25	14	4	7	53	32	46
5	Southampton	26	10	6	10	34	29	36
6	West Ham Utd.	26	9	7	10	39	32	34
7	Charlton Athletic	26	9	7	10	36	40	34
8	Tottenham	26	10	4	12	25	37	34
9	Chelsea	25	9	6	10	25	39	33
10	Nott'm. Forest	26	9	5	12	29	40	32
11	Leicester City	26	7	8	11	32	45	29
12	Wimbledon	26	8	3	15	34	52	27
13	Coventry City	26	6	7	13	29	42	25
14	Watford	26	3	8	15	25	49	17

AVON INSURANCE LEAGUE

PREMIER DIVISION

		P	W	D	L	F	A	Pts
1	Preston N.E.	24	14	2	8	46	40	44
2	Barnsley	24	12	5	7	43	31	41
3	Tranmere Rov.	24	12	5	7	40	32	41
4	Sheffield Utd.	24	10	9	5	38	31	39
5	Burnley	24	11	6	7	43	40	39
6	Rotherham Utd.	24	10	8	6	42	31	38
7	Wolves	24	11	4	9	25	22	37
8	Birmingham City	24	9	7	8	35	26	34
9	Huddersfield Town	24	7	10	7	36	34	31
10	Oldham Athletic	24	5	9	10	30	44	24
11	W.B.A.	24	5	8	11	20	29	23
12	Wrexham	24	5	6	13	41	49	21
13	Port Vale	24	3	5	16	19	49	14

DIVISION ONE

		P	W	D	L	F	A	Pts
1	Walsall	22	14	3	5	52	22	45
2	Bury	22	13	2	7	45	34	41
3	Scunthorpe Utd.	22	12	2	8	39	37	38
4	Grimsby Town	22	11	3	8	42	34	36
5	Stoke City	22	10	3	9	52	27	33
6	Doncaster Rov.	22	10	3	9	44	33	33
7	Shrewsbury Town	22	9	3	10	35	35	30
8	Lincoln City	22	7	8	7	21	34	29
9	Darlington	22	8	4	10	27	38	28
10	Blackpool	22	5	6	11	28	48	21
11	Stockport Co.	22	5	6	11	26	51	21
12	York City	22	5	3	14	19	37	18

DIVISION TWO

		P	W	D	L	F	A	Pts
1	Macclesfield Town	20	14	3	3	37	13	45
2	Hull City	20	13	4	3	53	27	43
3	Kidderminster Harriers	20	12	2	6	40	27	38
4	Notts Co.	20	9	6	5	36	22	33
5	Mansfield Town	20	9	4	7	31	31	31
6	Hartlepool Utd.	20	9	1	10	39	32	28
7	Wigan Athletic	20	7	4	9	36	34	25
8	Rochdale	20	6	4	10	29	35	22
9	Chesterfield	20	5	2	13	22	58	17
10	Halifax Town	20	4	3	13	23	45	15
11	Carlisle Utd.	20	3	5	12	17	39	14

PRESS AND JOURNAL HIGHLAND LEAGUE

		P	W	D	L	F	A	Pts
1	Peterhead	30	24	4	2	89	19	76
2	Huntly	30	23	3	4	86	38	72
3	Keith	30	22	4	4	92	41	70
4	Elgin City	30	21	1	8	71	39	64
5	Fraserburgh	30	18	6	6	86	39	60
6	Clachnacuddin	30	16	8	6	80	45	56
7	Cove Rangers	30	16	5	9	88	48	53
8	Forres Mechs.	30	11	6	13	60	60	39
9	Brora Rangers	30	11	5	14	61	63	38
10	Deveronvale	30	11	4	15	57	72	37
11	Rothes	30	8	5	17	46	64	29
12	Buckie Thistle	30	8	4	18	36	60	28
13	Lossiemouth	30	8	4	18	40	67	28
14	Wick Acad.	30	7	2	21	33	85	23
15	Nairn Co.	30	3	2	25	32	114	11
16	Fort William	30	1	1	28	24	127	4

LEAGUE OF WALES

		P	W	D	L	F	A	Pts
1	Barry Town	34	23	8	3	82	29	77
2	T.N.S.	34	21	7	6	65	33	70
3	Bangor City	34	21	6	7	83	38	69
4	Caersws	34	18	4	12	65	44	58
5	Afan Lido	34	18	4	12	42	36	58
6	Rhyl	34	17	5	12	53	45	56
7	Cwmbran Town	34	17	4	13	66	53	55
8	Connah's Quay	34	14	9	11	56	46	51
9	Aberystwyth Town	34	14	9	11	53	48	51
10	Carmarthen Town	34	13	9	12	51	37	48
11	Caernarfon	34	12	8	14	64	64	44
12	Port Talbot Town	34	12	7	15	44	55	43
13	Newtown	34	9	11	14	35	44	38
14	Flexsys Druids	34	8	8	18	49	79	32
15	Llanelli	34	8	7	19	41	64	31
16	Oswestry Town	34	8	6	20	39	84	30
17	Haverfordwest	34	6	10	18	47	76	28
18	Rhayader Town	34	3	6	25	29	89	15

NATIONAL REFEREES 2002-03

ARMSTRONG, Paul (Thatcham, Berks)
BAINES, Steve (Chesterfield)
▲ BARBER, Graham (Tring)
▲ BARRY, Neale (Roxby, N. Lincs)
BATES, Tony (Stoke-on-Trent)
BEEBY, Richard (Northampton)
▲ BENNETT, Steve (Orpington)
★ BOYESON, Carl (Hull)
BUTLER, Alan (Sutton-in-Ashfield, Notts)
CABLE, Lee (Woking)
CAIN, George (Seaforth, Merseyside)
CLATTENBURG, Mark (Chester-le-Street)
COOPER, Mark (Walsall)
COWBURN, Mark (Blackpool)
CRICK, David (Worcester Park, Surrey)
★ CROSSLEY, Phil (Bromley, Kent)
CURSON, Brian (Hinckley)
DANSON, Paul (Leicester)
▲ DEAN, Mike (Heswall, Wirral)
▲ DOWD, Phil (Stoke-on-Trent)
▲ DUNN, Steve (Bristol)
▲ DURKIN, Paul (Portland, Dorset)
▲ D'URSO, Andy (Billericay)
★ ELLERAY, David (Harrow-on-the-Hill)
★ EVANS, Eddie (Manchester)
FLETCHER, Mick (Wolverley, Worcs)
▲ FOY, Chris (St Helens)
FRANKLAND, Graham (Middlesbrough)
▲ GALLAGHER, Dermot (Banbury)
▲ HALL, Andy (Birmingham)
▲ HALSEY, Mark (Welwyn Garden City)
HEGLEY, Grant (Bishops Stortford)
HILL, Keith (Royston)
★ ILDERTON, Eddie (Cullercoats, Tyne & Wear)
JONES, Michael (Chester)
JORDAN, Bill (Tring)
JOSLIN, Phil (Newark)

KAYE, Alan (Wakefield)
▲ KNIGHT, Barry (Orpington)
LAWS, David (Whitley Bay)
LAWS, Graham (Whitley Bay)
LEAKE, Tony (Darwen)
★ MASON, Lee (Bolton)
MATHIESON, Scott (Stockport)
▲ MESSIAS, Matt (York)
OLIVIER, Ray (Sutton Coldfield)
PARKES, Trevor (Birmingham)
PEARSON, Roy (Peterlee)
★ PENN, Andy (Wall Heath, West Midlands)
PENTON, Clive (East Sussex)
PIKE, Mike (Barrow-in-Furness)
▲ POLL, Graham (Tring)
PROSSER, Phil (Abbeymead, Gloucs)
▲ PUGH, David (Bebington, Merseyside)
REJER, Paul (Droitwich Spa)
▲ RENNIE, Uriah (Sheffield)
▲ RILEY, Mike (Leeds)
ROBINSON, Paul (Hull)
ROSS, Joe (London)
RYAN, Michael (Preston)
SALISBURY, Graham (Preston)
STRETTON, Frazer (Nottingham)
▲ STYLES, Rob (Waterlooville, Hants.)
TAYLOR, Paul (Cheshunt)
★▲ THORPE, Mike (Ipswich)
TOMLIN, Steve (Lewes)
WALTON, Peter (Long Buckby, Northants)
WARREN, Mark (Walsall)
WEBB, Howard (Rotherham)
WEBSTER, Colin (Shotley Bridge, Durham)
▲ WILEY, Alan (Burntwood, Staffs.)
WILKES, Clive (Gloucester)
★ WILLIAMSON, Iain (Reading)
▲ WINTER, Jeff (Stockton-on-Tees)
▲ WOLSTENHOLME, Eddie (Blackburn)

(▲ Select group; ★ First season)

EUROPEAN CHAMPIONS LEAGUE 2001-02

First qualifying round, first leg: Barry Town 2 (Flynn 64, French 69), Shamkir 0. Att: 1,950. **Bohemians** 3 (Maher 1, Crowe 9, 56 pen), Levadia Maardu 0. Att: 4,200. Linfield 0, Torpedo Kutaisi 0. Att: 2,600.

First qualifying round, second leg: Levadia Maardu 0, **Bohemians** 0. Att: 750 (**Bohemians** won 3-0 on agg). Shamkir 0, **Barry Town** 1 (Phillips 57). Att: 7,000 (**Barry Town** won 3-0 on agg). Torpedo Kutaisi 1, **Linfield** 0. Att: 8,000 (Torpedo Kutaisi won 1-0 on agg).

First qualifying round (on aggregate): Haka 5, Valletta 0; Levski Sofia 4, Zeljeznicar 0; Serif Tiraspol 3, Araks 0; Skonto Riga 6, Dudelang 2; Slavia Mozyr 5, Vagur 0; Sloga Jugomagnat 1, Kaunas 1 (Sloga Jugomagnat won on away goal); Vllaznia 2, Reykjavik 2 (Vllaznia won on away goal).

Second qualifying round, first leg: Bohemians 1 (Crowe 24), Halmstads 2. Att: 4,225. FC Porto 8, **Barry Town** 0. Att: 43,050. Maribor 0, **Rangers** 3 (Flo 39, 74 pen, Nerlinger 56). Att: 8,000.

Second qualifying round, second leg: Barry Town 3 (Phillips 37, Flynn 38, Lloyd 90 pen), FC Porto 1. Att: 2,377 (FC Porto won 9-3 on agg). Halmstads 2, **Bohemians** 0. Att: 3,643 (Halmstads won 4-1 on agg). **Rangers** 3 (Flo 54, Caniggia 58, 73), Maribor 1. Att: 50,000 (**Rangers** won 6-1 on agg).

Second qualifying round (on aggregate): Anderlecht 6, Serif Tiraspol 1; Copenhagen 4, Torpedo Kutaisi 2; Galatasaray 6, Vllaznia 1; Hajduk Split 0, Ferencvaros 0 (Hajduk Split won 5-4 on pens); Inter Bratislava 2, Slavia Mozyr 0; Levski Sofia 1, Brann 1 (Levski Sofia won on away goal); Maccabi Haifa 5, Haka 0 (Maccabi Haifa fielded ineligible player – Haka awarded tie); Red Star Belgrade 3, Omonia Nicosia 2; Shaktar Donetsk 4, Lugano 2; Steaua Bucharest 5, Sloga Jugomagnat 1; Wisla Krakow 3, Skonto Riga 1.

Third qualifying round, first leg: Ajax 1, **Celtic** 3 (Petta 7, Agathe 20, Sutton 55). Att: 48,000. Haka 0, **Liverpool** 5 (Heskey 32, Owen 56, 66, 88, Hyypia 87). Att: 33,217. **Rangers** 0, Fenerbahce 0. Att: 49,472.

Third qualifying round, second leg: Celtic 0, Ajax 1. Att: 60,000 (**Celtic** won 3-2 on agg). Fenerbahce 2, **Rangers** 1 (Ricksen 73). Att: 30,000 (Fenerbahce won 2-1 on agg). **Liverpool** 4 (Fowler 37, Redknapp 50, Heskey 56, Wilson 83 og), Haka 1. Att: 31,602 (**Liverpool** won 9-1 on agg).

Third qualifying round (on aggregate): Anderlecht 4, Halmstads 3; Barcelona 5, Wisla Krakow 3; Bayer Leverkusen 3, Red Star Belgrade 0; Borussia Dortmund 5, Shakhtar Donetsk 1; Dynamo Kiev 5, Steaua Bucharest 1; FC Porto 5, Grasshoppers 2; Galatasaray 3, Levski Sofia 2; Lazio 5, Copenhagen 3; Lille 2, Parma 1; Lokomotiv Moscow 4, Innsbruck 1; Mallorca 2, Hajduk Split 1; Panathinaikos 3, Slavia Prague 1; Rosenborg 7, Inter Bratislava 3.

FIRST GROUP STAGE

GROUP A

September 11, 2001
Lokomotiv Moscow 1 (Maminov 18), **Anderlecht** 1 (Hendrikx 14). Att: 15,500.
Roma 1 (Totti 73 pen), **Real Madrid** 2 (Figo 50, Guti 63). Att: 70,000.

145

September 19, 2001
Anderlecht 0, **Roma** 0. Att: 30,000.
Real Madrid 4 (Munitis 38, Figo 64 pen, Roberto Carlos 80, Savio 86), **Lokomotiv Moscow** 0. Att: 54,000.

September 26, 2001
Real Madrid 4 (Celades 49, Raul 50, 68, Solari 79), **Anderlecht** 1 (Dindane 33). Att: 65,000.
Roma 2 (Chugainov 69 og, Totti 79), **Lokomotiv Moscow** 1 (Obradovic 59). Att: 40,000.

October 16, 2001
Anderlecht 0, **Real Madrid** 2 (Raul 19, McManaman 35). Att: 21,900.
Lokomotiv Moscow 0, **Roma** 1 (Cherevchenko 78 og). Att: 18,000.

October 24, 2001
Anderlecht 1 (Ilic 2), **Lokomotiv Moscow** 5 (Izmailov 13, Sennikov 28, Pimenov 58, Buznikin 63, 69). Att: 26,000.
Real Madrid 1 (Figo 75 pen), **Roma** 1 (Totti 34). Att: 70,000.

October 30, 2001
Lokomotiv Moscow 2 (Buznikin 30, Cherevchenko 50), **Real Madrid** 0. Att: 22,400.
Roma 1 (Delvecchio 52), **Anderlecht** 1 (Mornar 11). Att: 35,000.

FINAL TABLE

	P	W	D	L	F	A	Pts
REAL MADRID	6	4	1	1	13	5	13
ROMA	6	2	3	1	6	5	9
Lokomotiv Moscow	6	2	1	3	9	9	7
Anderlecht	6	0	3	3	4	13	3

GROUP B

September 11, 2001
Dynamo Kiev 2 (Melashchenko 15, Idahor 45), **Borussia Dortmund** 2 (Koller 56, Amoroso 74). Att: 60,000.
Liverpool 1 (Owen 29), **Boavista** 1 (Silva 3). Att: 30,015.
Liverpool (4-4-2): Dudek, Carragher, Henchoz, Hyypia, Vignal, Murphy (Riise 70), Gerrard, Hamann, McAllister, Owen, Heskey.

September 19, 2001
Boavista 3 (Sanchez 4, Silva 11, Duda 30), **Dynamo Kiev** 1 (Ghioane 5). Att: 10,000.
Borussia Dortmund 0, **Liverpool** 0. Att: 60,000.
Liverpool (4-4-2): Dudek, Carragher, Henchoz, Hyypia, Vignal, Murphy, Gerrard, Hamann, Riise (McAllister 75), Owen, Heskey.

September 26, 2001
Boavista 2 (Silva 24, Sanchez 39), **Borussia Dortmund** 1 (Amoroso 75). Att: 8,000.
Liverpool 1 (Litmanen 24), **Dynamo Kiev** 0. Att: 33,513.
Liverpool (4-4-2): Dudek, Carragher, Henchoz, Hyypia, Vignal, Gerrard, Hamann, Barmby (Murphy 61), Riise (McAllister 79), Litmanen (Fowler 64), Heskey.

October 16, 2001
Borussia Dortmund 2 (Ricken 50, Koller 68), **Boavista** 1 (Goulart 33). Att: 42,000.
Dynamo Kiev 1 (Ghioane 59), **Liverpool** 2 (Murphy 43, Gerrard 67). Att: 50,000.
Liverpool (4-4-1-1): Dudek, Carragher, Henchoz, Hyypia, Riise, Barmby (Berger 62), Gerrard, McAllister, Murphy, Smicer (Redknapp 78), Heskey.

October 24, 2001
Boavista 1 (Silva 60), **Liverpool** 1 (Murphy 17). Att: 6,000.
Liverpool (4-1-4-1): Dudek, Carragher, Henchoz, Hyypia (Wright 6), Riise, Hamann, Smicer, McAllister (Berger 76), Murphy, Heskey, Fowler.
Borussia Dortmund 1 (Rosicky 35), **Dynamo Kiev** 0. Att: 41,500.

October 30, 2001
Dynamo Kiev 1 (Melashchenko 49), **Boavista** 0. Att: 10,000.
Liverpool 2 (Smicer 15, Wright 82), **Borussia Dortmund** 0. Att: 41,507.
Liverpool (4-4-2): Dudek, Wright, Henchoz, Carragher, Riise, Gerrard (Redknapp 85), Murphy, Hamann, Smicer (Berger 65), Heskey, Owen (Fowler 76).

FINAL TABLE

	P	W	D	L	F	A	Pts
LIVERPOOL	6	3	3	0	7	3	12
BOAVISTA	6	2	2	2	8	7	8
Borussia Dortmund	6	2	2	2	6	7	8
Dynamo Kiev	6	1	1	4	5	9	4

GROUP C

September 11, 2001
Mallorca 1 (Engonga 11 pen), **Arsenal** 0. Att: 22,000.
Arsenal (4-4-2): Seaman, Lauren, Keown, Campbell, Cole, Pires (Parlour 78), Vieira, Van Bronckhorst, Ljungberg (Jeffers 71), Henry, Wiltord (Kanu 71). Sent-off: Cole.
Schalke 0, **Panathinaikos** 2 (Vlaovic 75, Basinas 80). Att: 52,000.

September 19, 2001
Arsenal 3 (Ljungberg 33, Henry 35, 47 pen), **Schalke** 2 (Van Hoogdalem 43, Mpenza 59). Att: 35,361.
Arsenal (4-4-2): Seaman, Lauren, Keown, Grimandi, Van Bronckhorst, Ljungberg, Parlow, Vieira, Pires (Inamoto 75), Henry (Upson 90), Wiltord (Bergkamp 71).
Panathinaikos 2 (Vlaovic 25, Konstantinou 28), **Mallorca** 0. Att: 17,000.

September 26, 2001
Panathinaikos 1 (Karagounis 24), **Arsenal** 0. Att: 14,500.
Arsenal (4-4-2): Seaman, Lauren, Keown, Upson, Cole, Ljungberg (Kanu 68), Parlour (Van Bronckhorst 52), Vieira, Pires, Henry, Wiltord (Jeffers 68).
Schalke 0, **Mallorca** 1 (Etoo 65). Att: 52,300.

October 16, 2001
Arsenal 2 (Henry 23, 52 pen), **Panathinaikos** 1 (Olisadebe 50). Att: 35,432.
Arsenal (4-4-2): Wright, Lauren, Upson, Campbell, Cole, Ljungberg, Vieira, Van Bronckhorst, Pires (Parlour 70), Wiltord (Bergkamp 70), Henry (Grimandi 89).
Mallorca 0, **Schalke** 4 (Van Hoogdalem 15, Hajto 22 pen, Asamoah 77, Sand 84). Att: 20,000.

October 24, 2001
Arsenal 3 (Pires 61, Bergkamp 63, Henry 90), **Mallorca** 1 (Novo 74). Att: 34,764.
Arsenal (4-4-2): Wright, Lauren, Keown, Campbell, Van Bronckhorst, Pires, Vieira, Grimandi (Parlour 85), Ljungberg (Kanu 79), Bergkamp (Wiltord 72), Henry.
Panathinaikos 2 (Olisadebe 31, Konstantinou 60), **Schalke** 0. Att: 17,000.

October 30, 2001
Mallorca 1 (Biagini 55), **Panathinaikos** 0. Att: 15,000.
Schalke 3 (Mulder 2, Vermant 60, Moller 64), **Arsenal** 1 (Wiltord 71). Att: 53,500.

Arsenal (4-4-2): Wright, Luzhny, Campbell (Keown 68), Upson (Stepanovs 66), Cole, Parlour, Grimandi, Edu, Pires, Kanu (Pennant 78), Wiltord. Sent-off: Luzhny.

FINAL TABLE

	P	W	D	L	F	A	Pts
PANATHINAIKOS	6	4	0	2	8	3	12
ARSENAL	6	3	0	3	9	9	9
Mallorca	6	3	0	3	4	9	9
Schalke	6	2	0	4	9	9	6

GROUP D

September 11, 2001
Galatasaray 1 (Karan 79), **Lazio** 0. Att: 20,000.
Nantes 4 (Andre 5, Quint 10 pen, Dalmat 44, Vahirua 75), **PSV Eindhoven** 1 (De Jong 90). Att: 28,000.

September 19, 2001
Lazio 1 (Fernando Couto 7), **Nantes** 3 (Fabbri 3, Armand 63, Ziani 82). Att: 30,000.
PSV Eindhoven 3 (Bruggink 38, Faber 53, Kezman 90), **Galatasaray** 1 (Kran 66). Att: 27,000.

September 26, 2001
Nantes 0, **Galatasaray** 1 (Yalcin 79). Att: 28,000.
PSV Eindhoven 1 (Hofland 39), **Lazio** 0. Att: 30,000.

October 16, 2001
Galatasaray 0, **Nantes** 0. Att: 22,000.
Lazio 2 (Fiore 38, Lopez 55 pen), **PSV Eindhoven** 1 (Kezman 56). Att: 18,471.

October 24, 2001
Lazio 1 (Stankovic 76), **Galatasaray** 0. Att: 25,000.
PSV Eindhoven 0, **Nantes** 0. Att: 28,500.

October 30, 2001
Galatasaray 2 (Yalcin 26, Arif 50), **PSV Eindhoven** 0. Att: 22,000.
Nantes 1 (Andre 72), **Lazio** 0. Att: 35,000.

FINAL TABLE

	P	W	D	L	F	A	Pts
NANTES	6	3	2	1	8	3	11
GALATASARAY	6	3	1	2	5	4	10
PSV Eindhoven	6	2	1	3	6	9	7
Lazio	6	2	0	4	4	7	6

GROUP E

September 18, 2001
Juventus 3 (Trezeguet 43, 55, Amoruso 90 pen), **Celtic** 2 (Petrov 67, Larsson 85 pen). Att: 39,945.
Celtic (3-5-2): Douglas, Balde, Mjallby, Valgaeren, Agathe, Lambert, Lennon, Petrov, Thomson (Petta 59), Sutton, Larsson.
Rosenborg 1 (Rushfeldt 90), **FC Porto** 2 (Pena 10, Deco 60). Att: 20,007.

September 25, 2001
Celtic 1 (Larsson 36), **FC Porto** 0. Att: 54,664.
Celtic (3-5-2): Douglas, Balde, Mjallby, Valgaeren, Agathe, Lennon, Lambert, Petrov (McNamara 88), Petta (Thompson 68), Sutton, Larsson.
Rosenborg 1 (Skammelsrud 88 pen), **Juventus** 1 (Del Piero 85). Att: 20,578.

October 10, 2001
Celtic 1 (Thompson 21), **Rosenborg** 0. Att: 54,000.
Celtic (3-5-2): Douglas, Balde, Mjallby, Valgaeren, Agathe, Lambert, Lennon, Petrov, Thompson (Guppy 66), Sutton, Larsson.
FC Porto 0, **Juventus** 0. Att: 40,228.

October 17, 2001
FC Porto 3 (Clayton 1, 61, Mario 45), **Celtic** 0. Att: 30,303.
Celtic (3-5-2): Douglas, Balde, Mjallby, Valgaeren, Agathe, Lambert, Lennon, Petrov (Sylla 68), Thompson (Moravcik 56), Hartson (Maloney 89), Larsson.
Juventus 1 (Trezeguet 25), **Rosenborg** 0: Att: 38,000.

October 23, 2001
Juventus 3 (Del Piero 32, Montero 47, Trezeguet 73), **FC Porto** 1 (Clayton 13). Att: 38,328.
Rosenborg 2 (Brattbakk 19, 36), **Celtic** 0. Att: 21,540.
Celtic (3-5-2): Douglas, Balde, Mjallby, Valgaeren, Agathe, Lambert, Lennon, Petrov (Moravcik 66), Thompson (Hartson 77), Sutton, Larsson.

October 31, 2001
Celtic 4 (Valgaeren 24, Sutton 45, 64, Larsson 57 pen), **Juventus** 3 (Del Piero 19, Trezeguet 51, 77). Att: 57,717.
Celtic (3-5-2): Douglas, Balde, Mjallby, Valgaeren, Agathe, Lambert, Lennon, Moravcik (Petrov 65), Petta, Sutton, Larsson.
FC Porto 1 (Pena 37), **Rosenborg** 0. Att: 31,429.

FINAL TABLE

	P	W	D	L	F	A	Pts
JUVENTUS	6	3	2	1	11	8	11
FC PORTO	6	3	1	2	7	5	10
Celtic	6	3	0	3	8	11	9
Rosenborg	6	1	1	4	4	6	4

GROUP F

September 18, 2001
Fenerbahce 0, **Barcelona** 3 (Kluivert 25, Andersson 28, Saviola 66). Att: 25,000.
Lyon 0, **Bayer Leverkusen** 1 (Kirsten 75). Att: 37,000.

September 25, 2001
Bayer Leverkusen 2 (Basturk 52, Neuville 69), **Barcelona** 1 (Luis Enrique 21). Att: 22,500.
Fenerbahce 0, **Lyon** 1 (Delmotte 89). Att: 16,000.

October 10, 2001
Barcelona 2 (Kluivert 79, Rivaldo 87 pen), **Lyon** 0. Att: 75,000.
Bayer Leverkusen 2 (Lucio 36, Ballack 59), **Fenerbahce** 1 (Revivo 6). Att: 22,500.

October 17, 2001
Barcelona 2 (Kluivert 12, Luis Enrique 38), **Bayer Leverkusen** 1 (Ramelow 32). Att: 70,000.

Lyon 3 (Govou 45, Carriere 56, Delmotte 69), **Fenerbahce** 1 (Derelioglu 39). Att: 37,000.

October 23, 2001
Fenerbahce 1 (Derelioglu 40), **Bayer Leverkusen** 2 (Schneider 21, Kirsten 34). Att: 13,000.
Lyon 2 (Luyindula 66, Carriere 88), **Barcelona** 3 (Kluivert 9, Rivaldo 18, Gerard 90). Att: 37,000.

October 31, 2001
Barcelona 1 (Rivaldo 90), **Fenerbahce** 0. Att: 44,100.
Bayer Leverkusen 2 (Sebescen 45, Berbatov 52), **Lyon** 4 (Carriere 32, 38, Nee 64, Govou 81). Att: 22,500.

FINAL TABLE

	P	W	D	L	F	A	Pts
BARCELONA	6	5	0	1	12	5	15
B. LEVERKUSEN	6	4	0	2	10	9	12
Lyon	6	3	0	3	10	9	9
Fenerbahce	6	0	0	6	3	12	0

GROUP G

September 18, 2001
Deportivo La Coruna 2 (Fran 22, Valeron 90), **Olympiakos** 2 (Giannakopoulos 80, Oforiquaye 82). Att: 26,000.
Manchester Utd. 1 (Beckham 90), **Lille** 0. Att: 64,827.
Manchester Utd. (4-4-1-1): Barthez, G. Neville (Silvestre 12), Blanc, Brown, Irwin, Beckham, Scholes, Keane, Giggs (Solskjaer 74), Veron, Van Nistelrooy.

September 25, 2001
Deportivo La Coruna 2 (Pandiani 86, Naybet 89 pen), **Manchester Utd.** 1 (Scholes 40). Att: 34,000.
Manchester Utd. (4-1-4-1): Barthez, G. Neville, Johnsen, Blanc, Irwin, Keane, Beckham (Cole 90), Scholes, Veron, Giggs, Van Nistelrooy (Solskjaer 90).
Lille 3 (Bakari 33, Cheyrou 43, Tafforeau 79), **Olympiakos** 1 (Giannakopoulos 90). Att: 40,000.

October 10, 2001
Lille 1 (Olufade 87), **Deportivo La Coruna** 1 (Valeron 49). Att: 40,000.
Olympiakos 0, **Manchester Utd.** 2 (Beckham 66, Cole 82). Att: 73,537.
Manchester Utd. (4-1-4-1): Barthez, G. Neville, Blanc, Johnsen, Irwin (Silvestre 90), Keane, Beckham, Veron (Cole 80), Scholes, Giggs, Van Nistelrooy (Solskjaer 84).

October 17, 2001
Manchester Utd. 2 (Van Nistelrooy 7, 40), **Deportivo La Coruna** 3 (Sergio 37, Tristan 38, 60). Att: 65,585.
Manchester Utd. (4-2-3-1): Barthez, G. Neville, Blanc, Johnsen (Brown 7), Irwin (Solskjaer 85), Keane, Veron, Beckham, Scholes (Cole 63), Giggs, Van Nistelrooy.
Olympiakos 2 (Alexandris 53, Niniadis 64), **Lille** 1 (Bassir 37). Att: 30,000.

October 23, 2001
Deportivo La Coruna 1 (Tristan 13 pen), **Lille** 1 (Cheyrou 19 pen). Att: 30,000.
Manchester Utd. 3 (Solskjaer 79, Giggs 88, Van Nistelrooy 90), **Olympiakos** 0. Att: 66,769.
Manchester Utd. (4-4-1-1): Barthez, G. Neville, Blanc, Brown, Irwin, Beckham, Veron, Scholes, Butt (Solskjaer 73), Giggs, Van Nistelrooy.

October 31, 2001
Lille 1 (Cheyrou 65), **Manchester Utd.** 1 (Solskjaer 6). Att: 37,400.
Manchester Utd. (4-1-4-1): Carroll, P. Neville, May (O'Shea 68), Silvestre, Irwin, Butt, Solskjaer, Beckham, Scholes, Fortune, Cole (Yorke 75).
Olympiakos 1 (Alexandris 51), **Deportivo La Coruna** 1 (Capdevila 84). Att: 25,000.

FINAL TABLE

	P	W	D	L	F	A	Pts
DEP. LA CORUNA	6	2	4	0	10	8	10
MANCHESTER UTD.	6	3	1	2	10	6	10
Lille	6	1	3	2	7	7	6
Olympiakos	6	1	2	3	6	12	5

GROUP H

September 18, 2001
Bayern Munich 0, **Sparta Prague** 0. Att: 20,000.
Spartak Moscow 2 (Robson 63, Bestchastnykh 69), **Feyenoord** 2 (Bosvelt 12, Tomasson 58). Att: 25,000.

September 25, 2001
Spartak Moscow 1 (Baranov 64), **Bayern Munich** 3 (Salihamidzic 16, Elber 41, 74). Att: 30,000.
Sparta Prague 4 (Hartiq 24, Labant 37 pen, Kincl 71, Michalik 74), **Feyenoord** 0. Att: 15,150.

October 10, 2001
Feyenoord 2 (Van Hooijdonk 40, Tomasson 45), **Bayern Munich** 2 (Elber 12, 50). Att: 40,000.
Sparta Prague 2 (Kincl 57, Sionko 88), **Spartak Moscow** 0. Att: 17,221.

Ocotober 17, 2001
Bayern Munich 5 (Pizarro 7, 23, Elber 34, 52, Zickler 90), **Spartak Moscow** 1 (Bestchastnykh 58). Att: 25,000.
Feyenoord 0, **Sparta Prague** 2 (Jarosik 43, Novotny 77). Att: 41,000.

October 23, 2001
Bayern Munich 3 (Van Gobbel 12 og, Santa Cruz 30, 90), **Feyenoord** 1 (Elmander 25). Att: 40,000.
Spartak Moscow 2 (Robson 5, Bestchastnykh 34), **Sparta Prague** 2 (Holub 29, Babnic 90). Att: 4,000.

October 31, 2001
Feyenoord 2 (Tomasson 5, Elmander 17), **Spartak Moscow** 1 (Bestchastnykh 13). Att: 40,000.
Sparta Prague 0, **Bayern Munich** 1 (Novotny og). Att: 19,369.

FINAL TABLE

	P	W	D	L	F	A	Pts
BAYERN MUNICH	6	4	2	0	14	5	14
SPARTA PRAGUE	6	3	2	1	10	3	11
Feyenoord	6	1	2	3	7	14	5
Spartak Moscow	6	0	2	4	7	16	2

SECOND GROUP STAGE

GROUP A

November 20, 2001
Bayern Munich 1 (Sergio 87), **Manchester Utd.** 1 (Van Nistelrooy 74). Att: 59,000.
Manchester Utd. (4-1-4-1): Barthez, G. Neville, Blanc, Brown, Irwin (Silvestre 45), Keane, Beckham, Veron, Scholes, Fortune, Van Nistelrooy (Yorke 85).
Boavista 1 (Sanchez 24), **Nantes** 0. Att: 21,000.

December 5, 2001
Manchester Utd. 3 (Van Nistelrooy 31, 62, Blanc 56), **Boavista** 0. Att: 66,274.
Manchester Utd. (4-4-2): Barthez, P. Neville, G. Neville (O'Shea 77), Blanc, Silvestre, Veron, Keane, Butt, Scholes (Fortune 84), Yorke, Van Nistelrooy (Solskjaer 88).
Nantes 0, **Bayern Munich** 1 (Paulo Sergio 65). Att: 19,500.

February 20, 2002
Boavista 0, **Bayern Munich** 0. Att: 14,000.
Nantes 1 (Moldovan 9), **Manchester Utd.** 1 (Van Nistelrooy 90 pen). Att: 38,285.
Manchester Utd. (4-4-1-1): Barthez, P. Neville (Forlan 77), G. Neville, Blanc, Silvestre, Beckham, Keane, Veron (Solskjaer 63), Giggs, Scholes, Van Nistelrooy.

February 26, 2002
Bayern Munich 1 (Santa Cruz 81), **Boavista** 0. Att: 30,000.
Manchester Utd. 5 (Beckham 19, Solakjaer 31, 78, Silvestre 38, Van Nistelrooy 64 pen), **Nantes** 1 (Da Rocha 17). Att: 66,492.
Manchester Utd. (4-4-2): Barthez, Irwin, G. Neville, Blanc (Johnsen 68), Silvestre, Beckham, Keane (Butt 75), Veron, Giggs, Van Nistelrooy (Forlan 68), Solskjaer.

March 13, 2002
Manchester Utd. 0, **Bayern Munich** 0. Att: 66,818.
Manchester Utd. (4-4-2): Barthez, G. Neville, Blanc, Johnsen, Silvestre, Beckham, Keane, Veron, Giggs, Van Nistelrooy, Solskjaer (Forlan 78).
Nantes 1 (Moldovan 43), **Boavista** 1 (Martelinho 79). Att: 28,000.

March 19, 2002
Bayern Munich 2 (Jeremies 57, Pizarro 87), **Nantes** 1 (Ahamada 53). Att: 32,000.
Boavista 0, **Manchester Utd.** 3 (Blanc 14, Solskjaer 29, Beckham 51 pen). Att: 13,223.
Manchester Utd. (4-4-2): Barthez, G. Neville, Blanc (O'Shea 73), Johnsen (P. Neville 73), Silvestre, Beckham, Butt, Scholes (Stewart 59), Giggs, Solskjaer, Forlan.

FINAL TABLE

	P	W	D	L	F	A	Pts
MANCHESTER UTD.	6	3	3	0	13	3	12
BAYERN MUNICH	6	3	3	0	5	2	12
Boavista	6	1	2	3	2	8	5
Nantes	6	0	2	4	4	11	2

GROUP B

November 20, 2001
Galatasaray 1 (Perez 22), **Roma** 1 (Emerson 90). Att: 22,000.
Liverpool 1 (Owen 27), **Barcelona** 3 (Kluivert 41, Rochemback 65, Overmars 84). Att: 41,521.
Liverpool (4-4-2): Dudek, Carragher, Henchoz, Hyypia, Riise, Murphy, Gerrard, McAllister (Berger 69), Smicer (Litmanen 80), Owen, Heskey.

December 5, 2001
Barcelona 2 (Saviola 49, 66), **Galatasaray** 2 (Karan 5, Fleurquin 41). Att: 49,300.
Roma 0, **Liverpool** 0. Att: 57,819.
Liverpool (4-4-2): Dudek, Carragher, Henchoz, Hyypia, Riise, Gerrard (Biscan 84), Hamann, Smicer (McAllister 63), Murphy (Berger 60), Owen, Heskey.

February 20, 2002
Barcelona 1 (Kluivert 82), **Roma** 1 (Panucci 57). Att: 85,000.
Liverpool 0, **Galatasaray** 0. Att: 41,605.
Liverpool (4-4-2): Kirkland, Xavier, Henchoz, Hyypia, Carragher (Smicer 67), Murphy, Gerrard (McAllister 72), Hamann, Riise, Owen, Heskey.

February 26, 2002
Galatasaray 1 (Niculescu 70), **Liverpool** 1 (Heskey 79). Att: 39,362.
Liverpool (4-4-2): Kirkland, Xavier, Henchoz, Hyypia, Carragher, Smicer (Litmanen 74), Murphy, Hamann, Riise, Owen, Heskey.
Roma 3 (Emerson 61, Montello 74, Tommasi 90), **Barcelona** 0. Att: 70,000.

March 13, 2002
Barcelona 0, **Liverpool** 0. Att: 75,362.
Liverpool (4-4-1-1): Dudek, Xavier, Henchoz, Hyypia, Carragher, Murphy, Gerrard, Hamann, Riise (Barmby 80), Litmanen (Smicer 70), Heskey (Baros 75).
Roma 1 (Cafu 50), **Galatasaray** 1 (Karan 44). Att: 58,000.

March 19, 2002
Galatasaray 0, **Barcelona** 1 (Luis Enrique 58). Att: 39,500.
Liverpool 2 (Litmanen 7 pen, Heskey 64), **Roma** 0. Att: 41,794.
Liverpool (4-3-1-2): Dudek, Xavier, Henchoz, Hyypia, Carragher, Gerrard, Murphy, Riise, Litmanen (Biscan 87), Smicer (McAllister 90), Heskey.

FINAL TABLE

	P	W	D	L	F	A	Pts
BARCELONA	6	2	3	1	7	7	9
LIVERPOOL	6	1	4	1	4	4	7
Roma	6	1	4	1	6	5	7
Galatasaray	6	0	5	1	5	6	5

GROUP C

November 21, 2001
Panathinaikos 0, **FC Porto** 0. Att: 18,000.
Sparta Prague 2 (Michalik 30, Sionko 72), **Real Madrid** 3 (Zidane 20, Morientes 36, 74). Att: 20,482.

December 4, 2001
FC Porto 0, **Sparta Prague** 1 (Sionko 76). Att: 25,766.
Real Madrid 3 (Helguera 40, Raul 67, 71), **Panathinaikos** 0. Att: 60,000.

February 19, 2002
Real Madrid 1 (Solari 83), **FC Porto** 0. Att: 64,855.
Sparta Prague 0, **Panathinaikos** 2 (Karagounis 39, Konstantinou 71). Att: 15,557.

February 27, 2002
FC Porto 1 (Capucho 28), **Real Madrid** 2 (Solari 7, Helguera 20). Att: 50,000.
Panathinaikos 2 (Konstantinou 15, 47), **Sparta Prague** 1 (Klein 89). Att: 17,500.

March 12, 2002
FC Porto 2 (Deco 12, Pena 54), **Panathinaikos** 1 (Kolkka 65). Att: 12,835.
Real Madrid 3 (Solari 60, Guti 64, Savio 70), **Sparta Prague** 0. Att: 40,000.

March 20, 2002
Panathinaikos 2 (Liberopoulos 9, Goumas 64), **Real Madrid** 2 (Morientes 11, Portillo 80). Att: 15,600.
Sparta Prague 2 (Sionko 63, Jarosik 71), **FC Porto** 0. Att: 10,521.

FINAL TABLE

	P	W	D	L	F	A	Pts
REAL MADRID	6	5	1	0	14	5	16
PANATHINAIKOS	6	2	2	2	7	8	8
Sparta Prague	6	2	0	4	6	10	6
FC Porto	6	1	1	4	3	7	4

GROUP D

November 21, 2001
Deportivo La Coruna 2 (Makaay 9, Tristan 25), **Arsenal** 0. Att: 32,800.
Arsenal (4-4-2): Wright (Taylor 46), Lauren, Campbell, Upson, Cole, Ljungberg, Vieira, Van Bronckhorst (Edu 79), Pires, Henry, Wiltord (Kanu 72).

November 29, 2001
Juventus 4 (Trezeguet 8, 60, Del Piero 37, Tudor 44), **Bayer Leverkusen** 0. Att: 5,000.

December 4, 2001
Arsenal 3 (Ljungberg 21, 88, Henry 27), **Juventus** 1 (Taylor 51 og). Att: 35,421.
Arsenal (4-4-2): Taylor, Lauren, Campbell, Upson, Cole (Keown 88), Ljungberg, Parlour, Vieira, Pires, Kanu (Bergkamp 69), Henry (Grimandi 84).
Bayer Leverkusen 3 (Ze Roberto 64, Neuville 67, Ballack 79), **Deportivo La Coruna** 0. Att: 22,500.

February 19, 2002
Bayer Leverkusen 1 (Kirsten 90), **Arsenal** 1 (Pires 56). Att: 22,200.
Arsenal (4-4-2): Seaman, Lauren, Stepanovs, Campbell, Van Bronckhorst, Wiltord (Edu 70), Parlour, Vieira, Pires; Kanu, Henry. Sent-off: Parlour.
Juventus 0, **Deportivo La Coruna** 0. Att: 16,000.

February 27, 2002
Arsenal 4 (Pires 5, Henry 7, Vieira 48, Bergkamp 83), **Bayer Leverkusen** 1 (Sebescen 86). Att: 35,019.
Arsenal (4-4-2): Seaman, Dixon, Stepanovs, Campbell, Lauren (Inamoto 84), Wiltord (Pennant 90), Grimandi (Edu 67), Vieira, Pires, Henry, Bergkamp.
Deportivo La Coruna 2 (Tristan 8, Djalminha 78), **Juventus** 0. Att: 30,000.

March 12, 2002
Arsenal 0, **Deportivo La Coruna** 2 (Valeron 30, Naybet 40). Att: 35,392.
Arsenal (4-4-2): Seaman, Lauren, Stepanovs, Campbell, Luzhny, Wiltord (Kanu 64), Grimandi (Ljungberg 64), Vieira, Pires, Bergkamp, Henry.
Bayer Leverkusen 3 (Butt 24 pen, Brdaric 71, Babic 90), **Juventus** 1 (Tudor 61). Att: 22,500.

March 20, 2002
Deportivo La Coruna 1 (Tristan 74), **Bayer Leverkusen** 3 (Ballack 33, Schneider 53, Neuville 85). Att: 30,000.
Juventus 1 (Zalayeta 76), **Arsenal** 0. Att: 8,562.

Arsenal (4-4-2): Seaman, Dixon, Campbell, Luzhny, Lauren (Cole 82), Ljungberg, Vieira, Edu (Wiltord 78), Pires, Kanu, Henry.

FINAL TABLE

	P	W	D	L	F	A	Pts
B. LEVERKUSEN	6	3	1	2	11	11	10
DEP. LA CORUNA	6	3	1	2	7	6	10
Arsenal	6	2	1	3	8	8	7
Juventus	6	2	1	3	7	8	7

QUARTER-FINALS

FIRST LEGS

April 2, 2002
Bayern Munich 2 (Effenberg 81, Pizarro 87), **Real Madrid** 1 (Geremi 12). Att: 60,000.
Deportivo La Coruna 0, **Manchester Utd.** 2 (Beckham 15, Van Nistelrooy 41). Att: 32,351.
Manchester Utd. (4-4-2): Barthez, G. Neville, Blanc, Johnsen, Silvestre, Beckham (P. Neville 90), Keane (Fortune 45), Butt, Scholes, Giggs, Van Nistelrooy (Solskjaer 75).

April 3, 2002
Liverpool 1 (Hyypia 44), **Bayer Leverkusen** 0. Att: 42,454.
Liverpool (4-4-2): Dudek, Carragher, Hyypia, Henchoz, Riise, Murphy, Gerrard, Hamann, Smicer (Berger 74), Owen (Litmanen 69), Heskey.
Panathinaikos 1 (Basinas 78 pen), **Barcelona** 0. Att: 15,800.

SECOND LEGS

April 9, 2002
Barcelona 3 (Luis Enrique 22, 49, Saviola 61), **Panathinaikos** 1 (Konstantinou 7). Att 82,000 (**Barcelona** won 3-2 on agg).
Bayer Leverkusen 4 (Ballack 15, 63, Berbatov 68, Lucio 84), **Liverpool** 2 (Xavier 42, Litmanen 79). Att: 22,500 (**Bayer Leverkusen** won 4-3 on agg).
Liverpool (4-4-2): Dudek, Xavier (Berger 75), Hyypia, Henchoz, Carragher, Murphy, Gerrard, Hamann (Smicer 61), Riise, Owen, Heskey (Litmanen 41).

April 10, 2002
Manchester Utd. 3 (Solskjaer 23, 56, Giggs 69), **Deportivo La Coruna** 2 (Blanc 44 og, Djalminha 90). Att: 65,875 (**Manchester Utd.** won 5-2 on agg).
Manchester Utd. (4-4-1-1): Barthez, G. Neville, Blanc, Johnsen (Brown 37), Silvestre, Beckham (Solskjaer 20), Butt, Veron (P. Neville 73), Fortune, Giggs, Van Nistelrooy.
Real Madrid 2 (Helguera 68, Guti 84), **Bayern Munich** 0. Att: 75,000 (**Real Madrid** won 3-2 on agg).

SEMI-FINALS

FIRST LEGS

April 23, 2002
Barcelona 0, **Real Madrid** 2 (Zidane 55, McManaman 90). Att: 98.000.

April 24, 2002
Manchester Utd. 2 (Zivkovic 30 og, Van Nistelrooy 67 pen), **Bayer Leverkusen** 2 (Ballack 62, Neuville 75). Att: 66,534.
Manchester Utd. (4-4-2): Barthez, G. Neville (P. Neville 17) (Irwin 87)), Blanc, Brown, Silvestre, Veron, Butt, Scholes (Keane 81), Giggs, Solskjaer, Van Nistelrooy.

SECOND LEGS

April 30, 2002
Bayer Leverkusen 1 (Neuville 45), **Manchester Utd.** 1 (Keane 28). Att: 22,500 (agg 3-3, **Bayer Leverkusen** won on away goals).
Manchester Utd. (4-5-1): Barthez, Brown (Forlan 81), Blanc, Johnsen (Irwin 59), Silvestre, Scholes (Solskjaer 61), Keane, Veron, Butt, Giggs, Van Nistelrooy.

May 1, 2002
Real Madrid 1 (Raul 43), **Barcelona** 1 (Helguera 48 og). Att: 73,000 (**Real Madrid** won 3-1 on agg).

EUROPEAN CUP FINAL

BAYER LEVERKUSEN 1, REAL MADRID 2
Hampden Park, (52,000), Wednesday, May 15, 2002

Bayer Leverkusen (4-1-4-1): Butt, Sebescen (Kirsten 65), Zivkovic, Lucio (Babic 90), Placente, Ramelow (capt), Schneider, Ballack, Basturk, Brdaric (Berbatov 39), Neuville. **Subs not used:** Juric, Vranjes, Dzaka, Kleine. **Scorer:** Lucio (14). **Coach:** Klaus Toppmoller.

Real Madrid (4-4-2): Cesar (Casillas 68), Salgado, Hierro (capt), Helguera, Roberto Carlos, Figo (McManaman 61), Makelele (Flavio Conceicao 73), Zidane, Solari, Raul, Morientes. **Subs not used:** Guti, Karanka, Munitis, Pavon. **Scorers:** Raul (8), Zidane (45). **Booked:** Salgado, Roberto Carlos. **Coach:** Vicente del Bosque.

Referee: U. Meier (Switzerland). **Half-time:** 1-2.

LEADING SCORERS

10 – Van Nistelrooy (Manchester Utd.); **8** Trezeguet (Juventus); **7** Henry (Arsenal), Solskjaer (Manchester Utd.); **6** Ballack (Bayer Leverkusen), Elber (Bayern Munich), Kluivert (Barcelona), Konstantinou (Panathinaikos), Raul (Real Madrid), Tristan (Deportivo La Coruna); **5** Beckham (Manchester Utd.), Luis Enrique (Barcelona), Neuville (Bayer Leverkusen); **4** Beschastnykh (Spartak Moscow), Carriere (Lyon), Del Piero (Juventus), Pizarro (Bayern Munich), Saviola (Barcelona), Silva (Boavista), Sionko (Sparta Prague), Solari (Real Madrid), Karan (Galatasaray).

SHORTAGE OF PREMIERSHIP STRIKERS

On the November weekend that the threatened players' strike was called off, there was an acute shortage of strikers on the mark in the Premiership. Just 10 goals were scored in 10 matches – the lowest total since its inception in 1992 – and four of those came in one match. The total equalled the all-time low for the top flight in 1923 when all 10 were scored by home teams. Results last season were: Arsenal 3, Manchester Utd. 1; Bolton Wand. 0, Fulham 0; Chelsea 0, Blackburn Rov. 0; Leeds Utd. 1, Aston Villa 1; Leicester City 0, Everton 0; Liverpool 1, Sunderland 0; Middlesbrough 0, Ipswich Town 0; Newcastle Utd. 1, Derby Co. 0; Southampton 1, Charlton Athletic 0; West Ham Utd. 0 Tottenham 1.

EUROPEAN CUP FINALS

1956	Real Madrid 4, Rheims 3 (Paris)
1957	Real Madrid 2, Fiorentina 0 (Madrid)
1958†	Real Madrid 3, AC Milan 2 (Brussels)
1959	Real Madrid 2, Rheims 0 (Stuttgart)
1960	Real Madrid 7, Eintracht Frankfurt 3 (Glasgow)
1961	Benfica 3, Barcelona 2 (Berne)
1962	Benfica 5, Real Madrid 3 (Amsterdam)
1963	AC Milan 2, Benfica 1 (Wembley)
1964	Inter Milan 3, Real Madrid 1 (Vienna)
1965	Inter Milan 1, Benfica 0 (Milan)
1966	Real Madrid 2, Partizan Belgrade 1 (Brussels)
1967	Celtic 2, Inter Milan 1 (Lisbon)
1968†	Manchester Utd. 4, Benfica 1 (Wembley)
1969	AC Milan 4, Ajax 1 (Madrid)
1970†	Feyenoord 2, Celtic 1 (Milan)
1971	Ajax 2, Panathinaikos 0 (Wembley)
1972	Ajax 2, Inter Milan 0 (Rotterdam)
1973	Ajax 1, Juventus 0 (Belgrade)
1974	Bayern Munich 4, Atletico Madrid 0 (replay Brussels, after a 1-1 draw, Brussels)
1975	Bayern Munich 2, Leeds Utd. 0 (Paris)
1976	Bayern Munich 1, St. Etienne 0 (Glasgow)
1977	Liverpool 3, Borussia Moenchengladbach 1 (Rome)
1978	Liverpool 1, Brugge 0 (Wembley)
1979	Nott'm. Forest 1, Malmo 0 (Munich)
1980	Nott'm. Forest 1, Hamburg 0 (Madrid)
1981	Liverpool 1, Real Madrid 0 (Paris)
1982	Aston Villa 1, Bayern Munich 0 (Rotterdam)
1983	SV Hamburg 1, Juventus 0 (Athens)
1984†	Liverpool 1, AS Roma 1 (Liverpool won 4-2 on penalties) (Rome)
1985	Juventus 1, Liverpool 0 (Brussels)
1986†	Steaua Bucharest 0, Barcelona 0 (Steaua won 2-0 on penalties) (Seville)
1987	Porto 2, Bayern Munich 1 (Vienna)
1988†	PSV Eindhoven 0, Benfica 0 (PSV won 6-5 on penalties) (Stuttgart)
1989	AC Milan 4, Steaua Bucharest 0 (Barcelona)
1990	AC Milan 1, Benfica 0 (Vienna)
1991†	Red Star Belgrade 0, Marseille 0 (Red Star won 5-3 on penalties) (Bari)
1992	Barcelona 1, Sampdoria 0 (Wembley)
1993	Marseille 1, AC Milan 0 (Munich)
1994	AC Milan 4, Barcelona 0 (Athens)
1995	Ajax 1, AC Milan 0 (Vienna)
1996†	Juventus 1, Ajax 1 (Juventus won 4-2 on penalties) (Rome)
1997	Borussia Dortmund 3, Juventus 1 (Munich)
1998	Real Madrid 1, Juventus 0 (Amsterdam)
1999	Manchester Utd. 2, Bayern Munich 1 (Barcelona)
2000	Real Madrid 3, Valencia 0 (Paris)
2001	Bayern Munich 1, Valencia 1 (Bayern Munich won 5-4 on penalties) (Milan)
2002	Real Madrid 2, Bayer Leverkusen 1, (Glasgow)

(† After extra time)

UEFA CUP 2001-02

PRE-TOURNAMENT INTERTOTO CUP (selected results)

FIRST ROUND

AIK Solna 3, **Carmarthen Town** 0 (3-0h, 0-0a); FK Sartid 5, **Dundee** 2 (5-2h, 0-0a); Metalurgs Liepaja 3, **Cork City** 1 (2-1h, 1-0a); Tiligul Tiraspol 4, **Cliftonville** 1 (3-1h, 1-0a).

THIRD ROUND, FIRST LEG

Slaven Belupo 2 (Cmac 60, Gersak 90), **Aston Villa** 1 (Ginola 90). Att: 3,000. Lokeren 0, **Newcastle Utd.** 4 (Quinn 13, Ameobi 23, 39, Lua Lua 85). Att: 6,000.

THIRD ROUND, SECOND LEG

Aston Villa 2 (Hendrie 19, 41), Slaven Belupo 0. Att: 27,580 (**Aston Villa** won 3-2 on agg). **Newcastle Utd.** 1 (Bellamy 60), Lokeren 0. Att: 29,021 (**Newcastle Utd.** won 5-0 on agg).

SEMI-FINALS, FIRST LEG

Rennes 2 (Lucas 20, Chapuis 77), **Aston Villa** 1 (Vassell 90). Att: 8,000. 1860 Munich 2 (Agostino 56, Tapalovic 67), **Newcastle Utd.** 3 (Solano 11, 55 pen, Hughes 82). Att: 15,000.

SEMI-FINALS, SECOND LEG

Aston Villa 1 (Dublin 5), Rennes 0. Att: 30,782 (agg 2-2, **Aston Villa** won on away goal). **Newcastle Utd.** 3 (Speed 5, Lua Lua 80, Solano 90 pen), 1860 Munich 1 (Schroth 42). Att: 36,635 (**Newcastle Utd.** won 6-3 on agg).

FINALS, FIRST LEG

Basle 1 (Gimenez 75), **Aston Villa** 1 (Merson 59). Att: 29,879. Paris St-Germain 0, Brescia 0. Att: 20,000. Troyes 0, **Newcastle Utd.** 0. Att: 10,414.

FINALS, SECOND LEG

Aston Villa 4 (Vassell 45, Angel 55, 79, Ginola 83), Basle 1 (Chipperfield 30). Att: 39,593 (**Aston Villa** won 5-2 on agg). Brescia 1, Paris St-Germain 1. Att: 20,000 (agg 1-1, Paris St-Germain won on away goal). **Newcastle Utd.** 4 (Solano 2, Ameobi 65, Speed 69 pen, Hughes 90), Troyes 4 (Leroy 25, Gousse 28, Boutal 47, 61). Att: 36,577 (Agg 4-4, Troyes won on away goals).

QUALIFYING ROUND

Brondby 5, **Shelbourne** 0 (2-0h, 3-0a); **Kilmarnock** 2, **Glenavon** 0 (1-0h, 1-0a); Liteks Lovetch 3, **Longford** 1 (2-0h, 1-1a); Midtjylland 5, **Glentoran** 1 (1-1h, 4-0a); Polonia Warsaw 6, **TNS** 0 (4-0h, 2-0a); Slovan Bratislava 5, **Cwmbran** 0 (1-0h, 4-0a).

QUALIFYING ROUND (on aggregate)

AEK Athens 8, Grevenmacher 0; Apollon Limassol 5, Tirana 4; Birkirkara 1, Lokomotiv Tbilisi 1 (Birkirkara won on away goal); Borisov 5, Dinamo Tbilisi 2; Brasov 7, Mika Ashtarak 1; Bruges 10, Akranes 1; CSKA Sofia 5, Shakhter Soligorsk 2; Debrecen 3,

Nistru Otaci 1; Dinamo Bucharest 4, Dinamo Tirana 1; Dynamo Zagreb 2, Flora Tallinn 0; Elfsborg 5, Trans Narva 3; Fylkir 3, Pogon Szczecin 2; Gaziantepspor 4, Zimbru Chisinau 1; Gorica 1, Neftchi 0; Graz 6, Torshavn 2; Hapoel Tel Aviv 5, Ararat Yerevan 0; Helsingborg 5, MyPa 2; HJK Helsinki 3, Ventspils 1; CSKA Kiev 4, Jokerit 0; Legia Warsaw 6, Etzella Ettelbruck 1; Maccabi Tel Aviv 7, Zalgiris Vilnius 0; Maritimo 2, Sarajavo 0; Obilic 5, Gotu 1; Olimpija Ljubljana 7, Shafa 0; Olympiakos Nicosia 6, Dunaferr 4; Osijek 2, Dinaburg 2 (Osijek won on away goals); Partizan Belgrade 8, Santa Coloma 1; Puchov 4, Sliema Wanderers 2; Rapid Bucharest 12, Atlantas 0; Rapid Vienna 3, Cosmos 0; Ruzomberok 3, Belshina Bobruisk 1; St Gallen 4, Pelister 3; Viking 2, Brotnjo 1; Standard Liege 6, Vardar 1; Varteks 9, Vaduz 4.

FIRST ROUND, FIRST LEG

AEK Athens 2 (Tsartas 54 pen, Nikolaidis 66), **Hibernian** 0. Att: 15,525. Aston Villa 2 (Angel 54, 70), Varteks 3 (Bjelanovic 44, 86, Karic 64). Att: 27,132. **Chelsea** 3 (Gudjohnsen 45, 74, Lampard 90), Levski Sofia 0. Att: 20,812. **Ipswich Town** 1 (Bramble 85), Torpedo Moscow 1 (Vyasmikin 14). Att: 21,201. **Kilmarnock** 1 (Dargo 73), Viking 1 (Sanne 45). Att: 6,322. Maritimo 1 (Bruno 33), **Leeds Utd.** 0. Att: 10,500.

FIRST ROUND, SECOND LEG

Hibernian 3 (Luna 52, 82, Zitelli 114), AEK Athens 2 (Tsartas 92, 105). Att: 16,647 (aet AEK Athens won 4-3 on agg). **Leeds Utd.** 3 (Keane 20, Kewell 37, Bakke 62), Maritimo 0. Att: 38,125 (**Leeds Utd.** won 3-1 on agg). Levski Sofia 0, **Chelsea** 2 (Terry 32, Gudjohnsen 45). Att: 10,000 (**Chelsea** won 5-0 on agg). Torpedo Moscow 1 (Viamizkin 66), **Ipswich Town** 2 (George 47, Stewart 54 pen). Att: 5,000 (**Ipswich Town** won 3-2 on agg). Varteks 0, **Aston Villa** 1 (Hadji 90). Att: 10,000 (Agg 3-3, Varteks won on away goals). Viking 2 (Sanne 1, Nevland 17), **Kilmarnock** 0. Att: 4,599 (Viking won 3-1 on agg).

FIRST ROUND (on aggregate)

*Anzhi Makhachkala 0, **Rangers** 1 (Konteman 85); AC Milan 6, Borisov 0; Ajax 5, Apollon Limassol 0; Bordeaux 6, Debrecen 4; Brondby 4, Olimpija Ljubljana 2; Bruges 9, Olympiakos Nicosia 3; Celta Vigo 7, Sigma Olomouc 4; CSKA Kiev 3, Red Star Belgrade 2; CSKA Sofia 4, Shakhtar Donetsk 2; Dinamo Moscow 1, Birkirkara 0; Dukla Pribram 5, Sedan 3; Fiorentina 2, Dnipro 1; FC Copenhagen 4, FK Obilic 2; FC Twente 4, Polonia Warsaw 1; Freiburg 2, Matador Puchov 1; Grasshoppers 6, Dinamo Bucharest 2; Halmstad 2, Genclerbirligi 1; Hapoel Tel Aviv 2, Gaziantepspor 1; Helsingborg 3, Odd Grenland 3 (Helsingborg won on away goals); Hertha Berlin 3, Westerlo 0; Inter Milan 6, Brasov 0; Legia Warsaw 10, Elfsborg 2; Liteks Lovetch 3, Inter Bratislava 1; Maccabi Tel Aviv 3, Dinamo Zagreb 3 (Maccabi Tel Aviv won on away goals); Osijek 3, Gorica 1; PAOK Salonika 4, Karnten 0; ** Paris St-Germain 3, Rapid Bucharest 0; Parma 3, HJK Helsinki 0; Partizan Belgrade 2, Rapid Vienna 5, Partizan Belgrade 2; Real Zaragoza 5, Silkeborg 1; Roda 6, Fylkir 1; Servette 2, Slavia Prague 1; Slovan Liberec 2, Slovan Bratislava 1; Sporting Lisbon 6, Midtjylland 2; St Gallen 3, Steaua Bucharest 3, Standard Liege 4, Strasbourg 2; Tirol 1, Viktoria Zizkov 0; Troyes 6, Ruzemberok 2; Union Berlin 4, Haka 1; Utrecht 6, Graz 3; Valencia 6, Chernomorets 0; Wisla Krakow 3, Hajduk Split 2.

* One-off match in Warsaw after UEFA ruled that Makhachkala was too near hostilities in Chechnya.

** Paris St-Germain awarded tie following second leg floodlit failure – Rapid did not have requisite back-up generator.

SECOND ROUND, FIRST LEG

Hapoel Tel Aviv 2 (Gershon 89 pen, Klashenco 90), **Chelsea** 0. Att: 11,500. Ipswich **Town** 0, Helsingborg 0. Att: 22,254. Leeds Utd. 4 (Viduka 6, 44, Bowyer 23, 46), Troyes 2 (Loko 31, 81). Att: 40,015. Rangers 3 (Amoruso 9, Ball 61, De Boer 80), Dynamo Moscow 1 (Gusev 90). Att: 45,008.

SECOND ROUND, SECOND LEG

Chelsea 1 (Zola 64), Hapoel Tel Aviv 1 (Osterc 36). Att: 28,433 (Hapoel won 3-1 on agg). Dynamo Moscow 1 (Gusev 27), **Rangers** 4 (De Boer 8, Ferguson 16, Flo 42, Lovenkrands 79). Att: 6,000 (**Rangers** won 7-2 on agg). Helsingborg 1 (Eklund 8), **Ipswich Town** 3 (Hreidarsson 69, Stewart 81, 88). Att: 9,500 (**Ipswich Town** won 3-1 on agg). Troyes 3 (Amzine 8, Hamed 38, Rothen 58), **Leeds Utd.** 2 (Viduka 14, Keane 76). Att: 14,500 (**Leeds Utd.** won 6-5 on agg).

SECOND ROUND (on aggregate)

AC Milan 3, CSKA Sofia 0; AEK Athens 5, Osijek 3; Bordeaux 4, Standard Liege 0; Brondby 6, Varteks 3; Bruges 7, CSKA Kiev 0; FC Copenhagen 1, Ajax 0; Fiorentina 4, Tirol 2; Freiburg 4, St Gallen 2; Grashoppers 6, FC Twente 5; Hertha Berlin 3, Viking 0; Inter Milan 2, Wisla Krakow 1; Liteks Lovetch 2, Union Berlin 0; PAOK Salonika 8, Dukla Pribram 3; Paris St-Germain 6, Rapid Vienna 2; Parma 3, Utrecht 1; Roda 5, Maccabi Tel Aviv 2; Servette 1, Real Zarazoza 0; Slovan Liberec 4, Celta Vigo 3; Sporting Lisbon 7, Halmstad 1; Valencia 7, Legia Warsaw 2.

THIRD ROUND, FIRST LEG

Grasshoppers 1 (Chapuisat 17), **Leeds Utd.** 2 (Harte 73, Smith 79). Att: 15,000. **Ipswich Town** 1 (Armstrong 81), Inter Milan 0. Att: 24,569. **Rangers** 0, Paris St-Germain 0. Att: 49,223. Valencia 1 (Vicente 75), **Celtic** 0. Att: 38,000.

THIRD ROUND, SECOND LEG

Celtic 1 (Larsson 45), Valencia 0. Att: 57,299 (aet, agg 1-1, Valencia won 5-4 on pens). Inter Milan 4 (Vieri 18, 34, 70, Kallon 40), **Ipswich Town** 1 (Armstrong 79 pen). Att: 25,358 (Inter Milan won 4-2 on agg). **Leeds Utd.** 2 (Kewell 19, Keane 45), Grasshoppers 2 (Nunez 45, 90). Att: 40.014 (**Leeds Utd.** won 4-3 on agg). Paris St-Germain 0, **Rangers** 0 (aet, agg 0-0, **Rangers** won 4-3 on pens)

THIRD ROUND (on aggregate)

AC Milan 3, Sporting Lisbon 1; AEK Athens 4, Liteks Lovetch 3; Borussia Dortmund 2, FC Copenhagen 0; Feyenoord 3, Freiburg 2; Hapoel Tel Aviv 3, Lokomotiv Moscow 1; Lille 3, Fiorentina 0; Lyon 4, Bruges 4 (Lyon won on away goals); Parma 4, Brondby 1; PSV Eindhoven 6, PAOK Salonika 4; Roda 2, Bordeaux 1; Servette 3, Hertha Berlin 0; Slovan Liberec 5, Mallorca 2.

FOURTH ROUND, FIRST LEG

PSV Eindhoven 0, **Leeds Utd.** 0. Att: 31,000. **Rangers** 1 (Ferguson 81 pen), Feyenoord 1 (Ono 72). Att: 49,041.

FOURTH ROUND, SECOND LEG

Feyenoord 3 (Van Hooijdonk 37, 45, Kalou 46), **Rangers** 2 (McCann 28, Ferguson 54 pen). Att: 43,000 (Feyenoord won 4-3 on agg). **Leeds Utd.** 0, PSV Eindhoven 1 (Vennegoor 90). Att: 39,755. (PSV Eindhoven won 1-0 on agg).

FOURTH ROUND (on aggregate)

AC Milan 1, Roda 1 (aet, AC Milan won 3-2 on pens); Borussia Dortmund 1, Lille 1 (Borussia Dortmund won on away goal); Hapoel Tel Aviv 2, Parma 1; Inter Milan 5, AEK Athens 2; Slovan Liberec 5, Lyon 2; Valencia 5, Servette 2.

QUARTER-FINALS (on aggregate)

AC Milan 2, Hapoel Tel Aviv 1; Borussia Dortmund 4, Slovan Liberec 0; Feyenoord 1, PSV Eindhoven 1 (aet, Feyenoord won 5-4 on pens); Inter Milan 2, Valencia 1.

SEMI-FINALS, FIRST LEGS

Borussia Dortmund 4 (Amoroso 8 pen, 34, 39, Heinrich 62), AC Milan 0. Att: 52,000. Inter Milan 0, Feyenoord 1 (Cordoba 50 og). Att: 39,662.

SEMI-FINALS, SECOND LEGS

AC Milan 3 (Inzaghi 11, Chamot 19, Serginho 90 pen), Borussia Dortmund 1 (Ricken 90). Att: 15,301 (Borussia Dortmund won 5-3 on agg). Feyenoord 2 (Van Hooijdonk 17, Tomasson 34), Inter Milan 2 (Zanetti 82, Kallon 90 pen). Att: 45,000 (Feyenoord won 3-2 on agg).

UEFA CUP FINAL

BORUSSIA DORTMUND 2, FEYENOORD 3

Rotterdam, (45,000), Wednesday, May 8, 2002

Borussia Dortmund (4-2-1-3): Lehmann, Evanilson, Worns, Kohler (capt), Dede, Reuter, Ricken (Heinrich 69), Rosicky, Ewerthon (Addo 61), Koller, Amoroso. **Subs not used:** Laux, Stevic, Oliseh, Madouni, Sorensen. **Scorers:** Amoroso (47 pen), Koller (58). **Booked:** Amoroso, Dede, Rosicky. **Sent-off:** Kohler. **Coach:** Matthias Sammer.

Feyenoord (4-3-3): Zoetebier, Gyan, Van Wonderen, Paauwe, Rzasa, Bosvelt (capt), Tomasson, Ono (De Haan 75), Kalou (Elmander 75), Van Hooijdonk, Van Persie (Leonardo 62). **Subs not used:** Timmer, Aros, Korneev, Collen. **Scorers:** Van Hooijdonk (33 pen, 50), Tomasson (50). **Booked:** Rzasa, Paauwe, De Haan, Van Persie. **Coach:** Bert Van Maarwijk.

Referee: V. Melo Pereira (Portugal). **Half-time:** 2-0.

UEFA CUP FINALS

1972	Tottenham beat Wolves 3-2 on agg. (2-1a, 1-1h)
1973	Liverpool beat Borussia Moenchengladbach 3-2 on agg. (3-0h, 0-2a)
1974	Feyenoord beat Tottenham 4-2 on agg. (2-2a, 2-0h)
1975	Borussia Moenchengladbach beat Twente Enschede 5-1 on agg. (0-0h, 5-1a)
1976	Liverpool beat Brugge 4-3 on agg. (3-2h, 1-1a)
1977	Juventus beat Atletico Bilbao on away goals after 2-2 agg. (1-0h, 1-2a)
1978	PSV Eindhoven beat Bastia 3-0 on agg. (0-0a, 3-0h)
1979	Borussia Moenchengladbach beat Red Star Belgrade 2-1 on agg. (1-1a, 1-0h)
1980	Eintracht Frankfurt beat Borussia Moenchengladbach on away goals after 3-3 agg. (2-3a, 1-0h)
1981	Ipswich Town beat AZ 67 Alkmaar 5-4 on agg. (3-0h, 2-4a)
1982	IFK Gothenburg beat SV Hamburg 4-0 on agg. (1-0h, 3-0a)
1983	Anderlecht beat Benfica 2-1 on agg. (1-0h, 1-1a)
1984	Tottenham beat Anderlecht 4-3 on penalties after 2-2 agg. (1-1a, 1-1h)
1985	Real Madrid beat Videoton 3-1 on agg. (3-0a, 0-1h)
1986	Real Madrid beat Cologne 5-3 on agg. (5-1h, 0-2a)

1987	IFK Gothenburg beat Dundee Utd. 2-1 on agg. (1-0h, 1-1a)
1988	Bayer Leverkusen beat Espanol 3-2 on penalties after 3-3 agg. (0-3a, 3-0h)
1989	Napoli beat VfB Stuttgart 5-4 on agg. (2-1h, 3-3a)
1990	Juventus beat Fiorentina 3-1 on agg. (3-1h, 0-0a)
1991	Inter Milan beat AS Roma 2-1 on agg. (2-0h, 0-1a)
1992	Ajax beat Torino on away goals after 2-2 agg. (2-2a, 0-0h)
1993	Juventus beat Borussia Dortmund 6-1 on agg. (3-1a, 3-0h)
1994	Inter Milan beat Salzburg 2-0 on agg. (1-0a, 1-0h)
1995	Parma beat Juventus 2-1 on agg. (1-0h, 1-1a)
1996	Bayern Munich beat Bordeaux 5-1 on agg. (2-0h, 3-1a)
1997	FC Schalke beat Inter Milan 4-1 on penalties after 1-1 agg. (1-0h, 0-1a)
1998	Inter Milan beat Lazio 3-0 (one match only) – Paris
1999	Parma beat Marseille 3-0 (one match only) – Moscow
2000	Galatasaray beat Arsenal on penalties after 0-0 (one match only) – Copenhagen
2001	Liverpool beat Alvares 5-4 on golden goal (one match only) – Dortmund
2002	Feyenoord beat Borussia Dortmund 3-2 (one match only) – Rotterdam

FAIRS CUP FINALS

(As UEFA Cup previously known)

1958	Barcelona beat London 8-2 on agg. (2-2a, 6-0h)
1960	Barcelona beat Birmingham 4-1 on agg. (0-0a, 4-1h)
1961	AS Roma beat Birmingham City 4-2 on agg. (2-2a, 2-0h)
1962	Valencia beat Barcelona 7-3 on agg. (6-2h, 1-1a)
1963	Valencia beat Dynamo Zagreb 4-1 on agg. (2-1a, 2-0h)
1964	Real Zaragoza beat Valencia 2-1 (Barcelona)
1965	Ferencvaros beat Juventus 1-0 (Turin)
1966	Barcelona beat Real Zaragoza 4-3 on agg. (0-1h, 4-2a)
1967	Dynamo Zagreb beat Leeds Utd. 2-0 on agg. (2-0h, 0-0a)
1968	Leeds Utd. beat Ferencvaros 1-0 on agg. (1-0h, 0-0a)
1969	Newcastle Utd. beat Ujpest Dozsa 6-2 on agg. (3-0h, 3-2a)
1970	Arsenal beat Anderlecht 4-3 on agg. (1-3a, 3-0h)
1971	Leeds Utd. beat Juventus on away goals after 3-3 agg. (2-2a, 1-1h)

CUP-WINNERS' CUP FINALS

1961	Fiorentina beat Rangers 4-1 on agg. (2-0 Glasgow first leg, 2-1 Florence second leg)
1962	Atletico Madrid beat Fiorentina 3-0 (replay Stuttgart, after a 1-1 draw, Glasgow)
1963	Tottenham beat Atletico Madrid 5-1 (Rotterdam)
1964	Sporting Lisbon beat MTK Budapest 1-0 (replay Antwerp, after a 3-3 draw, Brussels)
1965	West Ham Utd. beat Munich 1860 2-0 (Wembley)
1966†	Borussia Dortmund beat Liverpool 2-1 (Glasgow)
1967†	Bayern Munich beat Rangers 1-0 (Nuremberg)
1968	AC Milan beat SV Hamburg 2-0 (Rotterdam)
1969	Slovan Bratislava beat Barcelona 3-2 (Basle)
1970	Manchester City beat Gornik Zabrze 2-1 (Vienna)
1971†	Chelsea beat Real Madrid 2-1 (replay Athens, after a 1-1 draw, Athens)

1972	Rangers beat Moscow Dynamo 3-2 (Barcelona)
1973	AC Milan beat Leeds Utd. 1-0 (Salonika)
1974	Magdeburg beat AC Milan 2-0 (Rotterdam)
1975	Dynamo Kiev beat Ferencvaros 3-0 (Basle)
1976	Anderlecht beat West Ham Utd. 4-2 (Brussels)
1977	SV Hamburg beat Anderlecht 2-0 (Amsterdam)
1978	Anderlecht beat Austria WAC 4-0 (Paris)
1979†	Barcelona beat Fortuna Dusseldorf 4-3 (Basle)
1980†	Valencia beat Arsenal 5-4 on penalties after a 0-0 draw (Brussels)
1981	Dynamo Tbilisi beat Carl Zeiss Jena 2-1 (Dusseldorf)
1982	Barcelona beat Standard Liege 2-1 (Barcelona)
1983†	Aberdeen beat Real Madrid 2-1 (Gothenburg)
1984	Juventus beat Porto 2-1 (Basle)
1985	Everton beat Rapid Vienna 3-1 (Rotterdam)
1986	Dynamo Kiev beat Atletico Madrid 3-0 (Lyon)
1987	Ajax beat Lokomotiv Leipzig 1-0 (Athens)
1988	Mechelen beat Ajax 1-0 (Strasbourg)
1989	Barcelona beat Sampdoria 2-0 (Berne)
1990	Sampdoria beat Anderlecht 2-0 (Gothenburg)
1991	Manchester Utd. beat Barcelona 2-1 (Rotterdam)
1992	Werder Bremen beat Monaco 2-0 (Lisbon)
1993	Parma beat Royal Antwerp 3-1 (Wembley)
1994	Arsenal beat Parma 1-0 (Copenhagen)
1995†	Real Zaragoza beat Arsenal 2-1 (Paris)
1996	Paris St. Germain beat Rapid Vienna 1-0 (Brussels)
1997	Barcelona beat Paris St. Germain 1-0 (Rotterdam)
1998	Chelsea beat VfB Stuttgart 1-0 (Stockholm)
1999	Lazio beat Real Mallorca 2-1 (Villa Park, Birmingham)

(† After extra time)

INTER-CONTINENTAL CUP

BAYERN MUNICH 1, BOCA JUNIORS 0 (aet)

Toyko, (60,000), Tuesday, November 27, 2001

Bayern Munich (3-5-2): Kahn, R. Kovac (Jancker 76), Fink, Sagnol, Kuffour, N. Kovac, Hargreaves (Sforza 76), Pizarro (Thiam 118), Lizarazu, Paulo Sergio, Elber. **Scorer:** Kuffour (109). **Booked:** Kuffour, Hargreaves, Elber.

Boca Juniors (3-5-2): Cordoba, Martinez (Calvo 17), Schiavi, Burdisso, Rodriguez, Traverso, Serna, Riquelme, Villareal (Pinto 99), Delgado, Schelotto. **Booked:** Serna, Delgado, Rodriguez, Schelotto. **Sent-off:** Delgado (46).

Referee: K. Nielsen (Denmark). **Half-time:** 0-0.

COMPLETE RESULTS

Year	Winners	Runners-up	Score		
1960	Real Madrid (Spa.)	Penarol (Uru.)	0-0	5-1	
1961	Penarol (Uru.)	Benfica (Por.)	0-1	2-1	5-0
1962	Santos (Bra.)	Benfica (Por.)	3-2	5-2	
1963	Santos (Bra.)	AC Milan (Ita.)	2-4	4-2	1-0
1964	Inter Milan (Ita.)	Independiente (Arg.)	0-1	2-0	1-0

1965	Inter Milan (Ita.)	Independiente (Arg.)	3-0 0-0
1966	Penarol (Uru.)	Real Madrid (Spa.)	2-0 2-0
1967	Racing (Arg.)	Celtic (Sco.)	0-1 2-1 1-0
1968	Estudiantes (Arg.)	Manchester Utd. (Eng.)	1-0 1-1
1969	AC Milan (Ita.)	Estudiantes (Arg.)	3-0 1-2
1970	Feyenoord (Hol.)	Estudiantes (Arg.)	2-2 1-0
1971	Nacional (Uru.)	Panathanaikos (Gre.)*	1-1 2-1
1972	Ajax (Hol.)	Independiente (Arg.)	1-1 3-0
1973	Independiente (Arg.)	Juventus (Ita.)*	1-0 #
1974	Atletico Madrid (Spa.)*	Independiente (Arg.)	0-1 2-0
1975	Not played		
1976	Bayern Munich (W.Ger.)	Cruzeiro (Bra.)	2-0 0-0
1977	Boca Juniors (Arg.)	Borussia Mönchengladbach (W.Ger.)*	2-2 3-0
1978	Not played		
1979	Olimpia Asuncion (Par.)	Malmö (Swe.)*	1-0 2-1
1980	Nacional (Arg.)	Nott'm. Forest (Eng.)	1-0
1981	Flamengo (Bra.)	Liverpool (Eng.)	3-0
1982	Penarol (Uru.)	Aston Villa (Eng.)	2-0
1983	Porto Alegre (Bra.)	SV Hamburg (W.Ger.)	2-1
1984	Independiente (Arg.)	Liverpool (Eng.)	1-0
1985	Juventus (Ita.)	Argentinos Juniors (Arg.)	2-2 (aet)
	(Juventus won 4-2 on penalties)		
1986	River Plate (Arg.)	Steaua Bucharest (Rum.)	1-0
1987	Porto (Por.)	Penarol (Uru.)	2-1 (aet)
1988	Nacional (Uru.)	PSV Eindhoven (Hol.)	1-1 (aet)
	(Nacional won 7-6 on penalties)		
1989	AC Milan (Ita.)	Nacional (Col.)	1-0 (aet)
1990	AC Milan (Ita.)	Olimpia Asuncion (Par.)	3-0
1991	Red Star (Yug.)	Colo Colo (Chi.)	3-0
1992	Sao Paulo (Bra.)	Barcelona (Spa.)	2-1
1993	Sao Paulo (Bra.)	AC Milan (Ita.)	3-2
1994	Velez Sarsfield (Arg.)	AC Milan (Ita.)	2-0
1995	Ajax (Hol.)	Gremio (Bra.)	0-0 (aet)
	(Ajax won 4-3 on penalties)		
1996	Juventus (Ita.)	River Plate (Arg.)	1-0
1997	Borussia Dortmund (Ger.)	Cruzeiro (Arg.)	2-0
1998	Real Madrid (Spa.)	Vasco da Gama (Bra.)	2-1
1999	Manchester Utd. (Eng.)	Palmeiras (Bra.)	1-0
2000	Boca Juniors (Arg.)	Real Madrid (Spa.)	2-1
2001	Bayern Munich (Ger.)	Boca Juniours (Arg.)	1-0

Played as a single match in Tokyo since 1980
* European Cup runners-up. # One match only.
Summary: 40 contests; South America 21 wins, Europe 19 wins.

EUROPEAN SUPER CUP

BAYERN MUNICH 2, LIVERPOOL 3

Monaco, (15,000), Friday, August 24, 2001

Bayern Munich (3-5-2): Kahn, R. Kovac, Thiam, Linke, Sagnol, Sforza (N. Kovac 66), Hargreaves, Salihamidzic (Santa Cruz 72), Lizarazu, Pizzaro (Jancker 66), Elber. **Subs not used:** Dreher, Fink, Kuffour, Zickler. **Scorers:** Salihamidzic (57), Jancker (81).

Liverpool (4-4-2): Westerveld, Babbel, Hyypia (capt), Henchoz, Carragher, Gerrard (Biscan 66), Hamann, McAllister, Riise (Murphy 69), Owen (Fowler 83), Heskey. **Subs not used:** Arphexad, Redknapp, Vignal, Litmanen. **Scorers:** Riise (22), Heskey (45), Owen (46). **Booked:** Hamann.

Referee: V. Melo Pereira (Portugal). **Half-time:** 0-2.

QUOTE UNQUOTE

'Football is a mix of sport and entertainment and it's our opinion that this proposal took away the sporting element and left only entertainment' – Nationwide Conference spokesman on the decision to refuse Stevenage Borough permission to take part in a Channel 4 programme in which fans would have influenced team selection.

'Watching Owen and Heskey run at me was one of the most awseome sights I have seen' – **Andy Marshall**, Ipswich Town goalkeeper, after a 6-0 drubbing by Liverpool.

'It isn't unknown for games to be thrown deliberately at this time of year by way of favours' – **Susan Reynolds**, wife of Darlington chairman George Reynolds, straying beyond criticism of poor team performances and prompting a walk-out by players attending a fans' forum.

'I've just seen Fu Manchu with a gun to his head. I think his business plan has gone down the pan' – **Steve McMahon**, Blackpool manager, after his side beat Cambridge United 4-1 in the LDV Vans Trophy Final and spoiled the efforts of feng shui expert Paul Darby to lift the jinx of the Millennium Stadium's south dressing room.

'Slavery is finished . . . the time when clubs could agree on transfers without a player's consent is over' – **Olivier Dacourt** on reports that Leeds United had agreed to sell him to Lazio for £16m.

'It is not a good idea for the winners to have a place in Europe' – **Arsene Wenger**, Arsenal manager, arguing against the Worthington Cup holders qualifying for the UEFA Cup.

'All we need is a new stadium, a new training ground, half a new team. Apart from that we're not in bad shape' – **Harry Redknapp** after taking over as Portsmouth manager.

'I hope the boards of those companies realise they have a contractual, moral and social obligation to football' – **David Burns**, chief executive of the Football League, spelling out to Carlton and Granada the threat to the game posed by the collapse of ITV Digital's television agreement.

'The world went mad in that week and you're seeing the consequences now' – **Greg Dyke**, director-general of the BBC, recalling the summer of 2000 when television companies paid £2.3bn. for broadcasting rights.

EUROPEAN TABLES

BELGIUM

		P	W	D	L	F	A	Pts
1	Genk	34	20	12	2	85	43	72
2	Bruges	34	22	4	8	74	41	70
3	Anderlecht	34	18	12	4	71	37	66
4	Ghent	34	16	10	8	62	51	58
5	Standard Liege	34	15	12	7	57	38	57
6	Mouscron	34	17	5	12	68	40	56
7	Lokeren	34	15	10	9	43	33	55
8	St Truiden	34	16	5	13	52	47	53
9	Germinal	34	11	16	7	68	51	49
10	Molenbeek	34	13	5	16	50	59	44
11	La Louviere	34	12	8	14	41	52	44
12	Charleroi	34	11	6	17	40	63	39
13	Lommel	34	10	9	15	54	66	39
14	Westerlo	34	9	9	16	49	61	36
15	Lierse	34	9	8	17	55	65	35
16	Antwerp	34	7	10	17	47	67	31
17	Eendracht Aalst	34	4	9	21	32	73	21
18	Beveren	34	2	8	24	30	91	14

Leading scorers: 30 Sonck (Genk); 25 Kpaka (Germinal); 21 Dagano (Genk); 20 Lange (Bruges); 17 Kaklamanos (Ghent), Mbonabucya (St Truiden); 16 Goots (Antwerp), Zewlakow (Mouscron); 15 Mendoza (Bruges).
Cup Final: Bruges 3, Mouscron 1.

FRANCE

		P	W	D	L	F	A	Pts
1	Lyon	34	20	6	8	62	32	66
2	Lens	34	18	10	6	55	30	64
3	Auxerre	34	16	11	7	48	38	59
4	Paris S.G.	34	15	13	6	43	24	58
5	Lille	34	15	11	8	39	32	56
6	Bordeaux	34	14	8	12	34	31	50
7	Troyes	34	13	8	13	40	35	47
8	Sochaux	34	12	10	12	41	40	46
9	Marseille	34	11	11	12	34	39	44
10	Nantes	34	12	7	15	35	41	43
11	Bastia	34	12	5	17	38	44	41
12	Rennes	34	11	8	15	40	51	41
13	Montpellier	34	9	13	12	28	31	40
14	Sedan	34	8	15	11	35	39	39
15	Monaco	34	9	12	13	36	41	39
16	Guingamp	34	9	8	17	34	57	35
17	Metz	34	9	6	19	31	47	33
18	Lorient	34	7	10	17	43	64	31

Leading scorers: 22 Cisse (Auxerre), Pauleta (Bordeaux); 19 Darcheville (Lorient); 15 Frau (Sochaux); 14 Anderson (Lyon), Gousse (Troyes), Nonda (Monaco), Vairelles (Bastia); 12 Moreira (Lens).
Cup Final: Bastia 0, Lorient 1.

GERMANY

		P	W	D	L	F	A	Pts
1	Borussia Dortmund	34	21	7	6	62	33	70
2	Bayer Leverkusen	34	21	6	7	77	38	69
3	Bayern Munich	34	20	8	6	65	25	68
4	Hertha Berlin	34	18	7	9	61	38	61
5	Schalke	34	18	7	9	52	36	61
6	Werder Bremen	34	17	5	12	54	43	56
7	Kaiserslautern	34	17	5	12	62	53	56
8	Stuttgart	34	13	11	10	47	43	50
9	1860 Munich	34	15	5	14	59	59	50
10	Wolfsburg	34	13	7	14	57	49	46
11	Hamburg	34	10	10	14	51	57	40
12	Borussia M'gladbach	34	9	12	13	41	53	39
13	Cottbus	34	9	8	17	36	60	35
14	Hansa Rostock	34	9	7	18	35	54	34
15	Nurnberg	34	10	4	20	34	57	34
16	Freiburg	34	7	9	18	37	64	30
17	Cologne	34	7	8	19	26	61	29
18	St Pauli	34	4	10	20	37	70	22

Leading scorers: 18 Amoroso (Borussia Dortmund), Max (1860 Munich); 17 Ballack (Bayer Leverkusen), Elber (Bayern Munich); 16 Ailton (Werder Bremen); 14 Klose (Kaiserslautern), Pizzaro (Bayern Munich); 13 Neuville (Bayer Leverkusen); 12 Kirsten (Bayer Leverkusen), Van Lent (Borussia M'gladbach).
Cup Final: Bayer Leverkusen 2, Schalke 4.

HOLLAND

		P	W	D	L	F	A	Pts
1	Ajax	34	22	7	5	73	34	73
2	PSV Eindhoven	34	20	8	6	77	32	68
3	Feyenoord	34	19	7	8	68	29	64
4	Heerenveen	34	17	9	8	57	27	60
5	Vitesse	34	16	12	6	45	34	60
6	Breda	34	15	9	10	55	52	54
7	Utrecht	34	14	9	11	60	51	51
8	Waalwijk	34	14	6	14	49	44	48
9	Nijmegen	34	13	6	15	38	59	45
10	Alkaar	34	12	7	15	43	45	43
11	Willem II	34	10	13	11	54	61	43
12	Twente	34	10	12	12	41	41	42
13	Roda	34	11	8	15	33	45	41
14	De Graafschap	34	10	7	17	43	55	37
15	Groningen	34	10	7	17	40	59	37
16	Den Bosch	34	8	9	17	40	55	33
17	Sparta	34	4	12	18	26	75	24
18	Fortuna Sittard	34	3	8	23	27	71	17

Leading scorers: 24 Van Hooijdonk (Feyenoord); 22 Vennegoor (PSV Eindhoven); 17 Tomasson (Feyenoord); 16 Landzaat (Willem II); 15 Allback (Heerenveen), Gluscevic (Utrecht), Kezman (PSV Eindhoven); 14 Van den Eede (Den Bosch), Van der Vaart (Ajax).
Cup Final: Ajax 3, Utrecht 2.

ITALY

		P	W	D	L	F	A	Pts
1	Juventus	34	20	11	3	64	23	71
2	Roma	34	19	13	2	58	24	70
3	Inter Milan	34	20	9	5	62	35	69
4	AC Milan	34	14	13	7	47	33	55
5	Chievo	34	14	12	8	57	52	54
6	Lazio	34	14	11	9	50	37	53
7	Bologna	34	15	7	12	40	40	52
8	Perugia	34	13	7	14	38	46	46
9	Atalanta	34	12	9	13	41	50	45
10	Parma	34	12	8	14	43	47	44
11	Torino	34	10	13	11	37	39	43
12	Piacenza	34	11	9	14	49	43	42
13	Brescia	34	9	13	12	43	52	40
14	Udinese	34	11	7	16	41	52	40
15	Verona	34	11	6	17	41	53	39
16	Lecce	34	6	10	18	36	56	28
17	Fiorentina	34	5	7	22	29	63	22
18	Venezia	34	3	9	22	30	61	18

Leading scorers: 24 Hubner (Piacenza), Trezeguet (Juventus); 22 Vieri (Inter Milan); 20 Di Vaio (Parma); 18 Maniero (Venezia); 16 Del Piero (Juventus), Doni (Atalanta); 14 Muzzi (Udinese), Shevcheko (AC Milan); 13 Crespo (Lazio); Marazzina (Chievo/Verona), Toni (Brescia).
Cup Final: Juventus 2, Parma 2 (on agg, Parma won on away goal).

PORTUGAL

		P	W	D	L	F	A	Pts
1	Sporting Lisbon	34	22	9	3	74	25	75
2	Boavista	34	21	7	6	53	20	70
3	FC Porto	34	21	5	8	65	34	68
4	Benfica	34	17	12	5	66	37	63
5	Belenenses	34	17	6	11	54	44	57
6	Maritimo	34	17	5	12	48	35	56
7	U. Leiria	34	15	10	9	52	35	55
8	Paços Ferreira	34	12	10	12	41	44	46
9	Braga	34	10	12	12	43	43	42
10	Guimaraes	34	11	9	14	35	41	42
11	Beira Mar	34	10	9	15	48	56	39
12	Setúbal	34	9	11	14	40	46	38
13	Gil Vicente	34	10	8	16	42	56	38
14	Santa Clara	34	9	10	15	32	46	37
15	Varzim	34	8	8	18	27	55	32
16	Salgueiros	34	8	6	20	29	70	30
17	Farense	34	7	7	20	29	63	28
18	Alverca	34	7	6	21	39	67	27

Leading scorers: 42 Jardel (Sporting Lisbon); 21 Derlei (Leiria); 18 Fary (Beira); 16 Henrique (Setubal); 15 Barata (Braga), Gaucho (Maritimo); 14 Leonardo (Pacos); 13 Deco (FC Porto), Mantorras (Benfica).
Cup Final: Leixoes 0, Sporting Lisbon 1.

SPAIN

		P	W	D	L	F	A	Pts
1	Valencia	38	21	12	5	51	27	75
2	Dep. La Coruna	38	20	8	10	65	41	68
3	Real Madrid	38	19	9	10	69	44	66
4	Barcelona	38	18	10	10	65	37	64
5	Celta Vigo	38	16	12	10	64	46	60
6	Real Betis	38	15	14	9	42	34	59
7	Alaves	38	17	3	18	41	44	54
8	Sevilla	38	14	11	13	51	40	53
9	Athletic Bilbao	38	14	11	13	54	66	53
10	Malaga	38	13	14	11	44	44	53
11	Rayo Vallecano	38	13	10	15	46	52	49
12	Valladolid	38	13	9	16	45	58	48
13	Real Sociedad	38	13	8	17	48	54	47
14	Espanyol	38	13	8	17	47	56	47
15	Villarreal	38	11	10	17	46	55	43
16	Mallorca	38	11	10	17	40	52	43
17	Osasuna	38	10	12	16	36	49	42
18	Las Palmas	38	9	13	16	40	50	40
19	Tenerife	38	10	8	20	32	58	38
20	Real Zaragoza	38	9	10	19	35	54	37

Leading scorers: 21 Tristan (Deportivo La Coruna); 18 Kluivert (Barcelona), Morientes (Real Madrid); 17 Catanha (Celta Vigo), Saviola (Barcelona), Tamudo (Espanyol); 15 Fernando (Valladolid), Urzaiz (Athletic Bilbao).
Cup Final: Deportivo La Coruna 2, Real Madrid 1.

QUOTE UNQUOTE

'David, this job now, dealing with players and how powerful they are, keeping them happy and the media and how people are so impatient to get results . . . it is bad for your health' – **Gerard Houllier**, Liverpool manager, talking to Leeds United's David O'Leary before being taken ill and having life-saving heart surgery.

'He looked at me and said: 'I fancy it, the time is right' ' – **Phil Thompson**, assistant manager, on the moment Gerard Houllier decided to return to the Liverpool dug-out.

'I don't think anybody could go through such an experience without saying: Oh my God, I'm miraculously alive. It's wonderful to be here' – **Gerard Houllier**.

'You would not pick a player who was less than 100 per cent fit, so make sure you are before you go back to work' – a treasured message for Gerard Houllier among the thousands he received while recovering.

'Over 100 goals scored, over 50 conceded . . . I guess you could say it's my style' – **Kevin Keegan** after leading Manchester City to the Division One title

'The most outstanding player I've ever worked with, bar none' – **Kevin Keegan** on his Algerian midfielder Ali Benarbia.

EUROPEAN CHAMPIONSHIP 2004

England will break new ground in their qualifying group for the 2004 European Championship in Portugal. But there are some familiar faces and the prospect of tough times ahead for the rest of the home countries.

The draw matched England with Slovakia, Macedonia and Liechtenstein, teams they have never played before. Their other group seven opponents, Turkey, have been beaten seven times in eight meetings between the two countries in World Cup and European Championship qualifiers. The other game was drawn.

England did not concede a goal in any of those matches and were twice 8-0 winners – the first time in Istanbul in 1984 (Bryan Robson 3, Tony Woodcock 2, John Barnes 2, Viv Anderson) and then at Wembley in 1987 (Gary Lineker 3, John Barnes 2, Bryan Robson, Peter Beardsley, Neil Webb).

The countries last met in Izmir in 1993 when goals by David Platt and Paul Gascoigne gave England a 2-0 victory. Turkey are a much more formidable proposition these days, having just finished third in the World Cup Finals.

Berti Vogts, successor to Craig Brown, will lead Scotland against Germany, the team he coached to victory in Euro 96. A runners-up spot, at least, looks a distinct possibility for the new coach, with Iceland, Lithuania and Faroe Islands completing group five. But Northern Ireland, paired with Spain, Ukraine and Greece, and Wales, who meet Italy, Yugoslavia and Finland, have it all to do. The Republic of Ireland's biggest challenge for the top spot is likely to come from Russia.

Qualifying begins on September 7/8, 2002, with the final round of matches on October 11/12, 2003. Group winners qualify for the Finals, along with the winners of five play-off games between the 10 runners-up. The first legs of three are on November 15/16, 2003, and the return fixtures on November 18/19. The draw for the Finals is on November 30, 2003 and they kick off on June 12, 2004, when Portugal, who qualify as hosts, will be in action in the Das Antas Stadium, Oporto. The Final is on July 4 in Benfica's new stadium in Lisbon.

QUALIFYING DRAW

Group 1: France, Slovenia, Israel, Cyrprus, Malta.
Group 2: Romania, Denmark, Norway, Bosnia, Luxembourg.
Group 3: Czech Republic, Holland, Austria, Moldova, Belarus.
Group 4: Sweden, Poland, Hungary, Latvia, San Marino.
Group 5: Germany, **Scotland**, Iceland, Lithuania, Faroe Islands.
Group 6: Spain, Ukraine, Greece, **Northern Ireland**, Armenia.
Group 7: Turkey, **England**, Slovakia, Macedonia, Liechtenstein.
Group 8: Belgium, Croatia, Bulgaria, Estonia, Andorra.
Group 9: Italy, Yugoslavia, Finland, **Wales**, Azerbaijan.
Group 10: **Republic of Ireland**, Russia, Switzerland, Georgia, Albania.

PREVIOUS FINALS

1960	*USSR	2	Yugoslavia	1	(Paris)
1964	Spain	2	USSR	1	(Madrid)
1968	***Italy	2	Yugoslavia	0	(Rome)
1972	West Germany	3	USSR	0	(Brussels)
1976	**Czechoslovakia	2	West Germany	2	(Belgrade)
1980	West Germany	2	Belgium	1	(Rome)
1984	France	2	Spain	0	(Paris)
1988	Holland	2	USSR	0	(Munich)
1992	Denmark	2	Germany	0	(Gothenburg)
1996	+Germany	2	Czech Republic	1	(Wembley)
2000	+France	2	Italy	1	(Rotterdam)

(***Replay after 1-1; **Czechoslovakia won 5-3 on pens; *After extra-time; +Golden goal winner)

BRITISH AND IRISH INTERNATIONALS
2001-02

(* denotes new cap)

WORLD CUP 2002 – QUALIFYING

GERMANY 1, ENGLAND 5
Munich, (66,000), Saturday, September 1, 2001

Germany (3-4-1-2): Kahn, Worns (Asamoah 46), Nowotny, Linke, Rehmer, Hamann, Ballack (Klose 67), Bohme, Deisler, Jancker, Neuville (Kehl 78). **Scorer:** Jancker (6). **Booked:** Hamann.

England (4-4-2): Seaman (Arsenal), G. Neville (Manchester Utd.), Campbell (Arsenal), Ferdinand (Leeds Utd.), Cole (Arsenal), Beckham (Manchester Utd.), Scholes (Manchester Utd.) (Carragher, Liverpool, 84), Gerrard (Liverpool) (Hargreaves, Bayern Munich, 77), Barmby (Liverpool) (McManaman, Real Madrid, 65), Owen (Liverpool), Heskey (Liverpool). **Scorers:** Owen (12, 48, 66), Gerrard (45), Heskey (74). **Booked:** Heskey.

Referee: P. Collina (Italy). **Half-time:** 1-2.

SCOTLAND 0, CROATIA 0
Hampden Park, (47,384), Saturday, September 1, 2001

Scotland (3-4-3): Sullivan (Tottenham), Weir (Everton), Elliott (Leicester City), Matteo (Leeds Utd.), Dailly (West Ham Utd.), Lambert (Celtic), Burley (Derby Co.), Naysmith (Everton) (Gemmill, Everton, 84), Hutchison (Sunderland), Booth (Twente Enschede) (Dodds, Rangers, 72), McCann (Rangers) (Cameron, Wolves, 52). **Booked:** Elliott, McCann.

Croatia (3-4-2-1): Pletikosa, Tudor, Stimac, Kovac, Zivkovic, Soldo, Tomas (Biscan 84), Jarni, Prosinecki (Vugrinec 78), Stanic (Suker 71), Balaban. **Booked:** Soldo, Stanic, Tudor.

Referee: L. Michel (Slovakia). **Half-time:** 0-0.

WALES 0, ARMENIA 0
Millennium Stadium, (18,000), Saturday, September 1, 2001

Wales (4-3-2-1): P. Jones (Southampton), Delaney (Aston Villa), Melville (Fulham), Symons (Fulham), Jenkins (Huddersfield Town) (Barnard, Barnsley, 80), Davies (Tottenham), Savage (Leicester City), Robinson (Wolves) (M. Jones, Leicester City, 80), Bellamy (Newcastle Utd.), Giggs (Manchester Utd.), Roberts (Norwich City). **Booked:** Melville.

Armenia (3-5-2): Berezovski, Sukiasyan, Hovsepyan, Vardanyan, A. Dokhoyan, Petrosyan (Demirtshyan 90), Khachatryan, Voskanyan (Harutyunyan 67), K. Dokhoyan, Shahgeldyan (Simonyan 75), Movsisyan. **Booked:** Hovsepyan.

Referee: J. Attard (Malta). **Half-time:** 0-0.

DENMARK 1, NORTHERN IRELAND 1
Copenhagen, (41,569), Saturday, September 1, 2001

Denmark (4-4-2): Sorensen (Kjaer 11), Helveg, Laursen, Henriksen, Heintze, Rommedahl, Tofting, Nielsen (Frandsen 68), Gronkjaer, Tomasson (Nygaard 78), Sand. **Scorer:** Rommedahl (3). **Booked:** Rommedahl, Laursen.

Northern Ireland (4-5-1): Taylor (Fulham), Griffin (Dundee Utd.), Murdock (Preston N.E.), A. Hughes (Newcastle Utd.), Kennedy (Wigan Athletic), Gillespie (Blackburn Rov.), Magilton (Ipswich Town), Mulryne (Norwich City), Horlock (Manchester City), M. Hughes (Wimbledon) (Elliott, Motherwell, 70), Healy (Preston N.E.). **Scorer:** Mulryne (73). **Booked:** Murdock, Gillespie.

Referee: R. Wojcik (Poland). **Half-time:** 1-0.

REPUBLIC OF IRELAND 1, HOLLAND 0
Lansdowne Road, (49,000), Saturday, September 1, 2001

Rep. of Ireland (4-4-2): Given (Newcastle Utd.), Kelly (Leeds Utd.), Dunne (Manchester City), Staunton (Aston Villa), Harte (Leeds Utd.), McAteer (Blackburn Rov.) (O'Brien, Newcastle Utd., 90), Roy Keane (Manchester Utd.), Holland (Ipswich Town), Kilbane (Sunderland), Duff (Blackburn Rov.) (Quinn, Sunderland, 88), Robbie Keane (Leeds Utd.) (Finnan, Fulham, 58). **Scorer:** McAteer (68). **Booked:** Kelly. **Sent-off:** Kelly (58).

Holland (4-4-1-1): Van der Sar, Melchiot, Stam, Hofland, Numan (Van Hooijdonk 63), Zenden (Hasselbaink 55), Van Bommel, Cocu, Overmars (Van Bronckhorst 71), Kluivert, Van Nistelrooy. **Booked:** Hofland, Zenden, Melchiot, Kluivert.

Referee: H. Krug (Germany). **Half-time:** 0-0.

ENGLAND 2, ALBANIA 0
St James' Park, (51,046), Wednesday, September 5, 2001

England (4-4-2): Seaman (Arsenal), G. Neville (Manchester Utd.), Campbell (Arsenal), Ferdinand (Leeds Utd.), Cole (Arsenal), Beckham (Manchester Utd.), Scholes (Manchester Utd.), Gerrard (Liverpool) (Carragher, Liverpool, 81), Barmby (Liverpool) (McManaman, Real Madrid, 62), Owen (Liverpool), Heskey (Liverpool) (Fowler, Liverpool, 53). **Scorers:** Owen (44), Fowler (88). **Booked:** Gerrard.

Albania (3-5-2): Strakosha, Xhumba, Cipi, Fakaj, Dede, Bella, Vata, Hasi (Bushaj 46), Murait, Rraklli (Mukaj 61), Bogdani (Tare 54). **Booked:** Murati.

Referee: J. Marin (Spain). **Half-time:** 2-0.

BELGIUM 2, SCOTLAND 0
Brussels, (48,500), Wednesday, September 5, 2001

Belgium (4-4-1-1): De Vlieger, Deflandre, De Boeck, Van Meir, Van Kerckhoven, Verheyen, Vanderhaege, Walem (Simons 88), Goor, Wilmots, Sonck (Peeters 83). **Scorers:** Van Kerckhoven (28), Goor (90). **Booked:** De Boeck.

Scotland (3-5-2): Sullivan (Tottenham), Weir (Everton) (Cameron, Wolves, 74), Elliott (Leicester City), Dailly (West Ham Utd.), Boyd (Celtic) (Booth, Twente Enschede, 57), Burley (Derby Co.) (McNamara, Celtic, 83), Lambert (Celtic), Matteo (Leeds Utd.), Naysmith (Everton), Hutchison (West Ham Utd.), Dodds (Rangers). **Booked:** Booth.

Referee: M. Mejuto (Spain). **Half-time:** 1-0.

NORWAY 3, WALES 2
Oslo, (18,211), Wednesday, September 5, 2001

Norway (4-5-1): Myhre, Basma, Berg, R. Johnsen, Riise, Sorensen (F. Johnsen 46), R. Strand, Rudi, Leonhardsen (P. Strand 90), Solskjaer, Iversen (Carew 5). **Scorers:** R. Johnsen (17), Carew (65), F. Johnsen (83). **Booked:** Leonhardsen, Solskjaer.

Wales (4-3-2-1): P. Jones (Southampton), Delaney (Aston Villa), Page (Watford), Symons (Fulham), Jenkins (Huddersfield Town), Davies (Tottenham) (J. Robinson, Charlton Athletic, 77), Savage (Leicester City), C. Robinson (Wolves) (M. Jones, Leicester City, 84), Bellamy (Newcastle Utd.), Giggs (Manchester Utd.), Hartson (Celtic) (Blake, Blackburn Rov., 83). **Scorers:** Savage (10), Bellamy (27). **Booked:** Savage, Gibbs. **Sent-off:** Giggs (85).

Referee: F. Stuchlik (Austria). **Half-time:** 1-2.

NORTHERN IRELAND 3, ICELAND 0
Windsor Park, (6,625), Wednesday, September 5, 2001

Northern Ireland (4-5-1): Taylor (Fulham), Griffin (Dundee Utd.), A. Hughes (Newcastle Utd.), *McCartney (Sunderland), Kennedy (Wigan Athletic), Gillespie (Blackburn Rov.) (McVeigh, Norwich City, 88), Mulryne (Norwich City), Magilton (Ipswich Town), M. Hughes (Wimbledon), Horlock (Manchester City), Healy (Preston N.E.). **Scorers:** Healy (48), M. Hughes (58), McCartney (60).

Iceland (4-3-3): Arason, Helgason (Helguson, 62), Sverrisson. Hreidarsson, Vidarsson, Gudjonsson, Marteinsson, Gretarsson, Sigurdsson (Baldvinsson 86), Sigthorsson, Gudjohnsen.

Referee: A. Hanacsek (Hungary). **Half-time:** 0-0.

ENGLAND 2, GREECE 2
Old Trafford, (66,009), Saturday, October 6, 2001

England (4-4-2): Martyn (Leeds Utd.), G. Neville (Manchester Utd.), Keown (Arsenal), Ferdinand (Leeds Utd.), Ashley Cole (Arsenal) (McManaman, Real Madrid, 78), Beckham (Manchester Utd.), Gerrard (Liverpool), Scholes (Manchester Utd.), Barmby (Liverpool) (Andy Cole, Manchester Utd., 46), Heskey (Liverpool), Fowler (Liverpool) (Sheringham, Tottenham, 66). **Scorers:** Sheringham (68), Beckham (90). **Booked:** Scholes.

Greece (5-3-2): Nikopolidis, Patsatzoglou, Dabizas, Konstantinidis, Vokolos, Fissas, Charisteas (Lakis 73), Zagorakis (Basinas 56), Karagounis, Kassapis, Nikolaidis (Macnlas 85). **Scorers:** Charisteas (36), Nikolaidis (69). **Booked:** Zagorakis

Referee: D. Jol (Holland). **Half-time:** 0-1.

SCOTLAND 2, LATVIA 1
Hampden Park, (23,228), Saturday, October 6, 2001

Scotland (3-4-1-2): Sullivan (Tottenham), Weir (Everton), Elliott (Leicester City) (*Rae, Dundee, 71), Dailly (West Ham Utd.), Nicholson (Dunfermline) (Booth, Twente Enschede, 63), Burley (Derby Co.), Cameron (Wolves), Davidson (Leicester City), Hutchison (West Ham Utd.) (*Severin, Hearts, 76), *Freedman (Crystal Palace), McCann (Rangers). **Scorers:** Freedman (44), Weir (53). **Booked:** Weir.

Latvia (4-4-2): Kolinko, Isakovs, Zakresevskis, Stepanovs, Blagonadezdins, Bleidelis (Kolesnicenko 76), Laizans, Astafjevs, Rubins (Dobrecovs 82), Pahars, Verpakovskis. **Scorer:** Rubins (21). **Booked:** Zakresevskis.

Referee: T. Hauge (Norway). **Half-time:** 1-1.

WALES 1, BELARUS 0
Millennium Stadium, (12,000), Saturday, October 6, 2001

Wales (4-4-2): P. Jones (Southampton), Delaney (Aston Villa), Melville (Fulham), Symons (Fulham) (Page, Sheffield Utd., 17), Speed (Newcastle Utd.), J. Robinson (Charlton Athletic), Davies (Tottenham), Pembridge (Everton), M. Jones (Leicester City) (C. Robinson, Wolves, 65), Bellamy (Newcastle Utd.), Hartson (Celtic) (Roberts, Norwich City, 90). **Scorer:** Hartson (47).

Belarus (3-4-1-2): Tumilovich, Lukhvich, Yakhimovic, Shtanyuk, Gurenko, Shuneiko, Kulchy, Yaskovich, Baranov (Gleb 67), Vasilyuk (Ryndyuk 44), Katchuro.

Referee: P. Rodomonti (Italy). **Half-time:** 0-0.

MALTA 0, NORTHERN IRELAND 1
Valletta, (1,000), Saturday, October 6, 2001

Malta (3-5-2): Muscat, Debono, Said, Spiteri, Carabott, Agius, Theuma (Mallia 65), Zahra (Suda 80), Chetcuti, Mifsud, Nwoko. **Booked:** Chetcuti.

Northern Ireland (4-4-1-1): Taylor (Fulham), Griffin (Dundee Utd.), McCartney (Sunderland), Murdock (Preston N.E.), Kennedy (Wigan Athletic), Johnson (Blackburn Rov.), Magilton (Ipswich Town), Horlock (Manchester City), Elliott (Motherwell) (Quinn, W.B.A., 80), Hughes (Wimbledon), Healy (Preston N.E.) (*McCann, West Ham Utd., 80). **Scorer:** Healy (57 pen).

Referee: M. Schuttengruber (Austria). **Half-time:** 0-0.

REPUBLIC OF IRELAND 4, CYPRUS 0
Lansdowne Road, (35,000), Saturday, October 6, 2001

Rep. of Ireland (4-4-2): Given (Newcastle Utd.), Finnan (Fulham), Breen (Coventry City), Staunton (Aston Villa), Harte (Leeds Utd.), Kennedy (Wolves) (Carsley, Coventry City, 65), Roy Keane (Manchester Utd.), Holland (Ipswich Town), Kilbane (Sunderland) (McPhail, Leeds Utd., 85), Quinn (Sunderland) (Morrison, Crystal Palace, 70), Connolly (Wimbledon). **Scorers:** Harte (3), Quinn (11), Connolly (63), Roy Keane (68).

Cyprus (4-1-4-1): Panayiotou, Konnafis (Louka 70), Melanarkitis, Daskalakis, Kotsonis, Nikolaou, Theodotou, Okkas (Themistocleous 85), Satsias, Christodoulou, Ylasoymi (Kontolefterou 90). **Booked:** Okkas, Melanarkitis.

Referee: J. Roca (Spain). **Half-time:** 2-0.

WORLD CUP PLAY-OFF, FIRST LEG

REPUBLIC OF IRELAND 2, IRAN 0
Lansdowne Road, (35,000), Saturday, November 10, 2001

Rep. of Ireland (4-4-2): Given (Newcastle Utd.), Finnan (Fulham), Breen (Coventry City), Staunton (Aston Villa), Harte (Leeds Utd.), McAteer (Sunderland) (Kelly, Leeds Utd., 84), Roy Keane (Manchester Utd.), Holland (Ipswich Town), Kilbane (Sunderland), Quinn (Sunderland), Robbie Keane (Leeds Utd.). **Scorers:** Harte (45 pen), Robbie Keane (50).

Iran (3-5-2): Mirzapour, Peyrovani, Golmohammadi, Rezaei, Mahdavikia, Bagheri, Kavianpour, Minavand, Vahedinikbahkt (Khaziravi 46), Karimi, Daei. **Booked:** Peyrovani, Golmohammadi.

Referee: A. Pereira da Silva (Brazil). **Half-time:** 1-0.

WORLD CUP PLAY-OFF, SECOND LEG

IRAN 1, REPUBLIC OF IRELAND 0
Tehran, (100,000), Thursday, November 15, 2001

Iran (3-4-3): Mirzapour, Peyrovani, Golmohammadi, Rezaei, Mahdavikia, Bagheri, Kavianpour, Minavand, Vahedinikbahkt, Karimi, Daei. **Scorer:** Golmohammadi (90). **Booked:** Golmohammadi, Bagheri.

Rep. of Ireland (4-4-2): Given (Newcastle Utd.), Finnan (Fulham), Breen (Coventry City), Staunton (Aston Villa), Harte (Leeds Utd.), McAteer (Sunderland), Kinsella (Charlton Athletic), Holland (Ipswich Town), Kilbane (Sunderland) (Kelly, Leeds Utd., 79), Connolly (Wimbledon), Robbie Keane (Leeds Utd.) (Morrison, Crystal Palace, 76). **Booked:** McAteer, Robbie Keane.

Referee: W. Vega (Costa Rica). **Half-time:** 0-0.

FRIENDLY INTERNATIONALS

ENGLAND 0, HOLLAND 2
White Hart Lane, (35,238), Wednesday, August 15, 2001

England (4-4-2): Martyn (Leeds Utd.) (James, Aston Villa, 46) (Wright, Arsenal, 49), G. Neville (Manchester Utd.) (Mills, Leeds Utd., 46), Brown (Manchester Utd.) (Southgate, Middlesbrough, 46), Keown (Arsenal) (Ehiogu, Middlesbrough, 49), Ashley Cole

(Arsenal) (Powell, Charlton Athletic, 46), Beckham (Manchester Utd.) (Lampard, Chelsea, 46), Carragher (Liverpool), Scholes (Manchester Utd.) (Carrick, West Ham Utd., 46), *Hargreaves (Bayern Munich) (Barmby, Liverpool, 46), Andy Cole (Manchester Utd.) (Smith, Leeds Utd., 69), Fowler (Liverpool) (Owen, Liverpool, 46). **Booked:** Neville, Carragher.

Holland (4-3-3): Van der Sar (Walerrius 46), Reiziger, Stam (Melchiot 46), Hofland, Van Bronckhorst, Cocu, Kluivert (Van Hooijdonk, 89), Van Bommel (Landzaat 72), Zenden (Makaay 46), Van Nistelrooy (Hasselbaink 46), Overmars (Davids 46). **Scorers:** Van Bommel (38), Van Nistelrooy (39). **Booked:** Kluivert.

Referee: A. Fisk (Sweden). **Half-time:** 0-2.

REPUBLIC OF IRELAND 2, CROATIA 2
Lansdowne Road, (27,000), Wednesday, August 15, 2001

Rep. of Ireland (4-4-2): Given (Newcastle Utd.) (A. Kelly, Blackburn Rov., 46), G. Kelly (Leeds Utd.) (*O'Shea, Manchester Utd., 84), Dunne (Manchester City) (O'Brien, Newcastle Utd., 46), Staunton (Aston Villa), Harte (Leeds Utd.) (McPhail, Leeds Utd., 46), *Reid (Millwall) (Finnan, Fulham, 46), Carsley (Coventry City), Roy Keane (Manchester Utd.) (McAteer, Blackburn Rov., 46), Kennedy (Wolves) (Kilbane, Sunderland, 46), Robbie Keane (Leeds Utd.) (*Morrison, Crystal Palace, 52), Duff (Blackburn Rov.) (Connolly, Wimbledon, 52). **Scorers:** Duff (21), Morrison (77).

Croatia (3-1-4-2): Pletikosa, Kovac, Tudor, Simic (Tomas 74), Soldo (Prosinecki 74), Stanic (Biscan 46), Kovac (Bjelica 82), Rapaic (Zivkovic 46), Jarni (Saric 62), Balaban (Vugrinec 46), Boksic (Suker 74). **Scorers:** Vugrinec (46), Suker (90 pen). **Booked:** Soldo.

Referee: A. Schluchter (Switzerland). **Half-time:** 1-0.

ENGLAND 1, SWEDEN 1
Old Trafford, (64,413), Saturday, November 10, 2001

England (4-4-2): Martyn (Leeds Utd.), G. Neville (Manchester Utd.) (Mills, Leeds Utd., 59), Ferdinand (Leeds Utd.), Southgate (Middlesbrough), Carragher (Liverpool) (P. Neville, Manchester Utd., 86), Beckham (Manchester Utd.), Butt (Manchester Utd.) (*Murphy, Liverpool, 59), Scholes (Manchester Utd.) (Lampard, Chelsea, 86), *Sinclair (West Ham Utd.) (Fowler, Liverpool, 59), Phillips (Sunderland) (Anderton, Tottenham, 59), Heskey (Liverpool) (Sheringham, Tottenham, 59). **Scorer:** Beckham (28 pen).

Sweden (4-4-2): Hedman (Kihlstedt 45), C. Andersson, Michael Svensson, Mjallby (Jakobsson 62), Edman, Alexandersson (Soderstrom 83), Linderoth (D. Andersson 45), Mild, Magnus Svensson (Anders Svensson, 46), Ibrahimovic (Osmanovski, 74), Allback. **Scorer:** Mild (44).

Referee: C. Colombo (France). **Half-time:** 1-1.

HOLLAND 1, ENGLAND 1
Amsterdam, (48,500), Wednesday, February 13, 2002

Holland (4-4-2): Van der Sar, Ricksen, Reiziger, F. de Boer (Paauwe 67), Van Bronckhorst, R de Boer (Sikora 59), Van Bommel (Davids 46), Cocu (Boateng 46), Overmars (Makaay 88), Van Nistelrooy (Hasselbaink 64), Kluivert. **Scorer:** Kluivert (26).

England (4-3-3): Martyn (Leeds Utd.) (James, West Ham Utd., 46), G. Neville (Manchester Utd.) (P. Neville, Manchester Utd., 77), Ferdinand (Leeds Utd.), Campbell (Arsenal) (Southgate, Middlesbrough, 46), *Bridge (Southampton) (Powell, Charlton Athletic, 46), Beckham (Manchester Utd.), Gerrard (Liverpool) (Lampard, Chelsea, 77), Scholes (Manchester Utd.) (Butt, Manchester Utd., 77), *Vassell (Aston Villa) (Cole West Ham Utd., 77), *Ricketts (Bolton Wand.) (Phillips, Sunderland, 46), Heskey (Liverpool). **Scorer:** Vassell (61).

Referee: L. Duhamel (France). **Half-time:** 1-0.

WALES 1, ARGENTINA 1
Millenium Stadium, (62,500), Wednesday, February 13, 2002

Wales (4-4-2): Jones (Southampton) (Crossley, Middlesbrough, 46), Delaney (Aston Villa), Page (Sheffield Utd.), Melville (Fulham), Speed (Newcastle Utd.), Davies (Tottenham), Pembridge (Everton) (C. Robinson, Wolves, 90), Savage (Leicester City), Giggs (Manchester Utd.) (J. Robinson, Charlton Athletic, 61), Bellamy (Newcastle Utd.), Hartson (Celtic). **Scorer:** Bellamy (34). **Booked:** Savage, Page, Hartson.

Argentina (3-4-1-2): Saja, Placente, Chamot, Vivas, Gonzalez, Sorin, Veron, Hussain, Riquelme (Aimar 74), Caniggia (Galletti 90), Cruz (Saviola 74). **Scorer:** Cruz (61). **Booked:** Chamot, Veron, Hussain.

Referee: P. McKeon (Ireland). **Half-time:** 1-0.

POLAND 4, NORTHERN IRELAND 1
Limassol, Cyprus, (221) Wednesday, February 13, 2002

Poland (4-4-2): Majdan (Bledzewski 90), Krzynowek, J. Bak, Michal Zewlakow (Rzasa 60), Waldoch, Kozminski, Swierczewski (Zdebel 46), Iwan (Smolarek 46), Kryszalowicz, (Zielinski 82), Kaluzny (A. Bak 46), Olisadebe (Marcin Zewlakow 46). **Scorers:** Kryszalowicz (6, 67), Kaluzny (11), Marcin Zewlakow (69). **Booked:** Waldoch, Swierczewski.

Northern Ireland (4-4-1-1): Taylor (Fulham), Griffin (Dundee Utd.) (McCartney, Sunderland, 46), A. Hughes (Newcastle Utd.), Kennedy (Wigan Athletic) (McCann, West Ham Utd., 82), Lomas (West Ham Utd.), Johnson (Blackburn Rov.) (McVeigh, Norwich City, 66), Mulryne (Norwich City) (Lennon, Celtic, 46), Magilton (Ipswich Town) (*Duff, Cheltenham Town, 82), Gillespie (Blackburn Rov.), M. Hughes (Wimbledon), Healy (Preston N.E.) (Elliott, Motherwell, 60). **Scorer:** Lomas (18). **Booked:** Gillespie, Elliott.

Referee: T. Papaioannou (Cyprus). **Half-time:** 2-1.

REPUBLIC OF IRELAND 2, RUSSIA 0
Lansdowne Road, (44,000), Wednesday, February 13, 2002

Rep. of Ireland (4-4-2): Given (Newcastle Utd.) (Kiely, Charlton Athletic, 46), Finnan (Fulham) (McAteer, Sunderland, 72) (Quinn, Sunderland, 90), O'Brien (Newcastle Utd.) (Dunne, Manchester City, 46), Cunningham (Wimbledon) (Breen, Coventry City, 46), Harte (Leeds Utd.) (Staunton, Aston Villa, 72), Reid (Millwall) (Kelly, Leeds Utd., 46), Roy Keane (Manchester Utd.) (Holland, Ipswich Town, 86), *Healy (Celtic) (Carsley, Everton, 46), Kilbane (Sunderland) (Kennedy, Manchester City, 46), Robbie Keane (Leeds Utd.) (*Sadlier, Millwall, 72), Duff (Blackburn Rov.) (Morrison, Crystal Palace, 46). **Scorers:** Reid (3), Robbie Keane (20).

Russia (4-5-1): Nigmatullin, Khlestov (Daev 90), Nikiforov (Chugainov 66), Onopko, Kovtun, Karpin, Khokhlov (Izmailov 53), Mostovoi, Titov, Alenichev (Semak 72), Beschastnykh.

Referee: D. Gallagher (England). **Half-time:** 2-0.

ENGLAND 1, ITALY 2
Elland Road, (36,635), Wednesday, March 27, 2002

England (4-4-2): Martyn (Leeds Utd.) (James, West Ham Utd., 46), Mills (Leeds Utd.) (P. Neville, Manchester Utd., 46), Southgate (Middlesbrough) (Ehiogu, Middlesbrough, 46), Campbell (Arsenal) (*King, Tottenham, 46), Bridge (Southampton) (G. Neville, Manchester Utd., 86), Beckham (Manchester Utd.) (Murphy, Liverpool, 46), Lampard (Chelsea) (Hargreaves, Bayern Munich, 46), Butt (Manchester Utd.) (Cole, West Ham Utd., 46), Sinclair (West Ham Utd.) (Sheringham, Tottenham, 70), Owen (Liverpool) (Fowler, Liverpool, 46), Heskey (Liverpool) (Vassell, Aston Villa, 46). **Scorer:** Fowler (63). **Booked:** Heskey, James.

Italy (4-4-1-1): Buffon, Cannavro, Nesta (Adani 81), Materazzi (Iuliano 57), Panucci (Coco 75), Zambrotta, Di Biagio (Gattuso 57), Zanetti (Albertini 57), Doni (Tommasi 75), Totti (Montella 46), Delvecchio (Maccarone 75). **Scorer:** Montella (67, 90 pen). **Booked:** Nesta.

Referee: H. Frandel (Germany). **Half-time:** 0-0.

FRANCE 5, SCOTLAND 0
Paris, (80,000), Wednesday, March 27, 2002

France (4-2-3-1): Barthez, Candela (Karembeu 63), Leboeuf, Desailly (Silvestre 46), Lizarazu, Vieira (Makelele 59), Petit, Wiltord (Marlet 63), Zidane (Djorkaeff 80), Henry, Trezeguet. **Scorers:** Zidane (12), Trezeguet (23, 42), Henry (32), Marlet (87). **Booked:** Lizarazu.

Scotland (4-3-3): Sullivan (Tottenham), Weir (Everton), Dailly (West Ham Utd.), *Caldwell (Newcastle Utd.), *Crainey (Celtic), Lambert (Celtic), Cameron (Wolves) (Holt, Norwich City, 46) (McNamara, Celtic, 74), Matteo (Leeds Utd.), Freedman (Crystal Palace) (Gemmill, Everton, 46), Crawford (Dunfermline) (*Thompson, Dundee Utd., 63), McCann (Rangers).

Referee: J. Granat (Poland). **Half-time:** 4-0.

WALES 0, CZECH REPUBLIC 0
Millennium Stadium, Wednesday, March 27, 2002

Wales (4-3-2-1): Ward (Nott'm. Forest) (Coyne, Grimsby Town, 46), Delaney (Aston Villa), Melville (Fulham), Page (Sheffield Utd.), *Gabbidon (Cardiff City), Davies (Tottenham), Savage (Leicester City) (*Evans, Brentford, 73), Robinson (Charlton Athletic), Koumas (Tranmere Rov.), Blake (Wolves) (Trollope, Fulham, 62), Hartson (Celtic) (Taylor, Burnley, 73). **Booked:** Blake.

Czech Republic (4-4-2): Cech, Fukal, Ujifalusi, Novotny, Jankulovski (Holenak 82), Poborsky, Galasek, Rosicky, Smicer, Lokvenc, Stajner.

Referee: C. Larsen (Denmark). **Half-time:** 0-0.

LIECHTENSTEIN 0, NORTHERN IRELAND 0
Vaduz, (1,080), Wednesday, March 27, 2002

Liechenstein (5-4-1): Jehle (Heebe 45), Telser, Hasler, Zech, Michael Stocklasa, Gigon, Nigg (Burgmeier 72), Martin Stocklasa, M. Beck, T.Beck, Buchel. **Booked:** M. Beck, Gigon.

Northern Ireland (4-4-2): Taylor (Fulham) (Carroll, Manchester Utd., 45), Lomas (West Ham Utd.), Williams (Wimbledon), McCartney (Sunderland), McCann (West Ham Utd.) (*Holmes, Wrexham, 70), Gillespie (Blackburn Rov.), Magilton (Ipswich Town), Mulryne (Norwich City), Johnson (Birmingham City), Healy (Preston N.E.) (Elliott, Motherwell, 83), *Feeney (Bournemouth) (Hughes, Wimbledon, 57). **Booked:** Gillespie, Healy. **Sent-off:** Lomas.

Referee: K. Rogalla (Switzerland). **Half-time:** 0-0.

REPUBLIC OF IRELAND 3, DENMARK 0
Lansdowne Road, (42,000), Wedenesday, March 27, 2002

Rep.of Ireland (4-4-2): Kiely (Charlton Athletic) (*Colgan, Hibernian, 65), Kelly (Leeds Utd.), Cunningham (Wimbledon), Staunton (Aston Villa), Harte (Leeds Utd.), McAteer (Sunderland) (Reid, Millwall, 65), Kinsella (Charlton Athletic) (Healy, Celtic, 63), Holland (Ipswich Town), Duff (Blackburn Rov.) (Dunne, Manchester City, 83), Morrison (Crystal Palace), Robbie Keane (Leeds Utd.) (Connolly, Wimbledon, 75). **Scorers:** Harte (19), Robbie Keane (54), Morrison (90).

Denmark (4-4-2): Sorensen (Kjaer 46), Rytter, Laursen, Henriksen, Heintze (Jensen 80), Poulsen, B. Nielsen, A. Nielsen (Madsen 46), Gronkjaer, Rommedahl (Lovenkrands 67), Sand.

Referee: B. Lawlor (Wales). Half-time: 1-0.

ENGLAND 4, PARAGUAY 0
Anfield, (42,713), Wednesday, April 17, 2002

England (4-4-2): Seaman (Arsenal), G. Neville (Manchester Utd.) (Lampard, Chelsea, 68), Keown (Arsenal) (Mills, Leeds Utd., 46), Southgate (Middlesbrough) (Carragher, Liverpool, 68), Bridge (Southampton) (P. Neville, Manchester Utd., 68), Gerrard (Liverpool) (Sinclair, West Ham Utd., 46), Butt (Manchester Utd.) (Hargreaves, Bayern Munich, 46), Scholes (Manchester Utd.) (Murphy, Liverpool, 46), Dyer (Newcastle Utd.) (Cole, West Ham Utd., 46), Vassell (Aston Villa) (Sheringham, Tottenham, 68), Owen (Liverpool) (Fowler, Liverpool, 46). **Scorers:** Owen (7), Murphy (47), Vassell (55), Ayala (81 og).

Paraguay (4-4-2): Taverelli, Arce, Ayala, Gamarra (Cesar Caceres 80), Caniza, Struway, Gavilan (Sanabria 55), Paredes, Bonet (Moringo 80), Cardozo (Baez 46), Santa Cruz.

Referee: C. Bolgnino (Italy). Half-time: 1-0.

SCOTLAND 1, NIGERIA 2
Pittodrie, (20,465), Wednesday, April 17, 2002

Scotland (4-1-3-2): *Douglas (Celtic), *Stockdale (Middlesbrough) (*Alexander, Preston N.E., 46), Weir (Everton), Dailly (West Ham Utd.), Crainey (Celtic), *Williams (Nott'm. Forest) (*Stewart, Manchester Utd., 64), *McNaughton (Aberdeen), Lambert (Celtic), Gemmill (Everton) (Caldwell, Newcastle Utd., 46), Thompson (Dundee Utd.) (*O'Connor, Hibernian, 74), McCann (Rangers) (Johnston, Middlesbrough, 78). **Scorer:** Dailly (7).

Nigeria (4-3-1-2): Ejide (Bankole 46), Sodje (Ifeajigwa 85), Yobo, Okoronkwo, Christopher (Adepoju 78), Okocha, Ejiofor, Utaka, Kanu, Aghahowa, Ogbeche. **Scorers:** Aghahowa (40, 69).

Referee: T. Ovredo (Norway). Half-time: 1-1.

NORTHERN IRELAND 0, SPAIN 5
Windsor Park, (11,103), Wednesday, April 17, 2002

Northern Ireland (4-4-1-1): Taylor (Fulham) (Carroll, Manchester Utd., 46), Nolan (Wigan Athletic), Hughes (Newcastle Utd.), Williams (Wimbledon), McCartney (Sunderland), Gillespie (Blackburn Rov.) (*McCourt, Rochdale, 77), Johnson (Birmingham City), Horlock (Manchester City), Elliott (Motherwell), Healy (Preston N.E.), Feeney (Bournemouth) (*McEvilly, Rochdale, 63).

Spain (4-4-2): Canizares (Casillas 74), Puyol, Hierro (Sergio 74), Nadal (Torres 46), Juanfran, Joaquin (Helguera 46), Albelda (Mendieta 46), Baraja, De Pedro (Valeron 46), Morientes, Raul. **Scorers:** Raul (23, 54), Baraja (47), Puyol (69), Morientes (78).

Referee: K. Clark (Scotland). Half-time: 0-1.

REPUBLIC OF IRELAND 2, UNITED STATES 1
Lansdowne Road, (39,000), Wednesday, April 17, 2002

Rep. of Ireland (4-4-2): Given (Newcastle Utd.), Finnan (Fulham) (Kelly, Leeds Utd., 46), Breen (Coventry City) (Doherty, Tottenham, 71), O'Brien (Newcastle Utd.) (Cunningham, Wimbledon, 46), Harte (Leeds Utd.) (Staunton, Aston Villa, 46), Delap (Southampton), Kinsella (Charlton Athletic) (Holland, Ipswich Town, 46), Healy (Celtic), Kilbane (Sunderland) (Reid, Millwall, 46), Robbie Keane (Leeds Utd.) (Morrison, Crystal Palace, 83), Duff (Blackburn Rov.) (Connolly, Wimbledon, 46). **Scorers:** Kinsella (6), Doherty (83).

United States (4-4-2): Friedel (Keller 46), Sanneh, Pope, Berhalter (Vanney 46), Agoos, Reyna (Hejduk 71), Armas, O'Brien (Lewis 46), Stewart (Donovan 46), McBride (Moore 46), Mathis (Wolff 63). **Scorer:** Pope (34).

Referee: P. Leuba (Switzerland). **Half-time:** 1-1.

WALES 1, GERMANY 0
Millennium Stadium, (35,000), Tuesday, May 14, 2002

Wales (4-3-2-1): Crossley (Middlesbrough), Delaney (Aston Villa), Melville (Fulham), Page (Sheffield Utd.), Speed (Newcastle Utd.), Davies (Tottenham), Savage (Leicester City), Pembridge (Everton), *Earnshaw (Cardiff City) (Coleman, Fulham, 90), Giggs (Manchester Utd.), Hartson (Celtic). **Scorer:** Earnshaw (46). **Booked:** Speed, Delaney.

Germany (4-4-2): Kahn, Heinrich, Linke, Metzelder, Ziege (Bode 63) Deisler (Asamoah 63), Jeremies, Hamann (Kehl 72), Frings, Klose, Bierhoff (Jancker 71). **Booked:** Frings, Heinrich, Asamoah.

Referee: R.Olsen (Norway). **Half-time:** 0-0.

SOUTH KOREA 4, SCOTLAND 1
Busan, (55,000), Thursday, May 16, 2002

South Korea (3-1-3-3): Kim Byung-ji, Hong Myung-bo (Yoon Jong-hwan 65), Choi Jin-cheul (Lee Min-sung 46), Kim Tae-young, Lee Young-pyo, Lee Eul-yong, Yoo Sang-chul, Song Chong-gug, Lee Chun-soo (Cha Doo-ri 72), Hwang Sun-hong (Ahn Jung-hwan 46), Park Ji-sung (Choi Tai-uk 72). **Scorers:** Lee Chun-soo (15), Ahn Jung-hwan (57, 87), Yoon Jong-hwan (67). **Booked:** Park Ji-sung.

Scotland (4-4-2): Sullivan (Tottenham), Ross (Rangers), Dailly (West Ham Utd.), Weir (Everton), Alexander (Preston N.E.) (Stockdale, Middlesbrough, 62), Johnston (Sunderland) (*Kyle, Sunderland, 66), Caldwell (Newcastle Utd.), Gemmill (Everton), O'Connor (Hibernian) (Williams, Nott'm. Forest, 46), Stewart (Manchester Utd.) (Severin, Hearts,46), *Dobie (W.B.A.). **Scorer:** Dobie (74).

Referee: N. Santhan (Singapore). **Half-time:** 1-0.

REPUBLIC OF IRELAND 1, NIGERIA 2
Lansdowne Road, (42,652), Thursday, May 16, 2002

Rep. of Ireland (4-4-2): Given (Newcastle Utd.), Finnan (Fulham), Cunningham (Wimbledon), Staunton (Aston Villa), Harte (Leeds Utd.), McAteer (Sunderland) (Reid, Millwall, 46), Roy Keane (Manchester Utd.) (Kinsella, Charlton Athletic, 63), Holland (Ipswich Town), Kilbane (Sunderland) (Kelly, Leeds Utd., 61), Robbie Keane (Leeds Utd.) (Morrison, Crystal Palace, 61), Duff (Blackburn Rov.) (Connolly, Wimbledon, 61). **Scorer:** Reid (69).

Nigeria (4-4-2): Shorunmu, Yobo, Udeze, Sodje, West, Ikedia, Okocha (Oruma 65), Kanu, Opabunmi, Ogbeche, Aghahowa. **Scorers:** Aghahowa (13), Sodje (47).

Referee: L. Dos Santos (Portugal). **Half-time:** 0-1.

SCOTLAND 0, SOUTH AFRICA 2
Hong Kong, (3,007), Monday, May 20, 2002

Scotland (3-5-2): Douglas (Celtic), Weir (Everton), Dailly (West Ham Utd.), Caldwell (Newcastle Utd.) (*Wilkie, Dundee, 46), Stockdale (Middlesbrough) (Alexander, Preston N.E., 69), Williams (Nott'm. Forest) (Severin, Hearts, 78), Gemmill (Everton) (Stewart, Manchester Utd., 86), Johnston (Middlesbrough) (*McFadden, Motherwell, 62), Ross (Rangers), Dobie (W.B.A.), Kyle (Sunderland).

South Africa (4-4-2): Vonk, A. Mokoena (Nzama 62), Radebe, Issa, Carnell, Zuma (Koumantarakis 82), Sibaya, Fortune (Buckley 84), Pule (Arendse 69), McCarthy, T. Mokoena. **Scorers:** T. Mokoena (32), Koumantarakis (90).

Referee: Chan Siu-kee (Hong Kong). **Half-time:** 0-1.

SOUTH KOREA 1, ENGLAND 1
Seoguipo, (39,876), Tuesday, May 21, 2002

South Korea (4-2-3-1): Lee Woon-jae, Song Chong-gug, Choi Jin-cheul, Hong Myung-bo, Lee Young-pyo, Kim Nam-il (Lee Min-sung 89), Park Ji-sung, Yoo Sang-chul, Choi Tai-uk (Cha Du-ri 76), Lee Chun-soo, Seol Ki-hyeon (Ahn Jung-hwan). **Scorer:** Park Ji-sung (52).

England (4-3-3): Martyn (Leeds Utd.) (James, West Ham Utd., 46), Mills (Leeds Utd.) (Brown, Manchester Utd., 68), Ferdinand (Leeds Utd.) (Southgate, Middlesbrough, 46), Campbell (Arsenal) (Keown, Arsenal, 46), A. Cole (Arsenal) (Bridge, Southampton, 46), Murphy (Liverpool) (Sinclair, West Ham Utd., 46), Hargreaves (Bayern Munich), Scholes (Manchester Utd.) (J. Cole, West Ham Utd., 46), Vassell (Aston Villa), Owen (Liverpool) (Sheringham, Tottenham, 46), Heskey (Liverpool). **Scorer:** Owen (26).

Referee: A. Supian (Malaysia). **Half-time:** 0-1.

ENGLAND 2, CAMEROON 2
Kobe, Japan, (36,424), Sunday, May 26, 2002

England (4-4-2): Martyn (Leeds Utd.) (James, West Ham Utd., 46), Brown (Manchester Utd.), Ferdinand (Leeds Utd.) (Keown, Arsenal, 46), Campbell (Arsenal) (Southgate, Middlesbrough, 46), Bridge (Southampton), Cole (West Ham Utd.), Hargreaves (Bayern Munich), Scholes (Manchester Utd.) (Mills, Leeds Utd., 46), Heskey (Liverpool) (Sinclair, West Ham Utd., 46), Owen (Liverpool) (Sheringham, Tottenham, 46), Vassell (Aston Villa) (Fowler, Leeds Utd., 75). **Scorers:** Vassell (12), Fowler (90).

Cameroon (3-5-2): Alioum (Songo'o 78), Kalla (Mettomo 55), Song (Ndo 68), Tchato, Geremi (Alnoudji 65), Lauren (Epalle 58), Foe (Djemba-Djemba 73), Olembe (Kome 52), Wome (Njanka 60), Mboma (N'Diefi 66), Eto'o (Suffo 58). **Scorers:** Eto'o (5), Geremi (58).

Referee: Y. Katayama (Japan). **Half-time:** 1-1.

EUROPEAN U-21 CHAMPIONSHIP – QUALIFYING ROUND

GERMANY 1, ENGLAND 2
Freiburg, (15,000), Friday, August 31, 2001

England: Taylor (Arsenal), Wright (Liverpool), King (Tottenham), Barry (Aston Villa), Bridge (Southampton), Greening (Middlesbrough), Davis (Fulham), Prutton (Nott'm. Forest), Chadwick (Manchester Utd.) (Defoe, West Ham Utd., 70), Vassell (Aston Villa) (Jeffers, Arsenal, 57), Cole (West Ham Utd.) (Parker, Charlton Athletic, 75).

Scorers – Germany: Metzelder (90). **England:** Cole (55), Jeffers (90). **Half-time:** 0-0.

SCOTLAND 1, CROATIA 1
McDiarmid Park, (5,104), Friday, August 31, 2001

Scotland: Langfield (Dundee), McCunnie (Dundee Utd.) (Maloney, Celtic, 85), Cummings (Chelsea), S. Caldwell (Newcastle Utd.), G. Caldwell (Newcastle Utd.), Murray (Hibernian), Young (Aberdeen) (Fowler, Kilmarnock, 77), Easton (Dundee Utd.), Miller (Rangers), Severin (Hearts), McManus (Hibernian) (Paterson, Dundee Utd., 62).

Scorers – Scotland: Miller (90 pen). **Croatia:** Bilic (58). **Half-time:** 0-0. **Sent-off:** S. Caldwell, Vrajkovic (Croatia).

WALES 1, ARMENIA 1
Merthyr Tydfil, (1,564), Friday, August 31, 2001

Wales: Walsh (Wrexham), Hillier (Tottenham), Gabbidon (Cardiff City), Day (Manchester City), Price (Hull City) (De-Vulgt, Swansea City, 87), Gibson (Sheffield Wed.), Valentine (Everton), S. Thomas (Wrexham) (Phillips, Swansea City, 70), Maxwell (Cardiff City) (Low, Cardiff City, 74), Roberts (Swansea City), J. Thomas (Blackburn Rov.)

Scorers – Wales: Day (41 pen). **Armenia:** Erzrvmyan (68). **Half-time:** 1-0.

DENMARK 2, NORTHERN IRELAND 0
Odense, (3,541), Friday, August 31, 2001

Northern Ireland: Miskelly (Oldham Athletic), Kelly (Derry City), McCartney (Sunderland) (Capaldi, Birmingham City, 63), McAreavey (Swindon Town) (McFlynn, Woking, 71), Simms (Hartlepool Utd.), Holmes (Wrexham), Carlisle (Crystal Palace) (Carson, Dundee Utd., 77), Toner (Tottenham), Feeney (Bournemouth), Kirk (Hearts), McCann (West Ham Utd.).

Scorers – Denmark: Skoubo (58), Jorgensen (71). **Half-time:** 0-0.

REPUBLIC OF IRELAND 1, HOLLAND 1
Waterford, (4,750), Friday, August 31, 2001

Rep. of Ireland: Murphy (Tranmere Rov.), B. Quinn (Coventry City), O'Shea (Manchester Utd.), Gavin (Middlesbrough), Foy (Nott'm. Forest), Healy (Celtic), Butler (Sunderland), Byrne (West Ham Utd.) (A. Quinn, Sheffield Wed., 46), Sadlier (Millwall), Barrett (Arsenal), McPhail (Leeds Utd.).

Scorers – Rep. of Ireland: Barrett (8). **Holland:** Van der Vaart (12). **Half-time:** 1-1.

ENGLAND 5, ALBANIA 0
Riverside Stadium, (23,118), Tuesday, September 4, 2001

England: Taylor (Arsenal), Wright (Liverpool), King (Tottenham), Barry (Aston Villa), Bridge (Southampton), Davis (Fulham) (Wilson, Middlesbrough, 75), Greening (Middlesbrough), Parker (Charlton Athletic) (Pennant, Arsenal, 70), Chadwick (Manchester Utd.) (Johnson, Derby Co., 63), Jeffers (Arsenal), Defoe (West Ham Utd.).

Scorers – England: Jeffers (17, 59, 90), Defoe (71), Greening (89). **Half-time:** 1-0.

BELGIUM 0, SCOTLAND 0
St-Truiden, (1,500), Tuesday, September 4, 2001

Scotland: Esson (Aberdeen), Fowler (Kilmarnock), Cummings (Chelsea), McGuire (Aberdeen), G. Caldwell (Newcastle Utd.), Murray (Hibernian), Mason (Dunfermline), Easton (Dundee Utd.) (Williams, Nott'm. Forest, 46), Miller (Rangers), Severin (Hearts), McManus (Hibernian) (Maloney, Celtic, 76).

Half-time: 0-0.

NORWAY 2, WALES 0
Drammen, (1,427), Tuesday, September 4, 2001

Wales: Walsh (Wrexham) (Jones, Swansea City, 29), Hillier (Tottenham), Price (Hull City), Gabbidon (Cardiff City), Day (Manchester City), Valentine (Everton) (Low, Cardiff City, 73), Roberts (Swansea City), Gibson (Sheffield Wed.), J. Thomas (Blackburn Rov.) (Gall, Bristol Rov., 65), S. Thomas (Wrexham), Maxwell (Cardiff City).

Scorers – Norway: Ludvigsen (3), George (45). **Half-time:** 2-0.

NORTHERN IRELAND 1, ICELAND 3
Lurgan, (837), Tuesday, September 4, 2001

Northern Ireland: Miskelly (Oldham Athletic), Kelly (Derry City), Capaldi (Birmingham City), Close (Middlesbrough) (McAreavey, Swindon Town), Simms (Hartlepool Utd.), Holmes (Wrexham), Carlisle (Crystal Palace) (McFynn, Woking), Toner (Tottenham), Kirk (Hearts) (Feeney, Bournemouth), Hamilton (Portadown), McCann (West Ham Utd.)

Scorers – Northern Ireland: McCann (10). **Iceland:** Simms (58 og), Adalsteinsson (76), Gunnarsson (90). **Half-time:** 1-0.

ENGLAND 2, GREECE 1
Ewood Park, (29,164), Friday, October 5, 2001

England: Kirkland (Liverpool), Young (Charlton Athletic), King (Tottenham), Barry (Aston Villa), Bridge (Southampton), Pennant (Arsenal), Carrick (West Ham Utd.), Dunn (Blackburn Rov.), Greening (Middlesbrough) (Prutton, Nott'm. Forest, 73), Vassell (Aston Villa), Defoe (West Ham Utd.) (Christie, Derby Co., 73).

Scorers – England: Defoe (10), Christie (85). **Greece:** Papadopoulos (90 pen). **Half-time:** 1-0.

SCOTLAND 1, LATVIA 0
Broadwood Stadium, (2,455), Friday, October 5, 2001

Scotland: Stewart (Kilmarnock), Fowler (Kilmarnock) (Canero, Kilmarnock, 69), Hammell (Motherwell) (McNaughton, Aberdeen, 46), McGuire (Aberdeen), G. Caldwell (Newcastle Utd.), McCracken (Dundee Utd.), Stewart (Manchester Utd.), Murray (Hibernian), McManus (Hibernian), Maloney (Celtic) (McPhee, Port Vale, 85), Mackie (Aberdeen).

Scorers – Scotland: McNaughton (81). **Half-time:** 0-0.

WALES 1, BELARUS 2
Ninian Park, (1,374), Friday, October 5, 2001

Wales: Walsh (Wrexham), De-Vulgt (Swansea City) (Maxwell, Cardiff City, 50), Price (Hull City), Valentine (Everton), Day (Manchester City), Phillips (Swansea City), Low (Cardiff City), Gibson (Sheffield Wed.), J. Thomas (Blackburn Rov.), S. Thomas (Wrexham) (Gall, Bristol Rov., 81), Roberts (Swansea City) (Williams, Crystal Palace, 87).

Scorers – Wales: Williams (90). **Belarus:** Sokal (12), Kutuzau (32). **Sent-off:** Rahavik (Croatia). **Half-time:** 0-2.

MALTA 2, NORTHERN IRELAND 2
Ta'Qali, (508), Friday, October 5, 2001

Northern Ireland: Miskelly (Oldham Athletic), Dickson (Wigan Athletic), Holmes (Wrexham), Kelly (Derry City), Simms (Hartlepool Utd.), McCann (West Ham Utd.) (McAreavey, Swindon Town), Carlisle (Crystal Palace), Toner (Tottenham) (Close, Middlesbrough), Boyle (Leeds Utd.) (Morrison, Sheffield Wed.), Hamilton (Portadown), Capaldi (Birmingham City).

Scorers – Malta: Mattocks (15), Debono (88). **Northern Ireland:** Boyle (14), McCann (61). **Sent-off:** Dickson. **Half-time:** 1-1.

REPUBLIC OF IRELAND 3, CYPRUS 0
Longford, (1,700), Friday, October 5, 2001

Rep. of Ireland: Roche (Nott'm. Forest), Thompson (Nott'm. Forest) (Shelley, Bohemians, 84), Goodwin (Celtic), O'Shea (Manchester Utd.), Foy (Nott'm. Forest), Butler (Sunderland), Miller (Celtic), Byrne (West Ham Utd.), Doyle (Celtic) (Keane, Preston N.E., 78), Reid (Nott'm. Forest), Barrett (Arsenal) (Burgess, Blackburn Rov., 67).

Scorers – Rep. of Ireland: Doyle (53, 60), Reid (64). **Half-time:** 0-0.

PLAY-OFF, FIRST LEG

HOLLAND 2, ENGLAND 2
Utrecht, (14,500), Friday, November 9, 2001

England: Kirkland (Liverpool), Young (Charlton Athletic), Terry (Chelsea) (Barry, Aston Villa, 80), King (Tottenham), Bridge (Southampton), Pennant (Arsenal), Carrick (West Ham Utd.), Davis (Fulham), Dunn (Blackburn Rov.), Christie (Derby Co.) (Ameobi, Newcastle Utd., 30), Defoe (West Ham Utd.).

Scorers – Holland: Van der Vaart (21), Kuyt (37). **England:** Davis (45), Dunn (57). **Half-time:** 2-1.

PLAY-OFF, SECOND LEG

ENGLAND 1, HOLLAND 0
Pride Park, (32,418), Tuesday, November 13, 2001

England: Kirkland (Liverpool), Young (Charlton Athletic), Terry (Chelsea), King (Tottenham), Bridge (Southampton), Pennant (Arsenal) (Greening, Middlesbrough, 69), Carrick (West Ham Utd.), Davis (Fulham), Dunn (Blackburn Rov.), Defoe (West Ham Utd.), Ameobi (Newcastle Utd.).

Scorer – England: Carrick (72). **Half-time:** 0-0.

TOULON TOURNAMENT

REPUBLIC OF IRELAND 0, JAPAN 2
Nimes, (1,200), Tuesday, May 7, 2002

Rep. of Ireland: Murphy (Tranmere Rov.), Douglas (Blackburn Rov.), Goodwin (Celtic), O'Callaghan (Barnsley), Foy (Nott'm. Forest), Byrne (West Ham Utd.), Miller (Celtic), Doyle (Celtic) (Gamble, Reading, 74), Barrett (Arsenal), Daly (Stockport Co.) (Heffernan, Notts Co., 55), Reid (Nott'm. Forest) (Cash, Nott'm. Forest, 65).

Scorers – Japan: Yamase (33), Nakayama (38). **Half-time:** 0-2.

REPUBLIC OF IRELAND 0, ITALY 2
Toulon, (2,000), Thursday, May 9, 2002

Rep. of Ireland: Murphy (Tranmere Rov.), S. Byrne (West Ham Utd.), Goodwin (Celtic), C. Byrne (Sunderland), Tierney (Manchester Utd.), Cash (Nott'm. Forest), Miller (Celtic), Gamble (Reading), Keane (Preston N.E.), Barrett (Arsenal), Reid (Nott'm. Forest) (Daly, Stockport Co., 76).

Scorer – Italy: Pellicori (51, 52). **Half-time:** 0-0.

REPUBLIC OF IRELAND 1, SOUTH AFRICA 2
Frejus, (1,500) Monday, May 13, 2002

Rep. of Ireland: Murphy (Tranmere Rov.), Byrne (West Ham Utd.), Goodwin (Celtic), O'Shea (Manchester Utd.), Tierney (Manchester Utd.), Butler (Sunderland), Miller (Celtic), Gamble (Reading) (Doyle, Celtic, 63), Keane (Preston N.E.), Heffernan (Notts Co.) (Daly, Stockport Co., 50), Reid (Nott'm. Forest).

Scorers – Republic of Ireland: Reid (28). **South Africa:** Handricks (37), Kometsi (75). **Half-time:** 1-1.

REPUBLIC OF IRELAND 2, GERMANY 2

La Seyne, (2,000) Wednesday, May 15, 2002

Rep. of Ireland: Stack (Arsenal), S. Byrne (West Ham Utd.), Goodwin (Celtic), O'Shea (Manchester Utd.) (C. Byrne, Sunderland, 55), Foy (Nott'm. Forest), Butler (Sunderland), Miller (Celtic), Gamble (Reading), Keane (Preston N.E.), Barrett (Arsenal), Reid (Nott'm. Forest) (O'Callaghan, Barnsley, 70).

Scorers – Republic of Ireland: O'Shea (43), Reid (54). **Germany:** Tiffert (47), Auer (70). **Sent-off:** Goodwin. **Half-time:** 1-0.

FRIENDLY INTERNATIONALS

ENGLAND 4, HOLLAND 0

Madejski Stadium, (19,467), Tuesday, August 14, 2001

England: Taylor (Arsenal) (Bywater, West Ham Utd., 64), Young (Charlton Athletic) (Wright, Liverpool, 46), Terry (Chelsea) (Riggott, Derby Co., 64), Barry (Aston Villa) (Bramble, Ipswich Town, 46), Bridge (Southampton) (Johnson, Derby Co., 46), Greening (Middlesbrough) (Pennant, Arsenal, 67), Dunn (Blackburn Rov.) (Prutton, Nott'm. Forest, 43), Davis (Fulham) (Parker, Charlton Athletic, 46), Chadwick (Manchester Utd.) (Wilson, Middlesbrough, 64), Vassell (Aston Villa) (Defoe, West Ham Utd., 48), Jeffers (Arsenal) (Christie, Derby Co., 46).

Scorers – England: Vassell (6), Defoe (50, 90), Christie (87). **Half-time:** 1-0.

SLOVENIA 0, ENGLAND 1

Nova Gorica, (350), Tuesday, February 12, 2002

England: Robinson (Leeds Utd.) (Weaver, Manchester City, 60), Wright (Liverpool) (Knight, Fulham, 61), Konchesky (Charlton Athletic), Riggott (Derby Co.), Barry (Aston Villa), Pennant (Arsenal), Parker (Charlton Athletic) (Prutton, Nott'm. Forest, 46), Jenas (Newcastle Utd.), Dunn (Blackburn Rov.) (Etherington, Tottenham, 46), Defoe (West Ham Utd.) (Ameobi, Newcastle Utd., 61), Christie (Derby Co.).

Scorer – England: Ameobi (65). **Half-time:** 0-0.

NORTHERN IRELAND 0, GERMANY 1

Windsor Park, (1,200), Tuesday, February 12, 2002

Northern Ireland: Morris (W.B.A.) (Blayney, Southampton), Baird (Southampton), Capaldi (Birmingham City), Clyde (Wolves), Simms (Hartlepool Utd.) (Buchanan, Bolton Wand.), Melaugh (Aston Villa), Close (Middlesbrough), McFlynn (Margate) (Hunter, Linfield), Braniff (Millwall) (McVeigh, Ayr Utd.), Black (Morecambe) (McCann, Rangers), McCourt (Rochdale) (Curran, Everton).

Scorer – Germany: Auer (54). **Half-time:** 0-0.

ENGLAND 1, ITALY 1

Valley Parade, (21,642), Tuesday, March 26, 2002

England: Robinson (Leeds Utd.) (Bywater, West Ham Utd., 79), Wright (Liverpool), Knight (Fulham) (Gardner, Tottenham, 79), Barry (Aston Villa), Samuel (Aston Villa), Wright-Phillips (Manchester City) (Pennant, Arsenal, 46), Prutton (Nott'm. Forest), Jenas (Newcastle Utd.) (Parker, Charlton Athletic, 46), Etherington (Tottenham) (Crouch, Portsmouth, 60), Defoe (West Ham Utd.), Smith (Leeds Utd.).

Scorers – England: Barry (59). **Italy:** Maccarone (15). **Half-time:** 0-1.

REPUBLIC OF IRELAND 3, DENMARK 2

Cork, (8,000), Tuesday, March 26, 2002

Rep. of Ireland: Murphy (Tranmere Rov.), Shelley (Bohemians), Goodwin (Celtic), O'Shea (Manchester Utd.) (O'Callaghan, Barnsley, 54), Foy (Nott'm. Forest), Miller (Celtic), Mattis (Huddersfield Town) (Gamble, Reading, 46), Doyle (Celtic), Butler (Sunderland), Burgess (Blackburn Rov.) (Daly, Stockport Co., 70), Reid (Nott'm. Forest) (Byrne, Sunderland, 70).

Scorers – Republic of Ireland: Goodwin (21), Burgess (52), Gamble (89). **Denmark:** Hakansson (72 pen), Larsaen (82). **Half-time:** 1-0.

ENGLAND 0, PORTUGAL 1

Britannia Stadium, (28,000), Tuesday, April 16, 2002

England: Robinson (Leeds Utd.) (Kirkland, Liverpool, 46), Wright (Liverpool) (Young, Charlton Athletic, 70), Riggott (Derby Co.), Barry (Aston Villa), Konchesky (Charlton Athletic), Dunn (Blackburn Rov.) (Pennant, Arsenal, 46), Davis (Fulham) (Jenas, Newcastle Utd., 55), Carrick (West Ham Utd.), Johnson (Leeds Utd.) (Defoe, West Ham Utd., 77), Smith (Leeds Utd.) (Zamora, Brighton & H.A., 70), Christie (Derby Co.) (Crouch, Aston Villa, 46).

Scorer – Portugal: Tonel (39). **Half-time:** 0-1.

AUSTRIA 3, REPUBLIC OF IRELAND 3

Kindberg-Styria, (900), Tuesday, April 16, 2002

Rep. of Ireland: Stack (Arsenal), Shelley (Bohemians) (Callaghan, Barnsley, 28), Goodwin (Celtic), O'Shea (Manchester Utd.), Foy (Nott'm. Forest), Byrne (West Ham Utd.), Miller (Celtic), Doyle (Celtic) (Keane, Preston N.E., 78), Butler (Sunderland), Heffernan (Notts Co.) (Cash, Nott'm. Forest, 50), Reid (Nott'm. Forest).

Scorers – Austria: Lasnik (62), Pircher (80), Parapatits (88). **Republic of Ireland:** Byrne (12), Heffernan (16), Reid (58). **Half-time:** 0-2.

EUROPEAN U-21 CHAMPIONSHIP QUALIFYING TABLES

GROUP 1

	P	W	D	L	F	A	P
Switzerland	8	4	4	0	22	10	16
Yugoslavia	8	4	3	1	22	11	15
Russia	8	4	3	1	23	9	15
Slovenia	8	2	2	4	10	10	8
Luxembourg	8	0	0	8	1	38	0

GROUP 3

	P	W	D	L	F	A	P
Czech Republic	10	9	0	1	28	5	27
Bulgaria	10	5	3	2	16	17	18
Denmark	10	4	3	3	18	12	15
Iceland	10	3	2	5	13	17	11
Northern Ireland	10	2	2	6	12	21	8
Malta	10	0	4	6	5	20	4

GROUP 2

	P	W	D	L	F	A	P
Portugal	8	6	1	1	22	4	19
Holland	8	5	2	1	20	7	17
Rep. of Ireland	8	4	1	3	10	7	13
Cyprus	8	3	0	5	9	17	9
Estonia	8	0	0	8	2	28	0

GROUP 4

	P	W	D	L	F	A	P
Turkey	10	7	2	1	19	6	23
Sweden	10	5	4	1	19	6	19
Slovakia	10	4	4	2	13	7	16
Moldova	10	2	3	5	6	13	9
Azerbaijan	10	2	3	5	4	17	9
Macedonia	10	1	2	7	6	18	5

GROUP 5

	P	W	D	L	F	A	P
Ukraine	10	6	1	3	14	13	19
Poland	10	5	3	2	20	14	18
Norway	10	6	0	4	21	12	18
Belarus	10	5	1	4	21	14	16
Armenia	10	4	2	4	10	15	14
Wales	10	0	1	9	4	22	1

GROUP 6

	P	W	D	L	F	A	P
Belgium	6	4	1	1	8	2	13
Croatia	6	3	2	1	9	6	11
Scotland	6	2	2	2	6	6	8
Latvia	6	0	1	5	3	12	1

GROUP 7

	P	W	D	L	F	A	P
France	8	6	2	0	16	6	20
Spain	8	5	1	2	13	7	16
Israel	8	4	0	4	16	13	12
Austria	8	2	2	4	7	14	8
Bosnia	8	0	1	7	5	17	1

GROUP 8

	P	W	D	L	F	A	P
Italy	8	6	1	1	14	5	19
Romania	8	5	1	2	13	5	16
Hungary	8	5	0	3	12	9	15
Lithuania	8	2	0	6	5	17	6
Georgia	8	1	0	7	9	17	3

GROUP 9

	P	W	D	L	F	A	P
England	8	5	2	1	18	8	17
Greece	8	5	1	2	14	6	16
Germany	8	5	1	2	18	7	16
Finland	8	1	1	6	7	20	4
Albania	8	1	1	6	3	19	4

Play-offs to decide championship finalists (on agg): Belgium 4, Sweden 3; Czech Republic 1, Croatia 1 (Czech Republic won on away goal); **England** 3, Holland 2; France 5, Romania 0; Greece 4, Turkey 2; Italy 5, Poland 2; Portugal 2, Spain 2 (Portugal won on away goal); Switzerland 4, Ukraine 2.

FINALS – SWITZERLAND (MAY 16-28, 2002)

Having topped their qualifying section and then beaten Holland in the play-offs to qualify for the finals, England opened the Championship with a victory over the host nation. But they suffered defeats in two other matches and failed to go through from their group.

Peter Crouch, the 6ft 6in striker who joined Aston Villa from Portsmouth towards the end of the season, and 5ft 7in West Ham United starlet Jermain Defoe rewarded manager David Platt for his choice of strikers with the goals which brought a hard-earned 2-1 win over Switzerland.

Platt switched to playing Crouch up front on his own for the next game, but it was Italy who had most influential attacker in Massimo Maccarone. His second, decisive goal came six minutes from the end, with England looking for a point from Gareth Barry's equalising volley created by David Dunn's excellent play.

Two goals – one penalty – conceded in the first 20 minutes left them with a lot to do against Portugal. Alan Smith pulled one back two minutes from half-time and the match could have gone either way until his team conceded a third with 20 minutes remaining.

Italy, favourites to retain the title, lost out in the semi-finals to a golden goal scored by the Czech Republic, who went on to succeed them as champions with a 3-1 win on penalties against France after the final finished goalless.

ENGLAND 2, SWITZERLAND 1
Group A – Zurich, (16,000), Friday, May 17, 2002

England (4-4-2): Robinson (Leeds Utd.), Young (Charlton Athletic), Riggott (Derby Co.), Barry (Aston Villa), Konchesky (Charlton Athletic), Pennant (Arsenal), Davis (Fulham) (Prutton, Nott'm. Forest, 34), Dunn (Blackburn Rov.), Smith (Leeds Utd.), Defoe (West Ham Utd.) (Parker, Charlton Athletic, 64), Crouch (Aston Villa) (Ameobi, Newcastle Utd., 78).

Scorers – England: Defoe (3), Crouch (53). **Switzerland:** Frei (58). **Half-time:** 1-0.

ENGLAND 1, ITALY 2
Group A – Basle, (5,000), Monday, May 20, 2002

England (4-5-1): Robinson (Leeds Utd.), Young (Charlton Athletic), Knight (Fulham), Riggott (Derby Co.), Konchesky (Charlton Athletic), Smith (Leeds Utd.), Prutton (Nott'm. Forest) (Pennant, Arsenal, 84), Davis (Fulham), Dunn (Blackburn Rov.), Barry (Aston Villa) (Zamora, Brighton & H.A., 88), Crouch (Aston Villa) (Defoe, West Ham Utd., 46).

Scorers – England: Barry (64). **Italy:** Maccarone (58, 84). **Sent-off:** Bonera (Italy). **Half-time:** 0-0.

ENGLAND 1, PORTUGAL 3
Goup A – Zurich, (6,000), Wednesday, May 22, 2002

England (4-4-2): Robinson (Leeds Utd.), Young (Charlton Athletic), Knight (Fulham), Barry (Aston Villa), Konchesky (Charlton Athletic), Pennant (Arsenal) (Parker, Charlton Athletic, 76), Dunn (Blackburn Rov.), Prutton (Nott'm. Forest), Greening (Middlesbrough) (Ameobi, Newcastle Utd., 31), Defoe (West Ham Utd.) (Zamora, Brighton & H.A., 66), Smith (Leeds Utd.).

Scorers – England: Smith (43). **Portugal:** Teixeira (7), Makukula (20 pen), Viana (69). **Half-time:** 1-2.

Other results – Group A: Italy 1, Portugal 1; Portugal 0, Switzerland 2; Italy 0, Switzerland 0.
Group B: Belgium 2, Greece 1; Czech Republic 0, France 2; Belgium 0, Czech Republic 1; Greece 1, France 3; Belgium 0, France 2; Czech Republic 1, Greece 1.

GROUP A

	P	W	D	L	F	A	P
ITALY	3	1	2	0	3	2	5
SWITZERLAND	3	1	1	1	3	2	4
Portugal	3	1	1	1	4	4	4
England	3	1	0	2	4	6	3

GROUP B

	P	W	D	L	F	A	P
FRANCE	3	3	0	0	7	1	9
CZECH REPUBLIC	3	1	1	1	2	3	4
Belgium	3	1	0	2	2	4	3
Greece	3	0	1	2	3	6	1

Semi-finals: Czech Republic 3, Italy 2 (aet, golden goal); France 2, Switzerland 0. **Final** (May 28, Basle): Czech Republic 0, France 0 (aet, Czech Republic won 3-1 on pens).

OTHER BRITISH INTERNATIONAL RESULTS
ENGLAND

For matches played between the Home nations please see p. 3.

v. ALBANIA

		E	A
1989	Tirana (W.C.)	2	0
1989	Wembley (W.C.)	5	0
2001	Tirana (W.C.)	3	1
2001	Newcastle (W.C.)	2	0

v. ARGENTINA

		E	A
1951	Wembley	2	1
1953*	Buenos Aires	0	0
1962	Rancagua (W.C.)	3	1
1964	Rio de Janeiro	0	1
1966	Wembley (W.C.)	1	0
1974	Wembley	2	2
1977	Buenos Aires	1	1
1980	Wembley	3	1
1986	Mexico City (W.C.)	1	2
1991	Wembley	2	2
1998†	St Etienne (W.C.)	2	2
2000	Wembley	0	0
2002	Sapporo (W.C.)	1	0

(* Abandoned after 21 mins. – rain)
(† England lost 3-4 on pens.)

v. AUSTRALIA

		E	A
1980	Sydney	2	1
1983	Sydney	0	0
1983	Brisbane	1	0
1983	Melbourne	1	1
1991	Sydney	1	0

v. AUSTRIA

		E	A
1908	Vienna	6	1
1908	Vienna	11	1
1909	Vienna	8	1
1930	Vienna	0	0
1932	Chelsea	4	3
1936	Vienna	1	2
1951	Wembley	2	2
1952	Vienna	3	2
1958	Boras (W.C.)	2	2
1961	Vienna	1	3
1962	Wembley	3	1
1965	Wembley	2	3
1967	Vienna	1	0
1973	Wembley	7	0
1979	Vienna	3	4

v. BELGIUM

		E	B
1921	Brussels	2	0
1923	Highbury	6	1
1923	Antwerp	2	2
1924	West Bromwich	4	0
1926	Antwerp	5	3
1927	Brussels	9	1
1928	Antwerp	3	1
1929	Brussels	5	1
1931	Brussels	4	1
1936	Brussels	2	3
1947	Brussels	5	2
1950	Brussels	4	1
1952	Wembley	5	0
1954	Basle (W.C.)	4	4
1964	Wembley	2	2
1970	Brussels	3	1
1980	Turin (E.C.)	1	1
1990	Bologna (W.C.)	1	0
1998*	Casablanca	0	0
1999	Sunderland	2	1

(* England lost 3-4 on pens.)

v. BOHEMIA

		E	B
1908	Prague	4	0

v. BRAZIL

		E	B
1956	Wembley	4	2
1958	Gothenburg (W.C.)	0	0
1959	Rio de Janeiro	0	2
1962	Vina del Mar (W.C.)	1	3
1963	Wembley	1	1
1964	Rio de Janeiro	1	5
1969	Rio de Janeiro	1	2
1970	Guadalajara (W.C.)	0	1
1976	Los Angeles	0	1
1977	Rio de Janeiro	0	0
1978	Wembley	1	1
1981	Wembley	0	1
1984	Rio de Janeiro	2	0
1987	Wembley	1	1
1990	Wembley	1	0
1992	Wembley	1	1
1993	Washington	1	1
1995	Wembley	1	3
1997	Paris (T.F.)	0	1
2000	Wembley	1	1
2002	Shizuoka (W.C.)	1	2

v. BULGARIA

		E	B
1962	Rancagua (W.C.)	0	0
1968	Wembley	1	1
1974	Sofia	1	0
1979	Sofia (E.C.)	3	0

		E	B
1979	Wembley (E.C.)	2	0
1996	Wembley	1	0
1998	Wembley (E.C.)	0	0
1999	Sofia (E.C.)	1	1

v. CAMEROON

		E	C
1990	Naples (W.C.)	3	2
1991	Wembley	2	0
1997	Wembley	2	0
2002	Kobe (Japan)	2	2

v. CANADA

		E	C
1986	Vancouver	1	0

v. CHILE

		E	C
1950	Rio de Janeiro (W.C.)	2	0
1953	Santiago	2	1
1984	Santiago	0	0
1989	Wembley	0	0
1998	Wembley	0	2

v. CHINA

		E	C
1996	Beijing	3	0

v. C.I.S.
(formerly Soviet Union)

		E	C
1992	Moscow	2	2

v. COLOMBIA

		E	C
1970	Bogota	4	0
1988	Wembley	1	1
1995	Wembley	0	0
1998	Lens (W.C.)	2	0

v. CROATIA

		E	C
1995	Wembley	0	0

v. CYPRUS

		E	C
1975	Wembley (E.C.)	5	0
1975	Limassol (E.C.)	1	0

v. CZECH REPUBLIC

		E	C
1998	Wembley	2	0

v. CZECHOSLOVAKIA

		E	C
1934	Prague	1	2
1937	Tottenham	5	4
1963	Bratislava	4	2
1966	Wembley	0	0
1970	Guadalajara (W.C.)	1	0
1973	Prague	1	1

		E	C
1974	Wembley (E.C.)	3	0
1975*	Bratislava (E.C.)	1	2
1978	Wembley (E.C.)	1	0
1982	Bilbao (W.C.)	2	0
1990	Wembley	4	2
1992	Prague	2	2

(* Aband. 0-0, 17 mins. prev. day – fog)

v. DENMARK

		E	D
1948	Copenhagen	0	0
1955	Copenhagen	5	1
1956	W'hampton (W.C.)	5	2
1957	Copenhagen (W.C.)	4	1
1966	Copenhagen	2	0
1978	Copenhagen (E.C.)	4	3
1979	Wembley (E.C.)	1	0
1982	Copenhagen (E.C.)	2	2
1983	Wembley (E.C.)	0	1
1988	Wembley	1	0
1989	Copenhagen	1	1
1990	Wembley	1	0
1992	Malmo (E.C.)	0	0
1994	Wembley	1	0
2002	Niigata (W.C.)	3	0

v. EAST GERMANY

		E	EG
1963	Leipzig	2	1
1970	Wembley	3	1
1974	Leipzig	1	1
1984	Wembley	1	0

v. ECUADOR

		E	Ec
1970	Quito	2	0

v. EGYPT

		E	Eg
1986	Cairo	4	0
1990	Cagliari (W.C.)	1	0

v. F.I.F.A.

		E	F
1938	Arsenal	3	0
1953	Wembley	4	4
1963	Wembley	2	1

v. FINLAND

		E	F
1937	Helsinki	8	0
1956	Helsinki	5	1
1966	Helsinki	3	0
1976	Helsinki (W.C.)	4	1
1976	Wembley (W.C.)	2	1
1982	Helsinki	4	1
1984	Wembley (W.C.)	5	0
1985	Helsinki (W.C.)	1	1
1992	Helsinki	2	1
2000	Helsinki (W.C.)	0	0

		E	F
2001	Liverpool (W.C.)	2	1

v. FRANCE

		E	F
1923	Paris	4	1
1924	Paris	3	1
1925	Paris	3	2
1927	Paris	6	0
1928	Paris	5	1
1929	Paris	4	1
1931	Paris	2	5
1933	Tottenham	4	1
1938	Paris	4	2
1947	Arsenal	3	0
1949	Paris	3	1
1951	Arsenal	2	2
1955	Paris	0	1
1957	Wembley	4	0
1962	Sheffield Wed. (E.C.)	1	1
1963	Paris (E.C.)	2	5
1966	Wembley (W.C.)	2	0
1969	Wembley	5	0
1982	Bilbao (W.C.)	3	1
1984	Paris	0	2
1992	Wembley	2	0
1992	Malmo (E.C.)	0	0
1997	Montpellier (T.F.)	1	0
1999	Wembley	0	2
2000	Paris	1	1

v. GEORGIA

		E	G
1996	Tbilisi (W.C.)	2	0
1997	Wembley (W.C.)	2	0

v. GERMANY/WEST GERMANY

		E	G
1930	Berlin	3	3
1935	Tottenham	3	0
1938	Berlin	6	3
1954	Wembley	3	1
1956	Berlin	3	1
1965	Nuremberg	1	0
1966	Wembley	1	0
1966	Wembley (W.C.F.)	4	2
1968	Hanover	0	1
1970	Leon (W.C.)	2	3
1972	Wembley (E.C.)	1	3
1972	Berlin (E.C.)	0	0
1975	Wembley	2	0
1978	Munich	1	2
1982	Madrid (W.C.)	0	0
1982	Wembley	1	2
1985	Mexico City	3	0
1987	Dusseldorf	1	3
1990*	Turin (W.C.)	1	1
1991	Wembley	0	1
1993	Detroit	1	2

		E	G
1996†	Wembley (E.C.)	1	1
2000	Charleroi (E.C.)	1	0
2000	Wembley (W.C.)	0	1
2001	Munich (W.C.)	5	1

(* England lost 3-4 on pens.)
(† England lost 5-6 on pens.)

v. GREECE

		E	G
1971	Wembley (E.C.)	3	0
1971	Athens (E.C.)	2	0
1982	Salonika (E.C.)	3	0
1983	Wembley (E.C.)	0	0
1989	Athens	2	1
1994	Wembley	5	0
2001	Athens (W.C.)	2	0
2001	Manchester Utd. (W.C.)	2	2

v. HOLLAND

		E	H
1935	Amsterdam	1	0
1946	Huddersfield	8	2
1964	Amsterdam	1	1
1969	Amsterdam	1	0
1970	Wembley	0	0
1977	Wembley	0	2
1982	Wembley	2	0
1988	Wembley	2	2
1988	Dusseldorf (E.C.)	1	3
1990	Cagliari (W.C.)	0	0
1993	Wembley (W.C.)	2	2
1993	Rotterdam (W.C.)	0	2
1996	Wembley (E.C.)	4	1
2001	Tottenham	0	2
2002	Amsterdam	1	1

v. HUNGARY

		E	H
1908	Budapest	7	0
1909	Budapest	4	2
1909	Budapest	8	2
1934	Budapest	1	2
1936	Highbury	6	2
1953	Wembley	3	6
1954	Budapest	1	7
1960	Budapest	0	2
1962	Rancagua (W.C.)	1	2
1965	Wembley	1	0
1978	Wembley	4	1
1981	Budapest (W.C.)	3	1
1981	Wembley (W.C.)	1	0
1983	Wembley (E.C.)	2	0
1983	Budapest (E.C.)	3	0
1988	Budapest	0	0
1990	Wembley	1	0
1992	Budapest	1	0
1996	Wembley	3	0
1999	Budapest	1	1

v. ICELAND

		E	I
1982	Reykjavik	1	1

v. REPUBLIC OF IRELAND

		E	RI
1946	Dublin	1	0
1950	Everton	0	2
1957	Wembley (W.C.)	5	1
1957	Dublin (W.C.)	1	1
1964	Dublin	3	1
1977	Wembley	1	1
1978	Dublin (E.C.)	1	1
1980	Wembley (E.C.)	2	0
1985	Wembley	2	1
1988	Stuttgart (E.C.)	0	1
1990	Cagliari (W.C.)	1	1
1990	Dublin (E.C.)	1	1
1991	Wembley (E.C.)	1	1
1995*	Dublin	0	1

(* Abandoned 27 mins. – crowd riot)

v. ISRAEL

		E	I
1986	Tel Aviv	2	1
1988	Tel Aviv	0	0

v. ITALY

		E	I
1933	Rome	1	1
1934	Arsenal	3	2
1939	Milan	2	2
1948	Turin	4	0
1949	Tottenham	2	0
1952	Florence	1	1
1959	Wembley	2	2
1961	Rome	3	2
1973	Turin	0	2
1973	Wembley	0	1
1976	New York	3	2
1976	Rome (W.C.)	0	2
1977	Wembley (W.C.)	2	0
1980	Turin (E.C.)	0	1
1985	Mexico City	1	2
1989	Wembley	0	0
1990	Bari (W.C.)	1	2
1996	Wembley (W.C.)	0	1
1997	Nantes (T.F.)	2	0
1997	Rome (W.C.)	0	0
2000	Turin	0	1
2002	Leeds	1	2

v. JAPAN

		E	J
1995	Wembley	2	1

v. KUWAIT

		E	K
1982	Bilbao (W.C.)	1	0

v. LUXEMBOURG

		E	L
1927	Luxembourg	5	2
1960	Luxembourg (W.C.)	9	0
1961	Arsenal (W.C.)	4	1
1977	Wembley (W.C.)	5	0
1977	Luxembourg (W.C.)	2	0
1982	Wembley (E.C.)	9	0
1983	Luxembourg (E.C.)	4	0
1998	Luxembourg (E.C.)	3	0
1999	Wembley (E.C.)	6	0

v. MALAYSIA

		E	M
1991	Kuala Lumpur	4	2

v. MALTA

		E	M
1971	Valletta (E.C.)	1	0
1971	Wembley (E.C.)	5	0
2000	Valletta	2	1

v. MEXICO

		E	M
1959	Mexico City	1	2
1961	Wembley	8	0
1966	Wembley (W.C.)	2	0
1969	Mexico City	0	0
1985	Mexico City	0	1
1986	Los Angeles	3	0
1997	Wembley	2	0
2001	Derby	4	0

v. MOLDOVA

		E	M
1996	Kishinev	3	0
1997	Wembley (W.C.)	4	0

v. MOROCCO

		E	M
1986	Monterrey (W.C.)	0	0
1998	Casablanca	1	0

v. NEW ZEALAND

		E	NZ
1991	Auckland	1	0
1991	Wellington	2	0

v. NIGERIA

		E	N
1994	Wembley	1	0
2002	Osaka (W.C.)	0	0

v. NORWAY

		E	N
1937	Oslo	6	0
1938	Newcastle	4	0
1949	Oslo	4	1
1966	Oslo	6	1
1980	Wembley (W.C.)	4	0
1981	Oslo (W.C.)	1	2
1992	Wembley (W.C.)	1	1

		E	N
1993	Oslo (W.C.)	0	2
1994	Wembley	0	0
1995	Oslo	0	0

v. PARAGUAY

		E	P
1986	Mexico City (W.C.)	3	0
2002	Liverpool	4	0

v. PERU

		E	P
1959	Lima	1	4
1961	Lima	4	0

v. POLAND

		E	P
1966	Everton	1	1
1966	Chorzow	1	0
1973	Chorzow (W.C.)	0	2
1973	Wembley (W.C.)	1	1
1986	Monterrey (W.C.)	3	0
1989	Wembley (W.C.)	3	0
1989	Katowice (W.C.)	0	0
1990	Wembley (E.C.)	2	0
1991	Poznan (E.C.)	1	1
1993	Chorzow (W.C.)	1	1
1993	Wembley (W.C.)	3	0
1996	Wembley (W.C.)	2	1
1997	Katowice (W.C.)	2	0
1999	Wembley (E.C.)	3	1
1999	Warsaw (E.C.)	0	0

v. PORTUGAL

		E	P
1947	Lisbon	10	0
1950	Lisbon	5	3
1951	Everton	5	2
1955	Oporto	1	3
1958	Wembley	2	1
1961	Lisbon (W.C.)	1	1
1961	Wembley (W.C.)	2	0
1964	Lisbon	4	3
1964	Sao Paulo	1	1
1966	Wembley (W.C.)	2	1
1969	Wembley	1	0
1974	Lisbon	0	0
1974	Wembley (E.C.)	0	0
1975	Lisbon (E.C.)	1	1
1986	Monterrey (W.C.)	0	1
1995	Wembley	1	1
1998	Wembley	3	0
2000	Eindhoven (E.C.)	2	3

v. ROMANIA

		E	R
1939	Bucharest	2	0
1968	Bucharest	0	0
1969	Wembley	1	1
1970	Guadalajara (W.C.)	1	0

		E	R
1980	Bucharest (W.C.)	1	2
1981	Wembley (W.C.)	0	0
1985	Bucharest (W.C.)	0	0
1985	Wembley (W.C.)	1	1
1994	Wembley	1	1
1998	Toulouse (W.C.)	1	2
2000	Charleroi (E.C.)	2	3

v. SAN MARINO

		E	SM
1992	Wembley (W.C.)	6	0
1993	Bologna (W.C.)	7	1

v. SAUDI ARABIA

		E	SA
1988	Riyadh	1	1
1998	Wembley	0	0

v. SOUTH AFRICA

		E	SA
1997	Manchester Utd.	2	1

v. SOUTH KOREA

		E	SK
2002	Seoguipo	1	1

v. SOVIET UNION
(see also C.I.S.)

		E	SU
1958	Moscow	1	1
1958	Gothenburg (W.C.)	2	2
1958	Gothenburg (W.C.)	0	1
1958	Wembley	5	0
1967	Wembley	2	2
1968	Rome (E.C.)	2	0
1973	Moscow	2	1
1984	Wembley	0	2
1986	Tbilisi	1	0
1988	Frankfurt (E.C.)	1	3
1991	Wembley	3	1

v. SPAIN

		E	S
1929	Madrid	3	4
1931	Arsenal	7	1
1950	Rio de Janeiro (W.C.)	0	1
1955	Madrid	1	1
1955	Wembley	4	1
1960	Madrid	0	3
1960	Wembley	4	2
1965	Madrid	2	0
1967	Wembley	2	0
1968	Wembley (E.C.)	1	0
1968	Madrid (E.C.)	2	1
1980	Barcelona	2	0
1980	Naples (E.C.)	2	1
1981	Wembley	1	2
1982	Madrid (W.C.)	0	0
1987	Madrid	4	2
1992	Santander	0	1

		E	S
1996*	Wembley (E.C.)	0	0
2001	Aston Villa	3	0

(* England won 4-2 on pens.)

v. SWEDEN

		E	S
1923	Stockholm	4	2
1923	Stockholm	3	1
1937	Stockholm	4	0
1948	Arsenal	4	2
1949	Stockholm	1	3
1956	Stockholm	0	0
1959	Wembley	2	3
1965	Gothenburg	2	1
1968	Wembley	3	1
1979	Stockholm	0	0
1986	Stockholm	0	1
1988	Wembley (W.C.)	0	0
1989	Stockholm (W.C.)	0	0
1992	Stockholm (E.C.)	1	2
1995	Leeds	3	3
1998	Stockholm (E.C.)	1	2
1999	Wembley (E.C.)	0	0
2001	Manchester Utd.	1	1
2002	Saitama (W.C.)	1	1

v. SWITZERLAND

		E	S
1933	Berne	4	0
1938	Zurich	1	2
1947	Zurich	0	1
1949	Arsenal	6	0
1952	Zurich	3	0
1954	Berne (W.C.)	2	0
1962	Wembley	3	1
1963	Basle	8	1
1971	Basle (E.C.)	3	2
1971	Wembley (E.C.)	1	1
1975	Basle	2	1
1977	Wembley	0	0
1980	Wembley (W.C.)	2	1
1981	Basle (W.C.)	1	2
1988	Lausanne	1	0
1995	Wembley	3	1
1996	Wembley (E.C.)	1	1
1998	Berne	1	1

v. TUNISIA

		E	T
1990	Tunis	1	1
1998	Marseille (W.C.)	2	0

v. TURKEY

		E	T
1984	Istanbul (W.C.)	8	0
1985	Wembley (W.C.)	5	0
1987	Izmir (E.C.)	0	0
1987	Wembley (E.C.)	8	0
1991	Izmir (E.C.)	1	0
1992	Wembley (E.C.)	1	0
1992	Wembley (W.C.)	4	0
1993	Izmir (W.C.)	2	0

v UKRAINE

		E	U
2000	Wembley	2	0

v. URUGUAY

		E	U
1953	Montevideo	1	2
1954	Basle (W.C.)	2	4
1964	Wembley	2	1
1966	Wembley (W.C.)	0	0
1969	Montevideo	2	1
1977	Montevideo	0	0
1984	Montevideo	0	2
1990	Wembley	1	2
1995	Wembley	0	0

v. U.S.A.

		E	USA
1950	Belo Horizonte (W.C.)	0	1
1953	New York	6	3
1959	Los Angeles	8	1
1964	New York	10	0
1985	Los Angeles	5	0
1993	Boston	0	2
1994	Wembley	2	0

v. YUGOSLAVIA

		E	Y
1939	Belgrade	1	2
1950	Arsenal	2	2
1954	Belgrade	0	1
1956	Wembley	3	0
1958	Belgrade	0	5
1960	Wembley	3	3
1965	Belgrade	1	1
1966	Wembley	2	0
1968	Florence (E.C.)	0	1
1972	Wembley	1	1
1974	Belgrade	2	2
1986	Wembley (E.C.)	2	0
1987	Belgrade (E.C.)	4	1
1989	Wembley	2	1

ENGLAND'S RECORD

England's first international was a 0-0 draw against Scotland in Glasgow, on the West of Scotland cricket ground, Partick, on November 30, 1872. Now, 130 years on, their complete International record, at the start of 2002-03, is:

P	W	D	L	F	A
794	445	195	154	1790	812

ENGLAND "B" TEAM RESULTS

(England score shown first)

Year	Opponent			Year	Opponent		
1949	Finland (A)	4	0	1979	N. Zealand (H)	4	1
1949	Holland (A)	4	0	1980	U.S.A. (H)	1	0
1950	Italy (A)	0	5	1980	Spain (H)	1	0
1950	Holland (H)	1	0	1980	Australia (H)	1	0
1950	Holland (H)	0	3	1981	Spain (A)	2	3
1950	Luxembourg (A)	2	1	1984	N. Zealand (H)	2	0
1950	Switzerland (H)	5	0	1987	Malta (A)	2	0
1952	Holland (H)	1	0	1989	Switzerland (A)	2	0
1952	France (A)	1	7	1989	Iceland (A)	2	0
1953	Scotland (A)	2	2	1989	Norway (A)	1	0
1954	Scotland (H)	1	1	1989	Italy (H)	1	1
1954	Germany (A)	4	0	1989	Yugoslavia (H)	2	1
1954	Yugoslavia (A)	1	2	1990	Rep. of Ireland (A)	1	4
1954	Switzerland (A)	0	2	1990	Czechoslovakia (H)	2	0
1955	Germany (H)	1	1	1990	Algeria (A)	0	0
1955	Yugoslavia (H)	5	1	1991	Wales (A)	1	0
1956	Switzerland (H)	4	1	1991	Iceland (H)	1	0
1956	Scotland (A)	2	2	1991	Switzerland (H)	2	1
1957	Scotland (H)	4	1	1991	Spanish XI (A)	1	0
1978	W. Germany (A)	2	1	1992	France (H)	3	0
1978	Czechoslovakia (A)	1	0	1992	Czechoslovakia (A)	1	0
1978	Singapore (A)	8	0	1992	C.I.S. (H)	1	1
1978	Malaysia (A)	1	1	1994	N. Ireland (H)	4	2
1978	N. Zealand (A)	4	0	1995	Rep. of Ireland (A)	2	0
1978	N. Zealand (A)	3	1	1998	Chile (A)	1	2
1978	N. Zealand (A)	4	0	1998	Russia (H)	4	1
1979	Austria (A)	1	0				

GREAT BRITAIN V. REST OF EUROPE (F.I.F.A.)

		GB	RofE			GB	RofE
1947	Glasgow	6	1	1955	Belfast	1	4

SCOTLAND

v. ARGENTINA

		S	A			S	A
1977	Buenos Aires	1	1	1985*	Melbourne (W.C.)	0	0
1979	Glasgow	1	3	1996	Glasgow	1	0
1990	Glasgow	1	0	2000	Glasgow	0	2
				(* World Cup play-off)			

v. AUSTRALIA

		S	A
1985*	Glasgow (W.C.)	2	0

v. AUSTRIA

		S	A
1931	Vienna	0	5

		S	A
1933	Glasgow	2	1
1937	Vienna	1	1
1950	Glasgow	0	1
1951	Vienna	0	4
1954	Zurich (W.C.)	0	1
1955	Vienna	4	1
1956	Glasgow	1	1
1960	Vienna	1	4
1963*	Glasgow	4	1
1968	Glasgow (W.C.)	2	1
1969	Vienna (W.C.)	0	2
1978	Vienna (E.C.)	2	3
1979	Glasgow (E.C.)	1	1
1994	Vienna	2	1
1996	Vienna (W.C.)	0	0
1997	Glasgow (W.C.)	2	0

(* Abandoned after 79 minutes)

v. BELARUS

		S	B
1997	Minsk (W.C.)	1	0
1997	Aberdeen (W.C.)	4	1

v. BELGIUM

		S	B
1947	Brussels	1	2
1948	Glasgow	2	0
1951	Brussels	5	0
1971	Liege (E.C.)	0	3
1971	Aberdeen (E.C.)	1	0
1974	Brugge	1	2
1979	Brussels (E.C.)	0	2
1979	Glasgow (E.C.)	1	3
1982	Brussels (E.C.)	2	3
1983	Glasgow (E.C.)	1	1
1987	Brussels (E.C.)	1	4
1987	Glasgow (E.C.)	2	0
2001	Glasgow (W.C.)	2	2
2001	Brussels (W.C.)	0	2

v. BOSNIA

		S	B
1999	Sarajevo (E.C.)	2	1
1999	Glasgow (E.C.)	1	0

v. BRAZIL

		S	B
1966	Glasgow	1	1
1972	Rio de Janeiro	0	1
1973	Glasgow	0	1
1974	Frankfurt (W.C.)	0	0
1977	Rio de Janeiro	0	2
1982	Seville (W.C.)	1	4
1987	Glasgow	0	2
1990	Turin (W.C.)	0	1
1998	St. Denis (W.C.)	1	2

v. BULGARIA

		S	B
1978	Glasgow	2	1
1986	Glasgow (E.C.)	0	0
1987	Sofia (E.C.)	1	0
1990	Sofia (E.C.)	1	1
1991	Glasgow (E.C.)	1	1

v. CANADA

		S	C
1983	Vancouver	2	0
1983	Edmonton	3	0
1983	Toronto	2	0
1992	Toronto	3	1

v. CHILE

		S	C
1977	Santiago	4	2
1989	Glasgow	2	0

v. C.I.S.
(formerly Soviet Union)

		S	C
1992	Norrkoping (E.C.)	3	0

v. COLOMBIA

		S	C
1988	Glasgow	0	0
1996	Miami	0	1
1998	New York	2	2

v. COSTA RICA

		S	C
1990	Genoa (W.C.)	0	1

v. CROATIA

		S	C
2000	Zagreb (W.C.)	1	1
2001	Glasgow (W.C.)	0	0

v. CYPRUS

		S	C
1968	Nicosia (W.C.)	5	0
1969	Glasgow (W.C.)	8	0
1989	Limassol (W.C.)	3	2
1989	Glasgow (W.C.)	2	1

v. CZECH REPUBLIC

		S	C
1999	Glasgow (E.C.)	1	2
1999	Prague (E.C.)	2	3

v. CZECHOSLOVAKIA

		S	C
1937	Prague	3	1
1937	Glasgow	5	0
1961	Bratislava (W.C.)	0	4
1961	Glasgow (W.C.)	3	2
1961*	Brussels (W.C.)	2	4
1972	Porto Alegre	0	0
1973	Glasgow (W.C.)	2	1
1973	Bratislava (W.C.)	0	1
1976	Prague (W.C.)	0	2

	S	C
1977 Glasgow (W.C.)	3	1
(* World Cup play-off)		

v. DENMARK

	S	D
1951 Glasgow	3	1
1952 Copenhagen	2	1
1968 Copenhagen	1	0
1970 Glasgow (E.C.)	1	0
1971 Copenhagen (E.C.)	0	1
1972 Copenhagen (W.C.)	4	1
1972 Glasgow (W.C.)	2	0
1975 Copenhagen (E.C.)	1	0
1975 Glasgow (E.C.)	3	1
1986 Neza (W.C.)	0	1
1996 Copenhagen	0	2
1998 Glasgow	0	1

v. EAST GERMANY

	S	EG
1974 Glasgow	3	0
1977 East Berlin	0	1
1982 Glasgow (E.C.)	2	0
1983 Halle (E.C.)	1	2
1986 Glasgow	0	0
1990 Glasgow	0	1

v. ECUADOR

	S	E
1995 Toyama, Japan	2	1

v. EGYPT

	S	E
1990 Aberdeen	1	3

v. ESTONIA

	S	E
1993 Tallinn (W.C.)	3	0
1993 Aberdeen	3	1
1996 Tallinn (W.C.) .... * No result		
1997 Monaco (W.C.)	0	0
1997 Kilmarnock (W.C.)	2	0
1998 Edinburgh (E.C.)	3	2
1999 Tallinn (E.C.)	0	0
(* Estonia absent)		

v. FAROE ISLANDS

	S	F
1994 Glasgow (E.C.)	5	1
1995 Toftir (E.C.)	2	0
1998 Aberdeen (E.C.)	2	1
1999 Toftir (E.C.)	1	1

v. FINLAND

	S	F
1954 Helsinki	2	1
1964 Glasgow (W.C.)	3	1
1965 Helsinki (W.C.)	2	1
1976 Glasgow	6	0
1992 Glasgow	1	1

	S	F
1994 Helsinki (E.C.)	2	0
1995 Glasgow (E.C.)	1	0
1998 Edinburgh	1	1

v. FRANCE

	S	F
1930 Paris	2	0
1932 Paris	3	1
1948 Paris	0	3
1949 Glasgow	2	0
1950 Paris	1	0
1951 Glasgow	1	0
1958 Orebro (W.C.)	1	2
1984 Marseilles	0	2
1989 Glasgow (W.C.)	2	0
1990 Paris (W.C.)	0	3
1997 St. Etienne	1	2
2000 Glasgow	0	2
2002 Paris	0	5

v. GERMANY/ WEST GERMANY

	S	G
1929 Berlin	1	1
1936 Glasgow	2	0
1957 Stuttgart	3	1
1959 Glasgow	3	2
1964 Hanover	2	2
1969 Glasgow (W.C.)	1	1
1969 Hamburg (W.C.)	2	3
1973 Glasgow	1	1
1974 Frankfurt	1	2
1986 Queretaro (W.C.)	1	2 *
1992 Norrkoping (E.C.)	0	2
1993 Glasgow	0	1
1999 Bremen	1	0

v. GREECE

	S	G
1994 Athens (E.C.)	0	1
1995 Glasgow	1	0

v. HOLLAND

	S	H
1929 Amsterdam	2	0
1938 Amsterdam	3	1
1959 Amsterdam	2	1
1966 Glasgow	0	3
1968 Amsterdam	0	0
1971 Amsterdam	1	2
1978 Mendoza (W.C.)	3	2
1982 Glasgow	2	1
1986 Eindhoven	0	0
1992 Gothenburg (E.C.)	0	1
1994 Glasgow	0	1
1994 Utrecht	1	3
1996 Birmingham (E.C.)	0	0
2000 Arnhem	0	0

v. HUNGARY

		S	H
1938	Glasgow	3	1
1955	Glasgow	2	4
1955	Budapest	1	3
1958	Glasgow	1	1
1960	Budapest	3	3
1980	Budapest	1	3
1987	Glasgow	2	0

v. ICELAND

		S	I
1984	Glasgow (W.C.)	3	0
1985	Reykjavik (W.C)	1	0

v. IRAN

		S	I
1978	Cordoba (W.C.)	1	1

v. REPUBLIC OF IRELAND

		S	RI
1961	Glasgow (W.C.)	4	1
1961	Dublin (W.C.)	3	0
1963	Dublin	0	1
1969	Dublin	1	1
1986	Dublin (E.C.)	0	0
1987	Glasgow (E.C.)	0	1
2000	Dublin	2	1

v. ISRAEL

		S	I
1981	Tel Aviv (W.C.)	1	0
1981	Glasgow (W.C.)	3	1
1986	Tel Aviv	1	0

v. ITALY

		S	I
1931	Rome	0	3
1965	Glasgow (W.C.)	1	0
1965	Naples (W.C.)	0	3
1988	Perugia	0	2
1992	Glasgow (W.C.)	0	0
1993	Rome (W.C.)	1	3

v. JAPAN

		S	J
1995	Hiroshima	0	0

v. LATVIA

		S	L
1996	Riga (W.C.)	2	0
1997	Glasgow (W.C.)	2	0
2000	Riga (W.C.)	1	0
2001	Glasgow (W.C.)	2	1

v. LITHUANIA

		S	L
1998	Vilnius (E.C.)	0	0
1999	Glasgow (E.C.)	3	0

v. LUXEMBOURG

		S	L
1947	Luxembourg	6	0
1986	Glasgow (E.C.)	3	0
1987	Esch (E.C.)	0	0

v. MALTA

		S	M
1988	Valletta	1	1
1990	Valletta	2	1
1993	Glasgow (W.C.)	3	0
1993	Valletta (W.C.)	2	0
1997	Valletta	3	2

v. MOROCCO

		S	M
1998	St. Etienne (W.C.)	0	3

v. NEW ZEALAND

		S	NZ
1982	Malaga (W.C.)	5	2

v. NIGERIA

		S	N
2002	Aberdeen	1	2

v. NORWAY

		S	N
1929	Bergen	7	3
1954	Glasgow	1	0
1954	Oslo	1	1
1963	Bergen	3	4
1963	Glasgow	6	1
1974	Oslo	2	1
1978	Glasgow (E.C.)	3	2
1979	Oslo (E.C.)	4	0
1988	Oslo (W.C.)	2	1
1989	Glasgow (W.C.)	1	1
1992	Oslo	0	0
1998	Bordeaux (W.C.)	1	1

v. PARAGUAY

		S	P
1958	Norrkoping (W.C.)	2	3

v. PERU

		S	P
1972	Glasgow	2	0
1978	Cordoba (W.C.)	1	3
1979	Glasgow	1	1

v. POLAND

		S	P
1958	Warsaw	2	1
1960	Glasgow	2	3
1965	Chorzow (W.C.)	1	1
1965	Glasgow (W.C.)	1	2
1980	Poznan	0	1
1990	Glasgow	1	1
2001	Bydgoszcz	1	1

v. PORTUGAL

		S	P
1950	Lisbon	2	2
1955	Glasgow	3	0
1959	Lisbon	0	1
1966	Glasgow	0	1
1971	Lisbon (E.C.)	0	2
1971	Glasgow (E.C.)	2	1
1975	Glasgow	1	0
1978	Lisbon (E.C.)	0	1
1980	Glasgow (E.C.)	4	1
1980	Glasgow (W.C.)	0	0
1981	Lisbon (W.C.)	1	2
1992	Glasgow (W.C.)	0	0
1993	Lisbon (W.C.)	0	5

v. ROMANIA

		S	R
1975	Bucharest (E.C.)	1	1
1975	Glasgow (E.C.)	1	1
1986	Glasgow	3	0
1990	Glasgow (E.C.)	2	1
1991	Bucharest (E.C.)	0	1

v. RUSSIA

		S	R
1994	Glasgow (E.C.)	1	1
1995	Moscow (E.C.)	0	0

v. SAN MARINO

		S	SM
1991	Serravalle (E.C.)	2	0
1991	Glasgow (E.C.)	4	0
1995	Serravalle (E.C.)	2	0
1995	Glasgow (E.C.)	5	0
2000	Serravalle (W.C.)	2	0
2001	Glasgow (W.C.)	4	0

v. SAUDI ARABIA

		S	SA
1988	Riyadh	2	2

v. SOUTH AFRICA

		S	SA
2002	Hong Kong	0	2

v. SOUTH KOREA

		S	SK
2002	Busan	1	4

v. SOVIET UNION
(see also C.I.S. and RUSSIA)

		S	SU
1967	Glasgow	0	2
1971	Moscow	0	1
1982	Malaga (W.C.)	2	2
1991	Glasgow	0	1

v. SPAIN

		S	Sp
1957	Glasgow (W.C.)	4	2
1957	Madrid (W.C.)	1	4

		S	Sp
1963	Madrid	6	2
1965	Glasgow	0	0
1975	Glasgow (E.C.)	1	2
1975	Valencia (E.C.)	1	1
1982	Valencia	0	3
1985	Glasgow (W.C.)	3	1
1985	Seville (W.C.)	0	1
1988	Madrid	0	0

v. SWEDEN

		S	Swe
1952	Stockholm	1	3
1953	Glasgow	1	2
1975	Gothenburg	1	1
1977	Glasgow	3	1
1980	Stockholm (W.C.)	1	0
1981	Glasgow (W.C.)	2	0
1990	Genoa (W.C.)	2	1
1995	Solna	0	2
1996	Glasgow (W.C.)	1	0
1997	Gothenburg (W.C.)	1	2

v. SWITZERLAND

		S	Sw
1931	Geneva	3	2
1948	Berne	1	2
1950	Glasgow	3	1
1957	Basle (W.C.)	2	1
1957	Glasgow (W.C.)	3	2
1973	Berne	0	1
1976	Glasgow	1	0
1982	Berne (E.C.)	0	2
1983	Glasgow (E.C.)	2	2
1990	Glasgow (E.C.)	2	1
1991	Berne (E.C.)	2	2
1992	Berne (W.C.)	1	3
1993	Aberdeen (W.C.)	1	1
1996	Birmingham (E.C.)	1	0

v. TURKEY

		S	T
1960	Ankara	2	4

v. U.S.A.

		S	USA
1952	Glasgow	6	0
1992	Denver	1	0
1996	New Britain, Conn	1	2
1998	Washington	0	0

v. URUGUAY

		S	U
1954	Basle (W.C.)	0	7
1962	Glasgow	2	3
1983	Glasgow	2	0
1986	Neza (W.C.)	0	0

v. YUGOSLAVIA

		S	Y
1955	Belgrade	2	2

		S	Y
1956	Glasgow	2	0
1958	Vaasteras (W.C.)	1	1
1972	Belo Horizonte	2	2
1974	Frankfurt (W.C.)	1	1
1984	Glasgow	6	1

		S	Y
1988	Glasgow (W.C.)	1	1
1989	Zagreb (W.C.)	1	3

v. ZAIRE

		S	Z
1974	Dortmund (W.C.)	2	0

WALES

v. ALBANIA

		W	A
1994	Cardiff (E.C.)	2	0
1995	Tirana (E.C.)	1	1

v. ARGENTINA

		W	A
1992	Gifu (Japan)	0	1
2002	Cardiff	1	1

v. ARMENIA

		W	A
2001	Yerevan (W.C.)	2	2
2001	Cardiff (W.C.)	0	0

v. AUSTRIA

		W	A
1954	Vienna	0	2
1955	Wrexham	1	2
1975	Vienna (E.C.)	1	2
1975	Wrexham (E.C.)	1	0
1992	Vienna	1	1

v. BELARUS

		W	B
1998	Cardiff (E.C.)	3	2
1999	Minsk (E.C.)	2	1
2000	Minsk (W.C.)	1	2
2001	Cardiff (W.C.)	1	0

v. BELGIUM

		W	B
1949	Liege	1	3
1949	Cardiff	5	1
1990	Cardiff (E.C.)	3	1
1991	Brussels (E.C.)	1	1
1992	Brussels (W.C.)	0	2
1993	Cardiff (W.C.)	2	0
1997	Cardiff (W.C.)	1	2
1997	Brussels (W.C.)	2	3

v. BRAZIL

		W	B
1958	Gothenburg (W.C.)	0	1
1962	Rio de Janeiro	1	3
1962	Sao Paulo	1	3
1966	Rio de Janeiro	1	3
1966	Belo Horizonte	0	1
1983	Cardiff	1	1
1991	Cardiff	1	0
1997	Brasilia	0	3
2000	Cardiff	0	3

v. BULGARIA

		W	B
1983	Wrexham (E.C.)	1	0
1983	Sofia (E.C.)	0	1
1994	Cardiff (E.C.)	0	3
1995	Sofia (E.C.)	1	3

v. CANADA

		W	C
1986	Toronto	0	2
1986	Vancouver	3	0

v. CHILE

		W	C
1966	Santiago	0	2

v. COSTA RICA

		W	C
1990	Cardiff	1	0

v. CYPRUS

		W	C
1992	Limassol (W.C.)	1	0
1993	Cardiff (W.C.)	2	0

v. CZECHOSLOVAKIA
(see also R.C.S.)

		W	C
1957	Cardiff (W.C.)	1	0
1957	Prague (W.C.)	0	2
1971	Swansea (E.C.)	1	3
1971	Prague (E.C.)	0	1
1977	Wrexham (W.C.)	3	0
1977	Prague (W.C.)	0	1
1980	Cardiff (W.C.)	1	0
1981	Prague (W.C.)	0	2
1987	Wrexham (E.C.)	1	1
1987	Prague (E.C.)	0	2

v. CZECH REPUBLIC

		S	CR
2002	Cardiff	0	0

v. DENMARK

		W	D
1964	Copenhagen (W.C.)	0	1
1965	Wrexham (W.C.)	4	2
1987	Cardiff (E.C.)	1	0
1987	Copenhagen (E.C.)	0	1
1990	Copenhagen	0	1
1998	Copenhagen (E.C.)	2	1
1999	Anfield (E.C.)	0	2

v. EAST GERMANY

		W	EG
1957	Leipzig (W.C.)	1	2
1957	Cardiff (W.C.)	4	1
1969	Dresden (W.C.)	1	2
1969	Cardiff (W.C.)	1	3

v. ESTONIA

		W	E
1994	Tallinn	2	1

v. FAROE ISLANDS

		W	FI
1992	Cardiff (W.C.)	6	0
1993	Toftir (W.C.)	3	0

v. FINLAND

		W	F
1971	Helsinki (E.C.)	1	0
1971	Swansea (E.C.)	3	0
1986	Helsinki (E.C.)	1	1
1987	Wrexham (E.C.)	4	0
1988	Swansea (W.C.)	2	2
1989	Helsinki (W.C.)	0	1
2000	Cardiff	1	2

v. FRANCE

		W	F
1933	Paris	1	1
1939	Paris	1	2
1953	Paris	1	6
1982	Toulouse	1	0

v. GEORGIA

		W	G
1994	Tbilisi (E.C.)	0	5
1995	Cardiff (E.C.)	0	1

v. GERMANY/ WEST GERMANY

		W	G
1968	Cardiff	1	1
1969	Frankfurt	1	1
1977	Cardiff	0	2
1977	Dortmund	1	1
1979	Wrexham (E.C.)	0	2
1979	Cologne (E.C.)	1	5
1989	Cardiff (W.C.)	0	0
1989	Cologne (W.C.)	1	2
1991	Cardiff (E.C.)	1	0
1991	Nuremberg (E.C.)	1	4
1995	Dusseldorf (E.C.)	1	1
1995	Cardiff (E.C.)	1	2
2002	Cardiff	1	0

v. GREECE

		W	G
1964	Athens (W.C.)	0	2
1965	Cardiff (W.C.)	4	1

v. HOLLAND

		W	H
1988	Amsterdam (W.C.)	0	1
1989	Wrexham (W.C.)	1	2
1992	Utrecht	0	4
1996	Cardiff (W.C.)	1	3
1996	Eindhoven (W.C.)	1	7

v. HUNGARY

		W	H
1958	Sanviken (W.C.)	1	1
1958	Stockholm (W.C.)	2	1
1961	Budapest	2	3
1963	Budapest (E.C.)	1	3
1963	Cardiff (E.C.)	1	1
1974	Cardiff (E.C.)	2	0
1975	Budapest (E.C.)	2	1
1986	Cardiff	0	3

v. ICELAND

		W	I
1980	Reykjavik (W.C.)	4	0
1981	Swansea (W.C.)	2	2
1984	Reykjavik (W.C.)	0	1
1984	Cardiff (W.C.)	2	1
1991	Cardiff	1	0

v. IRAN

		W	I
1978	Tehran	1	0

v. REPUBLIC OF IRELAND

		W	RI
1960	Dublin	3	2
1979	Swansea	2	1
1981	Dublin	3	1
1986	Dublin	1	0
1990	Dublin	0	1
1991	Wrexham	0	3
1992	Dublin	1	0
1993	Dublin	1	2
1997	Cardiff	0	0

v. ISRAEL

		W	I
1958	Tel Aviv (W.C.)	2	0
1958	Cardiff (W.C.)	2	0
1984	Tel Aviv	0	0
1989	Tel Aviv	3	3

v. ITALY

		W	I
1965	Florence	1	4
1968	Cardiff (W.C.)	0	1
1969	Rome (W.C.)	1	4
1988	Brescia	1	0
1996	Terni	0	3
1998	Anfield (E.C.)	0	2
1999	Bologna (E.C.)	0	4

200

v. JAMAICA

		W	J
1998	Cardiff	0	0

v. JAPAN

		W	J
1992	Matsuyama	1	0

v. KUWAIT

		W	K
1977	Wrexham	0	0
1977	Kuwait City	0	0

v. LUXEMBOURG

		W	L
1974	Swansea (E.C.)	5	0
1975	Luxembourg (E.C.)	3	1
1990	Luxembourg (E.C.)	1	0
1991	Luxembourg (E.C.)	1	0

v. MALTA

		W	M
1978	Wrexham (E.C.)	7	0
1979	Valletta (E.C.)	2	0
1988	Valletta	3	2
1998	Valletta	3	0

v. MEXICO

		W	M
1958	Stockholm (W.C.)	1	1
1962	Mexico City	1	2

v. MOLDOVA

		W	M
1994	Kishinev (E.C.)	2	3
1995	Cardiff (E.C.)	1	0

v. NORWAY

		W	N
1982	Swansea (E.C.)	1	0
1983	Oslo (E.C.)	0	0
1984	Trondheim	0	1
1985	Wrexham	1	1
1985	Bergen	2	4
1994	Cardiff	1	3
2000	Cardiff (W.C.)	1	1
2001	Oslo (W.C.)	2	3

v. POLAND

		W	P
1973	Cardiff (W.C.)	2	0
1973	Katowice (W.C.)	0	3
1991	Radom	0	0
2000	Warsaw (W.C.)	0	0
2001	Cardiff (W.C.)	1	2

v. PORTUGAL

		W	P
1949	Lisbon	2	3
1951	Cardiff	2	1
2000	Chaves	0	3

v. QATAR

		W	Q
2000	Doha	1	0

v. R.C.S.
(formerly Czechoslovakia)

		W	RCS
1993	Ostrava (W.C.)	1	1
1993	Cardiff (W.C.)	2	2

v. REST OF UNITED KINGDOM

		W	UK
1951	Cardiff	3	2
1969	Cardiff	0	1

v. ROMANIA

		W	R
1970	Cardiff (E.C.)	0	0
1971	Bucharest (E.C.)	0	2
1983	Wrexham	5	0
1992	Bucharest (W.C.)	1	5
1993	Cardiff (W.C.)	1	2

v. SAN MARINO

		W	SM
1996	Serravalle (W.C.)	5	0
1996	Cardiff (W.C.)	6	0

v. SAUDI ARABIA

		W	SA
1986	Dahran	2	1

v. SOVIET UNION

		W	SU
1965	Moscow (W.C.)	1	2
1965	Cardiff (W.C.)	2	1
1981	Wrexham (W.C.)	0	0
1981	Tbilisi (W.C.)	0	3
1987	Swansea	0	0

v. SPAIN

		W	S
1961	Cardiff (W.C.)	1	2
1961	Madrid (W.C.)	1	1
1982	Valencia	1	1
1984	Seville (W.C.)	0	3
1985	Wrexham (W.C.)	3	0

v. SWEDEN

		W	S
1958	Stockholm (W.C.)	0	0
1988	Stockholm	1	4
1989	Wrexham	0	2
1990	Stockholm	2	4
1994	Wrexham	0	2

v. SWITZERLAND

		W	S
1949	Berne	0	4
1951	Wrexham	3	2
1996	Lugano	0	2
1999	Zurich (E.C.)	0	2
1999	Wrexham (E.C.)	0	2

v. TUNISIA

		W	T
1998	Tunis	0	4

v. TURKEY

		W	T
1978	Wrexham (E.C.)	1	0
1979	Izmir (E.C.)	0	1
1980	Cardiff (W.C.)	4	0
1981	Ankara (W.C.)	1	0
1996	Cardiff (W.C.)	0	0
1997	Istanbul (W.C.)	4	6

v. UKRAINE

		W	U
2001	Cardiff (W.C.)	1	1
2001	Kiev (W.C.)	1	1

v. URUGUAY

		W	U
1986	Wrexham	0	0

v. YUGOSLAVIA

		W	Y
1953	Belgrade	2	5
1954	Cardiff	1	3
1976	Zagreb (E.C.)	0	2
1976	Cardiff (E.C.)	1	1
1982	Titograd (E.C.)	4	4
1983	Cardiff (E.C.)	1	1
1988	Swansea	1	2

NORTHERN IRELAND

v. ALBANIA

		NI	A
1965	Belfast (W.C.)	4	1
1965	Tirana (W.C.)	1	1
1983	Tirana (E.C.)	0	0
1983	Belfast (E.C.)	1	0
1992	Belfast (W.C.)	3	0
1993	Tirana (W.C.)	2	1
1996	Belfast (W.C.)	2	0
1997	Zurich (W.C.)	0	1

v. ALGERIA

		NI	A
1986	Guadalajara (W.C.)	1	1

v. ARGENTINA

		NI	A
1958	Halmstad (W.C.)	1	3

v. ARMENIA

		NI	A
1996	Belfast (W.C.)	1	1
1997	Yerevan (W.C.)	0	0

v. AUSTRALIA

		NI	A
1980	Sydney	2	1
1980	Melbourne	1	1
1980	Adelaide	2	1

v. AUSTRIA

		NI	A
1982	Madrid (W.C.)	2	2
1982	Vienna (E.C.)	0	2
1983	Belfast (E.C.)	3	1
1990	Vienna (E.C.)	0	0
1991	Belfast (E.C.)	2	1
1994	Vienna (E.C.)	2	1
1995	Belfast (E.C.)	5	3

v. BELGIUM

		NI	B
1976	Liege (W.C.)	0	2
1977	Belfast (W.C.)	3	0
1997	Belfast	3	0

v. BRAZIL

		NI	B
1986	Guadalajara (W.C.)	0	3

v. BULGARIA

		NI	B
1972	Sofia (W.C.)	0	3
1973	Sheffield (W.C.)	0	0
1978	Sofia (E.C.)	2	0
1979	Belfast (E.C.)	2	0
2001	Sofia (W.C.)	3	4
2001	Belfast (W.C.)	0	1

v. CANADA

		NI	C
1995	Edmonton	0	2
1999	Belfast	1	1

v. CHILE

		NI	C
1989	Belfast	0	1
1995	Edmonton, Canada	0	2

v. COLOMBIA

		NI	C
1994	Boston, USA	0	2

v. CYPRUS

		NI	C
1971	Nicosia (E.C.)	3	0
1971	Belfast (E.C.)	5	0
1973	Nicosia (W.C.)	0	1
1973	Fulham (W.C.)	3	0

v. CZECHOSLOVAKIA/ CZECH REPUBLIC

		NI	C
1958	Halmstad (W.C.)	1	0
1958	Malmo (W.C.)	2	1

	NI	C
2001 Belfast (W.C.)	0	1
2001 Teplice (W.C.)	1	3

v. DENMARK

	NI	D
1978 Belfast (E.C.)	2	1
1979 Copenhagen (E.C.)	0	4
1986 Belfast	1	1
1990 Belfast (E.C.)	1	1
1991 Odense (E.C.)	1	2
1992 Belfast (W.C.)	0	1
1993 Copenhagen (W.C.)	0	1
2000 Belfast (W.C.)	1	1
2001 Copenhagen (W.C.)	1	1

v. FAROE ISLANDS

	NI	FI
1991 Belfast (E.C.)	1	1
1991 Landskrona, Sw. (E.C.)	5	0

v. FINLAND

	NI	F
1984 Pori (W.C.)	0	1
1984 Belfast (W.C.)	2	1
1998 Belfast (E.C.)	1	0
1999 Helsinki (E.C.)	1	4

v. FRANCE

	NI	F
1951 Belfast	2	2
1952 Paris	1	3
1958 Norrkoping (W.C.)	0	4
1982 Paris	0	4
1982 Madrid (W.C.)	1	4
1986 Paris	0	0
1988 Belfast	0	0
1999 Belfast	0	1

v. GERMANY/
WEST GERMANY

	NI	G
1958 Malmo (W.C.)	2	2
1960 Belfast (W.C.)	3	4
1961 Berlin (W.C.)	1	2
1966 Belfast	0	2
1977 Cologne	0	5
1982 Belfast (E.C.)	1	0
1983 Hamburg (E.C.)	1	0
1992 Bremen	1	1
1996 Belfast	1	1
1997 Nuremberg (W.C.)	1	1
1997 Belfast (W.C.)	1	3
1999 Belfast (E.C.)	0	3
1999 Dortmund (E.C.)	0	4

v. GREECE

	NI	G
1961 Athens (W.C.)	1	2
1961 Belfast (W.C.)	2	0
1988 Athens	2	3

v. HOLLAND

	NI	H
1962 Rotterdam	0	4
1965 Belfast (W.C.)	2	1
1965 Rotterdam (W.C.)	0	0
1976 Rotterdam (W.C.)	2	2
1977 Belfast (W.C.)	0	1

v. HONDURAS

	NI	H
1982 Zaragoza (W.C.)	1	1

v. HUNGARY

	NI	H
1988 Budapest (W.C.)	0	1
1989 Belfast (W.C.)	1	2
2000 Belfast	0	1

v. ICELAND

	NI	I
1977 Reykjavik (W.C.)	0	1
1977 Belfast (W.C.)	2	0
2000 Reykjavik (W.C.)	0	1
2001 Belfast (W.C.)	3	0

v. REPUBLIC OF IRELAND

	NI	RI
1978 Dublin (E.C.)	0	0
1979 Belfast (E.C.)	1	0
1988 Belfast (W.C.)	0	0
1989 Dublin (W.C.)	0	3
1993 Dublin (W.C.)	0	3
1993 Belfast (W.C.)	1	1
1994 Belfast (E.C.)	0	4
1995 Dublin (E.C.)	1	1
1999 Dublin	1	0

v. ISRAEL

	NI	I
1968 Jaffa	3	2
1976 Tel Aviv	1	1
1980 Tel Aviv (W.C.)	0	0
1981 Belfast (W.C.)	1	0
1984 Belfast	3	0
1987 Tel Aviv	1	1

v. ITALY

	NI	I
1957 Rome (W.C.)	0	1
1957 Belfast (W.C.)	2	2
1958 Belfast (W.C.)	2	1
1961 Bologna	2	3
1997 Palermo	0	2

v. LATVIA

	NI	L
1993 Riga (W.C.)	2	1
1993 Belfast (W.C.)	2	0
1995 Riga (E.C.)	1	0
1995 Belfast (E.C.)	1	2

v. LIECHTENSTEIN

		NI	L
1994	Belfast (E.C.)	4	1
1995	Eschen (E.C.)	4	0
2002	Vaduz	0	0

v. LITHUANIA

		NI	L
1992	Belfast (W.C.)	2	2
1993	Vilnius (W.C.)	1	0

v. LUXEMBOURG

		NI	L
2000	Luxembourg	3	1

v. MALTA

		NI	M
1988	Belfast (W.C.)	3	0
1989	Valletta (W.C.)	2	0
2000	Ta'Qali	3	0
2000	Belfast (W.C.)	1	0
2001	Valletta (W.C.)	1	0

v. MEXICO

		NI	M
1966	Belfast	4	1
1994	Miami	0	3

v. MOLDOVA

		NI	M
1998	Belfast (E.C.)	2	2
1999	Kishinev (E.C.)	0	0

v. MOROCCO

		NI	M
1986	Belfast	2	1

v. NORWAY

		NI	N
1974	Oslo (E.C.)	1	2
1975	Belfast (E.C.)	3	0
1990	Belfast	2	3
1996	Belfast	0	2
2001	Belfast	0	4

v. POLAND

		NI	P
1962	Katowice (E.C.)	2	0
1962	Belfast (E.C.)	2	0
1988	Belfast	1	1
1991	Belfast	3	1
2002	Limassol (Cyprus)	1	4

v. PORTUGAL

		NI	P
1957	Lisbon (W.C.)	1	1
1957	Belfast (W.C.)	3	0
1973	Coventry (W.C.)	1	1
1973	Lisbon (W.C.)	1	1
1980	Lisbon (W.C.)	0	1
1981	Belfast (W.C.)	1	0
1994	Belfast (E.C.)	1	2
1995	Oporto (E.C.)	1	1
1997	Belfast (W.C.)	0	0
1997	Lisbon (W.C.)	0	1

v. ROMANIA

		NI	R
1984	Belfast (W.C.)	3	2
1985	Bucharest (W.C.)	1	0
1994	Belfast	2	0

v. SLOVAKIA

		NI	S
1998	Belfast	1	0

v. SOVIET UNION

		NI	SU
1969	Belfast (W.C.)	0	0
1969	Moscow (W.C.)	0	2
1971	Moscow (E.C.)	0	1
1971	Belfast (E.C.)	1	1

v. SPAIN

		NI	S
1958	Madrid	2	6
1963	Bilbao	1	1
1963	Belfast	0	1
1970	Seville (E.C.)	0	3
1972	Hull (E.C.)	1	1
1982	Valencia (W.C.)	1	0
1985	Palma, Majorca	0	0
1986	Guadalajara (W.C.)	1	2
1988	Seville (W.C.)	0	4
1989	Belfast (W.C.)	0	2
1992	Belfast (W.C.)	0	0
1993	Seville (W.C.)	1	3
1998	Santander	1	4
2002	Belfast	0	5

v. SWEDEN

		NI	S
1974	Solna (E.C.)	2	0
1975	Belfast (E.C.)	1	2
1980	Belfast (W.C.)	3	0
1981	Stockholm (W.C.)	0	1
1996	Belfast	1	2

v. SWITZERLAND

		NI	S
1964	Belfast (W.C.)	1	0
1964	Lausanne (W.C.)	1	2
1998	Belfast	1	0

v. THAILAND

		NI	T
1997	Bangkok	0	0

v. TURKEY

		NI	T
1968	Belfast (W.C.)	4	1
1968	Istanbul (W.C.)	3	0
1983	Belfast (E.C.)	2	1
1983	Ankara (E.C.)	0	1
1985	Belfast (W.C.)	2	0
1985	Izmir (W.C.)	0	0
1986	Izmir (E.C.)	0	0
1987	Belfast (E.C.)	1	0
1998	Istanbul (E.C.)	0	3
1999	Belfast (E.C.)	0	3

v. UKRAINE

		NI	U
1996	Belfast (W.C.)	0	1
1997	Kiev (W.C.)	1	2

v. URUGUAY

		NI	U
1964	Belfast	3	0
1990	Belfast	1	0

v. YUGOSLAVIA

		NI	Y
1975	Belfast (E.C.)	1	0
1975	Belgrade (E.C.)	0	1
1982	Zaragoza (W.C.)	0	0
1987	Belfast (E.C.)	1	2
1987	Sarajevo (E.C.)	0	3
1990	Belfast (E.C.)	0	2
1991	Belgrade (E.C.)	1	4
2000	Belfast	1	2

REPUBLIC OF IRELAND

v. ALBANIA

		RI	A
1992	Dublin (W.C.)	2	0
1993	Tirana (W.C.)	2	1

v. ALGERIA

		RI	A
1982	Algiers	0	2

v. ANDORRA

		RI	A
2001	Barcelona (W.C.)	3	0
2001	Dublin (W.C.)	3	1

v. ARGENTINA

		RI	A
1951	Dublin	0	1
1979*	Dublin	0	0
1980	Dublin	0	1
1998	Dublin	0	2
(* Not regarded as full Int.)			

v. AUSTRIA

		RI	A
1952	Vienna	0	6
1953	Dublin	4	0
1958	Vienna	1	3
1962	Dublin	2	3
1963	Vienna (E.C.)	0	0
1963	Dublin (E.C.)	3	2
1966	Vienna	0	1
1968	Dublin	2	2
1971	Dublin (E.C.)	1	4
1971	Linz (E.C.)	0	6
1995	Dublin (E.C.)	1	3
1995	Vienna (E.C.)	1	3

v. BELGIUM

		RI	B
1928	Liege	4	2

		RI	B
1929	Dublin	4	0
1930	Brussels	3	1
1934	Dublin (W.C.)	4	4
1949	Dublin	0	2
1950	Brussels	1	5
1965	Dublin	0	2
1966	Liege	3	2
1980	Dublin (W.C.)	1	1
1981	Brussels (W.C.)	0	1
1986	Brussels (E.C.)	2	2
1987	Dublin (E.C.)	0	0
1997*	Dublin (W.C.)	1	1
1997*	Brussels (W.C.)	1	2
(* World Cup play-off)			

v. BOLIVIA

		RI	B
1994	Dublin	1	0
1996	East Rutherford, N.J.	3	0

v. BRAZIL

		RI	B
1974	Rio de Janeiro	1	2
1982	Uberlandia	0	7
1987	Dublin	1	0

v. BULGARIA

		RI	B
1977	Sofia (W.C.)	1	2
1977	Dublin (W.C.)	0	0
1979	Sofia (E.C.)	0	1
1979	Dublin (E.C.)	3	0
1987	Sofia (E.C.)	1	2
1987	Dublin (E.C.)	2	0

v. CAMEROON

		RI	C
2002	Niigata (W.C.)	1	1

v. CHILE

		RI	C
1960	Dublin	2	0
1972	Recife	1	2
1974	Santiago	2	1
1982	Santiago	0	1
1991	Dublin	1	1

v. CHINA

		RI	C
1984	Sapporo	1	0

v. CROATIA

		RI	C
1996	Dublin	2	2
1998	Dublin (E.C.)	2	0
1999	Zagreb (E.C.)	0	1
2001	Dublin	2	2

v. CYPRUS

		RI	C
1980	Nicosia (W.C.)	3	2
1980	Dublin (W.C.)	6	0
2001	Nicosia (W.C.)	4	0
2001	Dublin (W.C.)	4	0

v. CZECHOSLOVAKIA/ CZECH REPUBLIC

		RI	C
1938	Prague	2	2
1959	Dublin (E.C.)	2	0
1959	Bratislava (E.C.)	0	4
1961	Dublin (W.C.)	1	3
1961	Prague (W.C.)	1	7
1967	Dublin (E.C.)	0	2
1967	Prague (E.C.)	2	1
1969	Dublin (W.C.)	1	2
1969	Prague (W.C.)	0	3
1979	Prague	1	4
1981	Dublin	3	1
1986	Reykjavik	1	0
1994	Dublin	1	3
1996	Prague	0	2
1998	Olomouc	1	2
2000	Dublin	3	2

v. DENMARK

		RI	D
1956	Dublin (W.C.)	2	1
1957	Copenhagen (W.C.)	2	0
1968*	Dublin (W.C.)	1	1
1969	Copenhagen (W.C.)	0	2
1969	Dublin (W.C.)	1	1
1978	Copenhagen (E.C.)	3	3
1979	Dublin (E.C.)	2	0
1984	Copenhagen (W.C.)	0	3
1985	Dublin (W.C.)	1	4
1992	Copenhagen (W.C.)	0	0
1993	Dublin (W.C.)	1	1
2002	Dublin	3	0

(* Abandoned after 51 mins. – fog)

v. ECUADOR

		RI	E
1972	Natal	3	2

v. EGYPT

		RI	E
1990	Palermo (W.C.)	0	0

v. ESTONIA

		RI	E
2000	Dublin (W.C.)	2	0
2001	Tallinn (W.C.)	2	0

v. FINLAND

		RI	F
1949	Dublin (W.C.)	3	0
1949	Helsinki (W.C.)	1	1
1990	Dublin	1	1
2000	Dublin	3	0

v. FRANCE

		RI	F
1937	Paris	2	0
1952	Dublin	1	1
1953	Dublin (W.C.)	3	5
1953	Paris (W.C.)	0	1
1972	Dublin (W.C.)	2	1
1973	Paris (W.C.)	1	1
1976	Paris (W.C.)	0	2
1977	Dublin (W.C.)	1	0
1980	Paris (W.C.)	0	2
1981	Dublin (W.C.)	3	2
1989	Dublin	0	0

v. GERMANY/ WEST GERMANY

		RI	G
1935	Dortmund	1	3
1936	Dublin	5	2
1939	Bremen	1	1
1951	Dublin	3	2
1952	Cologne	0	3
1955	Hamburg	1	2
1956	Dublin	3	0
1960	Dusseldorf	1	0
1966	Dublin	0	4
1970	Berlin	1	2
1979	Dublin	1	3
1981	Bremen	0	3
1989	Dublin	1	1
1994	Hanover	2	0
1995*	Dublin	1	0
2002	Ibaraki (W.C.)	1	1

(*v. W. Germany 'B')

v. GREECE

		RI	G
2000	Dublin	0	1

v. HOLLAND

		RI	H
1932	Amsterdam	2	0

		RI	H
1934	Amsterdam	2	5
1935	Dublin	3	5
1955	Dublin	1	0
1956	Rotterdam	4	1
1980	Dublin (W.C.)	2	1
1981	Rotterdam (W.C.)	2	2
1982	Rotterdam (E.C.)	1	2
1983	Dublin (E.C.)	2	3
1988	Gelsenkirchen (E.C.)	0	1
1990	Palermo (W.C.)	1	1
1994	Tilburg	1	0
1994	Orlando (W.C.)	0	2
1995*	Liverpool (E.C.)	0	2
1996	Rotterdam	1	3
(* Qual. Round play-off)			
2000	Amsterdam (W.C.)	2	2
2001	Dublin (W.C.)	1	0

v. HUNGARY

		RI	H
1934	Dublin	2	4
1936	Budapest	3	3
1936	Dublin	2	3
1939	Cork	2	2
1939	Budapest	2	2
1969	Dublin (W.C.)	1	2
1969	Budapest (W.C.)	0	4
1989	Budapest (W.C.)	0	0
1989	Dublin (W.C.)	2	0
1992	Gyor	2	1

v. ICELAND

		RI	I
1962	Dublin (E.C.)	4	2
1962	Reykjavik (E.C.)	1	1
1982	Dublin (E.C.)	2	0
1983	Reykjavik (E.C.)	3	0
1986	Reykjavik	2	1
1996	Dublin (W.C.)	0	0
1997	Reykjavik (W.C.)	4	2

v. IRAN

		RI	I
1972	Recife	2	1
2001*	Dublin (W.C.)	2	0
2001*	Tehran (W.C.)	0	1
(*Qual. Round play-off)			

v. ISRAEL

		RI	I
1984	Tel Aviv	0	3
1985	Tel Aviv	0	0
1987	Dublin	5	0

v. ITALY

		RI	I
1926	Turin	0	3
1927	Dublin	1	2
1970	Florence (E.C.)	0	3

		RI	I
1971	Dublin (E.C.)	1	2
1985	Dublin	1	2
1990	Rome (W.C.)	0	1
1992	Boston, USA	0	2
1994	New York (W.C.)	1	0

v. LATVIA

		RI	L
1992	Dublin (W.C.)	4	0
1993	Riga (W.C.)	2	0
1994	Riga (E.C.)	3	0
1995	Dublin (E.C.)	2	1

v. LIECHTENSTEIN

		RI	L
1994	Dublin (E.C.)	4	0
1995	Eschen (E.C.)	0	0
1996	Eschen (W.C.)	5	0
1997	Dublin (W.C.)	5	0

v. LITHUANIA

		RI	L
1993	Vilnius (W.C.)	1	0
1993	Dublin (W.C.)	2	0
1997	Dublin (W.C.)	0	0
1997	Zalgiris (W.C.)	2	1

v. LUXEMBOURG

		RI	L
1936	Luxembourg	5	1
1953	Dublin (W.C.)	4	0
1954	Luxembourg (W.C.)	1	0
1987	Luxembourg (E.C.)	2	0
1987	Luxembourg (E.C.)	2	1

v. MACEDONIA

		RI	M
1996	Dublin (W.C.)	3	0
1997	Skopje (W.C.)	2	3
1999	Dublin (E.C.)	1	0
1999	Skopje (E.C.)	1	1

v. MALTA

		RI	M
1983	Valletta (E.C.)	1	0
1983	Dublin (E.C.)	8	0
1989	Dublin (W.C.)	2	0
1989	Valletta (W.C.)	2	0
1990	Valletta	3	0
1998	Dublin (E.C.)	1	0
1999	Valletta (E.C.)	3	2

v. MEXICO

		RI	M
1984	Dublin	0	0
1994	Orlando (W.C.)	1	2
1996	New Jersey	2	2
1998	Dublin	0	0
2000	Chicago	2	2

v. MOROCCO

		RI	M
1990	Dublin	1	0

v. NIGERIA

		RI	N
2002	Dublin	1	2

v. NORWAY

		RI	N
1937	Oslo (W.C.)	2	3
1937	Dublin (W.C.)	3	3
1950	Dublin	2	2
1951	Oslo	3	2
1954	Oslo	2	1
1955	Oslo	3	1
1960	Dublin	3	1
1964	Oslo	4	1
1973	Oslo	1	1
1976	Dublin	3	0
1978	Oslo	0	0
1984	Oslo (W.C.)	0	1
1985	Dublin (W.C.)	0	0
1988	Oslo	0	0
1994	New York (W.C.)	0	0
1999	Dublin	2	0

v. POLAND

		RI	P
1938	Warsaw	0	6
1938	Dublin	3	2
1958	Katowice	2	2
1958	Dublin	2	2
1964	Cracow	1	3
1964	Dublin	3	2
1968	Dublin	2	2
1968	Katowice	0	1
1970	Dublin	1	2
1970	Poznan	0	2
1973	Wroclaw	0	2
1973	Dublin	1	0
1976	Poznan	2	0
1977	Dublin	0	0
1978	Lodz	0	3
1981	Bydgoscz	0	3
1984	Dublin	0	0
1986	Warsaw	0	1
1988	Dublin	3	1
1991	Dublin (E.C.)	0	0
1991	Poznan (E.C.)	3	3

v. PORTUGAL

		RI	P
1946	Lisbon	1	3
1947	Dublin	0	2
1948	Lisbon	0	2
1949	Dublin	1	0
1972	Recife	1	2
1992	Boston, USA	2	0
1995	Dublin (E.C.)	1	0
1995	Lisbon (E.C.)	0	3

		RI	P
1996	Dublin	0	1
2000	Lisbon (W.C.)	1	1
2001	Dublin (W.C.)	1	1

v. ROMANIA

		RI	R
1988	Dublin	2	0
1990*	Genoa	0	0
1997	Bucharest (W.C.)	0	1
1997	Dublin (W.C.)	1	1

(* Rep. won 5-4 on pens.)

v. RUSSIA
(See also Soviet Union)

		RI	R
1994	Dublin	0	0
1996	Dublin	0	2
2002	Dublin	2	0

v. SAUDI ARABIA

		RI	SA
2002	Yokohama (W.C.)	3	0

v. SOUTH AFRICA

		RI	SA
2000	New Jersey	2	1

v. SOVIET UNION
(See also Russia)

		RI	SU
1972	Dublin (W.C.)	1	2
1973	Moscow (W.C.)	0	1
1974	Dublin (E.C.)	3	0
1975	Kiev (E.C.)	1	2
1984	Dublin (W.C.)	1	0
1985	Moscow (W.C.)	0	2
1988	Hanover (E.C.)	1	1
1990	Dublin	1	0

v. SPAIN

		RI	S
1931	Barcelona	1	1
1931	Dublin	0	5
1946	Madrid	1	0
1947	Dublin	3	2
1948	Barcelona	1	2
1949	Dublin	1	4
1952	Madrid	0	6
1955	Dublin	2	2
1964	Seville (E.C.)	1	5
1964	Dublin (E.C.)	0	2
1965	Dublin (W.C.)	1	0
1965	Seville (W.C.)	1	4
1965	Paris (W.C.)	0	1
1966	Dublin (E.C.)	0	0
1966	Valencia (E.C.)	0	2
1977	Dublin	0	1
1982	Dublin (E.C.)	3	3
1983	Zaragoza (E.C.)	0	2
1985	Cork	0	0

	RI	S
1988 Seville (W.C.)	0	2
1989 Dublin (W.C.)	1	0
1992 Seville (W.C.)	0	0
1993 Dublin (W.C.)	1	3
2002* Suwon (W.C.)	1	1

(*Rep. lost 3-2 on pens.)

v. SWEDEN

	RI	S
1949 Stockholm (W.C.)	1	3
1949 Dublin (W.C.)	1	3
1959 Dublin	3	2
1960 Malmo	1	4
1970 Dublin (E.C.)	1	1
1970 Malmo (E.C.)	0	1
1999 Dublin	2	0

v. SWITZERLAND

	RI	S
1935 Basle	0	1
1936 Dublin	1	0
1937 Berne	1	0
1938 Dublin	4	0
1948 Dublin	0	1
1975 Dublin (E.C.)	2	1
1975 Berne (E.C.)	0	1
1980 Dublin	2	0
1985 Dublin (W.C.)	3	0
1985 Berne (W.C.)	0	0
1992 Dublin	2	1

v. TRINIDAD & TOBAGO

	RI	T&T
1982 Port of Spain	1	2

v. TUNISIA

	RI	T
1988 Dublin	4	0

v. TURKEY

	RI	T
1966 Dublin (E.C.)	2	1
1967 Ankara (E.C.)	1	2
1974 Izmir (E.C.)	1	1
1975 Dublin (E.C.)	4	0
1976 Ankara	3	3
1978 Dublin	4	2
1990 Izmir	0	0
1990 Dublin (E.C.)	5	0
1991 Istanbul (E.C.)	3	1
1999 Dublin (E.C.)	1	1
1999 Bursa (E.C.)	0	0

v. URUGUAY

	RI	U
1974 Montevideo	0	2
1986 Dublin	1	1

v. U.S.A.

	RI	USA
1979 Dublin	3	2
1991 Boston	1	1
1992 Dublin	4	1
1992 Washington	1	3
1996 Boston	1	2
2000 Foxboro	1	1
2002 Dublin	2	1

v. YUGOSLAVIA

	RI	Y
1955 Dublin	1	4
1988 Dublin	2	0
1998 Belgrade (E.C.)	0	1
1999 Dublin (E.C.)	2	1

THREE RED CARDS IN SIX MATCHES

Kristian O'Leary was sent off three times in six Third Division appearances for Swansea City between September and November last season. The Wales U-21 defender saw red for deliberate handball against Shrewsbury Town, for a tackle in the match with Southend United and for a second bookable offence against Hartlepool Utd. Tomas Repka was dismissed twice in his first three games for West Ham United. after joining the club from Fiorentina, and walked again in the Czech Republic's World Cup qualifier with Belgium. Darren Sheridan (Oldham Athletic) was sent off four times last season, twice in the League and once in the F.A. Cup and Worthington Cup. Ray Parlour (Arsenal), Craig Short (Blackburn Rovers), Alan Reeves (Swindon Town) and Paul Stoneman (Halifax Town) were all sent off three times.

INTERNATIONAL APPEARANCES
SINCE THE WAR (1946-2002)

(As at start of season 2002-03. In year shown, 2002 = season 2001-02 etc.
*Also a pre-war International player. Totals include appearances as substitute).

ENGLAND

A'Court, A. (Liverpool, 1958-9) 5
Adams, T. (Arsenal, 1987-2001) 66
Allen, A. (Stoke City, 1960) 3
Allen, C. (Q.P.R., Tottenham,
  1984-8) 5
Allen, R. (W.B.A., 1952-5) 5
Anderson, S. (Sunderland, 1962) 2
Anderson, V. (Nott'm Forest, Arsenal,
  Manchester Utd., 1979-88) 30
Anderton, D. (Tottenham,
  1994-2002) 30
Angus, J. (Burnley, 1961) 1
Armfield, J. (Blackpool, 1959-66) 43
Armstrong, D. (Middlesbrough,
  Southampton, 1980-4) 3
Armstrong, K. (Chelsea, 1955) 1
Astall, G. (Birmingham City, 1956) 2
Astle, J. (W.B.A., 1969-70) 5
Aston, J. (Manchester Utd.,
  1949-51) 17
Atyeo, J. (Bristol City, 1956-7) 6

Bailey, G. (Manchester Utd., 1985) 2
Bailey, M. (Charlton Athletic,
  1964-5) 2
Baily, E. (Tottenham, 1950-3) 9
Baker, J. (Hibernian, Arsenal,
  1960-6) 8
Ball, A. (Blackpool, Everton, Arsenal,
  1965-75) 72
Ball, M. (Everton, 2001) 1
Banks, G. (Leicester City, Stoke City,
  1963-72) 73
Banks, T. (Bolton Wand., 1958-9) 6
Bardsley, D. (Q.P.R., 1993) 2
Barham, M. (Norwich City, 1983) 2
Barlow, R. (W.B.A., 1955) 1
Barmby, N. (Tottenham, Middlesbrough,
  Everton, Liverpool, 1995-2002) 23
Barnes, J. (Watford, Liverpool,
  1983-96) 79
Barnes, P. (Manchester City, W.B.A.,
  Leeds Utd., 1978-82) 22
Barrass, M. (Bolton Wand., 1952-3) ... 3
Barrett, E. (Oldham Athletic, Aston Villa,
  1991-3) 3
Barton, W. (Wimbledon, Newcastle Utd.,
  1995) 3
Barry, G. (Aston Villa, 2000-01) 6

Batty, D. (Leeds Utd., Blackburn Rov.,
  Newcastle Utd., Leeds Utd.,
  1991-2000) 42
Baynham, R. (Luton Town, 1956) 3
Beardsley, P. (Newcastle Utd., Liverpool,
  Newcastle Utd., 1986-96) 59
Beasant, D. (Chelsea, 1990) 2
Beattie, K. (Ipswich Town, 1975-8) 9
Beckham, D. (Manchester Utd.,
  1997-2002) 54
Bell, C. (Manchester City, 1968-76) . 48
Bentley, R. (Chelsea, 1949-55) 12
Berry, J. (Manchester Utd., 1953-6) 4
Birtles, G. (Nott'm Forest, 1980-1) 3
Blissett, L. (Watford, AC Milan,
  1983-4) 14
Blockley, J. (Arsenal, 1973) 1
Blunstone, F. (Chelsea, 1955-7) 5
Bonetti, P. (Chelsea, 1966-70) 7
Bould, S. (Arsenal, 1994) 2
Bowles, S. (Q.P.R., 1974-7) 5
Boyer, P. (Norwich City, 1976) 1
Brabrook, P. (Chelsea, 1958-60) 3
Bracewell, P. (Everton, 1985-6) 3
Bradford, G. (Bristol Rov., 1956) 1
Bradley, W. (Manchester Utd., 1959) .. 3
Bridge, W. (Southampton, 2002) 7
Bridges, B. (Chelsea, 1965-6) 4
Broadbent, P. (Wolves, 1958-60) 7
Broadis, I. (Manchester City, Newcastle
  Utd., 1952-4) 14
Brooking, T. (West Ham Utd.,
  1974-82) 47
Brooks, J. (Tottenham, 1957) 3
Brown, A. (W.B.A., 1971) 1
Brown, K. (West Ham Utd., 1960) 1
Brown, W. (Manchester Utd.,
  1999-2002) 6
Bull, S. (Wolves, 1989-91) 13
Butcher, T. (Ipswich Town, Rangers,
  1980-90) 77
Butt, N. (Manchester Utd.,
  1997-2002) 20
Byrne, G. (Liverpool, 1963-6) 2
Byrne, J. (Crystal Palace, West Ham
  Utd., 1962-5) 11
Byrne, R. (Manchester Utd.,
  1954-8) 33

NORTHERN IRELAND

SCOTLAND

WALES

REPUBLIC OF IRELAND

228

INTERNATIONAL GOALSCORERS 1946-2002

(As at start of season 2002-03)

ENGLAND

Whiteside	9	
Dougan	8	
Healy	8	
Irvine, W	8	
O'Neill, M (1972-85)	8	
McAdams	7	
Taggart, G	7	
Wilson, S	7	
Gray	6	
McLaughlin	6	
Nicholson, J	6	
Wilson, K	6	
Cush	5	
Hamilton, W	5	
Hughes, M	5	
Magilton	5	
McIlroy, S	5	
Simpson	5	
Smyth, S	5	
Walsh, D	5	
Anderson, T	4	
Hamilton, B	4	
McGrath	4	
McMorran	4	
O'Neill, M. (1989-96)	4	
Brotherston	3	
Harvey, M	3	
Lockhart	3	
Lomas	3	
McDonald	3	
McMordie	3	
Morgan, S	3	
Mulryne	3	
Nicholl, C	3	
Quinn, S.J.	3	
Spence, D	3	
Tully	3	
Blanchflower, D	2	
Casey	2	
Clements	2	
Doherty, P	2	
Harkin	2	
Finney	2	
Lennon	2	
McMahon	2	
Neill, W	2	
O'Neill, J	2	
Peacock	2	
Penney	2	
Stewart, I	2	
Barr	1	
Black	1	
Blanchflower, J	1	
Brennan	1	
Campbell, W	1	
Caskey	1	
Cassidy	1	
Cochrane, T	1	
Crossan, E	1	

D'Arcy	1
Doherty, L	1
Elder	1
Elliott	1
Ferguson	1
Ferris	1
Gillespie	1
Griffin	1
Hill, C	1
Humphries	1
Hunter, A	1
Hunter, B	1
Johnston	1
Jones, J	1
McCartney	1
McClelland (1961)	1
McCrory	1
McCurdy	1
McGarry	1
McVeigh	1
Moreland	1
Morrow	1
Nelson	1
Nicholl, J	1
O'Boyle	1
O'Kane	1
Patterson, D	1
Rowland	1
Stevenson	1
Walker	1
Welsh	1
Whitley, Jeff	1
Williams	1
Wilson, D	1

SCOTLAND

Dalglish	30
Law	30
Reilly	22
McCoist	19
Johnston, M	14
Collins, J	12
Gilzean	12
Steel	12
Jordan	11
Collins, R	10
Johnstone, R	10
Stein	10
Gallacher	9
McStay	9
Mudie	9
St. John	9
Brand	8
Gemmill, A	8
Leggat	8
Robertson, J (1978-84)	8
Wilson, D	8
Dodds	7

Durie	7
Gray, A	7
Wark	7
Booth	6
Brown, A	6
Cooper	6
Gough	6
Liddell	6
Rioch	6
Waddell	6
Henderson, W	5
Hutchison	5
Macari	5
Masson	5
McAllister G.	5
McQueen	5
Murdoch	5
Nevin	5
Nicholas	5
O'Hare	5
Scott, A	5
Strachan	5
Young, A	5
Archibald	4
Caldow	4
Hamilton	4
Hartford	4
Herd, D.	4
Jackson, D	4
Johnstone, J	4
Lorimer	4
Mackay, D	4
Mason	4
McGinlay	4
McKinlay, W.	4
McLaren	4
Smith, G	4
Souness	4
Baxter	3
Bremner, W	3
Burley, C	3
Chalmers	3
Gibson	3
Graham, G	3
Greig	3
Hendry	3
Lennox	3
MacDougall	3
McInally, A	3
McNeill	3
McPhail	3
Morris	3
Robertson, J (1991-5)	3
Sturrock	3
White	3
Baird, S	2
Bauld	2
Cameron	2

Dailly	2	
Flavell	2	
Fleming	2	
Graham, A	2	
Harper	2	
Hewie	2	
Holton	2	
Hopkin	2	
Houliston	2	
Jess	2	
Johnstone, A.	2	
Johnstone, D.	2	
McClair	2	
McGhee	2	
McMillan	2	
Pettigrew	2	
Ring	2	
Robertson, A	2	
Shearer, D	2	
Aitken, R	1	
Bannon	1	
Bett	1	
Bone	1	
Boyd	1	
Brazil	1	
Buckley	1	
Burns	1	
Calderwood	1	
Campbell, R	1	
Combe	1	
Conn	1	
Craig	1	
Crawford	1	
Curran	1	
Davidson	1	
Dobie	1	
Docherty	1	
Duncan, M	1	
Elliott	1	
Ferguson, B	1	
Fernie	1	
Freedman	1	
Gray, F	1	
Gemmell, T	1	
Henderson, J	1	
Howie	1	
Hughes, J	1	
Hunter, W	1	
Hutchison, T	1	
Jackson, C	1	
Jardine	1	
Johnstone, L	1	
Linwood	1	
Mackay, G	1	
MacLeod	1	
McAvennie	1	
McCall	1	
McCalliog	1	
McCann	1	

McKenzie	1	
McKimmie	1	
McKinnon	1	
McLean	1	
McLintock	1	
McSwegan	1	
Miller, W	1	
Mitchell	1	
Morgan	1	
Mulhall	1	
Murray, J	1	
Narey	1	
Ormond	1	
Orr	1	
Parlane	1	
Provan, D	1	
Quinn	1	
Ritchie, P	1	
Sharp	1	
Stewart, R	1	
Thornton	1	
Wallace, I	1	
Weir, A	1	
Weir, D	1	

WALES

Rush	28	
Allchurch, I	23	
Ford	23	
Saunders	22	
Hughes, M	16	
Charles, John	15	
Jones, C	15	
Toshack	13	
James, L	10	
Davies, R.T.	8	
James, R	8	
Vernon	8	
Davies, R.W.	7	
Flynn	7	
Giggs	7	
Walsh, I	7	
Charles, M	6	
Curtis, A	6	
Griffiths, A	6	
Hartson	6	
Medwin	6	
Pembridge	6	
Clarke, R	5	
Leek	5	
Bellamy	4	
Blake	4	
Coleman	4	
Deacy	4	
Edwards, I	4	
Speed	4	
Tapscott	4	
Thomas, M	4	

Woosnam	4	
Allen, M	3	
Bodin	3	
Bowen, M	3	
England	3	
Melville	3	
Palmer, D	3	
Rees, R	3	
Robinson, J	3	
Davies, G	2	
Durban, A	2	
Dwyer	2	
Edwards, G	2	
Giles, D	2	
Godfrey	2	
Griffiths, M	2	
Hodges	2	
Horne	2	
Jones, Barrie	2	
Jones, Bryn	2	
Lowrie	2	
Nicholas	2	
Phillips, D	2	
Reece, G	2	
Robinson	2	
Savage	2	
Slatter	2	
Symons	2	
Yorath	2	
Barnes	1	
Blackmore	1	
Bowen, D	1	
Boyle, T	1	
Burgess, R	1	
Charles, Jeremy	1	
Earnshaw	1	
Evans, I	1	
Foulkes	1	
Harris, C	1	
Hewitt, R	1	
Hockey	1	
Jones, A	1	
Jones, D	1	
Jones, J	1	
Krzywicki	1	
Lovell	1	
Mahoney	1	
Moore, G.	1	
O'Sullivan	1	
Paul	1	
Powell, A	1	
Powell, D	1	
Price, P	1	
Roberts, P	1	
Smallman	1	
Williams, A	1	
Williams, G.E	1	
Williams, G.G	1	
Young	1	

REP. OF IRELAND

Quinn, N	21	Holland	4	Morrison	2
Stapleton	20	Irwin	4	O'Connor	2
Aldridge	19	McGee	4	O'Farrell	2
Cascarino	19	Martin, M	4	O'Reilly, J	2
Givens	19	O'Neill, K	4	Reid	2
Cantwell	14	Robinson	4	Ambrose	1
Daly	13	Tuohy	4	Anderson	1
Keane, Robbie	13	Carey, J	3	Carroll	1
Brady	9	Coad	3	Dempsey	1
Keane, Roy	9	Conway	3	Doherty	1
Kelly, D	9	Dunne, R	3	Duffy	1
Sheedy	9	Farrell	3	Finnan	1
Connolly	8	Fogarty	3	Fitzgerald, J	1
Curtis	8	Haverty	3	Fullam, J	1
Grealish	8	Kennedy, Mark	3	Galvin	1
Harte	8	Kilbane	3	Glynn	1
McGrath, P	8	Kinsella	3	Grimes	1
Fitzsimons	7	McAteer	3	Holmes	1
Ringstead	7	Ryan, R	3	Hughton	1
Staunton	7	Waddock	3	Kavanagh	1
Townsend	7	Walsh, M	3	Kernaghan	1
Breen G	6	Whelan	3	Mancini	1
Coyne	6	Conroy	2	McCann	1
Houghton	6	Dennehy	2	McPhail	1
McEvoy	6	Duff	2	Mooney	1
Martin, C	6	Eglington	2	Moroney	1
Moran	6	Fallon	2	Mulligan	1
Cummins	5	Fitzgerald, P	2	O'Callaghan, K	1
Fagan, F	5	Foley	2	O'Keefe	1
Giles	5	Gavin	2	O'Leary	1
Lawrenson	5	Hale	2	O'Neill, F	1
Rogers	5	Hand	2	Ryan, G	1
Sheridan	5	Hurley	2	Slaven	1
Treacy	5	Kelly, G	2	Sloan	1
Walsh, D	5	Leech	2	Strahan	1
Byrne, J	4	McCarthy	2	Waters	1
		McLoughlin	2		

FAIR PLAY BY MILLWALL'S MCLAUGHLIN

Millwall reserve-team manager Joe McLaughlin ordered his team to let Bournemouth equalise in an Avon Insurance Combination match. McLaughlin wanted to make amends for a goal scored unintentionally by Mark Hicks after Bournemouth had put the ball out of play for treatment to two of their players. Attempting to return it to goalkeeper Michael Menetrier, Hicks miscued, the ball hit a divot and went into the net. Millwall won the match 2-1.

NAP HAND FOR JONES AND GORDON

Two players scored scored five goals in a match last season – Lee Jones for Wrexham in the 5-0 victory over Cambridge United and Cardiff City's Gavin Gordon in a 7-1 LDV Vans Trophy win over Rushden and Diamonds.

RECORDS SECTION
Compiled by Albert Sewell

INDEX

GOALSCORING
(† Football League pre 1992-3. * Home team)

Highest: *Arbroath 36, Bon Accord (Aberdeen) 0, in **Scottish Cup** 1st Round, Sept. 12, 1885. On same day, also in Scottish Cup 1st Round, Dundee Harp beat Aberdeen Rov. 35-0.

Internationals: England 15, *France 0, in Paris, 1906 (Amateur); England 13 *Ireland 0, in Belfast, Feb. 18, 1882 (record in U.K.); *England 9, Scotland 3, at Wembley, Apr. 15, 1961; Biggest England win at Wembley: 9-0 v Luxembourg (E.Champ), Dec. 15, 1982.

Other record wins: Scotland: 11-0 v Ireland (Glasgow, Feb. 23, 1901); **Northern Ireland:** 7-0 v Wales (Belfast, Feb. 1, 1930); **Wales:** 11-0 v Ireland (Wrexham, Mar. 3, 1888); **Rep. of Ireland:** 8-0 v Malta (E. Champ., Dublin, Nov. 16, 1983).

Record International defeats: England: 1-7 v Hungary (Budapest, May 23, 1954); **Scotland:** 3-9 v England (Wembley, April 15, 1961); **Ireland:** 0-13 v England (Belfast, Feb. 18, 1882); **Wales:** 0-9 v Scotland (Glasgow, March 23, 1878); **Rep. of Ireland:** 0-7 v Brazil (Uberlandia, May 27, 1982).

World Cup: Qualifying round – Australia 31, American Samoa 0, world record Int. score (April 11, 2001); Australia 22, Tonga 0 (April 9, 2001); Iran 19, Guam 0 (Nov. 25, 2000); Maldives 0, Iran 17 (June 2, 1997). **Finals – highest scores:** Hungary 10, El Salvador 1 (Spain, June 15, 1982); Hungary 9, S. Korea 0 (Switzerland, June 17, 1954); Yugoslavia 9, Zaire 0 (W. Germany, June 18, 1974).

European Championship: Qualifying round – France 10, Azerbaijan 0 (Auxerre, Sept. 6, 1995). **Finals – highest score:** Holland 6, Yugoslavia 1 (Quarter-final, Rotterdam, June 25, 2000).

F.A. Cup: *Preston N.E. 26, Hyde 0, 1st Round, Oct. 15, 1887.

League Cup: *West Ham Utd. 10, Bury 0 (2nd Round, 2nd Leg, Oct 25, 1983); *Liverpool 10, Fulham 0 (2nd Round, 1st Leg, Sept. 23, 1986). **Record Aggregates:** Liverpool 13, Fulham 2 (10-0h, 3-2a), Sept. 23-Oct. 7, 1986; West Ham Utd. 12, Bury 1 (2-1a, 10-0h), Oct. 4-25, 1983; Liverpool 11, Exeter City 0 (5-0h, 6-0a), Oct 7-28, 1981.

F.A. Premier League (beginning 1992-3): *Manchester Utd. 9, Ipswich Town 0, Mar. 4, 1995. **Record away win:** Manchester Utd. 8, *Nott'm. Forest 1, Feb. 6, 1999.

Highest aggregate scores in Premier League – 9: Manchester Utd. 9, Ipswich Town 0, Mar. 4, 1995; Nott'm. Forest 1, Manchester Utd. 8, Feb. 6, 1999; Blackburn Rov. 7, Sheff. Wed. 2, Mar. 11, 1999; Southampton 6, Manchester Utd. 3, Oct. 26, 1996; Tottenham 7, Southampton 2, Mar. 11, 2000.

†Football League (First Division): *Aston Villa 12, Accrington 2, Mar. 12, 1892; *Tottenham 10, Everton 4, Oct. 11, 1958 (highest 1st Div. aggregate this century); *W.B.A. 12, Darwen 0, Apr. 4, 1892; *Nott'm. Forest 12, Leicester Fosse 0, Apr. 21, 1909. **Record away wins:** Sunderland 9, *Newcastle Utd. 1, Dec. 5, 1908; Wolves 9, *Cardiff City 1, Sept. 3, 1955.

New First Division (beginning 1992-3): *Bolton Wand. 7, Swindon Town 0, Mar. 8, 1997; Sunderland 7, Oxford Utd. 0, Sept. 19, 1998. **Record away win:** Birmingham City 7, *Stoke City 0, Jan. 10, 1998; Birmingham City 7, *Oxford Utd. 0, Dec. 12, 1998.

†**Second Division:** *Manchester City 11, Lincoln City 3, Mar. 23, 1895; *Newcastle Utd. 13, Newport County 0, Oct. 5, 1946; *Small Heath 12, Walsall Town Swifts 0, Dec. 17, 1892; *Darwen 12, Walsall 0, Dec. 26, 1896; *Small Heath 12, Doncaster Rov. 0, Apr. 11, 1903. **Record away win:** Sheffield Utd. 10, *Burslem Port Vale 0, Dec. 10, 1892.

New Second Division (beginning 1992-3): *Hartlepool Utd. 1, Plymouth Argyle 8, May 7, 1994.

†**Third Division:** *Gillingham 10, Chesterfield 0, Sept. 5, 1987; *Tranmere Rov. 9, Accrington Stanley 0, Apr. 18, 1959; *Brighton & H.A. 9, Southend Utd. 1, Nov. 22, 1965; *Brentford 9, Wrexham 0, Oct. 15, 1963. **Record away win:** Fulham 8, *Halifax Town 0, Sept. 16, 1969.

New Third Division (beginning 1992-3): *Barnet 1, Peterborough Utd. 9, Sept. 5, 1998.

†**Third Division (North):** *Stockport Co. 13, Halifax Town 0 (still joint biggest win in F. League – see Div. 2) Jan. 6, 1934; *Tranmere Rov. 13, Oldham Athletic 4, Dec. 26, 1935. *(17 is highest Football League aggregate score)*. **Record away win:** Barnsley 9, *Accrington Stanley 0, Feb. 3, 1934.

†**Third Division (South):** *Luton Town 12, Bristol Rov. 0, Apr. 13, 1936; *Gillingham 9, Exeter City 4, Jan. 7, 1951. **Record away win:** Walsall 8, *Northampton Town 0, Apr. 8, 1947.

†**Fourth Division:** *Oldham Athletic 11, Southport 0, Dec. 26, 1962; *Hartlepool Utd. 10, Barrow 1, Apr. 4, 1959; *Wrexham 10, Hartlepool Utd. 1, Mar. 3, 1962. **Record away win:** Rotherham Utd. 8, *Crewe Alexandra 1, Sept. 8, 1973.

Scottish Premier Division – Highest aggregate: 11 goals – Celtic 8, Hamilton 3, Jan. 3, 1987; Motherwell 5, Aberdeen 6, Oct. 20, 1999. **Other highest team scores:** Aberdeen 8, Motherwell 0 (Mar. 26, 1979); Kilmarnock 1, Rangers 8 (Sept. 6, 1980); Hamilton 0, Celtic 8 (Nov. 5, 1988).

Scottish League Div. 1: *Celtic 11, Dundee 0, Oct. 26, 1895. **Record away win:** Hibs 11, *Airdrie 1, Oct. 24, 1959.

Scottish League Div. 2: *Airdrieonians 15, Dundee Wanderers 1, Dec. 1, 1894.

Record British score since 1900: Stirling Albion 20, Selkirk 0 (Scottish Cup 1st. Round, Dec. 8, 1984). Winger Davie Thompson (7 goals) was one of 9 Stirling players to score.

FOOTBALL LEAGUE – BEST IN SEASON (Before restructure in 1992)

Div.		Goals	Games
1	W.R. (Dixie) Dean, Everton, 1927-8	60	39
2	George Camsell, Middlesbrough, 1926-7	59	37
3(S)	Joe Payne, Luton Town, 1936-7	55	39
3(N)	Ted Harston, Mansfield Town, 1936-7	55	41
3	Derek Reeves, Southampton, 1959-60	39	46
4	Terry Bly, Peterborough Utd., 1960-1	52	46

(Since restructure in 1992)

Div.		Goals	Games
1	Guy Whittingham, Portsmouth, 1992-3	42	46
2	Jimmy Quinn, Reading, 1993-4	35	46
3	Graeme Jones, Wigan Athletic, 1996-7	31	40

F.A. PREMIER LEAGUE – BEST IN SEASON

Andy Cole **34 goals** (Newcastle Utd. – 40 games, 1993-4); Alan Shearer **34 goals** (Blackburn Rov. – 42 games, 1994-5).

FOOTBALL LEAGUE – BEST MATCH HAULS
(Before restructure in 1992)

Div.		Goals
1	Ted Drake (Arsenal), away to Aston Villa, Dec. 14, 1935	7
	James Ross (Preston N.E.) v Stoke City, Oct 6, 1888	7
2	*Neville (Tim) Coleman (Stoke City) v Lincoln City, Feb. 23, 1957 .	7
	Tommy Briggs (Blackburn Rov.) v Bristol Rov., Feb. 5, 1955	7

3(S)	Joe Payne (Luton Town) v Bristol Rov., April 13, 1936	10
3(N)	Robert ('Bunny') Bell (Tranmere Rov.) v Oldham Athletic, Dec. 26, 1935 – he also missed a penalty	9
3	Barrie Thomas (Scunthorpe Utd.) v Luton Town, April 24, 1965	5
	Keith East (Swindon Town) v Mansfield Town, Nov. 20, 1965	5
	Steve Earle (Fulham) v Halifax Town, Sept. 16, 1969	5
	Alf Wood (Shrewsbury Town) v Blackburn Rov., Oct. 2, 1971	5
	Tony Caldwell (Bolton Wand.) v Walsall, Sept 10, 1983	5
	Andy Jones (Port Vale) v Newport Co., May 4, 1987	5
4	Bert Lister (Oldham Athletic) v Southport, Dec. 26, 1962	6

* Scored from the wing

(SINCE RESTRUCTURE IN 1992)

Div.	Goals
1	4 in match – John Durnin (Oxford Utd. v Luton Town, 1992-3); Guy Whittingham (Portsmouth v Bristol Rov. 1992-3); Craig Russell (Sunderland v Millwall, 1995-6).
2	5 in match – Paul Barnes (Burnley v Stockport Co., 1996-7); Robert Taylor (all 5, Gillingham at Burnley, 1998-9); Lee Jones (all 5, Wrexham v Cambridge Utd., 2001-02).
3	5 in match – Tony Naylor (Crewe Alexandra v Colchester Utd., 1992-3); Steve Butler (Cambridge Utd. v Exeter City, 1993-4); Guiliano Grazioli (Peterborough Utd. at Barnet, 1998-9).

F.A. PREMIER LEAGUE – BEST MATCH HAUL

5 goals in match: Andy Cole (Manchester Utd. v Ipswich Town, 1994-5); Alan Shearer (Newcastle Utd. v Sheffield Wed., 1999-2000).

SCOTTISH LEAGUE

Div.		Goals
Prem.	Kenny Miller (Rangers) v St. Mirren, Nov. 4, 2000	5
	Paul Sturrock (Dundee Utd.) v Morton, Nov. 20, 1984	5
1	Jimmy McGrory (Celtic) v Dunfermline Athletic, Jan. 14, 1928	8
1	Owen McNally (Arthurlie) v Armadale, Oct. 1, 1927	8
2	Jim Dyet (King's Park) v Forfar Athletic, Jan. 2, 1930, on his debut for the club	8
2	John Calder (Morton) v Raith Rov., April 18, 1936	8
2	Norman Haywood (Raith Rov.) v Brechin, Aug. 20, 1937	8

SCOTTISH LEAGUE – BEST IN SEASON

Prem.	Brian McClair (Celtic, 1986-7)	35
1	William McFadyen (Motherwell, 1931-2)	53
2	*Jimmy Smith (Ayr, 1927-8 – 38 appearances)	66

(*British record)

CUP FOOTBALL

Scottish Cup: John Petrie (Arbroath) v Bon Accord, at Arbroath, 1st Round, Sept. 12, 1885	13
F.A. Cup: Ted MacDougall (Bournemouth) v Margate, 1st Round, Nov. 20, 1971	9
F.A. Cup Final: Billy Townley (Blackburn Rov.) v Sheffield Wed., at Kennington Oval, 1890; Jimmy Logan (Notts Co.) v Bolton Wand., at Everton, 1894; Stan Mortensen (Blackpool) v Bolton Wand., at Wembley, 1953	3
League Cup: Frank Bunn (Oldham Athletic) v Scarborough (3rd Round), Oct. 25, 1989	6

Scottish League Cup: Jim Fraser (Ayr) v Dumbarton, Aug. 13, 1952 .... **5**
Jim Forrest (Rangers) v Stirling Albion, Aug. 17, 1966 .... **5**
Scottish Cup: Most goals in match since war: **10** by **Gerry Baker** (St. Mirren) in 15-0
win (1st. Round) v Glasgow Univ., Jan 30, 1960; **9** by his brother **Joe Baker** (Hibernian) in 15-1 win (2nd. Round) v Peebles Rov., Feb. 11, 1961.

AGGREGATE LEAGUE SCORING RECORDS

Goals
* Arthur Rowley (1947-65, WBA, Fulham, Leicester City, Shrewsbury Town) **434**
† Jimmy McGrory (1922-38, Celtic, Clydebank) **410**
Hughie Gallacher (1921-39, Airdrieonians, Newcastle Utd., Chelsea, Derby Co.,
Notts Co., Grimsby Town, Gateshead) **387**
William ('Dixie') Dean (1923-37, Tranmere Rov., Everton, Notts County) **379**
Hugh Ferguson (1916-30, Motherwell, Cardiff City, Dundee) **362**
■ Jimmy Greaves (1957-71, Chelsea, Tottenham, West Ham Utd.) **357**
Steve Bloomer (1892-1914, Derby Co., Middlesbrough, Derby Co.) **352**
George Camsell (1923-39, Durham City, Middlesbrough) **348**
Dave Halliday (1920-35, St. Mirren, Dundee, Sunderland, Arsenal, Manchester City,
Clapton Orient) **338**
John Aldridge (1979-98, Newport, Oxford Utd., Liverpool, Tranmere Rov.) **329**
John Atyeo (1951-66, Bristol City) **315**
Joe Smith (1908-29, Bolton Wand., Stockport Co.) **315**
Victor Watson (1920-36, West Ham Utd., Southampton) **312**
Harry Johnson (1919-36, Sheffield Utd., Mansfield Town) **309**
Bob McPhail (1923–1939, Airdrie, Rangers) **306**
(* **Rowley** scored 4 for WBA, 27 for Fulham, 251 for Leicester City, 152 for Shrewsbury
Town. ■ **Greaves's** 357 is record top-division total (he also scored 9 League goals for
AC Milan). **Aldridge** also scored 33 League goals for Real Sociedad. † **McGrory** scored
397 for Celtic, 13 for Clydebank.)

Most League goals for one club: 349 – Dixie Dean (Everton 1925-37); 326 – George
Camsell (Middlesbrough 1925-39); 315 – John Atyeo (Bristol City 1951-66); 306 – Vic
Watson (West Ham Utd. 1920-35); 291 – Steve Bloomer (Derby Co. 1892-1906,
1910-14); 259 – Arthur Chandler (Leicester City 1923-35); 255 – Nat Lofthouse
(Bolton Wand. 1946-61); 251 – Arthur Rowley (Leicester City 1950-58).

Over 500 Goals: Jimmy McGrory (Celtic, Clydebank and Scotland) scored a total of 550
goals in his first-class career (1922-38).

Over 1,000 goals: Brazil's **Pele** is reputedly the game's all-time highest scorer with 1,282
goals in 1,365 matches (1956-77), but many of them were scored in friendlies for
his club, Santos. He scored his 1,000th goal, a penalty, against Vasco da Gama in
the Maracana Stadium, Rio, on November 19, 1969. Pele (born Oct. 23, 1940)
played regularly for Santos from the age of 16. During his career, he was sent off only
once. He played 95 'A' Internationals for Brazil and in their World Cup-winning teams
in 1958 and 1970. ● Pele (Edson Arantes do Nascimento) was subsequently Brazil's
Minister for Sport. He never played at Wembley, apart from being filmed there scoring
a goal for a commercial. Aged 57, Pele received an 'honorary knighthood' (Knight
Commander of the British Empire) from the Queen at Buckingham Palace on
December 3, 1997.

MOST LEAGUE GOALS IN SEASON: DEAN'S 60

W.R. ('Dixie') Dean, Everton centre-forward, created a League scoring record in 1927-8
with an aggregate of 60 in 39 First Division matches. He also scored three goals in F.A.
Cup-ties, and 19 in representative games (total for the season 82).
  George Camsell, of Middlesbrough, previously held the record with 59 goals in 37
Second Division matches in 1926-7, his total for the season being 75.

SHEARER'S RECORD 'FIRST'

Alan Shearer (Blackburn Rov.) is the only player to score more than 30 top-division goals
in 3 successive seasons since the war: 31 in 1993-4, 34 in 1994-5, 31 in 1995-6.

David Halliday (Sunderland) topped 30 First Div. goals in 4 consecutive seasons with totals of 38, 36, 36 and 49 from 1925-26 to 1928-29.

MOST GOALS IN A MATCH

TOP SCORE by a player in a first-class club match is **13** in the Scottish Cup and **10** in the Football League.

September 12, 1885: John Petrie set the all-time British individual record for a first-class match when, in Arbroath's 36-0 win against Bon Accord (Scottish Cup first round), he scored 13

April 13, 1936: Joe Payne set the still-existing individual record on his debut as a centre-forward, for Luton Town v Bristol Rov. (Div. III South). In a 12-0 win he scored 10

December 26, 1935: Robert ('Bunny') Bell for Tranmere Rov. v Oldham Athletic (Div. III North) beat Drake's 12-day-old record in a 13-4 win by scoring 9

October 6, 1888: James Ross for Preston N.E. (7-0 v Stoke City) set a League record in its first season by scoring all 7

December 14, 1935: Ted Drake for Arsenal in 7-1 win away to Aston Villa (Div. 1). Scored six goals with his first six shots and in all equalled Ross's Football League record by scoring 7

February 5, 1955: Tommy Briggs for Blackburn Rov. v Bristol Rov. set Second Division record during 8-3 win by scoring 7

February 23, 1957: Neville ('Tim') Coleman for Stoke City v Lincoln City (8-0) in Second Division set a record as a winger by scoring 7

OTHER BIG HAULS

Eric Gemmell for Oldham Athletic v Chester City in Third Division North (11-2), January 19, 1952, and **Albert Whitehurst** for Bradford City v Tranmere Rov. (Third Division North) (8-0), March 6, 1929; both scored **seven**.

W.H. (Billy) Minter scored **seven** goals for St. Albans City in replayed F.A. Cup 4th Qualifying Round against Dulwich Hamlet, November 22, 1922. Dulwich won 8-7, and Minter's seven is still the most goals scored in one match by a player in a losing side.

Denis Law scored **seven** but only one counted and he finished a loser in Manchester City's F.A. Cup 4th Round tie at Luton Town in 1961. The original match on January 28 was washed out (69 mins.) when City led 6-2 (Law 6). He scored a seventh when the game was played again, but Luton Town won 3-1.

Louis Page, England outside-left, when tried for the first time as centre-forward, accomplished the **double hat-trick** for Burnley in a First Division match against Birmingham City, at St. Andrews, April 10, 1926. Burnley won 7-1.

Davie Wilson, Rangers outside-left, scored **six** goals from centre-forward at Falkirk in Scottish league, March 17, 1962. Result: 7-1.

Geoff Hurst was the last player to score **six** in a League match, in West Ham Utd.'s 8-0 win v Sunderland (Div. 1) on October 19, 1968.

ROWLEY'S ALL-TIME RECORD

Arthur Rowley is English football's **top club scorer** with a total of 464 goals for WBA, Fulham, Leicester City and Shrewsbury Town (1947-65). They comprised 434 in the League, 26 F.A. Cup, 4 League Cup.

Jimmy Greaves is second with a total of 420 goals for Chelsea, AC Milan, Tottenham and West Ham Utd., made up of 366 League, 35 F.A. Cup, 10 League Cup and 9 in Europe. He also scored nine goals for Italian club AC Milan.

John Aldridge, Tranmere Rovers manager, retired as a player at the end of the season 1997-98 with a career total of 329 Football League goals for Newport, Oxford Utd., Liverpool and Tranmere Rov. (1997-98). In all competitions for those clubs he scored 410 goals in 737 apps. He also scored 45 goals in 63 games for Spanish club Real Sociedad.

MOST GOALS IN INTERNATIONAL FOOTBALL

THIRTEEN BY
Archie Thompson for Australia v American Samoa in World Cup (Oceania Group qualifier) at Coff's Harbour, New South Wales, April 11, 2001. Result: 31-0.

SEVEN BY
Stanley Harris for England v France in Amateur International in Paris, November 1, 1906. Result: 15-0.

SIX BY
Nat Lofthouse for Football League v Irish League, at Wolves, September 24, 1952. Result: 7-1.
Joe Bambrick for Ireland against Wales, in Belfast, February 1, 1930. Result: 7-0.
W.C. Jordan in Amateur International for England v France, at Park Royal, March 23, 1908. Result: 12-0.
Vivian Woodward for England v Holland in Amateur International, at Chelsea, December 11, 1909. Result: 9-1.

FIVE BY
Steve Bloomer for England v Wales (Cardiff City) March 16, 1896. Result: 9-1.
Hughie Gallacher for Scotland against Ireland (Belfast), February 23, 1929. Result: 7-3.
Willie Hall for England v Ireland, at Old Trafford, Manchester, November 16, 1938. Five in succession (first three in 3½ mins. – fastest International hat-trick). Result: 7-0.
Malcolm Macdonald for England v Cyprus (Wembley) April 16, 1975. Result: 5-0.
Hughie Gallacher for Scottish League against Irish League (Belfast) November 11, 1925. Result: 7-3.
Barney Battles for Scottish League against Irish League (Firhill Park, Glasgow) October 31, 1928. Result: 8-2.
Bobby Flavell for Scottish League against Irish League (Belfast) April 30, 1947. Result: 7-4.
Joe Bradford for Football League v Irish League (Everton) September 25, 1929. Result: 7-2.
Albert Stubbins for Football League v Irish League (Blackpool) October 18, 1950. Result: 6-3.
Brian Clough for Football League v Irish League (Belfast) September 23, 1959. Result: 5-0.

LAST ENGLAND PLAYER TO SCORE . . .

3 goals: Michael Owen v Germany (5-1), World Cup qual., Munich, Sept. 1, 2001.
4 goals: Ian Wright v San Marino (7-1), World Cup qual., Bologna, Nov. 17, 1993.
5 goals: Malcolm Macdonald v Cyprus (5-0), Eur. Champ. qual., Wembley, Apr. 16, 1975.

INTERNATIONAL TOP SHOTS

		Goals	Games
England	– Bobby Charlton (1958-70)	49	106
N. Ireland	– Colin Clarke (1986-92)	13	38
Scotland	– Denis Law (1958-74)	30	55
	– Kenny Dalglish (1971-86)	30	102
Wales	– Ian Rush (1980-96)	28	73
Rep. of I.	– Niall Quinn (1986-2002)	21	91

ENGLAND'S TOP MARKSMEN
(As at start of season 2002-03)

	Goals	Games
Bobby Charlton (1958-70)	49	106
Gary Lineker (1984-92)	48	80

Jimmy Greaves (1959-67)	44	57
Tom Finney (1946-58)	30	76
Nat Lofthouse (1950-58)	30	33
Alan Shearer (1992-2000)	30	63
Vivian Woodward (1903-11)	29	23
Steve Bloomer (1895-1907)	28	23
David Platt (1989-96)	27	62
Bryan Robson (1979-91)	26	90
Geoff Hurst (1966-72)	24	49
Stan Mortensen (1947-53)	23	25
Tommy Lawton (1938-48)	22	23
Mike Channon (1972-77)	21	46
Kevin Keegan (1972-82)	21	63
Martin Peters (1966-74)	20	67
George Camsell (1929-36)	18	9
'Dixie' Dean (1927-32)	18	16
Johnny Haynes (1954-62)	18	56
Roger Hunt (1962-69)	18	34
Michael Owen (1998-2002)	18	41
Tommy Taylor (1953-57)	16	19
Tony Woodcock (1978-86)	16	42

CONSECUTIVE GOALS FOR ENGLAND

Steve Bloomer scored in **TEN** consecutive appearances (19 goals) for **England** between March 1895 and March 1899.

In modern times, **Paul Mariner** (Ipswich Town) scored in five consecutive **England** appearances (7 goals) between November 1981 and June 1982.

'GOLDEN GOAL' DECIDERS

The Football League, in an experiment to avoid penalty shoot-outs, introduced a new 'golden goal' system in the 1994-95 **Auto Windscreens Shield** to decide matches in the knock-out stages of the competition in which scores were level after 90 minutes. The first goal scored in overtime ended play.

Iain Dunn (Huddersfield Town) became the first player in British football to settle a match by this sudden-death method. His 107th-minute goal beat Lincoln City 3-2 on Nov. 30, 1994, and to mark his 'moment in history' he was presented with a golden football trophy.

The AWS Final of 1995 was decided when **Paul Tait** headed the only goal for Birmingham City against Carlisle Utd. 13 minutes into overtime – the first time a match at Wembley had been decided by the 'golden goal' formula.

First major International tournament match to be decided by sudden death was the Final of the **1996 European Championship** at Wembley in which Germany beat Czech Rep. 2-1 by **Oliver Bierhoff's** goal in the 95th minute.

In the **1998 World Cup Finals** (2nd Round), host country France beat Paraguay 1-0 on **Laurent Blanc's** Golden Goal (114 mins.).

France won the **2000 European Championship** with Golden Goals in the semi-final, 2-1 v Portugal (Zinedine Zidane pen, 117 mins), and in the Final, 2-1 v Italy (David Trezeguet, 103 mins).

Galatasary (Turkey) won the **European Super Cup** 2-1 against Real Madrid (Monaco, August 25, 2000) with a 103rd min Golden Goal, a penalty.

Liverpool won the **UEFA Cup** 5-4 against Alaves with a 117th min Golden Goal, an own goal, in the Final in Dortmund (May 19, 2001).

In the **2002 World Cup Finals**, 3 matches were decided by Golden Goals: in the 2nd Round Senegal beat Sweden 2-1 (Henri Camara, 104 mins) and South Korea beat Italy 2-1 (Ahn Jung – hwan, 117 mins); in the Quarter-final, Turkey beat Senegal 1-0 (Ilhan Mansiz, 94 mins).

PREMIERSHIP TOP SHOTS (1992-2002)

Alan Shearer	204	Andy Cole	145

Les Ferdinand	132	Dwight Yorke	108
Robbie Fowler	132	Matthew Le Tissier	101
Teddy Sheringham	117	(As at start of season 2002-03)	
Ian Wright	113		

LEAGUE GOAL RECORDS

The highest goal-scoring aggregates in the Football League, Premier and Scottish League are as follows:

FOR

	Goals	Games	Club	Season
Prem.	97	38	Manchester Utd.	1999-2000
Div. 1	128	42	Aston Villa	1930-1
New Div. 1	108	46	Manchester City	2001-02
Div. 2	122	42	Middlesbrough	1926-7
New Div. 2	89	46	Millwall	2000-01
Div. 3(S)	127	42	Millwall	1927-8
Div. 3(N)	128	42	Bradford City	1928-9
Div. 3	111	46	Q.P.R.	1961-2
New Div. 3	96	46	Luton Town	2001-02
Div. 4	134	46	Peterborough Utd.	1960-1
Scot. Prem.	101	44	Rangers	1991-2
Scot. L. 1	132	34	Hearts	1957-8
Scot. L. 2	142	34	Raith Rov.	1937-8
Scot. L. 3 (Modern)	*87	36	Ross County	1998-9

AGAINST

	Goals	Games	Club	Season
Prem.	100	42	Swindon Town	1993-4
Div. 1	125	42	Blackpool	1930-1
New Div. 1	102	46	Stockport Co.	2001-02
Div. 2	141	34	Darwen	1898-9
New Div. 2	102	46	Chester City	1992-3
Div. 3(S)	135	42	Merthyr T.	1929-30
Div. 3(N)	136	42	Nelson	1927-8
Div. 3	123	46	Accrington S.	1959-60
New Div. 3	113	46	Doncaster Rov.	1997-8
Div. 4	109	46	Hartlepool Utd.	1959-60
Scot. Prem.	100	36	Morton	1984-5
Scot. Prem.	100	44	Morton	1987-8
Scot. L. 1	137	38	Leith A.	1931-2
Scot. L. 2	146	38	Edinburgh City	1931-2
Scot. L. 3 (Modern)	82	36	Albion Rov.	1994-5

BEST DEFENSIVE RECORDS – *Denotes under old offside law

Div.	Goals Agst.	Games	Club	Season
Prem.	17	38	Arsenal	1998-9
1	16	42	Liverpool	1978-9
1	*15	22	Preston N.E.	1888-9
New Div. 1	28	46	Sunderland	1998-9
2	18	28	Liverpool	1893-4
2	*22	34	Sheffield Wed.	1899-1900
2	24	42	Birmingham City	1947-8

2	24	42	Crystal Palace	1978-9
New Div. 2	32	46	Fulham	1998-9
3(S)	*21	42	Southampton	1921-2
3(S)	30	42	Cardiff City	1946-7
3(N)	*21	38	Stockport Co.	1921-2
3(N)	21	46	Port Vale	1953-4
3	30	46	Middlesbrough	1986-7
New Div. 3	20	46	Gillingham	1995-6
4	25	46	Lincoln City	1980-1

SCOTTISH LEAGUE

Div.	Goals Agst.	Games	Club	Season
Prem.	18	38	Celtic	2001-02
1	*12	22	Dundee	1902-3
1	*14	38	Celtic	1913-14
2	20	38	Morton	1966-7
2	*29	38	Clydebank	1922-3
2	29	36	East Fife	1995-6
New Div. 3	21	36	Brechin	1995-6

TOP SCORERS (LEAGUE ONLY)

		Goals	Div.
2001-02	Shaun Goater (Manchester City	28	1
	Bobby Zamora (Brighton & H.A.)	28	2
2000-01	Bobby Zamora (Brighton & H.A.)	28	3
1999-2000	Kevin Phillips (Sunderland)	30	Prem.
1998-9	Lee Hughes (W.B.A.)	31	1
1997-8	Pierre van Hooijdonk (Nott'm Forest)	29	1
	Kevin Phillips (Sunderland)	29	1
1996-7	Graeme Jones (Wigan Athletic)	31	3
1995-6	Alan Shearer (Blackburn Rov.)	31	Prem.
1994-5	Alan Shearer (Blackburn Rov.)	34	Prem.
1993-4	Jimmy Quinn (Reading)	35	2
1992-3	Guy Whittingham (Portsmouth)	42	2
1991-2	Ian Wright (Crystal Palace 5, Arsenal 24)	29	1
1990-1	Teddy Sheringham (Millwall)	33	2
1989-90	Mick Quinn (Newcastle Utd.)	32	2
1988-9	Steve Bull (Wolves)	37	3
1987-8	Steve Bull (Wolves)	34	4
1986-7	Clive Allen (Tottenham)	33	1
1985-6	Gary Lineker (Everton)	30	1
1984-5	Tommy Tynan (Plymouth Argyle)	31	3
	John Clayton (Tranmere Rov.)	31	4
1983-4	Trevor Senior (Reading)	36	4
1982-3	Luther Blissett (Watford)	27	1
1981-2	Keith Edwards (Hull City 1, Sheffield Utd. 35)	36	4
1980-1	Tony Kellow (Exeter City)	25	3
1979-80	Clive Allen (Queens Park Rangers)	28	2
1978-9	Ross Jenkins (Watford)	29	3
1977-8	Steve Phillips (Brentford)	32	4
	Alan Curtis (Swansea City)	32	4
1976-7	Peter Ward (Brighton & H.A.)	32	3
1975-6	Dixie McNeil (Hereford)	35	3
1974-5	Dixie McNeil (Hereford)	31	3
1973-4	Brian Yeo (Gillingham)	31	4
1972-3	Bryan (Pop) Robson (West Ham Utd.)	28	1

1971-2	Ted MacDougall (Bournemouth)	35	3
1970-1	Ted MacDougall (Bournemouth)	42	4
1969-70	Albert Kinsey (Wrexham)	27	4
1968-9	Jimmy Greaves (Tottenham)	27	1
1967-8	George Best (Manchester Utd.)	28	1
	Ron Davies (Southampton)	28	1
1966-7	Ron Davies (Southampton)	37	1
1965-6	Kevin Hector (Bradford P.A.)	44	4
1964-5	Alick Jeffrey (Doncaster Rov.)	36	4
1963-4	Hugh McIlmoyle (Carlisle Utd.)	39	4
1962-3	Jimmy Greaves (Tottenham)	37	1
1961-2	Roger Hunt (Liverpool)	41	2
1960-1	Terry Bly (Peterborough Utd.)	52	4

100 LEAGUE GOALS

Manchester City, First Div. champions in 2001-02, scored 108 goals.

Bolton Wanderers, First Div. Champions in 1996-7, reached exactly 100 goals, the first side to complete a century in League football since 103 by Northampton Town (Div. 4 Champions) in 1986-7.

Last League Champions to reach **100** League goals: **Tottenham** (115 in 1960-1). Last century of goals in the top division: **111** by runners-up **Tottenham** in 1962-3.

In **1930-1**, the Championship top three all scored a century of League goals: 1 Arsenal (127), 2 Aston Villa (128), 3 Sheffield Wed. (102).

100 GOALS AGAINST

Swindon Town, relegated with 100 goals against in 1993-4, were the first top-division club to concede a century of League goals since **Ipswich Town** (121) went down in 1964. Most goals conceded in the top division: 125 by **Blackpool** in 1930-31, but they avoided relegation.

THE DAY IT RAINED GOALS

Saturday, February 1, 1936 has a permanent place in the Football League records, because on that afternoon the **44** matches played in the four divisions produced **209** goals – the most that have ever been scored on one day. They piled up like this: 46 in Div.1; 46 in Div.2; 68 in Div.3 North; 49 in Div.3 South. Three players scored four each and nine scored three each. Two matches in the Northern Section provided no fewer than 23 goals – Chester City 12, York City 0, and Crewe Alexandra 5, Chesterfield 6. There was only one 0-0 result (Aldershot v Bristol City, Div. 3 South).

● The previous record was set four years earlier on January 2, 1932, when 205 goals were scored in 43 League matches: 56 in Div.1, 49 in Div.2, 57 in Div.3 South and 43 in Div.3 North.

MOST GOALS IN TOP DIV. ON ONE DAY

This record has stood since December 26, 1963, when **66 goals** were scored in the ten First Division matches played.

MOST F.A. PREMIER LEAGUE GOALS ON ONE DAY

47, in nine matches on May 8, 1993 (last day of season).

FEWEST PREMIERSHIP GOALS IN ONE WEEK-END

10, in 10 matches on November 24/25, 2001

FEWEST FIRST DIV. GOALS ON ONE DAY

For full/near full programme: **Ten goals**, all by home clubs, in ten matches on April 28, 1923 (day of Wembley's first F.A. Cup Final).

SCORERS IN 8 CONSECUTIVE PREMIERSHIP MATCHES

Rudd van Nistelrooy (Manchester Utd., season 2001-02).

SCORER IN 13 CONSECUTIVE LEAGUE MATCHES

Tom Phillipson for Wolves (Div. 2, season 1926-7).

SCORER FOR 5 PREMIERSHIP CLUBS

Stan Collymore is the only player to do this – for Nott'm. Forest, Liverpool, Aston Villa, Leicester City and Bradford City.

SCORERS IN MOST CONSECUTIVE LEAGUE FIXTURES

Chesterfield, in 46 successive matches in Div. 3 (North) for a year between Christmas Day 1929 and the end of the sequence on December 27, 1930.
   Arsenal scored in all 38 matches as Premiership title winners in season 2001-02.

SIX-OUT-OF-SIX HEADERS

When **Oxford Utd.** beat Shrewsbury Town 6-0 (Div. 2) on April 23, 1996, all six goals were headers.

FIVE IN A MATCH

Latest players to score 5 goals in a top-division match: **Tony Woodcock** (for Arsenal in 6-2 win away to Aston Villa) and **Ian Rush** (Liverpool 6, Luton Town 0), both on October 29, 1983; **Andy Cole** (Manchester Utd. 9, Ipswich Town 0) on March 4, 1995; **Alan Shearer** (Newcastle Utd. 8, Sheffield Wed. 0) on September 19, 1999.

ALL–ROUND MARKSMAN

Alan Cork scored in four divisions of the Football League and in the F.A. Premier League in his 18-season career with Wimbledon, Sheffield Utd., and Fulham (1977-95).

MOST CUP GOALS

F.A. Cup – most goals in one season: 20 by Jimmy Ross (Preston N.E., runners-up 1887-8); 15 by Albert (Sandy) Brown (Tottenham, winners 1900-1).
   Most F.A. Cup goals in individual careers: 48 by Harry Cursham (Notts Co. 1880-87); this century: 44 by Ian Rush (39 for Liverpool, 4 for Chester City, 1 for Newcastle Utd. 1979-98). Denis Law was the previous highest F.A. Cup scorer this century with 41 goals for Huddersfield Town, Manchester City and Manchester Utd. (1957-74).
   Most F.A. Cup Final goals by individual: 5 by Ian Rush for Liverpool (2 in 1986, 2 in 1989, 1 in 1992).

HOTTEST CUP HOT-SHOT

Geoff Hurst scored 21 cup goals in season 1965-66: 11 League Cup, 4 F.A. Cup and 2 Cup-Winners' Cup for West Ham Utd., and 4 in the World Cup for England.

SCORERS IN EVERY ROUND

Twelve players have scored in **every round** of the F.A. Cup in one season, from opening to Final inclusive: **Archie Hunter** (Aston Villa, winners 1887); **Sandy Brown** (Tottenham, winners 1901); **Harry Hampton** (Aston Villa, winners 1905); **Harold Blackmore** (Bolton Wand., winners 1929); **Ellis Rimmer** (Sheffield Wed., winners 1935); **Frank O'Donnell** (Preston N.E., beaten 1937); **Stan Mortensen** (Blackpool, beaten 1948); **Jack Milburn** (Newcastle Utd., winners 1951); **Nat Lofthouse** (Bolton Wand., beaten 1953); **Charlie Wayman** (Preston N.E., beaten 1954); **Jeff Astle** (W.B.A., winners 1968); **Peter Osgood** (Chelsea, winners 1970).
   Blackmore and the next seven completed their 'set' in the Final at Wembley; Osgood did so in the Final replay at Old Trafford.
   Only player to score in every **Football League Cup** round possible in one season: **Tony Brown** for W.B.A., winners 1965-6, with 9 goals in 10 games (after bye in Round 1).

TEN IN A ROW

Dixie McNeill scored for Wrexham in **ten successive** F.A. Cup rounds (18 goals): 11 in Rounds 1-6, 1977-8; 3 in Rounds 3-4, 1978-9; 4 in Rounds 3-4, 1979-80.

Stan Mortensen (Blackpool) scored 25 goals in 16 F.A. Cup rounds out of 17 (1946-51).

TOP MATCH HAULS IN F.A. CUP

Ted MacDougall scored nine goals in the F.A. Cup first round on November 20, 1971, when Bournemouth beat Margate 11-0. On November 23, 1970 he had scored six in an 8-1 first round replay against Oxford City.

Other six-goal F.A. Cup scorers include **George Hilsdon** (Chelsea v Worksop, 9-1, 1907-8), **Ronnie Rooke** (Fulham v Bury, 6-0, 1938-9), **Harold Atkinson** (Tranmere Rov. v Ashington, 8-1, 1952-3), **George Best** (Manchester Utd. v Northampton Town 1969-70, 8-2 away), and **Duane Darby** (Hull City v Whitby, 8-4, 1996-7).

Denis Law scored all six for Manchester City at Luton Town (6-2) in an F.A. Cup 4th Round tie on January 28, 1961, but none of them counted – the match was abandoned (69 mins.) because of a waterlogged pitch. He also scored City's goal when the match was played again, but they lost 3-1.

Tony Philliskirk scored **five** when Peterborough Utd. beat Kingstonian 9-1 in an F.A. Cup 1st Round replay on November 25, 1992, but had then been wiped from the records. With the score at 3-0, the Kingstonian goalkeeper was concussed by a coin thrown from the crowd and unable to play on. The F.A. ordered the match to be replayed at Peterborough Utd. behind closed doors, and Kingstonian lost 1-0.

QUICKEST GOALS AND RAPID SCORING

Six seconds after kick-off by **Albert Mundy** for Aldershot v Hartlepool Utd., October 25, 1958; **Barrie Jones** for Notts County v Torquay Utd., March 31, 1962; **Keith Smith** for Crystal Palace v Derby Co., December 12, 1964.

9.6 seconds by **John Hewitt** for Aberdeen at Motherwell, 3rd Round, January 23, 1982 (fastest goal in Scottish Cup history).

A goal in **4 seconds** was claimed by **Jim Fryatt**, for Bradford P.A. v Tranmere Rov. (Div. 4, April 25, 1965), and by **Gerry Allen** for Whitstable Town v Danson (Kent League, March 3,1989). Backed by filmed evidence, **Damian Mori** scored in 4 seconds for Adelaide City v Sydney Utd. (Australian National League, December 6, 1995).

Colin Cowperthwaite reputedly scored in 3½ seconds for Barrow v Kettering (Alliance Premier League) on December 8, 1979, but the timing was unofficial.

Phil Starbuck scored for Huddersfield Town only **3 seconds** after entering the field as 54th min. substitute at home to Wigan Athletic (Div. 2) on Easter Monday, April 12, 1993. A corner-kick was delayed, awaiting his arrival, and he scored with a header.

Malcolm Macdonald scored after **5 seconds** (officially timed) in Newcastle Utd.'s 7-3 win in a pre-season friendly at St. Johnstone on July 29, 1972. From the kick-off, the ball was passed to him, and Macdonald, spotting the goalkeeper off his line, smashed a shot over him and into the net.

Scored first kick: **Billy Foulkes** (Newcastle Utd.) for Wales v England at Cardiff City, October 20, 1951, in his first International match.

Six goals in seven minutes in Preston N.E.'s record 26-0 F.A. Cup 1st Round win v Hyde, October 15, 1887.

Five in 20 minutes: **Frank Keetley** in Lincoln City's 9-1 win over Halifax Town in Div. III (North), January 16, 1932; **Brian Dear** for West Ham Utd. v W.B.A. (6-1, Div.1) April 16, 1965.

Four in five minutes: by **John McIntyre** for Blackburn Rov. v Everton (Div. 1), September 16, 1922; **W.G. (Billy) Richardson** for W.B.A. v West Ham Utd. (Div. 1), November 7, 1931.

Three in three minutes: **Billy Lane** for Watford v Clapton Orient (Div.3S), December 20, 1933; **Johnny Hartburn** for Leyton Orient v Shrewsbury Town (Div. 3S), January 22, 1955; **Gary Roberts** for Brentford v Newport, (Freight Rover Trophy, South Final), May 17, 1985; **Gary Shaw** for Shrewsbury Town v Bradford City (Div. 3), December 22, 1990.

Three in 2½ minutes: Jimmy Scarth for Gillingham v Leyton Orient (Div. 3S), November 1, 1952.

Two in nine seconds: Jamie Bates with last kick of first half, **Jermaine McSporran** 9 seconds into second half when Wycombe Wand. beat Peterborough Utd. 2-0 at home (Div. 2) on September 23, 2000.

Arsenal scored six goals in 18 minutes (71-89 mins.) in 7-1 home win v Sheffield Wed., February 15, 1992.

Sunderland scored eight goals in 28 minutes at Newcastle Utd. (9-1 Div 1), December 5, 1908. Newcastle went on to win the championship.

Southend Utd. scored all seven goals in 29 minutes in 7-0 win at home to Torquay Utd. (Leyland Daf Cup, Southern quarter-final), February 26, 1991. Score was 0-0 until 55th. minute.

Six goals in first 19 minutes by Tranmere Rov. when they beat Oldham Athletic 13-4 (Div. 3 North) on December 26, 1935.

Notts Co. scored six second-half goals in 12 minutes (Tommy Lawton 3, Jackie Sewell 3) when they beat Exeter City 9-0 (Div. 3 South) at Meadow Lane on October 16, 1948.

World's fastest goal: 2.8 seconds, direct from kick-off, by Argentinian **Ricardo Olivera** for Rio Negro v Soriano (Uruguayan League), December 26, 1998.

Fastest International goal: 8.3 secs. by **Davide Gualtieri** for San Marino v England (World Cup qual., Bologna, November 17, 1993).

Fastest International Hat-trick: 3 minutes 15 seconds by **Masashi Nakayami** for Japan in 9-0 win v Brunei in Macao (Asian Cup), February 16, 2000.

Fastest International hat-trick in British matches: 3½ minutes by **Willie Hall** for England v N. Ireland at Old Trafford, Manchester, November 16, 1938. (Hall scored 5 in 7-0 win); 4½ minutes by **Arif Erdem** for Turkey v N. Ireland, European Championship, at Windsor Park, Belfast, on September 4, 1999.

Fastest International goal by substitute: 5 seconds by **John Jensen** for Denmark v Belgium (Eur. Champ.), October 12, 1994.

Fastest England goals: 27 seconds by **Bryan Robson** v. France in World Cup at Bilbao, Spain on June 16, 1982; at Wembley: 38 seconds by **Bryan Robson** v Yugoslavia, December 13, 1989; 42 seconds by **Gary Lineker** v Malaysia in Kuala Lumpur, June 12, 1991.

Fastest goal by England substitute: 10 seconds by **Teddy Sheringham** v Greece (World Cup qualifying match) at Old Trafford, October 6, 2001.

Fastest F.A. Cup Final goals: 30 seconds by **John Devey**, for Aston Villa v W.B.A., 1895; at Wembley: 42 seconds by **Roberto di Matteo**, for Chelsea v Middlesbrough, 1997.

Fastest League Cup Final goal: 3 minutes by **Derek Lythgoe** for Norwich City v Rochdale, 1962.

Fastest goal in cup final: 4.07 seconds by 14-year-old **Owen Price** for Ernest Bevin College, Tooting, beaten 3-1 by Barking Abbey in Heinz Ketchup Cup Final at Arsenal Stadium on May 18, 2000. Owen, on Tottenham's books, scored from inside his own half when the ball was played back to him from kick-out.

Fastest F.A. Cup hat-tricks: In 3 minutes by **Billy Best** for Southend Utd. v Brentford (2nd. Round, December 7, 1968); 2 minutes 20 seconds by **Andy Locke** for Nantwich v Droylesden (1st. Qual. Round, September 9, 1995).

F.A. Premier League – fastest scoring: Four goals in 4 minutes, 44 seconds by Tottenham at home to Southampton on Sunday, February 7, 1993.

Fastest First Division hat-tricks since war: Graham Leggat, 3 goals in 3 minutes (first half) when Fulham beat Ipswich Town 10-1 on Boxing Day, 1963; Nigel Clough, 3 goals in 4 minutes (81, 82, 85 pen) when Nott'm Forest beat Q.P.R. 4-0 on Sunday, December 13, 1987.

F.A. Premier League – fastest hat-trick: 4½ minutes (26, 29, 31) by **Robbie Fowler** in Liverpool 3, Arsenal 0 on Sunday, August 28, 1994.

Fastest Premier League goals: 10 seconds by **Ledley King** for Tottenham away to Bradford City, December 9, 2000; 13 seconds by **Chris Sutton** for Blackburn Rov. at Everton, April 1, 1995; 13 seconds by **Dwight Yorke** for Aston Villa at Coventry City, September 30, 1995.

Fastest top-division goal: 7 seconds by **Bobby Langton** for Preston N.E. v Manchester City (Div. 1), August 25, 1948.

Fastest Premier League goal by substitute: 13 seconds by **Jamie Cureton** for Norwich City v Chelsea, December 10, 1994.

Four in 13 minutes by Premier League substitute: Ole Gunnar Solskjaer for Manchester Utd. away to Nott'm. Forest, Feb. 6, 1999.

Fastest new-First Division goal: 10 seconds by **Keith O'Neill** for Norwich City v Stoke City, April 12, 1997.

Fastest Scottish hat-trick: 2½ mins. by **Ian St. John** for Motherwell away to Hibernian (Scottish League Cup), August 15, 1959.

Fastest all-time hat-trick: Reported at 1 min. 50 secs. by **Eduardo Maglioni** for Independiente against Gimnasia de la Plata in Argentina, March 18, 1973.

Fastest goal in Women's Football: 7 seconds by **Angie Harriott** for Launton Ladies v Thame Utd. (Southern League, Prem. Div.), season 1998-9.

FASTEST GOALS IN WORLD CUP FINAL SERIES

10.8 secs. by **Hakan Sukur** for Turkey against South Korea in 3rd/4th-place match at Taegu, June 29, 2002.

15 secs. by **Vaclav Masek** for Czechoslovakia v Mexico (in Vina, Chile, 1962).

27 secs. by **Bryan Robson** for England v France (in Bilbao, Spain, 1982).

TOP MATCH SCORES SINCE WAR

By English clubs: 13-0 by Newcastle Utd. v Newport (Div. 2, Oct. 1946); **13-2** by Tottenham v Crewe Alexandra (F.A. Cup 4th. Rd. replay, Feb. 1960); **13-0** by Chelsea v Jeunesse Hautcharage, Lux. (Cup-Winners' Cup 1st. Rd., 2nd. Leg, Sept. 1971).

By Scottish club: 20-0 by Stirling Albion v Selkirk (E. of Scotland League) in Scottish Cup 1st. Rd. (Dec. 1984). That is the highest score in British first-class football since Preston N.E. beat Hyde 26-0 in F.A. Cup, Oct. 1887.

GOALS BY WINGERS

		Season	Matches	Goals
	Football League	(Div. I)		
Cliff Bastin (Arsenal)		1932-3	42	33
	Scottish League	(Div. I)		
Bob Ferrier (Motherwell)		1929-30	27	32
	Scottish League	(Div. II)		
Ken Dawson (Falkirk)		1935-6	34	39

GOALS BY GOALKEEPERS

Goalkeepers who have scored with long clearances include:

Pat Jennings for Tottenham away to Manchester Utd. (goalkeeper Alex Stepney) in the F.A. Charity Shield on August 12, 1967.

Peter Shilton for Leicester City at Southampton (goalkeeper Campbell Forsyth) on October 14, 1967 (Div. 1).

Ray Cashley for Bristol City at home to Hull City (goalkeeper Jeff Wealands) on September 18, 1973 (Div. 2).

Steve Sherwood for Watford away to Coventry City (goalkeeper Raddy Avramovic) on January 14, 1984 (Div. 1).

Steve Ogrizovic for Coventry City away to Sheffield Wed. (goalkeeper Martin Hodge) on October 25, 1986 (Div. 1).

Andy Goram for Hibernian at home to Morton (goalkeeper David Wylie) on May 7, 1988 (Scottish Premier Div.).

Andy McLean, on Irish League debut, for Cliftonville v Linfield (goalkeeper George Dunlop) on August 20, 1988.

Alan Paterson for Glentoran against Linfield (goalkeeper George Dunlop) on November 30, 1988 (Irish League Cup Final at The Oval, Belfast). His long punt (87 mins) gave Glentoran a 2-1 victory – the only instance of a goalkeeper scoring the winning goal in a senior cup final in the UK.

Ray Charles for East Fife at Stranraer (goalkeeper Bernard Duffy) on February 28, 1990 (Scottish Div. 2).

Iain Hesford scored Maidstone's winner (3-2 v Hereford, Div. 4, November 2, 1991) with long kick-out that went first bounce past Tony Elliott in opposite goal.

Chris Mackenzie for Hereford at home to Barnet (goalkeeper Mark Taylor) in Div. 3, August 12, 1995.

Aston Villa's **Mark Bosnich** scored the last goal (a penalty) when Australia beat Solomon Islands 13-0 in World Cup Oceania Zone qualifier in Sydney on June 11, 1997.

With a free-kick from his own half, Notts Co. goalkeeper **Steve Mildenhall** scored past Mansfield Town 'keeper Kevin Pilkington for the winning goal (4-3,away) in the Worthington Cup 1st Round on August 21, 2001.

Most goals by a goalkeeper in a League season: 5 (all penalties) by **Arthur Birch** for Chesterfield (Div. 3 North), 1923-4.

Arthur Wilkie, Reading's goalkeeper at home to Halifax Town (Div. 3) on August 31, 1962, injured a hand, then played as a forward and scored twice in a 4-2 win.

Alex Stepney was Manchester Utd.'s joint top scorer for two months in season 1973-4 with two penalties.

Alan Fettis, N. Ireland goalkeeper, scored twice for Hull City in Div. 2 in season 1994-5: as a substitute in 3-1 home win v Oxford Utd. (Dec. 17) and, when selected outfield, with last-minute winner (2-1) at Blackpool on May 6.

Peter Schmeichel, Manchester Utd.'s goalkeeper, headed an 89th minute equaliser (2-2) from Ryan Giggs' corner in the UEFA Cup 1st. Round, 2nd leg against Rotor Volgograd (Russia) on September 26, 1995, but United lost the tie on away goals.

On October 20, 2001, **Schmeichel** became the first goalkeeper to score in the Premiership when, following a corner, he volleyed Aston Villa's second goal in their 3-2 defeat at Everton.

In League matches for Swansea City, **Roger Freestone** scored with a penalty at Oxford Utd. (Div. 2, April 30, 1995) and, in 1995-6 (Div. 2) with penalties at home to Shrewsbury Town (August 12) and Chesterfield (August 26).

Goalkeeper **Jimmy Glass**, on loan from Swindon Town, scored the winner that kept Carlisle Utd. in the Football League on May 8, 1999. With only ten seconds of injury time left, he went upfield for a corner and shot the goal that beat Plymouth Argyle 2-1 at Brunton Park. It preserved Carlisle Utd.'s League existence since 1928 and sent Scarborough down to the Conference.

Tony Roberts (Dagenham & Redbridge), only known goalkeeper to score from open play in the F.A. Cup, away to Basingstoke in 4th Qual. Round on October 27, 2001. His last-minute equaliser (2-2) forced a replay, which Dagenham won 3-0 and went on to the 3rd Round proper.

Jose Luis Chilavert, Paraguay's Int. goalkeeper, scored a hat-trick of penalties when his club Velez Sarsfield beat Ferro Carril Oeste 6-1 in the Argentine League on November 28, 1999.

OWN GOALS

Most by player in one season: 5 by **Robert Stuart** (Middlesbrough) in 1934-35.

Two in match by one player: Chris Nicholl (Aston Villa) scored all 4 goals in 2-2 draw away to Leicester City (Div. 1), March 20, 1976; **Jamie Carragher** (Liverpool) in first half at home to Manchester Utd. (2-3) in Premiership, September 11, 1999.

Fastest own goals: 8 seconds by **Pat Kruse** of Torquay Utd., for Cambridge Utd. (Div. 4), January 3, 1977; in **First Division**, 16 seconds by **Steve Bould** (Arsenal) away to Sheffield Wed., February 17, 1990.

Late own-goal man: Frank Sinclair (Leicester City) put through his own goal in the 90th minute of Premiership matches away to Arsenal (L1-2) and at home to Chelsea (D2-2) in August 1999.

Half an own goal each: Chelsea's second goal in a 3-1 home win against Leicester City on December 18, 1954 was uniquely recorded as 'shared own goal'. Leicester City defenders **Stan Milburn** and **Jack Froggatt**, both lunging at the ball in an attempt to clear, connected simultaneously and sent it rocketing into the net.

MOST SCORERS IN MATCH

Liverpool set a Football League record with **EIGHT** scorers when they beat Crystal Palace 9-0 (Div.1) on September 12, 1989. Their marksmen were: Steve Nicol (7 and 88 mins), Steve McMahon (16), Ian Rush (45), Gary Gillespie (56), Peter Beardsley (61), John Aldridge pen. (67), John Barnes (79) and Glenn Hysen (82).

Fifteen years earlier, **Liverpool** had gone one better with **NINE** different scorers when they achieved their record win, 11-0 at home to Stromsgodset (Norway) in the Cup-Winners' Cup 1st. round, 1st leg on September 17, 1974.

Eight players scored for **Swansea City** when they beat Sliema, Malta, 12-0 in the Cup-Winners' Cup 1st round, 1st leg on September 15, 1982.

Nine **Stirling Albion** players scored in the 20-0 win against Selkirk in the Scottish Cup 1st. Round on December 8, 1984.

LONG SCORING RUNS

The record in England is held by **Bill Prendergast**, who scored in 13 consecutive League and Cup appearances for Chester (Div. 3 North, Sept.-Dec., 1938).

Dixie Dean scored in 12 consecutive games (23 goals) for Everton in Div. 2 in 1930-1.

Danish striker **Finn Dossing** scored in 15 consecutive matches (Scottish record) for Dundee Utd. (Div. 1) in 1964-5.

Marco Negri (Rangers) scored in all the first 10 Premier games of 1997-8, a total of 12 goals.

Jermaine Defoe, 18, on loan from West Ham Utd., equalled a single-season post-war record by scoring for Bournemouth in 10 consecutive matches (Div. 2), October-January 2000-01. **Billy McAdams** did likewise for Manchester City (1957-8), as did **Ron Davies** for Southampton (1966-7).

John Aldridge (Liverpool) scored in 10 successive First Division matches – the last game of season 1986-7 and the first nine in 1987-8.

Kevin Russell (Wrexham) scored in nine consecutive matches in Div. 4, March-May, 1988.

Ruud van Nistelrooy (Manchester Utd.) holds the record for scoring in most consecutive Premiership matches – 8 (11 goals) in December-January, 2001-02.

Ian Wright scored on 12 successive first-team appearances, including 7 Premiership, for Arsenal (Sept. 15-Nov. 23, 1994).

50-GOAL PLAYERS

With **52** goals for **Wolves** in 1987-8 (34 League, 12 Sherpa Van Trophy, 3 Littlewoods Cup, 3 F.A. Cup), **Steve Bull** became the first player to score 50 in a season for a League club since **Terry Bly** for 4th Division newcomers Peterborough Utd. in 1960-1. Bly's 54 comprised 52 League goals and 2 in the F.A. Cup, and included 7 hat-tricks, still a post-war League record.

Bull was again the country's top scorer with 50 goals in season 1988-9: 37 League, 2 Littlewoods Cup and 11 Sherpa Van Trophy.

Between Bly and Bull, the highest individual scoring total for a season was 49 by two players: Ted MacDougall (Bournemouth 1970-1, 42 League, 7 F.A. Cup) and Clive Allen (Tottenham 1986-7, 33 League, 12 Littlewoods Cup, 4 F.A. Cup).

HOT SHOTS

Jimmy Greaves was First Division top scorer (League goals) six times in 11 seasons: 32 for Chelsea (1958-9), 41 for Chelsea (1960-1) and, for Tottenham, 37 in 1962-3, 35 in 1963-4, 29 in 1964-5 (joint top) and 27 in 1968-9.

Brian Clough (Middlesbrough) was the Second Division's leading scorer in three successive seasons: 40 goals in 1957-8, 42 in 1958-9 and 39 in 1959-60.

John Hickton (Middlesbrough) was top Div. 2 scorer three times in four seasons: 24 goals in 1967-8, 24 in 1969-70 and 25 in 1970-1.

MOST HAT-TRICKS

Nine by **George Camsell** (Middlesbrough) in Div. 2, 1926-7, is the record for one season. Most League hat-tricks in career: 37 by **Dixie Dean** for Tranmere Rov. and Everton (1924-38).

Most **top division** hat-tricks in a season since last war: six by **Jimmy Greaves** for Chelsea (1960-1). **Alan Shearer** scored five hat-tricks for Blackburn Rov. in the Premier League, season 1995-96.

Frank Osborne (Tottenham) scored three consecutive hat-tricks in Div. 1 in October-November 1925, against Liverpool, Leicester City (away) and West Ham Utd.

Tom Jennings (Leeds Utd.) scored hat-tricks in three successive First Div. matches (Sept-Oct. 1926): 3 goals v Arsenal, 4 at Liverpool, 4 v Blackburn Rov. Leeds Utd. were relegated at the end of the season.

Jack Balmer (Liverpool) scored only three hat-tricks in a 17-year career - in successive First Div. matches (Nov. 1946): 3 v Portsmouth, 4 at Derby Co., 3 v Arsenal.

Gilbert Alsop scored hat-tricks in three successive matches for Walsall in Div. 3 South in April 1939: 3 at Swindon Town, 3 v Bristol City and 4 v Swindon Town.

Alf Lythgoe scored hat-tricks in three successive games for Stockport Co. (Div. 3 North) in March 1934: 3 v Darlington, 3 at Southport and 4 v Wrexham.

TRIPLE HAT-TRICKS

There have been at least three instances of **3 hat-tricks being scored** for **one team** in a Football League match:-

April 21, 1909: Enoch West, Billy Hooper and Alfred Spouncer scored 3 apiece for Nott'm. Forest (12-0 v Leicester Fosse, Div. 1).

March 3, 1962: Ron Barnes, Wyn Davies and Roy Ambler registered hat-tricks in Wrexham's 10-1 win against Hartlepool Utd. (Div. 4).

November 7, 1987: Tony Adcock, Paul Stewart and David White each scored 3 goals for Manchester City in 10-1 win at home to Huddersfield Town (Div. 2).

For the first time in the Premiership, **three hat-tricks** were completed **on one day** (September 23, 1995): Tony Yeboah for Leeds Utd. at Wimbledon; Alan Shearer for Blackburn Rov. v Coventry City; and Robbie Fowler with 4 goals for Liverpool v Bolton Wand.

In the F.A. Cup, **Jack Carr**, **George Elliott** and **Walter Tinsley** each scored 3 in Middlesbrough's 9-3 first round win against Goole in Jan. 1915. **Les Allen** scored 5, **Bobby Smith** 4 and **Cliff Jones** 3 when Tottenham beat Crewe Alexandra 13-2 in a fourth-round replay in February 1960.

HAT-TRICKS v THREE 'KEEPERS

When West Ham Utd. beat Newcastle Utd. 8-1 (Div.1) at home on April 21, 1986 **Alvin Martin** scored 3 goals against different 'keepers: Martin Thomas injured a shoulder and was replaced, in turn, by outfield players Chris Hedworth and Peter Beardsley.

Jock Dodds of Lincoln City had done the same **against** West Ham Utd. on December 18, 1948, scoring past **Ernie Gregory**, **Tommy Moroney** and **George Dick**. The Hammers lost 3-4.

David Herd (Manchester Utd.) scored against three Sunderland goalkeepers (Jim Montgomery, Charlie Hurley and Johnny Parke) in 5-0 First Division home win on Nov. 26, 1966.

Brian Clark, of Bournemouth, scored against three Rotherham Utd. goalkeepers (Jim McDonagh,, Conal Gilbert and Michael Leng twice) in 7-2 win at Rotherham Utd. (Div. 3) on Oct. 10, 1972.

On Oct. 16, 1993 (Div.3) **Chris Pike** (Hereford) scored a hat-trick against different goalkeepers. Opponents Colchester Utd., beaten 5-0, became the first team in League history to have two 'keepers sent off in the same game.

Joe Bradford of Birmingham City scored three hat-tricks in eight days in September 1929-30. v Newcastle Utd. (won 5-1) on the 21st, 5 for the Football League v Irish League (7-2) on the 25th, and 3 in his club's 5-7 defeat away to Blackburn Rov. on the 28th.

TON UP – BOTH ENDS

Manchester City are the only club to **score and concede** a century of League goals in the same season. When fifth in the 1957-8 Championship, they scored 104 goals and gave away 100.

TOURNAMENT TOP SHOTS

Most individual goals in a World Cup Final series: 13 by **Just Fontaine** for France, in Sweden 1958.

MOST GOALS ON CLUB DEBUT

Jim Dyet scored **eight** in King's Park's 12-2 win against Forfar Athletic (Scottish Div. 2, Jan. 2, 1930).

Len Shackleton scored **six** times in Newcastle Utd.'s 13-0 win v Newport County (Div. 2, Oct. 5, 1946) in the week he joined them from Bradford Park Avenue.

MOST GOALS ON LEAGUE DEBUT

Five by **George Hilsdon**, for Chelsea (9-2) v Glossop, Div. 2 Sept. 1, 1906.

Alan Shearer, with three goals for Southampton (4-2) v Arsenal, April 9, 1988, became, at 17, the youngest player to score a First Division hat-trick on his full debut.

CLEAN-SHEET RECORDS

On the way to promotion from Div. 3 in season 1995-6, **Gillingham's** ever-present goalkeeper **Jim Stannard** set a clean-sheet record. In 46 matches, he achieved 29 shut-outs (17 at home, 12 away), beating the 28 by Ray Clemence for Liverpool (42 matches in Div. 1, 1978-9) and the previous best in a 46-match programme of 28 by Port Vale (Div. 3 North, 1953-4). In conceding only 20 League goals in 1995-6, Gillingham created a defensive record for the lower divisions.

Chris Woods, Rangers' England goalkeeper, set a British record in season 1986-7 by going 1,196 minutes without conceding a goal. The sequence began in the UEFA Cup match against Borussia Moenchengladbach on Nov. 26, 1986 and ended when Rangers were sensationally beaten 1-0 at home by Hamilton in the Scottish Cup 3rd. Round on Jan. 31, 1987 with a 70th.-minute goal by Adrian Sprott.

The previous British record of 1,156 minutes without a goal conceded was held by Aberdeen goalkeeper **Bobby Clark** (season 1970-1).

There have been three instances of clubs keeping 11 consecutive clean sheets in the Football League: Millwall (Div. 3 South, 1925-6), York City (Div. 3, 1973-4) and Reading (Div. 4, 1978-9). In his sequence, Reading goalkeeper **Steve Death** set the existing League shut-out record of 1,103 minutes.

Mark Leonard (Chesterfield) kept a clean sheet in 8 consecutive Div.3 away games (Jan-April 1994). Believed an away-match record in British football.

Sasa Ilic remained unbeaten for over 14 hours with 9 successive shut-outs (7 in FL Div. 1, 2 in play-offs) to equal a Charlton Athletic club record in Apr./May 1998. He had 12 clean sheets in 17 first team games after winning promotion from the reserves with 6 successive clean sheets.

Sebastiano Rossi kept a clean sheet in 8 successive away matches for AC Milan (Nov. 1993-Apr. 1994).

A world record of 1,275 minutes without conceding a goal was set in 1990-1 by **Abel Resino**, the Atletico Madrid goalkeeper. He was finally beaten by Sporting Gijon's Enrique in Atletico's 3-1 win on March 19, 1991.

In International football, the record is held by **Dino Zoff** with a shut-out for Italy (Sept. 1972 to June 1974) lasting 1,142 minutes.

LOW SCORING

Fewest goals by any club in season in Football League: **24** by **Stoke City** (Div. 1, 42 matches, 1984-5); **24** by **Watford** (Div. 2, 42 matches, 1971-2). In 46-match programme, **27** by **Stockport Co.** (Div. 3, 1969-70).

Arsenal were the lowest Premier League scorers in its opening season (1992-3) with 40 goals in 42 matches, but won both domestic cup competitions. In subsequent seasons the lowest Premier League scorers were **Ipswich Town** (35) in 1993-4, **Crystal Palace** (34) in 1994-5, and **Manchester City** (33) in 1995-6, before **Leeds Utd.** set the Premiership's existing fewest-goals record with 28 in 1996-7.

LONG TIME NO SCORE

Longest non-scoring sequences in Football League: 11 matches by **Coventry City** in 1919-20 (Div. 2); 11 matches by **Hartlepool Utd.** in 1992-3 (Div. 2). After beating

Crystal Palace 1-0 in the F.A. Cup 3rd round on Jan. 2, they went 13 games and 2 months without scoring (11 League, 1 F.A. Cup, 1 Autoglass Trophy). The sequence ended after 1,227 blank minutes with a 1-1 draw at Blackpool (League) on March 6.

In the **Premier League** (Oct.-Jan. season 1994-5) Crystal Palace failed to score in nine consecutive matches.

The British non-scoring record is held by Scottish club **Stirling Albion**: 14 consecutive matches (13 League, 1 Scottish Cup) and 1,292 minutes play, from Jan. 31, 1981 until Aug. 8, 1981 (when they lost 4-1 to Falkirk in the League Cup).

In season 1971-2, **Mansfield Town** did not score in any of their first nine home games in Div. 3. They were relegated on goal difference of minus two.

F.A. CUP CLEAN SHEETS

Most consecutive F.A. Cup matches without conceding a goal: 11 by **Bradford City**. The sequence spanned 8 rounds, from 3rd. in 1910-11 to 4th. Round replay in 1911-12, and included winning the Cup in 1911.

ATTENDANCES

GREATEST WORLD CROWDS

World Cup, Maracana Stadium, Rio de Janeiro, July 16, 1950. Final match (Brazil v Uruguay) attendance 199,850; receipts £125,000.

Total attendance in three matches (including play-off) between Santos (Brazil) and AC Milan for the Inter-Continental Cup (World Club Championship) 1963, exceeded 375,000.

BRITISH RECORD CROWDS

Most to pay: 149,547, Scotland v England, at Hampden Park, Glasgow, April 17, 1937. This was the first all-ticket match in Scotland (receipts £24,000).
At Scottish F.A. Cup Final: 146,433, Celtic v Aberdeen, at Hampden Park, April 24, 1937. Estimated another 20,000 shut out.
For British club match (apart from a Cup Final): 143,470, Rangers v Hibernian, at Hampden Park, March 27, 1948 (Scottish Cup semi-final).
F.A. Cup Final: 126,047, Bolton Wand. v West Ham Utd., at Wembley, April 28, 1923. Estimated 150,000 in stadium.
World Cup Qualifying Ties: 120,000, Cameroon v Morocco, Yaounde, November 29, 1981; 107,580, Scotland v Poland, Hampden Park, October 13, 1965.
European Cup: 135,826, Celtic v Leeds Utd. (semi-final, 2nd. leg) at Hampden Park, Glasgow, April 15, 1970.
European Cup Final: 127,621, Real Madrid v Eintracht Frankfurt, at Hampden Park, Glasgow, May 18, 1960.
European Cup-Winners' Cup Final: 100,000, West Ham Utd. v TSV Munich, at Wembley, May 19, 1965.
Scottish League: 118,567, Rangers v Celtic, January 2, 1939.
Scottish League Cup Final: 107,609, Celtic v Rangers, at Hampden Park, October 23, 1965.
Football League old format: First Div.: 83,260, Manchester Utd. v Arsenal, January 17, 1948 (at Maine Road); **Second Div.:** 70,302 Tottenham v Southampton, February 25, 1950; **Third Div. South:** 51,621 Cardiff City v Bristol City, April 7, 1947; **Third Div. North:** 49,655, Hull City v Rotherham Utd., December 25, 1948; **Third Div.:** 49,309, Sheffield Wed. v Sheffield Utd., December 26, 1979; **Fourth Div.:** 37,774, Crystal Palace v Millwall, March 31, 1961.
F.A. Premier League: 67, 683, Manchester Utd. v Middlesbrough, March 23, 2002.
Football League – New Div. 1: 41,214, Sunderland v Stoke City, April 25, 1998; **New Div. 2:** 32,471, Manchester City v York City, May 8, 1999; **New Div. 3:** 18,700, Preston N.E. v Exeter City, May 4, 1996.

In English Provinces: 84,569, Manchester City v Stoke City (F.A. Cup 6th Round), March 3, 1934.

Record for Under-21 International: 32,865 England v France at Derby Co., February 9, 1999.

Record for friendly match: 104,679, Rangers v Eintracht Frankfurt, at Hampden Park, Glasgow, October 17, 1961.

Record Football League aggregate (season): 41,271,414 (1948-9) – 88 clubs.

Record Football League aggregate (single day): 1,269,934, December 27, 1949.

Record average home League attendance for season: 67,543 by Manchester Utd. in 2000-01.

Long-ago League attendance aggregates: 10,929,000 in 1906-07 (40 clubs); 28,132,933 in 1937-8 (88 clubs).

Last 1m. crowd aggregate, League: 1,007,200, December 27, 1971.

Record Amateur match attendance: 100,000 for F.A. Amateur Cup Final, Pegasus v Harwich & Parkeston at Wembley, April 11, 1953.

Record Cup-tie aggregate: 265,199, at two matches between Rangers and Morton, in the Scottish Cup Final, 1947-8.

Abandoned match attendance records: In **England** – 63,480 at Newcastle Utd. v Swansea City F.A. Cup 3rd round, Jan. 10, 1953, abandoned 8 mins (0-0), fog.

In Scotland: 94,596 at Scotland v Austria (4-1), Hampden Park, May 8, 1963. Referee Jim Finney ended play (79 minutes) after Austria had two players sent off and one carried off.

What is still **Colchester Utd.'s** record crowd (19,072) was for the F.A. Cup 1st round tie v Reading on Nov. 27, 1948, abandoned 35 minutes (0-0), fog.

SMALLEST CROWDS

Lowest post-war League attendance: 450 Rochdale v Cambridge Utd. (Div. 3, February 2, 1974).

Lowest F.A. Premier League crowd: 3,039 for Wimbledon v Everton, Jan. 26, 1993 (smallest top-division attendance since war).

Lowest Saturday post-war top-division crowd: 3,231 for Wimbledon v Luton Town, Sept. 7, 1991 (Div. 1).

Lowest Football League crowds, new format – Div. 1: 3,086 Southend Utd. v Bristol City, February 10,1993; **Div. 2:** 1,077, Hartlepool Utd. v Cardiff City, March 22, 1994; **Div. 3:** 739, Doncaster Rov. v Barnet, March 3, 1998.

Other low First Division crowds since the war: 3,121 for Wimbledon v Sheffield W., Oct. 2, 1991; 3,231 for Wimbledon v Luton Town, Sept. 7, 1991; 3,270 for Wimbledon v Coventry City, Dec. 28, 1991; 3,496 for Wimbledon v Luton Town, Feb. 14, 1990.

Lowest top-division crowd at a major ground since the war: 4,554 for Arsenal v Leeds Utd. (May 5, 1966) - fixture clashed with live TV coverage of Cup-Winners' Cup Final (Liverpool v Borussia Dortmund).

Smallest League Cup attendance at top-division ground: 1,987 for Wimbledon v Bolton Wand. (2nd Round, 2nd Leg) Oct. 6, 1992.

Smallest Wembley crowds for England matches: 15,628 v Chile (Rous Cup, May 23, 1989 – affected by Tube strike); 20,038 v Colombia (Friendly, Sept. 6, 1995); 21,432 v Czech. (Friendly, Apr. 25, 1990); 21,142 v Japan (Umbro Cup, June 3, 1995); 23,600 v Wales (British Championship, Feb. 23, 1983); 23,659 v Greece (Friendly, May 17, 1994); 23,951 v East Germany (Friendly, Sept. 12, 1984); 24,000 v N. Ireland (British Championship, Apr. 4, 1984); 25,756 v Colombia (Rous Cup, May 24, 1988); 25,837 v Denmark (Friendly, Sept. 14, 1988).

Smallest Int. modern crowd: 221 for Poland v N. Ireland (4-1, friendly) at Limassol, Cyprus, on February 13, 2002. Played at neutral venue at Poland's World Cup training base.

Smallest Int. modern crowds at home: N.Ireland: 2,500 v Chile (Belfast, May 26, 1989 – clashed with ITV live screening of Liverpool v Arsenal Championship decider); **Scotland:** 7,843 v N.Ireland (Hampden Park, May 6, 1969); **Wales:** 2,315 v N.Ireland (Wrexham, May 27, 1982).

Smallest attendance for post-war England match: 2,378 v San Marino (World Cup) at Bologna (Nov. 17, 1993). Tie clashed with Italy v Portugal (World Cup) shown live on Italian TV.

Smallest paid attendance for British first-class match: 29 for Clydebank v East Stirling, CIS Scottish League Cup 1st Round, July 31, 1999. Played at Morton's Cappielow Park ground, shared by Clydebank, the match clashed with the Tall Ships Race which attracted 200,000 to the area.

F.A. CUP CROWD RECORD (OUTSIDE FINAL)

The first F.A. Cup-tie shown on closed-circuit TV (5th. Round, Saturday, March 11, 1967, kick-off 7pm) drew a total of 105,000 spectators to Goodison Park and Anfield. This is the biggest attendance for a single F.A. Cup match other than the Final. At Goodison, 64,851 watched the match 'for real', while 40,149 saw the TV version on eight giant screens at Anfield. Everton beat Liverpool 1-0.

LOWEST SEMI-FINAL CROWD

The smallest F.A. Cup semi-final attendance since the war was 17,987 for Manchester Utd. v Crystal Palace replay, at Villa Park on April 12, 1995. Crystal Palace supporters largely boycotted tie after a fan died in car-park clash outside pub in Walsall before first match. Previous lowest: 25,963 for Wimbledon v Luton Town, at Tottenham on April 9, 1988.

Lowest quarter-final crowd since the war: 8,735 for Chesterfield v Wrexham on March 9, 1997.

Smallest F.A. Cup 3rd. Round attendances for matches between League clubs: 1,833 for Chester City v Bournemouth (at Macclesfield Town) Jan. 5, 1991; 1,966 for Aldershot v Oxford Utd., Jan. 10, 1987.

PRE-WEMBLEY CUP FINAL CROWDS

AT CRYSTAL PALACE

1895	42,560	1902	48,036	1908	74,967
1896	48,036	Replay	33,050	1909	67,651
1897	65,891	1903	64,000	1910	76,980
1898	62,017	1904	61,734	1911	69,098
1899	73,833	1905	101,117	1912	54,434
1900	68,945	1906	75,609	1913	120,028
1901	110,802	1907	84,584	1914	72,778

AT OLD TRAFFORD

1915 50,000

AT STAMFORD BRIDGE

1920	50,018	1921	72,805	1922	53,000

RECEIPTS RECORDS

Wembley Stadium underwent its first considerable alteration during 1962-3 in preparation for the World Cup in 1966. Higher admission fees at the 1963 F.A. Cup Final resulted in 100,000 spectators paying a record £89,000.
This is how Wembley's receipts records subsequently rose:

1968 F.A. Cup Final (Everton v W.B.A.)	£110,000
1968 European Cup Final (Manchester Utd. v Benfica)	£120,000
1976 F.A. Cup Final (Southampton v Manchester Utd.)	£420,000
1978 F.A. Cup Final (Ipswich Town v Arsenal)	£500,000
1981 England v Hungary (World Cup)	£671,000
1982 F.A. Cup Final (Tottenham v Q.P.R.)	£886,000
(plus £605,000 for replay)	
1984 F.A. Cup Final (Everton v Watford)	£919,000
*1985 F.A. Cup Final (Manchester Utd. v Everton)	£1,100,000

```
1986  F.A. Cup Final (Liverpool v Everton) .......................................... £1,100,000
†1987  League Cup Final (Arsenal v Liverpool) ...................................... £1,000,000
1987  F.A. Cup Final (Coventry City v Tottenham) ............................... £1,286,737
1988  F.A. Cup Final (Wimbledon v Liverpool) ..................................... £1,422,814
1989  F.A. Cup Final (Liverpool v Everton) .......................................... £1,600,000
1990  League Cup Final (Nott'm Forest v Oldham Athletic) ................... £1,650,000
1990  F.A. Cup Final (Manchester Utd. v Crystal Palace – first match) .. £2,000,000
1991  League Cup Final (Manchester Utd. v Sheffield Wed.) ............... £2,000,000
1991  F.A. Cup Final (Nott'm F. v Tottenham) .................................... £2,016,000
1992  F.A. Cup Final (Liverpool v Sunderland) .................................... £2,548,174
1993  F.A. Cup Final (Arsenal v Sheffield W. – first match) .................. £2,818,000
       (Replay took receipts for both matches to £4,695,200)
1994  F.A. Cup Final record (Manchester Utd. v Chelsea) ................... £2,962,167
1997  League Cup Final record (Leicester City v Middlesbrough) .......... £2,750,000
1998  League Cup Final record (Chelsea v Middlesbrough) ................... £2,983,000
•2000  F.A. Cup Final record (Chelsea v Aston Villa) ............................ £3,100,000
```

(* Britain's first £1m. gate; †First £1m. gate for League Cup Final; • British club match receipts record)

Record England match receipts: £4,100,000 (v. Germany, Wembley, European Championship semi-final, June 26, 1992 – att: 75,862)

EARLY CUP FINAL RECEIPTS

```
1885  Blackburn Rov. v Queens Park ................................................... £442
1913  Aston Villa v Sunderland ......................................................... £9,406
1923  Bolton Wand. v West Ham Utd., first Wembley Final ................. £27,776
1939  Portsmouth v Wolves .............................................................. £29,000
1946  Derby Co. v Charlton Athletic .................................................. £45,000
```

WORLD RECORD MATCH RECEIPTS

£4,300,000 for **World Cup Final**, Argentina v West Germany (Rome, July 8, 1990).

INTERNATIONAL RECORDS
MOST APPEARANCES

Peter Shilton, England goalkeeper, then aged 40, retired from International football after the 1990 World Cup Finals with the European record number of caps – 125. Previous record (119) was set by **Pat Jennings**, Northern Ireland's goalkeeper from 1964-86, who retired on his 41st birthday during the 1986 World Cup in Mexico. Shilton's England career spanned 20 seasons from his debut against East Germany at Wembley on Nov. 25, 1970.

Four players have completed a century of appearances in full International matches for England. **Billy Wright,** of Wolves, was the first, retiring in 1959 with a total of 105 caps.

Bobby Charlton, of Manchester Utd., beat Wright's record in the World Cup match against West Germany in Leon, Mexico, in June 1970 and **Bobby Moore,** of West Ham Utd., overtook Charlton's 106 caps against Italy in Turin, in June 1973. Moore played 108 times for England, a record that stood until **Shilton** reached 109 against Denmark in Copenhagen (June 7, 1989).

Kenny Dalglish became Scotland's first 100-cap International v Romania (Hampden Park, March 26, 1986).

World's most-capped player: Mohamed Al-Deayea (Saudi Arabia goalkeeper), made his 165th International appearance, v Republic of Ireland (World Cup) at Yokohama, Japan, on June 11, 2002.

Most-capped European goalkeeper: Thomas Ravelli, 143 Internationals for Sweden (1981-97).

Gillian Coultard, (Doncaster Belles), England Women's captain, received a special presentation from Geoff Hurst to mark 100 caps when England beat Holland 1-0 at

Upton Park on October 30, 1997. She made her Int. debut at 18 in May 1981, and retired at the end of season 1999-2000 with a record 119 caps (30 goals).

BRITAIN'S MOST-CAPPED PLAYERS

(As at start of season 2002-03)

England

Peter Shilton	125
Bobby Moore	108
Bobby Charlton	106
Billy Wright	105

Scotland

Kenny Dalglish	102
Jim Leighton	91
Alex McLeish	77
Paul McStay	76
Tommy Boyd	71

Wales

Neville Southall	92
Dean Saunders	75
Peter Nicholas	73
Ian Rush	73
Mark Hughes	72
Joey Jones	72

Northern Ireland

Pat Jennings	119
Mal Donaghy	91
Sammy McIlroy	88

Republic of Ireland

Steve Staunton	102
Niall Quinn	91
Tony Cascarino	88
Paul McGrath	83
Pat Bonner	80
Ray Houghton	73
Liam Brady	72
Frank Stapleton	71
Andy Townsend	70

MOST ENGLAND CAPS IN ROW

Most consecutive International appearances: 70 by **Billy Wright**, for England from October 1951 to May 1959. He played 105 of England's first 108 post-war matches. **England captains most times: Billy Wright** and **Bobby Moore**, 90 each.

MOST PLAYERS FROM ONE CLUB IN ENGLAND SIDES

Arsenal supplied seven men (a record) to the England team v Italy at Highbury on November 14, 1934. They were: Frank Moss, George Male, Eddie Hapgood, Wilf Copping, Ray Bowden, Ted Drake and Cliff Bastin. In addition, Arsenal's Tom Whittaker was England's trainer.

Since then until 2002, the most players from one club in an England team was six from **Liverpool** against Switzerland at Wembley in September 1977. The side also included a Liverpool old boy, Kevin Keegan (Hamburg).

Seven **Arsenal** men took part in the England – France (0-2) match at Wembley on February 10, 1999. Goalkeeper David Seaman and defenders Lee Dixon, Tony Adams and Martin Keown lined up for England. Nicolas Anelka (2 goals) and Emmanuel Petit started the match for France and Patrick Vieira replaced Anelka.

Manchester Utd. equalled Arsenal's 1934 record by providing England with seven players in the World Cup qualifier away to Albania on March 28, 2001. Five started the match — David Beckham (captain), Gary Neville, Paul Scholes, Nicky Butt and Andy Cole — and two went on as substitutes: Wes Brown and Teddy Sheringham.

INTERNATIONAL SUBS RECORDS

Malta substituted all 11 players in their 1-2 home defeat against England on June 3, 2000. Six substitutes by England took the total replacements in the match to 17, then an International record.

Most substitutions in match by **England**: 11 in second half by Sven Goran Eriksson against Holland at Tottenham on August 15, 2001; 11 against Italy at Leeds on March 27, 2002; Italy sent on 8 players from the bench — the total of 19 substitutions was a record for an England match.

The **Republic of Ireland** sent on 12 second-half substitutes, using 23 players in all, when they beat Russia 2-0 in a friendly International in Dublin on February 13, 2002.

ENGLAND'S WORLD CUP-WINNERS

At Wembley, July 30, 1966, 4-2 v West Germany (2-2 after 90 mins), scorers Hurst 3, Peters. Team: Banks; Cohen, Wilson, Stiles, Charlton (J.), Moore (Captain), Ball, Hurst, Charlton (R.), Hunt, Peters. Manager **Alf Ramsey** fielded that same eleven in six successive matches (an England record): the World Cup quarter-final, semi-final and Final, and the first three games of the following season. England wore red shirts in the Final and Her Majesty the Queen presented the Cup to Bobby Moore. The players each received a £1,000 bonus, plus £60 World Cup Final appearance money, all less tax, and Ramsey a £6,000 bonus from the F.A. The match was shown live on TV (in black and white).

BRAZIL'S RECORD RUN

Brazil hold the record for the longest unbeaten sequence in International football: 45 matches from 1993-7. The previous record of 31 matches undefeated was held by Hungary between June 1950 and July 1954.

ENGLAND UNDER COVER

England played indoors for the first time when they beat Argentina 1-0 in the World Cup at the Sapporo Dome, Japan, on June 7, 2002.

ALL-SEATED INTERNATIONALS

The first **all-seated crowd** (30,000) for a full International in Britain saw **Wales** and **West Germany** draw 0-0 at Cardiff City Arms Park on May 31, 1989. The terraces were closed.

England's first all-seated International at Wembley was against Yugoslavia (2-1) on December 13, 1989 (attendance 34,796). The terracing behind the goals was closed for conversion to seating.

The first **full-house all-seated** International at Wembley was for England v Brazil (1-0) on March 28, 1990, when a capacity 80,000 crowd paid record British receipts of £1,200,000.

Cardiff's new **Millennium Stadium** set attendance records for **Wales** in consecutive friendly Internationals: 66,500 v Finland, March 28, 2000, then 72,500 v Brazil, May 23, 2000 — Britain's first indoor International.

FIRST BLACK CAPS

First black player for **England** in a senior International was Nott'm. Forest full-back **Viv Anderson** against Czechoslovakia at Wembley on November 29, 1978.

Aston Villa's **Ugo Ehiogu** was **England's** first black captain (U-21 v Holland at Portsmouth, April 27, 1993).

Paul Ince (Manchester Utd.) became the first black player to captain **England** in a **full International** (v U.S.A., Boston, June 9, 1993).

First black British International was **Eddie Parris** (Bradford Park Avenue) for Wales against N. Ireland in Belfast on December 5, 1931.

PLAYED FOR MORE THAN ONE COUNTRY

Multi-nationals in senior International football include: **Johnny Carey** (1938-53) – caps Rep. of Ireland 29, N. Ireland 7; **Ferenc Puskas** (1945-62) – caps Hungary 84, Spain 4; **Alfredo di Stefano** (1950-6) – caps Argentina 7, Spain 31; **Ladislav Kubala** (1948-58) – caps, Hungary 3, Czechoslovakia 11, Spain 19, only player to win full Int. honours with 3 countries. Kubala also played in a fourth Int. team, scoring twice for FIFA v England at Wembley in 1953.

Eleven players, including Carey, appeared for both N. Ireland and the Republic of Ireland in seasons directly after the last war.

Cecil Moore, capped by N. Ireland in 1949 when with Glentoran, played for USA v England in 1953.

Hawley Edwards played for England v Scotland in 1874 and for Wales v Scotland in 1876.

Jack Reynolds (Distillery and W.B.A.) played for both Ireland (5 times) and England (8) in the 1890s.

Bobby Evans (Sheffield Utd.) had played 10 times for Wales when capped for England, in 1910-11. He was born in Chester of Welsh parents.

In recent years several players have represented USSR and one or other of the breakaway republics. The same applies to Yugoslavia and its component states. **Josip Weber** played for Croatia in 1992 and made a 5-goal debut for Belgium in 1994.

3-GENERATION INTERNATIONAL FAMILY

When Bournemouth striker **Warren Feeney** was capped away to Liechtenstein on March 27, 2002, he became the third generation of his family to play for N. Ireland. He followed in the footsteps of his grandfather James (capped twice in 1950) and father Warren Snr. (1 in 1976).

FATHERS & SONS CAPPED BY ENGLAND

George Eastham senior (pre-war) and **George Eastham** junior; **Brian Clough** and **Nigel Clough**; **Frank Lampard** senior and **Frank Lampard** junior.

FATHER & SON SAME-DAY CAPS

Iceland made father-and-son Int. history when they beat Estonia 3-0 in Tallin on April 24, 1996. Arnor Gudjohnsen (35) started the match and was replaced (62 mins.) by his 17-year-old son Eidur.

SUCCESSIVE ENGLAND HAT-TRICKS

The last player to score a hat-trick in consecutive England matches was **Dixie Dean** on the summer tour in May 1927, against Belgium (9-1) and Luxembourg (5-2).

POSTWAR HAT-TRICKS v ENGLAND

November 25, 1953, scorer **Nandor Hidegkuti** (England 3, Hungary 6, Wembley); May 11, 1958, scorer **Aleksandar Petakovic** (Yugoslavia 5, England 0, Belgrade); May 17, 1959, scorer **Juan Seminario** (Peru 4, England 1, Lima); June 15, 1988, scorer **Marco Van Basten** (Holland 3, England 1, European Championship, Dusseldorf).

NO-SAVE GOALKEEPERS

Chris Woods did not have one save to make when England beat San Marino 6-0 (World Cup) at Wembley on February 17, 1993. He touched the ball only six times throughout the match.

Gordon Banks had a similar no-save experience when England beat Malta 5-0 (European Championship) at Wembley on May 12, 1971. Malta did not force a goal-kick or corner, and the four times Banks touched the ball were all from back passes.

FIFA PIONEERS

FIFA, now with a membership of 203 countries, was founded in Paris on May 21, 1904 by seven nations: Belgium, Denmark, France, Holland, Spain, Sweden and Switzerland.

UEFA FULL HOUSE

For the first time, clubs from all 51 member countries of **UEFA** competed in the Champions League or UEFA Cup in season 2000-1.

FIFA WORLD YOUTH CHAMPIONSHIP (UNDER-20)

Finals: 1977 (Tunis) Soviet Union 2, Mexico 2 (Soviet won 9-8 on pens.); **1979** (Tokyo) Argentina 3, Soviet Union 1; **1981** (Sydney) W. Germany 4, Qatar 0; **1983** (Mexico City) Brazil 1, Argentina 0; **1985** (Moscow) Brazil 1, Spain 0; **1987** (Santiago) Yugoslavia 1, W. Germany 1 (Yugoslavia won 5-4 on pens.); **1989** (Riyadh) Portugal 2, Nigeria 0; **1991** (Lisbon) Portugal 0, Brazil 0 (Portugal won 4-2 on pens.); **1993** (Sydney) Brazil 2, Ghana 1; **1995** (Qatar) Argentina 2, Brazil 0; **1997** (Kuala Lumpur) Argentina 2, Uruguay 1; **1999** (Lagos) Spain 4, Japan 0; **2001** (Buenos Aires) Argentina 3, Ghana 0; **2002**.

FAMOUS CLUB FEATS

The Double: There have been ten instances of a club winning the Football League/ Premiership title and the F.A. Cup in the same season. **Manchester Utd.** and **Arsenal** have each done so three times:-

Preston N.E. 1888-89; **Aston Villa** 1896-97; **Tottenham** 1960-61; **Arsenal** 1970-71, 1997-98, 2001-02; **Liverpool** 1985-86; **Manchester Utd.** 1993-94, 1995-96, 1998-99.

The Treble: Liverpool were the first English club to win three major competitions in one season when in 1983-84, Joe Fagan's first season as manager, they were League Champions, League Cup winners and European Cup winners.

Alex Ferguson's **Manchester Utd.** achieved an even more prestigious treble in 1998-99, completing the domestic double of Premiership and F.A. Cup and then winning the European Cup.

Liverpool completed a unique treble by an English club with three cup successes under Gerard Houllier in season 2000-01: the League Cup, F.A. Cup and UEFA Cup.

Liverpool the first English club to win five major trophies in one calendar year (February-August 2001): Worthington Cup, F.A. Cup, UEFA Cup, Charity Shield, UEFA Super Cup.

As Champions in season 2001-02, **Arsenal** set a Premiership record by winning the last 13 matches. They were the first top-division club since Preston N.E. in the League's inaugural season (1888-9) to maintain an unbeaten away record.

(See Scottish section for treble feats by Rangers and Celtic.)

Home Runs: Sunderland lost only one Div. 1 game out of 73 in five seasons, 1891 to 1896. **Brentford** won all 21 home games in 1929-30 in the Third Division (South). Others have won all home games in a smaller programme.

Record Home Run: Liverpool went 85 competitive first-team games unbeaten at home between losing 2-3 to Birmingham City on January 21, 1978 and 1-2 to Leicester City on January 31, 1981. They comprised 63 in the League, 9 League Cup, 7 in European competition and 6 F.A. Cup. Leicester were relegated that season.

Millwall were unbeaten at home in the League for 59 consecutive matches from 1964-67.

Third to First: Charlton Athletic, in 1936, became the first club to advance from the Third to First Division in successive seasons. **Queen's Park Rangers** were the second club to achieve the feat in 1968, and **Oxford Utd.** did it in 1984 and 1985 as Champions of each division. Subsequently, **Derby Co.** (1987), **Middlesbrough** (1988), **Sheffield Utd.** (1990) and **Notts Co.** (1991) climbed from Third Division to First in consecutive seasons.

Watford won successive promotions from the modern Second Division to the Premier League in 1997-8, 1998-9. **Manchester City** equalled the feat in 1998-9, 1999-2000.

Fourth to First: Northampton Town, in 1965 became the first club to rise from the Fourth to the First Division. **Swansea City** climbed from the Fourth Division to the First (three promotions in four seasons), 1977-8 to 1980-1. **Wimbledon** repeated the feat, 1982-3 to 1985-6 **Watford** did it in five seasons, 1977-8 to 1981-2. **Carlisle Utd.** climbed from Fourth Division to First, 1964-74.

Non-League to First: When **Wimbledon** finished third in the Second Division in 1986, they completed the phenomenal rise from non-League football (Southern League) to the First Division in nine years. Two years later they won the F.A. Cup.

Tottenham, in 1960-1, not only carried off the First Division Championship and the F.A. Cup for the first time this century but set up other records by opening with 11 successive wins, registering most First Division wins (31), most away wins in the League's history (16), and equalling Arsenal's First Division records of 66 points and 33 away points. They already held the Second Division record of 70 points (1919-20).

Arsenal, in 1993, became the first club to win both English domestic cup competitions (F.A. Cup and League Cup) in the same season. **Liverpool** repeated the feat in 2000-01.

Preston N.E., in season 1888-9, won the first League Championship without losing a match and the F.A. Cup without having a goal scored against them. Only other English club to remain unbeaten through a League season were **Liverpool** (Div. 2 Champions in 1893-4).

Bury, in 1903, also won the F.A. Cup without conceding a goal.

Everton won Div. 2, Div. 1 and the F.A. Cup in successive seasons, 1930-1, 1931-2, 1932-3.

Liverpool won the League Championship in 1964, the F.A. Cup in 1965 and the Championship again in 1966. In 1978 they became the first British club to win the European Cup in successive seasons. **Nott'm. Forest** repeated the feat in 1979 and 1980.

Liverpool won the League Championship six times in eight seasons (1976-83) under **Bob Paisley's** management.

Sir Alex Ferguson's **Manchester Utd.** have won the F.A. Premier League in seven of its first nine seasons (1993-2001). They were runners-up on the other two occasions, each time within a point of the Champions.

Most Premiership wins in season: 28 by Manchester Utd. (1999-2000).

Biggest points-winning margin by League Champions: 18 by Manchester Utd. (1999-2000).

COVENTRY UNIQUE

Coventry City are the only club to have played in the Premier League, all four previous divisions of the Football League and in both sections (North and South) of the old Third Division.

Grimsby Town were the other club to play in the four divisions of the Football League and its two Third Division sections.

FAMOUS UPS & DOWNS

Sunderland: Relegated in 1958 after maintaining First Division status since their election to the Football League in 1890. They dropped into Division 3 for the first time in 1987.

Aston Villa: Relegated with **Preston N.E.** to the Third Division in 1970.

Arsenal up: When the League was extended in 1919, Woolwich Arsenal (sixth in Division Two in 1914-15, last season before the war) were elected to Division One. Arsenal have been in the top division ever since.

Tottenham down: At that same meeting in 1919 Chelsea (due for relegation) retained their place in Division One but the bottom club (Tottenham) had to go down to Division Two.

Preston N.E. and Burnley down: Preston N.E., the first League Champions in season 1888-9, dropped into the Fourth Division in 1985. So did Burnley, also among the League's original members in 1888. In 1986, Preston N.E. had to apply for re-election.

Wolves' fall: Wolves, another of the Football League's original members, completed the fall from First Division to Fourth in successive seasons (1984-5-6).

Lincoln City out: Lincoln City became the first club to suffer automatic demotion from the Football League when they finished bottom of Div. 4, on goal difference, in season 1986-7. They were replaced by Scarborough, champions of the GM Vauxhall Conference. Lincoln City regained their place a year later.

Swindon Town up and down: In the 1990 play-offs, Swindon Town won promotion to the First Division for the first time, but remained in the Second Division because of financial irregularities.

MOST CHAMPIONSHIP WINS

Liverpool, by winning the First Division in 1976-7, established a record of 10 Championship victories. They later increased the total to 18. **Manchester Utd.** are second with 14 League titles (7 Football League, 7 Premier League).

LONGEST CURRENT MEMBERS OF TOP DIVISION

Arsenal (since 1919), **Everton** (1954), **Liverpool** (1962), **Manchester Utd.** (1975), **Southampton** (1978).

CHAMPIONS: FEWEST PLAYERS

Liverpool used only 14 players (five ever-present) when they won the League Championship in season 1965-6. **Aston Villa** also called on no more than 14 players to win the title in 1980-81, with seven ever-present.

CHAMPIONS WITH FEWEST DEFEATS

Arsenal (season 1990-01, 38 matches) are the only League Champions to lose only once since **Preston N.E.** were undefeated as the first title winners in 1888-9 (22 matches).

LEAGUE HAT-TRICKS

Huddersfield Town created a record in 1925-6 by winning the League Championship for the third year in succession.

Arsenal equalled this League hat-trick in 1933-4-5, **Liverpool** in 1982-3-4 and **Manchester United** in 1999-2000-01.

'SUPER DOUBLE' WINNERS

Since the war, there have been three instances of players appearing in and then managing F.A. Cup and Championship-winning teams:

Joe Mercer: Player in Arsenal Championship teams 1948, 1953 and in their 1950 F.A. Cup side; manager of Manchester City when they won Championship 1968, F.A. Cup 1969.

Kenny Dalglish: Player in Liverpool Championship-winning teams 1979, 1980, 1982, 1983, 1984, player-manager 1986, 1988, 1990; player-manager when Liverpool won F.A. Cup (to complete Double) 1986; manager of Blackburn Rov., Champions 1995.

George Graham: Played in Arsenal's Double-winning team in 1971, and as manager took them to Championship success in 1989 and 1991 and the F.A. Cup – League Cup double in 1993.

BACK FIRST TIME

The following clubs won promotion the season after losing their position in the First Division of the League (*as Champions):

Sheffield Wed. *1899-1900, *1951-2, *1955-6, *1958-9, 1990-1; **Bolton Wand.** 1899-1900, *1908-9, 1910-11; **W.B.A.** *1901-2; **Manchester City** *1902-3, *1909-10, 1950-1; **Burnley** *1897-8.

Small Heath 1902-3; **Liverpool** *1904-5; **Nott'm. Forest** *1906-7; **Preston N.E.** *1912-13, 1914-15; **Notts Co.** *1913-14; **Derby Co.** *1914-15.

Tottenham *1919-20, 1977-8; **Leeds Utd.** 1927-8, 1931-2; **Middlesbrough** *1928-9; **Everton** *1930-1; **Manchester Utd.** 1937-8, *1974-5; **Huddersfield Town** 1952-3.

Aston Villa *1959-60, 1987-8; **Chelsea** 1962-3; *1988-9; **Norwich City** 1974-5, 1981-2, *1985-6; **Wolves** 1976-7, 1982-3; **Birmingham City** 1979-80, 1984-5.

West Ham Utd., relegated in 1992, won promotion to the **Premier League** in 1993; *Crystal Palace and **Nott'm. Forest** both returned to the **Premiership** in 1994, a year after relegation; so did **Leicester City** in 1996, *Bolton Wand. in 1997, *Nott'm Forest and **Middlesbrough** in 1998, *Charlton Athletic in 2000 and *Manchester City in 2002.

ORIGINAL TWELVE

The original 12 members of the Football League (formed in 1888) were: **Accrington, Aston Villa, Blackburn Rov., Bolton Wand., Burnley, Derby Co., Everton, Notts Co., Preston N.E., Stoke City, W.B.A. and Wolves.**

Results on the opening day (September 8, 1888): Bolton Wand. 3, Derby Co. 6; Everton 2, Accrington 1; Preston N.E. 5, Burnley 2; Stoke City 0, W.B.A. 2; Wolves 1, Aston Villa 1. Preston N.E. had the biggest first-day crowd: 6,000. Blackburn Rov. and Notts Co. did not play that day. They kicked off a week later (September 15) – Blackburn Rov. 5, Accrington 5; Everton 2, Notts Co. 1.

FASTEST CLIMBS

Three promotions in four seasons by two clubs – **Swansea City:** 1978 third in Div.4; 1979 third in Div.3; 1981 third in Div.2; **Wimbledon:** 1983 Champions of Div.4; 1984 second in Div.3; 1986 third in Div.2.

MERSEYSIDE RECORD

Liverpool is the only city to have staged top-division football – through Everton and/or Liverpool – in **every season** since League football began in 1888.

EARLIEST RELEGATONS POST-WAR

From top division: **Q.P.R.** went down from the old First Division on March 29, 1969. From modern First Division: **Stockport Co.** on March 16, 2002, with 7 matches still to play.

LEAGUE RECORDS

MOST POINTS IN A SEASON

The following records applied before the introduction of three points for a win in the Football League in 1981-2.

Lincoln City set a **Football League** record in season 1975-6 with 74 points from 46 games (including 32 victories) in **Division 4.**

First Division: Liverpool (1978-9), 68 points from 42 matches.
Second Division: Tottenham (1919-20), 70 points from 42 matches.
Third Division: Aston Villa (1971-2) 70 points from 46 games.

Since 3 points for win (pre-Premier League):
First Division: Everton (1984-5) and Liverpool (1987-8) 90 points: **Second Division:** Chelsea (1988-9) 99 points; **Third Division:** Bournemouth (1986-7) 97 points; **Fourth Division:** Swindon Town (1985-6) 102 points.

Since change of League format:

Premier League: Manchester Utd. (1993-4) 92 points; **First Division**: Sunderland (1998-9) 105 points (record for any division); **Second Division**: Fulham (1998-9) 101 points; **Third Division**: Plymouth Arggle (2001-02) 102 points.
Fewest Points: Doncaster Rov. 8 points (of possible 68) in Second Division, 1904-5. Stirling Albion 6 points (of possible 60) in Scottish League Division A, 1954-5.

DOUBLE CHAMPIONS

Nine men have played in and managed League Championship-winning teams:
Ted Drake Player – Arsenal 1934, 1935, 1938. Manager – Chelsea 1955.
Bill Nicholson Player – Tottenham 1951. Manager – Tottenham 1961.
Alf Ramsey Player – Tottenham 1951. Manager – Ipswich Town 1962.
Joe Mercer Player – Everton 1939, Arsenal 1948, 1953. Manager – Manchester City 1968.
Dave Mackay Player – Tottenham 1961. Manager – Derby Co. 1975.
Bob Paisley Player – Liverpool 1947. Manager – Liverpool 1976, 1977, 1979, 1980, 1982, 1983.
Howard Kendall Player – Everton 1970. Manager – Everton 1985, 1987.
Kenny Dalglish Player – Liverpool 1979, 1980, 1982, 1983, 1984. Player-manager – Liverpool 1986, 1988, 1990. Manager – Blackburn Rov. 1995.
George Graham Player – Arsenal 1971. Manager – Arsenal 1989, 1991.

MOST LEAGUE CHAMPIONSHIP MEDALS

Kenny Dalglish: 9 – 8 for Liverpool (5 as player, 1979-80-82-83-84; 3 as player-manager, 1986-88-90); 1 for Blackburn Rov. (as manager, 1995). As a player he also won 4 Scottish Championship medals with Celtic (1972-73-74-77). **Phil Neal**: 8 for Liverpool (1976-77-79-80-82-83-84-86); **Alan Hansen**: 8 for Liverpool (1979-80-82-83-84-86-88-90).

CANTONA'S FOUR-TIMER

Eric Cantona played in four successive Championship-winning teams: Marseille 1990-1, Leeds Utd. 1991-2, Manchester Utd. 1992-3 and 1993-4.

ARRIVALS AND DEPARTURES

The following are the Football League arrivals and departures since 1923:

Year	In	Out
1923	Doncaster Rov.	Stalybridge Celtic
	New Brighton	
1927	Torquay Athletic	Aberdare Athletic
1928	Carlisle Utd.	Durham City
1929	York City	Ashington
1930	Thames	Merthyr Tydfil
1931	Mansfield Town	Newport County
	Chester City	Nelson
1932	Aldershot	Thames
	Newport County	Wigan Borough
1938	Ipswich Town	Gillingham
1950	Colchester Utd.	
	Gillingham	
	Scunthorpe Utd.	
	Shrewsbury Town	
1951	Workington	New Brighton
1960	Peterborough Utd.	Gateshead
1962	Oxford Utd.	Accrington Stanley (resigned)
1970	Cambridge Utd.	Bradford P.A.
1972	Hereford Utd.	Barrow
1977	Wimbledon	Workington
1978	Wigan Athletic	Southport
1987	Scarborough	Lincoln City

1988	Lincoln City	Newport County
1989	Maidstone Utd.	Darlington
1990	Darlington	Colchester Utd.
1991	Barnet	
1992	Colchester Utd.	Aldershot, Maidstone (resigned)
1993	Wycombe Wand.	Halifax Town
1997	Macclesfield Town	Hereford Utd.
1998	Halifax Town	Doncaster Rov.
1999	Cheltenham Town	Scarborough
2000	Kidderminster Harriers	Chester City
2001	Rushden & Diamonds	Barnet
2002	Boston Utd.	Halifax Town

Leeds City were expelled from Div. 2 in October, 1919; Port Vale took over their fixtures.

EXTENSIONS TO FOOTBALL LEAGUE

Clubs	Season	Clubs	Season
12 to 14	1891-2	44 to 66+	1920-1
14 to 28*	1892-3	66 to 86†	1921-2
28 to 31	1893-4	86 to 88	1923-4
31 to 32	1894-5	88 to 92	1950-1
32 to 36	1898-9	92 to 93	1991-2
36 to 40	1905-6	(Reverted to 92 when Aldershot closed,
40 to 44	1919-20	March 1992)

* Second Division formed. + Third Division (South) formed from Southern League clubs.
† Third Division (North) formed.
Football League reduced to 70 clubs and three divisions on the formation of the F.A.
Premier League in 1992; increased to 72 season 1994-5, when Premier League
reduced to 20 clubs.

RECORD RUNS

Nott'm. Forest hold the record unbeaten sequence in the English League – 42 matches
spanning the last 26 of season 1977-8 and the first 16 of 1978-9. The run began on
19, November 1977 and ended on December 9, 1978 when Forest lost 0-2 at
Liverpool. Their sequence comprised 21 wins and 21 draws.

Best debuts: Ipswich Town won the First Division at their first attempt in 1961-2.
Peterborough Utd. in their first season in the Football League (1960-1) not only won the
Fourth Division but set the all-time scoring record for the League of 134 goals. **Hereford
Utd.** were promoted from the Fourth Division in their first League season, 1972-3.
Wycombe Wand. were promoted from the Third Division (via the play-offs) in their first
League season, 1993-4.

Record winning sequence in a season: 14 consecutive League victories (all in Second
Division): **Manchester Utd.** 1904-5, **Bristol City** 1905-6 and **Preston N.E.** 1950-1.

Best winning start to League season: 13 successive victories in Div. 3 by **Reading**,
season 1985-6.

Best starts in 'old' First Division: 11 consecutive victories by **Tottenham** in 1960-1; 10
by **Manchester Utd.** in 1985-6. **Newcastle Utd.** won their first 11 matches in the **'new'
First Division** in 1992-3.

Longest unbeaten sequence (all competitions): 40 by **Nott'm. Forest**, March-December
1978. It comprised 21 wins, 19 draws (in 29 League matches, 6 League Cup, 4
European Cup, 1 Charity Shield).

Longest unbeaten start to League season: 29 matches – **Leeds Utd.,** Div 1 1973-4 (19
wins, 10 draws, goals 51-16); **Liverpool**, Div. 1 1987-8 (22 wins, 7 draws, goals
67-13).

Most consecutive League matches unbeaten in a season: 30 **Burnley** (21 wins, 9 draws,
goals 68-17), September 6, 1920 – March 25, 1921, Div. 1.

Longest winning sequence in Div. 1: 13 matches by **Tottenham** – last two of season
1959-60, first 11 of 1960-1.

Longest winning one-season sequences in Championship: 13 matches by **Preston N.E.** in 1891-2 (September 12–January 2); 13 by **Sunderland**, also in 1891-2 (November 14–April 2).

Premier League – best starts to season: 12 games unbeaten – **Nott'm. Forest** in 1995-6, **Arsenal** in 1997-8, **Aston Villa** in 1998-9.

Premier League – most consecutive wins: 13 by **Arsenal**, February-May, 2002.

Premier League's record unbeaten runs: 29 matches (20W, D9) by Manchester Utd. (Dec. 1998-Oct. 1999), ending with 5-0 defeat at Chelsea. In one season, 25 matches (15W, 10D) by Nott'm. Forest (Feb.-Nov. 1995). It ended with a 7-0 defeat at Blackburn.

Record home-win sequences: Bradford Park Avenue won 25 successive home games in Div. 3 North – the last 18 in 1926-7 and the first 7 the following season. Longest run of home wins in the top division is 21 by **Liverpool** – the last 9 of 1971-2 and the first 12 of 1972-3.

WORST SEQUENCES

Cambridge Utd. experienced the longest run without a win in Football League history in season 1983-4: 31 matches (21 lost, 10 drawn) between October 8 and April 23. They finished bottom of the Second Division.

Previous worst no-win League sequence was 30 by **Crewe Alexandra** (Div. 3 North) in season 1956-7.

Worst losing start to a League season: 12 consecutive defeats by **Manchester Utd.** (Div. 1) in 1930-1.

Worst Premier League start: Swindon Town 15 matches without win (6 draws, 9 defeats), 1993-4.

Worst Premier League sequence: Nott'm. Forest 19 matches without win (7 draws, 12 defeats), 1998-9.

Premier League – most consecutive defeats: 8 by **Ipswich Town** in 1994-5, **Manchester City** in 1995-6, **Crystal Palace** in 1997-8, **Charlton** in 1998-9, **Leicester City** in 2000-01.

Longest non-winning start to League season: 25 matches (4 draws, 21 defeats) by **Newport County**, Div. 4 (Aug. 15, 1970 – Jan. 9, 1971). Worst no-win League starts since then: 16 matches by **Burnley** (9 draws, 7 defeats in Div. 2, 1979-80); 16 by **Hull City** (10 draws, 6 defeats in Div. 2, 1989-90); 16 by **Sheffield Utd.** (4 draws, 12 defeats in Div. 1, 1990-91).

Most consecutive League defeats: 18 by **Darwen** (Div. 1) 1898-9. **In modern times**: 15 by **Walsall** (Div. 2, 1988-9), longest such sequence since last War.

Most League defeats in season: 34 by **Doncaster Rov.** (Div. 3) 1997-8.

Fewest League wins in season: 1 by **Loughborough Town** (Div. 2, season 1899-1900). They lost 27, drew 6, goals 18-100 and dropped out of the League. (See also Scottish section.)

Fewest home Leagues wins in season: 1 by **Loughborough Town** (Div. 2, 1899-1900), **Notts Co.** (Div. 1, 1904-5), **Woolwich Arsenal** (Div. 1, 1912-13), **Blackpool** (Div. 1, 1966-7), **Rochdale** (Div. 3, 1973-4).

Most home League defeats in season: 18 by **Cambridge Utd.** (Div. 3, 1984-5).

Away League defeats record: 24 in row by **Nelson** (Div. 3 North) – 3 in April 1930 followed by all 21 in season 1930-31. They then dropped out of the League.

Biggest defeat in Champions' season: During **Newcastle Utd.'s** Championship-winning season in 1908-9, they were beaten 9-1 at home by Sunderland on December 5.

WORST START BY EVENTUAL CHAMPIONS

Sunderland took only 2 points from their first 7 matches in season 1912-13 (2 draws, 5 defeats). They won 25 of the remaining 31 games to clinch their fifth League title.

UNBEATEN LEAGUE SEASON

Only two clubs have completed an English League season unbeaten: **Preston N.E.** (22 matches in 1888-9, the League's first season) and **Liverpool** (28 matches in Div. 2, 1893-4).

100 PER CENT HOME RECORDS

Five clubs have won every home League match in a season, four of them in the old Second Division: **Liverpool** (14) in 1893-4, **Bury** (15) in 1894-5, **Sheffield Wed.** (17) in 1899-1900 and **Birmingham City** (17) in 1902-3. The last club to do it, **Brentford**, won all 21 home games in Div. 3 South in 1929-30.

Rotherham Utd. just failed to equal that record in 1946-7. They won their first 20 home matches in Div. 3 North, then drew the last 3-3 v Rochdale.

WORST HOME RUNS

Most consecutive home League defeats: 8 by **Rochdale,** who took only 11 points in Div. 3 North in season 1931-2; 8 by **Stockport Co.** in season 2001-02.

Between November 1958 and October 1959 **Portsmouth** drew 2 and lost 14 out of 16 consecutive home games.

MOST AWAY WINS IN SEASON

Doncaster Rov. won 18 of their 21 away League fixtures when winning the Div. 3 North Championship in 1946-7.

AWAY WINS RECORD

Most **consecutive away League wins: 10 by Tottenham** (Div. 1) – 8 at start of 1960-1, after ending previous season with 2 away victories.

100 PER CENT HOME WINS ON ONE DAY

Div. 1 – All 11 home teams won on Feb. 13, 1926 and on Dec. 10, 1955. **Div. 2** – All 12 home teams won on Nov. 26, 1988. **Div. 3**, all 12 home teams won in the week-end programme of Oct. 18-19, 1968.

NO HOME WINS IN DIV. ON ONE DAY

Div. 1 – 8 away wins, 3 draws in 11 matches on Sept. 6, 1986. **Div. 2** – 7 away wins, 4 draws in 11 matches on Dec. 26, 1987. **Premier League** – 6 away wins, 5 draws in 11 matches on Dec. 26, 1994.

The week-end **Premiership** programme on Dec. 7-8-9, 1996 produced no home win in the ten games (4 aways, 6 draws). There was again no home victory (3 away wins, 7 draws) in the week-end **Premiership** fixtures on September 23-24, 2000.

MOST DRAWS IN A SEASON (FOOTBALL LEAGUE)

23 by **Norwich City** (Div. 1, 1978-9), **Exeter City** (Div. 4, 1986-7). **Cardiff City** and **Hartlepool Utd.** (both Div. 3, 1997-8). Norwich City played 42 matches, the others 46.

MOST DRAWS IN ONE DIV. ON ONE DAY

On September 18, 1948 **nine** out of 11 First Division matches were drawn.

MOST DRAWS IN PREMIER DIV. PROGRAMME

Over the week-ends of December 2-3-4, 1995, and September 23-24, 2000, seven out of the ten matches finished level.

HIGHEST-SCORING DRAWS IN LEAGUE

Leicester City 6, Arsenal 6 (Div. 1 April 21, 1930) and **Charlton Athletic 6, Middlesbrough 6** (Div 2. October 22, 1960)

Latest 6-6 draw in first-class football was between Tranmere Rov. and Newcastle Utd. in the Zenith Data Systems Cup 1st. Round on October 1, 1991. The score went from 3-3 at 90 minutes to 6-6 after extra time, and Tranmere Rov. won 3-2 on penalties.

Most recent 5-5 draws in top division: Southampton v Coventry City (Div. 1, May 4, 1982); Q.P.R. v Newcastle Utd. (Div. 1, Sept. 22, 1984).

DRAWS RECORDS

Most consecutive drawn matches in Football League: 8 by **Torquay Utd.** (Div. 3), Oct. 25 – Dec. 13, 1969.

Longest sequence of draws by the same score: six 1-1 results by **Q.P.R.** in season 1957-8.

Tranmere Rov. became the first club to play **five consecutive 0-0 League draws**, in season 1997-8.

IDENTICAL RECORDS

There is only **one instance** of two clubs in one division finishing a season with identical records. In 1907-8, **Blackburn Rov.** and **Woolwich Arsenal** were bracketed equal 14th. in the First Division with these figures: P38, W12, D12, L14, Goals 51-63, Pts. 36.

The total of **1195 goals** scored in the Premier League in season 1993-4 was **repeated** in 1994-5.

CHAMPIONS OF ALL DIVISIONS

Wolves and **Burnley** are the only clubs to have won the Championships of the old **Divisions 1, 2, 3 and 4**. Wolves were also **Champions** of the **Third Division North**.

UPS & DOWNS RECORD

Northampton Town went from **Fourth Division** to **First** and back again in nine seasons (1961-9). **Carlisle Utd.** did the same from 1974-87.

NIGHTMARE STARTS

Most goals conceded by a goalkeeper on League debut: 13 by **Steve Milton** when Halifax Town lost 13-0 at Stockport Co. (Div. 3 North) on January 6, 1934.

Post-war: 11 by Crewe Alexandra's new goalkeeper **Dennis Murray** (Div. 3 North) on September 29, 1951, when Lincoln City won 11-1.

RELEGATION ODD SPOTS

In season 1937-8, **Manchester City** were the highest-scoring team in the First Division with 80 goals (3 more than Champions Arsenal), but they finished in 21st place and were relegated – a year after winning the Championship. They scored more goals than they conceded (77).

Twelve years earlier, in 1925-6, City went down to Division 2 despite totalling 89 goals – still the most scored in any division by a relegated team. Manchester City also scored 31 F.A. Cup goals that season, but lost the Final 1-0 to Bolton Wanderers.

Cardiff City were relegated from Div. 1 in season 1928-9, despite conceding fewest goals in the division (59). They also scored fewest (43).

RELEGATION TREBLES

Two Football League clubs have been relegated three seasons in succession. **Bristol City** fell from First Division to Fourth in 1980-1-2, and **Wolves** did the same in 1984-5-6.

OLDEST CLUBS

Oldest Association Football Club is **Sheffield F.C.** (formed in 1857). The original minute book is still in existence.

The oldest Football League clubs are **Notts Co.**, 1862; **Nott'm. Forest**, 1865; and **Sheffield Wed.**, 1866.

FOUR DIVISIONS

In **May, 1957**, the Football League decided to re-group the two sections of the Third Division into Third and Fourth Divisions in **season 1958-9**.

The Football League was reduced to three divisions on the formation of the F.A. Premier League in **1992**.

THREE UP – THREE DOWN

The Football League Annual General Meeting of June 1973 agreed to adopt the promotion and relegation system of three up and three down.

The **new system** came into effect in **season 1973-4** and applied only to the first three divisions; four clubs were still relegated from the Third and four promoted from the Fourth.

It was the first change in the promotion and relegation system for the top two divisions in 81 years.

MOST LEAGUE APPEARANCES

Players with more than 700 Football League appearances (as at end of season 2001-02):

1005   **Peter Shilton** 1966-97 (286 Leicester City, 110 Stoke City, 202 Nott'm. Forest, 188 Southampton, 175 Derby Co., 34 Plymouth Argyle, 1 Bolton Wand., 9 Leyton Orient).

931   **Tony Ford** 1975-2002 (423 Grimsby Town, 9 Sunderland, 112 Stoke City, 114 W.B.A., 5 Bradford City, 76 Scunthorpe Utd., 103 Mansfield Town, 89 Rochdale).

824   **Terry Paine** 1956-77 (713 Southampton, 111 Hereford).

795   **Tommy Hutchison** 1968-91 (165 Blackpool, 314 Coventry City, 46 Manchester City, 92 Burnley, 178 Swansea City). In addition, 68 Scottish League apps. for Alloa 1965-68, giving career League app. total of 863.

782   **Robbie James** 1973-94 (484 Swansea City, 48 Stoke City, 87 Q.P.R., 23 Leicester City, 89 Bradford City, 51 Cardiff City).

777   **Alan Oakes** 1959-84 (565 Manchester City, 211 Chester City, 1 Port Vale).

770   **John Trollope** 1960-80 (all for Swindon Town, record total for one club).

764   **Jimmy Dickinson** 1946-65 (all for Portsmouth).

761   **Roy Sproson** 1950-72 (all for Port Vale).

760   **Mick Tait** 1974-97 (64 Oxford Utd., 106 Carlisle Utd., 33 Hull City, 240 Portsmouth, 99 Reading, 79 Darlington, 139 Hartlepool Utd.).

758   **Billy Bonds** 1964-88 (95 Charlton Athletic, 663 West Ham Utd.).

758   **Ray Clemence** 1966-88 (48 Scunthorpe Utd., 470 Liverpool, 240 Tottenham).

757   **Pat Jennings** 1963-86 (48 Watford, 472 Tottenham, 237 Arsenal).

757   **Frank Worthington** 1966-88 (171 Huddersfield Town, 210 Leicester City, 84 Bolton Wand., 75 Birmingham City, 32 Leeds Utd., 19 Sunderland, 34 Southampton, 31 Brighton & H.A., 59 Tranmere Rov., 23 Preston N.E., 19 Stockport Co.).

757   **Dave Beasant** 1980-2002 (340 Wimbledon, 20 Newcastle Utd., 6 Grimsby Town, 4 Wolves, 133 Chelsea, 88 Southampton, 139 Nott'm. F., 27 Portsmouth).

749   **Ernie Moss** 1968-88 (469 Chesterfield, 35 Peterborough Utd., 57 Mansfield Town, 74 Port Vale, 11 Lincoln City, 44 Doncaster Rov., 26 Stockport Co., 23 Scarborough, 10 Rochdale).

746   **Les Chapman** 1966-88 (263 Oldham Athletic, 133 Huddersfield Town, 70 Stockport Co., 139 Bradford City, 88 Rochdale, 53 Preston N.E.).

744   **Asa Hartford** 1967-90 (214 W.B.A., 260 Manchester City, 3 Nott'm. F., 81 Everton, 28 Norwich City, 81 Bolton Wand., 45 Stockport Co., 7 Oldham Athletic, 25 Shrewsbury Town).

743   **Alan Ball** 1963-84 (146 Blackpool, 208 Everton, 177 Arsenal, 195 Southampton, 17 Bristol Rov.).

743   **John Hollins** 1963-84 (465 Chelsea, 151 Q.P.R., 127 Arsenal).

743   **Phil Parkes** 1968-91 (52 Walsall, 344 Q.P.R., 344 West Ham Utd., 3 Ipswich Town).

737   **Steve Bruce** 1979-99 (205 Gillingham, 141 Norwich City, 309 Manchester Utd. 72 Birmingham City, 10 Sheffield Utd.).

732   **Mick Mills** 1966-88 (591 Ipswich Town, 103 Southampton, 38 Stoke City).

731   **Ian Callaghan** 1959-81 (640 Liverpool, 76 Swansea City, 15 Crewe
        Alexandra).

725   **Steve Perryman** 1969-90 (655 Tottenham, 17 Oxford Utd., 53 Brentford).

722   **Martin Peters** 1961-81 (302 West Ham Utd., 189 Tottenham, 207 Norwich
        City, 24 Sheffield Utd.).

718   **Mike Channon** 1966-86 (511 Southampton, 72 Manchester City, 4 Newcas-
        tle Utd., 9 Bristol Rov., 88 Norwich City, 34 Portsmouth).

718   **Phil Neal** 1968-89 (186 Northampton Town, 455 Liverpool, 77 Bolton
        Wand.).

716   **Ron Harris** 1961-83 (655 Chelsea, 61 Brentford).

716   **Mike Summerbee** 1959-79 (218 Swindon Town, 357 Manchester City, 51
        Burnley, 3 Blackpool, 87 Stockport Co.).

714   **Glenn Cockerill** 1976-98 (186 Lincoln City, 26 Swindon Town, 62 Sheffield
        Utd., 387 Southampton, 90 Leyton Orient, 40 Fulham, 23 Brentford).

705   **John Wile** 1968-86 (205 Peterborough Utd., 500 W.B.A.).

701   **Neville Southall** 1980-2000 (39 Bury, 578 Everton, 9 Port Vale, 9 South-
        end, 12 Stoke, 53 Torquay, 1 Bradford City).

● **Stanley Matthews** made 701 League apps. 1932-65 (322 Stoke City, 379 Blackpool),
incl. 3 for Stoke City at start of 1939-40 before season abandoned (war).

● Goalkeeper **John Burridge** made a total of 771 League appearances in a 28-season
career in English and Scottish football (1968-96). He played 691 games for 15 English
clubs (Workington, Blackpool, Aston Villa, Southend Utd., Crystal Palace, Q.P.R.,
Wolves, Derby Co., Sheffield Utd., Southampton, Newcastle Utd., Scarborough, Lincoln
City, Manchester City and Darlington) and 80 for 5 Scottish clubs (Hibernian,
Aberdeen, Dumbarton, Falkirk and Queen of the South).

LONGEST LEAGUE SEQUENCE

Harold Bell, centre-half of Tranmere Rov., was ever-present for the first nine post-war
seasons (1946-55), achieving a League record of 401 consecutive matches. Counting
F.A. Cup and other games, his run of successive appearances totalled 459.

   The longest League sequence since Bell's was 394 appearances by goalkeeper **Dave
Beasant** for Wimbledon, Newcastle Utd. and Chelsea. His nine-year run began on August
29, 1981 and was ended by a broken finger sustained in Chelsea's League Cup-tie
against Portsmouth on October 31, 1990. Beasant's 394 consecutive League games
comprised 304 for Wimbledon (1981-8), 20 for Newcastle Utd. (1988-9) and 70 for
Chelsea (1989-90).

   Phil Neal made 366 consecutive First Division appearances for Liverpool between
December 1974 and September 1983, a remarkable sequence for an outfield player in
top-division football.

EVER-PRESENT DEFENCE

The **entire defence** of Huddersfield Town played in all 42 Second Division matches in
season 1952-3, namely, Bill Wheeler (goal), Ron Staniforth and Laurie Kelly (full-
backs), Bill McGarry, Don McEvoy and Len Quested (half-backs). In addition, Vic
Metcalfe played in all 42 League matches at outside-left.

FIRST SUBSTITUTE USED IN LEAGUE

Keith Peacock (Charlton Athletic), away to Bolton Wand. (Div. 2) on August 21, 1965.

FROM PROMOTION TO CHAMPIONS

Clubs who have become Champions of England a year after winning promotion:
Liverpool 1905, 1906; **Everton** 1931, 1932; **Tottenham** 1950, 1951; **Ipswich Town**
1961, 1962; **Nott'm. Forest** 1977, 1978. The first four were placed top in both seasons:
Forest finished third and first.

THREE-NATION CHAMPION

Trevor Steven earned eight Championship medals, in three countries: two with Everton (1985, 1987); five with Rangers (1990, 1991, 1993, 1994, 1995) and one with Marseille in 1992.

LEEDS NO-WAY AWAY

Leeds Utd., in 1992-3, provided the first instance of a club failing to win an away League match as reigning Champions.

PIONEERS IN 1888 AND 1992

Three clubs among the twelve who formed the Football League in 1888 were also founder members of the F.A. Premier League: **Aston Villa**, **Blackburn Rov.** and **Everton**.

CHAMPIONS (MODERN) WITH TWO CLUBS – PLAYERS

Francis Lee (Manchester City 1968, Derby Co. 1975); **Ray Kennedy** (Arsenal 1971, Liverpool 1979, 1980, 1982); **Archie Gemmill** (Derby Co. 1972, 1975, Nott'm. F. 1978); **John McGovern** (Derby Co. 1972, Nott'm. F. 1978) **Larry Lloyd** (Liverpool 1973, Nott'm. F. 1978); **Peter Withe** (Nott'm. F. 1978, Aston Villa 1981); **John Lukic** (Arsenal 1989, Leeds Utd. 1992); **Kevin Richardson** (Everton 1985, Arsenal 1989); **Eric Cantona** (Leeds Utd. 1992, Manchester Utd. 1993, 1994, 1996, 1997); **David Batty** (Leeds Utd. 1992, Blackburn Rov. 1995); **Bobby Mimms** (Everton 1987, Blackburn Rov. 1995), **Henning Berg** (Blackburn Rov. 1995, Manchester United 1999, 2001).

CLUB CLOSURES

Four clubs have left the Football League in mid-season: **Leeds City** (expelled Oct. 1919); **Wigan Borough** (Oct. 1931, debts of £20,000); **Accrington Stanley** (March 1962, debts £62,000); **Aldershot** (March 1992, debts £1.2m.). **Maidstone Utd.**, with debts of £650,000, closed August 1992, on the eve of the season.

FOUR-DIVISION MEN

In season 1986-7, goalkeeper **Eric Nixon**, became the first player to appear in **all four divisions** of the Football League **in one season**. He served two clubs in Div. 1: Manchester City (5 League games) and Southampton (4); in Div. 2 Bradford City (3); in Div. 3 Carlisle Utd. (16); and in Div. 4 Wolves (16). Total appearances: 44.

Harvey McCreadie, a teenage forward, played in four divisions over two seasons inside a calendar year – from Accrington (Div. 3) to Luton Town (Div. 1) in January 1960, to Div. 2 with Luton Town later that season and to Wrexham (Div. 4) in November.

Tony Cottee played in all four divisions in season 2000-01, for Leicester City (Premiership), Norwich City (Div. 1), Barnet (Div. 3, player-manager) and Millwall (Div. 2).

FATHERS & SONS

When player-manager **Ian Bowyer** (39) and **Gary Bowyer** (18) appeared together in the Hereford Utd. side at Scunthorpe Utd. (Div.4, April 21, 1990), they provided the first instance of father and son playing in the same team in a Football League match for 39 years. Ian Bowyer played as substitute, and Gary scored Hereford's injury-time equaliser in a 3-3 draw.

Alec (39) and **David** (just 17) **Herd** were the previous father-and-son duo in League football – for **Stockport Co.**, 2-0 winners at Hartlepool Utd. (Div.3 North) on May 5, 1951.

When **Preston N.E.** won 2-1 at Bury in Div. 3 on January 13, 1990, the opposing goalkeepers were brothers: **Alan Kelly** (21) for Preston N.E. and **Gary** (23) for Bury. Their father, **Alan Kelly Senior** (who kept goal for Preston N.E. in the 1964 F.A. Cup Final and won 47 Rep. of Ireland caps) flew from America to watch the sons he taught to keep goal line up on opposite sides.

George Eastham Snr. (manager) and son **George Eastham Jnr.** were inside-forward partners for Ards in the Irish League in season 1954-5.

FATHER & SON BOTH CHAMPIONS

John Aston Snr. won a Championship medal with Manchester Utd. in 1952 and **John Aston Jnr.** did so with Utd. in 1967.

FATHER & SON RIVAL MANAGERS

When **Bill Dodgin senior** took Bristol Rov. to Fulham for an F.A. Cup 1st Round tie in Nov. 1970, the opposing manager was his son, **Bill junior**.

FATHER & SON ON OPPOSITE SIDES

It happened for the first time in F.A. Cup history (1st. Qual. Round on Sept. 14, 1996) when 21-year-old **Nick Scaife** (Bishop Auckland) faced his father **Bobby** (41), who played for Pickering. Both were in midfield. Home side Bishops won 3-1.

THREE BROTHERS IN SAME SIDE

Southampton provided the first instance for 65 years of three brothers appearing together in a First Division side when **Danny Wallace** (24) and his 19-year-old twin brothers **Rodney** and **Ray** played against Sheffield Wed.on October 22, 1988. In all, they made 25 appearances together for Southampton until September 1989.

A previous instance in Div. 1 was provided by the Middlesbrough trio, **William**, **John** and **George Carr** with 24 League appearances together from January 1920 to October 1923.

The **Tonner** brothers, **Sam**, **James** and **Jack**, played together in 13 Second Division matches for Clapton Orient in season 1919-20.

Brothers **David**, **Donald** and **Robert Jack** played together in Plymouth Argyle's League side in 1920.

TWIN TEAM-MATES (see also **Wallace twins** above)

Twin brothers **David** and Peter **Jackson** played together for three League clubs (Wrexham, Bradford City and Tranmere Rov.) from 1954-62.

The **Morgan** twins, **Ian** and **Roger**, played regularly in the Q.P.R. forward line from 1964-68.

The **Chambers** twins, **Adrian** and **James**, 19, played senior football together for the first time in W.B.A.'s League Cup team v Derby Co. (2nd Round) in September 2000.

SIR TOM DOES THE HONOURS

Sir Tom Finney, England and Preston N.E. legend, opened the Football League's new headquarters on their return to Preston on Feb. 23, 1999. Preston had been the League's original base for 70 years before they moved to Lytham St. Annes in 1959.

SHORTENED MATCHES

The 0-0 score in the **Bradford City v Lincoln City Third Division fixture** on May 11, 1985, abandoned through fire after 40 minutes, was subsequently confirmed as a result. It is the shortest officially completed League match on record, and was the fourth of only five instances in Football League history of the score of an unfinished match being allowed to stand.

The other occasions: **Middlesbrough 4, Oldham Athletic 1** (Div. 1, April 3, 1915), abandoned after 55 minutes when Oldham Athletic defender Billy Cook refused to leave the field after being sent off; **Barrow 7, Gillingham 0** (Div. 4, Oct. 9, 1961), abandoned after 75 minutes because of bad light, the match having started late because of Gillingham's delayed arrival.

A crucial **Manchester derby** (Div.1) was abandoned after 85 minutes, and the result stood, on April 27, 1974, when a pitch invasion at Old Trafford followed the only goal, scored for City by Denis Law, which relegated Manchester Utd., Law's former club.

Only instance of a first-class match in England being abandoned 'through shortage of players' occurred in the First Division at Bramall Lane on March 16, 2002. Referee Eddie Wolstenholme halted play after 82 minutes because Sheffield Utd. were reduced to 6 players against W.B.A. They had had 3 men sent off (goalkeeper and 2 substitutes), and with all 3 substitutes used and 2 players injured, were left with fewer than the required minimum of 7 on the field. Promotion contenders W.B.A. were leading 3-0, and the League ordered the result to stand.

The last 60 seconds of **Birmingham City v Stoke City** (Div. 3, 1-1, on Feb. 29, 1992) were played behind locked doors. The ground had been cleared after a pitch invasion.

A First Division fixture, **Sheffield Wed. v Aston Villa** (Nov. 26, 1898), was abandoned through bad light after 79½ mins. with Wed. leading 3-1. The Football League ruled that the match should be completed, and the remaining 10½ minutes were played **four months later** (Mar. 13, 1899), when Wed. added another goal to make the result 4-1.

F.A. CUP RECORDS

(See also Goalscoring section)

CHIEF WINNERS

Ten Times: Manchester Utd.
Eight Times: Tottenham, Arsenal.
Seven Times: Aston Villa.
Three Times in Succession: The Wanderers (1876-7-8) and Blackburn Rov. (1884-5-6).
Trophy Handed Back: The F.A. Cup became the Wanderers' absolute property in 1878, but they handed it back to the Association on condition that it was not to be won outright by any club.
In Successive Years by Professional Clubs: Blackburn Rov. (in 1890 and 1891); Newcastle Utd. (in 1951 and 1952); Tottenham (in 1961 and 1962) and Tottenham again (in 1981 and 1982).
Record Final-tie score: Bury 6, Derby Co. 0 (1903).
Most F.A. Cup wins at Wembley: Manchester Utd. 9, Arsenal 7, Tottenham 6, Newcastle Utd. 5, Liverpool 5.

F.A. CUP: SECOND DIVISION WINNERS

Notts Co. (1894), Wolves (1908), Barnsley (1912), West Bromwich Albion (1931), Sunderland (1973), Southampton (1976), West Ham Utd. (1980). When Tottenham won the Cup in 1901 they were a Southern League club.

'OUTSIDE' SEMI-FINALISTS

Wycombe Wand., in 2001, became only the eighth team from outside the top two divisions to reach the semi-finals, following Millwall (1937), Port Vale (1954), York City (1955), Norwich City (1959), Crystal Palace (1976), Plymouth Argyle (1984) and Chesterfield (1997). None reached the Final..

FOURTH DIVISION QUARTER-FINALISTS

Oxford Utd. (1964), Colchester Utd. (1971), Bradford City (1976), Cambridge Utd. (1990).

F.A. CUP – FOUR TROPHIES

The latest F.A. Cup, first presented at Wembley in 1992, is a replica of the one it replaced, which had been in existence since 1911. 'It was falling apart and was not going to last much longer,' said the FA.

The new trophy is the fourth F.A. Cup. These were its predecessors:
1895 First stolen from shop in Birmingham while held by Aston Villa. Never seen again.
1910 Second presented to Lord Kinnaird on completing 21 years as F.A. president.
1992 Third 'gracefully retired' after 80 years' service (1911-91).
There are three F.A. Cups currently in existence. The retired model is still used for promotional work. The present trophy stays with the winners until the following March. A third, identical Cup is secreted in the F.A. vaults as cover against loss of the existing trophy.

FINALISTS RELEGATED

Four clubs have reached the F.A. Cup Final in a season of relegation, and all lost at Wembley: Manchester City 1926, Leicester City 1969, Brighton & H.A. 1983, Middlesbrough 1997.

GIANT-KILLING IN F.A. CUP
(* Home team; R = Replay; Season 2002 = 2001-02)

2002	*Wigan Athletic 0	Canvey Island 1
2002	*Canvey Island 1	Nothampton T. 0
2002	*Dagenham & R ... 3	Exeter City 0R
2002	*Cardiff City 2	Leeds Utd. 1
2002	*Derby Co. 1	Bristol Rov. 3
2001	*Wycombe Wand. .. 2	Wolves 1
2001	*Wimbledon 2	Wycombe Wand. .. 2R
	(Wycombe Wand. won on pens).	
2001	*Leicester City ... 1	Wycombe Wand. .. 2
2001	*Brentford 1	Kingstonian 3
2001	*Yeovil 5	Colchester Utd. 1
2001	*Southend Utd. ... 0	Kingstonian 1
2001	*Nuneaton 1	Stoke City 0R
2001	*Hull City 0	Kettering 1R
2001	*Northwich Vic. ... 1	Bury 0R
2001	*Port Vale 1	Canvey Island 2R
2001	*Lincoln City 0	Dagenham & R. 1
2001	*Morecambe 2	Cambridge Utd. ... 1
2001	*Blackpool 0	Yeovil 1
2001	*Everton 0	Tranmere Rov. 3
2001	*Tranmere Rov. 4	Southampton 3R
2000	*Rushden & D 2	Scunthorpe Utd. ... 0
2000	*Chesterfield 1	Enfield 2
2000	*Hereford 1	York City 0
2000	*Ilkeston Town 2	Carlisle Utd. 1
2000	*Hereford 1	Hartlepool Utd. 0
1999	*Bedlington T 4	Colchester Utd. ... 1
1999	*Hednesford 3	Barnet 1
1999	*Mansfield Town .. 1	Southport 2
1999	*Rushden & D 1	Shrewsbury Town . 0
1999	*Southend Utd. ... 0	Doncaster Rov. 1
1999	*Yeovil Town 2	Northampton T 0
1999	*Aston Villa 0	Fulham 2
1998	*Hull City 0	Hednesford 2
1998	Lincoln City 3	Emley 3R
	(at H'field; Emley won on pens).	
1998	*Leyton O 1	Hendon 1R
1998	*Swindon Town 1	Stevenage 2
1998	*Stevenage 2	C'bridge Utd. 1
1997	*Millwall 0	Woking 1
1997	*Brighton & H.A. . 1	Sudbury Town ... 1R
	(Sudbury won on pens).	
1997	*Blackpool 0	Hednesford 1
1997	*Cambridge Utd. . 0	Woking 2
1997	*Leyton O. 1	Stevenage 2
1997	*Hednesford 1	York City 0
1997	*Chesterfield 1	Nott'm. Forest 0
1996	*Hitchin 2	Bristol Rov. 1
1996	*Woking 2	Barnet 1R
1996	*Bury 0	Blyth Spartans 2
1996	*Gravesend 2	Colchester Utd. 1

1995	*Kingstonian 2	Brighton & H.A. ... 1
1995	*Enfield 1	Cardiff City 0
1995	*Marlow 2	Oxford Utd. 0
1995	*Woking 1	Barnet 0R
1995	*Hitchin 4	Hereford 2R
1995	*Torquay Utd. 0	Enfield 1R
1995	*Altrincham 1	Wigan Athletic 0
1995	*Wrexham 2	Ipswich Town 1
1995	*Scarboro' 1	Port Vale 0
1994	*Colchester Utd. .. 3	Sutton 4
1994	*Yeovil 1	Fulham 0
1994	*Torquay Utd. 0	Sutton 1
1994	*Halifax Town 2	W.B.A. 1
1994	*Birmingham C. ... 1	Kid'minster 2
1994	*Stockport Co. 2	Q.P.R. 1
1994	*Liverpool 0	Bristol City 1R
1994	*Arsenal 1	Bolton Wand. 3R
1994	*Leeds Utd. 2	Oxford Utd. 3R
1994	*Luton Town 2	Newcastle Utd. . 0R
1994	*Kidderminster ... 1	Preston N.E. 0
1994	*Cardiff City 1	Manchester City .. 0
1993	*Hereford 1	Yeovil 2R
1993	*Torquay Utd. 2	Yeovil 5
1993	*Altrincham 2	Chester City 0R
1993	*Cardiff City 2	Bath 3
1993	*Chesterfield 2	Macclesfield 2R
	(Macclesfield Town won on pens).	
1993	*Marine 4	Halifax Town 1
1993	*Stafford 2	Lincoln City 1R
1993	*Hartlepool Utd. .. 1	Crystal Palace 0
1993	*Liverpool 0	Bolton Wand. 2R
1992	*Fulham 0	Hayes 2
1992	*Crawley 4	Northampton 2
1992	*Telford 2	Stoke City 1R
1992	*Aldershot 0	Enfield 1
1992	*Halifax Town 1	Witton A. 2R
1992	*Maidstone 1	Kettering 2
1992	*Walsall 0	Yeovil 1R
1992	*Farnborough 4	Torquay Utd. 3
1992	*Wrexham 2	Arsenal 1
1991	*Scarboro' 0	Leek 2
1991	*Northampton 0	Barnet 1R
1991	*Hayes 1	Cardiff City 0R
1991	*Chorley 2	Bury 1
1991	*Shrewsbury T 1	Wimbledon 0
1991	*W.B.A. 2	Woking 4
1990	*Aylesbury 1	Southend Utd. 0
1990	*Scarborough 0	Whitley Bay 1
1990	*Welling 1	Gillingham 0R
1990	*Whitley Bay 2	Preston N.E. 0
1990	*Northampton 0	Coventry City 1

276

1990	*Cambridge Utd. . 1	Millwall 0R
1989	*Sutton 2	Coventry City 1
1989	*Halifax Town 2	Kettering 3R
1989	*Kettering 2	Bristol Rov. 1
1989	*Bognor 2	Exeter City 1
1989	*Leyton Orient 0	Enfield 1R
1989	*Altrincham 3	Lincoln City 2
1989	*Wrexham 2	Runcorn 3R
1988	*Sutton 3	Aldershot 0
1988	*Peterborough 1	Sutton 3
1988	*Carlisle Utd. 2	Maccesfield 4
1988	*Macc'field 4	Rotherham Utd. ... 0
1988	*Chester City 0	Runcorn 1
1988	*Cambridge Utd. . 0	Yeovil 1
1987	*Caernarfon 1	Stockport Co. 0
1987	Chorley 3	Wolves 0R
	(at Bolton Wand.)	
1987	*Telford 3	Burnley 0
1987	*York City 1	Caernarfon 2R
1987	*Aldershot 3	Oxford Utd. 0
1987	*Wigan Athletic 1	Norwich City 0
1987	*Charlton Ath. 1	Walsall 2
1986	*Stockport Co. 0	Telford 1
1986	*Wycombe W. 2	Colchester Utd. 0
1986	*Dagenham 2	Cambridge Utd. 1
1986	*Blackpool 1	Altrincham 2
1986	*Birmingham C. 1	Altrincham 2
1986	*Peterboro' 1	Leeds Utd. 0
1985	*Telford 2	Lincoln City 1
1985	*Preston N.E. 1	Telford 4
1985	*Telford 2	Bradford City 1
1985	*Telford 3	Darlington 0R
1985	*Blackpool 0	Altrincham 1
1985	*Wimbledon 1	Nott'm. Forest ... 0R
1985	*Orient 2	W.B.A. 1
1985	*Dagenham 2	Peterborough 0
1985	*Swindon Town ... 1	Dagenham 2R
1985	*York City 1	Arsenal 0
1984	*Halifax Town 2	Whitby 0
1984	*Bournemouth 2	Manchester Utd. .. 0
1984	*Telford 3	Stockport Co. 0
1984	*Telford 3	Northampton 2R
1984	Telford 4	*Rochdale 1
1983	*Cardiff City 2	Weymouth 3
1981	*Exeter City 3	Leicester City 1R

1981	*Exeter City 4	Newcastle Utd. .. 0R
1980	*Halifax Town 1	Manchester City ... 0
1980	*Harlow 1	Leicester City ... 0R
1980	*Chelsea 0	Wigan Athletic 1
1979	*Newport 2	West Ham Utd. ... 1
1978	*Wrexham 4	Newcastle 1R
1978	*Stoke City 2	Blyth S 3
1976	*Leeds Utd. 0	Crystal Palace 1
1975	*Brighton & H.A. .. 0	Leatherhead 1
1975	*Burnley 0	Wimbledon 1
1972	*Hereford 2	Newcastle 1R
1971	*Colchester Utd. .. 3	Leeds Utd. 2
1969	*Mansfield Town .. 3	West Ham Utd. ... 0
1967	*Swindon Town ... 3	West Ham Utd. .. 0R
1967	*Manchester U. ... 1	Norwich City 2
1966	*Ipswich Town 2	Southport 3R
1965	*Peterboro' 2	Arsenal 1
1964	*Newcastle Utd. .. 1	Bedford Town 2
1964	*Aldershot 2	Aston Villa 1R
1961	*Coventry City 1	Kings Lynn 2
1961	*Chelsea 2	Crewe Alex. 2
1960	*Manchester City . 1	South'ton 5
1959	*Norwich City 3	Manchester U 0
1959	*Worcester 2	Liverpool 1
1959	*Tooting 3	Bournemouth 1
1959	*Tooting 2	Northampton 1
1958	*Newcastle Utd. .. 1	Scunthorpe Utd. .. 3
1957	*Wolves 0	Bournemouth 1
1957	*Bournemouth 3	Tottenham 1
1957	*Derby Co. 1	N. Brighton 3
1956	*Derby Co. 1	Boston United 6
1955	*York City 2	Tottenham 1
1955	*Blackpool 0	York City 2
1954	*Arsenal 1	Norwich City 2
1954	*Port Vale 1	Blackpool 0
1952	*Everton 1	Leyton Orient 3
1949	*Yeovil Town 2	Sunderland 1
1948	*Colchester Utd. .. 1	Huddersfield 0
1948	*Arsenal 0	Bradford City 1
1938	*Chelmsford 4	Southampton 1
1933	*Walsall 2	Arsenal 0
1922	*Everton 0	Crystal Palace 6

YEOVIL TOP GIANT-KILLERS

Yeovil's victories over Colchester Utd. and Blackpool in season 2000-01 gave them a total of 20 F.A. Cup wins against League opponents. They hold another non-League record by reaching the third round 13 times.

This is Yeovil's triumphant Cup record against League clubs: 1924-5 Bournemouth 3-2; 1934-5 Crystal Palace 3-0, Exeter City 4-1; 1938-9 Brighton & H.A. 2-1; 1948-9 Bury 3-1, Sunderland 2-1; 1958-9 Southend Utd. 1-0; 1960-1 Walsall 1-0; 1963-4 Southend Utd. 1-0, Crystal Palace 3-1; 1970-1 Bournemouth 1-0; 1972-3 Brentford 2-1; 1987-8 Cambridge Utd. 1-0; 1991-2 Walsall 1-0; 1992-3 Torquay Utd. 5-2, Hereford 2-1; 1993-4 Fulham 1-0; 1998-9 Northampton 2-0; 2000-01 Colchester Utd. 5-1, Blackpool 1-0.

NON-LEAGUE BEST IN F.A. CUP

Since League football began in 1888, three non-League clubs have reached the F.A. Cup Final. **Sheffield Wed.** (Football Alliance) were runners-up in 1890, as were **Southampton** (Southern League) in 1900 and 1902. **Tottenham** won the Cup as a Southern League team in 1901.

Otherwise, the **furthest progress** by non-League clubs has been to the **5th. Round** on 5 occasions: Colchester Utd. 1948, Yeovil 1949, Blyth Spartans 1978, Telford 1985 and Kidderminster 1994.

Greatest number of non-League sides to reach the **3rd. Round** is 6 in 1978: Blyth, Enfield, Scarborough, Tilbury, Wealdstone and Wigan Athletic.

Most to reach **Round 4**: 3 in 1957 (Rhyl, New Brighton, Peterborough Utd.) and 1975 (Leatherhead, Stafford and Wimbledon).

Five non-League clubs reaching **Round 3** in 2001 was a Conference record. They were Chester City, Yeovil, Dagenham & Redbridge, Morecambe and Kingstonian.

NON-LEAGUE 'LAST TIMES' IN F.A. CUP

Last time no non-League club reached Round 3: 1951. Last time only one did so: 1969 (Kettering Town). Last time only two: 2000 (Hereford and Rushden & Diamonds) and 2002 (Canvey Island and Dagenham & Redbridge).

TOP-DIVISION SCALPS

Victories in F.A. Cup by non-League clubs over top-division teams this century include:- 1900-1 (Final, replay); **Tottenham** 3, Sheffield Utd. 1 (Tottenham then in Southern League); 1919-20 **Cardiff City** 2, Oldham Athletic 0, and Sheffield Wed. 0, **Darlington** 2; 1923-4 **Corinthians** 1, Blackburn Rov. 0; 1947-8 **Colchester Utd.** 1, Huddersfield Town 0; 1948-9 **Yeovil Town** 2, Sunderland 1; 1971-2 **Hereford Utd.** 2, Newcastle Utd. 1; 1974-5 Burnley 0, **Wimbledon** 1; 1985-6 Birmingham City 1, **Altrincham** 2; 1988-9 **Sutton Utd.** 2, Coventry City 1.

MOST WEMBLEY FINALS

Eight players appeared in five F.A. Cup Finals at Wembley, replays excluded:-
* Joe Hulme (Arsenal: 1927, lost; 1930 won; 1932 lost; 1936 won; Huddersfield Town: 1938 lost).
* Johnny Giles (Manchester Utd.: 1963 won; Leeds Utd.: 1965 lost; 1970 drew at Wembley, lost replay at Old Trafford; 1972 won; 1973 lost).
* Pat Rice (all for Arsenal: 1971 won; 1972 lost; 1978 lost; 1979 won; 1980 lost).
* Frank Stapleton (Arsenal: 1978 lost; 1979 won; 1980 lost; Manchester Utd.: 1983 won; 1985 won).
* Ray Clemence (Liverpool: 1971 lost; 1974 won; 1977 lost; Tottenham: 1982 won; 1987 lost).
* Mark Hughes (Manchester Utd.: 1985 won; 1990 won; 1994 won; 1995 lost; Chelsea: 1997 won).
* John Barnes (Watford: 1984 lost; Liverpool: 1988 lost; 1989 won; 1996 lost; Newcastle Utd.: 1998, sub, lost): he was the first player to lose Wembley F.A. Cup Finals with three different clubs.
* Roy Keane (Nott'm Forest: 1991 lost; Manchester Utd.: 1994 won; 1995 lost; 1996 won; 1999 won).

Stapleton, Clemence and Hughes also played in a replay, making six actual F.A. Cup Final appearances for each of them.

Glenn Hoddle also made six F.A. Cup Final appearances at Wembley: 5 for Tottenham (incl. 2 replays), in 1981, 1982 and 1987, and 1 for Chelsea as sub in 1994.

▲Paul Bracewell played in four F.A. Cup Finals without being on the winning side – for Everton 1985, 1986, 1989, Sunderland 1992.

F.A. CUP SEMI-FINALS AT WEMBLEY

1991 Tottenham 3, Arsenal 1; **1993** Sheffield Wed. 2, Sheffield Utd. 1; Arsenal 1, Tottenham 0; **1994** Chelsea 2, Luton 0; Manchester Utd. 1, Oldham 1; **2000** Aston Villa beat Bolton 4-1 on pens. (after 0-0); Chelsea 2, Newcastle Utd 1.

FIRST F.A. CUP ENTRANTS (1871-2)

Barnes, Civil Service, Crystal Palace, Clapham Rov., Donnington School (Spalding), Hampstead Heathens, Harrow Chequers, Hitchin, Maidenhead, Marlow, Queen's Park (Glasgow), Reigate Priory, Royal Engineers, Upton Park and Wanderers. Total 15. Three scratched. **Record F.A. Cup entry 674 in 1921.**

CUP 'FIRSTS'

Out of country: Cardiff City, by defeating Arsenal 1-0 in the 1927 Final at Wembley, became the first and only club to take the F.A. Cup out of England.

All-English Winning XI: First club to win the F.A. Cup with all-English XI: Blackburn Olympic in 1883. Others since: W.B.A. in 1888 and 1931, Bolton Wand. (1958), Manchester City (1969), West Ham Utd. (1964 and 1975).

Non-English Winning XI: Liverpool in 1986 (Mark Lawrenson, born Preston N.E., was a Rep. of Ireland player).

Won both Cups: Old Carthusians won the F.A. Cup in 1881 and the F.A. Amateur Cup in 1894 and 1897. **Wimbledon** won Amateur Cup in 1963, F.A. Cup in 1988.

MOST GAMES NEEDED TO WIN F.A. CUP

Barnsley played a record 12 matches (20 hours' football) to win the F.A. Cup in season 1911-12. All six replays (one in Rd. 1, three in Rd. 4 and one in each of semi-final and Final) were brought about by goalless draws.

Arsenal played 11 F.A. Cup games when winning the trophy in 1979. Five of them were in the 3rd. Rd. against Sheffield Wed..

LONGEST F.A. CUP TIES

6 matches (11 hours): **Alvechurch v Oxford City** (4th. qual. round, 1971-2). Alvechurch won 1-0.

5 matches (9 hours, 22 mins – record for competition proper): **Stoke City v Bury** (3rd. round, 1954-5). Stoke City won 3-2.

5 matches: Chelsea v Burnley (4th. round, 1955-6). Chelsea won 2-0.

5 matches: Hull City v Darlington (2nd. round, 1960-1). Hull City won 3-0.

5 matches: Arsenal v Sheffield Wed. (3rd. round, 1978-9). Arsenal won 2-0.

Other marathons (qualifying comp., all 5 matches, 9 hours): **Barrow v Gillingham** (last qual. round, 1924-5) – winners Barrow; **Leyton v Ilford** (3rd. qual. round, 1924-5) – winners Leyton; **Falmouth Town v Bideford** (3rd. qual. round, 1973-4) – winners Bideford.

End of Cup Final replays: The F.A. decided that, with effect from 1999, there would be no Cup Final replays. In the event of a draw after extra time, the match would be decided on penalties.

F.A. Cup marathons ended in season 1991-2, when the penalty shoot-out was introduced to decide ties still level after one replay and extra time.

● In 1932-3 **Brighton & H.A.** (Div. 3 South) played 11 F.A. Cup games, including replays, and scored 43 goals, without getting past Rd 5. They forgot to claim exemption and had to play from 1st Qual. Round.

LONGEST ROUND

The longest round in F.A. Cup history was the **third round** in **season 1962-3**. It took 66 days to complete, lasting from January 5 to March 11, and included 261 postponements because of bad weather.

LONGEST UNBEATEN F.A. CUP RUN

23 matches by **Blackburn Rov.** In winning the Cup in three consecutive years (1884-5-6), they won 21 ties (one in a replay), and their first Cup defeat in four seasons was in a first round replay of the next competition.

RE-STAGED F.A. CUP TIES

Sixth round, March 9, 1974: Newcastle Utd. 4, Nott'm. Forest 3. Match declared void by F.A. and ordered to be replayed following a pitch invasion after Newcastle Utd. had a player sent off. Forest claimed the hold-up caused the game to change its pattern. The tie went to two further matches at Goodison Park (0-0, then 1-0 to Newcastle Utd.).

Third round, January 5, 1985: Burton Albion 1, Leicester City 6 (at Derby Co.). Burton goalkeeper Paul Evans was hit on the head by a missile thrown from the crowd, and continued in a daze. The F.A. ordered the tie to be played again, behind closed doors at Coventry City (Leicester City won 1- 0).

First round replay, November 25, 1992: Peterborough Utd. 9 (Tony Philliskirk 5), Kingstonian 1. Match expunged from records because, at 3-0 after 57 mins, Kingstonian were reduced to ten men when goalkeeper Adrian Blake was concussed by a 50 pence coin thrown from the crowd. The tie was re-staged on the same ground behind closed doors (Peterborough Utd. won 1-0).

Fifth round: Within an hour of Cup-holders Arsenal beating Sheffield Utd. 2-1 at Highbury on February 13, 1999, the Football Association took the unprecedented step of declaring the match void because an unwritten rule of sportsmanship had been broken. With United's Lee Morris lying injured, their goalkeeper Alan Kelly kicked the ball into touch. Play resumed with Arsenal's Ray Parlour throwing it in the direction of Kelly, but Nwankwo Kanu took possession and centred for Marc Overmars to score the 'winning' goal. After four minutes of protests by manager Steve Bruce and his players, referee Peter Jones confirmed the goal. Both managers absolved Kanu of cheating but Arsenal's Arsene Wenger offered to replay the match. With the F.A. immediately approving, it was re-staged at Highbury ten days later (ticket prices halved) and Arsenal again won 2-1.

F.A. CUP PRIZE MONEY

The makeover of the F.A. Cup competition took off in 2001-02 with the introduction of prize money round by round (semi-finals excepted). Cup winners Arsenal received £2,675,000.

Payments were made to winning clubs as follows: Extra Prelim. Round £500; Prelim. Round £1,000; 1st Qual. Round £7,500; 2nd Qual. Round £7,500; 3rd Qual. Round £10,000; 4th Qual. Round £20,000; 1st Round proper £20,000; 2nd Round £30,000; 3rd Round £50,000; 4th Round £75,000; 5th Round £150,000; 6th Round £400,000; Runners-up £1m; Winners £2m.

F.A. CUP FOLLIES 1999-2000

The F.A. broke with tradition by deciding the 3rd. Round should be moved from its regular January date and staged before Christmas. Criticism was strong, gates poor and the 3rd. Round in 2001-01 reverted to the New Year.

By allowing the holders Manchester Utd. to withdraw from the 1999-2000 Cup competition in order to play in FIFA's inaugural World Club Championship in Brazil in January, the F.A. were left with an odd number of clubs in the 3rd. Round. Their solution was a **'lucky losers'** draw among clubs knocked out in Round 2. Darlington, beaten at Gillingham, won it to re-enter the competition, then lost 2-1 away to Aston Villa.

WAR-TIME MARATHON

Match of 203 minutes: Stockport Co.'s second-leg tie with Doncaster Rov. in the Third Division North Cup, March 30, 1946, lasted 203 minutes and a replay was still necessary. Both legs were drawn 2-2 and Doncaster Rov. won the replay 4-0.

F.A. CUP FINAL HAT-TRICKS

There have been only three in the history of the competition: **Billy Townley** (Blackburn Rov., 1890), **Jimmy Logan** (Notts Co., 1894) and **Stan Mortensen** (Blackpool, 1953).

FIVE WINNING MEDALS

The Hon. Arthur Kinnaird (The Wanderers and Old Etonians), **Charles Wollaston** (The Wanderers) and **Jimmy Forrest** (Blackburn Rov.) each earned five F.A. Cup winners' medals. Kinnaird, later president of the F.A., played in nine of the first 12 F.A. Cup Finals, and was on the winning side three times for The Wanderers, in 1873 (captain), 1877, 1878 (captain), and twice as captain of Old Etonians (1879, 1882).

MOST F.A. CUP WINNERS' MEDALS AT WEMBLEY

4 – **Mark Hughes** (3 for Manchester Utd., 1 for Chelsea).

3 – **18 players: Dick Pym** (3 clean sheets in Finals), **Bob Haworth, Jimmy Seddon, Harry Nuttall, Billy Butler** (all Bolton Wand.); **David Jack** (2 Bolton Wand., 1 Arsenal); **Bob Cowell, Jack Milburn, Bobby Mitchell** (all Newcastle Utd.); **Dave Mackay** (Tottenham); **Frank Stapleton** (1 Arsenal, 2 Manchester Utd.); **Bryan Robson** (3 times winning captain), **Arthur Albiston, Gary Pallister** (all Manchester Utd.); **Bruce Grobbelaar, Steve Nicol, Ian Rush** (all Liverpool); **Roy Keane; Peter Schmeichel; Dennis Wise** (1 Wimbledon, 2 Chelsea).

MOST F.A. CUP APPEARANCES

88 by **Ian Callaghan** (79 for Liverpool, 7 for Swansea City, 2 for Crewe Alexandra); 87 by **John Barnes** (31 for Watford, 51 for Liverpool, 5 for Newcastle Utd.); 86 by **Stanley Matthews** (37 for Stoke City, 49 for Blackpool); 86 by **Peter Shilton** for six clubs (Leicester City, Stoke City, Nott'm. Forest, Southampton, Derby Co. and Plymouth Argyle); 84 by **Bobby Charlton** (80 for Manchester Utd., 4 for Preston N.E.).

THREE-CLUB FINALISTS

Three players have appeared in the F.A. Final for three clubs: **Harold Halse** for Manchester Utd. (1909), Aston Villa (1913) and Chelsea (1915); **Ernie Taylor** for Newcastle Utd. (1951), Blackpool (1953) and Manchester Utd. (1958); **John Barnes** for Watford (1984), Liverpool (1998, 1989, 1996) and Newcastle Utd. (1998).

CUP MAN WITH TWO CLUBS IN SAME SEASON

Stan Crowther, who played for Aston Villa against Manchester Utd. in the 1957 F.A. Cup Final, appeared for both Aston Villa and United. in the 1957-8 competition. United signed him directly after the Munich air crash and, in the circumstances, he was given special dispensation to play for them in the Cup, including the Final.

CAPTAIN'S CUP DOUBLE

Martin Buchan is the only player to have captained Scottish and English F.A. Cup-winning teams – Aberdeen in 1970 and Manchester Utd. in 1977.

MEDALS BEFORE AND AFTER

Two players appeared in F.A. Cup Final teams before and after the war: **Raich Carter** was twice a winner (Sunderland 1937, Derby Co. 1946) and **Willie Fagan** twice on the losing side (Preston N.E. 1937, Liverpool 1950).

DELANEY'S COLLECTION

Scotland winger **Jimmy Delaney** uniquely earned Scottish, English, N. Ireland and Rep. of Ireland cup medals. He was a winner with Celtic (1937), Manchester Utd. (1948) and Derry City (1954) and a runner-up with Cork City (1956).

STARS WHO MISSED OUT

Internationals who never won an F.A. Cup winner's medal include: **Tommy Lawton, Tom Finney, Johnny Haynes, Gordon Banks, George Best, Terry Butcher, Peter Shilton, Martin Peters, Nobby Stiles, Alan Ball** and **Malcolm Macdonald.**

CUP WINNERS AT NO COST

Not one member of **Bolton's** 1958 F.A. Cup-winning team cost the club a transfer fee. Five were Internationals and the eleven each joined the club for a £10 signing-on fee.

ALL-INTERNATIONAL CUP WINNERS

In **Manchester Utd.'s** 1985 Cup-winning team v Everton, all 11 players were full Internationals, as was the substitute who played. So were ten of Everton's team.

NO-CAP CUP WINNERS

Sunderland, in 1973, were the last F.A. Cup-winning team not to include an International player, although some were capped later.

HIGH-SCORING SEMI-FINALS

The **record team score** in F.A. Cup semi-finals is 6: 1891-2 WBA 6, Nott'm. Forest 2; 1907-8 Newcastle Utd. 6, Fulham 0; 1933-4 Manchester City 6, Aston Villa 1.

Most goals in semi-finals (aggregate): 17 in 1892 (4 matches) and 1899 (5 matches). In modern times: 15 in 1958 (3 matches, including Manchester Utd. 5, Fulham 3 – highest-scoring semi-final since last war); 16 in 1989-90 (Crystal Palace 4, Liverpool 3; Manchester Utd. v Oldham Athletic 3-3, 2-1. **All 16 goals** in those three matches were scored by **different players.**

Last hat-trick in an F.A. Cup semi-final was scored by **Alex Dawson** for Manchester Utd. in 5-3 replay win against Fulham at Highbury in 1958.

FOUR SPECIAL AWAYS

For the only time in F.A. Cup history, **all four quarter-finals** in season 1986-7 were won by the away team.

F.A. CUP – DRAWS RECORD

In season 1985-6, **seven** of the eight F.A. Cup 5th. Round ties went to replays – a record for that stage of the competition.

LUCK OF THE DRAW

In the F.A. Cup on Jan. 11, 1947, eight of **London's** ten Football League clubs involved in the 3rd. Round were drawn at home (including Chelsea v Arsenal). Only Crystal Palace played outside the capital (at Newcastle Utd.).

Contrast: In the 3rd. Round in Jan. 1992, Charlton Athletic were the only London club drawn at home (against Barnet), but the venue of the Farnborough v West Ham Utd. tie was reversed on police instruction. So Upton Park staged Cup-ties on successive days, with West Ham Utd. at home on the Saturday and Charlton Athletic (who shared the ground) on Sunday.

Arsenal were drawn away in every round on the way to reaching the F.A. Cup Finals of 1971 and 1972. **Manchester Utd.** won the Cup in 1990 without playing once at home.

The 1999 F.A. Cup finalists **Manchester Utd.** and **Newcastle Utd.** were both drawn at home every time in Rounds 3-6.

F.A. CUP: ALL TOP-DIVISION VICTIMS

Only instance of an F.A. Cup-winning club meeting top-division opponents in every round was provided by Manchester Utd. in 1947-8. They beat Aston Villa, Liverpool, Charlton Athletic, Preston N.E., then Derby Co. in the semi-final and Blackpool in the Final.

HOME ADVANTAGE

For the first time in F.A. Cup history, all eight ties in the 1992-3 5th. Round were won (no replays) by the **clubs drawn at home**. Only other instance of eight home wins at the 'last 16' stage of the F.A. Cup was in 1889-90, in what was then the 2nd. Round.

SIXTH-ROUND ELITE

For the first time in F.A. Cup 6th. Round history, dating from 1926, when the format of the competition changed, **all eight quarter-finalists** in 1995-6 were from the top division.

F.A. CUP SEMI-FINAL – DOUBLE DERBIES

There have been only two instances of both F.A. Cup semi-finals in the same year being local derbies: **1950** Liverpool beat Everton 2-0 (Maine Road), Arsenal beat Chelsea 1-0 after 2-2 draw (both at Tottenham); **1993** Arsenal beat Tottenham 1-0 (Wembley), Sheffield Wed. beat Sheffield Utd. 2-1 (Wembley).

TOP CLUB DISTINCTION

Since the Football League began in 1888, there has never been an F.A. Cup Final in which **neither club** represented the top division.

SPURS OUT – AND IN

Tottenham were banned, pre-season, from the 1994-5 F.A. Cup competition because of financial irregularities, but were readmitted on appeal and reached the semi-finals.

BROTHERS IN F.A. CUP FINAL TEAMS (Modern Times)

1950 Denis and Leslie Compton (Arsenal); **1952** George and Ted Robledo (Newcastle Utd.); **1967** Ron and Allan Harris (Chelsea); **1977** Jimmy and Brian Greenhoff (Manchester Utd.); **1996** and **1999** Gary and Phil Neville (Manchester Utd.)

F.A. CUP – FIRST SPONSORS

Littlewoods Pools became the first sponsors of the F.A. Cup in season 1994-5 in a £14m., 4-year deal.

French insurance giants **AXA** took over (season 1998-9) in a sponsorship worth £25m. over 4 years.

A TRADITION RETURNS

With effect this campaign, the F.A. Cup Final reverts to being played on the last Saturday of the season (May 17, 2003).

LEAGUE CUP RECORDS

(See also Goalscoring section)

Highest scores: West Ham Utd. 10-0 v Bury (2nd. Rd., 2nd. Leg 1983-4; agg. 12-1); Liverpool 10-0 v Fulham (2nd. Rd., 1st. Leg 1986-7; agg. 13-2).

Most League Cup goals (career): 49 Geoff Hurst (43 West Ham Utd., 6 Stoke City, 1960-75); 49 Ian Rush (48 Liverpool, 1 Newcastle Utd., 1981-98).

Highest scorer (season): 12 Clive Allen (Tottenham 1986-7 in 9 apps).

Most goals in match: 6 Frank Bunn (Oldham Athletic v Scarborough, 3rd. Rd., 1989-90).

Fewest goals conceded by winners: 3 by Leeds Utd. (1967-8), Tottenham (1970-1), Aston Villa (1995-6).

Most winner's medals: 5 Ian Rush (Liverpool).

Most appearances in Final: 6 Kenny Dalglish (Liverpool 1978-87), Ian Rush (Liverpool 1981-95).

Alan Hardaker Man of the Match Award was introduced in the 1990 Final, in recognition of the League's late secretary who proposed the competition in 1960.

League Cup sponsors: Milk Cup 1981-6, Littlewoods Cup 1987-90, Rumbelows Cup 1991-2, Coca-Cola Cup 1993-8. Bass Brewers took over from season 1998-9 with a 5-year sponsorship of the Worthington Cup worth £23m. It ends in 2003.

Norwich City unique: In 1985, Norwich City became (and they remain) the only club to win a major domestic cup and be relegated in the same season. They won the League's Milk Cup and went down from the old First Division.

Liverpool's League Cup records: Winners a record 6 times. **Ian Rush** only player to win 5 times. Rush also first to play in 8 winning teams in Cup Finals **at Wembley**, all with Liverpool (F.A. Cup 1986-89-92; League Cup 1981-82-83-84-95).

Britain's first under-cover Cup Final: Worthington (league) Cup Final between Blackburn Rov. and Tottenham at Cardiff's Millennium Stadium on Sunday, February 24, 2002. With rain forecast, the retractable roof was closed on the morning of the match.

DISCIPLINE

SENDINGS-OFF

After three consecutive seasons in which sendings-off in **English domestic football** were down, the red-card total rose from 375 in 2000-01 to 437 in 2001-02, surpassing the previous record of 425 in 1998-9.

Last season's total comprised 78 among Premiership clubs (66 League, 6 F.A. Cup, 6 Worthington Cup) and 359 players from Nationwide League clubs (329 League, 11 F.A. Cup, 16 Worthington Cup, 2 LDV Vans Trophy, 1 in play-offs).

Among Premiership clubs, Arsenal had most dismissals: 12 (6 Premiership, 3 Champions League, 2 F.A. Cup, 1 Worthington Cup). But they did not have a player sent off in the season's last 3 months.

Most sendings-off in season in **English top division:** 70 in Premiership, 1998-9.

November 20, 1982 was the **worst day** for dismissals **in football history** with 15 players sent off (3 League, 12 in the F.A. Cup first round). That was also the blackest day for disciplinary action in the F.A. Cup (previous worst – eight on January 9, 1915).

Most players sent off in **English League football on one day:** 16 on 16, 2002 (2 Prem. League, 14 Nationwide League).

Most players sent off in one **Football League programme:** 15 in week-end of Sat., Dec. 22 (11) and Sun., Dec. 23 (4), 1990.

Most players ordered off in **Anglo-Scottish football on one day:** 25, all League, on Oct. 16, 1999 (14 in England, 11 in Scotland).

● In the entire first season of post-war League football (1946-7) only 12 players were sent off, followed by 14 in 1949-50, and the total League dismissals for the first nine seasons were 104.

The worst pre-war total was 28 in each of seasons 1921-2 and 1922-3.

ENGLAND SENDINGS-OFF

David Batty became the eighth player England have had sent off in their Int. history (1872 to date) when he was shown the red card in the European Championship qualifier against Poland in Warsaw on Sept. 8, 1999. **Paul Scholes** is England's only dismissal **at Wembley:**

June 5, 1968 **Alan Mullery**	v Yugoslavia (Florence, Eur. Champ.)
June 6, 1973 **Alan Ball**	v Poland (Chorzow, World Cup qual.)
June 15, 1977 **Trevor Cherry**	v Argentina (Buenos Aires, friendly)
June 6, 1986 **Ray Wilkins**	v Morocco (Monterrey, World Cup Finals)
June 30, 1998 **David Beckham**	v Argentina (St. Etienne, World Cup Finals)
Sept. 5, 1998 **Paul Ince**	v Sweden (Stockholm, Eur. Champ. qual.)
June 5, 1999 **Paul Scholes**	v Sweden (Wembley, Eur. Champ. qual.)
Sept. 8, 1999 **David Batty**	v Poland (Warsaw, Eur. Champ. qual.)

Other countries: Most recent sendings-off of players representing the other Home Countries: **N. Ireland – Steve Lomas** v Liechtenstein (Friendly, Vaduz, March 2002); **Scotland – Matt Elliott** v Faroe Islands (European Champ., Toftir, June, 1999); **Wales – Ryan Giggs** v Norway (World Cup qual., Oslo, September 2001); **Rep. of Ireland – Gary Kelly** (v Holland World Cup qual., Dublin, September 2001).

England dismissals at other levels:-

U-23 (4): **Stan Anderson** (v Bulgaria, Sofia, May 19, 1957); **Alan Ball** (v Austria, Vienna, June 2, 1965); **Kevin Keegan** (v E. Germany, Magdeburg, June 1, 1972); **Steve Perryman** (v Portugal, Lisbon, Nov. 19, 1974).

U-21 (12): **Sammy Lee** (v Hungary, Keszthely, June 5, 1981); **Mark Hateley** (v Scotland, Hampden Park, April 19, 1982); **Paul Elliott** (v Denmark, Maine Road, Manchester, March 26, 1986); **Tony Cottee** (v W. Germany, Ludenscheid, September 8, 1987); **Julian Dicks** (v Mexico, Toulon, France, June 12, 1988); **Jason Dodd** (v Mexico, Toulon, May 29, 1991; 3 Mexico players also sent off in that match); **Matthew Jackson** (v France, Toulon, May 28, 1992); **Robbie Fowler** (v Austria, Kafkenberg, October 11, 1994); **Alan Thompson** (v Portugal, Oporto, September 2, 1995); **Terry Cooke** (v Portugal, Toulon, May 30, 1996); **Ben Thatcher** (v Italy, Rieti, October 10, 1997); **John Curtis** (v Greece, Heraklion, November 13, 1997); **Jody Morris** (v Luxembourg, Grevenmacher, October 13, 1998); **Stephen Wright** (v Germany, Derby Co., October 6, 2000); **Alan Smith** (v Finland, Valkeakoski, October 10, 2000); **Luke Young** and **John Terry** (v Greece, Athens, June 5, 2001).
England 'B' (1): **Neil Webb** (v Algeria, Algiers, December 11, 1990).

MOST DISMISSALS IN INTERNATIONAL MATCHES

19 (10 Chile, 9 Uruguay), June 25, 1975; **6** (2 Mexico, 4 Argentina), 1956; **6** (5 Ecuador, 1 Uruguay), Jan. 4, 1977 (4 Ecuadorians sent off in 78th min., match abandoned, 1-1); **5** (Holland 3, Brazil 2), June 6, 1999 in Goianio, Brazil.

INTERNATIONAL STOPPED THROUGH DEPLETED SIDE

Portugal v Angola (5-1), friendly International in Lisbon on November 14, 2001, abandoned (68 mins) because Angola were down to 6 players (4 sent off, 1 carried off, no substitutes left).

MOST 'CARDS' IN WORLD CUP FINALS MATCH

18 (16 yellow, 2 red, both colours equally shared) in Germany v Cameroon group qualifier, Shizuoka, Japan, June 11, 2002.

FIVE OFF IN ONE MATCH

For the first time since League football began in 1888, **five** players were sent off in one match (two Chesterfield, three Plymouth Argyle) in Div. 2 at Saltergate on **Feb. 22, 1997**. Four were dismissed (two from each side) in a goalmouth brawl in the last minute.

Second instance of **five** sent off in a League match was on **Dec. 2, 1997**: 4 Bristol Rov. players, 1 Wigan Athletic in Div. 2 match at Wigan. Four of those dismissals came in the 45th minute.

There have been nine instances of **four** Football League club players being sent off in one match:

Jan. 8, 1955 Crewe Alexandra v Bradford City (Div. 3 North), two players from each side.

Dec. 13, 1986 Sheffield Utd. (1 player) v Portsmouth (3) in Div. 2.

Aug. 18, 1987 Port Vale v Northampton Town (Littlewoods Cup 1st. Round, 1st. Leg), two players from each side.

Dec. 12, 1987 Brentford v Mansfield Town (Div. 3), two players from each side.

Sept. 6, 1992 First instance in British first-class football of **four players from one side** being sent off in one match. Hereford Utd.'s seven survivors, away to Northampton Town (Div. 3), held out for a 1-1 draw.

Mar. 1, 1977 Norwich City v Huddersfield Town (Div. 1), two from each side.

Oct. 4, 1977 Shrewsbury Town (1 player), Rotherham Utd. (3) in Div. 3.

Aug. 22, 1998 Gillingham v Bristol Rov. (Div. 2), two from each side, all after injury-time brawl.

Mar. 16, 2001 Bristol City v Millwall (Div. 2), two from each side.

Four Stranraer players were sent off away to Airdrie (Scottish Div. 1) on Dec. 3, 1994, and that Scottish record was equalled when **four Hearts men** were ordered off away to Rangers (Prem. Div.) on **Sept. 14, 1996**. Albion Rov. had **four players** sent off (3 in last 8 mins) away to Queen's Park (Scottish Div. 3) on **August 23, 1997**.

Modern instances of **three players from one side** being sent off:

Dec. 13, 1986 Portsmouth (away to Sheffield Utd., Div. 2); **Aug. 23, 1989** Falkirk (home to Hearts, Scottish Skol Cup 3rd. Round); **Apr. 20, 1992** Newcastle Utd. (away to Derby Co., Div. 2); **May 2, 1992** Bristol City (away to Watford, Div. 2); **Nov. 23, 1996**

Wycombe Wand. (home to Preston N.E., Div. 2); **Feb. 8, 1997** Darlington (away to Scarborough, Div. 3); **Oct. 4, 1997** Rotherham Utd. (away to Shrewsbury Town, Div. 3); **Mar. 28, 1998** Barnsley (home to Liverpool, Premiership); **Sept. 26, 1998** Southend Utd. (away to Swansea City, Div. 3); **May 1, 1999** West Ham Utd. (home to Leeds Utd., Premiership); **Oct. 9, 1999** Torquay Utd. away to Northampton Town (Div. 3); **Dec. 28, 1999** Cardiff City away to Cambridge Utd. (Div. 2); **Apr. 29, 2000** Halifax Town away to York City (Div. 3); **Apr. 16, 2001** Carlisle Utd. away to Scunthorpe Utd. (Div. 3); **May 1, 2002** Kidderminster away to Bristol Rov. (Div. 3); **May 16, 2002** Sheffield Utd. home to W.B.A. (Div. 1).

Aug. 24, 1994: Three Sheffield Utd. players, and one from Udinese, were sent off in the Anglo-Italian Cup at Bramall Lane on Aug. 24, 1994. In addition, Utd. manager Dave Bassett was ordered from the bench.

Most dismissals one team, one match: Five players of America Tres Rios in first ten minutes after disputed goal by opponents Itaperuna in Brazilian cup match in Rio de Janeiro on Nov. 23, 1991. Tie then abandoned and awarded to Itaperuna.

Eight dismissals in one match: Four on each side in S. American Super Cup quarter-final (Gremio, Brazil v Penarol, Uruguay) in Oct. 1993.

Five dismissals in one season – Dave Caldwell (2 with Chesterfield, 3 with Torquay Utd.) in 1987-88.

First instance of **four dismissals in Scottish match**: three **Rangers** players (all English – Terry Hurlock, Mark Walters, Mark Hateley) and **Celtic's** Peter Grant in Scottish Cup quarter-final at Parkhead on Mar. 17, 1991 (Celtic won 2-0).

Four players (3 Hamilton, 1 Airdrie) were sent off in Scottish Div. 1 match on Oct. 30, 1993.

Four players (3 Ayr, 1 Stranraer) were sent off in Scottish Div. 1 match on Aug. 27, 1994.

In Scottish Cup first round replays on Dec. 16, 1996, there were two instances of **three players of one side sent off**: Albion Rov. (away to Forfar) and Huntly (away to Clyde).

FASTEST SENDINGS-OFF

World record – 10 secs: Giuseppe Lorenzo (Bologna) for striking opponent in Italian League match v Parma, December 9, 1990.

Domestic – 13 secs: Kevin Pressman (Sheffield Wed. goalkeeper at Wolves, Div. 1, Sunday, Aug. 14, 2000); **19 secs: Mark Smith** (Crewe Alexandra goalkeeper at Darlington, Div. 3, Mar. 12, 1994). **In Div. 1 – 85 secs: Liam O'Brien** (Manchester Utd. at Southampton, Jan. 3, 1987). **Premier League – 72 secs: Tim Flowers** (Blackburn Rov. goalkeeper v Leeds Utd., Feb. 1, 1995).

In World Cup – 55 secs: Jose Batista (Uruguay v Scotland at Neza, Mexico, June 13, 1986).

In European competition – 90 secs: Sergei Dirkach (Dynamo Moscow v Ghent UEFA Cup 3rd round, 2nd leg, December 11, 1991).

Fastest F.A. Cup dismissal – 52 secs: Ian Culverhouse (Swindon Town defender, deliberate hand-ball on goal-line, away to Everton, 3rd. Round, Sunday Jan. 5, 1997).

Fastest League Cup dismissal – 33 secs: Jason Crowe (Arsenal substitute v Birmingham City, 3rd Round, Oct. 14, 1997).

Fastest Sending-off on debut: See Jason Crowe (above).

Fastest Sending-off of substitute – 0 secs: Walter Boyd (Swansea City) for striking opponent before ball in play after he went on (83 mins) at home to Darlington, Div. 3, Nov. 23, 1999.

MOST SENDINGS-OFF IN CAREER

21 – **Willie Johnston** (Rangers 7, WBA 6, Vancouver Whitecaps 4, Hearts 3, Scotland 1)

21 – **Roy McDonough** (13 in Football League, 8 non-league).

- **Career Red Cards** of modern players (at end of season 2001-02): **Steve Walsh** (Leicester City) 13, **Dennis Wise** (Chelsea) 11, **Roy Keane** (Manchester Utd.) 9, **Paul Gascoigne** (Middlesbrough) 8, **Mark Hughes** (Everton) 8.
- **Carlton Palmer** holds the unique record of having been sent off with each of his five Premiership clubs: Sheffield Wed., Leeds Utd., Southampton, Nott'm. Forest and Coventry City.

WEMBLEY SENDINGS-OFF

Manchester Utd.'s **Kevin Moran** is the only player to be sent off in the F.A. Cup Final (v Everton, 1985). His dismissal was one of 22 in major matches at Wembley:

Aug. 1948 **Branko Stankovic** (Yugoslavia) v Sweden, Olympic Games.
July 1966 **Antonio Rattin** (Argentina captain) v England, World cup q-final.
Aug. 1974 **Billy Bremner** (Leeds Utd.) and **Kevin Keegan** (Liverpool), Charity Shield.
Mar. 1977 **Gilbert Dresch** (Luxembourg) v England, World Cup.
May 1985 **Kevin Moran** (Manchester Utd.) v Everton, F.A. Cup Final.
Apr. 1993 **Lee Dixon** (Arsenal) v Tottenham, F.A. Cup semi-final.
May 1993 **Peter Swan** (Port Vale) v W.B.A., Div. 2 Play-off Final.
Mar. 1994 **Andrei Kanchelskis** (Manchester Utd.) v Aston Villa, League Cup Final.
May 1994 **Mike Wallace** and **Chris Beaumont** (Stockport Co.) v Burnley, Div. 2 Play-off Final.
June 1995 **Tetsuji Hashiratani** (Japan) v England, Umbro Cup.
May 1997 **Brian Statham** (Brentford) v Crewe Alexandra, Div. 2 Play-off Final.
Apr. 1998 **Capucho** (Portugal) v England, friendly.
Nov. 1998 **Ray Parlour** (Arsenal) and Tony Vareilles (Lens), Champions League.
Mar. 1999 **Justin Edinburgh** (Tottenham) v Leicester City, League Cup Final.
June 1999 **Paul Scholes** (England) v Sweden, European Championship qual.
Feb. 2000 **Clint Hill** (Tranmere) v Leicester City, League Cup Final.
Apr. 2000 **Mark Delaney** (Aston Villa) v Bolton Wand., F.A. Cup semi-final.
May 2000 **Kevin Sharp** (Wigan Athletic) v Gillingham, Div. 2 Play-off Final.
Aug. 2000 **Roy Keane** (Manchester Utd. captain) v Chelsea, Charity Shield.

WEMBLEY'S SUSPENDED CAPTAINS

Suspension prevented four **club captains** playing at Wembley in modern finals, in successive years.

Three were in F.A. Cup Finals – Glenn Roeder (Q.P.R., 1982), Steve Foster (Brighton & H.A., 1983) and Wilf Rostron (Watford, 1984) – and Sunderland's **Shaun Elliott** was barred from the 1985 Milk Cup Final.

Roeder was banned from Q.P.R.'s 1982 Cup Final replay against Tottenham, and Foster was ruled out of the first match in Brighton & H.A.'s 1983 Final against Manchester Utd.

BOOKINGS RECORDS

Most players of one Football League club booked in one match is **TEN** – members of the Mansfield Town team away to Crystal Palace in F.A. Cup third round, January 1963.

Fastest bookings – 3 seconds after kick-off, Vinnie Jones (Chelsea, home to Sheffield Utd., F.A. Cup fifth round, February 15, 1992); 5 seconds after kick-off: **Vinnie Jones** (Sheffield Utd., away to Manchester City, Div. 1, January 19, 1991). He was sent-off (54 mins) for second bookable offence.

FIGHTING TEAM-MATES

Charlton Athletic's **Mike Flanagan** and **Derek Hales** were sent off for fighting each other five minutes from end of F.A. Cup 3rd Round tie at home to Southern League Maidstone on Jan. 9, 1979.

Bradford City's **Andy Myers** and **Stuart McCall** had a fight during the 1-6 Premiership defeat at Leeds on Sunday, May 13, 2001.

On Sept. 28, 1994 the Scottish F.A. suspended Hearts players **Graeme Hogg** and **Craig Levein** for ten matches for fighting each other in a pre-season 'friendly' v Raith.

FOOTBALL'S FIRST BETTING SCANDAL

A Football League investigation into the First Division match which ended Manchester Utd 2, Liverpool 0 at Old Trafford on Good Friday, April 2, 1915 proved that the result had been 'squared' by certain players betting on the outcome. Four members of each team were suspended for life, but some of the bans were lifted when League football resumed in 1919 in recognition of the players' war service.

PLAYERS JAILED

Ten professional footballers found guilty of conspiracy to fraud by 'fixing' matches for betting purposes were given prison sentences at Nottingham Assizes on Jan. 26, 1965.

Jimmy Gauld (Mansfield Town), described as the central figure, was given four years. Among the others sentenced, Tony Kay (Sheffield Wed., Everton & England), Peter Swan (Sheffield Wed. & England) and David 'Bronco' Layne (Sheffield Wed.) were suspended from football for life by the F.A.

LONG SUSPENSIONS

The longest suspension in modern times for a player in British football was imposed on Manchester Utd.'s French international captain **Eric Cantona**, following his attack on a spectator as he left the pitch after being sent off at Crystal Palace (Prem. League) on Jan. 25, 1995. He was banned from football for 8 months.

The club immediately suspended him to the end of the season and fined him 2 weeks' wages (est. £20,000). Then, on a disrepute charge, the F.A. fined him £10,000 (February 1995) and extended the ban to September 30 (which FIFA confirmed as world wide).

A subsequent 2-weeks' jail sentence on Cantona for assault was altered, on appeal, to 120 hours' community service, which took the form of coaching schoolboys in the Manchester area.

Mark Dennis, the Q.P.R. defender, was sent off for the 11th time in his career away to Tottenham (Div. 1) on November 14, 1987. (Two of those dismissals were for after-match tunnel offences; in addition, Dennis had then been cautioned 64 times in ten seasons and answered two disrepute charges concerning newspaper articles).

On December 10, the F.A. imposed on him a 53-day suspension, which was amended on appeal (January 25) to an 8-match ban. This was the longest suspension of a Football League player since **Kevin Keegan** (Liverpool) and **Billy Bremner** (Leeds Utd.) were each banned for 5 weeks (10 matches) after being sent off in the F.A. Charity Shield at Wembley in August 1974.

On December 6, 1988 Dennis was sent off for **12th. time** (Q.P.R. v Fulham reserves) and fined £1,000.

Steve Walsh (Leicester City) has been sent off 13 times in his 18-season career (4 times with Wigan Athletic, 9 with Leicester City; 11 times in League, twice in F.A. Cup; 12 times away, once at home). His latest dismissal was away to Chelsea (F.A. Cup 5) on Jan. 30, 2000.

Before the disciplinary points system was introduced in season 1972-73, offenders were suspended for a specific number of weeks. Other lengthy suspensions imposed by the F.A. for on-field offences:

November 1969: Derek Dougan (Wolves) 8 weeks; **John Fitzpatrick** (Manchester Utd.) 8 weeks.

January 1970: Ronnie Rees (Nott'm Forest) 6 weeks; **George Best** (Manchester Utd.) 6 weeks.

January 1971: Peter Osgood (Chelsea) 8 weeks, following second trio of cautions in a year.

December 1971: Kevin Lewis (Manchester Utd.) 5 months; **Denis Hollywood** and **Brian O'Neil** (both Southampton) 9 weeks.

October 1987: Steve Walsh (Leicester City) 9 matches – original ban of 6 games (following the sixth sending-off of his career) increased to 9 when he reached 21 disciplinary points.

April 1988: Chris Kamara (Swindon Town) suspended to end of season (6 matches).

October 1988: Paul Davis (Arsenal) suspended for 9 matches, and fined a record £3,000, for breaking jaw of Glen Cockerill (Southampton) – off-ball incident caught on video.

January 1992: Frank Sinclair (Chelsea) suspended for 9 matches (fined £600) after being found guilty of assault on referee Paul Alcock (clash of heads) while playing for W.B.A. on loan.

January 1993: Alan Gough, Fulham goalkeeper, suspended for 42 days for assaulting referee in Autoglass Trophy match at Gillingham on December 8.

November 1994: Andy Townsend (Aston Villa) suspended for 6 matches (3 for 21 discip. points, 3 for sending-off).

October 26, 1997: Emmanuel Petit (Arsenal) pushes referee Paul Durkin when sent off at home to Aston Villa (Prem.). F.A. impose 3-match ban and £1,000 fine.

August 1998: F.A. suspend **David Batty** (Newcastle Utd.) for first 6 Prem. matches of season 1998-9 and fine him £1,500 for pushing referee David Elleray when sent off at Blackburn Rov. in last game of previous season.

October 1998: Paolo Di Canio (Sheff. Wed.) banned for 11 matches and fined £10,000 for pushing referee Paul Alcock after being sent off at home to Arsenal (Prem.), Sept. 26.

Seven-month ban: Frank Barson, 37-year-old Watford centre-half, sent off at home to Fulham (Div. 3 South) on September 29, 1928, was suspended by the F.A. for the remainder of the season.

Twelve-month ban: Oldham Athletic full-back **Billy Cook** was given a 12-month suspension for refusing to leave the field when sent off at Middlesbrough (Div. 1), on April 3, 1915. The referee abandoned the match with 35 minutes still to play, and the score (4-1 to Middlesbrough) was ordered to stand.

Long Scottish bans: September 1954: **Willie Woodburn**, Rangers and Scotland centre-half, suspended for rest of career after fifth sending-off in 6 years.

Billy McLafferty, Stenhousemuir striker, was banned (April 14) for 8½ months, to Jan. 1, 1993, and fined £250 for failing to appear at a disciplinary hearing after being sent off against Arbroath on Feb. 1.

Twelve-match ban: On May 12, 1994 Scottish F.A. suspended Rangers forward **Duncan Ferguson** for 12 matches for violent conduct v Raith on Apr. 16. On Oct. 11, 1995, Ferguson (then with Everton) sent to jail for 3 months for the assault (served 44 days); Feb. 1, 1996 Scottish judge quashed 7 matches that remained of SFA ban on Ferguson.

On September 29, 2001 the SFA imposed a **17-match suspension** on Forfar Athletic's former Scottish International **Dave Bowman** for persistent foul and abusive language when sent off against Stranraer on September 22. As his misconduct continued, he was shown **5 red cards** by the referee.

FINES ETC. – MODERN

2000 (January) F.A. fine Notts Co. manager **Gary Brazil** £250 and Bournemouth manager Mel Machin £100 for comments to referee Jeff Winter after F.A. Cup 1st Round replay, November 9. Football League fine **Barnet** £2,500 for late arrival at Hartlepool, November 2. F.A. ban **Ben Thatcher** (Wimbledon) for 2 matches for elbowing Sunderland's Nicky Summerbee, January 3 – on video evidence (player not sent off). F.A. fine West Ham Utd. captain **Steve Lomas** £6,000 for comments to officials after match at Chelsea, November 7. F.A. fine **Hull City** £2,500 for failing to assist with enquiries into running of club. F.A. suspend referee **Rob Harris** for month for 'not applying the rules' at Tranmere v Sunderland F.A. Cup (4), January 8, Tranmere having replaced a sent-off player with a substitute.

2000 (March) F.A. fine **Paul Gascoigne** (Middlesbrough) £5,000, with 3-match ban, for elbowing offence v Aston Villa (February 14) in which Gascoigne broke an arm (charged on video evidence – incident missed by match officials). F.A. fine **Paolo Di Canio** (West Ham Utd.) £5,000 for making gesture to opponent v Aston Villa (January 15). UEFA fine **Chelsea** £7,500 and **Marseilles** £37,000 for spectator misconduct (Champions League, February 29). F.A. fine **Leeds Utd.** and **Tottenham** £150,000 each for mass player-brawl at Elland Road (Premier League), February 12. F.A. fine Wolves striker **Ade Akinbiyi** £2,000 with 4-match suspension for head-butting Nott'm Forest player, February 26. Seven **Leicester City** men – players and officials, past or present – collectively fined £75,000 by F.A. for misconduct relating to distribution of tickets for 1999 Worthington Cup Final.

2000 (April) Football League fine **Bolton Wand.** £45,000 for poaching manager Sam Allardyce from Notts Co. F.A. fine **Emmanuel Petit** (Arsenal) £5,000 for obscene gesture to Aston Villa fans, March 5. F.A. fine **Steve Claridge** £900 for breach of rules when betting on his team to beat Barnsley, January 29 (they did by 3-0, Claridge hat-trick). F.A. fine **Chelsea** £50,000 for players' part in tunnel brawl at home to Wimbledon, February 12 (see also May). F.A. fine Chelsea captain **Dennis Wise** £7,500 for 'insulting behaviour' in same incident. F.A. fine Tranmere Rov. manager **John Aldridge** £750 for incident at Worthington Cup Final v Leicester and for comments to match officials after League matches v Birmingham and Portsmouth.

2000 (May) F.A. fine **Wimbledon** £50,000 and captain **Kenny Cunningham** £5,000 for their part in tunnel brawl at Chelsea, February 12 (see April).

2000 (July) UEFA fine **Portuguese F.A. £70,300** and ban 3 of their players from all European competitions, club and country, as sequel to fracas when France awarded penalty (handball by Everton's **Abel Xavier**) for Golden Goal decider in Euro 2000 semi-final. Suspensions: **Xavier** 9 months, **Nuno Gomes** 8 months, **Paulo Bento** 6 months. F.A. fine **Bryan Robson** (Middlesbrough manager) £7,500 for confrontation with referee after defeat at Coventry, April 15. F.A. fine **John Hartson** (Wimbledon) £5,000 on charge of abusive language to referee away to Bradford City, April 30.

2000 (October) F.A. fine **Paul Ince** (Middlesbrough) £15,000 for misconduct (abusive language at home to Derby Co., Sept. 6. F.A. fine **Gilles Grimandi** (Arsenal) £3,000 (1-match ban) for stamping on Gary McAllister (Liverpool), August 21. F.A. fine Swindon Town manager **Colin Todd** £2,500 for verbal assault on referee at Exeter (Worthington Cup, Sept. 5). UEFA fine **David Beckham** £4,000 for spitting towards referee in Manchester Utd.'s Champions League defeat away to PSV Eindhoven, Sept. 26. F.A. give Arsenal manager **Arsene Wenger** 12-match touchline ban and fine him 4 weeks' wages after 'tunnel row' with fourth official at Sunderland, August 19 (Wenger to appeal – see Feb. 2001). F.A. fine **Ipswich Town** £2,500 for sub-standard floodlights v Manchester Utd., August 22. F.A. fine **Neil Lennon** (Leicester City) £4,000 for ticket-selling offences (1999 Worthington Cup Final). F.A. fine **Crystal Palace** £20,000. **Nott'm. Forest** £15,000 for players' mass confrontation at Selhust Park, August 28. UEFA fine **Arsenal** £8,300 for offences at Champions League match away to Lazio. Oct. 17.

2000 (November) F.A. fine **Norwich City** £30,000 (reduced on appeal to £12,000 plus £12,000 suspended) and **Blackpool** £6,000 for players' mass brawl at Norwich (Worthington Cup, Sept. 19). F.A. fine Tranmere Rov. manager **John Aldridge** £2,500 with 14-day touchline ban for throwing water bottle away to Barnsley, Oct. 17. F.A. fine **Preston N.E.** and **Sheffield Utd.** £15,000 each after 19-player brawl at Preston, August 19 (Sheffield Utd. manager **Neil Warnock** fined £2,000). F.A. ban **Stan Collymore** (Bradford City) 3 matches for stamping on Paul Gascoigne when playing for Leicester City v Everton, Sept. 29 (incident investigated by F.A. video panel).

2000 (December) UEFA fine **Manchester Utd.** £2,000 for players' misconduct v PSV Eindhoven (Champions League), Oct. 18.

2001 (January) F.A. fine **Paul Jewell** (Sheffield Wed. manager) £1,000 for comments to referee at Birmingham (Worthington Cup), December 12.

2001 (February) Arsenal manager **Arsene Wenger's** appeal (see October) upheld – reprimanded and fine reduced to £10,000. **Patrick Vieira** fined £10,000 by F.A. (1-match ban) for kicking Olivier Dacourt, Leeds Utd., Nov. 26. **Matt Elliott** (Leicester City) fined £5,000 by F.A. and **Hassan Kachloul** (Southampton) £2,000 on 'improper conduct' charges F.A. fine **Colin Todd** (Derby Co. assistant-manager) £2,500, with 3-match touchline ban, for verbal abuse of match official when Swindon Town manager.

2001 (March) F.A. fine **Gary Neville** (Manchester Utd.) £30,000, with 2-match ban, for foul and abusive language to assistant-referee after F.A. Cup defeat v West Ham Utd., Jan. 28 (see April re appeal). F.A. fine **Jim Magilton** (Ipswich Town) £5,000, with 1-match ban, for comments to referee at Chelsea, Jan. 20. F.A. fine Wimbledon manager **Terry Burton** £5,000, with 2-match touchline ban, for comments to assistant-referee at F.A. Cup 4th Round replay at Wycombe Wand., Feb. 20.

2001 (April) F.A. fine Wycombe Wand. manager **Lawrie Sanchez** £2,000, with 3-match touchline ban, for comments to assistant-referee at F.A. Cup 6th Round win at Leicester, March 10. F.A. fine Ipswich Town defender **Hermann Hreidarsson** £1,500 for jumping into crowd to celebrate goal v Bradford City, March 4. F.A. fine **Gillingham** £15,000 and **Crystal Palace** £5,000 following 12-player brawl at Gillingham, Dec. 26. Football League tribunal docks **Chesterfield** (Div. 3 leaders) 9 points, plus £20,000 fine, for breach of transfer regulations and under-reporting gate receipts (subsequent appeal turned down). F.A. fine **Nott'm. Forest** and **Preston N.E.** £5,000 each after mass confrontation of players at Nottingham, November 4. F.A. Appeal Board reduce fine on **Gary Neville** (Manchester Utd.) – see March – to £7,000; 2-match ban stays. FIFA ban Scotland captain **Colin Hendry** from 6 Int. matches (reduced to 3 on appeal) for elbowing a San Marino player in World Cup qualifier at Hampden Park, March 28.

2001 (May) F.A. fine **Lee Hendrie** (Aston Villa) £5,000 for 'over-exuberant' celebration of winning goal at home to Leicester City, April 4.

2001 (August) F.A. impose fines (suspended to end of season) for poor disciplinary records in 2000-01: **Derby Co.** £100,000; **Everton** and **Sheffield Wed.** £50,000; **Millwall** and **Bury** £25,000; **Torquay Utd.** and **Exeter City** £12,500

2001 (September) F.A. find **Martin Keown** (Arsenal) £10,000 with 1-match ban for striking Mark Viduka (Leeds Utd.) at Highbury, May 5. UEFA fine **English F.A.** £2,400 for 4 England U-21 players being booked v Germany, August 31, UEFA fine **Newcastle Utd.** £2,800 for 3 bookings v Troyes (InterToto Cup), August 21. F.A. fine Birmingham City manager **Trevor Francis** £1,500 for protests at play-off semi-final v Preston N.E. in May.

2001 (November) F.A. fine **Mark Wright**, Oxford Utd. manager, £1,750 with 4-match touchline ban for abusive language to referee v Scunthorpe Utd., October 20.

2001 (December) F.A. fine Watford £5,000 and W.B.A. £2,500 for 16-player brawl, September 15.

2002 (January) F.A. find **David Ginola** (Aston Villa) £22,000 with 2-match ban for confrontation with 4th official when sent off v Leicester City, December 1. Football league fines: **Carlisle Utd.** £25,000 for fielding ineligible player v Mansfield Town, November 10; **Luton Town** £20,000 for failing to fulfil fixture at Kidderminster, December 1 (claiming 20 players ill or injured).

2002 (February) F.A. fines: **Portsmouth** £10,000 after 15 bookings in less than a month; **Wolves** £2,500 for players' misconduct v W.B.A., December 2; managers **Mark McGhee** (Millwall) £7,500 and **Steve Bruce** (Birmingham City) £5,000 for confrontations with referee, January 10.

2002 (March) F.A. fines: **Everton** £25,000 for disorderly conduct at Fulham, December 8 (£30,000 Fulham fine subsequently rescinded); **Mauricio Taricco** (Tottenham) £5,000 for improper conduct v Chelsea (Worthington Cup semi-final, 2nd leg). F.A. ban **Thierry Henry** (Arsenal) 3 domestic matches for improper conduct towards referee v Newcastle Utd., December 18. Premier League fine **Liverpool** £20,000 for illegal approach when signing **Christian Ziege** from Middlesbrough, August 2000; Ziege fined £20,000 for breach of rules.

2002 (April) F.A. fine Blackburn Rov. manager **Graeme Souness** £10,000 (1-match touchline ban) for verbal abuse of referee at Middlesbrough (F.A. Cup 5th Round, February 16).

2002 (May) F.A. fines: Derby Co. manager **John Gregory** £5,000 for improper conduct at Premiership match v Newcastle Utd., April 13. **Sheffield Utd.** £10,000 for players' misconduct at abandoned match v W.B.A., March 16; manager **Neil Warnock** £2,000, with 2-match ban for misconduct; 3 players punished – **Patrick Suffo** £3,000, with 3-match ban, **Keith Curle** £500 (2-match ban), **George Santos** 2-match ban. Wales F.A. fine **Cardiff City** £20,000 for crowd trouble v Leeds Utd. (F.A. Cup 3rd Round, January 6). N. Ireland manager **Sammy McIlroy** and assistant **Jim Harvey** each banned for 1 match and fined £4,000 by FIFA for misconduct at World Cup qualifier away to Malta, October 6.

2002 (June) **Portsmouth** fined £30,000 (suspended for year) by F.A. for receiving 8 red and 108 yellow cards last season.

TOP FINES

Clubs: £1,500,000 (increased from original £600,000) Tottenham, Dec. 1994; **£150,000** Leeds Utd., Mar. 2000; **£150,000** Tottenham, Mar. 2000; **£105,000** Chelsea, Jan. 1991; **£90,000** Tottenham, Jan. 1996; **£75,000** Chelsea, July 1988; **£75,000** Everton, Apr. 1994; **£60,000** Wimbledon, Jan. 1996; **£55,000** Birmingham City, Feb. 1994; **£50,000** Norwich City, June 1989; **£50,000** Arsenal, Nov. 1990; **£50,000** Barnet, Nov. 1992; **£50,000** Middlesbrough, Jan. 1997; **£50,000** Arsenal, Aug. 1997; **£50,000** Everton, July 1999; **£50,000** Chelsea, Apr. 2000; **£50,000** Wimbledon, May 2000.

Players: £45,000 Patrick Vieira (Arsenal), Oct. 1999; **£32,000** Robbie Fowler (Liverpool), Apr. 1999; **£22,000** David Ginola (Aston Villa), Jan. 2002; **£20,000** Vinnie Jones (Wimbledon), Nov. 1992; **£20,000** Patrick Vieira (Arsenal), Dec. 1998; **£20,000** John Hartson (Wimbledon – offence when with West Ham Utd.), Jan. 1999; **£20,000** Christian Ziege (ex-Liverpool), Mar. 2002; **£17,500** Ian Wright (West Ham Utd.), May 1999; **£15,000** Ian Wright (Arsenal), July 1997; **£15,000** Paul Ince (Middlesbrough), Oct. 2000; **£10,000** Paolo Di Canio (Sheff. Wed.), Oct. 1998; **£10,000** Faustino Asprilla (Newcastle Utd.), Apr. 1996; **£10,000** Eric Cantona (Manchester Utd.), Feb. 1995; **£10,000** Patrick Vieira (Arsenal), Feb. 2001; **£10,000** Martin Keown (Arsenal), Sept. 2001.

● In five seasons with Arsenal (1996-2001) Patrick Vieira was fined a total of £75,000 by the F.A. for offences that included six sendings-off.
Managers: £10,000 Arsene Wenger (Arsenal), Feb. 2001; **£10,000** Graeme Souness (Blackburn) Apr. 2002; **£7,500** Bryan Robson (Middlesbrough), July 2000; **£7,500** Mark McGhee (Millwall), Feb. 2002; **£5,000** Brian Clough (Nott'm. Forest), Feb. 1989; **£5,000** Ruud Gullit (Newcastle Utd.), Sept. 1999; **£5,000** John Gregory (Aston Villa), Nov. 1999; **£5,000** Steve Bruce (Birmingham), Feb. 2002.

MANAGERS

INTERNATIONAL RECORDS

(As at start of season 2002-03)

	P	W	D	L	F	A
Sven-Goran Eriksson	20	10	7	3	39	17
(England – appointed Coach Jan. 2001)						
Sammy McIlroy	18	5	3	10	19	29
(N. Ireland – appointed Jan. 2000)						
Berti Vogts	4	0	0	4	2	13
(Scotland – appointed Feb. 2002)						
*Mark Hughes	20	4	8	8	16	26
(Wales – appointed Aug. 1999)						

*Neville Southall joint acting-manager last match season 1998-9, first two 1999-2000 (W1, L2).

	P	W	D	L	F	A
Mick McCarthy	65	28	20	17	106	60
(Rep. of Ireland – appointed Feb. 1996)						

ENGLAND'S MANAGERS

		P	W	D	L
1946-62	**Walter Winterbottom**	139	78	33	28
1963-74	**Sir Alf Ramsey**	113	69	27	17
1974	**Joe Mercer,** caretaker	7	3	3	1
1974-77	**Don Revie**	29	14	8	7
1977-82	**Ron Greenwood**	55	33	12	10
1982-90	**Bobby Robson**	95	47	30	18
1990-93	**Graham Taylor**	38	18	13	7
1994-96	**Terry Venables,** coach	23	11	11	1
1996-99	**Glenn Hoddle,** coach	28	17	6	5
1999	**Howard Wilkinson,** caretaker	1	0	0	1
1999-2000	**Kevin Keegan,** coach	18	7	7	4
2000	**Howard Wilkinson,** caretaker	1	0	1	0
2000	**Peter Taylor,** caretaker	1	0	0	1
2001-2002	**Sven Goran Eriksson,** coach	20	10	7	3

INTERNATIONAL MANAGER CHANGES

England: Walter Winterbottom 1946-62 (initially coach); **Alf Ramsey** (Feb. 1963-May 1974); **Joe Mercer** (caretaker May 1974); **Don Revie** (July 1974-July 1977); **Ron Greenwood** (Aug. 1977-July 1982); **Bobby Robson** (July 1982-July 1990); **Graham Taylor** (July 1990-Nov. 1993); **Terry Venables,** coach (Jan. 1994-June 1996); **Glenn Hoddle,** coach (June 1996-Feb. 1999); **Howard Wilkinson** (caretaker Feb. 1999); **Kevin Keegan** coach (Feb. 1999-Oct. 2000); **Howard Wilkinson** (caretaker Oct. 2000); **Peter Taylor** (caretaker Nov. 2000); **Sven Goran Eriksson** (from Jan. 2001).

N. Ireland (modern): Billy Bingham (1967-Aug. 1971); **Terry Neill** (Aug. 1971-Mar. 1975); **Dave Clements** (player-manager Mar. 1975-1976); **Danny Blanchflower** (June 1976-Nov. 1979); **Billy Bingham** (Feb. 1980-Nov. 1993); **Bryan Hamilton** Feb. 1994-Feb. 1998); **Lawrie McMenemy** (since Feb. 1998); **Sammy McIlroy** (since Jan. 2000).

Scotland (modern): **Bobby Brown** (Feb. 1967-July 1971); **Tommy Docherty** (Sept. 1971- Dec. 1972); **Willie Ormond** (Jan. 1973-May 1977); **Ally MacLeod** (May 1977-Sept.1978); **Jock Stein** (Oct. 1978-Sept. 1985); **Alex Ferguson** (caretaker Oct. 1985-June 1986); **Andy Roxburgh**, coach (July 1986-Sept. 1993); **Craig Brown** (Sept. 1993-Oct. 2001); **Berti Vogts** (since Feb. 2002).

Wales (modern): **Mike Smith** (July 1974-Dec. 1979); **Mike England** (Mar. 1980-Feb. 1988); **David Williams** (caretaker Mar. 1988); **Terry Yorath** (Apr. 1988-Nov. 1993); **John Toshack** (Mar. 1994, one match); **Mike Smith** (Mar. 1994-June 1995); **Bobby Gould** (Aug. 1995-June 1999); **Mark Hughes** (since Aug. 1999).

Rep. of Ireland (modern): **Liam Tuohy** (Sept. 1971-Nov. 1972); **Johnny Giles** (Oct. 1973-Apr. 1980, initially player-manager); **Eoin Hand** (June 1980-Nov. 1985); **Jack Charlton** (Feb. 1986-Dec. 1995); **Mick McCarthy** (since Feb. 1996).

FIRST BLACK ENGLAND MANAGER

Chris Ramsey, 36, in charge of England's U-20 squad for the World Youth Championship in Nigeria, April 1999. He was Brighton & H.A.'s right-back in the 1983 F.A. Cup Final v Manchester Utd.

YOUNGEST LEAGUE MANAGER

Graham Taylor, aged 28 years, 3 months when appointed manager of Lincoln City in December 1972.

LONGEST-SERVING LEAGUE MANAGERS – ONE CLUB

Fred Everiss, secretary-manager of W.B.A. for 46 years (1902-48); since last war, **Sir Matt Busby**, in charge of Manchester Utd. for 25 seasons (1945-69, 1970-71; **Jimmy Seed** at Charlton Athletic for 23 years (1933-56).

1,000-TIME MANAGERS

Only four have managed in more than 1,000 English League games: **Alec Stock**, **Brian Clough**, **Jim Smith** and **Graham Taylor**. **Sir Matt Busby**, **Dario Gradi** and **Dave Bassett** have each managed more than 1,000 matches in all competitions.

SHORT-TERM MANAGERS

		Departed
3 Days	Bill Lambton (Scunthorpe Utd.)	April 1959
7 Days	Tim Ward (Exeter City)	March 1953
7 Days	Kevin Cullis (Swansea City)	February 1996
10 Days	Dave Cowling (Doncaster Rov.)	October 1997
10 Days	Peter Cormack (Cowdenbeath)	December 2000
13 Days	Johnny Cochrane (Reading)	April 1939
13 Days	Micky Adams (Swansea City)	October 1997
16 Days	Jimmy McIlroy (Bolton Wand.)	November 1970
20 Days	Paul Went (Leyton Orient)	October 1981
27 Days	Malcolm Crosby (Oxford Utd.)	January 1998
28 Days	Tommy Docherty (Q.P.R.)	December 1968
32 Days	Steve Coppell (Manchester City)	November 1996
41 Days	Steve Wicks (Lincoln City)	October 1995
44 Days	Brian Clough (Leeds Utd.)	September 1974
44 Days	Jock Stein (Leeds Utd.)	October 1978
48 Days	John Toshack (Wales)	March 1994
48 Days	David Platt (Sampdoria coach)	February 1999
49 Days	Brian Little (Wolves)	October 1986
61 Days	Bill McGarry (Wolves)	November 1985
63 Days	Dave Booth (Peterborough Utd.)	January 1991

● In May 1984, Crystal Palace named **Dave Bassett** as manager, but he changed his mind four days later, without signing the contract, and returned to Wimbledon.

● In an angry outburst after a play-off defeat in May 1992, Barnet chairman Stan Flashman sacked manager **Barry Fry** and re-instated him a day later.

EARLY-SEASON MANAGER SACKINGS

2000 Alan Buckley (Grimsby Town) 10 days; **1997** Kerry Dixon (Doncaster Rov.) 12 days; **1996** Sammy Chung (Doncaster Rov.) on morning of season's opening League match; **1996** Alan Ball (Manchester City) 12 days; **1994** Kenny Hibbitt (Walsall) and Kenny Swain (Wigan Athletic) 20 days; **1993** Peter Reid (Manchester City) 12 days; **1991** Don Mackay (Blackburn Rov.) 14 days; **1989** Mick Jones (Peterborough Utd.) 12 days; **1980** Bill McGarry (Newcastle Utd.) 13 days; **1979** Dennis Butler (Port Vale) 12 days; **1977** George Petchey (Leyton O.) 13 days; **1977** Willie Bell (Birmingham City) 16 days; **1971** Len Richley (Darlington) 12 days.

FEWEST MANAGERS

West Ham Utd. have had only nine managers in their 105-year history: Syd King, Charlie Paynter, Ted Fenton, Ron Greenwood, John Lyall, Lou Macari, Billy Bonds, Harry Redknapp and Glenn Roeder.

RECORD START FOR MANAGER

Arsenal were unbeaten in 17 League matches from the start of season 1947-8 under new manager Tom Whittaker.

MANAGER DOUBLES

Four managers have won the League Championship with different clubs: **Tom Watson**, secy-manager with Sunderland (1892-3-5) and Liverpool (1901); **Herbert Chapman** with Huddersfield Town (1923-4, 1924-5) and Arsenal (1930-1, 1932-3); **Brian Clough** with Derby Co. (1971-2) and Nott'm. Forest (1977-8); **Kenny Dalglish** with Liverpool (1985-6, 1987-8, 1989-90) and Blackburn Rov. (1994-5).

Managers to win the F.A. Cup with different clubs: **Billy Walker** (Sheffield Wed. 1935, Nott'm. Forest 1959); **Herbert Chapman** (Huddersfield Town 1922, Arsenal 1930).

Kenny Dalglish (Liverpool) and **George Graham** (Arsenal) completed the Championship/F.A. Cup double as both player and manager with a single club. **Joe Mercer** won the Championship as a player with Everton, the Championship twice and F.A. Cup as a player with Arsenal and both competitions as manager of Manchester City.

FIRST CHAIRMAN-MANAGER

On December 20, 1988, after two years on the board, Dundee Utd. manager **Jim McLean** was elected chairman, too. McLean, Scotland's longest-serving manager (appointed by Utd. on November 24, 1971), resigned at end of season 1992-3 (remained chairman).

Ron Noades was chairman-manager of Brentford from July 1998 – March 2001.

TOP DIVISION PLAYER–MANAGERS

Les Allen (Q.P.R. 1968-9); **Johnny Giles** (W.B.A. 1976-7); **Howard Kendall** (Everton 1981-2); **Kenny Dalglish** (Liverpool, 1985-90); **Trevor Francis** (Q.P.R., 1988-9); **Terry Butcher** (Coventry City, 1990-1); **Peter Reid** (Manchester City, 1990-93); **Trevor Francis** (Sheffield Wed., 1991-4); **Glenn Hoddle**, (Chelsea, 1993-5); **Bryan Robson** (Middlesbrough, 1994-7); **Ray Wilkins** (Q.P.R., 1994-6); **Ruud Gullit** (Chelsea, 1996-8); **Gianluca Vialli** (Chelsea, 1998-2000).

FOREIGN TRIUMPHS

Former Dutch Int. **Ruud Gullit** became the first foreign manager to win a major English competition when Chelsea took the F.A. Cup in 1997.

In season 1997-8 Chelsea won the Coca-Cola Cup and the Cup-Winners' Cup for Gullit's successor, the Italian **Gianluca Vialli**; Arsenal won the Premiership and F.A. Cup double under Frenchman **Arsene Wenger**; Dutchman **Wim Jansen** took Celtic to triumph in the Scottish Championship and Coca-Cola Cup.

Under Frenchman **Gerard Houllier**, Liverpool achieved a triple success in 2000-01, winning the Worthington Cup, F.A. Cup and UEFA Cup.

In 2001-02 **Arsene Wenger** took Arsenal to his second Premiership – F.A. Cup double in five seasons.

In 1998-9 Rangers completed the Scottish treble under Dutchman **Dick Advocaat**. In 1999-2000 Chelsea won the F.A. Cup under **Vialli** and Rangers completed the Scottish Premier League and S.F.A. Cup double for **Advocaat**.

MANAGERS OF POST-WAR CHAMPIONS

1947 George Kay (Liverpool); **1948** Tom Whittaker (Arsenal); **1949** Bob Jackson (Portsmouth); **1950** Bob Jackson (Portsmouth); **1951** Arthur Rowe (Tottenham); **1952** Matt Busby (Manchester Utd.); **1953** Tom Whittaker (Arsenal).

1954 Stan Cullis (Wolves); **1955** Ted Drake (Chelsea); **1956** Matt Busby (Manchester Utd.); **1957** Matt Busby (Manchester Utd.); **1958** Stan Cullis (Wolves); **1959** Stan Cullis (Wolves); **1960** Harry Potts (Burnley).

1961 *Bill Nicholson (Tottenham); **1962** Alf Ramsey (Ipswich Town); **1963** Harry Catterick (Everton); **1964** Bill Shankly (Liverpool); **1965** Matt Busby (Manchester Utd.); **1966** Bill Shankly (Liverpool); **1967** Matt Busby (Man Utd.).

1968 Joe Mercer (Manchester City); **1969** Don Revie (Leeds Utd.); **1970** Harry Catterick (Everton); **1971** *Bertie Mee (Arsenal); **1972** Brian Clough (Derby Co.); **1973** Bill Shankly (Liverpool); **1974** Don Revie (Leeds Utd.).

1975 Dave Mackay (Derby Co.); **1976** Bob Paisley (Liverpool); **1977** Bob Paisley (Liverpool); **1978** Brian Clough (Nott'm. Forest); **1979** Bob Paisley (Liverpool); **1980** Bob Paisley (Liverpool); **1981** Ron Saunders (Aston Villa).

1982 Bob Paisley (Liverpool); **1983** Bob Paisley (Liverpool); **1984** Joe Fagan (Liverpool); **1985** Howard Kendall (Everton); **1986** *Kenny Dalglish (Liverpool – player/manager); **1987** Howard Kendall (Everton).

1988 Kenny Dalglish (Liverpool – player/manager); **1989** George Graham (Arsenal); **1990** Kenny Dalglish (Liverpool); **1991** George Graham (Arsenal); **1992** Howard Wilkinson (Leeds Utd.); **1993** Alex Ferguson (Manchester Utd.).

1994 *Alex Ferguson (Manchester Utd.); **1995** Kenny Dalglish (Blackburn Rov.); **1996** *Alex Ferguson (Manchester Utd.); **1997** Alex Ferguson (Manchester Utd.); **1998** *Arsene Wenger (Arsenal); **1999** *Alex Ferguson (Manchester Utd.); **2000** Sir Alex Ferguson (Manchester Utd.); **2001** Sir Alex Ferguson; **2002** *Arsene Wenger (Arsenal).

(* Double winners)

SIR ALEX IS TOPS

With 24 major prizes **Sir Alex Ferguson** has the most successful managerial record with Scottish and English clubs combined. At **Aberdeen** (1978-86) he won ten top prizes: 3 Scottish Championships, 4 Scottish Cups, 1 Scottish League Cup, 1 Cup-Winners' Cup, 1 European Super Cup.

Manchester Utd. winning the Premiership again in 2001 made Sir Alex the outright most successful manager in English football, the first to win seven League titles, the first to win three in a row.

It was their 14th major trophy in the last 12 seasons: 1990 F.A. Cup, 1991 Cup-Winners' Cup, 1992 League Cup, 1993 League Championship, 1994 League Championship and F.A. Cup, 1996 Championship and F.A. Cup; 1997 Championship; 1999 Championship, F.A. Cup and European Cup; 2000 Championship; 2001 Championship.

Aged 57, he signed a new 3-year contract with Utd. (May 4, 1999), making him Britain's highest-paid manager, reputedly at £1.67m. a year.

BOB PAISLEY'S HONOURS

Bob Paisley won 13 major competitions for Liverpool (1974-83): 6 League Championships, 3 European Cups, 3 League Cups, 1 UEFA Cup.

MANAGERS WITH MOST F.A. CUP SUCCESSES

4 Sir Alex Ferguson (Manchester Utd.); **3** Charles Foweraker (Bolton Wand.), John Nicholson (Sheffield Utd.), Bill Nicholson (Tottenham).

RECORD FEE FOR MANAGER

Tottenham paid Leeds Utd. £3m. compensation when they appointed **George Graham** in October 1998.

RELEGATION 'DOUBLES'

Managers associated with two clubs relegated in same season: **John Bond** in 1985-6 (Swansea City and Birmingham City); **Ron Saunders** in 1985-6 (W.B.A. – and their reserve team – and Birmingham City); **Bob Stokoe** in 1986-7 (Carlisle Utd. and Sunderland); **Billy McNeill** in 1986-7 (Manchester City and Aston Villa); **Dave Bassett** in 1987-8 (Watford and Sheffield Utd.); **Mick Mills** in 1989-90 (Stoke City and Colchester Utd.).

WEMBLEY STADIUM

When, in 2000, the Football Association were campaigning at enormous expense to bring the 2006 World Cup to England, the spin was heavily on 'the new Wembley.' The fiasco it has become was beyond imagination.

Demolition of the old stadium was due to begin within weeks of England's World Cup qualifier against Germany (Oct. 2000), but by the end of the season plans discussed by F.A.-owned Wembley National Stadium Ltd., the F.A. and the Government had produced nothing but frustration and embarrassment.

Dilly-dallying over whether the project should house athletics added to the chaos, and a discussed loan of £430m. from city banks fell through. The F.A. said (June 2002) that work would begin on the new £715m. 90,000-seat Wembley complex and infrastructure with demolition of the old stadium starting in September.

ORIGINAL CONTRACT

The **Empire Stadium** was built at a cost of **£750,000**. Its construction included 25,000 tons of concrete, 2,000 tons of steel and 104 turnstiles. The original contract (May 1921) between the F.A. and the British Empire Exhibition was for the Cup Final to be played there for 21 years.

INVASION DAY

Memorable scenes were witnessed at the **first F.A. Cup Final at Wembley, April 28, 1923**, between **Bolton Wand.** and **West Ham Utd.**. An accurate return of the attendance could not be made owing to thousands breaking in, but there were probably more than 200,000 spectators present. The match was delayed for 40 minutes by the crowd invading the pitch. Official attendance was 126,047.

Gate receipts totalled £27,776. The two clubs and the Football Association each received £6,365 and the F.A. refunded £2,797 to ticket-holders who were unable to get to their seats. Cup Final admission has since been by ticket only.

ENGLAND'S WEMBLEY DEAL

Under an agreement signed in 1983, the Football Association were contracted to playing **England's home matches***, the F.A. Cup Final and Charity Shield at Wembley Stadium until 2002.

* Exceptions were v Sweden (Umbro Cup) at Elland Road, Leeds, on June 8, 1995 – first England home game played away from Wembley since Poland at Goodison Park on Jan. 5, 1966 – and the matches v S. Africa at Old Trafford on May 24, 1997 and Belgium at Sunderland on October 10, 1999.

England previously played elsewhere on their own soil on May 12, 1973, when they met N. Ireland on Everton's ground. Officially, that was a home fixture for Ireland, but the venue was switched from Belfast for security reasons.

REDUCED CAPACITY

Capacity of the all-seated **Wembley Stadium** was 78,000. The last 100,000 attendance was for the 1985 F.A. Cup Final between Manchester Utd. and Everton.

WEMBLEY'S FIRST UNDER LIGHTS

November 30, 1955 (England 4, Spain 1), when the floodlights were switched on after 73 minutes (afternoon match played in damp, foggy conditions).
   First Wembley International played throughout under lights: England 8, N. Ireland 3 on evening of November 20, 1963 (att: 55,000).

MOST WEMBLEY APPEARANCES BY PLAYER

57 by Peter Shilton (52 England, 2 League Cup Finals, 1 F.A. Cup Final, 1 Charity Shield, 1 Football League XI).

WEMBLEY HAT-TRICKS

Three players have scored hat-tricks in major cup finals at Wembley: **Stan Mortensen** for Blackpool v Bolton Wand. (F.A. Cup Final, 1953), **Geoff Hurst** for England v West Germany (World Cup Final, 1966) and **David Speedie** for Chelsea v Manchester City (Full Members Cup, 1985).

ENGLAND'S WEMBLEY DEFEATS

England have lost 18 matches to foreign opponents at Wembley:

Nov.	1953	3-6 v Hungary	Sept.	1983	0-1 v Denmark
Oct.	1959	2-3 v Sweden	June	1984	0-2 v Russia
Oct.	1965	2-3 v Austria	May	1990	1-2 v Uruguay
Apr.	1972	1-3 v W. Germany	Sept.	1991	0-1 v Germany
Nov.	1973	0-1 v Italy	June	1995	1-3 v Brazil
Feb.	1977	0-2 v Holland	Feb.	1997	0-1 v Italy
Mar.	1981	1-2 v Spain	Feb.	1998	0-2 v Chile
May	1981	0-1 v Brazil	Feb.	1999	0-2 v France
Oct.	1982	1-2 v W. Germany	Oct.	2000	0-1 v Germany

A further defeat came in **Euro 96**. After drawing the semi-final with Germany 1-1, England went out 6-5 on penalties.

FASTEST GOALS AT WEMBLEY

In first-class matches: **38 seconds** by Bryan Robson in England's 2-1 win against Yugoslavia on December 13, 1989; **44 seconds** by Bryan Robson for England in 4-0 win v N. Ireland on February 23, 1982; **42 seconds** by Roberto di Matteo for Chelsea in the 1997 F.A. Cup Final v Middlesbrough.
   Fastest goal in **any** match at Wembley: **20 seconds** by **Maurice Cox** for Cambridge University against Oxford on December 5, 1979.

FOUR WEMBLEY HEADERS

When **Wimbledon** beat Sutton Utd. 4-2 in the F.A. Amateur Cup Final at Wembley on May 4, 1963, Irish centre-forward **Eddie Reynolds** headed all four goals.

ENGLAND POSTPONEMENT

Fog at Wembley on November 21, 1979 caused England's European Championship match against Bulgaria to be postponed 24 hours.

WEMBLEY ONE-SEASON DOUBLES

In 1989, **Nott'm. Forest** became the first club to win two Wembley Finals in the same season (Littlewoods Cup and Simod Cup).

In 1993, **Arsenal** made history there as the first club to win the League (Coca-Cola) Cup and the F.A. Cup in the same season. They beat Sheffield Wed. 2-1 in both finals.

SUDDEN DEATH DECIDERS

First Wembley Final decided on sudden death (first goal scored in overtime): April 23, 1995 – **Birmingham City** beat Carlisle Utd. (1-0, Paul Tait 103 mins.) to win Auto Windscreens Shield.

First instance of a 'golden goal' deciding a major International tournament was at Wembley on June 30, 1996, when **Germany** beat the Czech Republic 2-1 in the European Championship Final with Oliver Bierhoff's goal in the 95th. minute.

MILLENNIUM STADIUM, CARDIFF

Wales' new national stadium is the ground its chairman **Glanmor Griffiths** proudly built. On the site of Cardiff Arms Park, world-famous home of Welsh Rugby, it cost £130m. (£50m. from Lottery grants), took two years to build with retractable roof and a 73,434 all-seated capacity. Facilities include 126 hospitality boxes, 380 wheelchair spaces, 112 turnstiles, 38 food outlets and 17 public bars.

The stadium opened on June 26, 1999 with Wales beating the reigning World rugby champions South Africa. The first soccer international there was Wales v Finland on March 29, 2000.

The first 11 soccer matches played at the Millennium Stadium were won by the team using the North dressing-room. Stoke City ended the sequence when they beat Brentford 2-0 in the Div. 2 play-off Final on May 11 last.

The Millennium Stadium has solved English football's problem caused by the closure of Wembley, staging all the major domestic Finals in seasons 2000-01, 2002-02.

In the F.A. Charity Shield fixture on Sunday, August 12, 2001, Liverpool and Manchester Utd. became the first British clubs to meet under a closed-in roof.

SHADOWS OVER SOCCER

DAYS OF TRAGEDY – CLUBS

Season 1988-9 brought the worst disaster in the history of British sport, with the death of *95 Liverpool supporters (200 injured) at the **F.A. Cup semi-final** against Nott'm. Forest at **Hillsborough, Sheffield**, on Saturday, April 15. The tragedy built up in the minutes preceding kick-off, when thousands surged into the ground at the Leppings Lane end. Many were crushed in the tunnel between entrance and terracing, but most of the victims were trapped inside the perimeter fencing behind the goal. The match was abandoned without score after six minutes' play. The dead included seven women and girls, two teenage sisters and two teenage brothers. The youngest victim was a boy of ten, the oldest 67-year-old Gerard Baron, whose brother Kevin played for Liverpool in the 1950 Cup Final. (*Total became 96 in March 1993, when Tony Bland died after being in a coma for nearly four years).

The two worst disasters in one season in British soccer history occurred at the end of 1984-5. On May 11, the last Saturday of the League season, 56 people (two of them visiting supporters) were burned to death – and more than 200 taken to hospital – when fire destroyed the main stand at the **Bradford City-Lincoln City** match at Valley Parade.

The wooden, 77-year-old stand was full for City's last fixture before which, amid scenes of celebration, the club had been presented with the Third Division Championship trophy. The fire broke out just before half-time and, within five minutes, the entire stand was engulfed.

Eighteen days later, on May 29, at the European Cup Final between **Liverpool** and **Juventus** at the Heysel Stadium, Brussels, 39 spectators (31 of them Italian) were crushed or trampled to death and 437 injured. The disaster occurred an hour before the scheduled kick-off when Liverpool supporters charged a Juventus section of the crowd at one end of the stadium, and a retaining wall collapsed.

The sequel was a 5-year ban by UEFA on English clubs generally in European competition, with a 6-year ban on Liverpool.

On May 26, 1985 ten people were trampled to death and 29 seriously injured in a crowd panic on the way into the **Olympic Stadium, Mexico City** for the Mexican Cup Final between local clubs National University and America.

More than 100 people died and 300 were injured in a football disaster at **Nepal's national stadium** in Katmandu in March 1988. There was a stampede when a violent hailstorm broke over the capital. Spectators rushed for cover, but the stadium exits were locked, and hundreds were trampled in the crush.

In South Africa, on January 13, 1991 40 black fans were trampled to death (50 injured) as they tried to escape from fighting that broke out at a match in the gold-mining town of Orkney, 80 miles from Johannesburg. The friendly, between top teams **Kaiser Chiefs** and **Orlando Pirates**, attracted a packed crowd of 20,000. Violence erupted after the referee allowed Kaiser Chiefs a disputed second-half goal to lead 1-0.

Disaster struck at the French Cup semi-final (May 5, 1992), with the death of 15 spectators and 1,300 injured when a temporary metal stand collapsed in the Corsican town of Bastia. The tie between Second Division **Bastia** and French Champions **Marseille** was cancelled. **Monaco**, who won the other semi-final, were allowed to compete in the next season's Cup-Winners' Cup.

A total of 318 died and 500 were seriously injured when the crowd rioted over a disallowed goal at the National Stadium in Lima, Peru, on May 24, 1964. **Peru** and **Argentina** were competing to play in the Olympic Games in Tokyo.

That remained sport's heaviest death toll until October 20, 1982, when (it was revealed only in July 1989) 340 Soviet fans were killed in Moscow's Lenin Stadium at the UEFA Cup second round first leg match between **Moscow Spartak** and **Haarlem (Holland)**. They were crushed on an open stairway when a last-minute Spartak goal sent departing spectators surging back into the ground.

Among other crowd disasters abroad: **June 1968** – 74 died in **Argentina**. Panic broke out at the end of a goalless match between River Plate and Boca Juniors at Nunez, Buenos Aires, when Boca supporters threw lighted newspaper torches on to fans in the tiers below.

February 1974 – 49 killed in **Egypt** in crush of fans clamouring to see Zamalek play Dukla Prague.

September 1971 – 44 died in **Turkey**, when fighting among spectators over a disallowed goal (Kayseri v Siwas) led to a platform collapsing.

The then worst disaster in the history of British football, in terms of loss of life, occurred at Glasgow Rangers' ground at **Ibrox Park**, January 2, 1971.

Sixty-six people were trampled to death (100 injured) as they tumbled down Stairway 13 just before the end of the **Rangers v Celtic** New Year's match. That disaster led to the 1975 Safety of Sports Grounds legislation.

The Ibrox tragedy eclipsed even the Bolton disaster in which 33 were killed and about 500 injured when a wall and crowd barriers collapsed near a corner-flag at the **Bolton Wand. v Stoke City** F.A. Cup sixth round tie on March 9, 1946. The match was completed after half an hour's stoppage.

In a previous crowd disaster at **Ibrox** on April 5, 1902, part of the terracing collapsed during the Scotland v England International and 25 people were killed. The match, held up for 20 minutes, ended 1-1, but was never counted as an official International.

Eight leading players and three officials of **Manchester Utd.** and eight newspaper representatives were among the 23 who perished in the air crash at Munich on February 6, 1958, during take-off following a European Cup-tie in Belgrade. The players were Roger Byrne, Geoffrey Bent, Eddie Colman, Duncan Edwards, Mark Jones, David Pegg, Tommy Taylor and Liam Whelan, and the officials were Walter Crickmer (secretary), Tom Curry (trainer) and Herbert Whalley (coach). The newspaper representatives were Alf Clarke, Don Davies, George Follows, Tom Jackson, Archie Ledbrooke, Henry Rose, Eric Thompson and Frank Swift (former England goalkeeper of Manchester City).

On May 14, 1949, the entire team of Italian Champions **Torino**, 8 of them Internationals, were killed when the aircraft taking them home from a match against Benfica in Lisbon crashed at Superga, near Turin. The total death toll of 28 included all the club's reserve players, the manager, trainer and coach.

On February 8, 1981, 24 spectators died and more than 100 were injured at a match **in Greece**. They were trampled as thousands of the 40,000 crowd tried to rush out of the stadium at Piraeus after Olympiakos beat AEK Athens 6-0.

On November 17, 1982, 24 people (12 of them children) were killed and 250 injured when fans stampeded at the end of a match at the Pascual Guerrero stadium in **Cali, Colombia**. Drunken spectators hurled fire crackers and broken bottles from the higher stands on to people below and started a rush to the exits.

On December 9, 1987, the 18-strong team squad of **Alianza Lima,** one of Peru's top clubs, were wiped out, together with 8 officials and several youth players, when a military aircraft taking them home from Puccalpa crashed into the sea off Ventillana, ten miles from Lima. The only survivor among 43 on board was a member of the crew.

On April 28, 1993, 18 members of **Zambia's International** squad and 5 ZFA officials died when the aircraft carrying them to a World Cup qualifying tie against Senegal crashed into the Atlantic soon after take-off from Libreville, Gabon.

On October 16, 1996, 81 fans were crushed to death and 147 seriously injured in the 'Guatemala Disaster' at the World Cup qualifier against Costa Rica in Mateo Flores stadium. The tragedy happened an hour before kick-off, allegedly caused by ticket forgery and overcrowding – 60,000 were reported in the 45,000-capacity ground – and safety problems related to perimeter fencing.

On July 9, 1996, 8 people died, 39 injured in riot after derby match between **Libya's two top clubs** in Tripoli. Al-Ahli had beaten Al-Ittihad 1-0 by a controversial goal.

On April 6, 1997, 5 spectators were crushed to death at **Nigeria's national stadium** in Lagos after the 2-1 World Cup qualifying victory over Guinea. Only two of five gates were reported open as the 40,000 crowd tried to leave the ground.

It was reported from the **Congo** (October 29, 1998) that a bolt of lightning struck a village match, killing all 11 members of the home team Benatshadi, but leaving the opposing players from Basangana unscathed. It was believed the surviving team wore better-insulated boots.

On January 10, 1999 eight fans died and 13 were injured in a stampede at **Egypt's Alexandria Stadium**. Some 25,000 spectators had pushed onto the ground. Despite the tragedy, the cup-tie between Al-Ittihad and Al-Koroum was completed.

Three people suffocated and several were seriously injured when thousands of fans forced their way into **Liberia's national stadium** in Monrovia at a goalless World Cup qualifying match against Chad on April 23, 2000. The stadium (capacity 33,000) was reported 'heavily overcrowded'.

On Sunday, July 9, 2000 12 spectators died from crush injuries when police fired tear gas into the 50,000 crowd after South Africa scored their second goal in a World Cup group qualifier against Zimbabwe in **Harare**. A stampede broke out as fans scrambled to leave the national stadium. Players of both teams lay face down on the pitch as fumes swept over them. FIFA launched an investigation and decided that the result would stand, with South Africa leading 2-0 at the time of the 84th-minute abandonment.

On April 11, 2001, at one of the biggest matches of the South African season, 43 died and 155 were injured in a crush at **Ellis Park, Johannesburg**. After tearing down a fence, thousands of fans surged into a stadium already packed to its 60,000 capacity for the Premiership derby between top Soweto teams Kaizer Chiefs and Orlando Pirates. The match was abandoned at 1-1 after 33 minutes. In January 1991, 40 died in a crowd crush at a friendly between the same clubs at Orkney, 80 miles from Johannesburg.

On April 29, 2001, seven people were trampled to death and 51 injured when a riot broke out at a match between two of Congo's biggest clubs, Lupopo and Mazembe at **Lubumbashi**, southern Congo.

On May 6, 2001, two spectators were killed in Iran and hundreds were injured when a glass fibre roof collapsed at the over-crowded Mottaqi Stadium at **Sari** for the match between Pirouzi and Shemshak Noshahr.

On May 9, 2001, in Africa's worst football disaster, 123 died and 93 were injured in a stampede at the national stadium in **Accra, Ghana**. Home team Hearts of Oak were leading 2-1 against Asante Kotoko five minutes from time, when Asanti fans started hurling bottles on to the pitch. Police fired tear gas into the stands, and the crowd panicked in a rush for the exits, which were locked. It took the death toll at three big matches in Africa in April/May to 173.

On August 12, 2001, two players were killed by lightning and ten severely burned at a **Guatemala** Third Division match between Deportivo Culquimulilla and Pueblo Nuevo Vinas.

DAYS OF TRAGEDY – PERSONAL

Sam Wynne, Bury right-back, collapsed five minutes before half-time in the First Division match away to Sheffield Utd. on April 30, 1927, and died in the dressing-room.

In the Rangers v Celtic League match on September 5, 1931, **John Thomson**, the 23-year-old Celtic and Scotland goalkeeper, sustained a fractured skull when diving at an opponent's feet just before half-time and died the same evening.

Sim Raleigh (Gillingham), injured in a clash of heads at home to Brighton & H.A. (Div. 3 South) on December 1, 1934, continued to play but collapsed in second half and died in hospital the same night.

James Thorpe, 23-year-old Sunderland goalkeeper, was injured during the First Division match at home to Chelsea on February 1, 1936 and died in a diabetic coma three days later.

Derek Dooley, Sheffield Wed. centre-forward and top scorer in 1951-52 in the Football League with 46 goals in 30 matches, broke a leg in the League match at Preston N.E. on February 14, 1953, and, after complications set in, had to lose the limb by amputation.

John White (27), Tottenham's Scottish International forward, was killed by lightning on a golf course at Enfield, North London in July, 1964.

Two players were killed by lightning during the **Army Cup Final** replay at Aldershot in April, 1948.

Tommy Allden (23), Highgate Utd. centre-half was struck by lightning during an Amateur Cup quarter-final with Enfield Town on February 25, 1967. He died the following day. Four other players were also struck but recovered.

Roy Harper died while refereeing the York City–Halifax Town (Div. 4) match on May 5, 1969.

Jim Finn collapsed and died from a heart attack while refereeing Exeter City v Stockport Co. (Div. 4) on September 16, 1972.

Scotland manager **Jock Stein**, 62, collapsed and died at the end of the Wales-Scotland World Cup qualifying match (1-1) at Ninian Park, Cardiff on September 10, 1985.

David Longhurst, 25-year-old York City forward, died after being carried off two minutes before half-time in the Fourth Division fixture at home to Lincoln City on September 8, 1990. The match was abandoned (0-0). The inquest revealed that Longhurst suffered from a rare heart condition.

Mike North collapsed while refereeing Southend Utd. v Mansfield Town (Div. 3) on April 16, 2001 and died shortly afterwards. The match was abandoned and re-staged on May 8, with the receipts donated to his family.

GREAT SERVICE

'For services to Association Football', **Stanley Matthews** (Stoke City, Blackpool and England), already a C.B.E., became the first professional footballer to receive a knighthood. This was bestowed in 1965, his last season.

Before he retired and five days after his 50th birthday, he played for Stoke City to set a record as the oldest First Division footballer (v. Fulham, February 6, 1965).

Over a brilliant span of 33 years, he played in 886 first-class matches, including 54 full Internationals (plus 31 in war time), 701 League games (including 3 at start of season 1939-40, which was abandoned on the outbreak of war) and 86 F.A. Cup-ties, and scored 95 goals. He was never booked in his career.

Sir Stanley died on February 23 2000, three weeks after his 85th birthday. His ashes were buried under the centre circle of Stoke's Britannia Stadium. After spending a number of years in Toronto, he made his home back in the Potteries in 1989, having previously returned to his home town, Hanley, Stoke-on-Trent in October, 1987 to unveil a life-size bronze statue of himself.

The inscription reads: 'Sir Stanley Matthews, CBE. Born Hanley, 1 February 1915. His name is symbolic of the beauty of the game, his fame timeless and international, his sportsmanship and modesty universally acclaimed. A magical player, of the people, for the people.'

On his home-coming in 1989, Sir Stanley was made President of Stoke City, the club he joined as a boy of 15 and served as a player for 20 years between 1931 and 1965, on either side of his spell with Blackpool.

In July 1992 FIFA honoured him with their 'Gold merit award' for outstanding services to the game.

Former England goalkeeper **Peter Shilton** has made more first-class appearances (1,387) than any other footballer in British history. He played his 1,000th. League game in Leyton Orient's 2-0 home win against Brighton & H.A. on Dec. 22, 1996 and in all played 9 times for Orient in his final season. He retired from International football after the 1990 World Cup in Italy with 125 caps, then a world record.

Shilton's career spanned 32 seasons, 20 of them on the International stage. He made his League debut for Leicester City in May 1966, two months before England won the World Cup.

His 1,387 first-class appearances comprise a record 1,005 in the Football League, 125 Internationals, 102 League Cup, 86 F.A. Cup, 13 for England U-23s, 4 for the Football League and 52 other matches (European Cup, UEFA Cup, World Club Championship, Charity Shield, European Super Cup, Full Members' Cup, Play-offs, Screen Sports Super Cup, Anglo-Italian Cup, Texaco Cup, Simod Cup, Zenith Data Systems Cup and Autoglass Trophy).

Shilton appeared more times at Wembley (57) than any other player: 52 for England, 2 League Cup Finals, 1 F.A. Cup Final, 1 Charity Shield match, and 1 for the Football League. He passed a century of League appearances with each of his first five clubs: Leicester City (286), Stoke City (110), Nott'm. Forest (202), Southampton (188) and Derby Co. (175) and subsequently played for Plymouth Argyle, Bolton Wand. and Leyton Orient.

His club honours, all gained with Nott'm. Forest: League Championship 1978, League Cup 1979, European Cup 1979 and 1980, PFA Player of Year 1978.

Four other British footballers have made more than 1,000 first-class appearances:

Ray Clemence, formerly with Tottenham, Liverpool and England, retired through injury in season 1987-8 after a goalkeeping career of 1,119 matches starting in 1965-6. Clemence played 50 times for his first club, Scunthorpe Utd.; 665 for Liverpool; 337 for Tottenham; his 67 representative games included 61 England caps.

A third great British goalkeeper, **Pat Jennings**, ended his career (1963-86) with a total of 1,098 first-class matches for Watford, Tottenham, Arsenal and N. Ireland. They were made up of 757 in the Football League, 119 full Internationals, 84 F.A. Cup appearances, 72 League/Milk Cup, 55 European club matches, 2 Charity Shield, 3 Other Internationals, 1 Under-23 cap, 2 Texaco Cup, 2 Anglo-Italian Cup and 1 Super Cup. Jennings played his 119th. and final International on his 41st birthday, June 12, 1986, against Brazil in Guadalajara in the Mexico World Cup.

Defender **Graeme Armstrong**, 42-year-old commercial manager for an Edinburgh whisky company and part-time assistant-manager and captain of Scottish Third Division club Stenhousemuir, made the 1000th first team appearance of his career in the Scottish Cup 3rd Round against Rangers at Ibrox on January 23, 1999. He was presented with the Man of the Match award before kick-off.

Against East Stirling on Boxing Day, he had played his 864th League game, breaking the British record for an outfield player set by another Scot, Tommy Hutchison, with Alloa, Blackpool, Coventry City, Manchester City, Burnley and Swansea City.

Armstrong's 24-year career, spent in the lower divisions of the Scottish League, began as a 1-match trialist with Meadowbank Thistle in 1975 and continued via Stirling Albion, Berwick Rangers, Meadowbank and, from 1992, Stenhousemuir.

Tony Ford became the first English outfield player to reach 1000 senior appearances in Rochdale's 1-0 win at Carlisle (Auto Windscreens Shield) on March 7, 2000. Grimsby-born, he began his 26-season midfield career with Grimsby Town and played for 7 other League clubs: Sunderland (loan), Stoke City, W.B.A., Bradford City (loan), Scunthorpe Utd., Mansfield Town and Rochdale. He retired, aged 42, in 2001 with a career record of 1072 appearances (121 goals) and his total of 931 League games is exceeded only by Peter Shilton's 1005.

EIGHT KNIGHTS OF SOCCER

In the Queen's Golden Jubilee Honours, on June 15, 2002, Newcastle Utd.'s 69-year-old manager **Bobby Robson** was awarded a knighthood for his services to football. He became the eighth player or manager to be so honoured.

The elite list reads: **Stanley Matthews** (1965), **Alf Ramsey** (1967), **Matt Busby** (1968), **Bobby Charlton** (1994), **Tom Finney** (1998), **Geoff Hurst** (1998) and **Alex Ferguson** (1999) and **Bobby Robson** (2002).

PENALTIES

The **penalty-kick** was introduced to the game, following a proposal to the Irish F.A. in 1890 by William McCrum, son of the High Sheriff for Co. Omagh, and approved by the International Football Board on June 2, 1891.

First penalty scored in a first-class match in England was by John Heath, for Wolves v Accrington Stanley (5-0 in Div. 1, September 14, 1891).

The greatest influence of the penalty has come since the 1970s, with the introduction of the shoot-out to settle deadlocked ties in various competitions.

Manchester Utd. were the first club to win a competitive match in British football via a shoot-out (4-3 v Hull City, Watney Cup semi-final, August 1970); in that penalty contest, George Best was the first player to score, Denis Law the first to miss.

In season 1991-2, penalty shoot-outs were introduced to decide **F.A. Cup ties** still level after one replay and extra time.

Wembley saw its first penalty contest in the 1974 Charity Shield. Since then many major matches across the world have been settled thus, including:-

1974	**F.A. Charity Shield** (Wembley): Liverpool beat Leeds Utd. 6-5 (after 1-1).
1976	**Eur. Champ. Final** (Belgrade): Czech. beat W. Germany 5-3 (after 2-2).
1980	**Cup-Winners' Cup Final** (Brussels): Valencia beat Arsenal 5-4 (0-0).
1980	**Eur. Champ. 3rd/4th place play-off** (Naples): Czechoslovakia beat Italy 9-8 (after 1-1).
1982	**World Cup s-final** (Seville): West Germany beat France 5-4 (after 3-3).
1984	**European Cup Final** (Rome): Liverpool beat AS Roma 4-2 (after 1-1).
1984	**UEFA Cup Final:** Tottenham (home) beat Anderlecht 4-3 (2-2 agg.).
1984	**Eur. Champ. s-final** (Lyon, France): Spain beat Denmark 5-4 (after 1-1).
1986	**European Cup Final** (Seville): Steaua Bucharest beat Barcelona 2-0 (0-0). Barcelona's four penalties were all saved.
1986	**World Cup q-finals** (in Mexico): France beat Brazil 4-3 (after 1-1); West Germany beat Mexico 4-1 (after 0-0); Belgium beat Spain 5-4 (after 1-1).
1987	**Freight Rover Trophy Final** (Wembley): Mansfield Town Town beat Bristol City 5-4 (after 1-1).
1987	**Scottish League (Skol) Cup Final** (Hampden Park): Rangers beat Aberdeen 5-3 (after 3-3).
1988	**European Cup Final** (Stuttgart): PSV Eindhoven beat Benfica 6-5 (after 0-0).
1988	**UEFA Cup Final:** Bayer Leverkusen (home) beat Espanyol 3-2 after 3-3 (0-3a, 3-0h).
1990	**Scottish F.A. Cup Final** (Hampden Park): Aberdeen beat Celtic 9-8 (0-0).
1990	**World Cup** (in Italy): 2nd. Round: Rep. of Ireland beat Romania 5-4 (after 0-0); q-final: Argentina beat Yugoslavia 3-2 (after 0-0); s-finals: Argentina beat Italy 4-3 (after 1-1); West Germany beat England 4-3 (1-1).
1991	**European Cup Final** (Bari): Red Star Belgrade beat Marseille 5-3 (after 0-0).
1991	**Barclays League Play-off** (4th. Div. Final – Wembley): Torquay Utd. beat Blackpool 5-4 (after 2-2).
1992	**F.A. Cup s-final** replay (Villa Park): Liverpool beat Portsmouth 3-1 (after 0-0).

1992	**Barclays League Play-off** (4th. Div. Final – Wembley): Blackpool beat Scunthorpe Utd. 4-3 (after 1-1).
1992	**Eur. Champ. s-final** (Gothenburg): Denmark beat Holland 5-4 (after 2-2).
1993	**Barclays League Play-off**: (3rd Div. Final – Wembley): York City beat Crewe Alexandra 5-3 (after 1-1).
1993	**F.A. Charity Shield** (Wembley): Manchester Utd. beat Arsenal 5-4 (after 1-1).
1994	**League (Coca-Cola) Cup s-final**: Aston Villa beat Tranmere Rov. 5-4 (after 4-4, 1-3a, 3-1h).
1994	**Autoglass Trophy Final** (Wembley): Swansea City beat Huddersfield Town 3-1 (after 1-1).
1994	**World Cup** (in U.S.A.): **2nd. Round**: Bulgaria beat Mexico 3-1 (after 1-1); q-final: Sweden beat Romania 5-4 (after 2-2); **Final**: Brazil beat Italy 3-2 (after 0-0).
1994	**Scottish League (Coca-Cola) Cup Final** (Ibrox Park): Raith beat Celtic 6-5 (after 2-2).
1995	**Cup-Winners' Cup s-final**: Arsenal beat Sampdoria away 3-2 (5-5 agg.)
1995	**Copa America Final** (Montevideo): Uruguay beat Brazil 5-3 (after 1-1).
1996	**European Cup Final** (Rome): Juventus beat Ajax 4-2 (after 1-1).
1996	**European U-21 Champ. Final** (Barcelona): Italy beat Spain 4-2 (after 1-1).
1996	**Eur. Champ. q-finals**: England beat Spain (Wembley) 4-2 after 0-0; France beat Holland (Anfield) 5-4 after 0-0; **s-finals**: Germany beat England (Wembley) 6-5 after 1-1; Czech Republic beat France (Old Trafford) 6-5 after 0-0.
1997	**Auto Windscreens Shield Final** (Wembley): Carlisle Utd. beat Colchester Utd. 4-3 (after 0-0)
1997	**UEFA Cup Final**: FC Schalke beat Inter Milan 4-1 (after 1-1 agg.).
1998	**Nationwide League play-off** (1st Div. Final Wembley): Charlton Athletic beat Sunderland 7-6 (after 4-4).
1998	**World Cup Finals**: Argentina beat England (2nd Round) 4-3 (after 2-2); France beat Italy (Q-final) 4-3 (after 0-0; Brazil beat Holland (S-final) 4-2 (after 1-1).
1999	**Nationwide League play-offs Div. 1 s-final**: Watford beat Birmingham City 7-6 away (after 1-1); **Div. 2 Final (Wembley)**: Manchester City beat Gillingham 3-1 (after 2-2).
1999	**Women's World Cup Final** (Rose Bowl, Pasedena, California) U.S.A. beat China 5-4 (after 0-0). **Third/Fourth place play-off** (same venue): Brazil beat Norway 5-4 (after 0-0).
2000	**African Nations Cup Final** (Lagos): Cameroon beat Nigeria 4-3 (after 0-0).
2000	**F.A. Cup s-final** (Wembley): Aston Villa beat Bolton Wand. 4-1 (after 0-0).
2000	**UEFA Cup Final** (Copenhagen): Galatasaray beat Arsenal 4-1 (after 0-0).
2000	**Eur. Champ. s-final** (Amsterdam): Italy beat Holland 3-1 (after 0-0). Holland missed 5 penalties in match – 2 in normal play, 3 in shoot-out. Italy survived with ten men after 33rd minute sending-off.
2000	**Olympic Final** (Sydney): Cameroon beat Spain 5-3 (after 2-2). Spain led 2-0, then had 2 men sent off.
2001	**League (Worthington) Cup Final** (Millennium Stadium, Cardiff): Liverpool beat Birmingham City 5-4 (after 1-1).
2001	**Champions League Final** (Milan): Bayern Munich beat Valencia 5-4 (after 1-1).
2002	**Eur. U-21 Champ. Final** (Basle): Czech Republic beat France 3-1 (after 0-0).
2002	**Nationwide League** play-off (1st Div. Final, Millennium Stadium, Cardiff): Birmingham City beat Norwich City 4-2 (after 1-1).
2002	**World Cup Finals**: Spain beat Rep. of Ireland (2nd Round) 3-2 (after 1-1); South Korea beat Spain (Q-final) 5-3 (after 0-0).

Footnote: Highest-recorded score in a penalty shoot-out between Football League clubs was **Aldershot's 11-10** victory at home to **Fulham** after their 1-1 draw in the Freight Rover Trophy Southern quarter-final on February 10, 1987. Seven spot-kicks were missed or saved in a record 28-penalty shoot-out at senior level.

In South America in 1992, in a 26-shot competition, **Newell's Old Boys** beat America 11-10 in the Copa Libertadores.

Longest-recorded penalty contest in first-class matches was in Argentina in 1988 – from 44 shots, **Argentinos Juniors** beat **Racing Club 20-19**. **Genclerbirligi** beat **Galatasaray** 17-16 in a Turkish Cup-tie in 1996. Only one penalty was missed.

Highest-scoring shoot-outs in **Int. football:** North Korea beat Hong Kong 11-10 (after 3-3 draw) in an Asian Cup match in 1975; and Ivory Coast beat Ghana 11-10 (after 0-0 draw) in African Nations Cup Final, 1992.

Most penalties needed to settle an adult game in Britain: 44 in Norfolk Primary Cup 4th Round replay, December 2000. Aston Villa side **Freethorpe** beat Foulsham 20-19 (5 kicks missed). All 22 players took 2 penalties each, watched by a crowd of 20. The sides had drawn 2-2, 4-4 in a tie of 51 goals.

ENGLAND'S CRUCIAL PENALTY SHOOT-OUTS

1990 World Cup Semi-final: Beaten 4-3 by West Germany.
1996 European Champ. Q-final: Beat Spain 4-2
1996 European Champ. S-final: Beaten 6-5 by Germany
1998 World Cup (2nd Round): Beaten 4-3 by Argentina.

INTERNATIONAL PENALTIES, MISSED

Four penalties out of five were missed when **Colombia** beat **Argentina** 3-0 in a Copa America group tie in Paraguay in July 1999. Martin Palmeiro missed three for Argentina and Colombia's Hamilton Ricard had one spot-kick saved.

In the European Championship semi-final against Italy in Amsterdam on June 29, 2000, **Holland** missed five penalties – two in normal time, three in the penalty contest which Italy won 3-1 (after 0-0). Dutch captain Frank de Boer missed twice from the spot.

F.A. CUP SHOOT-OUTS

In **11 seasons** since the introduction of this method to settle F.A. Cup ties (from Round 1) that are level after two matches, a total of **52 ties** in the competition proper have been decided by such means (5 in 1991-2, 6 in 1992-3, 4 in 1993-4, 4 in 1994-5, 4 in 1995-6; 3 in 1996-7, 12 in 1997-8, 5 in 1998-9, 4 in 1999-2000, 2 in 2000-01, 3 in 2001-02).

The **first** penalty contest in the F.A. Cup took place **30** years ago. In days of the play-off for third place, the 1972 match was delayed until the eve of the following season when losing semi-finalists **Birmingham City** and **Stoke City** met at St. Andrew's on Aug. 5. The score was 0-0 and Birmingham City won 4-3 on penalties.

Highest recorded F.A. Cup shoot-out went to 24 kicks, with Macclesfield Town beating Forest Green Rov. (away) 11-10 in 1st Round replay on November 28, 2001.

Shoot-out abandoned: The F.A. Cup 1st Round replay between Oxford City and Wycombe Wand. at Wycombe on November 9, 1999 was abandoned (1-1) after extra time because, as the penalty shoot-out was about to begin, a fire broke out under a stand. Wycombe won the second replay 1-0 at Oxford Utd.'s ground.

WEMBLEY'S MISSED CUP FINAL PENALTIES

John Aldridge (Liverpool) became the first player to miss a penalty in the F.A. Cup Final at Wembley – and the second in the competition's history (previously Charlie Wallace, of Aston Villa, in the 1913 Final against Sunderland at Crystal Palace) – when Wimbledon's Dave Beasant saved his shot in May 1988. Seven previous penalties had been scored in this Final at Wembley.

Another crucial penalty miss at Wembley was by Arsenal's **Nigel Winterburn,** Luton Town's Andy Dibble saving his spot-kick in the 1988 Littlewoods Cup Final, when a goal would have put Arsenal 3-1 ahead. Instead, they lost 3-2.

Winterburn was the third player to fail with a League Cup Final penalty at Wembley, following **Ray Graydon** (Aston Villa) against Norwich City in 1975 and **Clive Walker** (Sunderland), who shot wide in the 1985 Milk Cup Final, also against Norwich City (won 1-0). Graydon had his penalty saved by Kevin Keelan, but scored from the rebound and won the cup for Aston Villa (1-0).

Tottenham's **Gary Lineker** saw his penalty saved by Nott'm. Forest goalkeeper Mark Crossley in the 1991 F.A. Cup Final.

Derby Co.'s Martin Taylor saved a penalty from **Eligio Nicolini** in the Anglo-Italian Cup Final at Wembley on March 27, 1993, but Cremonese won 3-1.

LEAGUE PENALTIES RECORD

Most penalties in Football League match: Five – 4 to Crystal Palace (3 missed), 1 to Brighton & H.A. (scored) in Div. 2 match at Selhurst Park on March 27 (Easter Monday), 1989. Crystal Palace won 2-1. Three of the penalties were awarded in a 5-minute spell. The match also produced 5 bookings and a sending-off.

Other teams missing 3 penalties in a match: **Burnley** v Grimsby Town (Div. 2), February 13, 1909; **Manchester City** v Newcastle Utd. (Div. 1), January 17, 1912.

HOTTEST MODERN SPOT-SHOT

Matthew Le Tissier ended his career in season 2001-02 with the distinction of having netted 48 out of 49 first-team penalties for Southampton. He scored the last 27 after his only miss when Nott'm. Forest keeper Mark Crossley saved in a Premier League match at The Dell on March 24, 1993.

SPOT-KICK HAT-TRICKS

Danish International **Jan Molby**'s only hat-trick in English football, for Liverpool in their 3-1 win at home to Coventry City (Littlewoods Cup, 4th round replay, Nov. 26, 1986) comprised three goals from the penalty spot.

It was the first such hat-trick in a major match for two years – since **Andy Blair** scored three penalties for Sheffield Wed. against Luton Town (Milk Cup 4th. round, Nov. 20 1984).

Portsmouth's **Kevin Dillon** scored a penalty hat-trick in the Full Members Cup (2nd rd.) at home to Millwall (3-2) on Nov. 4, 1986.

Alan Slough scored a hat-trick of penalties in an away game and was on the losing side, when Peterborough Utd. were beaten 4-3 at Chester City (Div. 3, Apr. 29, 1978).

Penalty hat-tricks in **International football: Dimitris Saravakos** (in 9 mins.) for Greece v Egypt in 1990. He scored 5 goals in match; **Henrik Larsson**, among his 4 goals in Sweden's 6-0 home win v Moldova in World Cup qualifying match, June 6, 2001.

MOST PENALTY GOALS (LEAGUE) IN SEASON

Thirteen out of 13 by **Francis Lee** for Manchester City (Div. 1) in 1971-2. His goal total for the season was 33. In season 1988-9, **Graham Roberts** scored 12 League penalties for Second Division Champions Chelsea.

PENALTY-SAVE SEQUENCES

Ipswich Town goalkeeper **Paul Cooper** saved eight of the ten penalties he faced in 1979-80. **Roy Brown** (Notts Co.) saved six in a row in season 1972-3.

Andy Lomas, goalkeeper for Chesham Utd. (Diadora League) claimed a record eight **consecutive** penalty saves – three at the end of season 1991-2 and five in 1992-3.

Mark Bosnich (Aston Villa) saved five in two consecutive matches in 1993-4: three in Coca-Cola Cup semi-final penalty shoot-out v Tranmere Rov. (Feb. 26), then two in Premiership at Tottenham (Mar. 2).

MISSED PENALTIES SEQUENCE

Against Wolves in Div. 2 on Sept. 28, 1991, **Southend Utd.** missed their seventh successive penalty (five of them the previous season).

SCOTTISH RECORDS
(See also under 'Goals' & 'Discipline')

RANGERS' MANY RECORDS

Rangers' record-breaking feats include:-
League Champions: 49 times (once joint holders) – world record.

Winning every match in Scottish League (18 games, 1898-9 season).

Major hat-tricks: Rangers have completed the domestic treble (League Championship, League Cup and Scottish F.A. Cup) a record six times (1948-9, 1963-4, 1975-6, 1977-8, 1992-3, 1998-9).

League & Cup double: 16 times.

Nine successive Championships (1989-97). Four men played in all nine sides: Richard Gough, Ally McCoist, Ian Ferguson and Ian Durrant.

102 major trophies: Championships 49, Scottish Cup 30, League Cup 22, Cup-Winners' Cup 1.

CELTIC'S GRAND SLAM

Celtic's record in 1966-7 was the most successful by a British club in one season. They won the **Scottish League**, the **Scottish Cup**, the **Scottish League Cup** and became the first British club to win the **European Cup**. They also won the **Glasgow Cup**.

Celtic have 3 times achieved the Scottish treble (League Championship, League Cup and F.A. Cup), in 1966-7, 1968-9 and 2000-01 (in Martin O'Neill's first season as their manager). They became Scottish Champions for 2000-01 with a 1-0 home win against St. Mirren on April 7 – the earliest the title had been clinched for 26 years, since Rangers' triumph on March 29, 1975.

They have won the Scottish Cup most times (31), and have completed the League and Cup double 12 times.

Celtic won nine consecutive Scottish League titles (1966-74) under Jock Stein.

LARSSON SUPREME

After missing most of the previous campaign with a broken leg, Swedish International **Henrik Larsson**, with 53 goals in season 2000-01, set a post-war record for Celtic and equalled the Scottish Premier League record of 35 by Brian McClair (Celtic) in 1986-7. Larsson's 35 earned him Europe's Golden Shoe award.

SCOTTISH CUP HAT-TRICKS

Aberdeen's feat of winning the Scottish F.A. Cup in 1982-3-4 made them only the third club to achieve that particular hat-trick.

Queen's Park did it twice (1874-5-6 and 1880-1-2), and **Rangers** have won the Scottish Cup three years in succession on three occasions: 1934-5-6, 1948-9-50 and 1962-3-4.

SCOTTISH CUP FINAL DISMISSALS

Three players have been sent off in the Scottish F.A. Cup Final: **Jock Buchanan** (Rangers v. Kilmarnock, 1929), **Roy Aitken** (Celtic v Aberdeen, 1984) and **Walter Kidd** (Hearts captain v Aberdeen, 1986).

CELTIC'S RECORD 62

Celtic hold the Scottish League record run of success with 62 matches undefeated, from November 13, 1915 to April 21, 1917, when Kilmarnock won 2-0 at Parkhead.

Greenock Morton in 1963-4 were undefeated in home League matches, obtained a record 67 points out of 72 and scored 135 goals, clinching promotion from Div. 2 as early as February 29.

Queen's Park did not have a goal scored against them during the first seven seasons of their existence (1867-74, before the Scottish League was formed).

WORST HOME SEQUENCE

After gaining promotion to Div. 1 in 1992, **Cowdenbeath** went a record 38 consecutive home League matches without a win. They ended the sequence (drew 8, lost 30) when beating Arbroath 1-0 on April 2, 1994, watched by a crowd of 225.

ALLY'S RECORDS

Ally McCoist became the first player to complete 200 goals in the Premier Division when he scored Rangers' winner (2-1) at Falkirk on December 12, 1992. His first was against Celtic in September 1983, and he reached 100 against Dundee on Boxing Day 1987.

When McCoist scored twice at home to Hibernian (4-3) on December 7, 1996, he became Scotland's record post-war League marksman, beating Gordon Wallace's 264.

Originally with St. Johnstone (1978-81), he spent two seasons with Sunderland (1981-3), then joined Rangers for £200,000 in June 1983.

In 15 seasons at Ibrox, he scored 355 goals for Rangers (250 League), and helped them win 10 Championships (9 in succession), 3 Scottish Cups and earned a record 9 League Cup winner's medals. He won the European Golden Boot in consecutive seasons (1991-2, 1992-3).

His 9 Premier League goals in three seasons for Kilmarnock gave him a career total of 281 Scottish League goals when he retired at the end of 2000-01.

FIVE IN A MATCH

Paul Sturrock set an individual scoring record for the Scottish Premier Division with 5 goals in Dundee Utd.'s 7-0 win at home to Morton on November 17, 1984. **Marco Negri** equalled the feat with all 5 when Rangers beat Dundee Utd. 5-1 at Ibrox (Premier Division) on August 23, 1997, and **Kenny Miller** scored 5 in Rangers' 7-1 win at home to St. Mirren on November 4, 2000.

SEATS MILESTONE FOR CELTIC

In season 1998-9, **Celtic** became the first British club with an **all-seated** capacity of 60,000. That figure was exceeded by **Manchester Utd.** (61,629) in 1999-2000.

NEGRI'S TEN-TIMER

Marco Negri scored in Rangers' first ten League matches (23 goals) in season 1997-8 – a Premier Division record. The previous best sequence was 8 by Ally MacLeod for Hibernian in 1978.

DOUBLE SCOTTISH FINAL

Rangers v Celtic drew **129,643** and **120,073** people to the Scottish Cup Final and replay at Hampden Park, Glasgow, in 1963. Receipts for the two matches totalled £50,500.

MOST SCOTTISH CHAMPIONSHIP MEDALS

13 by **Sandy Archibald** (Rangers, 1918-34). Post-war record: **10** by **Bobby Lennox** (Celtic, 1966-79).

Alan Morton won **nine** Scottish Championship medals with Rangers in 1921-23-24-25-27-28-29-30-31. **Ally McCoist** played in the Rangers side that won nine successive League titles (1989-97).

Between 1927 and 1939 **Bob McPhail** helped Rangers win nine Championships, finish second twice and third once. He scored 236 League goals but was never top scorer in a single season.

SCOTTISH CUP – NO DECISION

The **Scottish F.A.** withheld their Cup and medals in 1908-9 after Rangers and Celtic played two drawn games at Hampden Park. Spectators rioted.

FEWEST LEAGUE WINS IN SEASON

Clydebank won only one of 36 matches in Div. 1, season 1999-2000. That victory did not come until March 7 (2-1 at home to Raith).

HAMPDEN'S £63M. REDEVELOPMENT

On completion of redevelopment costing £63m. **Hampden Park**, home of Scottish football and the oldest first-class stadium in the world, was re-opened full scale for the Rangers-Celtic Cup Final on May 29, 1999.

Work on the 'new Hampden' (capacity 52,000) began in 1992. The North and East stands were restructured (£12m.); a new South stand and improved West stand cost £51m. The Millennium Commission contributed £23m. and the Lottery Sports Fund provided a grant of £3.75m.

DEMISE OF AIRDRIE AND CLYDEBANK

In May 2002, First Division **Airdrieonians**, formed in 1878, went out of business. They had debts of £3m. Their place in the Scottish League was taken by **Gretna**, from the English Unibond League, who were voted into Div. 3. Second Division **Clydebank** folded in July 2002 and were taken over by the new **Airdrie United** club.

GREAT SCOTS

In February 1988, the Scottish F.A. launched a national **Hall of Fame**, initially comprising the first 11 Scots to make 50 International appearances, to be joined by all future players to reach that number of caps. Each member receives a gold medal, invitation for life at all Scotland's home matches, and has his portrait hung at Scottish F.A. headquarters in Glasgow.

MORE CLUBS IN 2000

The **Scottish Premier League** increased from 10 to 12 clubs in season 2000-1.

The **Scottish Football League** admitted two new clubs – Peterhead and Elgin City from the Highland League – to provide three divisions of 10 in 2000-1.

NOTABLE SCOTTISH 'FIRSTS'

- The father of League football was a Scot, **William McGregor**, a draper in Birmingham City. The 12-club Football League kicked off in September 1888, and McGregor was its first president.
- **Hibernian** were the first British club to play in the European Cup, by invitation. They reached the semi-final when it began in 1955-6.
- **Celtic** were Britain's first winners of the European Cup, in 1967.
- Scotland's First Division became the **Premier Division** in season 1975-6.
- Football's **first International** was staged at the West of Scotland cricket ground, Partick, on November 30, 1872: Scotland 0, England 0.
- Scotland introduced its **League Cup** in 1945-6, the first season after the war. It was another 15 years before the Football League Cup was launched.
- The Scottish F.A. Cup has been **sponsored** by Tennents for the last 13 seasons.
- Scotland pioneered the use in British football of **two substitutes** per team in League and Cup matches.
- The world's **record football score** belongs to Scotland: Arbroath 36, Bon Accord 0 (Scottish Cup first round) on September 12, 1885.
- The Scottish F.A. introduced the **penalty shoot-out** to their Cup Final in 1990.
- On Jan. 22, 1994 all six matches in the **Scottish Premier Division** ended as draws.
- Scotland's new Premier League introduced a **3-week shut-down** in January 1999 – first instance of British football adopting the winter break system that operates in a number of European countries.
- **Rangers** made history at home to St. Johnstone (Premier League, 0-0, March 4, 2000) when fielding a team entirely without Scottish players.

SCOTTISH CUP SHOCK RESULTS

1885-86 (1) Arbroath 36, Bon Accord 0
1921-22 (F) Morton 1, Rangers 0
1937-38 (F) East Fife 4, Kilmarnock 2 (replay, after 1-1)
1960-61 (F) Dunfermline 2, Celtic 0 (replay, after 0-0)

1966-67 (1) Berwick Rangers 1, Rangers 0
1979-80 (3) Hamilton 2, Keith 3
1984-85 (1) Stirling Albion 20, Selkirk 0
1984-85 (3) Inverness Thistle 3, Kilmarnock 0
1986-87 (3) Rangers 0, Hamilton 1
1994-95 (4) Stenhousemuir 2, Aberdeen 0
1998-99 (3) Aberdeen 0, Livingston 1
1999-2000 (3) Celtic 1, Inverness Caledonian Thistle 3

Scottish League (Coca-Cola) Cup Final shock
1994-95   Raith 2, Celtic 2 (Raith won 6-5 on pens.)

SCOTTISH DISCIPLINE (MODERN)

1989 (June) fine **Hearts** £93,000, following TV infringement at UEFA Cup q-final.
1990 (May) S.F.A. fine Rangers manager **Graeme Souness** record £5,000 for breaking touchline ban v Hearts on Feb. 17, and extend Souness trackside ban to May 1992.
1991 (February) S.F.A. fine **Rangers** £10,000 and order them to forfeit £13,000 sponsorship money for failing to carry out sponsors' agreement at Cup-tie v Dunfermline in January.
1991 (June) S.F.A. fine **Dundee Utd.** £12,000 for incidents involving referee at Scottish Cup Final defeat by Motherwell.
1992 (October) UEFA fine **Hibernian** £5,730 for crowd trouble at UEFA Cup match v Anderlecht.
1993 (March) UEFA fine **Rangers** £8,000 (later halved) for crowd misconduct away to Bruges in European Cup.
1993 (May) **Rangers** fined £5,000 by League under rule covering 'tapping' of players with other clubs.
1993 (August) S.F.A. fine **Airdrie** £10,000, **Dundee** £5,000 for poor disciplinary records, season 1992-3.
1993 (November) UEFA fine **Aberdeen** £4,500 for fan misconduct v Torino (CWC).
1994 (January) S.F.A. fine **Rangers** coach **John McGregor** £3,000 and ban him from touchline until year 2000 for using foul and abusive language to referee at reserve match.
1994 (August) Scottish League fine **Celtic** record £100,000 for poaching manager Tommy Burns from Kilmarnock.
1994 (August) S.F.A. fines for prev. season's disciplinary records: **Dundee** £10,000; **Cowdenbeath, East Fife, Stranraer** each £1,000.
1994 (November) S.F.A. fine **Celtic** manager **Tommy Burns** and assistant **Billy Stark** each £2,000 for breach of contract when leaving Kilmarnock.
1995 (March) S.F.A. fine **Celtic** manager **Tommy Burns** £1,000 and ban him from touchline for rest of season (verbal abuse of referee).
1995 (August) S.F.A. fine five clubs for poor disciplinary records in 1994-5: **Dundee Utd.** (£5,000), **Falkirk** (£5,000), **Cowdenbeath, East Fife** and **Stranraer** (each £2,000).
1996 (August) Scottish League fine **Ayr** £12,000 for fielding suspended players in Coca-Cola Cup.
1996 (October) S.F.A. fine **Tommy Burns** (Celtic manager) £3,000 for 'aggressive attitude' to referee in match v Kilmarnock, April 10.
1996 (November) UEFA fine **Celtic** £42,000 and **Alan Stubbs** £28,000 for using unlicensed agents in summer transfer from Bolton Wand.; UEFA ban **Paul Gascoigne** from 4 Champions' League games (sent off away to Ajax, Oct. 17); UEFA fine **Rangers** £2,500 for players' poor discipline v Ajax, Oct. 17.
1996 (December) Scottish League fine **Falkirk** £25,000 for fielding ineligible player and order match v St. Mirren to be replayed.
1997 (January) S.F.A. fine Celtic manager **Tommy Burns** £2,000 for verbal abuse of match officials v Rangers, Nov. 14.
1997 (February) Scottish League fine **Raith** £10,000 for fielding 3 Scandinavian trialists in match (rule permits maximum of 2).
1998 (April) S.F.A. fine Rangers manager **Walter Smith** £500 for comments to referee at match at Celtic, Nov. 19.

1999 (March) S.F.A. fine Rangers manager **Dick Advocaat** £1,000, with 'severe censure', for touchline misbehaviour at Dunfermline, Feb. 7.

1999 (August) Scottish Premier League fine **Celtic** £45,000 for their part in disturbances at home match with Rangers, May 2.

2000 (March) S.F.A. give **Ian Wright** 2-match ban (served with Burnley) for pushing fourth official when with Celtic (at Kilmarnock, Premier League, Jan. 23).

2000 (April) Scottish League deduct a record 15 points from **Hamilton Academical**, following their players (in protest over unpaid wages) refusing to turn up for Div. 2 fixture at Stenhousemuir on April 1. As a result, Hamilton relegated at end of season.

MISCELLANEOUS

NATIONAL ASSOCIATIONS FORMED

F.A. on Oct. 26 1863
F.A. of Wales 1876
Scottish F.A. 1873
Irish F.A. 1904
Federation of International Football Associations (FIFA) 1904

NATIONAL & INTERNATIONAL COMPETITIONS LAUNCHED

F.A. Cup 1871
Welsh Cup 1877
Scottish Cup 1873
Irish Cup 1880
Football League 1888
F.A. Premier League 1992
Scottish League 1890
Scottish Premier League 1998
Scottish League Cup 1945
Football League Cup 1960
Home International Championship 1883-4
World (Jules Rimet) Cup, at Montevideo 1930
European Championship 1958
European Cup 1955
Fairs/UEFA Cup 1955
Cup-Winners' Cup 1960
Youth International (16-18 age-groups) 1946-7
Olympic Games Tournament, at Shepherd's Bush 1908

INNOVATIONS

Size of Ball: Fixed in **1872**.

Shinguards: Introduced and registered by Sam Weller Widdowson (Nott'm. Forest & England) in **1874**.

Referee's Whistle: First used on Nott'm. Forest's ground in **1878**.

Professionalism: Legalised in England in the summer of **1885** as a result of agitation by Lancashire clubs.

Goal-nets: Invented and patented in **1890** by Mr. J. A. Brodie of Liverpool. They were first used in the North v South match in January, **1891**.

Referees and Linesmen: Replaced umpires and referees in January, **1891**.

Penalty-kick: Introduced at Irish F.A.'s request in the season **1891-2**. The penalty law ordering the goalkeeper to remain on the goal-line came into force in September, **1905**, and the order to stand on his goal-line until the ball is kicked arrived in **1929-30**.

White ball: First came into official use in **1951**.

Floodlighting: First F.A. Cup-tie (replay), Kidderminster Harriers v Brierley Hill Alliance, **1955**.

Heated pitch to beat frost tried by Everton at Goodison Park in **1958.**
First Soccer Closed-circuit TV: At Coventry City ground in October **1965** (10,000 fans saw their team win at Cardiff City, 120 miles away).
Substitutes (one per team) were first allowed in Football League matches at the start of season **1965-6.** Three substitutes (one a goalkeeper) allowed, two of which could be used, in Premier League matches, **1992-93.** The Football League introduced three substitutes for **1993-94.**
Three points for a win: This was introduced by the Football League in **1981-2,** by FIFA in World Cup games in 1994, and by the Scottish League in the same year.
Offside law amended, player 'level' no longer offside, and 'professional foul' made sending-off offence, **1990.**
Penalty shoot-outs introduced to decide F.A. Cup ties level after one replay and extra time, **1991-2.**
New back-pass rule – goalkeeper must not handle ball kicked to him by team-mate, **1992.**
Linesmen became 'referees' assistants', **1998.**
Goalkeepers not to hold ball longer than 6 seconds, **2000.**
Free-kicks advanced by ten yards against opponents failing to retreat, **2000.**

CUP AND LEAGUE DOUBLES

League Championship and F.A. Cup: Preston N.E., 1889; Aston Villa, 1897; Tottenham, 1961; Arsenal, 1971; Liverpool 1986; Manchester Utd. 1994, 1996; Arsenal 1998; Manchester Utd. 1999; Arsenal 2002.
F.A. Cup and Promotion: W.B.A., 1931.
F.A. Cup and Football League Cup: Arsenal, 1993; Liverpool, 2001 (also won UEFA Cup).
League Championship and Football League Cup: Nott'm Forest, 1978; Liverpool, 1982; Liverpool, 1983; Liverpool, 1984 (also won European Cup).
Scottish League Championship and Cup Double: Rangers, (15): 1928-30-34-35-49-50-53-63-64-76-78-92-93-96-2000. Celtic, (12): 1907-8-14-54-67-69-71-72-74-77-88-2001. Aberdeen, (1): 1984.
Scottish Treble (Championship, Cup, League Cup): Rangers 6 times (1949-64-76-78-93-99); Celtic 3 times (1967-69-2001) (also won European Cup in 1967).

DERBY DAYS: COMPLETE LEAGUE RESULTS

Arsenal v Tottenham: Played 130 (all in top div.); Arsenal 52 wins, Tottenham 45, Drawn 33.
Aston Villa v Birmingham City: Played 96; Aston Villa 39, Birmingham City 32, Drawn 25.
Everton v Liverpool: Played 166 (all in top div.); Liverpool 60, Everton 54, Drawn 52.
Ipswich Town v Norwich City: Played 68; Ipswich Town 33, Norwich City 24, Drawn 11.
Manchester City v Manchester Utd.: Played 126; United 49, City 32, Drawn 45.
Middlesbrough v Newcastle Utd.: Played 98; Newcastle Utd. 39, Middlesbrough 32, Drawn 27.
Newcastle Utd. v Sunderland: Played 124; Newcastle Utd. 44, Sunderland 41, Drawn 39 (incl. 1990 play-offs – Sunderland win and draw).
Middlesbrough v Sunderland: Played 120; Sunderland 53, Middlesbrough 36, Drawn 31.
Nott'm. Forest v Notts Co.: Played 86; Forest 35, County 28, Drawn 23.
Sheffield Utd. v Sheffield Wed.: Played 102; United 38, Wed. 31, Drawn 33.
Port Vale v Stoke City: Played 44; Stoke 17, Port Vale 13, Drawn 14.
Bristol City v Bristol Rovers: Played 86; City 33, Rovers 25, Drawn 28.
Celtic v Rangers: Played 264; Rangers 104, Celtic 81, Drawn 79.
Dundee v Dundee Utd.: Played 113; United 57, Dundee 34, Drawn 22.
Hearts v Hibernian: Played 225; Hearts 91, Hibernian 66, Drawn 68.

YOUNGEST AND OLDEST

Youngest Caps   *Age*
Norman Whiteside (N. Ireland v Yugoslavia, June 17, 1982)   **17** years **41** days
Ryan Green (Wales v Malta, June 3, 1998)   **17** years **226** days
James Prinsep (England v Scotland, April 5, 1879)   **17** years **252** days

Johnny Lambie (Scotland v Ireland, March 20, 1886) **17** years **92** days
Jimmy Holmes (Rep. of Ireland v Austria, May 30, 1971) **17** years **200** days

England's youngest cap since 1900: Michael Owen (v Chile, Wembley, February 11, 1998) 18 years 59 days.

Youngest England scorer: Michael Owen (18 years, 164 days) v Morocco, Wembley, May 27, 1998.

Youngest England captains: Bobby Moore (v Czech., away, May 29, 1963), 22 years, 47 days; Michael Owen (v Paraguay, Anfield, April 17, 2002), 22 years, 117 days.

Youngest player in World Cup Final: Pele (Brazil) aged 17 years, 237 days v Sweden in Stockholm, June 12, 1958.

Youngest player to appear in World Cup Finals: Norman Whiteside (N. Ireland v Yugoslavia in Spain – June 17, 1982, age 17 years and 42 days.

Youngest First Division player: Derek Forster (Sunderland goalkeeper v Leicester City, August 22, 1964) aged 15 years, 185 days.

Youngest First Division scorer: At 16 years and 57 days, schoolboy Jason Dozzell (substitute after 30 minutes for Ipswich Town at home to Coventry City on February 4, 1984). Ipswich Town won 3-1 and Dozzell scored their third goal.

Youngest F.A. Premier League player: Gary McSheffrey (Coventry City v Aston Villa, February 27, 1999), 16 years, 198 days.

Youngest F.A. Premier League scorer: Michael Owen (Liverpool v Wimbledon, May 6, 1997), 17 years, 145 days.

Youngest First Division hat-trick scorer: Alan Shearer, aged 17 years, 240 days, in Southampton's 4-2 home win v Arsenal (April 9, 1988) on his full debut. Previously, Jimmy Greaves (17 years, 309 days) with 4 goals for Chelsea at home to Portsmouth (7-4), Christmas Day, 1957.

Youngest to complete 100 Football League goals: Jimmy Greaves (20 years, 261 days) when he did so for Chelsea v Manchester City, November 19, 1960.

Youngest Football League scorer: Ronnie Dix (for Bristol Rov. v Norwich City, Div. 3 South, March 3, 1928) aged 15 years, 180 days.

Youngest players in Football League: Albert Geldard (Bradford Park Avenue v Millwall, Div. 2, September 16, 1929) aged 15 years, 158 days; Ken Roberts (Wrexham v Bradford Park Avenue, Div. 3 North, September 1, 1951) also 15 years, 158 days.

Youngest player in Scottish League: Goalkeeper Ronnie Simpson (Queens Park) aged 15 in 1946.

Youngest player in F.A. Cup: Andy Awford, Worcester City's England Schoolboy defender, aged 15 years, 88 days when he substituted in second half away to Boreham Wood (3rd. qual. round) on October 10, 1987.

Youngest player in F.A. Cup proper: Scott Endersby (15 years, 279 days) when he kept goal for Kettering Town v Tilbury in first round on November 26, 1977.

Youngest Wembley Cup Final captain: Barry Venison (Sunderland v Norwich City, Milk Cup Final, March 24, 1985 – replacing suspended captain Shaun Elliott) – aged 20 years, 220 days.

Youngest F.A. Cup-winning captain: Bobby Moore (West Ham Utd., 1964, v Preston N.E.), aged 23 years, 20 days.

Youngest F.A. Cup Final captain: David Nish was 21 years and 212 days old when he captained Leicester City against Manchester City at Wembley on April 26, 1969.

Youngest F.A. Cup Final player: James Prinsep (Clapham Rov. v Old Etonians, 1879) aged 17 years, 245 days.

Youngest F.A. Cup Final player since 1900: Paul Allen (West Ham Utd. v Arsenal, 1980) aged 17 years, 256 days.

Youngest F.A. Cup Final scorer: Norman Whiteside (Manchester Utd. v Brighton & H.A. in 1983 replay at Wembley), aged 18 years, 19 days.

Youngest F.A. Cup Final managers: Stan Cullis, Wolves (33) v Leicester City, 1949; Steve Coppell, Crystal Palace (34) v Manchester Utd., 1990; Ruud Gullit, Chelsea (34) v Mid'bro', 1997.

Youngest player in Football League Cup: Kevin Davies (Chesterfield sub at West Ham Utd., 2nd Round, 2nd Leg on September 22, 1993) aged 16 years, 180 days.

Youngest Wembley scorer: Norman Whiteside (Manchester Utd. v Liverpool, Milk Cup Final, March 26, 1983) aged 17 years, 324 days.

Youngest Wembley Cup Final goalkeeper: Chris Woods (18 years, 125 days) for Nott'm Forest v Liverpool, League Cup Final on March 18, 1978.

Youngest Wembley F.A. Cup Final goalkeeper: Peter Shilton (19 years, 219 days) for Leicester City v Manchester City, April 26, 1969.

Youngest senior International at Wembley: Salomon Olembe (sub for Cameroon v England, November 15, 1997), aged 16 years, 342 days.

Youngest winning manager at Wembley: Roy McDonough, aged 33 years. 6 months, 24 days as player-manager of Colchester Utd., F.A. Trophy winners on May 10, 1992.

Youngest scorer in full International: Mohamed Kallon (Sierra Leone v Congo, African Nations Cup, April 22, 1995), reported as aged 15 years, 192 days.

Youngest player sent off in World Cup Final series: Rigobert Song (Cameroon v Brazil, in USA, June 1994) aged 17 years, 358 days.

Youngest F.A. Cup Final referee: Kevin Howley, of Middlesbrough, aged 35 when in charge of Wolves v Blackburn Rov., 1960.

Youngest player in England U-23 team: Duncan Edwards (v. Italy, Bologna, January 20, 1954), aged 17 years, 112 days.

Youngest player in England U-21 team: Lee Sharpe (v. Greece, away, February 7, 1989), aged 17 years, 254 days.

Youngest player in Scotland U-21 team: Christian Dailly (v Romania, Hampden Park, Sept. 11, 1990), aged 16 years, 330 days.

Youngest player in senior football: Cameron Campbell Buchanan, Scottish-born outside right, aged 14 years, 57 days when he played for Wolves v W.B.A. in War-time League match, September 26, 1942.

Youngest player in peace-time senior match: Eamon Collins (Blackpool v Kilmarnock, Anglo-Scottish Cup quarter-final 1st. leg, September 9, 1980) aged 14 years, 323 days.

World's youngest player in top-division match: Centre-forward Fernando Rafael Garcia, aged 13, played for 23 minutes for Peruvian club Juan Aurich in 3-1 win against Estudiantes on May 19, 2001.

Oldest player to appear in Football League: New Brighton manager Neil McBain (51 years, 120 days) as emergency goalkeeper away to Hartlepool Utd. (Div. 3 North, March 15, 1947).

Other oldest post-war League players: Sir Stanley Matthews (Stoke City, 1965, 50 years, 5 days); Peter Shilton (Leyton Orient 1997, 47 years, 126 days); Alf Wood (Coventry City, 1958, 43 years, 199 days); Tommy Hutchison (Swansea City, 1991, 43 years, 172 days).

Oldest Football League debutant: Andy Cunningham, for Newcastle Utd. at Leicester City (Div. 1) on February 2, 1929, aged 38 years, 2 days.

Oldest player to appear in First Division: Sir Stanley Matthews (Stoke City v Fulham, February 6, 1965), aged 50 years, 5 days.

Oldest players in Premier League: Goalkeepers John Burridge (Manchester City v Q.P.R., May 14, 1995), aged 43 years, 5 months, 11 days; Steve Ogrizovic (Coventry City v Sheffield Wed., May 6, 2000), aged 42 years, 7 months, 24 days; Neville Southall (Bradford City v Leeds Utd., March 12, 2000), aged 41 years, 5 months, 26 days. Outfield: Gordon Strachan (Coventry City v Derby Co., May 3, 1997) aged 40 years, 2 months, 24 days.

Oldest F.A. Cup Final player: Walter (Billy) Hampson (Newcastle Utd. v Aston Villa on April 26, 1924), aged 41 years, 257 days.

Oldest F.A. Cup-winning team: Arsenal 1950 (average age 31 years, 2 months). Eight of the players were over 30, with the three oldest centre-half Leslie Compton 37, and skipper Joe Mercer and goalkeeper George Swindin, both 35.

Oldest World Cup-winning captain: Dino Zoff, Italy's goalkeeper v W. Germany in 1982 Final, aged 40 years, 92 days.

Oldest player capped by England: Stanley Matthews (v. Denmark, Copenhagen, May 15, 1957), aged 42 years, 103 days.

Oldest England scorer: Stanley Matthews (v N. Ireland, Belfast, October 6, 1956), aged 41 years, 248 days.

Oldest British International player: Billy Meredith (Wales v England at Highbury, March 15, 1920), aged 45 years, 229 days.

Oldest 'new cap': Arsenal centre-half Leslie Compton, at 38 years, 64 days when he made his England debut in 4-2 win against Wales at Sunderland on November 15, 1950. **For Scotland:** Goalkeeper Ronnie Simpson (Celtic) at 36 years, 186 days v England at Wembley, April 15, 1967.

Longest Football League career: This spanned 32 years and 10 months, by Stanley Matthews (Stoke City, Blackpool, Stoke City) from March 19, 1932 until February 6, 1965.

Smallest F.A. Cup-winning captain: 5ft. 4in. – Bobby Kerr (Sunderland v Leeds Utd., 1973).

SHIRT NUMBERING

Numbering players in Football League matches was made compulsory in 1939. Players wore numbered shirts (1-22) in the F.A. Cup Final as an experiment in 1933 (Everton 1-11 v Manchester City 12-22).

Squad numbers for players were introduced by the F.A. Premier League at the start of the season 1993-4. They were optional in the Football League until made compulsory in 1999-2000.

Names on shirts: For first time, players wore names as well as numbers on shirts in League Cup and F.A. Cup Finals, 1993.

SUBSTITUTES

In **1965**, the Football League, by 39 votes to 10, agreed that **one substitute** be allowed for an injured player at any time during a League match. First substitute used in Football League: Keith Peacock (Charlton Athletic), away to Bolton Wand. in Div. 2, August 21, 1965.

Two substitutes per team were approved for the League (Littlewoods) Cup and F.A. Cup in season 1986-7 and two were permitted in the Football League for the first time in 1987-8.

Three substitutes (one a goalkeeper), two of which could be used, introduced by the Premier League for 1992-3. The Football League followed suit for 1993-4.

Three substitutes (one a goalkeeper) were allowed at the World Cup Finals for the first time at US '94.

Three substitutes (any position) introduced by Premier League and Football League in 1995-6.

First substitute to score in F.A. Cup Final: Eddie Kelly (Arsenal v Liverpool, 1971).

The **first recorded use of a substitute was in 1889** (Wales v Scotland at Wrexham on April 15) when Sam Gillam arrived late – although he was a Wrexham player – and Allen Pugh (Rhostellyn) was allowed to keep goal until he turned up. The match ended 0-0.

When Dickie Roose, the Welsh goalkeeper, was injured against England at Wrexham, March 16, 1908, Dai Davies (Bolton Wand.) was allowed to take his place as substitute. Thus Wales used 12 players. England won 7-1.

END OF WAGE LIMIT

Freedom from the maximum wage system – in force since the formation of the Football League in 1888 – was secured by the Professional Footballers' Association in 1961. About this time Italian clubs renewed overtures for the transfer of British stars and Fulham's **Johnny Haynes** became the first British player to earn £100 a week.

THE BOSMAN RULING

On December 15, 1995 the **European Court of Justice** ruled that clubs had no right to transfer fees for out-of-contract players, and the outcome of the 'Bosman case' irrevocably changed football's player-club relationship. It began in 1990, when the contract of 26-year-old **Jean-Marc Bosman**, a midfield player with FC Liege, Belgium, expired. French club Dunkirk wanted him but were unwilling to pay the £500,000 transfer fee, so Bosman was compelled to remain with Liege. He responded with a lawsuit against his club and UEFA on the grounds of 'restriction of trade', and after five years at various court levels the European Court of Justice ruled not only in favour of Bosman but of all professional footballers.

The end of restrictive labour practices revolutionised the system. It led to a proliferation of transfers, rocketed the salaries of elite players who, backed by an increasing army of agents, found themselves in a vastly improved bargaining position as they moved from team to team, league to league, nation to nation. Removing the limit on the number of foreigners clubs could field brought an increasing ratio of such signings, not least in England and Scotland.

Bosman's one-man stand opened the way for footballers to become millionaires, but ended his own career. All he received for his legal conflict was 16 million Belgian francs (£312,000) in compensation, a testimonial of poor reward and martyrdom as the man who did most to change the face of football.

Celtic were the first British club to lose out, when Scottish International John Collins moved to Monaco in June 1996. Subsequent Bosman-free transfers involving British clubs include: Gianluca Vialli, Juventus to Chelsea (7/96); Michael Hughes, Strasbourg to West Ham Utd. (7/96); Gustavo Poyet, Real Zaragoza to Chelsea (5/97); Stefano Eranio, AC Milan to Derby Co. (5/97); Scott Booth, Aberdeen to Borussia Dortmund (6/97); David Connolly, Watford to Feyenoord (7/97); Jonathan Gould, Bradford City to Celtic (8/97); Brian Laudrup, Rangers to Chelsea (6/98); Shaka Hislop, Newcastle Utd. to West Ham Utd. (7/98); John Salako, Coventry City to Fulham (7/98); Rod Wallace, Leeds Utd. to Rangers (7/98); Gerry Taggart, Bolton Wand. to Leicester City (7/98); Mark Pembridge, Sheffield Wed. to Benfica (7/98); Mikael Forssell, HJK Helsinki to Chelsea (11/98); Steve McManaman, Liverpool to Real Madrid (7/99); Andy Melville, Sunderland to Fulham (5/99); Peter Schmeichel, Manchester Utd. to Sporting Lisbon (6/99); Kasey Keller, Leicester City to Rayo Vallencano, Spain (7/99); Ken Monkou, Southampton to Huddersfield Town (10/99); Markus Babbel, Bayern Munich to Liverpool (1/00); Pegguy Arphexad, Leicester City to Liverpool (7/00); Gary McAllister, Coventry City to Liverpool (7/00); Paul Okon, Fiorentina to Middlesbrough (7/00); Peter Atherton, Sheffield Wed. to Bradford City (7/00); Mark Crossley, Nott'm. Forest to Middlesbrough (7/00); Benito Carbone, Aston Villa to Bradford City (8/00); Winston Bogarde, Barcelona to Chelsea (8/00); Jari Litmanen, Barcelona to Liverpool (1/01); Teddy Sheringham, Manchester Utd. to Tottenham (6/01); Vivas Nelson, Arsenal to Inter Milan (6/01); Hassan Kachloul, Southampton to Aston Villa (6/01); Sol Campbell, Tottenham to Arsenal (6/01); Laurent Blanc, Inter Milan to Man. Utd. (8/01).

GREATEST SHOCKS

Excluding such tragedies as the Munich air crash (Feb. 1958), the Bradford City fire disaster (May 1985), Heysel (May 1985) and Hillsborough (April 1989), here in date order are, arguably, the greatest shocks in football history:

(1)	Jan. 1933	F.A. Cup 3rd. Round: Walsall 2, Arsenal 0.
(2)	Jan. 1949	F.A. Cup 4th. Round: Yeovil 2, Sunderland 1.
(3)	June 1950	World Cup Finals: U.S.A. 1, England 0 (Belo Horizonte, Brazil).
(4)	Nov. 1953	England 3, Hungary 6 (Wembley).
(5)	Sept. 1962	Cup-Winners' Cup 1st. Round, 1st. Leg: Bangor 2, Napoli 0.
(6)	Mar. 1966	World Cup stolen in London (found a week later).
(7)	June 1966	World Cup Finals: N. Korea 1, Italy 0 (Middlesbrough).
(8)	Jan. 1967	Scottish Cup 1st. Round: Berwick Rangers 1, Glasgow Rangers 0.
(9)	Mar. 1969	League Cup Final: Swindon Town 3, Arsenal 1.
(10)	Feb. 1971	F.A. Cup 5th. Round: Colchester Utd. 3, Leeds Utd. 2.
(11)	Jan. 1972	F.A. Cup 3rd. Round: Hereford Utd. 2, Newcastle Utd. 1.
(12)	May 1973	F.A. Cup Final: Sunderland 1, Leeds Utd. 0.
(13)	July 1974	Bill Shankly retires as Liverpool manager.
(14)	May 1976	F.A. Cup Final: Southampton 1, Manchester Utd. 0.
(15)	July 1977	England manager Don Revie defects to coach Utd. Arab Emirates.
(16)	June 1982	World Cup Finals: Algeria 2, West Germany 1 (Gijon, Spain).
(17)	Jan. 1984	F.A. Cup 3rd. Round: Bournemouth 2, Manchester Utd. (holders) 0.
(18)	May 1988	F.A. Cup Final: Wimbledon 1, Liverpool 0 .
(19)	June 1990	World Cup Finals: Cameroon 1, Argentina (World Champions) 0 (Milan).
(20)	Sept. 1990	European Championship (Qual. Round): Faroe Islands 1, Austria 0.
(21)	Feb. 1991	Kenny Dalglish resigns as Liverpool manager.
(22)	Jan. 1992	F.A. Cup 3rd. Round: Wrexham 2, Arsenal 1.
(23)	June 1992	European Championship Final: Denmark 2, Germany (World Champions) 0.

(24)	June 1993	U.S. Cup '93: U.S.A. 2, England 0 (Foxboro, Boston).
(25)	July 1994	World Cup Finals: Bulgaria 2, Germany 1 (New York City).
(26)	Feb. 1998	Concacaf Gold Cup: U.S.A. 1, Brazil 0 (Los Angeles).
(27)	July 1998	World Cup Q-final: Croatia 3 Germany 0.
(28)	July 1996	Olympic s-final (Athens, Georgia): Nigeria beat Brazil 4-3 with extra-time 'golden goal' (Brazil led 3-1 with 13 mins. left).
(29)	Feb. 2000	Scottish Cup 3rd. Round: Celtic 1, Inverness Cal. Thistle 3.
(30)	Nov. 2000	Scotland 0, Australia 2 (friendly, Hampden Park).
(31)	June 2001	Confed. Cup 3rd place play-off: Australia 1, Brazil 0 (Ulsan, S. Korea).
(32)	July 2001	Honduras 2, Brazil 0 (Copa America quarter-final).

OTHER INTERNATIONAL SHOCKS

(Read in conjunction with Greatest Shocks above)

1982	Spain 0, N. Ireland 1 (World Cup Finals in Spain).
1990	Scotland 0, Costa Rica 1 (World Cup Finals in Italy).
1990	Sweden 1, Costa Rica 2 (World Cup Finals in Italy).
1993	Argentina 0, Colombia 5 (World Cup qual. round).
1993	France 2, Israel 3 (World Cup qual. round).
1993	San Marino score fastest goal in Int. records: 8.3 secs. v England (World Cup qual. round).
1994	Moldova 3, Wales 2; Georgia 5, Wales 0 (both Euro. Champ. qual. round).
1995	Belarus 1, Holland 0 (European Champ. qual. round).
2001	Australia 1, France 0 (Confed. Cup, S. Korea). France won tournament.
2001	German 1, England 5 (World Cup qual. round).
2002	France 0, Senegal 1 (World Cup Finals, opening match, in S. Korea).
2002	France, World Cup holders, out without scoring.
2002	World Cup joint hosts South Korea beat Ital with Golden Goal and Spain on penalties.

GREAT RECOVERIES

On December 21, 1957, Charlton Athletic were losing 5-1 against Huddersfield Town (Div. 2) at The Valley with only 28 minutes left, and from the 15th minute, had been reduced to ten men by injury, but they won 7-6, with left-winger Johnny Summers scoring five goals. Huddersfield Town (managed by Bill Shankly) remain the only team to score six times in a League match and lose.

Among other notable comebacks: on November 12, 1904 (Div. 1), Sheffield Wed. were losing 0-5 at home to Everton, but drew 5-5. At Anfield on December 4, 1909 (Div.1), Liverpool trailed 2-5 to Newcastle Utd. at half-time, then won 6-5. On Boxing Day, 1927, in Div. 3 South, Northampton Town won 6-5 at home to Luton Town after being 1-5 down at half-time. On September 22, 1984 (Div. 1), Q.P.R. drew 5-5 at home to Newcastle Utd. after trailing 0-4 at half-time. On April 12, 1993 (Div. 1) Swindon Town were 1-4 down at Birmingham City with 30 minutes left, but won 6-4.

Other astonishing turnabouts in Div.1 include: Grimsby Town (3-5 down) won 6-5 at W.B.A. on Apr. 30, 1932; and Derby Co. beat Manchester Utd. 5-4 (from 1-4) on Sept. 5, 1936.

With 5 minutes to play, Ipswich Town were losing 3-0 at Barnsley (Div. 1, March 9, 1996), but drew 3-3.

On Sunday, Jan. 19, 1997 (Div. 1), Q.P.R. were 0-4 down away to Port Vale at half-time and still trailing 1-4 with 5 minutes left. They drew 4-4.

Celtic trailed 0-2, 1-3 and 2-4 away to Dunfermline (Scottish First Div., Nov. 19,1966) but won 5-4 with a last-minute goal.

Premier League comebacks: Jan. 4, 1994 – Liverpool were 3 down after 24 mins. at home to Manchester Utd., drew 3-3; Nov. 8, 1997 – Derby Co. led 3-0 after 33 mins. at Elland Road, but Leeds Utd. won 4-3 with last-minute goal; Sept. 29, 2001 – Manchester Utd. won 5-3 at Tottenham after trailing 3-0 at half-time.

Tranmere Rov. retrieved a 3-0 half-time deficit to beat Southampton 4-3 in an F.A. Cup fifth round replay at home on Feb. 20, 2001.

GOALS THAT WERE WRONGLY GIVEN

Tottenham's last-minute winner at home to Huddersfield (Div. 1) on April 2, 1952: Eddie Baily's corner-kick struck referee W.R. Barnes in the back, and the ball rebounded to Baily, who centred for Len Duquemin to head into the net. Baily had infringed the Laws by playing the ball twice, but the result (1-0) stood. Those two points helped Spurs to finish Championship runners-up; Huddersfield were relegated.

The second goal (66 mins) in **Chelsea's** 2-1 home win v Ipswich Town (Div. 1) on Sept. 26, 1970: Alan Hudson's low shot from just beyond the penalty-area hit the stanchion on the outside of goal and the ball rebounded on to the pitch. But instead of the goal-kick, referee Roy Capey gave a goal, on a linesman's confirmation. TV pictures proved otherwise. But the Football League quoted from the Laws of the Game: 'The referee's decision on all matters is final.' And though it was wrong, the goal stood and sent Chelsea on the way to victory.

MATCHES OFF

Worst day for postponements: Feb. 9, 1963, when 57 League fixtures in England and Scotland were frozen off. Only 7 Football League matches took place, and the entire Scottish programme was wiped out

Worst other weather-hit days:

Jan. 12, 1963 and Feb. 2, 1963 – on both those Saturdays, only 4 out of 44 Football League matches were played.

Jan. 1, 1979 – 43 out of 46 Football League fixtures postponed.

Jan. 17, 1987 – 37 of 45 scheduled Football League fixtures postponed; only 2 Scottish matches survived.

Feb. 8-9, 1991 – only 4 of the week-end's 44 Barclays League matches survived the freeze-up (4 of the postponements were on Friday night). In addition, 11 Scottish League matches were off.

Jan. 27, 1996 – 44 Cup and League matches in England and Scotland were frozen off. The ten matches played comprised 3 F.A. Cup (4th. Round), 1 in Div. 1, 5 in Scottish Cup (3rd. Round), 1 in Scottish Div. 2.

Fewest matches left on one day by postponements was during the Second World War – Feb. 3, 1940 when, because of snow, ice and fog only one out of 56 regional league fixtures took place. It resulted Plymouth Argyle 10, Bristol City 3.

The Scottish Cup second round tie between Inverness Thistle and Falkirk in season 1978-9 was **postponed 29 times** because of snow and ice. First put off on Jan. 6, it was eventually played on Feb. 22. Falkirk won 4-0.

Pools Panel's busiest days: Jan. 17, 1987 and Feb. 9, 1991 – on both dates they gave their verdict on 48 postponed coupon matches.

FEWEST 'GAMES OFF'

Season 1947-8 was the best since the war for Football League fixtures being played to schedule. Only **six** were postponed.

LONGEST SEASON

The latest that League football has been played in a season was **June 7, 1947** (six weeks after the F.A. Cup Final). The season was extended because of mass postponements caused by bad weather in mid-winter.

The latest the F.A. Cup competition has ever been completed was in season 1981-2, when Tottenham beat Q.P.R. 1-0 in a Final replay at Wembley on May 27.

Worst winter hold-up was in season 1962-3. The Big Freeze began on Boxing Day and lasted until March, with nearly 500 first-class matches postponed. The F.A. Cup 3rd. Round was the longest on record – it began with only three out of 32 ties playable on January 5 and ended 66 days and 261 postponements later on March 11. The Lincoln City-Coventry City tie was put off 15 times. The Pools Panel was launched that winter, on January 26, 1963.

Hottest day for a Football League programme is believed to have been Saturday, September 1, 1906, when temperatures across the country were over 90°.

LEAGUE SECRETARIES

Harry Lockett (1888-1902), **Tom Charnley** (1902-33), **Fred Howarth** (1933-57), **Alan Hardaker** (1957-79), **Graham Kelly** (1979-88), **David Dent** (1989-2001). **Andy Williamson** succeeded David Dent in June 2001, with the title Head of Operations
    Football League Chairman: Keith Harris (appointed July 2000). **Chief Executive:** David Burns (appointed October 2000).
    F.A. Premier League: Secretary: Mike Foster. Chairman: David Richards (Sheffield Wed.). Chief Executive: Richard Scudamore.

FOOTBALL ASSOCIATION SECRETARIES/ CHIEF EXECUTIVES

Ebenezer Morley (1863-66), **Robert Willis** (1866-68), **R.G. Graham** (1868-70), **Charles Alcock** (1870-95, paid from 1887), 1895-1934 **Sir Frederick Wall**, 1934-62 **Sir Stanley Rous**, 1962-73 **Denis Follows**, 1973-89 **Ted Croker** (latterly chief executive), 1989-99 **Graham Kelly** (chief executive). Since Jan. 1, 2000 **Adam Crozier** (chief executive).
    F.A. Chairman: Geoffrey Thompson (appointed June, 1999).

FOOTBALL'S SPONSORS

Football League: Canon 1983-6; Today Newspaper 1986-7; Barclays 1987-93; Endsleigh Insurance 1993-6; Nationwide Building Society 1996-2001 then extended to 2004.
League Cup: Milk Cup 1982-6; Littlewoods 1987-90; Rumbelows 1991-2; Coca-Cola Cup 1993-8; Worthington Cup 1998-2003.
Premier League: Carling 1993-2001; Barclaycard 2001-04.
F.A. Cup: Littlewoods 1994-8; AXA 1998-2002.

SOCCER HEADQUARTERS

Football Association: 25 Soho Square, London W1D 4FA (moved from Lancaster Gate, London W2, September 2000). Chief Executive: Adam Crozier.
F.A. Premier League: 16 Lancaster Gate, London W2 3LW. Chief Executive: Richard Scudamore.
Football Foundation: 25 Soho Square, London W1D 4FF. Chief Executive: Peter Lee.
Football League: Edward VII Quay, Navigation Way, Preston PR2 2YF. Head of Operations: Andy Williamson. **London Office:** 11 Connaught Place, London W2 2ET.
Professional Footballers' Association: 2 Oxford Utd. Court, Bishopsgate, Manchester M2 3WQ. Chief Executive: Gordon Taylor.
Scottish Football Association: 6 Park Gardens, Glasgow G3 7YF. Secretary: David Taylor.
Scottish Premier League: National Stadium, Hampden Park, Glasgow GU2 9BA. Chief Executive: Roger Mitchell.
Scottish Football League: 188 West Regent Street, Glasgow G2 4RY. Secretary: Peter Donald.
Irish Football Association: 20 Windsor Avenue, Belfast BT9 6EG. Secretary: David Bowen.
Irish Football League: 96 University Street, Belfast BT7 1HE. Secretary: Harry Wallace.
League of Ireland: 80 Merrion Square, Dublin 2. Secretary: Eamonn Morris.
Republic of Ireland F.A.: 80 Merrion Square, Dublin 2. Secretary: Brendan Menton.
Welsh Football Association: 3 Westgate Street, Cardiff City, S. Glamorgan CF1 1DD. Secretary: David Collins.
Football Conference: Collingwood House, Schooner Court, Crossways, Dartford, Kent DA2 6QQ.
FIFA: P.O. Box 85, 8030 Zurich, Switzerland.
UEFA: Chemin de la Redoute 54, Case Postale 303, CH-1260, Nyon, Geneva, Switzerland.

WORLD'S LARGEST STADIA

(Source: *FIFA NEWS***)**
Capacity 165,000: Maracana, Rio de Janeiro, Brazil; **150,000** Rungnado Stadium, Pyongyang, North Korea; **125,000** Magalhaes Pinto Stadium, Belo Horizonte, Brazil; **120,000** Morumbi Stadium, Sao Paulo, Brazil; Stadium of Light, Lisbon, Portugal; Krirangan Stadium, Salt Lake, Calcutta; Senayan Stadium, Jakarta, Indonesia; **119,000**

Castelao Stadium, Fortaleza, Brazil; **115,000** Arrudao Stadium, Recife, Brazil; Azteca Stadium, Mexico City; Nou Camp, Barcelona, Spain; **114,000** Bernabeu Stadium, Madrid; **100,000** Nasser Stadium, Cairo, Egypt; Azadi Stadium, Tehran, Iran; Red Star Stadium, Belgrade, Yugoslavia; Central Stadium, Kiev, USSR.

F.A. NATIONAL FOOTBALL CENTRE

This is due to open at Burton-upon-Trent in August 2003. On a site of 350 acres and built at a cost of £30m., it will comprise 14 pitches, sports science clinic, swimming pools, indoor training facilities and luxury accommodation. England teams at all levels will train there.

NEW HOMES OF SOCCER

Newly-constructed League grounds in Britain since the war: 1946 Hull City (Boothferry Park); 1950 Port Vale (Vale Park); 1955 Southend Utd. (Roots Hall); 1988 Scunthorpe Utd. (Glanford Park); 1988 St. Johnstone (McDiarmid Park); 1990 Walsall (Bescot Stadium); 1990 Wycombe Wand. (Adams Park); 1992 Chester City (Deva Stadium, Bumpers Lane); 1993 Millwall (New Den); 1994 Clyde (Broadwood Stadium); 1994 Huddersfield Town (Alfred McAlpine Stadium, Kirklees); 1994 Northampton Town (Sixfields Stadium); 1995 Middlesbrough (Riverside Stadium); 1997 Bolton Wand. (Reebok Stadium); 1997 Derby Co. (Pride Park); Stoke City (Britannia Stadium); Sunderland (Stadium of Light); 1998 Reading (Madejski Stadium); 1999 Wigan Athletic (JJB Stadium); 2001 Southampton (St. Mary's Stadium); 2001 Oxford Utd. (Kassam Stadium); 2002 Leicester City (Walkers Stadium).

GROUND-SHARING

Crystal Palace and **Charlton Athletic** (Selhurst Park, 1985-91); **Bristol Rov.** and **Bath City** (Twerton Park, Bath, 1986-96); **Partick Thistle** and **Clyde** (Firhill Park, Glasgow, 1986-91; in seasons 1990-1, 1991-2 **Chester City** shared **Macclesfield Town's** ground (Moss Rose). **Crystal Palace** and **Wimbledon** now share Selhurst Park, starting season 1991-2, when **Charlton Athletic** (tenants) moved to rent Upton Park from **West Ham Utd. Clyde** moved to Douglas Park, **Hamilton Academicals'** home, in 1991-2. **Stirling Albion** shared **Sten-housemuir's** ground, Ochilview Park, in 1992-3. In 1993-4, **Clyde** shared **Partick's** home until moving to their new ground. In 1994-5, **Celtic** shared Hampden Park with **Queen's Park** (while Celtic Park was redeveloped); **Hamilton** shared **Partick's** ground. **Airdrie** shared **Clyde's** Broadwood Stadium. **Bristol Rov.** left Bath City's ground at the start of season 1996-7, sharing Bristol Rugby Club's Memorial Ground. **Clydebank** shared **Dumbarton's** Boghead Park from 1996-7 until renting **Greenock Morton's** Cappielow Park in season 1999-2000. **Brighton** shared **Gillingham's** ground in seasons 1997-8, 1998-9.

ARTIFICIAL TURF

Q.P.R. were the first British club to install an artificial pitch, in 1981. They were followed by **Luton Town** in 1985, and **Oldham Athletic** and **Preston N.E.** in **1986**. Q.P.R. reverted to grass in 1988, as did Luton Town and promoted Oldham Athletic in season 1991-2 (when artificial pitches were banned in Div. 1). **Preston N.E.** were the last Football League club playing 'on plastic' in 1993-4, and their Deepdale ground was restored to grass for the start of 1994-5.

Stirling Albion were the **first Scottish club** to play on plastic, in season 1987-8.

F.A. SOCCER SCHOOL

The Football Association's **national soccer school**, at Lilleshall, aimed at providing the backbone of England's World Cup challenge in the 1990s, was opened by the Duke of Kent (President) on September 4, 1984. It was sponsored by GM Motors, and the first intake comprised 25 boys aged fourteen.

The School of Excellence produced England Internationals Nick Barmby, Andy Cole, Sol Campbell, Ian Walker and Michael Owen. It closed in 1999, to be replaced nationwide by academies at leading clubs.

DOUBLE RUNNERS-UP

There have been nine instances of clubs finishing **runner-up in both the League Championship and F.A. Cup in the same season**: 1928 Huddersfield Town; 1932 Arsenal; 1939 Wolves; 1962 Burnley; 1965 and 1970 Leeds Utd.; 1986 Everton; 1995 Manchester Utd; 2001 Arsenal.

CORNER-KICK RECORDS

Not a single corner-kick was recorded when **Newcastle Utd.** drew 0-0 at home to **Portsmouth** (Div.1) on December 5, 1931.

The record for **most corners** in a match for one side is believed to be **Sheffield Utd.'s 28** to West Ham Utd.'s 1 in Div.2 at Bramall Lane on October 14, 1989. For all their pressure, Sheffield Utd. lost 2-0.

Nott'm. Forest led Southampton 22-2 on corners (Premier League, Nov. 28, 1992) but lost the match 1-2.

Tommy Higginson (Brentford, 1960s) once passed back to his own goalkeeper from a corner kick.

Steve Staunton (Rep. of Ireland) is believed to be the only player to score direct from a corner in **two** Internationals.

OFFSIDES NIL

Not one offside decision was given in the **Brazil-Turkey** World Cup semi-final at Saitama, Japan, on June 26, 2002.

'PROFESSIONAL FOUL' DIRECTIVE

After the 1990 World Cup Finals, F.I.F.A. dealt with the **'professional foul'**, incorporating this directive into the Laws of the Game: 'If, in the opinion of the referee, a player who is moving towards his opponents' goal, with an obvious opportunity to score, is intentionally impeded by an opponent through unlawful means – thus denying the attacking player's team the aforesaid goalscoring opportunity – the offender should be sent from the field of play.'

SACKED AT HALF-TIME

Leyton Orient sacked **Terry Howard** on his 397th. appearance for the club – at half-time in a Second Division home defeat against Blackpool (Feb. 7, 1995) for 'an unacceptable performance'. He was fined two weeks' wages, given a free transfer and moved to Wycombe Wand.

Harald Schumacher, former Germany goalkeeper, was sacked as Fortuna Koln coach when they were two down at half-time against Waldhof Mannheim (Dec. 15, 1999). They lost 5-1.

MOST GAMES BY 'KEEPER FOR ONE CLUB

Alan Knight made 683 League appearances for Portsmouth, over 23 seasons (1978-2000), a record for a goalkeeper at one club. The previous holder was Peter Bonetti with 600 League games for Chelsea (20 seasons, 1960-79).

PLAYED TWO GAMES ON SAME DAY

Jack Kelsey played full-length matches for both club and country on Wed., November 26, 1958. In the afternoon he kept goal for Wales in a 2-2 draw against England at Villa Park, and he then drove to Highbury to help Arsenal win 3-1 in a prestigious floodlit friendly against Juventus.

On the same day, winger **Danny Clapton** played for England (against Wales and Kelsey) and then in part of Arsenal's match against Juventus.

On November 11, 1987, **Mark Hughes** played for Wales against Czechoslovakia (European Championship) in Prague, then flew to Munich and went on as substitute that night in a winning Bayern Munich team, to whom he was on loan from Barcelona.

On February 16, 1993 goalkeeper **Scott Howie** played in Scotland's 3-0 U-21 win v Malta at Tannadice Park, Dundee (k.o. 1.30pm) and the same evening played in Clyde's 2-1 home win v Queen of South (Div. 2).

Ryman League **Hornchurch**, faced by end-of-season fixture congestion, played **two matches on the same night** (May 1, 2001). They lost 2-1 at home to Ware and drew 2-2 at Clapton.

GOING PUBLIC

Manchester Utd. became the fourth British club (after Tottenham, Hibernian and Millwall) to 'go public' with a share issue in June 1991. Many other clubs have since "floated" on the Stock Exchange.

MEDIA INVEST IN TOP CLUBS

In season 1999-2000, satellite broadcaster **BSkyB** bought 9.9% share stakes in Manchester Utd. (£84m), Chelsea (£40m), Leeds Utd. (£13.8m), Manchester City (£12m) and a 5% share in Sunderland (£6.5m). **Granada TV** bought a £22m. stake in Liverpool. Cable giants **NTL** acquired 9.9% shares/sponsorship investment in Newcastle Utd. (£35m) and Aston Villa (£26m) and Leicester City (£12.5m). They agreed a £31m. sponsorship with Rangers.

RECORD CLUB LOSS

Fulham, brokered by Harrods owner Mohamed Al Fayed, made British football's record loss of £23.3m. in the year to June 30, 2001 (in which they won promotion to the Premiership as Div. 1 Champions). The club's debts rose to £61.7m. Previous highest loss was £18.7m. by Newcastle Utd. in 2000.

FIRST 'MATCH OF THE DAY'

BBC TV (recorded highlights): Liverpool 3, Arsenal 2 on August 22, 1964. **First complete match to be televised:** Arsenal 3, Everton 2 on August 29, 1936. **First League match televised in colour:** Liverpool 2, West Ham Utd. 0 on November 15, 1969.

'MATCH OF THE DAY' – BIGGEST SCORES

Football League: Tottenham 9, Bristol Rov. 0 (Div. 2, 1977-8). **Premier League:** Nott'm Forest 1, Manchester Utd. 8 (1998-9).

FIRST COMMENTARY ON RADIO

Arsenal 1, **Sheffield Utd.** 1 (Div. 1) broadcast on BBC, January 22, 1927.

OLYMPIC SOCCER WINNERS

1908 Great Britain (in London); **1912** Great Britain (Stockholm); **1920** Belgium (Antwerp); **1924** Uruguay (Paris); **1928** Uruguay (Amsterdam); **1932** No soccer in Los Angeles Olympics.
1936 Italy (Berlin); **1948** Sweden (London); **1952** Hungary (Helsinki); **1956** USSR (Melbourne); **1960** Yugoslavia (Rome); **1964** Hungary (Tokyo); **1968** Hungary (Mexico); **1972** Poland (Munich); **1976** E. Germany (Montreal); **1980** Czechoslovakia (Moscow); **1984** France (Los Angeles); **1988** USSR (Seoul); **1992** Spain (Barcelona); **1996** Nigeria (Atlanta); **2000** Cameroon (Sydney).
Highest scorer in Final tournament: Ferenc Bene (Hungary) 12 goals, 1964.
Record crowd for Olympic Soccer Final: 108,800 (France v Brazil, Los Angeles 1984).

MOST AMATEUR CUP WINS

Bishop Auckland set the F.A. Amateur Cup record with 10 wins, and in 1957 became the only club to carry off the trophy in three successive seasons. Five wins: Clapton and Crook Town. The competition was discontinued after the Final on April 20, 1974. (Bishop's Stortford 4, Ilford 1, at Wembley).

FOOTBALL FOUNDATION

This was formed (May 2000) to replace the **Football Trust**, which had been in existence since 1975 as an initiative of the Pools companies to provide financial support at all levels, from schools football to safety and ground improvement work throughout the game. The Foundation, chaired by **Tom Pendry** and with representatives of the Government, F.A. and Premier League on board, was empowered to distribute 5% of the Premiership's TV money to football's grass-roots level.

TESTIMONIALS

The first £1m. testimonial was **Sir Alex Ferguson's** at Old Trafford on October 11, 1999, when a full-house crowd of 54,842 saw a Rest of the World team beat Manchester Utd. 4-2. United's manager pledged that a large percentage of the receipts would go to charity.

Two nights after Manchester Utd. completed the Double in May, 1994, 42,079 packed Old Trafford for **Mark Hughes'** testimonial (1-3 Celtic). The estimated proceeds of £500,000 equalled the then testimonial record of **Ally McCoist's** match (Rangers 1, Newcastle Utd. 2) on August 3, 1993.

The match for **Bryan Robson**, Manchester Utd. and England captain, against Celtic at Old Trafford on Tuesday, November 20, 1990 was watched by a crowd of 41,658, and receipts of £300,000 were a then record for a testimonial.

Kenny Dalglish's testimonial (Liverpool v Real Sociedad) at Anfield on August 14, 1990 attracted 30,461 spectators, with receipts estimated at £150,000.

On December 4, 1990, **Willie Miller's** testimonial (Aberdeen v World XI) packed Pittodrie to its 22,500 capacity, and raised an estimated £150,000.

The match for 82-year-old **Sir Matt Busby**, between Manchester Utd. and a Rep. of Ireland XI at Old Trafford on Sunday, August 11, 1991 was watched by 35,410 (estimated benefit £250,000).

Ian Rush's testimonial brought an estimated £250,000 from a 25,856 crowd at Anfield on December 6, 1994 (Liverpool 6, Celtic 0).

Three lucrative testimonials were staged in May 1996. Arsenal's **Paul Merson** earned a reported £400,000 (a percentage to charity) from his match against an Int. XI at Highbury (May 9, att: 31,626); the Republic of Ireland's new manager **Mick McCarthy** received an estimated £300,000 from a 40,000 crowd who saw Celtic beaten 3-0 at Lansdowne Road, Dublin on May 26; and **Stuart Pearce** benefited by some £200,000 from a turn-out of 23,815 when Nott'm. Forest beat Newcastle Utd. 6-5 at the City Ground on May 8.

Testimonial sums reported in season 1996-7 included: **Bryan Gunn**, Norwich City goalkeeper, £250,000 for 21,000 sell-out v Manchester Utd., Nov. 4; **Brian McClair**, Manchester Utd., £380,000 v Celtic, April 14.

Among testimonials in 1997-8: A full-house 50,000 at Ibrox paid an estimated £500,000 for retiring manager **Walter Smith** (Rangers 1, Liverpool 0) on March 3, 1998.

Paul McGrath's testimonial at Lansdowne Road, Dublin (May 17, 1998) produced record receipts of £600,000. A crowd of 39,000 saw Jack Charlton's XI beat a Rep. Of Ireland XI 3-2.

A crowd of 49,468 attended Ibrox (Rangers 4, Middlesbrough 4) on March 2, 1999 for former Rangers player **Alan McLaren's** testimonial. His fund benefited by an estimated £500,000.

A capacity crowd of 36,733 packed St. James' Park, paying an estimated £250,000, for **Peter Beardsley's** testimonial (Newcastle Utd. 1, Celtic 3) on Jan. 27, 1999.

Among testimonials in 2000-01: **Denis Irwin** (Manchester Utd.) estimated receipts £1m. from Manchester Utd. 2, Manchester City 0, Old Trafford, (att. 45,158) August 16; **David Seaman** (Arsenal 0, Barcelona 2, (att. 33,297), May 22. He donated part of the £600,000 estimated receipts to the Willow Foundation Charity, set up by Bob Wilson, his goalkeeping coach at Highbury. The testimonial for **Tom Boyd** (Celtic) against Manchester Utd. (May 15, 2001) attracted a 57,000 crowd with receipts estimated at £1m.

In season 2001-02: For **Ryan Giggs**, a full-house 66,967 (record Testimonial attendance) paid £1m. to see Manchester Utd. 3, Celtic 4 on August 1. Undisclosed sums were donated to charities.

Receipts estimated at £500,000 were produced by the 35,887 crowd at Tottenham v Fiorentina (August 8) for **Bill Nicholson**, who managed Tottenham from 1958-74.

Gary Kelly's Testimonial (Leeds Utd. 1, Celtic 4) drew 26,440 at Elland Road on May 7, 2002, and receipts of £600,000 were donated to cancer charities.

Tony Adams' second Testimonial (1-1 v Celtic on May 13, 2002) two nights after Arsenal completed the Double, was watched by 38,021 spectators. Of £1m. receipts, he donated a substantial percentage to Sporting Chance, the charity that helps sportsmen/women with drink, drug, gambling problems.

Another one-club player, **Matthew Le Tissier**, ended his playing career at Southampton with 31.904 spectators (receipts £500,000) watching a 9-9 draw with an England XI on May 14, 2002.

On the same night, Sunderland and a Republic of Ireland XI drew 0-0 in front of 35,702 at the Stadium of Light. The beneficiary, **Nial Quinn**, was donating his entire Testimonial proceeds, estimated at £1m., to children's hospitals in Sunderland and Dublin, and to homeless children in Africa and Asia.

WHAT IT USED TO COST

Minimum admission to League football was one shilling in 1939. After the war, it was increased to 1s. 3d. in 1946; 1s. 6d. in 1951; 1s. 9d. in 1952; 2s. in 1955; 2s. 6d. in 1960; 4s. in 1965; 5s. in 1968; 6s. in 1970; and 8s. (40p) in 1972. After that, the fixed minimum charge was dropped.

Wembley's first Cup Final programme in 1923 cost three pence (1¼p in today's money). The programme for the 'farewell' F.A. Cup Final in May, 2000 was priced £10.

WHAT THEY USED TO EARN

In the 1930s, First Division players were on £8 a week (£6 in close season) plus bonuses of £2 win, £1 draw. The maximum wage went up to £12 when football resumed post-war in 1946 and had reached £20 by the time the limit was abolished in 1961.

ENGLAND TOP EURO-PRIZE WINNERS

There have been **130 European club competitions** since what is now the Champions' League was launched in season 1955-6; 47 for the European Cup, 44 for the Fairs/UEFA Cup and 39 for the Cup-Winners' Cup, which ended in 1999.

Despite the five-year enforced absence that followed the Heysel disaster in 1985, **English clubs** head the European prize list, Liverpool's success in the 2001 UEFA Cup taking the total to 27 triumphs: 9 in the Champions' Cup, 8 in the Cup-Winners' Cup and 10 in the Fairs/UEFA Cup.

Italy have won 26 Euro prizes, followed by Spain (25) and West Germany/Germany (16). The 130 winners have come from 17 countries.

England's 27 prizes are shared among 13 clubs: Liverpool 7 (4 EC, 3 UEFA); Manchester Utd. 3 (2 EC, 1 CWC); Tottenham 3 (1 CWC, 2 UEFA); Chelsea 2 (2 CWC); Leeds Utd. 2 (2 UEFA); Nott'm. Forest 2 (2 EC); Arsenal 2 (1 UEFA, 1 CWC); Aston Villa 1 (EC); Everton 1 (CWC); Ipswich Town 1 (UEFA); Manchester City 1 (CWC); Newcastle Utd. 1 (UEFA); West Ham Utd. 1 (CWC).

Scotland's three successes have been achieved by Celtic (EC); Rangers and Aberdeen (both CWC).

EUROPEAN TRIUMPHS, COUNTRY BY COUNTRY

	European Cup/ Champions League	Cup-Winners' Cup	Fairs Cup/ UEFA Cup	Total
England	9	8	10	27
Italy	9	7	10	26
Spain	10	7	8	25
West Germany/Germany	6	4	6	16
Holland	6	1	4	11
Belgium	–	3	1	4
Portugal	3	1	–	4
Scotland	1	2	–	3
USSR	–	3	–	3
France	1	1	–	2
Sweden	–	–	2	2
Yugoslavia	1	–	1	2
Czechoslovakia	–	1	–	1
East Germany	–	1	–	1

Hungary	–	–	1	1
Romania	1	–	–	1
Turkey	–	–	1	1
Total:	**47**	**39**	**44**	**130**

EUROPEAN TROPHY WINNERS – SUMMARY

European Cup (47 competitions, 21 different winners): **9** Real Madrid; **5** AC Milan; **4** Ajax Amsterdam, Liverpool; Bayern Munich; **2** Benfica, Inter Milan, Juventus, Manchester Utd., Nott'm. Forest; **1** Aston Villa, Barcelona, Borussia Dortmund, Celtic, Feyenoord, Hamburg SV, Marseille, PSV Eindhoven, FC Porto, Red Star Belgrade, Steaua Bucharest.

Cup-Winners' Cup (39 competitions, 32 different winners): **4** Barcelona; **2** Anderlecht, Chelsea, Dynamo Kiev, AC Milan; **1** Aberdeen, Ajax Amsterdam, Arsenal, Atletico Madrid, Bayern Munich, Borussia Dortmund, Dynamo Tbilisi, Everton, Fiorentina, Hamburg SV, Juventus, Lazio, Magdeburg, Manchester City, Manchester Utd., Mechelen, Paris St. Germain, Parma, Rangers, Real Zaragoza, Sampdoria, Slovan Bratislava, Sporting Lisbon, Tottenham, Valencia, Werder Bremen, West Ham Utd.

UEFA Cup (orig. Fairs Cup) (44 competitions, 28 different winners): **3** Barcelona, Inter Milan, Juventus, Liverpool; **2** Borussia Moenchengladbach, Feyenoord, IFK Gothenburg, Leeds Utd., Parma, Real Madrid, Tottenham, Valencia; **1** Ajax Amsterdam, Anderlecht, Arsenal, Bayer Leverkusen, Bayern Munich, Dynamo Zagreb, Eintracht Frankfurt, PSV Eindhoven, Ferencvaros, Ipswich Town, Napoli, Newcastle Utd., Real Zaragoza, AS Roma, FC Schalke, Galatasaray.

- Four clubs have won all three trophies – Barcelona, Bayern Munich, Juventus and Ajax.
- The Champions League was introduced into the European Cup in 1992-3 to counter the threat of a European Super League.

BRITAIN'S 30 TROPHIES IN EUROPE

Liverpool's success in the 2001-01 UEFA Cup took the number of **British** club triumphs in European Football to 30:

European Cup (10)	**Cup-Winners' Cup (10)**	**Fairs/UEFA Cup (10)**
1967 Celtic	1963 Tottenham	1968 Leeds Utd.
1968 Manchester Utd.	1965 West Ham Utd.	1969 Newcastle Utd.
1977 Liverpool	1970 Manchester City	1970 Arsenal
1978 Liverpool	1971 Chelsea	1971 Leeds Utd.
1979 Nott'm Forest	1972 Rangers	1972 Tottenham
1980 Nott'm Forest	1983 Aberdeen	1973 Liverpool
1981 Liverpool	1985 Everton	1976 Liverpool
1982 Aston Villa	1991 Manchester Utd.	1981 Ipswich Town
1984 Liverpool	1994 Arsenal	1984 Tottenham
1999 Manchester Utd.	1998 Chelsea	2001 Liverpool

END OF CUP-WINNERS' CUP

The **European Cup-Winners' Cup**, inaugurated in 1960-61, terminated with the 1999 final. The competition merged into a revamped, 121-club **UEFA Cup**.

Also with effect from season 1999-2000, the **European Cup/Champions League** was increased by 8 clubs to 32.

From its inception in 1955, the **European Cup** comprised only championship-winning clubs until 1998-9, when selected runners-up were introduced. Further expansion came in 1999-2000 with the inclusion of clubs finishing third in certain leagues and fourth in 2002.

EUROPEAN CLUB COMPETITIONS – SCORING RECORDS

European Cup – Record aggregate: 18-0 by Benfica v Dudelange (Lux) (8-0a, 10-0h), prelim. round, 1965-6.
Record single-match score: 12-0 by Feyenoord v KR Reykjavik (Ice), 1st. round, 1st. leg, 1969-70 (aggregate was 16-0).

Cup-Winners' Cup – *Record aggregate: 21-0 by Chelsea v Jeunesse Hautcharage (Lux) (8-0a, 13-0h), 1st. round, 1971-2.
   Record single-match score: 16-1 by Sporting Lisbon v Apoel Nicosia, 2nd. round, 1st. leg, 1963-4 (aggregate was 18-1).
UEFA Cup (prev. Fairs Cup) – *Record aggregate: 21-0 by Feyenoord v US Rumelange (Lux) (9-0h, 12-0a), 1st. round, 1972-3.
   Record single-match score: 14-0 by Ajax Amsterdam v Red Boys (Lux) 1st. round, 2nd leg, 1984-5 (aggregate also 14-0).
Record British score in Europe: 13-0 by Chelsea at home to Jeunesse Hautcharage (Lux) in Cup-Winners' Cup 1st. round, 2nd. leg, 1971-2. Chelsea's overall 21-0 win in that tie is highest aggregate by British club in Europe.
Individual scoring record for European tie (over two legs): **10 goals** (6 home, 4 away) by Kiril Milanov for Levski Spartak in 19-3 agg. win CWC 1st round v Lahden Reipas, 1976-7. Next highest: **8 goals** by Jose Altafini for AC Milan v US Luxembourg (European Cup, prelim. round, 1962-3, agg. 14-0) and by Peter Osgood for Chelsea v Jeunesse Hautcharage (Cup-Winners' Cup, 1st. round 1971-2, agg. 21-0). Altafini and Osgood each scored 5 goals at home, 3 away.
Individual single-match scoring record in European competition: **6 goals** by Mascarenhas for Sporting Lisbon in 16-1 Cup-Winner's Cup 2nd. round, 1st. leg win v Apoel, 1963-4; **6** by Lothar Emmerich for Borussia Dortmund in 8-0 CWC 1st. round, 2nd. leg win v Floriana 1965-6; **6** by Kiril Milanov for Levski Spartak in 12-2 CWC 1st. round, 1st. leg win v Lahden Reipas, 1976-7.
Most goals in single European campaign: 15 by Jurgen Klinsmann for Bayern Munich (UEFA Cup 1995-6).
Most goals (career total) by British player in European competition: 30 by Peter Lorimer (Leeds Utd., in 9 campaigns).

(*Joint record European aggregate)

EUROPEAN FOOTBALL – BIG RECOVERIES

In the 47-year history of European competition, only four clubs have survived a **4-goal** deficit after the first leg had been completed:
1961-2 (Cup-Winners' Cup 1st. Rd.): Leixoes (Portugal) beat Chaux de Fonds (Luxembourg) 7-6 on agg. (lost 2-6a, won 5-0h).
1962-3 (Fairs Cup 2nd. Rd.): Valencia (Spain) beat Dunfermline 1-0 in play-off in Lisbon after 6-6 agg. (Valencia won 4-0h, lost 2-6a).
1984-5 (UEFA Cup 2nd. Rd.): Partizan Belgrade beat Q.P.R. on away goals (lost 2-6 away, at Highbury, won 4-0 home).
1985-6 (UEFA Cup 3rd. Rd.): Real Madrid beat Borussia Moenchengladbach on away goals (lost 1-5a, won 4-0h) and went on to win competition.

In the **European Cup**, there are eight instances of clubs reaching the next round after **arrears of three goals** in the first leg:
1958-9 (Prel. Rd.) Schalke beat KB Copenhagen (0-3, 5-2, 3-1).
1965-6 (Q-final) Partizan Belgrade beat Sparta Prague (1-4, 5-0).
1970-1 (S-final) Panathinaikos beat Red Star Belgrade on away goal (1-4, 3-0).
1975-6 (2nd. Rd.) Real Madrid beat Derby Co. (1-4, 5-1).
1985-6 (S-final) Barcelona beat IFK Gothenburg on pens. (0-3, 3-0).
1988-9 (1st. Rd.) Werder Bremen beat Dynamo Berlin (0-3, 5-0).
1988-9 (2nd. Rd.) Galatasaray (Turkey) beat Neuchatel Xamax (Switz.) (0-3, 5-0).
1992-3 (1st. Rd.) **Leeds Utd.** beat VfB Stuttgart 2-1 in play-off in Barcelona. Over two legs, VfB won on away goal (3-0h, 1-4 away) but a third match was ordered because they broke 'foreigners' rule in team selection.

In the **Cup-Winners' Cup**, six clubs survived a **3-goal** deficit:
1963-4 (Q-final) Sporting Lisbon beat Manchester Utd. (1-4, 5-0).
1963-4 (S-final) MTK Budapest beat Celtic (0-3, 4-0).
1978-9 (2nd. Rd.) Barcelona beat Anderlecht on penalties. (0-3, 3-0).
1980-1 (1st. Rd.) Carl Zeiss Jena beat AS Roma (0-3, 4-0).
1984-5 (Q-final) Rapid Vienna beat Dynamo Dresden (0-3, 5-0).
1989-90 (1st. Rd.) Grasshoppers (Switz.) beat Slovan Bratislava (0-3, 4-0).

In the **Fairs Cup/UEFA Cup**, there have been more than 20 occasions when clubs have survived a deficit of **3 goals**, the most notable example being the 1988 UEFA Cup Final, which Bayer Leverkusen won 3-2 on pens., having lost the first leg 0-3 away to Espanol and won the return 3-0 to level the aggregate.

Apart from Leeds Utd., two other British clubs have won a European tie from a 3-goal, first leg deficit: **Kilmarnock** 0-3, 5-1 v Eintracht Frankfurt (Fairs Cup 1st. Round, 1964-5); **Hibernian** 1-4, 5-0 v Napoli (Fairs Cup 2nd. Round, 1967-8).

English clubs have three times gone out of the **UEFA Cup** after leading 3-0 from the first leg: 1975-6 (2nd. Rd.) **Ipswich Town** lost 3-4 on agg. to Bruges; 1976-7 (Q-final) **Q.P.R.** lost on pens. to AEK Athens after 3-3 agg; 1977-8 (3rd. Rd.) **Ipswich Town** lost on pens. to Barcelona after 3-3 agg.

HEAVIEST ENGLISH-CLUB DEFEATS IN EUROPE

(Single-leg scores)

European Cup: Ajax 5, Liverpool 1 (2nd. Rd.), Dec. 1966 (agg. 7-3); Real Madrid 5, Derby Co. 1 (2nd. Rd.), Nov. 1975 (agg. 6-5).
Cup-Winners' Cup: Sporting Lisbon 5, Manchester Utd. 0 (Q-final), Mar. 1964 (agg. 6-4).
Fairs/UEFA Cup: Bayern Munich 6, Coventry City 1 (2nd. Rd.), Oct. 1970 (agg. 7-3).
   Combined London team lost 6-0 (agg. 8-2) in first Fairs Cup Final in 1958.

SHOCK ENGLISH-CLUB DEFEATS

1968-69 (E. Cup, 1st. Rd.): Manchester City beaten by Fenerbahce, 1-2 agg.
1971-72 (CWC, 2nd. Rd.): Chelsea beaten by Atvidaberg on away goals.
1993-94 (E. Cup, 2nd. Rd.): Manchester Utd. beaten by Galatasaray on away goals.
1994-95 (UEFA Cup, 1st. Rd.): Blackburn Rov. beaten by Trelleborgs, 2-3 agg.
2000-01 (UEFA Cup, 1st. Rd.): Chelsea beaten by St. Gallen, Swit. 1-2 agg.

FIFA'S HALL OF CHAMPIONS

Ten retired players, honoured for 'sporting success that contributed to the positive image of the game' – Sir Stanley Matthews, Sir Bobby Charlton (England), Pele (Brazil), Franz Beckenbauer (W. Germany), Johan Cruyff (Holland), Alfredo di Stefano (Argentina), Eusebio (Portugal), Michel Platini (France), Ferenc Puskas (Hungary), Lev Yashin (Soviet Union). Managers: Sir Matt Busby (Manchester Utd.), Rinus Michels (Ajax Amsterdam).

The names were announced in January 1998.

P.F.A. FAIR PLAY AWARD (Bobby Moore Trophy from 1993)

1988	Liverpool	1996	Crewe Alexandra
1989	Liverpool	1997	Crewe Alexandra
1990	Liverpool	1998	Cambridge Utd.
1991	Nott'm. Forest	1999	Grimsby Town
1992	Portsmouth	2000	Crewe Alexandra
1993	Norwich City	2001	Crewe Alexandra
1994	Crewe Alexandra	2002	Crewe Alexandra
1995	Crewe Alexandra		

RECORD MEDALS SALE

West Ham Utd. bought (June 2000) the late **Bobby Moore's** collection of medals and trophies for £1.8m. at Christie's auction in London. It was put up for sale by his first wife Tina and included his World Cup winner's medal.

A No. 6 duplicate red shirt made for England captain **Bobby Moore** for the 1966 World Cup Final fetched £44,000 at an auction at Wolves' ground in Sept. 1999. Moore kept the shirt he wore in that Final and gave the replica to England physio Harold Shepherdson.

Sir Geoff Hurst's 1966 World Cup-winning shirt fetched a record £91,750 at Christie's on September 28, 2000. His World Cup Final cap fetched £37,600 and his Man of the Match trophy £18,800. Proceeds totalling £274,410 from the 129 lots went to Hurst's three daughters and charities of his choice, including the Bobby Moore Imperial Cancer Research Fund.

In August 2001, Sir Geoff sold his World Cup-winner's medal to his former club West Ham Utd. (for their museum) at a reported £150,000.

'The **Billy Wright Collection**' – caps, medals and other memorabilia from his illustrious career – fetched over £100,000 at Christie's in Glasgow on Nov. 21, 1996.

At the sale in Oct. 1993, trophies, caps and medals earned by **Ray Kennedy**, former England, Arsenal and Liverpool player, fetched a then record total of £88,407. Kennedy, who suffers from Parkinson's Disease, received £73,000 after commission.

The P.F.A. paid £31,080 for a total of 60 lots – including a record £16,000 for his 1977 European Cup winner's medal – to be exhibited at their Manchester museum. An anonymous English collector paid £17,000 for the medal and plaque commemorating Kennedy's part in the Arsenal Double in 1971.

Previous record for one player's medals, shirts etc. collection: £30,000 (**Bill Foulkes**, Manchester Utd. in 1992). The sale of **Dixie Dean**'s medals etc. in 1991 realised £28,000.

In March 2001, **Gordon Banks**' 1966 World Cup-winner's medal fetched a new record £124,750, and at auctions in season 2001-02: In London on Sept. 21, TV's Nick Hancock, a Stoke City fan, paid £23,500 for **Sir Stanley Matthews**' 1953 F.A. Cup-winner's medal. He also bought one of Matthews' England caps for £3,525 and paid £2,350 for a Stoke Div. 2 Championship medal (1963).

Dave Mackay's 1961 League Championship and F.A. Cup winner's medals sold for £18,000 at Sotherby's. Tottenham bought them for their museum.

A selection of England World Cup-winning manager **Sir Alf Ramsey**'s memorabilia – England caps, championship medals with Ipswich Town etc. – fetched more than £80,000 at Christie's. They were offered for sale by his family, and his former clubs Tottenham and Ipswich Town were among the buyers.

Ray Wilson's 1966 England World Cup-winning shirt fetched £80,750. Also in March, the No. 10 shirt worn by **Pele** in Brazil's World Cup triumph in 1970 was sold for a record £157,750 at Christies. It went to an anonymous telephone bidder.

VARSITY MATCH

Oxford and **Cambridge** have met 118 times. Cambridge lead by 46 wins to 45, with 27 draws. The fixture began in 1874.

LONGEST UNBEATEN CUP RUN

Liverpool established the longest unbeaten Cup sequence by a Football League club: 25 successive rounds in the League/Milk Cup between semi-final defeat by Nott'm. Forest (1-2 agg.) in 1980 and defeat at Tottenham (0-1) in the third round on October 31, 1984. During this period Liverpool won the tournament in four successive seasons, a feat no other Football League club has achieved in any competition.

NEAR £1M. RECORD DAMAGES

A High Court judge in Newcastle (May 7, 1999) awarded Bradford City's 28-year-old striker **Gordon Watson** record damages for a football injury: £909,143. He had had his right leg fractured in two places by Huddersfield Town's Kevin Gray on Feb. 1, 1997.

Huddersfield Town were 'proven negligent for allowing their player to make a rushed tackle'. The award was calculated at £202,643 for loss of earnings, £730,500 for 'potential career earnings' if he had joined a Premiership club, plus £26,000 to cover medical treatment and care.

Watson, awarded £50,000 in an earlier legal action, had a 6-inch plate inserted in the leg. He resumed playing for City in season 1998-9.

BIG HALF-TIME SCORES

Tottenham 10, Crewe Alexandra 1 (F.A. Cup 4th. Rd. replay, Feb. 3, 1960; result 13-2); Tranmere Rov. 8, Oldham Athletic 1 (Div. 3N., Dec. 26, 1935; result 13-4); Chester City 8, York City 0 (Div. 3N., Feb. 1, 1936; result 12-0; believed to be record half-time scores in League football).

Stirling Albion led Selkirk 15-0 at half-time (result 20-0) in the Scottish Cup 1st. Rd., Dec. 8, 1984.

World record half-time score: 16-0 when Australia beat American Samoa 31-0 (another world record) in the World Cup Oceania qualifying group at Coff's Harbour, New South Wales, on April 11, 2001.

● On March 4, 1933 Coventry City beat Q.P.R. (Div. 3 South) 7-0, having led by that score at half-time. This repeated the half-time situation in Bristol City's 7-0 win over Grimsby Town on Dec. 26, 1914.

● Only instance of club failing to win League match after leading 5-0 at half-time: Sheffield Wed. 5, Everton 5 (Div. 1, Nov. 12, 1904; Wed. scored 5 in first half, Everton 5 in second).

TOP SECOND-HALF TEAM

Most goals scored by a team in one half of a League match is eleven. Stockport Co. led Halifax Town 2-0 at half-time in Div. 3 North on Jan. 6, 1934 and won 13-0.

FIVE NOT ENOUGH

Last team to score 5 in League match and lose: Reading, beaten 7-5 at Doncaster Rov. (Div. 3, Sept. 25, 1982).

LONG SERVICE WITH ONE CLUB

Bill Nicholson, OBE, has been associated with Tottenham for 64 years – as a wing-half (1938-55), then the club's most successful manager (1958-74) with 8 major prizes, subsequently chief advisor and scout. Now 83, he is club president, is an honorary freeman of the borough, still lives close to the ground, has an executive suite named after him at the club, and the stretch of roadway from Tottenham High Road to the main gates has the nameplate Bill Nicholson Way.

Ted Bates is the Grand Old Man of Southampton with 65 years of unbroken service to the club and awarded the Freedom of the City in April, 2001. He joined Saints as an inside-forward from Norwich City in 1937, made 260 peace-time appearances for the club, became reserve-team trainer in 1953 and manager at the Dell for 18 years (1955-73), taking Southampton into the top division in 1966. He was subsequently chief executive, director and now, at 84, is club president.

Dario Gradi, MBE, 60, is the longest-serving manager in British football, having completed 19 seasons and more than 1,000 matches in charge of Crewe Alexandra (appointed June 1983). Never a League player, he previously managed Wimbledon and Crystal Palace. At Crewe, where he is also a director, his policy of finding and grooming young talent has earned the club more than £12m. in transfer fees.

Bob Paisley was associated with Liverpool for 57 years from 1939, when he joined them from Bishop Auckland, until he died in February 1996. He served them as player, trainer, coach, assistant-manager, manager, director and vice-president.

Ronnie Moran, who joined Liverpool in as a player 1952, retired from the Anfield coaching staff in season 1998-9.

Ernie Gregory served West Ham Utd. for 52 years as goalkeeper and coach. He joined them as boy of 14 from school in 1935, retired in May 1987.

Ted Sagar, Everton goalkeeper, 23 years at Goodison Park (1929-52, but only 16 League seasons because of War).

Alan Knight, goalkeeper, played 23 seasons (1977-2000) for his only club, Portsmouth.

Roy Sproson, defender, played 21 League seasons for his only club, Port Vale (1950-71).

Allan Ball, goalkeeper, 20 seasons with Queen of the South (1963-83).

Pat Bonner, goalkeeper, 19 seasons with Celtic (1978-97).

Danny McGrain, defender, 17 years with Celtic (1970-87).

TIGHT AT HOME

Fewest home goals conceded in League season (modern times): 4 by **Liverpool** (Div. 1, 1978-9); 4 by **Manchester Utd.** (Premier League, 1994-5) – both in 21 matches.

FOOTBALL POOLS

Littlewoods launched them in 1923 with a capital of £100. Coupons were first issued (4,000 of them) outside Manchester Utd.'s ground, the original 35 investors staking a total of £4-7s.-6d (pay-out £2-12s).

Vernons joined Littlewoods as the leading promoters. The Treble Chance, leading to bonanza dividends, was introduced in 1946 and the Pools Panel began in January 1963, to counter mass fixture postponements caused by the Big Freeze winter.

But business was hard hit by the launch of the National Lottery in 1994. Dividends slumped, the work-force was drastically cut and in June 2000 the Liverpool-based Moores family sold Littlewoods Pools in a £161m. deal.

The record prize remains the £2,924,622 paid to a Worsley, Manchester, syndicate in November 1994.

TRANSFER DEADLINE

This was introduced by the Football League in 1911, to prevent clubs in contention for honours or fighting relegation gaining an unfair advantage in the closing weeks.

The original deadline was March 16. It is now 5 p.m. on the fourth Thursday in March, after which only in exceptional circumstances (e.g. if a side has no fit goalkeeper) can a transferred player appear for his new club that season.

After the last war, frantic spending was the norm on deadline day, but in recent years last-day business has dwindled to a comparative trickle.

TEMPORARY TRANSFERS

These were introduced (originally limited to two per club) as 'permit loan transfers' by the Football League in 1967.

PROGRAMME PIONEERS

Chelsea pioneered football's magazine-style programme when they introduced a 16-page issue for their First Division match against Portsmouth on Christmas Day 1948. It cost sixpence (2½p).

TRIBUNAL-FEE RECORDS

Top tribunal fee: £2.5m for **Chris Bart-Williams** (Sheffield Wed. to Nott'm. Forest, June 1995).

Biggest discrepancy: Andy Walker, striker, Bolton Wand. to Celtic, June 1994: Bolton Wand. asked £2.2m, Celtic offered £250,000. Tribunal decided £550,000.

LONGEST THROW-IN?

That by Notts Co.'s **Andy Legg** was measured (season 1994-5) at 41 metres (45 yards) and claimed as the longest throw by any footballer in the world, until 1997-8, when **Dave Challinor** (Tranmere Rov.) reached 46.3 metres (50½ yards).

BALL JUGGLING: WORLD RECORD CLAIMS

Sam Ik (South Korea) juggled a ball non-stop for 18 hours, 11 minutes, 4 seconds in March 1995. Thai footballer **Sam-Ang Sowanski** juggled a ball for 15 hours without letting it touch the ground in Bangkok in April 2000.

SUBS' SCORING RECORD

Barnet's 5-4 home win v Torquay Utd. (Div. 3, Dec. 28, 1993) provided the first instance of **all four substitutes** scoring in a major League match in England.

FOOTBALL'S OLDEST ANNUAL

Now in its 116th edition, this publication began as the 16-page *Athletic News Football Supplement & Club Directory* in 1887. From the long-established *Athletic News*, it became the *Sunday Chronicle Annual* in 1946, the *Empire News* in 1956, the *News of the World & Empire News* in 1961 and, since 1965, the *News of the World Annual*.

TRANSFER TRAIL

For space reasons, it is no longer possible to include every million-pound transfer involving British clubs since the first such deal: **Trevor Francis** from Birmingham City to Nott'm. Forest (£1,180,000) in Feb. 1979. For the same reason, deals of below £5m are not included.

★	= British record fee at that time	H =	Record winger import
A	= Record all-British deal	J =	Record received for winger
B	= Record for goalkeeper	K =	Record for teenager
C	= Record for defender	L =	Most expensive foreign import
D	= Record deal between English and Scottish clubs	M =	Record English-club signing
		N =	British record for striker
E	= Record fee paid by Scottish club	(• Fees as at time of transfer, i.e. not
F	= Record fee to Scottish club	including any subsequent increases)
G	= Record all-Scottish deal	(• Re dates, 1/00 = Jan 2000 etc)

	Player	From	To	Date	£
★LM	Juan Sebastian Veron	Lazio	Manchester Utd.	7/01	23,500,000
★	Nicolas Anelka	Arsenal	Real Madrid	8/99	22,500,000
J	Marc Overmars	Arsenal	Barcelona	7/00	22,500,000
N	Ruud van Nistelrooy	PSV Eindhoven	Manchester Utd.	4/01	19,000,000
AC	Rio Ferdinand	West Ham Utd.	Leeds Utd.	11/00	18,000,000
	Jaap Stam	Manchester Utd.	Lazio	8/01	15,250,000
★	Alan Shearer	Blackburn Rov.	Newcastle Utd.	7/96	15,000,000
	Jimmy F. Hasselbaink	Atl. Madrid	Chelsea	6/00	15,000,000
	Robbie Keane	Coventry City	Inter Milan	7/00	13,000,000
	Sylvain Wiltord	Bordeaux	Arsenal	8/00	13,000,000
	Nicolas Aneka	Paris St. Germain	Manchester City	5/02	13,000,000
	Dwight Yorke	Aston Villa	Manchester Utd.	8/98	12,600,000
	Juninho	Middlesbrough	Atl. Madrid	7/97	12,000,000
	Jimmy F. Hasselbaink	Leeds Utd.	Atl. Madrid	8/99	12,000,000
DE	Tore Andre Flo	Chelsea	Rangers	11/00	12,000,000
	Robbie Keane	Inter Milan	Leeds Utd.	12/00	12,000,000
	Steve Marlet	Lyon	Fulham	8/01	11,500,000
	Sergei Rebrov	Dynamo Kiev	Tottenham	5/00	11,000,000
	Frank Lampard	West Ham Utd.	Chelsea	6/01	11,000,000
	Robbie Fowler	Liverpool	Leeds Utd.	11/01	11,000,000
	Jaap Stam	PSV Eindhoven	Manchester Utd.	5/98	10,750,000
	Thierry Henry	Juventus	Arsenal	8/99	10,500,000
	Laurent Robert	Paris St. Germain	Newcastle Utd.	8/01	10,500,000
	Chris Sutton	Blackburn Rov.	Chelsea	7/99	10,000,000
	Emile Heskey	Leicester City	Liverpool	2/00	10,000,000
	El Hadji Diouf	Lens	Liverpool	6/02	10,000,000
	Juan Pablo Angel	River Plate (Arg.)	Aston Villa	1/01	9,500,000
F	Giovanni van Bronckhorst	Rangers	Arsenal	6/01	8,500,000
★	Stan Collymore	Nott'm Forest	Liverpool	6/95	8,500,000
K	Hugo Viana	Sporting Lisbon	Newcastle Utd.	6/02	8,500,000
	Dean Richards	Southampton	Tottenham	9/01	8,100,000
	Massimo Maccarone	Empoli	Middlesbrough	7/02	8,100,000
	Andrei Kanchelskis	Everton	Fiorentina	1/97	8,000,000
	Dietmar Hamann	Newcastle Utd.	Liverpool	7/99	8,000,000
	Ugo Ehiogu	Aston Villa	Middlesbrough	10/00	8,000,000
	Francis Jeffers	Everton	Arsenal	6/01	8,000,000
	Andy Cole	Manchester Utd.	Blackburn Rov.	12/01	8,000,000
B	Fabien Barthez	Monaco	Manchester Utd.	5/00	7,800,000
	Jesper Gronkjaer	Ajax Amsterdam	Chelsea	10/00	7,800,000
★	Dennis Bergkamp	Inter Milan	Arsenal	6/95	7,500,000
	Kevin Davies	Southampton	Blackburn Rov.	6/98	7,500,000

	John Hartson	West Ham Utd.	Wimbledon	1/99	7,500,000
	Emmanuel Petit	Barcelona	Chelsea	6/01	7,500,000
	Diego Forlan	Independiente (Arg.)	Manchester Utd.	1/02	7,500,000
	Olivier Dacourt	Lens	Leeds Utd.	5/00	7,200,000
★	Andy Cole	Newcastle Utd.	Manchester Utd.	1/95	7,000,000
	Fabrizio Ravanelli	Juventus	Middlesbrough	7/96	7,000,000
	Stan Collymore	Liverpool	Aston Villa	5/97	7,000,000
H	Marc Overmars	Ajax Amsterdam	Arsenal	6/97	7,000,000
	Duncan Ferguson	Everton	Newcastle Utd.	11/98	7,000,000
	Lauren	Real Mallorca	Arsenal	5/00	7,000,000
	Carl Cort	Wimbledon	Newcastle Utd.	7/00	7,000,000
	Edwin Van der Sar	Juventus	Fulham	8/01	7,000,000
	Boudewijn Zenden	Barcelona	Chelsea	8/01	7,000,000
	Seth Johnson	Derby Co.	Leeds Utd.	10/01	7,000,000
	Paul Merson	Middlesbrough	Aston Villa	8/98	6,750,000
	Corrado, Grabbi	Ternana	Blackburn Rov.	6/01	6,750,000
	Faustino Asprilla	Parma	Newcastle Utd.	2/96	6,700,000
★	David Platt	Bari	Juventus	6/92	6,500,000
	Olivier Dacourt	Everton	Lens	6/99	6,500,000
	Kieron Dyer	Ipswich Town	Newcastle Utd.	7/99	6,500,000
	Craig Bellamy	Coventry City	Newcastle Utd.	6/01	6,500,000
	Gareth Southgate	Aston Villa	Middlesbrough	7/01	6,500,000
	Michael Ball	Everton	Rangers	8/01	6,500,000
	John Hartson	Coventry City	Celtic	8/01	6,500,000
	William Gallas	Marseille	Chelsea	5/01	6,200,000
★	Paul Ince	Manchester Utd.	Inter Milan	6/95	6,000,000
	Les Ferdinand	Q.P.R.	Newcastle Utd.	6/95	6,000,000
	Les Ferdinand	Newcastle Utd.	Tottenham	7/97	6,000,000
	Faustino Asprilla	Newcastle Utd.	Parma	1/98	6,000,000
	Robbie Keane	Wolves	Coventry City	8/99	6,000,000
	Marc-Vivien Foe	West Ham Utd.	Lyon	5/00	6,000,000
	Chris Sutton	Chelsea	Celtic	7/00	6,000,000
	Mark Viduka	Celtic	Leeds Utd.	7/00	6,000,000
	Nick Barmby	Everton	Liverpool	7/00	6,000,000
	Emmanuel Petit	Arsenal	Barcelona	7/00	6,000,000
	Richard Wright	Ipswich Town	Arsenal	7/01	6,000,000
	Bosko Balaban	Dynamo Zagreb	Aston Villa	8/01	6,000,000
	Mikel Arteta	Barcelona	Rangers	7/02	5,800,000
	Nick Barmby	Middlesbrough	Everton	10/96	5,750,000
	Dion Dublin	Coventry City	Aston Villa	11/98	5,750,000
	Eyal Berkovic	West Ham Utd.	Celtic	7/99	5,750,000
	Neil Lennon	Leicester City	Celtic	12/00	5,700,000
	Mario Stanic	Parma	Chelsea	6/00	5,600,000
★	David Platt	Aston Villa	Bari	7/91	5,500,000
★	Paul Gascoigne	Tottenham	Lazio	6/92	5,500,000
	Fabrizio Ravanelli	Middlesbrough	Marseille	9/97	5,500,000
	Gary Speed	Everton	Newcastle Utd.	2/98	5,500,000
	Georgi Kinkladze	Manchester City	Ajax	5/98	5,500,000
	Andrei Kanchelskis	Fiorentina	Rangers	7/98	5,500,000
	Steve Stone	Nott'm Forest	Aston Villa	3/99	5,500,000
	Robert Pires	Marseille	Arsenal	7/00	5,500,000
	Christian Ziege	Middlesbrough	Liverpool	8/00	5,500,000
	Igor Biscan	Dynamo Zagreb	Liverpool	12/00	5,500,000
	Tomas Repka	Fiorentina	West Ham Utd.	9/01	5,500,000
	Pierluigi Casiraghi	Lazio	Chelsea	5/98	5,400,000
	Christian Dailly	Derby Co.	Blackburn Rov.	8/98	5,300,000
	Nick Barmby	Tottenham	Middlesbrough	8/95	5,250,000
	Dietmar Hamann	Bayern Munich	Newcastle Utd.	7/98	5,250,000
	David Platt	Juventus	Sampdoria	7/93	5,200,000

Lee Hughes	W.B.A.	Coventry City	8/01	5,000,001
Trevor Steven	Rangers	Marseille	8/91	5,000,000
Chris Sutton	Norwich City	Blackburn Rov.	7/94	5,000,000
Andrei Kanchelskis	Manchester Utd.	Everton	8/95	5,000,000
Paul Merson	Arsenal	Middlesbrough	7/97	5,000,000
Graeme Le Saux	Blackburn Rov.	Chelsea	8/97	5,000,000
Henning Berg	Blackburn Rov.	Manchester Utd.	8/97	5,000,000
Arthur Numan	PSV Eindhoven	Rangers	7/98	5,000,000
Elena Marcelino	Real Mallorca	Newcastle Utd.	6/99	5,000,000
Giovanni V. Bronckhorst	Feyenoord	Rangers	7/98	5,000,000
Michael Bridges	Sunderland	Leeds Utd.	7/99	5,000,000
Ben Thatcher	Wimbledon	Tottenham	7/00	5,000,000
Ade Akinbiyi	Wolves	Leicester City	7/00	5,000,000
Edu	Corinthians (Braz.)	Arsenal	1/01	5,000,000
Olof Mellberg	Racing Santander	Aston Villa	7/01	5,000,000
Don Hutchison	Sunderland	West Ham Utd.	8/01	5,000,000
Chris Kirkland	Coventry City	Liverpool	8/01	5,000,000
Jermaine Jenas	Nott'm. Forest	Newcastle Utd.	2/02	5,000,000
Peter Crouch	Portsmouth	Aston Villa	3/02	5,000,000
Salif Diao	Sedan (Fr.)	Liverpool	5/02	5,000,000
Titus Bramble	Ipswich Town	Newcastle Utd.	7/02	5,000,000
Joseph Yobo	Marseille	Everton	7/02	5,000,000

Record stages: Prior to Trevor Francis becoming the subject of the first £1m. transfer, this is how the record was broken, stage by stage from the time of the first £1,000 deal in 1905:

Player	From	To	Date	£
Alf Common	Sunderland	Middlesbrough	2/1905	1,000
Syd Puddefoot	West Ham Utd.	Falkirk	2/22	5,000
Warney Cresswell	S. Shields	Sunderland	3/22	5,500
Bob Kelly	Burnley	Sunderland	12/25	6,500
David Jack	Bolton Wand.	Arsenal	10/28	10,890
Bryn Jones	Wolves	Arsenal	8/38	14,500
Billy Steel	Morton	Derby Co.	9/47	15,000
Tommy Lawton	Chelsea	Notts Co.	11/47	20,000
Len Shackleton	Newcastle Utd.	Sunderland	2/48	20,500
Johnny Morris	Manchester Utd.	Derby Co.	2/49	24,000
Eddie Quigley	Sheffield Wed.	Preston N.E.	12/49	26,500
Trevor Ford	Aston Villa	Sunderland	10/50	30,000
Jackie Sewell	Notts Co.	Sheffield Wed.	3/51	34,500
Eddie Firmani	Charlton Athletic	Sampdoria	7/55	35,000
John Charles	Leeds Utd.	Juventus	4/57	65,000
Denis Law	Manchester City	Torino	6/61	100,000
Denis Law	Torino	Manchester Utd.	7/62	115,000
Allan Clarke	Fulham	Leicester City	6/68	150,000
Allan Clarke	Leicester City	Leeds Utd.	6/69	165,000
Martin Peters	West Ham Utd.	Tottenham	3/70	200,000
Alan Ball	Everton	Arsenal	12/71	220,000
David Nish	Leicester City	Derby Co.	8/72	250,000
Bob Latchford	Birmingham City	Everton	2/74	350,000
Graeme Souness	Middlesbrough	Liverpool	1/78	352,000
Kevin Keegan	Liverpool	Hamburg	6/77	500,000
David Mills	Middlesbrough	W.B.A.	1/79	516,000

• **World's first £1m. transfer:** Giuseppe Savoldi, Bologna to Napoli, July 1975.

TOP FOREIGN SIGNINGS

Player	From	To	Date	£
Zinedine Zidane	Juventus	Real Madrid	7/01	47,200,000

Luis Figo	Barcelona	Real Madrid	7/00	37,200,000
Hernan Crespo	Parma	Lazio	7/00	35,000,000
Gianluigi Buffon	Parma	Juventus	7/01	32,600,000
Christian Vieri	Lazio	Inter Milan	6/99	31,000,000
Gaizka Mendieta	Valencia	Lazio	7/01	28,500,000
Pavel Nedved	Lazio	Juventus	7/01	25,000,000
Rui Costa	Fiorentina	AC Milan	7/01	24,500,000
Gabriel Batistuta	Fiorentina	Roma	5/00	22,000,000
Lilian Thuram	Parma	Juventus	6/01	22,000,000
Nicolas Anelka	Real Madrid	Paris St. Germain	7/00	21,700,000
Filippo Inzaghi	Juventus	AC Milan	7/01	21,700,000
Denilson	Sao Paulo	Real Betis	7/97	21,400,000
Marcio Amoroso	Udinese	Parma	6/99	21,000,000
Antonio Cassano	Bari	Roma	3/01	20,000,000
Javier Saviola	River Plate	Barcelona	7/01	20,000,000
Juan Sebastian Veron	Parma	Lazio	6/99	19,800,000
Hidetoshi Nakata	Roma	Parma	7/01	19,100,000
Ronaldo	Barcelona	Inter Milan	6/97	18,000,000
Francesco Toldo	Fiorentina	Inter Milan	7/01	18,000,000
Christian Vieri	Atletico Madrid	Lazio	8/98	17,500,000
David Trezeguet	Monaco	Juventus	6/00	17,500,000
Savo Milosevic	Real Zaragoza	Parma	7/00	17,000,000
Andrei Shevchenko	Dynamo Kiev	AC Milan	6/99	15,700,000
Vincenzo Montella	Sampdoria	Roma	6/99	15,300,000
Clarence Seedorf	Real Madrid	Inter Milan	12/99	15,000,000
Mathias Almeyda	Lazio	Parma	7/00	14,800,000
Ronald de Boer	Ajax	Barcelona	1/99	14,000,000
Frank de Boer	Ajax	Barcelona	1/99	14,000,000
Claudio Lopez	Valencia	Lazio	7/00	14,000,000
Shabani Nonda	Rennes	Monaco	6/00	13,500,000
Gianluigi Lentini	Torino	AC Milan	7/92	13,000,000
Walter Samuel	Boca Juniors	Roma	6/00	13,000,000
Geovanni	Cruzeiro	Barcelona	6/01	12,700,000
Jose Mari Romero	Atletico Madrid	AC Milan	12/99	12,700,000
Gianluca Vialli	Sampdoria	Juventus	6/92	12,500,000
Ronaldo	PSV Eindhoven	Barcelona	7/96	12,500,000
Rivaldo	Dep. La Coruna	Barcelona	8/97	12,500,000

WORLD RECORD GOALKEEPER FEE

£32.6m for **Gianluigi Buffon** (Parma to Juventus, July 2001).

RECORD CONFERENCE FEE

£250,000: **Andy Clarke**, Barnet to Wimbledon, Feb 1991; **Barry Hayles**, Stevenage Borough to Bristol Rov., Aug. 1997; **Jason Roberts**, Hayes to Wolves, Sept. 1997.

RECORD FEE BETWEEN NON-LEAGUE CLUBS

£180,000 for **Justin Jackson**, Morecambe to Rushden & Diamonds (Conference), June 2000.

WORLD RECORD FEE FOR TEENAGER

£19m. for **Antonio Cassano**, 18, Bari to Roma, March 2001.

BRITISH RECORD FEES FOR TEENAGERS

£8.5. for **Hugo Viana,** aged 19, Sporting Lisbon to Newcastle Utd., June 2002.
£6m. for **Robbie Keane**, aged 19, Wolves to Coventry City, Aug. 1999.

FINAL WHISTLE – OBITUARIES 2001-02

JULY

BERTIE FELSTEAD, 106, who died in a Gloucester nursing home, was the last survivor of the World War I truce, on Christmas Day 1915, that produced the most incongruous game in football history. British and German soldiers emerged from trenches 100 yards apart beside the Somme in Northern France to play 50-a-side in the snow. He recalled: 'Somehow a ball was produced, I know not from where, and we had a kick-around that lasted about half an hour. Nothing was planned, it was spontaneous.' It ended with a major appearing and angrily barking out orders for us to return to the trenches, accompanied by a British artillery salvo.' Mr. Felstead, who served in the Royal Welch Fusiliers, was awarded the Legion d'Honneur in 1998.

NEIL MIDGLEY, 57, was a referee for 20 years and graduated to the top flight. He was on the FIFA panel, and took charge of the 1987 F.A. Cup Final between Coventry City and Tottenham. After retiring from the League list, he continued to serve the game as a referees' assessor for the Premier League and UEFA.

TOM SAUNDERS, 80, was the quiet man behind a dynasty of Liverpool managers. Locally-born and a schoolteacher by profession, he was appointed youth development officer by Bill Shankly in the late Sixties, and as a member of Anfield's famous Boot Room, stayed on the backroom staff until retiring in 1986. He was elected to the board in 1993.

AUGUST

AARON FLAHAVAN, 25, who played 93 times in goal for Portsmouth after graduating from the club's youth team, died in a late-night crash near Bournemouth after losing control of his car at high speed.

BOBBY JOHNSTONE, 71, was one of Manchester City's finest players, an inside-forward whose skills earned him the sobriquet 'Bobby Dazzler.' He was signed from Hibernian for £20,700 in March 1955 and played 138 times for City (50 goals) before returning to Hibs (£7,000) in 1959. He was the first player to score in successive F.A. Cup Finals, in 1955 and 1956, and won 4 of his 17 Scotland caps while at Maine Road. He ended his playing career with Oldham Athletic, helping them win promotion as Fourth Division runners-up in 1963.

NORMAN RIGBY, 78, became a legend of Peterborough United during 20 years' service to the club from 1949-69. A centre-half signed from Notts County, he captained the side to the Fourth Division title in their first season as a League club (1960-61), and was promoted from assistant-manager to manage them from 1967-69.

LES SEALEY, 43, Manchester United's goalkeeper in their first two successes under Alex Ferguson – the F.A. Cup in 1990 and the Cup-Winners' Cup a year later – died of a heart attack. He was a surprise replacement for Jim Leighton in United's Cup Final replay team against Crystal Palace, and the career of this larger-than-life character spanned 22 years and 564 matches with ten clubs: Coventry City, Luton Town, Manchester United (initially on loan), Blackpool, Birmingham City, Aston Villa, Plymouth Argyle, Bury, Leyton Orient and West Ham United, with whom he subsequently became goalkeeper-coach.

TOM STANIFORTH, 20, Sheffield Wednesday defender and emerging squad player, died suddenly in York. He was the son of former York City, Carlisle United and Plymouth Argyle striker Gordon Staniforth.

SEPTEMBER

BOBBY EVANS, 74, was the sturdy, red-haired half-back who made 535 appearances for Celtic in the first 16 post-war seasons and was capped 48 times by Scotland (1949-60). In the Fifties, he won Scottish Championship honours and the Scottish Cup and League Cup twice each, captaining Celtic in the 7-1 rout of Rangers in the 1958 League Cup Final. A £12,500 transfer in May 1960 took him from Parkhead to Chelsea for one year, the first of a series of short stays which continued with Newport County (player-manager 1961-63), Morton (1963-64), Third Lanark (1964-65) and Raith Rovers (1965-67), where he ended a 23-season career at the age of 40.

STAN HARLAND, 61, who captained Third Division Swindon Town to a 3-1 win against Arsenal in the 1969 League Cup Final, died at his Somerset home. Swindon (1966-71) were the third of this wing-half's four League clubs, preceded by Bradford City (1961-64) and Carlisle United (1964-66) and followed by Birmingham City (1971-72) in a career of 471 League appearances.

BRIAN MOORE, 69, one of football's outstanding broadcasters, died at his home at Benenden, Kent, a few hours before England's 5-1 World Cup qualifying victory over Germany. The son of a farm labourer, he was both commentator and fan (particularly of Gillingham, where he was a director for 7 years). He won a scholarship at Cranbrook School and came into the media with *The Times* (1958-61) via the Dixon's and Exchange Telegraph agencies, then joined BBC Radio, with whom he broadcast England's World Cup triumph in 1966. Two years later he was recruited by London Weekend Television, and for three decades was their principal voice of football as commentator and, at times, presenter. He covered 9 World Cups and more than 20 Cup Finals. His last match was the 1998 World Cup Final in France, but he did not put down the microphone for good, engaging in a series of conversation pieces on Sky TV with such eminences as Tom Finney, Dave Mackay and Cliff Jones. Four days after he died, a minute's silence was observed in his memory at the England-Albania match at Newcastle.

ALEX SCOTT, 64, was a flamboyant right-winger on both sides of the Border and capped 16 times by Scotland. With Rangers, he won 4 Scottish Championship medals, the League Cup twice and the Scottish Cup once in the Fifties and early Sixties. When it became known he was keen to move into English football, a fierce battle developed, a £45,000 bid by Everton finally winning the day over Tottenham in February 1963. At the end of his first season at Goodison Park, he earned a title medal, and he played in Everton's F.A. Cup-winning side in 1966. A successful four-season career at Goodison ended with a £20,000 transfer to Hibernian in September 1967.

OCTOBER

REG MATTHEWS, who died aged 68, became the world's costliest and highest-paid goalkeeper when transferred from Coventry City to Chelsea for £20,000 in November 1956. Fearless and with lightning reflexes, he was among the most daring 'keepers and with Coventry became the first player from the old Third Division to play for England (5 caps). In five years at Chelsea he made 148 apps. and after losing his place to Peter Bonetti left Stamford Bridge (£10,000) in October 1961 for Derby County where, in seven seasons, he played more than 250 games as one of the most popular players at the Baseball Ground.

BERTIE MEE, 82, became with Arsenal in 1970-71 only the second manager in the 20th Century to take a club to the League Championship and F.A. Cup double, thus emulating the feat of Bill Nicholson at Tottenham ten years earlier. In another parallel, he rose at Highbury, like Tom Whittaker in 1947, from club physio to manager, taking over in 1966 and holding the post for ten years. A pre-war left-winger with Derby County reserves and Mansfield Town, he returned from Army service with the Medical Corps to study football injuries and the treatment thereof, and replaced Billy Milne as Arsenal's trainer in 1960. A surprise choice to succeed Billy Wright in charge at Highbury, he was an outstanding man-manager and organiser, a shrewd delegater and strong disciplinarian ('the little general'). He chose Dave Sexton as his first coach, and when Sexton moved to Chelsea, replaced him with former Arsenal full-back Don Howe. They were a formidable combination, and over six seasons Arsenal were League Cup runners-up in 1968 and 1969, Fairs Cup winners 1970, League Champions and F.A. Cup winners 1971, F.A. Cup runners-up 1972 and League runners-up 1973. Resigning in 1976, Mee continued in football as assistant-manager to Graham Taylor at Watford, and served the club as general manager and then as a director until 1991.

ROY ULYETT, 87, who died at Southend, was the finest sports cartoonist of his generation. His working life in newspapers began as a 20-year-old with the London evening *Star* and was followed by more than 40 years with the *Daily Express*. He was a self-taught artist and, via pencil, pen and brush, amused the sporting world with more than 25,000 cartoons. With a humour that was never unkind, the man with the handlebar moustache and Sherlock Holmes pipe caricatured football most of all. He was awarded the OBE in 1989 for his fund-raising with the Grand Order of Water Rats, and his epitaph was 'he made people smile for a living.'

DECEMBER

GERALD ASHBY, 52, who died in his sleep, graduated from Worcester & District League football to the highest level of refereeing in Premier League, European and International matches. By profession an accountant, he was promoted from linesman to the referees' list in 1985 and served on the FIFA panel from 1992-94. His career highlight was to take charge of the 1995 F.A. Cup Final between Everton and Manchester United. On retiring, at 48, at the end of season 1997-98, he became a referees' assessor and, under the F.A., gave others the benefit of his experience by coaching match officials.

PETER (PEDRO) RICHARDS, 45, made more than 450 appearances at right-back for Notts County, his only League club (1974-86). He was a member of the side that won promotion to the old First Division in 1981.

WILLIE WOODBURN, 82, was a Rangers and Scotland centre-half whose temper earned him a reputation that lasted long beyond his playing days. He served the Ibrox club from 1937-54 (losing 6 years of his first-class career to the war), and in the early post-war years helped them win 4 Scottish Championships, the Scottish Cup 4 times and the League Cup twice, including Rangers' first domestic treble success in 1948-49. In a career that brought him 24 Scotland caps, he was sent off 4 times, and his final dismissal in a League Cup-tie against Stirling Albion in August 1954 led to his being suspended *sine die* by the SFA. The ban was lifted 3 years later, but at 37 it was too late for a comeback. He stayed close to the game by writing for the *News of the World*.

JANUARY

JEFF ASTLE, 59, was a goalscoring hero of Midlands football with West Bromwich Albion in the 1964-74 era. He was signed for £25,000 from Notts County, where Tommy Lawton taught him centre-forward play and particularly the art of far-post heading, and by the time he retired from the first-class game he had scored 171 goals in 353 matches for the 'Baggies.' He helped them win the League Cup in 1966, to reach the Final again a year later and then, in a Final for the third year running, shot the only goal against Everton in extra time to maintain his record of scoring in every F.A. Cup round that season. As First Division top scorer with 25 goals in 1969-70, he earned the first of 5 England caps and went to the 1970 World Cup in Mexico, where he missed famously against Brazil. He gave up the professional game at 32 and played non-League for Dunstable, Weymouth, Atherstone and Hillingdon Borough before retiring in 1977 to set up a thriving window-cleaning business at Burton-upon-Trent. His vans carried the legend: 'Astle Never Misses the Corners.' He remained a WBA fan, rarely missing a home match until illness overtook him two years before he died.

BOBBY BRENNAN, 76, was a Northern Ireland International inside-forward (5 caps) who left Distillery for a career in English football with Luton Town, Birmingham City, Fulham and Norwich City between 1947 and 1959. In 6 seasons with Norwich, he made 223 League appearances and scored 44 goals. He played in their F.A. Cup run to the semi-final in 1959 and in the side that won promotion to Division Two in 1959-60.

GEORG ERICSON, 82, was Sweden's national coach for 8 years and took them to the World Cup Final series in 1974 in West Germany and 1978 in Argentina.

CHARLIE MITTEN, 80, was the dashing, flamboyant, uncapped left-winger in Manchester United's first post-war 'famous five' forward line in company with Jimmy Delaney, Stan Pearson, Jack Rowley and Johnny Morris. After playing in the 1948 F.A. Cup-winning team against Blackpool, he defected to Colombian club Santa Fe for a £10,000 signing-on fee and £100 a week, money undreamed of in British football by players on

£8 a week. On return to England, he was suspended for 6 months and fined £250, and subsequently played 4 seasons for Fulham (1952-56) and as Mansfield Town's player-manager (1956-58). He managed Newcastle United from 1958-61, and after leaving the game managed Manchester's White City greyhound stadium and then a sports promotion business in the city.

BRIAN THURLOW, 65, was a whole-hearted right-back for Norwich City from 1955-64, making 224 first-team appearances, including a run of 121 consecutively. Locally born, he was, at 22 the youngest member of the Canaries side that reached the F.A. Cup semi-final in 1959.

VAVA (full name Edvaldo Izidio Netto), 67, was Brazil's centre-forward in World Cup-winning teams of 1958 and 1962, scoring twice in the Final against Sweden and the third goal when they beat Czechoslovakia to retain the title 4 years later. He died in Rio after a history of heart trouble. He began at 15 with Recife, next played for Vasco da Gama and moved to Atletico Madrid after the 1958 World Cup. He returned home to join Palmeiras of Sao Paulo, was assistant coach to Brazil at the 1982 World Cup and later took charge of the Qatar national team.

FEBRUARY

JOHN BROMLEY, OBE, 68, the charismatic controller of ITV Sport, brought a new dimension to football coverage when he introduced the experts' panel – Malcolm Allison, Pat Crerand, Derek Dougan and Bob McNab – at the 1970 World Cup. He began in sports journalism as a junior football reporter with the *Daily Herald* in 1957, moved to the *Daily Mirror* and then in 1965 away from Fleet Street to the lure of television. He launched ITV's *World of Sport* show to compete on Saturday afternoons with BBC's *Grandstand*, and by 1972 was Head of Sport at London Weekend TV, where he introduced Sunday's *Big Match* programme, fronted by Jimmy Hill and Brian Moore. After leaving ITV he became a consultant with Sky TV and wrote as a sports TV critic for the *Daily Telegraph*. A prodigious worker for charities, he fought a long battle with cancer. In an obituary in *The Independent*, Ken Jones wrote: 'His room at a London hospital had the atmosphere of a private club; good wine, good company, laughter and lively reminiscence.' Typical Brommers to the end.

ERNIE BUTLER, 82, was Portsmouth's goalkeeper in the immediate post-war years, making 222 First Division appearances for the club from 1946-53.

BILL HARVEY, 82, was unique in Grimsby Town's history as their only manager to have been born in the town. He never played League football, began in management with Luton Town (1962-64), then coached Swindon Town and Bristol City on his way back home to Grimsby, where he was in charge of Town from January 1968 to January 1969.

BERT HEAD, 85, began in football as a full-back and centre-half for Torquay Utd. from 1936 until moving to Bury in 1952. He managed Swindon Town (1955-65), Bury (1965-66) and Crystal Palace (1966-73), taking Palace to the top flight for the first time in 1969. In his time at Swindon, he produced such fine young players as Mike Summerbee, Ernie Hunt, Don Rogers and Rod Thomas.

NANDOR HIDEGKUTI, 79, who died in Budapest, was the deep-lying centre-forward in the Hungary side that thrashed a bemused England 6-3 at Wembley (where he scored a hat-trick) in November 1953 and 7-1 in Budapest the following May. Those defeats revolutionised English football's approach to training and tactics, with Don Revie the first England centre-forward to drop deep and attack from midfield. Hidegkuti won 3 League titles with the MTK club and scored 39 goals in 68 matches for Hungary. He later coached in Italy (making Fiorentina the first holders of the Cup-Winners' Cup in 1961), Hungary, United Arab Emirates and Egypt.

DUGGIE REID, 84, was the gangling, raw-boned Scottish centre-forward whose fierce shooting helped Portsmouth to achieve back-to-back League Championship triumphs in seasons 1948-49 and 1949-50. From a penalty-kick against Manchester City, he once hammered the ball through the net and into his home crowd, but more than brawn took him to a total of 134 League and F.A. Cup goals, including 7 hat-tricks, in more than 300 appearances for the club. Born in Kilbride, he played for Stockport County from

1936 until his transfer to Portsmouth in 1946 for £7,000, a sum which raised eyebrows far beyond Fratton Park. He concluded his playing career at centre-half, then gave Portsmouth yeoman service for another 20 years as groundsman until he retired in 1978. He also ran a hostel for the club's young players in Southsea.

SIR WALTER WINTERBOTTOM, OBE, CBE, 88, was the first and longest-serving manager of the England team from 1946-62. The least envied, too, in that he had to submit his selected team for approval by the amateurs in the F.A. International Committee. He took England to the World Cups of 1950-54-58-62, put down the country's ground rules for coaching and initiated the Youth and U-23 teams. A pre-war defender with Manchester United from 1936, he served in the RAF in World War II, attaining the rank of Wing Commander. His England record read 139 matches, 78 wins, 33 draws, 28 defeats, and when he retired as manager it was widely thought that he would succeed his mentor Sir Stanley Rous as F.A. secretary, but his vast football knowledge was spurned at Lancaster Gate. He joined the Central Council for Physical Recreation, later served on the Sports Council and was knighted for his services to British sport on retirement in 1978.

MARCH

KENNETH WOLSTENHOLME, 81, was the BBC's voice of football for nearly a quarter of a century, and he immortalised England's World Cup triumph in 1966, with the most famous words in sports broadcasting as Geoff Hurst completed his hat-trick in the last seconds: 'Some people are on the pitch. They think it's all over . . . it is now.' Long established as a football reporter in radio, he was the commentator on the first *Match of the Day* highlights programme in August 1964 (Liverpool 3, Arsenal 2) and stayed with the BBC until 1971. Overall he covered 5 World Cups, 16 European Cup Finals and 23 consecutive FA Cup Finals. Born near Bolton, he worked on local newspapers until called up for the RAF, in which as a bomber pilot he flew more than 100 missions over Occupied Europe and was awarded the DFC and bar. Back from war service, he went into broadcasting in Manchester – the start of a long career for the most distinctive voice in football reporting. He died at Torquay. Among the many who paid tribute, Sir Bobby Charlton said: '1966 was not just about England. It was about Kenneth Wolstenholme as well. He's there forever and so are his words.' The BBC's Barry Davies said: 'He set commentary standards for everyone and taught us all a lot. He found the right words for the most important moment in the history of English football. In 1966, I was very much the new boy and he was the godfather. He had been commenting on every televised football match since 1948. That famous line from 1966 will never die. It didn't entirely do justice to his career, but it did justice to the art of commentary and will never be bettered. He was the BBC first choice for so long and left far too early.'

APRIL

BILLY AYRE, 49, was typical of those who make their living in football's lower leagues. As a player, he won two FA Trophy Finals at Wembley with Scarborough, and his career continued with Hartlepool United, Halifax Town, Mansfield Town and back with Halifax, where he began in management (1986-90). In 4 years at Blackpool, he took them out of the bottom division via the play-offs in 1992, managed Cardiff City in 1999-2000 and was mourned as Bury's first-team coach.

ISAAC (IKE) CLARKE, 87, scored the winning goal against Bolton that clinched Portsmouth's first League title in 1949. The Tipton-born marksman began with West Bromwich Albion in 1937 and moved to Fratton Park (£7,000) in November 1947. He scored 58 times in 129 appearances for Portsmouth and was their top scorer with 31 goals when they won a second successive Championship in 1950. He player-managed Yeovil Town from 1953-57.

SIR DAVID HILL-WOOD, 75, followed long family tradition as a lifelong Arsenal fan. He joined the FA Council in 1978 and served on the finance committee for 20 years, becoming chairman in 1988.

RON PHILLIPS, 55, made 145 League appearances as a Bolton winger from 1966-75, and subsequently played for Chesterfield, Bury and Chester until retiring in 1981.

MAY

GRAHAM BENT, 57, graduated from Welsh Schoolboy International winger to join Aston Villa as an apprentice and played League football for Wrexham in the mid-Sixties.

ROY PAUL, 82, was Manchester City's F.A. Cup-winning captain against Birmingham City in 1956 and at wing-half also captained Wales in an International career of 33 caps from 1949-57. Born at Ton Pentre, he began in League football with Swansea City in 1946 and moved to Maine Road (£25,000) in July 1950. In 7 seasons he played a total of 275 League matches for Manchester City.

LADISLAO KUBALA, 74, was voted 'best player in Barcelona's history' during the club's centenary celebrations in 1999. He joined them in 1950 from a team of East European refugees which he formed after escaping the Communist regime, and started as he was to go on for Barcelona, scoring 6 goals and creating 5 in his first 2 games. He helped them win 4 League titles, 5 Spanish Cups and 2 Fairs Cups, and he retired in season 1961-62 with a record of 256 goals in 329 matches for the club. He was capped by 3 countries, first by his native Hungary (where he played for Ferencvaros), 11 times by Czechoslovakia (Slovan Bratislava) and 19 for Spain. He coached Spain in 68 matches from 1969-80.

VALERY LOBANOVSKY, 63, coach to Dynamo Kiev and formerly to the Soviet Union and Ukraine national teams. Recognised as one of Eastern Europe's most successful coaches, he took Dynamo to 5 League titles and 2 Cup-Winners' Cup triumphs between 1974 and 1986. He guided the Soviet Union to runners-up place in the 1988 European Championship and coached Ukraine from 1999-2001. Tens of thousands of people gathered in Kiev for his state funeral.

STANLEY REED, 93, director and former Wimbledon chairman, was the club's last link with the successful 'Crazy Gang' era. Previously a director of Chelsea, he exuded old-world charm and was affectionately known by Vinnie Jones and company as 'Lord Reed.'

JUNE

SAID BELQOLA, 45-year-old Moroccan, was nominated 'the best Arab referee' after taking charge of the 1998 World Cup Final between France and Brazil. He died during the 2002 Finals, and as a mark of respect match officials wore black armbands at matches played the following week-end in Japan and South Korea.

FRANK NICKLIN, 80, who died at Bedford, was the first sports editor (1969-81) of the relaunched *Sun* and widely regarded as the 'inventor of tabloid sports journalism.' Born at Ilkeston, he began as a reporter with the *Derby Evening Telegraph* – he was a lifelong follower of Derby County – and returned from RAF service as a fighter pilot to become sports editor of the *Manchester Evening News, Sunday People* and *Daily Herald*. He was an ideas man, a master of design and layout, and his sports pages helped send *The Sun*'s circulation past 4 million. After leaving the paper, he was with Hayters sports agency for 12 years, subsequently as a director, until retiring.

FRITZ WALTER, 81, became Germany's first World Cup-winning captain when, in the 1954 Final in Switzerland, they beat Hungary 3-2 after suffering a shock 8-3 defeat in the opening round against the same opponents. He earned 61 caps for West Germany (33 goals), and spent his entire career with hometown team Kaiserslautern, inspiring them to German Championship successes in 1951 and 1953, and over 21 years achieved the phenomenal record of 306 goals in 379 appearances. When he retired in 1959, he left football for a new career, helping offenders rehabilitate their lives after leaving prison. But football never forgot him, and on his 65th birthday in 1985 Kaiserslautern named their ground the Fritz Walter Stadium. He died as Germany were on the way to their seventh World Cup Final.

Compiled by Albert Sewell

(Sources: Association of Football Statisticians, World Soccer, club websites, national and provincial newspapers)

MILESTONES OF SOCCER

1848 First code of rules compiled at Cambridge Univ.
1857 Sheffield F.C., world's oldest football club, formed.
1862 Notts Co. (oldest League club) formed.
1863 Football Association founded – their first rules of game agreed.
1871 F.A. Cup introduced.
1872 First official International: Scotland 0, England 0. Corner-kick introduced.
1873 Scottish F.A. formed; Scottish Cup introduced.
1874 Shinguards introduced. Oxford v Cambridge, first match.
1875 Crossbar introduced (replacing tape).
1876 F.A. of Wales formed.
1877 Welsh Cup introduced.
1878 Referee's whistle first used.
1880 Irish F.A. founded; Irish Cup introduced.
1883 Two-handed throw-in introduced.
1885 Record first-class score (Arbroath 36, Bon Accord 0 – Scottish Cup). Professionalism legalised.
1886 International Board formed.
1887 Record F.A. Cup score (Preston N.E. 26, Hyde 0).
1888 Football League founded by Wm. McGregor. First matches on Sept. 8.
1889 Preston N.E. win Cup and League (first club to complete Double).
1890 Scottish League and Irish League formed.
1891 Goal-nets introduced. Penalty-kick introduced.
1892 Inter-League games began. Football League Second Division formed.
1893 F.A. Amateur Cup launched.
1894 Southern League formed.
1895 F.A. Cup stolen from Birmingham shop window – never recovered.
1897 First Players' Union formed. Aston Villa win Cup and League.
1898 Promotion and relegation introduced.
1901 Maximum wage rule in force (£4 a week). Tottenham first professional club to take F.A. Cup South. First six-figure attendance (110,802) at F.A. Cup Final.
1902 Ibrox Park disaster (25 killed). Welsh League formed.
1904 F.I.F.A. founded (7 member countries).
1905 First £1,000 transfer (Alf Common, Sunderland to Middlesbrough).
1907 Players' Union revived.
1908 Transfer fee limit (£350) fixed in January and withdrawn in April.
1911 New F.A. Cup trophy – in use to 1991. Transfer deadline introduced.
1914 King George V first reigning monarch to attend F.A. Cup Final.
1916 Entertainment Tax introduced.
1919 League extended to 44 clubs.
1920 Third Division (South) formed.
1921 Third Division (North) formed.
1922 Scottish League (Div. II) introduced.
1923 Beginning of football pools. First Wembley Cup Final.
1924 First International at Wembley (England 1, Scotland 1). Rule change allows goals to be scored direct from corner-kicks.
1925 New offside law.
1926 Huddersfield Town complete first League Championship hat-trick.
1927 First League match broadcast (radio): Arsenal v Sheff. Utd. (Jan 22). First radio broadcast of Cup Final (winners Cardiff City). Charles Clegg, president of F.A., becomes first knight of football.
1928 First £10,000 transfer – David Jack (Bolton Wand. to Arsenal). W.R. ('Dixie') Dean (Everton) creates League record – 60 goals in season. Britain withdraws from F.I.F.A.
1930 Uruguay first winners of World Cup.
1931 W.B.A. win Cup and promotion.
1933 Players numbered for first time in Cup Final (1-22).

1934 Sir Frederick Wall retires as F.A. secretary; successor Stanley Rous. Death of Herbert Chapman (Arsenal manager).

1935 Arsenal equal Huddersfield Town's Championship hat-trick record. Official two-referee trials.

1936 Joe Payne's 10-goal League record (Luton Town 12, Bristol Rov. 0).

1937 British record attendance: 149,547 at Scotland v England match.

1938 First live TV transmission of F.A. Cup Final. F.A.'s 75th anniversary. Football League 50th Jubilee. New pitch marking – arc on edge of penalty-area. Laws of Game re-drafted by Stanley Rous. Arsenal pay record £14,500 fee for Bryn Jones (Wolves).

1939 Compulsory numbering of players in Football League. First six-figure attendance for League match (Rangers v Celtic, 118,567). All normal competitions suspended for duration of Second World War.

1944 Death of Sir Frederick Wall (84), F.A. secretary 1896-1934.

1945 Scottish League Cup introduced.

1946 British associations rejoin F.I.F.A. Bolton Wand. disaster (33 killed) during F.A. Cup tie with Stoke City. Walter Winterbottom appointed England's first director of coaching.

1947 Great Britain beat Rest of Europe 6-1 at Hampden Park, Glasgow. First £20,000 transfer – Tommy Lawton, Chelsea to Notts Co.

1949 Stanley Rous, secretary F.A., knighted. England's first home defeat outside British Champ. (0-2 v Eire).

1950 Football League extended from 88 to 92 clubs. World record crowd (203,500) at World Cup Final, Brazil v Uruguay, in Rio. Scotland's first home defeat by foreign team (0-1 v Austria).

1951 White ball comes into official use.

1952 Newcastle Utd. first club to win F.A. Cup at Wembley in successive seasons.

1953 England's first Wembley defeat by foreign opponents (3-6 v Hungary).

1954 Hungary beat England 7-1 in Budapest.

1955 First F.A. Cup match under floodlights (prelim. round replay, Sept. 14): Kidderminster Harriers v Brierley Hill Alliance.

1956 First F.A. Cup ties under floodlights in competition proper (Jan. 7). First League match by floodlight (Feb. 22, Portsmouth v Newcastle Utd.). Real Madrid win the first European Cup.

1957 Last full Football League programme on Christmas Day. Entertainment Tax withdrawn.

1958 Manchester Utd. air crash at Munich (Feb. 6). League re-structured into four divisions.

1959 Football League establish fixtures copyright; pools must pay for use.

1960 Record transfer fee: £55,000 for Denis Law (Huddersfield Town to Manchester City). Wolves miss Cup, miss Double and Championship hat-trick by one goal. For fifth time in ten years F.A. Cup Final team reduced to ten men by injury. F.A. recognise Sunday football. Football League Cup launched.

1961 Tottenham complete the first Championship-F.A. Cup double this century. Maximum wage (£20 a week) abolished in High Court challenge by George Eastham. First British £100-a-week wage paid (by Fulham to Johnny Haynes). First £100,000 British transfer – Denis Law, Manchester City to Torino. Sir Stanley Rous elected president of F.I.F.A.

1962 Manchester Utd. raise record British transfer fee to £115,000 for Denis Law.

1963 F.A. Centenary. Football League's 75th anniversary. Season extended to end of May due to severe winter. First pools panel. English "retain and transfer" system ruled illegal in High Court test case.

1964 Rangers' second great hat-trick – Scottish Cup, League Cup and League. Football League and Scottish League guaranteed £500,000 a year in new fixtures copyright agreement with Pools. First televised 'Match of the Day' (BBC2): Liverpool 3, Arsenal 2 (August 22).

1965 Bribes scandal – ten players jailed (and banned for life by F.A.) for match-fixing 1960-3. Stanley Matthews knighted in farewell season. Arthur Rowley (Shrewsbury Town) retires with record of 434 League goals. Substitutes allowed for injured players in Football League matches (one per team).

1966 England win World Cup (Wembley).

1967 Alf Ramsey, England manager, knighted; O.B.E. for captain Bobby Moore. Celtic become first British team to win European Cup. First substitutes allowed in F.A. Cup Final (Tottenham v Chelsea) but not used. Football League permit loan transfers (two per club).

1968 First F.A. Cup Final televised live in colour (BBC2 – W.B.A. v Everton). Manchester Utd. first English club to win European Cup.

1971 Arsenal win League Championship and F.A. Cup.

1973 Football League introduce 3-up, 3-down promotion/relegation between Divisions 1, 2 and 3 and 4-up, 4-down between Divisions 3 and 4.

1974 First F.A. Cup ties played on Sunday (Jan. 6). League football played on Sunday for first time (Jan. 20). Last F.A. Amateur Cup Final. Joao Havelange (Brazil) succeeds Sir Stanley Rous as F.I.F.A. president.

1975 Scottish Premier Division introduced.

1976 Football League introduce goal difference (replacing goal average).

1977 Liverpool achieve the double of League Championship and European Cup. Don Revie defects to United Arab Emirates when England manager – successor Ron Greenwood.

1978 Freedom of contract for players accepted by Football League. P.F.A. lifts ban on foreign players in English football. Football League introduce Transfer Tribunal. Viv Anderson (Nott'm. Forest) first black player to win a full England cap. Willie Johnston (Scotland) sent home from World Cup Finals in Argentina after failing dope test.

1979 First all-British £500,000 transfer – David Mills, M'bro' to W.B.A. First British million pound transfer (Trevor Francis – B'ham to Nott'm. Forest). Andy Gray moves from Aston Villa to Wolves for a record £1,469,000 fee.

1981 Tottenham win 100th F.A. Cup Final. Liverpool first British side to win European Cup three times. Three points for a win introduced by Football League. Q.P.R. install Football League's first artificial pitch. Sept. 29, death of Bill Shankly, manager-legend of Liverpool 1959-74. Record British transfer – Bryan Robson (W.B.A. to Manchester Utd.), £1,500,000.

1982 Aston Villa become sixth consecutive English winners of European Cup. Tottenham retain F.A. Cup – first club to do so since Tottenham 1961 and 1962. Football League Cup becomes the (sponsored) Milk Cup.

1983 Liverpool complete the League Championship-Milk Cup double for second year running. Manager Bob Paisley retires. Aberdeen first club to do Cup-Winners' Cup and domestic Cup double. Football League clubs vote to keep own match receipts. Football League sponsored by Canon, Japanese camera and business equipment manufacturers – 3-year agreement starting 1983-4. Football League agree 2-year contract for live TV coverage of ten matches per season (5 Friday night, BBC, 5 Sunday afternoon, ITV).

1984 One F.A. Cup tie in rounds 3, 4, 5 and 6 shown live on TV (Friday or Sunday). Aberdeen take Scottish Cup for third successive season, win Scottish Championship, too. Tottenham win UEFA Cup on penalty shoot-out. Liverpool win European Cup on penalty shoot-out to complete unique treble with Milk Cup and League title (as well as Championship hat-trick). N. Ireland win the final British Championship. France win European Championship – their first honour. F.A. National Soccer School opens at Lilleshall. Britain's biggest score this century: Stirling Alb. 20, Selkirk 0 (Scottish Cup).

1985 Bradford City fire disaster – 56 killed. First £1m. receipts from match in Britain (F.A. Cup Final). Kevin Moran (Manchester Utd.) first player to be sent off in F.A. Cup Final. Celtic win 100th Scottish F.A. Cup Final. European Cup Final horror (Liverpool v Juventus, riot in Brussels) 39 die. UEFA ban all English clubs indefinitely from European competitions. No TV coverage at start of League season – first time since 1963 (resumption delayed until January 1986). Sept: first ground-sharing in League history – Charlton Athletic move from The Valley to Selhurst Park (Crystal Palace).

1986 Liverpool complete League and Cup double in player-manager Kenny Dalglish's first season in charge. Swindon Town (4th Div. Champions) set League points record (102). League approve reduction of First Division to 20 clubs by 1988. Everton chairman Philip Carter elected president of Football League. July 18, death of Sir Stanley Rous (91). 100th edition of *News of the World* Football Annual. League Cup sponsored for next three years by Littlewoods (£2m.). Football League voting majority (for rule changes) reduced from ¾ to ⅔. Wales move HQ from Wrexham to Cardiff

City after 110 years. Two substitutes in F.A. Cup and League (Littlewoods) Cup. Two-season League/TV deal (£6.2m.):- BBC and ITV each show seven live League matches per season, League Cup semi-finals and Final. Football League sponsored by *Today* newspaper. Luton Town first club to ban all visiting supporters; as sequel are themselves banned from League Cup. Oldham Athletic and Preston N.E. install artificial pitches, making four in F. League (following Q.P.R. and Luton Town).

1987 May: League introduce play-off matches to decide final promotion/relegation places in all divisions. Re-election abolished – bottom club in Div. 4 replaced by winners of GM Vauxhall Conference. Two substitutes approved for Football League 1987-8. Red and yellow disciplinary cards (scrapped 1981) re-introduced by League and F.A. Football League sponsored by Barclays. First Div. reduced to 21 clubs.

1988 Football League Centenary. First Division reduced to 20 clubs.

1989 Soccer gets £74m. TV deal: £44m. over 4 years, ITV; £30m. over 5 years, BBC/BSB. But it costs Philip Carter the League Presidency. Ted Croker retires as F.A. chief executive; successor Graham Kelly, from Football League. Hillsborough disaster: 95 die at F.A. Cup semi-final (Liverpool v Nott'm. Forest). Arsenal win closest-ever Championship with last kick. Peter Shilton sets England record with 109 caps.

1990 Nott'm. Forest win last Littlewoods Cup Final. Both F.A. Cup semi-finals played on Sunday and televised live. Play-off finals move to Wembley; Swindon Town win place in Div. 1, then relegated back to Div. 2 (breach of financial regulations) – Sunderland promoted instead. Pools betting tax cut from 42½ to 40%. England reach World Cup semi-final in Italy and win F.I.F.A. Fair Play Award. Peter Shilton retires as England goalkeeper with 125 caps (world record). Graham Taylor (Aston Villa) succeeds Bobby Robson as England manager. Int. Board amend offside law (player 'level' no longer offside). F.I.F.A. make "pro foul" a sending-off offence. English clubs back in Europe (Manchester Utd. and Aston Villa) after 5-year exile.

1991 First F.A. Cup semi-final at Wembley (Tottenham 3, Arsenal 1). Bert Millichip (F.A. chairman) and Philip Carter (Everton chairman) knighted. End of artificial pitches in Div. 1 (Luton Town, Oldham Athletic). Scottish League reverts to 12-12-14 format (as in 1987-8). Penalty shoot-out introduced to decide F.A. Cup ties level after one replay.

1992 Introduction of fourth F.A. Cup (previous trophy withdrawn). F.A. launch Premier League (22 clubs). Football League reduced to three divisions (71 clubs). Record TV-sport deal: BSkyB/BBC to pay £304m. for 5-year coverage of Premier League. ITV do £40m., 4-year deal with F. League. Channel 4 show Italian football live (Sundays). F.I.F.A. approve new back-pass rule (goalkeeper must not handle ball kicked to him by team-mate). New League of Wales formed. Record all-British transfer, £3.3m.: Alan Shearer (Southampton to Blackburn Rov.). Charlton Athletic return to The Valley after 7-year absence.

1993 Barclays end 6-year sponsorship of F. League. For first time both F.A. Cup semi-finals at Wembley (Sat., Sun.). Arsenal first club to complete League Cup/F.A. Cup double. Rangers pull off Scotland's domestic treble for fifth time. F.A. in record British sports sponsorship deal (£12m. over 4 years) with brewers Bass for F.A. Carling Premiership, from Aug. Brian Clough retires after 18 years as Nott'm. Forest manager; as does Jim McLean (21 years manager of Dundee Utd.). Football League agree 3-year, £3m. sponsorship with Endsleigh Insurance. Premier League introduce squad numbers with players' names on shirts. Record British transfer: Duncan Ferguson, Dundee Utd. to Rangers (£4m.). Record English-club signing: Roy Keane, Nott'm. Forest to Manchester Utd. (£3.75m.). Graham Taylor resigns as England manager after World Cup exit (Nov.). Death in Feb. of Bobby Moore (51), England World-Cup winning captain 1966.

1994 Death of Sir Matt Busby (Jan.). Terry Venables appointed England coach (Jan.). Manchester Utd. complete the Double. Last artificial pitch in English football goes – Preston N.E. revert to grass, summer 1994. Bobby Charlton knighted. Scottish League format changes to four divisions of ten clubs. Record British transfer: Chris Sutton, Norwich City to Blackburn Rov. (£5m.). Sept: F.A. announce first sponsorship of F.A. Cup – Littlewoods Pools (4-year, £14m. deal, plus £6m. for Charity Shield). Death of Billy Wright, 70 (Sept).

1995 New record British transfer: Andy Cole, Newcastle Utd. to Manchester Utd. (£7m.). First England match abandoned through crowd trouble (v Rep. of Ireland, Dublin). Blackburn Rov. Champions for first time since 1914. Premiership reduced to

20 clubs. British transfer record broken again (June): Stan Collymore, Nott'm. Forest to Liverpool (£8½m.). Starting season 1995-6, teams allowed to use 3 substitutes per match, not necessarily including a goalkeeper. Dec: European Court of Justice upholds Bosman ruling, barring transfer fees for players out of contract and removing limit on number of foreign players clubs can field.

1996 Death in Feb. of Bob Paisley (77), ex-Liverpool, most successful manager in English Football. F.A. appoint Chelsea manager Glenn Hoddle to succeed Terry Venables as England coach after Euro 96. Manchester Utd. first English club to achieve Double twice (and in 3 seasons). Football League completes £125m., 5-year TV deal with BSkyB starting 1996-7. England stage European Championship, reach semi-finals, lose on pens to tournament winners Germany. Keith Wiseman succeeds Sir Bert Millichip as F.A. Chairman. Linesmen become known as "referees' assistants". Coca-Cola Cup experiment with own disciplinary system (red, yellow cards). Alan Shearer football's first £15m. player (Blackburn Rov. to Newcastle Utd.). Nigeria first African country to win Olympic soccer. Nationwide Building Society sponsor Football League in initial 3-year deal worth £5.25m. Peter Shilton first player to make 1000 League apps.

1997 Howard Wilkinson appointed English football's first technical director. England's first home defeat in World Cup (0-1 v Italy). Ruud Gullit (Chelsea) first foreign coach to win F.A. Cup. Rangers equal Celtic's record of 9 successive League titles. Manchester Utd. win Premier League for fourth time in 5 seasons. New record World Cup score: Iran 17, Maldives 0 (qual. round). Season 1997-8 starts Premiership's record £36m., 4-year sponsorship extension with brewers Bass (Carling).

1998 In French manager Arsene Wenger's second season at Highbury, Arsenal become second English club to complete the Double twice. Chelsea also win two trophies under new player-manager Gianluca Vialli (Coca-Cola Cup, Cup Winners' Cup). France win 16th World Cup competition. In breakaway from Scottish League, top ten clubs form new Premiership under SFA, starting season 1998-9. Football League celebrates its 100th season, 1998-9. New F.A. Cup sponsors – French insurance giants AXA (25m., 4-year deal). League Cup becomes Worthington Cup in £23m., 5-year contract with brewers Bass. Nationwide Building Society's sponsorship of Football League extended to season 2000-1.

1999 F.A. buy Wembley Stadium (£103m.) for £320m. redevelopment (Aug. 2000-March 2003) as new national stadium (Lottery Sports fund contributes £110m.) Scotland's new Premier League takes 3-week mid-season break in January. Sky screen Oxford Utd. v Sunderland (Div. 1, Feb. 27) as first pay-per-view match on TV. F.A. sack England coach Glenn Hoddle; Fulham's Kevin Keegan replaces him at £1m. a year until 2003. Sir Alf Ramsey, England's World Cup-winning manager, dies aged 79. With effect 1999, F.A. Cup Final to be decided on day (via penalties, if necessary). Hampden Park re-opens for Scottish Cup Final after £63m. refit. Alex Ferguson knighted after Manchester Utd. complete Premiership, F.A. Cup, European Cup treble. Starting season 1999-2000, UEFA increase Champions League from 24 to 32 clubs. End of Cup-Winners' Cup (merged into 121-club UEFA Cup). F.A. allow holders Manchester Utd. to withdraw from F.A. Cup to participate in FIFA's inaugural World Club Championship in Brazil in January. Chelsea first British club to field an all-foreign line-up at Southampton (Pre., Dec. 26). F.A. vote (December) in favour of streamlined 14-man board of directors to replace its 92-member council.

2000 Scot Adam Crozier takes over as F.A. chief executive, Jan. 1. Wales move to Cardiff City's £125m. Millennium Stadium (v Finland, March 29). Brent Council approve plans for new £475m. Wembley Stadium (completion target spring 2003); demolition of old stadium to begin after England v Germany (World Cup qual., Oct. 7). Fulham Ladies become Britain's first female professional team. F.A. Premiership and Nationwide League to introduce (season 2000-01) rule whereby referees advance free-kick by 10 yards and caution player who shows dissent, delays kick or fails to retreat 10 yards. Scottish football increased to 42 League clubs in 2000-01 (12 in Premier League and 3 division of ten; Peterhead and Elgin City elected from Highland League). France win eleventh European Championship – first time a major Int. tournament has been jointly hosted (Holland/Belgium). England's £10m. bid to stage 2006 World Cup fails; vote goes to Germany. England manager Kevin Keegan resigns

(Oct. 7) after 1-0 World Cup defeat by Germany in Wembley's last International. Oct. 30: Lazio's Swedish coach Sven Goran Eriksson agrees to become England head coach.

2001 January: Scottish Premier League experiment with split into two 5-game mini leagues (6 clubs in each) after 33 matches completed. July: New transfer system agreed by FIFA/UEFA is ratified. August: Barclaycard begin £48m., 3-year sponsorship of the Premiership, and Nationwide's contract with the Football League is extended by a further 3 years (£12m.). ITV, after winning auction against BBC's Match of the Day, begin £183m., 3-season contract for highlights of Premiership matches; BSkyB's live coverage (66 matches per season) for next 3 years will cost £1.1bn. BBC and BSkyB pay £400m. (3-year contract) for live coverage of F.A. Cup and England home matches. ITV and Ondigital pay £315m. to screen Nationwide League and Worthington Cup matches. In new charter for referees, top men can earn up to £60,000 a season in Premiership. Real Madrid break world transfer record, buying Zinedine Zidane from Juventus for £47.2m. F.A. introduce prize money, round by round, in F.A. Cup.

2002 February: Scotland appoint their first foreign manager, Germany's former national coach Bertie Vogts replacing Craig Brown. April: Collapse of ITV Digital deal, with Football League owed £178m., threatens lower-division clubs. May: Arsenal complete Premiership/F.A. Cup Double for second time in 5 seasons, third time in all. June: Newcastle Utd. manager Bobby Robson knighted in Queen's Jubilee Honours. Brazil win World Cup for fifth time.

QUOTE UNQUOTE

'It was my best day in racing. Unfortunately my little football team had to spoil it' – **Sir Alex Ferguson** after Manchester United's home defeat by Bolton Wanderers put the damper on his horse Rock of Gibraltar's victory in the £116,000 Dewhurst Stakes at Newmarket.

'I accept that this type of challenge is not in order and should have no part in the game' – **Graeme Le Saux**, Chelsea defender, making a public apology for a two-footed tackle on Leeds United's Danny Mills.

'My girls have had a great day and so has their dad' – **Alan Shearer** after scoring one of the finest goals of his career on the day his two daughters were Newcastle United club mascots for the game against Aston Villa.

'Enough is enough' – **Sol Campbell** after being vilified by Tottenham fans on his return to White Hart Lane with Arsenal.

FIVE CLUBS IN THREE-AND-A-HALF YEARS
FOR
BRUCE

When Steve Bruce took over at Birmingham City last season, it was his fifth managerial job in three-and-a-half years following spells at Sheffield United. (resigned), Huddersfield Town (sacked), Wigan Athletic (resigned) and latterly Crystal Palace (resigned).

ENGLISH LEAGUE ROLL-CALL

REVIEWS, APPEARANCES & SCORERS 2001-02

(figures in brackets = appearances as substitute)

F.A. BARCLAYCARD PREMIER LEAGUE

ARSENAL

Arsenal delivered their second League and F.A. Cup double in five seasons with style and staying power, not to mention the sense of satisfaction attached to clinching it with a 1-0 victory over Manchester United. Overcoming injuries to key players like David Seaman, Tony Adams, Martin Keown and Robert Pires, Arsene Wenger's side accumulated a formidable array of statistics to justify their success. They scored in every Premiership game, were unbeaten away from home, won their final 13 fixtures and had the top scorer in Thierry Henry with 24 goals to his credit. Four days before winning at Old Trafford, Arsenal beat Chelsea 2-0 in the F.A. Cup Final. The next challenge is Europe, where defeat by Deportivo La Coruna at Highbury effectively cost them a place in the Champions League quarter-finals.

Adams, T	10	Jeffers, F	2(4)	Seaman, D	17
Aliadiere, J	–(1)	Kanu, N	9(14)	Stepanovs, I	6
Bergkamp, D	22(11)	Keown, M	21(1)	Taylor, S	9(1)
Campbell, S	29(2)	Lauren	27	Upson, M	10(4)
Cole, A	29	Ljungberg, F	24(1)	Van Bronckhorst, G	13(8)
Dixon, L	3(10)	Luzhny, O	15(3)	Vieira, P	35(1)
Edu	8(6)	Parlour, R	25(2)	Wiltord, S	23(10)
Grimandi, G	11(15)	Pires, R	27(1)	Wright, R	12
Henry, T	31(2)				

League goals (79): Henry 24, Ljungberg 12, Wiltord 10, Bergkamp 9, Pires 9, Kanu 3, Campbell 2, Cole 2, Jeffers 2, Lauren 2, Vieira 2, Edu 1, Van Bronckhorst 1.
F.A. Cup goals (17): Bergkamp 3, Kanu 2, Ljungberg 2, Parlour 2, Wiltord 2, Adams 1, Campbell 1, Edu 1, Henry 1, Pires 1, Opponents 1. **Worthington Cup goals (6):** Wiltord 4, Edu 1, Kanu 1. **Champions League goals (17):** Henry 7, Ljungberg 3, Pires 3, Bergkamp 2, Wiltord 1, Vieira 1.
Average home League attendance: 38,054. **Player of Year:** Robert Pires.

ASTON VILLA

The most significant aspects of Aston Villa's season were the resignation of John Gregory and Graham Taylor's decision to return to management after nine months of retirement. On the field, Villa under-achieved, losing to Varteks of Croatia in the UEFA Cup, surrendering a two-goal lead to Manchester United in the F.A. Cup and finishing eighth in the Premiership. Taylor started to change things around before the end of the season, paying £4m. for 6ft 6in Peter Crouch in an attempt to repeat the success his teams once enjoyed with two more big front men, George Reilly and Ian Ormondroyd.

Alpay, O	14	Enckelman, P	9	Samuel, J	17(6)
Angel, J-P	26(3)	Ginola, D	–(5)	Schmeichel, P	29
Balaban, B	–(8)	Hadji, M	17(6)	Staunton, S	30(3)
Barry, G	16(4)	Hendrie, L	25(4)	Stone, S	14(8)
Boateng, G	37	Hitzlsperger, T	11(1)	Taylor, I	7(9)
Crouch, P	7	Kachloul, H	17(5)	Vassell, D	30(6)
Delaney, M	30	Mellberg, O	32	Wright, A	23
Dublin, D	9(12)	Merson, P	18(3)		

League goals (46): Angel 12, Vassell 12, Dublin 4, Taylor 3, Crouch 2, Hadji 2, Hendrie 2, Kachloul 2, Merson 2, Boateng 1, Hitzlsperger 1, Schmeichel 1, Stone 1, Opponents 1.

F.A. Cup goals (2): Taylor 1, Opponents 1. **Worthington Cup goals (1):** Dublin 1. **InterToto Cup goals (10):** Angel 2, Ginola 2, Hendrie 2, Vassell 2, Dublin 1, Merson 1. **UEFA Cup goals (3):** Angel 2, Hadji 1.
Average home League attendance: 35,011. **Player of Year:** Juan Pablo Angel.

BLACKBURN ROVERS

Blackburn had little time to savour their first trophy success for 74 years – a 2-1 win over favourites Tottenham in the final of the Worthington Cup. They were deep in relegation trouble and the next match was against fellow strugglers Bolton Wanderers. That finished 1-1 and was followed by wins over Aston Villa and Ipswich Town which suggested Rovers were too good to go down. Sure enough, they lost only one of the final seven games and climbed to mid-table, Graeme Souness's signing of Andy Cole from Manchester United having proved a shrewd move.

Bent, M .... 1(8)	Friedel, B 36	Kelly, A 2
Berg, H 34	Gillespie, K .... 21(11)	Mahon, A .... 10(3)
Bjornebye, S 23	Grabbi, C .... 10(4)	McAteer, J .... 1(3)
Blake, N .... –(3)	Hakan Unsal .... 7(1)	Neill, L 31
Cole, A 15	Hignett, C .... 4(16)	Ostenstad, E .... 2(2)
Curtis, J 10	Hughes, M .... 4(17)	Short, C .... 21(1)
Duff, D .... 31(1)	Jansen, M .... 34(1)	Taylor, M .... 12(7)
Dunn, D .... 26(3)	Johansson, N .... 14(6)	Tugay, K .... 32(1)
Flitcroft, G .... 26(3)	Johnson, D .... 6(1)	Yordi .... 5(3)

League goals (55): Jansen 10, Cole 9, Duff 7, Dunn 7, Hignett 4, Gillespie 3, Tugay 3, Yordi 2, Berg 1, Blake 1, Flitcroft 1, Grabbi 1, Hughes 1, Johnson 1, Mahon 1, Neill 1, Opponents 2.
F.A. Cup goals (5): Cole 1, Dunn 1, Grabbi 1, Hignett 1, Johansson 1. **Worthington Cup goals (18):** Jansen 6, Cole 3, Hignett 3, Duff 1, Dunning, D 1, Hughes 1, Johansson 1, Johnson 1, Short 1.
Average home League attendance: 25,976. **Player of Year:** Damien Duff.

BOLTON WANDERERS

Most neutrals tipped Bolton to go straight back down, even after a splendid start which put them on top-of-the-table with 10 points from four matches. That they kept their nerve in a tense run-in was testimony to the faith Sam Allardyce had in his team and to the players he brought in. When Michael Ricketts lost his scoring touch at a crucial time, World Cup winner Youri Djorkaeff exerted a major influence, while a hat-trick by Fredi Bobic in a six-pointer against Ipswich Town delivered the single most important victory for the team.

Banks, S 1	Gardner, R .... 29(2)	Pedersen, H .... 5(6)
Barness, A .... 19(6)	Hansen, B .... 10(7)	Poole, K 3
Bergsson, G 30	Hendry, C 3	Richardson, L .... –(1)
Bobic, F .... 14(2)	Holdsworth, D .... 9(22)	Ricketts, M .... 26(11)
Charlton, S .... 35(1)	Jaaskelainen, J 34	Smith, J .... –(1)
Diawara, D .... 4(5)	Johnson, J .... 4(6)	Southall, N .... 10(8)
Djorkaeff, Y 12	Konstantinidis, K 3	Tofting, S 6
Espartero, M .... –(3)	Marshall, I .... –(2)	Wallace, R .... 14(5)
Farrelly, G .... 11(7)	N'Gotty, A .... 24(2)	Warhurst, P 25
Frandsen, P .... 25(4)	Nolan, K .... 34(1)	Whitlow, M .... 28(1)

League goals (44): Ricketts 12, Nolan 8, Bobic 4, Djorkaeff 4, Frandsen 3, Gardner 3, Wallace 3, Holdsworth 2, Bergsson 1, Hansen 1, N'Gotty 1, Southall 1, Opponents 1.
F.A. Cup goals (4): Bergsson 1, Pedersen 1, Ricketts 1, Opponents 1. **Worthington Cup goals (7):** Holdsworth 2, Ricketts 2, Nishizawa 1, Pedersen 1, Wallace 1.
Average home League attendance: 25,098. **Player of Year:** Simon Charlton.

CHARLTON ATHLETIC

Considering that they were without key players like Richard Rufus, Claus Jensen and Mark Kinsella for long spells through injury, Charlton did well to finish comfortably clear of danger. A run of eight undefeated matches against London rivals – before Arsenal won 3-0 at the Valley to reverse a 4-2 embarrassment at Highbury – was particularly satisfying. Less so was the way the season tailed off without a victory in the last eight matches – or a 2-1 home defeat by Walsall in the fourth round of the F.A. Cup.

Bartlett, S .... 10(4)	Kiely, D 38	Powell, C .... 35(1)
Bart-Williams, C .... 10(6)	Kinsella, M .... 14(3)	Robinson, J .... 16(12)
Brown, S .... 11(3)	Kishishev, R .... –(3)	Rufus, R 10
Costa, J .... 22(2)	Konchesky, P ...... 22(12)	Salako, J .... 2(1)
Euell, J .... 31(5)	Lisbie, K .... 10(12)	Stuart, G 31
Fish, M 25	MacDonald, C .... –(2)	Svensson, M .... 6(6)
Fortune, J .... 14(5)	Parker, S .... 36(2)	Todd, A .... 3(2)
Jensen, C .... 16(2)	Peacock, G .... 1(4)	Young, L 34
Johansson, J .... 21(9)		

League goals (38): Euell 11, Johansson 5, Lisbie 5, Stuart 3, Bartlett 2, Brown 2, Bart-Williams 1, Jensen 1, Konchesky 1, MacDonald 1, Parker 1, Powell 1, Robinson 1, Rufus 1, Opponents 2.
F.A. Cup goals (3): Stuart 2, Euell 1. **Worthington Cup goals (5):** Brown 1, Euell 1, Fortune 1, Konchesky 1, Robinson 1.
Average home League attendance: 24,096. **Player of Year:** Dean Kiely.

CHELSEA

On their day, with Jimmy Floyd Hasselbaink and Eidur Gudjohnsen rampaging up front, Chelsea were a match for anyone. Witness a 3-0 win at Old Trafford and a 4-0 home success against Liverpool. The problem was that the highs were so often followed by the lows, which inevitably caught up with this curious team whose sixth place proved disappointing. Arsenal deprived them of a third F.A. Cup win in six seasons, while there were embarrassing defeats by Tottenham (5-1) in the Worthington Cup and Hapoel Tel Aviv in the UEFA Cup when several of their players declined to travel to Israel.

Babayaro, C 18	Gallas, W .... 27(3)	Le Saux, G .... 26(1)
Bosnich, M 5	Gronkjaer, J .... 11(2)	Melchiot, M .... 35(2)
Cole, C .... 2(1)	Gudjohnsen, E ...... 26(6)	Morris, J .... 2(3)
Cudicini, C .... 27(1)	Hasselbaink, J 35	Petit, E .... 26(1)
Dalla Bona, S .... 16(8)	Huth, R .... –(1)	Stanic, M .... 18(9)
De Goey, E 6	Jokanovic, S .... 12(8)	Terry, J .... 32(1)
Desailly, M 24	Keenan, J .... –(1)	Zenden, B .... 13(9)
Ferrer, A .... 2(2)	Lampard, F .... 34(3)	Zola, G .... 19(16)
Forssell, M .... 2(20)		

League goals (66): Hasselbaink 23, Gudjohnsen 14, Lampard 5, Dalla Bona 4, Forssell 4, Zenden 3, Zola 3, Melchiot 2, Cole 1, Desailly 1, Gallas 1, Le Saux 1, Petit 1, Stanic 1, Terry 1, Opponents 1.
F.A. Cup goals (16): Gudjohnsen 3, Hasselbaink 3, Forssell 3, Terry 2, Gallas 1, Lampard 1, Le Saux 1, Stanic 1, Zola 1, **Worthington Cup goals (8):** Gudjohnsen 3, Hasselbaink 3, Forssell 2. **UEFA Cup goals (6):** Gudjohnsen 3, Lampard 1, Terry 1, Zola 1.
Average home League attendance: 39,072.

DERBY COUNTY

A tale of three managers and relegation at Pride Park, where Fabrizio Ravanelli experienced a familiar sinking feeling on his return to English football. Colin Todd succeeded veteran Jim Smith and was sacked after three months in the job, clearing the way for John Gregory to come in six days after he walked out at Aston Villa. Two quick wins and a point against Manchester United suggested Gregory might be the saviour.

But Derby's failings ran too deep to be rectified in the time he had, with seven defeats in the last eight matches confirming the drop. There was also an embarrassing 3-1 F.A. Cup home defeat by Bristol Rovers.

Barton, W 14	Feuer, I 2	Oakes, A 20
Boertien, P .... 23(9)	Foletti, P .... 1(1)	O'Neil, B .... 8(2)
Bolder, A .... 2(9)	Grenet, F .... 12(3)	Poom, M 15
Burley, C 11	Higginbotham, D 37	Powell, D 23
Burton, D .... 8(9)	Jackson, R .... 6(1)	Ravanelli, F .... 30(1)
Carbonari, H 3	Johnson, S 7	Riggott, C 37
Carbone, B 13	Kinkladze, G ...... 13(11)	Robinson, M .... –(2)
Christie, M .... 27(8)	Lee, R 13	Strupar, B .... 8(4)
Daino, D 2	Mawene, Y 17	Twigg, G .... –(1)
Ducrocq, P 19	Morris, L .... 9(6)	Valakari, S .... 6(3)
Elliott, S .... 2(4)	Murray, A .... 3(3)	Zavagno, L 26
Evatt, I .... 1(2)		

League goals (33): Christie 9, Ravanelli 9, Morris 4, Strupar 4, Burton 1, Carbone 1, Higginbotham 1, Kinkladze 1, Mawene 1, Powell 1, Robinson 1.
F.A. Cup goals (1): Ravanelli 1. **Worthington Cup goals (5):** Burton 2, Burley 1, Kinkladze 1, Ravanelli 1.
Average home League attendance: 30,091. **Player of Year:** Danny Higginbotham.

EVERTON

When Everton lost patience with Walter Smith, they were staring at relegation and had just given a tepid performance against Middlesbrough in the quarter-finals of the F.A. Cup. Enter Preston's David Moyes to effect a transformation, with a team scratching around for goals starting to score regularly. There were wins over Fulham (2-1) and Derby County (4-3), and despite a 6-2 setback at Newcastle, Moyes organised a 3-1 victory over fellow-strugglers Bolton Wanderers which insulated his team from another dip in results at the end of the season.

Alexandersson, N .... 28(3)	Gemmill, S .... 31(1)	Pistone, A 25
Blomquist, J .... 10(5)	Gerrard, P 13	Radzinski, T .... 23(4)
Cadamarteri, D .... 2(1)	Ginola, D .... 2(3)	Simonsen, S 25
Campbell, K .... 21(2)	Gravesen, T .... 22(3)	Stubbs, A .... 29(2)
Carsley, L 8	Hibbert, T .... 7(3)	Tal, I .... 1(6)
Chadwick, N .... 2(7)	Linderoth, T .... 4(4)	Unsworth, D .... 28(5)
Clarke, P .... 5(2)	Moore, J-M .... 3(13)	Watson, S .... 24(1)
Cleland, A .... –(3)	Naysmith, G .... 23(1)	Weir, D 36
Ferguson, D .... 17(5)	Pembridge, M .... 10(4)	Xavier, A .... 11(1)
Gascoigne, P .... 8(10)		

League goals (45): Ferguson 6, Radzinksi 6, Campbell 4, Watson 4, Weir 4, Chadwick 3, Unsworth 3, Alexandersson 2, Gravesen 2, Moore 2, Stubbs 2, Blomqvist 1, Carsley 1, Gascoigne 1, Gemmill 1, Pembridge 1, Pistone 1, Opponents 1.
F.A. Cup goals (7): Campbell 3, Ferguson 1, Radzinski 1, Stubbs 1, Opponents 1.
Worthington Cup goals (1): Ferguson 1.
Average home League attendance: 33,602. **Player of Year:** David Weir.

FULHAM

Despite an outlay of £34m. on new players, Fulham had a difficult first season in the Premiership. The main problem was in attack, with £11.5m. Steve Marlet and Louis Saha both scoring infrequently. That eventually led to run of nine matches without a win, which threatened danger until another Frenchman, Steed Malbranque, scored a surprise winner at Leeds. His team followed that up with victory over Bolton Wanderers to ease clear. In the F.A. Cup, Fulham overcame First, Second and Third Division opposition before losing somewhat unluckily to Chelsea in the semi-finals.

Betsy, K .... –(1)	Brevett, R .... 34(1)	Collins, J .... 29(4)
Boa Morte, L .... 15(8)	Clark, L .... 5(4)	Davis, S .... 25(5)

Finnan, S 38	Legwinski, S .... 30(3)	Saha, L .... 28(8)
Goldbaek, B .... 8(5)	Lewis, E 1	Stolcers, A .... –(5)
Goma, A .... 32(1)	Malbranque, S .... 33(4)	Symons, K .... 2(2)
Harley, J .... 5(5)	Marlet, S .... 21(5)	Taylor, M .... 1(1)
Hayles, B .... 27(8)	Melville, A 35	Van der Sar, E 37
Knight, Z .... 8(2)	Ouaddou, A .... 4(4)	Willock, C .... –(2)

League goals (36): Hayles 8, Malbranque 8, Saha 8, Marlet 6, Legwinski 3, Boa Morte 1, Goldbaek 1, Opponents 1.
F.A. Cup goals (8): Marlet 3, Hayles 2, Legwinski 1, Malbranque 1, Opponents 1.
Worthington Cup goals (8): Hayles 2, Boa Morte 1, Brevett 1, Collins 1, Legwinski 1, Malbranque 1, Saha 1.
Average home League attendance: 19,343. **Player of Year:** Steve Finnan.

IPSWICH TOWN

A year after qualifying for Europe and earning George Burley the Manager of the Year award, Ipswich dropped back into the First Division. Having won only one of the first 17 matches, they were transformed by a haul of 21 points out of the next 24 and seemed to be heading for safety. Then Liverpool handed out a 6-0 drubbing at Portman Road to precipitate another slide. This time Ipswich were unable to halt it. Marcus Stewart's lean spell in front of goal after he returned from a broken jaw was a key factor and a 5-0 defeat at Anfield completed their downfall. There were two UEFA Cup successes before they ran into a Christian Vieri hat-trick for Inter Milan.

Ambrose, D .... –(1)	George, F .... 21(4)	Naylor, R .... 5(9)
Armstrong, A .... 21(11)	Holland, M 38	Peralta, S .... 16(6)
Bent, D .... 2(3)	Hreidarsson, H 38	Reuser, M .... 18(6)
Bent, M .... 22(3)	Le Pen, U .... –(1)	Sereni, M 25
Bramble, T .... 16(2)	Magilton, J .... 16(8)	Stewart, M .... 20(8)
Branagan, K .... –(1)	Makin, C 30	Venus, M 29
Clapham, J .... 22(10)	Marshall, A 13	Wilnis, F .... 6(8)
Counago, P .... 1(12)	McGreal, J 27	Wright, J .... 24(5)
Gaardsoe, T .... 3(1)	Miller, T .... 5(3)	

League goals (41): Bent, M 9, George 6, Stewart 6, Armstrong 4, Holland 3, Peralta 3, Clapham 2, Bent, D 1, Gaardsoe 1, Hreidarsson 1, McGreal 1, Naylor 1, Reuser 1, Venus 1, Wright 1.
F.A. Cup goals (5): Peralta 2, Bent, M 1, Magilton 1, Stewart 1. **Worthington Cup goals (4):** Reuser 2, Armstrong 1, Bent, D 1. **UEFA Cup goals (8):** Stewart 3, Armstrong 2, Bramble 1, George 1, Hreidarsson 1.
Average home League attendance: 24,434. **Player of Year:** Mark Venus.

LEEDS UNITED

A traumatic season for Leeds, with the fall-out from the retrial of Jonathan Woodgate and Lee Bowyer clouding everything. David O'Leary's side went into 2002 a point off the top, but defeat by Cardiff City in the F.A. Cup on an unpleasant afternoon at Ninian Park took its toll. Nine games without a win included a UEFA Cup fourth round defeat by PSV Eindhoven, who scored in the last minute at Elland Road to go through. Goals from Robbie Fowler, an £11m. signing from Liverpool, put Leeds back on track before a home defeat by Fulham ended their Champions League hopes. O'Leary was sacked and in came Terry Venables from the TV studio to replace him.

Bakke, E .... 20(7)	Harte, I .... 34(2)	Maybury, A .... –(1)
Batty, D .... 30(6)	Johnson, S .... 12(2)	McPhail, S .... –(1)
Bowyer, L .... 24(1)	Keane, R .... 16(9)	Mills, D 28
Dacourt, O .... 16(1)	Kelly, G .... 19(1)	Smith, A .... 19(4)
Duberry, M 3	Kewell, H .... 26(1)	Viduka, M 33
Ferdinand, R 31	Martyn, N 38	Wilcox, J .... 4(9)
Fowler, R 22	Matteo, D 32	Woodgate, J .... 11(2)

League goals (53): Fowler 12, Viduka 11, Kewell 8, Bowyer 5, Harte 5, Smith 4, Keane 3, Bakke 2, Mills 1, Opponents 2.
F.A. Cup goals (1): Viduka 1. **Worthington Cup goals (6):** Keane 3, Bakke 1, Kewell 1, Viduka 1. **UEFA Cup goals (13):** Keane 3, Viduka 3, Bowyer 2, Kewell 2, Bakke 1, Harte 1, Smith 1.
Average home League attendance: 39,751. **Player of Year:** Rio Ferdinand.

LEICESTER CITY

Fears that Leicester would still have a hangover from the previous season when they won only one of their last 10 games in the wake of an F.A. Cup defeat by Wycombe Wanderers, were immediately confirmed. A 5-0 home defeat by promoted Bolton Wanderers on the opening day, followed by a 4-0 reverse at Arsenal, set the tone for their last campaign at Filbert Street before a move to a 32,000-capacity new stadium. Peter Taylor was sacked and before relegation was confirmed his successor, Dave Bassett, made way for Micky Adams.

Akinbiyi, A .... 16(5)	Impey, A .... 20(7)	Savage, R 35
Ashton, J .... 3(4)	Izzet, M .... 29(2)	Scowcroft, J .... 21(3)
Benjamin, T .... 4(7)	Jones, M .... 6(4)	Sinclair, F .... 33(2)
Davidson, C .... 29(1)	Laursen, J 10	Stevenson, J .... -(6)
Deane, B .... 13(2)	Lewis, J .... 4(2)	Stewart, J .... 9(3)
Delaney, D .... 2(1)	Marshall, L .... 29(6)	Sturridge, D .... 8(1)
Dickov, P .... 11(1)	Oakes, S .... 16(5)	Taggart, G .... -(1)
Elliott, M 31	Piper, M .... 14(2)	Walker, I 35
Flowers, T .... 3(1)	Reeves, N .... 1(4)	Williamson, T .... -(1)
Gunnlaugsson, A .... -(2)	Rogers, A .... 9(4)	Wise, D .... 15(2)
Heath, M .... 3(2)	Rowett, G .... 9(2)	Wright, T .... -(1)

League goals (30): Deane 6, Scowcroft 5, Dickov 4, Izzet 4, Sturridge 3, Akinbiyi 2, Jones 1, Oakes 1, Piper 1, Stevenson 1, Wise 1, Opponents 1.
F.A. Cup goals (2): Scowcroft 2. **Worthington Cup goals (1):** Akinbiyi 1.
Average home League attendance: 19,835. **Player of Year:** Robbie Savage.

LIVERPOOL

Liverpool's progress under Gerard Houllier continued, despite the manager succumbing to the pressures of the job and undergoing 11 hours of life-saving heart surgery which kept him away from Anfield for five months. In his absence, Phil Thompson did sterling work keeping his team in the hunt for the championship and for Champions League success. Liverpool outpaced Manchester United to finish runners-up to Arsenal, their highest Premiership place, and reached the quarter-finals in Europe before a defence which had conceded just three goals in the previous 14 matches let in four to Bayer Leverkusen.

Anelka, N .... 13(7)	Gerrard, S .... 26(2)	Owen, M .... 25(4)
Arphexad, P .... 1(1)	Hamann, D 31	Redknapp, J .... 2(2)
Babbel, M 2	Henchoz, S 37	Riise, J A .... 34(4)
Barmby, N .... 2(4)	Heskey, E .... 26(9)	Smicer, V .... 13(9)
Berger, P .... 12(9)	Hyypia, S 37	Vignal, G .... 3(1)
Biscan, I .... 4(1)	Kirkland, C 1	Xavier, A .... 9(1)
Carragher, J 33	Litmanen, J .... 8(13)	Westerveld, S 1
Dudek, J 35	McAllister, G .... 14(11)	Wright, S .... 10(2)
Fowler, R .... 8(2)	Murphy, D .... 31(5)	

League goals (67): Owen 19, Heskey 9, Riise 7, Murphy 6, Anelka 4, Litmanen 4, Smicer 4, Fowler 3, Gerrard 3, Hyypia 3, Berger 1, Hamann 1, Redknapp 1, Xavier 1, Opponents 1.
F.A. Cup goals (3): Owen 2, Anelka 1. **Worthington Cup goals (1):** McAllister 1

MANCHESTER UNITED

A rare, trophy-less season for Sir Alex Ferguson, despite an outlay of £47m. on Ruud van Nistelrooy and Juan Sebastian Veron. Van Nistelrooy did everything expected of him with 36 goals in all competitions. Veron, in contrast, had a patchy season, although it was in defence where United were most vulnerable. A run of eight straight wins put them back in the title running, but a home defeat by Middlesbrough – who had earlier knocked them out of the F.A. Cup – handed the initiative to Arsenal. Ferguson's hopes of Champions League success in his native Glasgow ended with a semi-final defeat by Bayer Leverkusen.

Barthez, F 32	Giggs, R .... 18(7)	Silvestre, M .... 31(4)
Beckham, D .... 23(5)	Irwin, D .... 10(2)	Solskjaer, O .... 23(7)
Blanc, L 29	Johnsen, R .... 9(1)	Stam, J 1
Brown, W .... 15(2)	Keane, R 28	Stewart, M .... 2(1)
Butt, N .... 20(5)	May, D 2	Van Der Gouw, R ..... –(1)
Carroll, R .... 6(1)	Neville, G .... 31(3)	Van Nistelrooy, R ... 29(3)
Chadwick, L .... 5(3)	Neville, P .... 21(7)	Veron, J .... 24(2)
Cole, A .... 7(4)	O'Shea, J .... 4(5)	Wallwork, R .... –(1)
Forlan, D .... 6(7)	Scholes, P .... 30(5)	Yorke, D .... 4(6)
Fortune, Q .... 8(6)		

League goals (87): Van Nistelrooy 23, Solskjaer 17, Beckham 11, Scholes 8, Giggs 7, Veron 5, Cole 4, Keane 3, Neville, P 2, Blanc 1, Butt 1, Fortune 1, Johnsen 1, Yorke 1, Opponents 2.
F.A. Cup goals (3): Van Nistelrooy 2, Solskjaer 1. **Worthington Cup goals:** None.
Charity Shield goal (1): Van Nistelrooy 1. **Champions League goals (31):** Van Nistelrooy 10, Solskjaer 7, Beckham 5, Giggs 2, Blanc 2, Cole 1, Keane 1, Scholes 1, Silvestre 1, Opponents 1.
Average home League attendance: 67,557. **Player of Year:** Ruud van Nistelrooy.

MIDDLESBROUGH

Middlesbrough lost their first four matches and faltered again towards the end of the year when scoring only once in six games. But they found a marksman in Noel Whelan, some enterprise from the on-loan Benito Carbone and improved significantly in the second half of the season. A sweet victory for Steve McClaren at Old Trafford confirmed his team's rise, along with a place in the semi-finals of the F.A. Cup, where Arsenal were fortunate to prevail through an own goal by Gianluca Festa. Four straight defeats after that cost McClaren's team a top-half finish.

Beresford, M .... –(1)	Gavin, J .... 5(4)	Queudrue, F 28
Boksic, A .... 20(2)	Gordon, D .... –(1)	Richard, H .... 6(3)
Campbell, A .... –(4)	Greening, J 36	Schwarzer, M 21
Carbone, B 13	Hudson, M .... –(2)	Southgate, G 37
Cooper, C .... 14(4)	Ince, P 31	Stamp, P .... 3(3)
Crossley, M .... 17(1)	Job, J-D .... 3(1)	Stockdale, R .... 26(2)
Deane, B .... 6(1)	Johnston, A .... 13(4)	Vickers, S 2
Debeve, M .... 1(3)	Marinelli, C .... 12(8)	Whelan, N .... 18(1)
Downing, S .... 2(1)	Murphy, D .... –(5)	Wilkshire, L .... 6(1)
Ehiogu, U 29	Mustoe, R .... 31(5)	Wilson, M .... 2(8)
Festa, G 8	Nemeth, S .... 11(10)	Windass, D .... 8(19)
Fleming, C 8	Okon, P .... 1(3)	

League goals (35): Boksic 8, Whelan 4, Nemeth 3, Cooper 2, Ince 2, Marinelli 2, Mustoe 2, Queudrue 2, Carbone 1, Deane 1, Ehiogu 1, Festa 1, Greening 1, Johnston 1, Southgate 1, Stockdale 1, Windass 1, Opponents 1.
F.A. Cup goals (8): Whelan 3, Campbell 1, Ehiogu 1, Ince 1, Nemeth 1, Opponents 1.
Worthington Cup goals (4): Nemeth 2, Murphy 1, Wilson 1.
Average home League attendance: 28,458. **Player of Year:** Gareth Southgate.

NEWCASTLE UNITED

Bobby Robson's repeated assertion that his side were not ready for the championship began to look like pure psychology until successive defeats by Arsenal and Liverpool underlined the true order at the top. A sixth round F.A. Cup loss to Arsenal followed. Nevertheless, it was a season of considerable progress for Newcastle. They started it in the InterToto Cup and finished it with a Champions League place after securing fourth spot. Alan Shearer rounded off the campaign in style with his 200th Premiership goal, scoring 27 in all competitions and later came a knighthood for the manager.

Acuna, C	10(6)	Distin, S	20(8)	Lua Lua, L	4(16)
Ameobi, S	4(11)	Dyer, K	15(3)	McClen, J	3
Barton, W	4(1)	Elliott, R	26(1)	O'Brien, A	31(3)
Bassedas, C	1(1)	Given, S	38	Robert, L	34(2)
Bellamy, C	26(1)	Griffin, A	3(1)	Shearer, A	36(1)
Bernard, O	4(12)	Hughes, A	34	Solano, N	37
Cort, C	6(2)	Jenas, J	6(6)	Speed, G	28(1)
Dabizas, N	33(2)	Lee, R	15(1)		

League goals (74): Shearer 23, Bellamy 9, Robert 8, Solano 7, Speed 5, Acuna 3, Bernard 3, Dabizas 3, Dyer 3, Lua Lua 3, O'Brien 2, Cort 1, Elliott 1, Lee 1, Opponents 1.
F.A. Cup goals (8): Shearer 2, Acuna 1, Hughes 1, McClen 1, O'Brien 1, Robert 1, Solano 1. **Worthington Cup goals (9):** Bellamy 4, Ameobi 2, Shearer 2, Robert 1.
InterToto Cup goals (15): Solano 4, Ameobi 3, Hughes 2, Speed 2, Lua Lua 2, Bellamy 1, Quinn, W 1.
Average home League attendance: 51,372.

SOUTHAMPTON

In the splendid new surroundings of the St Mary's Stadium, Southampton were steered to safety by Gordon Strachan, a manager well-acquainted with life in the lower reaches from his time at Coventry. The controversy surrounding the dismissal of Stuart Gray to make way for him followed Southampton's spat with Tottenham over the transfer of Dean Richards. But Strachan calmed things down, made his side difficult to beat and with the experience of the former Coventry pair Paul Williams and Paul Telfer to the fore, they finished 11th, moving up four places by beating Newcastle United on the final day.

Beattie, J	24(4)	Fernandes, F	6(5)	Ormerod, B	8(10)
Benali, F	–(3)	Jones, P	36	Pahars, M	33(3)
Bleidelis, I	–(1)	Le Tissier, M	–(4)	Petrescu, D	–(2)
Bridge, W	38	Lundekvam, C	34	Richards, D	4
Davies, K	18(5)	Marsden, C	27(1)	Ripley, S	1(4)
Delap, R	24(4)	McDonald, S	–(2)	Rosler, U	3(1)
Delgado, A	–(1)	Monk, G	1(1)	Svensson, A	33(1)
Dodd, J	26(3)	Moss, N	2	Telfer, P	27(1)
Draper, M	1(1)	Murray, P	–(1)	Tessem, J	7(15)
El Khalej, T	12(2)	Oakley, M	26(1)	Williams, P	27(1)

League goals (46): Pahars 14, Beattie 12, Svensson 4, Marsden 3, Davies 2, Delap 2, Tessem 2, El Khalej 1, Fernandes 1, Oakley 1, Ormerod 1, Telfer 1, Opponents 2.
F.A. Cup goals (1): Pahars 1. **Worthington Cup goals (7):** Beattie 2, Svensson 2, Davies 1, El Khalej 1, Pahars 1.
Average home League attendance: 30,632. **Player of Year:** Chris Marsden/Wayne Bridge.

SUNDERLAND

Two spectacular goals by the former Rangers player Claudio Reyna against Leicester City eased Sunderland's relegation fears, but safety was not confirmed until the last day of a poor season. It prompted a club apology to the fans, who continued to pack the Stadium of Light, for failing to build on two successive seventh-place finishes. Sunderland scored fewer goals (29) than anyone, while first hurdle defeats by West Bromwich Albion in the F.A. Cup and Sheffield Wednesday in the Worthington Cup added to the pressure on Peter Reid.

Arca, J .... 20(2)	Kyle, K .... –(6)	Rae, A .... 1(2)
Bellion, D .... –(9)	Laslandes, L .... 5(7)	Reyna, C 17
Bjorklund, J .... 11(1)	Macho, J 4	Schwarz, S .... 18(2)
Butler, T .... 2(5)	Mboma, P .... 5(4)	Sorensen, T 34
Craddock, J 30	McAteer, J 26	Thirlwell, P .... 11(3)
Gray, M 35	McCann, G 29	Thome, E 12
Haas, B 27	McCartney, G ...... 12(6)	Varga, S 9
Hutchison, D 2	Phillips, K 37	Williams, D .... 23(5)
Kilbane, K .... 24(4)	Quinn, N .... 24(14)	

League goals (29): Phillips 11, Quinn 6, Reyna 3, Kilbane 2, McAteer 2, Arca 1, Craddock 1, Mboma 1, Schwarz 1, Thome 1.
F.A. Cup goals (1): Phillips 1. **Worthington Cup goals (2):** Phillips 1, Laslandes 1.
Average home League attendance: 46,744. **Player of Year:** Jody Craddock.

TOTTENHAM

Tottenham were true to their Cup traditions until a double blow meant there would be no silverware from the season. First they lost 2-1 to underdogs Blackburn Rovers in the final of the Worthington Cup. Then a Chelsea side overwhelmed in those semi-finals turned the tables by winning 4-0 at White Hart Lane in the sixth round of the F.A. Cup. Tottenham headed the pack outside the top six in the Premiership before a poor finish to the season produced only one win in five games and meant they were overtaken by West Ham United and Aston Villa.

Anderton, D .... 33(2)	Gardner, A .... 11(4)	Richards, D 24
Bunjevcevic, G ..... 5(1)	Iversen, S .... 12(6)	Sheringham, T ...... 33(1)
Clemence, S .... 4(2)	Keller, K 9	Sherwood, T .... 15(4)
Davies, S .... 22(9)	King, L 32	Sullivan, N 29
Doherty, G .... 4(3)	Leonhardsen, O .... 2(5)	Taricco, M 30
Etherington, M ...... 3(8)	Perry, C .... 30(3)	Thatcher, B .... 11(1)
Ferdinand, L ...... 22(3)	Poyet, G .... 32(2)	Thelwell, A .... –(2)
Freund, S .... 19(1)	Rebrov, S .... 9(21)	Ziege, C 27

League goals (49): Poyet 10, Sheringham 10, Ferdinand 9, Ziege 5, Anderton 4, Davies 4, Iversen 4, Richards 2, Rebrov 1.
F.A. Cup goals (10): Poyet 3, Anderton 1, Etherington 1, Ferdinand 1, Iversen 1, Sheringham 1, Ziege 1, Opponents 1. **Worthington Cup goals (21):** Ferdinand 5, Davies 3, Rebrov 3, Iversen 2, Sheringham 2, Anderton 1, King 1, Poyet 1, Sherwood 1, Ziege 1, Opponents 1.
Average home League attendance: 35,000. **Player of Year:** Neil Sullivan.

WEST HAM UNITED

The knives were out for Glenn Roeder, Harry Redknapp's successor as manager, when a 5-0 defeat at Everton was followed by a 7-1 thrashing at Blackburn. Paolo Di Canio, for one, expressed deep concern at the direction of the club. But West Ham kept faith with Roeder and three successive wins calmed the nerves. His side conceded five on two more occasions – one a 5-3 mini-classic against Manchester United – but still did enough to finish at the head of the teams outside the top six.

Byrne, S .... –(1)	Carrick, M 30	Courtois, L .... 5(2)
Camara, T .... –(1)	Cole, J .... 29(1)	Dailly, C 38

Defoe, J .... 14(21)	Kitson, P .... 3(4)	Repka, T 31
Di Canio, P 26	Labant, V .... 7(5)	Schemmel, S 35
Foxe, H .... 4(2)	Lomas, S .... 14(1)	Sinclair, T 34
Garcia, R .... 2(6)	McCann, G .... –(3)	Soma, R .... 1(2)
Hislop, S 12	Minto, S 5	Song, R 5
Hutchison, D 24	Moncur, J .... 7(12)	Todorov, S .... 2(4)
James, D 26	Pearce, I .... 8(1)	Winterburn, N .... 29(2)
Kanoute, F 27		

League goals (48): Kanoute 11, Defoe 10, Di Canio 9, Sinclair 5, Lomas 4, Kitson 3, Carrick 2, Pearce 2, Hutchison 1, Schemmel 1.
F.A. Cup goals (6): Defoe 4, Cole 1, Kanoute 1. **Worthington Cup goals:** None.
Average home League attendance: 31,356. **Player of Year:** Sebastien Schemmel.

NATIONWIDE LEAGUE – FIRST DIVISION

BARNSLEY

Barnsley seemed to have turned the corner after Steve Parkin arrived from Rochdale in November to replace Nigel Spackman as manager. They went on a run of 12 matches without defeat, thanks in no small measure to Mike Sheron's goals, and mid-table security seemed to beckon. Then Sheron went off the boil, his defence started leaking goals again and successive defeats by Manchester City and Norwich City sealed relegation for a club who were in the Premiership four seasons earlier.

Barker, C .... 43(1)	Gallen, K .... 8(1)	Naylor, R .... 7(1)
Barnard, D .... 34(4)	Ghent, M 1	Neil, A .... 17(8)
Bedeau, A .... –(3)	Gibbs, P 4	O'Callaghan, B .... 1(5)
Bertos, L .... 2(2)	Gorre, D .... 14(5)	Oster, J 2
Betsy, K 10	Jones, G 25	Parkin, J 4
Chettle, S .... 31(1)	Jones, L .... 2(11)	Rankin, I .... 2(7)
Christie, J .... –(1)	Kay, A .... –(1)	Regan, C .... 6(4)
Corbo, M .... –(1)	Lumsden, C 32	Sand, P .... 4(2)
Crooks, L .... 20(6)	Marriott, A .... 17(1)	Scothern, A .... –(1)
Donovan, K .... 28(4)	McSwegan, G .... 1(4)	Sheron, M .... 23(10)
Dyer, B .... 42(2)	Miller, K 28	Tinkler, E .... 8(8)
Fallon, R .... 2(7)	Morgan, C 42	Ward, M .... 12(3)
Flynn, M 7	Mulligan, D .... 27(1)	

League goals (59): Dyer 14, Sheron 12, Barnard 7, Lumsden 7, Morgan 4, Barker 3, Gallen 2, Gorre 2, Neil 2, Donovan 1, Jones, G 1, Rankin 1, Sand 1, Opponents 2.
F.A. Cup goals (2): Barnard 1, Dyer 1. **Worthington Cup goals (5):** Dyer 3, Jones, L 1, Tinkler 1.
Average home League attendance: 13,322. **Player of Year:** Bruce Dyer.

BIRMINGHAM CITY

Steve Bruce led Birmingham back to the top division after 16 years in the most dramatic fashion. A last-minute goal by Stern John accounted for Millwall in the play-off semi-finals, then 18-year-old substitute Darren Carter completed a 4-2 penalty shoot-out success after the final against Norwich City ended 1-1. It was the reward for the way Bruce reshaped the team after taking over as manager from Trevor Francis and for a 10-match unbeaten run to the end of the season which took Birmingham into the top six when the odds were stacked against them.

Bak, A. .... 2(2)	Eaden, N .... 24(5)	Holdsworth, D .... 3(1)
Bennett, I 18	Ferrari, C .... –(4)	Horsfield, G .... 33(7)
Bragstad, P 3	Fleming, C 6	Hutchinson, J .... –(3)
Burrows, D .... 9(3)	Furlong, P .... 2(9)	Hyde, G .... 1(4)
Carter, D .... 12(1)	Gill, J 14	Hughes, B .... 27(4)
Devlin, P .... 11(2)	Grainger, M .... 39(1)	Hughes, M 3

356

John, S	15	Luntala, T	9(6)	Sonner, D	10(5)
Johnson, A	9(14)	Marcelo	17(4)	Tebily, O	7
Johnson, D	5(3)	McCarthy, J	3(1)	Vaesen, N	22(1)
Johnson, M	30(2)	Mooney, T	29(4)	Vickers, S	13(1)
Kelly, A	6	O'Connor, M	24	Williams, T	4
Kenna, J	21	Purse, D	35(1)	Woodhouse, C	18(10)
Lazaridis, S	22(10)				

Play-offs – Appearances: Grainger 3, Horsfield 3, Hughes, B 3, John 3, Kenna 3, Mooney 3, Tebily 3, Vaesen 3, Devlin 2, Purse 2, Vickers 2, Carter 1(1), Johnson, D 1, Johnson, M 1, Lazaridis – (3), Johnson, A –(2).
League goals (70): Mooney 13, Marcelo 12, Horsfield 11, Hughes, B 7, John 7, Grainger 4, Johnson, A 3, Purse 3, Carter 1, Devlin 1, Eaden 1, Furlong 1, Johnson, D 1, Johnson, M 1, Sonner 1, Vickers 1, Opponents 2. **Play-off goals (3):** Horsfield 1, Hughes, B 1, John 1.
F.A. Cup goals: None. **Worthington Cup goals (6):** Hughes, B 2, Mooney 2, Johnson, A 1, Johnson, M 1.
Average home League attendance: 21,978. **Player of Year:** Geoff Horsfield.

BRADFORD CITY

Bradford City flattered to deceive on their return to Division One after two seasons in the top flight. They kicked off with three straight wins, then lapsed into inconsistent home form which Nicky Law, who came from Chesterfield to take over from Jim Jefferies as manager mid-way through the season, was unable to correct. There were 12 defeats at Valley Parade – only Stockport County suffered more on their own ground – so it wasn't surprising that Bradford finished below half-way.

Atherton, P	1	Grayson, S	7	McCall, S	42(1)
Blake, R	19(7)	Halle, L	31(1)	Molenaar, R	21
Bower, M	9(1)	Jacobs, W	37(1)	Muggleton, C	4
Cadamarteri, D	14	Jess, E	43(2)	Myers, A	28(4)
Caldwell, S	9	Jorgensen, C	13(5)	Sharpe, L	11(7)
Carbone, B	10(1)	Juanjo	5(12)	Tod, A	25(5)
Combe, A	16	Kearney, T	5	Walsh, G	17(1)
Davison, A	9	Lawrence, J	13(8)	Ward, A	27
Emanuel, L	8(2)	Lee, A	–(1)	Wetherall, D	17(2)
Etherington, M	12(1)	Locke, G	26(5)	Whalley, G	21(2)
Grant, G	4(6)	Makel, L	2(11)		

League goals (69): Jess 14, Blake 10, Ward 10, Carbone 5, Tod 4, McCall 3, Bower 2, Cadamarteri 2, Lawrence 2, Locke 2, Myers 2, Sharpe 2, Wetherall 2, Etherington 1, Grant 1, Halle 1, Jacobs 1, Jorgensen 1, Juanjo 1, Opponents 3.
F.A. Cup goals: None **Worthington Cup goals (7):** Blake 2, Tod 2, Lawrence 1, McCall 1, Ward 1.
Average home League attendance: 15,488. **Player of Year:** Andy Myers.

BURNLEY

So near, yet so far from the play-offs. Two late Paul Gascoigne free-kicks in the final game of the season against Coventry City were saved by Magnus Hedman, Burnley were restricted to a 1-0 win and Norwich City edged them out of the top six by a single goal. Burnley were top going into the New Year, but could not maintain the momentum and the signing of Gascoigne from Everton on a short-term contract failed to resurrect the team's fortunes during the run-in.

Armstrong, G	11(7)	Briscoe, L	43(1)	Gascoigne, P	3(3)
Ball, K	37(5)	Cook, P	25(3)	Gnohere, A	31(3)
Beresford, M	13	Cox, I	32(2)	Grant, A	26(2)
Blake, R	1(9)	Davis, S	22(1)	Johnrose, L	–(5)
Branch, G	8(2)	Ellis, T	–(10)	Johnson, D	8

Little, G .... 31(6)	Moore, I .... 41(5)	Taylor, G .... 35(5)
Maylett, B .... –(10)	Mullin, J .... –(4)	Thomas, M .... 10(2)
McGregor, M 1	Papadopoulos, D .... –(6)	Weller, P .... 29(9)
Michopoulos, N 33	Payton, A .... –(17)	West, D .... 43(1)
Moore, A .... 23(6)		

League goals (70): Taylor 16, Moore, I 11, Little 9, Briscoe 5, Cook 5, Johnson 5, Payton 4, Moore, A 3, Gnohere 3, Armstrong 2, Cox 2, Weller 2, Davis 1, Ellis 1, Opponents 1.
F.A. Cup goals (5): Moore, I 3, Little 1, Moore, A 1. **Worthington Cup goals (2):** McGregor 1, Moore, A 1.
Average home League attendance: 15,947. **Player of Year:** Dean West.

COVENTRY CITY

A turbulent season at Highfield Road, where manager Gordon Strachan left by mutual consent after five matches, his successor Roland Nilsson was sacked after six months and in between chairman Bryan Richardson was ousted in a boardroom coup. A run of 11 League matches without defeat under Nilsson more than compensated for a poor start to the season. But once that purple patch came to an end, Coventry were too inconsistent for a play-off place. Gary McAllister's return as player-manager improved the mood of supporters.

Antonelius, T .... 3(2)	Goram, A .... 6(1)	Nilsson, R 9
Betts, R .... 4(5)	Guerrero, I .... 3(1)	Normann, R .... –(2)
Bothroyd, J .... 24(7)	Hall, M .... 27(2)	O'Neill, K .... 7(4)
Breen, J 30	Healy, C 17	Pead, C 1
Carbonari, H 5	Hedman, M 34	Quinn, B .... 18(4)
Carsley, L .... 25(1)	Hughes, L .... 35(3)	Safri, Y .... 32(1)
Chippo, Y .... 29(5)	Joachim, J .... 4(12)	Shaw, R .... 29(3)
Davenport, C .... 1(2)	Kirkland, C 1	Strachan, G .... –(1)
Delorge, L .... 21(7)	Konjic, M 38	Thompson, D .... 35(2)
Edworthy, M .... 18(2)	Martinez, J .... 5(6)	Trollope, P .... 5(1)
Eustace, J .... 5(1)	McSheffrey, G .... 1(7)	Williams, P .... 4(1)
Flowers, T 5	Mills, L .... 19(1)	Zuniga, Y .... 1(6)
Fowler, L .... 5(8)		

League goals (59): Hughes 14, Thompson 12, Bothroyd 6, Mills 5, Chippo 4, Delorge 4, Martinez 3, Carsley 2, Healey 2, Konjic 2, Hall 1, Joachim 1, McSheffrey 1, Safri 1, Opponents 1.
F.A. Cup goals: None. **Worthington Cup goals (2):** Carsley 1, Thompson 1.
Average home League attendance: 16,150. **Player of Year:** David Thompson.

CREWE ALEXANDRA

Dario Gradi's success in keeping this homespun club in Division One against the odds came to an end because of a run of 11 games from mid-March which failed to produce a victory. During the run-in they had fixtures in hand on those teams directly above them, but failed to take advantage. So it was a disappointing end to the season for the longest-serving manager in English football, who had earlier reached 1,000 games in charge at Gresty Road since his appointment in 1983.

Ashton, D .... 29(2)	Jack, R .... 24(9)	Smith, S .... 41(1)
Bankole, A 28	Jones, S .... 1(5)	Sorvel, N .... 31(7)
Barrett, G .... 2(1)	Little, C .... 8(9)	Street, K .... 2(7)
Brammer, D .... 29(1)	Lunt, K 45	Tait, P .... 3(9)
Charnock, P .... 21(2)	Macauley, S 9	Thomas, G .... 8(6)
Collins, W .... 13(7)	McCready, C .... –(1)	Vaughan, D .... 11(2)
Foster, S .... 29(5)	Navarro, A 7	Walker, R .... –(1)
Grant, J 1	Richards, M .... 1(3)	Walton, D .... 29(2)
Hulse, R .... 40(1)	Rix, R .... 6(15)	Whalley, G 7
Ince, C .... 18(1)	Sodje, E .... 34(2)	Wright, D .... 29(1)

League goals (47): Hulse 12, Ashton 7, Jack 7, Foster 5, Lunt 5, Brammer 2, Sodje 2, Thomas 2, Charnock 1, Little 1, Smith 1, Street 1, Walton 1.
F.A. Cup goals (7): Ashton 3, Foster 1, Rix 1, Thomas 1, Vaughan 1. **Worthington Cup goals (6):** Brammer 1, Hulse 1, Little 1, Richards 1, Smith 1, Walton 1.
Average home League attendance: 7,128. **Player of Year:** Efe Sodje.

CRYSTAL PALACE

Crystal Palace were prospering, with Clinton Morrison and Dougie Freedman scoring plenty of goals, until manager Steve Bruce set his heart on taking over at Birmingham City after the departure of Trevor Francis from St Andrews. Francis replaced him in a bizarre managerial 'swop' and later signed the much-criticised Ade Akinbiyi from Leicester City. Things were never the same. A 5-2 defeat at Grimsby started a poor run-in, during which Palace failed to score on six occasions, and they finished 10th.

Akinbiyi, A .... 9(5)	Freedman, D .... 39(1)	Murphy, S 11
Austin, D .... 27(8)	Gooding, S .... –(1)	Popovic, T 20
Benjamin, T .... 5(1)	Granville, D 16	Riihilahti, A 45
Berhalter, G .... 6(8)	Gray, J .... 35(8)	Rodger, S .... 29(7)
Black, T .... 5(20)	Harrison, C .... 4(2)	Routledge, W .... –(2)
Carasso, C .... –(1)	Hopkin, D .... 13(7)	Rubins, A .... –(7)
Clarke, M 28	Kabba, S .... 1(3)	Smith, J .... 28(4)
Edwards, C 9	Kirovski, J .... 25(11)	Symons, K 9
Fan Zhiyi 2	Kolinko, A .... 18(1)	Thomson, S .... 10(13)
Fleming, C 17	Morrison, C 45	Vickers, S 6
Frampton, A .... 1(1)	Mullins, H 43	

League goals (70): Morrison 22, Freedman 20, Kirovski 5, Riihilahti 5, Smith 4, Hopkin 3, Akinbiyi 2, Gray 2, Popovic 2, Benjamin 1, Berhalter 1, Rodger 1, Opponents 2.
F.A. Cup goals: None. **Worthington Cup (7):** Black 2, Morrison 2, Freedman 1, Riihilahti 1, Rodger 1.
Average home League attendance: 18,120. **Player of Year:** Dougie Freedman.

GILLINGHAM

Competing against clubs with far greater resources, Gillingham continued to hold their own under the guidance of Andy Hessenthaler and with Marlon King's goals proving a major influence. They held on securely to a mid-table position and made an impact in the F.A. Cup, winning at Wolves, ending the run of Bristol Rovers and then causing a few ripples at Highbury. Ty Gooden scored a delightful goal before Arsenal were forced to bring on Thierry Henry and Robert Pires for a 5-2 win.

Ashby, B 28	Ipoua, G .... 20(20)	Perpetuini, D .... 25(9)
Bartram, V 36	James, K .... –(9)	Rose, R .... 2(1)
Brown, J 10	King, M .... 38(4)	Samuel, J .... 7(1)
Browning, M .... 38(3)	Nosworthy, N 29	Saunders, M .... 6(13)
Butters, G .... 21(2)	Onuora, I .... 31(2)	Shaw, P .... 27(10)
Edge, R 14	Osborn, S .... 23(5)	Smith, P 46
Gooden, T .... 20(5)	Patterson, M .... 17(3)	Spiller, D .... –(1)
Hessenthaler, A ...... 10(7)	Pennock, A .... 9(1)	Taylor, R .... 3(8)
Hope, C 46		

League goals (64): King 17, Onuora 11, Ipoua 8, Shaw 7, Hope 4, Osborn 4, Browning 3, Ashby 2, Smith 2, Butters 1, Gooden 1, Perpetuini 1, Saunders 1, Opponents 2.
F.A. Cup goals (4): Gooden 1, King 1, Shaw 1, Opponents 1. **Worthington Cup goals (4):** King 2, Ipoua 1, Onuora 1.
Average home League attendance: 8,601. **Player of Year:** Paul Smith.

GRIMSBY TOWN

What a roller-coaster season for Grimsby, who were top of the table after six games and then won only one of their next 20 in the League. Paul Groves, appointed player-manager when Lennie Lawrence was sacked, also found victories hard to come by until the arrival of Andy Todd on loan from Charlton Athletic. Suddenly the goals flowed – 5-2 against Crystal Palace, 6-2 against Wimbledon and a 3-1 success over Burnley in the last home game which ensured survival. All that and a 2-1 triumph over holders Liverpool in the Worthington Cup at Anfield.

Allen, B .... 19(9)	Coyne, D 45	Pouton, A 35
Beharall, D .... 13(1)	Croudson, S 1	Pringle, M 2
Boulding, M .... 24(11)	Falconer, W .... 1(1)	Raven, P .... 4(5)
Broomes, M .... 13(2)	Ford, S .... 8(5)	Robinson, P .... 1(4)
Burnett, W .... 18(14)	Gallimore, A 38	Rowan, J .... 19(5)
Busscher, R .... –(1)	Groves, P 43	Smith, D 4
Butterfield, D .... 43(3)	Jeffrey, M .... 4(14)	Taylor, R 4
Campbell, S .... 32(1)	Jevons, P .... 25(6)	Thompson, C .... 4(4)
Chapman, B .... 12(5)	Livingstone, S .... –(3)	Todd, A 12
Coldicott, S .... 19(7)	McDermott, J 24	Ward, I 1
Cooke, T 3	Neilson, A .... 8(2)	Willems, M .... 27(3)

League goals (50): Boulding 11, Jevons 6, Pouton 5, Allen 4, Rowan 4, Campbell 3, Todd 3, Burnett 2, Groves 2, Butterfield 2, Cooke 1, Ford 1, Jeffrey 1, Smith 1, Taylor 1, Willems 1, Opponents 2.
F.A. Cup goals: None. **Worthington Cup goals (7):** Broomes 2, Jevons 2, Allen 1, Jeffrey 1, Rowan 1.
Average home League attendance: 6,430. **Player of Year:** Danny Coyne.

MANCHESTER CITY

Kevin Keegan led Manchester City back to the Premiership in typically cavalier fashion. They scored four or more goals on nine occasions, finished with a total of 108 and clinched the title with a Darren Huckerby hat-trick in a 5-1 win over Barnsley. The fact that City conceded 52 emphasised what entertainment they served up – one way or another. Shaun Goater led the way with 32 in all competitions, Huckerby finished with 26 and Paulo Wanchope 13 despite missing more than half the season. But many rated Algerian midfielder Ali Benarbia the team's star man.

Benarbia, A 38	Horlock, K .... 33(9)	Pearce, S 38
Berkovic, E .... 20(5)	Howey, S 34	Ritchie, P .... –(8)
Charvet, L 3	Huckerby, D .... 30(10)	Shuker, C .... –(2)
Colosimo, S .... –(6)	Jensen, N .... 16(2)	Sun Jihai .... 2(5)
Dickov, P .... –(7)	Killen, C .... –(3)	Tiatto, D .... 36(1)
Dunne, R .... 41(2)	Macken, J .... 4(4)	Toure, A .... –(1)
Edghill, R .... 9(2)	Mears, T .... –(1)	Wanchope, P .... 14(1)
Etuhu, D .... 11(1)	Mettomo, L .... 17(6)	Weaver, N .... 24(1)
Goater, S 42	Mike, L .... 1(1)	Whitley, J .... –(2)
Grant, A .... 2(1)	Nash, C .... 22(1)	Wiekens, G .... 24(5)
Granville, D .... 12(4)	Negouai, C .... 2(3)	Wright-Phillips, S ... 31(4)
Haaland, A .... –(3)		

League goals (108): Goater 28, Huckerby 20, Wanchope 12, Benarbia 8, Wright-Phillips 8, Horlock 7, Berkovic 6, Macken 5, Howey 3, Pearce 3, Dunne 1, Granville 1, Jensen 1, Mettomo 1, Negouai 1, Tiatto 1, Opponents 2.
F.A. Cup goals (6): Goater 2, Berkovic 1, Horlock 1, Huckerby 1, Wanchope 1.
Worthington Cup goals (10): Huckerby 5, Goater 2, Dickov 1, Shuker 1, Opponents 1.
Average home League attendance: 33,058. **Player of Year:** Ali Benarbia.

MILLWALL

Evergreen Steve Claridge scored 17 goals and Dion Dublin proved an influential loan signing for the final month of the season as promoted Millwall exceeded all expectations by reaching the play-offs. When Mark McGhee's team went on to hold Birmingham City 1-1 at St Andrews, hopes were high of a place in the final. But they were dashed by a last-minute Stern John goal at the New Den and disappointment turned to disgust as 47 police officers were injured in violent scenes at the end of the game.

Bircham, M .... 22(2)	Hearn, C .... –(2)	Phillips, M 1
Braniff, K .... –(1)	Ifill, P .... 27(13)	Reid, S .... 33(2)
Bull, R .... 20(6)	Kinet, C .... 11(6)	Ryan, R .... 32(5)
Cahill, T 43	Lawrence, M .... 24(2)	Sadlier, R .... 36(1)
Claridge, S .... 39(2)	Livermore, D 43	Savarese, G .... –(1)
Dublin, D 5	McPhail, S 3	Stamp, P .... –(1)
Dunne, A .... –(1)	Moody, P .... –(1)	Sweeney, P .... –(1)
Dyche, S 35	Naylor, R .... 2(1)	Tuttle, D 5
Green, R .... 12(1)	Neill, L .... 2(2)	Ward, D .... 10(4)
Gueret, W .... –(1)	Nethercott, S 46	Warner, T 46
Harris, N .... 9(12)	Odunsi, A .... –(2)	

Play-offs – Appearances: Bull 2, Cahill 2, Dublin 2, Ifill 2, Lawrence 2, Livermore 2, Nethercott 2, Reid 2, Ward 2, Warner 2, Claridge 1(1).
League goals (69): Claridge 17, Sadlier 14, Cahill 13, Reid 5, Harris 4, Ifill 4, Dyche 3, Kinet 3, Nethercott 3, Dublin 2, Neill 1. **Play-off goals (1):** Dublin 1.
F.A. Cup goals (2): Sadlier 2. **Worthington Cup goals (3):** Claridge 1, Moody 1, Sadlier 1.
Average home League attendance: 13,253. **Player of Year:** Steve Claridge.

NORWICH CITY

Norwich City came up on the rails to collect 17 points from their final seven matches and claim the final play-off spot from Burnley by a single goal. Then a last-minute header by Malky Mackay gave them the cushion of a 3-1 to defend successfully in the second leg of the semi-final against Wolves. When Iwan Roberts, who missed most of the second half of the season through injury, opened the scoring in the first-minute of extra-time against Birmingham City in the final, the Premiership beckoned. Instead, Norwich conceded an equaliser and their dream died when losing out 4-2 in a penalty shoot-out.

Abbey, Z 6	Holt, G 46	Nedergaard, S .... 37(3)
Benjamin, T .... 3(3)	Kenton, D .... 30(3)	Nielsen, D .... 22(1)
Crichton, P .... 5(1)	Libbra, M .... 17(17)	Notman, A .... 6(23)
Drury, A 35	Llewellyn, C .... 5(8)	Rivers, M .... 19(13)
Easton, C .... 10(4)	Mackay, M 44	Roberts, A .... 4(1)
Emblen, N .... 1(1)	McGovern, B .... 5(4)	Roberts, I .... 29(2)
Fleming, C 46	McVeigh, P .... 37(5)	Russell, D .... 13(10)
Green, R 41	Mulryne, P .... 39(1)	Sutch, D .... 6(13)

Play-offs – Appearances: Drury 3, Easton 3, Fleming 3, Green 3, Holt 3, Kenton 3, Mackay 3, McVeigh 3, Mulryne 3, Rivers 3, Nielsen 3, Notman –(3), Roberts, I –(3), Sutch –(2), Libbra –(1).
League goals (60): Roberts, I 13, McVeigh 8, Nielsen 8, Libbra 7, Mulryne 6, Kenton 4, Mackay 3, Holt 2, Nedergaard 2, Rivers 2, Easton 1, Opponents 3. **Play-off goals (4):** Mackay 1, McVeigh 1, Rivers 1, Roberts, I 1. **F.A. Cup goals:** None. **Worthington Cup goals:** None.
Average home League attendance: 18,628. **Player of Year:** Gary Holt.

NOTTINGHAM FOREST

The sale of 18-year-old Jermaine Jenas to Newcastle United for £5m., followed quickly by Stern John's move to Birmingham City, underlined Forest's financial plight. It was a difficult first season for Paul Hart, who moved up from youth team manager when David

Platt took over the England U-21 team. But his youthful team played some attractive football at times to keep City Ground attendances healthy, with an average of more than 21,000 despite the lack of success.

Bart-Williams, C 17	Harewood, M .... 20(8)	Prutton, D 43
Bopp, E .... 12(7)	Hjelde, J 42	Reid, A .... 19(10)
Brennan, J 41	Jenas, J 28	Rogers, A 3
Cash, B .... -(5)	John, S .... 20(6)	Scimeca, R .... 35(2)
Dawson, K 3	Johnson, A .... -(1)	Summerbee, N 17
Dawson, M 1	Johnson, D .... 17(5)	Thompson, J 8
Doig, C 8	Jones, G .... 2(3)	Vaughan, A .... 5(3)
Edds, G .... -(1)	Lester, J .... 23(9)	Ward, D 46
Edwards, C .... 2(4)	Louis-Jean, M .... 37(1)	Westcarr, C .... -(8)
Foy, K 2	Proudlock, A 3	Williams, G 44
Gray, A .... 8(8)		

League goals (50): John 13, Harewood 11, Lester 5, Jenas 4, Bart-Williams 3, Johnson, D 3, Prutton 3, Summerbee 2, Bopp 1, Doig 1, Gray 1, Jones 1, Louis-Jean 1, Opponents 1.
F.A. Cup goals: None. **Worthington Cup goals (3):** Bart-Williams 1, John 1, Lester 1.
Average home League attendance: 21,699. **Player of Year:** Gareth Williams.

PORTSMOUTH

A testing season at Fratton Park started with defeat by Colchester United in the Worthington Cup. It continued with inconsistent League form and a quick F.A. exit at the hands of Leyton Orient. Then chairman Milan Mandaric threatened not to pay his players and coaching staff becauser of poor results. Finally, manager Graham Rix was sacked and replaced by director of football Harry Redknapp. Peter Crouch scored 19 goals before he was sold to Aston Villa for a club-record £5m., while Robert Prosinecki supplied some memorable moments.

Barrett, N .... 23(3)	Hiley, S .... 28(5)	Prosinecki, R .... 30(3)
Beasant, D 27	Howe, E 1	Quashie, N .... 33(2)
Biagini, L .... 6(2)	Ilic, S 7	Rudonja, M .... 2(1)
Bradbury, L .... 17(5)	Kawaguchi, Y 11	Summerbell, M 5
Brady, G .... 1(5)	Lovell, S .... 8(11)	Tardif, C 1
Burchill, M .... 5(1)	Miglioranzi, S .... 1(2)	Thogersen, T .... 2(3)
Buxton, L .... 27(2)	Mills, L 2	Tiler, C .... 7(1)
Cooper, S .... 3(4)	Moore, D 2	Todorov, S 3
Crouch, P 37	O'Neil, G .... 27(6)	Vincent, J .... 29(5)
Crowe, J .... 18(4)	Panopoulos, M .... 1(1)	Vine, R .... 3(8)
Curtis, T .... 3(6)	Pettefer, C .... 1(1)	Waterman, D .... 8(1)
Derry, S 12	Pitt, C .... 29(10)	Wilson, S 5
Edinburgh, J 7	Primus, L .... 21(1)	Zamperini, A 16
Harper, K .... 37(2)		

League goals (60): Crouch 18, Prosinecki 9, Bradbury 7, Burchill 4, Pitt 3, Barrett 2, Biagini 2, Lovell 2, Primus 2, Quashie 2, Zamperini 2, Crowe 1, Edinburgh 1, Harper 1, O'Neil 1, Todorov 1, Vincent 1, Opponents 1.
F.A. Cup goals (1): Opponents 1. **Worthington Cup goals (1):** Crouch 1.
Average home League attendance: 15,121. **Player of Year:** Robert Prosinecki.

PRESTON NORTH END

Preston could probably have been forgiven for not sustaining their bid for a play-off place following the departure to Everton of manager David Moyes, 10 days after striker Jon Macken's move to Manchester City. Instead the team, under caretaker Kelham O'Hanlon, displayed commendable resolve to stay in touch and it took a defeat by Crystal Palace in their penultimate match to rule them out of contention. Former Scotland coach Craig Brown came in as the new manager.

Ainsworth, G	3(2)	Gallacher, K	1(4)	Macken, J	28(3)
Alexander, G	45	Gregan, S	40(1)	McKenna, P	37(1)
Anderson, I	16(15)	Gudjonsson, T	4(3)	Moilanen, T	23(1)
Barry-Murphy, B	2(2)	Healy, D	35(9)	Murdock, C	22(1)
Basham, S	–(15)	Hendry, C	2	Rankine, M	24(2)
Cartwright, L	34(2)	Jackson, M	12(1)	Reid, P	–(1)
Cresswell, R	27(13)	Keane, M	17(3)	Robinson, S	–(2)
Eaton, A	6(6)	Kidd, R	5(1)	Skora, E	2(2)
Edwards, R	36	Lucas, D	23(1)	Wijnhard, C	6
Etuhu, D	16	Lucketti, C	40		

League goals (71): Cresswell 13, Healy 10, Macken 8, Alexander 6, Anderson 5, McKenna 4, Rankine 4, Etuhu 3, Lucketti 3, Wijnhard 3, Edwards 2, Keane 2, Murdock 2, Ainsworth 1, Basham 1, Cartwright 1, Gallacher 1, Gregan 1, Reid 1.
F.A. Cup goals (5): Cresswell 2, Alexander 1, Macken 1, Skora 1. **Worthington Cup goals (4):** Cresswell 1, Gallacher 1, Jackson 1, Macken 1.
Average home League attendance: 14,887. **Player of Year:** Richard Cresswell.

ROTHERHAM UNITED

Another remarkable performance by Ronnie Moore and his team after climbing from the Third to the First Division in successive seasons. Few would have bet against relegation when Rotherham were rock bottom after failing to win any of their first 10 games. But they battled their way out of immediate danger and then dug deep again at the end of the season to secure draws against five of the top seven teams, including Manchester City and West Bromwich Albion, before staying up on goal difference.

Barker, R	11(24)	Lee, A	37(1)	Robins, M	34(7)
Beech, C	2(6)	Lowndes, N	2	Scott, R	35(3)
Branston, G	10	McIntosh, M	39	Sedgwick, C	39(5)
Bryan, M	19	Miranda, J	2	Swailes, C	44
Byfield, D	3	Monkhouse, A	21(17)	Talbot, M	36(2)
Daws, N	21(14)	Mullin, J	27(7)	Warne, P	14(11)
Gray, I	–(1)	Pollitt, M	46	Watson, K	19
Hurst, P	45				

League goals (52): Robins 15, Lee 9, Swailes 6, McIntosh 4, Barker 3, Scott 3, Byfield 2, Monkhouse 2, Mullin 2, Beech 1, Branston 1, Daws 1, Sedgwick 1, Talbot 1, Watson 1.
F.A. Cup goals (4): Mullin 2, Barker 1, Warne 1. **Worthington Cup goals (2):** Lee 1, Robins 1.
Average home League attendance: 7,476. **Player of Year:** Martin McIntosh.

SHEFFIELD UNITED

A black day in mid-March blighted the season at Bramall Lane. Referee Eddie Wolstenholme took the unprecedented step of abandoning the match against West Bromwich Albion with United reduced to six men by the dismissals of three players and injuries. The Football League ruled that Albion's 3-0 lead should stand as a result. United badly needed something positive to start repairing the damage. Successive wins over Millwall and Burnley did the trick, but an overall shortage of goals cast them adrift in mid-table.

Asaba, C	26(3)	Javary, J-P	6(1)	Peschisolido, P	19(10)
Brown, M	36	Killeen, L	–(1)	Phelan, T	8
Cryan, C	–(1)	Kozluk, R	6(2)	Sandford, L	5(1)
Curle, K	30(2)	Littlejohn, A	1(2)	Santos, G	14(16)
Devlin, P	14(5)	Lovell, S	3(2)	Smith, G	1(6)
De Vogt, W	5(1)	Mallon, R	–(1)	Suffo, P	10(10)
D'Jaffo, L	23(9)	Montgomery, N	14(17)	Tonge, M	27(3)
Doane, B	14	Murphy, S	27	Tracey, S	41
Ford, R	20(5)	Ndlovu, P	41(4)	Uhlenbeek, G	19(1)
Furlong, P	4	Nicholson, S	21(4)	Ullathorne, R	14
Jagielka, P	14(9)	Page, R	43	Ward, M	–(1)

League goals (53): Asaba 7, Brown 6, D'Jaffo 5, Peschisolido 5, Ndlovu 4, Suffo 4, Jagielka 3, Nicholson 3, Tonge 3, Devlin 2, Furlong 2, Montgomery 2, Santos 2, Curle 1, Doane 1, Javary 1, Lovell 1, Opponents 1.
F.A. Cup goals (2): Brown 1, Ndlovu 1. **Worthington Cup goals (4):** Devlin 1, D'Jaffo 1, Ndlovu 1, Suffo 1.
Average home League attendance: 18,034. **Player of Year:** Michael Brown.

SHEFFIELD WEDNESDAY

Another uncomfortable season at Hillsborough, where Wednesday suffered too many defeats – before and after Terry Yorath replaced Peter Shreeves as manager – to breathe easily. A single point – along with a slightly superior goal difference – was all that separated them from the bottom three. The season's bright spot was a run to the semi-finals of the Worthington Cup during which they accounted for Sunderland and Aston Villa before losing 6-3 over two legs to the eventual winners Blackburn Rovers.

Armstrong, C .... 7(1)	Hamshaw, M .... 13(8)	Morrison, O .... 11(13)
Bonvin, P .... 7(16)	Haslam, S .... 39(2)	O'Donnell, P .... 6(2)
Bromby, L 26	Heald, P 5	Palmer, C 10
Broomes, M .... 18(1)	Hendon, I 9	Pressman, K 40
Burrows, D 8	Hinchcliffe, A 1	Quinn, A .... 35(3)
Crane, T .... 4(11)	Johnson, D 7	Roberts, S .... –(1)
Di Piedi, M .... 2(10)	Johnson, T 8	Sibon, G .... 31(4)
Djordjic, B .... 4(1)	Kuqi, S 17	Soltvedt, T 38
Donnelly, S .... 14(9)	Lescott, A .... 2(5)	Stringer, C 1
Ekoku, E .... 21(6)	Maddix, D .... 33(3)	Westwood, A .... 25(1)
Gallacher, K .... –(4)	McCarthy, J 4	Windass, D 2
Geary, D .... 29(3)	McLaren, P .... 29(6)	

League goals (49): Sibon 12, Ekoku 7, Kuqi 6, Bonvin 4, Donnelly 4, Johnson, T 3, Johnson, D 2, McLaren 2, Morrison 2, Quinn 2, Bromby 1, Di Piedi 1, Maddix 1, Soltvedt 1, Westwood 1.
F. A. Cup goals (1): Hamshaw 1. **Worthington Cup goals (17):** Ekoku 5, Soltvedt 2, Bonvin 1, Crane 1, Di Piedi 1, Hamshaw 1, Maddix 1, McLaren 1, Morrison 1, O'Donnell 1, Sibon 1, Westwood 1,
Average home League attendance: 20,870. **Player of Year:** Derek Geary.

STOCKPORT COUNTY

Stockport turned to the much-travelled player Carlton Palmer when manager Andy Kilner paid the price for only one win in the first 15 matches. Palmer was encouraged by a point gained at Watford followed by victory over Norwich City. But the task was immense, 17 more games went by before his re-shaped team including several youngsters won again and they were the first in the country to be relegated. Some consolation came with improved end-of-season form which included a 2-1 victory over Manchester City.

Arphexad, P 3	Fradin, K .... 18(2)	Ross, N .... 2(1)
Beckett, L .... 17(2)	Gibb, A .... 40(1)	Sandford, L 7
Briggs, K .... 30(2)	Hancock, G .... –(1)	Smith, D .... 9(2)
Bryngelsson, F 3	Hardiker, J .... 11(1)	Sneekes, R .... 8(1)
Byrne, M .... 1(4)	Hardy, N .... 4(6)	Spencer, J .... 1(1)
Carratt, P .... –(2)	Holt, D .... –(1)	Taylor, S .... 19(8)
Challinor, D 18	Helin, P .... 10(3)	Thomas, A .... 7(3)
Clare, R .... 21(2)	Hurst, G .... 12(3)	Turner, S .... 4(2)
Clark, P .... 12(2)	Jones, L .... 21(3)	Van Blerk, J 13
Daly, J .... 11(2)	Kuqi, S .... 15(3)	Welsh, A .... 9(6)
Delaney, D .... 10(2)	Lescott, A 17	Wilbraham, A .... 19(2)
Dibble, A 13	McLachlan, F 2	Wild, P 1
Ellison, K .... 6(5)	McSheffrey, G .... 3(2)	Williams, C .... 1(4)
Flowers, T 4	Palmer, C .... 20(1)	Wiss, J .... 7(4)
Flynn, M 26	Roget, L .... 20(2)	Woodthorpe, C ..... 22(12)

League goals (42): Beckett 7, Kuqi 5, Hurst 4, Taylor 4, Hardiker 3, Palmer 3, Wilbraham 3, Flynn 2, Fradin 2, Hardy 2, Daly 1, Delaney 1, McLachlan 1, McSheffrey 1, Roget 1, Ross 1, Opponents 1.
F.A. Cup goals (1): Daly 1. Worthington Cup goals (4): Taylor 3, Kuqi 1.
Average home League attendance: 6,245. Player of Year: Keith Briggs.

WALSALL

A 2-1 F.A. Cup win at Charlton enabled Colin Lee to make an instant impact after taking over as manager when Ray Graydon was dismissed. The job of steering promoted Walsall away from relegation took a little longer. They went into the Easter Monday programme in the bottom three, but a crucial 3-2 away win over Nottingham Forest followed by maximum points against Stockport County and Sheffield United carried them clear without having to rely on results on the last day of the season.

Andre, C 5	Curtis, T .... 3(1)	O'Connor, M .... 12(1)
Angell, B .... 13(7)	Gadsby, M .... 17(5)	Ofodile, A .... –(1)
Aranalde, Z .... 43(2)	Garrocho, C .... 2(2)	Roper, I .... 24(3)
Barras, A .... 25(1)	Goodman, D .... 7(10)	Scott, D .... –(1)
Bennett, T .... 34(6)	Harper, L 3	Shields, G 7
Biancalani, F .... 13(5)	Hawley, K .... –(1)	Simpson, F .... 21(7)
Birch, G .... –(1)	Herivelto, M .... 11(13)	Thogersen, T 7
Brightwell, I .... 25(2)	Holdsworth, D 9	Tillson, A .... 8(1)
Byfield, D .... 24(13)	Keates, D .... 6(7)	Uhlenbeek, G 5
Carbon, M 22	Leitao, J .... 24(14)	Walker, J 43
Chettle, S 6	Marcelo 9	Wrack, D .... 40(3)
Corica, S 13	Matias, P .... 25(5)	

League goals (51): Leitao 8, Matias 5, Barras 4, Byfield 4, Herivelto 4, Wrack 4, Angell 3, Corica 3, Aranalde 2, Biancalani 2, Simpson 2, Thogersen 2, Carbon 1, Goodman 1, Holdsworth 1, Keates 1, Marcelo 1, O'Connor 1, Tillson 1, Opponents 1.
F.A. Cup goals (5): Leitao 2, Bennett 1, Byfield 1. Worthington Cup goals (4): Barras 1, Byfield 1, Erivelto 1, Wrack 1.
Average home League attendance: 6,830. Player of Year: James Walker.

WATFORD

Gianluca Vialli's first season as manager at Vicarage Road promised much but never delivered. It started on the wrong foot with a 3-0 defeat by Manchester City and apart from doubles over Coventry City and Crystal Palace, Watford were too often found wanting when coming up against the more fancied sides. The best part of a campaign which ended with a position below half-way was a run to the quarter-finals of the Worthington Cup before a 4-0 defeat by Sheffield Wednesday. Vialli lost his job to be replaced by coach Ray Lewington.

Baardsen, E 14	Glass, S .... 29(2)	Norville, J .... –(2)
Blondeau, P .... 24(1)	Hand, J .... 4(6)	Okon, P .... 14(1)
Brown, W .... 10(1)	Helguson, H .... 11(23)	Panayi, J .... –(3)
Chamberlain, A 32	Hughes, S .... 11(4)	Pennant, J 9
Cook, L .... 6(4)	Hyde, M .... 37(2)	Robinson, P 38
Cox, N .... 39(1)	Issa, P .... 12(3)	Smith, T .... 35(5)
Doyley, L .... 11(9)	Mahon, G 6	Vega, R .... 23(4)
Fisken, G .... 12(5)	McNamee, A .... 2(5)	Vernazza, P 21
Foley, D 1	Nielsen, A .... 19(3)	Ward, D .... –(1)
Galli, F .... 27(1)	Noble, D .... 5(10)	Webber, D .... 4(1)
Gayle, M .... 28(8)	Noel-Williams, G .. 15(14)	Wooter, N .... 7(10)
Gibbs, P .... –(1)		

League goals (62): Smith 11, Helguson 6, Nielsen 6, Noel-Williams 6, Gayle 4, Hyde 4, Brown 3, Glass 3, Robinson 3, Cox 2, Pennant 2, Webber 2, Fisken 1, Galli 1, Issa 1, McNamee 1, Noble 1, Vega 1, Wooter 1, Opponents 3.

F.A. Cup goals (2): Noel-Williams 1, Gayle 1. **Worthington Cup goals (11):** Gayle 2, Noel-Williams 2, Hyde 2, Vega 2, Fisken 1, Robinson 1, Vernazza 1.
Average home League attendance: 14,896. **Player of Year:** Alec Chamberlain.

WEST BROMWICH ALBION

Gary Megson led Albion back to the top flight after 16 years with a tremendous end-of-season run. A play-off place looked to the best they could hope for when trailing Wolves by 10 points with nine games remaining. But as their rivals wilted, Albion won seven and drew two to finish runners-up to Manchester City, thanks largely to the meanest of defences more than compensating for the absence of key striker Jason Roberts for more than half the campaign. A 2-0 clincher against Crystal Palace on the final day was the 24th clean sheet Albion achieved in their 46 games.

Appleton, M 18	Dobie, S .... 32(11)	McInnes, D 45
Balis, I .... 32(2)	Fox, R .... 2(18)	Moore, D .... 31(1)
Benjamin, T .... –(3)	Gilchrist, P 43	Quinn, J .... 1(6)
Butler, A .... 14(5)	Hoult, R 45	Roberts, J .... 12(2)
Chambers, A .... 24(8)	Jensen, B 1	Rosler, U 5
Chambers, J .... 1(4)	Johnson, A .... 28(4)	Sigurdsson, L .... 42(1)
Clement, N 45	Jordao .... 19(6)	Taylor, R .... 18(16)
Cummings, W .... 6(8)	Lyttle, D .... 13(10)	Varga, S .... 3(1)
Dichio, D .... 26(1)		

League goals (61): Dobie 11, Dichio 9, Roberts 7, Taylor 7, Clement 6, Jordao 5, Johnson 4, McInnes 3, Balis 2, Moore 2, Benjamin 1, Fox 1, Rosler 1, Sigurdsson 1, Opponents 1.
F.A. Cup goals (3): Clement 2, Johnson 1. **Worthington Cup goals (3):** Dobie 2, Jordao 1.
Average home League attendance: 20,910. **Player of Year:** Russell Hoult.

WIMBLEDON

Tired legs brought Wimbledon's late bid for a play-off place to a halt after they had responded to a 6-2 setback at Grimsby by winning three games on the trot to close the gap on the teams above them. A fourth match in the space of eight days proved too much, a 2-1 home defeat by Bradford City ending their chances. The high spot was the double over champions Manchester City, something no other team achieved. But uncertainty about a move to Milton Keynes – now confirmed – clouded much of the season which ended on a sour note with the dismissal of manager Terry Burton. Goalkeeper coach Stuart Murdoch took over.

Agyemang, P .... 17(15)	Francis, D .... 21(2)	McAnuff, J .... 22(15)
Ainsworth, G .... –(2)	Gier, R 3	Mild, H .... 8(1)
Andersen, T .... 27(3)	Gore, S .... –(1)	Morgan, L .... 4(7)
Ardley, N .... 27(2)	Hawkins, P .... 25(4)	Nielsen, D .... 6(6)
Brown, W 17	Heald, P 4	Nowland, A .... 1(6)
Byrne, D .... –(1)	Holloway, D 32	Roberts, A 18
Connolly, D 35	Hughes, M .... 24(2)	Robinson, P .... –(1)
Cooper, K .... 39(1)	Jupp, D .... 1(1)	Reo-Coker, N .... –(1)
Cunningham, K 34	Karlsson, P .... 1(6)	Shipperley, N .... 36(5)
Darlington, J .... 25(4)	Kimble, A .... 7(1)	Williams, M .... 4(1)
Davis, K 40	Leigertwood, M 1	Willmott, C .... 25(2)
Feuer, I .... 2(3)		

League goals (63): Connolly 18, Shipperley 12, Cooper 10, Agyemang 4, McAnuff 4, Hughes 4, Ardley 3, Nielsen 2, Roberts 1, Brown 1, Francis 1, Morgan 1, Willmott 1, Opponents 1.
F.A. Cup goals: None. **Worthington Cup goals (1):** Williams 1.
Average home League attendance: 6,976. **Player of Year:** Kenny Cunningham.

WOLVERHAMPTON WANDERERS

When big-spending Wolves went into the final part of the season 10 points ahead of West Bromwich Albion for the second automatic promotion spot, a long-awaited return to the top flight looked inevitable. But with Dean Sturridge running out of goals after scoring 20 in 23 matches and his team running out of steam, they were overhauled by their fast-finishing neighbours. In the first play-off semi-final, Wolves conceded a last-minute goal to lose 3-1 at Norwich and found the deficit too much to retrieve in the return leg.

Andrews, K .... 4(7)	Halle, G .... 4(1)	Oakes, M 46
Blake, N .... 38(1)	Kennedy, M 35	Pollet, L .... 5(3)
Branch, M .... 5(2)	Ketsbaia, T .... –(2)	Proudlock, A .... 12(7)
Butler, P 43	Lescott, J 44	Rae, A .... 31(5)
Camara, A .... 23(4)	Miller, K .... 5(15)	Robinson, C .... 15(8)
Cameron, C .... 38(3)	Muscat, K 37	Roussel, C .... 6(11)
Connelly, S .... 5(3)	Naylor, L .... 26(1)	Sinton, A .... 3(3)
Cooper, K .... 4(1)	Ndah, G .... 1(14)	Sturridge, D 27
Dinning, A 4	Newton, S 45	

Play-offs – Appearances: Blake 2, Butler 2, Camara 2, Cameron 2, Cooper 2, Halle 2, Lescott 2, Newton 2, Oakes 2, Rae 2, Sturridge 2, Miller –(2), Kennedy –(1), Proudlock –(1).
League goals (76): Sturridge 20, Blake 11, Newton 8, Rae 7, Cameron 5, Kennedy 5, Lescott 5, Proudlock 3, Miller 2, Robinson 2, Roussel 2, Butler 1, Ndah 1, Sinton 1, Opponents 3. **Play-off goals (2):** Cooper 1, Sturridge 1.
F.A. Cup goals: None. **Worthington Cup goals (1):** Dinning 1.
Average home League attendance: 23,796. **Player of Year:** Alex Rae.

NATIONWIDE LEAGUE – SECOND DIVISION

BLACKPOOL

A season of consolidation for Steve McMahon's promoted side was rounded off by success in the LDV Vans Trophy. Blackpool showed a liking for the Millennium Stadium, where they had accounted for Leyton Orient 4-2 in the previous year's Play-off Final, proving too strong by a 4-1 margin for Cambridge United. When 20-goal Brett Ormerod left for Southampton in a £1.75m. move in December, John Murphy took over the responsibility of chief marksman, finishing with 20 to his credit in all competitions.

Barnes, P 30	Hills, J .... 30(7)	Ormerod, B 21
Blinkhorn, M .... –(3)	Hughes, I .... 13(7)	Parkinson, G .... 13(2)
Bullock, M .... 37(6)	Jaszczun, T .... 36(4)	Payton, A 4
Caldwell, S 6	MacKenzie, N .... 6(8)	Pullen, J 16
Clarke, C .... 10(1)	Marshall, I 21	Reid, B 26
Clarkson, P .... 1(1)	Milligan, J .... 9(8)	Simpson, P .... 25(7)
Coid, D .... 24(3)	Milligan, M 1	Taylor, S .... 13(4)
Collins, L .... 24(8)	Murphy, J .... 33(4)	Thompson, P .... 10(3)
Day, R .... 4(5)	Murphy, N 1	Walker, R .... 16(5)
Dunning, D 5	O'Kane, J .... 34(4)	Wellens, R .... 31(5)
Fenton, G .... 6(9)		

League goals (66): Murphy, J 13, Ormerod 13, Walker 8, Fenton 5, Hills 5, O'Kane 4, Coid 3, Bullock 2, Collins 2, Taylor 2, Hughes 1, MacKenzie 1, Marshall 1, Payton 1, Simpson 1, Thompson 1, Wellens 1, Opponents 2.
F.A. Cup goals (9): Ormerod 2, Murphy, J 2, Hills 1, Jaszczun 1, MacKenzie 1, Simpson 1, Opponents 1. **Worthington Cup goals (3):** Ormerod 3. **LDV Vans Trophy goals (23):** Murphy, J 5, Bullock 3, Walker 3, MacKenzie 2, Ormerod 2, Taylor 2, Caldwell 1, Clarke 1, Hills 1, Parkinson 1, Wellens 1, Opponents 1.
Average home League attendance: 5,730. **Player of Year:** John Hills.

AFC BOURNEMOUTH

What made relegation even more disappointing was the fact that Bournemouth were playing in the smart new surroundings of a redeveloped Dean Court. A 5-1 win there against Northampton Town came immediately after a point won at Reading and suggested they were capable of climbing out of trouble. Instead, the next six games yielded only three points and it was Northampton who did enough to avoid the drop. One win away from home all season was a major factor in Bournemouth's demise.

Birmingham, D .... 3(1)	Hayter, J .... 43(1)	Narada, B .... 4(4)
Broadhurst, K .... 22(1)	Holmes, D .... 34(3)	O'Connor, G .... 12(16)
Cooke, S .... 6(1)	Howe, E 38	Purches, S 41
Elliott, W .... 40(6)	Huck, W .... (7)	Smith, J .... 1(2)
Eribenne, C .... 6(18)	Hughes, R .... 16(6)	Stewart, G 45
Feeney, W .... 35(2)	Kandol, T .... 3(9)	Stock, B .... 19(7)
Fletcher, C 35	Maher, S .... 28(3)	Thomas, D .... 3(9)
Fletcher, S .... 1(1)	McAnespie, K .... 3(4)	Tindall, J 44
Ford, J .... 5(2)	Melligan, J .... 7(1)	Young, N .... 10(1)
Foyewa, A .... 1(7)	Menetrier, M 1	

League goals (56): Feeney 13, Holmes 9, Elliott 8, Hayter 7, Fletcher, C 5, Howe 4, Tindall 3, Hughes 2, Purches 2, Stock 2, McAnespie 1.
F.A. Cup goals (3): Hayter 1, Hughes 1, Fletcher, S 1. **Worthington Cup goals:** None. **LDV Vans Trophy goals (1):** Kandol 1.
Average home League attendance: 5,068. **Player of Year:** Warren Feeney.

BRENTFORD

So near, yet so far. Brentford were 13 minutes away from the second automatic promotion place when Jamie Cureton scored an equaliser on the final day of the season at Griffin Park to send Reading up instead. Steve Coppell's side accounted for Huddersfied Town in the play-off semi-finals, but Ben Burgess conceded an own goal in the final and Lloyd Owusu were unable to continue their prolific partnership and it was Stoke City who enjoyed the breaks to win 2-0. Brentford won admiration all round for achieving so much with so few resources, but that was not enough for Coppell, who resigned because of the financial constraints and who was replaced by coach Wally Downes.

Anderson, I .... 33(2)	Hunt, S .... 34(1)	Powell, D 41
Boxall, D .... (5)	Hutchinson, E .... 2(7)	Price, J 15
Bryan, D .... (1)	Ingimarsson, I 46	Rowlands, M .... 13(10)
Burgess, B 43	Lovett, J 2	Sidwell, S .... 29(1)
Caceres, A 5	Mahon, G .... 34(1)	Smith, P 18
Dobson, M .... 38(1)	McCammon, M .... 1(13)	Tabb, J .... (3)
Evans, P 40	O'Connor, K .... 12(13)	Theobald, P .... 5(1)
Gibbs, P .... 23(4)	Owusu, L .... 43(1)	Williams, M .... (20)
Gottksalksson, O 28	Partridge, S .... (1)	

Play-offs – Appearances: Anderson 3, Burgess 3, Dobson 3, Evans 3, Hunt 3, Ingimarsson 3, Owusu 3, Powell 3, Rowlands 3, Sidwell 3, Smith 3, O'Connor (2), McCammon (1).
League goals (77): Owusu 20, Burgess 17, Evans 14, Rowlands 7, Ingimarsson 6, Hunt 4, Sidwell 4, Gibbs 2, Powell 1, Price 1, Williams 1. **Play-off goals (2):** Owusu 1, Powell 1.
F.A. Cup goals (3): Burgess 1, Dobson 1, Gibbs 1. **Worthington Cup goals (2):** O'Connor 1, Owusu 1. **LDV Vans Trophy goals:** None.
Average home League attendance: 6,713. **Player of Year:** Ivar Ingimarsson.

BRIGHTON & HOVE ALBION

Peter Taylor led Brighton to the championship, then walked out a fortnight later unhappy about what he saw as the direction of the club. It was Taylor's second departure, having become the first Premiership casualty when Leicester City sacked him. His decision somewhat overshadowed Brighton's second successive title, a tremendous turnaround for a club who four years earlier were homeless, broke and in danger of going out of the League. Bobby Zamora followed up 31 goals in the previous campaign with a total of 32 as his team outpaced Reading and Brentford in the home straight. The manager's job went to youth director Matin Hinshelwood.

Brooker, P .... 30(11)	Lehmann, D .... 3(4)	Pitcher, G .... 2(7)
Carpenter, R 45	Lewis, J .... 14(1)	Rogers, P .... 19(6)
Crosby, A .... –(2)	Mayo, K .... 30(3)	Royce, S 6
Cullip, D 44	McPhee, C 2	Steele, L .... 20(17)
Gray, W .... 3(1)	Melton, S .... 5(5)	Virgo, A .... 4(2)
Hadland, P .... –(2)	Morgan, S 42	Watson, P 45
Hart, G .... 34(5)	Oatway, C .... 27(5)	Webb, D .... 7(5)
Jones, N .... 29(7)	Packham, W 1	Wicks, M 2
Kuipers, M 39	Pethick, R .... 13(11)	Zamora, R .... 40(1)
Lee, D .... –(2)		

League goals (66): Zamora 28, Steele 9, Watson 5, Brooker 4, Hart 4, Carpenter 3, Lewis 3, Jones 2, Gray 1, Melton 1, Morgan 1, Oatway 1, Rogers 1, Webb 1, Opponents 2.
F.A. Cup goals (3): Zamora 2, Cullip 1. **Worthington Cup goals (2):** Zamora 2. **LDV Vans Trophy goals (5):** Melton 2, Lehmann 1, Pitcher 1, Steele 1.
Average home League attendance: 6,597. **Player of Year:** Bobby Zamora.

BRISTOL CITY

Even allowing for the fact that they had played more games than their rivals, Bristol City's position at the top of the table at the turn of the year carried with it considerable optimism. Danny Wilson's side, however, were unable to maintain that momentum. A 2-0 home defeat by Brentford was a key loss, a demanding Easter against Reading and Brighton cost them further ground and a 5-1 defeat at Blackpool ended all hope of a play-off place, City finishing in seventh position.

Amankwaah, K .... 18(6)	Goodridge, G .... –(2)	Roberts, C 4
Bell, M .... 41(1)	Hill, M 40	Robinson, S 6
Brown, A .... 34(2)	Hulbert, R .... 4(7)	Rodrigues, D .... –(4)
Brown, M .... 1(9)	Jones, D .... 1(1)	Rosenior, L .... –(1)
Burnell, J .... 26(4)	Jones, S .... 17(6)	Singh, H 3
Carey, L .... 34(1)	Lever, N .... 26(3)	Stowell, M 25
Clist, S .... 9(11)	Matthews, L .... 6(15)	Summerbell, M 5
Coles, D .... 20(3)	Murray, S .... 34(3)	Thorpe, T .... 36(6)
Doherty, T .... 27(7)	Peacock, L .... 28(3)	Tinnion, B .... 35(3)
Fortune, C .... –(1)	Phillips, S .... 21(1)	Woodman, C .... 5(1)

League goals (68): Thorpe 16, Peacock 15, Murray 8, Bell 7, Jones, S 5, Matthews 3, Tinnion 3, Amankwaah 1, Brown, A 1, Clist 1, Coles 1, Doherty 1, Hill 1, Lever 1, Robinson 1, Opponents 3.
F.A. Cup goals: None. **Worthington Cup goals (4):** Amankwaah 1, Clist 1, Jones, S 1, Thorpe 1. **LDV Vans Trophy goals (8):** Matthews 2, Peacock 2, Amankwaah 1, Bell 1, Murray 1, Thorpe 1.
Average home League attendance: 11,227. **Player of Year:** Matthew Hill.

BURY

It was a traumatic season for Bury, who went into administration with large debts and who at one time looked to be going out of business. It was little better on the field where injuries, suspensions and a lack of goals contributed to relegation. A total of 43 was the smallest in the division and only once did they score two successive victories. A 2-0 Easter success against promotion-seeking Brentford offered some hope, but three defeats to finish the season cast them adrift.

Armstrong, C 11	Bhutia, B 3	Borley, D .... 16(5)
Barrass, M .... 6(1)	Billy, C .... 19(2)	Bullock, D .... 2(2)

Clarkson, P	4	Jarrett, J	32(5)	Redmond, S	26
Clegg, G	25(6)	Kenny, P	41	Reid, P	23(5)
Collins, S	26(3)	Lawson, I	12(12)	Seddon, G	23(12)
Connell, L	9(4)	Murphy, M	5(4)	Singh, H	11(1)
Evans, G	1	Nelson, M	28(2)	Stuart, J	24
Forrest, M	31(3)	Newby, J	46	Swailes, D	26(2)
Garner, G	5(2)	Nugent, D	1(4)	Syros, G	9
Gunby, S	–(1)	O'Shaughnessy, P	–(2)	Unsworth, L	34(1)
Hill, N	3(2)	Preece, A	4(9)		

League goals (43): Seddon 7, Newby 6, Clegg 4, Lawson 4, Billy 3, Borley 3, Reid 3, Jarrett 2, Nelson 2, Singh 2, Forrest 1, Preece 1, Redmond 1, Syros 1, Stuart 1, Swailes 1, Unsworth 1.
F.A. Cup goals (2): Seddon 1, Singh 1. **Worthington Cup goals (1):** Reid 1. **LDV Vans Trophy goals (3):** Lawson 1, Newby 1, Swailes 1.
Average home League attendance: 3,914. **Player of Year:** Jon Newby.

CAMBRIDGE UNITED

After flirting with relegation in the two previous seasons, Cambridge never really recovered from a poor start which brought only one win in 10 and they finished bottom. John Beck resigned as manager in November and after a spell as caretaker, John Taylor was given the job full-time. But a run of 13 games without a win from February onwards ruled out any chance of a rescue act. The one bright spot was a place in the LDV Vans Trophy Final, although that too ended in disappointment with a 4-1 defeat by Blackpool.

Alcide, C	7(1)	Guttridge, L	27(2)	Revell, A	7(17)
Angus, S	41	Jackman, D	5(2)	Richardson, M	4(2)
Ashbee, I	38	Kandol, T	2(2)	Scully, A	19(6)
Austin, K	4(2)	Kelly, L	1(1)	Tann, A	24(1)
Bridges, D	1(6)	Kitson, D	30(3)	Taylor, S	–(3)
Byrne, D	3(1)	Marshall, S	4(3)	Traore, D	2(5)
Chillingworth, D	10(2)	McAnespie, S	–(1)	Tudor, S	31(1)
Clements, M	–(1)	Murray, F	21	Walling, D	20
Cowan, T	3(2)	Mustoe, N	–(5)	Wanless, P	28(1)
Duncan, A	20(3)	One, A	18(14)	Warner, P	11(1)
Fleming, T	28(6)	Perez, L	42	Youngs, T	36(6)
Goodhind, W	11(3)	Prokas, R	8(1)		

League goals (47): Youngs 11, Kitson 9, Wanless 6, One 4, Tudor 3, Ashbee 2, Chillingworth 2, Guttridge 2, Revell 2, Scully 2, Bridges 1, Cowan 1, Jackman 1, Prokas 1.
F.A. Cup goals (1): Tudor 1. **Worthington Cup goals (1):** Alcide 1. **LDV Vans Trophy goals (10):** One 5, Chillingworth 1, Guttridge 1, Kitson 1, Tudor 1, Wanless 1.
Average home League attendance: 3,505. **Player of Year:** Adam Tann.

CARDIFF CITY

The big spenders of the division, with nearly £4.5m. invested in players, went into the play-offs in the best-possible shape. After Lennie Lawrence replaced Alan Cork as manager, Cardiff put together a 13-match unbeaten run – including a 7-1 win at Oldham which left them within a point of the second automatic promotion place. There was a 2-1 success against Stoke City in the first leg of the semi-finals, but then it all went wrong, with Cardiff conceding a last-minute goal in the return and a second in extra-time. So the season's highlight – crowd trouble apart – remained a 2-1 F.A. Cup win over Leeds United.

Alexander, N	46	Bowen, J	21(4)	Collins, J	2(5)
Boland, W	40(2)	Brayson, P	16(19)	Croft, G	3(3)
Bonner, M	25(4)	Campbell, A	8	Earnshaw, R	28(2)

370

Fortune-West, L .... 18(18)	Jeanne, L .... –(2)	Nugent, K 1
Gabbidon, D 44	Jones, G .... –(1)	Prior, S .... 33(4)
Gordon, D 7	Kavanagh, G 43	Simpkins, M .... 13(4)
Gordon, G .... 12(3)	Legg, A .... 27(8)	Thorne, P .... 23(3)
Hamilton, D .... 14(4)	Low, J .... 11(11)	Weston, R .... 35(2)
Hughes, D .... 1(1)	Maxwell, L .... 5(12)	Young, S .... 30(3)

Play-offs – Appearances: Alexander 2, Boland 2, Bonner 2, Croft 2, Earnshaw 2, Fortune-West 2, Kavanagh 2, Prior 2, Thorne 2, Weston 2, Young 2, Campbell –(2), Bowen –(1), Collins –(1), Maxwell –(1).
League goals (75): Kavanagh 13, Earnshaw 11, Fortune-West 9, Thorne 8, Campbell 7, Bowen 5, Young 4, Brayson 3, Gabbidon 3, Gordon, G 3, Legg 2, Prior 2, Boland 1, Collins 1, Croft 1, Maxwell 1, Opponents 1. **Play-off goals (2):** Earnshaw 1, Fortune-West 1.
F.A. Cup goals (9): Earnshaw 2, Kavanagh 2, Brayson 1, Fortune-West 1, Gordon, G 1, Hamilton 1, Young 1. **Worthington Cup goals (1):** Earnshaw 1. **LDV Vans Trophy goals (8):** Gordon, G 5, Bonner 1, Giles, M 1, Nugent 1.
Average home League attendance: 12,522. **Player of Year:** Willie Boland.

CHESTERFIELD

Chesterfield, whose first match after being promoted resulted in a 6-3 home defeat by Colchester United, banked enough points to comfortably offset an end-of-season slide. Five successive defeats before, during and after Easter, could otherwise have been costly for a side who lost manager Nicky Law to Bradford City mid-way through the campaign. Dave Rushbury, the club physio, was eventually given the job after two months as caretaker.

Abbey, N 46	Hewitt, J 1	Parrish, S .... 11(9)
Allott, A .... 19(2)	Hitzlsperger, T 5	Payne, S 44
Beckett, L .... 20(1)	Howard, J .... 12(8)	Pearce, G .... 5(2)
Blatherwick, S .... 4(1)	Howson, S 13	Reeves, D .... 20(2)
Booty, M 40	Hurst, G .... 22(1)	Richardson, L .... 13(1)
Breckin, I 42	Hyde, G .... 8(1)	Rowland, K .... 6(3)
Buchanan, W 3	Ingledow, J .... 12(4)	Rushbury, A .... –(3)
Burt, J .... 18(6)	Innes, M .... 22(1)	Walsh, D .... – (1)
D'Auria, D .... 10(4)	Jones, M .... 1(5)	Williams, D .... 19(4)
Ebdon, M .... 29(2)	Moore, L .... 1(1)	Willis, R .... 11(13)
Edwards, R .... 30(1)	O'Hare, A 19	

League goals (53): Hurst 9, Burt 7, Beckett 6, Howard 5, Allott 4, Reeves 4, Willis 4, Booty 2, Ebdon 2, Innes 2, Breckin 1, D'Auria 1, Edwards 1, Howson 1, Hyde 1, Parrish 1, Payne 1, Richardson 1.
F.A. Cup goals (4): Beckett 2, D'Auria 1, Opponents 1. **Worthington Cup goals (1):** Rowland 1. **LDV Vans Trophy goals (2):** D'Auria 1, Reeves 1.
Average home League attendance: 4,391. **Player of Year:** Ian Breckin and Steve Payne (joint).

COLCHESTER UNITED

Colchester opened with a 6-3 win over Chesterfield and shared top spot after the first six matches produced 13 points. It was always going to be difficult maintaining that sort of form over the course of the season against teams with far greater resources, but neither did they ever look like being drawn into a relegation struggle. There was no improvement in the club's poor F.A. Cup form of recent seasons, defeat in the first round coming this time on penalties against York City.

Barrett, G .... 19(1)	Chambers, T .... –(1)	Fitzgerald, S .... 36(1)
Blatsis, C 7	Clark, S .... 19(2)	Gregory, D .... 15(1)
Bowry, R .... 27(9)	Coote, A .... 5(14)	Halls, J 6
Brown, S 19	Duguid, R .... 36(5)	Izzet, K .... 36(4)
Canham, M .... –(1)	Dunne, J .... 6(2)	Johnson, G .... 19(1)

Johnson, R .... 13(3)	McGleish, S .... 44(2)	Rapley, K .... 26(9)
Keith, J .... 33(8)	Morgan, D .... 1(29)	Stockwell, M .... 45(1)
Knight, R 1	Opara, L .... –(1)	White, A .... 28(5)
MacDonald, C .... 2(2)	Pinault, T .... 37(5)	Woodman, A 26

League goals (65): McGleish 15, Rapley 9, Stockwell 9, Barrett 4, Coote 4, Duguid 4, Keith 4, Izzett 3, White 3, Dunne 2, Bowry 1, Johnson, G 1, Johnson, R 1, MacDonald 1, Opponents 4.
F.A. Cup goals (2): Duguid 1, McLeish 1. **Worthington Cup goals (3):** Izzet 1, Keith 1, Stockwell 1. **LDV Vans Trophy goals (2):** Izzet 1, Stockwell 1.
Average home League attendance: 3,838. **Player of Year:** Karl Duguid.

HUDDERSFIELD TOWN

Boosted by a steady stream of goals from Leon Knight, on loan from Chelsea, relegated Huddersfield stayed ahead of Bristol City to claim the fourth play-off place, eventually by a comfortable margin. But Knight's sending-off against Oldham Athletic left them short of options for the semi-final with Brentford. They were held to a 0-0 at home and despite a second minute strike by Andy Booth in the return, finally lost out 2-1 to a goal from the London side's leading marksman Lloyd Owusu. Manger Lou Macari paid the price, Mick Wadsworth taking over soon after losing his job with Oldham Athletic.

Armstrong, C .... 7(4)	Gray, K 44	Lucketti, C 2
Baldry, S .... 3(1)	Hay, C .... 19(12)	Macari, P .... –(6)
Beech, C .... 6(3)	Heary, T .... 21(11)	Margetson, M 46
Booth, A .... 30(6)	Holland, C .... 35(2)	Mattis, D .... 21(8)
Clarke, N 36	Ifil, J .... 1(1)	Moses, A .... 13(4)
Delaney, D .... 1(1)	Irons, K .... 34(7)	Schofield, D .... 39(1)
Evans, G 35	Jenkins, S 40	Thorrington, A .... 29(2)
Facey, D .... 11(2)	Knight, L 31	Wijnhard, C .... 2(11)

Play-offs – Appearances: Booth 2, Evans 2, Facey 2, Gray 2, Heary 2, Holland 2, Ifil 2, Irons 2, Margetson 2, Thorrington 2, Jenkins 1, Moses 1, Hay –(2).
League goals (65): Knight 16, Booth 11, Schofield 8, Irons 7, Thorrington 6, Hay 5, Facey 2, Armstrong 1, Beech 1, Clarke 1, Gray 1, Holland 1, Jenkins 1, Mattis 1, Wijnhard 1, Opponents 2. **Play-off goals (1):** Booth 1.
F.A. Cup goals (2): Knight 1, Moses 1. **Worthington Cup goals:** None. **LDV Vans Trophy goals (9):** Schofield 4, Booth 2, Hay 1, Holland 1, Wijnhard 1.
Average home League attendance: 10,880. **Player of Year:** Leon Knight.

NORTHAMPTON TOWN

Seven defeats in the first eight matches cost manager Kevin Wilson his job. By the turn of the year Northampton were still bottom – nine points away from safety – under his successor Kevin Broadhurst. The outlook was bleak until Jamie Forrester began to score some important goals. Five points were gained from successive matches against promotion-minded Stoke City, Bristol City and Brentford, a 3-0 win over Notts County confirmed the improvement and they went on to complete an excellent recovery by finishing the season five points clear of the bottom two.

Asamoah, D .... 3(36)	Gabbiadini, M .... 30(5)	McGregor, P .... 37(2)
Burgess, D 36	Hargreaves, C .... 38(1)	Morison, S .... –(1)
Carruthers, C .... 6(7)	Hodge, J .... 4(15)	Parkin, S .... 31(9)
Cavill, A .... –(1)	Hope, R .... 35(8)	Sampson, I .... 24(3)
Dempsey, P .... 13(7)	Hunt, J 38	Sollitt, A .... 8(2)
Evatt, I .... 10(1)	Hunter, R .... 38(2)	Spedding, D .... 22(1)
Forrester, J .... 40(3)	Lavin, G 2	Welch, K 38
Frain, J .... 25(2)	Marsh, C 26	Wolleaston, R .... 2(5)

League goals (54): Forrester 17, Gabbiadini 7, Hope 6, Hunt 4, Hunter 4, Parkin 4, Asamoah 3, Hargreaves 3, McGregor 3, Burgess 1, Carruthers 1, Hodge 1.

F.A. Cup goals (2): Gabbiadini 2. **Worthington Cup goals (3):** Forrester 1, McGregor 1, Parkin 1. **LDV Vans Trophy goals (2):** Hunt 1, McGregor 1.
Average home League attendance: 5,252. **Player of Year:** Chris Hargreaves.

NOTTS COUNTY

Bill Dearden must have wondered what he had let himself in for after resigning as Mansfield Town manager to take over from Gary Brazil at Meadow Lane in January. County gained only two points from a run of 10 matches and relegation looked inevitable. Then Danny Allsopp struck a rich seam of goals to spark a run of four straight victories after which his team did not look back. Allsopp finished the season with 20 to his credit – 29 in all competitions – as County climbed six points clear of the bottom four.

Allsopp, D 43	Hackworth, T .... 9(23)	Owers, G .... 26(4)
Baraclough, I .... 30(3)	Hamilton, I .... 6(3)	Quinn, J 6
Bolland, P .... 16(3)	Heffernan, P .... 18(5)	Richardson, I .... 25(3)
Brough, M .... 14(7)	Holmes, R 1	Richardson, L ...... 16(1)
Cas, M .... 39(1)	Ireland, C .... 26(1)	Riley, P .... 3(3)
Caskey, D .... 39(3)	Jorgensen, H .... –(2)	Stallard, M .... 21(5)
Chilvers, L 9	Liburd, R .... 22(3)	Stone, D .... 5(1)
Fenton, N .... 41(1)	McNamara, N .... –(4)	Warren, M .... 12(5)
Garden, S 21	Mildenhall, S .... 25(1)	Whitley, J 6
Grayson, S 10	Nicholson, K .... 15(9)	Wilkie, L 2

League goals (59): Allsopp 20, Cas 6, Caskey 5, Heffernan 5, Stallard 4, Baraclough 3, Fenton 3, Quinn 3, Liburd 2, Richardson, I 2, Chilvers 1, Grayson 1, Hackworth 1, Ireland 1, Nicholson 1, Owers 1.
F.A. Cup goals (3): Allsopp 2, Owers 1. **Worthington Cup goals (6):** Allsopp 4, Mildenhall 1, Stallard 1. **LDV Vans Trophy goals (5):** Allsopp 3, Caskey 1, Hackworth 1.
Average home League attendance: 5,955. **Player of Year:** Danny Allsopp.

OLDHAM ATHLETIC

An up-and-down season for Oldham, who sacked Andy Ritchie after a run of five matches without a win in October when he refused to move 'upstairs.' Mick Wadsworth, former assistant manager at Newcastle and Southampton, got the team winning again and kept them within reach of a place in the play-offs until a 7-1 home defeat by Cardiff City at the start of a demanding run-in showed that they were not up to it. To their credit, Oldham came back to finish as joint top scorers in the division with Brentford on 77, but then there was another change of manager, with coach Iain Dowie replacing Wadsworth.

Adebola, D 5	Duxbury, L .... 34(6)	McNiven, S .... 32(3)
Allott, M .... 9(6)	Eyre, J .... 11(9)	Miskelly, D 4
Appleby, M .... 16(1)	Eyres, D .... 40(5)	Murray, P .... 23(1)
Armstrong, C .... 31(1)	Garnett, S .... 4(4)	Prenderville, B ..... 10(2)
Balmer, S .... 35(1)	Gill, W 3	Rachubka, P 16
Baudet, J .... 13(7)	Goram, A 4	Reeves, D .... 11(2)
Beharall, D 18	Griffin, A .... –(1)	Richards, M .... 3(2)
Boshell, D .... 2(2)	Haining, W .... 1(3)	Rickers, P .... 13(11)
Carss, A .... 7(7)	Hall, C 4	Sheridan, D .... 25(3)
Clegg, M .... 5(1)	Hardy, L .... –(1)	Sheridan, J .... 24(3)
Colusso, C .... 6(7)	Holden, D .... 20(3)	Smart, A .... 14(7)
Corazzin, C .... 24(9)	Innes, M .... –(5)	Tipton, M .... 11(11)
Dudley, C .... 6(3)	Kelly, G 2	

League goals (77): Eyres 9, Corazzin 9, Balmer 6, Smart 6, Eyre 5, Murray 5, Tipton 5, Allott 4, Duxbury 4, Reeves 3, Appleby 2, Colusso 2, Holden 2, Rickers 2, Sheridan, D 2, Sheridan, J 2, Baudet 1, Beharall 1, Carss 1, Dudley 1, Hall 1, Oppponents 4.
F.A. Cup goals (6): Eyres 3, Duxbury 2, Sheridan, J. 1. **Worthington Cup goals:** None. **LDV Vans Trophy goals (5):** Duxbury 1, Eyre 1, Eyres 1, Richards 1, Smart 1.
Average home League attendance: 5,810. **Player of Year:** David Eyres.

PETERBOROUGH UNITED

On their day, Peterborough were a match for most, scoring six against Bournemouth, five against Tranmere Rovers and four against Bristol City and Q.P.R. But a barren spell of eight matches without a win sent them into the New Year with not much chance of making up ground on the leading group. High point of the season was a rousing F.A. Cup fourth round tie against Newcastle United at London Road in which they gave Bobby Robson some anxious moments before going down 4-2.

Bullard, J .... 36(4)	Forinton, H .... 13(4)	MacDonald, G .... 7(1)
Clarke, A .... 19(9)	Forsyth, R .... 30(2)	McKenzie, L .... 28(2)
Clarke, L .... –(1)	French, D .... 1(9)	Oldfield, D .... 27(3)
Connor, D .... –(1)	Gill, M .... 11(1)	Pearce, D .... 8(1)
Cowan, T .... 4(1)	Green, F .... 12(11)	Rea, S .... 27(3)
Cullen, J .... 10(3)	Hanlon, R .... –(1)	Shields, T .... 6(9)
Danielsson, H ...... 20(11)	Hooper, D .... 7(6)	Steele, L 2
Edwards, A 44	Jelleyman, G .... 6(4)	Toner, C 6
Farrell, D .... 35(3)	Joseph, M 44	Tyler, M 44
Fenn, N .... 25(11)	Kimble, A 3	Williams, T .... 31(3)

League goals (64): McKenzie 18, Bullard 8, Farrell 6, Fenn 6, Clarke, A 5, Green 3, Danielsson 2, Edwards 2, Forinton 2, Gill 2, Joseph 2, Williams 2, Cowan 1, Cullen 1, French 1, MacDonald 1, Oldfield 1, Rea 1.
F.A. Cup goals (9): Clarke, A 2, Farrell 2, Bullard 1, Danielsson 1, Fenn 1, McKenzie 1, Opponents 1. **Worthington Cup goals (4):** Clarke, A 1, Fenn 1, Forsyth 1, Opponents 1.
LDV Vans Trophy goals (4): Bullard 2, Green 1, McKenzie 1.
Average home League attendance: 5,544. **Player of Year:** Jimmy Bullard.

PORT VALE

An excellent run of form, starting early in the New Year, enabled Port Vale to make up considerable ground on the top six. They beat Brentford, Stoke City and Q.P.R. on the way to accumulating 22 points out of 24, but then the goals dried up to such an extent that Vale scored only five in their final 11 games and they finished just below mid-table. Speculation about the future of manager Brian Horton, linked with the then-vacant job at Preston, ended when he signed a new contract.

Armstrong, I .... 20(11)	Carragher, M 41	Maye, D .... –(2)
Atangana, S .... 1(1)	Cummins, M 46	McClare, S .... 19(4)
Birchall, C .... –(1)	Delaney, D .... 3(1)	McPhee, S 44
Bridge-Wilkinson,	Dodd, A .... 5(4)	O'Callaghan, G .... 8(3)
M .... 15(4)	Donnelly, P .... 1(5)	Osborn, S 7
Brisco, N .... 34(3)	Durnin, J .... 18(1)	Paynter, W .... 2(5)
Brooker, S 41	Gibson, J 1	Rowland, S 25
Burgess, R .... 1(1)	Goodlad, M 43	Torpey, S .... –(1)
Burns, L .... 30(4)	Hardy, P 8	Walsh, M .... 27(1)
Burton, S .... 33(4)	Ingram, R .... 22(2)	Webber, D .... 2(2)
Byrne, P 1	Killen, C .... 8(1)	

League goals (51): McPhee 11, Brooker 9, Cummins 8, Bridge-Wilkinson 6, Killen 6, Armstrong 3, O'Callaghan 3, Dodd 1, Durnin 1, Hardy 1, McClare 1, Rowland 1.
F.A. Cup goals (3): Brooker 1, Burgess 1, Cummins 1. **Worthington Cup goals (2):** McPhee 2. **LDV Vans Trophy goals (5):** Armstrong 2, Brooker 1, Burton 1, McPhee 1.
Average home League attendance: 5,210. **Player of Year:** Mark Goodlad.

QUEENS PARK RANGERS

With club finances dictating that Ian Holloway operate on a shoestring budget, the prospect of Rangers regaining Division One status at the first attempt was always an unlikely one, despite the return of Loftus Road favourites Kevin Gallen and Gavin Peacock. Four successive wins around Easter offered a glimmer of hope. But a goalless draw against Brentford in front of an 18,000 crowd at Loftus Road, and results elsewhere, decided otherwise. All of leading scorer Andy Thomson's 21 goals came in League matches.

Agogo, J ....–(2)	Evans, R 11	Pacquette, R ....8(8)
Ben Askar, A 18	Fitzgerald, B ....–(1)	Palmer, S 46
Bignot, M ....41(4)	Foley, D ....3(2)	Peacock, G ....19(1)
Bonnot, A ....17(5)	Forbes, T 43	Perry, M ....13(3)
Bruce, P 13	Gallen, K 25	Plummer, C 1
Burgess, O 4	Griffiths, L ....23(7)	Rose, M ....37(2)
Connolly, K ....24(9)	Koejoe, S ....–(2)	Shittu, D 27
Daly, W 1	Langley, R ....15(3)	Taylor, R 3
Day, C 16	Leaburn, C ....–(1)	Thomas, J 4
De Ornelas, F ....1(1)	McEwen, D ....2(3)	Thomson, A ....29(8)
Digby, F 19	Murphy, D ....10(2)	Wardley, S ....5(5)
Doudou ....20(16)	Oli, D ....–(2)	Warren, C ....8(6)

League goals (60): Thomson 21, Gallen 7, Connolly 4, Palmer 4, Dodou 3, Griffiths 3, Langley 3, Rose 3, Pacquette 2, Peacock 2, Shittu 2, Bignot 1, Bruce 1, Burgess 1, Foley 1, Thomas 1, Opponents 1.
F.A. Cup goals: None. **Worthington Cup goals (1):** Opponents 1. **LDV Vans Trophy goals:** None.
Average home League attendance: 11,748. **Player of Year:** Terrell Forbes.

READING

On a dramatic final day of the season, Reading squeezed into the runners-up spot behind Brighton thanks to a goal 13 minutes from time by substitute Jamie Cureton. It earned a 1-1 result at Brentford and meant that they, and not the London side, went up automatically. With 10 games remaining, Reading were top-of-the-table and held a big lead over both rivals. But the winning touch deserted them to such an extent that nine of those games were drawn and it became touch and go whether they would be able to bring First Division football to the impressive Madejski Stadium.

Ashdown, J 1	Igoe, S ....27(8)	Savage, B ....–(1)
Branch, P ....–(2)	Jones, K ....10(6)	Shorey, N 32
Butler, M ....14(3)	Mackie, J 27	Smith, A ....12(1)
Cureton, J ....24(14)	Murty, G 43	Smith, N ....3(11)
Forster, N ....36(6)	Parkinson, P ....32(1)	Tyson, N ....–(1)
Gamble, J ....2(4)	Roberts, B 6	Viveash, A 18
Hahnemann, M 6	Robinson, M 14	Watson, K 12
Harper, J ....19(7)	Roget, L 1	Whitbread, A 14
Henderson, D ....2(36)	Rougier, A ....20(13)	Whitehead, P 33
Hughes, A ....34(5)	Salako, J 31	Williams, A ....33(2)

League goals (70): Forster 18, Cureton 15, Henderson 7, Hughes 6, Salako 6, Butler 2, Mackie 2, Parkinson 2, Smith, A 2, Harper 1, Igoe 1, Smith, N 1, Rougier 1, Viveash 1, Watson 1, Williams 1, Opponents 1.
F.A. Cup goals (1): Cureton 1. **Worthington Cup goals (4):** Henderson 2, Parkinson 1, Smith, A 1. **LDV Vans Trophy goals (3):** Henderson 2, Smith, N 1.
Average home League attendance: 14,114. **Player of Year:** Graeme Murty.

STOKE CITY

Two victories in Cardiff in the space of 11 days brought Stoke the First Division place their status, stadium and support demanded. A third successive failure in the play-offs looked on the cards until James O'Connor's 89th minute equaliser and Souleymane Oulare's extra-time winner turned their semi-final at Ninian Park on its head. Then Deon Burton's strike followed by an own goal accounted for Brentford at the Millennium Stadium. But the celebrations turned sour the following week when manager Gudjon Thordarson's back-me-or-sack me message to the club's owners prompted his dismissal. He was replaced by Cheltenham Town's Steve Cotterill.

Brightwell, I .... 3(1)   Gunnarsson, B .... 21(2)   Oulare, S .... –(1)
Burton, D .... 11(1)   Gunnlaugsson, A 9   Rowson, D .... 8(5)
Clarke, C .... 42(1)   Handyside, P 34   Shtaniuk, S 40
Cooke, A .... 26(9)   Henry, K .... 9(15)   Smart, A .... –(2)
Cutler, N 36   Hoekstra, P .... 20(4)   Thomas, W 40
Dadason, R .... 6(5)   Iwelumo, C .... 22(16)   Thordarson, S .... 3(18)
Dinning, A 5   Marteinsson, P .... 2(1)   Thorne, P 5
Flynn, M .... 11(2)   Miles, J .... –(1)   Vandeurzen, J .... 37(3)
Goodfellow, M .... 11(12)   Neal, L .... 6(5)   Ward, G 10
Gudjonsson, B 46   O'Connor, J 43   Wilson, B .... –(1)

Play-offs – Appearances: Clarke 3, Cutler 3, Dinning 3, Gudjonsson 3, Handyside 3, Iwelumo 3, O'Connor 3, Thomas 3, Shtaniuk 3, Burton 2(1), Gunnlaugsson 2, Cooke 1 (2), Goodfellow 1, Vandeurzen –(3), Brightwell –(1), Dadason –(1), Oulare –(1).
League goals (67): Iwelumo 10, Cooke 9, Goodfellow 5, Gunnarsson 5, Dadason 4, Thordarson 4, Thorne 4, Vandeurzen 4, Gudjonsson 3, Gunnlaugsson 3, Hoekstra 3, Burton 2, O'Connor 2, Shtaniuk 2, Thomas 2, Clarke 1, Opponents 4. **Play-off goals (5):** Burton 2, O'Connor 1, Oulare 1, Opponents 1.
F.A. Cup goals (6): Gunnarsson 2, Cooke 1, Gudjonsson 1, Handyside 1, Iwelumo 1.
Worthington Cup goals: None. **LDV Vans Trophy goals (2):** Iwelumo 1, Neal 1.
Average home League attendance: 13,965.

SWINDON TOWN

A season of comings and goings at the County Ground started with the dismissal of Andy King and the arrival of former Liverpool manager Roy Evans as director of football and ex-Anfield defender Neil Ruddock as player-coach. It continued with the takeover of the club by a consortium headed by former champion jockey Willie Carson, the departure of Evans and Ruddock and the return of King as manager. Failure to score in 20 matches meant Swindon could not aspire to higher than a mid-table position.

Brayley, B .... –(7)   Griemink, B 45   Osei-Kuffour, J .... 4(7)
Carlisle, W .... 10(1)   Gurney, A 43   Reeves, A .... 24(1)
Cobian, J .... –(1)   Herring, I .... –(1)   Robinson, M .... 7(2)
Davies, G .... –(2)   Hewlett, M .... 38(1)   Robinson, S .... 36(3)
Davis, S .... 15(6)   Heywood, M .... 42(2)   Ruddock, N .... 14(1)
Duke, D .... 36(6)   Howe, B .... 33(6)   Sabin, E .... 33(1)
Edwards, N .... 2(4)   Invincible, D .... 40(4)   Williams J .... –(1)
Edwards, P .... 14(6)   McAreavey, P .... 8(11)   Willis, A .... 19(3)
Foley, D .... 5(2)   McKinney, R 1   Young, A .... 7(7)
Grazioli, G .... 24(7)   O'Halloran, K 6

League goals (46): Grazioli 8, Gurney 7, Invincible 6, Sabin 5, Heywood 3, Carlisle 2, Duke 2, O'Halloran 2, Osei-Kuffour 2, Reeves 2, Foley 1, Hewlett 1, Howe 1, Ruddock 1, Willis 1, Young 1, Opponents 1.
F.A. Cup goals (6): Invincible 2, Edwards, P 1, Heywood 1, Howe 1, Ruddock 1.
Worthington Cup goals (2): Howe 1, O'Halloran 1. **LDV Vans Trophy goals:** None.
Average home League attendance: 6,354. **Player of Year:** Matt Heywood.

TRANMERE ROVERS

Tranmere's affinity with Cup competitions continued during former Everton stalwart Dave Watson's first season in management. Rovers reached the fifth round of the F.A. Cup before losing 4-0 to Tottenham, who also knocked them out of the Worthington Cup by the same score at the third round stage. In the League, Tranmere had to be satisfied with a period of consolidation rather than a concerted effort to return to Division One at the first attempt, a shortage of goals in the second half of the campaign proving a problem.

Achterberg, J 25   Allison, W .... 13(14)   Challinor, D 6
Allen, G .... 30(1)   Barlow, S .... 31(7)   Flynn, S .... 30(1)

Harrison, D 1	Jobson, R 1	Parkinson, A .... 14(17)
Haworth, S 12	Koumas, J 38	Price, J .... 20(4)
Hay, A .... 2(1)	Mellon, M .... 23(4)	Rideout, P .... 14(1)
Hazell, R 6	Morgan, A .... 1(1)	Roberts, G 45
Henry, N 39	Murphy, J .... 21(1)	Sharps, I .... 25(4)
Hill, C 30	Navarro, A 21	Thornton, S .... 9(2)
Hinds, R .... 6(4)	N'Diaye, S .... 6(5)	Yates, S .... 36(1)
Hume, I .... 1(13)	Nixon, E .... -(1)	

League goals (63): Barlow 14, Koumas 8, Price 7, Flynn 5, Haworth 5, Allison 4, Rideout 4, Yates 3, Hill 2, N'Diaye 2, Parkinson 2, Roberts 2, Allen 1, Henry 1, Mellon 1, Navarro 1, Thornton 1.
F.A. Cup goals (16): Koumas 4, Price 4, Flynn 3, Allison 1, Barlow 1, Navarro 1, Rideout 1, Yates 1, **Worthington Cup goals (7):** Barlow 2, Flynn 2, Henry 1, Koumas 1, Mellon 1. **LDV Vans Trophy goals:** None.
Average home League attendance: 8,655. **Player of Year:** Sean Flynn.

WIGAN ATHLETIC

No team in the country experienced more contrasting fortunes in back-to-back matches than Wigan, who beat Stoke City 6-1 and then four days later lost 1-0 at home to Canvey Island in the first round of the F.A. Cup. The two results summed up a season in which the big spenders were as good as anyone on their day but rarely showed any consistency. The result was another major outlay, this time on Bristol Rovers striker Nathan Ellington for a fee that could eventually reach £1.2m.

Adamczuk, D 3	Green, S .... 35(4)	McLoughlin, A .... 1(2)
Ashcroft, L .... 14(2)	Haworth, S .... 19(8)	McMillan, S 29
Brannan, G .... 31(2)	Jackson, M 26	Mitchell, P .... 16(7)
Bukran, G 1	Jarrett, J 5	Nolan, I .... 5(3)
Cook, P 6	Kenna, J 6	Pendlebury, I 4
Croft, G 7	Kennedy, P .... 29(2)	Roberts, N .... 5(12)
Dalglish, P .... 17(12)	Kerr, S 8	Santus, P .... -(1)
De Vos, J .... 19(1)	Kilford, I .... 7(13)	Sharp, K .... 1(1)
De Zeeuw, A 42	Liddell, A .... 33(1)	Stillie, D 13
Dinning, A .... 32(1)	McCulloch, L ...... 24(10)	Teale, G .... 22(1)
Ellington, N 3	McGibbon, P 18	Traynor, G .... -(1)
Filan, J 25		

League goals (66): Liddell 17, Haworth 10, McCulloch 6, De Vos 5, Dinning 5, Roberts 4, Ashcroft 3, Green 3, Dalglish 2, De Zeeuw 2, Ellington 2, Cook 1, Kenna 1, McGibbon 1, Teale 1, Opponents 3.
F.A. Cup goals: None. **Worthington Cup goals (2):** Brannan 1, Haworth 1. **LDV Vans Trophy goals (1):** Opponents 1.
Average home League attendance: 5,771. **Player of Year:** Arjan De Zeeuw.

WREXHAM

If Wrexham hoped for a change of fortune with a change of manager, they were sadly disappointed. Denis Smith started with seven points from his first three games in charge when Brian Flynn departed after 12 years in the job. But only once after that did his team manage back-to-back victories. A 3-1 success against Port Vale raised hopes briefly, but another poor run of one point from five games, taking in Easter, ruled out hopes of beating the drop. They were relegated, ironically, on the day they beat Cambridge United 5-0 with Lee Jones scoring all five.

Barrett, P .... 10(5)	Edwards, C .... 10(16)	Hill, K 12
Bennett, D .... 5(1)	Evans, M .... -(4)	Holmes, S .... 39(1)
Blackwood, M ...... 21(10)	Faulconbridge, C ... 36(1)	Jones, L .... 3(1)
Carey, B .... 16(2)	Ferguson, D .... 37(1)	Lawrence, D .... 29(3)
Chalk, M .... 17(7)	Gibson, R .... 11(7)	Miller, W 5

Moody, A .... –(1)	Rogers, K 27	Thomas, S .... 30(8)
Morgan, C .... –(2)	Rovde, M 12	Trundle, L .... 30(6)
Morrell, A .... 13(12)	Russell, K .... 8(2)	Walsh, D .... 7(2)
Pejic, S .... 11(1)	Sam, H .... 15(14)	Warren, D 5
Phillips, W 27	Sharp, K .... 12(3)	Whitley, J 34
Roberts, S 24		

League goals (56): Faulconbridge 13, Trundle 8, Edwards 5, Jones 5, Sam 5, Chalk 3, Ferguson 3, Thomas 3, Blackwood 2, Carey 2, Lawrence 2, Morrell 2, Hill 1, Phillips 1, Roberts 1.
F.A. Cup goals: None. **Worthington Cup goals (2):** Faulconbridge 1, Russell 1. **LDV Vans Trophy goals (5):** Morrell 2, Trundle 2, Thomas 1.
Average home League attendance: 3,811. **Player of Year:** Jim Whitley.

WYCOMBE WANDERERS

Wycombe's season tailed off disappointingly after they had looked capable of mounting a challenge for a place in the play-offs. A run of one win in 10 matches was responsible, leaving them just above mid-table at the end. After reaching the semi-finals the previous season, Lawrie Sanchez's side again had their best moments in the F.A. Cup, holding Fulham at Adams Park in round three and making the Premiership team work hard for a 1-0 victory in the replay.

Baird, A .... 1(5)	Johnson, R 7	Rogers, M .... 39(2)
Brown, S .... 31(8)	Leach, M 1	Ryan, K .... 12(23)
Bulman, D .... 37(9)	Lee, M .... 2(5)	Senda, D .... 38(5)
Carroll, D .... 1(11)	Lopez, C 1	Simpson, M 43
Cousins, J .... 13(6)	Marsh, C .... –(1)	Taylor, M 46
Currie, D .... 44(2)	McCarthy, P 28	Thomson, A 3
Devine, S .... 19(1)	McSporran, J .... 19(13)	Townsend, B 2
Emblen, P .... 5(7)	Phelan, L .... –(1)	Tuttle, D 4
Harris, R .... 2(1)	Rammell, A 27	Vinnicombe, C 42
Holligan, G .... 11(9)	Roberts, S .... 18(8)	Walker, R .... 10(2)

League goals (58): Rammell 11, Brown 8, McSporran 7, Bulman 5, Devine 5, Currie 4, Holligan 4, McCarthy 3, Walker 3, Rogers 2, Emblen 1, Johnson 1, Ryan 1, Simpson 1, Vinnicombe 1, Opponents 1.
F.A. Cup goals (9): Currie 3, Rammell 2, Brown 1, Bulman 1, McSporran 1, Walker 1.
Worthington Cup goals: None. **LDV Vans Trophy goals (2):** Emblen 1, Holligan 1.
Average home League attendance: 6,681. **Player of Year:** Martin Taylor.

NATIONWIDE LEAGUE – THIRD DIVISION

BRISTOL ROVERS

Rovers looked a decent bet to make an immediate return to the Second Division, particularly after opening with three wins. But a dreadful spell of one goal in 10 matches undermined their season. Manager Gerry Francis resigned for personal reasons, his successor Garry Thompson was sacked after four months and in came Ray Graydon to try to improve on the season's second-from-bottom finish. The bright spot was a 3-1 F.A. Cup victory at Derby, earned by one of three hat-tricks Nathan Ellington registered before a £1.2m. move to Wigan Athletic.

Arndale, N .... –(1)	Ellington, N 27	Howie, S 46
Astafjevs, V .... 14(5)	Foran, M .... 30(1)	Jones, S .... 14(5)
Bryant, S .... 8(1)	Foster, S 33	Lopez, C 6
Bubb, A .... 3(10)	Gall, K .... 25(6)	Lopez, R .... 5(2)
Cameron, M .... 10(15)	Gilroy, D .... 2(2)	Mauge, R .... 14(1)
Carlisle, W 5	Hammond, E .... 3(4)	McKeever, M .... 6(2)
Challis, T .... 28(1)	Hillier, D 27	Ommel, S .... 18(5)
Clarke, J .... –(1)	Hogg, L .... 22(1)	Plummer, D .... 12(3)

Pritchard, D .... 1(4)	Smith, M .... 17(2)	Trought, M .... 17(3)
Quinn, J 6	Thomas, J 7	Walters, M .... 7(19)
Richards, J .... –(1)	Thomson, A .... 29(2)	Weare, R .... 9(1)
Ross, N .... 2(3)	Toner, C 6	Wilson, C 38
Shore, A 9		

League goals (40): Ellington 15, Ommel 8, Cameron 4, Gall 3, Foran 2, Astafjevs 1, Foster 1, Hillier 1, Quinn 1, Thomas 1, Thomson 1, Weare 1, Opponents 1.
F.A. Cup goals (8): Ellington 4, Astafjevs 1, Hogg 1, Ommel 1, Walters 1. **Worthington Cup goals (1):** Hillier 1. **LDV Vans Trophy goals (5):** Ellington 2, Cameron 1, Hogg 1, Ommel 1.
Average home League attendance: 6,564. **Player of Year:** Scott Howie.

CARLISLE UNITED

After narrowly avoiding relegation to the Conference in the previous three seasons, Carlisle enjoyed the relative luxury of a place well away from danger. They went into the New Year joint bottom with Halifax Town, but a 6-1 win over Leyton Orient launched a run of only one defeat in nine matches. The season, however, ended in turmoil. Manager Roddy Collins – brother of former world champion boxer Steve Collins – was sacked for 'upsetting' owner Michael Knighton over comments about a club takeover, and not a single goal came in the final five games.

Allan, J .... 10(19)	Harkin, M .... 2(2)	Rogers, D .... 26(1)
Andrews, L .... 37(2)	Hews, S .... 4(1)	Rooke, S .... –(1)
Bell, S .... 3(2)	Hopper, T .... 20(9)	Skinner, S .... 1(5)
Berkley, A .... 2(3)	Hore, J .... –(3)	Slaven, J .... –(2)
Birch, M 42	Jack, M .... 16(16)	Soley, S .... 19(2)
Dickinson, M .... –(1)	Keen, P 36	Stevens, I .... 23(3)
Elliott, S 6	Maddison, L .... 5(2)	Thurston, M 1
Foran, R 37	McAughtrie, C .... 2(3)	Thwaites, A .... –(1)
Friars, S .... –(1)	McDonagh, W .... 7(5)	Weaver, L 10
Green, S 16	McGill, B .... 27(1)	Whitehead, S .... 29(3)
Haddow, A 4	Morley, D .... 14(4)	Willis, R .... –(1)
Hadland, P 4	Murphy, P .... 39(1)	Winstanley, M 36
Halliday, S .... 28(15)		

League goals (49): Foran 14, Stevens 8, Halliday 7, Soley 4, Green 3, Allan 2, Hews 2, McGill 2, Hadland 1, Hopper 1, McAughtrie 1, McDonagh 1, Rogers 1, Whitehead 1, Winstanley 1.
F.A. Cup goals (2): Foran 1, Soley 1. **Worthington Cup:** None. **LDV Vans Trophy goals (1):** Foran 1.
Average home League attendance: 3,204. **Player of Year:** Lee Andrews.

CHELTENHAM TOWN

From the Dr Martens League to the Conference to the Nationwide League Second Division in six seasons has been Cheltenham's rise under one of the game's brightest young managers, Steve Cotterill. A late loss of form cost them automatic promotion this time, but they overcame Hartlepool United on penalties in the play-off semi-finals and beat Rushden & Diamonds 3-1 in the final. Reaching the fifth round of the F.A. Cup confirmed the quality of a side for whom Julian Alsop and Tony Naylor scored 44 goals between them. But success came at a price, with Cotterill moving to Stoke City. Coach Graham Allner replaced him.

Alsop, J .... 38(3)	Grayson, N .... 13(20)	Jackson, M .... –(1)
Banks, C 38	Griffin, A .... 21(3)	Jones, S .... 2(3)
Book, S 39	Higgs, S .... –(1)	Lee, M .... 2(3)
Brough, J .... 9(12)	Hill, K .... 2(3)	McAuley, H .... 3(4)
Devaney, M .... 8(17)	Hopkins, G .... –(3)	Milton, R .... 37(2)
Duff, M 45	Howarth, N .... 18(8)	Muggleton, C 7
Finnigan, J 12	Howells, L 31	Naylor, A .... 43(1)

Tyson, N .... 1(7)	Walker, R .... 11(1)	Williams, L .... 36(2)
Victory, J .... 45(1)	White, J .... –(4)	Yates, M 45

Play-offs – Appearances: Alsop 3, Book 3, Duff 3, Finnigan 3, Griffin 3, Victory 3, Walker 3, Yates 3, Devaney 2(1), Williams 2(1), Naylor 2, Grayson 1(2), Lee 1(1), Milton 1.
League goals (66): Alsop 20, Naylor 12, Victory 7, Yates 7, Duff 3, Williams 3, Finnigan 2, Howells 2, Milton 2, Brough 1, Devaney 1, Grayson 1, Howarth 1, Tyson 1, Walker 1, White 1, Opponents 1. **Play-off goals (5):** Alsop 1, Devaney 1, Finnigan 1, Grayson 1, Williams 1.
F.A. Cup goals (12): Naylor 5, Alsop 4, Devaney 1, Howells 1, Milton 1. **Worthington Cup goals (1):** Grayson 1. **LDV Vans Trophy goals (3):** Alsop 1, Naylor 1, Victory 1.
Average home League attendance: 4,073. **Player of Year:** Julian Alsop.

DARLINGTON

Darlington move to a splendid new 25,000-capacity stadium still a Third Division club after an indifferent season in which the low spot was a toss-up between a 7-1 defeat at Scunthorpe and a players' walk-out at a fans' forum following comments by the chairman's wife Susan Reynolds about 'games being thrown at this time of the year.' Tommy Taylor went straight from Leyton Orient to the manager's job after Gary Bennett resigned and at least had the satisfaction of finishing above his former side.

Atkinson, B 35	Finch, K .... 11(1)	Marcelle, C .... –(3)
Betts, S 29	Ford, M .... 34(1)	Marsh, A 1
Brightwell, D 22	Harper, S .... 15(8)	McGurk, D .... 10(2)
Brumwell, P .... 16(6)	Healy, B .... 1(1)	Mellanby, D .... 22(2)
Caldwell, G 4	Heckingbottom, P ... 40(2)	Naylor, G 6
Campbell, P .... 8(8)	Hodgson, R .... 24(12)	Pearson, G 9
Chillingworth, D ...... 2(2)	Jackson, K .... 1(10)	Porter, C 7
Clark, I 28	Jeannin, A 11	Reed, A 7
Collett, A 28	Kilty, M .... 1(1)	Rundle, A .... 5(7)
Conlon, B 35	Liddle, C 31	Sheeran, M .... 1(21)
Convery, M .... 6(11)	Maddison, N .... 24(6)	Wainwright, N .... 32(3)

League goals (60): Clark 13, Conlon 10, Ford 7, Sheeran 6, Mellanby 5, Wainwright 4, Heckingbottom 2, Liddle 2, Hodgson 2, Atkinson 1, Campbell 1, Chillingworth 1, Harper 1, Healy 1, Maddison 1, Pearson 1, Naylor 1.
F.A. Cup goals (5): Wainwright 2, Campbell 1, Chillingworth 1, Conlon 1. **Worthington Cup goals:** None. **LDV Vans Trophy goals (2):** Brumwell 1, Opponents 1.
Average home League attendance: 3,827. **Player of Year:**

EXETER CITY

A difficult season at St James Park, where Noel Blake was sacked as manager after the first nine matches of the season yielded only one win. The chance of a money-spinning F.A. Cup run went by the board with a 3-0 defeat by Conference side Dagenham & Redbridge. Then the club's financial problems resulted in the players not being paid for a time. All things considered, Blake's successor John Cornforth did a reasonable job securing what would have been a mid-table position but for a poor finish in which his team failed to win in six games.

Afful, L .... –(2)	Elliott, S .... –(1)	Read, P .... 3(12)
Ampadu, K .... 33(3)	Flack, S .... 27(9)	Richardson, J .... 5(13)
Barlow, M .... 26(4)	Fraser, S .... 10(2)	Roberts, C .... 34(3)
Birch, G .... 5(10)	Goff, S 2	Roscoe, A .... 35(3)
Breslan, G .... 21(12)	Gregg, M 2	Tomlinson, G .... 25(7)
Buckle, P .... 19(6)	Gross, M 1	Van Heusden, A 33
Burrows, M .... 6(3)	Kerr, D 5	Walker, A 1
Campbell, J .... 14(2)	McCarthy, S .... 18(8)	Watson, A .... 42(1)
Cronin, G .... 24(6)	McConnell, B .... 30(2)	Whitworth, N .... 12(3)
Curran, C .... 35(2)	Moor, R .... –(2)	Zabek, L 2
Diallo, C .... –(2)	Power, G .... 36(1)	

League goals (48): Roberts 11, Roscoe 7, Flack 6, McCarthy 6, Tomlinson 5, McConnell 3, Breslan 2, Buckle 1, Campbell 1, Curran 1, Kerr 1, Power 1, Watson 1, Opponents 2.
F.A. Cup goals (3): Curran 1, Roscoe 1, Tomlinson 1. **Worthington Cup goals:** None. **LDV Vans Trophy goals (1):** Opponents 1.
Average home League attendance: 3,312. **Player of Year:** Barry McConnell.

HALIFAX TOWN

When Paul Bracewell became the first managerial casualty of the season after only four League games, the writing was on the wall at The Shay. Alan Little, his successor, had a measure of success in addressing the promotion's chronic lack of goals before a run of 12 matches without a win starting in late January took its toll. A 4-1 victory over promotion-chasing Cheltenham Town offered a glimmer of hope of survival. But Halifax had left themselves with too much to do. After finishing one off the bottom 12 months earlier, they were relegated to the Conference for the second time in nine years and Little went soon afterwards.

Bushell, S 25	Jones, G .... 20(15)	Richards, M 5
Butler, L .... 21(1)	Jules, M .... 34(1)	Richardson, B 24
Clarke, C 24	Kerrigan, S .... 23(7)	Smith, C .... –(2)
Clarke, M .... 22(8)	Ludden, D 2	Smith, G .... 11(2)
Crookes, P 1	Middleton, C .... 21(8)	Stoneman, P 32
Farrell, A .... 7(2)	Midgley, C .... 12(12)	Swales, S .... 20(4)
Fitzpatrick, I .... 26(3)	Mitchell, G .... 41(2)	Winder, N .... –(1)
Harsley, P 45	Oleksewycz, S .... –(2)	Wood, J .... 10(6)
Heinemann, N 3	Redfearn, N .... 27(3)	Woodward, A .... 29(1)
Herbert, R .... 11(1)	Reilly, A .... –(2)	Wright, P .... 3(11)
Houghton, S 7		

League goals (39): Harsley 11, Fitzpatrick 8, Redfearn 6, Jones 4, Midgley 3, Middleton 2, Bushell 1, Clarke, M 1, Stoneman 1, Swales 1, Woodward 1.
F.A. Cup goals (3): Harsley 1, Middleton 1, Wood 1. **Worthington Cup goals:** None. **LDV Vans Trophy goals:** None.
Average home League attendance: 2,114. **Player of Year:** Paul Harsley.

HARTLEPOOL UNITED

More heartbreak for Hartlepool, who suffered a third successive defeat in the play-off semi-finals. This time it came in a penalty shoot-out with Cheltenham Town after the teams were locked at 2-2 on aggregate over the two legs. But they deserved credit for turning the season round after being bottom at the beginning of November. Maximum points from their last five games pushed them into the top seven, with a 7-1 victory over Swansea City proving all-important when it came down to goal difference.

Arnison, P .... 11(8)	Hollund, M 3	Smith, P .... 30(1)
Barron, M 39	Humphreys, R .... 42(4)	Stephenson, P .... 23(6)
Bass, J .... 19(1)	Lee, G .... 38(1)	Sweeney, A .... –(2)
Boyd, A .... 10(18)	Lormor, A .... 4(13)	Tinkler, M .... 39(1)
Clark, I 5	Ormerod, A 2	Watson, G .... 31(1)
Clarke, D .... 24(9)	Parkin, J .... –(1)	Westwood, C 35
Coppinger, J 14	Robinson, M .... 33(4)	Widdrington, T 24
Easter, J .... –(12)	Sharp, J .... 13(2)	Williams, A 43
Henderson, K .... 13(10)	Simms, G .... 6(4)	Williams, E .... 5(3)

Play-offs – Appearances: Barron 2, Clarke 2, Humphreys 2, Lee 2, Smith 2, Watson 2, Williams, A 2, Williams, E 2, Westwood 2, Stephenson 1(1), Arnison 1, Boyd 1, Robinson 1, Henderson –(2).
League goals (74): Watson 18, Boyd 9, Tinkler 9, Clarke 7, Humphreys 5, Lee 5, Williams, E 4, Smith 3, Clark 2, Coppinger 2, Easter 2, Henderson 2, Widdrington 2, Barron 1, Bass 1, Lormor 1, Westwood 1. **Play-off goals (2):** Arnison 1, Williams, E 1.
F.A. Cup goals (1): Clarke 1. **Worthington Cup goals:** None. **LDV Vans Trophy goals:** None.
Average home League attendance: 3,566. **Player of Year:** Graeme Lee.

HULL CITY

A season which held considerable promise for Hull fell away badly after Christmas. They were handily placed for a promotion challenge until the flow of goals from Gary Alexander and Lawrie Dudfield dried up, the wins became infrequent and manager Brian Little departed after a difference of opinion with chairman Adam Pearson. Caretaker Billy Russell could not regain the initiative and Jan Molby came in too late from Kidderminster Harriers to make any difference. Of their last 13 games, Hull won only one.

Alexander, G 43	Holt, A .... 24(6)	Price, M .... –(1)
Beresford, D .... 33(8)	Johnsson, J .... 38(2)	Reddy, M .... 1(4)
Bloomer, M .... –(3)	Lee, D .... 2(9)	Roberts, N .... 3(3)
Bradshaw, G 3	Lightbourne, K .... 3(1)	Rowe, R .... 5(9)
Caceres, A .... 1(3)	Matthews, R .... 9(6)	Sneekes, R .... 17(5)
Dudfield, L .... 32(6)	Mohan, N .... 26(1)	Tait, P .... –(2)
Edwards, M .... 38(1)	Morley, B .... 1(2)	Van Blerk, J 10
Folan, C .... –(1)	Musselwhite, P 20	Whitmore, T ...... 23(11)
Glennon, M 26	Norris, D .... 3(3)	Whittle, J .... 35(1)
Goodison, I .... 14(2)	Petty, B .... 22(4)	Wicks, M 14
Greaves, M .... 25(1)	Philpott, L .... 9(2)	Williams, R .... 26(3)

League goals (57): Alexander 17, Dudfield 12, Johnsson 4, Reddy 4, Matthews 3, Rowe 2, Whitmore 2, Williams 2, Beresford 1, Bradshaw 1, Edwards 1, Greaves 1, Lee 1, Mohan 1, Norris 1, Philpott 1, Van Blerk 1, Opponents 2.
F.A. Cup goals (7): Alexander 2, Dudfield 2, Johnsson 1, Matthews 1, Opponents 1.
Worthington Cup goals (3): Alexander 1, Greaves 1, Whitmore 1. **LDV Vans Trophy goals (5):** Alexander 3, Whitmore 1, Whittle 1.
Average home League attendance: 9,505. **Player of Year:** Gary Alexander.

KIDDERMINSTER HARRIERS

It may have been a coincidence, but Kidderminster's chances of making the play-offs were effectively ended by a 2-1 defeat by Bristol Rovers three days after Jan Molby left to become manager of Hull City. The fact that they also had three players sent off in that game added to the disappointment. Kidderminster were never far away from the leading group and there was a feeling that one final push would have put them there. Caretaker Ian Britton was confirmed as manager at the end of the season.

Appleby, R .... 18(1)	Davies, B 9	Montgomery, G 2
Ayres, L .... 5(1)	Doyle, D .... –(1)	Medou-Otye, P 2
Bennett, D .... 39(3)	Ducros, A .... 7(7)	Nixon, E 2
Bird, A .... 14(12)	Foster, I .... 21(12)	Sall, A 27
Blake, M .... 23(1)	Hadley, S .... 5(5)	Shail, M 4
Brock, S 42	Henriksen, B .... 24(1)	Shilton, S .... 12(12)
Broughton, D ...... 23(15)	Hinton, C 41	Smith, A .... 33(3)
Clarkson, I .... 36(3)	Joy, I .... 13(3)	Stamps, S .... 36(1)
Corbett, A .... –(1)	Larkin, C .... 31(2)	Williams, D .... 37(1)
Danby, J .... –(3)	Lewis, M .... –(2)	

League goals (56): Bennett 8, Broughton 8, Larkin 8, Henriksen 8, Larkin 6, Appleby 4, Blake 4, Bird 2, Ducros 2, Sall 2, Smith 2, Williams 1, Opponents 1.
F.A. Cup goals: None. **Worthington Cup goals (2):** Bird 2. **LDV Vans Trophy goals (1):** Larkin 1.
Average home League attendance: 2,984. **Player of Year:** Craig Hinton.

LEYTON ORIENT

Four successive wins in September gave way to six matches without a victory and resulted in the resignation of Tommy Taylor, the longest-serving manager in Division Three with nearly five years' service at Brisbane Road. When coach Paul Brush succeeded him, Orient's fortunes continued to see-saw before a productive pre-Easter spell removed any relegation worries. The season was given impetus by an F.A. Cup run during which they won 4-1 at Portsmouth before falling by the same score to a Paul Gascoigne-inspired Everton in the fourth round at Goodison Park.

Barnard, D .... 6(4)	Gray, W .... 13(2)	McElhom, B .... –(2)
Barrett, S 32	Hadland, P .... –(5)	McGhee, D .... 39(1)
Bayes, A .... 12(1)	Harris, A 45	McLean, A .... 4(23)
Beall, M .... 7(4)	Hatcher, D .... 2(6)	Minton, J .... 32(1)
Brazier, M 8	Herrera, R 2	Morris, G 2
Canham, S .... 23(1)	Houghton, S .... 10(11)	Newton, A 10
Castle, S .... –(1)	Hutchings, C .... 9(1)	Nugent, K .... 7(2)
Christie, I .... 9(6)	Ibehre, J .... 21(7)	Oakes, S 11
Constantine, L .... 9(1)	Jones, B 16	Partridge, D .... 6(1)
Dorrian, C .... 2(1)	Joseph, M .... 29(1)	Smith, D 45
Downer, S .... 11(1)	Leigertwood, M 8	Tate, C .... 1(6)
Fletcher, G .... 3(6)	Lockwood, M .... 20(4)	Watts, S .... 22(8)
Gough, N .... 1(10)	Martin, J .... 29(2)	

League goals (55): Watts 9, Gray 5, Houghton 5, Minton 5, Canham 4, Ibehre 4, Christie 3, Constantine 3, Lockwood 2, Martin 2, McGhee 2, Smith 2, Gough 1, Hadland 1, Harris 1, Hutchings 1, Joseph 1, McLean 1, Newton 1, Nugent 1, Opponents 1.
F.A. Cup goals (8): Watts 3, Canham 1, Christie 1, Gray 1, Ibehre 1, Smith 1. **Worthington Cup goals (2):** Houghton 1, Minton 1. **LDV Vans Trophy goals (2):** McLean 1, Smith 1.
Average home League attendance: 4,539. **Player of Year:** Scott Barrett.

LINCOLN CITY

The demise of Halifax Town meant there was no late scrambling to avoid the drop into the Conference. That was the only real satisfaction Lincoln derived from a season in which they slipped to third from bottom after failing to win any of their last 11 matches. The campaign ended with the club in administration and the departure of manager Alan Buckley because of financial worries caused by the collapse of ITV Digital. Buckley's assistant, Keith Alexander, replaced him.

Bailey, M 18	Cameron, D .... 23(21)	Marriott, A 43
Barnett, J .... 23(3)	Camm, M .... 5(11)	Mayo, P .... 11(3)
Battersby, A .... 28(11)	Finnigan, J .... 21(2)	Morgan, P .... 32(2)
Betts, R .... 1(2)	Gain, P .... 35(7)	Pettinger, P 3
Bimson, S .... 34(1)	Hamilton, I 26	Sedgemore, B ...... 33(10)
Black, K .... 30(1)	Holmes, S .... 18(2)	Smith, P .... 6(2)
Bloomer, M .... 4(1)	Horrigan, D .... –(1)	Thorpe, L 37
Brown, G .... 32(4)	Logan, R .... –(2)	Walker, J .... 24(7)
Buckley, A .... 19(12)		

League goals (44): Thorpe 13, Cameron 6, Battersby 5, Black 5, Holmes 4, Walker 3, Barnett 2, Gain 2, Sedgemore 2, Morgan 1, Opponents 1.
F.A. Cup goals (3): Cameron 1, Hamilton 1, Holmes 1. **Worthington Cup goals (1):** Battersby 1. **LDV Vans Trophy goals (1):** Cameron 1.
Average home League atttendance: 3,222. **Player of Year:** Justin Walker.

LUTON TOWN

After successive defeats by Rochdale and Scunthorpe United in mid-February, there was a question mark about whether Joe Kinnear's side could stay the course for automatic promotion. They answered it emphatically with a club-record 12 successive victories which ensured the runners-up spot behind Plymouth Argyle and an immediate return to the Second Division. Leading their total of 96 goals – bettered only by Manchester City – was Steve Howard, who scored 19 of his 24 in the second half of the campaign. In most other seasons a team compiling 97 points would have been crowned champions.

Bayliss, D .... 15(3)	Coyne, C .... 29(2)	Dryden, R .... 2(1)
Boyce, E .... 30(7)	Crowe, D .... 32(2)	Emberson, C 33
Brkovic, A .... 17(4)	Douglas, S .... 2(7)	Forbes, A .... 15(25)

Fotiadis, A .... –(8)	Johnson, M .... 11(7)	Perrett, R .... 39(1)
George, L .... 2(2)	Kabba, S .... –(3)	Skelton, A 9
Griffiths, C 10	Locke, A .... 1(2)	Spring, M 42
Hillier, I .... 11(12)	Mansell, L .... 6(5)	Stirling, J 1
Holmes, P .... 4(3)	McSwegan, G .... 2(1)	Street, K .... 1(1)
Howard, S 42	Neilson, A 8	Taylor, M 43
Hughes, P .... 12(10)	Nicholls, K 42	Valois, J .... 32(2)
Hunter, I .... –(1)	Ovendale, M 13	

League goals (96): Howard 24, Crowe 15, Taylor 9, Griffiths 7, Nicholls 6, Spring 6, Valois 6, Forbes 4, Coyne 3, Hughes 3, Perrett 3, Brkovic 1, Fotiadis 1, Hillier 1, Holmes 1, Johnson 1, Mansell 1, Skelton 1, Opponents 1.
F.A. Cup goals (2): Brkovic 1, Forbes 1. **Worthington Cup:** None. **LDV Vans Trophy goals (2):** Brennan 1, Thomson 1.
Average home League attendance: 6,852. **Player of Year:** Matthew Taylor.

MACCLESFIELD TOWN

Macclesfield Town went into the record books by winning the longest-ever F.A. Cup penalty shoot-out 11-10 against Conference side Forest Green – a result which helped pave the way for a money-spinning third round tie against West Ham United. In the League, they prospered away from Moss Rose with eight victories. Home form, however, was below par and resulted in a mid-table position for David Moss, who took over when Gil Prescott resigned after two months of the season.

Abbey, G .... 15(2)	Lambert, R .... 32(3)	Smith, J .... 7(1)
Adams, D .... 38(1)	Lightbourne, K ...... 22(7)	Smith, D 8
Askey, J .... 1(17)	Macauley, S 12	Tinson, D 46
Bullock, M .... 2(1)	Martin, L .... 8(1)	Tipton, M .... 12(1)
Byrne, C .... 26(6)	McAvoy, A .... 4(6)	Tracey, R .... 10(10)
Came, S 1	Munroe, K .... 19(11)	Welch, M 6
Eyre, R .... 12(2)	O'Neill, P .... 7(4)	Whitehead, D .... 1(1)
Glover, L .... 38(5)	Priest, C .... 32(1)	Whitaker, D .... 15(1)
Hitchen, S .... 28(2)	Ridler, D .... 37(2)	Wilson, S 38
Keen, K .... 29(1)	Shuttleworth, B .... –(3)	Woolley, M .... –(3)

League goals (41): Glover 9, Lambert 8, Byrne 6, Lightbourne 4, Tipton 3, Smith, J 2, Tracey 2, Whittaker 2, Askey 1, Hitchen 1, Priest 1, Tinson 1, Opponents 1.
F.A. Cup goals (7): Byrne 2, Glover 2, Lambert 2, Keen 1. **Worthington Cup goals (1):** Glover 1. **LDV Vans Trophy goals (1):** Glover 1.
Average home League attendance: 2,127. **Player of Year:** Danny Adams.

MANSFIELD TOWN

Jubilant scenes on the final day of the season at Field Mill, where Mansfield claimed the third automatic promotion spot with a 2-0 win over Carlisle United in front of a crowd of more than 8,000. They overtook Cheltenham Town after snapping out of a lean run-up to Easter which brought only one point from five matches. It was a successful first taste of management for Stuart Watkiss, who took over when Bill Dearden left for Notts County in mid-season. Individual honours went to 28-goal Chris Greenacre, the division's top scorer in all competitions.

Asher, A .... 1(9)	Harris, R .... –(6)	Reddington, S .... 34(4)
Bacon, D .... 1(7)	Hassell, B 43	Robinson, L 36
Barrett, A .... 26(3)	Jervis, D .... –(3)	Sellars, S .... 5(1)
Bingham, M .... 1(1)	Kelly, D .... 11(6)	Tankard, A .... 22(8)
Bradley, S .... 7(9)	Lawrence, L 32	Wheatcroft, P .... 1(1)
Clarke, J 1	Murray, A 13	White, A .... 16(6)
Corden, W 46	Pemberton, M ...... 33(5)	White, J .... 6(1)
Disley, C .... 31(5)	Pilkington, K 45	Williams, L .... –(2)
Greenacre, C .... 43(1)	Piper, M 8	Williamson, L .... 44(2)

League goals (72): Greenacre 21, Corden 8, Disley 7, Murray 7, Kelly 4, Pemberton 4, White, A 4, Bradley 3, Williamson 3, Lawrence 2, Tankard 2, Bacon 1, Hassell 1, Piper 1, Reddington 1, Sellars 1, Opponents 2.
F.A. Cup goals (6): Greenacre 5, Corden 1. **Worthington Cup goals (3):** Greenacre 2, White, A 1. **LDV Vans Trophy goals:** None.
Average home League attendance: 4,919. **Player of Year:** Bobby Hassell.

OXFORD UNITED

Oxford moved out of the cramped Manor Ground to a new stadium, but there was never any prospect of a move back to the Second Division. League results were poor and their Cup form offered no consolation with first round defeats in the F.A. Cup, Worthington Cup and LDV Vans Trophy. Manager Mark Wright resigned after being fined by the F.A. for abusive language towards a referee and was replaced by Ian Atkins, whose team were 16th at the turn of the year and slipped to 21st at the end of the campaign – the club's lowest-ever in the League.

Beauchamp, J .... 2(1)	King, S .... 1(1)	Richardson, J .... 16(2)
Bolland, P 20	Knight, R 3	Ricketts, S .... 19(10)
Bound, M 22	Louis, J .... –(1)	Savage, D 42
Brooks, J .... 18(7)	Maddison, L 11	Scott, A .... 25(5)
Crosby, A .... 22(1)	McCaldon, I 28	Stockley, S .... 39(2)
Douglas, S .... 1(3)	Moody, P .... 29(6)	Tait, P .... 13(1)
Folland, R .... –(10)	Morley, D .... 16(2)	Thomas, M .... 13(1)
Gray, P .... 14(7)	Omoyinmi, E .... 11(12)	Waterman, D .... 4(1)
Guyett, S .... 20(2)	Patterson, D 2	Whitehead, D .... 30(10)
Hackett, C .... 5(10)	Powell, P .... 33(3)	Woodman, A 15
Hatswell, W 21	Quinn, R .... 11(5)	

League goals (53): Moody 13, Brooks 10, Scott 8, Gray 4, Powell 4, Morley 3, Omoyinmi 3, Thomas 2, Beauchamp 1, Bolland 1, Crosby 1, Ricketts 1, Savage 1, Whitehead 1.
F.A. Cup goals: None. **Worthington Cup goals (1):** Scott 1. **LDV Vans Trophy goals:** None.
Average home League attendance: 6,257. **Player of Year:** Jamie Brooks.

PLYMOUTH ARGYLE

Plymouth Argyle had the distinction of becoming the first team in the country to make sure of promotion and went on to become Third Division champions with a record 102 points after making light of a poor start to the season. Their first three matches yielded a single point, but it was not until December 22 that Paul Sturrock's side lost again and they continued in the same vein in the New Year. Success was founded on a resolute defence which conceded only 28 goals, and was rewarded with five-figure crowds at a redeveloped Home Park, topped by more than 18,000 for the last game against Cheltenham Town.

Adams, S .... 40(6)	Evans, M .... 30(8)	McGlinchey, B .... 26(3)
Adamson, C 1	Evers, S .... 3(4)	Phillips, M .... 37(2)
Banger, N .... 3(7)	Friio, D 41	Stonebridge, I ...... 29(13)
Bent, J .... 16(5)	Gritton, M .... –(2)	Sturrock, B .... 4(15)
Beswetherick, J ..... 27(5)	Heaney, N .... 1(7)	Taylor, C .... –(1)
Broad, J .... 1(6)	Hodges, L .... 42(3)	Wills, K .... 13(5)
Coughlan, G 46	Keith, M .... 13(10)	Worrell, D 42
Crowe, D .... –(1)	Larrieu, R 45	Wotton, P 46

League goals (71): Coughlan 11, Keith 9, Friio 8, Stonebridge 8, Evans 7, Hodges 6, Phillips 6, Wotton 5, Bent 3, Adams 2, Banger 2, McGlinchey 1, Sturrock 1, Opponents 2.
F.A. Cup goals (7): Friio 2, Phillips 2, Bent 1, Stonebridge 1, Wotton 1. **Worthington Cup goals:** None. **LDV Vans Trophy goals (1):** Friio 1.
Average home League attendance: 8,788. **Player of Year:** Graham Coughlhan.

ROCHDALE

John Hollins kept Rochdale in the hunt after Steve Parkin left to manage Barnsley and a productive finish to the season, during which Paul Simpson scored some important goals, was almost rewarded with the third automatic promotion place. Simpson was on the mark again in a 2-2 draw secured in the first leg of the play-off semi-final at Rushden and Diamonds. But despite scoring first in the return, Rochdale were unable to maintain the advantage and a 2-1 defeat left them reflecting on what might have been. Hollins went after failing to agree a new contract and Simpson replaced him.

Atkinson, G .... 8(3)	Evans, W 43	McCourt, P ...... 10(13)
Banks, S 15	Flitcroft, D .... 21(14)	McEvilly, L .... 13(5)
Bayliss, D 9	Ford, A 17	McLoughlin, A .... 15(3)
Coleman, S .... 8(3)	Gilks, M 19	Oliver, M 45
Connor, P .... 11(6)	Griffiths, G 41	Platt, C .... 41(2)
Doughty, M .... 32(4)	Hahnemann, M 5	Simpson, P 7
Duffy, L .... 1(5)	Jobson, R .... 34(1)	Todd, L .... 8(2)
Dunning, D .... 4(1)	Jones, G 20	Townson, K ...... 17(24)
Durkan, K .... 16(14)	Jones, S .... 6(3)	Ware, P .... 4(4)
Edwards, N 7	McAuley, S 23	Wheatcroft, P 6

Play-offs – Appearances: Doughty 2, Edwards 2, Evans 2, Flitcroft 2, Griffiths 2, Jobson 2, McEvilly 2, McLoughlin 2, Oliver 2, Simpson 2, Townson 1(1), Platt 1, Coleman –(1), Connor –(1), McCourt –(1).
League goals (65): Townson 14, Oliver 7, Platt 7, Jones, G 5, Simpson 5, Griffiths 4, McCourt 4, McEvilly 4, Jobson 3, Wheatcroft 3, Ford 2, Coleman 2, Connor 1, Doughty 1, Durkan 1, McLoughlin 1, Jones, S 1, Opponents 1. **Play-off goals (3):** McEvilly 1, Simpson 1, Opponents 1.
F.A. Cup goals (2): Doughty 1, Oliver 1. **Worthington Cup goals (3):** Townson 2, Ford 1.
LDV Vans Trophy goals (3): Jones, G 1, Platt 1, Townson 1.
Average home League attendance: 3,430. **Player of Year:** Gareth Griffiths.

RUSHDEN AND DIAMONDS

Brian Talbot would have settled for consolidation by his side in their first season in the Nationwide League. Instead, the new boys exceeded all expectations by reaching the play-offs with the help of a flood of goals by Onandi Lowe and the creative influence of fellow Jamaican Paul Hall. They overcame Rochdale over two legs – Lowe scoring for the 20th time in 28 matches – and although former Conference rivals Cheltenham Town proved too strong in the final, Rushden could reflect on a job well done with the prospect of good times ahead.

Angell, B .... 3(2)	Hall, P 34	Rodwell, J .... 8(1)
Bell, D .... –(1)	Hanlon, R .... 33(2)	Sambrook, A .... 25(1)
Brady, J .... 9(13)	Hunter, B 23	Setchell, G .... 13(9)
Burgess, A .... 28(4)	Jackson, J 5	Sigere, J M .... 4(3)
Butterworth, G .... 28(1)	Lee, C 1	Solkhon, B .... –(1)
Carey, S .... 7(1)	Lowe, O 25	Talbot, D .... 2(1)
Carr, D .... 1(0)	McElhatton, M ...... 4(3)	Thomson, P .... 1(1)
Darby, D .... 17(13)	Mills, G .... 3(6)	Tillson, A 14
Dempster, J .... –(2)	Mustafa, T .... 21(2)	Turley, W 43
Douglas, S .... 4(4)	Partridge, S .... 26(11)	Underwood, P 40
Duffy, R .... 1(7)	Patmore, W 4	Warburton, R 1
Folan, C .... 1(5)	Pennock, A .... 3(2)	Wardley, S 18
Gray, S 12	Peters, M 40	Wormull, S .... 4(1)

Play-offs – Appearances: Butterworth 3, Hall 3, Lowe 3, Mustafa 3, Partridge 3, Peters 3, Tillson 3, Turley 3, Underwood 3, Wardley 3, Burgess 2, Gray 1(1), Angell –(2), Brady –(1).

League goals (69): Lowe 19, Hall 8, Darby 7, Hanlon 6, Partridge 5, Burgess 4, Wardley 4, Angell 2, Brady 1, Butterworth 1, Duffy 1, Hunter 1, McElhatton 1, Mustafa 1, Patmore 1, Setchell 1, Sigere 1, Thomson 1, Opponents 4. Play-off goals (5): Hall 2, Butterworth 1, Lowe 1, Wardley 1.
F.A. Cup goals (2): Hanlon 2. Worthington Cup goals (3): Darby 1, Mustafa 1, Peters 1.
LDV Vans Trophy goals (1): Hall 1.
Average home League attendance: 4,403. Player of Year: Paul Underwood.

SCUNTHORPE UNITED

With a month of the season remaining, Scunthorpe looked a good bet for a play-off place and even harboured ambitions of a late run for an automatic promotion place. But five games produced only two points and a last-minute winner against York City on the final day was not enough to prevent them losing out to Hartlepool United on goal difference. Ironically, a 7-1 success over Darlington had helped them build up a healthy difference, until Hartlepool's 7-1 victory over Swansea City in their penultimate match altered the picture.

Anderson, M .... –(1)	Evans, T 42	Pepper, N .... –(1)
Barwick, T .... 7(3)	Grant, K .... 3(1)	Quailey, B .... 15(15)
Beagrie, P .... 39(1)	Graves, W .... 16(1)	Ridley, L .... 2(2)
Bradshaw, C .... 18(3)	Hodges, L .... 26(9)	Sheldon, G .... 6(8)
Brough, S .... 5(14)	Jackson, M 45	Sparrow, M .... 20(4)
Calvo-Garcia, A .... 33(1)	Jeffrey, M .... 4(2)	Stanton, N .... 39(3)
Carruthers, M .... 30(3)	Kell, R 16	Thom, S .... 17(3)
Cotterill, J .... 8(2)	McCombe, J .... 11(6)	Torpey, S .... 37(2)
Croudson, S 4	McGibbon, P 6	Vaughan, A 5
Dawson, A 44	Parton, A 1	Wilcox, R .... 6(3)
Dudley, C .... 1(3)		

League goals (74): Carruthers 13, Torpey 12, Beagrie 11, Quailey 8, Calvo-Garcia 6, Hodges 6, Graves 3, Jackson 3, Sheldon 2, Thom 2, Bradshaw 1, Brough 1, Grant 1, Jeffrey 1, Kell 1, McCombe 1, Sparrow 1, Opponents 1.
F.A. Cup goals (7): Carruthers 3, Calvo-Garcia 2, Hodges 1, McCombe 1. Worthington Cup goals: None. LDV Vans Trophy goals (7): Beagrie 2, Torpey 2, Carruthers 1, Hodges 1, McCombe 1.
Average home League attendance: 3,791. Player of Year: Alex Calvo-Garcia.

SHREWSBURY TOWN

Three straight wins at a crucial time of the season lifted Shrewsbury into a play-off place and raised confidence for the final match against Luton Town at Gay Meadow. They had beaten most of the other leading teams at home, but despite a stream of corners and 22-goal Luke Rodgers being denied by a goal-line clearance, the afternoon ended in disappointment for a sell-out crowd as runners-up Luton ended promotion aspirations with a 2-0 victory.

Aiston, S .... 22(13)	Jagielka, S .... 25(6)	Rioch, G 38
Atkins, M 42	Jemson, N 28	Rodgers, L 38
Cartwright, M 14	Jenkins, I .... 3(2)	Thompson, A .... 13(1)
Drysdale, L .... 22(4)	Lormor, A 7	Tolley, J .... 19(4)
Dunbavin, I .... 32(2)	Lowe, R .... 22(16)	Tretton, A .... 15(3)
Fallon, R .... 8(3)	Moss, D .... 23(8)	Walker, J .... –(3)
Freestone, C .... 3(4)	Murphy, C .... –(4)	Wilding, P .... 12(10)
Guinan, S .... 4(1)	Murray, K .... 25(8)	Woan, I 14
Heathcote, M .... 33(1)	Redmile, M 44	

League goals (64): Rodgers 22, Jemson 10, Lowe 7, Jagielka 5, Woan 3, Aiston 2, Atkins 2, Heathcote 2, Lormor 2, Moss 2, Murray 2, Redmile 2, Rioch 2, Tolley 1.
F.A. Cup goals: None. Worthington Cup goals (1): Jemson 1. LDV Vans Trophy goals: None.
Average home League attendance: 3,836. Player of Year: Luke Rodgers.

SOUTHEND UNITED

When David Webb resigned as manager two months into the season, saying he was no longer able to put 100 per cent into the job after a health scare, Southend turned to former club captain Rob Newman to fill the position. Newman presided over an a largely uneventful season in which his side neither threatened to put pressure on the leading group nor came close to being sucked into trouble, although he did have the satisfaction of scoring a couple of goals when he returned to playing.

Alderton, R	–(2)	Forbes, S	3(10)	Rawle, M	25(5)
Barry-Murphy, B	8	Gay, D	5(1)	Richards, T	9(8)
Beard, M	5(9)	Harris, J	2(3)	Risbridger, G	–(1)
Belgrave, B	32(2)	Holness, D	1(1)	Searle, D	41(2)
Bramble, T	32(3)	Hutchings, C	28(1)	Selley, I	14
Broad, S	30(2)	Johnson, L	24(4)	Smith, B	–(1)
Clark, A	1(2)	Kerrigan, D	6(5)	Szmid, M	1(1)
Clark, S	8(3)	Lunan, J	–(1)	Thurgood, S	34(5)
Cort, L	43(2)	Maher, K	36	Wallace, A	–(2)
D'Sane, R	1(1)	McSweeney, D	13(8)	Webb, D	10(6)
Flahavan, D	41	Newman, R	10(1)	Whelan, P	43(1)

League goals (51): Bramble 9, Belgrave 5, Maher 5, Rawle 5, Whelan 5, Cort 4, Hutchings 4, Broad 2, Johnson 2, Newman 2, Richards 2, Webb 2, Barry-Murphy 1, Searle 1, Clark S 1, Opponents 1.
F.A. Cup goals (7): Bramble 3, Belgrave 2, Rawle 1, Whelan 1. **Worthington Cup goals:** None. **LDV Vans Trophy goals (4):** Bramble 1, Hutchings 1, Rawle 1, Webb 1.
Average home League attendance: 3,994. **Player of Year:** Darryl Flahavan.

SWANSEA CITY

Never any prospect of Swansea regaining their Second Division status, but no shortage of activity off the field at the Vetch. John Hollins went after six matches, his successor Colin Addison lasted six months and there was a take-over of the club by a consortium led by their former defender and Wales stalwart Mel Nurse. The F.A. Cup provided a rare high spot – a 4-0 win over Q.P.R. Low point was a 7-1 defeat by Hartlepool United in the penultimate match of the season.

Appleby, R	3(7)	Freestone, R	43	Roberts, S	13
Bound, M	18	Howard, M	42	Romo, D	3(7)
Brodie, S	21(4)	Jenkins, L	14(1)	Sharp, N	22(3)
Casey, R	6(10)	Jones, J	3	Sidibe, M	26(5)
Coates, J	44(1)	Keegan, M	–(2)	Smith, J	7(1)
Cusack, N	33(2)	Lacey, D	5(11)	Todd, C	28(4)
De-Vulgt, L	7(3)	Mazzina, N	3	Tyson, N	7(4)
Draper, C	–(2)	Mumford, A	28(4)	Watkin, S	25(6)
Evans, S	4	O'Leary, K	30(1)	Williams, J	26(15)
Evans, T	16	Phillips, G	29(6)		

League goals (53): Watkin 8, Sidibe 7, Coates 5, Mumford 5, Roberts 5, Williams 4, Todd 3, Bound 2, Brodie 2, Cusack 2, O'Leary 2, Phillips 2, Howard 1, Jenkins 1, Lacey 1, Romo 1, Sharp 1, Tyson 1.
F.A. Cup goals (5): Cusack 2, Sidibe 1, Watkin 1, Williams 1. **Worthington Cup goals:** None. **LDV Vans Trophy goals (1):** Coates 1.
Average home League attendance: 3,692. **Player of Year:** Andrew Mumford.

TORQUAY UNITED

Another dramatic end to the season for Torquay, whose victory at Barnet 12 months previously had determined who would drop into the Conference. This time it was former England defender Roy McFarland resigning as manager after refusing to fire his assistant David Preece in a cost-cutting exercise resulting from the ITV Digital collapse.

McFarland's team enjoyed their best spell either side of Easter when going six matches without conceding a goal before a 4-2 home defeat by relegated Halifax Town. Leroy Rosenior took over from McFarland.

Aggrey, J 2	Greyling, A .... –(2)	Nicholls, M .... 4(5)
Ashford, R .... 1(1)	Hankin, S 27	O'Brien, M .... –(1)
Banger, N 1	Hanson, C 6	Parker, K .... –(2)
Bedeau, A .... 9(12)	Hazell, R 19	Preece, D .... 4(2)
Benefield, J .... 3(5)	Healy, B 2	Rees, J .... 26(7)
Brabin, G 6	Herrera, R .... 2(1)	Richardson, M .... 18(12)
Brandon, C .... 22(5)	Hill, K .... 40(4)	Roach, N .... 5(7)
Brown, D 2	Hockley, M 12	Russell, A 33
Canoville, L .... 10(2)	Holmes, P .... 17(1)	Russell, L .... 7(4)
Dearden, K 46	Law, G .... –(5)	Tully, S .... 17(1)
Douglin, T .... 5(1)	Logan, R 16	Williams, E .... 8(17)
Fowler, J 14	MacDonald, C 5	Williamson, M 3
Goodridge, G .... 9(8)	Martin, A 5	Woods, S 38
Graham, D .... 31(5)	McNeil, M 16	Woozley, D .... 15(1)

League goals (46): Graham 8, Russell, A 6, Richardson 6, Bedeau 4, Logan 4, Brandon 3, Hill 3, Woods 2, Ashford 1, Canoville 1, Fowler 1, Goodridge 1, Nicholls 1, Rees 1, Roach 1, Williams 1, Opponents 2.
F.A. Cup goals (1): Hill 1. **Worthington Cup goals (2):** Brandon 1, Graham 1. **LDV Vans Trophy goals:** None.
Average home League attendance: 2,563. **Player of Year:** Kevin Dearden.

YORK CITY

A difficult season on and off the field for York, who were in danger of going out of business until motor racing tycoon John Batchelor took over the reins at the club in mid-March. Three wins out of five at the outset suggested a measure of League success, but York failed to maintain the momentum and spent most of the time hovering just above the danger zone before 13 points from the last five matches improved their position.

Basham, M .... 26(3)	Fielding, J 9	Parkin, J 18
Brackstone, S .... 6(3)	Fox, C .... 5(7)	Potter, G 37
Brass, C 41	Grant, L .... –(1)	Proctor, M .... 40(1)
Bullock, L .... 39(1)	Hobson, G .... 14(2)	Rhodes, B 1
Cooper, R .... 23(2)	Hocking, M .... 29(4)	Richardson, N .... 17(5)
Darlow, K .... 1(1)	Howarth, R .... 1(1)	Salvati, M .... 1(7)
Duffield, P .... 7(4)	Jones, S .... 7(1)	Smith, C .... 12(3)
Edmondson, D .... 34(2)	Maley, S .... 11(2)	Stamp, N .... 5(2)
Emmerson, S .... –(5)	Mathie, A .... 11(12)	Wise, S .... 3(3)
Evans, M .... 1(1)	Nogan, L .... 40(2)	Wood, L .... 12(2)
Fettis, A 45	O'Kane, A .... 11(1)	

League goals (54): Proctor 14, Nogan 13, Bullock 8, Duffield 3, Basham 2, Brass 2, Mathie 2, Parkin 2, Potter 2, Cooper 1, Fielding 1, Jones 1, Salvati 1, Opponents 2.
F.A. Cup goals (5): Potter 2, Brass 1, Richardson 1, Opponents 1. **Worthington Cup goals (2):** Brass 1, Bullock 1. **LDV Vans Trophy goals:** None.
Average home League attendance: 3,144. **Player of Year:** Alan Fettis.

HAT-TRICK FOR F.A. CUP SUBSTITUTE

Lee Poland came on as a substitute and scored a hat-trick to give Altrincham a 4-1 win over Lancaster City in an F.A. Cup first round replay.

SCOTTISH LEAGUE ROLL CALL

APPEARANCES & SCORERS 2001-02

(Figures in brackets = appearances as substitute)

PREMIER LEAGUE

ABERDEEN

Ground: Pittodrie Stadium, Aberdeen AB24 5QH. **Capacity:** 22,199.
Telephone: 01224 650400. **Colours:** Red with white. **Nickname:** Dons.

Anderson, R .... 17(7)	Mackie, D .... 27(7)	Solger, T .... 10(5)
Belabed, R .... –(1)	McAllister, J .... 26(3)	Thornley, B .... 15(9)
Bett, C .... 1(2)	McGuire, P 38	Tiernan, F .... 11(12)
Bisconti, R 31	McNaughton, K ...... 33(1)	Whyte, D .... 30(1)
Clark, C .... 1(7)	Mike, L .... 7(2)	Winters, R 34
Dadi, E .... 20(8)	O'Donoghue, R .... –(1)	Young, Darren 32
Esson, R .... 7(2)	Peat, M 1	Young, Derek .... 24(8)
Guntveit, C .... 16(3)	Preece, D .... 7(1)	Zerouali, H .... 6(12)
Kjaer, P 23	Rutkiewicz, K .... 1(3)	

League goals (51): Winters 13, Mackie 8, Zerouali 8, Dadi 4, McGuire 3, Mike 3, Thornley 3, Young, Derek 3, Anderson 1, Bisconti 1, Guntveit 1, Rutkiewicz 1, Solberg 1, Young, Darren 1.
Tennents Cup goals (4): McAllister 1, Thornley 1, Winters 1, Young, Darren 1. **CIS Cup goals (3):** Dadi 1, Mackie 1. Thornley 1.

CELTIC

Ground: Celtic Park, Glasgow G40 3RE. **Capacity:** 60,832.
Telephone: 0141 556 2611. **Colours:** Green and white. **Nickname:** Bhoys.

Agathe, D 20	Kharine, D .... 2(1)	Petrov, S .... 26(2)
Balde, B 22	Lambert, P .... 33(1)	Petta, B .... 12(6)
Boyd, T 9	Larsson, H 33	Smith, J .... 3(8)
Crainey, S .... 10(5)	Lennon, N .... 32(1)	Sutton, C 18
Douglas, R 35	Lynch, S 1	Sylla, M .... 7(2)
Gould, J 1	Maloney, S .... 3(13)	Tebily, O .... 8(3)
Guppy, S .... 10(6)	McNamara, J .... 9(11)	Thompson, A .... 22(3)
Hartson, J .... 26(5)	Mjallby, J 35	Valgaeren, J 20
Healy, C .... 2(2)	Moravcik, L .... 16(7)	Wieghorst, M .... 2(1)
Kennedy, J 1		

League goals (94): Larsson 29, Hartson 19, Moravcik 6, Petrov 6, Thompson 6, Lambert 5, Maloney 5, Sutton 4, Mjallby 3, Balde 2, Lynch 2, Valgaeren 2, Agathe 1, Lennon 1, Smith 1, Sylla 1, Opponents 1.
Tennents Cup goals (14): Balde 2, Hartson 2, Larsson 2, Thompson 2, Maloney 1, Petrov 1, Petta 1, Sylla 1, Wieghorst 1, Opponents 1. **CIS Cup goals (11):** Maloney 4, Hartson 3, Balde 2, Healy 1, Tebily 1. **Champions League goals (11):** Larsson 3, Sutton 3, Agathe 1, Petrov 1, Petta 1, Thompson 1, Valgaeren 1. **UEFA Cup goals (1):** Larsson 1.

DUNDEE

Ground: Dens Park, Dundee DD3 7JY. **Capacity:** 12,371.
Telephone: 01382 889966. **Colours:** Navy blue and white. **Nickname:** Dark Blues.

Artero, J .... 12(9)	Beith, G .... 1(2)	Caballero, F .... 28(4)
Beghetto, M 21	Boylan, C .... –(1)	Carranza, B .... 23(3)

Coyne, C .... –(2)	Langfield, J 21	Robertson, M .... 7(9)
Del Rio, W .... 31(2)	Mackay, D .... 13(4)	Romano, A .... 17(4)
Fan Zhiyi 14	Marrocco, M 12	Sara, J .... 25(3)
Forbes, B .... 2(2)	Milne, S .... 15(14)	Smith, B .... 36(2)
Garrido, B .... 8(10)	Naveda, B .... –(2)	Speroni, J 17
Gatti, L .... –(4)	Nemsadze, G .... 10(1)	Torres, Q 19
Kemas, K .... 2(10)	Rae, G 36	Traverso, G .... –(2)
Ketsbaia, T 22	Robb, S .... –(1)	Wilkie, L 8
Khizanishvili, Z 18		

League goals (41): Sara 11, Caballero 6, Ketsbaia 6, Rae 6, Milne 5, Fan Zhiyi 2, Carranza 1, Kemas 1, Mackay 1, Nemsadze 1, Torres 1.
Tennents Cup goals (4): Fan Zhiyi 1, Milne 1, Sara 1, Torres 1. **CIS Cup goals (3):** Boylan 1, Caballero 1, Milne 1.

DUNDEE UNITED

Ground: Tannadice Park, Dundee DD3 7JW. **Capacity:** 14,209.
Telephone: 01382 833166. **Colours:** Tangerine and black. **Nickname:** Terrors.

Aljofree, H 27	Hannah, D .... 16(4)	O'Donnell, S .... 1(5)
Buchan, M .... 6(1)	Jarvie, P .... –(1)	Ogunmade, D .... –(2)
Carson, S .... 6(7)	Lauchlan, J 33	Partridge, D 13
Cocozza, M .... 1(1)	Lilley, D .... 19(7)	Paterson, J .... 12(16)
Duff, S 9	McConalogue, S ..... 5(7)	Thompson, S .... 20(11)
Easton, C .... 33(3)	McCracken, D .... 16(3)	Venetis, A .... 14(10)
Fullarton, J 11	McCunnie, J .... 27(1)	Wilson, M 1
Gallacher, P 38	McIntyre, J .... 16(3)	Winters, D .... 4(9)
Griffin, D 29	Miller, C .... 31(3)	Wright, S .... 8(1)
Hamilton, J .... 20(4)	O'Brien, R .... 2(6)	

League goals (38): Lilley 6, McIntyre 6, Thompson 6, Hamilton 5, Miller 4, Easton 3, Aljofree 2, Griffin 2, McConalogue 1, Paterson 1, Venetis 1, Opponents 1.
Tennents Cup goals (9): Aljofree 3, Thompson 2, Winters 2, Easton 1, Miller 1. **CIS Cup goals (6):** Thompson 2, Easton 1, Griffin 1, Hamilton 1, Paterson 1.

DUNFERMLINE

Ground: East End Park, Dunfermline KY12 7RB. **Capacity:** 12,558.
Telephone: 01383 724295. **Colours:** Black and white. **Nickname:** Pars.

Blair, B .... –(1)	MacPherson, A .... 22(2)	Panopoulos, M .... 7(2)
Bullen, L .... 25(6)	Mason, G .... 33(2)	Petrie, S .... 14(9)
Crawford, S 36	McGarty, M .... –(2)	Potter, J .... 2(2)
Dair, J .... 17(11)	McGroarty, C .... 17(5)	Rossi, Y .... 9(1)
De Gier, J 12	McLeish, K .... 1(1)	Ruitenbeek, M 29
Doesburg, M .... 4(5)	N'Diaye, S .... 6(3)	Thomson, S M 33
Ferguson, I 20	Nicholls, D .... 12(11)	Thomson, S Y 8
Hampshire, S .... 13(11)	Nicholson, B .... 36(1)	Skerla A 35
Karnebeek, A .... 3(2)	Nish, C .... 2(12)	Skinner, J .... 18(8)
Kilgannon, S .... 3(6)		

League goals (41): Crawford 7, Nicholson 7, Thomson, S M 6, De Gier 5, Bullen 4, Hampshire 3, Mason 2, Petrie 2, Dair 1, N'Diaye 1, Nicholls 1, Skerla 1, Opponents 1.
Tennents Cup goals (3): Crawford 2, Thomson, S M 1. **CIS Cup goals (4):** Mason 2, Hampshire 1, Nicholson 1.

HEARTS

Ground: Tynecastle, Edinburgh EH 11 2NL. **Capacity:** 18,008.
Telephone: 0131 200 7200. **Colours:** Maroon. **Nickname:** Jam Tarts.

Adam, S .... 12(7)	Boyack, S .... 6(12)	Cameron, C 4

Davidson, R .... –(2)	Maybury, A 27	Pressley, S 30
Flogel, T .... 29(3)	McCann, A .... 4(2)	Severin, S .... 24(3)
Fuller, R 27	McKenna, K ...... 31(2)	Simmons, S ...... 24(10)
Fulton, S .... 27(8)	McKenzie, R 6	Sloan, R .... 4(2)
Gronlund, T .... 22(1)	McMullan, P .... –(1)	Tod, A 3
Hamill, J .... 1(2)	McSwegan, G .... 1(4)	Tomaschek, R .... 6(1)
Juanjo .... 5(4)	Milne, K .... 3(1)	Wales, G .... 21(11)
Kirk, A .... 4(16)	Neilson, R 2	Webster, A .... 25(2)
Mahe, S 35	Niemi, A 32	Weir, J .... 3(7)

League goals (52): McKenna 9, Fuller 8, Wales 5, Simmons 5, Adam 3, Cameron 3, Fulton . 3, Severin 3, Gronlund 2, Juanjo 2, Mahe 2, Pressley 2, Kirk 1, Sloan 1, Tod 1, Webster 1.
Tennents Cup goals (3): Fuller 2, Wales 1. **CIS Cup goals:** None.

HIBERNIAN

Ground: Easter Road, Edinburgh EH7 5QG. **Capacity:** 16,032.
Telephone: 0131 661 2159. **Colours:** Green and white. **Nickname:** Hibees.

Andrews, L .... –(2)	Hilland, P 3	Orman, J 30
Arpinon, F .... 16(4)	Hurtado, E .... 4(8)	Reid, A .... –(2)
Brebner, G .... 23(5)	Jack, M .... 28(3)	Riordan, D .... 1(5)
Brewster, C .... 23(2)	Laursen, U .... 23(1)	Sauzee, F 10
Caig, A 8	Luna, F .... 16(9)	Smart, A .... 2(3)
Caldwell, G .... 10(1)	Martin, L 1	Smith, G 30
Colgan, N 30	McManus, T .... 14(7)	Townsley, D .... 7(11)
Daquin, F .... 1(1)	Murray, I .... 30(2)	Whittaker, S .... –(1)
De la Cruz, U ...... 25(7)	Nicol, K .... –(2)	Wiss, J .... 6(5)
Dempsie, A .... 2(1)	O'Connor, G ...... 14(5)	Zitelli, D .... 7(14)
Fenwick, P 22	O'Neil, J 32	

League goals (51): O'Connor 9, Luna 6, Townsley 5, O'Neil 4, Sauzee 4, Brewster 3, Fenwick 3, McManus 3, Arpinon 2, Brebner 2, De la Cruz 2, Murray 2, Hurtado 1, Laursen 1, Orman 1, Smart 1, Opponents 2.
Tennents Cup goals (5): Brebner 1, Hurtado 1, Luna 1, Smith 1, Zitelli 1. **CIS Cup goals (4):** Brewster 2, Luna 1, McManus 1. **UEFA Cup goals (3):** Luna 2, Zitelli 1.

KILMARNOCK

Ground: Rugby Park, Kilmarnock KA1 2DP. **Capacity:** 18,128.
Telephone: 01563 545300. **Colours:** White and blue. **Nickname:** Killie.

Baker, M 6	Fowler, J .... 22(6)	McLaren, A .... 13(14)
Boyd, K .... 11(17)	Hay, G 26	Meldrum, C .... 2(1)
Calderon, A .... 9(8)	Hessey, S .... 13(2)	Mitchell, A .... 33(1)
Canero, P .... 31(1)	Innes, C 20	Murray, S .... 16(3)
Canning, M .... –(1)	Jaconelli, E .... –(3)	Ngonge, M .... 7(2)
Cocard, C .... 4(6)	Johnson, T .... 7(3)	Pizzo, M .... 10(3)
Dargo, C .... 25(4)	Mahood, A 33	Reilly, M .... –(2)
Di Giacomo, P ..... 15(8)	Marshall, G 36	Sanjuan, J .... 18(2)
Dillon, S .... 1(1)	McCutcheon, G ...... 2(1)	Shields, G 5
Dindeleux, F 27	McDonald, G .... 1(5)	Vareille, J 3
Durrant, I .... –(1)	McGowne, K 22	

League goals (44): Johnson 7, Dargo 6, Boyd 5, McLaren 4, Di Giacomo 3, Mitchell 3, Ngonge 3, Mahood 2, Murray 2, Calderon 1, Cocard 1, Dindeleux 1, Hay 1, Innes 1, McGowne 1, Pizzo 1, Opponents 2.
Tennents Cup goals (3): Canero 1, Mitchell 1, Sanjuan 1. **CIS Insurance Cup goals:** None.
UEFA Cup goals (3): Dargo 1, Innes 1, Mitchell 1.

LIVINGSTON

Ground: West Lothian Courier Stadium, Livingston EH54 7DN. **Capacity:** 10,004.
Telephone: 01506 417000. **Colours:** Gold and black. **Nickname:** Livvy's Lions.

Anderson, J .... 12(1)	Deas, P 1	McEwan, D .... –(1)
Andrews, M 33	Del Nero, S .... –(1)	Petersen, M .... 2(1)
Aurellio, D .... 5(9)	Fernandez, D .... 30(3)	Quino, F .... 34(2)
Bingham, M .... 31(6)	Hart, M .... 14(7)	Rubio, O 33
Bollan, G .... 20(1)	Jokovic, N .... –(3)	Santini, D 21
Brinquin, P 23	Keith, M .... –(1)	Tosh, S .... 21(10)
Brittain, R .... –(2)	Lovell, S .... 26(1)	Toure-Maman, S ...... 3(6)
Broto, J 17	Lowndes, N .... 7(14)	Wilson, B .... 32(5)
Caputo, M .... 4(17)	Makel, L .... 9(4)	Xausa, D .... 19(9)
Culkin, N 27	McCulloch, M .... –(2)	

League goals (50): Quino 8, Wilson 8, Xausa 7, Bingham 6, Fernandez 6, Andrews 3, Lovell 3, Lowndes 3, Tosh 2, Aurellio 1, Brinquin 1, Rubio 1, Opponents 1.
Tennents Cup goals (4): Bingham 2, Fernandez 1, Wilson 1. **CIS Cup goals (9):** Caputo 4, Wilson 2, Bingham 1, Lovell 1, Tosh 1.

MOTHERWELL

Ground: Fir Park, Motherwell ML1 2QN. **Capacity:** 13,742.
Telephone: 01698 333333. **Colours:** Claret and amber. **Nickname:** Well.

Adams, D .... 19(9)	Forrest, E .... 9(4)	McFadden, J .... 20(4)
Bernhard, F .... 2(1)	Ferrere, D .... 7(3)	Nicholas, S .... 5(11)
Brown, M 19	Hammell, S .... 37(1)	Pearson, S .... 19(8)
Clarke, D .... –(1)	Harvey, P .... –(2)	Ramsay, D .... 2(1)
Corrigan, M .... 26(4)	Kelly, D 19	Ready, K .... 35(1)
Cosgrove, S .... –(2)	Kinniburgh, W 1	Soloy, Y .... 11(1)
Deloumeaux, E .... 22(1)	Lasley, K .... 25(3)	Strong, G .... 31(1)
Dubourdeau, F 4	Lehmann, D .... 10(1)	Tarrant, N .... 2(3)
Dow, A .... 7(2)	Leitch, D 26	Twaddle, K .... 7(5)
Elliott, S .... 30(7)	Martinez, R .... 8(8)	Woods, S .... 15(1)
Fagan, S .... –(2)	McDonald, K .... –(1)	Wright, K .... –(1)

League goals (49): Elliott 10, McFadden 10, Kelly 6, Lehmann 4, Ferrere 3, Ready 3, Adams 2, Lasley 2, Nicholas 2, Pearson 2, Strong 2, Dow 1, Hammell 1, Soloy 1, Opponents 1.
Tennents Cup goals (1): Elliott 1. **CIS Cup goals (1):** Kelly 1.

RANGERS

Ground: Ibrox, Glasgow G51 2XD. **Capacity:** 52,025.
Telephone: 0141 580 8500. **Colours:** Royal blue. **Nickname:** Gers.

Amoruso, L 28	Gibson, J .... –(1)	Miller, K .... –(3)
Arveladze, S .... 21(1)	Hughes, S .... 12(5)	Mols, M .... 8(7)
Ball, M .... 5(2)	Johnston, A 1	Moore, C 18
Brighton, J 1	Kanchelskis, A .... 6(4)	Nerlinger, C .... 7(1)
Burke, C .... 1(1)	Klos, S 36	Numan, A .... 28(2)
Caniggia, C .... 16(8)	Konterman, B 26	Penttila, T .... –(1)
De Boer, R .... 19(6)	Latapy, R .... 14(2)	Reyna, C 10
Dodds, W .... 5(6)	Lovenkrands, P ...... 10(9)	Ricksen, F 31
Dowie, A .... –(1)	Malcolm, R .... 6(1)	Ross, M .... 19(2)
Ferguson, B .... 21(1)	McCann, N .... 13(12)	Vidmar, T .... 23(1)
Flo, T .... 25(5)	McGregor, A 2	Wilson, S 6

League goals (82): Flo 18, Arveladze 11, De Boer 8, McCann 6, Caniggia 5, Latapy 5, Amoruso 4, Ricksen 4, Moore 3, Dodds 2, Konterman 2, Lovenkrands 2, Mols 2, Reyna 2, Burke 1, Ferguson 1, Hughes 1, Kanchelskis 1, Nerlinger 1, Numan 1, Vidmar 1, Opponents 1.
Tennents Cup goals (19): Dodds 4, Arveladze 3, Lovenkrands 3, Ferguson 2, Flo 2, Nerlinger 2, Amoruso 1, Kanchelskis 1, Konterman 1. **CIS Cup goals (11):** Arveladze 3, Caniggia 2, Ferguson 1, Flo 1, Konterman 1, Lovenkrands 1, Numan 1, Reyna 1.
Champions League goals (7): Flo 3, Caniggia 2, Nerlinger 1, Ricksen 1. **UEFA Cup goals (11):** Ferguson 3, De Boer 2, Amoruso 1, Ball 1, Flo 1, Konterman 1, Lovenkrands 1, McCann 1.

ST. JOHNSTONE

Ground: McDiarmid Park, Perth PH1 2SJ. **Capacity:** 10,723.
Telephone: 01738 459090. **Colours:** Royal blue. **Nickname:** Saints.

Connolly, P .... 21(8)	Jones, G .... 7(6)	McCulloch, M .... 4(2)
Cuthbert, K .... 11(1)	Kane, P 15	Miller, A 18
Dasovic, N .... 22(2)	Kemble, B 14	Murray, G 38
Djebaili, R .... 4(9)	Lovenkrands, T .... 28(1)	Panther, E .... 5(2)
Dods, D 32	Lynch, M 20	Parker, K .... 14(7)
Falconer, W .... 16(9)	MacDonald, P .... 12(10)	Roy, L 2
Ferry, M .... -(2)	Maher, M .... 4(6)	Russell, C .... 7(6)
Forsyth, R .... 15(1)	Main, A 7	Sylla, M 1
Fotheringham, M ..... 2(4)	McBride, J .... 15(6)	Weir, J 17
Hartley, P 32	McClune, D .... 5(2)	Youssouf, S 5
Jackson, D .... 6(3)	McCluskey, S .... 19(4)	

League goals (24): Hartley 4, Falconer 3, MacDonald 3, Connolly 2, Dods 2, Lovenkrands 1, Jackson 1, Jones 1, McBride 1, Murray 1, Parker 1, Russell 1, Weir 1, Youssouf 1.
Tennents Cup goals: None. **CIS Cup goals (4):** MacDonald 2, Dods 1, Hartley 1.

FIRST DIVISION

AIRDRIE

Ground: Shyberry Excelsior Stadium, Airdrie ML6 8QZ. **Capacity:** 10,171.
Telephone: 01236 622000. **Colours:** White, red and black. **Nickname:** Diamonds.

Armstong, P .... 30(2)	Henry, J .... 21(1)	McPherson, C .... 29(3)
Beesley, D .... 4(5)	James, K 34	Reilly, M 6
Bennett, N .... 9(1)	MacDonald, S .... 4(6)	Roberts, M .... 34(2)
Coyle, O 36	McAlpine, J .... -(1)	Ronald, P .... -(5)
Docherty, S .... 11(8)	McCulloch, S 4	Smith, T .... 26(5)
Dunn, R .... -(14)	McDonald, C .... -(4)	Stewart, A .... 25(2)
Ferguson, A 26	McFarlane, N 28	Taylor, S .... 24(7)
Gardner, R .... 8(14)	McManus, A 28	Vareille, J .... 9(3)

League goals (59): Coyle 23, Roberts 12, Taylor 8, McFarlane 3, McPherson 3, Smith 2, Vareille 2, Armstrong 1, Gardner 1, James 1, McDonald 1, Opponents 2.
Tennents Cup goals: None. **CIS Cup goals (5):** Coyle 1, James 1, McFarlane 1, Roberts 1, Opponents 1. **Bell's Cup goals (11):** Coyle 3, Roberts 3, McPherson 2, Taylor 2, James 1.

ARBROATH

Ground: Gayfield Park, Arbroath DD11 1QB. **Capacity:** 4,020.
Telephone: 01241 872157. **Colours:** Maroon and white. **Nickname:** Red Lichties.

Arbuckle, D .... -(2)	Cargill, A .... 29(2)	Fallon, S 3
Bayne, G .... 33(1)	Cusick, J .... 23(5)	Florence, S .... 25(1)
Brownlie, P .... 26(5)	Durno, P .... -(1)	Gardner, J .... 3(7)

Graham, E 1	McAulay, J .... 7(11)	Ritchie, I 31
Heenan, K .... 9(11)	McGlashan, J 32	Roddie, A .... 3(1)
Henslee, G .... 2(1)	McInally, D .... 17(3)	Rowe, G 31
Hinchcliffe, C 35	McKinnon, C .... 20(8)	Swankie, G .... 3(5)
Mackay, D 5	Mercer, J .... 6(10)	Tait, J 31
Mallan, S .... 14(8)	Moffat, S .... 6(2)	Wight, C 1

League goals (42): Mallan 6, McGlashan 6, Bayne 5, McKinnon 5, Ritchie 5, Cargill 4, Cusick 4, Rowe 3, Brownlie 1, Heenan 1, McAulay 1, Opponents 1.
Tennents Cup goals: None. **CIS Cup goals:** None. **Bell's Cup goals (1):** Brownlie 1.

AYR UNITED

Ground: Somerset Park, Ayr KA8 9NB. **Capacity:** 10,185.
Telephone: 01292 263435. **Colours:** White and black. **Nickname:** Honest Men.

Annand, E .... 21(7)	Hughes, J 30	Robertson, J 36
Bradford, J .... –(10)	Kean, S .... 4(4)	Scally, N .... 5(2)
Chaplain, S .... 4(4)	Lovering, P .... 27(5)	Sharp, L .... 9(12)
Crabbe, S 20	McEwan, C .... 15(7)	Sheerin, P .... 33(1)
Craig, D .... 27(1)	McGinlay, P 27	Smyth, M 4
Dodds, J 1	McLaughlin, B .... 8(11)	Stevenson, C .... –(1)
Duffy, C .... 21(1)	Molloy, T .... –(1)	Teale, G 18
Dunlop, M 1	Moss, D 5	Twaddle, K 1
Grady, J .... 24(7)	Nelson, C 35	Wilson, M .... 20(6)

League goals (53): Annand 14, Grady 8, Sheerin 6, McGinlay 5, Teale 4, Crabbe 3, Kean 3, Robertson 2, Wilson 2, Hughes 1, Lovering 1, McEwan 1, McLaughlin 1, Moss 1, Scally 1.
Tennents Cup goals (13): Crabbe 3, Annand 2, Grady 2, McGinlay 2, Sheerin 2, Robertson 1, Opponents 1. **CIS Cup goals (10):** Annand 4, Grady 2, McGinlay 1, Robertson 1, Sharp 1, Teale 1. **Bell's Cup goals (5):** Annand 1, Bradford 1, McGinlay 1, Sheerin 1, Teale 1.

CLYDE

Ground: Broadwood Stadium, Cumbernauld G68 9NE. **Capacity:** 8,029.
Telephone: 01236 451511. **Colours:** White and red. **Nickname:** Bully Wee.

Aitken, C .... 2(3)	Grant, A .... –(1)	McLaughlin, M .... 12(2)
Bingham, C .... 10(6)	Hagen, D .... 16(12)	McPhee, B 4
Budienauckas, K ...... 10(2)	Halliwell, B .... 24(1)	Mensing, S 23
Carrigan, B 9	Hinds, L .... 24(7)	Millen, A 31
Convery, M .... 13(15)	Kane, A .... 1(9)	Mitchell, J 31
Cranmer, C .... 8(5)	Kane, P .... 4(1)	Murray, D 9
Crawford, B .... 8(9)	Keogh, P .... 28(3)	Okikiolu, S .... 2(1)
De Gregorio, R .... 4(4)	Kernaghan, A 15	Potter, J 6
Dunn, D .... 22(5)	McClay, A .... 3(1)	Ross, J 27
Fraser, J 22	McCusker, R .... –(1)	Smith, B .... 25(1)
Graham, M 2	McDowell, M .... 1(2)	

League goals (51): Keogh 10, Hinds 9, Mitchell 6, Carrigan 4, Fraser 3, Millen 3, Convery 2, Crawford 2, Hagen 2, Ross 2, Kernaghan 1, McCusker 1, McLaughlin 1, McPhee 1, Mensing 1, Potter 1, Opponents 2.
Tennents Cup goals (2): Hinds 1, Mensing 1. **CIS Cup goals (3):** Crawford 3. **Bell's Cup goals (9):** Kane, A 2, Keogh 2, Ross 2, Convery 1, McCusker 1, Mitchell 1.

FALKIRK

Ground: Brockville Park, Falkirk FK1 5AX. **Capacity:** 7,576.
Telephone: 01324 624121. **Colours:** Navy blue and white. **Nickname:** Bairns.

Brown, K 5	Christie, K 29	Convery, J 3

Craig, S .... 19(9)	McAllister, K .... 21(7)	Pearson, C .... 1(1)
Denham, G 9	McQuilken, J 35	Rennie, S .... 28(2)
Deuchar, K .... 3(10)	McStay, G .... 8(9)	Rodgers, A .... 4(9)
Henry, J 9	Miller, L 27	Tano, P .... 4(2)
Hill, D 5	Morris, I .... 18(15)	Waddell, R .... 17(12)
Hogarth, M 31	Moss, D 3	Watson, S .... 4(2)
Kerr, M .... 28(2)	Murray, N 8	Wilkie, L 9
Lawrie, A 34	Oponga, C 3	Wright, P .... 12(2)
Mair, L .... 19(1)		

League goals (49): Miller 11, Morris 5, Christie 4, Craig 4, Kerr 3, Rennie 3, Waddell 3, Henry 2, Lawrie 2, McQuilken 2, Wilkie 2, Wright 2, Brown 1, Deuchar 1, McAllister 1, Rodgers 1, Watson 1, Opponents 1.
Tennents Cup goals (1): Rodgers 1. **CIS Cup goals (2):** Craig 1, Lawrie 1. **Bell's Cup goals (4):** Watson 2, Craig 1, Kerr 1.

INVERNESS CALEDONIAN THISTLE

Ground: Caledonian Stadium, Inverness IV1 1FF. **Capacity:** 6,280.
Telephone: 01463 222880. **Colours:** Royal blue, red and white. **Nickname:** Caley Thistle.

Bagan, D .... 10(7)	MacDonald, N ....–(10)	Robson, B .... 33(1)
Bavidge, M .... 23(10)	Mann, R 34	Stewart, G .... 3(15)
Bradshaw, P 2	McBain, R 33	Teasdale, M .... 14(3)
Calder, J .... 9(1)	McCaffrey, S 32	Tokely, R 34
Christie, C .... 30(2)	Munro, G 18	Walker, N 27
Duncan, R .... 25(6)	Ritchie, P .... 29(5)	Wyness, D .... 35(1)
Golabek, S .... 5(10)		

League goals (60): Wyness 18, Ritchie 15, Mann 7, Bavidge 4, Tokely 3, Bagan 2, Christie 2, McBain 2, Robson 2, Duncan 1, MacDonald 1, Munro 1, Stewart 1, Opponents 1.
Tennents Cup goals (7): Wyness 3, Bagan 1, Ritchie 1, Robson 1, Tokely 1. **CIS Cup goals (7):** Ritchie 2, Robson 2, Bavidge 1, Teasdale 1, Tokely 1. **Bell's Cup goals (5):** Ritchie 2, Bavidge 1, Christie 1, Wyness 1.

PARTICK THISTLE

Ground: Firhill Stadium, Glasgow G20 7AL. **Capacity:** 14,538.
Telephone: 0141 579 1971. **Colours:** Red, yellow and black. **Nickname:** Jags.

Archibald, A .... 31(2)	Fleming, D .... 24(5)	McAnespie, S ....–(1)
Arthur, K .... 22(1)	Gibson, A .... 1(3)	McCulloch, M .... 14(2)
Britton, G .... 24(9)	Gow, G 5	McDowell, M ....–(4)
Budinauckas, K 4	Hardie, M .... 22(9)	McKinstry, J .... 21(2)
Burns, A 13	Howie, W ....–(1)	McLean, S .... 23(5)
Cameron, M .... 6(2)	Huxford, R .... 2(4)	Nicholls, M 1
Connaghan, D 8	Javary, J-P ....–(1)	Paterson, S 36
Constantine, L 2	Kelly, P .... 9(1)	Roddie, A .... 1(2)
Craigan, S .... 31(1)	Klein, D 5	Smith, J ....–(1)
Deas, P 25	Lennon, D .... 32(2)	Walker, P .... 12(14)
Dolan, J .... 19(7)	Lyle, D ....–(2)	Watson, S 1
Elliot, B .... 2(5)		

League goals (61): Britton 12, Hardie 11, McLean 9, Fleming 7, Burns 4, Lennon 4, Walker 4, Archibald 2, Dolan 2, McKinstry 2, Cameron 1, Elliot 1, McCulloch 1, Opponents 1.
Tennents Cup goals (10): Hardie 2, McLean 2, Paterson 2, Walker 2, Britton 1, Gibson 1.
CIS Cup goals (6): Lennon 2, McLean 2, Hardie 1, McDowell 1. **Bell's Cup goals (10):** Britton 2, Fleming 2, Hardie 2, Lennon 2, McCallum, D 1, McDowell 1.

RAITH ROVERS

Ground: Stark's Park, Kirkaldy KY1 1SA. **Capacity:** 10,104.
Telephone: 01592 263514. **Colours:** Navy blue and white. **Nickname:** Rovers.

Brown, I 1	Henderson, R 8	Monin, S 27
Browne, P .... 33(1)	Javary, J-P 7	Nanou, W .... 13(9)
Clark, A .... 1(11)	Jones, M .... 8(7)	Novo, N 33
Clark, J .... 1(2)	Matheson, R .... 13(2)	O'Boyle, G .... 2(3)
Crabbe, S 11	McCulloch, G .... 25(1)	Paquito .... 14(1)
Davidson, H .... 10(1)	McGarty, M .... 3(5)	Quesana, A .... 14(3)
Dennis, S 26	Millar, M 8	Smith, A 32
Ellis, L .... 19(2)	Miller, J .... 3(2)	Stein, J .... 22(7)
Hampshire, P .... 4(2)	Miller, W 3	Zoco, J .... 18(1)
Henderson, D .... 28(1)	Miotto, S 9	

League goals (50): Novo 18, Smith 12, Crabbe 6, Henderson, D 3, Dennis 2, Stein 2, Clark, A 1, Davidson 1, Jones 1, Miller, J 1, Nanou 1, Paquito 1, Quesana 1.
Tennents Cup goals: None. **CIS Cup goals (3):** Henderson, D 1, Novo 1, Smith 1. **Bell's Cup goals (6):** Novo 3, Dennis 1, Matheson 1, Zoco 1.

ROSS COUNTY

Ground: Victoria Park, Dingwall IV15 9QW. **Capacity:** 5,800.
Telephone: 01349 860860. **Colours:** Navy blue and white. **Nickname:** County.

Anselin, C .... 7(3)	Fridge, L 1	Mackay, S .... 3(10)
Blackley, D .... –(1)	Gethins, C .... 11(13)	MacDonald, K .... –(1)
Bone, A .... 27(3)	Gilbert, K 15	Maxwell, I 35
Boukraa, K .... 10(6)	Gonzalez, R .... 2(1)	McCormick, M .... 11(9)
Bullock, T 33	Hastings, R .... 26(2)	McQuade, J .... 5(2)
Campbell, C .... –(2)	Hislop, S .... 29(4)	Perry, M 36
Canning, M 7	Holmes, D .... 2(1)	Prest, M .... 2(6)
Cowie, D .... 14(4)	Irvine, B .... 29(1)	Robertson, H 36
Dlugonski, B 3	Jack, D .... –(1)	Tarrant, N .... 2(4)
Ferguson, S .... 26(2)	Lilley, D .... 5(1)	Webb, S .... 15(4)
Fraser, J 4		

League goals (51): Hislop 14, Bone 9, Gethins 6, Robertson 6, Ferguson 4, McCormick 3, Boukraa 2, Irvine 2, Campbell 1, Gilbert 1, Prest 1, Opponents 2.
Tennents Cup goals (1): Perry 1. **CIS Cup goals (6):** Bone 2, Boukraa 2, Irvine 1, Mackay 1. **Bell's Cup goals (4):** Hislop 3, McQuade 1.

ST. MIRREN

Ground: St Mirren Park, Paisley PA3 2EJ. **Capacity:** 10,622.
Telephone: 0141 889 2558. **Colours:** Black and white. **Nickname:** Buddies.

Baltacha, S .... 9(4)	McCann, R .... –(1)	Robertson, K .... 1(2)
Bowman, G .... 17(2)	McGarry, S .... 11(11)	Robinson, R .... –(1)
Burns, A .... 16(6)	McGinty, B .... 20(1)	Ross, I .... 23(2)
Dempster, J .... –(1)	McGowan, J 24	Roy, L 25
Gillies, R .... 27(3)	McKenzie, S .... 26(2)	Rudden, P .... 2(4)
Guy, G .... –(1)	McKnight, P .... 6(7)	Strang, S 1
Hillcoat, J 9	McLaughlin, B 31	Turner, T .... 8(2)
Keogh, L .... –(1)	Murray, H .... 27(5)	Walker, S 34
Kerr, C .... 11(5)	Nicolson, I .... 17(6)	Wreh, C .... –(3)
Lappin, S .... –(1)	Quitongo, J .... 33(1)	Yardley, M .... 16(7)
Lowing, D 2		

League goals (43): McGinty 6, Gillies 5, McLaughlin 5, Quitongo 5, Ross 5, Yardley 4, Walker 3, McGarry 2, Nicolson 2, Baltacha 1, Burns 1, Kerr 1, McGowan 1, Opponents 2.
Tennents Cup goals: None. **CIS Cup goals (1):** Quitongo 1. **Bell's Cup goals (1):** Yardley 1.

SECOND DIVISION

ALLOA ATHLETIC

Ground: Recreation Park, Alloa FK10 1RR. **Capacity:** 3,100.
Telephone: 01259 722695. **Colours:** Black and gold. **Nickname:** Wasps.

Anderson, D .... 7(3)	Fisher, J .... 26(3)	Seaton, A .... 21(6)
Brown, T .... 8(3)	Hamilton, R .... 24(10)	Soutar, D 31
Christie, M .... 16(6)	Hutchison, G .... 32(3)	Thomson, S .... 31(1)
Cowan, M .... 8(2)	Irvine, W .... 2(5)	Valentine, C 33
Curran, H .... 19(12)	Kerr, C 1	Walker, R .... 23(9)
Donnachie, S .... 2(11)	Knox, K 28	Watson, S 17
Evans, G .... 7(3)	Little, I .... 29(4)	Whalen, S 5
Evans, J .... 4(2)	Raeside, R .... 22(1)	

League goals (55): Hutchison 14, Hamilton 7, Seaton 6, Knox 5, Little 5, Curran 4,
Raeside 3, Walker 3, Donnachie 2, Fisher 2, Brown 1, Christie 1, Thomson 1, Watson 1.
Tennents Cup goals (4): Evans, G 2, Hutchison 1, Little 1. **CIS Cup goals (4):** Curran 1,
Little 1, Thomson 1, Walker 1. **Bell's Cup goals (10):** Evans, G 2, Little 2, Curran 1,
Fisher 1, Hamilton 1, Hutchison 1, Irvine 1, Opponents 1.

BERWICK RANGERS

Ground: Shielfield Park, Berwick-upon-Tweed TD15 2EF. **Capacity:** 4,131.
Telephone: 01289 307424. **Colours:** Black and gold. **Nickname:** Borderers.

Anthony, M .... 23(3)	Harvey, J .... 1(3)	O'Connor, G 6
Bennett, N .... 25(2)	Huxford, R .... 11(3)	Rae, D .... -(2)
Bradley, M .... 17(12)	Mathers, P 6	Ritchie, I 4
Brannigan, K 5	May, E .... 3(3)	Robertson, S .... 8(1)
Crawford, D .... 1(2)	McCulloch, W 24	Ronald, P .... 7(4)
Duthie, M 1	McDonald, C .... 7(5)	Smith, A 5
Farrell, G .... 21(1)	McDowell, M .... 10(6)	Smith, D .... 19(8)
Feroz, C .... 20(2)	McNicholl, G .... 13(3)	Thomas, K .... 3(1)
Forrest, G .... 25(5)	Murie, D 35	Whelan, J .... 6(2)
Glancy, M .... 6(3)	Neil, M .... 19(4)	Wood, G 28
Gray, D .... 1(3)	Neill, A 36	

League goals (44): Wood 10, McDowell 7, Anthony 5, Bennett 4, Smith, D 4, Feroz 4,
Forrest 2, Brannigan 1, Duthie 1, Glancy 1, Neil 1, Neill 1, Robertson 1, Smith, A 1,
Thomas 1.
Tennents Cup goals (1): Feroz 1. **CIS Cup goals:** None. **Bell's Cup goals (3):** Glancy 1,
Ritchie 1, Wood 1.

CLYDEBANK

Bossy, F .... 27(2)	Kinnaird, P .... -(3)	Mooney, G .... 2(1)
Brannigan, K .... -(1)	Klein, D .... 1(1)	Nicholls, M .... 5(6)
Burke, A .... 17(10)	Lavety, B .... 7(1)	O'Neill, M 19
Carrigan, B .... 7(3)	McColligan, B .... 25(2)	Paton, E .... 31(4)
Dick, J .... 4(5)	McGowan, N .... 31(1)	Robertson, S .... 9(2)
Falconer, W 1	McGrillen, P .... 19(14)	Shaw, G 1
Ferguson, D 28	McKinlay, W 8	Shields, P .... 13(3)
George, L 2	McKinnon, R 20	Smith, H 26
Gow, A .... 3(2)	McNally, M .... 18(1)	Stirling, J 1
Graham, A .... 9(10)	McPeak, T 3	Vella, S 9
Hamilton, B 27	McVey, L .... 5(2)	Whiteford, A .... 10(4)
Jackson, D .... 7(6)	Miller, J .... 1(1)	

League goals (44): Burke 9, Paton 8, McGrillen 7, O'Neill 4, Lavety 3, Shields 3,
Graham 2, Jackson 2, Ferguson 1, McGolligan 1, McKinnon 1, Opponents 3.
Tennents Cup goals (1): Paton 1. **CIS Cup goals:** None. **Bell's Cup goals (1):** Burke 1.

COWDENBEATH

Ground: Central Park, Cowdenbeath KY4 9QQ. **Capacity:** 4,370.
Telephone: 01383 610166. **Colours:** Royal blue and white. **Nickname:** Blue Brazil.

Banks, A 1	Huggon, R .... 2(3)	Raynes, S .... 12(3)
Boyle, J .... 34(1)	King, T 9	Renwick, M 7
Brown, G 35	Kwik Ajet, W 1	Robertson, S 1
Burns, J .... 1(1)	Lawrence, A .... 21(2)	Sullivan, V .... 2(2)
Byle, K .... 1(2)	Martin, J 4	Swift, S .... 31(2)
Carver, F	Mauchlen, J .... 13(9)	Welsh, B .... 1(1)
Campbell, A .... 12(2)	McMillan, C .... –(5)	White, D 30
Crabbe, G .... 1(1)	Miller, C .... –(1)	Wilson, K 32
Dixon, J .... 5(5)	Milne, K 9	Wilson, P 1
Elliott, J .... 6(6)	Moffat, A 3	Winter, C 25
French, H .... 33(1)	Neeson, C .... 11(3)	Wright, K .... 13(12)
Gibb, S 1	O'Connor, G 19	Young, C .... 7(8)
Gordon, C 12		

League goals (49): Brown 16, Wright 9, French 4, Mauchlen 4, White 3, Lawrence 2, Swift 2, Crabbe 1, Dixon 1, Elliott 1, King 1, Wilson 1, Winter 1, Young 1, Opponents 2.
Tennents Cup goals: None. **CIS Cup goals (2):** Wilson 2. **Bell's Cup goals:** None.

FORFAR ATHLETIC

Ground: Station Park, Forfar DD8 3BT. **Capacity:** 4,602.
Telephone: 01307 463576. **Colours:** Sky blue and navy. **Nickname:** Loons.

Bett, C 8	Horn, R .... 20(1)	Rattray, A 29
Bowman, D .... 11(1)	Lunan, P .... 16(9)	Sellars, B 24
Brown, M 36	Mallan, S 3	Stewart, W .... 22(10)
Byers, K .... 34(1)	McCloy, B .... 25(1)	Taylor, S .... 1(2)
Christie, S .... 12(19)	McCulloch, S 9	Tosh, P 30
Donaldson, E .... 10(5)	McWilliams .... –(2)	Walker, D .... –(3)
Farnan, C .... 1(7)	Milne, K 23	Williams, D .... 5(5)
Good, I 26	Moffat, B .... 17(6)	Yardley, M 4
Henry, J .... 18(3)	Morris, R .... 12(7)	

League goals (51): Tosh 19, Byers 9, Christie 5, Sellars 5, Moffat 3, Stewart 3, Yardley 3, Horn 1, McCulloch 1, Opponents 1.
Tennents Cup goals (9): Sellars 3, Tosh 3, Byers 2, Yardley 1. **CIS Cup goals (1):** Tosh 1.
Bell's Cup goals (2): Good 1, Moffat 1.

HAMILTON ACADEMICALS

Ground: New Douglas Park, Hamilton ML3 OBN. **Capacity:** 5,330.
Telephone: 01698 286103. **Colours:** Red and white. **Nickname:** Accies.

Armstrong, G .... 5(2)	Lurinsky, A .... 1(2)	Nelson, M .... 27(4)
Bonnar, M .... 26(1)	MacFarlane, I 15	Nicholls, M 2
Callaghan, S 32	MacLaren, R .... 11(4)	O'Neil, K .... 3(13)
Cunnington, E 19	Martin, M .... 18(5)	Potter, G .... 14(3)
Davidson, S .... –(1)	McCreadie, I .... 6(1)	Renicks, S .... 29(1)
Elfallah .... 1(3)	McDonald, P .... 15(4)	Russell, A .... 7(5)
Gaughan, P 17	McFarlane, D .... 11(4)	Sherry, J .... 13(3)
Goram, A 1	McNiven, D .... 25(1)	Stewart, C 2
Graham, A .... 25(7)	McPhee, B .... 15(2)	Sweeney, S .... 24(2)
Herbert, M 5	Moore, M .... 25(5)	Walker, J .... –(3)
Kwick Ajet, W .... 2(3)		

League goals (49): Moore 12, Callaghan 7, McNiven 6, McFarlane 5, Bonnar 3, McPhee 3, MacFarlane 2, Martin 2, Nicholls 2, Armstrong 1, Gaughan 1, Graham 1, Russell 1, Sherry 1, Sweeney 1, Opponents 1.

Tennents Cup goals (5): McPhee 2, Callaghan 1, McFarlane 1, McNiven 1. **CIS Cup goals (1):** Moore 1. **Bell's Cup goals:** None.

MORTON

Ground: Cappielow Park, Greenock PA15 2TY. **Capacity:** 11,550.
Telephone: 01475 723571. **Colours:** Royal blue, white and yellow. **Nickname:** Ton.

Aitken, C .... 7(12)	Greacen, S 15	Moffat, C .... 2(1)
Bannerman, S 31	Hawke, W 19	Moore, A .... 11(4)
Bottiglieri, E .... 15(11)	Kearney, D .... 2(3)	O'Connor, S .... 20(1)
Cannie, P 7	Kerr, D .... 21(1)	Redmond, G .... 2(16)
Carmichael, D .... 1(3)	Maisano, M 11	Reid, A 9
Collins, D 32	Mapes, C .... 2(1)	Renwick, M 2
Correia, A .... 1(1)	McAneny, P .... 5(1)	Riddell, S .... 1(3)
Coyle, C 33	McGregor, A 32	Ross, K .... 3(1)
Curran, H .... 9(1)	McMillan, A .... –(2)	Tweedie, G .... 19(12)
Frail, S 24	McPherson, D 16	Uotonen, J 1
Gibson, J .... 14(8)	Miller, S .... 16(4)	Wright, P 13

League goals (48): Bannerman 8, O'Connor 8, Tweedie 5, McPherson 4, Miller 4, Wright 4, Bottiglieri 2, Cannie 2, Hawke 2, Kerr 2, Reid 2, Aitken 1, Gibson 1, Moore 1, Redmond 1, Uotonen 1.
Tennents Cup goals (1): Aitken 1. **CIS Cup goals:** None. **Bell's Cup goals (1):** O'Connor 1.

QUEEN OF THE SOUTH

Ground: Palmerston Park, Dumfries DG2 9BA. **Capacity:** 6,412.
Telephone: 01387 254853. **Colours:** Royal blue and white. **Nickname:** Doonhamers.

Aitken, A .... 25(1)	Donald, B .... 6(5)	Moore, A .... 2(8)
Allan, D .... 11(2)	Feroz, C 8	O'Boyle, G 7
Anderson, D .... 15(1)	Glancy, M .... 2(1)	O'Connor, S .... 4(3)
Armstrong, G .... –(2)	Gray, A .... 34(1)	O'Neill, J .... 27(5)
Atkinson, P .... 23(4)	Hawke, W 6	Paterson, M .... 1(1)
Bowey, S .... 5(2)	Hogg, A 2	Poston, T 1
Campbell, J .... 3(1)	Hollier, P .... –(3)	Robertson, S .... –(1)
Connell, G .... 26(5)	Lyle, D 13	Scott, C 33
Connelly, G .... 26(4)	McAlpine, J .... 27(4)	Sunderland, J .... 2(6)
Connolly, S .... 1(1)	McDowell, M 2	Thomson, J .... 32(1)
Crawford, J .... 16(2)	McKeown, D .... 2(1)	Walker, L .... –(2)
Davidson, S .... 7(9)	McMahon, D .... –(1)	Weatheston, P .... 26(6)
Dawson, S .... –(1)		

League goals (64): O'Neill 19, Weatherson 16, Lyle 6, McAlpine 6, Atkinson 3, O'Boyle 3, Davidson 2, O'Connor 2, Bowey 1, Connelly 1, Feroz 1, Gray 1, Moore 1, Opponents 2.
Tennents Cup goals (2): O'Neill 2. **CIS Cup goals (1):** Feroz 4. **Bell's Cup goals:** None.

STENHOUSEMUIR

Ground: Ochilview Park, Stenhousemuir FK5 5QL. **Capacity:** 2,066.
Telephone: 01324 562992. **Colours:** Maroon and white. **Nickname:** Warriors.

Abbott, G .... 8(1	Donaldson, E .... 13(2)	Irvine, W .... 11(9)
Carlin, A 17	English, I .... 25(6)	Jackson, C 32
Clyde, B .... 1(1)	Ferguson, I 24	Jarvie, P 5
Connaghan, D 4	Forrest, F .... 2(1)	McGurk, R 4
Cormack, P .... 13(3)	Graham, B .... 16(8)	McKeown, D 25
Davidson, G 10	Graham, M 10	Miller, P .... –(3)
Dick, J 1	Graham, S .... –(1)	Milne, D .... 20(1)
Donald, B .... 4(7)	Grant, M 4	Mooney, M .... 11(6)
Donald, G .... 20(3)	Harvey, P .... 2(1)	Murphy, S .... 3(2)

Sandison, J .... 8(2)	Stone, M 35	Wilson, M 15
Shanks, P .... 1(1)	Storrar, A .... 27(7)	Wood, C .... 15(6)
Shearer, G .... –(4)	Vella, S .... 10(2)	

League goals (33): Irvine 7, English 6, Ferguson 6, Donald 5, Graham, D 2, Mooney 2, Jackson 1, Milne 1, Stone 1, Storrar 1, Wood 1.
Tennents Cup goals: None. CIS Cup goals (2): Abbott 1, Ferguson 1. **Bell's Cup goals (1):** Mooney 1.

STRANRAER

Ground: Stair Park, Stranraer DG9 8BS. **Capacity:** 5,600.
Telephone: 01776 703271. **Colours:** Royal blue and white. **Nickname:** Blues.

Aitken, S 36	George, D .... 3(3)	O'Neil, S .... –(1)
Blair, P .... 11(10)	Glancy, M .... 5(1)	Paterson, A .... 10(3)
Bradford, J 3	Grace, A .... 16(5)	Rodosthenous, M ..... –(1)
Dempster, J .... 3(2)	Harty, I .... 28(2)	Shaw, G .... 27(2)
Duthie, M 2	Hodge, S .... 21(3)	Sherry, M .... 1(1)
Farrell, D .... 21(2)	Jenkins, A .... 13(11)	Stewart, C 1
Finlayson, K .... 24(6)	Johnstone, D 8	Stirling, J .... 11(2)
Gallagher, M .... 2(6)	Kerr, P 2	Weir, M .... 1(7)
Gallagher, P .... –(2)	McDonald, B 32	Wingate, D 34
Gaughan, K .... 15(4)	McGeown, M 35	Wright, F .... 31(2)

League goals (48): Harty 16, Finlayson 7, Shaw 4, Aitken 3, Wright 3, Grace 2, Hodge 2, Kerr 2, Wingate 2, Blair 1, Farrell 1, Gaughan 1, Glancy 1, Jenkins 1, McDonald 1, Opponents 1.
Tennents Cup goals (1): Harty 1. **CIS Insurance Cup goals (3):** Harty 1, Finlayson 1, Shaw 1. **Bell's Cup goals (10):** Gallagher, M 3, Wright 2, Finlayson 1, Gaughan 1, Harty 1, Jenkins 1, Johnstone 1.

THIRD DIVISION

ALBION ROVERS

Ground: Cliftonhill Stadium, Coatbridge ML5 3RB. **Capacity:** 2,496.
Telephone: 01236 606334. **Colours:** Yellow, red and black. **Nickname:** Wee Rov.

Bonar, P .... 19(2)	Harty, M .... 23(4)	Rankin, I .... –(3)
Booth, M 31	Ingram, N .... –(2)	Rodden, P .... –(2)
Carr, D .... 5(9)	Lumsden, T 22	Shearer, S .... 9(1)
Coulter, J 1	McCormick, S .... 11(6)	Silvestro, C .... 15(3)
Coulter, R .... 10(2)	McKenna, G .... 25(9)	Smith, J 20
Diack, I .... 19(7)	McKenzie, J .... 18(5)	Stirling, J 4
Donnelly, K .... 2(2)	McLean, C .... 19(8)	Struthers, W 1
Easton, S .... 25(2)	McLees, J .... –(2)	Tait, T 15
Fahey, C 27	McMullan, R .... 8(19)	Waldie, C .... 35(1)
Hamilton, S .... 32(1)	Murdoch, S .... –(3)	

League goals (51): McLean 11, Booth 8, Diack 7, Harty 5, McKenzie 3, Bonar 2, Carr 2, McMullan 2, Silvestro 2, Smith 2, Donnelly 1, Hamilton 1, McCormick 1, McKenna 1, Stirling 1, Waldie 1, Opponents 1.
Tennents Cup goals (3): McLean 2, Harty 1. **CIS Cup goals: None. Bell's Cup goals (3):** Bonar 1, Hamilton 1, McMullan, 1.

BRECHIN CITY

Ground: Glebe Park, Brechin DD9 6BJ. **Capacity:** 3,060.
Telephone: 01356 622856. **Colours:** Red, white and black. **Nickname:** City.

Bain, K .... 29(2)	Cairns, M 26	Craig, D .... 2(3)
Black, R .... 29(4)	Campbell, P .... 11(10)	Dewar, G .... –(3)
Cairney, H 32	Clark, D .... 24(3)	Donnachie, B .... 3(5)

Ewart, J .... 4(2)	King, C 36	O'Boyle, G .... 4(1)
Fotheringham, K 32	Leask, M .... 1(7)	Riley, P .... 13(9)
Grant, R .... 23(2)	McAllister, S .... 1(1)	Smith, D .... 17(4)
Henderson, A .... –(6)	McKeown, K 10	Smith, J 30
Honeyman, B .... 6(12)	Miller, G 26	Templeman, C .... 34(1)
Kernaghan, A 3		

League goals (67): Templeman 15, Grant 10, Bain 7, King 7, Fotheringham 6, Smith, J 6, Clark 4, Honeyman 3, Campbell 2, Miller 2, O'Boyle 2, Black 1, Leask 1, Smith, D 1.
Tennents Cup goals (4): O'Boyle 2, Fotheringham 1, Grant 1. **CIS Cup goals:** None. **Bell's Cup goals (11):** Smith, D 3, Fotheringham 3, Grant 2, Bain 1, Kernaghan 1, Templeman 1.

DUMBARTON

Ground: Boghead Park, Dumbarton G82 2JA. **Capacity:** 2,020.
Telephone: 01389 762569. **Colours:** Yellow and black. **Nickname:** Sons.

Bonar, S .... 19(11)	Dunn, R .... 11(2)	McKelvie, D .... 2(20)
Brittain, C .... 27(5)	Flannery, P .... 32(1)	McKeown, J .... 23(11)
Brown, A 35	Hillcoat, J 12	Murdoch, S 5
Bruce, J 10	Jack, S .... 25(3)	O'Neill, M .... 26(3)
Connelly, J 2	Lauchlan, M .... 9(2)	Robertson, J .... 28(6)
Crilly, M .... 29(1)	Lynes, C .... 5(15)	Stewart, D 17
Dickie, M 23	McCann, K .... 19(1)	Wight, J 22
Dillon, J .... 15(18)		

League goals (59): Flannery 18, Crilly 10, Robertson 8, Brown 7, Dunn 4, Brittain 2, McCann 2, O'Neill 2, Bonar 1, Dillon 1, Lauchlan 1, Lynes 1, McKeown 1, Stewart 1.
Tennents Cup goals (1): McKeown 1. **CIS Cup goals (2):** Brown 1, Flannery 1. **Bell's Cup goals:** None.

EAST FIFE

Ground: Bayview Stadium, Methil KY8 3RW. **Capacity:** 1,992.
Telephone: 01333 426323. **Colours:** Gold and black. **Nickname:** Fifers.

Allan, J .... 18(13)	Gilbert, G .... 3(2)	Nairn, J .... 13(7)
Bailey, L .... 27(3)	Godfrey, R 36	Oliver, N 15
Brown, S .... –(1)	Graham, R .... 12(4)	Ovenstone, J .... 6(2)
Clyde, B 1	Herkes, J .... 19(11)	Rae, G .... 3(2)
Coulston, D 4	Lofting, A .... 2(8)	Spink, D .... 1(2)
Courts, C .... –(2)	MacDonald, A .... –(1)	Tejero, A 1
Cunningham, G ...... 28(4)	McManus, P .... 32(2)	Thompson, J 12
Gallagher, J 35	Mortimer, P 35	Wilson, W 36
Gibson, K 24	Munro, K 33	

League goals (39): McManus 11, Bailey 4, Cunningham 3, Gibson 3, Mortimer 3, Allan 2, Gallagher 2, Graham 2, Herkes 2, Gilbert 1, Munro 1, Nairn 1, Oliver 1, Wilson 1, Opponents 2.
Tennents Cup goals (4): McManus 3, Bailey 1. **CIS Cup goals (1):** McManus 1. **Bell's Cup goals (2):** Graham 1, McManus 1.

EAST STIRLINGSHIRE

Ground: Firs Park, Falkirk FK2 7AY. **Capacity:** 781.
Telephone: 01324 623583. **Colours:** Black and white. **Nickname:** Shire.

Aitken, A .... –(2)	Kristjansson, T 1	McCheyne, G 22
Ferguson, B .... 22(2)	Lorimer, D .... 23(5)	McDonald, G 3
Gordon, K .... 23(9)	Lyle, D .... 16(1)	McDonald, I .... 22(2)
Hall, M .... 21(2)	Mauchen 2	McGhee, G .... 24(2)
Hay, D 27	Maughan, R .... 27(3)	McKechnie, G .... 15(4)
Hunter, M .... 1(8)	McAuley, S .... 31(2)	McLaren .... 1(4)

McLaughlin, P 2	Russell, G 30	Tolland, M .... 4(1)
McShane 7	Scott, A .... 19(4)	Ure, D .... 13(5)
Menelaws, D 7	Todd, C .... 8(1)	Wood, D .... –(2)
Robertson, S 1	Todd, C .... 24(6)	

League goals (51): Gordon 11, Lyle 10, McKechnie 6, Menelaws 5, Lorimer 3, Ure 3, Maughan 2, McAuley 2, McCheyne 2, Ferguson 1, Hall 1, McDonald, I 1, McGhee 1, Scott 1, Todd 1, Opponents 1.
Tennents Cup goals (2): Lyle 1, Opponents 1. **CIS Cup goals:** None. **Bell's Cup goals:** None.

ELGIN CITY

Ground: Borough Briggs, Elgin IV30 1AP. **Capacity:** 4,962.
Telephone: 01343 551114. **Colours:** Black and white. **Nickname:** Black and Whites.

Bremner, F .... 1(1)	James, R 10	Pirie, M 33
Campbell, C .... 22(6)	Kelly, J .... 12(7)	Rae, D .... 5(1)
Craig, D .... 11(16)	MacDonald, J .... 19(6)	Rae, M 1
Craig, R .... 4(7)	MacDonald, S .... 17(1)	Ross, D .... 28(1)
Dlugonski, B 22	Mackay, S 20	Rutherford, R .... 4(5)
Furphy, W .... 12(1)	Mailer, C .... 16(2)	Sanderson, M .... 15(1)
Gilzean, I .... 33(1)	McBride, R .... 25(1)	Teasdale, M 10
Hamilton, A 2	McGlashan, C .... 11(3)	Tully, C 33
Hind, D .... 23(4)	Morrison, M 6	Watt, G .... –(1)

League goals (45): Gilzean 12, Kelly 6, James 4, Tully 4, Campbell 3, Hind 2, MacKay 2, Ross 2, Craig 1, Dlugonski 1, MacDonald, S 1, Mailer 1, McBride 1, Rae 1, Rutherford 1, Sanderson 1, Teasdale 1, Opponents 1.
Tennents Cup goals: None. **CIS Cup goals (2):** Gilzean 1, McGlashan 1. **Bell's Cup goals:** None.

MONTROSE

Ground: Links Park, Montrose DD10 8QD. **Capacity:** 3,292.
Telephone: 01674 673200. **Colours:** Royal blue and white. **Nickname:** Gable Endies.

Allison, J .... 26(5)	Johnston, G 31	McQuillan, J 27
Brand, R .... 22(2)	Kerrigan, S .... 23(2)	Mitchell, J .... 6(12)
Butter, J 4	Laidlaw, S .... 18(14)	Muirhead, D .... 1(1)
Christie, G 33	Leask, M .... 6(1)	Sharp, G .... –(1)
Conway, F .... 20(1)	Lowe, B .... 1(4)	Sharp, R 25
Craib, M .... 11(1)	Magee, K .... 5(4)	Stewart, S 4
Craig, D .... 24(3)	McGlynn, G .... 32(2)	Thomas, K 3
Ferguson, S .... 34(2)	McKellar, J .... 12(11)	Webster, K 1
Hutcheon, A .... 3(22)	McKinnon, R 20	Yates, M .... 2(2)

League goals (43): Laidlaw 13, Kerrigan 7, Conway 3, Ferguson 3, Brand 2, Christie 2, Johnston 2, McKellar 2, McKinnon 2, Sharp, R 2, Allison 1, Leask 1, Magee 1, Mitchell 1, Stewart 1.
Tennents Cup goals (4): Laidlaw 3, Lowe 1. **CIS Cup goals:** None. **Bell's Cup goals:** None.

PETERHEAD

Ground: Balmoor Stadium, Peterhead AB42 IEU. **Capacity:** 3,250.
Telephone: 01779 478256. **Colours:** Royal blue and white. **Nickname:** Blue Toon.

Bissett, K .... 11(15)	Duffy, J .... 2(3)	McQuade, J 3
Brown, S .... –(2)	Findlay, C .... 5(9)	McSkimming, S .... 4(4)
Buchanan, R 1	Johnston, M .... 29(6)	Murray, I .... –(1)
Canning, M 21	King, S .... 24(4)	Pirie, I 25
Clark, G .... –(2)	Livingstone, R .... 24(4)	Robertson, K .... 7(2)
Clark, S .... 19(6)	Mackay, S .... 32(3)	Simpson, M 33
Cooper, C .... 21(4)	Mathers, P 10	Slater, M .... 6(1)

Smith, G .... 28(1)   Tindal, K 33   Yeats, C .... 17(14)
Stewart, L .... 32(1)   Wood, M .... 7(1)
League goals (63): Stewart 19, Johnston 18, Yeats 5, Tindal 4, Cooper 3, Mackay 3, Robertson 3, Bissett 2, Wood 2, Clark, S 1, Findlay 1, Livingstone 1, McSkimming 1.
Tennents Cup goals: None. **CIS Cup goals:** None. **Bells Cup goals (2):** Stewart 2.

QUEENS PARK

Ground: Hampden Park, Glasgow G42 9BA. **Capacity:** 52,025.
Telephone: 0141 632 1275. **Nickname:** Spiders.

Borland, P 21   Fisher, Colin .... –(2)   Orr, G .... –(1)
Brown, J .... 7(10)   Gallagher,M .... 10(2)   Orr, S .... 1(2)
Bruce, J .... 11(2)   Gallagher, P .... 4(3)   Patterson, P .... 9(4)
Canning, S .... 27(9)   Gemmill, J .... 7(4)   Proudfoot, K .... 2(1)
Carberry, A .... 2(1)   Jackson, R .... 18(11)   Quinn, A .... 33(2)
Caven, R 16   Marshall, S .... 22(2)   Rae, D .... 5(1)
Clarke, P .... –(1)   Martin, W .... 9(16)   Sinclair, R .... 11(1)
Collins, N 28   McPhee, G .... 2(2)   Smith, A 2
Cunningham, J .... 7(1)   McVey, L .... 6(1)   Smith, G 22
Dunning, A .... 7(3)   Miller, B .... 2(4)   Stevenson, C 18
Ewing, C .... 5(2)   Miller, G 7   Whelan, J 21
Ferry, D .... 26(1)   Miller, K 3   White, J 7
Fisher, Chris .... 6(8)   Mitchell, A 12
League goals (38): Canning 5, Jackson 5, Whelan 4, Gemmill 3, Martin 3, Quinn 3, Caven 2, Dunning 2, Gallagher,M 2, Marshall 2, Fisher, Chris 1, Fisher, Colin 1, Ferry 1, Fisher 1, Miller 1, Proudfoot 1, Opponents 1.
Tennents Cup goals (2): Jackson 2. **CIS Cup goals:** None. **Bells Cup goals:** None.

STIRLING ALBION

Ground: Forthbank Stadium, Stirling FK7 7UJ. **Capacity:** 3,808.
Telephone: 01786 450399. **Colours:** White and navy. **Nickname:** Albion.

Bailey, L .... –(1)   Goldie, D 12   Morrison, G .... 16(2)
Beveridge, R .... 1(1)   Hay, P .... 29(3)   Munro, G .... 11(12)
Brannigan, K 19   Heighton, H 3   Nugent, P 22
Butler, D 3   Henderson, N 14   O'Brien, D .... 9(3)
Davies, D 1   Higgins, G .... 9(4)   Raeside, R 6
Cosgrove, S .... 9(1)   Hutchison, S .... 3(2)   Reid, C 33
Cremin, B .... 2(3)   Kearney, D .... 8(1)   Reilly, S 27
Crozier, B 13   Kelly, G .... 2(2)   Ross, D .... 4(19)
De Gergorio, R 1   McCallion, K .... 13(9)   Stuart, W .... 6(10)
Devine, S .... 24(1)   McLellan, K .... 21(5)   Williams, A .... 29(3)
Edwards, C .... 4(2)   Middleton, G 2   Wilson, D .... –(1)
Geraghty, M .... 24(2)   Moriarty, T 13   Zujovic, G .... 2(1)
League goals (45): Williams 17, Geraghty 7, Devine 5, Henderson 4, Higgins 3, Ross 3, Brannigan 1, Cremin 1, Goldie 1, Hay 1, Nugent 1, Opponents 1.
Tennents Cup goals (2): Munro 1, Williams 1. **CIS Cup goals (5):** Williams 4, Munro 1.
Bell's Cup goals (1): Henderson 1.

NEW CLUBS ELECTED
AIRDRIE UNITED

Ground: New Broomfield Stadium, Airdrie ML6 8QZ. **Capacity:** 10,171.
Telephone: 01236 622000. **Colours:** White and Red. **Nickname:** Diamonds.

GRETNA

Ground: Raydale Park, Getna. **Capacity:** 2,200.
Telephone: 01461 337602. **Colours:** Black and white. **Nickname:** Black and whites.

F.A. BARCLAYCARD PREMIERSHIP

CLUB DETAILS AND PLAYING STAFFS 2002–03

(At time of going to press)

ARSENAL

Ground: Arsenal Stadium, Highbury, London, N5 1BU.
Telephone: 020 7704 4000 **Clubcall:** 09064 744000. **Club Nickname:** The Gunners.
First-choice colours: Red white shirts; white shorts; white stockings.
Record transfer fee: £13,000,000 to Bordeaux for Sylvain Wiltord, August 2000.
Record fee received: £25,000,000 from Barcelona for Marc Overmars, July 2000.
Record attendance: At Highbury: 73,295 v Sunderland March 1935. At Wembley: 73,707 v Lens (Champions League) November 1998.
Capacity for 2002-03: 38,500. **Sponsors:** O_2.
League Championship: winners 1930-31, 1932-33, 1933-34, 1934-35, 1937-38, 1947-48, 1952-53, 1970-71, 1988-89, 1990-91, 1997-98, 2001-02.
F.A. Cup: winners 1930, 1936, 1950, 1971, 1979, 1993, 1998, 2002.
League Cup: winners 1987, 1993.
European Competitions: winners Fairs Cup: 1969-70, Cup Winners Cup: 1993-94.
Finishing positions in Premiership: 1992-93 10th, 1993-94 4th, 1994-95 12th, 1995-96 5th, 1996-97 3rd, 1997-98 1st, 1998-99 2nd, 1999-2000 2nd, 2000-01 2nd, 2001-02 1st.
Biggest win: 12-0 v Loughborough Town, Div. 2, 12.3.1900.
Biggest defeat: 0-8 v Loughborough Town, Div. 2, 12.12.1896.
Highest League scorer in a season: Ted Drake, 42, 1934-35.
Most League goals in aggregate: Cliff Bastin, 150, 1930-47.
Most capped player: Kenny Sansom (England) 77.
Longest unbeaten League sequence: 26 matches (April 1990).
Longest sequence without a League win: 23 (September 1912).

Name	Height ft. in.	Previous club	Birthplace	Birthdate
Goalkeepers				
Seaman, David	6. 4	Q.P.R.	Rotherham	19.09.63
Taylor, Stuart	6. 4	–	Romford	28.11.81
Wright, Richard	6. 2	Ipswich Town	Ipswich	5.11.77
Defenders				
Adams, Tony	6. 3	–	Romford	10.10.66
Campbell, Sol	6. 1	Tottenham	Newham	18.09.74
Cole, Ashley	5. 8	–	Stepney	20.12.80
Cygan, Pascal	6. 5	Lille	Lens	29.04.74
Halls, John	6. 0	–	Islington	14.02.82
Juan	5.11	Sao Paulo	Sao Paulo	6.02.82
Keown, Martin	6. 1	Everton	Oxford	24.07.66
Luzhny, Oleg	5.10	Dynamo Kiev	Kiev	5.08.68
Stepanovs, Igors	6. 4	FC Skonto	Ogre, Lat.	21.01.76
Svard, Sebastian	5.10	FC Copenhagen	Denmark	15.01.83
Tavlaridis, Stathis	6. 1	Iraklis Saloniki	Greece	25.01.80
Upson, Matthew	6. 1	Luton Town	Eye	18.04.79
Midfielders				
Edu	6. 1	Corinthians	Sao Paulo	15.05.78
Lauren	5.11	Real Mallorca	Londi Kribi, Cam.	19.01.77
Ljungberg, Fredrik	5.11	Halmstads	Halmstad	16.04.77
Parlour, Ray	5.10	–	Romford	7.03.73
Pennant, Jermaine	5. 9	Notts Co.	Nottingham	5.01.83
Pires, Robert	6. 1	Marseille	Reims	29.10.73

Van Bronckhorst, Giovanni	5.10	Rangers	Rotterdam	5.02.75
Vieira, Patrick	6. 4	AC Milan.	Dakar, Sen.	23.06.76
Forwards				
Aliadiere, Jeremie	6. 0	–	Rambouillet, Fra.	30.03.83
Bergkamp, Dennis	6. 0	Inter Milan	Amsterdam	18.05.69
Henry, Thierry	6. 2	Juventus	Paris	17.08.77
Itonga, Carlin	5.10	–	Zaire	11.12.82
Jeffers, Francis	5. 9	Everton	Liverpool	25.01.81
Kanu, Nwankwo	6. 5	Inter Milan	Owerri, Nig.	1.08.76
Wiltord, Sylvain	5. 9	Bordeaux	Neuilly, Fra.	10.05.74

ASTON VILLA

Ground: Villa Park, Trinity Road, Birmingham, B6 6HE.
Telephone: 0121 327 2299 **Clubcall:** 09068 121148. **Club Nickname:** Villans.
First-choice colours: Claret and blue shirts; white shorts; claret and blue stockings.
Record transfer fee: £9,500,000 to River Plate for Juan Pablo Angel, January 2001.
Record fee received: £12,600,000 for Dwight Yorke from Manchester Utd., August 1998.
Record attendance: 76,588 v Derby Co. (F.A. Cup 6) 2 March 1946.
Capacity for 2002-03: 46,602. **Sponsors:** MG Rover.
League Championship: winners 1893-94, 1895-96, 1896-97, 1898-99, 1899-1900, 1909-10, 1980-81.
F.A. Cup: winners 1887, 1895, 1897, 1905, 1913, 1920, 1957.
League Cup: winners 1961, 1975, 1977, 1994, 1996.
European Competitions: Winners European Cup 1981-82, European Super Cup 1982-83.
Finishing positions in Premiership: 1992-93 2nd, 1993-94 10th, 1994-95 18th, 1995-96 4th, 1996-97 5th, 1997-98 7th, 1998-99 6th, 1999-2000 6th, 2000-01 8th, 2001-02 8th.
Biggest win: 12-2 v Accrington, Div. 1, 12.3.1892, 11-1 v Charlton Athletic, Div. 2, 24.11.1959, 10-0 v Sheffield Wed., Div. 1, 5.10.1912 and v Burnley, Div. 1, 29.8.1925.
Biggest defeat: 0-7 in five League matches from Blackburn Rov., Div. 1, 19.10.1889 to Manchester Utd., Div. 1, 24.10.1964.
Highest League scorer in a season: 'Pongo' Waring, 49, 1930-31.
Most League goals in aggregate: Harry Hampton, 215, 1904-1915.
Most capped player: Paul McGrath (Ireland) 51.
Longest unbeaten League sequence: 15 matches (January 1897, December 1909 and March 1949).
Longest sequence without a League win: 12 matches (November 1973 and December 1986).

Name	Height ft. in.	Previous club	Birthplace	Birthdate
Goalkeepers				
Enckelman, Peter	6. 2	Jalkapallo TPS	Turku, Fin.	10.03.77
Myhill, Boaz	6. 3	–	California	9.11.82
Postma, Stefan	6. 1	De Graafschap	Holland	10.06.76
Defenders				
Alpay, Ozalan	6. 2	Fenerbahce	Izmir	29.05.73
Barry, Gareth	6. 0	–	Hastings	23.2.81
Bewers, Jonathan	5. 9	–	Kettering	10.09.82
Delaney, Mark	6. 1	Cardiff City	Haverfordwest	13.05.71
Mellberg, Olof	6. 1	Racing Santander	Stockholm	9.03.77
Samuel, JLloyd	5.11	–	Trinidad	24.05.79
Staunton, Steve	6. 1	Liverpool	Drogheda	19.01.69
Wright, Alan	5. 4	Blackburn Rov.	Ashton-under-Lyne	28.09.71
Midfielders				
Boateng, George	5. 9	Coventry City	Nkawka, Gha.	5.09.75
Cooke, Stephen	5. 7	–	Walsall	15.02.83
Hadji, Moustapha	6. 0	Coventry City	Ifrane, Mor.	16.11.71

Hendrie, Lee	5.10	–	Birmingham	18.05.77
Hitzlsperger, Thomas	6. 0	Bayern Munich	Munich	5.04.82
Kachloul, Hassan	6. 2	Southampton	Agadir	19.02.73
McLaugh, Gavin	5. 7	–	Derry	9.07.81
Stone, Steve	5. 8	Nott'm. Forest	Gateshead	20.08.71
Taylor, Ian	6. 1	Sheffield Wed.	Birmingham	4.06.68
Forwards				
Allback, Marcus	5.11	Heerenveen	Gothenburg	5.07.73
Angel, Juan Pablo	5.11	River Plate	Medellin, Col.	21.10.75
Balaban, Bosko	5.11	Dinamo Zagreb	Rijeka	15.10.78
Boulding, Michael	5.10	Grimsby Town	Sheffield	8.02.75
Crouch, Peter	6. 6	Portsmouth	Macclesfield	30.01.81
Dublin, Dion	6. 2	Coventry City	Leicester	22.04.69
Merson, Paul	6. 0	Middlesbrough	London	20.03.68
Moore, Stefan	5.11	–	Birmingham	28.09.83
Vassell, Darius	5. 7	–	Birmingham	13.06.80

BIRMINGHAM CITY

Ground: St Andrews, Birmingham City B9, 4NH.
Telephone: 07091 112 5837. **Clubcall:** 09068 121188. **Club nickname:** Blues.
First-choice colours: Blue shirts, blue shorts, white stockings.
Record transfer fee: £2,500,000 to Leicester City for Robbie Savage, June 2002.
Record fee received: £2,500,000 from Coventry City for Gary Breen, January 1997.
Record attendance: 66,844 v Everton (F.A. Cup 5) 11 February, 1967.
Capacity for 2002-03: 30,007. **Sponsors:** Phones 4U.
League championship: 6th 1955-56.
F.A. Cup: runners-up 1931, 1956.
League Cup: winners 1963.
European Competitions: runners-up Fairs Cup 1959-60, 1960-61.
Biggest win: 12-0 v Walsall, Div. 2, 17.12.1892, 12-0 v Doncaster Rov., Div. 2, 11.4.1903.
Biggest defeat: 1-9 v Sheffield Wed., Div. 1, 13.12.30. 1-9 v Blackburn Rov., Div. 1, 5.11.1895.
Highest League scorer in a season: Joe Bradford, 29, 1927-28.
Most League goals in aggregate: Joe Bradford, 249, 1920-35.
Most capped player: Malcolm Page, 28, Wales.
Longest unbeaten League sequence: 20 matches (January 1995).
Longest sequence without a League win: 17 matches (January 1986).

Name	Height ft. in.	Previous club	Birthplace	Birthdate
Goalkeepers				
Bennett, Ian	6. 0	Peterborough Utd.	Worksop	10.10.71
Vaesen, Nico	6. 1	Huddersfield Town	Ghent	28.09.69
Defenders				
Capaldi, Tony	6. 0	–	Porsgrunn, Nor.	12.08.81
Cisse, Aliou	6. 2	Paris St-Germain	Senegal	24.03.76
Cunningham, Kenny	5.11	Wimbledon	Dublin	28.06.71
Eaden, Nicky	5. 9	Barnsley	Sheffield	12.12.72
Gill, Jerry	5.11	Yeovil Town	Clevedon	8.09.70
Grainger, Martin	5.10	Brentford	Enfield	23.08.72
Johnson, Michael	5.11	Notts Co.	Nottingham	4.07.73
Kenna, Jeff	5.11	Blackburn Rov.	Dublin	27.08.70
Purse, Darren	6. 2	Oxford Utd.	Stepney	14.02.76
Tebily, Olivier	6. 0	Celtic	Abidjan, Iv. Coast	19.12.75
Vickers, Steve	6. 1	Middlesbrough	Bishop Auckland	13.10.67
Williams, Tommy	5.11	Peterborough Utd.	Carshalton	8.07.80
Midfielders				
Devlin, Paul	5. 9	Sheffield Utd.	Birmingham	14.04.72
Hyde, Graham	5. 7	Sheffield Wed.	Doncaster	10.11.70

Name	Height ft. in.	Previous club	Birthplace	Birthdate
Hughes, Bryan	5. 9	Wrexham	Liverpool	19.06.76
Johnson, Damien	5.10	Blackburn Rov.	Lisburn	18.11.78
Lazaridis, Stan	5. 9	West Ham Utd.	Perth, Aus.	16.08.72
Luntala, Tresor	5. 9	Rennes	Dreux, Fra.	31.05.82
Savage, Robbie	5.11	Leicester City	Wrexham	18.10.74
Williams, Jacques	5. 9	–	Liverpool	25.04.81
Woodhouse, Curtis	5. 8	Sheffield Utd.	Beverley	17.04.80
Forwards				
Furlong, Paul	6. 0	Chelsea	Wood Green	27.01.69
Horsfield, Geoff	6. 1	Fulham	Barnsley	1.11.73
John, Stern	6. 1	Nott'm. Forest	Canefarm, Trin.	30.10.76
Johnson, Andrew	5. 7	–	Bedford	10.02.81
Mooney, Tommy	5.11	Watford	Billingham	11.08.71

BLACKBURN ROVERS

Ground: Ewood Park, Blackburn BB2 4JF.
Telephone: 01254 698888 **Clubcall:** 09068 121179. **Club Nickname:** Rovers.
First-choice colours: Blue and white shirts; white shorts; white stockings.
Record transfer fee: £8,000,000 to Manchester Utd. for Andy Cole, December 2001.
Record fee received: £15,000,000 from Newcastle Utd. for Alan Shearer, July 1996.
Record attendance: 62,522 v Bolton Wand., F.A. Cup 6th Rd, 2 March 1929.
Capacity for 2002-03: 31,367. **Sponsors:** AMD.
League championship: winners 1911-12, 1913-14, 1994-95.
F.A. Cup: winners 1884, 1885, 1886, 1890, 1891, 1928.
League Cup: winners 2002.
European Competitions: Champions League 1st group stage 1995-96.
Finishing positions in Premiership: 1992-93 4th, 1993-94 2nd, 1994-95 1st, 1995-96 7th, 1996-97 13th, 1997-98 6th, 1998-99 19th, 2001-02 10th.
Biggest win: 9-0 v Middlesbrough, Div. 2, 6.11.1954. Also 11-0 v Rossendale, F.A. Cup 1st Rd, 13.10.1884.
Biggest defeat: 0-8 v Arsenal, Div. 1, 25.2.1933.
Highest League scorer in a season: Ted Harper, 43, 1925-26.
Most League goals in aggregate: Simon Garner, 168, 1978-92.
Most capped player: Bob Crompton (England) 41.
Longest unbeaten League sequence: 23 matches (September 1987).
Longest sequence without a League win: 16 matches (November 1978).

Name	Height ft. in.	Previous club	Birthplace	Birthdate
Goalkeepers				
Friedel, Brad	6. 3	Liverpool	Lakewood, USA	18.05.71
Kelly, Alan	6. 2	Birmingham City	Preston	11.08.68
Miller, Alan	6. 3	W.B.A.	Epping	29.03.70
Defenders				
Berg, Henning	6. 0	Manchester Utd.	Eidsvoll, Nor.	1.09.69
Bjornebye, Stig-Inge	5.10	Liverpool	Elverum, Nor.	11.12.69
Curtis, John	5.10	Manchester Utd.	Nuneaton	3.09.78
Greer, Gordon	6. 2	Clyde	Glasgow	17.08.82
Hakan Unsal	6. 1	Galatasaray	Sinop, Turkey	14.05.73
Johansson, Nils-Eric	6. 1	Nurnberg	Stockholm	13.01.80
Sebastian-Pelzer, Marc	5.10	Kaiserslautern	Germany	
Short, Craig	6. 2	Everton	Bridlington	25.06.68
Neill, Lucas	6. 1	Millwall	Sydney	9.03.78
Taylor, Martin	6. 4	–	Ashington	9.11.79
Midfielders				
Douglas, Jon	5.10	Celtic	Clones	22.11.81
Dunning, Darren	5. 6	–	Scarborough	8.01.81
Dunn, David	5.10	–	Blackburn	27.12.79
Flitcroft, Gary	6. 0	Manchester City	Bolton	6.11.72
Gillespie, Keith	5.10	Newcstle Utd.	Larne	18.02.75

Hignett, Craig	5. 9	Barnsley	Liverpool	12.01.70
Mahon, Alan	5. 9	Sporting Lisbon	Dublin	4.04.78
O'Brien, Burton	5.11	St Mirren	South Africa	10.06.81
Todd, Andy	5.10	Charlton Athletic	Derby	21.09.74
Tugay, Kerimoglu	5. 9	Rangers	Istanbul	24.08.70
Forwards				
Cole, Andy	5.10	Manchester Utd.	Nottingham	15.10.71
Duff, Damien	5. 8	–	Ballyboden	2.03.79
Grabbi, Corrado	5.11	Ternana	Turin	29.07.75
Jansen, Matt	5.11	Crystal Palace	Carlisle	20.10.77
Ostenstad, Egil	5.11	Southampton	Haugesund, Nor.	2.01.72
Richards, Marc	5.10	–	Wolverhampton	8.07.82

BOLTON WANDERERS

Ground: Reebok Stadium, Burnden Way, Lostock, Bolton BL6 6JW.
Telephone: 01204 673673 **Clubcall:** 09068 121153. **Club Nickname:** The Trotters.
First-choice colours: White and navy shirts; navy shorts; white stockings.
Record transfer fee: £3,500,000 to Wimbledon for Dean Holdsworth, October 1997.
Record fee received: £4,500,000 from Liverpool for Jason McAteer, September 1995.
Record attendance: At Reebok Stadium: 27,351 v Arsenal (Premier League) 29 April 2002. At Burnden Park: 69,912 v Manchester City, F.A. Cup 5th Rd, 18 February 1933.
Capacity for 2001-02: 27,500. **Sponsors:** Reebok.
League championship: 3rd 1891-92, 1920-21, 1924-25.
F.A. Cup: winners 1923, 1926, 1929, 1958.
League Cup: runners-up 1995.
Finishing positions in Premiership: 1995-96 20th, 1997-98 18th, 2001-02 16th.
Biggest win: 8-0 v Barnsley, Div. 2, 6.10.1934. Also 13-0 v Sheffield Utd., F.A. Cup 2nd Rd, 1.2.1890.
Biggest defeat: 1-9 v Preston N.E., F.A. Cup 2nd Rd, 10.12.1887.
Highest League scorer in a season: Joe Smith, 38, 1920-21.
Most League goals in aggregate: Nat Lofthouse, 255, 1946-61.
Most capped player: Mark Fish (South Africa) 34.
Longest unbeaten League sequence: 23 matches (October 1990).
Longest sequence without a League win: 26 matches (April 1902).

Name	Height ft. in.	Previous club	Birthplace	Birthdate
Goalkeepers				
Banks, Steve	5.11	Blackpool	Hillingdon	9.02.72
Jaaskelainen, Jussi	6. 4	VPS	Vaasa, Fin	17.04.75
Poole, Kevin	5.10	Birmingham City	Bromsgrove	21.07.63
Defenders				
Barness, Anthony	5.11	Charlton Athletic	Lewisham	25.03.73
Bergsson, Gudni	6. 1	Tottenham	Reykjavik	21.07.65
Charlton, Simon	5. 8	Birmingham City	Huddersfield	25.10.71
Hendry, Colin	6. 1	Coventry City	Keith	7.11.65
N'Gotty, Bruno	6. 2	Marseille	Lyon	10.06.71
Warhurst, Paul	6. 0	Crystal Palace	Stockport	26.09.69
Whitlow, Mike	6. 0	Leicester City	Northwich	13.01.68
Midfielders				
Bulent, Akin	6. 1	Galatasaray	Turkey	28.08.79
Farrelly, Gareth	6. 0	Everton	Dublin	28.08.75
Forschelet, Gerald	6. 2	Cannes	Tahiti	–
Frandsen, Per	6. 1	Blackburn Rov.	Copenhagen	6.02.70
Nolan, Kevin	6. 1	–	Liverpool	24.06.82
Gardner, Ricardo	5. 9	Harbour View	St. Andrews, Jam.	25.09.78
Pedersen, Henrik	6. 1	Silkeborg	Denmark	10.06.75
Okocha, Jay-Jay	5.10	Paris St-Germain	Enugu, Nig.	14.08.73
Smith, Jeff	5.10	Bishop Auckland	Middlesbrough	28.06.80

Southall, Nicky	5.10	Gillingham	Middlesbrough	28.01.72
Tofting, Stig	5.10	Hamburg	Aarhus	14.08.69
Forwards				
Baldacchino, Ryan	5. 9	Blackburn Rov.	Leicester	13.01.81
Bobic, Fredi	6. 3	Borussia Dortmund	Maribor, Slov.	30.10.71
Djorkaeff, Youri	5.11	Kaiserslautern	Lyon	3.09.68
Facey, Delroy	6. 0	Huddersfield Town	Huddersfield	22.04.80
Hansen, Bo	6. 1	Brondby	Denmark	16.06.72
Holdsworth, Dean	5.11	Wimbledon	Walthamstow	8.11.68
Kaprilion, Mickael	5.10	Martigues	Marseilles	6.10.80
Norris, David	5. 7	Boston Utd.	Peterborough	22.02.81
Ricketts, Michael	6. 2	Walsall	Birmingham	4.12.78

CHARLTON ATHLETIC

Ground: The Valley, Floyd Road, Charlton, London, SE7 8BL.
Telephone: 0208 333 4000. **Club Nickname:** Addicks.
First-choice colours: Red shirts; white shorts; red stockings.
Record transfer fee: £4,750,000 to Wimbledon for Jason Euell, July 2001.
Record fee received: £4,000,000 from Leeds Utd. for Danny Mills, July 1999.
Record attendance: 75,031 v Aston Villa (F.A. Cup 5) 12 February 1938.
Capacity for 2002-03: 26,819 (26,000 by December 2001). **Sponsors:** all:sports.
League Championship: 2nd 1936-37.
F.A. Cup: winners 1947.
League Cup: 4th rnd 1963, 1966, 1979, 2001.
Finishing positions in Premiership: 1998-99 18th, 2000-01 9th, 2001-02 14th.
Biggest win: 8-1 v Middlesbrough, Div. 1, 12 September 1953.
Biggest defeat: 1-11 v Aston Villa, Div. 2, 14 November 1959.
Highest League scorer in a season: Ralph Allen, 32, Div. 3 (south), 1934-35.
Most League goals in aggregate: Stuart Leary, 153, 1953-62.
Most capped player: Mark Kinsella (Rep. of Ireland) 32.
Longest unbeaten League sequence: 15 matches (December 1980).

Name	Height ft. in.	Previous club	Birthplace	Birthdate
Goalkeepers				
Kiely, Dean	6. 1	Bury	Salford	10.10.70
Rachubka, Paul	6. 1	Manchester Utd.	San Luis, USA	21.05.81
Roberts, Ben	6. 2	Middlesbrough	Bishop Auckland	22.06.75
Defenders				
Brown, Steve	6. 1		Brighton	13.05.72
Fish, Mark	6. 3	Bolton Wand.	Cape Town	14.03.74
Fortune, Jonathan	6. 2		Islington	28.08.80
Kishishev, Radostin	5.11	Liteks Lovech	Burgas, Bul.	30.07.74
Konchesky, Paul	5.10		Barking	15.05.81
Powell, Chris	5.10	Derby Co.	Lambeth	8.09.69
Rowett, Gary	6. 0	Leicester City	Bromsgrove	6.03.74
Rufus, Richard	6. 1		Lewisham	12.01.75
Young, Luke	6. 0	Tottenham	Harlow	19.07.79
Midfielders				
Bart-Williams, Chris	5.11	Nott'm. Forest	Freetown, S.L	16.06.74
Jensen, Claus	5.11	Bolton Wand.	Nykobing, Den.	29.04.77
Kinsella, Mark	5. 9	Colchester Utd.	Dublin	12.08.72
Parker, Scott	5. 7		Lambeth	13.10.80
Robinson, John	5.10	Brighton & H.A.	Bulawayo	29.08.71
Stuart, Graham	5. 9	Sheffield Utd.	Tooting	24.10.70
Forwards				
Bartlett, Shaun	6. 1	FC Zurich	Cape Town	31.10.72
Euell, Jason	5.11	Wimbledon	Lambeth	6.02.77
Johansson, Jonatan	6. 2	Rangers	Stockholm	16.08.75
Lisbie, Kevin	5.10		Hackney	17.10.78

| Pringle, Martin | 6.2 | Benfica | Gothenburg | 18.11.70 |
| Svensson, Matt | 6.0 | Crystal Palace | Boras, Swe. | 24.09.74 |

CHELSEA

Ground: Stamford Bridge Stadium, London SW6 1HS.
Telephone: 0207 385 5545 **Clubcall:** 09068 121159. **Club Nickname:** The Blues.
First-choice colours: Blue shirts; blue shorts; white stockings.
Record transfer fee: £15,000,000 to Atletico Madrid for Jimmy Floyd Hasselbaink, June 2000.
Record fee received: £12,000,000 from Rangers for Tore Andre Flo, November 2000.
Record attendance: 82,905 v Arsenal, Div. 1, 12 October 1935.
Capacity for 2002-03: 42,449. **Sponsors:** Emirates.
League Championship: winners 1954-55.
F.A. Cup: winners 1970, 1997, 2000.
League Cup: winners 1965, 1998.
European Competitions: winners Cup Winners' Cup 1970-71, 1997-98.
Finishing positions in Premiership: 1992-93 11th, 1993-94 14th, 1994-95 11th, 1995-96 11th, 1996-97 6th, 1997-98 4th, 1998-99 3rd, 1999-2000 5th, 2000-01 6th, 2001-02 6th.
Biggest win: 7-0 in four League matches from Lincoln City, Div. 2, 29.10.1910 to Walsall, Div. 2, 4.2.1989. Also 9-2 v Glossop N.E. Div. 2, 1.9.1906.
Biggest defeat: 1-8 v Wolves, Div. 1, 26.9.1923. Also 0-7 v Leeds Utd., Div. 1, 7.10.1967 and v Nott'm For. Div. 1, 20.4.1991.
Highest League scorer in a season: Jimmy Greaves, 41, 1960-61.
Most League goals in aggregate: Bobby Tambling, 164, 1958-70.
Most capped player: Dan Petrescu (Romania) 43.
Longest unbeaten League sequence: 27 matches (October 1988).
Longest sequence without a League win: 21 matches (November 1987).

Name	Height ft. in.	Previous club	Birthplace	Birthdate
Goalkeepers				
Bosnich, Mark	6. 2	Manchester Utd.	Sydney	13.01.72
Cudicini, Carlo	6. 1	Castel Di Sangro	Milan	6.09.73
De Goey, Ed	6. 6	Feyenoord	Gouda, Hol.	20.12.66
Evans, Rys	6. 1	–	Swindon	27.01.82
Defenders				
Babayaro, Celestine	5. 9	Anderlecht	Kaduna, Nig.	29.08.78
Bogarde, Winston	6. 2	Barcelona	Rotterdam	22.10.70
Desailly, Marcel	6. 0	AC Milan	Accra	7.09.68
Ferrer, Albert	5. 6	Barcelona	Barcelona	6.06.70
Gallas, William	6. 1	Marseille	Asnieres, Fra.	17.08.77
Le Saux, Graeme	5.10	Blackburn Rov.	Jersey	17.10.68
Melchiot, Mario	6. 2	Ajax	Amsterdam	4.11.76
Terry, John	6. 1	–	Barking	7.12.80
Midfielders				
De Lucas, Enrique	5. 9	Espanyol	Barcelona	17.08.78
Gronkjaer, Jesper	6. 1	Ajax	Nuuk, Den.	12.08.77
Lampard, Frank	6. 0	West Ham Utd.	Romford	20.06.78
Morris, Jody	5. 6	–	London	22.12.78
Petit, Emmanuel	6. 1	Barcelona	Dieppe	22.09.70
Stanic, Mario	6. 2	Parma	Sarajevo	10.04.72
Forwards				
Cole, Carlton	6. 3	–	Surrey	12.10.83
Gudjohnsen, Eidur	6. 0	Bolton Wand.	Reykjavik	15.09.78
Hasselbaink, Jimmy Floyd	6. 0	Atletico Madrid	Paramaribo, Sur.	27.03.72
Forssell, Mickael	6. 0	Helsinki	Steinfurt, Ger.	15.03.81
Knight, Leon	5. 4	–	London	16.09.82
Zenden, Boudewijn	5.10	Barcelona	Maastricht	15.08.76
Zola, Gianfranco	5. 6	Parma	Sardinia	5.07.66

EVERTON

Ground: Goodison Park, Liverpool L4 4EL.
Telephone: 0151 330 2200 **Clubcall:** 09068 121199. **Club Nickname:** Toffees.
First-choice colours: Blue shirts; white shorts; blue stockings.
Record transfer fee: £5,750,000 to Middlesbrough for Nick Barmby.
Record fee received: £8,000,000 from Arsenal for Francis Jeffers, June 2001.
Record attendance: 78,299 v Liverpool, Div. 1, September 1948.
Capacity for 2002-03: 40,170. **Sponsors:** TBC.
League Championship: winners 1890-91, 1914-15, 1927-28, 1931-31, 1938-39, 1962-63, 1969-70, 1984-85, 1986-87.
F.A. Cup: winners 1906, 1933, 1966, 1984, 1995.
League Cup: runners up 1977, 1984.
European Competitions: winners Cup-Winners' Cup 1984-85.
Finishing positions in Premiership: 1992-93 13th, 1993-94 17th, 1994-95 15th 1995-96 6th 1996-97 15th 1997-98 17th 1998-99 14th, 1999-2000 13th, 2000-01 16th, 2001-02 15th.
Biggest win: 9-1 v Manchester City, Div. 1, 3.9.1906, v Plymouth Argyle, Div. 2, 27.12.1930. Also 11-2 v Derby Co., F.A. Cup 1st rd, 18.1.1890.
Biggest defeat: 4-10 v Tottenham, Div. 1, 11.10.1958.
Highest League scorer in a season: Ralph 'Dixie' Dean, 60, 1927-28.
Most League goals in aggregate: Ralph 'Dixie' Dean, 349, 1925-37.
Most capped player: Neville Southall (Wales) 92.
Longest unbeaten League sequence: 20 matches (April 1978).
Longest sequence without a League win: 14 matches (March 1937).

Name	Height ft. in.	Previous club	Birthplace	Birthdate
Goalkeepers				
Gerrard, Paul	6. 2	Oldham Athletic	Heywood	22.01.73
Simonsen, Steve	6. 3	Tranmere Rov.	South Shields	3.04.79
Defenders				
Clarke, Peter	5.11	–	Southport	3.01.82
Hibbert, Tony	5.10	–	Liverpool	20.02.81
Linderoth, Tobias	5. 8	Stabaek	Marseille	21.04.79
Naysmith, Gary	5.11	Hearts	Edinburgh	16.11.78
Stubbs, Alan	6. 2	Celtic	Kirkby	6.10.71
Pistone, Alessandro	5.11	Newcastle Utd.	Milan	27.07.75
Unsworth, David	6. 1	Aston Villa	Chorley	16.10.73
Watson, Steve	6. 0	Aston Villa	North Shields	1.04.74
Weir, David	6. 2	Hearts	Falkirk	10.05.70
Yobo, Joseph	5. 9	Marseille	Nigeria	6.09.80
Midfielders				
Alexandersson, Niclas	6. 2	Sheffield Wed.	Halmstad, Swe.	29.12.71
Carsley, Lee	5. 9	Coventry City	Birmingham	28.02.74
Gemmill, Scot	5. 9	Nott'm. Forest	Paisley	2.01.71
Gravesen, Thomas	5. 9	Hamburg	Vejle, Den.	11.03.76
McLeod, Kevin	5.10	–	Liverpool	12.09.80
Pembridge, Mark	5. 7	Sheffield Wed.	Merthyr Tydfil	28.11.70
Tal, Idan	5. 8	Maccabi	Petach-Tikva, Isr.	13.09.75
Forwards				
Campbell, Kevin	6. 1	Trabzonspor	Lambeth	4.02.70
Ferguson, Duncan	6. 4	Newcastle Utd.	Stirling	27.12.71
Moore, Joe-Max	5. 9	New England Rev.	Tulsa	23.02.71
Radzinski, Tomasz	5. 9	Anderlecht	Poznan, Pol.	14.12.73

FULHAM

Ground (sharing): Loftus Road, South Africa Road, London W12 7PA.
Training ground: Motspur Park, New Malden, Surrey KT3 6PT.

Telephone: 0208 336 7400 **Clubcall:** 09068 440044. **Club Nickname:** Cottagers.
First-choice colours: White shirts; black shorts; white stockings.
Record transfer fee: £11,500,000 to Lyon for Steve Marlet, August 2001.
Record fee received: £2,250,000 from Birmingham City for Geoff Horsfield, July 2000.
Record attendance: 49,335 v Millwall, Division 2, 8 October 1938.
Capacity for 2002-03: 19,161 (at Loftus Road). **Sponsors:** –.
League championship: 10th 1959-60.
F.A. Cup: runners-up 1975.
League Cup: 5th Rd. 1968, 1971, 2000.
Finishing positions in Premiership: 2001-02 13th.
Biggest win: 10-1 v Ipswich Town, Div. 1, 26.12.63.
Biggest defeat: 0-10 v Liverpool, League Cup 2nd Rd 1st leg, 23.9.86.
Highest League scorer in a season: Frank Newton, 43, 1931-32.
Most League goals in aggregate: Gordon Davies, 159, 1978-84 and 1986-91.
Most capped player: Johnny Haynes (England) 56.
Longest unbeaten League sequence: 15 matches (January 1999).
Longest sequence without a League win: 15 matches (February 1950).

Name	Height ft. in.	Previous club	Birthplace	Birthdate
Goalkeepers				
Herrera, Martin	6. 1	Alaves	Rio Puerton, Arg.	13.09.70
Taylor, Maik	6. 3	Southampton	Hildeshein, Ger.	4.09.71
Thompson, Glyn	6. 2	Shrewsbury Town	Telford	24.02.81
Van der Sar, Edwin	6. 6	Juventus	Voorhout, Hol.	29.10.70
Defenders				
Brevett, Rufus	5. 8	Q.P.R.	Derby	24.09.69
Coleman, Chris	6. 2	Blackburn Rov.	Swansea	10.06.70
Finnan, Steve	5.10	Notts Co.	Limerick	20.04.76
Goma, Alain	6. 0	Newcastle Utd.	Sault, Fra.	5.10.72
Hudson, Mark	6. 3	Swindon Town	Guildford	30.03.82
Knight, Zat	6. 6	–	Solihull	2.05.80
McAnespie, Kieran	5.11	St Johnstone	–	–
Melville, Andrew	6. 1	Sunderland	Swansea	29.11.68
Ouaddou, Abdeslam	6. 3	Nancy	Ksar-Askour, Mor.	1.11.78
Midfielders				
Clark, Lee	5. 8	Sunderland	Wallsend	27.10.72
Collins, John	5. 8	Everton	Galashiels	31.01.68
Davis, Sean	5.11	–	Clapham	20.09.79
Harley, Jon	5. 9	Chelsea	Maidstone	26.09.79
Legwinski, Sylvain	6. 1	Bordeaux	Clermont-Ferrand	10.06.73
Lewis, Eddie	5.10	San Jose	Cerritos, USA	17.05.74
Malbranque, Steed	5. 8	Lyon	Mouscron, Bel.	6.01.80
Forwards				
Boa Morte, Luis	5. 9	Southampton	Lisbon	4.08.77
Hayles, Barry	5.10	Bristol Rov.	London	17.05.72
Marlet, Steve	5.11	Lyon	Pithiviers, Fra.	1.10.74
Saha, Louis	6. 1	Metz	Paris	8.08.78
Sava, Facundo	6. 1	Gimnasia	Ituzaingo, Arg.	7.03.74
Stolcers, Andrejs	5.11	Shakhtar Donetsk	Latvia	7.08.74

LEEDS UNITED

Ground: Elland Road, Leeds LS11 OES.
Telephone: 0113 226 6000 **Clubcall:** 09068 121180. **Club Nickname:** Whites.
First-choice colours: White shirts, shorts and stockings (all with royal blue trim).
Record transfer fee: £18,000,000 to West Ham Utd. for Rio Ferdinand, November 2000.
Record fee received: £12,000,000 from Atletico Madrid for Jimmy Floyd Hasselbaink, August 1999.
Record attendance: 57,892 v Sunderland, 15 March 1967.

Capacity for 2002-03: 40,296. **Sponsors:** Strongbow.
League Championship: winners 1968-69, 1973-74, 1991-92.
F.A. Cup: winners 1972.
League Cup: winners 1968.
European Competitions: winners Fairs Cup 1967-68, 1970-71. Runners-up European Cup 1974-75, Cup-Winners' Cup 1972-73.
Finishing positions in Premiership: 1992-93 17th, 1993-94 5th, 1994-95 5th, 1995-96 13th, 1996-97 11th, 1997-98 5th, 1998-99 4th, 1999-2000 3rd, 2000-01 4th, 2001-02 5th.
Biggest win: 8-0 v Leicester City, Div. 1, 7.4.1934.
Biggest defeat: 1-8 v Stoke City, Div. 1, 27.8.1934.
Highest League scorer in a season: John Charles, 42 1953-54.
Most League goals in aggregate: Peter Lorimer, 168, 1965-79 and 1983-86.
Most capped player: Billy Bremner (Scotland) 54.
Longest unbeaten League sequence: 34 matches (October 1968).
Longest sequence without a League win: 17 matches (February 1947).

Name	Height ft. in.	Previous club	Birthplace	Birthdate
Goalkeepers				
Allaway, Shaun	6. 2	Reading	Reading	16.02.83
Martyn, Nigel	6. 2	Crystal Palace	St Austell	11.08.66
Milosevic, Dejan	6. 3	Perth Glory	Carlton, Aus.	26.06.78
Robinson, Paul	6. 4	–	Beverley	15.10.79
Defenders				
Duberry, Michael	6. 1	Chelsea	Enfield	14.10.75
Harte, Ian	6. 0	–	Drogheda	31.08.77
Kelly, Gary	5. 8	Home Farm	Drogheda	9.07.74
Matteo, Dominic	6. 1	Liverpool	Dumfries	24.04.74
Mills, Danny	6. 0	Charlton Athletic	Norwich	18.05.77
Radebe, Lucas	6. 1	Kaizer Chiefs,	Johannesburg	12.04.69
Richardson, Frazer	5.10	–	Rotherham	29.10.82
Woodgate, Jonathan	6. 2	–	Middlesbrough	22.01.80
Midfielders				
Bakke, Eirik	6. 1	Sogndal	Sogndal, Nor.	13.09.77
Batty, David	5. 8	Newcastle Utd.	Leeds	2.12.68
Bowyer, Lee	5. 9	Charlton Athletic	London	3.01.77
Burns, Jacob		Parramatta		
Cansdell-Sherriff, Shane	6. 0	–	Sydney	10.11.82
Dacourt, Olivier	5.10	Lens	Montreuil, Fra.	25.09.74
Johnson, Seth	5.10	Derby Co.	Birmingham	12.03.79
McMaster, Jamie	5.10	–	New South Wales	29.11.82
McPhail, Stephen	5.10	–	London	9.12.79
Wilcox, Jason	6. 0	Blackburn Rov.	Bolton	15.07.71
Forwards				
Bridges, Michael	6. 1	Sunderland	North Shields	5.08.78
Fowler, Robbie	5.11	Liverpool	Liverpool	9.04.75
Keane, Robbie	5. 9	Inter Milan	Dublin	8.07.80
Kewell, Harry	6. 0	–	Sydney	22.09.78
Singh, Harpal	5. 7	–	Bradford	15.09.81
Smith, Alan	5. 9	–	Leeds	28.10.80
Viduka, Mark	6. 2	Celtic	Australia	9.10.75

LIVERPOOL

Ground: Anfield Road, Liverpool L4 OTH.
Telephone: 0151 263 2361 **Clubcall:** 09068 121184. **Club Nickname:** Reds or Pool.
First-choice colours: Red shirts; red shorts; red stockings.
Record transfer fee: £11,000,000 to Leicester City for Emile Heskey, February 2000.
Record fee received: £11,000,000 from Leeds Utd. for Robbie Fowler, November 2001.
Record attendance: 61,905 v Wolves, (F.A. Cup 4), 2 February 1952.

Capacity for 2002-03: 45,362. **Sponsors:** Carlsberg/Reebok.
League Championship: winners 1900-01, 1905-06, 1921-22, 1922-23, 1946-47, 1963-64, 1965-66, 1972-73, 1975-76, 1976-77, 1978-79, 1979-80, 1981-82, 1982-83, 1983-84, 1985-86, 1987-88, 1989-90.
F.A. Cup: winners 1965, 1974, 1986, 1989, 1992, 2001.
League Cup: winners 1981, 1982, 1983, 1984, 1995, 2001.
European Competitions: winners European Cup 1976-77, 1977-78, 1980-81, 1983-84 UEFA Cup 1972-73, 1975-76, 2000-01 European Super Cup 1977.
Finishing positions in Premiership:1992-93 6th, 1993-94 8th, 1994-95 4th, 1995-96 3rd, 1996-97 4th, 1997-98 3rd, 1998-99 7th, 1999-2000 4th, 2000-01 3rd, 2001-02 2nd.
Biggest win: 10-1 v Rotherham Utd., Div. 2, 18.2.1896. Europe: 11-0 v Stromsgodset, CWC, 17.9.1974.
Biggest defeat: 1-9 v Birmingham City, Div. 2, 11.12.1954.
Highest League scorer in a season: Roger Hunt, 41, 1961-62.
Most League goals in aggregate: Roger Hunt, 245, 1959-69.
Most capped player: Ian Rush (Wales) 67.
Longest unbeaten League sequence: 31 matches (May 1987).
Longest sequence without a League win: 14 (December 1953).

Name	Height ft. in.	Previous club	Birthplace	Birthdate
Goalkeepers				
Arphexad, Pegguy	6. 2	Leicester City	Abymes, Fra.	18.05.73
Dudek, Jerzy	6. 1	Feyenoord	Rybnik, Pol.	23.03.73
Kirkland, Chris	6. 3	Coventry City	Leicester	2.05.81
Defenders				
Babbel, Markus	6. 0	Bayern Munich	Munich	8.09.72
Culshaw, Paul	6. 2	–	Liverpool	17.09.81
Diarra, Alou	6. 3	Bayern Munich	France	15.07.81
Heggem, Vegard	5.11	Rosenborg	Trondheim	13.07.75
Henchoz, Stephane	6. 1	Blackburn Rov.	Billens, Swi.	7.09.74
Hyypia, Sami	6. 4	Willem II	Porvoo, Fin.	7.10.73
Traore, Djimi	6. 1	Laval	Saint-Ouen, Fra.	1.03.80
Vignal, Gregory	5.11	Montpellier	Montpellier	19.07.81
Wright, Stephen	6. 0	–	Liverpool	8.02.80
Xavier, Abel	6. 2	Everton	Mozambique	30.11.72
Midfielders				
Barmby, Nick	5. 6	Everton	Hull City	11.02.74
Berger, Partik	6. 1	Borussia Dortmund	Prague	10.11.73
Biscan, Igor	6. 3	Croatia Zagreb	Zagreb	4.05.78
Carragher, Jamie	6. 1	–	Liverpool	28.01.78
Cheyrou, Bruno	6. 1	Lille	Suresnes, Fra.	10.05.78
Diomede, Bernard	5. 9	Auxerre	Bourges, Fra.	23.01.74
Gerrard, Steven	6. 1	–	Whiston	30.05.80
Hamann, Dietmar	6. 2	Newcastle Utd.	Waldasson, Ger.	27.08.73
Murphy, Danny	5. 9	Crewe Alexandra	Chester	18.03.77
Partridge, Richie	5. 8	–	Dublin	12.09.80
Riise, John Arne	6. 1	Monaco	Molde, Nor.	24.09.80
Smicer, Vladimir	5.10	Lens	Degin, Cz.	24.05.73
Warnock, Stephen	5.10	–	Ormskirk	12.12.81
Forwards				
Baros, Milan	6. 1	Banik Ostrava	Czech Rep.	28.10.81
Diouf, El-Hadji	6. 0	Lens	Dakar	15.01.81
Heskey, Emile	6. 1	Leicester City	Leicester	11.01.78
Litmanen, Jari	6. 0	Barcelona	Lahti, Fin.	20.02.71
Owen, Michael	5. 8	–	Chester	14.12.79
Sjolund, Daniel	5.11	West Ham Utd.	Mariehamn, Fin.	22.04.83

MANCHESTER CITY

Ground: Maine Road, Moss Side, Manchester M14 7WN.
Telephone: 0161 232 3000. **Clubcall:** 09068 121191.**Club nickname:** City.
First-choice-colours: Laser blue shirts, white shorts, blue/navy stockings.
Record transfer fee: £13,000,000 to Paris St-Germain for Nicolas Anelka, June 2002
Record fee received: £4,925,000 from Ajax for Georgi Kinkladze, May 1998.
Record attendance: 84,569 v Stoke City (F.A. Cup 6) 3 March, 1934 (British record for any game outside London or Glasgow).
Capacity for 2002-03: 34,996. **Sponsors:** First Advice.
League Championship: winners 1936-37, 1967-68.
F.A. Cup: winners 1904, 1934, 1956, 1969.
European Competitions: winners Cup Winners' Cup 1969-70.
Finishing positions in Premiership: 1992-93 9th, 1993-94 16th, 1994-95 17th, 1995-96 18th, 2000-01: 18th.
Biggest win: 10-1 Huddersfield Town, Div. 2, 7.11.87.
Biggest defeat: 1-9 v Everton, Div. 1, 3.9.1906.
Highest League scorer in a season: Tommy Johnson, 38, 1928-29.
Most League goals in aggregate: Tommy Johnson, 158, 1919-30.
Most capped player: Colin Bell, 48, England.
Longest unbeaten League sequence: 22 matches (April 1947).
Longest sequence without a League win: 17 matches (April 1980).

Name	Height ft. in.	Previous club	Birthplace	Birthdate
Goalkeepers				
Murphy, Brian	5. 9	–	Waterford	7.05.83
Nash, Carlo	6. 5	Stockport Co.	Bolton	13.09.73
Schmeichel, Peter	6. 4	Aston Villa	Gladsaxe, Den.	18.11.63
Weaver, Nicky	6. 3	Mansfield Town	Sheffield	2.03.79
Defenders				
Bischoff, Mikkel	6. 3	AB Copenhagen	Denmark	3.02.82
Charvet, Laurent	5.11	Newcastle Utd.	Beziers, Fra.	8.05.73
Distin, Sylvain	6. 4	Paris St-Germain	France	6.12.77
Dunne, Richard	6. 2	Everton	Dublin	21.09.79
Horlock, Kevin	6. 2	Swindon Town	Erith	1.11.72
Howey, Steve	6. 2	Newcastle Utd.	Sunderland	26.10.71
Mettomo, Lucien	6. 0	St Etienne	Cameroon	19.04.77
Ritchie, Paul	5.11	Rangers	Kirkcaldy	21.08.75
Sun Jihai	5.10	Dalian Wanda	China	30.09.77
Tiatto, Danny	5. 8	Stoke City	Melbourne	22.05.73
Wiekens, Gerard	6. 1	Veendam	Tolhuiswyk, Hol.	25.02.73
Midfielders				
Benarbia, Ali	5. 8	Paris St-Germain	Oran, Alg.	8.10.68
Berkovic, Eyal	5. 7	Celtic	Haifa	2.04.72
Dunfield, Terry	5.10		Vancouver	20.02.82
Haaland, Alfie	6. 1	Leeds Utd.	Stavanger	23.11.72
Jensen, Niclas	5.10	FC Copenhagen	Denmark	17.08.74
Negouai, Christian	6. 4	Charleroi	Martinique	20.01.75
Shuker, Chris	5. 5	–	Liverpool	9.05.82
Whitley, Jeff	5.10	–	Zambia	28.01.79
Forwards				
Anelka, Nicolas	6. 0	Paris St-Germain	Versailles	14.03.79
Goater, Shaun	6. 0	Bristol City	Bermuda	25.02.70
Huckerby, Darren	5.11	Leeds Utd.	Nottingham	23.04.76
Killen, Chris	5.11	–	Wellington, NZ	8.10.81
Macken, Jonathan	5.10	Preston N.E.	Manchester	7.09.77
Wanchope, Paulo	6. 4	West Ham Utd.	Costa Rica	31.07.76
Wright-Phillips, Shaun	5. 6	–	Greenwich	25.10.81

MANCHESTER UNITED

Ground: Old Trafford Stadium, Sir Matt Busby Way, Manchester, M16 ORA.
Telephone: 0161 872 1661 **Clubcall:** 09068 121161.
Club Nickname: The Red Devils.
First-choice colours: Red shirts, white shorts, black stockings.
Record transfer fee: £23,500,000 to Lazio for Juan Sebastian Veron, July 2001.
Record fee received: £15,250,000 from Lazio for Jaap Stam, August 2001.
Record attendance: Club: 70,504 v Aston Villa, 27 December 1920, F.A. Cup (semi-final): 76,962, Wolves v Grimsby Town, 25 March, 1939. Note: 83,260 saw Manchester Utd. v Arsenal, Div. 1, 17 January 1948 at Maine Road. Old Trafford was out of action through bomb damage.
Capacity for 2002-03: 68,936. **Sponsors:** Vodafone.
League Championship: winners 1907-08, 1910-11, 1951-52, 1955-56, 1956-7, 1964-65, 1966-67, 1992-93, 1993-94, 1995-96, 1996-97, 1998-99, 1999-2000, 2000-01.
F.A. Cup: winners 1909, 1948, 1963, 1977, 1983, 1985, 1990, 1994, 1996, 1999.
League Cup: winners 1992.
European Competitions: winners European Cup 1967-68, 1998-99, Cup-Winners' Cup 1990-91, European Super Cup 1991.
Finishing positions in Premiership: 1992-93 1st, 1993-94 1st, 1994-95 2nd, 1995-96 1st, 1996-97 1st, 1997-98 2nd, 1998-99 1st, 1999-2000 1st, 2000-01 1st, 2001-02 3rd.
Biggest win: (while Newton Heath) 10-1 v Wolves, Div.1, 15.10.1892, (as Manchester Utd.) 9-0 v Ipswich Town, FAPL, 4.3.1995. Europe: 10-0 v Anderlecht, European Cup prelim. round, 26.9.1956.
Biggest defeat: 0-7 v Wolves Div 2, 26.12.1931, v Aston Villa, Div. 1, 27.12.1930 and v Blackburn Rov. Div. 1, 10.4.1926.
Highest League scorer in a season: Dennis Viollet, 32, 1959-60.
Most League goals in aggregate: Bobby Charlton, 199, 1956-73.
Most capped player: Bobby Charlton (England) 106.
Longest unbeaten League sequence: 26 matches (February 1956).
Longest sequence without a League win: 16 matches (November 1928 and April 1930).

Name	Height ft. in.	Previous club	Birthplace	Birthdate
Goalkeepers				
Barthez, Fabien	5.11	Monaco	Lavelanet, Fra.	28.06.71
Carroll, Roy	6. 2	Wigan Athletic	Enniskillen	30.09.77
Steele, Luke	6. 2	Peterborough Utd.	Peterborough	24.09.84
Defenders				
Blanc, Laurent	6. 2	Inter Milan	Ales, Fra.	19.11.65
Brown, Wes	6. 1	–	Manchester	13.10.79
May, David	5.11	Blackburn Rov.	Oldham	24.06.70
Neville, Gary	5.11	–	Bury	18.02.75
Neville, Phillip	5.11	–	Bury	21.01.77
O'Shea, John	6. 3	Waterford Bohemians	Waterford	30.04.81
Silvestre, Mikael	6. 0	Inter Milan	Chambray, Fra.	9.08.77
Midfielders				
Beckham, David	6. 0	–	Leytonstone	2.05.75
Butt, Nicky	5.10	–	Manchester	21.01.75
Djordjic, Bojan	5.10	Brommapojkarna	Belgrade	6.02.82
Fortune, Quinton	5. 9	Atletico Madrid	Cape Town	21.05.77
Giggs, Ryan	5.11	–	Cardiff	29.11.73
Keane, Roy	5.11	Nott'm. Forest	Cork	10.08.71
Scholes, Paul	5. 7	–	Salford	16.11.74
Stewart, Michael	5.11	–	Edinburgh	26.02.81
Veron, Juan Sebastian	6. 1	Lazio	Buenos Aires	9.03.75
Forwards				
Chadwick, Luke	5.11	–	Cambridge	18.11.80
Forlan, Diego	5. 8	Independiente	Montevideo	19.05.79

Solskjaer, Ole Gunnar	5.10	Molde	Kristiansund, Nor.	26.02.73
Van Nistelrooy, Ruud	6. 2	PSV Eindhoven	Oss, Hol.	1.07.76
Webber, Danny	5. 9	–	Manchester	28.12.81
Yorke, Dwight	5.10	Aston Villa	Canaan, Tob.	3.11.71

MIDDLESBROUGH

Ground: Cellnet Riverside Stadium, Middlesbrough, Cleveland TS3 6RS.
Telephone: 01642 877700 **Clubcall:** 09068 121181. **Club Nickname:** Boro.
First-choice colours: Red and white shirts; white and red shorts; white and red stockings.
Record transfer fee: £8,150,000 to Empoli for Massimo Maccarone, July 2002.
Record fee received: £12,000,000 from Atletico Madrid for Juninho, July 1997.
Record attendance: At Riverside Stadium: 34,800 v Leeds Utd. (Premier League) 26
  February 2000. At Ayresome Park: 53,596 v Newcastle Utd. (Div.1) December 1949.
Capacity for 2002-03: 35,100. **Sponsors:** Dial-a-Phone.
League Championship: 3rd 1913-14.
F.A. Cup: runners-up 1997.
League Cup: runners-up 1997, 1998.
Finishing positions in Premiership: 1992-93 21th 1995-96 12th, 1996-97 19th
  1998-99 9th, 1999-2000 12th, 2000-001 14th, 2001-02 12th.
Biggest win: 9-0 v Brighton & H.A., Div 2, 23.8.1958.
Biggest defeat: 0-9 v Blackburn Rov., Div 2, 6.11.1954.
Highest League scorer in a season: George Camsell, 59, 1926-27.
Most League goals in aggregate: George Camsell, 326, 1925-39.
Most capped player: Wilf Mannion (England) 26.
Longest unbeaten League sequence: 24 matches (September 1973).
Longest sequence without a League win: 19 matches (October 1981).

Name	Height ft. in.	Previous club	Birthplace	Birthdate
Goalkeepers				
Crossley, Mark	6. 0	Nott'm. Forest	Barnsley	16.06.69
Jones, Bradley	6. 3	–	Armadale, Aus.	19.03.82
Russell, Sam	6. 0	–	Middlesbrough	4.10.82
Schwarzer, Mark	6. 4	Bradford City	Sydney	6.10.72
Defenders				
Cooper, Colin	5.11	Nott'm. Forest	Sedgefield	28.02.67
Ehiogu, Ugo	6. 2	Aston Villa	Hackney	3.11.72
Festa, Gianluca	5.11	Inter Milan	Cagliari	15.03.69
Gavin, Jason	6. 0	–	Dublin	14.03.80
Murphy, David	5.11	–	Hartlepool	1.03.84
Queudrue, Franck	5.10	Lens	Paris	27.08.78
Southgate, Gareth	6. 0	Aston Villa	Watford	3.09.70
Stockdale, Robbie	6. 0	–	Redcar	30.11.79
Midfielders				
Debeve, Mickael	5. 9	Lens	Abbeville, Fra.	1.12.70
Hudson, Mark	5.10	–	Bishop Auckland	24.10.80
Marinelli, Carlos	5. 8	Boca Juniors	Buenos Aires	4.03.82
Nemeth, Szilard		Inter Bratislava		8.08.77
Parnaby, Stuart	5.11	–	Durham	19.07.82
Stamp, Phil	5.11	–	Middlesbrough	12.12.75
Wilkshire, Luke	5. 8	–	Wollongong, Aus.	2.10.81
Wilson, Mark	6. 0	Manchester Utd.	Scunthorpe	9.02.79
Forwards				
Boksic, Alen	6. 1	Lazio	Makarska, Cro.	31.01.70
Greening, Jonathan	6. 0	Manchester Utd.	Scarborough	2.01.79
Job, Joseph-Desire	5.11	Lens	Venissieux, Fra.	1.12.77
Johnston, Allan	5.11	Rangers	Glasgow	14.12.73
Maccarone, Massimo	5.10	Empoli	Galliate, Ita.	6.09.79
Nemeth, Szilard	5.10	Inter Bratislava	Komarno, Slov.	8.08.77

| Whelan, Noel | 6. 2 | Coventry City | Leeds | 30.12.74 |
| Windass, Dean | 5.10 | Bradford City | Hull | 1.04.69 |

NEWCASTLE UNITED

Ground: St James' Park, Newcastle-upon-Tyne, NE1 4ST.
Telephone: 0191 201 8400 **Clubcall:** 09068 121190. **Club Nickname:** Magpies.
First-choice colours: Black and white shirts; black shorts; black stockings.
Record transfer fee: £15,000,000 to Blackburn Rov. for Alan Shearer, July 1996.
Record fee received: £8,000,000 from Liverpool for Dietmar Hamann, July 1999.
Record attendance: 68,386 v Chelsea (Div. 1) September 1930.
Capacity for 2002-03: 52,193. **Sponsors:** NTL.
League Championship: winners 1904-05, 1906-07, 1908-09, 1926-27.
F.A. Cup: winners 1910, 1924, 1932, 1951, 1952, 1955.
League Cup: runners-up 1976.
European Competitions: winners Fairs Cup 1968-69, Anglo-Italian Cup 1972-73.
Finishing positions in Premiership: 1993-94 3rd 1994-95 6th 1995-96 2nd 1996-97 2nd 1997-98 13th 1998-99 13th, 1999-2000 11th, 2000-01 11th, 2001-02 4th.
Biggest win: 13-0 v Newport County, Div. 2, 5.10.1946.
Biggest defeat: 0-9 v Burton Wanderers, Div. 2, 15.4.1895.
Highest League scorer in a season: Hughie Gallacher, 36, 1926-27.
Most League goals in aggregate: Jackie Milburn, 177, 1946-57.
Most capped player: Alf McMichael (Northern Ireland) 40.
Longest unbeaten League sequence: 14 matches (April 1950).
Longest sequence without a League win: 21 matches (January 1978).

Name	Height ft. in.	Previous club	Birthplace	Birthdate
Goalkeepers				
Given, Shay	6. 1	Blackburn Rov.	Lifford, Ire.	20.04.76
Harper, Steve	6. 2	–	Easington	14.03.75
Karelse, John	6. 3	NAC Breda	Kapelle, Hol.	17.05.70
Defenders				
Bernard, Olivier	5. 7	Lyon	Paris	14.10.79
Bramble, Titus	6. 1	Ipswich Town	Ipswich	31.07.81
Caldwell, Gary	6. 0	–	Stirling	12.04.82
Caldwell, Stephen	6. 3	–	Stirling	12.09.80
Dabizas, Nikos	6. 1	Olympiakos	Amyndaeo, Gre.	3.08.73
Elliott, Robbie	5.10	Bolton Wand.	Newcastle	25.12.73
Griffin, Andrew	5. 9	Stoke City	Billinge	7.03.79
Hughes, Aaron	6. 1	–	Cookstown	8.11.79
Marcelino, Elena	6. 2	Real Mallorca	Gijon	26.09.71
O'Brien, Andy	5.10	Bradford City	Harrogate	29.06.79
Quinn, Wayne	5.10	Sheffield Utd.	Truro	19.11.76
Midfielders				
Acuna, Clarence	5. 7	Univ. de Chile	Coya Rancagua	8.02.75
Bassedas, Christian	5. 8	Velez Sarsfield	Buenos Aires	16.02.73
Dyer, Kieron	5. 7	Ipswich Town	Ipswich	29.12.78
Gavilan, Diego	5. 7	Cerro Porteno	Asuncion	1.03.80
Green, Stuart	5.10	–	Whitehaven	15.06.81
Jenas, Jermaine	6. 0	Nott'm. Forest	Nottingham	18.02.83
Kerr, Brian	5. 7	–	Motherwell	12.10.81
McClen, Jamie	5. 8	–	Newcastle	13.05.79
Robert, Laurent	5.10	Paris St-Germain	Saint-Benoit, Fra.	21.05.75
Solano, Nolberto	5. 8	Boca Juniors	Callao, Per.	12.12.74
Speed, Gary	5.10	Everton	Deeside	8.09.69
Viana, Hugo	5.10	Sporting Lisbon	Portugal	15.01.83
Forwards				
Ameobi, Shola	6. 3	–	Zaria, Nig.	12.10.81
Bellamy, Craig	5. 8	Coventry City	Cardiff	13.01.79
Chopra, Michael	5.10	–	Newcastle	23.12.83

Cort, Carl	6. 4	Wimbledon	Southwark	1.11.77
Lua Lua, Lomana	5. 8	Colchester Utd.	Zaire	28.12.80
Shearer, Alan	5.11	Blackburn Rov.	Newcastle	13.08.70

SOUTHAMPTON

Ground: The Friends Provident St Mary's Stadium, Britannia Road, Southampton, Hampshire SO14 5FP.
Telephone: 0870 220 0000 **Clubcall:** 09068 121178. **Club Nickname:** Saints.
First-choice colours: Red and white shirts; black shorts; white stockings.
Record transfer fee: £4,000,000 to Derby Co. for Rory Delap, July 2001.
Record fee received: £7,500,000 from Blackburn Rov. for Kevin Davies, June 1998.
Record attendance: At The Dell: 31,044 v Manchester Utd. (Div. 1) October 1969. At St Mary's: 31,973 v Newcastle Utd. (Premier League) 11 May 2002.
Capacity for 2002-03: 32,689. **Sponsors:** Friends Provident.
League Championship: 2nd 1983-84.
F.A. Cup: winners 1976.
League Cup: runners-up 1979.
European Competitions: Fairs Cup round 3, 1969-70, Cup-Winners' Cup round 3(QF), 1976-77.
Finishing positions in Premiership: 1992-93 18th, 1993-94 18th, 1994-95 10th, 1995-96 17th, 1996-97 16th, 1997-98 12th, 1998-99 17th, 1999-2000 15th, 2000-01 10th, 2001-02 11th.
Biggest win: 8-0 v Northampton Town, Div. 3S, 24.12.1921.
Biggest defeat: 0-8 v Tottenham, Div. 2, 28.3.1936 and v Everton Div. 1, 20.11.1971.
Highest League scorer in a season: Derek Reeves, 39, 1959-60.
Most League goals in aggregate: Mike Channon, 185, 1966-77, 1979-82.
Most capped player: Peter Shilton (England) 49.
Longest unbeaten League sequence: 19 matches (September 1921).
Longest sequence without a League win: 20 matches (August 1969).

Name	Height ft. in.	Previous club	Birthplace	Birthdate
Goalkeepers				
Jones, Paul	6. 3	Stockport Co.	Chirk	18.04.67
Moss, Neil	6. 3	Bournemouth	New Milton	10.05.75
Defenders				
Benali, Francis	5. 9	–	Southampton	30.12.68
Bridge, Wayne	5.10	–	Southampton	5.08.80
Dodd, Jason	5. 8	–	Bath	2.11.70
El Khalej, Tahar	6. 2	Benfica	Morocco	16.06.68
Lundekvam, Claus	6. 4	Brann	Austevoll, Nor.	22.03.73
Monk, Garry	6. 0	Torquay Utd.	Bedford	6.03.79
Svensson, Michael	6. 2	Troyes	Sweden	25.011.75
Williams, Paul	5.11	Coventry City	Burton	26.03.71
Midfielders				
Bleidelis, Imants	5. 9	Skonto Riga	Latvia	16.08.75
Delap, Rory	6. 1	Derby Co.	Sutton Coldfield	6.07.76
Draper, Mark	5.10	Aston Villa	Long Eaton	11.11.70
Fernandes, Fabrice	5. 9	Rennes	Paris	29.10.79
Marsden, Chris	6. 0	Birmingham City	Sheffield	3.01.69
Oakley, Matthew	5.10	–	Peterborough	17.08.77
Svensson, Anders	5.10	Elfsborg	Sweden	17.07.76
Telfer, Paul	5. 9	Coventry City	Edinburgh	21.10.71
Tessem, Jo	6. 2	Molde	Orlandet, Nor.	28.02.72
Forwards				
Beattie, James	6. 1	Blackburn Rov.	Lancaster	27.02.78
Davies, Kevin	6. 0	Blackburn Rov.	Sheffield	26.03.77
Delgado, Agustin	6. 3	Necaxa	Ibarra, Ecu.	23.12.74
Ela Eyene, Jacinto	5. 8	Espanyol	Ecua. Guinea	2.05.82
McDonald, Scott	5. 8	–	Melbourne	21.08.83

| Ormerod, Brett | 5.11 | Blackpool | Blackburn | 18.10.76 |
| Pahars, Marian | 5. 8 | Skonton Riga | Riga, Lat. | 5.08.76 |

SUNDERLAND

Ground: Stadium of Light, Sunderland, Tyne and Wear SR5 1SU.
Telephone: 0191 551 5000. **Clubcall:** 09068 121140. **Club Nickname:** Black Cats.
First-choice colours: Red and white shirts; black shorts, black stockings.
Record transfer fee: £4,500,000 to Chelsea for Emerson Thome, August 2000.
Record fee received: £5,000,000 from Leeds Utd. for Michael Bridges, July 1999.
Capacity for 2002-03: 48,300. **Sponsors:** Reg Vardy.
Record attendance: At Stadium of Light: 48,305 v Manchester Utd. (Premier League) 13
  October 2001. At Roker Park: 75,118 v Derby Co. (F.A. Cup 6) 8 March 1933.
League Championship: winners 1891-92, 1892-93, 1894-95, 1901-02, 1912-13,
  1935-36.
F.A. Cup: winners 1937, 1973.
League Cup: runners-up 1985.
European Competitions: Cup-Winners' Cup R2, 1973-74.
Finishing positions in Premiership: 1996-97 18th, 1999-2000 7th, 2000-01 7th,
  2001-02 17th.
Biggest win: 9-1 v Newcastle Utd. Div. 1, 5.12.1908. **F.A. Cup:** 11-1 v Fairfield, round
  one, 2.2.1895.
Biggest defeat: 0-8 v Sheffield Wed., Div. 1, 26.12.1911, v West Ham Utd., Div. 1,
  19.10.1968, v Watford, Div. 1, 25.9.1982.
Highest League scorer in a season: Dave Halliday, 43, 1928-29.
Most League goals in aggregate: Charlie Buchan, 209, 1911-25.
Most capped player: Charlie Hurley (Ireland) 38.
Longest unbeaten League sequence: 19 matches (May 1998).
Longest sequence without a League win: 14 matches (April 1985).

Name	Height ft. in.	Previous club	Birthplace	Birthdate
Goalkeepers				
Ingham, Michael	6. 4	–	Belfast	7.09.80
Macho, Jurgen	6. 4	FC Vienna	Vienna	24.08.77
Myhre, Thomas	6. 2	Besiktas	Sarpsborg, Nor.	16.10.73
Sorensen, Thomas	6. 4	Odense	Odense	12.06.76
Defenders				
Babb, Phil	6. 0	Sporting Lisbon	Lambeth	30.11.70
Bjorklund, Joachim	6. 1	Venezia	Vaxjo, Swe.	15.03.71
Byrne, Clifford	6. 0	–	Dublin	26.04.82
Clark, Ben	6. 2	–	Shotley Bridge	24.01.83
Craddock, Jody	6. 0	Cambridge Utd.	Redditch	25.07.75
Gray, Michael	5. 7	–	Sunderland	3.08.74
Haas, Bernt	6. 2	Grasshoppers Zurich	Switzerland	8.04.78
Harrison, Steve	5.11	–	Hexham	3.02.82
Maley, Mark	6. 0	–	Newcastle	26.01.81
McCartney, George	5.11	–	Belfast	28.04.81
Mercimek, Baki	6. 1	Haarlem	Holland	18.09.72
Ramsden, Simon	5.11	–	Bishop Auckland	17.12.81
Thome, Emerson	6. 1	Chelsea	Porto Alegre, Bra.	30.03.72
Varga, Stanislav	6. 5	Slovan Bratislava	Lipany, Slovak.	8.10.72
Williams, Darren	5.10	York City	Middlesbrough	28.04.77
Midfielders				
Arca, Julio	5. 9	Argentinos Jnrs.	Quilmes Bernal, Arg.	31.01.81
Butler, Thomas	5. 7	–	Dublin	25.04.81
Kilbane, Kevin	6. 2	W.B.A.	Preston	1.02.77
McAteer, Jason	5.11	Blackburn Rov.	Birkenhead	18.06.71
McCann, Gavin	6. 1	Everton	Blackpool	10.01.78
Medina, Nicolas	5. 9	Argentinos Jnrs.	Buenos Aires	17.02.82
Oster, John	5. 9	Everton	Boston	8.12.78

Peeters, Tom	5.10	Mechelen	Bornem, Bel.	25.09.78
Reyna, Claudio	5. 9	Rangers	New Jersey	20.07.73
Thirlwell, Paul	5.11	–	Gateshead	13.02.79
Thornton, Sean	5.10	Tranmere Rov.	Dreogheda	18.05.83
Forwards				
Bellion, David	6. 0	Cannes	Paris	27.11.82
Kyle, Kevin	6. 3	Ayr Boswell	Stranraer	7.06.81
Laslandes, Lilian	6. 1	Bordeaux	Paulliac, Fra.	4.09.71
Phillips, Kevin	5. 8	Watford	Hitchin	25.07.73
Quinn, Niall	6. 5	Manchester City	Dublin	6.10.66
Shields, Dene	5. 9	Raith Rov.	Edinburgh	16.09.82

TOTTENHAM HOTSPUR

Ground: 748 High Road, Tottenham, London N17 OAP.
Telephone: 0208 365 5000 **Clubcall:** 09068 100500. **Club Nickname:** Spurs.
First-choice colours: White shirts, navy shorts, white stockings.
Record transfer fee: £11,000,000 to Dynamo Kiev for Sergei Rebrov, May 2000.
Record fee received: £5,500,000 from Lazio for Paul Gascoigne, May 1992.
Record attendance: 75,038 v Sunderland (F.A. Cup 6) 5 March 1938.
Capacity for 2002-03: 36,289. **Sponsors:** Thomson.
League Championship: winners 1950-51, 1960-61.
F.A. Cup: winners 1901, 1921, 1961, 1962, 1967, 1981, 1982, 1991.
League Cup: winners 1971, 1973, 1999.
European Competitions: winners Cup-Winners' Cup 1962-63, UEFA Cup 1971-72, 1983-84.
Finishing positions in Premiership: 1992-93 8th, 1993-94 15th, 1994-95 7th, 1995-96 8th, 1996-97 10th, 1997-98 14th, 1998-99 11th, 1999-2000 10th, 2000-01 12th, 2001-02 9th.
Biggest win: 9-0 v Bristol Rov., Div.2, 22.10.1977, F.A. Cup 13-2 v Crewe Alexandra, round four replay, 3.2.1960, Europe 9-0 v Keflavik, UEFA Cup, round one, 28.9.1971.
Biggest defeat: 0-7 v Liverpool, Div.1, 2.9.1979.
Highest League scorer in a season: Jimmy Greaves, 37, 1962-63.
Most League goals in aggregate: Jimmy Greaves, 220, 1961-70.
Most capped player: Pat Jennings (Northern Ireland) 74.
Longest unbeaten League sequence: 22 matches (August 1949).
Longest sequence without a League win: 16 matches (December 1934).

Name	Height ft. in.	Previous club	Birthplace	Birthdate
Goalkeepers				
Keller, Kasey	6. 1	Rayo Vallecano	Olympia, USA	29.11.69
Kelly, Gavin	6. 0	–	Hammersmith	3.06.81
Sullivan, Neil	6. 1	Wimbledon	Sutton	24.02.70
Defenders				
Bunjevcevic, Goran	6. 2	Red Star Belgrade	Karlovac, Cro.	17.02.73
Carr, Stephen	5. 8	–	Dublin	29.08.76
Doherty, Gary	6. 1	Luton Town	Carndonagh	31.01.80
Gardner, Anthony	6. 5	Port Vale	Stafford	19.09.80
King, Ledley	6. 2	–	Bow	12.10.80
Perry, Chris	5. 8	Wimbledon	Carshalton	26.04.73
Richards, Dean	6. 2	Southampton	Bradford	9.06.74
Taricco, Mauricio	5. 8	Ipswich Town	Buenos Aires	10.03.73
Thatcher, Ben	5.10	Wimbledon	Swindon	30.11.75
Thelwell, Alton	5.11	–	Holloway	5.09.80
Ziege, Christian	6. 1	Liverpool	Berlin	1.02.72
Midfielders				
Acimovic, Milenko	5.10	Red Star Belgrade	Slovenia	15.02.77
Anderton, Darren	6. 1	Portsmouth	Southampton	3.03.72
Blondel, Jonathan	5. 7	Mouscron	Belgium	3.04.84

Clemence, Stephen	5.11	–	Liverpool	31.03.78
Davies, Simon	5.11	Peterborough Utd.	Haverfordwest	23.10.79
Etherington, Matthew	6. 0	Peterborough Utd.	Truro	14.08.81
Freund, Steffen	5. 9	Borussia Dortmund	Brandenburg	19.01.70
Jackson, Johnnie	5.11	–	Camden	15.08.82
Korsten, Willem	5.11	Vitesse Arnhem	Boxtel, Hol.	21.01.75
Leonhardsen, Oyvind	5.10	Liverpool	Kristiansund, Nor.	17.08.70
Piercy, John	5.11	–	Forest Gate	18.09.79
Poyet, Gustavo	6. 1	Chelsea	Montevideo	15.11.67
Redknapp, Jamie	6. 0	Liverpool	Barton-on-Sea	25.06.73
Ricketts, Rohan	5.11	Arsenal	Clapham	22.12.82
Sherwood, Tim	6. 1	Blackburn Rov.	St Albans	2.02.69
Forwards				
Ferdinand, Les	5.11	Newcastle Utd.	Ladbroke Grove	8.12.66
Ferguson, Steve	5.10	East Fife	–	1.04.82
Iversen, Steffen	5.10	Rosenborg	Oslo	10.11.76
Rebrov, Sergei	5. 8	Dynamo Kiev	Donetsk, Ukr.	3.06.74
Sheringham, Teddy	6. 0	Manchester Utd.	Highams Park	2.04.66

WEST BROMWICH ALBION

Ground: The Hawthorns, Halfords Lane, West Bromwich B71 4LF.
Telephone: 0121 525 8888. **Clubcall:** 09068 121193. **Club nickname:** Baggies.
First-choice colours: Navy blue and white striped shirts, white shorts, white stockings.
Record transfer fee: £2,100,000 to Bristol Rov. for Jason Roberts, July 2000.
Record fee received: £5,000,001 from Coventry City for Lee Hughes, August 2001.
Record attendance: 64,815 v Arsenal (F.A. Cup 6), 6 March, 1937.
Capacity for 2002-03: 28,003. **Sponsors:** West Bromwich Building Society.
League Championship: winners 1919-20.
F.A. Cup: winners 1888, 1892, 1931, 1954, 1968.
League Cup: winners 1966.
European Competitions: quarter-finalists Cup Winners' Cup 1968-69, quarter-finalists UEFA Cup 1978-79.
Finishing positions in Premiership: None.
Biggest win: 12-0 v Darwen, Div. 1, 4.4.1892.
Biggest defeat: 3-10 v Stoke City, Div. 1, 4.2.37.
Highest League scorer in a season: Ginger Richardson, 39, 1935-36.
Most League goals in aggregate: Tony Brown, 218, 1963-79.
Most capped player: Stuart Williams, 33, Wales.
Longest unbeaten League sequence: 17 matches (December 1957).
Longest sequence without a League win: 14 matches (February 1996).

Name	Height ft. in.	Previous club	Birthplace	Birthdate
Goalkeepers				
Adamson, Chris	6. 0	–	Ashington	4.11.78
Hoult, Russell	6. 4	Portsmouth	Ashby de la Zouch	22.11.72
Jensen, Brian	6. 3	AZ Alkmaar	Copenhagen	8.06.75
Murphy, Joe	6. 2	Tranmere Rov.	Dublin	21.08.81
Defenders				
Balis, Igor	6. 0	Spartak Trnava	Slovakia	5.01.70
Butler, Tony	6. 2	Port Vale	Stockport	28.09.72
Chambers, Adam	5.10	–	West Bromwich	20.11.80
Chambers, James	5.10	–	West Bromwich	20.11.80
Clement, Neil	6. 0	Chelsea	Reading	3.10.78
Gilchrist, Phil	6. 0	Leicester City	Stockton	25.08.73
Lyttle, Des	5. 9	Watford	Wolverhampton	24.09.71
Moore, Darren	6. 2	Portsmouth	Birmingham	22.04.74
Sigurdsson, Larus	6. 0	Stoke City	Akureyri, Ice.	4.06.73
Wallwork, Ronnie	5.10	Manchester Utd.	Manchester	10.09.77

Midfielders

	Height ft. in.	Previous club		Birthdate
Appleton, Michael	5. 8	Preston N.E.	Salford	12.04.75
Briggs, Mark	6. 1	–	Wolverhampton	16.02.82
Collins, Matt	5.10	–	Hitchin	10.02.82
Dobie, Scott	6. 0	Carlisle Utd.	Workington	10.10.78
Johnson, Andy	6. 1	Norwich City	Bristol	2.05.74
Jordao	6. 3	Sporting Braga	Malange, Ang.	30.08.71
McInnes, Derek	5. 8	Toulouse	Paisley	7.05.71
Oliver, Adam	5. 9	–	Sandwell	25.10.80
Turner, Matt	5. 6	Nott'm. Forest	Nottingham	29.12.81

Forwards

Dichio, Danny	6. 4	Sunderland	Hammersmith	19.10.74
Dobie, Scott	6. 1	Carlisle Utd.	Workington	10.10.78
Roberts, Jason	6. 1	Bristol Rov.	Park Royal, Gren.	25.01.78
Scott, Mark	6. 1	–	Birmingham	16.06.82
Taylor, Bob	5.11	Bolton Wand.	Easington	3.02.67

WEST HAM UNITED

Ground: Boleyn Ground, Green Street, Upton Park, London E13 9AZ.
Telephone: 0208 548 2748 **Clubcall:** 09065 861966.
Club Nickname: Hammers.
First-choice colours: Claret and sky blue shirts; white shorts; white stockings.
Record transfer fee: £5,500,000 to Fiorentina for Tomas Repka, September 2001.
Record fee received: £18,000,000 from Leeds Utd. for Rio Ferdinand, November 2000.
Record attendance: 43,322 v Tottenham, Div. 1, October 1970.
Capacity for 2002-03: 35,595. **Sponsors:** Fila/Dr Martens.
League Championship: 3rd 1985-86.
F.A. Cup: winners 1964, 1975, 1980.
League Cup: runners-up 1966, 1981.
European Competitions: winners Cup-Winners' Cup 1964-65.
Finishing positions in Premiership: 1993-94 13th 1994-95 14th 1995-96 10th 1996-97 14th 1997-98 8th 1998-99 5th, 1999-2000 9th, 2000-01 15th, 2001-02 7th.
Biggest win: 8-0 v Rotherham Utd., Div 2, 8.3.1958 and v Sunderland, Div 1, 19.10.1968. League Cup 10-0 v Bury, round 2, 25.10.1984.
Biggest defeat: 0-7 v Sheff. Wed., Div 1, 28.11.1959, v Everton, Div 1, 22.10.1927 and v Barnsley, Div 2, 1.9.1919.
Highest League scorer in a season: Vic Watson, 42, 1929-30.
Most League goals in aggregate: Vic Watson, 298, 1920-35.
Most capped player: Bobby Moore (England) 108.
Longest unbeaten League sequence: 27 matches (December 1980).
Longest sequence without a League win: 17 matches (January 1976).

Name	Height ft. in.	Previous club	Birthplace	Birthdate
Goalkeepers				
James, David	6. 5	Aston Villa	Welwyn Garden City	1.08.70
Van der Gouw, Raimond	6. 3	Manchester Utd.	OldenZall, Hol.	24.03.63
Defenders				
Byrne, Shaun	5. 9	–	Taplow	21.01.81
Charles, Gary	5. 9	Benfica	Newham	13.04.70
Dailly, Christian	6. 0	Blackburn Rov.	Dundee	23.10.73
Iriekpen, Ezomo	6. 1	–	London	14.05.82
Labant, Vladimir	6. 2	Sparta Prague	Slovakia	6.08.74
Minto, Scott	5.10	Benfica	Heswall	6.08.71
Pearce, Ian	6. 3	Blackburn Rov.	Bury St Edmunds	7.05.74
Repka, Tomas	6. 2	Fiorentina	Slavicin Zlin, Cz.	2.01.74
Schemmel, Sebastien	5.10	Metz	Nancy	2.06.75
Soma, Ragnvald	6. 2	Byrne	Byrne, Nor.	10.11.79
Winterburn, Nigel	5. 8	Arsenal	Coventry	11.12.63

Midfielders

Name	Height ft. in.	Previous club	Birthplace	Birthdate
Carrick, Michael	6. 0	–	Wallsend	28.07.81
Cole, Joe	5. 7	–	Islington	8.11.81
Courtois, Laurent	5. 7	Toulouse	Lyon	11.09.78
Hutchison, Don	6. 1	Sunderland	Gateshead	9.05.71
Lomas, Steve	6. 0	Manchester City	Hanover	18.01.74
McCann, Grant	5.10	–	Belfast	14.04.80
Moncur, John	5. 8	Swindon Town	Mile End	22.09.66
Sinclair, Trevor	5.10	Q.P.R.	Dulwich	2.03.73

Forwards

Name	Height ft. in.	Previous club	Birthplace	Birthdate
Camara, Titi	6. 0	Liverpool	Donka, Guin.	17.11.72
Defoe, Jermaine	5. 7	–	Beckton	7.10.82
Di Canio, Paolo	5. 9	Sheffield Wed.	Rome	9.07.68
Garcia, Richard	5.11	–	Perth, Aus.	9.04.81
Kanoute, Frederic	6. 3	Lyon	Sainte-Foy, Fra.	2.09.77

NATIONWIDE LEAGUE PLAYING STAFFS
2002-03 DIVIVISION ONE

BRADFORD CITY

Ground: Valley Parade, Bradford BD8 7DY.
Telephone: 01254 773355. **Clubcall:** 09068 888640. **Club nickname:** Bantams.
First-choice colours: Claret and amber shirts; black shorts; claret and amber stockings.
Main Sponsor: JCT 600. **Capacity for 2002-03:** 25,164.
Record attendance: 39,146 v Burnley (F.A. Cup 4) 11 March, 1911.

Name	Height ft. in.	Previous club	Birthplace	Birthdate
Goalkeepers				
Davison, Aidan	6. 1	Grimsby Town	Sedgefield	11.05.68
Walsh, Gary	6. 3	Middlesbrough	Wigan	21.03.68
Defenders				
Atherton, Peter	5.11	Sheffield Wed.	Wigan	6.04.70
Bower, Mark	5.10	–	Bradford	23.01.80
Emanuel, Lewis	5. 8	–	Bradford	4.10.83
Jacobs, Wayne	5. 9	Rotherham Utd.	Sheffield	3.02.69
Morgan, Robert	6. 2	–	Bradford	16.01.83
Molenaar, Robert	6. 2	Leeds Utd.	Zaandam, Hol.	27.02.69
Tod, Andy	6. 0	Dunfermline	Dunfermline	4.11.71
Wetherall, David	6. 4	Leeds Utd.	Sheffield	14.03.71
Midfielders				
Fishlock, Craig	5.10	–	Middlesbrough	23.02.83
Jorgensen, Claus	5.10	Bournemouth	Holstebro, Den.	27.04.76
Kearney, Thomas	5.11	Everton	Liverpool	7.10.81
Lawrence, Jamie	5.10	Leicester City	Balham	8.03.70
Lee, Andrew	5. 7	–	Bradford	18.08.82
Locke, Gary	6. 1	Hearts	Edinburgh	16.06.75
Myers, Andy	5. 9	Chelsea	Hounslow	3.11.73
Standing, Michael	5.10	Aston Villa	Shoreham	20.03.81
Forwards				
Cadamarteri, Danny	5. 9	Everton	Bradford	12.10.79
Carbone, Benito	5. 6	Aston Villa	Begnara, Ita.	14.08.71
Forrest, Danny	5.11	–	Keighley	23.10.84
Jess, Eoin	5.10	Aberdeen	Aberdeen	13.12.70
Juanjo	5. 9	Hearts	Barcelona	4.05.77
Ward, Ashley	6. 1	Blackburn Rov.	Manchester	24.11.70

BRIGHTON AND HOVE ALBION

Ground: Withdean Stadium, Tongdean Lane, Brighton BN1 5JD.
Telephone: 01273 778855. **Clubcall:** 09068 800609. **Club nickname:** Seagulls.
First-choice colours: Blue and white shirts; white shorts; white stockings.
Main sponsor: Skint. **Capacity for 2002-03:** 6,988.
Record attendance: (Goldstone Ground) 36,747 v Fulham (Div. 2) 27 December, 1958;
  (Withdean Stadium) 6,995 v Halifax Town (Div. 3) 2 December, 2000.

Name	Height ft. in.	Previous club	Birthplace	Birthdate
Goalkeepers				
Kuipers, Michel	6. 2	Bristol Rov.	Amsterdam	26.06.74
Packham, Will	6. 2	–	Brighton	13.01.81
Defenders				
Cullip, Danny	6. 0	Brentford	Ascot	17.09.76
Mayo, Kerry	5. 9	–	Cuckfield	21.09.77
Pethick, Robbie	5.10	Bristol Rov.	Tavistock	8.09.70
Virgo, Adam	6. 1	–	Brighton	25.01.83
Watson, Paul	5. 8	Brentford	Hastings	4.01.75
Midfielders				
Carpenter, Richard	6. 0	Cardiff City	Sheppey	30.09.72
Hammond, Dean	5.11	–	Sussex	7.03.83
Jones, Nathan	5. 6	Southend Utd.	Cardiff	28.05.73
Lee, David	5.11	Hull City	Basildon	28.03.80
Melton, Steve	5.11	Stoke City	Lincoln	3.10.78
Oatway, Charlie	5. 7	Brentford	Hammersmith	28.11.73
Pitcher, Geoff	5. 5	Kingstonian	Sutton	15.08.75
Rogers, Paul	6. 0	Wigan Athletic	Portsmouth	21.03.65
Wilkinson, Simon	5. 9	–	Portsmouth	12.09.81
Forwards				
Brooker, Paul	5. 8	Fulham	Hammersmith	25.11.76
Hart, Gary	5. 9	Stansted	Harlow	21.09.76
Marney, Daniel	5. 9	–	Sidcup	2.10.81
McPhee, Chris	5.11	–	Eastbourne	20.03.83
Zamora, Bobby	5.11	Bristol Rov.	Barking	16.01.81

BURNLEY

Ground: Turf Moor, Burnley BB10 4BX.
Telephone: 01282 700000. **Clubcall:** 09068 121153. **Club nickname:** Clarets.
First-choice colours: Claret and blue shirts; white shorts; white, claret and blue
  stockings.
Main sponsor: Lanway. **Capacity for 2002-03:** 22,500.
Record attendance: 54,775 v Huddersfield Town (F.A. Cup 4) 23 February, 1924.

Name	Height ft. in.	Previous club	Birthplace	Birthdate
Goalkeepers				
Michopolous, Nik	6. 3	PAOK Salonika	Khardsa, Gre.	20.02.70
Defenders				
Armstrong, Gordon	6. 0	Bury	Newcastle	15.07.67
Briscoe, Lee	6. 0	–	Pontefract	30.09.75
Davis, Steve	6. 2	Luton Town	Hexham	30.10.68
Cox, Ian	6. 1	Bournemouth	Croydon	25.03.71
Gnohere, Arthur	6. 0	Caen	Ivory Coast	20.11.78
McGregor, Mark	5.11	Wrexham	Chester	16.02.77
West, Dean	5.10	Bury	Wakefield	5.12.72
Midfielders				
Branch, Graham	6. 2	Stockport Co.	Liverpool	12.02.72
Cook, Paul	5.11	Stockport Co.	Liverpool	22.03.67
Grant, Tony	5.11	Manchester City	Liverpool	14.11.74

Name	Height ft. in.	Previous club	Birthplace	Birthdate
Little, Glen	6. 3	Glentoran	Wimbledon	15.10.75
Maylett, Bradley	5. 8	–	Manchester	24.12.80
Weller, Paul	5. 8	–	Brighton	6.03.75
Forwards				
Blake, Robbie	5. 9	Bradford City	Middlesbrough	4.03.76
Ellis, Tony	5.11	Rochdale	Salford	20.10.64
Moore, Alan	5.10	Middlesbrough	Dublin	25.11.74
Moore, Ian	5.11	Nott'm. Forest	Birkenhead	26.08.76
Papadopoulos, Dimitrios	6. 0	Akratitos	Kazakhstan	20.09.81
Payton, Andy	5. 9	Huddersfield Town	Burnley	23.10.67
Shandran, Anthony	5. 9	–	Newcastle	17.09.81
Taylor, Gareth	6. 1	Manchester City	Weston-s-Mare	25.02.73

COVENTRY CITY

Ground: Highfield Road Stadium, King Richard Street, Coventry CV2 4FW
Telephone: 0247 623 4000. **Club nickname:** Sky Blues.
First-choice colours: Sky blue shirts; navy blue shorts; sky blue stockings.
Main sponsor: Subaru. **Capacity for 2002-03:** 23,633.
Record attendance: 51,455 v Wolves (Div. 2) 29 April, 1967.

Name	Height ft. in.	Previous club	Birthplace	Birthdate
Goalkeepers				
Hedman, Magnus	6. 3	AIK Stockholm	Stockholm	19.03.73
Hyldgaard, Morten	6. 6	Ikast	Herning, Den.	26.01.78
Montgomery, Gary	6. 2	–	–	10.08.82
Defenders				
Gordon, Dean	6. 0	Middlesbrough	Thornton Heath	10.02.73
Guerrero, Ivan	5. 7	Club Deportivo	Honduras	30.11.77
Konjic, Muhamed	6. 3	Monaco	Bosnia	14.05.70
Shaw, Richard	5. 9	Crystal Palace	Brentford	11.09.68
Midfielders				
Chippo, Youssef	5.11	FC Porto	Boujaad, Mor.	10.06.73
Delorge, Laurent	5.10	Ghent	Leuven, Bel.	21.07.79
Eustace, John	5.11	–	Solihull	3.11.79
McAllister, Gary	6. 1	Liverpool	Motherwell	25.12.64
Normann, Runar	5.11	Lillestrom	Harstad, Nor.	1.03.78
O'Neill, Keith	6. 1	Middlesbrough	Dublin	16.02.76
Quinn, Barry	6. 0	–	Dublin	9.05.79
Safri, Youssef	6. 2	Raja Casablanca	Morocco	1.03.77
Strachan, Gavin	5.10	–	Aberdeen	23.12.78
Thompson, David	5. 7	Liverpool	Birkenhead	12.09.77
Forwards				
Bothroyd, Jay	6. 3	Arsenal	Islington	7.05.82
Hughes, Lee	5.10	W.B.A.	Smethwick	22.05.76
Joachim, Julian	5. 6	Aston Villa	Boston	20.09.74
Martinez, Jairo	5. 9	Club Deportivo	Honduras	14.05.78
McSheffrey, Gary	5. 8	–	Coventry	13.08.72
Zuniga, Ysrael	5. 9	Melgar	Lima, Per.	27.08.76

CRYSTAL PALACE

Ground: Selhurst Park, London SE25 6PU.
Telephone: 0208 768 6000. **Club nickname:** Eagles.
First-choice colours: Red and blue shirts; red shorts, red stockings.
Main sponsor: Churchill. **Capacity for 2002-03:** 26,500.
Record attendance: 51,482 v Burnley (Div. 2) 11 May, 1979.

Name	Height ft. in.	Previous club	Birthplace	Birthdate
Goalkeepers				
Clarke, Matt	6. 3	Bradford City	Sheffield	3.11.73
Kolinko, Alex	6. 2	Skonto Riga	Riga	18.06.75
Defenders				
Austin, Dean	5.11	Tottenham	Hemel Hempstead	26.04.70
Berhalter, Gregg	6. 0	Cambuur	New Jersey	1.08.73
Butterfield, Danny	5.10	Grimsby Town	Boston	21.11.79
Fleming, Curtis	5.11	Middlesbrough	Manchester	8.10.68
Frampton, Andrew	5.11	–	Wimbledon	3.09.79
Granville, Danny	5.11	Manchester City	Islington	19.01.75
Harrison, Craig	6. 0	Middlesbrough	Gateshead	10.11.77
Popovic, Tony	6. 0	Hiroshima	–	4.07.73
Smith, Jamie	5. 8	Wolves	Birmingham	17.09.74
Symons, Kit	6. 2	Fulham	Basingstoke	8.03.71
Midfielders				
Black, Tommy	5. 7	Arsenal	Chigwell	26.11.79
Gray, Julian	6. 1	Arsenal	Lewisham	21.09.79
Hopkin, David	5. 9	Bradford City	Greenock	21.08.70
Mullins, Hayden	6. 0	–	Reading	27.03.79
Riihilahti, Aki	5.11	Valerenga	Helsinki	9.09.76
Rubins, Andrejs	5. 9	Skonto Riga	Riga	26.11.78
Thomson, Steve	5. 8	–	Glasgow	23.01.78
Forwards				
Akinbiyi, Ade	6. 1	Leicester City	Hackney	10.10.74
Freedman, Dougie	5. 9	Nott'm. Forest	Glasgow	21.01.74
Kabba, Stephen	5. 8	–	Lambeth	7.03.81
Morrison, Clinton	6. 1	–	Tooting	14.05.79
Routledge, Wayne	5.11	–	Sidcup	7.01.85

DERBY COUNTY

Ground: Pride Park, Derby DE24 8XL.
Telephone: 01332 667503. **Clubcall:** 09068 121187. **Club nickname:** Rams.
First-choice colours: White shirts; black shorts; white stockings.
Main sponsor: Marstons Pedigree. **Capacity for 2002-03:** 33,597.
Record attendance: At Pride Park: 33,597 England v Mexico, 25 May, 2001, At Baseball Ground: 41, 826 v Tottenham (Div. 1) 20 September, 1969.

Name	Height ft. in.	Previous club	Birthplace	Birthdate
Goalkeepers				
Grant, Lee	6. 2	–	Hemel Hempstead	27.01.83
Oakes, Andy	6. 3	Hull City	Crewe	11.01.77
Poom, Mart	6. 4	Tallinn Flora	Tallinn, Est.	3.02.72
Defenders				
Barton, Warren	6. 0	Newcastle Utd.	Islington	19.03.69
Boertien, Paul	5.10	Carlisle Utd.	Carlisle	21.01.79
Bragstad, Bjorn	6. 4	Rosenborg	Trondheim	5.01.71
Carbonari, Horacio	6. 3	Rosario Central	Rosario, Arg.	2.05.73
Elliott, Steve	6. 1	–	Derby	29.10.76
Evatt, Ian	6. 3	–	Coventry	23.11.81
Grenet, Francois	5.11	Bordeaux	Bordeaux	8.03.75
Higginbotham, Danny	6. 1	Manchester Utd.	Manchester	29.12.78
Hunt, Lewis	5.11	–	Birmingham	25.08.82
Jackson, Richard	5. 7	Scarborough	Whitby	18.04.80
Mawene, Youl	6. 1	Lens	Caen	16.07.79
McKeown, Gareth	6. 0	–	Northern Ireland	14.07.83
Riggott, Chris	6. 2	–	Derby	1.09.80
Zavagno, Luciano	6. 0	Troyes	Rosario, Arg.	6.08.77

428

Midfielders

Bolder, Adam	5. 8	Hull City	Hull	25.10.80
Burley, Craig	6. 1	Celtic	Ayr	24.09.71
Kinkladze, Georgi	5. 6	Ajax	Tblisi	29.12.68
Lee, Robert	5.10	Newcastle Utd.	Plaistow	1.02.66
McArdle, Fiachra	5. 9	–	Newry	18.08.83
Murray, Adam	5. 8	–	Birmingham	30.09.81
O'Halloran, Matt	5. 9	–	–	18.11.82
O'Neil, Brian	6. 2	Wolfsburg	Glasgow	6.09.72
Powell, Darryl	6. 0	Portsmouth	Lambeth	15.11.71
Valakari, Simo	5.10	Motherwell	Helsinki	28.04.73

Forwards

Burton, Deon	5. 9	Portsmouth	Reading	25.10.76
Christie, Malcolm	6. 0	Nuneaton Borough	Peterborough	11.04.79
Morris, Lee	5. 9	Sheffield Utd.	Driffield	30.04.80
Robinson, Marvin	6. 0	–	Crewe	11.04.80
Ravanelli, Fabrizio	5.11	Lazio	Perugia	12.11.68
Strupar, Branko	6. 3	Genk	Zagreb	9.02.70
Tudgay, Marcus	5.10	–	Sussex	3,02,83
Twigg, Gary	5.10	–	Glasgow	19.03.84

GILLINGHAM

Ground: Priestfield Stadium, Redfern Avenue, Gillingham ME7 4DD.
Telephone: 01634 851854. **Clubcall:** 09068 332211. **Club nickname:** Gills.
First-choice colours: Blue, red and white shirts, shorts and stockings.
Main sponsor: Sea France. **Capacity for 2002-03:** 11,000.
Record attendance: 23,002 v Q.P.R. (F.A. Cup 3) 10 January, 1948.

Name	Height ft. in.	Previous club	Birthplace	Birthdate
Goalkeepers				
Bartram, Vince	6. 2	Arsenal	Birmingham	7.08.68
Brown, Jason	6. 0	Charlton Athletic	Bermondsey	18.05.82
Defenders				
Ashby, Barry	6. 2	Brentford	Park Royal	2.11.70
Butters, Guy	6. 3	Portsmouth	Hillingdon	30.10.69
Edge, Roland	5.10	–	Chatham	25.11.78
Hope, Chris	6. 1	Scunthorpe Utd.	Sheffield	14.11.72
Patterson, Mark	5. 9	Plymouth Argyle	Leeds	13.09.68
Pennock, Adrian	6. 1	Bournemouth	Ipswich	27.03.71
Rose, Richard	5.11	–	Tonbridge	8.09.82
White, Ben	6. 1	–	Hastings	2.06.82
Midfielders				
Browning, Marcus	6. 0	Huddersfield Town	Bristol	22.04.71
Gooden, Ty	5. 8	Swindon Town	Canvey Island	23.10.72
Hessenthaler, Andy	5. 7	Watford	Gravesend	17.06.75
Lovell, Mark	5.10	–	Bromley	16.07.83
Nosworthy, Nayron	6. 1	–	Brixton	11.10.80
Osborn, Simon	5. 9	Tranmere Rov.	Croydon	19.01.72
Perpetuini, David	5. 9	Watford	Hitchin	26.09.79
Phillips, Michael	5. 8	–	Camberwell	22.01.83
Saunders, Mark	5.11	Plymouth Argyle	Reading	23.07.71
Smith, Paul	5.11	Brentford	East Ham	18.09.71
Spiller, Daniel	5.10	–	–	10.01.81
Forwards				
Ipoua, Guy	6. 1	Scunthorpe Utd.	Douala, Cam.	14.01.76
James, Kevin	5. 9	Charlton Athletic	Southwark	3.01.80
Johnson, Tommy	5.11	Kilmarnock	Newcastle	15.01.71
King, Marlon	6. 1	Barnet	Dulwich	26.04.80
Shaw, Paul	5.11	Millwall	Burnham	4.09.73
Wallace, Rod	5. 7	Bolton Wand.	Lewisham	2.10.69

GRIMSBY TOWN

Ground: Blundell Park, Cleethorpes, DN35 7PY.
Telephone: 01472 605050. **Clubcall:** 09068 555855. **Club nickname:** Mariners.
First-choice colours: Black and white shirts; black shorts; black stockings.
Main sponsor: Dixon Motors. **Capacity for 2002-03:** 10,033.
Record attendance: 31,651 v Wolves (F.A. Cup 5) 20 February, 1937.

Name	Height ft. in.	Previous club	Birthplace	Birthdate
Goalkeepers				
Coyne, Danny	6. 1	Tranmere Rov.	Prestatyn	27.08.73
Croudson, Steve	6. 0	–	Grimsby	14.09.79
Defenders				
Chapman, Ben	5. 6	–	Scunthorpe	2.03.79
Gallimore, Tony	5.11	Carlisle Utd.	Stoke	21.02.72
McDermott, John	5. 7	–	Middlesbrough	3.02.69
Raven, Paul	6. 1	W.B.A.	Salisbury	28.07.70
Midfielders				
Burnett, Wayne	5.11	Huddersfield Town	Lambeth	4.09.71
Campbell, Stuart	5.10	Leicester City	Corby	9.12.77
Coldicott, Stacy	5. 8	W.B.A	Worcester	29.04.74
Ford, Simon	5.10	Charlton Athletic	–	–
Groves, Paul	5.11	W.B.A.	Derby	28.02.66
Pouton, Alan	6. 0	York City	Newcastle	1.02.77
Willems, Menno	6. 0	Vitesse Arnhem	Amsterdam	10.03.77
Forwards				
Allen, Bradley	5. 8	Charlton Athletic	Harold Wood	13.09.71
Cooke, Terry	5. 8	Manchester City	Marston Green	5.08.76
Jeffrey, Michael	5.10	Kilmarnock	Liverpool	11.08.71
Jevons, Phil	5.11	Everton	Liverpool	1.08.79
Livingstone, Steve	6. 1	Chelsea	Middlesbrough	8.09.68
Rowan, Jonathan	5.10	–	Grimsby	29.11.81
Taylor, Robert	6. 1	Wolves	Norwich	30.04.71
Thompson, Chris	5.11	Liverpool	–	–

IPSWICH TOWN

Ground: Portman Road, Ipswich IP1 2DA.
Telephone: 01473 400500. **Club nickname:** Blues/Town.
First-choice colours: Blue shirts; white shorts; blue stockings.
Main sponsor: TXU Energi. **Capacity for 2002-03:** 30,000.
Record attendance: 38,010 v Leeds Utd. (F.A. Cup 6) 8 March, 1975.

Name	Height ft. in.	Previous club	Birthplace	Birthdate
Goalkeepers				
Branagan, Keith	6. 0	Bolton Wand.	Fulham	10.07.66
Marshall, Andy	6. 2	Norwich City	Bury	14.04.75
Salmon, Mike	6. 2	Charlton Athletic	Leyland	14.07.64
Sereni, Matteo	6. 1	Sampdoria	Italy	11.02.75
Defenders				
Brown, Wayne	6. 0	–	Banbury	20.08.77
Clapham, Jamie	5. 9	Tottenham	Lincoln	7.12.75
Croft, Gary	5. 8	Blackburn Rov.	Stafford	17.02.74
Gaardsoe, Thomas	6. 2	Aalborg	Denmark	23.11.79
Hreidarsson, Hermann	6. 1	Wimbledon	Iceland	11.07.74
Makin, Chris	5.11	Sunderland	Manchester	8.05.73
McGreal, John	5.11	Tranmere Rov.	Liverpool	2.06.72
Miller, Justin	6. 0	–	Johannesburg	16.12.80
Venus, Mark	6. 1	Wolves	Hartlepool	6.04.67
Wilnis, Fabian	5.10	De Graafschap.	Surinam	23.08.70

Midfielders

Name	Height ft. in.	Previous club	Birthplace	Birthdate
Abidallah, Nabil	5. 7	Ajax	Amsterdam	5.08.82
George, Finidi	6. 2	Real Mallorca	Port Harcourt, Nig.	15.04.71
Holland, Matt	5. 9	Bournemouth	Bury	11.04.74
Karic, Amir	5.11	Maribor	Oramovica, Slov.	31.12.73
Le Pen, Ulrich	5. 9	Lorient	France	21.01.74
Magilton, Jim	6. 0	Sheffield Wed.	Belfast	6.05.69
Miller, Tommy	6. 1	Hartlepool Utd.	Easington	8.01.79
Nicholls, Ashley	5.11	–	Ipswich	30.10.81
Wright, Jermaine	5. 9	Crewe Alexandra	Greenwich	21.10.75

Forwards

Name	Height ft. in.	Previous club	Birthplace	Birthdate
Armstrong, Alun	6. 0	Middlesbrough	Gateshead	22.02.75
Bent, Darren	6. 0	–	Cambridge	6.02.84
Bent, Marcus	6. 2	Blackburn Rov.	Hammersmith	19.05.78
Counago, Pablo	6. 0	Celta Vigo	Pontevedra, Spa.	9.08.79
Graaven, Guillermo	6. 0	Ajax	Amsterdam	17.01.82
Logan, Richard	6. 0	–	Bury St. Edmunds	4.01.82
Naylor, Richard	6. 1	–	Leeds	28.02.77
Reuser, Martijn	5. 7	Vitesse Arnhem	Amsterdam	1.02.75
Stewart, Marcus	5.10	Huddersfield Town	Bristol	7.11.72

LEICESTER CITY

Ground: Walkers Stadium, Leicester LE2 7FL
Telephone: 0870 040 6000. **Club nickname:** Foxes.
First-choice colours: Blue shirts, shorts and stockings.
Main sponsor: LG Electronics. **Capacity for 2002-03:** 32,500.
Record attendance: At Filbert Street: 47,298 v Tottenham (F.A. Cup 5) 18 February, 1928.

Goalkeepers

Name	Height ft. in.	Previous club	Birthplace	Birthdate
Flowers, Tim	6. 2	Blackburn Rov.	Kenilworth	3.02.67
Price, Michael	6. 0	–	Newcastle	4.03.83
Royce, Simon	6. 2	Charlton Athletic	Forest Gate	9.09.71
Walker, Ian	6. 1	Tottenham	Watford	31.10.71

Defenders

Name	Height ft. in.	Previous club	Birthplace	Birthdate
Davidson, Callum	5.10	Blackburn Rov.	Stirling	25.06.76
Delaney, Damien	6. 2	Cork City	Cork	20.07.81
Elliott, Matt	6. 3	Oxford Utd.	Roehampton	1.11.68
Heath, Matt	5.11	–	Leicester	11.01.81
Rogers, Alan	5.10	Nott'm. Forest	Liverpool	3.01.77
Sinclair, Frank	5.10	Chelsea	Lambeth	3.12.71
Taggart, Gerry	6. 2	Bolton Wand.	Belfast	18.10.70

Midfielders

Name	Height ft. in.	Previous club	Birthplace	Birthdate
Ashton, Jonathan	5.10	–	Nuneaton	4.10.82
Impey, Andy	5. 8	West Ham Utd.	Hammersmith	13.09.71
Izzet, Muzzy	5.10	Chelsea	Hackney	31.10.74
Jones, Matthew	5.11	Leeds Utd.	Llanelli	1.09.80
Lewis, Junior	5. 9	Gillingham	Wembley	9.10.73
Marshall, Lee	6. 2	Norwich City	Islington	21.01.79
McCann, Tim	5. 9	–	Belfast	22.03.80
Oakes, Stefan	5.11	–	Leicester	6.09.78
Reeves, Martin	5.11	–	Birmingham	7.09.81
Stevenson, Jonathan	5.10	–	Leicester	13.10.82
Stewart, Jordan	6. 0	–	Birmingham	3.03.82
Wise, Dennis	5. 6	Chelsea	Kensington	16.12.66

Forwards

Name	Height ft. in.	Previous club	Birthplace	Birthdate
Benjamin, Trevor	6. 2	Cambridge Utd.	Kettering	8.02.79
Deane, Brian	6. 3	Middlesbrough	Leeds	7.02.68
Dickov, Paul	5. 5	Manchester City	Glasgow	1.11.72

	Height			
	ft. in.			
Eadie, Darren	5. 7	Norwich City	Chippenham	10.06.75
Piper, Matt	6. 1	–	Leicester	29.09.81
Scowcroft, Jamie	6. 1	Ipswich Town	Bury St. Edmunds	15.11.75
Wright, Tommy	5.11	–	Leicester	28.09.84

MILLWALL

Ground: The New Den, Zampa Road, London SE16 3LN.
Telephone: 0207 232 1222. **Clubcall:** 09068 400300. **Club nickname:** Lions.
First-choice colours: Blue shirts; white shorts; blue stockings.
Main sponsor: 24 Seven. **Capacity for 2002-03:** 19,252.
Record attendance: (The Den) 48,672 v Derby Co. (F.A. Cup 5) 20 February, 1937.
  (New Den) 20,093 v Arsenal (F.A. Cup 3) 10 January, 1994.

Name	Height ft. in.	Previous club	Birthplace	Birthdate
Goalkeepers				
Gueret, Willy	6. 1	Le Mans	Guadaloupe	3.08.73
Harpur, Chad	5.10	Leeds	Johannesburg	3.09.82
Warner, Tony	6. 4	Liverpool	Liverpool	11.05.74
Defenders				
Bull, Ronnie	5. 8	–	Hackney	26.12.80
Dolan, Joe	6. 3	Chelsea	Harrow	27.05.80
Dunne, Alan	5.10	–	Dublin	23.08.82
Lawrence, Matt	6. 1	Wycombe Wand.	Northampton	19.06.74
Nethercott, Stuart	6. 0	Tottenham	Ilford	21.03.73
Robinson, Paul	6. 1	–	Barnet	7.01.82
Ryan, Robbie	5.10	Huddersfield Town	Dublin	16.05.77
Tuttle, David	6. 2	Barnsley	Reading	6.02.73
Phillips, Mark	6. 2	–	Lambeth	27.01.82
Rees, Matthew	6. 3	–	Swansea	2.09.82
Ward, Darren	6. 3	Watford	Harrow	13.09.78
Midfielders				
Booth, Stuart	5.11	–	London	7.12.83
Cahill, Tim	5.10	Sydney Utd.	Sydney	6.12.79
Hearn, Charley	5.11	–	Ashford	5.11.83
Hicks, Mark	5. 8	–	Belfast	24.07.81
Ifill, Paul	6. 0	–	Brighton	20.10.79
Livermore, David	6. 0	Arsenal	Edmonton	20.05.80
Odunsi, Leke	5. 9	–	Walworth	5.12.80
Reid, Steven	5.11	–	Kingston	10.03.81
Forwards				
Braniff, Kevin	5.11	–	Belfast	4.03.83
Claridge, Steve	6. 0	Portsmouth	Portsmouth	10.04.66
Harris, Neil	5.11	Cambridge City	Orsett	12.07.77
May, Ben	6. 1	–	Gravesend	10.03.84
Sadlier, Richard	6. 2	Belvedere	Dublin	14.01.79

NORWICH CITY

Ground: Carrow Road, Norwich NR1 1JE.
Telephone: 01603 760760. **Club nickname:** Canaries.
First-choice colours: Yellow and green shirts; green and yellow shorts; yellow stockings.
Main sponsor: Digital Phone. **Capacity for 2002-03:** 21,472.
Record attendance: 43,984 v Leicester City (F.A. Cup 6) 30 March, 1963.

Name	Height ft. in.	Previous club	Birthplace	Birthdate
Goalkeepers				
Crichton, Paul	6. 1	Burnley	Pontefract	3.10.68
Green, Robert	6. 3	–	Chertsey	18.01.80
Lee-Barrett, Arran	6. 0	Ipswich	Ipswich	28.02.84

Defenders

Name	Height ft. in.	Previous club	Birthplace	Birthdate
Blois, Lewis	5.11	–	London	14.12.81
Drury, Adam	5.10	Peterborough Utd.	Cambridge	29.08.78
Easton, Clint	5.11	Watford	Barking	1.11.77
Fleming, Craig	5.11	Oldham Athletic	Halifax	6.10.71
Heckingbottom, Paul	6. 0	Darlington	Barnsley	17.07.77
Holt, Gary	5.10	Kilmarnock	Irvine	9.03.73
Kenton, Darren	5.11	–	Wandsworth	13.09.78
Mackay, Malky	6. 3	Celtic	Bellshill	19.02.72
Sutch, Daryl	5.11	–	Lowestoft	11.09.71

Midfielders

Name	Height ft. in.	Previous club	Birthplace	Birthdate
Emblen, Neil	6. 1	Wolves	Bromley	19.06.71
Llewellyn, Chris	6. 0	–	Merthyr	28.08.79
McGovern, Brian	6. 3	Arsenal	Dublin	28.04.80
Mulryne, Phil	5. 8	Manchester Utd.	Belfast	1.01.78
Nedergaard, Steen	6. 0	Odense	Alborg, Den.	25.02.70
Oxby, Andrew	5. 7	–	London	20.11.83
Russell, Darel	6. 0	–	Mile End	22.10.80

Forwards

Name	Height ft. in.	Previous club	Birthplace	Birthdate
Abbey, Zema	6. 1	Cambridge Utd.	Luton	17.04.77
Bloomfield, Danny	5.10	Felixstowe	Ipswich	28.07.82
Giallanza, Gaetano	6. 0	Nantes	Basle	6.06.74
Libbra, Marc	6. 3	Toulouse	Toulon	5.08.72
McVeigh, Paul	5. 6	Tottenham	Belfast	6.12.77
Nielsen, David	5.11	Wimbledon	Denmark	1.12.76
Notman, Alex	5. 7	Manchester Utd.	Edinburgh	10.12.79
Rivers, Mark	5.10	Crewe Alexandra	Crewe	26.11.75
Roberts, Iwan	6. 3	Wolves	Bangor	26.06.68

NOTTINGHAM FOREST

Ground: City Ground, Nottingham NG2 5FJ.
Telephone: 0115 982 4444. **Clubcall:** 09068 121174. **Club nickname:** Forest.
First-choice colours: Red shirts; white shorts; red stockings.
Main sponsor: Pinnacle Insurance. **Capacity for 2002-03:** 30,602.
Record attendance: 49,945 v Manchester Utd. (Div. 1) 28 October, 1967.

Name	Height ft. in.	Previous club	Birthplace	Birthdate
Goalkeepers				
Formann, Pascal	6. 0	Chelsea	Werne, Ger.	16.11.82
Roche, Barry	6. 4	–	Dublin	6.04.82
Ward, Darren	5.11	Notts Co.	Worksop	11.05.74
Defenders				
Brennan, Jim	5. 9	Bristol City	Toronto	8.05.77
Dawson, Kevin	6. 0	–	Northallerton	18.06.81
Doig, Chris	6. 2	–	Dumfries	13.02.81
Edwards, Christain	6. 2	Swansea City	Caerphilly	23.11.75
Foy, Keith	5.11	–	Crumlin	30.12.81
Hjelde, Jon Olav	6. 2	Rosenborg	Levanger, Nor.	30.07.72
Louis-Jean, Matthieu	5. 9	Le Havre	Mont-St-Aignan, Fra.	22.02.76
Vaughan, Tony	6. 1	Manchester City	Manchester	11.10.75
Walker, Des	5.11	Sheffield Wed.	Hackney	26.11.65
Midfielders				
Bopp, Eugen	6. 0	–	Kiev	5.09.83
Cash, Brian	5.10	–	Dublin	24.11.82
Jones, Gary	6. 3	Tranmere Rov.	Chester	10.05.75
Prutton, David	6. 1	–	Hull	12.09.81
Reid, Andy	5. 7	–	Dublin	29.07.82
Scimeca, Ricardo	6. 1	Aston Villa	Leamington Spa	13.06.75
Thompson, John	6. 1	–	Dublin	12.10.82
Williams, Gareth	5.11	–	Glasgow	16.12.81

Forwards

Name	Height ft. in.	Previous club	Birthplace	Birthdate
Freeman, David	5.10	Cherry Orchard	Dublin	25.11.79
Harewood, Marlon	6. 1	–	Hampstead	25.08.79
Johnson, David	5. 6	Ipswich Town	Kingston, Jam.	15.08.76
Lester, Jack	5.10	Grimsby Town	Sheffield	8.10.75
Westcarr, Craig	5.11	–	Nottingham	29.01.85

PORTSMOUTH

Ground: Fratton Park, Frogmore Road, Portsmouth PO4 8RA.
Telephone: 02392 731204. **Club nickname:** Pompey.
First-choice colours: Blue shirts; white shorts; red stockings. **Capacity for 2002-03:** 19,000.
Record attendance: 51,385 v Derby Co. (F.A. Cup 6) 26 February, 1949.

Name	Height ft. in.	Previous club	Birthplace	Birthdate
Goalkeepers				
Beasant, Dave	6. 4	Tottenham	Willesden	20.03.59
Hislop, Shaka	6. 4	West Ham Utd.	Hackney	22.02.69
Kawaguchi, Yoshikatsu	5.10	Yokohama	Shizuoka	15.08.75
Tardif, Chris	5.11	–	Guernsey	20.06.81
Defenders				
Buxton, Lewis	5.11	–	Cowes	10.12.83
Cooper, Shaun	5. 9	–	Newport, IOW	5.10.83
Crowe, Jason	5. 9	Arsenal	Sidcup	30.09.78
De Zeeuw, Arjan	6. 1	Wigan Athletic	Castricum, Hol.	16.04.70
Foxe, Hayden	6. 2	West Ham Utd.	Australia	23.06.77
Hiley, Scott	5. 9	Southampton	Plymouth	27.09.68
Howe, Eddie	5. 9	Bournemouth	Amersham	29.11.77
Primus, Linvoy	5.11	Reading	Forest Gate	14.07.73
Tiler, Carl	6. 1	Charlton Athletic	Sheffield	11.02.70
Vincent, Jamie	5.11	Huddersfield Town	Wimbledon	18.06.75
Midfielders				
Barrett, Neil	5. 9	Chelsea	Tooting	29.12.81
Courville, Uliano	5.11	Monaco	Mantes La Jolie, Fra.	8.08.78
Curtis, Tom	5. 8	Chesterfield	Exeter City	1.03.73
Derry, Shaun	5.11	Sheffield Utd.	Nottingham	6.12.77
Harper, Kevin	5. 6	Derby Co.	Oldham	15.01.76
Mapeza, Norman	6. 0	Altay Izmir	Zimbabwe	12.04.72
Miglioranzi, Stefani	6. 2	–	Pacos De Caldas, Bra.	20.09.77
O'Neil, Gary	5. 9	–	Beckenham	18.05.83
Pettefer, Carl	5. 7	–	Taplow	22.03.81
Quashie, Nigel	6. 0	Nott'm. Forest	Peckham	20.07.78
Taylor, Matthew	5.11	Luton Town	Oxford	27.11.81
White, Tom	5.10	–	Chichester	30.10.81
Forwards				
Allen, Rory	5.11	Tottenham	Beckenham	17.10.77
Bradbury, Lee	6. 0	Crystal Palace	Cowes	3.07.75
Burchill, Mark	5. 8	Celtic	Bellshill	18.08.80
Lovell, Steve	6. 1	Bournemouth	Amersham	6.12.80
Nightingale, Luke	5.11	–	Portsmouth	22.12.80
Pitt, Courtney	5. 8	Chelsea	London	17.12.81
Todorov, Svetoslav	5.11	West Ham Utd.	Bulgaria	31.12.78
Vine, Rowan	5.11	–	Portsmouth	1.12.81

PRESTON NORTH END

Ground: Deepdale, Sir Tom Finney Way, Preston PR1 6RU.
Telephone: 01772 902020. **Club nickname:** Lilywhites.
First-choice colours: White shirts; dark blue shorts; white stockings.

Main sponsor: NewReg.com. **Capacity for 2002-03:** 22,227.
Record attendance: 42,684 v Arsenal (Div. 1) 23 April, 1938.

Name	Height ft. in.	Previous club	Birthplace	Birthdate
Goalkeepers				
Lucas, David	6. 1	–	Preston	23.11.77
Lonergan, Andrew	6. 4	–	Preston	19.10.83
Moilanen, Tepi	6. 5	Jaro	Oulu, Fin.	12.12.73
Defenders				
Alexander, Graham	5.11	Luton Town	Coventry	10.10.71
Eaton, Adam	5.10	Everton	Wigan	2.05.80
Jackson, Michael	5.11	Bury	Chester	4.12.73
Lucketti, Chris	6. 0	Huddersfield Town	Littleborough	28.09.71
Mears, Tyrone	5.10	Manchester City	Stockport	18.02.83
Murdock, Colin	6. 1	Manchester Utd.	Ballymena	2.07.75
Midfielders				
Anderson, Iain	5. 5	Toulouse	Glasgow	23.07.77
Bailey, John	5. 8	–	Manchester	2.07.84
Barry-Murphy, Brian	5.10	Cork City	Cork	27.07.78
Cartwright, Lee	5. 8	–	Rossendale	19.09.72
Edwards, Rob	5.11	Bristol City	Kendal	1.07.73
Etuhu, Dickson	6. 2	Manchester City	Kano, Nig.	8.06.82
Gregan, Sean	6. 0	Darlington	Middlesbrough	29.03.74
Keane, Michael	5. 6	–	Dublin	29.12.82
McKenna, Paul	5. 8	–	Chorley	20.10.77
Rankine, Mark	5. 9	Wolves	Doncaster	30.09.69
Skora, Eric	5.10	–	France	20.08.81
Forwards				
Abbott, Pawel	5.10	LKS Lodz	York	2.12.77
Basham, Steve	5. 9	Southampton	Southampton	2.12.77
Cresswell, Richard	6. 0	Leicester City	Bridlington	20.09.77
Fuller, Ricardo	6. 3	Tivoli Gardens	Kingston, Jam.	31.10.79
Healy, David	5. 8	Manchester Utd.	Downpatrick	5.08.79
O'Neil, Joe	6. 0	–	Blackburn	28.10.82
Wright, Mark	5.10	–	Chorley	4.09.81

READING

Ground: Madejski Stadium, Junction 11 M4, Reading RG2 0FL.
Telephone: 0118 968 1100. **Club nickname:** Royals.
First-choice colours: Blue and white shirts; white shorts; white stockings.
Main sponsor: Westcoast. **Capacity for 2002-03:** 25,000.
Record attendance: (Elm Park) 33,042 v Brentford (F.A. Cup 5) 17 February, 1927.
(Madejski Stadium) 22,034 v Wigan Athletic (Div. 2 play-off) 16, May, 2001.

Name	Height ft. in.	Previous club	Birthplace	Birthdate
Goalkeepers				
Ashdown, Jamie	6. 3	–	Reading	30.11.80
Talia, Frank	6. 1	Sheffield Utd.	Melbourne	20.07.72
Whitehead, Phil	6. 3	W.B.A.	Halifax	17.12.69
Defenders				
Allaway, Ricky	6. 2	–	Reading	16.02.83
Mackie, John	6. 0	Sutton	London	5.07.76
Shorey, Nicky	5. 9	Leyton Orient	Romford	19.02.81
Smith, Alex	5. 8	Port Vale	Liverpool	15.02.76
Viveash, Adrian	6. 2	Walsall	Swindon	30.09.69
Whitbread, Adrian	6. 2	Portsmouth	Epping	22.10.71
Williams, Adrian	6. 2	Wolves	Reading	16.08.71
Midfielders				
Campion, Adam	5. 9	–	Ascot	4.10.82

Gamble, Joe	5. 7	Cork City	Cork	14.01.82
Harper, James	5.11	Arsenal	Chelmsford	9.11.80
Hughes, Andy	5.11	Notts Co.	Manchester	2.01.78
Igoe, Sammy	5. 6	Portsmouth	Spelthorne	30.09.75
Murty, Graeme	5.10	York City	Saltburn	13.11.74
Newman, Ricky	5.10	Millwall	Guildford	5.08.70
Parkinson, Phil	6. 0	Bury	Chorley	1.12.67
Salako, John	5.10	Charlton Athletic	Nigeria	11.02.69
Watson, Kevin	5.10	Rotherham Utd.	Hackney	3.01.74
Forwards				
Butler, Martin	5.11	Cambridge Utd.	Dudley	15.09.74
Cureton, Jamie	5. 7	Bristol Rov.	Bristol	28.08.75
Forster, Nicky	5. 9	Birmingham City	Caterham	8.09.73
Henderson, Darius	6. 1	–	Doncaster	7.09.81
Rougier, Tony	6. 0	Port Vale	Tobago	17.07.71
Savage, Bas	6. 3	Walton & Hersham	London	7.01.82
Tyson, Nathan	6. 0	–	Reading	4.05.82

ROTHERHAM UNITED

Ground: Millmoor, Rotherham S60 1HR.
Telephone: 01709 512434. **Clubcall**: 09068 121637. **Club nickname**: Millers.
First-choice colours: Red and white shirts; red shorts; red and white stockings.
Main sponsor: T Mobile. **Capacity for 2002-03**: 11,486.
Record attendance: 25,000 v Sheffield Wed. (Div. 2) 26 January, 1952 and v Sheffield Wed. (Div. 2) 13 December, 1952.

Name	Height ft. in.	Previous club	Birthplace	Birthdate
Goalkeepers				
Gray, Ian	6. 2	Stockport Co.	Manchester	25.02.75
Pollitt, Mike	6. 3	Chesterfield	Bolton	29.02.72
Defenders				
Artell, David	6. 2	–	Rotherham	22.11.80
Beech, Chris	5. 9	Cardiff City	Congleton	5.11.75
Branston, Guy	6. 2	Leicester City	Leicester	9.01.79
Hurst, Paul	5. 4	–	Sheffield	25.09.74
Swailes, Chris	6. 2	Bury	Gateshead	19.10.70
Jones, Rhodri	6. 0	Manchester Utd.	Cardiff	19.01.82
Midfielders				
Bryan, Marvin	5.10	Bury	Paddington	2.08.75
Daws, Nick	5.11	Bury	Salford	15.03.70
Garner, Darren	5. 9	Plymouth Argyle	Plymouth	10.12.71
Hudson, Danny	5. 9	–	Mexborough	25.06.79
McIntosh, Martin	6. 3	Hibernian	East Kilbride	19.03.71
Miranda, Jose	5.10	–	Lisbon	20.04.74
Talbot, Stuart	5.11	Port Vale	Birmingham	14.06.73
Forwards				
Barker, Richard	5.11	Macclesfield Town	Sheffield	30.05.75
Byfield, Darren	5.11	Walsall	Sutton Coldfield	29.09.76
Lee, Alan	6. 2	Burnley	Galway	21.08.78
Monkhouse, Andy	6. 0	–	Leeds	23.10.80
Mullin, John	6. 0	Burnley	Bury	11.08.75
Robins, Mark	5. 8	Walsall	Ashton-under-Lyne	22.12.69
Scott, Rob	6. 1	Fulham	Epsom	15.08.73
Sedgwick, Chris	6. 1	–	Sheffield	28.04.80
Warne, Paul	5. 8	Wigan Athletic	Norwich	8.05.73

SHEFFIELD UNITED

Ground: Bramall Lane, Sheffield, S2 4SU.
Telephone: 0114 221 5757. **Clubcall**: 09068 888650. **Club nickname**: Blades.

First-choice colours: Red and white shirts; white shorts and stockings.
Main Sponsor: Desun. **Capacity for 2002-03:** 30,413.
Record attendance: 68,287 v Leeds Utd. (F.A. Cup 5) 15 February, 1936.

Name	Height ft. in.	Previous club	Birthplace	Birthdate
Goalkeepers				
Blackwell, Kevin	–	–	–	–
De Vogt, Wilko	6. 0	Utrecht	Breda	17.09.75
Tracey, Simon	6. 0	Wimbledon	Woolwich	9.12.67
Defenders				
Croissant, Benoit	6. 0	Troyes	Virity Francois, Fra.	9.08.80
Curle, Keith	6. 0	Wolves	Bristol	14.11.63
Doane, Ben	5.10	–	Sheffield	22.12.79
Jagielka, Phil	5.11	–	Manchester	17.08.82
Kozluk, Rob	6. 0	Derby Co.	Sutton-in-Ashfield	5.08.77
Murphy, Shaun	6. 1	W.B.A.	Sydney	5.11.70
Nicholson, Shane	5.10	Stockport Co.	Newark	3.06.70
Page, Robert	6. 0	Watford	Llwynpia	3.09.74
Sandford, Lee	6. 0	Stoke City	London	22.04.68
Thompson, Lee	5.10	–	Dublin	23.03.81
Ullathorne, Rob	5. 8	Leicester City	Wakefield	11.10.71
Yates, Steve	5.11	Tranmere Rov.	Bristol	29.02.70
Midfielders				
Brown, Michael	5. 9	Manchester City	Hartlepool	25.01.77
Burley, Adam	5.10	–	Sheffield	27.11.80
Ford, Bobby	5. 8	Oxford Utd.	Bristol	22.09.74
Javary, Jean-Phillipe	5.11	Plymouth Argyle	Montpellier	10.01.78
McCall, Stuart	5. 7	Bradford City	Leeds	10.06.64
Montgomery, Nick	5. 9	–	Leeds	28.10.81
Ndlovu, Peter	5. 8	Birmingham City	Bulawayo	25.02.73
Santos, George	6. 3	W.B.A.	Marseille	15.08.70
Smith, Grant	5.11	–	Irvine	5.05.80
Tonge, Michael	5.11	–	Manchester	7.04.83
Uhlenbeek, Gus	5.10	Fulham	Surinam	20.08.70
Forwards				
Asaba, Carl	6. 2	Gillingham	London	28.01.73
Boussatta, Dries	5. 8	Alkmaar	Amsterdam	23.12.72
Devlin, Paul	5. 8	Birmingham City	Birmingham	14.04.72
Mallon, Ryan	5. 9	–	Sheffield	22.03.83
Onuora, Iffy	6. 1	Gillingham	Glasgow	28.07.67
Peschisolido, Paul	5. 7	Fulham	Scarborough, Can.	25.05.71
Suffo, Patrick	5. 8	Nantes	Ebolowa, Cam.	17.01.78
Ten Heuvel, Laurens	6. 0	Telstar	Amsterdam	6.06.76
Ward, Mark	6. 1	–	Sheffield	21.01.82

SHEFFIELD WEDNESDAY

Ground: Hillsborough, Sheffield S6 1SW.
Telephone: 0114 221 2121. **Club nickname:** Owls.
First-choice colours: Blue and white shirts; black shorts; blue and black stockings.
Capacity for 2002-03: 39,814.
Record attendance: 72,841 v Manchester City (F.A. Cup 5) 17 February, 1934.

Name	Height ft. in.	Previous club	Birthplace	Birthdate
Goalkeepers				
Stringer, Chris	6. 6	–	Sheffield	19.09.83
Pressman, Kevin	6. 1	–	Fareham	6.11.67
Defenders				
Armstrong, Craig	5.11	Huddersfield Town	South Shields	23.05.75
Beswetherick, Jon	5.11	Plymouth Argyle	Liverpool	15.01.78

Bromby, Leigh	5. 6	–	Dewsbury	2.06.80
Burrows, David	5.10	Birmingham City	Dudley	25.10.68
Connolly, Calem	5. 8	–	Leeds	12.02.82
Geary, Derek	5. 7	–	Dublin	19.06.80
Hendon, Ian	6. 0	Northampton Town	Ilford	5.12.71
Maddix, Danny	5.11	Q.P.R.	Ashford	11.10.67
Westwood, Ashley	6. 0	Bradford City	Bridgnorth	31.08.76
Midfielders				
Crane, Tony	6. 4	–	Liverpool	8.09.82
Donnelly, Simon	5. 8	Celtic	Glasgow	1.12.74
Evans, Paul	5. 8	Brentford	Oswestry	1.09.74
Hamshaw, Matthew	5.10	–	Rotherham	1.01.82
Haslam, Steve	5.11	–	Sheffield	6.09.79
McLaren, Paul	6. 1	Luton Town	High Wycombe	17.11.76
O'Donnell, Phil	5.11	Celtic	Bellshill	23.03.72
Soltvedt, Trond	6. 0	Southampton	Voss, Nor.	15.02.67
Wilson, Laurie	5.10	–	Brighton	5.12.84
Forwards				
Di Piedi, Michelle	6. 6	–	Italy	
Ekoku, Efan	6. 2	Grasshoppers Zur.	Manchester	8.06.67
Kuqi, Shefki	5.10	Stockport Co.	Albania	10.11.76
Morrison, Owen	5. 7	–	Londonderry	8.12.81
Owusu, Lloyd	6. 1	Brentford	Slough	12.12.76
Quinn, Alan	5. 9	–	Dublin	13.06.79
Shaw, Jon	6. 1	–	Sheffield	10.11.83
Sibon, Gerald	6. 5	Ajax	Emmen, Hol.	19.04.74

STOKE CITY

Ground: Britannia Stadium, Stanley Matthews Way, Stoke-on-Trent ST4 7EG.
Telephone: 01782 592222. **Clubcall:** 09068 121040. **Club nickname:** Potters.
First-choice colours: Red and white shirts; white shorts; red and white stockings.
Main sponsor: Britannia. **Capacity for 2002-03:** 28,218.
Record attendance: (Victoria Ground) 51,380 v Arsenal (Div. 1) 29 March, 1937.
(Britannia Stadium) 27,109 v Liverpool (League Cup 4) 29 November, 2000.

Name	Height ft. in.	Previous club	Birthplace	Birthdate
Goalkeepers				
Alcock, Danny	5.11	–	Staffs	15.02.84
Cutler, Neil	6. 1	Aston Villa	Birmingham	3.09.76
Viander, Jani	6. 4	HJK Helsinki	Tuusula, Fin.	18.08.75
Defenders				
Clarke, Clive	6. 0	–	Dublin	14.01.80
Commons, Kris	5. 6	–	Notts	30.08.83
Handyside, Peter	6. 1	Grimsby Town	Dumfries	31.07.74
Owen, Gareth	6. 1	–	Staffs	21.09.82
Shtaniuk, Sergei	6. 3	Dynamo Moscow	Minsk	11.01.72
Thomas, Wayne	6. 2	Torquay Utd.	Gloucester	17.05.79
Wilkinson, Andy	5.11	–	Stone	6.08.84
Wilson, Brian	5.10	–	Manchester	9.05.83
Midfielders				
Gudjonsson, Bjarni	5. 8	Genk	Reykavik	26.02.79
Gunnarsson, Brynjar	6. 1	Orgryte	Reykavik	16.10.75
Henry, Karl	6. 1	–	Wolverhampton	26.11.82
Hoekstra, Peter	6. 3	Ajax	Assen	4.04.73
Marteinsson, Petur	6. 1	Stabaek	Reykjavik	14.07.73
Neal, Lewis	5.11	–	Leicester	14.07.81
O'Connor, James	5. 8	–	Dublin	1.09.79
Rowson, David	5.10	Åberdeen	Aberdeen	14.09.76
Short, Chris	5.10	Sheffield Utd.	Munster, Ger.	9.05.70
Vandeurzen, Jurgen	5. 7	Turnhout	Genk	26.01.74

Forwards

Name	Height ft. in.	Previous club	Birthplace	Birthdate
Albrigtsen, Ole	5. 9	Vesteralen	Sortland, Nor.	21.04.75
Cooke, Andy	5.11	Burnley	Stoke	20.01.74
Goodfellow, Marc	5.10	–	Swadlincote	20.09.81
Greenacre, Chris	5.11	Mansfield Town	Halifax	23.12.77
Hall, Laurence	6. 0	–	Nottingham	26.03.84
Iwelumo, Chris	6. 4	Aarhus	Coatbridge	1.08.78
Miles, John	5.10	Liverpool	Fazackerly	28.09.81
Oulare, Souleymane	5.11	Genk	Guinea	16.10.72
Thordarson, Stefan	6. 1	Bayer Uerdingen	Reykjavik	27.03.75

WALSALL

Ground: Bescot Stadium, Bescot Crescent, Walsall WS1 4SA.
Telephone: 01922 622791. **Clubcall:** 09068 555800. **Club nickname:** Saddlers.
First-choice colours: Red, white and black shirts and shorts; red stockings.
Main Sponsor: Banks's. **Capacity for 2002-03:** 11,200.
Record attendance: (Fellows Park) 25,433 v Newcastle Utd. (Div. 2) 29 August, 1961.
(Bescot Stadium) 10,628 England v Sitzerland B intl. 20 May, 1991. Club: 9,517 v Manchester City (Div. 2) 23 January, 1999.

Name	Height ft. in.	Previous club	Birthplace	Birthdate
Goalkeepers				
Walker, James	5.11	Notts Co.	Sutton-in-Ashfield	9.07.73
Defenders				
Aranalde, Zigor	6. 1	Logrones	Guipuzcoa, Spa.	28.02.73
Barras, Tony	6. 0	Reading	Billingham	29.03.71
Bazeley, Darren	5.11	Wolves	Northampton	5.10.72
Carbon, Matt	6. 2	W.B.A.	Nottingham	8.06.75
Gadsby, Matthew	6. 1	–	Sutton Coldfield	6.09.79
Hay, Danny	6. 4	Leeds Utd.	Auckland	15.05.75
Roper, Ian	6. 4	–	Nuneaton	20.06.77
Midfielders				
Birch, Gary	5.10		Birmingham	8.10.81
Corica, Steve	5. 8	Hiroshima	Cairns, Aus.	24.03.73
Garrocho, Carlos	5.11	Leca	Angola	26.01.74
Herivelto, Moreira	5.10	Cruzeiro	Brazil	23.08.75
Keates, Dean	5. 6	–	Walsall	30.06.78
Matias, Pedro	6. 0	Tranmere Rov.	Madrid	11.10.73
O'Connor, Martyn	5. 9	Birmingham City	Walsall	10.12.67
Wright, Mark	5.11	–	Wolverhampton	24.02.82
Forwards				
Goodman, Don	5.10	Motherwell	Leeds	9.05.66
Hawley, Karl	5. 8	–	Walsall	6.12.81
Leitao, Jorge	5.11	Farense	Oporto	14.01.74
Rodrigues, Dani	5.11	Southampton	Madeira	3.03.80
Wrack, Darren	5. 9	Grimsby Town	Cleethorpes	5.05.76
Zdrilic, David	6. 0	Unterhaching	Sydney	13.04.74

WATFORD

Ground: Vicarage Road Stadium, Vicarage Road, Watford WD1.
Telephone: 01923 496000. **Clubcall:** 09068 104104. **Club nickname:** Hornets.
First-choice colours: Yellow shirts; black shorts; black stockings.
Main sponsor: Toshiba. **Capacity for 2002-03:** 20,836.
Record attendance: 34,099 v Manchester Utd. (F.A. Cup 4) February, 1969.

Name	Height ft. in.	Previous club	Birthplace	Birthdate
Goalkeepers				
Baardsen, Espen	6. 5	Tottenham	San Rafael, USA	7.12.77

Name	ft. in.	Previous club	Birthplace	Birthdate
Chamberlain, Alec	6. 2	Sunderland	March	20.06.64
Lee, Richard	5.11	–	Oxford	5.10.82
Defenders				
Cox, Neil	6. 0	Bolton Wand.	Scunthorpe	8.10.71
Doyley, Lloyd	5.10	–	Whitechapel	1.12.82
Dyche, Sean	6. 0	Millwall	Kettering	28.06.71
Gibbs, Nigel	5. 7	–	St Albans	20.11.65
Ifil, Jerel	6. 1	–	London	27.06.82
Langston, Matthew	6. 3	–	Brighton	2.04.81
Mahon, Gavin	6. 0	Brentford	Birmingham	2.01.77
Matthews, Barrie	5. 9	–	Cinderford	1.02.83
Neill, Tom	6. 0	–	Harrow	13.11.81
Panayi, James	6. 1	–	Hammersmith	24.01.80
Robinson, Paul	5. 9	–	Watford	14.12.78
Williams, Nick	6. 1	–	Cheltenham	16.02.83
Midfielders				
Cook, Lee	5. 9	–	Hammersmith	3.08.82
Fisken, Gary	6. 0	–	Watford	27.10.81
Glass, Stephen	5. 7	Newcastle Utd.	Dundee	23.05.76
Hughes, Stephen	6. 0	Everton	Reading	18.09.76
Hyde, Micah	5.11	Cambridge Utd.	Newham	10.11.74
Johnson, Richard	5.10	–	Kurri-Kurri, Aus.	27.04.74
McNamee, Anthony	5. 6	–	Kensington	13.07.84
Nielsen, Allan	5. 9	Tottenham	Esbjerg	13.03.71
Noble, David	5.11	Arsenal	Hitchin	2.02.82
Swonnell, Sam	5.10	–	Brentwood	13.09.82
Wooter, Nordin	5. 7	Real Zaragoza	Surinam	24.08.76
Forwards				
Foley, Dominic	6. 2	Wolves	Cork	7.07.76
Forde, Fabian	6. 0	–	Harrow	26.10.81
Gayle, Marcus	6. 1	Rangers	Hammersmith	27.09.70
Godfrey, Elliott	5.10	–	Toronto	22.02.83
Helguson, Heidar	5.10	Lillestrom	Akureyri, Ice.	22.08.77
Noel-Williams, Gifton	6. 4	–	Islington	21.01.80
Norville, Jason	5.11	–	Trinidad	9.09.83
Patterson, Simon	6. 4	–	Harrow	4.09.82
Smith, Tommy	5.10	–	Hemel Hempstead	22.05.80
Wright, Nick	5.10	Carlisle Utd.	Derby	15.10.75

WIMBLEDON

Ground: Selhurst Park, London SE25 6PY.
Telephone: 0208 771 2233. **Clubcall:** 09068 121175. **Club nickname:** Dons.
First-choice colours: Dark blue shirts, shorts and stockings.
Main sponsor: Maximuscle. **Capacity for 2002-03:** 26,297.
Record attendance: 30,115 v Manchester Utd. (Prem. League) 9 May, 1993.

Name	Height ft. in.	Previous club	Birthplace	Birthdate
Goalkeepers				
Davis, Kelvin	6. 1	Luton Town	Bedford	29.09.76
Gore, Shane	6. 1	–	–	28.10.81
Heald, Paul	6. 2	Leyton Orient	Wath-on-Dearne	20.09.68
Defenders				
Byrne, Des	5.10	Patrick's Athletic	Dublin	10.04.81
Gier, Rob	5.11	–	Ascot	6.01.80
Hawkins, Peter	6. 0	–	Maidstone	19.09.78
Holloway, Darren	6. 0	Sunderland	Crook	3.10.77
Jupp, Duncan	6. 0	Fulham	Guildford	25.01.75
Leigertwood, Mikele	6. 1	–	Enfield	12.11.82
Willmott, Chris	5.11	Luton Town	Bedford	30.09.77
Williams, Mark	6. 0	Watford	Stalybridge	28.09.70

Midfielders

Name	Height ft. in.	Previous club	Birthplace	Birthdate
Andersen, Trond	6. 0	Molde	Kristiansund, Nor.	6.01.75
Darlington, Jermaine	5. 7	Q.P.R.	Hackney	11.04.74
Francis, Damien	6. 0	–	Wandsworth	27.02.79
Hughes, Michael	5. 6	West Ham Utd.	Larne	2.08.71
Karlsson, Per	5.10	IFK Gothenburg	Gothenburg	20.05.78
Mild, Hakan	6. 0	IFK Gothenburg	Trollhattan, Swe.	14.06.71
Nowland, Adam	5.11	Blackpool	Preston	6.07.81
Tapp, Alex	5. 9	–	Redhill	7.06.82

Forwards

Agyemang, Patrick	6. 1	–	Walthamstow	29.09.80
Connolly, David	5. 8	Feyenoord	Willesden	6.06.77
Gray, Wayne	5.10	–	Camberwell	7.11.80
McAnuff, Joel	5.11	–	Edmonton	9.11.81
Morgan, Lionel	5.11	–	Tottenham	17.02.83
Robinson, Paul	5.10	Newcastle Utd.	Sunderland	20.11.78
Shipperley, Neil	6. 0	Barnsley	Chatham	30.10.74

WOLVES

Ground: Molineux, Waterloo Road, Wolverhampton WV1 4QR.
Telephone: 01902 655000. **Clubcall:** 09068 121103. **Club nickname:** Wolves.
First-choice colors: Gold and black shirts; black and gold shorts; black and gold stockings.
Main sponsor: Doritos. **Capacity for 2002-03:** 28,500.
Record attendance: 61,315 v Liverpool (F.A. Cup 5) 11 February, 1939.

Name	Height ft. in.	Previous club	Birthplace	Birthdate
Goalkeepers				
Murray, Matt	6. 4	–	Lichfield	2.05.81
Oakes, Michael	6. 1	Aston Villa	Northwich	30.10.73
Defenders				
Butler, Paul	6. 3	Sunderland	Manchester	2.11.72
Camara, Mohamed	5.11	Le Havre	Guinea	25.06.75
Connolly, Sean	5.10	Stockport Co.	Sheffield	26.06.70
Lescott, Joleon	6. 2	–	Birmingham	16.08.82
Naylor, Lee	5. 8	–	Walsall	19.03.80
Pollet, Ludovic	5.11	Le Havre	Vieux-Conde, Fra.	7.08.73
Midfielders				
Andrews, Keith	6. 0	–	Dublin	18.09.80
Cameron, Colin	5. 8	Hearts	Kirkcaldy	23.10.72
Cooper, Kevin	5. 8	Wimbledon	Derby	8.02.75
Ingimarsson, Ivar	6. 0	Brentford	Iceland	20.08.77
Kennedy, Mark	5.11	Manchester City	Dublin	15.05.76
Melligan, John	5. 9	–	Dublin	11.02.82
Rae, Alex	5.10	Sunderland	Glasgow	30.09.69
Larkin, Colin	5. 9	–	Dundalk	27.04.82
Newton, Shaun	5. 8	Charlton Athletic	Camberwell	20.08.75
Forwards				
Blake, Nathan	5.11	Blackburn Rov.	Cardiff	27.01.72
Branch, Michael	5.10	Everton	Liverpool	18.10.78
Miller, Kenny	5.10	Rangers	Edinburgh	23.12.79
Ndah, George	6. 1	Swindon Town	Dulwich	23.12.74
Proudlock, Adam	6. 0	–	Wellington	9.05.81
Roussel, Cedric	6. 2	Coventry City	Mons, Bel.	6.01.78
Sturridge, Dean	5. 8	Leicester City	Birmingham	26.07.73

DIVISION TWO

BARNSLEY

Ground: Oakwell, Barnsley S71 1ET.
Telephone: 01226 211211. **Clubcall:** 09068 121152. **Club nickname:** Tykes.
First-choice colours: Red shirts; white shorts; red stockings.
Main Sponsor: isoft. **Capacity for 2002-03:** 23,115.
Record attendance: 40,255 v Stoke City (F.A. Cup 5) 15 February, 1936.

Name	Height ft. in.	Previous club	Birthplace	Birthdate
Goalkeepers				
Ghent, Matthew	6. 3	Aston Villa	Burton	5.10.80
Marriott, Andy	6. 0	Sunderland	Sutton-in-Ashfield	11.10.70
Parry, Craig	5.11	–	Barnsley	15.03.84
Defenders				
Crooks, Lee	6. 2	Manchester City	Wakefield	14.01.78
Dudgeon, James	6. 2	–	Newcastle	19.03.81
Flynn, Mike	6. 1	Stockport Co.	Oldham	23.02.69
Gibbs, Paul	5.11	Brentford	Great Yarmouth	26.10.72
Miller, Chris	5. 8	–	Paisley	19.11.82
Morgan, Chris	6. 1	–	Barnsley	9.11.77
O'Callaghan, Brian	6. 1	–	Limerick	24.02.81
Regan, Carl	6. 0	Everton	Liverpool	14.01.80
Midfielders				
Bertos, Leo	5. 8	Wellington	Wellington, NZ	20.12.81
Betsy, Kevin	6. 1	Fulham	Seychelles	20.03.78
Dixon, Kevin	5. 8	Leeds Utd.	Easington	27.06.80
Donovan, Kevin	5.10	Grimsby Town	Halifax	17.12.71
Gorre, Dean	5. 7	Huddersfield Town	Paramaribo, Sur.	10.09.70
Hayward, Steve	5.11	Fulham	Walsall	8.09.71
Jones, Gary	5.11	Rochdale	Birkenhead	3.06.77
Lumsdon, Chris	5.11	Sunderland	Newcastle	15.12.79
Mulligan, David	5. 5	–	Liverpool	24.03.82
Neil, Alex	5. 9	Airdrie	Bellshill	9.06.81
Ward, Mitch	5. 8	Everton	Sheffield	19.06.71
Forwards				
Austin, Neil	5.10	–	Barnsley	26.04.83
Barrowclough, Carl	5. 7	–	Doncaster	25.09.81
Dyer, Bruce	5.11	Crystal Palace	Ilford	13.04.75
Fallon, Rory	6. 2	–	Gisborne, NZ	20.03.82
Kay, Antony	5.11	–	Barnsley	21.10.82
Rankin, Isaiah	5.10	Bradford City	Edmonton	22.05.78
Sheron, Mike	5.10	Q.P.R.	Liverpool	11.01.72

BLACKPOOL

Ground: Bloomfield Road, Blackpool FY1 6JJ.
Telephone: 01253 405331. **Clubcall:** 09068 121648. **Club nickname:** Seasiders.
First-choice colours: Tangerine shirts, shorts and stockings.
Main sponsor: Electricity Direct. **Capacity for 2002-03:** 13,000.
Record attendance: 38,098 v Wolves (Div. 1) 17 September, 1955

Name	Height ft. in.	Previous club	Birthplace	Birthdate
Goalkeepers				
Barnes, Phil	6. 1	Rotherham Utd.	Rotherham	2.03.79
Defenders				
Clarke, Chris	6. 3	Halifax Town	Leeds	18.12.80
Gordon, Dale	5. 9	–	Ballymena	12.08.83

Heffernan, Guy	5.11	–	Barrow	1.03.84
Hills, John	5. 9	Everton	Blackpool	21.04.78
Hughes, Ian	5.10	Bury	Bangor	2.08.74
Jaszczun, Tommy	5.10	Aston Villa	Kettering	16.09.77
MacKenzie, Neil	6. 2	Kidderminster Harr.	Birmingham	15.04.76
Maden, Wayne	6. 2	–	Blackpool	24.03.83
O'Kane, John	5.10	Bolton Wand.	Nottingham	15.11.74
Reid, Brian	6. 2	Dunfermline	Paisley	15.06.70
Midfielders				
Bullock, Martin	5. 4	Barnsley	Derby	5.03.75
Burns, Jamie	5. 9	–	Blackpool	6.03.84
Coid, Danny	5.11	–	Liverpool	3.10.81
Collins, Lee	5. 8	Swindon Town	Bellshill	3.02.74
Milligan, Jamie	5. 6	Everton	Blackpool	3.01.80
Wellens, Richard	5. 9	Manchester Utd.	Manchester	26.03.80
Forwards				
Blinkhorn, Matthew	6. 0	–	Blackpool	2.03.85
Fenton, Graham	5.10	St Mirren	Wallsend	22.05.74
Murphy, John	6. 2	Chester City	Whiston	18.10.76
Taylor, Scott	5.10	Stockport Co.	Chertsey	5.05.76
Walker, Richard	6. 0	Aston Villa	Birmingham	8.11.77

BRENTFORD

Ground: Griffin Park, Braemar Road, Brentford TW7 6RD.
Telephone: 0208 847 2511. **Clubcall:** 09068 121108. **Club nickname:** Bees.
First-choice colours: Red and white shirts; black shorts; red stockings.
Main sponsor: GMB. **Capacity for 2002-03:** 12,750.
Record attendance: 39,626 v Preston N.E. (F.A. Cup 6) 5 March, 1938.

Name	Height ft. in.	Previous club	Birthplace	Birthdate
Goalkeepers				
Gottskalksson, Olafur	6. 1	Hibernian	Iceland	12.03.68
Julian, Alan	6. 0	–	Northern Ireland	11.03.83
Defenders				
Anderson, Ijah	5. 8	Southend Utd.	Hackney	30.12.75
Dobson, Michael	6. 0	–	London	9.04.80
Evans, Stephen	6. 0	Crystal Palace	Caerphilly	25.09.80
Fieldwick, Lee	5.11	–	–	6.09.82
Lovett, Jay	6. 1	Crawley Town	Brighton	22.01.78
Marshall, Scott	6. 1	Southampton	Edinburgh	1.05.73
Powell, Darren	6. 3	Hampton	Hammersmith	10.03.76
Somner, Matt	5.11	–	London	8.12.82
Midfielders				
Hunt, Stephen	5. 8	Crystal Palace	Laois	1.08.81
Hutchinson, Eddie	6. 1	Sutton Utd.	Kingston	23.02.82
Rowlands, Martin	5. 9	Farnborough	Hammersmith	8.02.79
Smith, Jay	5.10	–	Hammersmith	29.12.81
Tabb, Jay	5. 6	–	London	21.02.84
Williams, Mark	5. 9	–	Chatham	19.10.81
Forwards				
McCammon, Mark	6. 3	Charlton Athletic	Barnet	7.08.78
O'Connor, Kevin	5.11	–	Blackburn	24.02.82
Peters, Mark	5. 8	Southampton	Frimley	4.10.83

BRISTOL CITY

Ground: Ashton Gate, Bristol BS3 2EJ.
Telephone: 0117 963 0630. **Clubcall:** 09068 121176. **Club nickname:** Robins.
First-choice colours: red shirts, shorts and stockings.

Main sponsor: DAS Legal Expenses Insurance. **Capacity for 2002-03:** 21,497.
Record attendance: 43,335 v Preston N.E. (F.A. Cup 5) 16 February 1935.

Name	Height ft. in.	Previous club	Birthplace	Birthdate
Goalkeepers				
Mercer, Billy	6. 1	Chesterfield	Liverpool	22.05.69
Phillips, Steve	6. 1	–	Bath	6.05.78
Stowell, Mike	6. 2	Wolves	Portsmouth	19.04.65
Defenders				
Amankwaah, Kevin	6. 1	–	Harrow	19.05.82
Bell, Michael	5. 8	Wycombe Wand.	Newcastle	15.11.71
Burnell, Joe	5. 9	–	Bristol	10.10.80
Carey, Louis	5.10	–	Bristol	20.01.77
Coles, Danny	6. 0	–	Bristol	30.10.81
Fortune, Clayton	5.11	–	Forest Gate	10.11.82
Hill, Matthew	5. 8	–	Bristol	26.03.81
Jones, Darren	6. 0	–	Newport	26.11.83
Lever, Mark	6. 1	Grimsby Town	Beverley	29.03.70
Millen, Keith	6. 2	Watford	Croydon	26.09.66
Woodman, Craig	5. 9	–	Tiverton	22.12.82
Midfielders				
Brown, Aaron	5.10	–	Bristol	14.03.80
Clist, Simon	5. 9	Tottenham	Bournemouth	13.06.81
Doherty, Thomas	5. 8	–	Bristol	17.03.79
Hulbert, Robin	5.10	Swindon Town	Plymouth	14.03.80
Murray, Scott	5. 8	Aston Villa	Aberdeen	26.05.74
Tinnion, Brian	6. 2	Bradford City	Durham	23.03.68
Forwards				
Beadle, Peter	6. 2	Notts Co.	Lambeth	13.05.72
Brown, Marvin	5. 8	–	Bristol	6.07.83
Correia, Albano	6. 0	–	Guinea Bissau	18.10.81
Matthews, Lee	6. 2	Leeds Utd.	Middlesbrough	6.01.79
Peacock, Lee	5. 9	Manchester City	Paisley	9.10.76
Roberts, Christian	5.10	Exeter City	Cardiff	22.10.79

CARDIFF CITY

Ground: Ninian Park, Sloper Road, Cardiff CF1 8SX.
Telephone: 02920 221001. **Club nickname:** Bluebirds.
First-choice colours: Royal blue and white shirts, shorts and stockings.
Main sponsor: Ken Thorne Group. **Capacity for 2002-03:** 21,500.
Record attendance: 61,566 Wales v England, 14 October, 1961. Club: 57,800 v Arsenal (Div. 1) 22 April, 1953.

Name	Height ft. in.	Previous club	Birthplace	Birthdate
Goalkeepers				
Alexander, Neil	6. 1	Livingston	Edinburgh	10.03.78
Kendall, Lee	5.10	Crystal Palace	Newport	8.01.81
Walton, Mark	6. 4	Brighton & H.A.	Merthyr Tydfil	1.06.69
Defenders				
Barker, Chris	6. 0	Barnsley	Sheffield	2.03.80
Bonner, Mark	5.10	Blackpool	Ormskirk	7.06.74
Evans, Kevin	6. 2	Leeds Utd.	Carmarthen	16.12.80
Gabbidon, Daniel	5.10	W.B.A.	Cwmbran	8.08.79
Hughes, David	6. 4	Shrewsbury Town	Wrexham	1.02.78
Jordan, Andrew	6. 1	Bristol City	Manchester	14.12.79
Prior, Spencer	6. 3	Manchester City	Southend	22.04.71
Simpkins, Mick	6. 0	Chesterfield	Sheffield	28.11.78
Weston, Rhys	6. 1	Arsenal	Kingston	27.10.80
Young, Scott	6. 1	–	Llwynpia	14.01.76

Midfielders

Boland, Willie	5. 9	Coventry City	Ennis	6.08.75
Jones, Gethin	5.11	Carmarthen	Llanbyther	8.08.81
Hamilton, Des	5.10	Newcastle Utd.	Bradford	15.08.76
Hughes, Ceri	5.10	Portsmouth	Pontypridd	26.02.71
Kavanagh, Graham	5.10	Stoke City	Dublin	2.12.73
Legg, Andrew	5. 8	Reading	Swansea	28.07.66
Maxwell, Layton	5. 8	Liverpool	Rhyl	3.10.79
Whalley, Gareth	5.10	Bradford City	Manchester	19.12.73

Forwards

Bowen, Jason	5. 7	Reading	Merthyr Tydfil	24.08.72
Campbell, Andy	6. 0	Middlesbrough	Middlesbrough	18.04.79
Collins, James	5.11	–	Newport	23.08.83
Earnshaw, Robert	5. 8	–	Zambia	6.04.81
Fortune-West, Leo	6. 3	Rotherham Utd.	Stratford	9.04.71
Gordon, Gavin	6. 3	Lincoln City	Manchester	29.06.79
Low, Josh	6. 1	Leyton Orient	Bristol	15.02.79
Nogan, Kurt	6. 1	Preston N.E.	Cardiff	9.09.70
Thorne, Peter	6. 0	Stoke City	Manchester	21.06.73

CHELTENHAM TOWN

Ground: Whaddon Road, Cheltenham GL52 5NA.
Telephone: 01242 573558. **Clubcall:** 09066 555833. **Club nickname:** Town.
First-choice colours: Red and white shirts; white shorts; red stockings.
Main Sponsor: Towergate Insurance. **Capacity for 2002-03:** 7,407.
Record attendance: 8,326 v Reading (F.A. Cup 1) 17 November, 1956.

Name	Height ft. in.	Previous club	Birthplace	Birthdate
Goalkeepers				
Book, Steve	6. 2	Forest Green Rov.	Bournemouth	7.07.69
Defenders				
Banks, Chris	6. 2	Bath City	Stone	22.11.65
Brough, John	6. 0	Hereford Utd.	Ilkeston	8.01.73
Duff, Michael	5.11	–	Belfast	11.01.78
Duff, Shane	6. 1	–	Wroughton	2.04.82
Griffin, Anthony	5.11	Bournemouth	Bournemouth	22.03.79
Hill, Keith	6. 1	Rochdale	Bolton	17.05.69
Howarth, Neil	6. 2	Macclesfield Town	Farnworth	15.11.71
Jones, Steve	5.11	Swansea City	Bristol	25.12.70
Victory, Jamie	5. 8	Bournemouth	London	14.11.75
Walker, Richard	5.11	Hereford Utd.	Derby	9.11.71
Midfielders				
Devaney, Martin	5.11	Coventry City	Cheltenham	1.06.80
Finnigan, John	5. 8	Lincoln City	Wakefield	20.03.76
Howells, Lee	5. 8	Brisbane Utd.	Freemantle	14.10.68
Milton, Russell	5.11	Dover Athletic	Folkestone	12.01.69
Williams, Lee	5. 7	Mansfield Town	Birmingham	3.02.73
Yates, Mark	6. 0	Kidderminster Harr.	Birmingham	24.01.70
Forwards				
Alsop, Julian	6. 4	Swansea City	Nuneaton	28.05.73
McAuley, Hugh	5.10	Leek Town	Plymouth	13.05.77
Naylor, Tony	5. 7	Port Vale	Manchester	29.03.68

CHESTERFIELD

Ground: Recreation Ground, Chesterfield S40 4SX.
Telephone: 01246 209765. **Clubcall:** 09068 555818. **Club nickname:** Spireites.
First-choice colours: Blue shirts; white shorts; blue stockings.
Main Sponsor: Gordon Lamb. **Capacity for 2002-03:** 6,897.
Record attendance: 30,698 v Newcastle Utd. (Div. 2) 7 April, 1939.

Name	Height ft. in.	Previous club	Birthplace	Birthdate
Goalkeepers				
Muggleton, Carl	6. 2	Cheltenham Town	Leicester	13.09.68
Richmond, Andy	6. 0	–	–	9.01.83
Defenders				
Blatherwick, Steve	6. 1	Burnley	Nottingham	20.09.73
Booty, Martyn	5.10	Southend Utd.	Leicester	30.05.71
Dawson, Kevin	6. 0	Nott'm. Forest	Northallerton	18.06.81
Payne, Steve	5.11	–	Castleford	1.08.75
Rowland, Keith	5.10	Q.P.R.	Portadown	1.09.71
Midfielders				
Brandon, Chris	5. 7	Torquay Utd.	Bradford	7.04.76
D'Auria, David	5.10	Hull City	Swansea	26.03.70
Davies, Gareth	6. 1	–	–	4.02.83
Ebdon, Marcus	5.10	Peterborough Utd.	Pontypool	17.10.70
Edwards, Rob	5. 9	Huddersfield Town	Middleton	23.02.70
Howson, Stuart	6. 1	Blackburn Rov.	Chorley	30.09.81
Innes, Mark	5.10	Oldham Athletic	Bellshill	27.09.78
Richardson, Lee	5.11	Huddersfield Town	Halifax	12.03.69
Rushbury, Andy	5.10	–	Carlisle	7.03.83
Forwards				
Allott, Mark	5.11	Oldham Athletic	Middleton	3.10.77
Burt, Jamie	5.10	Whitby Town	Blyth	29.09.79
Howard, Jonathan	5.11	Rotherham Utd.	Sheffield	7.10.71
Hurst, Glyn	5.10	Stockport Co.	Barnsley	17.01.76

COLCHESTER UNITED

Ground: Layer Road, Colchester CO2 7JJ.
Telephone: 01206 508800. **Clubcall:** 0906 5862345 **Club nickname:** U's.
First-choice-colours: Blue and white shirts; blue shorts, blue stockings.
Main sponsor: Tiptree. **Capacity for 2002-03:** 7,303.
Record attendance: 19,072 v Reading (F.A. Cup 1) 27 November, 1948.

Name	Height ft. in.	Previous club	Birthplace	Birthdate
Goalkeepers				
Brown, Simon	6. 2	Tottenham	Chelmsford	3.12.76
Williamson, Glenn	6. 0	–	Enfield	22.12.82
Defenders				
Dunne, Joe	5. 8	Dover Athletic	Dublin	25.05.73
Fitzgerald, Scott	6. 0	Millwall	Westminster	13.08.69
Hadrava, David	5.10	–	Newbury Park	26.02.83
Keith, Joey	5. 7	West Ham Utd.	Plaistow	1.10.78
White, Alan	6. 0	Luton Town	Darlington	22.03.76
Midfielders				
Bowry, Bobby	5. 9	Millwall	Croydon	19.05.71
Canham, Marc	5. 9	–	Wefburg, Ger.	11.09.82
Duguid, Karl	5.11	–	Hitchin	21.03.78
Gregory, David	5.11	Peterborough Utd.	Colchester	23.01.70
Izzet, Kemal	5. 8	Charlton Athletic	Whitechapel	29.09.80
Johnson, Gavin	5.11	Dunfermline	Stowmarked	10.10.70
Keeble, Chris	5.10	Ipswich Town	Colchester	17.09.78
Pinault, Thomas	5.11	Cannes	Grasse, Fra.	4.12.81
Stockwell, Micky	5. 9	Ipswich Town	Chelmsford	14.02.65
Forwards				
Chambers, Triston	5.10	–	Enfield	25.12.82
Coote, Adrian	6. 2	Norwich City	Great Yarmouth	30.09.78
McGleish, Scott	5. 9	Barnet	Barnet	10.02.74
Morgan, Dean	5.10	–	Enfield	3.10.83

| Opara, Lloyd | 5.11 | – | Enfield | 6.01.84 |
| Rapley, Kevin | 5. 9 | Notts Co. | Reading | 21.09.77 |

CREWE ALEXANDRA

Ground: Gresty Road, Crewe CW2 6EB.
Telephone: 01270 213014. **Clubcall:** 09068 121647. **Club nickname:** Railwaymen.
First-choice colours: Red shirts; white shorts; red stockings.
Main Sponsor: LC Charles. **Capacity for 2002-03:** 10,100.
Record attendance: 20,000 v Tottenham (F.A. Cup 4) 30 January,1960.

Name	Height ft. in.	Previous club	Birthplace	Birthdate
Goalkeepers				
Bankole, Ade	6. 3	Q.P.R.	Lagos	9.09.69
Ince, Clayton	6. 2	–	Trinidad	13.07.72
Defenders				
Foster, Stephen	5.11	–	Warrington	10.09.80
Liddle, Gareth	6. 0	–	Crewe	10.08.82
Macauley, Steve	6. 1	Fleetwood Town	Lytham	4.03.69
McCready, Chris	6. 0	–	Chester	5.07.81
Sodje, Efetobore	6. 2	Luton Town	Greenwich	5.10.72
Vaughan, David	5. 6	–	Rhuddlan	18.02.83
Walton, David	6. 2	Shrewsbury Town	Bellingham	10.04.73
Walker, Richard	6. 1	–	Stafford	17.09.80
Wright, David	5.11	–	Warrington	1.05.80
Midfielders				
Brammer, Dave	5.10	Port Vale	Bromborough	28.02.75
Charnock, Phil	5.10	Liverpool	Southport	14.02.75
Collins, Wayne	5.10	Fulham	Manchester	4.03.69
Lumsdon, Chris	5.10	Sunderland	Newcastle	15.12.79
Lunt, Kenny	5. 8	–	Runcorn	20.11.79
Rix, Ben	5.10	–	Wolverhampton	11.12.83
Street, Kevin	5. 9	–	Crewe	25.11.79
Sorvel, Neil	6. 0	Macclesfield Town	Whiston	2.03.73
Forwards				
Hulse, Rob	6. 0	–	Crewe	25.10.79
Jack, Rodney	5. 7	Torquay Utd.	St Vincent	28.09.72
Little, Colin	5. 9	Hyde Utd.	Wythenshaw	4.11.72

HUDDERSFIELD TOWN

Ground: McAlpine Stadium, Leeds Road, Huddersfield HD1 6PX.
Telephone: 01484 484100. **Clubcall:** 09068 121635. **Club nickname:** Terriers.
First-choice colours: Blue and white shirts; white shorts; white and blue stockings.
Main sponsor: Primetime Recruitment. **Capacity for 2002-03:** 24,554.
Record attendance: (Leeds Road) 67,037 v Arsenal (F.A. Cup 6) 27 February, 1932;
  (McAlpine Stadium) 23,678 v Liverpool (F.A. Cup 3) 12 December, 1999.

Name	Height ft. in.	Previous club	Birthplace	Birthdate
Goalkeepers				
Evans, Paul	6. 4	Jomo Cosmos	Newcastle, SA	16.09.73
Margetson, Martyn	6. 0	Southend Utd.	West Neath	8.09.71
Senior, Phil	5.11	–	Huddersfield	30.10.82
Defenders				
Clarke, Nathan	6. 2	–	Halifax	30.11.83
Dyson, John	6. 1	–	Mirfield	18.12.71
Evans, Gareth	6. 0	Leeds Utd.	Leeds	15.02.81
Heary, Thomas	5.10	Sheriff FC	Dublin	14.02.79
Jenkins, Steve	5.11	Swansea City	Merthyr Tydfil	16.07.72
Lucketti, Chris	6. 1	Bury	Littleborough	21.09.71

Name	Height ft. in.	Previous club	Birthplace	Birthdate
Moses, Ade	6. 0	Barnsley	Doncaster	4.05.75
Youds, Eddie	6. 2	Charlton Athletic	Liverpool	3.05.70
Midfielders				
Baldry, Simon	5.10	–	Huddersfield	12.02.78
Holland, Chris	6. 1	Birmingham City	Whalley	11.09.75
Irons, Kenny	5.10	Tranmere Rov.	Liverpool	4.11.70
Mattis, Dwayne	5.10	–	Huddersfield	31.07.81
Scott, Paul	5.11	–	Wakefield	5.11.79
Senior, Michael	5. 9	–	Huddersfield	3.03.81
Smith, Martin	5.11	Sheffield Utd.	Sunderland	13.11.74
Thorrington, John	5. 8	Manchester Utd.	Johannesburg	10.07.79
Forwards				
Booth, Andy	6. 1	Sheffield Wed.	Huddersfield	6.12.73
Brown, Nat	6. 2	–	Sheffield	15.06.81
Hay, Chris	6. 1	Swindon Town	Glasgow	28.08.74
Macari, Paul	5.10	Sheffield Utd.	Manchester	23.08.76
Schofield, Danny	5.10	Brodsworth	Doncaster	10.04.80

LUTON TOWN

Ground: Kenilworth Road, Maple Road, Luton LU4 8AW.
Telephone: 01582 411622. **Clubcall:** 09068 121123. **Club nickname:** Hatters.
First-choice colours: White, orange and black shirts; black, orange and white shorts; black and white stockings.
Main Sponsor: SKF (UK). **Capacity for 2002-03:** 9,975.
Record attendance: 30,069 v Blackpool (F.A. Cup 6) 4 March, 1959.

Name	Height ft. in.	Previous club	Birthplace	Birthdate
Goalkeepers				
Emberson, Carl	6. 1	Walsall	Epsom	13.07.73
Ovendale, Mark	6. 2	Bournemouth	Leicester	22.11.73
Defenders				
Bayliss, David	5.10	Rochdale	Liverpool	8.06.76
Boyce, Emmerson	5.11	–	Aylesbury	24.09.79
Coyne, Chris	6. 3	Dundee	Brisbane	28.12.78
Johnson, Marvin	6. 1	–	Wembley	29.10.68
Perrett, Russell	6. 3	Cardiff City	Barton-on-Sea	18.06.73
Midfielders				
Forbes, Adrian	5. 7	Norwich City	Greenford	23.01.79
Hillier, Ian	6. 0	Tottenham	Neath	26.12.79
Holmes, Peter	5.11	Sheffield Wed.	Bishop Auckland	18.11.80
Hughes, Paul	6. 0	Southampton	Hammersmith	19.04.76
Neilson, Alan	5.11	Grimsby Town	Wegburg, Ger.	26.09.72
Mansell, Lee	5.10	–	Gloucester	23.09.82
Nicholls, Kevin	5.11	Wigan Athletic	Newham	2.01.79
Robinson, Steve	5. 9	Preston N.E.	Lisburn	10.12.74
Skelton, Aaron	5.10	Colchester Utd.	Welwyn GC	22.11.74
Spring, Matthew	5.11	–	Harlow	17.11.79
Standen, Dean	5.10	Welling Utd.	London	23.03.82
Forwards				
Berkovic, Ahmet	5. 7	Leyton Orient	Dubrovnic	23.09.74
Crowe, Dean	5. 5	Stoke City	Stockport	6.06.79
Douglas, Stuart	5. 8	–	Enfield	9.04.78
Fotiadis, Andrew	5.11	–	Hitchin	6.09.77
Griffiths, Carl	5.10	Leyton Orient	Oswestry	15.07.71
Howard, Steve	6. 2	Northampton Town	Durham	10.05.76
Thorpe, Tony	5. 9	Bristol City	Leicester	10.04.74
Valois, Jean-Louis	5.11	Lille	France	15.10.73

MANSFIELD TOWN

Ground: Field Mill, Quarry Lane, Mansfield NG18 5DA.
Telephone: 01623 623567. **Club nickname:** Stags.
First-choice colours: Amber and royal blue shirts; amber shorts; amber and blue stockings.
Main sponsor: Vodka Kick. **Capacity for 2002-03:** 10,000.
Record attendance: 24,467 v Nott'm. Forest (F.A. Cup 3) 10 January, 1953.

Name	Height ft. in.	Previous club	Birthplace	Birthdate
Goalkeepers				
Bingham, Michael	6. 0	Blackburn Rov.	Preston	25.05.81
Pilkington, Kevin	6. 1	Port Vale	Hitchin	8.03.74
Defenders				
Jervis, David	5. 8	–	Worksop	18.01.82
Robinson, Les	5. 9	Oxford Utd.	Shirebrook	1.03.67
Reddington, Stuart		Chelsea	Lincoln	21.02.78
Scott, Dion	5.11	–	Birmingham	24.12.80
Tankard, Allen	5.10	Port Vale	Islington	21.05.69
Midfielders				
Corden, Wayne	5. 9	Port Vale	Leek	1.11.75
Disley, Craig	5. 9	–	Worksop	24.08.81
Hassell, Bobby	5. 9	–	Derby	4.06.80
Lawrence, Liam	5. 9	–	Worksop	14.12.81
Sellars, Scott	5. 8	Huddersfield Town	Sheffield	27.11.65
Sisson, Michael	5. 9	–	Sutton-in-Ashfield	24.11.78
Williamson, Lee	5. 9	–	Derby	7.06.82
Forwards				
Bacon, Danny	5. 9	–	Mansfield	20.09.80
Bradley, Shayne	5.11	Southampton	Gloucester	8.12.79
White, Andy	6. 4	–	Derby	6.11.81

NORTHAMPTON TOWN

Ground: Sixfields Stadium, Upton Way, Northampton NN5 5QA.
Telephone: 01604 757773. **Club nickname:** Cobblers.
First-choice colours: Claret and white shirts; white shorts; claret stockings.
Main sponsor: Nationwide. **Capacity for 2002-03:** 7,653.
Record attendance: (County Ground) 24,523 v Fulham (Div. 1) 23 April, 1966.
(Sixfields Stadium) 7,557 v Manchester City (Div. 2) 26 September, 1998.

Name	Height ft. in.	Previous club	Birthplace	Birthdate
Goalkeepers				
Harper, Lee	6. 1	Walsall	Chelsea	30.10.71
Welch, Keith	6. 2	Bristol City	Bolton	3.10.68
Defenders				
Burgess, Daryl	5.11	W.B.A.	Birmingham	24.01.68
Hope, Richard	6. 2	Darlington	Stockton	22.06.78
Lavin, Gerard	5.10	Bristol City	Corby	5.02.74
Marsh, Chris	5.11	Wycombe Wand.	Sedgley	14.01.70
Sampson, Ian	6. 2	Sunderland	Wakefield	14.11.68
Spedding, Duncan	6. 1	Southampton	Frimley	7.09.77
Midfielders				
Frain, John	5. 9	Birmingham City	Birmingham	8.10.68
Hargreaves, Chris	5.11	Plymouth Argyle	Cleethorpes	12.05.72
Harsley, Paul	5.10	Halifax Town	Scunthorpe	29.05.78
Hunter, Roy	5.10	W.B.A.	Saltburn	29.10.73
Lincoln, Greg	5. 9	Arsenal	Cheshunt	23.03.80
Rickers, Paul	5.10	Oldham Athletic	Pontefract	9.05.75

Forwards

Name	Height	Previous club	Birthplace	Birthdate
Asamoah, Derek	5. 6	Slough Town	Ghana	1.05.81
Forrester, Jamie	5. 6	Walsall	Bradford	1.11.74
Gabbiadini, Marco	5.10	Darlington	Nottingham	20.01.68
McGregor, Paul	5.10	Plymouth Argyle	Liverpool	17.12.74
Stamp, Darryn	6. 2	Scarborough	Beverley	21.09.78

NOTTS COUNTY

Ground: Meadow Lane, Nottingham NG2 3HJ.
Telephone: 0115 952 9000. **Clubcall:** 09068 443131. **Club nickname:** Magpies.
First-choice colours: Black and white shirts; black shorts; black stockings.
Main sponsor: Aaron Scargill. **Capacity for 2002-03:** 20,300.
Record attendance: 47,310 v York City (F.A. Cup 6) 12 March, 1955.

Name	Height ft. in.	Previous club	Birthplace	Birthdate
Goalkeepers				
Deeney, Saul	6. 1	–	Derry	12.03.83
Mildenhall, Steve	6. 5	Swindon Town	Swindon	13.05.78
Defenders				
Baraclough, Ian	6. 1	Q.P.R	Leicester	4.12.70
Cas, Marcel	5.11	Roosendaal	Holland	30.04.72
Fenton, Nick	6. 1	Manchester City	Preston	23.11.79
Holmes, Richard	5.10	–	Grantham	7.11.80
Ireland, Craig	6. 2	Dundee	Dundee	29.11.75
Liburd, Richard	5. 9	Carlisle Utd.	Nottingham	26.09.73
Richardson, Ian	6. 0	Birmingham City	Barking	22.10.70
Riley, Paul	5. 9	–	Nottingham	29.09.82
Midfielders				
Bolland, Paul	5.11	Bradford City	Bradford	23.12.79
Brough, Michael	6. 0	–	Nottingham	1.08.81
Caskey, Darren	5. 8	Reading	Basildon	21.08.74
Hughes, Andrew	5.11	Oldham Athletic	Manchester	2.01.78
Nicholson, Kevin	5. 9	Notts Co.	Derby	2.10.80
Forwards				
Allsopp, Danny	6. 0	Manchester City	Melbourne	10.08.78
Hackworth, Tony	6. 1	Leeds Utd.	Durham	19.05.80
Heffernan, Paul	5.10	Newtown	Dublin	29.12.81
Stallard, Mark	6. 0	Wycombe Wand.	Derby	24.10.74

OLDHAM ATHLETIC

Ground: Boundary Park, Oldham OL1 2PA.
Telephone: 0161 624 4972. **Clubcall:** 09068 121142. **Club nickname:** Latics.
First-choice colours: Blue and white shirts, shorts and stockings.
Main sponsor: Torex Foundation. **Capacity for 2002-03:** 13,700.
Record attendance: 47,761 v Sheffield Wed. (F.A. Cup 4) 25 January, 1930.

Name	Height ft. in.	Previous club	Birthplace	Birthdate
Goalkeepers				
Kelly, Gary	5.11	Bury	Fulwood	3.08.66
Miskelly, David	6. 0	–	Newtonards	3.09.79
Pogliacomi, Leslie	6. 5	–	Australia	3.05.76
Defenders				
Armstrong, Chris	5. 9	Bury	Newcastle	5.08.82
Balmer, Stuart	6. 1	Wigan Athletic	Falkirk	20.09.69
Baudet, Julien	6. 2	Toulouse	St Martin, Fra.	13.01.79
Beharall, David	6. 2	Newcastle Utd.	Newcastle	8.03.79
Clegg, Michael	5. 8	Manchester Utd.	Ashton-under-Lyne	3.07.77
Garnett, Shaun	6. 2	Swansea City	Wallasey	22.11.69

Name	Height ft. in.	Previous club	Birthplace	Birthdate
Graham, Richard	6. 2	–	Dewsbury	28.11.74
Haining, Will	5.11	–	Glasgow	2.10.82
Hall, Fitz	6. 4	Chesham Utd.	Walthamstow	20.12.80
Hill, Clint	6. 0	Tranmere Rov.	Liverpool	19.10.78
Holden, Dean	6. 0	Bolton Wand.	Salford	15.09.79
Midfielders				
Appleby, Matty	5.10	Barnsley	Middlesbrough	16.04.72
Boshell, Danny	5.10	–	Bradford	30.05.81
Carss, Tony	5.11	Carlisle Utd.	Alnwick	31.03.76
Duxbury, Lee	5.10	Bradford City	Keighley	7.10.69
Gill, Wayne	5. 6	Tranmere Rov.	Chorley	28.11.75
Murray, Paul	5. 8	Southampton	Carlisle	31.08.76
Sheridan, Darren	5. 6	Wigan Athletic	Manchester	8.12.67
Sheridan, John	5.10	Bolton Wand.	Stretford	1.10.64
Smith, Ben	5. 8	–	Oldham	25.08.82
Forwards				
Andrews, Wayne	5.10	Chesham Utd.	Paddington	25.11.77
Clegg, George	5.10	Manchester Utd.	Manchester	16.11.80
Corazzin, Carlo	5.10	Northampton Town	Canada	25.12.71
Eyre, John	6. 0	Hull City	Hull	9.10.74
Eyres, David	5.11	Preston N.E.	Liverpool	26.02.64
Reeves, David	6. 0	Chesterfield	Birkenhead	19.11.67

PETERBOROUGH UNITED

Ground: London Road, Peterborough PE2 8AL.
Telephone: 01733 563947. **Clubcall:** 09068 121654. **Club nickname:** Posh.
First-choice colours: Royal blue shirts; white shorts; blue stockings. **Capacity for 2002-03:** 14,330.
Record attendance: 30,096 v Swansea City (F.A. Cup 5) 20 February, 1965.

Name	Height ft. in.	Previous club	Birthplace	Birthdate
Goalkeepers				
Connor, Daniel	6. 2	–	Dublin	31.01.81
Tyler, Mark	5.11	–	Norwich	2.04.77
Defenders				
Edwards, Andy	6. 2	Birmingham City	Epping	17.09.71
Jelleyman, Gareth	5.10	–	Holywell	14.11.80
Joseph, Marc	6. 0	Cambridge Utd.	Leicester	10.11.76
Laurie, Steve	5.10	West Ham Utd.	Melbourne	30.10.82
MacDonald, Gary	6. 1	Havant & W'ville	Iselone, Ger.	25.10.79
Murray, Daniel	6. 2	–	Kettering	16.05.82
Newton, Adam	5.10	West Ham Utd.	Ascot	14.12.80
Pearce, Dennis	5.10	Notts Co.	Wolverhampton	10.09.74
Rae, Simon	6. 1	Birmingham City	Coventry	20.09.76
Midfielders				
Bullard, Jimmy	5.10	West Ham Utd.	Newham	23.10.78
Cullen, Jon	6. 0	Sheffield Utd.	Durham	10.01.73
Danielsson, Helgi	5.11	Reykjavik	Fylkir, Ice.	13.07.81
Forsyth, Richard	5.11	Blackpool	Dudley	3.10.70
French, Daniel	5.11	–	Peterborough	25.11.79
Gill, Matthew	6. 0	–	Cambridge	8.11.80
Oldfield, David	6. 0	Stoke City	Perth	30.05.68
Shields, Tony	5. 7	–	Londonderry	4.06.80
Forwards				
Clarke, Andy	5.10	Wimbledon	Islington	22.07.67
Clarke, Lee	5.11	Yaxley	Peterborough	28.07.83
Farrell, David	5. 9	Wycombe Wand.	Birmingham	11.11.71
Fenn, Neale	5.11	Tottenham	Edmonton	18.01.77
Forinton, Howard	5.11	Birmingham City	Boston	18.09.75
Green, Francis	5.11	Ilkeston Town	Derby	23.04.80

| Lee, Jason | 6. 3 | Chesterfield | Newham | 9.05.71 |
| McKenzie, Leon | 5.10 | Crystal Palace | Croydon | 17.05.78 |

PLYMOUTH ARGYLE

Ground: Home Park, Plymouth PL2 3DQ.
Telephone: 01752 562561. **Clubcall:** 0906 7090090 **Club nickname:** Pilgrims.
First-choice colours: Green shirts, shorts and stockings.
Main Sponsor: Ginsters. **Capacity for 2002-03:** 20,134.
Record attendance: 42,684 v Aston Villa (Div. 2) 10 October, 1936.

Name	Height ft. in.	Previous club	Birthplace	Birthdate
Goalkeepers				
Larrieu, Romain	6. 2	Valence	Mont de Marsan, Fra.	31.08.76
Defenders				
Adams, Steve	6. 0	–	Plymouth	25.09.80
Coughlan, Graham	6. 2	Livingston	Dublin	18.11.74
Taylor, Craig	6. 1	Swindon Town	Plymouth	24.01.74
Worrell, David	5.11	Dundee Utd.	Dublin	12.01.78
Wotton, Paul	5.11	–	Plymouth	17.08.77
Midfielders				
Bent, Jason	5. 9	Colorado Rapids	Toronto	8.03.77
Beresford, David	5. 5	Hull City	Middleton	11.11.76
Friio, David	5.10	Valence	Thionville, Fra.	17.02.73
Hodges, Lee	6. 0	Reading	Epping	4.09.73
Leadbitter, Chris	5. 9	Torquay Utd.	Middlesbrough	17.10.67
McGlinchey, Brian	5. 7	Gillingham	Derry	26.10.77
Morrison-Hill, Jamie	5. 8	–	Plymouth	8.06.81
Sturrock, Blair	5.10	Dundee Utd.	Dundee	25.08.81
Wills, Kevin	5. 7	–	Torquay	15.10.80
Forwards				
Evans, Mickey	6. 0	Bristol Rov.	Plymouth	1.01.73
Gritton, Martin	6. 1	Porthleven	Glasgow	1.06.78
Heaney, Neil	5.10	Dundee Utd.	Middlesbrough	3.11.71
Lowndes, Nathan	5.11	Livingston	Salford	6.02.77
Phillips, Martin	5. 9	Portsmouth	Exeter	13.03.76
Stonebridge, Ian	6. 0	–	London	30.08.81

PORT VALE

Ground: Vale Park, Hamil Road, Burslem, Stoke-on-Trent ST6 1AW.
Telephone: 01782 814134. **Club nickname:** Valiants.
First-choice colours: White shirts, shorts and stockings.
Main sponsor: Tunstall Assurance. **Capacity for 2002-03:** 18,982.
Record attendance: 50,000 v Aston Villa (F.A. Cup 5) 20 February, 1960.

Name	Height ft. in.	Previous club	Birthplace	Birthdate
Goalkeepers				
Delaney, Dean	6. 0	Everton	Dublin	15.09.80
Goodlad, Mark	6. 0	Nott'm. Forest	Barnsley	9.09.80
Defenders				
Burns, Liam	5.11	–	Belfast	30.10.78
Burton, Sagi	6. 2	Sheffield Utd.	Birmingham	25.11.77
Carragher, Matthew	5. 9	Wigan Athletic	Liverpool	14.01.76
Collins, Sam	6. 3	Bury	Pontefract	6.06.77
Donnelly, Paul	5.11	–	Staffordshire	16.02.81
Hardy, Phil	5. 7	Wrexham	Chester	9.04.73
Ingram, Rae	5.11	Macclesfield Town	Manchester	6.12.74
Rowland, Steve	5.10	–	Wrexham	2.11.81

| Walsh, Michael | 6. 0 | Scunthorpe Utd. | Rotherham | 5.08.77 |

Midfielders

Boyd, Mark	5. 9	Newcastle Utd.	Carlisle	22.10.81
Bridge-Wilkinson, Marc	5. 6	Derby Co.	Nuneaton	16.03.79
Brisco, Neil	6. 0	Manchester City	Billinge	26.01.78
Byrne, Paul	5. 9	–	Newcastle, SA	26.11.82
Cummins, Michael	6. 0	Middlesbrough	Dublin	1.06.78
Dodd, Ashley	5.10	Manchester Utd.	Stafford	7.01.82
Gibson, Alex	5. 9	Stoke City	Stafford	12.08.82
McClare, Sean	5.11	Barnsley	Rotherham	12.01.78
McPhee, Stephen	5. 7	Coventry City	Glasgow	5.06.81
Simpson, Ben	5. 8	–	Liverpool	30.12.81
Taylor, Paul	5.11	–	Stoke City	16.09.80

Forwards

Armstrong, Ian	5.11	Liverpool	Fazackerley	16.11.81
Brooker, Steve	5.10	Watford	Newport Pagnell	21.05.81
Durnin, John	5.10	Kidderminster Harr.	Bootle	18.08.65
Paynter, Billy	6. 0	–	Liverpool	13.07.84

QUEENS PARK RANGERS

Ground: Loftus Road Stadium, South Africa Road, London W12 7PA.
Telephone: 0208 743 0262. **Clubcall:** 09068 121162. **Club nickname:** Hoops.
First-choice colours: Blue and white shirts; white shorts; white stockings.
Main sponsor: JD Sports. **Capacity for 2002-03:** 19,001.
Record attendance: 35,353 v Leeds Utd. (Div. 1) 27 April, 1974.

Name	Height ft. in.	Previous club	Birthplace	Birthdate
Goalkeepers				
Culkin, Nick	6. 2	Manchester Utd.	York	6.07.78
Day, Chris	6. 3	Watford	Walthamstow	28.07.75
Digby, Fraser	6. 1	Swindon Town	Sheffield	23.01.67
Defenders				
Ben Askar, Aziz	6. 0	Lavallois	Gontier, Fra.	30.03.76
Bignot, Marcus	5.10	Bristol Rov.	Birmingham	22.08.74
Carlisle, Clarke	6. 1	Blackpool	Preston	14.10.79
Duncan, Lyndon	5. 9	–	Ealing	12.01.83
Forbes, Terrell	5.10	West Ham Utd.	London	17.08.81
Murphy, Danny	5. 6	–	London	4.12.82
Padula, Gino	5.10	Wigan Athletic	Argentina	–
Palmer, Steve	6. 1	Watford	Brighton	31.03.68
Perry, Mark	5.11	–	Perivale	19.10.78
Plummer, Chris	6. 2	–	Isleworth	12.10.76
Rose, Matthew	5.11	Arsenal	Dartford	24.09.75
Shittu, Danny	6. 3	Charlton Athletic	Lagos	2.09.80
Midfielders				
Barr, Hamid	5.10	Fisher Athletic	Lewisham	29.09.76
Bircham, Marc	5.10	Millwall	Wembley	11.05.78
Bruce, Paul	5.11	–	Lambeth	18.02.78
Burgess, Oliver	5.11	–	Ascot	12.10.81
Cochrane, Justin	5.11	–	Hackney	26.01.82
Langley, Richard	5.10	–	London	27.12.79
Walshe, Ben	5.11	–	Hammersmith	24.05.83
Forwards				
Agogo, Junior	5.10	–	Accra	1.08.79
Connolly, Karl	5.10	Wrexham	Prescot	9.02.70
Doudou	5. 8	Monaco	Kinshasa	11.09.80
Fitzgerald, Brian	5. 9	–	Perivale	23.10.83
Gallen, Kevin	5.11	Barnsley	Hammersmith	21.09.75
Griffiths, Leroy	5.11	Hampton	London	30.12.76
Koejoe, Sammy	5. 9	SV Saltzburg	Surinam	2.12.69

| Pacquette, Richard | 6. 0 | – | Paddington | 28.01.83 |
| Thomson, Andy | 5.10 | Gillingham | Motherwell | 1.04.71 |

STOCKPORT COUNTY

Ground: Edgeley Park, Hardcastle Road, Edgeley, Stockport SK3 9DD.
Telephone: 0161 286 8888. **Clubcall:** 09068 121638. **Club nickname:** County.
First-choice colours: Royal blue shirts, shorts and stockings.
Main Sponsor: Scandia Lager. **Capacity for 2002-03:** 11,000.
Record attendance: 27,833 v Liverpool (F.A. Cup 5) 11 February, 1950.

Name	Height ft. in.	Previous club	Birthplace	Birthdate
Goalkeepers				
Jones, Lee	6. 3	Bristol Rov.	Pontypridd	9.08.70
Turner, Sam	6. 1	Charlton Athletic	Pontypool	9.09.80
Defenders				
Challinor, Dave	6. 1	Tranmere Rov.	Chester	2.10.75
Clark, Peter	6. 1	Carlisle Utd.	Romford	16.12.79
Goodwin, Jim	5. 9	Celtic	Waterford	20.11.81
Hancock, Glynn	6. 0	–	Biddulph	24.05.82
Hardiker, John	6. 0	Morecambe	Preston	7.07.82
Kielthy, Anthony	6. 0	–	Manchester	6.04.83
Thomas, Andrew	5. 8	–	Stockport	2.12.82
Midfielders				
Bennett, Tom	5.11	Wolves	Falkirk	12.12.69
Briggs, Keith	6. 0	–	Glossop	11.12.81
Clare, Robert	5.10	–	Belper	28.02.83
Eames, Haydn	5. 9	Manchester Utd.	Stockport	13.10.83
Elderton, Ryan	5.10	Preston N.E.	Morecambe	3.11.83
Gibb, Ali	5. 9	Northampton Town	Salisbury	17.02.76
Helin, Petri	–	Luton Town	Helsinki	14.12.69
Lambert, Rickie	5.10	Macclesfield Town	Liverpool	16.02.82
Lescott, Aaron	5. 8	Sheffield Wed.	Birmingham	2.12.78
McLachlan, Fraser	5.11	–	Manchester	9.11.82
Ogden, Michael	5.10	Bradford Park	Worsley	28.04.82
Palmer, Carlton	6. 3	Coventry City	Birmingham	5.12.65
Pemberton, Martin	5.11	Mansfield Town	Bradford	1.02.76
Forwards				
Beckett, Luke	5.11	Chesterfield	Sheffield	25.11.76
Byrne, Mark	5. 9	–	Billinge	8.05.83
Daly, Jon	6. 3	–	Dublin	8.01.83
Ellison, Kevin	5.11	Leicester City	Liverpool	23.02.79
Fradin, Karim	5.11	Nice	Hyeres, Fra.	2.02.72
Welsh, Andy	5. 8	–	Manchester	24.11.83
Wilbraham, Aaron	6. 3	–	Knutsford	21.10.79
Wild, Peter	5. 9	–	Stockport	12.10.82

SWINDON TOWN

Ground: County Ground, County Road, Swindon SN1 2ED.
Telephone: 01793 430430. **Club nickname:** Robins.
First-choice colours: Red shirts; white shorts; red stockings.
Main sponsor: Nationwide Building Society. **Capacity for 2002-03:** 15,500.
Record attendance: 32,000 v Arsenal (F.A. Cup 3) 15 January, 1972.

Name	Height ft. in.	Previous club	Birthplace	Birthdate
Goalkeepers				
Griemink, Bart	6. 4	Peterborough Utd.	Holland	29.03.72
Farr, Craig	6. 0	–	–	–

Defenders				
Cobian, Juan	5. 9	Aberdeen	Buenos Aires	11.09.75
Collins, Chris	–	–	–	–
Davies, Gareth	6. 1	Reading	Hereford	11.12.73
Gurney, Andy	5.11	Reading	Bristol	25.01.74
Heywood, Matthew	6. 3	Burnley	Chatham	26.08.79
Reeves, Alan	6. 0	Wimbledon	Birkenhead	19.11.67
Robinson, Mark	5. 9	Newcastle Utd.	Rochdale	21.11.68
Ruddock, Neil	6. 2	Crystal Palace	Wandsworth	9.05.68
Williams, James	5. 9		Liverpool	15.07.80
Willis, Adam	5.11	Coventry City	Nuneaton	21.09.76
Midfielders				
Duke, David	5.10	Sunderland	Inverness	7.11.78
Edwards, Nathan	5.11		Lincoln	8.04.83
Halliday, Kevin	5.11	–	Swindon	8.07.83
Hewlett, Matt	6. 2	Bristol City	Bristol	25.02.76
Howe, Bobby	5. 7	Nott'm. Forest	Newcastle	6.11.73
Invincible, Danny	6. 0	Marconi	Brisbane	31.03.79
O'Halloran, Keith	5. 9	St. Johnstone	Dublin	27.03.77
Robinson, Steve	5. 9	Birmingham City	Nottingham	17.10.75
Forwards				
Herring, Ian	–	–	–	–
Sabin, Eric	6. 1	Wasquehall	Sarcelles, Fra.	22.08.74
Young, Alan	5. 7	–	Swindon	12.08.83

TRANMERE ROVERS

Ground: Prenton Park, Prenton, Wirral CH42 9PY.
Telephone: 0151 608 4194. **Clubcall:** 09068 121646. **Club nickname:** Rovers.
First-choice colours: White and blue shirts, shorts and stockings.
Mian Sponsor: Wirral Borough Council. **Capacity for 2002-03:** 16,587.
Record attendance: 24,424 v Stoke City (F.A. Cup 4) 5 February, 1972.

Name	Height ft. in.	Previous club	Birthplace	Birthdate
Goalkeepers				
Achterberg, John	6. 1	PSV Eindhoven	Utrecht	8.07.71
Nixon, Eric	6. 4	Wigan Athletic	Manchester	4.10.62
Defenders				
Allen, Graham	6. 0	Everton	Bolton	8.04.77
Baker, Phil	5.11	–	Birkenhead	4.11.82
Gray, Kevin	6. 0	Huddersfield Town	Sheffield	7.01.72
Hinds, Richard	6. 2	–	Sheffield	22.08.80
Olsen, James	6. 2	Liverpool	Liverpool	23.10.81
Roberts, Gareth	5. 8	Panionios, Gre.	Wrexham	6.02.78
Taylor, Ryan	5. 8	–	Liverpool	19.08.84
Midfielders				
Flynn, Sean	5. 8	W.B.A.	Birmingham	13.03.68
Harrison, Danny	5.11	–	Liverpool	4.11.82
Koumas, Jason	5.10	–	Wrexham	25.09.79
Mellon, Micky	5.10	Burnley	Paisley	18.03.72
Navarro, Alan	5.10	Liverpool	Liverpool	31.05.81
Price, Jason	6. 2	Brentford	Pontypridd	12.04.77
Sharps, Ian	6. 3	–	Warrington	23.10.80
Forwards				
Barlow, Stuart	5.10	Wigan Athletic	Liverpool	16.07.68
Haworth, Simon	6. 1	Wigan Athletic	Cardiff	30.03.77
Hay, Alex	5.10	–	Birkenhead	14.10.83
Hume, Iain	5. 7	–	Edinburgh	30.10.83
Parkinson, Andy	5. 8	Liverpool	Liverpool	27.05.76

WIGAN ATHLETIC

Ground: JJB Stadium, Robin Park, Wigan WN5 0UZ.
Telephone: 01942 774000. **Clubcall:** 09068 121655. **Club nickname:** Latics.
First-choice colours: Blue, white and green shirts; blue and white shorts; white and blue stockings.
Main sponsor: JJB Sports. **Capacity for 2002-03:** 25,000.
Record attendance: (Springfield Park) 27,500 v Hereford Utd. (F.A. Cup 2) 12 December, 1953. (JJB Stadium) 15,993 v Preston N.E. (Div. 2) 4 April, 2000.

Name	Height ft. in.	Previous club	Birthplace	Birthdate
Goalkeepers				
Filan, John	5.11	Blackburn Rov.	Sydney	8.02.70
Kerr, Stewart	6. 2	Celtic	Bellshill	13.11.74
Defenders				
Breckin, Ian	6. 0	Chesterfield	Rotherham	24.02.75
Charnock, Kieron	5.11	–	Preston	3.08.84
De Vos, Jason	6. 0	Dundee Utd.	Ontario	2.01.74
Green, Scott	5.10	Bolton Wand.	Walsall	15.01.70
Jackson, Matt	6. 0	Norwich City	Leeds	19.10.71
McMillan, Steve	5. 8	Motherwell	Edinburgh	19.01.76
Mitchell, Paul	5. 9	–	Manchester	26.08.81
Nolan, Ian	6. 0	Bradford City	Liverpool	9.07.70
Pendlebury, Ian	6. 0	–	Bolton	3.09.83
Midfielders				
Brannan, Ged	6. 0	Motherwell	Prescot	15.01.72
Dinning, Tony	5.11	Wolves	Wallsend	4.12.75
Flynn, Michael	5.11	Barry Town	–	–
Jarrett, Jason	6. 0	Bury	Bury	14.09.79
Kennedy, Peter	5.10	Watford	Lisburn	10.09.73
Santus, Paul	5.10	–	Wigan	8.09.83
Teale, Gary	5.11	Ayr Utd.	Glasgow	21.07.78
Traynor, Greg	5.10	–	Salford	17.10.84
Forwards				
Ashcroft, Lee	5. 9	Grimsby Town	Preston	7.09.72
Liddell, Andy	5. 8	Barnsley	Leeds	28.06.73
McCulloch, Lee	6. 1	Motherwell	Bellshill	14.05.78
Roberts, Neil	5.10	Wrexham	Wrexham	7.04.78
Ellington, Nathan	5.10	Bristol Rov.	Bradford	2.07.81

WYCOMBE WANDERERS

Ground: Adams Park, Hillbottom Road, High Wycombe HP1 4HJ.
Telephone: 01494 472100. **Clubcall:** 09003 446855. **Club nickname:** Chairboys.
First-choice colours: Light and dark blue shirts; dark blue shorts; light blue stockings.
Main sponsor: Integrity Software. **Capacity for 2002-03:** 10,000.
Record attendance: 9,921 v Fulham (F.A. Cup 3) 8 January, 2002.

Name	Height ft. in.	Previous club	Birthplace	Birthdate
Goalkeepers				
Osborn, Mark	6. 0	–	Bletchley	19.06.81
Taylor, Martin	6. 0	Derby Co.	Tamworth	9.12.66
Defenders				
Johnson, Roger	6. 3	–	Ashford	28.04.83
McCarthy, Paul	5.10	Brighton & H.A.	Cork	4.08.71
Rogers, Mark	5.11	Vancouver	Guelph, Can.	3.11.78
Thomson, Andy	6. 3	Bristol Rov.	Swindon	28.03.74
Townsend, Ben	5.10	–	Reading	8.10.81
Vinnicombe, Chris	5. 9	Burnley	Exeter	20.10.70

Midfielders

Name	Height ft. in.	Previous club	Birthplace	Birthdate
Brown, Steve	5.10	Northampton Town	Northampton	6.07.66
Bulman Danny	5. 9	Ashford Town	Ashford	21.04.79
Currie, Darren	5. 9	Barnet	Hampstead	29.11.74
Harris, Richard	5.11	Crystal Palace	Croydon	23.10.80
Lee, Martyn	5. 6	–	Guildford	10.08.80
Ryan, Keith	5.10	Berkhamstead	Northampton	25.06.70
Simpson, Michael	5. 8	Notts Co.	Nottingham	28.02.74
Simpemba, Ian	5.11	–	Dublin	–

Forwards

Name	Height ft. in.	Previous club	Birthplace	Birthdate
Devine, Sean	5.11	Barnet	Lewisham	6.09.72
Faulconbridge, Craig	6. 1	Wrexham	Nuneaton	20.04.78
Holligan, Gavin	5.10	West Ham Utd.	Lambeth	30.06.80
McSporran, Jermaine	5.10	Oxford City	Manchester	1.01.77
Rammell, Andy	5.11	Walsall	Nuneaton	10.02.67
Senda, Danny	5.10	Southampton	Harrow	17.04.81

DIVISION THREE

AFC BOURNEMOUTH

Ground: Dean Court, Bournemouth BH7 7AF.
Telephone: 01202 395381. **Club nickname:** Cherries.
First-choice colours: Red and black shirts; black shorts; black stockings.
Main sponsor: Seward. **Capacity for 2002-03:** 8,525.
Record attendance: 28,799 v Manchester Utd. (F.A. Cup 6) 2 March, 1957.

Name	Height ft. in.	Previous club	Birthplace	Birthdate
Goalkeepers				
Menetrier, Michael	6. 3	Metz	Reims	23.08.78
Stewart, Gareth	6. 0	Blackburn Rov.	Preston	3.02.80
Defenders				
Bernard, Narada	5. 2	Arsenal	Bristol	30.01.81
Broadhurst, Karl	6. 1	–	Portsmouth	18.03.80
Maher, Shaun	6. 3	Bohemians	Dublin	10.06.78
Purches, Steve	5.11	West Ham Utd.	Ilford	14.01.80
Young, Neil	5. 9	Tottenham	Harlow	31.08.73
Midfielders				
Elliott, Wade	5. 9	Bashley	Southampton	14.12.78
Fletcher, Carl	5.10	–	Camberley	7.04.80
Grant, Peter	5.10	Reading	Glasgow	30.08.65
Thomas, Danny	5. 7	Leicester City	Leamington Spa	1.05.81
Tindall, Jason	6. 1	Charlton Athletic	Stepney	15.11.77
Stock, Brian	5.11	–	Winchester	24.12.81
Forwards				
Eribenne, Chuck	5.10	Coventry City	Westminster	2.11.80
Feeney, Warren	5.10	Leeds Utd.	Belfast	17.01.81
Fletcher, Steve	6. 2	Hartlepool Utd.	Hartlepool	26.06.72
Foyewa, Amos	5. 8	West Ham Utd.	Nigeria	26.12.81
Hayter, James	5. 9	–	Newport, IOW	9.04.79
Holmes, Derek	6. 2	Ross Co.	Scotland	11.10.78
O'Connor, Garreth	5. 7	Bohemians	Dublin	10.11.78

BOSTON UNITED

Ground: York Street, Boston, PE21 6HN.
Telephone: 01205 364406. **Clubcall:** 09068 121539. **Club nickname:** Pilgrims.

First-choice colours: Amber and black shirts; black and amber shorts; black and yellow socks.
Main sponsor: Finn Forest. **Capacity for 2002-03**: 6,643.

Name	Height ft. in.	Previous club	Birthplace	Birthdate
Goalkeepers				
Bastock, Paul	5.11	Kettering Town	Leamington Spa	19.05.70
Defenders				
Ellender, Paul	5.10	Scarborough	Scunthorpe	21.10.74
Monington, Mark	6. 1	Rochdale	Bilsthorpe	21.10.70
Rodwell, Jim	5.11	Rushden & Diamonds	Lincoln	20.11.70
Thompson, Neil	6. 0	Scarborough	Beverley	2.10.63
Warburton, Ray	6. 0	Rushden & Diamonds	Rotherham	7.10.67
Midfielders				
Clifford, Mark	5.10	Ilkeston Town	Nottingham	11.09.77
Costello, Peter	5.11	Kettering Town	Halifax	31.10.69
Gould, James	5. 9	Northampton Town	Rushden	15.01.82
Rusk, Simon	5.10	Cambridge Utd. City	–	17.12.81
Forwards				
Angel, Mark	5.10	Darlington	Newcastle	23.08.75
Clare, Daryl	5. 9	Grimsby Town	Jersey	1.08.78
Elding, Anthony	6. 0	–	Boston	16.04.82
Weatherstone, Simon	5.10	Oxford Utd.	Reading	26.01.80

● At time of going to press Boston United were appearing before F.A. for alleged financial irregularities.

BRISTOL ROVERS

Ground: Memorial Ground, Filton Avenue, Horfield, Bristol BS7 0AQ.
Telephone: 0117 977 2000. **Clubcall**: 09068 121131. **Club nickname**: Pirates.
First-choice colours: Blue and white shirts; white and blue shorts; blue stockings.
Main sponsor: Cowlin Contruction. **Capacity for 2002-03**: 11,916.
Record attendance: (Eastville) 38,472 v Preston N.E. (F.A. Cup 4) 30 January, 1960.
(Memorial Ground) 11,433 v Sunderland (League Cup 3) 31 October, 2000.

Name	Height ft. in.	Previous club	Birthplace	Birthdate
Goalkeepers				
Clarke, Ryan	6. 3	–	Bristol	30.04.82
Howie, Scott	6. 2	Reading	Motherwell	4.01.72
Defenders				
Andreasson, Marcus	6. 4	Osters	Liberia	13.07.78
Challis, Trevor	5. 8	Q.P.R.	Paddington	23.10.75
Foran, Mark	6. 3	Crewe Alexandra	Aldershot	30.10.73
Foster, Steve	6. 1	Mansfield Town	Mansfield	3.12.74
Jones, Scott	5.10	Barnsley	Sheffield	1.05.75
Smith, Mark	6. 0	–	Bristol	13.09.79
Trought, Michael	6. 2	–	Bristol	19.10.80
Uddin, Anwar	5.10	Sheffield Wed.	–	1.11.81
Midfielders				
Astafjevs, Vitalys	5.11	Skonto Riga	Riga, Lat.	3.04.71
Bryant, Simon	5. 8	–	Bristol	22.11.82
Carlisle, Wayne	6. 0	Crystal Palace	Lisburn	9.09.79
Hillier, David	5.10	Portsmouth	Blackheath	19.12.69
Hogg, Lewis	5.11	–	Bristol	13.09.82
Lopez, Carlos	5.10	Getafe	Madrid	–
Pritchard, David	5. 7	Telford	Wolverhampton	27.05.72
Plummer, Dwayne	5.11	Chesham Utd.	Bristol	12.05.78
Walters, Mark	5.10	Swindon Town	Birmingham	2.06.64
Wilson, Che	5.11	Norwich City	Ely	17.01.79

Forwards

Name	Height ft. in.	Previous club	Birthplace	Birthdate
Cameron, Martin	5.11	Alloa Athletic	Dunfermline	16.06.78
Ellis, Clinton	5.10	–	Ealing	7.07.77
Gall, Kevin	5. 9	Newcastle Utd.	Merthyr	4.02.82
Gilroy, David	5.11	–	–	23.12.82
McKeever, Mark	5.10	Sheffield Wed.	Londonderry	16.11.78
Ommel, Sergio	5.10	Reykjavik	Den Haag, Hol.	2.09.77
Richards, Justin	5.10	W.B.A.	West Bromwich	16.10.80
Tait, Paul	6. 1	Crewe Alexandra	Newcastle	24.10.74

BURY

Ground: Gigg Lane, Bury BL9 9HR.
Telephone: 0161 764 4881. **Clubcall:** 0900 809003. **Club nickname:** Shakers.
First-choice colours: White shirts; royal blue shorts; royal blue stockings.
Main Sponsor: Bury Metropolitan Council. **Capacity for 2002-03:** 11,576.
Record attendance: 35,000 v Bolton Wand. (F.A. Cup 3) 9 January, 1960.

Name	Height ft. in.	Previous club	Birthplace	Birthdate
Goalkeepers				
Garner, Glyn	6. 2	Llanelli	Pontypool	9.12.76
Kenny, Patrick	6. 1	Bradford City	Halifax	17.05.78
Rowe, Sebastian	6. 1	–	Manchester	18.08.84
Defenders				
Barrass, Matthew	5.11	–	Bury	28.02.80
Billy, Chris	5.11	Notts Co.	Huddersfield	2.01.73
Evans, Gary	5. 9	–	Doncaster	13.09.82
Hill, Nicky	5.11	–	Accrington	26.02.81
Nelson, Michael	6. 2	Bishop Auckland	Gateshead	15.03.82
Redmond, Steve	5.11	Oldham Athletic	Liverpool	2.11.67
Stuart, Jamie	5.10	Millwall	Southwark	15.10.76
Swailes, Danny	6. 3	–	Bolton	1.04.79
Tarsus, Edward	5. 9	Doncaster Rov.	Leeds	3.11.82
Unsworth, Lee	5.11	Crewe Alexandra	Eccles	25.02.73
Midfielders				
Connell, Lee	6. 0	–	Bury	24.02.69
Forrest, Martyn	5.10	–	Bury	2.01.79
Gunby, Steve	5.11	–	Boston	14.04.84
O'Shaughnessy, Paul	6. 4	–	Bury	3.10.81
Forwards				
Borley, David	5. 9	–	Newcastle	14.04.83
Clegg, George	5.10	Manchester Utd.	Manchester	16.11.80
Lawson, Ian	5.11	Stockport Co.	Huddersfield	4.11.77
Newby, Jon	6. 0	Liverpool	Warrington	28.11.78
Preece, Andy	6. 1	Blackpool	Evesham	27.03.67

CAMBRIDGE UNITED

Ground: Abbey Stadium, Newmarket Road, Cambridge CB5 8LN.
Telephone: 01223 566500. **Clubcall:** 09068 555885. **Club nickname:** U's.
First-choice colours: Amber and black shirts; black shorts; black and amber stockings.
Main sponsor: Quicksilver/Kershaw. **Capacity for 2002-03:** 9,007.
Record attendance: 14,000 v Chelsea (Friendly) 1 May, 1970.

Name	Height ft. in.	Previous club	Birthplace	Birthdate
Goalkeepers				
Marshall, Shaun	6. 1	–	Fakenham	3.10.78
Perez, Lionel	5.11	Newcastle Utd.	Bagnols Coze, Fra.	24.04.67
Thornton, Rob	5.11	–	Bedford	21.11.83

Defenders

Angus, Stevland	5.11	West Ham Utd.	Essex	16.09.80
Butterworth, Adam	6. 1	Torquay Utd.	Paignton	9.08.82
Cowan, Tom	5. 9	Burnley	Bellshill	28.08.69
Duncan, Andy	5.11	Manchester Utd.	Hexham	20.10.77
Goodhind, Warren	5.11	Barnet	Johannesburg	16.08.77
McNeil, Martin	6. 1	–	Rutherglen	28.09.80
Murray, Fred	5.10	Blackburn Rov.	Tipperary	22.05.82
Nacca, Francesco	5. 6	–	Valencia	9.11.81
Rush, Graham	5.11	–	Cambridge	8.09.82
Tann, Adam	6. 1	–	Fakenham	12.05.82
Warner, Phil	5.10	Southampton	Southampton	2.02.79

Midfielders

Bridges, David	6. 0	–	Huntingdon	22.09.82
Fleming, Terry	5. 9	Plymouth Argyle	Birmingham	5.01.73
Guttridge, Luke	5. 5	Torquay Utd.	Barnstaple	27.03.82
Mustoe, Neil	5. 9	Wigan Athletic	Gloucester	5.11.76
Prokas, Richard	5. 9	Carlisle Utd.	Penrith	22.01.76
Scully, Tony	5. 7	Q.P.R.	Dublin	12.06.76
Tudor, Shane	5. 7	Wolves	Wolverhampton	10.02.82
Wanless, Paul	6. 1	Lincoln City	Banbury	14.12.73

Forwards

Alcide, Colin	6. 2	York City	Huddersfield	14.04.72
Chillingworth, Daniel	6. 0	–	Cambridge	13.09.81
Kitson, David	6. 3	Arlesey Town	Hitchin	21.01.80
One, Armand	6. 4	Nantes	Paris	15.03.83
Revell, Alex	6. 3	–	Cambridge	7.07.83
Traore, Demba	6. 2	–	Stockholm	22.04.82
Youngs, Tom	5. 9	–	Bury St Edmunds	31.08.79

CARLISLE UNITED

Ground: Brunton Park, Warwick Road, Carlisle CA1 1LL.
Telephone: 01228 526237. **Club nickname:** Cumbrians.
First-choice colours: Blue shirts; blue shorts; blue stockings.
Main sponsor: Eddie Stobart. **Capacity for 2002-03:** 13,481.
Record attendance: 27,500 v Birmingham City (F.A. Cup 3) 5 January, 1957, and v Middlesbrough (F.A. Cup 5) 7 January, 1970.

Name	Height ft. in.	Previous club	Birthplace	Birthdate
Goalkeepers				
Weaver, Luke	6. 3	Sunderland	Woolwich	26.06.79
Defenders				
Andrews, Lee	6. 0	–	Carlisle	23.04.83
Birch, Mark	5.10	Northwich Victoria	Stoke	5.01.77
Dickinson, Mike	5.11	–	Newcastle	4.05.84
Maddison, Lee	5.11	Dundee	Bristol	5.10.72
May, Kyle	6. 0	–	Carlisle	7.09.82
McDonagh, Will	6. 1	Bohemians	Dublin	14.03.83
Thwaites, Adam	6. 0	–	Carlisle	8.12.81
Whitehead, Stuart	6. 0	Bolton Wand.	Bromsgrove	17.07.76
Midfielders				
Bell, Stuart	5.10	–	Carlisle	15.03.84
Galloway, Mick	5.11	Chesterfield	Nottingham	13.10.74
Murphy, Peter	5.11	Blackburn Rov.	Dublin	27.10.80
Slaven, John	5.11	–	Edinburgh	8.10.85
Thurston, Mark	6. 2	–	Carlisle	10.02.80
Forwards				
Foran, Richie	6. 1	Shelbourne	Dublin	16.06.80
Nixon, Marc	5.11	–	Hexham	19.01.84
Wake, Brian	5.10	Tow Law Town	–	–

DARLINGTON

Ground: Feethams, Darlington DL1 5JB.
Telephone: 01325 240240. **Club nickname:** Quakers.
First-choice colours: White shirts; black shorts; white stockings.
Main sponsor: Darlington Building Society. **Capacity for 2002-03:** 8,383.
Record attendance: 21,023 v Bolton Wand. (League Cup 3) 14 November, 1960.

Name	Height ft. in.	Previous club	Birthplace	Birthdate
Goalkeepers				
Collett, Andy	6. 0	Bristol Rov.	Middlesbrough	28.10.73
Finch, Keith	5.11	–	Easington	6.05.82
Porter, Chris	6. 2	Southend Utd.	Middlesbrough	10.11.79
Defenders				
Betts, Simon	5.11	–	Middlesbrough	3.03.73
Brightwell, David	6. 2	Hull City	Lutterworth	7.01.71
Brumwell, Phil	5. 8	Hull City	Darlington	8.08.75
Clarke, Matthew	6. 3	Halifax Town	Leeds	18.12.80
Ford, Mark	5. 8	Torquay Utd.	Pontefract	10.10.75
Harper, Steve	5.10	Hull City	Newcastle-u-Lyme	3.02.69
Liddle, Craig	5.11	Middlesbrough	Chester-le-Street	21.10.71
McGurk, David	5.11	–	Middlesbrough	30.09.82
Naylor, Glenn	5.10	York City	York	11.08.72
Reed, Adam	6. 0	Blackburn Rov.	Darlington	18.02.75
Midfielders				
Atkinson, Brian	5. 9	Sunderland	Darlington	19.01.71
Campbell, Paul	6. 1	–	Middlesbrough	29.01.80
Clark, Ian	5.11	Hartlepool Utd.	Stockton	23.10.74
Hodgson, Richard	5.10	Scunthorpe Utd.	Sunderland	1.10.79
Keltie, Clark	6. 1	–	Newcastle	31.08.83
Kilty, Mark	6. 0	–	Sunderland	24.06.81
Pearson, Gary	5.10	Durham City	Easington	7.12.76
Maddison, Neil	5.10	Middlesbrough	Darlington	2.10.69
Mellanby, Danny	5.10	Bishop Auckland	Bishop Auckland	17.07.79
Wainwright, Neil	6. 0	Sunderland	Warrington	4.11.77
Waller, Russell	5.11	Enfield City	Adelaide	6.02.84
Forwards				
Conlon, Barry	6. 2	York City	Drogheda	1.10.78
Convery, Mark	5. 6	Sunderland	Newcastle	29.05.81
Marcelle, Clint	5. 4	Hull City	Trinidad	9.11.68
Marsh, Adam	5.11	Worksop Town	Derby	20.02.82
Rundle, Adam	5.11	–	Durham	8.07.84
Sheeran, Mark	5.10	–	Newcastle	9.08.82

EXETER CITY

Ground: St James Park, Exeter EX4 6PX.
Telephone: 01392 254073. **Clubcall:** 0891 121634. **Club nickname:** Grecians.
First-choice colours: Red and white shirts; white shorts; red stockings.
Main sponsor: Jewson. **Capacity for 2002-03:** 6,000.
Record attendance: 20,894 v Sunderland (F.A. Cup 6) 4 March, 1931.

Name	Height ft. in.	Previous club	Birthplace	Birthdate
Goalkeepers				
Fraser, Stuart	6. 0	Stoke City	Cheltenham	1.08.78
Van Heusden, Arjan	6. 4	Cambridge Utd.	Alphen, Hol.	11.12.72
Defenders				
Burrows, Mark	6. 3	Coventry City	Kettering	14.08.80
Curran, Chris	5.11	Plymouth Argyle	Birmingham	17.09.71
Power, Graeme	5.11	Bristol Rov.	Harrow	7.03.77

Name	Height ft. in.	Previous club	Birthplace	Birthdate
McConnell, Barry	5.11	–	Exeter	1.01.77
Watson, Alex	5.11	Torquay Utd.	Liverpool	5.04.68
Whitworth, Neil	6. 2	Hull City	Wigan	12.04.72
Midfielders				
Ampadu, Kwame	5.10	Leyton Orient	Bradford	20.12.70
Barlow, Martin	5. 7	Plymouth Argyle	Barnstaple	25.06.71
Breslan, Geoff	5. 9	–	Torquay	8.04.80
Cronin, Glenn	5. 8	–	Dublin	14.09.81
Richardson, Jay	5. 9	Chelsea	Keston	14.11.79
Roscoe, Andy	5.10	Mansfield Town	Liverpool	4.06.73
Zabek, Lee	6. 0	Bristol Rov.	Bristol	13.10.78
Forwards				
Afful, Leslie	5. 4	–	Liverpool	4.02.84
Coppinger, James	5. 7	Newcastle Utd.	Middlesbrough	10.01.81
Flack, Steve	6. 1	Cardiff City	Cambridge	29.05.71
McCarthy, Sean	6. 1	Plymouth Argyle	Bridgend	12.09.67
Read, Paul	5.10	Luton Town	Harlow	25.09.73
Sheldon, Gareth	5.11	Scunthorpe Utd.	Birmingham	31.01.80
Tomlinson, Graeme	5.10	Macclesfield Town	Watford	10.12.75

HARTLEPOOL UNITED

Ground: Victoria Park, Clarence Road, Hartlepool TS24 8BZ.
Telephone: 01429 272584. **Club nickname:** Pool.
First-choice colours: Dark blue and white shirts; dark blue shorts; dark blue stockings.
Main Sponsor: DNO. **Capacity for 2002-03:** 7,222.
Record attendance: 17,426 v Manchester Utd. (F.A. Cup 3) 5 January, 1957.

Name	Height ft. in.	Previous club	Birthplace	Birthdate
Goalkeepers				
Hollund, Martin	6. 2	Brann Bergen	Stord, Nor.	11.08.74
Williams, Anthony	6. 1	Blackburn Rov.	Ogwr	20.09.77
Defenders				
Barron, Michael	5.11	Middlesbrough	Lumley	22.12.74
Bass, Jonathan	6. 0	Birmingham City	Weston-s-Mare	1.01.76
Lee, Graeme	6. 2	–	Middlesbrough	31.05.78
Robinson, Mark	5. 9	–	Guisborough	24.07.81
Sharp, James	6. 2	Andover Town	Reading	2.01.76
Westwood, Chris	5.11	Wolves	Dudley	13.02.77
Midfielders				
Arnison, Paul	5.10	Newcastle Utd.	Hartlepool	18.09.77
Clarke, Darrell	5.10	Mansfield Town	Mansfield	16.12.77
Simms, Gordon	6. 2	Wolves	Larne	23.03.81
Smith, Paul	6. 0	Burnley	Leeds	22.07.76
Stephenson, Paul	5.10	York City	Wallsend	2.01.68
Sweeney, Anthony	6. 0	–	Stockton	5.09.83
Tinkler, Mark	5.11	Southend Utd.	Bishop Auckland	24.10.74
Widdrington, Tommy	5. 9	Port Vale	Newcastle	1.10.71
Forwards				
Boyd, Adam	5. 9	–	Hartlepool	25.05.82
Easter, Jermaine	5. 9	Wolves	Cardiff	15.01.82
Henderson, Kevin	5.11	Burnley	Ashington	8.06.74
Humphreys, Richie	5.11	Cambridge Utd.	Sheffield	30.11.77
Lormor, Tony	6. 0	Mansfield Town	Ashington	29.10.70
Watson, Gordon	5.10	Bradford City	Sidcup	20.03.71
Williams, Eifion	5.11	Torquay Utd.	Bangor	15.11.75

HULL CITY

Ground: Boothferry Park, Hull HU4 6EU.
Telephone: 01482 575263. **Clubcall:** 09068 888688. **Club nickname:** Tigers.

First-choice colours: Amber and black shirts; black and amber shorts; amber and black stockings.
Main Sponsor: Bonus Electrical. **Capacity for 2002-03:** 15,756.
Record attendance: 55,019 v Manchester Utd. (F.A. Cup 6) 28 February, 1949.

Name	Height ft. in.	Previous club	Birthplace	Birthdate
Goalkeepers				
Glennon, Matthew	6. 2	Bolton Wand.	Stockport	8.10.78
Musselwhite, Paul	6. 2	Port Vale	Portsmouth	22.12.68
Defenders				
Bloomer, Matthew	6. 1	Grimsby Town	Cleethorpes	30.11.78
Edwards, Mike	6. 0	–	North Ferriby	25.04.80
Goodison, Ian	6. 3	Olympic Gdns.	Kingston, Jam.	21.11.72
Greaves, Mark	6. 1	Brigg Town	Hull	22.01.75
Holt, Andy	6. 1	Oldham Athletic	Stockport	21.05.78
Mohan, Nicky	6. 1	Stoke City	Middlesbrough	6.10.70
Petty, Ben	6. 0	Stoke City	Birmingham	22.03.77
Price, Michael	5. 9	Everton	Wrexham	29.04.82
Smith, Shaun	5.10	Crewe Alexandra	Leeds	9.04.71
Strong, Greg	6. 2	Motherwell	Bolton	5.09.75
Whittle, Justin	6. 1	Stoke City	Derby	18.03.71
Wicks, Matthew	6. 2	Brighton & H.A.	Reading	8.09.78
Midfielders				
Appleby, Richie	5. 8	Kidderminster Harr.	Middlesbrough	18.09.75
Ashbee, Ian	6. 0	Cambridge Utd.	Birmingham	6.09.76
Beresford, David	5. 5	Huddersfield Town	Middleton	11.11.76
Bradshaw, Gary	5. 6	–	Hull City	30.12.82
Caceres, Adrian	5.10	Southampton	Buenos Aires	10.01.82
Elliott, Stuart	6. 0	Motherwell		
Kerr, Scott	5. 9	Bradford City	Leeds	11.12.81
Mann, Neil	5.10	Grantham Town	Nottingham	19.11.72
Morley, Ben	5. 9	–	Hull	22.12.80
Philpott, Lee	5.10	Lincoln City	Barnet	21.02.70
Williams, Ryan	5. 4	Chesterfield	Mansfield	31.08.78
Whitmore, Theodore	6. 2	Seba Utd.	Montego Bay, Jam.	5.08.72
Forwards				
Alexander, Gary	5.11	Swindon Town	Lambeth	15.08.79
Dudfield, Lawrie	6. 1	Leicester City	Southwark	7.05.80
Rowe, Rodney	5. 8	Gillingham	Huddersfield	30.07.75

KIDDERMINSTER HARRIERS

Ground: Aggborough Stadium, Hoo Road, Kidderminster DY10 1NB.
Telephone: 01562 823931. **Clubcall:** 09066 555815. **Club nickname:** Harriers.
First-choice colours: Red shirts, shorts and stockings.
Main sponsor: OGL Computer. **Capacity for 2001-02:** 6,229.
Record attendance: 9,155 v Hereford Utd. (F.A. Cup 1) 27 November, 1948.

Name	Height ft. in.	Previous club	Birthplace	Birthdate
Goalkeepers				
Brock, Stuart	6. 0	Aston Villa	Sandwell	29.09.76
Danby, John	6. 0	–	Stoke	20.09.83
Defenders				
Ayres, Lee	6. 1	–	Birmingham	28.08.82
Clarkson, Ian	5.11	Northampton Town	Solihull	4.12.70
Hinton, Craig	5.11	Birmingham City	Wolverhampton	26.11.77
Joy, Ian	5.10	Montrose	San Diego	14.07.81
Sall, Abdou	6. 4	Toulouse	Senegal	1.11.80
Shilton, Sam	5.11	Hartlepool Utd.	Nottingham	21.07.78
Smith, Adrian	5.10	Bromsgrove Rov.	Birmingham	11.08.73

Name	Height ft. in.	Previous club	Birthplace	Birthdate
Stamps, Scott	5.10	Colchester Utd.	Smethwick	20.03.75
Midfielders				
Blake, Mark	5.11	Mansfield Town	Nottingham	16.12.70
Bennett, Dean	5.10	Bromsgrove Rov.	Wolverhampton	13.12.77
Davies, Ben	5.10	Walsall	Birmingham	27.05.81
Doyle, Daire	5.10	Coventry City	Dublin	18.10.80
Ducros, Andy	5. 4	Nuneaton	Evesham	16.09.77
Faulds, Peter	5. 7	–	Birmingham	28.08.82
Parrish, Sean	5.10	Chesterfield	Wrexham	14.03.72
Webb, Paul	5. 9	Shrewsbury Town	Wolverhampton	30.11.67
Williams, Danny	6. 1	Wrexham	Wrexham	12.07.79
Forwards				
Broughton, Drewe	6. 3	Peterborough Utd.	Hitchin	25.10.78
Bird, Tony	5.10	Swansea City	Cardiff	1.09.74
Corbett, Andrew	6. 0	–	Worcester	20.02.82
Foster, Ian	5. 7	Barrow	Liverpool	11.11.76
Henriksen, Bo	5.10	Herfolge	Denmark	7.02.75

LEYTON ORIENT

Ground: Matchroom Stadium, Brisbane Road, London E10 5NE.
Telephone: 0208 926 1111. **Clubcall:** 09068 121150. **Club nickname:** O's.
First-choice colours: Red and white shirts; red shorts; white stockings.
Main Sponsor: Matchroom Sport. **Capacity for 2002-03:** 10,927.
Record attendance: 34,345 v West Ham Utd. (F.A. Cup 4) 25 January 1964.

Name	Height ft. in.	Previous club	Birthplace	Birthdate
Goalkeepers				
Barrett, Scott	5.11	Cambrdge Utd.	Ilkeston	2.04.63
Morris, Glenn	6. 0	–	Woolwich	20.12.83
Defenders				
Barnard, Donny	6. 0	–	Forest Gate	1.07.84
Harris, Andrew	5.10	Southend Utd.	Springs	26.02.77
Jones, Billy	6. 0	–	Gillingham	26.06.83
Joseph, Matthew	5. 7	Cambridge Utd.	Bethnal Green	30.09.72
Lockwood, Matthew	5. 9	Bristol Rov.	Rochford	17.10.76
McGhee, David	5.11	Brentford	Sussex	19.06.76
Smith, Dean	6. 0	Hereford Utd.	West Bromwich	19.03.71
Stephens, Kevin	5.10	–	Enfield	28.07.84
Midfielders				
Brazier, Matthew	5. 8	Cardiff City	Ilford	2.07.76
Canham, Scott	5. 7	Brentford	Newham	5.11.74
Downer, Simon	5.10	–	Romford	19.10.81
Hutchings, Carl	6. 0	Southend Utd.	Hammersmith	24.09.74
Martin, John	5. 5	–	Bethnal Green	15.07.81
Toner, Ciaran	6. 1	Tottenham	Craigavon	30.06.81
Forwards				
Fletcher, Gary	6. 0	Northwich Victoria	Liverpool	4.06.81
Forbes, Boniek	5.10	–	Guinea Bissau	30.09.83
Hatcher, Daniel	5.10	–	Newport, IOW	24.12.83
Ibehre, Jabo	6. 2	–	Islington	28.01.83
McLean, Aaron	5. 6	–	Hammersmith	25.05.83
Nugent, Kevin	6. 1	Cardiff City	Edmonton	10.04.69
Tate, Christopher	6. 0	Scarborough	York City	27.12.77
Thorpe, Lee	6. 0	Lincoln City	Wolverhampton	14.12.75
Watts, Steve	6. 1	Fisher Athletic	Lambeth	11.07.76

LINCOLN CITY

Ground: Sincil Bank, Lincoln LN5 8LD.
Telephone: 01522 880011. **Clubcall:** 09066 555900. **Club nickname:** Imps

First-choice colours: Red and white shirts; black shorts; red and white stockings.
Main sponsor: Alstom. Capacity for 2002-03: 10,200.
Record attendance: 23,196 v Derby Co. (League Cup 4) 15 November, 1967.

Name	Height ft. in.	Previous club	Birthplace	Birthdate
Goalkeepers				
Marriott, Alan	6. 0	Tottenham	Bedford	3.09.78
Pettinger, Paul	6. 0	Rotherham Utd.	Sheffield	1.10.75
Defenders				
Bimson, Stuart	5.10	Bury	Liverpool	29.09.69
Futcher, Ben	6. 7	Stalybridge Celtic	Bradford	20.02.81
Morgan, Paul	5.11	Preston N.E.	Belfast	23.10.78
Weaver, Simon	5.11	Nuneaton	–	20.12.77
Midfielders				
Bailey, Mark	5. 8	Northwich Victoria	Stoke	12.08.76
Black, Kingsley	5.10	Lincoln City	Luton	22.06.68
Buckley, Adam	5. 9	Grimsby Town	Nottingham	2.08.79
Camm, Mark	5. 8	Sheffield Utd.	Mansfield	1.10.81
Gain, Peter	6. 1	Tottenham	Hammersmith	2.11.76
Hamilton, Ian	5.10	Notts Co.	Stevenage	14.12.67
Logan, Richard	6. 1	Scunthorpe Utd.	Barnsley	24.05.69
Mayo, Paul	5.11	Nott'm. Forest	Hammersmith	13.10.81
Schofield, John	5. 6	Hull City	Barnsley	16.05.65
Sedgemore, Ben	6. 0	Macclesfield Town	Wolverhampton	5.08.75
Smith, Paul	5.11	Nott'm. Forest	Hastings	23.01.76
Forwards				
Battersby, Tony	6. 0	Bury	Doncaster	30.08.75
Cropper, Dene	6. 2	Sheffield Wed.	–	5.01.83
Yeo, Simon	5.10	Hyde Utd.	–	20.10.73

MACCLESFIELD TOWN

Ground: Moss Rose, London Road, Macclesfield SK11 7SP.
Telephone: 01625 264686. Clubcall: 09066 555835. Club nickname: Silkmen.
First-choice colours: Blue shirts and shorts; white stockings.
Main sponsor: James Irlam. Capacity for 2002-03: 6,712.
Record attendance: 9,003 v Winsford Town (Cheshire Senior Cup 2) 14 February, 1948.

Name	Height ft. in.	Previous club	Birthplace	Birthdate
Goalkeepers				
Martin, Lee	6. 0	Halifax Town	Huddersfield	9.09.68
Wilson, Steve	5.10	Hull City	Hull	24.04.74
Defenders				
Abbey, George	5.10	Port Harcourt	Port Harcourt, Nig.	20.10.73
Bamber, Michael	5. 7	Blackpool	Preston	1.10.80
Byrne, Chris	5. 9	Stockport Co.	Manchester	9.02.75
Came, Shaun	6. 3	–	Crewe	15.06.83
Carr, Michael	5.10	–	–	6.12.83
Hitchen, Steve	5. 8	Blackburn Rov.	Salford	28.11.76
Munroe, Karl	6. 1	Swansea City	Manchester	23.09.79
O'Neill, Paul	6. 2	–	Farnworth	17.06.82
Ridler, David	6. 0	Wrexham	Liverpool	12.03.76
Tinson, Darren	6. 0	Northwich Victoria	Birmingham	15.11.69
Midfielders				
Adams, Danny	5. 6	Altrincham	Manchester	3.01.76
Eyre, Richard	5.11	Port Vale	Poynton	5.09.76
Hardy, Lee	6. 0	Oldham Athletic	Blackpool	26.11.81
McAvoy, Andy	6. 0	Hartlepool Utd.	Middlesbrough	28.08.79
Priest, Chris	5.10	Chester City	Leigh	18.10.73
Whitaker, Dan	5.10	–	Manchester	14.11.80

Forwards

Aldridge, Paul	5.11	Tranmere Rov.	Liverpool	2.12.81
Askey, John	6. 0	Port Vale	Stoke	4.11.64
Glover, Lee	5.11	Rotherham Utd.	Kettering	24.04.70
Lightbourne, Kyle	6. 2	Stoke City	Bermuda	29.09.68
Tipton, Matthew	5.10	Oldham Athletic	Conway	29.06.80

OXFORD UNITED

Ground: The Kassam Stadium, Grenoble Road, Oxford OX4 4XP.
Telephone: 01865 337500. **Club nickname:** U's.
First-choice colours: Yellow shirts; navy shorts and stockings.
Main Sponsor: Buildbase. **Capacity for 2002-03:** 12,500.
Record attendance: (Manor Ground) 22,730 v Preston N.E. (F.A. Cup 6) 29 February, 1964.

Name	Height ft. in.	Previous club	Birthplace	Birthdate
Goalkeepers				
McCaldon, Ian	6. 1	Livingston	Liverpool	14.09.74
Woodman, Andy	6. 1	Colchester Utd.	Camberwell	11.08.71
Defenders				
Bound, Matthew	6. 2	Swansea City	Melksham	6.11.72
Crosby, Andy	6. 2	Brighton & H.A.	Rotherham	3.03.73
Guyett, Scott	6. 2	Southport	Ascot	20.01.76
King, Simon	5.11	–	Oxford	11.04.83
McNiven, Scott	5.10	Oldham Athletic	Leeds	2.05.78
Ricketts, Sam	6. 1	–	Wendover	11.10.81
Robinson, Matt	5.11	Reading	Exeter	23.12.74
Stockley, Sam	5. 8	Barnet	Tiverton	5.09.77
Waterman, David	5.11	Portsmouth	Guernsey	16.05.77
Midfielders				
Brooks, Jamie	5. 9	–	Oxford	12.08.80
Hackett, Chris	6. 1	–	Oxford	1.03.83
Hunt, James	5. 8	Northampton Town	Derby	17.02.76
Powell, Paul	5. 7	–	Wallingford	30.06.78
Savage, Dave	6. 1	Northampton Town	Dublin	30.07.73
Whitehead, Dean	5. 8	–	Oxford	12.01.82
Forwards				
Louis, Jefferson	6. 2	–	Harrow	22.02.79
Moody, Paul	6. 3	Millwall	Portsmouth	13.06.67
Omoyinmi, Manny	5. 6	West Ham Utd.	Nigeria	28.12.77
Scott, Andy	6. 1	Brentford	Epsom	2.08.72
Steele, Lee	5. 8	Brighton & H.A.	Liverpool	7.12.73

ROCHDALE

Ground: Spotland, Wilbutts Lane, Rochdale OL11 5DS.
Telephone: 01706 644648. **Club nickname:** Dale.
First-choice colours: Blue shirts, shorts and stockings.
Main Sponsor: Keytech. **Capacity for 2002-03:** 10,203.
Record attendance: 24,231 v Notts Co. (F.A. Cup 2) 10 December, 1949.

Name	Height ft. in.	Previous club	Birthplace	Birthdate
Goalkeepers				
Edwards, Neil	5. 8	Stockport Co.	Aberdare	5.12.70
Gilks, Matthew	6. 1	–	Rochdale	4.06.82
Defenders				
Coleman, Simon	6. 0	Southend Utd.	Mansfield	13.06.68
Doughty, Matthew	5.11	Chester City	Warrington	2.11.81

Duffy, Lee	5.10	–	Oldham	24.07.82
Evans, Wayne	5.10	Walsall	Welshpool	25.08.71
Griffiths, Gareth	6. 4	Wigan Athletic	Winsford	10.04.70
Grand, Simon	5.10	–	Chorley	23.02.84
Hill, Steven	5.10	–	Prescott	12.11.82
McAuley, Sean	5.11	Scunthorpe Utd.	Sheffield	23.06.72
Midfielders				
Atkinson, Graeme	5. 8	Scarborough	Hull	11.11.71
Beech, Chris	5.10	Huddersfield Town	Blackpool	16.09.74
Durkan, Kieron	5.10	Macclesfield Town	Chester	1.12.73
Flitcroft, David	5.11	Chester City	Bolton	14.01.74
McCourt, Patrick	5.10	–	Derry	16.12.83
Oliver, Michael	5.10	Darlington	Middlesbrough	2.08.75
Simpson, Paul	5. 6	Blackpool	Carlisle	26.07.66
Forwards				
Connor, Paul	6. 2	Stoke City	Bishop Auckland	12.01.79
Platt, Clive	6. 3	Walsall	Wolverhampton	27.10.77
Townson, Kevin	5. 6	–	Kirkby	19.04.83

RUSHDEN AND DIAMONDS

Ground: Nene Park, Diamond Way, Irthlingborough NN9 5QF.
Telephone: 01933 652000. **Clubcall:** 09068 440033. **Club nickname:** Diamonds.
First-choice colours: White shirts; blue shorts; white socks.
Main sponsor: Dr Martens. **Capacity for 2002-03:** 6,441.
Record attendance: 6,431 (v Leeds Utd. F.A. Cup 3) 4 January, 1999.

Name	Height ft. in.	Previous club	Birthplace	Birthdate
Goalkeepers				
Turley, Billy	6. 3	Northampton Town	Wolverhampton	15.07.73
Defenders				
Dempster, John	6. 0	–	Kettering	1.04.83
Gray, Stuart	5.10	Reading	Harrogate	18.12.73
Hunter, Barry	6. 4	Reading	Coleraine	18.11.68
Mustafa, Tarkan	5.11	Kingstonian	Islington	28.08.73
Peters, Mark	6. 0	Mansfield Town	St Asaph	6.07.72
Sambrook, Andrew	5.10	Gillingham	Chatham	13.07.79
Setchell, Gary	6. 0	Kettering Town	Kings Lynn	8.05.75
Solkhon, Brett	5.11	Arsenal	Canvey Island	12.09.82
Talbot, Daniel	5. 9	Arsenal	Enfield	30.01.84
Tillson, Andy	6. 2	Walsall	Huntingdon	30.06.66
Underwood, Paul	5.11	Enfield	Wimbledon	16.08.73
Midfielders				
Bell, David	5.10	–	Kettering	21.01.84
Burgess, Andy	6. 2	Luton Town	Bedford	10.08.81
Hall, Paul	5. 8	Walsall	Manchester	3.07.72
Hanlon, Ritchie	6. 1	Peterborough Utd.	Kenton	25.05.78
McElhatton, Michael	5.11	Scarborough	Killarney	16.04.75
Mills, Gary	5. 9	Northampton Town	Sheppey	20.05.81
Wardley, Stuart	5.11	Q.P.R.	Cambridge	10.09.75
Forwards				
Darby, Duane	5.11	Notts Co.	Birmingham	17.10.73
Duffy, Robert	6. 1	Swansea City	Swansea	2.12.82
Lowe, Onandi	6. 3	Kansas City	Kingston, Jam.	2.12.74
Partridge, Scott	5. 9	Brentford	Leicester	13.10.74

SCUNTHORPE UNITED

Ground: Glanford Park, Doncaster Road, Scunthorpe DN15 8TD.
Telephone: 01724 848077. **Club nickname:** Iron.

First-choice colours: White, claret and blue shirts; blue and white shorts; white, claret and blue stockings.
Main sponsor: Mercedes/H & L Garages. **Capacity for 2002-03:** 9,183.
Record attendance: (Old Show Ground) 23,935 v Portsmouth (F.A. Cup 4) 30 January, 1954. (Glanford Park) 8,775 v Rotherham Utd. (Div. 4) 1, May 1989.

Name	Height ft. in.	Previous club	Birthplace	Birthdate
Goalkeepers				
Evans, Tom	6. 1	Crystal Palace	Doncaster	13.12.76
Defenders				
Dawson, Andrew	5. 9	Nott'm Forest	Northallerton	20.10.78
Cotterill, James	5.11	–	Barnsley	3.08.82
McCombe, Jamie	6. 5	–	Scunthorpe	1.01.83
Ridley, Lee	5.10	–	Scunthorpe	5.12.81
Ridley, Steve	5.10	–	Scunthorpe	30.04.83
Stanton, Nathan	5. 9	–	Nottingham	6.05.81
Wilcox, Russ	6. 0	Preston N.E.	Hemsworth	25.03.64
Midfielders				
Beagrie, Peter	5. 9	Bradford City	Middlesbrough	28.11.65
Calvo Garcia, Alex	5.11	Eibar, Spa.	Ordiza	1.01.72
Graves, Wayne	5. 8	–	Scunthorpe	18.09.80
Jackson, Mark	5.11	Leeds Utd.	Barnsley	30.09.77
Kell, Richard	6. 1	Torquay Utd.	Bishop Auckland	15.09.79
Sparrow, Matthew	5.10	–	London	3.10.81
Forwards				
Brough, Scott	5. 6	–	Doncaster	10.02.83
Carruthers, Martin	5.10	Southend Utd.	Nottingham	7.08.72
Torpey, Steve	6. 3	Bristol City	Islington	8.12.70
Wheatcroft, Paul	5. 9	Bolton Wand.	Bolton	22.11.80

SHREWSBURY TOWN

Ground: Gay Meadow, Shrewsbury SY2 5AL.
Telephone: 01743 360111. **Clubcall:** 09068 121194. **Club nickname:** Shrews.
First-choice colours: Royal blue and amber shirts, shorts and stockings.
Main sponsor: RMW Electrical Services. **Capacity for 2002-03:** 8,000.
Record attendance: 18,917 v Walsall (Div. 3) 26 April, 1961.

Name	Height ft. in.	Previous club	Birthplace	Birthdate
Goalkeepers				
Cartwright, Mark	6. 2	Brighton & H.A.	Chester	13.01.73
Dunbavin, Ian	6. 1	Liverpool	Knowsley	27.05.80
Hart, Tim	6. 1	–	Coventry	20.09.82
Defenders				
Evans, Nick	5. 8	–	Newport	12.06.84
Heathcote, Mick	6. 2	Plymouth Argyle	Durham	10.09.65
Moss, Darren	5.11	Chester City	Wrexham	24.05.81
Redmile, Matthew	6. 4	Notts Co.	Nottingham	12.11.76
Thompson, Andy	5. 5	Cardiff City	Cannock	9.11.67
Wilding, Peter	6. 1	Telford Utd.	Shrewsbury	28.11.68
Midfielders				
Aiston, Sam	5. 9	Sunderland	Newcastle	21.11.76
Atkins, Mark	6. 0	Hull City	Doncaster	14.08.68
Courtney, Chris	5. 8	–	Hereford	14.05.84
Drysdale, Leon	5. 9	–	Walsall	3.02.81
Murray, Karl	5.11	–	Islington	24.06.82
Silgrams, James	5. 8	–	Manchester	30.09.82
Tolley, Jamie	6. 1	–	Shrewsbury	12.05.83
Woan, Ian	5.10	Swindon Town	Heswall	14.12.67

Forwards

Name		Previous club	Birthplace	Birthdate
Jagielka, Steve	5. 8	Stoke City	Manchester	10.03.78
Jemson, Nigel	5.11	Oxford Utd.	Preston	10.08.69
Lowe, Ryan	5.11	Burscough	Liverpool	18.09.78
Murphy, Chris	5. 6	–	Leamington	8.03.83
Rodgers, Luke	5. 6	–	Birmingham	1.01.82
Stevens, Ian	5.10	Carlisle Utd.	Malta	21.10.66

SOUTHEND UNITED

Ground: Roots Hall, Victoria Avenue, Southend SS2 6NQ.
Telephone: 01702 304050. **Clubcall:** 09068 121105. **Club nickname:** Shrimpers.
First-choice colours: Navy blue shirts, shorts and stockings.
Main sponsor: Martin Dawn. **Capacity for 2002-03:** 12,310.
Record attendance: 31,033 v Liverpool (F.A. Cup 3) 10 January, 1979.

Name	Height ft. in.	Previous club	Birthplace	Birthdate
Goalkeepers				
Flahavan, Darryl	5.11	Woking	Southampton	9.09.77
Gay, Daniel	6. 1	Norwich City	Kings Lynn	5.08.82
Defenders				
Cort, Leon	6. 2	Millwall	Southwark	11.09.79
Lunan, Daniel	6. 1	–	Farnborough	14.03.84
Newman, Rob	6. 2	Norwich City	Bradford on Avon	13.12.63
Searle, Damon	5. 9	Carlisle	Cardiff	26.10.71
Midfielders				
Alderton, Rio	6. 0	Millwall	Colchester	12.08.82
Beard, Mark	5. 8	Kingstonian	Roehampton	8.10.74
Broad, Stephen	6. 0	Chelsea	Epsom	10.06.80
Clark, Anthony	5.11	West Ham Utd.	Camden	5.10.84
Clark, Steve	6. 1	–	London	10.02.82
Maher, Kevin	5.11	Tottenham	Ilford	17.10.76
Maye, Danny	5. 9	Port Vale	Leicester	14.07.82
McSweeney, David	6. 0	–	Basildon	28.12.81
Thurgood, Stuart	5. 7	Simuzu Pulse	Enfield	2.07.83
Whelan, Philip	6. 4	Oxford Utd.	Stockport	7.03.72
Forwards				
Belgrave, Barrington	6. 0	Yeovil Town	Bedford	16.09.80
Bramble, Tesfaye	6. 1	Cambridge City	Ipswich	20.07.80
Rawle, Mark	5.11	Boston Utd.	Leicester	24.07.79
Webb, Daniel	6. 0	Southampton	Poole	2.07.83

SWANSEA CITY

Ground: Vetch Field, Swansea SA1 3SU.
Telephone: 01792 474114. **Club nickname:** Swans.
First-choice colours: White shirts, shorts and stockings.
Main sponsor: The Travel House. **Capacity for 2002-03:** 11,837.
Record attendance: 32,786 v Arsenal (F.A. Cup 4) 17 February, 1968.

Name	Height ft. in.	Previous club	Birthplace	Birthdate
Goalkeepers				
Freestone, Roger	6. 3	Chelsea	Newport	19.08.68
Defenders				
Evans, Terry	5. 7	Barry Town	Pontypridd	8.01.76
Howard, Michael	5. 9	Tranmere Rov.	Birkenhead	2.12.78
Jackson, Michael	5. 7	Cheltenham Town	Cheltenham	26.06.80
Moss, David	6. 0	Falkirk	Doncaster	15.11.68
Mumford, Andrew	6. 1	Llanelli	Neath	18.06.81
Murphy, Matt	5.10	Bury	Northampton	20.08.71

Sharp, Neil	6. 1	Merthyr Tydfil	Hemel Hempstead	19.01.78
O'Leary, Kristian	5.11	–	Neath	30.08.77
Smith, Jason	6. 3	Tiverton Town	Birmingham	6.09.74
Midfielders				
De-Vulgt, Leigh	5. 9	–	Swansea	17.03.81
Cusack, Nick	6. 0	Fulham	Rotherham	24.12.65
Jenkins, Lee	5. 9	–	Pontypool	28.06.79
Lacey, Damien	5. 9	–	Bridgend	3.08.77
Phillips, Gareth	5. 8	–	Pontypridd	18.08.79
Reid, Paul	5. 9	Bury	Oldbury	19.01.68
Forwards				
Thomas, Jason	6. 0	Blackburn Rov.	Swansea	16.01.79
Watkin, Steve	5.10	Wrexham	Wrexham	16.06.71
Williams, John	6. 2	Darlington	Birmingham	11.05.68

TORQUAY UNITED

Ground: Plainmoor, Torquay TQ1 3PS.
Telephone: 01803 328666. **Club nickname:** Gulls.
First-choice colours: Yellow and navy shirts, shorts and stockings.
Main sponsor: Sparkworld. **Capacity for 2002-03:** 6,283.
Record attendance: 21,908 v Huddersfield Town (F.A. Cup 4) 29 January, 1955.

Name	Height ft. in.	Previous club	Birthplace	Birthdate
Goalkeepers				
Dearden, Kevin	5.11	Wrexham	Luton	8.03.70
Griffiths, Kenny	6. 0	–	Torquay	8.11.83
Northmore, Ryan	6. 1	–	Plymouth	5.09.80
Defenders				
Canoville, Lee	6. 1	Arsenal	Ealing	14.03.81
Douglin, Troy	6. 2	–	Coventry	7.05.82
Hankin, Sean	5.11	Crystal Palace	Camberley	28.02.81
Hazell, Reuben	5.11	Tranmere Rov.	Birmingham	24.04.79
Hockley, Matthew	5.11	–	Paignton	5.06.82
Holmes, Paul	5.11	W.B.A.	Sheffield	18.02.68
Woods, Steve	5.11	Chesterfield	Davenham	5.12.76
Woozley, David	6. 0	Crystal Palace	Ascot	6.12.79
Midfielders				
Ashington, Ryan	5. 9	–	Torquay	28.03.83
Benefield, Jimmy	5.11	–	Bristol	6.05.83
Fowler, Jason	6. 0	Cardiff City	Bristol	20.08.74
Hill, Kevin	5. 8	Torrington	Exeter	6.03.76
Russell, Alex	5. 9	Cambridge Utd.	Crosby	17.03.73
Tully, Stephen	5. 7	–	Paignton	10.02.80
Forwards				
Bedeau, Tony	5.10	–	Hammersmith	24.03.79
Graham, David	5.10	Dunfermline	Edinburgh	6.10.78
Richardson, Marcus	6. 3	Cambridge Utd.	Reading	31.08.77

WREXHAM

Ground: Racecourse Ground, Mold Road, Wrexham LL11 2AH.
Telephone: 01978 262129. **Club nickname:** Robins.
First-choice-colours: Red shirts; white shorts; red stockings.
Main sponsor: Gap Personnel. **Capacity for 2002-03:** 15,500.
Record attendance: 34,445 v Manchester Utd. (F.A. Cup 4) 26 January, 1957.

Name	Height ft. in.	Previous club	Birthplace	Birthdate
Goalkeepers				
Dibble, Andy	6. 2	Stockport Co.	Cwmbran	8.05.65
Rodgers, Kristian	5.11	–	Chester	2.10.80

Whitfield, Paul	6. 0	–	St Asaph	6.05.82
Defenders				
Bennett, Dan	6. 1	Swindon Town	Great Yarmouth	7.01.78
Carey, Brian	6. 3	Leicester City	Cork	31.05.68
Holmes, Shaun	5. 9	Manchester City	Londonderry	27.12.80
Lawrence, Dennis	5.11	Defence Force	Trinidad	18.01.74
Morgan, Craig	6. 0	–	St Asaph	18.06.85
Roberts, Stephen	6. 2	–	Wrexham	24.02.80
Midfielders				
Barrett, Paul	5. 9	Newcastle Utd.	Newcastle	13.04.78
Campbell, Luke	5. 9	–	Llandudno	18.12.82
Edwards, Carlos	6. 0	–	Tobago	24.10.78
Edwards Paul	5.10	Swindon Town	Manchester	1.01.80
Evans, Mark	6. 0	–	Chester	16.09.82
Ferguson, Darren	5.10	Sparta Rotterdam	Glasgow	9.02.72
Gibson, Robin	5. 7	–	Crewe	15.11.79
Pejic, Shaun	6. 0	–	Hereford	16.11.82
Phillips, Wayne	5.11	Stockport Co.	Bangor	15.12.70
Thomas, Steve	5.10	–	Hartlepool	23.06.79
Whitley, Jim	5. 9	Manchester City	Zambia	14.04.75
Forwards				
Jones, Lee	5. 8	Barnsley	Wrexham	29.05.73
Morrell, Andy	5.11	Newcastle Blue Star	Doncaster	28.09.74
Sam, Hector	5.10	CL Financial San Juan	Trinidad	25.02.78
Trundle, Lee	6. 0	Rhyl	Liverpool	10.10.76

YORK CITY

Ground: Bootham Crescent, York YO3 7AQ.
Telephone: 01904 624447. **Club nickname:** Minstermen.
First-choice colours: Red shirts, shorts and stockings.
Main sponsor: Evening Press. **Capacity for 2002-03:** 9,456.
Record attendance: 28,123 v Huddersfield Town (F.A. Cup 6) 5 March 1938.

Name	Height ft. in.	Previous club	Birthplace	Birthdate
Goalkeepers				
Fettis, Alan	6. 2	Blackburn Rov.	Newtownards	1.02.71
Howarth, Russell	6. 1	–	York	27.03.82
Defenders				
Basham, Mike	6. 2	Barnet	Barking	27.09.73
Cooper, Richard	5. 9	Nott'm. Forest	Nottingham	27.09.79
Edmondson, Darren	6. 0	Huddersfield Town	Ulverston	4.11.71
Hobson, Gary	6. 2	Chester City	North Ferriby	12.11.72
Hocking, Matt	5.11	Hull City	Boston	30.01.78
Potter, Graham	6. 1	W.B.A.	Solihull	20.05.75
Richardson, Nick	6. 0	Chester City	Halifax	11.04.67
Smith, Chris	5.11	Reading	Derby	30.06.81
Stamp, Neville	5.11	Reading	Reading	7.07.81
Thompson, Marc	5.10	–	York	15.01.82
Midfielders				
Brass, Chris	5. 9	Burnley	Easington	24.07.75
Bullock, Lee	6. 1	–	Stockton	22.05.81
Fox, Christian	5.11	–	Auchenbrae	11.04.81
O'Kane, Aiden	5. 8	Cliftonville	Belfast	24.11.79
Wilding, Craig	5.10	Chesterfield	–	30.10.81
Forwards				
Duffield, Peter	5. 6	Darlington	Middlesbrough	4.02.69
Mathie, Alex	5.11	Dundee Utd.	Bathgate	20.12.68
Nogan, Lee	5.11	Luton Town	Cardiff	21.05.69

SCOTTISH LEAGUE SQUADS 2002-03

BANK OF SCOTLAND PREMIER LEAGUE

ABERDEEN: Russell Anderson, Callum Bett, Robert Bisconti, Allan Carella, Chris Clark, Eugene Dadi, Eric Deloumeaux, Laurent D'Jaffo, Bobby Duncan, Ryan Esson, Duncan Jones, Terry Kidd, Peter Kjaer, Darren Mackie, James McAllister, Philip McGuire, Callum McKenzie, Kevin McNaughton, Scott Michie, Leon Mike, Ross O'Donoghue, Mark Peat, David Preece, Kevin Rutkiewicz, Ben Thornley, Fergus Tiernan, Murray Watson, Robbie Winters, Darren Young, Derek Young. **Manager:** Ebbe Skovdahl.

CELTIC: Didier Agathe, Bobo Balde, Stephane Bonnes, Tom Boyd, John Convery, Barry Corr, Steven Crainey, Robert Douglas, David Fernandez, Mark Fotheringham, James Gallagher, Jonathan Gould, Steve Guppy, John Hartson, Colin Healy, Michael Herbet, John Kennedy, Dmitri Kharin, Paul Lambert, Henrik Larsson, Neil Lennon, Simon Lynch, Shaun Maloney, Ryan McCann, John McGovern, Jackie McNamara, Liam Miller, Johan Mjallby, David Moore, Lubo Moravcik, Stilian Petrov, Bobby Petta, Rafael, Paul Shields, Jamie Smith, Chris Sutton, Mohammed Sylla, Alan Thompson, Joos Valgaeren, David Van Zanten, Ross Wallace. **Manager:** Martin O'Neill.

DUNDEE: Javier Artero, Massimo Beghetto, Gavin Beith, Ivano Bonetti, Colin Boylan, Fabian Caballero, Beto Carranza, Walter Del Rio, James Earlie, Fan Zhiyi, Umberto Fatello, Barry Forbes, Alberto Garrido, Michael Hankinson, Jonathan Kelly, Khaled Kemas, Temuri Ketsbaia, Zura Khizanishvili, James Langfield, David Mackay, Lee Mair, Marcello Marrocco, Steven Milne, Georgi Nemsadze, Nacho Novo, Gavin Rae, Steven Robb, Mark Robertson, Alessandro Romano, Juan Sara, Barry Smith, Derek Soutar, Julian Speroni, Graham Thomson, Quique Torres, Gerardo Traverso, Mauro Vargiu, Lee Wilkie, Michael Yates, Marco de Marchi. **Manager:** Jim Duffy.

DUNDEE UNITED: Hasney Aljofree, Steven Carson, Marc Cocozza, Alan Combe, Hugh Davidson, Stuart Duff, Craig Easton, Paul Gallagher, Danny Griffin, Jim Hamilton, Paul Jarvie, Jim Lauchlan, Jean Licina, Derek Lilley, Stephen McConalogue, David McCracken, Jamie McCunnie, Kevin McGowne, Jim McIntyre, Charlie Miller, Stephen O'Donnell, Ogunmade, David Partridge, James Paterson, Allan Smart, Steve Thompson, Jon Thompson, Anastasios Venetis, Mark Wilson, David Winters, Stephen Wright. **Manager:** Alex Smith.

DUNFERMLINE ATHLETIC: Brian Blair, Steve Boyle, Craig Brewster, Lee Bullen, Stephen Crawford, Owen Coyle, Gary Dempsey, Jason Dair, Dean Fleming, George Fotheringham, Steve Hampshire, Ross Harrower, Andre Karnebeek, Sean Kilgallon, Angus MacPherson, Gary Mason, Mark McGarty, Chris McGroarty, Kevin McLeish, David Moss, David Nicholls, Barry Nicholson, Colin Nish, Stewart Petrie, Youssef Rossi, Marco Ruitenbeek, Andrius Skerla, Derek Stillie, Gary Sutherland, Scott M Thomson, Scott Walker. **Manager:** Jimmy Calderwood.

HEARTS: Steven Boyack, Ryan Davidson, Mark de Vries, David Dunn, Craig Gordon, Joe Hamill, Liam Fox, Neil Janczyk, Mathu King, Andy Kirk, John Knox, Stephane Mahe, Alan Maybury, Austin McCann, Neil MacFarlane, David McGeown, Kevin McKenna, Roddy McKenzie, Paul McLaughlan, Ross McLeod, Paul McMullan, Robbie Neilson, Antti Niemi, Steven Pressley, Graeme Sawers, Scott Severin, Robert Sloan, Elliot Smith, Stephen Simmons, Kevin Twaddle, Gary Wales, Andy Webster, Graham Weir, Lee Windrum, James Winning, Paul Kaczan. **Manager:** Craig Levein.

HIBERNIAN: Lyndon Andrews, Frederic Arpinon, Grant Brebner, Craig Brewster, Tony Caig, Gary Caldwell, Nick Colgan, Tony Craig, Ulises de la Cruz, Frederic Dacquin, Allan Dempsie, Mark Dempsie, Mathias Doumbe, Paul Fenwick, Paul Hilland, Mathias Jack, Ulrik Laursen, Francisco Luna, Tom McManus, Ian Murray, Kevin Nicol, Garry O'Connor, John O'Neill, Alen Orman, Liam O'Sullivan, Alan Reid, Derek Riordan, Gary Smith, Derek Townsley, Steven Whittaker, Jarkko Wiss. **Manager:** Bobby Williamson.

KILMARNOCK: Chris Boyle, Kris Boyd, Peter Canero, Mark Canning, Craig Dargo, Paul Di Gacomo, Frederic Dindeleux, James Fowler, Steve Fulton, Garry Hay, Robbie Henderson, Sean Hessey, Chris Innes, Alan Mahood, Gordon Marshall, Gary

McCutcheon, Gary McDonald, Andrew McLaren, Barry McLaughlin, Gary McSwegan, Colin Meldrum, Alistair Mitchell, Stephen Murray, Jesus Garcia Sanjuan, Greg Shields, Graeme Smith, Colin Stewart. **Manager:** Jim Jefferies.

LIVINGSTON: Marvin Andrews, David Bingham, Gary Bollan, Darren Brady, Philippe Brinquin, Richard Brittain, Javier Sanchez Broto, Tom Courts, Emmanuel Dorado, Scott Findlay, Stewart Greacen, Michael Hart, Nocko Jokovic, Stuart Lovell, Lee Makel, David McEwan, David McGuire, David Ormiston, Morten Petersen, Quino, Rubio, Didier Santini, Sebastien Socie, Cherif Toure-Maman, Stephen Whaley, Barry Wilson, David Xausa. **Manager:** James Leishman.

MOTHERWELL: Derek Adams, Andrew Bell, Martyn Corrigan, John Crawley, Brian Dempsie, Francois Dubourdeau, Shaun Fagan, Steven Hammell, William Kinniburgh, Keith Lasley, Dirk Lehmann, Scott Leitch, Kevin MacDonald, James McFadden, Stephen Pearson, Douglas Ramsey, Barry Tulloch, Steve Woods. **Manager:** Terry Butcher.

PARTICK THISTLE: Alan Archibald, Kenny Arthur, Joe Boyle, Andy Brand, Billy Brawley, Gerry Britton, Jamie Buchan, Kevin Budinauckas, Alex Burns, Stephen Craigan, Barry Elliot, Jamie Dolan, Derek Fleming, Andy Gibson, Martin Hardie, Willie Howie, Danny Lennon, David Lilley, Ian Morris, David McCallum, James McKinstry, Scott McLean, Colin Miller, Kenny Milne, Jamie Mitchell, Scott Paterson, Steven Pinkowski, Mark Thomson, Ricky Waddell, Paul Walker, Derek Whyte. **Manager:** John Lambie.

RANGERS: Dariusz Adamczuk, Lorenzo Amoruso, Mikel Arteta, Shota Arveladze, Michael Ball, John Brighton, Chris Burke, Claudio Caniggia, Iain Chalmers, Jesper Christiansen, Ronald de Boer, Billy Dodds, Andrew Dowie, Barry Ferguson, Tore Andre Flo, Billy Gibson, Jim Gibson, Alex Hauser, Stephen Hughes, Stefan Klos, Bert Konterman, Russell Latapy, Peter Leven, Peter Lovenkrands, Robert Malcolm, Steve McAdam, Neil McCann, Ryan McCann, Allan McGregor, Paul McHale, Michael Mols, Craig Moore, Kevin Muscat, Christian Nerlinger, Arthur Numan, Tero Penttila, Paul Reid, Fernando Ricksen, Maurice Ross, Ben Stevens, Kirk Willoughby, Scott Wilson, David Young. **Manager:** Alex McLeish.

BELL'S FIRST DIVISION

ALLOA ATHLETIC: James Adamson, Gilbert Allan, Graeme Armstrong, Stewart Bovill, Charles Brigain, Tom Brown, Max Christie, Mark Cowan, Harry Curran, Gareth Evans, Jim Evans, Derek Ferguson, Jimmy Fisher, James Gilmour, Ross Hamilton, Gareth Hutchison, Barry Kane, Keith Knox, Ian Little, Billy McDonald, James McQueen, Kevin Mitchell, David Pew, Robert Raeside, Andy Seaton, Steven Thomson, Craig Valentine, Richard Walker, Gregg Watson. **Manager:** Terry Christie.

ARBROATH: Paul Brownlie, Andy Cargill, Denis Cunningham, John Cusick, Paul Durno, Steve Fallon, Craig Ferox, Steve Florence, Jim Gardner, Garry Gow, Ewan Graham, Kevin Heenan, Greg Henslee, Craig Hinchcliffe, Steve Kirk, Steve Mallan, John McAulay, Murray McDowell, John McGlashan, David McInally, Stephen Moffat, Innes Ritchie, Andy Roddie, George Rowe, Darren Spink, Gavin Swankie, Jordan Tait. **Manager:** John Brownlie.

AYR UNITED: Eddie Annand, Aaron Black, John Bradford, Mark Campbell, Scott Chaplain, Scott Crabbe, David Craig, John Dodds, Neil Duffy, Lee Duncan, Michael Dunlop, James Grady, Brian Hamilton, Stewart Kean, Paul Lovering, Craig McEwan, Pat McGinlay, Allan McManus, Aidan McVeigh, Thomas Molloy, Craig Nelson, Iain Nicolson, Neil Scally, Lee Sharp, Paul Sheerin, Marc Smyth, Craig Stevenson, Marvyn Wilson. **Manager:** Gordon Dalziel.

CLYDE: Steve Convery, David Dunn, Willie Falconer, John Fraser, David Hagen, Bryn Halliwell, Leigh Hinds, Andy Kane, Paul Kane, Pat Keogh, Alan Kernaghan, Andy McClay, Mark McLaughlin, Simon Mensing, Andy Millen, Kevin Miller, John Potter, Jack Ross, Brian Smith. **Manager:** Alan Kernaghan.

FALKIRK: Neil Adams, Kevin Christie, Owen Coyle, Steven Craig, Philip Creaney, Stuart Cringean, Allan Ferguson, Alan Gray, Darren Hill, John Hughes, Kevin James, Mark Kerr, Andy Lawrie, Mark McHendry, Scott McLean, Craig McPherson, Jamie

McQuilken, Lee Miller, Neil Murray, Chic Pearson, Steven Rennie, Grant Richardson, Andy Rodgers, Patrice Tano, Steve Tosh. **Manager:** Ian McCall.

INVERNESS CALEDONIAN THISTLE: David Bagan, Charlie Christie, Russell Duncan, Stuart Golabek, Bobby Mann, Roy McBain, Stuart McCaffrey, Grant Munro, Paul Ritchie, Barry Robson, Alexander Rodgers, Graeme Stewaret, Ross Tokely, Nicky Walker, Dennis Wyness. **Manager:** Steve Paterson.

QUEEN OF THE SOUTH: Andrew Aitken, Derek Allan, Derek Anderson, Paddy Atkinson, Steve Bowey, Jamie Campbell, Jon Crawford, Barry Donald, Alan Gray, Derek Lyle, Joe McAlpine, Brian McColligan, Brian McLaughlin, Shaun O'Connor, Jon O'Neill, Eric Paton, Colin Scott, James Thomson, Peter Weatherson. **Manager:** John Connolly.

ROSS COUNTY: Graham Bayne, Alex Bone, Tony Bullock, Martin Canning, Don Cowie, Paul Deas, Les Fridge, Connor Gethins, Kenny Gilbert, Richard Hastings, Steve Hislop, Brian Irvine, Steven Mackay, Mark McCulloch, Mark Perry, Hugh Robertson, Sean Webb. **Manager:** Neale Cooper.

ST JOHNSTONE: Paddy Connolly, Brendan Crozier, Kevin Cuthbert, Craig Devlin, Darren Dods, Mark Ferry, Ross Forsyth, Martyn Fotheringham, Paul Hartley, Darren Jackson, Graeme Jones, Martin Lauchlan, Tommy Lovenkrands, Peter MacDonald, Martin Maher, Alan Main, Stuart Malcolm, Ian Maxwell, David McClune, Stuart McCluskey, Marc McCulloch, Grant Murray, Emmanuel Panther, Keigan Parker, Mark Reilly, John Robertson, Craig Russell, Ryan Stevenson, Jim Weir, Sammy Youssouf. **Manager:** Sandy Clark.

ST MIRREN: Sergei Baltacha, Greig Denham, Chris Dolan, Colin Drew, Ricky Gillies, Graham Guy, John Hillcoat, David Jack, Chris Kerr, Simon Lappin, David Lowing, James Mason, Steven McGarry, Brian McGinty, Jamie McGowan, Scott McKenzie, Junior Mendes, Hugh Murray, Kris Robertson, Ryan Robinson, Ian Ross, Ludovic Roy, Paul Rudden, Scott Simpson, Scott Strang, Christopher Wreh, Mark Yardley. **Manager:** Tom Hendrie.

BELL'S SECOND DIVISION

AIRDRIE UNITED: Paul Armstrong, Neil Bennett, Owen Coyle, Stephen Docherty, Allan Ferguson, Lee Gardner, John Henry, Kevin James, Stuart MacDonald, Neil MacFarlane, Allan McManus, Craig McPherson, Mark Roberts, Paul Ronald, Tony Smith, Sandy Stewart, Stuart Taylor, Jerome Vareille. **Manager:** Sandy Stewart.

BERWICK RANGERS: Neil Bennett, Mark Bradley, Graham Connell, Gordon Connelly, Eddie Forrest, Gordon Forrest, Ian Ferguson, Ross Godfrey, Dale Gray, Grant McNicholl, David Murie, Martin Neil, Alan Neill, Anthony Smith, Darren Smith, Henry Smith, Garry Wood. **Manager:** Paul Smith.

BRECHIN CITY: Roddy Black, Harry Cairney, Mark Cairns, Paul Campbell, Derek Clark, Barry Donnachie, Kevin Fotheringham, Graham Gibson, Roddy Grant, David Hay, Robbie Henderson, Ben Honeyman, Chris Jackson, Charlie King, Chris King, Gregor McKechnie, Kevin McKeown, Greg Miller, Paul Riley, Daryn Smith, Jamie Smith, Chris Templeman. **Manager:** Dick Campbell.

COWDENBEATH: Alan Banks, Derek Barnes, Graham Brown, Kevin Byle, Andy Campbell, Grant Carnie, Fraser Carver, Gerry Crabbe, John Dixon, Steven Duff, John Elliott, Allan Fleming, Hamish French, Scott Gibb, Kevin Gordon, Russell Huggon, James Lakie, John Martin, Ian Mauchlen, Ross McBride, Wes Mitchell, Gary O'Connor, Scott Reilly, Michael Renwick, Mark Somerville, Vinnie Sullivan, Colin Waugh, David White, Keith Wilson, Craig Winter, Keith Wright, Craig Young. **Manager:** Keith Wright.

DUMBARTON: Steve Bonar, Craig Brittain, Andy Brown, Mark Crilly, Michael Dickie, John Dillon, Robert Dunn, Paddy Flannery, Steve Grindlay, Stephen Jack, Craig Lynes, Kevin McCann, Danny McKelvie, John McKeown, Martin O'Neill, Joe Robertson, David Stewart, John Wight. **Manager:** David Winnie.

FORFAR ATHLETIC: Marin Bavidge, Michael Brown, Kevin Byers, Neal Ferrie, Darren Henderson, Robbie Horn, Paul Lunan, Brian McCloy, Scott McCulloch, Gregor McMaster, Kevin Milne, Barrie Moffat, Alan Rattray, Barry Sellars, George Shaw, Willie Stewart, Scott Taylor, Paul Tosh, David Williams. **Manager:** Neil Cooper.

HAMILTON ACADEMICALS: Gareth Armstrong, Martin Bonnar, Stuart Callaghan, Eddie Cunnington, Bill Davidson, Ian Dobbins, Alan Frame, Paul Gaughan, Alasdair Graham, David Grant, Chris Hillcoat, Gary Johnstone, Wale Kwick Ajet, Alex Lurinsky, Ian MacFarlane, Ross MacLaren, Michael Martin, Ally Maxwell, Iain McCreadie, Paul McDonald, David McNiven, Brian McPhee, John McShane, Michael Moore, Mark Nelson, Kris O'Neil, Graham Potter, Allan Russell, Jim Sherry, Sean Sweeney. Stewart Thomson. **Manager:** Dave McPherson.

RAITH ROVERS: Kenny Black, Ian Brown, Paul Browne, Antonio Calderon, Andy Clark, Jamie Clark, Shaun Dennis, Laurie Ellis, Paul Hampshire, Mark Jones, Ross Matheson, Greig McCulloch, Marc Millar, Willie Miller, Simon Miotto, Adam Moffat, Samuel Monin, Wilfred Nanou, Paquito, Martin Prest, Alvero Quesana, John Rushford, Andy Smith, Jay Stein, Jamie Sweeney, David Wilson, Jorge Zoco. **Manager:** Antonio Calderon.

STENHOUSEMUIR: Mark Booth, John Burrows, Andy Carlin, Brian Crawford, Kevin Donnelly, Stuart Easton, Isaac English, David Graham, Steve Graham, Fraser Forrest, Aaron Gillespie, Steve Hamilton, Martin Harty, Jamie McKenzie, David McFarlane, Gerry McKenna, Des McKeown, Ally McMillan, Martin Mooney, Scott Murphy, James Sandison, Paul Shanks, Gary Shearer, Michael Stone, Colin Waldie, Mark Wilson. **Manager:** John McVeigh.

STRANRAER: Stephen Aitken, David Farrell, Kevin Finlayson, Kevin Gaughan, Alex Grace, Ian Harty, Sandy Hodge, Allan Jenkins, Paul Kerr, Willie McCulloch, Steve Renwicks, Derek Wingate, Fraser Wright. **Manager:** Billy McLaren.

BELL'S THIRD DIVISION

ALBION ROVERS: Yannis Begue, Paul Bonar, David Carr, Sean Clark, James Coulter, Ian Diack, Chris Fahey, Tom Hanlon, Stuart Ingram, Todd Lumsden, Kevin McBride, James McKenzie, Charles McLean, Ryan McMullan, Stephen McMullen, Ian Rankin, Scott Shearer, Chris Silvestro, Jordan Smith, William Struthers, David Sutherland. **Manager:** Peter Hetherston.

EAST FIFE: John Allison, Steven Brown, Jimmy Butter, Conrad Courts, Grant Cunningham, Kenny Deuchar, Euan Donaldson, Craig Farnan, Gordon Gilbert, James Graham, James Herkes, Aaron MacDonald, Paul McManus, Craig McMillan, Jim Moffat, Paul Mortimer, Jimmy Nairn, John Ovenstone, Dean Walker. **Manager:** Jim Moffat.

EAST STIRLINGSHIRE: Alan Aitken, Ross Carlow, John Clarke, Scott Cormack, Browne Ferguson, Murray Hunter, David Lorimer, Roddy Maughan, Sean McAuley, Gary McDonald, Ian McDonald, Graham McGhee, Chris McKenzie, Paul McLaughlin, Dean McPherson, Neil Miller, Ciaran Quinn, Brian Ross, Gordon Russell, Kenny Sariley, Andy Scott, James Spence, Steven Stewart, Christopher Todd, Douglas Todd, Michael Tolland, Joe Tortolano, Derek Ure, John Wilson, David Wood. **Manager:** Brian Ross.

ELGIN CITY: David Blackhall, Fraser Bremner, Connor Campbell, David Craig, Richard Craig, Willie Furphy, Graham Grant, Garry Hamilton, David Hind, Ricky James, Steve MacDonald, Russell McBride, Colin McGlashan, Darren McGonnachie, Craig Milne, Michael Morrison, Martin Pirie, Michael Rae, David Ross, Mike Sanderson, Lee Shanks, Mark Sim, Steve Sim, Andrew Smith, Stuart Strathdee, Mike Teasdale, Craig Tully, Graeme Wilson. **Manager:** Alex Caldwell.

GRETNA: Lee Armstrong, Phil Coxall, Mark Dobie, Gary Harding, Matt Henney, David Hewson, David Mathieson, David Mawson, Vince Parker, Geoff Paterson, Gavin Skelton, Steve Skinner, Gary Wills, David Wylie, Kane Young. **Manager:** Rowan Alexander.

MONTROSE: Ronnie Adam, Ralph Brand, Graeme Christie, Frank Conway, David Craig, Stuart Ferguson, Keith Gibson, Ian Gilzean, Paul Glennie, Andrew Hutcheon, Grant Johnson, Steve Kerrigan, Moray Leask, Graeme McCheyne, Colin McDonald, Gary McGlynn, Ray McKinnon, John McQuillan, Jonathan Mitchell, Chris Ogboke, Barry Park, David Robertson, Graeme Sharp, Ray Sharp, Keith Webster, John Young. **Manager:** John Sheran.

MORTON: Scott Bannerman, Mel Bottiglieri, Darren Cairney, Phil Cannie, Derek Carmichael, Derek Collins, Craig Coyle, Stephen Frail, Warren Hawke, David McGregor, David McPherson, Marco MaisanO, Alex Williams, **Manager:** Peter Cormack.

PETERHEAD: Kevin Bissett, Scott Brown, Ross Buchanan, Scott Clark, Craig Cooper, John Duffy, Andy Gibson, Billy Herd, Martin Johnston, Steve King, Richard Livingstone, Stuart Mackay, Vince Marrs, Paul Mathers, Shaun McSkimming, Ivor Pirie, Kevin Rennie, Keith Robertson, Mark Simpson, Mark Slater, Greig Smith, Iain Stewart, Lee Sweeney, Kevin Tindal. **Manager:** Ian Wilson.

QUEEN'S PARK: Damiano Agostini, Paul Borland, Jim Bruce, Steven Canning, Ross Clark, Neil Collins, Allan Dunning, Danny Ferry, John Gallagher, John Gemmell, Stuart Jack, Ross Jackson, Gordon Lappin, Darren Magee, Stephen Marshall, Willie Martin, Tony Mitchell, David Menelaws, Tony Quinn, Richard Sinclair, Johnny Whelan, Jamie White. **Manager:** John McCormack.

STIRLING ALBION: Lee Bailey, Ross Beveridge, Kenny Brannigan, Andy Buchanan, David Butler, Blair Cremin, Stuart Devine, Paul Hay, Gary Higgins, Steve Hutchison, Ross Johnston, Gary Kelly, Kenneth McLellan, Allan Moore, Gareth Munro, Paul Nugent, David O'Brien, Chris Reid, Steve Reilly, Ryan Scobie, Greig Scott, William Stuart, Ian Turner, Andy Whitefoot, Douglas Wilson, Mark Wilson, Stephen Wilson, **Manager:** Allan Moore.

WORLD CUP PLAY-OFF WOE

Nine British-based players suffered World Cup disappointment with Australia, who were beaten 3-0 by Uruguay in the second leg of the South America/Oceania qualifying play-off after winning the home match 1-0. The team for the game in Montevideo was: Schwarzer (Middlesbrough), Muscat (Wolves), Moore (Rangers), Murphy (Sheffield Utd.), Vidmar (Rangers), Emerton (Feyenoord), Okon (Middlesbrough), Skoko (Genk), Lazaridis (Birmingham City), Viduka (Leeds Utd.), Kewell (Leeds Utd.). It was the fourth time in five World Cup play-offs that Australia had been beaten. Four years earlier, coached by Terry Venables, they lost on away goals to Iran.

CHAMPIONS LEAGUE FINAL FOR OLD TRAFFORD

Old Trafford will stage the 2003 European Cup Final, the first Premiership ground to host club football's biggest match. Wembley has hosted the final five times and Hampden Park twice, the second time last season.

NEWCASTLE END THEIR LONDON HOODOO

Newcastle United ended a run of 29 matches – including two F.A. Cup Finals – without a win in London by beating Arsenal 3-1 with goals by Andy O'Brien, Alan Shearer (pen) and Laurent Robert. Their previous victory in the capital was against Crystal Palace in November 1997.

FIFA WORLD PLAYER OF YEAR TOP TEN

Top ten placings for the FIFA World Player of 2001 award were: 1 Luis Figo (Real Madrid) 250 pts, 2 David Beckham (Manchester Utd.) 238, 3 Raul (Real Madrid) 96, 4 Zinedine Zidane (Real Madrid) 94, 5 Rivaldo (Barcelona) 92, 6 Juan Veron (Manchester Utd.) 71, 7 Oliver Kahn (Bayern Munich) 65, 8 Michael Owen (Liverpool) 61, 9 Andriy Shevchenko (AC Milan) 46, 10 Francesco Totti (Roma) 40.

Top ten for the European Player of 2001 were: 1 Owen 176, 2 Raul 140, 3 Kahn 114, 4 Beckham 102, 5 Totti 57, 6 Figo 56, 7 Rivaldo 20, 8 Shevchenko 18, 9 Zidane and Thierry Henry (Arsenal) 14.

LEAGUE FIXTURES 2002-2003

Saturday, 10 August
Nationwide League Division One
Burnley v Brighton & H.A.
Coventry City v Sheffield Utd.
Derby Co. v Reading
Leicester City v Watford
Millwall v Rotherham Utd.
Norwich City v Grimsby Town
Portsmouth v Nott'm. Forest
Preston N.E. v Crystal Palace
Sheffield Wed. v Stoke City
Walsall v Ipswich Town
Wimbledon v Gillingham

Nationwide League Division Two
Bristol City v Blackpool
Cheltenham Town v Wigan Athletic
Colchester Utd. v Stockport Co.
Huddersfield Town v Brentford
Luton Town v Peterborough Utd.
Mansfield Town v Plymouth Argyle
Northampton Town v Crewe Alexandra
Notts Co. v Wycombe Wand.
Oldham Athletic v Cardiff City
Port Vale v Tranmere Rov.
Q.P.R. v Chesterfield
Swindon Town v Barnsley

Nationwide League Division Three
Boston Utd. v Bournemouth
Cambridge Utd. v Darlington
Carlisle Utd. v Hartlepool Utd.
Hull City v Southend Utd.
Kidderminster Harr. v Lincoln City
Macclesfield Town v York City
Oxford Utd. v Bury
Rochdale v Leyton Orient
Scunthorpe Utd. v Wrexham
Shrewsbury Town v Exeter City
Swansea City v Rushden & D'monds
Torquay Utd. v Bristol Rov.

Sunday, 11 August
Nationwide League Division One
Bradford City v Wolves

Tuesday, 13 August
Nationwide League Division One
Brighton & H.A. v Coventry City
Crystal Palace v Bradford City
Gillingham v Derby Co.
Grimsby Town v Wimbledon

Reading v Sheffield Wed.
Rotherham Utd. v Norwich City
Sheffield Utd. v Portsmouth
Watford v Millwall
Wolves v Walsall

Nationwide League Division Two
Barnsley v Cheltenham Town
Blackpool v Luton Town
Brentford v Bristol City
Cardiff City v Port Vale
Chesterfield v Swindon Town
Crewe Alexandra v Notts Co.
Peterborough Utd. v Oldham Athletic
Plymouth Argyle v Huddersfield Town
Stockport Co. v Q.P.R.
Tranmere Rov. v Colchester Utd.
Wigan Athletic v Mansfield Town
Wycombe Wand. v Northampton Town

Nationwide League Division Three
Bournemouth v Kidderminster Harr.
Bristol Rov. v Hull City
Bury v Cambridge Utd.
Darlington v Swansea City
Exeter City v Scunthorpe Utd.
Hartlepool Utd. v Boston Utd.
Leyton Orient v Macclesfield Town
Lincoln City v Rochdale
Rushden & D'monds v Torquay Utd.
Southend Utd. v Carlisle Utd.
Wrexham v Oxford Utd.
York City v Shrewsbury Town

Wednesday, 14 August
Nationwide League Division One
Nott'm. Forest v Preston N.E.
Stoke City v Leicester City

Saturday, 17 August
F.A. Barclaycard Premiership
Blackburn Rov. v Sunderland
Charlton Athletic v Chelsea
Everton v Tottenham
Fulham v Bolton Wand.
Leeds Utd. v Manchester City
Manchester Utd. v W.B.A.
Newcastle Utd. v West Ham Utd.
Southampton v Middlesbrough

Nationwide League Division One
Brighton & H.A. v Norwich City
Crystal Palace v Portsmouth

Gillingham v Millwall
Grimsby Town v Derby Co.
Nott'm. Forest v Sheffield Wed.
Reading v Coventry City
Rotherham Utd. v Preston N.E.
Sheffield Utd. v Walsall
Stoke City v Bradford City
Watford v Wimbledon
Wolves v Burnley

Nationwide League Division Two
Barnsley v Q.P.R.
Blackpool v Swindon Town
Brentford v Oldham Athletic
Cardiff City v Northampton Town
Chesterfield v Port Vale
Crewe Alexandra v Colchester Utd.
Peterborough Utd. v Huddersfield Town
Plymouth Argyle v Luton Town
Stockport Co. v Notts Co.
Tranmere Rov. v Cheltenham Town
Wigan Athletic v Bristol City
Wycombe Wand. v Mansfield Town

Nationwide League Division Three
Bournemouth v Cambridge Utd.
Bristol Rov. v Rochdale
Bury v Swansea City
Darlington v Oxford Utd.
Exeter City v Hull City
Hartlepool Utd. v Macclesfield Town
Leyton Orient v Scunthorpe Utd.
Lincoln City v Carlisle Utd.
Rushden & D'monds v Kidderminster H.
Southend Utd. v Shrewsbury Town
Wrexham v Boston Utd.
York City v Torquay Utd.

Sunday, 18 August
F.A. Barclaycard Premiership
Arsenal v Birmingham City
Aston Villa v Liverpool

Nationwide League Division One
Ipswich Town v Leicester City

Friday, 23 August
F.A. Barclaycard Premiership
Chelsea v Manchester Utd.

Nationwide League Division Two
Northampton Town v Blackpool

Saturday, 24 August
F.A. Barclaycard Premiership
Birmingham City v Blackburn Rov.
Bolton Wand. v Charlton Athletic
Liverpool v Southampton
Manchester City v Newcastle Utd.
Middlesbrough v Fulham
Sunderland v Everton

Tottenham v Aston Villa
W.B.A. v Leeds Utd.
West Ham Utd. v Arsenal

Nationwide League Division One
Bradford City v Grimsby Town
Burnley v Sheffield Utd.
Coventry City v Crystal Palace
Derby Co. v Wolves
Leicester City v Reading
Millwall v Ipswich Town
Norwich City v Gillingham
Portsmouth v Watford
Preston N.E. v Stoke City
Sheffield Wed. v Rotherham Utd.
Walsall v Nott'm. Forest
Wimbledon v Brighton & H.A.

Nationwide League Division Two
Bristol City v Wycombe Wand.
Cheltenham Town v Plymouth Argyle
Colchester Utd. v Brentford
Huddersfield Town v Crewe Alexandra
Luton Town v Barnsley
Mansfield Town v Chesterfield
Notts Co. v Wigan Athletic
Oldham Athletic v Tranmere Rov.
Port Vale v Stockport Co.
Q.P.R. v Peterborough Utd.
Swindon Town v Cardiff City

Nationwide League Division Three
Boston Utd. v Lincoln City
Cambridge Utd. v Leyton Orient
Carlisle Utd. v Bristol Rov.
Hull City v Bury
Kidderminster Harr. v Exeter City
Macclesfield Town v Wrexham
Oxford Utd. v Southend Utd.
Rochdale v Darlington
Scunthorpe Utd. v York City
Shrewsbury Town v Rushden & D'monds
Swansea City v Bournemouth
Torquay Utd. v Hartlepool Utd.

Monday, 26 August
Nationwide League Division One
Brighton & H.A. v Walsall
Gillingham v Preston N.E.
Grimsby Town v Portsmouth
Ipswich Town v Bradford City
Rotherham Utd. v Derby Co.
Sheffield Utd. v Millwall
Stoke City v Norwich City
Watford v Coventry City

Nationwide League Division Two
Barnsley v Notts Co.
Blackpool v Oldham Athletic
Brentford v Swindon Town
Cardiff City v Luton Town

Peterborough Utd. v Colchester Utd.
Plymouth Argyle v Bristol City
Stockport Co. v Mansfield Town
Tranmere Rov. v Huddersfield Town
Wigan Athletic v Port Vale
Wycombe Wand. v Q.P.R.

Nationwide League Division Three
Bury v Shrewsbury Town
Exeter City v Torquay Utd.
Hartlepool Utd. v Hull City
Leyton Orient v Kidderminster Harr.
Lincoln City v Macclesfield Town
Rushden & D'monds v Scunthorpe Utd.
Southend Utd. v Cambridge Utd.
Wrexham v Rochdale
York City v Boston Utd.

Tuesday, 27 August
F.A. Barclaycard Premiership
Arsenal v W.B.A.
Charlton Athletic v Tottenham
Leeds Utd. v Sunderland

Nationwide League Division One
Crystal Palace v Leicester City
Reading v Burnley
Wolves v Sheffield Wed.

Nationwide League Division Two
Chesterfield v Northampton Town
Crewe Alexandra v Cheltenham Town

Nationwide League Division Three
Bournemouth v Oxford Utd.
Bristol Rov. v Swansea City
Darlington v Carlisle Utd.

Wednesday, 28 August
F.A. Barclaycard Premiership
Aston Villa v Manchester City
Blackburn Rov. v Liverpool
Everton v Birmingham City
Fulham v West Ham Utd.
Newcastle Utd. v Bolton Wand.
Southampton v Chelsea

Nationwide League Division One
Nott'm. Forest v Wimbledon

Saturday, 31 August
F.A. Barclaycard Premiership
Birmingham City v Leeds Utd.
Manchester City v Everton
Middlesbrough v Blackburn Rov.
Sunderland v Manchester Utd.
Tottenham v Southampton
W.B.A. v Fulham
West Ham Utd. v Charlton Athletic

Nationwide League Division One
Bradford City v Rotherham Utd.
Burnley v Crystal Palace
Coventry City v Nott'm. Forest
Derby Co. v Stoke City
Leicester City v Gillingham
Millwall v Grimsby Town
Norwich City v Watford
Portsmouth v Brighton & H.A.
Walsall v Reading
Wimbledon v Wolves

Nationwide League Division Two
Bristol City v Tranmere Rov.
Cheltenham Town v Cardiff City
Colchester Utd. v Wigan Athletic
Huddersfield Town v Blackpool
Luton Town v Chesterfield
Mansfield Town v Crewe Alexandra
Northampton Town v Barnsley
Notts Co. v Brentford
Oldham Athletic v Wycombe Wand.
Port Vale v Peterborough Utd.
Q.P.R. v Plymouth Argyle
Swindon Town v Stockport Co.

Nationwide League Division Three
Boston Utd. v Bury
Cambridge Utd. v Rushden & D'monds
Carlisle Utd. v Exeter City
Hull City v Leyton Orient
Kidderminster Harr. v Darlington
Macclesfield Town v Bournemouth
Oxford Utd. v Hartlepool Utd.
Rochdale v Southend Utd.
Scunthorpe Utd. v Bristol Rov.
Shrewsbury Town v Lincoln City
Swansea City v York City
Torquay Utd. v Wrexham

Sunday, 1 September
F.A. Barclaycard Premiership
Bolton Wand. v Aston Villa
Chelsea v Arsenal

Nationwide League Division One
Preston N.E. v Ipswich Town
Sheffield Wed. v Sheffield Utd.

Monday, 2 September
F.A. Barclaycard Premiership
Liverpool v Newcastle Utd.

Tuesday, 3 September
F.A. Barclaycard Premiership
Manchester Utd. v Middlesbrough

Saturday, 7 September
Nationwide League Division One
Bradford City v Coventry City
Derby Co. v Burnley
Gillingham v Portsmouth
Grimsby Town v Ipswich Town
Millwall v Brighton & H.A.
Norwich City v Sheffield Utd.
Rotherham Utd. v Reading
Sheffield Wed. v Crystal Palace
Stoke City v Nott'm. Forest
Watford v Walsall
Wimbledon v Leicester City
Wolves v Preston N.E.

Nationwide League Division Two
Blackpool v Tranmere Rov.
Brentford v Luton Town
Bristol City v Northampton Town
Colchester Utd. v Cheltenham Town
Crewe Alexandra v Chesterfield
Huddersfield Town v Barnsley
Mansfield Town v Q.P.R.
Notts Co. v Oldham Athletic
Plymouth Argyle v Cardiff City
Stockport Co. v Peterborough Utd.
Swindon Town v Port Vale
Wigan Athletic v Wycombe Wand.

Nationwide League Division Three
Bury v York City
Cambridge Utd. v Hull City
Carlisle Utd. v Rochdale
Darlington v Wrexham
Exeter City v Bournemouth
Kidderminster Harr. v Boston Utd.
Lincoln City v Scunthorpe Utd.
Macclesfield Town v Bristol Rov.
Oxford Utd. v Torquay Utd.
Rushden & D'monds v Southend Utd.
Shrewsbury Town v Leyton Orient
Swansea City v Hartlepool Utd.

Tuesday, 10 September
F.A. Barclaycard Premiership
Arsenal v Manchester City
Middlesbrough v Sunderland

Wednesday, 11 September
F.A. Barclaycard Premiership
Aston Villa v Charlton Athletic
Blackburn Rov. v Chelsea
Fulham v Tottenham
Liverpool v Birmingham City
Manchester Utd. v Bolton Wand.
Newcastle Utd. v Leeds Utd.
Southampton v Everton
West Ham Utd. v W.B.A.

Saturday, 14 September
F.A. Barclaycard Premiership
Bolton Wand. v Liverpool
Charlton Athletic v Arsenal
Chelsea v Newcastle Utd.
Everton v Middlesbrough
Leeds Utd. v Manchester Utd.
Sunderland v Fulham
W.B.A. v Southampton

Nationwide League Division One
Brighton & H.A. v Gillingham
Burnley v Stoke City
Coventry City v Grimsby Town
Crystal Palace v Wolves
Leicester City v Derby Co.
Nott'm. Forest v Watford
Portsmouth v Millwall
Preston N.E. v Sheffield Wed.
Reading v Wimbledon
Sheffield Utd. v Rotherham Utd.
Walsall v Bradford City

Nationwide League Division Two
Barnsley v Plymouth Argyle
Cardiff City v Stockport Co.
Cheltenham Town v Bristol City
Chesterfield v Wigan Athletic
Luton Town v Notts Co.
Northampton Town v Huddersfield Town
Oldham Athletic v Mansfield Town
Peterborough Utd. v Crewe Alexandra
Port Vale v Colchester Utd.
Q.P.R. v Swindon Town
Tranmere Rov. v Brentford
Wycombe Wand. v Blackpool

Nationwide League Division Three
Boston Utd. v Oxford Utd.
Bournemouth v Bury
Bristol Rov. v Exeter City
Hartlepool Utd. v Darlington
Hull City v Carlisle Utd.
Leyton Orient v Lincoln City
Rochdale v Shrewsbury Town
Scunthorpe Utd. v Kidderminster Harr.
Southend Utd. v Macclesfield Town
Torquay Utd. v Cambridge Utd.
Wrexham v Swansea City
York City v Rushden & D'monds

Sunday, 15 September
F.A. Barclaycard Premiership
Birmingham City v Aston Villa
Manchester City v Blackburn Rov.

Nationwide League Division One
Ipswich Town v Norwich City

Monday, 16 September
F.A. Barclaycard Premiership
Tottenham v West Ham Utd.

Tuesday, 17 September
Nationwide League Division One
Brighton & H.A. v Stoke City
Burnley v Millwall
Crystal Palace v Derby Co.
Leicester City v Bradford City
Portsmouth v Wimbledon
Preston N.E. v Watford
Sheffield Utd. v Grimsby Town
Walsall v Rotherham Utd.

Nationwide League Division Two
Barnsley v Blackpool
Cardiff City v Brentford
Cheltenham Town v Swindon Town
Chesterfield v Stockport Co.
Luton Town v Mansfield Town
Northampton Town v Colchester Utd.
Oldham Athletic v Bristol City
Peterborough Utd. v Plymouth Argyle
Port Vale v Notts Co.
Q.P.R. v Huddersfield Town
Tranmere Rov. v Wigan Athletic
Wycombe Wand. v Crewe Alexandra

Nationwide League Division Three
Bournemouth v Rushden & D'monds
Bristol Rov. v Bury
Hartlepool Utd. v Lincoln City
Hull City v Macclesfield Town
Leyton Orient v Oxford Utd.
Rochdale v Cambridge Utd.
Scunthorpe Utd. v Carlisle Utd.
Southend Utd. v Kidderminster Harr.
Torquay Utd. v Shrewsbury Town
Wrexham v Exeter City
York City v Darlington

Wednesday, 18 September
Nationwide League Division One
Coventry City v Sheffield Wed.
Ipswich Town v Wolves
Nott'm. Forest v Gillingham
Reading v Norwich City

Nationwide League Division Three
Boston Utd. v Swansea City

Saturday, 21 September
F.A. Barclaycard Premiership
Arsenal v Bolton Wand.
Liverpool v W.B.A.
Manchester Utd. v Tottenham
Middlesbrough v Birmingham City
Southampton v Charlton Athletic
West Ham Utd. v Manchester City

Nationwide League Division One
Bradford City v Burnley
Derby Co. v Preston N.E.
Gillingham v Sheffield Utd.
Grimsby Town v Nott'm. Forest
Millwall v Walsall
Norwich City v Portsmouth
Rotherham Utd. v Brighton & H.A.
Sheffield Wed. v Leicester City
Stoke City v Ipswich Town
Watford v Crystal Palace
Wimbledon v Coventry City
Wolves v Reading

Nationwide League Division Two
Blackpool v Port Vale
Brentford v Wycombe Wand.
Bristol City v Q.P.R.
Colchester Utd. v Oldham Athletic
Crewe Alexandra v Tranmere Rov.
Huddersfield Town v Luton Town
Mansfield Town v Cheltenham Town
Notts Co. v Cardiff City
Plymouth Argyle v Chesterfield
Stockport Co. v Barnsley
Swindon Town v Northampton Town
Wigan Athletic v Peterborough Utd.

Nationwide League Division Three
Bury v Hartlepool Utd.
Cambridge Utd. v York City
Carlisle Utd. v Boston Utd.
Darlington v Bournemouth
Exeter City v Leyton Orient
Kidderminster Harr. v Rochdale
Lincoln City v Southend Utd.
Macclesfield Town v Scunthorpe Utd.
Oxford Utd. v Hull City
Rushden & D'monds v Wrexham
Shrewsbury Town v Bristol Rov.
Swansea City v Torquay Utd.

Sunday, 22 September
F.A. Barclaycard Premiership
Aston Villa v Everton
Blackburn Rov. v Leeds Utd.
Newcastle Utd. v Sunderland

Monday, 23 September
F.A. Barclaycard Premiership
Fulham v Chelsea

Tuesday, 24 September
Nationwide League Division One
Ipswich Town v Burnley

Saturday, 28 September
F.A. Barclaycard Premiership
Birmingham City v Newcastle Utd.
Bolton Wand. v Southampton

Charlton Athletic v Manchester Utd.
Chelsea v West Ham Utd.
Everton v Fulham
Leeds Utd. v Arsenal
Manchester City v Liverpool
Sunderland v Aston Villa
Tottenham v Middlesbrough

Nationwide League Division One
Brighton & H.A. v Grimsby Town
Burnley v Wimbledon
Coventry City v Millwall
Ipswich Town v Derby Co.
Leicester City v Wolves
Nott'm. Forest v Rotherham Utd.
Portsmouth v Bradford City
Preston N.E. v Norwich City
Reading v Stoke City
Sheffield Utd. v Watford
Walsall v Sheffield Wed.

Nationwide League Division Two
Barnsley v Wigan Athletic
Cardiff City v Crewe Alexandra
Cheltenham Town v Notts Co.
Chesterfield v Blackpool
Luton Town v Swindon Town
Northampton Town v Mansfield Town
Oldham Athletic v Huddersfield Town
Peterborough Utd. v Brentford
Port Vale v Bristol City
Q.P.R. v Colchester Utd.
Tranmere Rov. v Stockport Co.
Wycombe Wand. v Plymouth Argyle

Nationwide League Division Three
Boston Utd. v Cambridge Utd.
Bournemouth v Carlisle Utd.
Bristol Rov. v Kidderminster Harr.
Hartlepool Utd. v Rushden & D'monds
Hull City v Swansea City
Leyton Orient v Darlington
Rochdale v Macclesfield Town
Scunthorpe Utd. v Shrewsbury Town
Southend Utd. v Exeter City
Torquay Utd. v Lincoln City
Wrexham v Bury
York City v Oxford Utd.

Sunday, 29 September
Nationwide League Division One
Crystal Palace v Gillingham

Monday, 30 September
F.A. Barclaycard Premiership
W.B.A. v Blackburn Rov.

Saturday, 5 October
F.A. Barclaycard Premiership
Aston Villa v Leeds Utd.
Fulham v Charlton Athletic
Middlesbrough v Bolton Wand.
Newcastle Utd. v W.B.A.
Southampton v Manchester City
West Ham Utd. v Birmingham City

Nationwide League Division One
Bradford City v Preston N.E.
Derby Co. v Walsall
Gillingham v Coventry City
Grimsby Town v Reading
Millwall v Nott'm. Forest
Norwich City v Leicester City
Rotherham Utd. v Portsmouth
Sheffield Wed. v Burnley
Stoke City v Crystal Palace
Watford v Brighton & H.A.
Wimbledon v Ipswich Town
Wolves v Sheffield Utd.

Nationwide League Division Two
Blackpool v Cheltenham Town
Brentford v Barnsley
Bristol City v Chesterfield
Colchester Utd. v Wycombe Wand.
Crewe Alexandra v Q.P.R.
Huddersfield Town v Port Vale
Mansfield Town v Tranmere Rov.
Notts Co. v Peterborough Utd.
Plymouth Argyle v Northampton Town
Stockport Co. v Luton Town
Swindon Town v Oldham Athletic
Wigan Athletic v Cardiff City

Nationwide League Division Three
Bury v Southend Utd.
Cambridge Utd. v Wrexham
Carlisle Utd. v Torquay Utd.
Darlington v Bristol Rov.
Exeter City v York City
Kidderminster Harr. v Hull City
Lincoln City v Bournemouth
Macclesfield Town v Boston Utd.
Oxford Utd. v Scunthorpe Utd.
Rushden & D'monds v Leyton Orient
Shrewsbury Town v Hartlepool Utd.
Swansea City v Rochdale

Sunday, 6 October
F.A. Barclaycard Premiership
Arsenal v Sunderland
Blackburn Rov. v Tottenham
Liverpool v Chelsea

Monday, 7 October
F.A. Barclaycard Premiership
Manchester Utd. v Everton

Saturday, 12 October
Nationwide League Division One
Bradford City v Derby Co.
Burnley v Walsall
Coventry City v Norwich City
Crystal Palace v Reading
Ipswich Town v Sheffield Wed.
Millwall v Wimbledon
Nott'm. Forest v Brighton & H.A.
Preston N.E. v Leicester City
Rotherham Utd. v Gillingham
Sheffield Utd. v Stoke City
Watford v Grimsby Town
Wolves v Portsmouth

Nationwide League Division Two
Barnsley v Bristol City
Cardiff City v Wycombe Wand.
Chesterfield v Tranmere Rov.
Huddersfield Town v Notts Co.
Luton Town v Cheltenham Town
Northampton Town v Brentford
Peterborough Utd. v Mansfield Town
Plymouth Argyle v Wigan Athletic
Port Vale v Oldham Athletic
Q.P.R. v Blackpool
Stockport Co. v Crewe Alexandra
Swindon Town v Colchester Utd.

Nationwide League Division Three
Boston Utd. v Torquay Utd.
Bournemouth v Hartlepool Utd.
Bristol Rov. v Lincoln City
Bury v Darlington
Carlisle Utd. v Shrewsbury Town
Exeter City v Rushden & D'monds
Hull City v Rochdale
Kidderminster Harr. v Macclesfield Town
Oxford Utd. v Swansea City
Scunthorpe Utd. v Cambridge Utd.
Southend Utd. v York City
Wrexham v Leyton Orient

Friday, 18 October
Nationwide League Division Two
Colchester Utd. v Chesterfield

Saturday, 19 October
F.A. Barclaycard Premiership
Blackburn Rov. v Newcastle Utd.
Everton v Arsenal
Fulham v Manchester Utd.
Leeds Utd. v Liverpool
Manchester City v Chelsea
Sunderland v West Ham Utd.
Tottenham v Bolton Wand.
W.B.A. v Birmingham City

Nationwide League Division One
Derby Co. v Nott'm. Forest
Gillingham v Watford
Grimsby Town v Rotherham Utd.
Leicester City v Burnley
Norwich City v Millwall
Portsmouth v Coventry City
Reading v Ipswich Town
Sheffield Wed. v Bradford City
Stoke City v Wolves
Walsall v Preston N.E.
Wimbledon v Crystal Palace

Nationwide League Division Two
Blackpool v Cardiff City
Brentford v Port Vale
Bristol City v Swindon Town
Cheltenham Town v Q.P.R.
Crewe Alexandra v Plymouth Argyle
Mansfield Town v Huddersfield Town
Notts Co. v Northampton Town
Oldham Athletic v Luton Town
Tranmere Rov. v Barnsley
Wigan Athletic v Stockport Co.
Wycombe Wand. v Peterborough Utd.

Nationwide League Division Three
Cambridge Utd. v Oxford Utd.
Darlington v Boston Utd.
Hartlepool Utd. v Wrexham
Leyton Orient v Bournemouth
Lincoln City v Exeter City
Macclesfield Town v Carlisle Utd.
Rochdale v Scunthorpe Utd.
Rushden & D'monds v Bury
Shrewsbury Town v Kidderminster Harr.
Swansea City v Southend Utd.
Torquay Utd. v Hull City
York City v Bristol Rov.

Sunday, 20 October
F.A. Barclaycard Premiership
Charlton Athletic v Middlesbrough

Nationwide League Division One
Brighton & H.A. v Sheffield Utd.

Monday, 21 October
F.A. Barclaycard Premiership
Aston Villa v Southampton

Friday, 25 October
Nationwide League Division Three
Southend Utd. v Hartlepool Utd.

Saturday, 26 October
F.A. Barclaycard Premiership
Arsenal v Blackburn Rov.
Birmingham City v Manchester City
Chelsea v W.B.A.

Liverpool v Tottenham
Manchester Utd. v Aston Villa
Middlesbrough v Leeds Utd.
Newcastle Utd. v Charlton Athletic

Nationwide League Division One
Bradford City v Norwich City
Burnley v Portsmouth
Coventry City v Walsall
Crystal Palace v Brighton & H.A.
Ipswich Town v Gillingham
Millwall v Derby Co.
Nott'm. Forest v Leicester City
Preston N.E. v Reading
Rotherham Utd. v Stoke City
Sheffield Utd. v Wimbledon
Watford v Sheffield Wed.
Wolves v Grimsby Town

Nationwide League Division Two
Barnsley v Wycombe Wand.
Cardiff City v Tranmere Rov.
Chesterfield v Notts Co.
Huddersfield Town v Colchester Utd.
Luton Town v Wigan Athletic
Northampton Town v Cheltenham Town
Peterborough Utd. v Bristol City
Plymouth Argyle v Blackpool
Port Vale v Crewe Alexandra
Q.P.R. v Oldham Athletic
Stockport Co. v Brentford
Swindon Town v Mansfield Town

Nationwide League Division Three
Boston Utd. v Rochdale
Bournemouth v York City
Bristol Rov. v Leyton Orient
Bury v Macclesfield Town
Carlisle Utd. v Swansea City
Exeter City v Darlington
Hull City v Rushden & D'monds
Kidderminster Harr. v Cambridge Utd.
Oxford Utd. v Shrewsbury Town
Scunthorpe Utd. v Torquay Utd.
Wrexham v Lincoln City

Sunday, 27 October
F.A. Barclaycard Premiership
Southampton v Fulham
West Ham Utd. v Everton

Monday, 28 October
F.A. Barclaycard Premiership
Bolton Wand. v Sunderland

Tuesday, 29 October
Nationwide League Division One
Brighton & H.A. v Ipswich Town
Gillingham v Wolves
Grimsby Town v Burnley

Leicester City v Coventry City
Norwich City v Nott'm. Forest
Portsmouth v Preston N.E.
Reading v Bradford City
Walsall v Crystal Palace
Wimbledon v Rotherham Utd.

Nationwide League Division Two
Blackpool v Stockport Co.
Brentford v Plymouth Argyle
Bristol City v Huddersfield Town
Cheltenham Town v Port Vale
Colchester Utd. v Barnsley
Crewe Alexandra v Luton Town
Mansfield Town v Cardiff City
Notts Co. v Swindon Town
Oldham Athletic v Northampton Town
Tranmere Rov. v Peterborough Utd.
Wigan Athletic v Q.P.R.
Wycombe Wand. v Chesterfield

Nationwide League Division Three
Cambridge Utd. v Carlisle Utd.
Darlington v Scunthorpe Utd.
Hartlepool Utd. v Bristol Rov.
Leyton Orient v Southend Utd.
Lincoln City v Bury
Macclesfield Town v Oxford Utd.
Rochdale v Exeter City
Rushden & D'monds v Boston Utd.
Shrewsbury Town v Hull City
Swansea City v Kidderminster Harr.
Torquay Utd. v Bournemouth
York City v Wrexham

Wednesday, 30 October
Nationwide League Division One
Derby Co. v Sheffield Utd.
Sheffield Wed. v Millwall
Stoke City v Watford

Friday, 1 November
Nationwide League Division Two
Mansfield Town v Colchester Utd.

Nationwide League Division Three
Hartlepool Utd. v York City

Saturday, 2 November
F.A. Barclaycard Premiership
Birmingham City v Bolton Wand.
Blackburn Rov. v Aston Villa
Fulham v Arsenal
Leeds Utd. v Everton
Liverpool v West Ham Utd.
Manchester Utd. v Southampton
W.B.A. v Manchester City

Nationwide League Division One
Brighton & H.A. v Bradford City
Coventry City v Rotherham Utd.

Grimsby Town v Gillingham
Ipswich Town v Crystal Palace
Nott'm. Forest v Sheffield Utd.
Portsmouth v Leicester City
Preston N.E. v Burnley
Reading v Millwall
Sheffield Wed. v Derby Co.
Walsall v Stoke City
Watford v Wolves
Wimbledon v Norwich City

Nationwide League Division Two
Brentford v Blackpool
Bristol City v Notts Co.
Cardiff City v Peterborough Utd.
Cheltenham Town v Huddersfield Town
Chesterfield v Barnsley
Northampton Town v Luton Town
Oldham Athletic v Stockport Co.
Port Vale v Q.P.R.
Tranmere Rov. v Plymouth Argyle
Wigan Athletic v Crewe Alexandra
Wycombe Wand. v Swindon Town

Nationwide League Division Three
Boston Utd. v Exeter City
Bournemouth v Bristol Rov.
Cambridge Utd. v Swansea City
Carlisle Utd. v Oxford Utd.
Darlington v Lincoln City
Hull City v Scunthorpe Utd.
Leyton Orient v Bury
Macclesfield Town v Shrewsbury Town
Rochdale v Rushden & D'monds
Southend Utd. v Wrexham
Torquay Utd. v Kidderminster Harr.

Sunday, 3 November
F.A. Barclaycard Premiership
Charlton Athletic v Sunderland
Tottenham v Chelsea

Monday, 4 November
F.A. Barclaycard Premiership
Newcastle Utd. v Middlesbrough

Saturday, 9 November
F.A. Barclaycard Premiership
Arsenal v Newcastle Utd.
Aston Villa v Fulham
Bolton Wand. v W.B.A.
Chelsea v Birmingham City
Everton v Charlton Athletic
Manchester City v Manchester Utd.
Middlesbrough v Liverpool
Southampton v Blackburn Rov.
West Ham Utd. v Leeds Utd.

Nationwide League Division One
Bradford City v Wimbledon
Burnley v Coventry City
Crystal Palace v Nott'm. Forest
Derby Co. v Portsmouth
Gillingham v Reading
Leicester City v Walsall
Millwall v Preston N.E.
Norwich City v Sheffield Wed.
Rotherham Utd. v Watford
Sheffield Utd. v Ipswich Town
Stoke City v Grimsby Town
Wolves v Brighton & H.A.

Nationwide League Division Two
Barnsley v Cardiff City
Blackpool v Wigan Athletic
Colchester Utd. v Bristol City
Crewe Alexandra v Brentford
Huddersfield Town v Wycombe Wand.
Luton Town v Port Vale
Notts Co. v Mansfield Town
Peterborough Utd. v Chesterfield
Plymouth Argyle v Oldham Athletic
Q.P.R. v Northampton Town
Stockport Co. v Cheltenham Town
Swindon Town v Tranmere Rov.

Nationwide League Division Three
Bristol Rov. v Southend Utd.
Bury v Torquay Utd.
Exeter City v Hartlepool Utd.
Kidderminster Harr. v Carlisle Utd.
Lincoln City v Hull City
Oxford Utd. v Rochdale
Rushden & D'monds v Darlington
Scunthorpe Utd. v Boston Utd.
Shrewsbury Town v Cambridge Utd.
Swansea City v Macclesfield Town
Wrexham v Bournemouth
York City v Leyton Orient

Sunday, 10 November
F.A. Barclaycard Premiership
Sunderland v Tottenham

Saturday, 16 November
F.A. Barclaycard Premiership
Arsenal v Tottenham
Birmingham City v Fulham
Blackburn Rov. v Everton
Chelsea v Middlesbrough
Leeds Utd. v Bolton Wand.
Liverpool v Sunderland
Manchester City v Charlton Athletic
Newcastle Utd. v Southampton
W.B.A. v Aston Villa

Nationwide League Division One
Brighton & H.A. v Derby Co.
Coventry City v Wolves
Gillingham v Sheffield Wed.
Grimsby Town v Preston N.E.
Millwall v Leicester City
Norwich City v Crystal Palace
Nott'm. Forest v Bradford City
Portsmouth v Stoke City
Rotherham Utd. v Burnley
Sheffield Utd. v Reading
Watford v Ipswich Town
Wimbledon v Walsall

Sunday, 17 November
F.A. Barclaycard Premiership
West Ham Utd. v Manchester Utd.

Friday, 22 November
Nationwide League Division Two
Cardiff City v Chesterfield

Saturday, 23 November
F.A. Barclaycard Premiership
Aston Villa v West Ham Utd.
Bolton Wand. v Chelsea
Everton v W.B.A.
Fulham v Liverpool
Manchester Utd. v Newcastle Utd.
Middlesbrough v Manchester City
Southampton v Arsenal
Sunderland v Birmingham City
Tottenham v Leeds Utd.

Nationwide League Division One
Bradford City v Sheffield Utd.
Burnley v Norwich City
Crystal Palace v Grimsby Town
Derby Co. v Wimbledon
Ipswich Town v Coventry City
Leicester City v Rotherham Utd.
Preston N.E. v Brighton & H.A.
Reading v Watford
Sheffield Wed. v Portsmouth
Stoke City v Millwall
Walsall v Gillingham
Wolves v Nott'm. Forest

Nationwide League Division Two
Brentford v Wigan Athletic
Crewe Alexandra v Blackpool
Huddersfield Town v Swindon Town
Luton Town v Q.P.R.
Mansfield Town v Bristol City
Northampton Town v Port Vale
Notts Co. v Colchester Utd.
Oldham Athletic v Cheltenham Town
Peterborough Utd. v Barnsley
Plymouth Argyle v Stockport Co.
Wycombe Wand. v Tranmere Rov.

Nationwide League Division Three
Bristol Rov. v Wrexham
Carlisle Utd. v Bury
Exeter City v Cambridge Utd.
Hull City v Boston Utd.
Kidderminster Harr. v Oxford Utd.
Leyton Orient v Hartlepool Utd.
Lincoln City v Rushden & D'monds
Macclesfield Town v Torquay Utd.
Rochdale v York City
Scunthorpe Utd. v Swansea City
Shrewsbury Town v Darlington
Southend Utd. v Bournemouth

Sunday, 24 November
F.A. Barclaycard Premiership
Charlton Athletic v Blackburn Rov.

Saturday, 30 November
F.A. Barclaycard Premiership
Arsenal v Aston Villa
Birmingham City v Tottenham
Blackburn Rov. v Fulham
Chelsea v Sunderland
Leeds Utd. v Charlton Athletic
Manchester City v Bolton Wand.
Newcastle Utd. v Everton
W.B.A. v Middlesbrough

Nationwide League Division One
Brighton & H.A. v Reading
Coventry City v Preston N.E.
Gillingham v Stoke City
Grimsby Town v Leicester City
Millwall v Bradford City
Norwich City v Derby Co.
Nott'm. Forest v Ipswich Town
Portsmouth v Walsall
Rotherham Utd. v Wolves
Sheffield Utd. v Crystal Palace
Watford v Burnley
Wimbledon v Sheffield Wed.

Nationwide League Division Two
Barnsley v Oldham Athletic
Blackpool v Notts Co.
Bristol City v Crewe Alexandra
Cheltenham Town v Brentford
Chesterfield v Huddersfield Town
Colchester Utd. v Plymouth Argyle
Port Vale v Mansfield Town
Q.P.R. v Cardiff City
Stockport Co. v Wycombe Wand.
Swindon Town v Peterborough Utd.
Tranmere Rov. v Luton Town
Wigan Athletic v Northampton Town

Nationwide League Division Three
Boston Utd. v Leyton Orient
Bournemouth v Scunthorpe Utd.

Bury v Exeter City
Cambridge Utd. v Macclesfield Town
Darlington v Southend Utd.
Hartlepool Utd. v Kidderminster Harr.
Oxford Utd. v Lincoln City
Rushden & D'monds v Bristol Rov.
Swansea City v Shrewsbury Town
Torquay Utd. v Rochdale
Wrexham v Hull City
York City v Carlisle Utd.

Sunday, 1 December
F.A. Barclaycard Premiership
Liverpool v Manchester Utd.

Monday, 2 December
F.A. Barclaycard Premiership
West Ham Utd. v Southampton

Saturday, 7 December
F.A. Barclaycard Premiership
Aston Villa v Newcastle Utd.
Bolton Wand. v Blackburn Rov.
Charlton Athletic v Liverpool
Everton v Chelsea
Fulham v Leeds Utd.
Manchester Utd. v Arsenal
Middlesbrough v West Ham Utd.
Southampton v Birmingham City
Sunderland v Manchester City

Nationwide League Division One
Bradford City v Gillingham
Burnley v Nott'm. Forest
Crystal Palace v Millwall
Derby Co. v Watford
Ipswich Town v Rotherham Utd.
Leicester City v Sheffield Utd.
Preston N.E. v Wimbledon
Reading v Portsmouth
Sheffield Wed. v Brighton & H.A.
Stoke City v Coventry City
Walsall v Grimsby Town
Wolves v Norwich City

Sunday, 8 December
F.A. Barclaycard Premiership
Tottenham v W.B.A.

Saturday, 14 December
F.A. Barclaycard Premiership
Aston Villa v W.B.A.
Charlton Athletic v Manchester City
Everton v Blackburn Rov.
Fulham v Birmingham City
Manchester Utd. v West Ham Utd.
Middlesbrough v Chelsea
Southampton v Newcastle Utd.
Tottenham v Arsenal

Nationwide League Division One
Bradford City v Nott'm. Forest
Burnley v Rotherham Utd.
Crystal Palace v Norwich City
Derby Co. v Brighton & H.A.
Ipswich Town v Watford
Leicester City v Millwall
Preston N.E. v Grimsby Town
Reading v Sheffield Utd.
Sheffield Wed. v Gillingham
Stoke City v Portsmouth
Walsall v Wimbledon
Wolves v Coventry City

Nationwide League Division Two
Brentford v Chesterfield
Cardiff City v Bristol City
Crewe Alexandra v Barnsley
Huddersfield Town v Stockport Co.
Luton Town v Colchester Utd.
Mansfield Town v Blackpool
Northampton Town v Tranmere Rov.
Notts Co. v Q.P.R.
Oldham Athletic v Wigan Athletic
Peterborough Utd. v Cheltenham Town
Plymouth Argyle v Swindon Town
Wycombe Wand. v Port Vale

Nationwide League Division Three
Bristol Rov. v Oxford Utd.
Carlisle Utd. v Wrexham
Exeter City v Swansea City
Hull City v Darlington
Kidderminster Harr. v York City
Leyton Orient v Torquay Utd.
Lincoln City v Cambridge Utd.
Macclesfield T. v Rushden & D'monds
Rochdale v Hartlepool Utd.
Scunthorpe Utd. v Bury
Shrewsbury Town v Bournemouth
Southend Utd. v Boston Utd.

Sunday, 15 December
F.A. Barclaycard Premiership
Sunderland v Liverpool

Monday, 16 December
F.A. Barclaycard Premiership
Bolton Wand. v Leeds Utd.

Friday, 20 December
Nationwide League Division One
Brighton & H.A. v Leicester City

Nationwide League Division Two
Stockport Co. v Northampton Town

Nationwide League Division Three
Hartlepool Utd. v Scunthorpe Utd.
York City v Lincoln City

Saturday, 21 December
F.A. Barclaycard Premiership
Arsenal v Middlesbrough
Birmingham City v Charlton Athletic
Blackburn Rov. v Manchester Utd.
Chelsea v Aston Villa
Leeds Utd. v Southampton
Newcastle Utd. v Fulham
W.B.A. v Sunderland
West Ham Utd. v Bolton Wand.

Nationwide League Division One
Coventry City v Derby Co.
Gillingham v Burnley
Grimsby Town v Sheffield Wed.
Millwall v Wolves
Norwich City v Walsall
Nott'm. Forest v Reading
Portsmouth v Ipswich Town
Rotherham Utd. v Crystal Palace
Sheffield Utd. v Preston N.E.
Watford v Bradford City
Wimbledon v Stoke City

Nationwide League Division Two
Barnsley v Mansfield Town
Blackpool v Peterborough Utd.
Bristol City v Luton Town
Cheltenham Town v Wycombe Wand.
Chesterfield v Oldham Athletic
Colchester Utd. v Cardiff City
Port Vale v Plymouth Argyle
Q.P.R. v Brentford
Swindon Town v Crewe Alexandra
Tranmere Rov. v Notts Co.
Wigan Athletic v Huddersfield Town

Nationwide League Division Three
Boston Utd. v Shrewsbury Town
Bournemouth v Hull City
Bury v Rochdale
Cambridge Utd. v Bristol Rov.
Darlington v Macclesfield Town
Oxford Utd. v Exeter City
Rushden & D'monds v Carlisle Utd.
Swansea City v Leyton Orient
Torquay Utd. v Southend Utd.
Wrexham v Kidderminster Harr.

Sunday, 22 December
F.A. Barclaycard Premiership
Liverpool v Everton

Monday, 23 December
F.A. Barclaycard Premiership
Manchester City v Tottenham

Thursday, 26 December
F.A. Barclaycard Premiership
Birmingham City v Everton
Bolton Wand. v Newcastle Utd.
Chelsea v Southampton
Liverpool v Blackburn Rov.
Manchester City v Aston Villa
Middlesbrough v Manchester Utd.
Sunderland v Leeds Utd.
Tottenham v Charlton Athletic
W.B.A. v Arsenal
West Ham Utd. v Fulham

Nationwide League Division One
Bradford City v Stoke City
Burnley v Wolves
Coventry City v Reading
Derby Co. v Grimsby Town
Leicester City v Ipswich Town
Millwall v Gillingham
Norwich City v Brighton & H.A.
Portsmouth v Crystal Palace
Preston N.E. v Rotherham Utd.
Sheffield Wed. v Nott'm. Forest
Walsall v Sheffield Utd.
Wimbledon v Watford

Nationwide League Division Two
Bristol City v Plymouth Argyle
Cheltenham Town v Crewe Alexandra
Colchester Utd. v Peterborough Utd.
Huddersfield Town v Tranmere Rov.
Luton Town v Cardiff City
Mansfield Town v Stockport Co.
Northampton Town v Chesterfield
Notts Co. v Barnsley
Oldham Athletic v Blackpool
Port Vale v Wigan Athletic
Q.P.R. v Wycombe Wand.
Swindon Town v Brentford

Nationwide League Division Three
Boston Utd. v York City
Cambridge Utd. v Southend Utd.
Carlisle Utd. v Darlington
Hull City v Hartlepool Utd.
Kidderminster Harr. v Leyton Orient
Macclesfield Town v Lincoln City
Oxford Utd. v Bournemouth
Rochdale v Wrexham
Scunthorpe Utd. v Rushden & D'monds
Shrewsbury Town v Bury
Swansea City v Bristol Rov.
Torquay Utd. v Exeter City

Saturday, 28 December
F.A. Barclaycard Premiership
Aston Villa v Middlesbrough
Blackburn Rov. v West Ham Utd.
Charlton Athletic v W.B.A.

Everton v Bolton Wand.
Fulham v Manchester City
Leeds Utd. v Chelsea
Manchester Utd. v Birmingham City
Southampton v Sunderland

Nationwide League Division One
Brighton & H.A. v Burnley
Crystal Palace v Preston N.E.
Gillingham v Wimbledon
Grimsby Town v Norwich City
Ipswich Town v Walsall
Nott'm. Forest v Portsmouth
Reading v Derby Co.
Rotherham Utd. v Millwall
Sheffield Utd. v Coventry City
Stoke City v Sheffield Wed.
Watford v Leicester City
Wolves v Bradford City

Nationwide League Division Two
Barnsley v Port Vale
Blackpool v Colchester Utd.
Brentford v Mansfield Town
Chesterfield v Cheltenham Town
Crewe Alexandra v Oldham Athletic
Peterborough Utd. v Northampton Town
Plymouth Argyle v Notts Co.
Stockport Co. v Bristol City
Tranmere Rov. v Q.P.R.
Wigan Athletic v Swindon Town
Wycombe Wand. v Luton Town

Nationwide League Division Three
Bournemouth v Rochdale
Bristol Rov. v Boston Utd.
Bury v Kidderminster Harr.
Darlington v Torquay Utd.
Exeter City v Macclesfield Town
Hartlepool Utd. v Cambridge Utd.
Leyton Orient v Carlisle Utd.
Lincoln City v Swansea City
Rushden & D'monds v Oxford Utd.
Southend Utd. v Scunthorpe Utd.
Wrexham v Shrewsbury Town
York City v Hull City

Sunday, 29 December
F.A. Barclaycard Premiership
Arsenal v Liverpool
Newcastle Utd. v Tottenham

Nationwide League Division Two
Cardiff City v Huddersfield Town

Wednesday, 1 January 2003
F.A. Barclaycard Premiership
Arsenal v Chelsea
Aston Villa v Bolton Wand.
Blackburn Rov. v Middlesbrough
Charlton Athletic v West Ham Utd.

Everton v Manchester City
Fulham v W.B.A.
Leeds Utd. v Birmingham City
Manchester Utd. v Sunderland
Newcastle Utd. v Liverpool
Southampton v Tottenham

Nationwide League Division One
Brighton & H.A. v Wimbledon
Crystal Palace v Coventry City
Gillingham v Norwich City
Grimsby Town v Bradford City
Ipswich Town v Millwall
Nott'm. Forest v Walsall
Reading v Leicester City
Rotherham Utd. v Sheffield Wed.
Sheffield Utd. v Burnley
Stoke City v Preston N.E.
Watford v Portsmouth
Wolves v Derby Co.

Nationwide League Division Two
Barnsley v Northampton Town
Blackpool v Huddersfield Town
Brentford v Colchester Utd.
Cardiff City v Swindon Town
Chesterfield v Luton Town
Crewe Alexandra v Mansfield Town
Peterborough Utd. v Q.P.R.
Plymouth Argyle v Cheltenham Town
Stockport Co. v Port Vale
Tranmere Rov. v Oldham Athletic
Wigan Athletic v Notts Co.
Wycombe Wand. v Bristol City

Nationwide League Division Three
Bournemouth v Swansea City
Bristol Rov. v Torquay Utd.
Bury v Hull City
Darlington v Rochdale
Exeter City v Kidderminster Harr.
Hartlepool Utd. v Carlisle Utd.
Leyton Orient v Cambridge Utd.
Lincoln City v Boston Utd.
Rushden & D'monds v Shrewsbury Town
Southend Utd. v Oxford Utd.
Wrexham v Macclesfield Town
York City v Scunthorpe Utd.

Saturday, 4 January
Nationwide League Division Two
Bristol City v Brentford
Cheltenham Town v Barnsley
Colchester Utd. v Tranmere Rov.
Huddersfield Town v Plymouth Argyle
Luton Town v Blackpool
Mansfield Town v Wigan Athletic
Northampton Town v Wycombe Wand.
Notts Co. v Crewe Alexandra
Oldham Athletic v Peterborough Utd.

Port Vale v Cardiff City
Q.P.R. v Stockport Co.
Swindon Town v Chesterfield

Nationwide League Division Three
Boston Utd. v Hartlepool Utd.
Cambridge Utd. v Bury
Carlisle Utd. v Southend Utd.
Hull City v Bristol Rov.
Kidderminster Harr. v Bournemouth
Macclesfield Town v Leyton Orient
Oxford Utd. v Wrexham
Rochdale v Lincoln City
Scunthorpe Utd. v Exeter City
Shrewsbury Town v York City
Swansea City v Darlington
Torquay Utd. v Rushden & D'monds

Saturday, 11 January
F.A. Barclaycard Premiership
Birmingham City v Arsenal
Bolton Wand. v Fulham
Chelsea v Charlton Athletic
Liverpool v Aston Villa
Manchester City v Leeds Utd.
Middlesbrough v Southampton
Sunderland v Blackburn Rov.
Tottenham v Everton
W.B.A. v Manchester Utd.
West Ham Utd. v Newcastle Utd.

Nationwide League Division One
Bradford City v Crystal Palace
Burnley v Ipswich Town
Coventry City v Brighton & H.A.
Derby Co. v Gillingham
Leicester City v Stoke City
Millwall v Watford
Norwich City v Rotherham Utd.
Portsmouth v Sheffield Utd.
Preston N.E. v Nott'm. Forest
Sheffield Wed. v Reading
Walsall v Wolves
Wimbledon v Grimsby Town

Nationwide League Division Two
Bristol City v Wigan Athletic
Cheltenham Town v Tranmere Rov.
Colchester Utd. v Crewe Alexandra
Huddersfield Town v Peterborough Utd.
Luton Town v Plymouth Argyle
Mansfield Town v Wycombe Wand.
Northampton Town v Cardiff City
Notts Co. v Stockport Co.
Oldham Athletic v Brentford
Port Vale v Chesterfield
Q.P.R. v Barnsley
Swindon Town v Blackpool

Nationwide League Division Three
Boston Utd. v Wrexham
Cambridge Utd. v Bournemouth
Carlisle Utd. v Lincoln City
Hull City v Exeter City
Kidderminster H. v Rushden & D'monds
Macclesfield Town v Hartlepool Utd.
Oxford Utd. v Darlington
Rochdale v Bristol Rov.
Scunthorpe Utd. v Leyton Orient
Shrewsbury Town v Southend Utd.
Swansea City v Bury
Torquay Utd. v York City

Friday, 17 January
Nationwide League Division Three
Bournemouth v Macclesfield Town

Saturday, 18 January
F.A. Barclaycard Premiership
Arsenal v West Ham Utd.
Aston Villa v Tottenham
Blackburn Rov. v Birmingham City
Charlton Athletic v Bolton Wand.
Everton v Sunderland
Fulham v Middlesbrough
Leeds Utd. v W.B.A.
Manchester Utd. v Chelsea
Newcastle Utd. v Manchester City
Southampton v Liverpool

Nationwide League Division One
Brighton & H.A. v Portsmouth
Crystal Palace v Burnley
Gillingham v Leicester City
Grimsby Town v Millwall
Ipswich Town v Preston N.E.
Nott'm. Forest v Coventry City
Reading v Walsall
Rotherham Utd. v Bradford City
Sheffield Utd. v Sheffield Wed.
Stoke City v Derby Co.
Watford v Norwich City
Wolves v Wimbledon

Nationwide League Division Two
Barnsley v Luton Town
Blackpool v Northampton Town
Brentford v Notts Co.
Cardiff City v Cheltenham Town
Chesterfield v Mansfield Town
Crewe Alexandra v Huddersfield Town
Peterborough Utd. v Port Vale
Plymouth Argyle v Q.P.R.
Stockport Co. v Swindon Town
Tranmere Rov. v Bristol City
Wigan Athletic v Colchester Utd.
Wycombe Wand. v Oldham Athletic

Nationwide League Division Three
Bristol Rov. v Scunthorpe Utd.
Bury v Boston Utd.
Darlington v Kidderminster Harr.
Exeter City v Carlisle Utd.
Hartlepool Utd. v Oxford Utd.
Leyton Orient v Hull City
Lincoln City v Shrewsbury Town
Rushden & D'monds v Cambridge Utd.
Southend Utd. v Rochdale
Wrexham v Torquay Utd.
York City v Swansea City

Saturday, 25 January
Nationwide League Division Two
Bristol City v Stockport Co.
Cheltenham Town v Chesterfield
Colchester Utd. v Blackpool
Huddersfield Town v Cardiff City
Luton Town v Wycombe Wand.
Mansfield Town v Brentford
Northampton Town v Peterborough Utd.
Notts Co. v Plymouth Argyle
Oldham Athletic v Crewe Alexandra
Port Vale v Barnsley
Q.P.R. v Tranmere Rov.
Swindon Town v Wigan Athletic

Nationwide League Division Three
Boston Utd. v Bristol Rov.
Cambridge Utd. v Hartlepool Utd.
Carlisle Utd. v Leyton Orient
Hull City v York City
Kidderminster Harr. v Bury
Macclesfield Town v Exeter City
Oxford Utd. v Rushden & D'monds
Rochdale v Bournemouth
Scunthorpe Utd. v Southend Utd.
Swansea City v Lincoln City
Torquay Utd. v Darlington

Sunday, 26 January
Nationwide League Division Three
Shrewsbury Town v Wrexham

Tuesday, 28 January
F.A. Barclaycard Premiership
Birmingham City v Manchester Utd.
Bolton Wand. v Everton
Middlesbrough v Aston Villa
Sunderland v Southampton
W.B.A. v Charlton Athletic

Wednesday, 29 January
F.A. Barclaycard Premiership
Chelsea v Leeds Utd.
Liverpool v Arsenal
Manchester City v Fulham
Tottenham v Newcastle Utd.

West Ham Utd. v Blackburn Rov.

Friday, 31 January
Nationwide League Division Three
Bournemouth v Boston Utd.

Saturday, 1 February
F.A. Barclaycard Premiership
Arsenal v Fulham
Aston Villa v Blackburn Rov.
Bolton Wand. v Birmingham City
Chelsea v Tottenham
Everton v Leeds Utd.
Manchester City v W.B.A.
Middlesbrough v Newcastle Utd.
Southampton v Manchester Utd.
Sunderland v Charlton Athletic
West Ham Utd. v Liverpool

Nationwide League Division One
Bradford City v Ipswich Town
Burnley v Reading
Coventry City v Watford
Derby Co. v Rotherham Utd.
Leicester City v Crystal Palace
Millwall v Sheffield Utd.
Norwich City v Stoke City
Portsmouth v Grimsby Town
Preston N.E. v Gillingham
Sheffield Wed. v Wolves
Walsall v Brighton & H.A.
Wimbledon v Nott'm. Forest

Nationwide League Division Two
Barnsley v Swindon Town
Blackpool v Bristol City
Brentford v Huddersfield Town
Cardiff City v Oldham Athletic
Chesterfield v Q.P.R.
Crewe Alexandra v Northampton Town
Peterborough Utd. v Luton Town
Plymouth Argyle v Mansfield Town
Stockport Co. v Colchester Utd.
Tranmere Rov. v Port Vale
Wigan Athletic v Cheltenham Town
Wycombe Wand. v Notts Co.

Nationwide League Division Three
Bristol Rov. v Carlisle Utd.
Bury v Oxford Utd.
Darlington v Cambridge Utd.
Exeter City v Shrewsbury Town
Hartlepool Utd. v Torquay Utd.
Leyton Orient v Rochdale
Lincoln City v Kidderminster Harr.
Rushden & D'monds v Swansea City
Southend Utd. v Hull City
Wrexham v Scunthorpe Utd.

Sunday, 2 February
Nationwide League Division Three
York City v Macclesfield Town

Saturday, 8 February
F.A. Barclaycard Premiership
Birmingham City v Chelsea
Blackburn Rov. v Southampton
Charlton Athletic v Everton
Fulham v Aston Villa
Leeds Utd. v West Ham Utd.
Liverpool v Middlesbrough
Manchester Utd. v Manchester City
Newcastle Utd. v Arsenal
Tottenham v Sunderland
W.B.A. v Bolton Wand.

Nationwide League Division One
Brighton & H.A. v Wolves
Coventry City v Burnley
Grimsby Town v Stoke City
Ipswich Town v Sheffield Utd.
Nott'm. Forest v Crystal Palace
Portsmouth v Derby Co.
Preston N.E. v Millwall
Reading v Gillingham
Sheffield Wed. v Norwich City
Walsall v Leicester City
Watford v Rotherham Utd.
Wimbledon v Bradford City

Nationwide League Division Two
Brentford v Crewe Alexandra
Bristol City v Colchester Utd.
Cardiff City v Barnsley
Cheltenham Town v Stockport Co.
Chesterfield v Peterborough Utd.
Mansfield Town v Notts Co.
Northampton Town v Q.P.R.
Oldham Athletic v Plymouth Argyle
Port Vale v Luton Town
Tranmere Rov. v Swindon Town
Wigan Athletic v Blackpool
Wycombe Wand. v Huddersfield Town

Nationwide League Division Three
Boston Utd. v Scunthorpe Utd.
Bournemouth v Wrexham
Cambridge Utd. v Shrewsbury Town
Carlisle Utd. v Kidderminster Harr.
Darlington v Rushden & D'monds
Hartlepool Utd. v Exeter City
Hull City v Lincoln City
Leyton Orient v York City
Macclesfield Town v Swansea City
Rochdale v Oxford Utd.
Southend Utd. v Bristol Rov.
Torquay Utd. v Bury

Friday, 14 February
Nationwide League Division Two
Colchester Utd. v Mansfield Town

Saturday, 15 February
Nationwide League Division One
Bradford City v Brighton & H.A.
Burnley v Preston N.E.
Crystal Palace v Ipswich Town
Derby Co. v Sheffield Wed.
Gillingham v Grimsby Town
Leicester City v Portsmouth
Millwall v Reading
Norwich City v Wimbledon
Rotherham Utd. v Coventry City
Sheffield Utd. v Nott'm. Forest
Stoke City v Walsall
Wolves v Watford

Nationwide League Division Two
Barnsley v Chesterfield
Blackpool v Brentford
Crewe Alexandra v Wigan Athletic
Huddersfield Town v Cheltenham Town
Luton Town v Northampton Town
Notts Co. v Bristol City
Peterborough Utd. v Cardiff City
Plymouth Argyle v Tranmere Rov.
Q.P.R. v Port Vale
Stockport Co. v Oldham Athletic
Swindon Town v Wycombe Wand.

Nationwide League Division Three
Bristol Rov. v Bournemouth
Bury v Leyton Orient
Exeter City v Boston Utd.
Kidderminster Harr. v Torquay Utd.
Lincoln City v Darlington
Oxford Utd. v Carlisle Utd.
Rushden & D'monds v Rochdale
Scunthorpe Utd. v Hull City
Shrewsbury Town v Macclesfield Town
Swansea City v Cambridge Utd.
Wrexham v Southend Utd.
York City v Hartlepool Utd.

Friday, 21 February
Nationwide League Division Two
Cardiff City v Plymouth Argyle

Saturday, 22 February
F.A. Barclaycard Premiership
Birmingham City v Liverpool
Bolton Wand. v Manchester Utd.
Charlton Athletic v Aston Villa
Chelsea v Blackburn Rov.
Everton v Southampton
Leeds Utd. v Newcastle Utd.
Manchester City v Arsenal
Sunderland v Middlesbrough

Tottenham v Fulham
W.B.A. v West Ham Utd.

Nationwide League Division One
Brighton & H.A. v Millwall
Burnley v Derby Co.
Coventry City v Bradford City
Crystal Palace v Sheffield Wed.
Ipswich Town v Grimsby Town
Leicester City v Wimbledon
Nott'm. Forest v Stoke City
Portsmouth v Gillingham
Preston N.E. v Wolves
Reading v Rotherham Utd.
Sheffield Utd. v Norwich City
Walsall v Watford

Nationwide League Division Two
Barnsley v Huddersfield Town
Cheltenham Town v Colchester Utd.
Chesterfield v Crewe Alexandra
Luton Town v Brentford
Northampton Town v Bristol City
Oldham Athletic v Notts Co.
Peterborough Utd. v Stockport Co.
Port Vale v Swindon Town
Q.P.R. v Mansfield Town
Tranmere Rov. v Blackpool
Wycombe Wand. v Wigan Athletic

Nationwide League Division Three
Boston Utd. v Kidderminster Harr.
Bournemouth v Exeter City
Bristol Rov. v Macclesfield Town
Hartlepool Utd. v Swansea City
Hull City v Cambridge Utd.
Leyton Orient v Shrewsbury Town
Rochdale v Carlisle Utd.
Scunthorpe Utd. v Lincoln City
Southend Utd. v Rushden & D'monds
Torquay Utd. v Oxford Utd.
Wrexham v Darlington
York City v Bury

Saturday, 1 March
F.A. Barclaycard Premiership
Arsenal v Charlton Athletic
Aston Villa v Birmingham City
Blackburn Rov. v Manchester City
Fulham v Sunderland
Liverpool v Bolton Wand.
Manchester Utd. v Leeds Utd.
Middlesbrough v Everton
Newcastle Utd. v Chelsea
Southampton v W.B.A.
West Ham Utd. v Tottenham

Nationwide League Division One
Bradford City v Walsall
Derby Co. v Leicester City
Gillingham v Brighton & H.A.

Grimsby Town v Coventry City
Millwall v Portsmouth
Rotherham Utd. v Sheffield Utd.
Sheffield Wed. v Preston N.E.
Stoke City v Burnley
Watford v Nott'm. Forest
Wimbledon v Reading
Wolves v Crystal Palace

Nationwide League Division Two
Blackpool v Wycombe Wand.
Brentford v Tranmere Rov.
Bristol City v Cheltenham Town
Colchester Utd. v Port Vale
Crewe Alexandra v Peterborough Utd.
Huddersfield Town v Northampton Town
Mansfield Town v Oldham Athletic
Notts Co. v Luton Town
Plymouth Argyle v Barnsley
Stockport Co. v Cardiff City
Swindon Town v Q.P.R.
Wigan Athletic v Chesterfield

Nationwide League Division Three
Bury v Bournemouth
Cambridge Utd. v Torquay Utd.
Carlisle Utd. v Hull City
Darlington v Hartlepool Utd.
Exeter City v Bristol Rov.
Kidderminster Harr. v Scunthorpe Utd.
Lincoln City v Leyton Orient
Macclesfield Town v Southend Utd.
Oxford Utd. v Boston Utd.
Rushden & D'monds v York City
Shrewsbury Town v Rochdale
Swansea City v Wrexham

Sunday, 2 March
Nationwide League Division One
Norwich City v Ipswich Town

Tuesday, 4 March
Nationwide League Division One
Bradford City v Leicester City
Gillingham v Nott'm. Forest
Grimsby Town v Sheffield Utd.
Millwall v Burnley
Rotherham Utd. v Walsall
Watford v Preston N.E.
Wimbledon v Portsmouth
Wolves v Ipswich Town

Nationwide League Division Two
Blackpool v Barnsley
Brentford v Cardiff City
Bristol City v Oldham Athletic
Colchester Utd. v Northampton Town
Crewe Alexandra v Wycombe Wand.
Huddersfield Town v Q.P.R.
Mansfield Town v Luton Town

Notts Co. v Port Vale
Plymouth Argyle v Peterborough Utd.
Stockport Co. v Chesterfield
Wigan Athletic v Tranmere Rov.

Nationwide League Division Three
Bury v Bristol Rov.
Cambridge Utd. v Rochdale
Carlisle Utd. v Scunthorpe Utd.
Darlington v York City
Exeter City v Wrexham
Kidderminster Harr. v Southend Utd.
Lincoln City v Hartlepool Utd.
Macclesfield Town v Hull City
Oxford Utd. v Leyton Orient
Rushden & D'monds v Bournemouth
Shrewsbury Town v Torquay Utd.
Swansea City v Boston Utd.

Wednesday, 5 March
Nationwide League Division One
Derby Co. v Crystal Palace
Norwich City v Reading
Sheffield Wed. v Coventry City
Stoke City v Brighton & H.A.

Nationwide League Division Two
Swindon Town v Cheltenham Town

Friday, 7 March
Nationwide League Division Three
Hartlepool Utd. v Bury

Saturday, 8 March
Nationwide League Division One
Brighton & H.A. v Rotherham Utd.
Burnley v Bradford City
Coventry City v Wimbledon
Crystal Palace v Watford
Ipswich Town v Stoke City
Leicester City v Sheffield Wed.
Nott'm. Forest v Grimsby Town
Portsmouth v Norwich City
Preston N.E. v Derby Co.
Reading v Wolves
Sheffield Utd. v Gillingham
Walsall v Millwall

Nationwide League Division Two
Barnsley v Stockport Co.
Cardiff City v Notts Co.
Cheltenham Town v Mansfield Town
Chesterfield v Plymouth Argyle
Luton Town v Huddersfield Town
Northampton Town v Swindon Town
Oldham Athletic v Colchester Utd.
Peterborough Utd. v Wigan Athletic
Port Vale v Blackpool
Q.P.R. v Bristol City
Tranmere Rov. v Crewe Alexandra

Wycombe Wand. v Brentford

Nationwide League Division Three
Boston Utd. v Carlisle Utd.
Bournemouth v Darlington
Bristol Rov. v Shrewsbury Town
Hull City v Oxford Utd.
Leyton Orient v Exeter City
Rochdale v Kidderminster Harr.
Scunthorpe Utd. v Macclesfield Town
Southend Utd. v Lincoln City
Torquay Utd. v Swansea City
Wrexham v Rushden & D'monds
York City v Cambridge Utd.

Friday, 14 March
Nationwide League Division Two
Tranmere Rov. v Cardiff City

Saturday, 15 March
F.A. Barclaycard Premiership
Aston Villa v Manchester Utd.
Blackburn Rov. v Arsenal
Charlton Athletic v Newcastle Utd.
Everton v West Ham Utd.
Fulham v Southampton
Leeds Utd. v Middlesbrough
Manchester City v Birmingham City
Sunderland v Bolton Wand.
Tottenham v Liverpool
W.B.A. v Chelsea

Nationwide League Division One
Brighton & H.A. v Nott'm. Forest
Derby Co. v Bradford City
Gillingham v Rotherham Utd.
Grimsby Town v Watford
Leicester City v Preston N.E.
Norwich City v Coventry City
Portsmouth v Wolves
Reading v Crystal Palace
Sheffield Wed. v Ipswich Town
Stoke City v Sheffield Utd.
Walsall v Burnley
Wimbledon v Millwall

Nationwide League Division Two
Blackpool v Plymouth Argyle
Brentford v Stockport Co.
Bristol City v Peterborough Utd.
Cheltenham Town v Northampton Town
Colchester Utd. v Huddersfield Town
Crewe Alexandra v Port Vale
Mansfield Town v Swindon Town
Notts Co. v Chesterfield
Oldham Athletic v Q.P.R.
Wigan Athletic v Luton Town
Wycombe Wand. v Barnsley

Nationwide League Division Three
Cambridge Utd. v Kidderminster Harr.
Darlington v Exeter City
Hartlepool Utd. v Southend Utd.
Leyton Orient v Bristol Rov.
Lincoln City v Wrexham
Macclesfield Town v Bury
Rochdale v Boston Utd.
Rushden & D'monds v Hull City
Shrewsbury Town v Oxford Utd.
Swansea City v Carlisle Utd.
Torquay Utd. v Scunthorpe Utd.
York City v Bournemouth

Tuesday, 18 March
Nationwide League Division One
Bradford City v Sheffield Wed.
Burnley v Leicester City
Crystal Palace v Wimbledon
Ipswich Town v Reading
Millwall v Norwich City
Preston N.E. v Walsall
Rotherham Utd. v Grimsby Town
Sheffield Utd. v Brighton & H.A.
Watford v Gillingham
Wolves v Stoke City

Nationwide League Division Two
Barnsley v Tranmere Rov.
Cardiff City v Blackpool
Chesterfield v Colchester Utd.
Huddersfield Town v Mansfield Town
Luton Town v Oldham Athletic
Northampton Town v Notts Co.
Peterborough Utd. v Wycombe Wand.
Plymouth Argyle v Crewe Alexandra
Port Vale v Brentford
Q.P.R. v Cheltenham Town
Stockport Co. v Wigan Athletic

Nationwide League Division Three
Bournemouth v Leyton Orient
Bristol Rov. v York City
Bury v Rushden & D'monds
Carlisle Utd. v Macclesfield Town
Exeter City v Lincoln City
Hull City v Torquay Utd.
Kidderminster Harr. v Shrewsbury Town
Oxford Utd. v Cambridge Utd.
Scunthorpe Utd. v Rochdale
Southend Utd. v Swansea City
Wrexham v Hartlepool Utd.

Wednesday, 19 March
Nationwide League Division One
Coventry City v Portsmouth
Nott'm. Forest v Derby Co.

Nationwide League Division Two
Swindon Town v Bristol City

Nationwide League Division Three
Boston Utd. v Darlington

Friday, 21 March
Nationwide League Division Two
Cardiff City v Mansfield Town

Saturday, 22 March
F.A. Barclaycard Premiership
Arsenal v Everton
Birmingham City v W.B.A.
Bolton Wand. v Tottenham
Chelsea v Manchester City
Liverpool v Leeds Utd.
Manchester Utd. v Fulham
Middlesbrough v Charlton Athletic
Newcastle Utd. v Blackburn Rov.
Southampton v Aston Villa
West Ham v Sunderland

Nationwide League Division One
Bradford City v Reading
Burnley v Grimsby Town
Coventry City v Leicester City
Crystal Palace v Walsall
Ipswich Town v Brighton & H.A.
Millwall v Sheffield Wed.
Nott'm. Forest v Norwich City
Preston N.E. v Portsmouth
Rotherham Utd. v Wimbledon
Sheffield Utd. v Derby Co.
Watford v Stoke City
Wolves v Gillingham

Nationwide League Division Two
Barnsley v Colchester Utd.
Chesterfield v Wycombe Wand.
Huddersfield Town v Bristol City
Luton Town v Crewe Alexandra
Northampton Town v Oldham Athletic
Peterborough Utd. v Tranmere Rov.
Plymouth Argyle v Brentford
Port Vale v Cheltenham Town
Q.P.R. v Wigan Athletic
Stockport Co. v Blackpool
Swindon Town v Notts Co.

Nationwide League Division Three
Boston Utd. v Rushden & D'monds
Bournemouth v Torquay Utd.
Bristol Rov. v Hartlepool Utd.
Bury v Lincoln City
Carlisle Utd. v Cambridge Utd.
Exeter City v Rochdale
Hull City v Shrewsbury Town
Kidderminster Harr. v Swansea City
Oxford Utd. v Macclesfield Town
Scunthorpe Utd. v Darlington
Southend Utd. v Leyton Orient
Wrexham v York City

Friday, 28 March
Nationwide League Division Three
Swansea City v Oxford Utd.

Saturday, 29 March
Nationwide League Division One
Brighton & H.A. v Crystal Palace
Derby Co. v Millwall
Gillingham v Ipswich Town
Grimsby Town v Wolves
Leicester City v Nott'm. Forest
Norwich City v Bradford City
Portsmouth v Burnley
Reading v Preston N.E.
Sheffield Wed. v Watford
Stoke City v Rotherham Utd.
Walsall v Coventry City
Wimbledon v Sheffield Utd.

Nationwide League Division Two
Blackpool v Q.P.R.
Brentford v Northampton Town
Bristol City v Barnsley
Cheltenham Town v Luton Town
Colchester Utd. v Swindon Town
Crewe Alexandra v Stockport Co.
Mansfield Town v Peterborough Utd.
Notts Co. v Huddersfield Town
Oldham Athletic v Port Vale
Tranmere Rov. v Chesterfield
Wigan Athletic v Plymouth Argyle
Wycombe Wand. v Cardiff City

Nationwide League Division Three
Cambridge Utd. v Scunthorpe Utd.
Darlington v Bury
Hartlepool Utd. v Bournemouth
Leyton Orient v Wrexham
Lincoln City v Bristol Rov.
Macclesfield Town v Kidderminster Harr.
Rochdale v Hull City
Rushden & D'monds v Exeter City
Shrewsbury Town v Carlisle Utd.
Torquay Utd. v Boston Utd.
York City v Southend Utd.

Friday, 4 April
Nationwide League Division Two
Northampton Town v Wigan Athletic

Saturday, 5 April
F.A. Barclaycard Premiership
Aston Villa v Arsenal
Bolton Wand. v Manchester City
Charlton Athletic v Leeds Utd.
Fulham v Blackburn Rov.
Manchester Utd. v Liverpool
Middlesbrough v W.B.A.
Southampton v West Ham Utd.
Sunderland v Chelsea

Tottenham v Birmingham City

Nationwide League Division One
Bradford City v Millwall
Burnley v Watford
Crystal Palace v Sheffield Utd.
Derby Co. v Norwich City
Ipswich Town v Nott'm. Forest
Leicester City v Grimsby Town
Preston N.E. v Coventry City
Reading v Brighton & H.A.
Sheffield Wed. v Wimbledon
Stoke City v Gillingham
Walsall v Portsmouth
Wolves v Rotherham Utd.

Nationwide League Division Two
Brentford v Cheltenham Town
Cardiff City v Q.P.R.
Crewe Alexandra v Bristol City
Huddersfield Town v Chesterfield
Luton Town v Tranmere Rov.
Mansfield Town v Port Vale
Notts Co. v Blackpool
Oldham Athletic v Barnsley
Peterborough Utd. v Swindon Town
Plymouth Argyle v Colchester Utd.
Wycombe Wand. v Stockport Co.

Nationwide League Division Three
Bristol Rov. v Rushden & D'monds
Carlisle Utd. v York City
Exeter City v Bury
Hull City v Wrexham
Kidderminster Harr. v Hartlepool Utd.
Leyton Orient v Boston Utd.
Lincoln City v Oxford Utd.
Macclesfield Town v Cambridge Utd.
Rochdale v Torquay Utd.
Scunthorpe Utd. v Bournemouth
Shrewsbury Town v Swansea City
Southend Utd. v Darlington

Sunday, 6 April
F.A. Barclaycard Premiership
Everton v Newcastle Utd.

Saturday, 12 April
F.A. Barclaycard Premiership
Arsenal v Southampton
Birmingham City v Sunderland
Blackburn Rov. v Charlton Athletic
Chelsea v Bolton Wand.
Leeds Utd. v Tottenham
Liverpool v Fulham
Manchester City v Middlesbrough
Newcastle Utd. v Manchester Utd.
W.B.A. v Everton
West Ham Utd. v Aston Villa

Nationwide League Division One
Brighton & H.A. v Preston N.E.
Coventry City v Ipswich Town
Gillingham v Walsall
Grimsby Town v Crystal Palace
Millwall v Stoke City
Norwich City v Burnley
Nott'm. Forest v Wolves
Portsmouth v Sheffield Wed.
Rotherham Utd. v Leicester City
Sheffield Utd. v Bradford City
Watford v Reading
Wimbledon v Derby Co.

Nationwide League Division Two
Barnsley v Peterborough Utd.
Blackpool v Crewe Alexandra
Bristol City v Mansfield Town
Cheltenham Town v Oldham Athletic
Chesterfield v Cardiff City
Colchester Utd. v Notts Co.
Port Vale v Northampton Town
Q.P.R. v Luton Town
Stockport Co. v Plymouth Argyle
Swindon Town v Huddersfield Town
Tranmere Rov. v Wycombe Wand.
Wigan Athletic v Brentford

Nationwide League Division Three
Boston Utd. v Hull City
Bournemouth v Southend Utd.
Bury v Carlisle Utd.
Cambridge Utd. v Exeter City
Darlington v Shrewsbury Town
Hartlepool Utd. v Leyton Orient
Oxford Utd. v Kidderminster Harr.
Rushden & D'monds v Lincoln City
Swansea City v Scunthorpe Utd.
Torquay Utd. v Macclesfield Town
Wrexham v Bristol Rov.
York City v Rochdale

Friday, 18 April
Nationwide League Division Two
Northampton Town v Stockport Co.

Saturday, 19 April
F.A. Barclaycard Premiership
Aston Villa v Chelsea
Bolton Wand. v West Ham Utd.
Charlton Athletic v Birmingham City
Everton v Liverpool
Fulham v Newcastle Utd.
Manchester Utd. v Blackburn Rov.
Middlesbrough v Arsenal
Southampton v Leeds Utd.
Sunderland v W.B.A.
Tottenham v Manchester City

Nationwide League Division One
Bradford City v Watford
Burnley v Gillingham
Crystal Palace v Rotherham Utd.
Derby Co. v Coventry City
Ipswich Town v Portsmouth
Leicester City v Brighton & H.A.
Preston N.E. v Sheffield Utd.
Reading v Nott'm. Forest
Sheffield Wed. v Grimsby Town
Stoke City v Wimbledon
Walsall v Norwich City
Wolves v Millwall

Nationwide League Division Two
Brentford v Q.P.R.
Cardiff City v Colchester Utd.
Crewe Alexandra v Swindon Town
Huddersfield Town v Wigan Athletic
Luton Town v Bristol City
Mansfield Town v Barnsley
Notts Co. v Tranmere Rov.
Oldham Athletic v Chesterfield
Peterborough Utd. v Blackpool
Plymouth Argyle v Port Vale
Wycombe Wand. v Cheltenham Town

Nationwide League Division Three
Bristol Rov. v Cambridge Utd.
Carlisle Utd. v Rushden & D'monds
Exeter City v Oxford Utd.
Hull City v Bournemouth
Kidderminster Harr. v Wrexham
Leyton Orient v Swansea City
Lincoln City v York City
Macclesfield Town v Darlington
Rochdale v Bury
Scunthorpe Utd. v Hartlepool Utd.
Shrewsbury Town v Boston Utd.
Southend Utd. v Torquay Utd.

Monday, 21 April
F.A. Barclaycard Premiership
Arsenal v Manchester Utd.
Birmingham City v Southampton
Blackburn Rov. v Bolton Wand.
Chelsea v Everton
Leeds Utd. v Fulham
Liverpool v Charlton Athletic
Manchester City v Sunderland
Newcastle Utd. v Aston Villa
W.B.A. v Tottenham
West Ham Utd. v Middlesbrough

Nationwide League Division One
Brighton & H.A. v Sheffield Wed.
Coventry City v Stoke City
Gillingham v Bradford City
Grimsby Town v Walsall
Millwall v Crystal Palace

Norwich City v Wolves
Nott'm. Forest v Burnley
Portsmouth v Reading
Rotherham Utd. v Ipswich Town
Sheffield Utd. v Leicester City
Watford v Derby Co.

Nationwide League Division Two
Barnsley v Crewe Alexandra
Blackpool v Mansfield Town
Cheltenham Town v Peterborough Utd.
Chesterfield v Brentford
Colchester Utd. v Luton Town
Port Vale v Wycombe Wand.
Q.P.R. v Notts Co.
Stockport Co. v Huddersfield Town
Swindon Town v Plymouth Argyle
Tranmere Rov. v Northampton Town
Wigan Athletic v Oldham Athletic

Nationwide League Division Three
Boston Utd. v Southend Utd.
Bury v Scunthorpe Utd.
Cambridge Utd. v Lincoln City
Darlington v Hull City
Hartlepool Utd. v Rochdale
Oxford Utd. v Bristol Rov.
Rushden & D'monds v Macclesfield T.
Swansea City v Exeter City
Torquay Utd. v Leyton Orient
Wrexham v Carlisle Utd.
York City v Kidderminster Harr.

Tuesday, 22 April
Nationwide League Division One
Wimbledon v Preston N.E.

Nationwide League Division Two
Bristol City v Cardiff City

Nationwide League Division Three
Bournemouth v Shrewsbury Town

Saturday, 26 April
F.A. Barclaycard Premiership
Birmingham City v Middlesbrough
Bolton Wand. v Arsenal
Charlton Athletic v Southampton
Chelsea v Fulham
Everton v Aston Villa
Leeds Utd. v Blackburn Rov.
Manchester City v West Ham Utd.
Sunderland v Newcastle Utd.
Tottenham v Manchester Utd.
W.B.A. v Liverpool

Nationwide League Division One
Brighton & H.A. v Watford
Burnley v Sheffield Wed.
Coventry City v Gillingham
Crystal Palace v Stoke City

Ipswich Town v Wimbledon
Leicester City v Norwich City
Nott'm. Forest v Millwall
Portsmouth v Rotherham Utd.
Preston N.E. v Bradford City
Reading v Grimsby Town
Sheffield Utd. v Wolves
Walsall v Derby Co.

Nationwide League Division Two
Barnsley v Brentford
Cardiff City v Wigan Athletic
Cheltenham Town v Blackpool
Chesterfield v Bristol City
Luton Town v Stockport Co.
Northampton Town v Plymouth Argyle
Oldham Athletic v Swindon Town
Peterborough Utd. v Notts Co.
Port Vale v Huddersfield Town
Q.P.R. v Crewe Alexandra
Tranmere Rov. v Mansfield Town
Wycombe Wand. v Colchester Utd.

Nationwide League Division Three
Boston Utd. v Macclesfield Town
Bournemouth v Lincoln City
Bristol Rov. v Darlington
Hartlepool Utd. v Shrewsbury Town
Hull City v Kidderminster Harr.
Leyton Orient v Rushden & D'monds
Rochdale v Swansea City
Scunthorpe Utd. v Oxford Utd.
Southend Utd. v Bury
Torquay Utd. v Carlisle Utd.
Wrexham v Cambridge Utd.
York City v Exeter City

Saturday, 3 May
F.A. Barclaycard Premiership
Arsenal v Leeds Utd.
Aston Villa v Sunderland
Blackburn Rov. v W.B.A.
Fulham v Everton
Liverpool v Manchester City
Manchester Utd. v Charlton Athletic
Middlesbrough v Tottenham
Newcastle Utd. v Birmingham City
Southampton v Bolton Wand.
West Ham Utd. v Chelsea

Nationwide League Division Two
Blackpool v Chesterfield
Brentford v Peterborough Utd.
Bristol City v Port Vale
Colchester Utd. v Q.P.R.
Crewe Alexandra v Cardiff City
Huddersfield Town v Oldham Athletic
Mansfield Town v Northampton Town
Notts Co. v Cheltenham Town
Plymouth Argyle v Wycombe Wand.

Stockport Co. v Tranmere Rov.
Swindon Town v Luton Town
Wigan Athletic v Barnsley

Nationwide League Division Three
Bury v Wrexham
Cambridge Utd. v Boston Utd.
Carlisle Utd. v Bournemouth
Darlington v Leyton Orient
Exeter City v Southend Utd.
Kidderminster Harr. v Bristol Rov.
Lincoln City v Torquay Utd.
Macclesfield Town v Rochdale
Oxford Utd. v York City
Rushden & D'monds v Hartlepool Utd.
Shrewsbury Town v Scunthorpe Utd.
Swansea City v Hull City

Sunday, 4 May
Nationwide League Division One
Bradford City v Portsmouth
Derby Co. v Ipswich Town
Gillingham v Crystal Palace

Grimsby Town v Brighton & H.A.
Millwall v Coventry City
Norwich City v Preston N.E.
Rotherham Utd. v Nott'm. Forest
Sheffield Wed. v Walsall
Stoke City v Reading
Watford v Sheffield Utd.
Wimbledon v Burnley
Wolves v Leicester City

Sunday, 11 May
F.A. Barclaycard Premiership
Birmingham City v West Ham Utd.
Bolton Wand. v Middlesbrough
Charlton Athletic v Fulham
Chelsea v Liverpool
Everton v Manchester Utd.
Leeds Utd. v Aston Villa
Manchester City v Southampton
Sunderland v Arsenal
Tottenham v Blackburn Rov.
W.B.A. v Newcastle Utd.

SCOTTISH LEAGUE FIXTURES 2002-2003

Reproduced under copyright licence no. Print/All/3004
(Copyright © The Scottish Football League 2002)
(Copyright © The Scottish Premier League 2002)

Saturday, 3 August
Bank of Scotland Premier League
Celtic v Dunfermline
Dundee v Hearts
Hibernian v Aberdeen
Kilmarnock v Rangers
Livingston v Motherwell
Partick v Dundee Utd.

Bell's First Division
Arbroath v Ross County
Ayr v Falkirk
Inverness CT v Alloa
Queen of South v Clyde
St Mirren v St Johnstone

Bell's Second Division
Brechin v Berwick
Airdrie Utd. v Forfar
Cowdenbeath v Hamilton
Raith v Stranraer
Stenhousemuir v Dumbarton

Bell's Third Division
East Stirling v Montrose
Gretna v Morton
Peterhead v East Fife
Queens Park v Elgin
Stirling v Albion

Saturday, 10 August
Bank of Scotland Premier League
Aberdeen v Celtic
Dundee Utd. v Kilmarnock
Dunfermline v Livingston
Hearts v Hibernian
Motherwell v Partick
Rangers v Dundee

Bell's First Division
Alloa v Arbroath
Clyde v Ayr
Falkirk v St Mirren
Ross County v Queen of South
St Johnstone v Inverness CT

Bell's Second Division
Berwick v Raith
Dumbarton v Brechin
Forfar v Stenhousemuir
Hamilton v Airdrie Utd.
Stranraer v Cowdenbeath

Bell's Third Division
Albion v Peterhead
East Fife v East Stirling
Elgin v Gretna
Montrose v Queens Park
Morton v Stirling

Saturday, 17 August
Bank of Scotland Premier League
Celtic v Dundee Utd.
Dunfermline v Dundee
Hibernian v Rangers
Kilmarnock v Motherwell

Bell's First Division
Arbroath v Clyde
Ayr v Ross County
Inverness CT v Falkirk
Queen of South v St Johnstone
St Mirren v Alloa

Bell's Second Division
Brechin v Hamilton
Airdrie Utd. v Stranraer
Cowdenbeath v Forfar
Raith v Dumbarton
Stenhousemuir v Berwick

Bell's Third Division
East Stirling v Albion
Gretna v Montrose
Peterhead v Morton
Queens Park v East Fife
Stirling v Elgin

Sunday, 18 August
Bank of Scotland Premier League
Aberdeen v Hearts
Partick v Livingston

Saturday, 24 August
Bank of Scotland Premier League
Dundee v Hibernian
Hearts v Dunfermline
Livingston v Kilmarnock
Partick v Celtic

Bell's First Division
Alloa v Falkirk
Arbroath v St Johnstone
Clyde v St Mirren
Inverness CT v Ross County
Queen of South v Ayr

Bell's Second Division
Brechin v Forfar
Cowdenbeath v Raith
Dumbarton v Airdrie Utd.
Hamilton v Berwick
Stenhousemuir v Stranraer

Bell's Third Division
East Fife v Montrose
Elgin v Peterhead
Morton v Queens Park
Gretna v Albion
Stirling v East Stirling

Sunday, 25 August
Bank of Scotland Premier League
Dundee Utd. v Motherwell
Rangers v Aberdeen

Saturday, 31 August
Bank of Scotland Premier League
Dundee Utd. v Dundee
Dunfermline v Rangers
Hearts v Kilmarnock
Motherwell v Hibernian

Bell's First Division
Ayr v Arbroath
Falkirk v Queen of South
Ross County v Clyde
St Johnstone v Alloa
St Mirren v Inverness CT

Bell's Second Division
Berwick v Dumbarton
Airdrie Utd. v Cowdenbeath
Forfar v Hamilton
Raith v Stenhousemuir
Stranraer v Brechin

Bell's Third Division
Albion v East Fife
East Stirling v Morton
Montrose v Elgin
Peterhead v Stirling
Queens Park v Gretna

Sunday, 1 September
Bank of Scotland Premier League
Aberdeen v Partick
Celtic v Livingston

Wednesday, 11 September
Bank of Scotland Premier League
Aberdeen v Dundee Utd.
Dundee v Livingston
Hibernian v Dunfermline
Kilmarnock v Partick
Motherwell v Celtic
Rangers v Hearts

Saturday, 14 September
Bank of Scotland Premier League
Celtic v Hibernian
Dundee Utd. v Dunfermline
Hearts v Motherwell
Kilmarnock v Aberdeen
Livingston v Rangers
Partick v Dundee

Bell's First Division
Arbroath v St Mirren
Ayr v St Johnstone
Clyde v Alloa
Queen of South v Inverness CT
Ross County v Falkirk

Bell's Second Division
Berwick v Stranraer
Brechin v Cowdenbeath
Dumbarton v Forfar
Raith v Airdrie Utd.
Stenhousemuir v Hamilton

Bell's Third Division
Elgin v East Fife
Morton v Albion
Gretna v Peterhead
Queens Park v East Stirling
Stirling v Montrose

Saturday, 21 September
Bank of Scotland Premier League
Dundee v Celtic
Dunfermline v Motherwell
Hearts v Dundee Utd.
Hibernian v Kilmarnock
Livingston v Aberdeen

Bell's First Division
Alloa v Ayr
Falkirk v Clyde
Inverness CT v Arbroath
St Johnstone v Ross County
St Mirren v Queen of South

Bell's Second Division
Airdrie Utd. v Brechin
Cowdenbeath v Stenhousemuir
Forfar v Berwick
Hamilton v Raith
Stranraer v Dumbarton

Bell's Third Division
Albion v Elgin
East Fife v Stirling
East Stirling v Gretna
Montrose v Morton
Peterhead v Queens Park

Sunday, 22 September
Bank of Scotland Premier League
Rangers v Partick

Saturday, 28 September
Bank of Scotland Premier League
Aberdeen v Dunfermline
Celtic v Kilmarnock
Dundee Utd. v Rangers
Hibernian v Livingston
Motherwell v Dundee
Partick v Hearts

Bell's First Division
Ayr v St Mirren
Clyde v Inverness CT
Falkirk v St Johnstone
Queen of South v Arbroath
Ross County v Alloa

Bell's Second Division
Berwick v Cowdenbeath
Dumbarton v Hamilton
Raith v Brechin
Stenhousemuir v Airdrie Utd.
Stranraer v Forfar

Bell's Third Division
East Stirling v Elgin
Montrose v Peterhead
Morton v East Fife
Gretna v Stirling
Queens Park v Albion

Saturday, 5 October
Bank of Scotland Premier League
Dundee v Kilmarnock
Dunfermline v Partick
Hibernian v Dundee Utd.
Livingston v Hearts
Motherwell v Aberdeen

Bell's First Division
Alloa v Queen of South
Arbroath v Falkirk
Inverness CT v Ayr
St Johnstone v Clyde
St Mirren v Ross County

Bell's Second Division
Brechin v Stenhousemuir
Airdrie Utd. v Berwick
Cowdenbeath v Dumbarton
Forfar v Raith
Hamilton v Stranraer

Bell's Third Division
Albion v Montrose
East Fife v Gretna
Elgin v Morton
Peterhead v East Stirling
Stirling v Queens Park

Sunday, 6 October
Bank of Scotland Premier League
Celtic v Rangers

Saturday, 19 October
Bank of Scotland Premier League
Aberdeen v Dundee
Dundee Utd. v Livingston
Hearts v Celtic
Kilmarnock v Dunfermline
Partick v Hibernian
Rangers v Motherwell

Bell's First Division
Alloa v Inverness CT
Clyde v Queen of South
Falkirk v Ayr
Ross County v Arbroath
St Johnstone v St Mirren

Bell's Second Division
Brechin v Dumbarton
Airdrie Utd. v Hamilton
Cowdenbeath v Stranraer
Raith v Berwick
Stenhousemuir v Forfar

Bell's Third Division
East Stirling v East Fife
Gretna v Elgin
Peterhead v Albion
Queens Park v Montrose
Stirling v Morton

Saturday, 26 October
Bank of Scotland Premier League
Aberdeen v Hibernian
Dundee Utd. v Partick
Dunfermline v Celtic
Hearts v Dundee
Motherwell v Livingston
Rangers v Kilmarnock

Bell's First Division
Arbroath v Alloa
Ayr v Clyde
Inverness CT v St Johnstone
Queen of South v Ross County
St Mirren v Falkirk

Bell's Second Division
Berwick v Brechin
Dumbarton v Stenhousemuir
Forfar v Airdrie Utd.
Hamilton v Cowdenbeath
Stranraer v Raith

Bell's Third Division
Albion v Stirling
East Fife v Peterhead
Elgin v Queens Park
Montrose v East Stirling
Morton v Gretna

Saturday, 2 November
Bank of Scotland Premier League
Celtic v Aberdeen
Dundee v Rangers
Hibernian v Hearts
Kilmarnock v Dundee Utd.
Livingston v Dunfermline
Partick v Motherwell

Bell's First Division
Alloa v St Johnstone
Arbroath v Ayr
Clyde v Ross County
Inverness CT v St Mirren
Queen of South v Falkirk

Bell's Second Division
Brechin v Stranraer
Cowdenbeath v Airdrie Utd.
Dumbarton v Berwick

Hamilton v Forfar
Stenhousemuir v Raith

Bell's Third Division
East Fife v Albion
Elgin v Montrose
Morton v East Stirling
Gretna v Queens Park
Stirling v Peterhead

Saturday, 9 November
Bank of Scotland Premier League
Dundee Utd. v Celtic
Hearts v Aberdeen
Livingston v Partick
Motherwell v Kilmarnock
Rangers v Hibernian

Bell's First Division
Ayr v Queen of South
Falkirk v Alloa
Ross County v Inverness CT
St Johnstone v Arbroath
St Mirren v Clyde

Bell's Second Division
Berwick v Hamilton
Airdrie Utd. v Dumbarton
Forfar v Brechin
Raith v Cowdenbeath
Stranraer v Stenhousemuir

Bell's Third Division
Albion v Gretna
East Stirling v Stirling
Montrose v East Fife
Peterhead v Elgin
Queens Park v Morton

Sunday, 10 November
Bank of Scotland Premier League
Dundee v Dunfermline

Saturday, 16 November
Bank of Scotland Premier League
Aberdeen v Rangers
Celtic v Partick
Dunfermline v Hearts
Hibernian v Dundee
Kilmarnock v Livingston
Motherwell v Dundee Utd.

Bell's First Division
Alloa v Clyde
Falkirk v Ross County
Inverness CT v Queen of South
St Johnstone v Ayr
St Mirren v Arbroath

Bell's Second Division
Airdrie Utd. v Raith
Cowdenbeath v Brechin
Forfar v Dumbarton
Hamilton v Stenhousemuir

Stranraer v Berwick

Bell's Third Division
Albion v Morton
East Fife v Elgin
East Stirling v Queens Park
Montrose v Stirling
Peterhead v Gretna

Saturday, 23 November
Bank of Scotland Premier League
Dundee v Dundee Utd.
Hibernian v Motherwell
Kilmarnock v Hearts
Livingston v Celtic
Partick v Aberdeen
Rangers v Dunfermline

Bell's First Division
Arbroath v Inverness CT
Ayr v Alloa
Clyde v Falkirk
Queen of South v St Mirren
Ross County v St Johnstone

Bell's Second Division
Berwick v Forfar
Brechin v Airdrie Utd.
Dumbarton v Stranraer
Raith v Hamilton
Stenhousemuir v Cowdenbeath

Bell's Third Division
Elgin v Albion
Morton v Montrose
Gretna v East Stirling
Queens Park v Peterhead
Stirling v East Fife

Saturday, 30 November
Bank of Scotland Premier League
Celtic v Motherwell
Dundee Utd. v Aberdeen
Dunfermline v Hibernian
Hearts v Rangers
Livingston v Dundee
Partick v Kilmarnock

Bell's First Division
Alloa v Ross County
Arbroath v Queen of South
Inverness CT v Clyde
St Johnstone v Falkirk
St Mirren v Ayr

Bell's Second Division
Berwick v Airdrie Utd.
Dumbarton v Cowdenbeath
Raith v Forfar
Stenhousemuir v Brechin
Stranraer v Hamilton

Bell's Third Division
East Stirling v Peterhead
Montrose v Albion
Morton v Elgin
Gretna v East Fife
Queens Park v Stirling

Wednesday, 4 December
Bank of Scotland Premier League
Aberdeen v Kilmarnock
Dundee v Partick
Dunfermline v Dundee Utd.
Hibernian v Celtic
Motherwell v Hearts
Rangers v Livingston

Saturday, 7 December
Bank of Scotland Premier League
Aberdeen v Motherwell
Dundee Utd. v Hibernian
Hearts v Livingston
Kilmarnock v Dundee
Partick v Dunfermline
Rangers v Celtic

Bell's First Division
Ayr v Inverness CT
Clyde v St Johnstone
Falkirk v Arbroath
Queen of South v Alloa
Ross County v St Mirren

Saturday, 14 December
Bank of Scotland Premier League
Dundee v Motherwell
Dunfermline v Aberdeen
Hearts v Partick
Kilmarnock v Celtic
Livingston v Hibernian
Rangers v Dundee Utd.

Bell's First Division
Alloa v St Mirren
Clyde v Arbroath
Falkirk v Inverness CT
Ross County v Ayr
St Johnstone v Queen of South

Bell's Second Division
Brechin v Raith
Airdrie Utd. v Stenhousemuir
Cowdenbeath v Berwick
Forfar v Stranraer
Hamilton v Dumbarton

Bell's Third Division
Albion v Queens Park
East Fife v Morton
Elgin v East Stirling
Peterhead v Montrose
Stirling v Gretna

Saturday, 21 December
Bank of Scotland Premier League
Aberdeen v Livingston
Celtic v Dundee
Dundee Utd. v Hearts
Kilmarnock v Hibernian
Motherwell v Dunfermline
Partick v Rangers

Bell's First Division
Arbroath v Ross County
Ayr v Falkirk
Inverness CT v Alloa
Queen of South v Clyde
St Mirren v St Johnstone

Bell's Second Division
Brechin v Berwick
Airdrie Utd. v Forfar
Cowdenbeath v Hamilton
Raith v Stranraer
Stenhousemuir v Dumbarton

Bell's Third Division
East Stirling v Montrose
Gretna v Morton
Peterhead v East Fife
Queens Park v Elgin
Stirling v Albion

Thursday, 26 December
Bank of Scotland Premier League
Celtic v Hearts
Dundee v Aberdeen
Dunfermline v Kilmarnock
Hibernian v Partick
Livingston v Dundee Utd.
Motherwell v Rangers

Saturday, 28 December
Bell's First Division
Ayr v Arbroath
Falkirk v Queen of South
Ross County v Clyde
St Johnstone v Alloa
St Mirren v Inverness CT

Bell's Second Division
Berwick v Stenhousemuir
Dumbarton v Raith
Forfar v Cowdenbeath
Hamilton v Brechin
Stranraer v Airdrie Utd.

Bell's Third Division
Albion v East Stirling
East Fife v Queens Park
Elgin v Stirling
Montrose v Gretna
Morton v Peterhead

Sunday, 29 December
Bank of Scotland Premier League
Celtic v Dunfermline
Dundee v Hearts
Hibernian v Aberdeen
Kilmarnock v Rangers
Livingston v Motherwell
Partick v Dundee Utd.

Wednesday, 1 January 2003
Bell's First Division
Alloa v Falkirk
Arbroath v St Johnstone
Clyde v St Mirren
Inverness CT v Ross County
Queen of South v Ayr

Bell's Second Division
Brechin v Forfar
Cowdenbeath v Raith
Dumbarton v Airdrie Utd.
Hamilton v Berwick
Stenhousemuir v Stranraer

Bell's Third Division
East Fife v Montrose
Elgin v Peterhead
Morton v Queens Park
Gretna v Albion
Stirling v East Stirling

Thursday, 2 January
Bank of Scotland Premier League
Aberdeen v Celtic
Dundee Utd. v Kilmarnock
Dunfermline v Livingston
Hearts v Hibernian
Motherwell v Partick
Rangers v Dundee

Saturday, 4 January
Bell's First Division
Arbroath v St Mirren
Ayr v St Johnstone
Clyde v Alloa
Queen of South v Inverness CT
Ross County v Falkirk

Saturday, 11 January
Bell's First Division
Alloa v Ayr
Falkirk v Clyde
Inverness CT v Arbroath
St Johnstone v Ross County
St Mirren v Queen of South

Bell's Second Division
Berwick v Dumbarton
Airdrie Utd. v Cowdenbeath
Forfar v Hamilton
Raith v Stenhousemuir
Stranraer v Brechin

Bell's Third Division
Albion v East Fife
East Stirling v Morton
Montrose v Elgin
Peterhead v Stirling
Queens Park v Gretna

Saturday, 18 January
Bell's First Division
Alloa v Queen of South
Arbroath v Falkirk
Inverness CT v Ayr
St Johnstone v Clyde
St Mirren v Ross County

Bell's Second Division
Berwick v Stranraer
Brechin v Cowdenbeath
Dumbarton v Forfar
Raith v Airdrie Utd.
Stenhousemuir v Hamilton

Bell's Third Division
Elgin v East Fife
Morton v Albion
Gretna v Peterhead
Queens Park v East Stirling
Stirling v Montrose

Tuesday, 28 January
Bank of Scotland Premier League
Partick v Livingston

Wednesday, 29 January
Bank of Scotland Premier League
Aberdeen v Hearts
Celtic v Dundee Utd.
Dunfermline v Dundee
Hibernian v Rangers
Kilmarnock v Motherwell

Saturday, 1 February
Bank of Scotland Premier League
Dundee v Hibernian
Hearts v Dunfermline
Livingston v Kilmarnock
Partick v Celtic

Bell's First Division
Ayr v St Mirren
Clyde v Inverness CT
Falkirk v St Johnstone
Queen of South v Arbroath
Ross County v Alloa

Bell's Second Division
Airdrie Utd. v Brechin
Cowdenbeath v Stenhousemuir
Forfar v Berwick
Hamilton v Raith
Stranraer v Dumbarton

Bell's Third Division
Albion v Elgin
East Fife v Stirling
East Stirling v Gretna
Montrose v Morton
Peterhead v Queens Park

Sunday, 2 February
Bank of Scotland Premier League
Dundee Utd. v Motherwell
Rangers v Aberdeen

Saturday, 8 February
Bank of Scotland Premier League
Aberdeen v Partick
Celtic v Livingston
Dundee Utd. v Dundee
Dunfermline v Rangers
Hearts v Kilmarnock
Motherwell v Hibernian

Bell's First Division
Arbroath v Clyde
Ayr v Ross County
Inverness CT v Falkirk
Queen of South v St Johnstone
St Mirren v Alloa

Bell's Second Division
Berwick v Cowdenbeath
Dumbarton v Hamilton
Raith v Brechin
Stenhousemuir v Airdrie Utd.
Stranraer v Forfar

Bell's Third Division
East Stirling v Elgin
Montrose v Peterhead
Morton v East Fife
Gretna v Stirling
Queens Park v Albion

Saturday, 15 February
Bank of Scotland Premier League
Aberdeen v Dundee Utd.
Dundee v Livingston
Hibernian v Dunfermline
Kilmarnock v Partick
Motherwell v Celtic
Rangers v Hearts

Bell's First Division
Alloa v Arbroath
Clyde v Ayr
Falkirk v St Mirren
Ross County v Queen of South
St Johnstone v Inverness CT

Bell's Second Division
Brechin v Stenhousemuir
Airdrie Utd. v Berwick
Cowdenbeath v Dumbarton
Forfar v Raith

Hamilton v Stranraer

Bell's Third Division
Albion v Montrose
East Fife v Gretna
Elgin v Morton
Peterhead v East Stirling
Stirling v Queens Park

Saturday, 22 February
Bell's Second Division
Berwick v Raith
Dumbarton v Brechin
Forfar v Stenhousemuir
Hamilton v Airdrie Utd.
Stranraer v Cowdenbeath

Bell's Third Division
Albion v Peterhead
East Fife v East Stirling
Elgin v Gretna
Montrose v Queens Park
Morton v Stirling

Saturday, 1 March
Bank of Scotland Premier League
Celtic v Hibernian
Dundee Utd. v Dunfermline
Hearts v Motherwell
Kilmarnock v Aberdeen
Livingston v Rangers
Partick v Dundee

Bell's First Division
Alloa v St Johnstone
Arbroath v Ayr
Clyde v Ross County
Inverness CT v St Mirren
Queen of South v Falkirk

Bell's Second Division
Brechin v Hamilton
Airdrie Utd. v Stranraer
Cowdenbeath v Forfar
Raith v Dumbarton
Stenhousemuir v Berwick

Bell's Third Division
East Stirling v Albion
Gretna v Montrose
Peterhead v Morton
Queens Park v East Fife
Stirling v Elgin

Saturday, 8 March
Bank of Scotland Premier League
Celtic v Rangers
Dundee v Kilmarnock
Dunfermline v Partick
Hibernian v Dundee Utd.
Livingston v Hearts
Motherwell v Aberdeen

Bell's First Division
Ayr v Queen of South
Falkirk v Alloa
Ross County v Inverness CT
St Johnstone v Arbroath
St Mirren v Clyde

Bell's Second Division
Berwick v Hamilton
Airdrie Utd. v Dumbarton
Forfar v Brechin
Raith v Cowdenbeath
Stranraer v Stenhousemuir

Bell's Third Division
Albion v Gretna
East Stirling v Stirling
Montrose v East Fife
Peterhead v Elgin
Queens Park v Morton

Saturday, 15 March
Bank of Scotland Premier League
Aberdeen v Dundee
Dundee Utd. v Livingston
Hearts v Celtic
Kilmarnock v Dunfermline
Partick v Hibernian
Rangers v Motherwell

Bell's First Division
Arbroath v Inverness CT
Ayr v Alloa
Clyde v Falkirk
Queen of South v St Mirren
Ross County v St Johnstone

Bell's Second Division
Brechin v Stranraer
Cowdenbeath v Airdrie Utd.
Dumbarton v Berwick
Hamilton v Forfar
Stenhousemuir v Raith

Bell's Third Division
East Fife v Albion
Elgin v Montrose
Morton v East Stirling
Gretna v Queens Park
Stirling v Peterhead

Saturday, 22 March
Bell's Second Division
Berwick v Forfar
Brechin v Airdrie Utd.
Dumbarton v Stranraer
Raith v Hamilton
Stenhousemuir v Cowdenbeath

Bell's Third Division
Elgin v Albion
Morton v Montrose
Gretna v East Stirling
Queens Park v Peterhead

Stirling v East Fife

Saturday, 5 April
Bank of Scotland Premier League
Dundee v Celtic
Dunfermline v Motherwell
Hearts v Dundee Utd.
Kilmarnock v Hibernian
Livingston v Aberdeen
Rangers v Partick

Bell's First Division
Alloa v Clyde
Falkirk v Ross County
Inverness CT v Queen of South
St Johnstone v Ayr
St Mirren v Arbroath

Bell's Second Division
Airdrie Utd. v Raith
Cowdenbeath v Brechin
Forfar v Dumbarton
Hamilton v Stenhousemuir
Stranraer v Berwick

Bell's Third Division
Albion v Morton
East Fife v Elgin
East Stirling v Queens Park
Montrose v Stirling
Peterhead v Gretna

Saturday, 12 April
Bank of Scotland Premier League
Aberdeen v Dunfermline
Celtic v Kilmarnock
Dundee Utd. v Rangers
Hibernian v Livingston
Motherwell v Dundee
Partick v Hearts

Bell's First Division
Alloa v Ross County
Arbroath v Queen of South
Inverness CT v Clyde
St Johnstone v Falkirk
St Mirren v Ayr

Bell's Second Division
Berwick v Airdrie Utd.
Dumbarton v Cowdenbeath
Raith v Forfar
Stenhousemuir v Brechin
Stranraer v Hamilton

Bell's Third Division
East Stirling v Peterhead
Montrose v Albion
Morton v Elgin
Gretna v East Fife
Queens Park v Stirling

Saturday, 19 April
Bell's First Division
Ayr v Inverness CT
Clyde v St Johnstone
Falkirk v Arbroath
Queen of South v Alloa
Ross County v St Mirren

Bell's Second Division
Brechin v Raith
Airdrie Utd. v Stenhousemuir
Cowdenbeath v Berwick
Forfar v Stranraer
Hamilton v Dumbarton

Bell's Third Division
Albion v Queens Park
East Fife v Morton
Elgin v East Stirling
Peterhead v Montrose
Stirling v Gretna

Saturday, 26 April
Bell's First Division
Alloa v Inverness CT
Clyde v Queen of South
Falkirk v Ayr
Ross County v Arbroath
St Johnstone v St Mirren

Bell's Second Division
Berwick v Brechin
Dumbarton v Stenhousemuir
Forfar v Airdrie Utd.
Hamilton v Cowdenbeath
Stranraer v Raith

Bell's Third Division
Albion v Stirling
East Fife v Peterhead
Elgin v Queens Park
Montrose v East Stirling
Morton v Gretna

Saturday, 3 May
Bell's First Division
Arbroath v Alloa
Ayr v Clyde
Inverness CT v St Johnstone
Queen of South v Ross County
St Mirren v Falkirk

Bell's Second Division
Brechin v Dumbarton
Airdrie Utd. v Hamilton
Cowdenbeath v Stranraer
Raith v Berwick
Stenhousemuir v Forfar

Bell's Third Division
East Stirling v East Fife
Gretna v Elgin
Peterhead v Albion
Queens Park v Montrose

Stirling v Morton

Saturday, 10 May
Bell's First Division
Alloa v St Mirren
Clyde v Arbroath
Falkirk v Inverness CT
Ross County v Ayr
St Johnstone v Queen of South

Bell's Second Division
Berwick v Stenhousemuir
Dumbarton v Raith

Forfar v Cowdenbeath
Hamilton v Brechin
Stranraer v Airdrie Utd.

Bell's Third Division
Albion v East Stirling
East Fife v Queens Park
Elgin v Stirling
Montrose v Gretna
Morton v Peterhead

NATIONWIDE FOOTBALL CONFERENCE
FIXTURES 2002-03

Saturday, 17 August
Burton Albion v Scarborough
Chester City v Kettering Town
Dag. & Red. v Leigh RMI.
Doncaster Rov. v Barnet
Halifax Town v Telford Utd.
Hereford Utd. v Farnborough Town
Margate v Morecambe
Southport v Nuneaton Borough
Stevenage Borough v Northwich Victoria
Woking v Forest Green Rov.
Yeovil Town v Gravesend & Northfleet

Monday, 19 August
Telford Utd. v Chester City

Tuesday, 20 August
Barnet v Yeovil Town
Farnborough Town v Stevenage Borough
Forest Green Rov. v Hereford Utd.
Gravesend and Northfleet v Dag. & Red.
Kettering Town v Margate
Leigh RMI. v Doncaster Rov.
Morecambe v Halifax Town
Northwich Victoria v Burton Albion
Nuneaton Borough v Woking
Scarborough v Southport

Saturday, 24 August
Barnet v Chester City
Farnborough Town v Halifax Town
Forest Green Rov. v Southport
Gravesend & Northfleet v Hereford Utd.
Kettering Town v Woking
Leigh RMI. v Burton Albion
Morecambe v Yeovil Town
Northwich Victoria v Margate
Nuneaton Borough v Stevenage Borough
Scarborough v Dag. & Red.
Telford Utd v Doncaster Rov.

Monday, 26 August
Burton Albion v Barnet
Chester City v Scarborough
Dag. & Red. v Telford Utd.
Doncaster Rov. v Farnborough Town
Halifax Town v Northwich Victoria
Hereford Utd. v Morecambe
Margate v Forest Green Rov.
Southport v Kettering Town
Stevenage Borough v Gravesend &
  Northfleet
Woking v Leigh RMI
Yeovil Town v Nuneaton Borough

Saturday, 31 August
Barnet v Halifax Town
Farnborough Town v Dag. & Red.
Forest Green Rov. v Chester City
Gravesend & Northfleet v Southport
Kettering Town v Yeovil Town
Leigh RMI v Margate
Morecambe v Stevenage Borough
Northwich Victoria v Doncaster Rov.
Nuneaton Borough v Hereford Utd.
Scarborough v Woking
Telford Utd. v Burton Albion

Monday, 2 September
Stevenage Borough v Telford Utd.

Tuesday, 3 September
Burton Albion v Forest Green Rov.
Chester City v Morecambe
Dag. & Red. v Nuneaton Borough
Doncaster Rov. v Kettering Town
Halifax Town v Scarborough
Hereford Utd. v Northwich Victoria
Margate v Barnet
Southport v Leigh RMI
Woking v Gravesend & Northfleet
Yeovil Town v Farnborough Town

Friday, 6 September
Chester City v Leigh RMI

Saturday, 7 September
Barnet v Telford Utd.
Burton Albion v Halifax Town
Doncaster Rov. v Dag. & Red.
Gravesend & Northfleet v Nuneaton Borough
Margate v Stevenage Borough
Morecambe v Forest Green Rov.
Scarborough v Kettering Town
Southport v Farnborough Town
Woking v Hereford Utd.
Yeovil Town v Northwich Victoria

Saturday, 14 September
Dag. & Red. v Burton Albion
Farnborough Town v Scarborough
Forest Green Rov. v Gravesend and
   Northfleet
Halifax Town v Doncaster Rov.
Hereford Utd. v Chester City
Kettering Town v Morecambe
Leigh RMI v Barnet
Northwich Victoria v Woking
Nuneaton Borough v Margate
Stevenage Borough v Yeovil Town
Telford Utd. v Southport

Monday, 16 September
Telford Utd v Scarborough

Tuesday, 17 September
Barnet v Farnborough Town
Burton Albion v Gravesend & Northfleet
Dag. & Red. v Kettering Town
Doncaster Rov. v Southport
Forest Green Rov. v Stevenage Borough
Halifax Town v Chester City
Hereford Utd. v Yeovil Town
Leigh RMI v Nuneaton Borough
Northwich Victoria v Morecambe
Woking v Margate

Saturday, 21 September
Chester City v Dag. & Red.
Farnborough Town v Leigh RMI
Gravesend & Northfleet v Telford Utd.
Kettering Town v Northwich Victoria
Margate v Doncaster Rov.
Morecambe v Woking
Nuneaton Borough v Forest Green Rov.
Scarborough v Barnet
Southport v Burton Albion
Stevenage Borough v Hereford Utd.
Yeovil Town v Halifax Town

Monday, 23 September
Stevenage Borough v Barnet

Tuesday, 24 September
Chester City v Burton Albion
Farnborough Town v Forest Green Rov.

Gravesend & Northfleet v Doncaster Rov.
Kettering Town v Hereford Utd.
Margate v Dag. & Red.
Morecambe v Telford Utd.
Nuneaton Borough v Northwich Victoria
Scarborough v Leigh RMI
Southport v Halifax Town
Yeovil Town v Woking

Saturday, 28 September
Barnet v Morecambe
Burton Albion v Margate
Dag. & Red. v Southport
Doncaster Rov. v Chester City
Forest Green Rov. v Kettering Town
Halifax Town v Nuneaton Borough
Hereford Utd. v Scarborough
Leigh RMI v Yeovil Town
Northwich Victoria v Gravesend & Northfleet
Telford Utd. v Farnborough Town
Woking v Stevenage Borough

Saturday, 5 October
Forest Green Rov. v Barnet
Gravesend & Northfleet v Scarborough
Hereford Utd. v Dag. & Red.
Kettering Town v Telford Utd.
Margate v Chester City
Morecambe v Leigh RMI
Northwich Victoria v Farnborough Town
Nuneaton Borough v Doncaster Rov.
Stevenage Borough v Halifax Town
Woking v Burton Albion
Yeovil Town v Southport

Monday, 7 October
Telford Utd. v Forest Green Rov.

Tuesday, 8 October
Barnet v Gravesend & Northfleet
Burton Albion v Yeovil Town
Chester City v Nuneaton Borough
Dagenham & Redbridge v Woking
Doncaster Rov. v Stevenage Borough
Farnborough Town v Margate
Halifax Town v Kettering Town
Leigh RMI v Hereford Utd.
Scarborough v Morecambe
Southport v Northwich Victoria

Friday, 11 October
Burton Albion v Hereford Utd.
Doncaster Rov. v Forest Green Rov.

Saturday, 12 October
Barnet v Nuneaton Borough
Dag. & Red. v Morecambe
Farnborough Town v Kettering Town
Halifax Town v Margate
Leigh RMI v Stevenage Borough
Southport v Woking

Sunday, 13 October
Chester City v Gravesend and Northfleet
Scarborough v Northwich Victoria
Telford Utd. v Yeovil Town

Saturday, 19 October
Forest Green Rov. v Scarborough
Gravesend & Northfleet v Leigh RMI
Hereford Utd. v Halifax Town
Kettering Town v Barnet
Margate v Southport
Morecambe v Farnborough Town
Northwich Victoria v Dag. & Red.
Nuneaton Borough v Telford Utd.
Stevenage Borough v Burton Albion
Woking v Chester City
Yeovil Town v Doncaster Rov.

Saturday, 2 November
Barnet v Northwich Victoria
Burton Albion v Morecambe
Chester City v Yeovil Town
Dag. & Red. v Forest Green Rov.
Doncaster Rov. v Hereford Utd.
Farnborough Town v Nuneaton Borough
Halifax Town v Gravesend & Northfleet
Leigh RMI v Kettering Town
Scarborough v Margate
Southport v Stevenage Borough
Telford Utd. v Woking

Saturday, 9 November
Forest Green Rov. v Halifax Town
Gravesend & Northfleet v Farnborough Town
Hereford Utd. v Southport
Kettering Town v Burton Albion
Margate v Telford Utd.
Morecambe v Doncaster Rov.
Northwich Victoria v Leigh RMI
Nuneaton Borough v Scarborough
Stevenage Borough v Chester City
Woking v Barnet
Yeovil Town v Dag. & Red.

Saturday, 23 November
Barnet v Forest Green Rov.
Burton Albion v Woking
Chester City v Margate
Dag. & Red. v Hereford Utd.
Doncaster Rov. v Nuneaton Borough
Farnborough Town v Northwich Victoria
Halifax Town v Stevenage Borough
Leigh RMI v Morecambe
Scarborough v Gravesend & Northfleet
Southport v Yeovil Town
Telford Utd. v Kettering Town

Saturday, 30 November
Doncaster Rov. v Woking
Farnborough Town v Burton Albion
Halifax Town v Dag. & Red.
Hereford Utd. v Barnet

Kettering Town v Nuneaton Borough
Leigh RMI v Telford Utd.
Morecambe v Gravesend & Northfleet
Northwich Victoria v Forest Green Rov.
Southport v Chester City
Stevenage Borough v Scarborough
Yeovil Town v Margate

Saturday, December 7
Barnet v Southport
Burton Albion v Doncaster Rov.
Chester City v Farnborough Town
Dag. & Red. v Stevenage Borough
Forest Green Rov. v Leigh RMI
Gravesend & Northfleet v Kettering Town
Margate v Hereford Utd.
Nuneaton Borough v Morecambe
Scarborough v Yeovil Town
Telford Utd. v Northwich Victoria
Woking v Halifax Town

Saturday, 14 December
Dag. & Red. v Doncaster Rov.
Farnborough Town v Southport
Forest Green Rov. v Morecambe
Halifax Town v Burton Albion
Hereford Utd. v Woking
Kettering Town v Scarborough
Leigh RMI v Chester City
Northwich Victoria v Yeovil Town
Nuneaton Borough v Gravesend & Northfleet
Stevenage Borough v Margate
Telford Utd. v Barnet

Saturday, 21 December
Barnet v Leigh RMI
Burton Albion v Dag. & Red.
Chester City v Hereford Utd.
Doncaster Rov. v Halifax Town
Gravesend & Northfleet v Forest Green Rov.
Margate v Nuneaton Borough
Morecambe v Kettering Town
Scarborough v Farnborough Town
Southport v Telford Utd.
Woking v Northwich Victoria
Yeovil Town v Stevenage Borough

Thursday, 26 December
Barnet v Dag. & Red.
Farnborough Town v Woking
Forest Green Rov. v Yeovil Town
Gravesend & Northfleet v Margate
Kettering Town v Stevenage Borough
Leigh RMI v Halifax Town
Morecambe v Southport
Northwich Victoria v Chester City
Nuneaton Borough v Burton Albion
Scarborough v Doncaster Rov.
Telford Utd. v Hereford Utd.

Saturday, 28 December
Burton Albion v Northwich Victoria
Chester City v Telford Utd.
Dag. & Red. v Gravesend & Northfleet
Doncaster Rov. v Leigh RMI
Halifax Town v Morecambe
Hereford Utd. v Forest Green Rov.
Margate v Kettering Town
Southport v Scarborough
Stevenage Borough v Farnborough Town
Woking v Nuneaton Borough
Yeovil Town v Barnet

Wednesday, 1 January
Burton Albion v Nuneaton Borough
Chester City v Northwich Victoria
Dag. & Red. v Barnet
Doncaster Rov. v Scarborough
Halifax Town v Leigh RMI
Hereford Utd. v Telford Utd.
Margate v Gravesend & Northfleet
Southport v Morecambe
Stevenage Borough v Kettering Town
Woking v Farnborough Town
Yeovil Town v Forest Green Rov.

Saturday, 4 January
Barnet v Doncaster Rov.
Farnborough Town v Hereford Utd.
Forest Green Rov. v Woking
Gravesend & Northfleet v Yeovil Town
Kettering Town v Chester City
Leigh RMI v Dag. & Red.
Morecambe v Margate
Northwich Victoria v Stevenage Borough
Nuneaton Borough v Southport
Scarborough v Burton Albion
Telford Utd. v Halifax Town

Saturday, 18 January
Burton Albion v Leigh RMI
Chester City v Barnet
Dag. & Red. v Scarborough
Doncaster Rov. v Telford Utd.
Halifax Town v Farnborough Town
Hereford Utd. v Gravesend & Northfleet
Margate v Northwich Victoria
Southport v Forest Green Rov.
Stevenage Borough v Nuneaton Borough
Woking v Kettering Town
Yeovil Town v Morecambe

Saturday, 25 January
Barnet v Burton Albion
Farnborough Town v Doncaster Rov.
Forest Green Rov. v Margate
Gravesend & Northfleet v Stevenage
  Borough
Kettering Town v Southport
Leigh RMI v Woking
Morecambe v Hereford Utd.

Northwich Victoria v Halifax Town
Nuneaton Borough v Yeovil Town
Scarborough v Chester City
Telford Utd. v Dag. & Red.

Saturday, 8 February
Burton Albion v Telford Utd.
Chester City v Forest Green Rov.
Dag. & Red. v Farnborough Town
Doncaster Rov. v Northwich Victoria
Halifax Town v Barnet
Hereford Utd. v Nuneaton Borough
Margate v Leigh RMI
Southport v Gravesend & Northfleet
Stevenage Borough v Morecambe
Woking v Scarborough
Yeovil Town v Kettering Town

Saturday, 15 February
Barnet v Margate
Farnborough Town v Yeovil Town
Forest Green Rov. v Burton Albion
Gravesend & Northfleet v Woking
Kettering Town v Doncaster Rov.
Leigh RMI v Southport
Morecambe v Chester City
Northwich Victoria v Hereford Utd.
Nuneaton Borough v Dag. & Red.
Scarborough v Halifax Town
Telford Utd. v Stevenage Borough

Saturday, 22 February
Barnet v Scarborough
Burton Albion v Southport
Dag. & Red. v Chester City
Doncaster Rov. v Margate
Forest Green Rov. v Nuneaton Borough
Halifax Town v Yeovil Town
Hereford Utd. v Stevenage Borough
Leigh RMI v Farnborough Town
Northwich Victoria v Kettering Town
Telford Utd. v Gravesend & Northfleet
Woking v Morecambe

Saturday, 1 March
Chester City v Halifax Town
Farnborough Town v Barnet
Gravesend & Northfleet v Burton Albion
Kettering Town v Dag. & Red.
Margate v Woking
Morecambe v Northwich Victoria
Nuneaton Borough v Leigh RMI
Scarborough v Telford Utd.
Southport v Doncaster Rov.
Stevenage Borough v Forest Green Rov.
Yeovil Town v Hereford Utd.

Saturday, 8 March
Barnet v Stevenage Borough
Burton Albion v Chester City
Dag. & Red. v Margate
Doncaster Rov. v Gravesend & Northfleet

Forest Green Rov. v Farnborough Town
Halifax Town v Southport
Hereford Utd. v Kettering Town
Leigh RMI v Scarborough
Northwich Victoria v Nuneaton Borough
Telford Utd. v Morecambe
Woking v Yeovil Town

Saturday, 15 March
Chester City v Doncaster Rov.
Farnborough Town v Telford Utd.
Gravesend & Northfleet v Northwich Victoria
Kettering Town v Forest Green Rov.
Margate v Burton Albion
Morecambe v Barnet
Nuneaton Borough v Halifax Town
Scarborough v Hereford Utd.
Southport v Dag. & Red.
Stevenage Borough v Woking
Yeovil Town v Leigh RMI

Saturday, 22 March
Barnet v Hereford Utd.
Burton Albion v Farnborough Town
Chester City v Southport
Dag. & Red. v Halifax Town
Forest Green Rov. v Northwich Victoria
Gravesend & Northfleet v Morecambe
Margate v Yeovil Town
Nuneaton Borough v Kettering Town
Scarborough v Stevenage Borough
Telford Utd. v Leigh RMI
Woking v Doncaster Rov.

Friday, 28 March
Doncaster Rov. v Burton Albion
Yeovil Town v Scarborough

Saturday, 29 March
Farnborough Town v Chester City
Halifax Town v Woking
Hereford Utd. v Margate
Kettering Town v Gravesend & Northfleet
Leigh RMI v Forest Green Rov.
Morecambe v Nuneaton Borough
Southport v Barnet
Stevenage Borough v Dag. & Red.

Sunday, 30 March
Northwich Victoria v Telford Utd.

Saturday, 5 April
Forest Green Rov. v Doncaster Rov.
Gravesend & Northfleet v Chester City
Hereford Utd. v Burton Albion
Kettering Town v Farnborough Town
Margate v Halifax Town
Morecambe v Dag. & Red.

Northwich Victoria v Scarborough
Nuneaton Borough v Barnet
Stevenage Borough v Leigh RMI
Woking v Southport
Yeovil Town v Telford Utd.

Saturday, 12 April
Barnet v Kettering Town
Burton Albion v Stevenage Borough
Chester City v Woking
Dag. & Red. v Northwich Victoria
Doncaster Rov. v Yeovil Town
Farnborough Town v Morecambe
Halifax Town v Hereford Utd.
Leigh RMI v Gravesend & Northfleet
Scarborough v Forest Green Rov.
Southport v Margate
Telford Utd. v Nuneaton Borough

Saturday, 19 April
Forest Green Rov. v Telford Utd.
Gravesend & Northfleet v Barnet
Hereford Utd. v Leigh RMI
Kettering Town v Halifax Town
Margate v Farnborough Town
Morecambe v Scarborough
Northwich Victoria v Southport
Nuneaton Borough v Chester City
Stevenage Borough v Doncaster Rov.
Woking v Dag. & Red.
Yeovil Town v Burton Albion

Monday, 21 April
Barnet v Woking
Burton Albion v Kettering Town
Chester City v Stevenage Borough
Dag. & Red. v Yeovil Town
Doncaster Rov. v Morecambe
Farnborough Town v Gravesend & Northfleet
Halifax Town v Forest Green Rov.
Leigh RMI v Northwich Victoria
Scarborough v Nuneaton Borough
Southport v Hereford Utd.
Telford Utd. v Margate

Saturday, 26 April
Forest Green Rov. v Dag. & Red.
Gravesend & Northfleet v Halifax Town
Hereford Utd. v Doncaster Rov.
Kettering Town v Leigh RMI
Margate v Scarborough
Morecambe v Burton Albion
Northwich Victoria v Barnet
Nuneaton Borough v Farnborough Town
Stevenage Borough v Southport
Woking v Telford Utd.
Yeovil Town v Chester City